Rand H. Morimoto, Ph.D., MCSE
Michael Noel, MCSE, MVP
Andrew Abbate, MCSE
Chris Amaris, MCSE, CISSP
Mark Weinhardt, MCSE

W9-CGY-235

Microsoft®
Exchange
Server 2007

UNLEASHED

SAMS   800 East 96th Street, Indianapolis, Indiana 46240 USA

Microsoft® Exchange Server 2007 Unleashed

International Standard Book Number: 0-672-32920-4

Library of Congress Cataloging-in-Publication Data

Microsoft Exchange server 2007 unleashed / Rand H. Morimoto ... [et al.].

p. cm.

ISBN-13: 978-0-672-32920-3

ISBN-10: 0-672-32920-4

1. Microsoft Exchange server. 2. Client/server computing. I. Morimoto, Rand.

QA76.9.C55M5296 2006

005.7'1376—dc22

2006038777

Printed in the United States of America

Third Printing: May 2007

Trademarks

All terms mentioned in this book that are known to be trademarks or service marks have been appropriately capitalized. Sams Publishing cannot attest to the accuracy of this information. Use of a term in this book should not be regarded as affecting the validity of any trademark or service mark.

Warning and Disclaimer

Every effort has been made to make this book as complete and as accurate as possible, but no warranty or fitness is implied. The information provided is on an "as is" basis. The authors and the publisher shall have neither liability nor responsibility to any person or entity with respect to any loss or damages arising from the information contained in this book.

Bulk Sales

Sams Publishing offers excellent discounts on this book when ordered in quantity for bulk purchases or special sales. For more information, please contact

U.S. Corporate and Government Sales
1-800-382-3419
corpsales@pearsontechgroup.com

For sales outside of the U.S., please contact

International Sales
international@pearsoned.com

The Safari® Enabled icon on the cover of your favorite technology book means the book is available through Safari Bookshelf. When you buy this book, you get free access to the online edition for 45 days. Safari Bookshelf is an electronic reference library that lets you easily search thousands of technical books, find code samples, download chapters, and access technical information whenever and wherever you need it.

To gain 45-day Safari Enabled access to this book:

· Go to http://www.samspublishing.com/safarienabled
· Complete the brief registration form
· Enter the coupon code **1VFR-KPSE-3ZQU-R6EN-W8RZ**

If you have difficulty registering on Safari Bookshelf or accessing the online edition, please e-mail customer-service@safaribooksonline.com.

Editor-in-Chief
Karen Gettman

Senior Acquisitions Editor
Neil Rowe

Development Editor
Mark Renfrow

Managing Editor
Gina Kanouse

Project Editor
Betsy Harris

Copy Editor
Karen Annett

Indexers
Ken Johnson
Lisa Stumpf

Proofreader
Kathy Bidwell

Technical Editor
Brian Barber

Publishing Coordinator
Cindy Teeters

Cover Designer
Gary Adair

Composition
Bronkella Publishing LLC

Contributing Writers
Alec Minty, MCSE, MVP

Jeff Guillet, MCSE:Messaging, MCSA:Messaging, MCP+I

Kim Amaris, PMP

Ross Mistry, MCSE, MCDBA, MCSA

Scott Chimner, MCSE, TCSE, A+

Contents at a Glance

Table of Contents

**31   Continuous Backups, Clustering, and Network Load Balancing in
          Exchange Server 2007   1045**

Understanding Clustering 1046

Deploying a Cluster Continuous Replication Mailbox Cluster 1047

    Requirements for CCR 1048

    Preparing the Operating System 1048

    Creating the File Witness Share 1049

    Creating the Cluster 1050

    Adding the Second Node to the Cluster 1051

    Configuring the MNS Quorum 1052

    Installing Exchange Server 2007 on the Active Node 1053

    Installing Exchange Server 2007 on the Passive Node 1054

    Special Considerations for CCR 1055

    Other Advantages of Clustering 1057

Single Copy Clusters 1057

    Requirements of SCC 1057

    Preparing the Operating System 1058

    Configuring the Shared Storage 1059

    Creating the Cluster 1059

    Adding the Second Node 1061

    Creating the Distributed Transaction Coordinator 1062

    Installing Exchange Server 2007 on the Active Node 1062

    Installing Exchange Server 2007 on the Passive Node 1064

    Special Considerations for SCC 1066

    Other Advantages of SCC 1066

Comparing and Contrasting CCR Versus SCC 1067

Managing a Windows Server 2003 Cluster 1068

    Managing the Cluster from the Command Line 1068

    Managing the Cluster from the GUI 1069

    Backing Up the Cluster 1072

Load Balancing in Exchange Server 2007 1073

    NLB Modes and Port Configuration Overview 1073

    NLB Network Card Configurations 1073

    Configuring Network Load Balancing with Client
        Access Servers 1074

About the Authors

Rand H. Morimoto, Ph.D., MBA, MCSE, MVP   Rand Morimoto has been in the computer industry for more than 25 years and has authored, coauthored, or been a contributing writer for over a dozen books on Windows Server 2003, Security, Exchange Server 2003, BizTalk Server, and Remote and Mobile Computing. Rand is the president of Convergent Computing, an IT-consulting firm in the San Francisco Bay area that has been one of the key early adopter program partners with Microsoft, implementing beta versions of Microsoft Exchange Server 2007, SharePoint 2007, and Windows Longhorn Server in production environments more than 2 years before the initial product releases. Besides speaking at over 50 conferences and conventions around the world in the past year on tips, tricks, and best practices on planning, migrating, and implementing Exchange Server 2007, Rand is one of four cybersecurity advisors to the White House.

Michael Noel, MCSE+I, CISSP, MCSA, MVP   Michael Noel has been involved in the computer industry for nearly two decades, and has significant real-world experience with enterprise Exchange Server environments. Michael has authored several major publications such as *Microsoft Exchange Server 2003 Unleashed, Microsoft ISA Server 2006 Unleashed, Microsoft SharePoint 2007 Unleashed, Microsoft Windows Server 2003 Unleashed*, and many more with a total worldwide circulation of more than 100,000 copies. Currently a principal consultant at Convergent Computing in the San Francisco Bay area, Michael's writings are leveraged from his real-world experience designing, deploying, and administering Exchange Server environments.

Andrew Abbate, MCSE, MCSA   Andrew Abbate is a 14-year veteran of consulting and IT with a wealth of practical knowledge on Exchange. Starting with his first migration of MS Mail to Exchange 4.0 through early adopter migrations to Exchange 2007, Andrew has worked with some of the largest and most complex Exchange environments in North America. In addition to his Exchange background, Andrew has written several other books covering topics such as Windows Server 2003, Active Directory, and Information Security. Andrew currently enjoys the position of Senior Consultant at Convergent Computing, where he continues to consult with both large and small clients to help improve their IT practices.

Chris Amaris, MCSE, MVP, CISSP/ISSAP, CHS III   Chris Amaris is the Chief Technology Officer and cofounder of Convergent Computing. He has more than 20 years experience consulting for Fortune 500 companies, leading companies in the technology selection, design, planning, and implementation of complex information technology projects. Chris has worked with Microsoft Exchange since the early beta days of version 4.0. He specializes in messaging, security, performance tuning, systems management, and migration. A Certified Information Systems Security Professional (CISSP) with an Information System Security Architecture Professional (ISSAP) concentration, Certified Homeland Security (CHS III), Windows 2003 MCSE, Novell CNE, Banyan CBE, and Certified Project Manager, Chris is also an author, writer, and technical editor for a number of IT books, including

Network Security for Government and Corporate Executives, Microsoft Windows Server 2003 Unleashed, Microsoft Exchange Server 2003 Unleashed, and *Microsoft Operations Manager 2005 Unleashed.* Chris presents on messaging, operations management, security, and information technology topics worldwide.

Mark Weinhardt, MCSE   Mark Weinhardt has worked in various aspects of the computing industry for more than 20 years. Coming from a military background, Mark understands the importance of implementing and maintaining proper communications and has preserved that mentality with his transition to the private sector. Mark has been a consultant with Convergent Computing since 1994. With an infectious enthusiasm for technology, Mark has performed Windows and Exchange implementations and migrations for companies throughout northern California.

Dedication

I dedicate this book to Kelly and Chip, thank you for trying your best at everything you do!

—Rand H. Morimoto, Ph.D., MBA, MCSE, MVP

This book is dedicated to my sister Anna. Your spirit, intelligence, and compassion would make anyone proud to be your brother.

—Michael Noel, MCSE+I, CISSP, MCSA, MVP

I dedicate this book to my niece and nephew, Katelyn and Nathan. You always remind me that I need to keep life in perspective and recognize what is truly important.

—Andrew Abbate, MCSE, MCSA

I dedicate this book to my wife, Sophia, whose love and support I cherish. And to my children, Michelle, Megan, Zoe, Zachary, and Ian, for whose sake all the hard work is worthwhile. I also want to dedicate the book to my late father, Jairo Amaris, who taught me to think on many different levels.

—Chris Amaris, MCSE, MVP, CISSP/ISSAP, CHS III

I dedicate this book to my parents, John and Pat Weinhardt, who always stood tall, and who taught me the importance of honesty and compassion in a world that is sometimes lacking in both, to my dear family and friends who are always there when I call, and to my step-children, Tyson and Nicole Cogley—I hope I continue to make you proud.

—Mark Weinhardt, MCSE

Acknowledgments

Rand H. Morimoto, Ph.D., MBA, MCSE, MVP   I want to thank our editor, Neil Rowe, who has been wonderful to work with and very supportive of the work I do for Sams Publishing! It's a lot of work to get a book of this scope out the door—glad to have another one done!

I also wanted to thank our dozens of early adopter clients who, in many cases, were our guinea pigs as we worked together years before Exchange 2007 shipped, helping build field experience and knowledge of the technology that ended up in the pages of this book. And a big thanks out to all of the consultants at Convergent Computing who got up to speed on Exchange 2007 long, long ago to help our customers with their migrations and implementations in the various early adopter program stages.

To Andrew and Kelly, now that this book is done, you actually might find daddy in bed when you wake up in the middle of the night instead of down on the couch writing at all hours of the night. And thank you mom for your constant love and support! For all those afternoons and evenings that you struggled to help me get my homework done because I couldn't string together words into a sentence to write a book report, I guess after all these years and several books later, I can finally say I figured it out.

Michael Noel, MCSE+I, CISSP, MCSA   There is never enough space on this page to thank everyone who contributed to this book, but I'll try. First and foremost, thanks to Rand Morimoto and my coauthors Andrew, Chris, and Mark for the collaboration in getting this one out the door. Sometimes it seems like it will never get written, but having a team like we have makes it that much easier.

A big thanks to our editor, Neil Rowe at Sams Publishing, for working with me again on this book (and the other books I always seem to be simultaneously working on). You make it much easier to get the impossible done, and for that I thank you.

And of course, thanks once again to my family for putting up with the late nights, missed meals, and grumpiness that accompanies "crunch time" with these books. Marina, Julia, Val, Liza, Mila, and everyone else! You fill my life with utter happiness!

Andrew Abbate, MCSE, MCSA   Book writing is a lot like mountain biking; it doesn't seem worth the effort while you are pedaling uphill but after that part is over, you really get to enjoy the fruits of your efforts. Unlike mountain biking, book writing is really a team effort and, therefore, I'd like to thank the other members of the team who made this possible. First, a big thanks to Sams Publishing for giving us yet another opportunity to write a book on a topic that holds a lot of interest for us. You allow us to reach a much larger audience than we'd be able to help alone and for that, we are grateful. I'd like to thank Rand, Mark, Mike, and Chris for always being available to bounce an idea or two off of. I've always believed that you learn more by sharing knowledge than you get from gathering it.

I'd also like to thank my friends for being understanding when I said I had to write instead of hanging out and I want to thank the "Dirt Monkeys" (you know who you are...) for dragging me out to the trails on occasion to maintain my balance between work and play.

Chris Amaris, MCSE, MVP, CISSP/ISSAP, CHS III   I would like to thank Rand Morimoto for leading the troops once again into the battle of book writing and on to victory in that battle by having the book finally completed. His leadership and strategic guidance keep us all on track and focused on what we need to do. His ability to work without sleep leaves me in awe.

And I would especially like to thank my immediate and extended family for putting up with my absent mindedness, short temper, and lack of communication while writing. And for picking up the slack and keeping on track while I spent the long hours toiling away at the keyboard.

Mark Weinhardt, MCSE   First, I would like to thank Rand Morimoto for the opportunity to foray once again into the writing biz...it is always a pleasure to work for (and with) you. I would also like to thank my coauthor, Andrew Abbate, who pushed me to get in the lab and get my work done—even on the days when I would much rather have felt the wind in my hair on the single-tracks of the Bay Area wilderness.

To my family, thank you for understanding as I put much of my personal life on hold (once again) for this endeavor—it was a journey that I would not have missed. And to my friends (on both coasts), whichever side of the country I may be on at the time, you are all in my heart and my thoughts. Peace on all of you...

We Want to Hear from You!

As the reader of this book, *you* are our most important critic and commentator. We value your opinion and want to know what we're doing right, what we could do better, what areas you'd like to see us publish in, and any other words of wisdom you're willing to pass our way.

As a senior acquisitions editor for Sams Publishing, I welcome your comments. You can email or write me directly to let me know what you did or didn't like about this book—as well as what we can do to make our books better.

Please note that I cannot help you with technical problems related to the topic of this book. We do have a User Services group, however, where I will forward specific technical questions related to the book.

When you write, please be sure to include this book's title and author as well as your name, email address, and phone number. I will carefully review your comments and share them with the author and editors who worked on the book.

Email: feedback@samspublishing.com

Mail: Neil Rowe
         Senior Acquisitions Editor
         Sams Publishing
         800 East 96th Street
         Indianapolis, IN 46240 USA

For more information about this book or another Sams Publishing title, visit our website at www.samspublishing.com. Type the ISBN (excluding hyphens) or the title of a book in the Search field to find the page you're looking for.

Introduction

In the past 12 years, we have written a book on every version of Exchange since its inception built on at least two years of early adopter beta experience. This book, *Microsoft Exchange Server 2007 Unleashed*, is the latest of our efforts. However, unlike the past two major releases of Exchange (2000 and 2003), Microsoft Exchange Server 2007, although very similar, had enough differences that it required complete rethinking of the way we wrote this book.

Rather than being just an email and calendaring product, Microsoft added a handful of new server roles to Exchange Server 2007 to improve security and reliability. In addition, Exchange 2007 is Microsoft's entry into the world of unified messaging. Exchange 2007 not only added a Unified Messaging server role, but Exchange is now the backbone of an entire unified communications strategy that Microsoft will be building on over the next several years. Beyond just email and calendaring, Exchange Server 2007 now lays the foundation for voice and mobile communications.

Just a decade ago, email was just one of a number of different ways people communicated. Early implementations of Exchange (v4.0, v5.0) had organizations tolerant if a server was down for a day or two. Today, email has become an extremely important, if not primary, method of communications for organizations. Downtime on an Exchange server can bring an entire organization to its knees. With Exchange 2007 adding voice mail and mobile communications into the messaging environment, an Exchange 2007 server and environment can no longer tolerate failures caused by viruses and spam, nor system downtime caused by server crashes or database corruption.

You will find that the improvements Microsoft has made to Exchange 2007 are not only evolutionary improvements, but highly critical if not absolutely essential to Microsoft's responsibility to help organizations maintain a safe, secure, and reliable communications infrastructure. This book covers all of the aspects of Exchange 2007 from introducing the technologies, to properly planning and designing Exchange, to the implementation, management, and support of an Exchange 2007 environment built on tips, tricks, and best practices from over two years of early adopter implementations in the field.

This book is organized into 10 parts, each part focusing on core Exchange Server 2007 areas, with several chapters making up each part:

- **Part I: Microsoft Exchange Server 2007 Overview**—This part provides an introduction to Exchange Server 2007, not only from the perspective of a general technology overview, but also to note what is truly new in Exchange 2007 that made it compelling enough for organizations to implement the technology in beta in a production environment. This part also covers best practices of planning, prototype testing, and migration techniques.

- **Part II: Planning and Designing an Exchange Server 2007 Environment**—This part covers the design of an underlying Windows Server 2003 and Active Directory environment in addition to the Exchange Server 2007 unified communications environment. Because organizations of varying sizes have different needs and requirements, as appropriate, this part addresses core Exchange 2007 design plans and concepts appropriate for most organizations, and specific attention is given to enterprise-level design and planning considerations for some of the largest Exchange implementations in the world. This part also covers the integration of Exchange 2007 in a non-Windows environment as well as tips, tricks, and best practices at getting a Windows Server 2003 Active Directory, DNS, and domain structure properly planned and architected.

- **Part III: Implementing Exchange Server 2007 Services**—This part covers the core implementation of Exchange 2007 as well as the new Edge Services role that has been added to the Exchange organizational structure to provide protection against viruses and spam. In addition, this section has a chapter on the Exchange Management Script based on PowerShell, the new Microsoft scripting solution that is the basis of the configuration, administration, and operations of Exchange 2007.

- **Part IV: Securing an Exchange Server 2007 Environment**—Security is on everyone's mind these days, and it was absolutely critical to have several chapters that covered security. The chapters of this part of the book include client-level, server-level, and transport-level security that is at the backbone of security for a network environment. A dedicated chapter on email encryption was necessary to cover the use of certificate-based encryption technologies to enable an organization the ability to provide person-to-person encrypted message communications. In addition, chapters on Microsoft ISA Server 2006 enhancing security at the edge and a chapter on enterprise policy environment addressing regulatory compliance security enhancements added to Exchange 2007 round out this extensive part on security.

- **Part V: Migrations and Coexistence with Exchange Server 2007**—This part is dedicated to migrations, Client Access servers (CASs), and Hub Transport servers.

This part provides a chapter specifically on migrating from Windows 2000 Server to Windows Server 2003 for organizations that have yet to complete their migration to a base Windows 2003 environment. And, of course, this part includes a chapter on migrating from Exchange 2000 Server and Exchange Server 2003 to the new Exchange 2007 unified communications environment. Because Microsoft does not provide migrations from Exchange Server 5.5 to Exchange 2007, nor does it provide in-place upgrades to Exchange 2007, there are fewer options to choose from, which means that the method you are left with needs to be planned, tested, and executed with the utmost care to minimize, if not eliminate, any interruption to users. This part of the book includes a chapter that covers the planning and implementation of the CAS role and the Hub Transport role, two new roles to Exchange 2007 that are critical to the new Exchange 2007 organizational environment.

▶ **Part VI: Exchange Server 2007 Administration and Management**—In this part, five chapters focus on the administration and management of an Exchange Server 2007 environment. The administration and management of mailboxes, distribution lists, sites, and administration have been greatly enhanced in Exchange Server 2007. Although you can continue to perform many of the tasks the way you did in the past, because of significant changes in replication, background transaction processing, secured communications, integrated mobile communications, and changes in Windows Server 2003 Active Directory, there are better ways to work with Exchange Server 2007. These chapters drill down into specialty areas helpful to administrators of varying levels of responsibility.

▶ **Part VII: Unified Communications in an Exchange Server 2007 Environment**— This section is completely new to Exchange 2007 with the addition of the Unified Messaging role, new mobility functionality, and tight integration with SharePoint 2007. As mentioned earlier in this introduction, Exchange 2007 not only added voice mail to Exchange, but the addition of voice integration takes Exchange 2007 far beyond just an email and calendaring solution. This addition takes Exchange into an area where communications is conducted on personal computers, mobile handheld devices, and from remote kiosks and terminal systems. The chapters in this part of the book highlight all of the new technologies and integration capabilities that make Exchange 2007 the core foundation to the future of an organization's communications infrastructure.

▶ **Part VIII: Client Access to Exchange Server 2007**—This part of the book focuses on the enhancements to the Outlook Web Access client, various Outlook client capabilities, and Outlook for non-Windows systems. Outlook Web Access is no longer just a simple browser client, but one that can effectively be a full primary user client to Exchange, including access to network file shares, an entry point to SharePoint shares, and a remote voice mail collection point. Being that Exchange 2007 now includes voice and mobile communications as a major component of the Exchange environment, client access as well as the distribution, management, and support of the client becomes even more important.

▶ **Part IX: Data Protection and Disaster Recovery of Exchange Server 2007**—As organizations implement Exchange 2007 and make it their central store for email, calendars, contacts, voice and fax communications, and mobile communications, it is no longer an option to set up and support an environment where downtime is even a possibility. This part of the book covers clustering and the new continuous backup technologies built in to Exchange 2007 intended to keep Exchange 2007 operating in a nonstop environment. Additional chapters in this part address backing up and restoring Exchange data, along with the recovery of an Exchange 2007 environment in the event of a disaster.

▶ **Part X: Optimizing Exchange Server 2007 Environments**—This last part of the book addresses optimization in terms of server and Exchange 2007 organizational environment optimization, as well as storage systems (SAN/NAS) optimization. Optimization goes far beyond simply tuning an Exchange server with the appropriate amount of RAM and disk space, but takes on a whole new area of load balancing data storage across external storage subsystems where information is managed and replicated separately.

The real-world experience we have had in working with Exchange Server 2007 and our commitment to writing this book based on years of field experience in early adopter Exchange 2007 environments enables us to relay to you information that we hope will be valuable in your successful planning, implementation, and migration to an Exchange Server 2007 environment.

PART I

Microsoft Exchange Server 2007 Overview

IN THIS PART

Exchange Server 2007 Technology Primer

Microsoft Exchange Server 2007 is the latest release of the messaging and communications system from Microsoft built on the Windows operating system. This chapter introduces you to "What is Exchange 2007?" not just from the perspective of what's new in Exchange 2007 compared to previous versions, but also from the perspective of those who are new to Exchange. This chapter discusses the background of Exchange, the previous versions, and the general concepts of the Exchange messaging system, so that regardless of whether you are an Exchange 2000 or 2003 expert, or you are new to working with Exchange, you are prepared to dive into the remainder of this book on planning, testing, implementing, administering, managing, and supporting an Exchange 2007 environment.

What Is Exchange Server 2007?

At its core, Microsoft Exchange Server 2007 is an email, calendaring, and address book system that runs on a centralized Windows Server 2003 server system. However with the release of Exchange 2007, now the sixth major release of Exchange in the 12-year history of the product, Microsoft has made significant improvements in the areas of security, reliability, scalability, mobility, and unified communications. For those Exchange experts who are already very familiar with the product, you might choose to skip this section, jump to the "Exchange Server 2007 Versions and Licensing" section (because Microsoft has a slightly different way of licensing Exchange 2007), and then jump to the "What's New in Exchange Server 2007" section to discover the latest and greatest in Exchange 2007.

So back to the basics of Exchange, with a centralized Exchange server holding mail messages, calendar appointments, contacts, and other user information, the Exchange environment provides a server-based storage of information. Users throughout the organization connect to the Exchange server from Microsoft Outlook, from a web browser, or from a variety of other client systems to get access to their email and other information.

For larger organizations, multiple Exchange servers can be added to the environment hosting mailbox information of the users. Microsoft has split the roles of servers in an Exchange environment, where some servers are dedicated for antivirus and antispam filtering, and other servers are dedicated to routing messages throughout the organization. The "Understanding Exchange Server 2007 Server Roles and Mail Flow" section discusses these roles in more detail.

Understanding the Evolution of Exchange

For those new to Microsoft Exchange, this section covers the history of the Exchange product line. Sometimes as a newcomer to a technology, it's hard to jump right into the technology because everyone working with the technology refers to previous versions without taking into consideration that some people might not remember what was in the last revision, or in the product a couple of revisions back. So, this section is intended to give you a little history of Exchange so that the version numbers and major notable features and functions make sense.

Exchange Server 4.0

The first version of Microsoft Exchange, despite the 4.0 designation, was Exchange Server 4.0. Some people ask, "What happened to Exchange Server 1.0, 2.0, and 3.0?" For a bit of trivia, prior to Exchange Server 4.0, Microsoft had MS-Mail 3.0 (and MS-Mail 2.0); prior to that, it was a product called Network Courier Mail that Microsoft bought in the early 1990s.

Microsoft Exchange 4.0 had nothing in common with MS-Mail 3.0; they were completely different products and different technologies. The first rollouts of Exchange 4.0 back in 1996 were on Windows NT Server 3.51, which anyone with old NT 3.x experience knows that it was a challenging operating system to keep fully operational. "Blue screens" in which the operating system would just lock up were common. Anything that caused a system error usually resulted in a blue screen, which meant that every patch, update, service pack addition, installation of antivirus software, and so on frequently caused complete server failures.

However, Exchange 4.0 was a major breakthrough, and organizations started to migrate from MS-Mail to Exchange Server 4.0. One of the biggest reasons organizations were migrating to Exchange 4.0 was that in 1996, the Internet was just opening up to the public. The specifications for the World Wide Web had just been released. Organizations were connecting systems to the Internet, and one of the first real applications that took advantage of the Internet was Microsoft Exchange 4.0. Organizations were able to connect their Exchange 4.0 server to the Internet and easily and simply send and receive emails to anyone else with an Internet-connected email system. MS-Mail 3.0 at the time had a Simple Mail Transfer Protocol (SMTP) gateway; however, it worked more on a scheduled dial-up basis, whereas Exchange 4.0 had a persistent connection to, typically, Integrated Services Digital Network (ISDN) or 56-KB frame connections to the Internet. And with Windows NT 4.0 shipping and being a much more solid infrastructure to work from, Exchange Server 4.0 was much more reliable than MS-Mail was for centralized organizationwide email communications.

Exchange Server 5.0

Exchange Server 5.0 came out in 1997 and was built to run on Windows NT 4.0, which proved to add more reliability to the Exchange Server product. In addition, Exchange 5.0 supported the first version of Outlook that to this day has a similar mailbox folder concept with the Inbox, Sent Items, Calendar, Contacts, and other common folders duplicated by mail systems throughout the industry. With the support for the Microsoft Outlook (97) client, Exchange also included calendaring directly within the Exchange product. In Exchange 5.0, the calendaring product was Schedule+, which was an add-on to Exchange 4.0, meaning that a user's email and calendaring weren't tied together, so Exchange 5.0 tied email, calendaring, and address books all together. With a service pack to Exchange 5.0, Microsoft also released the first version of Outlook Web Access (OWA) so that those who accessed the new World Wide Web could get remote access to their email on Exchange. Back in 1997, this was a big thing as web mail was a new concept, and Exchange 5.0 had web mail built in to the messaging product.

Exchange 5.0 also had better third-party support for things such as fax gateways, unified voice mail add-in products, and document-sharing tools, leveraging shared public folders in Exchange. With better reliability, third-party product support, and a growing base of customers now migrating from MS-Mail and cc:Mail to Exchange, the Microsoft Exchange marketshare started to skyrocket.

Exchange Server 5.5

In 1998, Microsoft released Exchange 5.5, which some organizations are still running in their networking environment. With Exchange 5.5, Microsoft worked out the bugs and quirks of their first two revisions of the Exchange product, and significantly better integration occurred between email, calendar, contacts, and tasks than in previous releases of Exchange. Microsoft also expanded the support for a larger Exchange database used to store messages, so instead of being limited to 16GB of mail with earlier releases of Exchange, organizations could upgrade to the Enterprise Edition of Exchange 5.5 that provided more than 16GB of data storage. With larger storage capabilities, Exchange 5.5 greatly supported large corporate, government, and organizational messaging environments.

Along with Exchange 5.5, OWA was improved to provide a faster and easier-to-use web client. The concept of site connectors was expanded with Exchange 5.5 to provide a larger enterprise Exchange environment with distribution of administration, message routing, and multilanguage support. Most organizations that hadn't migrated off of Exchange 5.5 earlier had made their migration to Exchange 2000 and 2003. Exchange 5.5 for the most part is now out of environments or will soon be migrated to Exchange 2003 in anticipation of the organization ultimately migrating to Exchange 2007.

Exchange 2000 Server

Exchange 2000 Server came out in 2000 right after the release of Windows 2000 Server and the first version of Microsoft Active Directory. The biggest change in Exchange 2000 is that it used Active Directory for the Global Address List (GAL), instead of Windows NT having its list of network logon users and Exchange 5.5 having its own directory of email users. Active Directory combined a network and email user account into one single account, making the administration and management of Exchange much simpler. Exchange 2000 also went to an ActiveX version of the OWA client instead of a straight Hypertext Markup Language (HTML) version of the web access, thus providing users with drag-and-drop capabilities, pull-down bars, and other functionality that made the web access function much easier for remote users.

Exchange 2000, which is required to run on top of Windows 2000, became much more reliable than Exchange 5.5, which ran on top of Windows NT 4.0. However, because Exchange 5.5 can run on top of Windows 2000, many organizations made the shift to Exchange 5.5 on top of Windows 2000. These organizations also gained better performance and reliability, which is why many organizations did not migrate from Exchange 5.5. However, Windows 2000 provided Exchange 2000 a stable operating system platform from the beginning. Also by 2000, Novell's popularity was dramatically decreasing and organizations were migrating from Novell GroupWise to Exchange 2000, so the Microsoft marketshare continued to grow.

Exchange Server 2003

Exchange 2003 was the most recent major product release prior to the current Exchange 2007 product line. Exchange 2003 added mobility for users to synchronize their Pocket PC mobile devices to Exchange. In addition, OWA got yet another major face-lift mirroring the OWA interface with the normal Microsoft Office Outlook desktop client. With better remote support, Exchange 2003 became more than an office-based messaging system—it also greatly enhanced an organization's ability to provide remote and mobile users with email anytime and anywhere.

Exchange 2003, running on top of Windows Server 2003, took advantage of additional operating system enhancements, making Exchange 2003 an even more reliable and manageable messaging system. Windows 2003 clustering finally worked so that organizations that put Exchange 2003 on top of Windows 2003 were able to do active-active and active-passive clustering. In addition, clustering went from two-node clusters to four-node clusters, providing even more redundancy and recoverability.

Exchange 2003 also introduced the concept of a recovery storage group (RSG) that allowed an organization to mount an Exchange database for test and recovery purposes. Prior to Exchange 2003, an Exchange database could only be mounted on an Exchange server, typically with the exact same server name and for the sole purpose of making the database accessible to users. The recovery storage group in Exchange 2003 allowed an Exchange database from another Exchange server to be mounted in an offline manner so that the Exchange administrator can extract corrupt or lost messages, or possibly even have the database in a "ready mode" to allow for faster recovery of a failed Exchange server.

1

Exchange Server 2003 Service Pack 2

Although not a major release of Exchange, it is significant to note the late major service pack for Exchange 2003, which is Exchange 2003 Service Pack 2. Exchange Service Pack 1 introduced cyclic redundancy check (CRC) error checking of the Exchange database. For 10 years, information written to Exchange was done without error checking, so prior to 2005, Microsoft Exchange had a bad reputation for having corruption in its databases any time the databases got too large. With the release of Exchange 2003 SP1, error checking brought Exchange to a whole new world in better reliability.

Exchange 2003 SP2 added to the reliability and security of Exchange by introducing support for SenderID message integrity checks as well as enhanced journaling of messages that captured a copy of messages in Exchange and locked the original copies of the messages in a tamperproof database that allowed for better support for regulatory compliance auditing and message integrity.

Exchange 2003 SP2 also added in direct push for mobile devices so that instead of having a Windows Mobile or Pocket PC device constantly "pull" messages down from Exchange, Exchange 2003 SP2 pushes messages to mobile devices, thus preventing constant polling by the mobile device, which increases battery life and enables Exchange and mobile devices to remain synchronized in real time.

Exchange Server 2007 Versions and Licensing

One major change to Exchange 2007 is that it only comes in an x64-bit version that requires Windows 2003 x64-bit to run as the core operating system. Although Exchange 2007 requires Windows 2003 x64-bit to run the Exchange server software, an organization can still run 32-bit Windows 2003 domain controllers, global catalog servers, and even Windows NT 4.0 and Windows 2000 member servers throughout the environment. Just the Exchange 2007 servers need to run x64-bit.

This means that organizations need to make sure their server hardware is x64-bit. Prior to the release of Exchange 2007, most organizations were buying x64-bit hardware anyway because many hardware vendors stopped shipping 32-bit hardware as much as a year to 18 months prior to the release of Exchange 2007. The benefit of x64-bit hardware is that you can still run 32-bit Windows and 32-bit software on the hardware until such time that you want to just reinstall 64-bit Windows and 64-bit software on the systems.

> **NOTE**
>
> Organizations with volume licensing agreements with Microsoft do not need to purchase or upgrade their Windows licenses from 32-bit to 64-bit. A Windows 2003 server license is a Windows 2003 server license, so regardless of whether the system is 32-bit or 64-bit, the organization's server licenses remain the same.

Choosing the Standard Edition of Exchange 2007

As with previous versions of Exchange, Microsoft has two different versions, a Standard Edition and an Enterprise Edition of the software. The Exchange Server 2007, Standard

Edition is the basic message server version of the software. The Standard Edition supports five data stores. The Standard Edition has full support for web access, mobile access, and server recovery functionality.

The Standard Edition is a good version of Exchange to support a messaging system for a small organization, or as a dedicated Edge Transport, Hub Transport, or Client Access server for a larger environment. Many small and medium-sized organizations find the capabilities of the Standard Edition sufficient for most messaging server services, and even large organizations use the Standard Edition for message routing servers or as the primary server in a remote office. The Standard Edition meets the needs of effectively any environment wherein a server with a limited database storage capacity is sufficient.

Expanding into the Exchange Server 2007 Enterprise Edition

The Exchange Server 2007, Enterprise Edition is focused at server systems that require more Exchange messaging databases and support for clustering for higher availability. With support for up to 50 databases per server, the Enterprise Edition of Exchange 2007 is the appropriate version of messaging system for organizations that have a lot of mailboxes or a lot of mail storage. The Enterprise Edition is also appropriate for an organization that wants to set up clustering for higher reliability and redundancy of the Exchange environment.

Table 1.1 summarizes the differences between the Standard and Enterprise Editions.

TABLE 1.1   Exchange 2007 Standard Versus Enterprise Editions

Exchange 2007 Function	Standard Edition	Enterprise Edition
Number of data stores supported	5	50
Clustering support	No	Yes
OS support	Windows 2003 x64-bit	Windows 2003 x64-bit

Exchange Enterprise CAL Versus Standard CAL

The basic differences of the Exchange Enterprise versus Standard server editions is the differing number of databases supported and higher availability clustering support. Beyond these basic differences, Exchange 2007 introduces an Enterprise client access license (CAL) and a Standard CAL. Either CAL can be used against either server edition and has no association between the server versions. Rather, the Enterprise CAL adds functionality such as providing the user a license for unified messaging (voice mail in Exchange 2007), per user journaling for archiving and compliance support, and the ability to use Exchange hosted services for message filtering (known as FrontBridge), or providing enhanced antispam and antivirus functionality using ForeFront Security for Exchange.

Organizations that had software assurance for Exchange will get upgraded to the Standard Exchange 2007 CAL, and those that want to add on unified messaging as well as the new journaling, antivirus, and antispam technologies can upgrade their licenses to the Enterprise CAL license.

What's New in Exchange Server 2007?

Exchange Server 2007, being the sixth major release of the Exchange Server product, adds to the existing technology base that more recent versions of Exchange, such as Exchange 2000 and Exchange 2003, had developed. Exchange administrators familiar with Exchange 2000 and 2003 will find that Exchange 2007 is about 70% to 80% the same; however, the 20% to 30% that is different is drastically different and requires some relearning of the changes.

What's the Same Between Exchange 2000/2003 and Exchange Server 2007?

The core infrastructure of Exchange 2000 and 2003 versus Exchange 2007 is basically the same. Microsoft continues to use the Jet EDB database as the main database store. Some time ago, it was rumored that Microsoft would migrate Exchange to run off SQL Server; however, neither Exchange 2007 nor versions coming out from Microsoft in the foreseeable future will change the basic EDB database structure.

Exchange 2007 still has the concept of a Mailbox server where EDBs are stored, and where user mailbox data resides. Storage groups remain the same where databases are created, and then databases are grouped together in storage groups to combine the management tasks of databases into common groupings.

Users can use the Microsoft Outlook client and can access Exchange using OWA, as shown in Figure 1.1, for browser-based access, as well as synchronize with Exchange from their Windows Mobile and Pocket PC mobile devices.

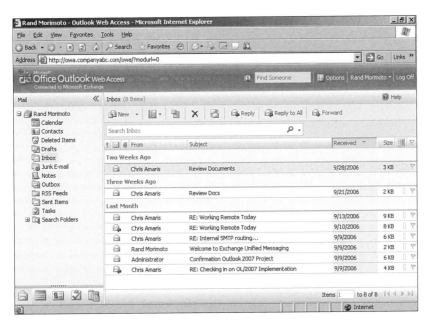

FIGURE 1.1   The new Outlook Web Access in Exchange Server 2007.

Exchange 2007 still uses the VSSBackup application programming interface (API) to freeze the state of the Exchange database to perform a backup of the Exchange database.

One of the most important things that the users of an Exchange 2007 environment who get migrated from Exchange 2000 or 2003 to Exchange 2007 will notice is nothing new or different from the end-user standpoint, assuming you keep the same Outlook client that the user has been using. A migration from Exchange 2000 and 2003 to Exchange 2007 does not require an upgrade to the Outlook 2007 client. Effectively, the user's mailbox is moved from an old server to a new server, and the user still has the exact same look, feel, and functionality as they had with Exchange 2000 and 2003. This seamless cutover of user mailboxes, covered in Chapter 16, "Migrating to Exchange Server 2007," makes user interruption a nonissue as part of the migration process. Users will notice enhanced features with the new OWA, and when their systems are upgraded to Outlook 2007.

What's Missing in Exchange Server 2007 That Was in Previous Versions?

A common question that is asked is "What is missing in Exchange 2007 that was in previous versions of Exchange?" Although the balance of this section of the chapter covers the new features—which could arguably be said to be missing because they have drastically changed—this portion of the chapter focuses on things that are completely gone or do not exist in Exchange 2007.

Relative to Exchange databases, the STM database has been removed, so Exchange is now back to just the EDB database as it was in Exchange 2000 and prior versions. Rather than completely removing the STM database, Microsoft incorporated the streaming data technology into the new EDB database, so instead of having two databases for each mailbox and trying to reconcile the storage of information within those two databases, the combined mailbox database is now the standard.

From an administration standpoint, the concept of administrative groups and routing groups has been completely removed. Administrative groups were introduced with Exchange 2000 as a method of grouping together users to identify who would manage and administer groups of mailboxes. Administrative groups were brought forward from Exchange 5.5 where administration was done based on sites connected by site connectors. In Exchange 2007, administration is now completely consolidated into an enterprise view of users and mailboxes. The administration of the users and mailboxes is handled as delegated rights of administrators, not by a group of users and servers. So, rather than grouping together servers and users into special containers, an administrator is merely assigned rights to manage specific users, mailboxes, servers, or preexisting containers.

As noted in the preceding paragraph, routing groups have also been removed. Rather than having to group servers by routing groups, Exchange 2007 has done away with separate routing groups within Exchange. Instead, the Active Directory Sites and Services now uses its configuration to determine organizational sites and the routing of message communications to those sites.

With the release of Exchange 2007, Microsoft has noted that public folders are being deemphasized, which basically means they are still there in Exchange 2007, but will be completely going away in a future version of Exchange. What you will find is when you install Exchange 2007 from scratch, public folders are not created at all. You need to manually add public folders to a Mailbox server and extend public folder access from the server system. During a migration, if the organization has public folders, they will continue to operate in Exchange 2007. Public folders, however, have not been improved in Exchange 2007. Their support is there, but no changes were made in the way public folders work or the features and functions of public folders. Microsoft has created excellent hooks between Exchange 2007 and SharePoint 2007 that allow a user to click on what used to be a folder for public folders, but instead a SharePoint share is rendered in the user's Outlook or OWA screen. You can do pretty much everything you were able to do with public folders with SharePoint 2007—and then some. More on SharePoint integration with Exchange 2007 is covered in Chapter 25, "Collaborating Within an Exchange Environment Using Microsoft Office SharePoint Portal Server 2007."

Several things have drastically changed in Exchange 2007, such as a completely new Exchange administration tool, a new Exchange server scripting language, and the removal of front-end and bridgehead servers with new server roles that will be covered in the next handful of sections.

Exploring the New Exchange Management Console

One of the first things an administrator will notice and have to relearn is the new Microsoft Exchange Management Console, or EMC tool, shown in Figure 1.2, which is used for administering and managing the Exchange 2007 environment. The Exchange Management Console looks nothing like the old Exchange Systems Manager. Microsoft made a drastic departure from the administrative tree structure used with Exchange for the past decade and, instead, revamped the entire structure to be focused to the way Exchange is managed and administered in the real world.

Rather than organizing users and servers by administrative groups and routing groups that broke up an organization and made it difficult for the enterprise Exchange administrators to see all users and all servers in the organization, Exchange 2007 now organizes objects as a whole. The administrator sees all users, all servers, and all resources in the Exchange organization in a single view. The Exchange administrator(s) can regroup users, computers, and resources into smaller delegation groups; however, this is done by filtering views, not by creating fixed containers and groupings. This filtering method of organization objects allows an organization the flexibility to simply change the groupings for administration, management, or operations without having to completely reorganize the entire Exchange architecture.

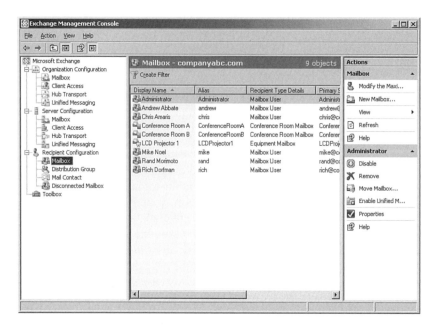

FIGURE 1.2   The new Exchange Management Console.

More on the Exchange Management Console is covered in Chapter 18, "Administering an Exchange Server 2007 Environment."

Providing Exchange Server 2007 on an x64-bit Platform Only

Another major change to Exchange 2007 is that it only runs on an x64-bit platform. Up until this version, Exchange ran primarily on a 32-bit platform, and although 64-bit has been supported, the way the core Exchange environment was designed, 64-bit didn't provide significant improvements until Exchange 2007 became available.

The Microsoft Exchange development team made the decision to go solely to a 64-bit environment because of the significant benefits that 64-bit Windows and 64-bit technologies provide in server scalability and management. One of the biggest problems with earlier versions of Exchange on a 32-bit platform is the support for only 4GB of memory on an Exchange server. Just a few years ago, no one thought 4GB of RAM was a limitation. However, with Exchange and the amount of messaging transactions an organization can send and receive, what is required for an Exchange server to process far exceeded the memory space available in just 4GB of RAM. Because the processing of messages, write transactions to disk, logging for rollback recoverability, and the addition of spam and virus protection takes away from available memory in the system, 4GB would be used up quite quickly.

To compensate for the lack of available memory in 32-bit Exchange, Microsoft Exchange 2003 and prior depended heavily on caching transactions to disk. As an example, for an organization with 5,000 users on an Exchange 2003 server in a large enterprise, the

Exchange 2003 server would have 4GB of RAM and need about 100GB of disk storage to have as available spool memory. In very large enterprises with tens of thousands of users, the Exchange servers could easily take up 500GB or even terabytes of disk space for spooling.

With 64-bit Windows and its support for 8TB of RAM memory, an Exchange 2007 server with 5,000 users now needs 32GB of RAM, but can do with just 5GB or less of spool disk space. Not only does the additional RAM memory eliminate the need for hundreds of gigabytes of spool disk space, the additional memory allows an Exchange 2007 server to support three to six times as many users per server, and provides a 50% to 80% increase in system efficiency of transactions.

Likely, the 64-bit operating system also has proven to provide better support for significantly larger Exchange EDB databases. Most organizations wouldn't think of having an Exchange 2000 or 2003 database greater than 80GB to 100GB in size; however, with a 64-bit operating system, Exchange 2007 supports databases that easily run in the hundreds of gigabyte size.

Server configuration and server optimization are covered in Chapter 3, "Understanding Core Exchange Server 2007 Design Plans," and in Chapter 34, "Optimizing an Exchange Server 2007 Environment."

Improvements in Exchange Server 2007 Relative to Security and Compliance

One of the improvement goals Microsoft has had with all of their products over the past few years has been to constantly improve the security in the products. More recently with all of the regulatory compliance laws and policies being implemented, Microsoft has focused a lot of security enhancements to address privacy, information archiving, and compliance support. The release of Exchange 2007 was no different—Microsoft added in several new enhancements in the areas of security and compliance support.

One of the additions to Exchange 2007 is the creation of an Edge Transport server role that supplements the traditional Exchange database server as a system in the Exchange organization environment. Whereas the Exchange database server holds user data, the Edge Transport server is dedicated to provide first line of defense relative to virus and spam blocking. Organizations with Exchange have had servers in their demilitarized zone (DMZ) typically as SMTP relay servers that collect messages, perform antivirus and anti-spam filtering, and route the messages internal to the organization. However, most of the message relay servers in the DMZ have typically had no tie back to Exchange, so when messages come in for email addresses for individuals who don't even exist in the organization, the DMZ mail relays didn't really have a way to know, so they blindly processed antispam and antivirus checks, and then forwarded messages on to the Exchange server. The Exchange server would realize when individuals did not exist and would bounce or delete the message. This meant that the Exchange server would still have to process hundreds if not thousands or tens of thousands of invalid messages.

The Edge Transport server role, covered in detail in Chapter 8, "Implementing Edge Services for an Exchange Server 2007 Environment," brings forward in a tightly encrypted format specific details out of Active Directory into the Edge Transport server (such as a valid list of email addresses), so that before a message is even processed for spam or virus filtering, the message determines if the recipient even exists in the organization. Only messages destined to valid recipients are processed for antispam and antivirus filtering. In many cases, this means that 50%, 60%, or even 70% of all messages are immediately deleted because a valid recipient does not exist in the organization. A simple rule of this type greatly improves the efficiency of Exchange for routing good messages, not spam.

Another major enhancement in Exchange 2007 is the addition of the Hub Transport server. For many, the Hub Transport server merely replaces the bridgehead server that handled routing in earlier versions of Exchange. However, the Hub Transport server in Exchange 2007 does more than just bridgehead routing, it also acts as the policy compliance management server. Policies can be configured in Exchange 2007 so that after a message is filtered for spam and viruses, the message goes to the policy server to be assessed whether the message meets or fits into any regulated message policy, and appropriate actions are taken. The same is true for outbound messages, that the messages go to the policy server, the content of the message is analyzed, and if the message is determined to meet specific message policy criteria, the message can be routed unchanged, or the message might be held or modified based on the policy. As an example, an organization might want any communications referencing a specific product code name or a message that has content that looks like private health information, such as Social Security number, date of birth, or health records of an individual, to be held so that encryption can be enforced on the message before it continues its route. More details on the role of policy compliance are in Chapter 14, "Understanding Enterprise Policy Enforcement Security," and information on the Hub Transport server role is covered in Chapter 17, "Implementing Client Access and Hub Transport Servers."

Other security enhancements in Exchange 2007 include default server-to-server Transport Layer Security (TLS) for server-to-server traffic so that message communications no longer transmits between Exchange servers unsecured. Even the Edge Transport and Hub Transport servers have the ability to check to see if a destination server supports TLS, and if it does support TLS communications, the transport out of Exchange 2007 is encrypted. More details on server encryption and transport communication encryption are discussed in Chapter 11, "Server and Transport-Level Security," and Chapter 13, "Securing Exchange Server 2007 with ISA Server."

Not new to Exchange 2007, but key in an organization's effort to maintain security and privacy of information is the ability to encrypt email messages and content at the client level. Exchange 2007 encrypts content between the Exchange 2007 server and an Outlook 2007 client by default, and provides full support for certificate-based Public Key Infrastructure (PKI) encryption of mail messages. More details on client-level security and encrypted email are covered in Chapter 10, "Client-Level Secured Messaging," and in Chapter 12, "Encrypting Email Communications with Exchange Server 2007."

Exchange Server 2007 as the Focal Point for Remote and Mobile Communications

Starting with Exchange Server 2003, Microsoft has added significant focus on support for remote and mobile access to Exchange. Remote and mobile access takes on two forms for Exchange: One is in the support of remote access users to Exchange with the improvement of the OWA client and mobile laptop user, and mobility is enhanced in the areas of access and synchronization with Windows Mobile and Pocket PC devices.

Remote access to Exchange has become extremely important as users want to access Exchange outside of the business office, potentially from a home computer, an Internet café kiosk system, or from a laptop they are carrying with them. OWA 2007 is now nearly feature complete compared to the full 32-bit Outlook 2007 client with full support for filters, spell checking, drag and drop of messages, out of office rules management, calendar and contact access, and the like. Many early adopters to Exchange 2007 have found the new OWA so feature complete that when they are remote, they only use OWA as their method to check and manage their messages. More on OWA in Exchange 2007 is covered in Chapter 28 "Leveraging the Capabilities of the Outlook Web Access (OWA) Client."

A new feature of OWA in Exchange 2007 is the remote document access feature. Remote document access is a new function that allows the administrator of a network to share internal network shares through OWA. Normally, for a user to access an internal Universal Naming Convention (UNC) such as \\server\share\, the user needs to be on the local area network (LAN) or they need to have a virtual private network (VPN) connection to securely connect to the network from a remote location. With remote document access, after a user is logged on to OWA, any network shares that the network administrators specifically allow to be accessed using remote document access can be accessed from the remote user, as shown in Figure 1.3. For organizations that have implemented remote document access in Exchange 2007, most have gotten rid of their need for VPNs because between OWA and remote document access, a user can access email, calendar, contacts, and internal file shares. From a security perspective, whatever file-level security has been enabled on the network shares relative to user access are activated as part of the remote access security for the user to the remote document access share privileges.

Additional remote access improvements in Exchange 2007 include just a name change of what used to be called RPC over HTTPS to what is now called Outlook Anywhere. RPC over HTTPS, or Outlook Anywhere, is the ability for a user running Outlook 2003 or Outlook 2007 to connect to an Exchange server using HTTPS and synchronize with the server using 128-bit encryption without using VPN access. The remote connection between the Outlook client and Exchange is encrypted so that the synchronization is protected. Although a VPN connection is no longer needed, Outlook Anywhere also does not require special ports or configurations to be opened up on firewalls or special settings to be configured. Outlook Anywhere uses the same connection address that the organization uses for OWA. So, if users normally type in https://owa.companyabc.com to get access to OWA, the Outlook Anywhere connection point for the Outlook user is also owa.companyabc.com. Between remote document access and Outlook Anywhere, an organization can seriously evaluate whether it needs to continue providing remote VPN access to the network, or possibly provide VPN access to a limited number of users whose remote access needs go beyond the requirements provided by OWA, remote document access, and Outlook Anywhere.

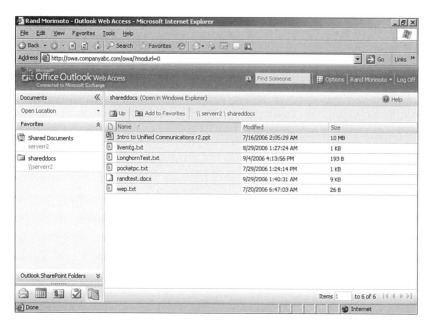

FIGURE 1.3   Remote document access in Exchange Server 2007.

On mobility, Microsoft has greatly enhanced the capabilities of remote access of users who have Windows Mobile and Pocket PC devices. Exchange 2007 had a significant improvement to ActiveSync that extends the direct push function that was included in Exchange 2003 SP2 that has the Exchange server push or send messages to Windows Mobile devices instead of having the Windows Mobile devices constantly poll the Exchange server for new messages. New to Exchange 2007 mobility is the ability for Windows Mobile systems to remotely search for old messages. In the past, a mobile device only had access to the messages that were synchronized by ActiveSync to the device, which usually meant 2–3 days of historical calendar appointments, and only the Inbox for messages. With Exchange 2007, a Windows Mobile device can now query all folders to which the user has access to find messages and download them to the mobile device at any time. In addition, just as OWA has the remote document access feature that brings down files from network shares without setting up a VPN connection, Exchange 2007 provides remote document access to Windows Mobile users. You can find more discussion on mobility in Exchange 2007 in Chapter 23, "Designing and Implementing Mobility in Exchange Server 2007."

Introducing Unified Messaging in Exchange Server 2007

One of the major additions to Exchange 2007 is the addition of unified messaging. Unified messaging is the ability for Exchange 2007 to be the voice mail server for an organization. Rather than having a separate voice mail system connected to the organization's phone system, Exchange 2007 can be integrated into the phone system to be able to take messages on incoming calls, and the messages are stored in the user's Exchange mailbox for playback from the phone or by accessing the message from within Outlook, OWA, or Windows Mobile, as shown in Figure 1.4.

Unified messaging is not new to Exchange; in fact, many organizations, including Cisco Systems, Siemens, Lucent Technologies, and so on, have had voice mail to Exchange add-ons for years. Microsoft claims to not be directly competing against organizations with unified messaging solutions for Exchange already, but rather wants to provide a better infrastructure to support a tightly integrated unified messaging system into Exchange 2007.

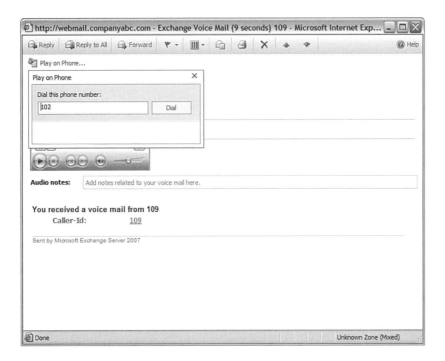

FIGURE 1.4   Voice mail client to Exchange Server 2007 unified messaging.

One of the benefits of unified messaging in Exchange is the concept of a single data store for inbound email messages, voice mail messages, and faxes. Rather than checking Outlook for emails, and calling into a phone voice mail system for voice messages, having all messages go in to Exchange provides a single point of message control. A single point for message access allows Exchange 2007 to provide anywhere access to all messages whether it is from an Outlook client, from OWA, or from a Windows Mobile device.

Unified messaging is significant in Exchange 2007 because it is the foundation that Microsoft will be using to provide unified communications across their entire product line. Over the next few years, Microsoft will more tightly integrate instant messaging (IM), voice over IP (VoIP) telephone integration, videoconferencing, data conferencing, and so forth into a complete, centralized communications system. Today, Microsoft has several new products they have introduced to the marketplace, including Office Communications Server 2007, Office Roundtable, and SharePoint 2007, that integrate technologies together in a unified communications backbone. Exchange 2007 is the first system that is core to the unified communications strategy that Microsoft is setting forward because Exchange is the point of connection for email, contacts, remote access, mobile access, and, now, voice and fax communications.

More information on unified messaging and the capabilities provided out of the box from Microsoft on unified messaging is in Chapter 24, "Designing and Configuring Unified Messaging in Exchange Server 2007."

Making Exchange Server 2007 Extremely Reliable and Recoverable

In addition to security and mobility as core areas in which Microsoft has invested heavily for all of their products, Microsoft has added significant improvements in making Exchange 2007 more reliable and more recoverable. As messaging has become critical to business communications, Exchange 2007 becomes an important component in making sure an organization can effectively communicate between employees as well as from employees to customers, to vendors, to business partners, and to the public. Add voice and fax communications into the new Exchange unified communications strategy, and it becomes even more important that Exchange 2007 is extremely reliable.

With Exchange 2007, Microsoft included a couple new continuous backup and replication technologies that effectively allow Exchange to now hold two copies of a user's mailbox information. In the past, Exchange only had one copy of a user's mailbox sitting in an Exchange database. In the event that the database holding the user's information became corrupt or the server holding the user's information failed, the way to get the user's mailbox back up and running was to typically restore the data to another server. Several hardware and software utility vendors have created snapshot technologies that replicate a user's mailbox information to another server; however, as much as the user's data can be available on another system in another site, the user's Outlook client was still pointing to the old Exchange server where the mailbox used to reside. So, as much as the data was available, business continuity couldn't continue until the user's Outlook profile was changed to redirect the user to the new location of the data.

Exchange 2007 now provides Local Continuous Replication (LCR) and Cluster Continuous Replication (CCR) that effectively has two copies of the user's information on the network. In the case of local continuous replication, the user's data is replicated on a separate drive within a single server, so effectively a server has two databases with a copy of the data stored in each of the databases. This is a good solution in the event of a drive failure, where the second drive and database are available to be mounted and made available to the user. However, in the event of a server or site failure, LCR does nothing to help the organization recover to another location.

CCR provides the replication of the user's mailbox across servers and sites so that if a user's mailbox is lost either because of a hard drive or database failure, a server failure, or the complete loss of a site, a replicated copy of the user's mailbox information resides on another server potentially in another site. Microsoft has made two key improvements in the method of replication: With LCR and CCR, the information is being replicated through a technology known as log shipping. Log shipping means that the 1-MB log files that note the information written to an Exchange server are transferred to another server, and the logs are replayed on that server to build up the content of the secondary system from data known to be accurate. If during a replication cycle a log file does not completely transfer to the remote system, individual log transactions are backed out of the replicated system and events are logged in Exchange to note that some data did not successfully write to the remote system. This means that only valid data is written to Exchange, and any data that did not transfer will either be requested to be resent, or at least a log is kept notifying the administrators that specific information was lost. Unlike bit-level transfers of data between source and destination, in the event of a system failure, bits don't transfer, and Exchange has no idea what the bits were, what to request for a resend of data, or how to notify an administrator what file or content the bits referenced. Microsoft's implementation of log shipping provides organizations a clean method of knowing what was replicated and what was not.

In addition, because log shipping is done with small 1-MB log files, Exchange 2007 replication can be conducted over relatively low-bandwidth connections. Dependent on the amount of data written to an Exchange server, a T1 line is usually adequate and, potentially, fractional T1 lines are enough to successfully keep a source and destination pair server up to date. More details on continuous backup are covered in Chapter 31, "Continuous Backups, Clustering, and Network Load Balancing in Exchange Server 2007," and in Chapter 33, "Recovering from a Disaster in an Exchange Server 2007 Environment."

Another major point about having data come live on a remote system is to redirect a user's Outlook clients to the location of their data. With Outlook 2007, shown in Figure 1.5, Microsoft no longer hard-codes the Mailbox server name to the user's Outlook profile, but rather has the user connect to the client access server (CAS) with merely the user's logon name and password, and the CAS parses Active Directory and Exchange and directs the user's Outlook 2007 client to the appropriate server that is currently hosting the user's mailbox. This automatic swap over at the client level provides the business continuity functionality that is needed in a server failover scenario.

Improving Configuration, Administration, and Management Through the Exchange Management Shell

New to Exchange 2007 is a command-line shell known as Exchange Management Shell, or EMS. The new command-line shell, shown in Figure 1.6, provides an administrator the ability to configure, administer, and manage an Exchange 2007 server environment using text commands instead of solely a graphical user interface (GUI). In fact with Exchange 2007, the GUI administration tool, Exchange Management Console, is nothing more than a front end to the Exchange Management Shell. Every GUI check box or pull-down function executes an EMS script in the back end. Experience with Exchange 2007 has shown that 80% to 90% of an administrator's tasks can be done through the graphic Exchange Management Console; however, on a regular basis, the Exchange administrator has to do things through the scripted interface because a GUI option does not exist. Throughout this book, the various chapters relating to administrative tasks note the EMS text command that needs to be run to perform certain tasks. Chapter 9, "Using the Windows PowerShell in an Exchange Server 2007 Environment," is dedicated to providing details on the Exchange Management Shell.

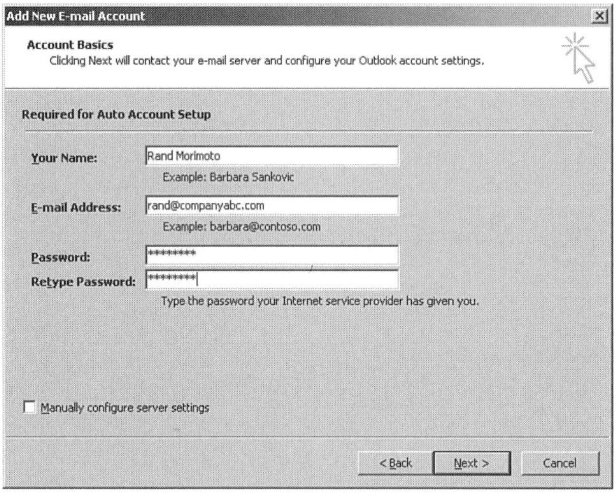

FIGURE 1.5   Automatic client configuration in Outlook 2007.

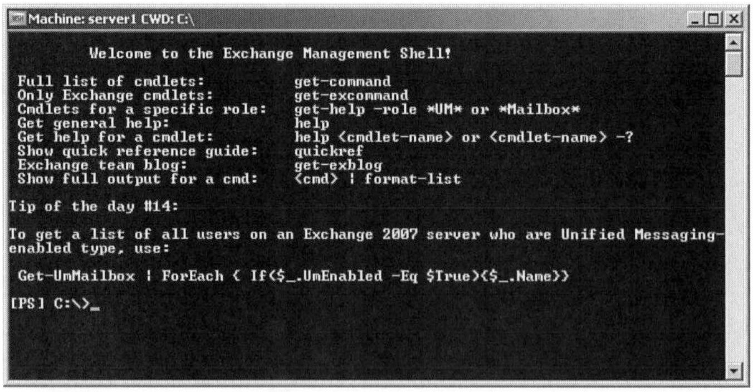

FIGURE 1.6   Sample Exchange Management Shell interface.

Exchange administrators have found that the EMS is very easy to use for day-to-day tasks. For example, tasks such as adding mailboxes or moving mailboxes used to require dozens of key clicks, but can now be scripted and simply cut/pasted into the EMS tool to be executed. As an example, a common task is moving a mailbox to a different database. Through the graphical management console, the task would take dozens of key clicks to move the mailboxes of a group of users. With EMS, it just takes a simple command such as:

```
Get-mailbox –server SERVER1 ¦ move-mailbox -targetdatabase
➥"SERVER2\Mailbox Database 1"
```

By creating a library of commands, an administrator can just search and replace words such as server names, usernames, or other object data, replace it in the command-line script, and then paste the script into EMS to have it execute. EMS is not only a necessity to do many tasks that are not available from the GUI, but it also makes administering and managing Exchange 2007 much easier for redundant tasks or for complex tasks that can be cut and pasted from a script library.

Understanding Exchange Server 2007 Server Roles and Mail Flow

As briefly introduced earlier in this chapter, Exchange 2007 now has several new server roles, where different servers have different specializations. Instead of just having a Mailbox server and a front-end server to host data and provide a connecting point for client systems, these server roles provide improvements in security with servers dedicated to antivirus and antispam functions, message routing and policy compliance functions, and voice mail communications.

Identifying Exchange Server 2007 Server Roles

Each server role in Exchange 2007 provides several functions. The five server roles in Exchange 2007, shown in Figure 1.7, are as follows:

- ▶ Edge Transport server role

- ▶ Hub Transport server role

- ▶ Client Access server role

- ▶ Mailbox server role

- ▶ Unified Messaging server role

The various server roles can be combined onto a single server with the exception of the Edge Transport server role. For security reasons, the Edge Transport server role must be installed on a server that provides no other Exchange server role functions, and is recommended to be a system that provides no other Windows functions to limit the attack surface on the Edge Transport server.

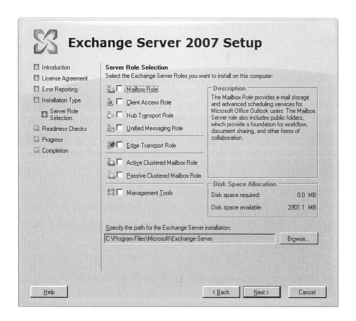

FIGURE 1.7   Server role selection option on Exchange 2007 installation.

Edge Transport Server Role

The Edge Transport server role is a dedicated server function that performs spam and virus filtering as the first point of entry of messages into an Exchange environment. Rather than having unwanted messages go directly to an Exchange back-end server taxing the database server with filtering of messages, the Edge Transport server off-loads this task. Rather than spam and virus filtering thousands of messages for recipients who do not exist in the environment, the Edge Transport server accesses and stores a copy of certain Active Directory data such as all valid Exchange 2007 email recipient mail addresses. This is so incoming messages can be checked against this Active Directory Application Mode (ADAM) directory and messages for recipients who do not exist in the organization are immediately deleted.

In addition, the Edge Transport server role performs a safelist aggregation function as well, where it gathers safelist information from Outlook clients and brings the safelists out to the edge. By bringing individual users' safelists to the edge, the Edge Transport server can now take into consideration individual user preferences to receive certain types of messages so that the messages are forwarded on to the recipient even if the Edge Server's antispam software would normally quarantine or delete the message.

After a first pass at deleting messages for nonexistent recipients, a spam and virus scan can then be run on the remaining messages. After being determined to be clean, the messages can be forwarded on to either a Hub Transport server or to an Exchange 2007 back-end server. More details on the Edge Transport server role are covered in Chapter 8.

Hub Transport Server Role

For those familiar with earlier versions of Exchange, the Hub Transport server role replaces what was formerly known as the bridgehead server. The function of the Hub Transport server is to intelligently route messages within an Exchange 2007 environment. By default, SMTP transport is very inefficient at routing messages to multiple recipients because it takes a message and sends multiple copies throughout an organization. As an example, if a message with a 5-MB attachment is sent to 10 recipients in an SMTP network, typically at the sendmail routing server, the 10 recipients are identified from the directory, and 10 individual 5-MB messages are transmitted from the sendmail server to the mail recipients even if all of the recipients' mailboxes reside on a single server.

The Hub Transport server takes a message destined to multiple recipients, identifies the most efficient route to send the message, and keeps the message intact for multiple recipients to the most appropriate endpoint. So, if all of the recipients are on a single server in a remote location, only one copy of the 5-MB message is transmitted to the remote server. At that server, the message is then broken apart with a copy of the message dropped into each of the recipient's mailboxes at the endpoint.

The Hub Transport server in Exchange 2007 does more than just intelligent bridgehead routing though, it also acts as the policy compliance management server. Policies can be configured in Exchange 2007 so that after a message is filtered for spam and viruses, the message goes to the policy server to be assessed whether the message meets or fits into any regulated message policy, and appropriate actions are taken. The same is true for outbound messages, that the messages go to the policy server, the content of the message is analyzed, and if the message is determined to meet specific message policy criteria, the message can be routed unchanged, or the message can be held or modified based on the policy. As an example, an organization might want any communications referencing a specific product code name, or a message that has content that looks like private health information, such as Social Security number, date of birth, or health records of an individual, to be held or encryption to be enforced on the message before it continues its route. More information on the role of policy compliance is found in Chapter 14, and information on the Hub Transport server role is found in Chapter 17.

Client Access Server Role

The Client Access server role in Exchange 2007 performs many of the tasks that were formerly performed by the Exchange front-end server such as providing a connecting point for client systems. A client system can be an Office Outlook client, a Windows Mobile handheld device, a connecting point for OWA, or a remote laptop user using Outlook Anywhere to perform an encrypted synchronization of their mailbox content.

Unlike a front-end server in previous versions of Exchange that effectively just passed user communications on to the back-end Mailbox server, the CAS does intelligent assessment of where a user's mailbox resides, and then provides the appropriate access and connectivity. This is because Exchange 2007 now has replicated mailbox technology (covered in the

"Making Exchange Server 2007 Extremely Reliable and Recoverable" section earlier in this chapter), where a user's mailbox can be active on a different server in the event of a primary mailbox server failure. By allowing the CAS server to redirect the user to the appropriate destination, there is more flexibility in providing redundancy and recoverability of mailbox access in the event of a system failure. More on the role of the Client Access server role is found in Chapter 17.

Mailbox Server Role

The Mailbox server role is merely a server that holds users' mailbox information. It is the server that has the Exchange EDB databases. However, rather than just being a database server, the Exchange 2007 Mailbox server role can be configured to perform several functions that keep the mailbox data online and replicated. For organizations that want to create high availability for Exchange data, the Mailbox server role systems would likely be clustered, and not just a local cluster with a shared drive (and, thus, a single point of failure on the data), but rather one that uses the new Exchange 2007 cluster continuous replication (CCR) technology.

Cluster continuous replication allows the Exchange server to replicate data transactions between Mailbox servers across a wide area network, or WAN. In the event of a primary Mailbox server failure, the secondary data source can be activated on a redundant server with a second copy of the data intact. Downtime and loss of data can be drastically minimized if not completely eliminated with the ability to replicate mailbox data on a real-time basis. You can find more details on Exchange 2007 Mailbox server recovery in Chapter 31.

Unified Messaging Server Role

A completely new role to Exchange from Microsoft is the Unified Messaging server role. Unified messaging is the ability for Exchange 2007 to be the voice mail server for an organization. Rather than having a separate voice mail system connected to the organization's phone system, an Exchange 2007 unified messaging server can be integrated into the phone system to be able to take messages on incoming calls, and the messages are stored in the users' Exchange mailboxes for playback from the phone or by accessing the message from within Outlook, OWA, or Windows Mobile.

Typically, the Unified Messaging server role will be set up on a dedicated server to isolate the tasks of mailbox management from unified voice communications and routing. However, the Unified Messaging server role can be combined as part of a limited server environment when the performance and separation of tasks is not required in the organization. You can find more information on unified messaging in Chapter 24.

How Messages Get to Exchange from the Internet

To follow the flow of messages in an Exchange 2007 environment with all of the various server roles, the following flow occurs:

1. An incoming message from the Internet first goes to the Edge Transport server.

2. The Edge Transport server performs first-level recipient validation as well as spam and virus filtering. The message is then passed on to the Hub Transport server.

3. The Hub Transport server performs compliance content assessment and then looks at the internal routing for messages and forwards the message to another Hub Transport server or directly to a Mailbox server.

4. The Mailbox server places the incoming message into the user's mailbox and notifies the user that a message has arrived.

5. The user launches Outlook, OWA, their Windows Mobile device, or another client system and connects to the Client Access server. The Client Access server confirms the destination point of the user's mailbox and provides the user access to their mailbox data.

6. In parallel, if a voice mail message comes in for a user, the Unified Messaging server processes the incoming voice message, and then takes the message and places the voice message into the user's mailbox residing on the Mailbox server for the recipient.

How Messages Route Within an Internal Exchange Environment

Internal messages are routed through Exchange in a similar manner. The process for a mail user to send a message to another mail user in the organization or to the Internet is as follows:

1. A message is created by a user in Outlook, on their Windows Mobile device, or on OWA where the user is connected to the Client Access server.

2. The message is stored on the user's Mailbox server as an Outbox message and, likely, a copy is stored in the user's Sent Items folder on the Mailbox server.

3. The Mailbox server then typically sends the message to a Hub Transport server that performs compliance content assessment and then looks at the internal routing for messages and forwards the message to another Hub Transport server, directly to a Mailbox server, or out to the Internet.

4. For internal messages, the Mailbox server places the incoming message into the user's mailbox and notifies the user that a message has arrived.

5. The message recipient launches Outlook, OWA, their Windows Mobile device, or another client system and connects to the Client Access server. The Client Access server confirms the destination point of the user's mailbox and provides the user access to their mailbox data.

Understanding the Importance of Active Directory for an Exchange Server 2007 Environment

Unlike previous versions of Exchange that leveraged Active Directory but still had separate components specific to routing of messages or separate administration roles, Exchange 2007 has done away with many of the Exchange-specific functions and now relies heavily on Active Directory. With Exchange 2007, the directory now provides the sole source for users, administrative roles, sites, server locations, and security functions. With this reliance on Active Directory, an Exchange 2007 environment needs to have a very reliable and properly configured Active Directory.

The Role of the Directory in an Exchange Server 2007 Environment

The directory in Active Directory is leveraged by Exchange 2007 to not only act as the lookup point for users' email addresses and contact information, but is now used as an authoritative directory to validate users within the organization. When messages come in from the Internet, rather than being processed for spam and virus filtering, a message is first checked to see if the recipient even exists in the environment. If the recipient is not in Active Directory, the message is quarantined or deleted completely, eliminating the task of processing messages for nonexistent recipients that takes up to 60%, 70%, and even 80% of a server's processing time.

Active Directory works in conjunction with Active Directory Application Mode, or ADAM, using a tool called EdgeSync on an Exchange 2007 Edge Transport server to move a portion of Active Directory to the edge in an encrypted, secure manner. In addition, Active Directory is leveraged on the Hub Transport server to process rules for compliance and regulatory content assessment. Using Active Directory user, group, organizational unit, site, domain, and forest level rules, content can be assessed and filtered at the Hub Transport server level.

The Role of Domain Name System (DNS) for Internal and External Message Routing

Exchange 2007 no longer maintains a separate message routing table nor does it provide a lookup table for servers within an Exchange environment. Rather, Exchange 2007 now uses DNS exclusively to determine name resolution and to identify servers and destination points from which to communicate. Unlike previous versions of Exchange that could still communicate using NetBIOS naming and Windows Internet Naming Service (WINS), Exchange 2007 solely depends on DNS. With the dependence on DNS in Exchange message transport and communications, it is extremely important that DNS is configured properly. More information on DNS is presented in Chapter 6, "Understanding Network Services and Active Directory Domain Controller Placement for Exchange Server 2007."

The Role of Sites in Exchange Server 2007

Exchange 2007 no longer has separate routing rules like routing groups for information on proper routing of messages within an Exchange environment. Rather, Exchange 2007 now uses Active Directory Sites and Services to determine how to route messages and to determine the most efficient route to transport messages within an organization. With the dependence on Active Directory Sites and Services in Exchange message transport and routing, it is extremely important that Active Directory Sites and Services be configured properly. You can find more details on Active Directory Sites and Services in Chapter 6.

Installing and Migrating to Exchange Server 2007

With an overview on what Exchange is and what is new in Exchange 2007, organizations usually turn to understanding how to plan, implement, or migrate to Exchange 2007, and how to administer, manage, and support the environment on an ongoing basis.

Installing Exchange Server 2007 from Scratch

Some organizations choose to install Exchange 2007 from scratch. This might occur for an organization that is new to email, or at least new to Exchange. This is common for an organization that had a different email platform, such as Lotus Notes, Novell GroupWise, or a sendmail/POP3/IMAP messaging system. Other times organizations implement Exchange from scratch is when an organization undergoes a major merger and consolidation and is better off creating the new environment from scratch rather than trying to consolidate or modify an existing environment.

Whatever the case might be, this book begins with design planning and implementation preparation tasks in Chapter 3. This is a good chapter for any size organization to plan and prepare for Exchange. For a larger organization, Chapter 4, "Architecting an Enterprise-Level Exchange Environment," covers the planning and implementation of Exchange 2007 with tips, tricks, and best practices specific to large enterprise environments.

After a design plan has been identified, Chapter 7, "Installing Exchange Server 2007," will help the implementer of Exchange walk through the steps of installing Windows Active Directory, Exchange 2007, and configure the basic server roles as necessary.

Migrating to Exchange Server 2007

For an organization that has an existing Exchange environment, the organization would likely migrate to Exchange 2007. The Exchange migration path is pretty limited. You cannot migrate directly from Exchange Server 5.5 or earlier directly into Exchange 2007. The only supported migrations from Microsoft are migrations from Exchange 2000 Server and Exchange Server 2003 to Exchange 2007. Furthermore, there is no support to perform an in-place upgrade of a server from Exchange 2000 or 2003 to Exchange 2007 primarily because Exchange 2007 runs on an x64-bit platform, and most Exchange servers running Exchange 2000 and 2003 are running on 32-bit platforms.

So because of this limited support, the process of migrating to Exchange 2007 is drastically simplified. There are specific tips, tricks, and best practices created in migrating from Exchange 2000 and Exchange 2003 to Exchange 2007 that help an organization more reliably and more effectively perform their migration. The steps for migration are outlined in Chapter 16.

Managing and Administering Exchange Server 2007

After an Exchange 2007 environment has been properly designed and implemented, the administrators of the organization need to be able to jump in and begin managing and administering the messaging environment. Because Exchange 2007 is more than just email message boxes and calendars, there is more to manage and administer. Chapter 18 goes through the top administrative tasks performed by Exchange administrators, such as adding users, deleting users, moving mailboxes, adding users to distribution lists, and so on. These tasks can now be performed both from the Exchange Management Console GUI and from the Exchange Management Shell command-line interface.

With Exchange 2007, a handful of ongoing management and maintenance tasks have proven to be important in keeping the Exchange environment operational. These management and maintenance tasks are covered in Chapter 19, "Exchange Server 2007 Management and Maintenance Practices." The tasks include daily, weekly, and monthly maintenance routines intended to keep Exchange operational on an ongoing basis.

Monitoring Exchange Using Microsoft Operations Manager (MOM)

Part of any best practice in network systems management is to monitor servers and services to ensure that the system is operating properly, and to provide proactive alerts if something is no longer operating. Chapter 20, "Using Microsoft Operations Manager to Monitor Exchange Server 2007," covers the MOM product used to monitor and alert on Exchange 2007 activities. There is a dedicated Exchange 2007 management pack that provides specific monitoring functions for Exchange 2007.

Summary

This chapter highlighted the new features, functions, migration tools, and management utilities in Exchange Server 2007 that will help administrators take advantage of the capabilities of the new messaging system. An upgrade to Exchange Server 2007 is more than just a simple upgrade from one messaging system to another, but should take into account the new ways Exchange 2007 will be leveraged as the depository for more than just email messages, but also voice and mobile communications.

Planning and implementing a new implementation or an upgrade to Exchange 2007 is an opportunity for the organization to make Exchange 2007 a highly reliable and fully recoverable communications infrastructure environment. The new capabilities of Exchange 2007 allow an organization to change the way users access the system remotely, improve security both in the background and at the client, and have the tools available to maintain, manage, and recover from a disaster.

The steps to proper planning and successful implementation are highlighted throughout this book, with tips, tricks, and best practices noted throughout the chapters.

Best Practices

The following are best practices from this chapter:

▶ Spend a moment to understand what is new in Exchange 2007 and how the focal point of Exchange 2007 as the infrastructure foundation for unified communications requires a rethinking of the current architecture and ultimate redesign of an organization's Exchange environment.

▶ Plan for the implementation of Exchange 2007 by reviewing the architecture recommendations for a basic Exchange configuration environment covered in Chapter 3, with more specific recommendations for larger enterprises covered in Chapter 4.

▶ Use the step-by-step installation procedures for implementing Exchange 2007 covered in Chapter 7.

▶ Use the step-by-step migration process covered in Chapter 16 to properly plan a migration from Exchange 2000 Server and Exchange Server 2003.

▶ Consider using the new Outlook Web Access 2007 not only as a web browser client, but possibly as the primary mail client for many users and as a replacement of the need for VPNs in an organization through the use of the remote document access technology in OWA.

▶ Leverage the Outlook Anywhere functionality to enable remote, full-client Outlook users connectivity to Exchange 2007 without the need to implement VPNs or other secured connection systems.

▶ Implement either Local Continuous Replication or Cluster Continuous Replication covered in Chapter 31 to create a more redundant Exchange environment for fast and fully supported recovery of Exchange mailboxes.

▶ Test the mailbox recovery process highlighted in Chapter 33 to ensure that if you need to recover from mailbox deletion or corruption, you have successfully tested the functionality.

▶ For better Exchange server management, administration, and reporting, review Chapters 18 and 19 on tips and techniques for managing and administering Exchange 2007.

▶ Leverage Microsoft Operations Manager to better proactively monitor and respond to Exchange 2007 operational problems before the problem impacts users.

▶ To minimize spam and unwanted messaging, enable Exchange 2007 Edge Transport servers to perform front-line filtering.

▶ Consider using the Exchange 2007 built-in remote and mobile capabilities for Windows Mobile phones and devices for the communication of messages, calendars, and contacts.

▶ Review exiting enterprise configurations for network settings that can be modified or reconfigured with an upgrade to Exchange 2007.

CHAPTER 2

Best Practices at Planning, Prototyping, Migrating, and Deploying Exchange Server 2007

Building a new messaging environment or upgrading an existing one can be both an exciting time and a stressful time for an administrator. Messaging has changed drastically over the years from an occasionally used way to send short messages to a complete collaboration tool that sends hundreds of times more messages each day than the U.S. Post Office. Users depend on Exchange to track their tasks, keep their appointments, store important pieces of information, and communicate quickly and easily with co-workers and vendors. As users become more dependent on these types of tools, their requirements increase in terms of accessibility and reliability. The ultimate goal of the end users is for email to be much like the telephone. They never want to have to think twice about whether they'll have access to it and whether they'll get a dial tone. Proper planning is the key to being able to deliver this level of functionality and reliability. This chapter helps the Exchange administrator to properly plan out their build or upgrade through standardized processes of planning, prototyping, and migrating or deploying Microsoft Exchange Server 2007.

Email has become a business-critical tool and, as such, the upgrade process should not be taken lightly. Although an upgrade from Exchange 2000 Server or Exchange Server 2003 might at first appear to be a simple process, its success relies on your understanding of current issues with the messaging environment, defining both the objectives of the upgrade and its potential effects on the user community. Adding more features and complexity to the messaging "ecosystem" might not result in ecstatic users, but reducing spam and the resulting impact on Inboxes might more than justify the cost of the upgrade. Reducing the number of milliseconds it takes to send an email probably won't get noticed, but being able to guarantee access to email anywhere and anytime should. Be aware of who your audience is for the upgrade and make sure you understand their existing pain points and how they use Exchange and Outlook. An enthusiastic user community tends to generate support and momentum for projects, which allows you to extend the functionality of the messaging system and increase the productivity of your users. Productive users result in happy management. Happy management results in project approval. It's a very positive circle to create.

Important decisions include whether the entire network operating system (NOS) needs to be upgraded (if Active Directory [AD] is not yet in place) or only a subset of it, and what other infrastructure components need to be changed or replaced. It is also very important to realize that Exchange 2007 is a 64-bit application and, therefore, needs a 64-bit operating system and 64-bit hardware to run. This means that some of your existing tools or integrated applications might or might not work. Testing cannot be underestimated in this process.

The examples used in this chapter assume that the environments being migrated are primarily based on Exchange 2000 or Exchange 2003, and except where noted that Active Directory is already in place. Please note that an Exchange environment must be in Exchange 2000 Native mode or higher. Exchange 2007 cannot be introduced into an organization that still has Exchange Server 5.5 servers. This would require migrating into a new forest and is discussed later in this chapter. The same process can be applied to other messaging migration projects, such as GroupWise or Notes. The migration process is covered in detail in Chapters 15, "Migrating from Windows 2000 Server to Windows Server 2003," and 16, "Migrating to Exchange Server 2007."

Initiation, Planning, Testing, and Pilot: The Four Phases to the Upgrade

This chapter presents a structured process for upgrading to Exchange Server 2007 and highlights some best practice recommendations to enhance the success of the project. The standard project management phases of *initiation*, *planning*, *testing*, and *implementation* can be used for organizations of any size and can be applied to most any information technology (IT) project. Transitioning each phase is a "go/no-go" step, in which the results of the phase are reviewed, and the decision makers determine whether the project should move forward. Any problems that were encountered are assessed to determine whether they require attention before moving forward. This ensures that issues identified are addressed, rather than being overlooked, to inevitably crop up at the worst possible moment. You can also use this go/no-go point to feedback results of the testing back into your plans. If you determine that something will be an issue when rolled out, take the fix for the issue and work it back into your process. Now retest with the altered procedure to make sure it works as expected. In this way, you will eventually reach a production rollout with no surprises.

Documentation Required During the Phases

A number of documents are produced during each phase to ensure that the phase is well defined and ultimately successful. In the initiation phase, the goals and requirements of the project can be identified and documented in a *Statement of Work* document. In the planning phase, more time and energy can be applied to detailing the end state of the migration into a *Design* document, including the majority of the technical decisions. Although this document paints the picture of what the end state will look like, the road map of how to get there is detailed in the *Project Schedule and Migration* documents. These documents are only drafts during this phase, because they need to be validated in the prototype phase before they can be considered "final."

The prototype phase validates that the new technologies will effectively meet the organization's needs, and determines whether modifications to the project are needed. Any additional documents that would help with the implementation process, such as *Server Build* documents, *Business Continuity* or *Disaster Recovery* documents, and checklists for workstation configurations are also created during the testing phase. Finally, the appropriate *Maintenance* documents are created during the prototype phase so that they can be properly tested without impacting production users. These phases and the documents to be created are discussed in more detail later in this chapter.

The following list summarizes the standard phases of an Exchange Server 2007 upgrade and the standard documents created in each phase:

- ▶ **Initiation phase**—Statement of Work document that reflects the goals and objectives of the key stakeholders of the project

- ▶ **Planning phase**—Design Document Draft, Migration Document Draft, and Migration Schedule Draft (Gantt chart)

- ▶ **Prototype phase**—Design Document Final, Migration Document Final, Migration Schedule Final (Gantt chart), Server Build Documents, Migration Checklists, Maintenance Documents, and Training Documents for end users and administrators

- ▶ **Implementation phase**—As-built documents for all servers

For smaller environments, not all of these items are required, but it's important to have each document created *before* it is needed, to avoid delays during the migration process. For example, having a Statement of Work document that is well constructed and agreed upon in the initiation phase clears the way for the creation of the Design document and Migration document. A detailed Migration Schedule Gantt chart facilitates scheduling of resources for the actual work and clarifies the roles and responsibilities. Remember to have the appropriate groups review the documentation and get their approval to consider the document "done." This avoids potential issues in which a group might change their minds and claim they never agreed to a design decision or migration process.

Initiation Phase: Defining the Scope and Goals

Upgrading to Exchange Server 2007 can be a simple process for basic messaging environments, or as challenging as a complete network operating system upgrade for more complex organizations. In most environments, Exchange is implemented on multiple servers, and an upgrade affects a number of other software applications. In fact, changes to the Exchange environment might affect the daily lives of the employees to a much greater extent than moving from Windows NT to Windows Server 2003 (or even more than an upgrade from a non-Microsoft environment) because they will most likely receive a new Outlook client and change the way they access email remotely. With an operating system upgrade, the end users often don't even know that anything has changed.

The upgrade process is also a great opportunity to help the business achieve its business objectives by leveraging the messaging components of the technology infrastructure and to help justify the never-ending IT expenses. Messaging, in essence, enables the sharing of information and access to data and other resources within the company to help the company deliver its products or services. With this critical purpose in mind, it makes sense to engage in a structured and organized process to determine the goals of the project, control the variables and risks involved, and make sure that a clear definition of the end state has been crafted. The Statement of Work is the key deliverable from this phase that paints the overall picture of the upgrade project and gains support from the key decision makers (and allocates an initial budget).

Be sure to take into account any regulatory compliances that you need to maintain. This includes things such as HIPAA, Sarbanes-Oxley, or the Gramm-Leach-Bliley Act. These types of regulatory compliances will likely influence your decisions about how your systems will be deployed and managed. It is much easier to account for these requirements during the planning phase than it is after you've deployed Exchange 2007.

The Scope of the Project

Before the entire Statement of Work can be written, time should be allocated to define the scope of the project. The scope of the project simply defines what is included in the project and what is not. For a simpler environment, this might be very easy to define—for example, an environment in which there is only one Exchange server used for email and scheduling, with a dedicated backup device and virus-protection software. If this organization has not migrated to Active Directory yet, the scope might expand to include the upgrade of additional servers or simply upgrade the single server. Depending on the version of Active Directory in place, there would likely be a schema updated in the scope as well. A desktop upgrade might be included in the scope of the project if the features and benefits of Outlook 2003 are desired. In any case, it's important to clarify this level of detail at the beginning of the planning process. "Scope creep" is a lot more manageable if it can be predicted in advance! If the scope starts to grow to be out of hand, consider breaking it up into multiple projects. For example, if you have a large upgrade to Exchange 2007, you can split off the upgrading of desktops to Outlook 2007 to be a separate project. This can also help prevent a project from stalling out because of too many dependencies on other groups or projects.

> **NOTE**
>
> An example of a scope of work for a small organization is as follows:
>
> ▶ Upgrade the Exchange 2000 Windows 2000 server to Exchange Server 2007 with Windows Server 2003 64-bit.
>
> ▶ Upgrade the tape backup and virus-protection software to Exchange Server 2007–compatible versions.
>
> ▶ Upgrade the Outlook client to Outlook 2007 on all workstations.
>
> ▶ Provide Outlook Web Access (OWA) access to all remote users.

In a larger company, "what's in" and "what's out" can be significantly more complicated. A company with multiple servers dedicated to Exchange functions—such as front-end and back-end servers, bridgehead servers, or servers dedicated to faxing or conferencing—requires the scope definition to get that much more detailed. Multiple sites and even different messaging systems complicate the scope, especially if the company has grown via mergers over the last few years. Odds are that larger environments will have a mix of hardware ranging in age from 0 to 3 years old. Given that most of the servers sold more than 1.5 years ago are likely not 64-bit capable, a large rollout of new servers is very likely.

> **NOTE**
>
> An example of a scope of work for a larger organization is as follows:
>
> ▶ Upgrade the four Exchange 2003 Windows 2003 servers to two Exchange Server 2007 CCR pairs on Windows Server 2003 64-bit.
>
> ▶ Replace the two Exchange 2003 Windows 2003 front-end servers with 64-bit hardware, Windows 2003 64-bit and install the Exchange 2007 Client Access server role.
>
> ▶ Migrate the Mailbox server locally attached databases to storage area network (SAN)–attached disks.
>
> ▶ Upgrade the enterprise tape backup and virus-protection software on all servers to the latest versions that are Windows Server 2003–compatible and Exchange Server 2007–compatible.
>
> ▶ Implement unified messaging on Exchange 2007.
>
> ▶ Upgrade the Outlook client to Outlook 2007. Provide OWA access to all remote users.

The scope of work might change as the initiation phase continues and in the more detailed planning phase as the Design and Migration documents are created and reviewed. This is especially true for more complex migration projects after the detailed planning phase is completed and the all-important budget is created. At this point, the scope might need to be reduced, so that the budget requested can be reduced.

It is in your best interest to circulate your plans among other groups not only to get their buy-in on the migration, but also to give them a chance to see how it might impact their projects. Often, the group managing the phone systems will look at a project like an Exchange 2007 upgrade and take the opportunity to make changes to their systems to further integrate with Exchange. Knowing about these integration plans early in your process makes it easier to accept them. Altering a deployed environment after the fact is almost always more expensive and more complicated. Do everything you can to keep your project stable and uneventful.

Identifying the Goals

As a next step in the initiation phase, it helps to spend time clearly identifying the goals of the project before getting too caught up in the technical details. All too often, everyone runs up the whiteboard and starts scribbling and debating technology before agreeing on the goals. Although this conversation is healthy and necessary, it should be part of the planning phase, after the high-level goals for the project and initial scope have been defined. Even if there is a very short timeline for the project, the goals—from high-level business objectives, to departmental goals, to the specific technology goals—should be specified.

It is important to have the correct audience in the goal-setting phase of the initiation phase. This will likely be the meeting with the largest attendance. Try to gather goals and objectives from groups such as the following:

- Information technology
- Help desk
- Upper management
- Business unit representatives
- Telecom
- Enterprise backup

By talking to this diverse group of people, you can capture existing pain points of the users and maintainers of the messaging environment and try to alleviate those issues. You can also get a much more accurate feel for how your end users actually utilize Exchange and ensure that you account for those items.

One of the biggest values you get out of clearly identifying your goals is that it simplifies the technical decisions that will be made later. Anytime there is contention around a given decision, you can always ask yourself "Does this decision support my originally stated goals?" and if not, it is probably not the right decision.

High-Level Business Goals

The vision statement of an organization is an excellent place to start because it tells the world where the company excels and what differentiates that company from its competitors. There will typically be several key objectives behind this vision, which are not so publicly stated, that can be related to the Exchange Server 2007 upgrade. These should be uncovered and clarified, or it will be difficult, if not impossible, to judge whether the project succeeds or fails from a business standpoint.

> **NOTE**
>
> High-level business goals that pertain to an Exchange Server 2007 upgrade can include better leveraging company knowledge and resources through efficient communications and collaboration, controlling IT costs to lower overhead and enable products to be more competitively priced, or improving security to meet governmental requirements. An IT group that understands these larger goals and can serve as an enabler for business practices through technology is an amazing asset to a company.

Although this process sounds basic, it might be more difficult if the company hasn't documented or updated its business objectives in some time (or *ever*). Different divisions of larger companies might even have conflicting business goals, which can make matters more complicated. High-level business goals of a company can also change rapidly, whether in response to changing economic conditions or as affected by a new key stakeholder or leader in the company. So even if a company has a standard vision statement in place, it is worth taking the time to review and ensure that it still accurately reflects the opinions of the key stakeholders.

This process helps clarify how the messaging upgrade fits into the overall company strategy and should help ensure that support will be there to approve the project and keep its momentum going. In this time of economic uncertainty, a project must be strategic and directly influence the delivery of the company's services and products; otherwise, the danger exists of a key stakeholder "pulling the plug" at the first sign of trouble or shifting attention to a more urgent project.

For example, a consulting organization might have a stated vision of providing the latest and greatest processes and information to its clients, and the internal goal could be to make its internal assets (data) available to all employees at all times to best leverage the knowledge gained in other engagements. The Exchange environment plays a key role in meeting this goal because employees have become so dependent on Outlook for communicating and organizing information and many of the employees rely on portable devices such as Pocket PCs devices.

A different company, one which specializes in providing low-cost products to the marketplace, might have an internal goal of cost control, which can be met by Exchange Server 2007 through reduction in the total server count and more cost-effective management to help reduce downtime. For this company, user productivity is measured carefully, and the enhancements in the Outlook 2007 client would contribute positively.

High-Level Messaging Goals

At this point, the business goals that will guide and justify the Exchange upgrade should be clearly defined, and the manner in which Exchange Server 2007's enhanced features will be valuable to the company are starting to become clear. The discussion can now turn to learning from key stakeholders what goals they have that are specific to the messaging environment that will be put in place and how Exchange 2007 might improve their day-to-day business processes.

The high-level goals tend to come up immediately, and be fairly vague in nature; but they can be clarified to determine the specific requirements. A CEO of the company might simply state "I need access to all of my email and calendar data from anywhere." The CTO of the same company might request "zero downtime of the Exchange servers and easy integration with other automated business systems." The CFO might want to "reduce the costs of the email system and associated technologies." If the managers in different departments are involved in the conversation, a second level of goals might well be expressed. The IT manager might want four-node clustering, the ability to restore a single user's mailbox, and reduced user complaints about spam and performance. The marketing manager might want better tools to organize the ever-increasing amount of "stuff" in his employees' Inboxes and mail folders.

Time spent gathering this information helps ensure that the project is successful and the technology goals match up with the business goals. It also matters who is spearheading the process and asking the questions because the answers might be very different if asked by the president of the company rather than an outside consultant who has no direct influence over the career of the interviewee. By involving the people whose employees will be most affected by the upgrade and listening to their needs, you can create very powerful allies in getting approval for the technology and hardware necessary to support their goals and objectives.

> **NOTE**
>
> An example of some high-level messaging goals include a desire to have no downtime of the Exchange servers, access to email and calendars from anywhere, better functionality of the OWA client, and increased virus and spam protection.

A specific trend or theme to look for in the expression of these goals is whether they are focused on fixing and stabilizing or on adding new functionality. When a company is fixated on simply "making things work properly," it might make sense to hold off on implementing a variety of new functionality (such as videoconferencing or providing Windows-powered mobile devices using the Pocket PC operating system) at the same time. Make sure you listen to your audience and design an environment that supports their needs and addresses their concerns. Avoid the pitfalls of enabling new functions simply because they seem "cool."

Business Unit or Departmental Messaging Goals

After these higher-level goals have been identified, the conversations can be expanded to include departmental managers and team leads. The results will start to reveal the complexity of the project and the details needed to complete the Statement of Work for the migration project. For an Exchange upgrade project to be completely successful, these individuals, as well as the end users, need to benefit in measurable ways.

Based on the business and technology goals identified thus far, the relative importance of different departments will start to become clear. Some organizations are IT-driven, especially if they are dependent on the network infrastructure to deliver the company's products and services. Others can survive quite well if technology isn't available for a day or even longer.

> **NOTE**
>
> Examples of some departmental goals include a desire to ensure encrypted transmission of human resource and personnel emails, an OWA client that has the same functionality as the Outlook client, and support for Smartphone and Windows Mobile devices. The IT department might also like better mailbox recovery tools and Exchange-specific management tools that can be used from Microsoft Operations Manager (MOM).

All departments use email, but the Sales department might also receive voice mails through the Outlook client and updates on product pricing, and, therefore, need the best possible reliability and performance. This includes ensuring that viruses don't make it into employee Inboxes and that spam be reduced as much as possible.

Certain key executives are rarely in the office and might not be happy with the existing OWA client. They might also carry BlackBerry wireless devices or Windows Mobile phones and need to make sure that they remain fully functional during and after the upgrade.

The Marketing department might use the email system for sharing graphics files via public folders, which have grown to an almost unmanageable size, but this enables them to share the data with strategic partners outside of the company. This practice won't change, and the amount of data to be managed will continue to grow over time.

The Finance and Human Resources departments might be concerned about security and want to make sure that all email information and attached files are as safe as possible when traveling within the organization, or being sent to clients over the Internet.

The IT department could have a very aggressive service level agreement (SLA) to meet and be interested in clustering, reducing the number of servers that need to be managed, and improving the management tools in place. In addition, Exchange Server 2007's integration with Active Directory will facilitate the management of users and groups and additions and changes to existing user information.

In the process of clarifying these goals, the features of the Exchange messaging system that are most important to the different departments and executives should become apparent.

A user focus group might also be helpful, which can be composed of employee volunteers and select managers, to engage in detailed discussions and brainstorming sessions. In this way, the end users can participate in the initial planning process and help influence the decisions that will affect their day-to-day work experience. New features offered by the

Outlook 2007 client include the Exchange Cached mode, optimized network traffic with data compression, and an improved Outlook 2007 client and OWA capabilities.

Other outcomes of these discussions should include an understanding of which stakeholders will be involved in the project and the goals that are primary for each person and each department. A sense of excitement should start to build over the possibilities presented by the new technologies that will be introduced to make managers' lives easier and workers' days more productive.

This process also serves an additional benefit of giving people a sense of how big the project really is and where they'll see the benefits that affect them the most. A major change like an Exchange upgrade should always be well communicated to the end-user community so that they will know what changes to expect, when to expect them, and how to prepare for them.

Initiation Phase: Creating the Statement of Work

Executives generally require a documented Statement of Work that reflects strategic thinking, an understanding of the goals and objectives of the organization, and a sense of confidence that the project will be successful and beneficial to the company. The document needs to be clear and specific and keep its audience in mind. This generally means not going into too much technical detail in the Statement of Work. This document also needs to give an estimate of the duration of the project, the costs involved, and the resources required. The document should be written such that it can be understood by someone who knows nothing about the technology that is being proposed.

The initial scope of work might have changed and evolved as discussions with the executives, managers, and stakeholders reveal problems that weren't obvious and requirements that hadn't been foreseen. Although the scope started out as a "simple Exchange upgrade," it might have expanded to include an upgrade to Active Directory, the addition of new features for remote access to the messaging environment, the rollout of new 64-bit capable servers or management, and business continuity features.

The following is a standard outline for the Statement of Work document:

1. Scope of Work

2. Goals and Objectives

3. Timeline and Milestones

4. Resources

5. Risks and Assumptions

6. Dependencies

7. Initial Budget

The following sections cover the different components of the Statement of Work. This document is arguably the most important in the entire process because it can convince the executives who hold the purse strings to move forward with the project—or, of course, to stop the project in its tracks.

Summarizing the Scope of Work

At this point in the initiation phase, a number of conversations have occurred that have clarified the basic scope of the project, the high-level business goals as they pertain to the messaging upgrade, and the more specific goals for each department and of key stakeholders. Armed with this wealth of information, the lead consultant on the project should now organize the data to include in the Statement of Work and get sign-off to complete the phase and move to the more detailed planning phase.

The Scope section of the Statement of Work document should answer these essential questions:

▶ How many Exchange and Windows servers need to be upgraded?

▶ Where do these servers reside?

▶ What additional applications need to be upgraded (especially backup, virus protection, disaster recovery, and remote access) as part of the project?

▶ What additional hardware needs to be upgraded or modified to support the new servers and applications (especially tape backup devices, SANs, routers)?

▶ Will laptop configurations be changed? If so, will you need physical access to them?

▶ Will the desktop configurations be changed?

The answers to these questions might still be unclear at this point, and require additional attention during the planning phase.

Summarizing the Goals

As discussed earlier, a number of conversations have been held previously on the topic of goals, so there might be a fairly long list of objectives at this point. A structure to organize these goals is suggested in the following list:

▶ Business continuity/disaster recovery (clustering, storage, backup, and restore)

▶ Performance (memory allocation improvements, public folders, email)

▶ Security (server, email)

▶ Mobility (Outlook Web Access, Pocket PC, and Smartphone support)

▶ Collaboration (real-time collaboration—replacement for Exchange instant messaging—SharePoint Portal)

▶ Serviceability (administration, management, deployment)

▶ Development (Collaboration Data Objects, managed application programming interface [API])

By using a framework such as this, any "holes" in the goals and objectives of the project will be more obvious. Some of the less-glamorous objectives, such as a stable network, data-recovery abilities, or protection from the hostile outside world, might not have been identified in the discussions. This is the time to bring up topics that might have been missed, before moving into the more detailed planning phase.

It might also be valuable to categorize portions of the upgrade as "fixes" for existing pain points as opposed to "new" capabilities that will be added to the environment.

Summarizing the Timeline and Milestones

A bulleted list of tasks is typically all that is needed to help define the time frame for the upgrade, although more complex projects will benefit from a high-level Gantt chart. The time frame should be broken down by phase to clarify how much time is to be allocated for the planning phase and testing phases. The actual implementation of the upgrade also should be estimated. A good rule of thumb at this point is that no task represented on the project plan should have a duration of less then 1 day. If it logically has a shorter duration, it's probably too detailed to call out at this point.

Depending on the complexity of the project, a time frame of 1 to 2 months could be considered a "short" time frame, with 2 to 4 months offering a more comfortable window for projects involving more servers, users, and messaging-related applications. Additional time should be included if an outside consulting firm will assist with part or the entire project. Be sure to account for things such as acquiring hardware, application testing, and shipping of hardware to remote locations. These types of items can often be overlooked yet they can easily add weeks to the timeline of a project like this.

Because every project is different, it's impossible to provide rules for how much time to allocate to which phase. Experience has shown that allocating additional time for the planning and testing phase helps the upgrade go more smoothly, resulting in a happier user base. If little or no planning is done, the testing phase will most likely miss key requirements for the success of the project. Remember also to allocate time during the process for training of the administrative staff and end users.

Be aware of your own internal processes and try to account for them. If your environment requires, for example, that the security group perform a security audit on any server before it is released into production, be sure to account for this in the timeline. Also be sure to let that other group know that you will be submitting a potentially large number of servers for them to audit so that they can also prepare their own resources to be ready for you. Careful teamwork and communication around these types of activities can save a lot of time overall.

The key to successfully meeting a short timeline is to understand the added risks involved and define the scope of the project so that the risks are controlled. This might include putting off some of the functionality that is not essential, or contracting outside assistance to speed up the process and leverage the experience of a firm that has performed similar upgrades many times. Hardware and software procurement can also pose delays, so for shorter time frames, they should be procured as soon as possible after the ideal configuration has been defined. Don't be afraid to make certain portions of the original project "out of scope" and spin them into separate projects. Keeping your project realistic makes it easier to complete successfully.

Summarizing the Resources Required

Typical roles that need to be filled for an Exchange Server 2003 upgrade project include the following:

- ▶ Project sponsor or champion
- ▶ Exchange Server 2007 design consultant
- ▶ Exchange Server 2007 technical lead
- ▶ Exchange Server 2007 consulting engineer
- ▶ Project manager
- ▶ Systems engineer(s)
- ▶ Technical writer
- ▶ Administrative trainer
- ▶ End-user trainer

The organization should objectively consider the experience and skills as well as available time of internal resources before deciding whether outside help is needed. For the most part, few companies completely outsource the whole project, choosing instead to leverage internal resources for the tasks that make sense and hiring external experts for the planning phase and testing phases. Often, internal resources simply can't devote 100% of their energy to planning and testing the messaging technologies because their daily duties get in the way. Contracted resources, on the other hand, are able to focus just on the messaging project. Most successful projects include a mix of internal and external resources. This allows the internal resources to gain valuable knowledge from the external resources and end up with a strong knowledge of their own environment from their direct involvement with the design and deployment.

The resulting messaging environment needs to be supported after the dust settles, so it makes sense for the administrative staff to receive training in the early phases of the upgrade (such as planning and testing) rather than after the implementation. Many consultants provide hands-on training during the testing and implementation phases. It is easier to perform most of the training in the prototype phase because you will have a working environment that doesn't have any users on it. This allows the administrative staff to practice moving mailboxes, recovering data and entire servers, and rebuilding servers from scratch without impacting any production users.

For larger projects, a team might be created for the planning phase, a separate team allocated for the testing phase, and a third team for the implementation. Ideally, the individuals who perform the testing participate in the implementation for reasons of continuity.

Implementation teams can benefit from less-experienced resources for basic server builds and workstation upgrades. By properly assigning the project tasks to the right resources, you can maximize the chances for overall success. By providing for a bit of overlap between tasks and resources, you can also cross-train your staff so that they can more easily support each other.

Summarizing the Risks and Assumptions

More time is spent discussing the details of the risks that could affect the successful outcome of the project during the planning phase; however, if there are immediately obvious risks, they should be included in the Statement of Work.

Basic risks could include the following:

▶ Existing Exchange problems, such as a corrupt database or lack of maintenance

▶ Lack of in-house expertise and bandwidth for the project

▶ Using existing hardware that might not have enough random access memory (RAM), storage capacity, processor speed, or the ability to support a 64-bit operating system

▶ Wide area network (WAN) or local area network (LAN) connectivity issues, making downtime a possibility

▶ A production environment that cannot experience any downtime or financial losses will occur

▶ Customized applications that interface with Exchange Server and that need to be tested and possibly rewritten for Exchange Server 2007

▶ Short timeline that will require cutting corners in the testing process

Summarizing the Initial Budget

The decision makers will want to start getting a sense for the cost of the project, at least for the planning phase of the project. Some information might already be quite clear, such as how many servers need to be purchased. If the existing servers are more than a few years old and don't support a 64-bit operating system, chances are they need to be replaced, and price quotes can easily be gathered for new machines. Software upgrades and licenses can also easily be gathered, and costs for peripheral devices such as tape drives or SANs should be included.

If external help is needed for the planning, testing, and implementation, some educated guesses should be made about the order of magnitude of these costs. Some organizations set aside a percentage of the overall budget for the planning phase, assuming outside assistance, and then determine whether they can do the testing and implementation on their own.

As mentioned previously, training should also not be forgotten for both the administrative staff and the end users.

Getting Approval on the Statement of Work

After the initial information has been presented in the Statement of Work format, formally present it and discuss it with the stakeholders. If the process has gone smoothly this far, the Statement of Work should be approved, or, if not, items that are still unclear can be clarified. After this document has been agreed upon, a great foundation is in place to move forward with the planning phase.

Planning Phase: Discovery

The planning phase enables the Exchange Server 2007 design consultant time to paint the detailed picture of what the end state of the upgrade will look like, and also to detail exactly how the network will evolve to this new state. The goals of the project are clear, what's in and what's out are documented, the resources required are defined, the timeline for the planning phase and an initial sketch of the risks are anticipated, and the budget is estimated.

Understanding the Existing Environment

If an organization has multiple Exchange servers in place, third-party add-on applications, multiple sites, complex remote access, or regulatory security requirements, it makes sense to perform a full network audit. If an outside company is spearheading the planning phase, this is its first real look at the configuration of the existing hardware and network, and it is essential to help create an appropriate end state and migration process. Standard questionnaires are helpful to collect data on the different servers that will be affected by the upgrade. Typically, these questionnaires are sent to the groups that manage the Exchange-related systems in various locations as they generally have the best information on those systems, including any issues or "quirks" they might have.

The discovery process typically starts with onsite interviews with the IT resources responsible for the different areas of the network and proceeds with a hands-on review of the network configuration. Focus groups or whiteboarding sessions can also help dredge up concerns or issues that might not have been shared previously. External consultants often generate better results because they have extensive experience with network reviews and analysis and with predicting the problems that can emerge midway through a project. Consider holding at least some of the interview sessions with only specific groups present. Sometimes, some groups don't want to bring up specific issues with other groups present.

Network performance can be assessed at the same time to predict the level of performance the end users will see and whether they are accessing email, public folders, or calendars from within the company, from home, or from an Internet kiosk in an airport. This is also a great time to get a baseline of system performance and bandwidth consumption. Having this baseline is very important and allows you to accurately rate the new environment. It can be very hard to deal with comments of "the new environment seems slower" if you have no previous performance data to compare it with.

Existing network security policies might be affected by the upgrade, and should be reviewed. If AD is being implemented, group policies—which define user and computer configurations and provide the ability to centralize logon scripts and printer access—can be leveraged.

Anyone using Exchange is familiar with the challenges of effectively managing the data that builds up, and in grooming and maintaining these databases. The existing database structure should be reviewed at least briefly so the Exchange Server 2007 design consultant understands where the databases reside, how many there are and their respective sizes, and whether regular maintenance has been performed. Serious issues with the database(s) crashing in the past should be covered. Methods of backing up this data should also be reviewed.

Desktop configurations should be reviewed if the upgrade involves an upgrade to the Outlook client. If there are a variety of different desktop configurations, operating systems, and models, the testing phase might need to expand to include these.

Disaster recovery plans or SLAs can be vital to the IT department's ability to meet the needs of the user community, and should be available for review at this time.

Remote and mobile connections to the messaging system should be reviewed in this phase as OWA is used by most organizations, as well as Terminal Services, or virtual private networks (VPNs). The features in Exchange Server 2007 might enable the organization to simplify this process; VPNs might not be needed if the design allows Outlook to be accessed via Hypertext Transfer Protocol Secure (HTTPS).

Although the amount of time required for this discovery process varies greatly, the goals are to fully understand the messaging infrastructure in place as the foundation on which the upgrade will be built. New information might come to light in this process that will require modifications to the Statement of Work document. Always review the initial documentation at the end of a phase so that any changes can be fed back into the processes and you can determine if any tests need to be repeated as a result of the changes.

Understanding the Geographic Distribution of Resources

If network diagrams exist, they should be reviewed to make sure they are up to date and contain enough information (such as server names, roles, applications managed, switches, routers, firewalls, IP address information, gateways, and so forth) to fully define the location and function of each device that plays a role in the upgrade. These diagrams can then be modified to show the end state of the project. Also critical to these network diagrams is an understanding of not only the bandwidth rating of the connection, but also the average utilization. Connection latency is also a useful piece of information because improvements in Outlook 2007 and Exchange 2007 might allow you to use configurations that were previously unavailable to you because of high latency on a WAN connection.

Existing utility servers—such as bridgehead servers, front-end servers, domain name system (DNS) naming servers, and Dynamic Host Configuration Protocol (DHCP) or Windows Internet Naming Service (WINS) servers—should be listed in these diagrams as well.

Has connectivity failure been planned for a partial or fully meshed environment? Connections to the outside world and other organizations need to be reviewed and fully understood at the same level, especially with an eye toward the existing security features. If this is an area that can be improved in the new Exchange 2007 design, be sure to track this as a goal of the project.

Companies with multiple sites bring added challenges to the table. As much as possible, the same level of information should be gathered on all the sites that will be involved in and affected by the messaging upgrade. Also, a *centralized* IT environment has different requirements from a *distributed* management model. It's important to fully understand these aspects of the environment to successfully plan for your upgrade.

If time permits, the number of support personnel in each location should be taken into account, as well as their ability to support the new environment. Some smaller sites might not have dedicated support staff and network monitoring, and management tools, such as MOM or Systems Management Server (SMS), might be required.

How is directory information replicated between sites, and what domain design is in place? If the company already has Active Directory in place, is a single domain with a simple organizational unit (OU) structure in place, or are there multiple domains with a complex OU structure? Global catalog placement should also be clarified. Did the existing Exchange environment span multiple administrative groups? Who managed what functions in each administrative group? Is this administrative model going to change in the new Exchange 2007 environment?

The answers to these questions directly shape the design of the solution, the testing phase, and the implementation process. Keep in mind, each decision made in the planning phase needs to support the original goals and objectives of the project. When in doubt, always return to these goals and ask yourself if a particular decision is in line with those goals.

Planning Phase: Creating the Design Document

When the initial discovery work is complete, you can turn your attention to the Design document itself, which paints a detailed picture of the end state of the messaging system upgrade. In essence, this document expands on the Statement of Work document and summarizes the process that was followed and the decisions that were made along the way. When possible, include a little information on what the options were and why a particular decision was made. This helps other people to understand why decisions were made if they were not directly involved in the design process.

The second key deliverable in the planning phase is the Migration document, which tells the story of how the end state will be reached. Typically, these documents are separate, because the Design document gives the "what" and "why" information, and the Migration document gives the "how" and "when" information. This is a good example of writing documents slightly differently based on who the audience will be.

Collaboration Sessions: Making the Design Decisions

Just as the planning phase kicked off with discovery efforts and review of the networking environment, the design phase will start with more meetings with the stakeholders and the project team for collaborative design discussions. This process covers the new features that Exchange Server 2007 offers and how these could be beneficial to the organization as a whole and to specific departments or key users in support of the already defined goals. Typically, several half-day sessions are required to discuss the new features and whether implementing them makes sense. Try to leave a bit of time between sessions to give participants a chance to let the information sink in and make sure there won't be any unintended side effects of a given decision.

By this point in the process, quite a bit of thought has already gone into what the end state will look like and that is reflected in the Statement of Work document. This means that everyone attending these sessions should be on the same page in terms of goals and expectations for the project. If they aren't, this is the time to resolve differing opinions, because the Design document is the plan of record for the results of the messaging upgrade.

The collaborative sessions should be led by someone with hands-on experience in designing and implementing Exchange Server 2007 solutions. This might be an in-house expert or it might be an external consultant. Agendas should be provided in advance to keep the sessions on track and enable attendees to prepare for specific questions. A technical writer should be invited to take notes and start to become familiar with the project as a whole because that individual will most likely be active in creating the Design document and additional documents required.

The specifics of the upgrade should be discussed in depth, especially the role that each server will play in the upgrade. A diagram is typically created during this process (or an existing Visio diagram updated) that defines the locations and roles of all Exchange 2007 servers and any legacy Exchange servers that need to be kept in place. This includes plans for the number of Mailbox servers, the number of Client Access servers needed to support the remote users, the placement of Edge Transport servers to allow for redundancy, and the placement of Hub Transport servers to ensure that mail can be routed efficiently.

The migration process should be discussed as well because it is likely to have the largest impact on the end users. This is the time to account for overlapping projects that might impact your Exchange 2007 rollout. Also pay careful attention to the availability of the resources you defined previously. You don't want any surprises, such as having your Exchange 2007 expert on vacation during the critical phases of your migration.

Disaster Recovery Options

Although a full disaster recovery assessment is most likely out of the scope of the messaging upgrade project, the topic should be covered at this phase in the project. Take this opportunity to review your existing disaster recovery plans for your existing environment and think about how it will need to change with the new design.

Most people would agree that the average organization would be severely affected if the messaging environment were to go offline for an extended period of time. Communications between employees would have to be in person or over the phone, document sharing would be more complex, communication with clients would be affected, and productivity of the remote workforce would suffer. Employees in the field rarely carry pagers any more, and some have even discarded their cell phones, so many employees would be hard to reach. This dependence on messaging makes it critical to adequately cover the topic of disaster recovery as it pertains to the Exchange messaging environment.

Existing SLAs should be reviewed and input gathered on the "real" level of disaster recovery planning and testing that has been completed. Few companies have spent the necessary time and energy to create plans of action for the different failures that could take place, such as power failures in one or more locations, Exchange database corruptions, or server failures. A complete disaster recovery plan should include offsite data and application access as well. For more details on items that should be considered, see Chapter 33, "Recovering from a Disaster in an Exchange Server 2007 Environment."

Design Document Structure

The Design document expands on the content created for the Statement of Work document defined previously, but goes into greater detail and provides historical information on the decisions that were made. This is helpful if questions come up later in the testing or implementation process, such as "Whose idea was that?" or "Why did we make that decision?"

The following is a sample table of contents for the Exchange Server 2007 Design document:

1. Executive Summary

2. Goals and Objectives

   ▶ Business Objectives

   ▶ Departmental Goals

3. Background

   ▶ Overview of Process

   ▶ Summary of Discovery Process

4. Exchange Design

   ▶ Exchange 2007 Design Diagram

   ▶ Exchange Mailbox Server Placement

   ▶ Exchange Client Access Server Placement

   ▶ Exchange Edge Transport Server Placement

▸ Exchange Hub Transport Server Placement

▸ Exchange Unified Messaging Server Placement

▸ Organization (definition of and number of Exchange organizations)

▸ Storage Groups (definition of and number of)

▸ Mixed Mode Versus Native Mode (choice and decision)

▸ Global Catalog Placement (definition and placement)

▸ Recipient Policies (definition and usage)

▸ Server Specifications (recommendations and decisions, role for each server defined, redundancy, disaster recovery options discussed)

▸ Virus Protection (selected product with configuration)

▸ Administrative Model (options defined, and decisions made for level of administration permitted by administrative group)

▸ System Policies (definition and decisions on which policies will be used)

▸ Exchange Monitoring (product selection and features described)

▸ Exchange Backup/Recovery (product selection and features described)

5. Budget Estimate

▸ Hardware and Software Estimate

Executive Summary

The Executive Summary should summarize the high-level solution for the reader in under one page by expanding upon the scope created previously. The importance of the testing phase can be explained and the budget summarized. The goal with this document is to really understand your audience. The executives probably don't care that you are implementing Cluster Continuous Replication, but they might be interested to hear that you are designing for "four 9s" of uptime.

Design Goals and Objectives

Goals and objectives have been discussed earlier in this chapter and should be distilled down to the most important and universal goals. They can be broken down by department if needed. The goals and objectives listed can be used as a checklist of sign-off criteria for the project. The project is complete and successful when the goals are all met.

Background

In the background section, the material gathered in the discovery portion of the planning phase should be included in summary form (details can always be attached as appendixes); also helpful is a brief narrative of the process the project team followed to assemble this document and make the decisions summarized in the design portion of the document.

Agreeing On the Design

When the document is complete, it should be presented to the project stakeholders and reviewed to make sure that it fully meets their requirements and to see whether any additional concerns come up. If there were significant changes since the initiation phase's Statement of Work document, they should be highlighted and reviewed at this point. Again, it is valuable in terms of time and effort to identify any issues at this stage in the project, especially when the Migration document still needs to be created.

Some organizations choose to use the Design document to get competitive proposals from service providers, and having this information levels the playing field and results in proposals that promise the same end results.

Creating the Migration Document

With the Design document completed and agreed to by the decision makers, the Migration document can now be created. There are always different ways to reach the desired Exchange Server 2007 configuration, and the Migration document presents the method best suited to the needs of the organization in terms of timeline, division of labor, and costs. Just like the Design document, the migration plan is based on the goals and objectives defined in the initiation and planning processes. The Migration document makes the project real; it presents specific information on "who does what" in the actual testing and migration process, assigns costs to the resources as applicable, and creates a specific timeline with milestones and due dates. Having accurate information in the migration timeline will make it much easier to ensure that resources, both people and hardware/software, are available in time.

The Migration document should present enough detail about the testing and upgrade process that the resources performing the work have guidance and understand the purpose and goals of each step. The Migration document is not a step-by-step handbook of how to configure the servers, implement the security features, and move mailboxes. The Migration document is still fairly high level, and the resources performing the work need real-world experience and troubleshooting skills.

Additional collaborative meetings might be needed at this point to brainstorm and decide both on the exact steps that will be followed and when the testing and upgrade will be. It is critical to plan the migration as carefully as possible and to always make the decisions that support the goals of the migration process. Remember, the primary goal of the migration isn't just to put a new system into place; your users won't appreciate the new functionality of Exchange 2007 if it was a painful process for them to get there.

Part V of this book, "Migrations and Coexistence with Exchange Server 2007," provides additional information about the various strategies and processes for moving from previous versions of Exchange to Exchange Server 2007.

The Project Schedule

A *project schedule* or *Gantt Chart* is a standard component of the Migration document, and it presents tasks organized by the order in which they need to be completed, in essence creating a detailed road map of how the organization will get from the current state, test the solution, and then implement it.

Other important information is included in the project schedule, such as resources assigned to each task, start dates and durations, key checkpoints, and milestones. Milestones by definition have no duration and represent events such as the arrival of hardware items, sign-off approval on a series of tasks, and similar events. Some additional time should be allocated (contingency time) if possible during the testing phase or between phases, in case stumbling blocks are encountered. This reduces the chances of having to shift the entire project back and potentially throw off the availability of resources.

A good rule of thumb is to have each task line represent at least 4 hours of activities; otherwise, the schedule can become too long and cumbersome. Another good rule is that a task should not be less than 1% of the total project, thus limiting the project to 100 lines. The project schedule is not intended to provide detailed information to the individuals performing the tasks, but to help schedule, budget, and manage the project. Tracking the completion of the project plan items versus time is a great way to quickly spot when you are at risk of falling behind and compromising the timeline.

To create a project schedule, a product such as Microsoft Project is recommended, which facilitates the process of starting with the high-level steps and then filling in the individual tasks. The high-level tasks should be established first and can include testing the server configurations and desktop designs and performing one or more pilot implementations, the upgrade or migration process, and the support phase.

Dependencies can also be created between tasks to clarify that Task 40 needs to be completed before Task 50 can start. A variety of additional tools and reports are built in to see whether resources are overburdened (for example, being expected to work 20 hours in one day), which can be used for *resource leveling*. A *baseline* can also be set, which represents the initial schedule, and then the *actuals* can be tracked and compared to the baseline to see whether the project is ahead or behind schedule.

Microsoft Project is also extremely useful in creating budgetary information and creating what-if scenarios to see how best to allocate the organization's budget for outside assistance, support, or training.

If the timeline is very short, the Gantt chart can be used to see if multiple tasks take place simultaneously or if this will cause conflicts.

Create the Migration Document

With the project schedule completed, the Migration document will come together quite easily because it essentially fills out the "story" told by the Gantt chart. Typically, the Migration document is similar to the structure of the Design document (another reason why many organizations want to combine the two), but the Design document relates the design decisions made and details the end state of the upgrade, and the Migration document details the process and steps to be taken.

The following is a sample table of contents for the Migration document:

1. Executive Summary

2. Goals and Objectives of the Migration Process

3. Background

4. Summary of Migration-Specific Decisions

5. Risks and Assumptions

6. Roles and Responsibilities

7. Timeline and Milestones

8. Training Plan

9. Migration Process

   ▶ Hardware and Software Procurement Process

   ▶ Prototype Proof of Concept Process

   ▶ Server Configuration and Testing

   ▶ Desktop Configuration and Testing

   ▶ Documentation Required from Prototype

   ▶ Pilot Phase(s) Detailed

   ▶ Migration/Upgrade Detailed

   ▶ Support Phase Detailed

   ▶ Support Documentation Detailed

10. Budget Estimate

   ▶ Labor Costs for Prototype Phase

   ▶ Labor Costs for Pilot Phase

   ▶ Labor Costs for Migration/Upgrade Phase

   ▶ Labor Costs for Support Phase

   ▶ Costs for Training

11. Project Schedule (Gantt Chart)

The following sections delve into the information that should be covered in each section. Part V of this book provides in-depth information on the steps involved in migrating to Exchange Server 2007 from Exchange 2003 or Exchange 2000.

Executive Summary

As with the Design document, the executive summary section summarizes what the Migration document covers, the scope of the project, and the budget requested. Again, keep in mind your audience for this summary and what they would be interested in. Avoid being too technical is this summary, focus on the high level of what they are getting from this project and when then can expect to get it.

Goals and Objectives of the Migration Process

The goals and objectives of the migration overlap with those of the overall project, but should focus also on what the goals are for use and development of internal resources and the experience of the user community. A goal of the overall project could be "no interruption of messaging services," and this would certainly be a goal to include in the Migration document. This is one of the reasons that many project management methodologies recommend always having an "end-user advocate" for this type of project.

Subphases of the Migration document have their own specific goals that might not have been included in the Design document. For example, a primary goal of the prototype phase, which takes place in a lab environment so it won't interfere with the production network, is to validate the design and to test compatibility with messaging-related applications. Other goals of the prototype phase can include hands-on training for the migration team, creating documents for configuration of the production servers, and creating and validating the functionality of the desktop configurations.

Background

A summary of the migration-specific decisions should be provided to answer questions such as "Why are we doing it that way?" Because there is always a variety of ways to implement new messaging technologies such as using built-in tools as opposed to using third-party tools. Because a number of conversations will have taken place during the planning phase to compare the merits of one method versus another, it is worth summarizing them early in the document for anyone who wasn't involved in those conversations.

Risks and Assumptions

Risks pertaining to the phases of the migration should be detailed, and, typically, are more specific than in the Design document. For example, a risk of the prototype phase might be that the hardware available won't perform adequately and needs to be upgraded. Faxing, virus protection, or backup software might not meet the requirements of the Design document and, therefore, need upgrading. Custom-designed messaging applications, or Exchange add-ons might turn out not to be Exchange Server 2007 compatible.

Roles and Responsibilities

The Design document focuses on the high-level "who does what"; the Migration document should be much more specific because the budget for labor services is part of this deliverable. Rather than just defining the roles (such as project sponsor, Exchange Server 2007 design specialist, Exchange Server 2007 technical lead, and project manager), the

Migration document specifically indicates the level of involvement of each resource throughout the prototype, pilot, and migration phases. The project sponsor should stay involved throughout the process, and regular project status meetings keep the team on the same page. At this point, everyone involved in the project should know exactly what they are and are not responsible for doing.

The project manager is expected to keep the project on time, on budget, and within scope, but generally needs support from the project sponsor and key stakeholders involved in the project. Depending on how the project manager role is defined, this individual might be either a full-time resource, overseeing the activities on a daily basis, or a part-time resource, measuring the progress, ensuring effective communications, and raising flags when needed. A cautionary note: Expecting the project manager to be a technical resource such as the Exchange Server 2007 technical lead can lead to a conflict of interest and generally does not yield the best results. Projects tend to be more successful if even 10% of an experienced project manager's time can be allocated to assist.

Timeline and Milestones
Specific target dates can be listed, and should be available directly from the project schedule already created. This summary can be very helpful to executives and managers, whereas the Gantt chart contains too much information. Constraints that were identified in the discovery process need to be kept in mind here because there might be important dates (such as the end of the fiscal year), seasonal demands on the company that black out certain date ranges, and key company events or holidays. Again, be aware of other large projects going on in your environment that might impact your timeline. There's no point trying to deploy new servers on the same weekend that the data center will be powered off for facility upgrades.

Training Plan
It is useful during the planning of any upgrade to examine the skill sets of the people who will be performing the upgrade and managing the new environment to see if there are any gaps that need to be filled with training. Often, training happens during the prototype testing process in a hands-on fashion for the project team with the alternate choice being classroom-style training, often provided by an outside company. Also ask yourself if the end users require training to use new client-side tools. Also pay attention to how the new environment will integrate into existing systems such as backup or monitoring. Determine if those groups need any training specific to interact with Exchange 2007 components.

Migration Process
The project schedule Gantt chart line items should be included and expanded upon so that it is clear to the resources doing the work what is expected of them. The information does not need to be on the level of step-by-step instructions, but it should clarify the process and results expected from each task. For example, the Gantt chart might indicate that an Exchange server needs to be configured, and in the Migration document, information would be added about which service pack is to be used for the NOS and for

Exchange, how the hard drives are to be configured, and which additional applications (virus protection, tape backup, faxing, network management) need to be installed.

If the Gantt chart lists a task of, for example, "Configure and test Outlook 2007 on sales workstation," the Migration document gives a similar level of detail: Which image should be used to configure the base workstation configuration, which additional applications and version of Office should be loaded, how the workstation is to be locked down, and what testing process should be followed (is it scripted or will an end user from the department do the testing).

Documentation also should be described in more detail. The Gantt chart might simply list "Create as-Built documents," with *as-built* defined as "document containing key server configuration information and screenshots so that a knowledgeable resource can rebuild the system from scratch."

Sign-off conditions for the prototype phase are important and should be included. Who needs to sign off on the results of the prototype phase to indicate that the goals were all met and that the design agreed upon is ready to be created in the production environment?

Similar levels of information are included for the pilot phase and the all-important migration itself. Typically during the pilot phase, all the upgraded functionality needs to be tested, including remote access to email, voice mail access, BlackBerry and personal information managers, and public folders. Be aware that pilot testing might require external coordination. For example, if you are testing access through OWA in Exchange 2007, you might need to acquire an additional external IP address and arrange to have an address record created in DNS to allow your external testers to reach it without having to disturb your existing OWA systems.

The migration plan should also account for support tasks that need to occur after the Exchange Server 2007 infrastructure is fully in place. If you are using an outside consulting firm for assistance in the design and implementation, you should make sure that they will leave staff onsite for a period of time immediately after the upgrade to be available to support user issues or to troubleshoot any technical issues that crop up.

If documentation is specified as part of the support phase, such as Exchange maintenance documents, disaster recovery plans, or procedural guides, expectations for these documents should be included to help the technical writers make sure the documents are satisfactory.

Budget Estimate

At this point in the process, the budgetary numbers should be within 10%–20% of the final costs, bearing in mind any risks already identified that could affect the budget. Breaking the budget into prototype, pilot, migration, support, and training sections helps the decision makers understand how the budget will be allocated and make adjustments if needed. No matter how much thought has gone into estimating the resources required and risks that could affect the budget, the later phases of the project might change based on the outcome of the prototype phase or the pilot phase.

The Prototype Phase

Depending on the design that was decided on by the organization, the prototype phase varies greatly in complexity and duration. It is still critical to perform a prototype, even for the simplest environments, to validate the design, test the mailbox migration process, and ensure that there won't be any surprises during the actual upgrade. The prototype lab should be isolated from the production network via a virtual LAN (VLAN) or physical separation to avoid interfering with the lives users.

The prototype phase also gives the project team a chance to get acquainted with the new features of Exchange Server 2007 and any new add-on applications that will be used and to configure the hardware in a low-stress environment. If an external company is assisting in this phase, informal or formal knowledge transfer should take place. Ideally, the prototype lab exactly mirrors the final messaging configuration so that training in this environment will be fully applicable to the administration and support skills needed after the upgrade.

Always take advantage of the unique opportunities granted to you in the prototype phase. Because the prototype is built as a replica of the planned production design, you can practice disaster recovery, server deployment, mailbox moves, and application integrations with no concerns about impacting users the way they would be in production.

What Is Needed for the Lab?

At a bare minimum, the lab should include a new Exchange Server 2007 server, one each of the standard desktop and laptop configurations, the tape drive that will be used to back up the public and private Information Stores, and application software as defined in the Design document. Connectivity to the Internet should be available for testing OWA and mobile access. You will also need at least one domain controller that is configured as a global catalog. The preferred method to deploy this domain controller is to promote a spare domain controller in production and after it has fully replicated, remove it from the network and move it to the lab network. After being isolated, seize the Flexible Single Master Operations (FSMO) roles on the lab domain controller. In production, use NTDSUTIL to perform a metadata cleanup to remove the references to the temporary domain controller. In this way, you have an accurate view of Active Directory for the prototype phase. This can be especially helpful because directory problems that would show up in a production migration will appear in the lab.

Existing data stores should be checked for integrity and then imported to Exchange Server 2007 to ensure that the process goes smoothly. Exchange Server 2007 comes with improved mailbox migration tools, which are more resistant to failure when corrupt mailboxes are encountered and are multithreaded for better performance.

> **NOTE**
>
> The recommended route for customers with Exchange 2000 or 2003 servers to get to Exchange 2007 is to install an Exchange 2007 server into the environment and move mailboxes. If hardware availability is limited, consider upgrading one location at a time

and use the "replaced" server as the new Exchange 2007 server in the next site. This assumes the hardware is capable of running Exchange 2007 and is appropriately sized.

If site consolidation or server consolidation are goals of the project, the prototype lab can be used for these purposes. Multiforest connectivity can now be tested, but this requires a Microsoft Identity Integration Services server in one or more of the forests to enable directory synchronization.

Exchange Server 2007 also comes with a number of new tools to aid in the testing and migration process, which are covered in detail in Chapters 15, 16, and 17. These include a prescriptive guide that walks through the deployment process, preparation tools that scan the topology and provide recommendations, and validation tools.

For more complex environments and larger companies, the lab should be kept in place even after the upgrade is completed. Although this requires the purchase of at least one additional Exchange server and related software, it provides a handy environment for testing patches and upgrades to the production environment, performing offline database maintenance, and in worst case scenarios, a server to scavenge from in times of dire need.

Depending on the complexity of the Exchange environment, this long-term lab might potentially be run in a virtual environment. Deploying the lab via VMware allows you to mimic the interactions of multiple servers and server roles on a single box. At the time of this writing, VMware Workstation 5.5 and VMware Server support 64-bit guest operating systems and, therefore, are viable options for an Exchange 2007 lab environment.

After the lab is configured to match the end state documented in the Design document, representative users from different departments with different levels of experience and feature requirements should be brought in and given a chance to play with the desktop configurations and test new features and remote access. Input should be solicited to see whether any changes need to be made to the client configurations or features offered, and to help get a sense for the training and support requirements.

Disaster Recovery Testing

Another important testing process that can be performed prior to implementation of the new solution on the live network is business continuity or disaster recovery testing. Ideally, this was covered in the design process and disaster recovery requirements were included in the design itself. Definitely take advantage of practicing your disaster recovery process in the prototype phase. This is likely your only opportunity to create and destroy servers without regard for impacting end users.

Documentation from the Prototype

During the prototype phase, a number of useful documents can be created that will be useful to the deployment team during the pilot and production upgrade phases, and to the administrators when the upgrade is complete.

As-built documents capture the key configuration information on the Exchange Server 2007 systems so that they can easily be replicated during the upgrade or rebuilt from scratch in case of catastrophic failure. Generally, the as-built documents include actual screenshots of key configuration screens to facilitate data entry. Having carefully prepared as-built documents allows you to go into production with a well-tested build process. Not unlike a disaster recovery situation, you want to simply follow your own instructions during the deployment; you don't want to have to learn as you go.

Assuming that disaster recovery requirements for the project were defined as suggested previously, this is a perfect time to summarize the testing that was performed in the lab and record the steps a knowledgeable administrator should take in the failure scenarios tested.

One last item of value to take out of the prototype phase is a well-documented list of any surprises that came up during the testing. If you tested the move mailbox process from an Exchange 2003 server that was restored from production and you had errors moving mailboxes, you can expect to have these exact same errors in the production move. If you were able to solve the issues in the lab, you should have well-documented notes on how to deal with the same error in production. Being prepared in this manner is the key to a smooth migration.

Final Validation of the Migration Document

When the testing is complete, the migration plan should be reviewed a final time to make sure that the testing process didn't reveal any showstoppers that will require a change in the way the upgrade will take place or in the components of the final messaging solution.

The end users who have had a chance to get their feet wet and play with the new Outlook 2007 client and learn about the new capabilities and enhanced performance of Exchange Server 2007 should be spreading the word by now, and the whole company should be excited for the upgrade!

The Pilot Phase: Deploying Services to a Limited Number of Users

With the testing completed, the Exchange Server 2007 upgrade team has all the tools needed for a successful upgrade, assuming the steps outlined so far in this chapter have been followed. The Design document is updated based on the prototype testing results so that the end state that the executives and decision makers are expecting has been conceptually proven. Unpleasant surprises or frantic midnight emails requesting more budget are nonexistent. The road map of how to get to the end state is created in detail, with the project schedule outlining the sequential steps to be taken and the Migration document providing the details of each step. Documentation on the exact server configurations and desktop configuration are created to assist the systems engineers who will be building and configuring the production hardware.

The project team has gained valuable experience in the safe lab environment, processes have been tested, and the team is brimming with confidence. End users representing the different departments, who tested and approved the proposed desktop configurations, are excited about the new features that will soon be available.

To be on the safe side, a rollback strategy should be clarified, in case unforeseen difficulties are encountered when the new servers are introduced to the network. Disaster recovery testing can also be done as part of the first pilot, so that the processes are tested with a small amount of data and a limited number of users.

The First Server in the Pilot

The pilot phase officially starts when the schema is extended and the first Exchange 2007 server is implemented in the production environment. The same testing and sign-off criteria that were used in the lab environment can be used to verify that the server is functioning properly and coexisting with the present Exchange servers. Surprises might be waiting that will require some troubleshooting because the production environment will add variables that weren't present in the lab, such as large quantities of data consuming bandwidth, non-Windows servers, network management applications, and applications that have nothing to do with messaging but might interfere with Exchange Server 2007.

The migration of the first group of mailboxes is the next test of the thoroughness of the preparation process. Depending on the complexity of the complete design, it might make sense to limit the functionality offered by the first pilot phase to basic Exchange Server 2007 functionality, and make sure that the foundation is stable before adding on the higher-end features, such as voice mail integration, mobile messaging, and faxing. The first server should have virus-protection software and tape backup software installed. Remote access via OWA is an important item to test as soon as possible because there can be complexities involved with demilitarized zone (DMZ) configurations and firewalls.

Choosing the Pilot Group

The first group of users, preferably more than 10, represents a sampling of different types of users. If all members of the first pilot group are in the same department, the feedback won't be as thorough and revealing as it could be if different users from different departments with varied needs and expectations are chosen. It's generally a good idea to avoid managers and executives in the first round, no matter how eager they are, because they will be more likely to be the most demanding, be the least tolerant of interruptions to network functionality, and have the most complex needs.

Although a great deal of testing has taken place already, these initial pilot users should understand that there will most likely be some fine-tuning that needs to take place after their workstations are upgraded; they should allocate time from their workdays to test the upgrades carefully with the systems engineer performing the upgrade. This will correctly set the expectation for the pilot users as well as allow the upgrade team to get the feedback they need before moving into the full migration.

After the initial pilot group is successfully upgraded and functional, the number of users can be increased because the upgrade team will be more efficient and the processes fine-tuned to where they are 99% error free.

For a multisite messaging environment, the pilot process should be carefully constructed to include the additional offices. It might make sense to fully implement Exchange Server 2007 and the related messaging applications in the headquarters before any of the other locations, but issues related to WAN connectivity might crop up later, and then the impact is greater than if a small pilot group is rolled out at HQ and several of the other offices. It is important to plan where the project team and help desk resources will be, and they ideally should travel to the other offices during those pilots, especially if no one from the other office participated in the lab testing phase. Be sure to have sufficient coverage for issues that might arise if the pilot groups span multiple time zones.

The help desk should be ready to support standard user issues, and the impact can be judged for the first few subphases of the pilot. Issues encountered can be collected and tracked in a knowledge base, and the most common issues or questions can be posted on the company intranet or in public folders, or used to create general training for the user community.

Gauging the Success of the Pilot Phase

When the pilot phase is complete, a sampling of the participants should be asked for input on the process and the results. Few companies do this on a formal basis, but the results can be very surprising and educational. Employees should be informed of when the upgrade will take place, that no data will be lost, and that someone will be there to answer questions immediately after the upgrade. Little changes to the workstation environment such as the loss of favorites or shortcuts, or a change in the network resources they have access to can be very distressing and result in disgruntled pilot testers. Your goal is for your employees to be happy about the upgrade experience after it's been done. Their opinions will reach the rest of your users and they'll be a lot more cooperative if they aren't expecting to have problems.

A project team meeting should be organized to share learning points and review the final outcome of the project. The company executives must now make the go-no-go decision for the full migration, so they must be updated on the results of the pilot process.

The Production Migration/Upgrade

When the pilot phase is officially completed and any lingering problems have been resolved with the upgrade process, there will typically be 10%–20% of the total user community upgraded. The project team will have all the tools it needs to complete the remainder of the upgrade without serious issues. Small problems with individual workstations or laptops will probably still occur but the help desk should be familiar with how to handle these issues by this point.

A key event at this point is the migration of large amounts of Exchange data. The public and private Information Stores should be analyzed with `eseutil` and `isinteg`, and complete backup copies should be made in case of serious problems. The project team should make sure that the entire user community is prepared for the migration and that training has been completed by the time a user's workstation is upgraded.

It is helpful to have a checklist for the tasks that need to be completed on the different types of workstations and laptops so that the same steps are taken for each unit, and any issues encountered can be recorded for follow-up if they aren't critical. Laptops will most likely be the most problematic because of the variation in models, features, and user requirements, and because the mobile employees often have unique needs when compared to workers who remain in the office. If home computers need to be upgraded with the Outlook 2007 client and if, for instance, the company VPN is being retired, these visits need to be coordinated.

As with the pilot phase, the satisfaction of the user community should be verified. New public folders or SharePoint discussions can be started, and supplemental training can be offered for users who might need some extra or repeat training.

> **TIP**
>
> If at all possible, get your users to clean up their mailboxes and clear their deleted items prior to the migration. Optimally, this would occur far enough in advance that the deleted items would be older than the retention period. This means that you would have much less data to migrate when the time comes. This can result in a very large time savings. Experience has shown that typically 50% of the data moved in an Exchange migration is Sent Items and Deleted Items.

Decommissioning the Old Exchange Environment

As mentioned previously, some upgrades require legacy Exchange servers to be kept online, if they are running applications that aren't ready or can't be upgraded right away to Exchange Server 2007. Even in environments where the Exchange 2003 or 2000 servers should be completely removed, this should not necessarily be done right away.

Supporting the New Exchange Server 2007 Environment

After the dust has settled and any lingering issues with users or functionality have been resolved, the project team can be officially disbanded and returned to their normal jobs. If they haven't been created already, Exchange Server Maintenance documents should be created to detail the daily, weekly, monthly, and quarterly steps to ensure that the environment is performing normally and the databases are healthy.

If the prototype lab is still in place, this is an ideal testing ground for these processes and for testing patches and new applications. By following the Exchange Server Maintenance documents and keeping up with regular maintenance tasks, you will be much less likely to have issues with your Exchange 2007 environment in the future.

Summary

Someone famous once said, "It's not the destination, it's the journey." In the case of an Exchange 2007 upgrade, or any project for that matter, it's both. This chapter has shown that the key to success in a major undertaking such as an Exchange 2007 upgrade is to follow a strong methodology that accounts for both the journey and the destination.

The use of a discovery phase allows the people who will be involved in the project to gather as much information as they can about the existing state of the environment as well as the needs of the environment. This prepares them to make design decisions that will allow them to support the needs of the business without putting the existing environment at risk.

A design phase allows the group to work interactively to design a new end state that best provides for the needs of the company. A key concept to keep in mind during a design phase is that there is no "one perfect design"—there is only a design that is most appropriate for you and your needs and limitations.

A prototype phase allows you to validate your design and your migration methodologies by testing them in a safe replica environment. This allows you to discover potential problems before they come up in a production migration. Always take advantage of the prototype phase to try out the "what-if" questions that will result in you and your team having a stronger knowledge of how the new environment will work.

The pilot phase allows you to try your migration steps in the real world with reduced exposure to problems through a controlled membership of pilot users. Take this opportunity to get feedback from the pilot users to update or modify your steps to reduce impact on users or administrators. Remember, if you need to make major changes after the pilot, run a second pilot and keep running pilots until you feel your process is sufficient. This shouldn't take too much feedback if you took full advantage of the prototype phase.

The implementation phase allows you to push through the migration full force and get all the users migrated to the new environment.

Utilize a support and retirement phase to make sure you have time to retire old servers and to make sure you have a bit of extra time with the enhanced support and help desk to make sure everyone is happy after the migration (at least happy about Exchange 2007).

By following this standard methodology, you will greatly increase the chances of having a smooth and uneventful migration. This will help build credibility for the IT organization and make it that much easier to get projects approved in the future.

Best Practices

The following are best practices from this chapter:

> ▶ An upgrade to Exchange 2007 should follow a process that keeps the project on schedule. Set up such a process with a four-phase approach, including initiation, planning, testing, and implementation.

▶ Documentation is important to keep track of plans, procedures, and schedules. Create some of the documentation that could be expected for an upgrade project, including a Statement of Work document, a Design document, a project schedule, and a Migration document.

▶ Key to the initiation phase is the definition of the scope of work. Create such a definition, identifying the key goals of the project.

▶ Make sure that the goals of the project are not just IT goals, but also include goals and objectives of the organization and business units of the organization. This ensures that business needs are tied to the migration initiative, which can later be quantified to determine cost savings or tangible business process improvements.

▶ Set milestones in a project that can ensure that key steps are being achieved and the project is progressing at an acceptable rate. Review any drastic variation in attaining milestone tasks and timelines to determine whether the project should be modified or changed, or the plans reviewed.

▶ Allocate skilled or qualified resources that can help the organization to better achieve technical success and keep it on schedule. Failure to include qualified personnel can have a drastic impact on the overall success of the project.

▶ Identify risks and assumptions in a project to provide the project manager the ability to assess situations and proactive work and avoid actions that might cause project failures.

▶ Plan the design around what is best for the organization, and then create the migration process to take into account the existing configuration of the systems within the organization. Although understanding the existing environment is important to the success of the project, an implementation or migration project should not predetermine the actions of the organization based on the existing enterprise configuration.

▶ Ensure that key stakeholders are involved in the ultimate design of the Exchange 2007 implementation. Without stakeholder agreement on the design, the project might not be completed and approved.

▶ Document decisions made in the collaborative design sessions as well as in the migration planning process to ensure that key decisions are agreed upon and accepted by the participants of the process. Anyone with questions on the decisions can ask for clarification before the project begins rather than stopping the project midstream.

▶ Test assumptions and validate procedures in the prototype phase. Rather than learning for the first time in a production environment that a migration will fail because an Exchange database is corrupt or has inconsistencies, the entire process can be tested in a lab environment without impacting users.

▶ Test the process in a live production environment with a limited number of users in the prototype phase. Although key executives (such as the CIO or IT director) want to be part of the initial pilot phase, it is usually not recommended to take such high-visibility users in the first phase. The pilot phase should be with users who will accept an incident of lost email or inability to send or receive messages for a couple of days while problems are worked out. In many cases, a prepilot phase could include the more tolerant users, with a formal pilot phase including insistent executives of the organization.

▶ Migrate, implement, or upgrade after all testing has been validated. The production process should be exactly that, a process that methodically follows procedures to implement or migrate mailboxes into the Exchange 2007 environment.

PART II

Planning and Designing an Exchange Server 2007 Environment

IN THIS PART

CHAPTER 3

Understanding Core Exchange Server 2007 Design Plans

The fundamental capabilities of Microsoft Exchange Server 2007 are impressive. Improvements to security, reliability, and scalability enhance an already road-tested and stable Exchange platform. Along with these impressive credentials comes an equally impressive design task. Proper design of an Exchange Server 2007 platform will do more than practically anything to reduce headaches and support calls in the future. Many complexities of Exchange might seem daunting, but with a proper understanding of the fundamental components and improvements, the task of designing the Exchange Server 2007 environment becomes manageable.

This chapter focuses specifically on the Exchange Server 2007 components required for design. Key decision-making factors influencing design are presented and tied into overall strategy. All critical pieces of information required to design Exchange Server 2007 implementations are outlined and explained. Enterprise Exchange design and planning concepts are expanded in Chapter 4, "Architecting an Enterprise-Level Exchange Environment."

Planning for Exchange Server 2007

Designing Exchange Server used to be a fairly simple task. When an organization needed email and the decision was made to go with Exchange Server, the only real decision to make was how many Exchange servers were needed. Primarily, organizations really needed only email and eschewed any "bells and whistles."

Exchange Server 2007, on the other hand, takes messaging to a whole new level. No longer do organizations require only an email system, but other messaging and unified communications functionality as well. After the productivity capabilities of an enterprise email platform have been demonstrated, the need for more productivity improvements arises. Consequently, it is wise to understand the integral design components of Exchange before beginning a design project.

Outlining Significant Changes in Exchange Server 2007

Exchange Server 2007 is the evolution of a product that has consistently been improving over the years from its roots. Since the Exchange 5.x days, Microsoft has released dramatic improvements with Exchange 2000 Server and later Exchange Server 2003. The latest version takes the functionality and reliability of Exchange to the next level, introducing several major enhancements and improvements.

The major areas of improvement in Exchange Server 2007 have focused on several key areas. The first is in the realm of user access and connectivity. The needs of many organizations have changed and they are no longer content with slow remote access to email and limited functionality when on the road. Consequently, many of the improvements in Exchange focus on various approaches to email access and connectivity. The improvements in this group focus on the following areas:

▶ **"Access anywhere" improvements**—Microsoft has focused a great deal of Exchange Server 2007 development time on new access methods for Exchange, including an enhanced Outlook Web Access (OWA) that works with a variety of Microsoft and third-party browsers, Microsoft ActiveSync improvements, new Outlook Voice Access (OVA), unified messaging support, and Outlook Anywhere (formerly known as RPC over HTTP). Having these multiple access methods greatly increases the design flexibility of Exchange, as end users can access email via multiple methods.

▶ **Protection and compliance enhancements**—Exchange Server 2007 now includes a variety of antispam, antivirus, and compliance mechanisms to protect the integrity of messaging data.

▶ **Admin tools improvements and Exchange Management Shell scripting**—The administrative environment in Exchange 2007 has been completely revamped and improved, and the scripting capabilities have been overhauled. It is now possible to script any administrative command from a command-line script. Indeed, the graphical user interface (GUI) itself sits on top of the scripting engine and simply fires scripts based on the task that an administrator chooses in the GUI. This allows for an unprecedented level of control.

▶ **Local Continuous Replication (LCR) and Cluster Continuous Replication (CCR)**—One of the most anticipated improvements to Exchange Server has been the inclusion of Local Continuous Replication (LCR) and Cluster Continuous Replication (CCR). These technologies allow for log shipping functionality for Exchange databases, allowing a replica copy of an Exchange database to be constantly built from new logs generated from the server. This gives administrators the ability to replicate in real time the data from a server to another server in a remote site or locally on the same server.

It is important to incorporate the concepts of these improvements into any Exchange design project because their principles often drive the design process.

Reviewing Exchange and Operating System Requirements

Exchange Server 2007 has some specific requirements, both hardware and software, that must be taken into account when designing. These requirements fall into several categories:

▶ Hardware

▶ Operating system

▶ Active Directory

▶ Exchange version

Each requirement must be addressed before Exchange Server 2007 can be deployed.

Reviewing Hardware Requirements

It is important to design Exchange hardware to scale out to the user load, which is expected for up to 3 years from the date of implementation. This helps retain the value of the investment put into Exchange. Specific hardware configuration advice is offered in later sections of this chapter.

Reviewing Operating System (OS) Requirements

Exchange Server 2007 is optimized for installation on Windows Server 2003. The increases in security and the fundamental changes to Internet Information Services (IIS) in Windows Server 2003 provide the basis for many of the improvements in Exchange Server 2007. The specific compatibility matrix, which indicates compatibility between Exchange versions and operating systems, is illustrated in Table 3.1.

TABLE 3.1   Exchange Version Compatibility

Version	Windows NT 4.0	Windows 2000	Windows 2003
Exchange 5.5	Yes	Yes	No
Exchange 2000	No	Yes	No
Exchange 2003	No	Yes	Yes
Exchange 2007	No	No	Yes*
64-bit SP1 or R2 editions only supported			

Understanding Active Directory (AD) Requirements

Exchange originally maintained its own directory. With the advent of Exchange 2000, however, the directory for Exchange was moved to the Microsoft Active Directory, the enterprise directory system for Windows. This gave greater flexibility and consolidated directories, but at the same time increased the complexity and dependencies for Exchange. Exchange Server 2007 uses the same model, with either Windows 2000 Server or Windows Server 2003 AD as its directory component.

Exchange 2007, while requiring an AD forest in all deployment scenarios, has certain flexibility when it comes to the type of AD it uses. It is possible to deploy Exchange in the following scenarios:

- **Single forest**—The simplest and most traditional design for Exchange is one where Exchange is installed within the same forest used for user accounts. This design also has the least amount of complexity and synchronization concerns to worry about.

- **Resource forest**—The Resource forest model in Exchange Server 2007 involves the deployment of a dedicated forest exclusively used for Exchange itself, and the only user accounts within it are those that serve as a placeholder for a mailbox. These user accounts are not logged onto by the end users, but rather the end users are given access to them across cross-forest trusts from their particular user forest to the Exchange forest. More information on this deployment model can be found in Chapter 4.

- **Multiple forests**—Different multiple forest models for Exchange are presently available, but they do require a greater degree of administration and synchronization. In these models, different Exchange organizations *live* in different forests across an organization. These different Exchange organizations are periodically synchronized to maintain a common Global Address List (GAL). More information on this deployment model can also be found in Chapter 4.

It is important to determine which design model will be chosen before proceeding with an Exchange deployment because it is complex and expensive to change the AD structure of Exchange after it has been deployed.

Outlining Exchange Version Requirements

As with previous versions of Exchange, there are separate Enterprise and Standard versions of the Exchange Server 2007 product. The Standard Edition supports all Exchange Server 2007 functionality with the exception of the following key components:

- **Unlimited Mailbox Store Size**—Exchange Server 2007 (both Standard Edition and Enterprise Edition) support an unlimited database store size. In previous versions of Exchange (2000 and 2003), the database was limited to 16GB or 75GB depending on the Exchange version being installed.

NOTE

There is no direct upgrade path from the Exchange Standard Edition to the Enterprise Edition. Only a mailbox migration procedure that can transfer mailboxes from a Standard Edition server to an Enterprise Edition server can accomplish an upgrade. Consequently, it is important to make an accurate determination of whether the Enterprise Edition of the software is needed.

▶ **Multiple mailbox database stores**—One of the key features of Exchange Server 2007 is the capability of the server to support multiple databases and storage groups with the Enterprise Edition of the software. Up to 50 storage groups and/or 50 databases per server are supported. This capability is not supported with the Standard Edition. Exchange Server 2007 supports up to 5 databases per server.

▶ **Clustering support**—Exchange Server 2007 clustering, including traditional Single Copy Clustering (shared storage) and the new Cluster Continuous Replication (CCR), is available only when using the Enterprise Edition of the software. Support for up to an eight-way active-passive cluster on Windows Server 2003 is available. Microsoft requires at least one passive node per cluster.

Scaling Exchange Server 2007

The days of the Exchange server "rabbit farm" are gone where it is no longer necessary to set up multiple Exchange server sites across an organization and watch them grow as usage of mail increases in the organization. Exchange 2000 originally provided the basis for servers that could easily scale out to thousands of users in a single site, if necessary. Exchange Server 2003 further improved the situation by introducing Messaging Application Programming Interface (MAPI) compression and RPC over HTTP. Exchange Server 2007 further improves the situation by improving RPC over HTTP (now called Outlook Anywhere) and allowing Mailbox servers to scale upward through 64-bit OS support.

Site consolidation concepts enable organizations that might have previously deployed Exchange servers in remote locations to have those clients access their mailboxes across wide area network (WAN) links or dial-up connections by using the enhanced Outlook 2003/2007 or OWA clients. This solves the problem that previously existed of having to deploy Exchange servers and global catalog (GC) servers in remote locations, with only a handful of users, and greatly reduces the infrastructure costs of setting up Exchange.

Having Exchange Server 2007 Coexist with an Existing Network Infrastructure

Exchange is built upon a standards-based model, which incorporates many industrywide compatible protocols and services. Internet standards—such as DNS, IMAP, SMTP, LDAP, and POP3—are built in to the product to provide coexistence with existing network infrastructure.

In a design scenario, it is necessary to identify any systems that require access to email data or services. For example, it might be necessary to enable a third-party monitoring application to relay mail off the Simple Mail Transfer Protocol (SMTP) engine of Exchange so that alerts can be sent. Identifying these needs during the design portion of a project is subsequently important.

Identifying Third-Party Product Functionality

Microsoft built specific hooks into Exchange Server 2007 to enable third-party applications to improve upon the built-in functionality provided by the system. For example, built-in support for antivirus scanning, backups, and unified messaging exist right out of the box, although functionality is limited without the addition of third-party software. The most common additions to Exchange implementation are the following:

▶ Antivirus

▶ Backup

▶ Phone/PBX integration

▶ Fax software

Understanding AD Design Concepts for Exchange Server 2007

After all objectives, dependencies, and requirements have been mapped out, the process of designing the Exchange Server 2007 environment can begin. Decisions should be made in the following key areas:

▶ AD design

▶ Exchange server placement

▶ Global catalog placement

▶ Client access methods

Understanding the AD Forest

Because Exchange Server 2007 relies on the Windows Server 2003 AD for its directory, it is therefore important to include AD in the design plans. In many situations, an AD implementation, whether based on Windows 2000 Server or Windows Server 2003, already exists in the organization. In these cases, it is necessary only to plan for the inclusion of Exchange Server into the forest.

> **NOTE**
>
> Exchange Server 2007 has several key requirements for AD. First, all domains must be in Windows 2000 or 2003 functional levels (no NT domain controllers). Second, it requires that the schema in an AD forest be extended for Windows Server 2003 RTM or R2 editions, and that the schema master domain controller be running either Windows Server 2003 SP1 or R2 edition. In addition, at least one global catalog server in each site where Exchange will be installed must be running Windows Server 2003 SP1 or R2.

If an AD structure is not already in place, a new AD forest must be established. Designing the AD forest infrastructure can be complex, and can require nearly as much thought into design as the actual Exchange Server configuration itself. Therefore, it is important to fully understand the concepts behind AD before beginning an Exchange 2007 design.

In short, a single "instance" of AD consists of a single AD forest. A forest is composed of AD trees, which are contiguous domain namespaces in the forest. Each tree is composed of one or more domains, as illustrated in Figure 3.1.

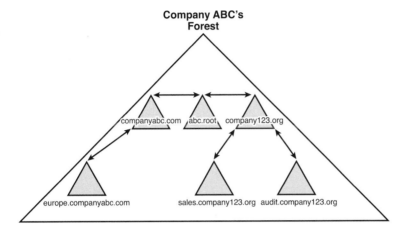

FIGURE 3.1   Multitree forest design.

Certain cases exist for using more than one AD forest in an organization:

   ▶ **Political limitations**—Some organizations have specific political reasons that force the creation of multiple AD forests. For example, if a merged corporate entity requires separate divisions to maintain completely separate information technology (IT) infrastructures, more than one forest is necessary.

   ▶ **Security concerns**—Although the AD domain serves as a de facto security boundary, the "ultimate" security boundary is effectively the forest. In other words, it is possible for user accounts in a domain in a forest to hack into domains within the same forest. Although these types of vulnerabilities are not common and are difficult to do, highly security-conscious organizations should implement separate AD forests.

   ▶ **Application functionality**—A single AD forest shares a common directory schema, which is the underlying structure of the directory and must be unique across the entire forest. In some cases, separate branches of an organization require that certain applications, which need extensions to the schema, be installed. This might not be possible or might conflict with the schema requirements of other branches. These cases might require the creation of a separate forest.

▶ **Exchange-specific functionality (resource forest)**—In certain circumstances, it might be necessary to install Exchange Server 2007 into a separate forest, to enable Exchange to reside in a separate schema and forest instance. An example of this type of setup is an organization with two existing AD forests that creates a third forest specifically for Exchange and uses cross-forest trusts to assign mailbox permissions.

The simplest designs often work the best. The same principle applies to AD design. The designer should start with the assumption that a simple forest and domain structure will work for the environment. However, when factors such as those previously described create constraints, multiple forests can be established to satisfy the requirements of the constraints.

Understanding the AD Domain Structure

After the AD forest structure has been chosen, the domain structure can be laid out. As with the forest structure, it is often wise to consider a single domain model for the Exchange 2007 directory. In fact, if deploying Exchange is the only consideration, this is often the best choice.

There is one major exception to the single domain model: the placeholder domain model. The placeholder domain model has an isolated domain serving as the root domain in the forest. The user domain, which contains all production user accounts, would be located in a separate domain in the forest, as illustrated in Figure 3.2.

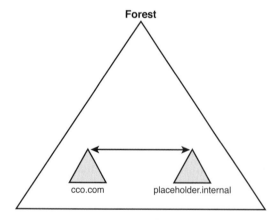

FIGURE 3.2   The placeholder domain model.

The placeholder domain structure increases security in the forest by segregating high-level schema-access accounts into a completely separate domain from the regular user domain. Access to the placeholder domain can be audited and restricted to maintain tighter control on the critical schema. The downside to this model, however, is the fact that the additional domain requires a separate set of domain controllers, which increases the infrastructure costs of the environment. In general, this makes this domain model less desirable for smaller organizations because the trade-off between increased cost and less security is too great. Larger organizations can consider the increased security provided by this model, however.

Reviewing AD Infrastructure Components

Several key components of AD must be installed within an organization to ensure proper Exchange Server 2007 and AD functionality. In smaller environments, many of these components can be installed on a single machine, but all need to be located within an environment to ensure server functionality.

Outlining the Domain Name System (DNS) Impact on Exchange Server 2007 Design

In addition to being tightly integrated with AD, Exchange Server 2007 is joined with the Domain Name System (DNS). DNS serves as the lookup agent for Exchange Server 2007, AD, and most new Microsoft applications and services. DNS translates common names into computer-recognizable IP addresses. For example, the name www.cco.com translates into the IP address of 12.155.166.151. AD and Exchange Server 2007 require that at least one DNS server be made available so that name resolution properly occurs.

Given the dependency that both Exchange Server 2007 and AD have on DNS, it is an extremely important design element. For an in-depth look at DNS and its role in Exchange Server 2007, see Chapter 6, "Understanding Network Services and AD Domain Controller Placement for Exchange Server 2007."

Reviewing DNS Namespace Considerations for Exchange

Given Exchange Server 2007's dependency on DNS, a common DNS namespace must be chosen for the AD structure to reside in. In multiple tree domain models, this could be composed of several DNS trees, but in small organization environments, this normally means choosing a single DNS namespace for the AD domain.

There is a great deal of confusion between the DNS namespace in which AD resides and the email DNS namespace in which mail is delivered. Although they are often the same, in many cases there are differences between the two namespaces. For example, CompanyABC's AD structure is composed of a single domain named abc.internal, and the email domain to which mail is delivered is companyabc.com. The separate namespace, in this case, was created to reduce the security vulnerability of maintaining the same DNS namespace both internally and externally (published to the Internet).

For simplicity, CompanyABC could have chosen companyabc.com as its AD namespace. This choice increases the simplicity of the environment by making the AD logon user principal name (UPN) and the email address the same. For example, the user Pete Handley is pete@companyabc.com for logon, and pete@companyabc.com for email. This option is the choice for many organizations because the need for user simplicity often trumps the higher security.

Optimally Locating Global Catalog Servers

Because all Exchange directory lookups use AD, it is vital that the essential AD global catalog information is made available to each Exchange server in the organization. For many small offices with a single site, this simply means that it is important to have a full global catalog server available in the main site.

The global catalog is an index of the AD database that contains a partial copy of its contents. All objects within the AD tree are referenced within the global catalog, which enables users to search for objects located in other domains. Every attribute of each object is not replicated to the global catalogs, only those attributes that are commonly used in search operations, such as first name and last name. Exchange Server 2007 uses the global catalog for the email-based lookups of names, email addresses, and other mail-related attributes.

Because full global catalog replication can consume more bandwidth than standard domain controller replication, it is important to design a site structure to reflect the available WAN link capacity. If a sufficient amount of capacity is available, a full global catalog server can be deployed. If, however, capacity is limited, universal group membership caching can be enabled to reduce the bandwidth load.

Understanding Multiple Forests Design Concepts Using Microsoft Identity Integration Server (MIIS) 2003

Microsoft Identity Integration Server 2003 enables out-of-the-box replication of objects between two separate AD forests. This concept becomes important for organizations with multiple Exchange implementations that want a common Global Address List for the company. Previous iterations of MIIS required an in-depth knowledge of scripting to be able to synchronize objects between two forests. MIIS 2003, on the other hand, includes built-in scripts that can establish replication between two Exchange Server 2007 AD forests, making integration between forests easier.

> **NOTE**
>
> The built-in scripts in MIIS 2003 enable synchronization only between two forests that have a full Exchange Server 2007 or Exchange Server 2003 schema. In other words, if synchronization between an Exchange 2000 forest or an Exchange 5.5 directory is required, customized scripts must be developed.

Determining Exchange Server 2007 Placement

Previous versions of Exchange essentially forced many organizations into deploying servers in sites with greater than a dozen or so users. With the concept of site consolidation in Exchange Server 2007, however, smaller numbers of Exchange servers can service clients in multiple locations, even if they are separated by slow WAN links. For small and medium-sized organizations, this essentially means that one or two servers should suffice for the needs of the organization, with few exceptions. Larger organizations require a larger number of Exchange servers, depending on the number of sites and users. Designing Exchange Server 2007 placement must take into account both administrative group and routing group structure. In addition, Exchange Server 2007 introduces new server role concepts, which should be understood so that the right server can be deployed in the right location.

Understanding Exchange Server 2007 Server Roles

Exchange Server 2007 introduced the concept of server roles to Exchange terminology. In the past, server functionality was loosely termed, such as referring to an Exchange server as an OWA or front-end server, bridgehead server, or a Mailbox or back-end server. In reality, there was no *set* terminology that was used for Exchange server roles. Exchange Server 2007, on the other hand, distinctly defines specific roles that a server can hold. Multiple roles can reside on a single server, or multiple servers can have the same role. By standardizing on these roles, it becomes easier to design an Exchange environment by designating specific roles for servers in specific locations.

The server roles included in Exchange Server 2007 include the following:

▶ **Client access server (CAS)**—The CAS role allows for client connections via nonstandard methods such as Outlook Web Access (OWA), Exchange ActiveSync, Post Office Protocol 3 (POP3), and Internet Message Access Protocol (IMAP). CAS servers are the replacement for Exchange 2000/2003 front-end servers and can be load balanced for redundancy purposes. As with the other server roles, the CAS role can coexist with other roles for smaller organizations with a single server, for example.

▶ **Edge Transport server**—The Edge Transport server role is unique to Exchange 2007, and consists of a standalone server that typically resides in the demilitarized zone (DMZ) of a firewall. This server filters inbound SMTP mail traffic from the Internet for viruses and spam, and then forwards it to internal Hub Transport servers. Edge Transport servers keep a local AD Application Mode (ADAM) instance that is synchronized with the internal AD structure via a mechanism called EdgeSync. This helps to reduce the surface attack area of Exchange.

▶ **Hub Transport server**—The Hub Transport server role acts as a mail bridgehead for mail sent between servers in one AD site and mail sent to other AD sites. There needs to be at least one Hub Transport server within an AD site that contains a server with the Mailbox role, but there can also be multiple Hub Transport servers to provide for redundancy and load balancing.

▶ **Mailbox server**—The Mailbox server role is intuitive; it acts as the storehouse for mail data in users' mailboxes and down-level public folders if required. It also directly interacts with Outlook MAPI traffic. All other access methods are proxied through the CAS servers.

▶ **Unified Messaging server**—The Unified Messaging server role is new in Exchange 2007 and allows a user's Inbox to be used for voice messaging and fax capabilities.

Any or all of these roles can be installed on a single server or on multiple servers. For smaller organizations, a single server holding all Exchange roles is sufficient. For larger organizations, a more complex configuration might be required. For more information on designing large and complex Exchange implementations, see Chapter 4.

Understanding Environment Sizing Considerations

In some cases with very small organizations, the number of users is small enough to warrant the installation of all AD and Exchange Server 2007 components on a single server. This scenario is possible, as long as all necessary components—DNS, a global catalog domain controller, and Exchange Server 2007—are installed on the same hardware. In general, however, it is best to separate AD and Exchange onto separate hardware wherever possible.

Identifying Client Access Points

At its core, Exchange Server 2007 essentially acts as a storehouse for mailbox data. Access to the mail within the mailboxes can take place through multiple means, some of which might be required by specific services or applications in the environment. A good understanding of what these services are and if and how your design should support them is warranted.

Outlining MAPI Client Access with Outlook 2007

The "heavy" client of Outlook, Outlook 2007, has gone through a significant number of changes, both to the look and feel of the application, and to the back-end mail functionality. The look and feel has been streamlined based on Microsoft research and customer feedback. Users of Outlook 2003 might be familiar with most of the layout, whereas users of Outlook 2000 and previous versions might take some getting used to the layout and configuration.

On the back end, Outlook 2007 improves the MAPI compression that takes place between an Exchange Server 2007 system and the Outlook 2007 client. The increased compression helps reduce network traffic and improve the overall speed of communications between client and server.

In addition to MAPI compression, Outlook 2007 expands upon the Outlook 2003 ability to run in cached mode, which automatically detects slow connections between client and server and adjusts Outlook functionality to match the speed of the link. When a slow link is detected, Outlook can be configured to download only email header information. When emails are opened, the entire email is downloaded, including attachments if necessary. This drastically reduces the amount of bits across the wire that is sent because only those emails that are required are sent across the connection.

The Outlook 2007 client is the most effective and full-functioning client for users who are physically located close to an Exchange server. With the enhancements in cached mode functionality, however, Outlook 2007 can also be effectively used in remote locations. When making the decision about which client to deploy as part of a design, you should keep these concepts in mind.

Accessing Exchange with Outlook Web Access (OWA)

The Outlook Web Access (OWA) client in Exchange Server 2007 has been enhanced and optimized for performance and usability. There is now very little difference between the full function client and OWA. With this in mind, OWA is now an even more efficient client for remote access to the Exchange server. The one major piece of functionality that OWA does not have, but the full Outlook 2007 client does, is offline mail access support. If this is required, the full client should be deployed.

Using Exchange ActiveSync (EAS)

Exchange ActiveSync (EAS) support in Exchange Server 2007 allows a mobile client, such as a Pocket PC device, to synchronize with the Exchange server, allowing for access to email from a handheld device. EAS also supports Direct Push technology, which allows for instantaneous email delivery to handheld devices running Windows Mobile 5.0 and the Messaging Security and Feature Pack (MSFP).

Understanding the Simple Mail Transport Protocol (SMTP)

The Simple Mail Transfer Protocol (SMTP) is an industry-standard protocol that is widely used across the Internet for mail delivery. SMTP is built in to Exchange servers and is used by Exchange systems for relaying mail messages from one system to another, which is similar to the way that mail is relayed across SMTP servers on the Internet. Exchange is dependent on SMTP for mail delivery and uses it for internal and external mail access.

By default, Exchange Server 2007 uses DNS to route messages destined for the Internet out of the Exchange topology. If, however, a user wants to forward messages to a smarthost before they are transmitted to the Internet, an SMTP connector can be manually set up to enable mail relay out of the Exchange system. SMTP connectors also reduce the risk and load on an Exchange server by off-loading the DNS lookup tasks to the SMTP smarthost. SMTP connectors can be specifically designed in an environment for this type of functionality.

Using Outlook Anywhere (Previously Known as RPC over HTTP)

One very effective and improved client access method to Exchange Server 2007 is known as Outlook Anywhere. This technology was previously referred to as RPC over HTTP(s) or Outlook over HTTP(s). This technology enables standard Outlook 2007 access across firewalls. The Outlook 2007 client encapsulates Outlook RPC packets into HTTP or HTTPS packets and sends them across standard web ports (80 and 443), where they are then extracted by the Exchange Server 2007 system. This technology enables Outlook to communicate using its standard RPC protocol, but across firewalls and routers that normally do not allow RPC traffic. The potential uses of this protocol are significant because many situations do not require the use of cumbersome VPN clients.

Configuring Exchange Server 2007 for Maximum Performance and Reliability

After decisions have been made about AD design, Exchange server placement, and client access, optimization of the Exchange server itself helps ensure efficiency, reliability, and security for the messaging platform.

Designing an Optimal Operating System Configuration for Exchange

As previously mentioned, Exchange Server 2007 only operates on the Windows Server 2003 operating system, and is scheduled to be able to run on the next version of the Windows Server operating system, currently referred to as Windows Longhorn. The enhancements to the operating system, especially in regard to security, make Windows Server 2003 the optimal choice for Exchange. Unless clustering (including Cluster Continuous Replication) is required, which is not common for smaller organizations, the Standard Edition of Windows Server 2003 can be installed as the OS.

> **NOTE**
>
> Contrary to popular misconception, the Enterprise Edition of Exchange can be installed on the Standard Edition of the operating system, and vice versa. Although there has been a lot of confusion on this concept, both versions of Exchange were designed to interoperate with either version of Windows.

Avoiding Virtual Memory Fragmentation Issues

The previous iterations of Windows Server have suffered from a problem with virtual memory (VM) fragmentation. The problem would manifest itself on systems with greater than 1GB of RAM, which run memory-intensive applications such as SQL Server or Exchange. The Advanced Server Edition of Windows 2000 Server enabled a workaround for this problem, in the form of a memory allocation switch that allocated additional memory for the user kernel.

Windows Server 2003 includes the capability of using this memory optimization technique in both the Standard and the Enterprise Editions of the software, so that the switch can now be used on any Windows Server 2003 system with more than 1GB of physical RAM. The switch is added to the end of the boot.ini file.

The /3GB switch tells Windows to allocate 3GB of memory for the user kernel, and the /USERVA=3030 switch optimizes the memory configuration, based on tests performed by Microsoft that determined the perfect number of megabytes to allocate for optimal performance and the least likely instance of VM fragmentation. This setting only applies to the 32-bit version of Windows 2003, so it would not apply to Exchange 2007 servers but would apply to 32-bit domain controllers and any other supporting 32-bit servers in an Exchange 2007 environment.

Configuring Disk Options for Performance

The single most important design element, which improves the efficiency and speed of Exchange, is the separation of the Exchange database and the Exchange logs onto a separate hard drive volume. Because of the inherent differences in the type of hard drive operations performed (logs perform primarily write operations, databases primarily read),

separating these elements onto separate volumes dramatically increases server performance. Keep these components separate in even the smallest Exchange server implementations. Figure 3.3 illustrates some examples of how the database and log volumes can be
configured.

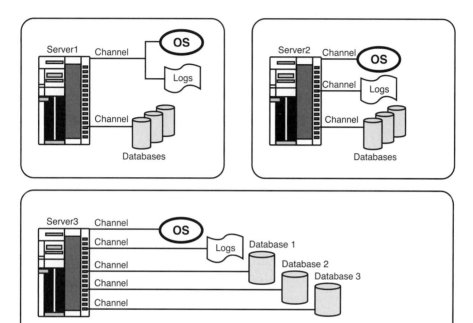

FIGURE 3.3   Database and log volume configuration.

On Server1, the OS and logs are located on the same mirrored C:\ volume and the database is located on a separate RAID-5 drive set. With Server2, the configuration is taken up
a notch, with the OS only on C:\, the logs on D:\, and the database on the RAID-5 E:\
volume. Finally, Server3 is configured in the optimal configuration, with separate volumes
for each database and a volume for the log files. The more advanced a configuration, the
more detailed and complex the drive configuration can get. However, the most important
factor that must be remembered is to separate the Exchange database from the logs wherever possible.

Working with Multiple Exchange Databases and Storage Groups

The Enterprise Edition of Exchange Server 2007 not only enables databases of larger than
75GB, it also enables the creation of multiple separate databases on a single server. This
concept gives great flexibility in design while enabling reduced downtime and increased
performance.

A storage group is a logical grouping of databases that share a single set of logs. Each Exchange Server 2007 Enterprise system can handle a maximum of 50 storage groups per server. Each storage group can contain a maximum of five databases each, although the total number of databases on a server cannot equal more than 50.

> **NOTE**
>
> If Cluster Continuous Replication (CCR) is to be used, it is important to note that CCR only supports a single database per storage group. Also, Microsoft recommends no more than 30 databases on a server running CCR.

In practice, however, each instance of a storage group that is created uses a greater amount of resources, so it is wise to create additional storage groups only if absolutely necessary. Multiple databases, on the other hand, can solve several problems:

▶ **Reduce database restore time**—Smaller databases take less time to restore from tape. This concept can be helpful if there is a group of users who require quicker recovery time (such as management). All mailboxes for this group could then be placed in a separate database to provide quicker recovery time in the event of a server or database failure.

▶ **Provide for separate mailbox limit policies**—Each database can be configured with different mailbox storage limits. For example, the standard user database could have a 200-MB limit on mailboxes, and the management database could have a 500-MB limit.

▶ **Mitigate risk by distributing user load**—By distributing user load across multiple databases, the risk of losing all user mail connectivity is reduced. For example, if a single database failed that contained all users, no one would be able to mail. If those users were divided across three databases, however, only one third of those users would be unable to mail in the event of a database failure.

> **NOTE**
>
> One disadvantage to multiple databases is that the concept of single-instance storage is lost across databases. Single-instance storage occurs when only one copy of an email message sent to multiple people is stored on the server, dramatically reducing the space needed to store mass mailings. Each separate database must keep a copy of mass mailings, however, which increases the aggregate total size of the databases.

Understanding Clustering for Exchange Server 2007

Exchange Server 2007 is configured to use Windows Server 2003 clustering for enhanced redundancy and increased uptime. Clustering is an expensive option, but one that will increase reliability of the Exchange Server 2007 implementation.

Clustering options with Exchange Server 2007 have significantly changed over those available in previous versions. Traditional, shared storage clustering is now referred to as a Single Copy Cluster. New options for clustering databases across geographical locations automatically using asynchronous synchronization of log files is now available and is referred to as Cluster Continuous Replication (CCR). More information on clustering with Exchange 2007 can be found in Chapters 4, "Architecting an Enterprise-Level Exchange Environment," and 31, "Continuous Backups, Clustering, and Network Load Balancing in Exchange Server 2007."

NOTE

Microsoft no longer supports a full active-active clustering configuration. Consequently, at least one cluster node should be configured as passive. With eight-way clustering, for example, this means that seven nodes can be active and one node must be passive.

Monitoring Design Concepts with Microsoft Operations Manager 2005

The enhancements to Exchange Server 2007 do not stop with the improvements to the product itself. New functionality has been added to the Exchange Management Pack for Microsoft Operations Manager (MOM) that enables MOM to monitor Exchange servers for critical events and performance data. The MOM Management Pack is preconfigured to monitor for Exchange-specific information and to enable administrators to proactively monitor Exchange servers. For more information on using MOM to monitor Exchange Server 2007, see Chapter 20, "Using Microsoft Operations Manager to Monitor Exchange Server 2007."

Securing and Maintaining an Exchange Server 2007 Implementation

One of the greatest advantages of Exchange Server 2007 is its emphasis on security. Along with Windows Server 2003, Exchange Server 2007 was developed during and after the Microsoft Trustworthy Computing initiative, which effectively put a greater emphasis on security over new features in the products. In Exchange Server 2007, this means that the OS and the application were designed with services "Secure by Default."

With Secure by Default, all nonessential functionality in Exchange must be turned on if needed. This is a complete change from the previous Microsoft model, which had all services, add-ons, and options turned on and running at all times, presenting much larger security vulnerabilities than was necessary. Designing security effectively becomes much easier in Exchange Server 2007 because it now becomes necessary only to identify components to turn on, as opposed to identifying everything that needs to be turned off.

In addition to being secure by default, Exchange Server 2007 server roles are built in to templates used by the Security Configuration Wizard (SCW), which was introduced in

Service Pack 1 for Windows Server 2003. Using the SCW against Exchange Server helps to reduce the surface attack area of a server.

Patching the Operating System Using Windows Software Update Services

Although Windows Server 2003 presents a much smaller target for hackers, viruses, and exploits by virtue of the Secure by Default concept, it is still important to keep the OS up to date against critical security patches and updates. Currently, two approaches can be used to automate the installation of server patches. The first method involves configuring the Windows Server 2003 Automatic Updates client to download patches from Microsoft and install them on a schedule. The second option is to set up an internal server to coordinate patch distribution and management. The solution that Microsoft supplies for this functionality is known as Windows Software Update Services (WSUS).

WSUS enables a centralized server to hold copies of OS patches for distribution to clients on a preset schedule. WSUS can be used to automate the distribution of patches to Exchange Server 2007 servers, so that the OS components will remain secure between service packs. WSUS might not be necessary in smaller environments, but can be considered in medium-sized to large organizations that want greater control over their patch management strategy.

Implementing Maintenance Schedules

Exchange still uses the Microsoft JET Database structure, which is effectively the same database engine that has been used with Exchange from the beginning. This type of database is useful for storing the type of unstructured data that email normally carries, and has proven to be a good fit for Exchange Server. Along with this type of database, however, comes the responsibility to run regular, scheduled maintenance on the Exchange databases on a regular basis.

Although online maintenance is performed every night, it is recommended that Exchange databases be brought offline on a quarterly or, at most, semiannual basis for offline maintenance. Exchange database maintenance utilities, `eseutil` and `isinteg`, should be used to compact and defragment the databases, which can then be mounted again in the environment.

Exchange databases that do not have this type of maintenance performed run the risk of becoming corrupt in the long term, and will also never be able to be reduced in size. Consequently, it is important to include database maintenance into a design plan to ensure data integrity.

Summary

Exchange Server 2007 offers a broad range of functionality and improvements to messaging and is well suited for organizations of any size. With proper thought for the major design topics, a robust and reliable Exchange email solution can be put into place that will perfectly complement the needs of any organization.

When Exchange design concepts have been fully understood, the task of designing the Exchange Server 2007 infrastructure can take place.

Best Practices

The following are best practices from this chapter:

▶ Use site consolidation strategies to reduce the number of Exchange servers to deploy.

▶ Separate the Exchange log and database files onto separate physical volumes whenever possible.

▶ Install Exchange Server 2007 on Windows Server 2003 R2 Edition when possible.

▶ Integrate an antivirus and backup strategy into Exchange Server design.

▶ Keep a local copy of the global catalog close to any Exchange servers.

▶ Implement quarterly or semiannual maintenance procedures against Exchange databases by using the `isinteg` and `eseutil` utilities.

▶ Keep the OS and Exchange up to date through service packs and software patches, either manually or via Windows Software Update Services.

▶ Keep the AD design simple, with a single forest and single domain, unless a specific need exists to create more complexity.

▶ Identify the client access methods that will be supported and match them with the appropriate Exchange Server 2007 technology.

▶ Implement DNS in the environment on the AD domain controllers.

CHAPTER 4

Architecting an Enterprise-Level Exchange Environment

Microsoft Exchange Server 2007 was designed to accommodate the needs of multiple organizations, from the small businesses to large, multinational corporations. In addition to the scalability features present in previous versions of Exchange, Exchange 2007 offers more opportunities to scale the back-end server environment to the specific needs of any group.

This chapter addresses specific design guidelines for midsize to large enterprise organizations. Throughout the chapter, specific examples of enterprise organizations are presented and general recommendations are made. This chapter assumes a base knowledge of design components that can be obtained by reading Chapter 3, "Understanding Core Exchange Server 2007 Design Plans."

Designing Active Directory for Exchange Server 2007

Active Directory (AD) is a necessary and fundamental component of any Exchange 2007 implementation. That said, organizations do not necessarily need to panic about setting up Active Directory in addition to Exchange, as long as a few straightforward design steps are followed. The following areas of Active Directory must be addressed to properly design and deploy Exchange 2007:

▶ Forest and domain design

▶ AD site and replication topology layout

▶ Domain controller and global catalog placement

▶ Domain name system (DNS) configuration

Understanding Forest and Domain Design

Because Exchange Server 2007 uses Active Directory for its underlying directory structure, it is necessary to link Exchange with a unique Active Directory forest.

In many cases, an existing Active Directory forest and domain structure is already in place in organizations considering Exchange 2007 deployment. In these cases, Exchange can be installed on top of the existing AD environment, and no additional AD design decisions need to be made. It is important to note that Exchange 2007 can only be installed in a Windows Server 2003 Active Directory forest; Windows 2000 Server forests are not supported.

In some cases, there might not be an existing AD infrastructure in place, and one needs to be deployed to support Exchange. In these scenarios, design decisions need to be made for the AD structure in which Exchange will be installed. In some specific cases, Exchange might be deployed as part of a separate forest by itself, as illustrated in Figure 4.1. This model is known as the Exchange Resource Forest model. This is often the case in an organization with multiple existing AD forests.

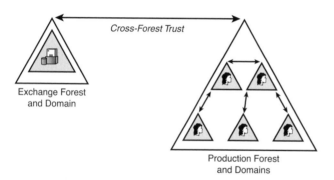

FIGURE 4.1   Understanding the Exchange Resource Forest model.

In any case, AD should be designed with simplicity in mind. A single-forest, single-domain model, for example, solves the needs of many organizations. If Exchange itself is all that is required of AD, this type of deployment is the best practice to consider.

> **NOTE**
>
> The addition of Exchange 2007 into an Active Directory forest requires an extension of the AD forest's Active Directory schema.
>
> Considerations for this factor must be taken into account when deploying Exchange onto an existing AD forest.

Microsoft has gotten serious recently about support for Exchange Server across multiple forests. This was previously an onerous task to set up, but the ability to synchronize between separate Exchange organizations has been simplified through the use of

Microsoft Identity Integration Server (MIIS) 2003. MIIS now comes with a series of preconfigured scripts to replicate between Exchange forests, enabling organizations which, for one reason or another, cannot use a common forest to unite the email structure through object replication.

Outlining AD Site and Replication Topology Layout

Active Directory sites should mirror existing network topology. Where there are pools of highly connected AD domain controllers, for example, Active Directory sites should be created to optimize replication. Smaller organizations have the luxury of a simplified AD site design. In general, the number of sites is small—or, in most cases, composed of a single physical location. Midsize and larger organizations might require the creation of multiple Active Directory sites to mirror the wide area network (WAN) connectivity of the organization.

Exchange 2007 no longer uses a separate replication mechanism (routing groups) from Active Directory, and Exchange replication takes place within the context of Active Directory sites. This makes proper AD site topology creation a critical component of an Exchange deployment.

Reviewing Domain Controller and Global Catalog Placement Concepts

In small or midsize organizations, you have effectively two options regarding domain controller placement. The first option involves using the same physical server for domain controller and Exchange Server duties. This option is feasible for smaller organizations because its impact on the server is minimal. This type of deployment strategy is not feasible for enterprise organizations, however, and the domain controller functions should be separated onto dedicated systems.

Configuring DNS

Because AD and Exchange are completely dependent on DNS for lookups and overall functionality, configuring DNS is an important factor to consider. In the majority of cases, DNS is installed on the domain controller(s), which enables the creation of Active Directory–integrated DNS zones. AD–integrated zones enable DNS data to be stored in AD with multiple read/write copies of the zone available for redundancy purposes. Although using other non-Microsoft DNS for AD is supported, it is not recommended.

The main decision regarding DNS layout is the decision about the namespace to be used within the organization. The DNS namespace is the same as the AD domain information, and it is difficult to change later. The two options in this case are to configure DNS to use either a published, external namespace that is easy to understand, such as cco.com, or an internal, secure namespace that is difficult to hack in to, such as cconet.internal. In general, the more security-conscious an organization, the more often the internal namespace will be chosen.

Determining Hardware and Software Components

Justifying hardware and software purchases is often a difficult task for organizations of any size. It is, therefore, important to balance the need for performance and redundancy with the available funds in the budget, and, thus, deploy the optimal Exchange Server hardware and software configuration.

Unlike previous versions of Exchange, Exchange 2007 requires the use of 64-bit capable systems, so it is critical to order the appropriate equipment when deploying Exchange 2007 systems.

Designing Server Number and Placement

Exchange scales very well to a large number of mailboxes on a single machine, depending on the hardware chosen for the Exchange server. Subsequently, Exchange 2007 is optimal for organizations that want to limit the amount of servers that are deployed and supported in an environment.

Exchange 2000 Server previously had one major exception to this concept, however. If multiple sites required high-speed access to an Exchange server, multiple servers were necessary for deployment. Exchange 2007, on the other hand, expands upon the concept of site consolidation, introduced in Exchange Server 2003. This concept enables smaller sites to use the Exchange servers in the larger sites through the more efficient bandwidth usage present in Outlook 2007 and Outlook 2003 and other mobile technologies.

Providing for Server Redundancy and Optimization

The ability of the Exchange server to recover from hardware failures is more than just a "nice-to-have" feature. Many server models come with an array of redundancy features, such as multiple fans and power supplies and mirrored disk capabilities. These features incur additional costs, however, so it is wise to perform a cost-benefit analysis to determine what redundancy features are required. Midsize and larger organizations should seriously consider robust redundancy options, however, because the increased reliability and uptime is often well worth the up-front costs.

Exchange 2007 further expands the redundancy options with the concept of Cluster Continuous Replication (CCR), which allows for a series of servers to each contain an active copy of a user's mailbox, allowing for immediate global cluster failover to any system. This concept is more fully explained in Chapter 31, "Continuous Backups, Clustering, and Network Load Balancing in Exchange Server 2007."

One of the most critical but overlooked performance strategies for Exchange is the concept of separating the Exchange logs and database onto separate physical drive sets. Because Exchange logs are very write-intensive, and the database is read-intensive, having these components on the same disk set would degrade performance. Separating these components onto different disk sets, however, is the best way to get the most out of Exchange.

In addition to separating the Exchange database onto a striped RAID5/RAID10(0+1) set, the Simple Mail Transfer Protocol (SMTP) component used by Exchange can be optimized by moving it to the same partition as the database or onto a dedicated partition. By default, the SMTP component is installed on the system (OS) partition, but can be easily moved after an Exchange server has been set up.

Reviewing Server Memory and Processor Recommendations

Exchange Server is a resource-hungry application that, left to its own devices, will consume a good portion of any amount of processor or memory that is given to it. The amount of processors and random access memory (RAM) required should reflect the budgetary needs of the organization. In general, midsize and larger organizations should consider multiprocessor servers and greater amounts of RAM—8GB or 16GB or more. This helps increase the amount of mailboxes that can be homed to any particular server.

> **NOTE**
>
> The rule of thumb when sizing an Exchange 2007 mailbox server is to start with 2GB of RAM for a server, then add 5MB of RAM for each mailbox that will be homed on it. For example, on a server with 3,000 mailboxes, at least 17GB of RAM would be required (2GB + (3000*.005GB)).

Outlining Server Operating System Considerations

The base operating system (OS) for Exchange, Windows Server 2003, comes in two versions, Enterprise and Standard. Some midsize and larger organizations could deploy the Enterprise Edition of the Windows Server 2003 product, namely for clustering support. If this functionality is not required, the Standard Edition of the OS is sufficient.

Designing Clustering and Advanced Redundancy Options

In larger organizations, the need to ensure a very high level of reliability is paramount. These organizations often require a level of uptime for their email that equates to "5 nines" of uptime, or 99.999% uptime per year. For this level of redundancy, a higher level of Exchange redundancy is required than the standard models. For these organizations, the clustering features built in to Windows Server 2003, Enterprise Edition and used by Exchange Server 2007, Enterprise Edition are ideal.

> **NOTE**
>
> It is now a Microsoft requirement that at least one node in a cluster be set up in Passive mode for the most effective failover strategy. For more information on using clustering with Exchange 2007, see Chapter 31.

Designing Exchange Server Roles in an Exchange Environment

Exchange 2007 was designed to be resilient and be able to adapt to a wide variety of deployment scenarios. Part of this design revolves around the concept that individual servers can play one or more roles for an organization. Each of these roles provides for specific functionality that is commonly performed by Exchange servers, such as Mailbox server or Client Access server (formerly referred to as an OWA server).

Central to the understanding of Exchange 2007 and how to design and architect it is the understanding of these individual roles. During the design process, understanding server roles is central to proper server placement.

The individual server roles in Exchange 2007 are as follows:

- ► Mailbox server role
- ► Client Access server role
- ► Edge Transport role
- ► Hub Transport role
- ► Unified Messaging role

Each of these roles is described in more detail in the subsequent sections.

Planning for the Mailbox Server Role

The Mailbox server role is the central role in an Exchange topology as it is the server that stores the actual mailboxes of the user. Therefore, Mailbox servers are often the most critical for an organization, and are given the most attention.

With the Enterprise Edition of Exchange, a Mailbox server can hold anywhere from 1 to 50 databases on it. Each of the databases are theoretically unlimited in size, although it is wise to keep an individual database limited to 100GB or less for performance and recovery scenarios.

> **NOTE**
>
> In large organizations, a single server or a cluster of servers is often dedicated to individual server roles. That said, a single server can also be assigned other roles, such as the Client Access server role, in the interest of consolidating the number of servers deployed. The only limitation to this is the Edge server role, which must exist by itself and cannot be installed on a server that holds other roles.

Planning for the Client Access Server Role

The Client Access server role in Exchange is the role that controls access to mailboxes from all clients that aren't Microsoft Outlook and that don't utilize Messaging Application

Programming Interface (MAPI) connections. It is the component that controls access to mailboxes via the following mechanisms:

▶ Outlook Web Access (OWA)

▶ Exchange ActiveSync

▶ Outlook Anywhere (formerly RPC over HTTP)

▶ Post Office Protocol 3 (POP3)

▶ Internet Message Access Protocol (IMAP4)

In addition, CAS systems also handle the following two special services in an Exchange topology:

▶ **Autodiscover service**—The Autodiscover service allows clients to determine their synchronization settings (such as Mailbox server and so on) by entering in their SMTP address and their credentials. It is supported across standard OWA connections.

▶ **Availability service**—The Availability service is the replacement for Free/Busy functionality in Exchange 2000/2003. It is responsible for making a user's calendar availability visible to other users making meeting requests.

Client access servers in Exchange 2007 are the equivalent of Exchange 2000/2003 front-end servers, but include additional functionality above and beyond what front-end servers performed. In addition, one major difference between the two types of servers is that client access servers in Exchange 2007 communicate via fast remote procedure calls (RPCs) between themselves and Mailbox servers. Exchange 2000/2003 servers used unencrypted Hypertext Transfer Protocol (HTTP) to communicate between the systems.

Planning for the Edge Transport Role

The Edge Transport role is new in Exchange 2007 and is a completely new concept. Edge Transport servers are standalone, workgroup members that are meant to reside in the demilitarized zone (DMZ) of a firewall. They do not require access to any internal resources, except for a one-way synchronization of specific configuration information from Active Directory via a process called EdgeSync.

Edge Transport servers hold a small instance of Active Directory Application Mode (ADAM), which is used to store specific configuration information, such as the location of Hub Transport servers within the topology. ADAM is a service that is often known as Active Directory Light, and can be thought of as a scaled-down version of a separate Active Directory forest that runs as a service on a machine.

The Edge Transport role is the role that provides for spam and virus filtering, as Microsoft has moved the emphasis on this type of protection to incoming and outgoing messages. Essentially, this role is a method in which Microsoft intends to capture some of the market taken by SMTP relay systems and virus scanners, which have traditionally been taken by third-party products provided by virus-scanning companies and UNIX sendmail hosts.

In large organizations, redundancy can be built in to Edge Transport services through simple DNS round-robin or with the use of a third-party, load-balancing service between requests sent to the servers.

Planning for the Hub Transport Role

The Hub Transport role is a server role that is responsible for the distribution of mail messages within an Exchange organization. There must be at least one Hub Transport role defined for each Active Directory site that contains a Mailbox server.

> **NOTE**
>
> The Hub Transport role can be added to a server running any other role, with only two exceptions. It cannot be added to a server that is an Edge Transport server, and it cannot be added to a server that is part of a cluster node.

Several special considerations exist for Hub Transport servers as follows:

- ▶ Multiple Hub Transport servers can be established in a site to provide for redundancy and load balancing.

- ▶ Exchange 2007 built-in protection features (antivirus and antispam) are not enabled by default on Hub Transport servers. Instead, they are enabled on Edge Transport servers. If needed, they can be enabled on a Hub Transport server by running a Management Shell script.

- ▶ Messaging policy and compliance features are enabled on Hub Transport servers and can be used to add disclaimers, control attachment sizes, encrypt messages, and block specific content.

Planning for the Unified Messaging Role

The Unified Messaging role in Exchange 2007 is a new concept for Exchange technologies. This role allows fax, voice mail, and email to be integrated into a user's mailbox.

The Unified Messaging role can be installed on multiple servers, although it is recommended that it only be installed when the infrastructure to support it exists in the organization. The Unified Messaging role requires integration with a third-party Private Branch Exchange (PBX) system. As Exchange 2007 progresses, this role will become more important.

Understanding a Sample Deployment Scenario

A better understanding of Exchange Server roles can be achieved by looking at sample deployment scenarios that utilize these roles. For example, Figure 4.2 illustrates a large enterprise deployment of Exchange that takes advantage of all of the unique server roles.

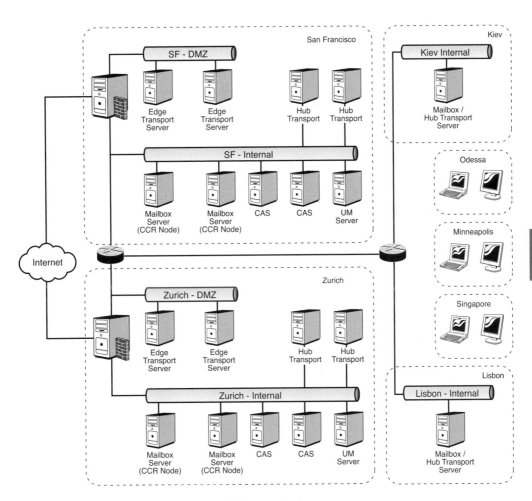

FIGURE 4.2   Examining an Enterprise Exchange deployment.

In this design, the following key deployment features are illustrated:

► Cluster Continuous Replication (CCR) clusters of Exchange Mailbox servers are distributed between the two main locations.

► Dedicated Hub Transport servers distribute mail between the two major sites in San Francisco and Zurich.

► Medium-sized sites such as Kiev and Lisbon make use of combined Mailbox/Hub Transport server systems.

► Client access servers are set up in the two main sites, to provide for two Internet presences for OWA and Outlook Anywhere.

► Edge Transport servers process inbound and outbound mail in the DMZ locations in San Francisco and Zurich.

▶ Unified Messaging servers exist in the main hub sites and are provided as a service for users in those locations. The servers are directly connected to PBX systems in those locations.

▶ Smaller sites such as Minneapolis, Odessa, and Singapore have their mailboxes hosted in the two hub locations and use the client access servers with Outlook Anywhere to access their mailboxes remotely.

Designing Exchange Infrastructure

After Active Directory and the physical OS has been chosen and deployed, the Exchange infrastructure can be set up and optimized for the specific needs of the organization. With these needs in mind, you can do several things to optimize an Exchange 2007 setup, as detailed in the following sections.

Determining the Exchange Version

When installing Exchange, the choice of Exchange version needs to be made. As with Windows Server 2003, there are two versions of Exchange, Standard and Enterprise. The Standard Edition enables all Exchange 2007 functionality except the following:

▶ Limited to 5 databases (as opposed to 50 databases for the Enterprise edition)

▶ Support for Single Copy Clusters

▶ Support for Cluster Continuous Replication (CCR)

Because these functions are only available with the Enterprise Edition of the Exchange Server 2007 product, the decision to choose the Standard Edition versus the Enterprise Edition of Exchange needs to be made at the time of server installation.

In addition to the ability to support more than five databases, the Enterprise Edition also allows for clustering support. In addition, the OS version must be Windows Server 2003 Enterprise or DataCenter Edition for clustering to be supported.

Determining Exchange Databases and Storage Groups Layout

As previously mentioned, the Enterprise Edition of Exchange enables the concept of multiple databases, up to a maximum of 50. This enables a greater amount of design freedom and gives administrators more flexibility. A maximum of 50 production storage groups can be created, and each storage group can contain up to five databases. This does not mean that a server can support 250 databases, however, as Exchange 2007 Enterprise Edition limits an administrator to 50 total databases across all storage groups on each server.

Outlining Exchange Recovery Options

Deploying Exchange requires considerable thought about backup and recovery solutions. Because Exchange is a live, active database, special considerations need to be taken into account when designing the backup strategy for email.

Microsoft designed Exchange 2007 to use the backup application programming interfaces (APIs) from Windows Server 2003. These APIs support the Volume Shadow Copy Service, which enables Exchange databases to be backed up through creation of a "shadow copy" of the entire disk at the beginning of the backup. The shadow copy is then used for the backup, so that the production disk is not affected.

NOTE

The Windows Server 2003 backup utility can be used to back up Exchange using the traditional online backup approach. Volume Shadow Copy requires a third-party solution that has been written to support the Windows Server 2003 backup and restore APIs.

Exchange 2007 also includes support for the concept of a recovery storage group, which is an additional storage group (available with either Standard or Enterprise Exchange) and which can be used on a running server to restore databases and mailboxes "on the fly." This streamlines the mailbox recovery process because restore servers are no longer a necessity. For more information on backup and recovery options, see Chapter 32, "Backing Up the Exchange Server 2007 Environment."

Considering Exchange Antivirus and Antispam Design

Viruses are a major problem for all organizations today. Email is especially vulnerable because it is typically unauthenticated and insecure. Consequently, design of an Exchange implementation should include consideration for antivirus options.

Exchange 2007 enhances the Virus Scanning Application Programming Interface (VSAPI) that was introduced in Exchange 2000 and improved in Exchange 2003. The enhanced VSAPI engine enables quarantine of email messages, as opposed to simply attachments, and enables virus scanning on gateway servers. Third-party virus products can be written to tie directly into the new VSAPI and use its functionality.

Spam, unsolicited email, has become another major headache for most organizations. In response to this, Exchange 2007 has some built-in antispam functionality that enables email messages to contain a spam rating. This helps determine which emails are legitimate, and can be used by third-party antispam products as well.

Monitoring Exchange

Email services are required in many organizations. The expectations of uptime and reliability are increasing, and end users are beginning to expect email to be as available as phone service. Therefore, the ability to monitor Exchange events, alerts, and performance data is optimal.

Exchange 2007 is a complex organism with multiple components, each busy processing tasks, writing to event logs, and running optimization routines. You can monitor Exchange using one of several methods, the most optimal being System Center Operations Manager 2007 (previously named Microsoft Operations Manager or MOM). SCOM 2007 is essentially a monitoring, alerting, and reporting product that gathers event information and performance data, and generates reports about Microsoft servers. An Exchange-specific management pack for SCOM contains hundreds of prepackaged counters and events for Exchange 2007. Use of the management pack is ideal in midsize and larger environments to proactively monitor Exchange.

Although close monitoring of multiple Exchange servers is best supported through the use of SCOM, this might not be the most ideal approach for smaller organizations because SCOM is geared toward medium and large organizations. Exchange monitoring for small organizations can be accomplished through old-fashioned approaches, such as manual reviews of event log information, performance counters using `perfmon`, and simple Simple Network Management Protocol (SNMP) utilities to monitor uptime.

Integrating Client Access into Exchange Server 2007 Design

Although the Exchange server is a powerful systems component, it is only half the equation for an email platform. The client systems comprise the other half, and are a necessary ingredient that should be carefully determined in advance.

Outlining Client Access Methods

Great effort has been put into optimizing and streamlining the client access approaches available in Exchange 2007. Not only have traditional approaches such as the Outlook client been enhanced, but support for nontraditional access with POP3 and IMAP clients is also available. The following options exist for client access with Exchange 2007:

▶ **Outlook MAPI**—The full Outlook client has been streamlined and enhanced. MAPI communications with Exchange 2007 systems have been compressed, and the addition of slow-link detection enables speedy mail retrieval for remote users. Outlook versions that support access to Exchange 2007 servers are limited to the 2002, 2003, and 2007 versions of Outlook.

▶ **Outlook Web Access (OWA)**—The Outlook Web Access (OWA) client is now nearly indistinguishable from the full Outlook client. The one major component missing is offline capability, but nearly every other Outlook functionality is part of OWA.

▶ **ActiveSync**—ActiveSync provides for synchronized access to email from a handheld device, such as a Pocket PC or other Windows Mobile device. It allows for real-time send and receive functionality to and from the handheld, through the use of push technology.

▶ **Outlook Anywhere**—Outlook Anywhere (previously known as RPC over HTTP) is a method by which a full Outlook client can dynamically send and receive messages directly from an Exchange server over an HTTP or Hypertext Transfer Protocol Secure (HTTPS) web connection. This allows for virtual private network (VPN)–free access to Exchange data, over a secured HTTPS connection.

▶ **Post Office Protocol 3 (POP3)**—The Post Office Protocol 3 (POP3) is a legacy protocol that is supported in Exchange 2007. POP3 enables simple retrieval of mail data via applications that use the POP3 protocol. Mail messages, however, cannot be sent with POP3 and must use the SMTP engine in Exchange. By default, POP3 is not turned on and must be explicitly activated.

▶ **Internet Message Access Protocol (IMAP)**—Legacy Interactive Mail Access Protocol (IMAP) access to Exchange is also available, which can enable an Exchange server to be accessed via IMAP applications, such as some UNIX mail clients. As with the POP3 protocol, IMAP support must be explicitly turned on.

NOTE

Exchange 2007 supports the option of disallowing MAPI access or allowing only specific Outlook clients MAPI access. This can be configured if an organization desires only OWA access to an Exchange server. It can also, for security reasons, stipulate that only Outlook 2007 and Outlook 2003 can access the Exchange server. The Registry key required for this functionality is the following:

```
Location:HKLM\System\CurrentControlSet\Services\MSExchangeIS\ParametersSystem
Value Name: Disable MAPI Clients
Data Type: REG_SZ
String: Version # (i.e. v4, v5, etc)
```

See Microsoft TechNet Article 288894 for more information:

```
http://support.microsoft.com/default.aspx?scid=KB;EN-US;288894
```

Each organization will have individual needs that determine which client or set of clients will be supported. In general, the full Outlook client offers the richest messaging experience with Exchange 2007, but many of the other access mechanisms, such as Outlook Web Access, are also valid. The important design consideration is identifying what will be supported, and then enabling support for that client or protocol. Any methods that will not be supported should be disabled or left turned off for security reasons.

Summary

Exchange 2007 offers a broad range of functionality and improvements to messaging and is well suited for organizations of any size. With proper thought into the major design topics, a robust and reliable Exchange email solution can be put into place that will perfectly complement the needs of organizations of any size.

In short, Exchange easily scales up to support thousands of users on multiple servers, and it also scales down very well. Single Exchange server implementations can easily support hundreds of users, even those that are scattered in various locations. This flexibility helps establish Exchange as the premier messaging solution for organizations of any size.

Best Practices

The following are best practices from this chapter:

▶ Try to create an Active Directory design that is as simple as possible. Expand the directory tree with multiple subdomains and forests at a later date if needed.

▶ Even if the organization has high bandwidth between sites, create a site to better control replication and traffic between sites.

▶ When possible, DNS in an organization should be Microsoft DNS; however, Windows Server 2003 (and Windows 2000 Server) also can be integrated with non-Microsoft DNS.

▶ Minimize the number of servers needed by consolidating services into as few systems as possible; however, after systems have been consolidated, take the leftover spare systems and create redundancy between systems.

CHAPTER 5

Integrating Exchange Server 2007 in a Non-Windows Environment

In many organizations, multiple technologies work side by side with Exchange. Certain organizations even have multiple messaging platforms in use. For some of these organizations, consolidation of these platforms into a single platform takes place, but for other organizations, consolidation is not an option, and coexistence in one form or another must be established.

Previous versions of Microsoft Exchange supported embedded connectors to competing messaging platforms, such as Novell GroupWise and Lotus Notes. Exchange Server 2007 servers, however, no longer support these connectors, and organizations are faced with the choice of leaving an Exchange 2003 server in place to support these connectors, or to find other methods of synchronizing address lists and other information between the various platforms.

Fortunately, Microsoft provides multiple tools to allow for synchronization between the directory component of Exchange, Active Directory (AD), and the various other products. This chapter focuses on the integration of AD with non-Windows environments, such as UNIX, Novell, and Lightweight Directory Access Protocol (LDAP) directories. Various tools, such as Microsoft Identity Integration Server (MIIS) 2003, that can be used to accomplish this are presented, and the pros and cons of each are analyzed.

Synchronizing Directory Information with Microsoft Identity Integration Server (MIIS) 2003

In most enterprises today, each individual application or system has its own user database or directory to track who is permitted to use that resource. Identity and access control data reside in different directories as well as applications such as specialized network resource directories, mail servers, human resource, voice mail, payroll, and many other applications.

Each has its own definition of the user's "identity" (for example, name, title, ID numbers, roles, membership in groups). Many have their own password and process for authenticating users. Each has its own tool for managing user accounts and, sometimes, its own dedicated administrator responsible for this task. In addition, most enterprises have multiple processes for requesting resources and for granting and changing access rights. Some of these are automated, but many are paper-based. Many differ from business unit to business unit, even when performing the same function.

Administration of these multiple repositories often leads to time-consuming and redundant efforts in administration and provisioning. It also causes frustration for users, requiring them to remember multiple IDs and passwords for different applications and systems. The larger the organization, the greater the potential variety of these repositories and the effort required to keep them updated.

In response to this problem, Microsoft developed Microsoft Metadirectory Services (MMS) to provide for identity synchronization between different directories. As the product improved, it was rereleased under the new name Microsoft Identity Integration Server (MIIS) 2003.

The use of MIIS 2003 for Exchange 2007 is particularly useful because it can synchronize information between the AD forest that contains Exchange and the other messaging systems in use within the organization.

Understanding MIIS 2003

MIIS is a system that manages and coordinates identity information from multiple data sources in an organization, enabling you to combine that information into a single logical view that represents all of the identity information for a given user or resource.

MIIS enables a company to synchronize identity information across a wide variety of heterogeneous directory and nondirectory identity stores. This enables customers to automate the process of updating identity information across heterogeneous platforms while maintaining the integrity and ownership of that data across the enterprise.

Password management capabilities enable end users or help desk staff to easily reset passwords across multiple systems from one easy-to-use web interface. End users and help desk staff no longer have to use multiple tools to change their passwords across multiple systems.

NOTE

There are actually two versions of MIIS. The first version, known as the Identity Integration Feature Pack for Microsoft Windows Server, is free to anyone licensed for Windows Server 2003 Enterprise Edition. It provides functionality to integrate identity information between multiple Active Directory forests or between Active Directory and Active Directory Application Mode (ADAM).

The second version requires a separate licensing scheme and also requires SQL Server 2000/2005 for the back-end database. This version is known as the Microsoft Identity Integration Server 2003—Enterprise Edition. It provides classic metadirectory functionality that enables administrators to synchronize and provision identity information across a wide variety of stores and systems.

Understanding MIIS 2003 Concepts

It is important to understand some key terms used with MIIS 2003 before comprehending how it can be used to integrate various directories. Keep in mind that the following terms are used to describe MIIS 2003 concepts but might also help give you a broader understanding of how metadirectories function in general:

▶ **Management agent (MA)**—A MIIS 2003 MA is a tool used to communicate with a specific type of directory. For example, an Active Directory MA enables MIIS 2003 to import or export data and perform tasks within Active Directory.

▶ **Connected directory (CD)**—A connected directory is a directory that MIIS 2003 communicates with using a configured MA. An example of a connected directory is a Microsoft Exchange Server 5.5 directory database.

▶ **Connector namespace (CS)**—The connector namespace is the replicated information and container hierarchy extracted from or destined to the respective connected directory.

▶ **Metaverse namespace (MV)**—The metaverse namespace is the authoritative directory data created from the information gathered from each of the respective connector namespaces.

▶ **Metadirectory**—Within MIIS 2003, the metadirectory is made up of all the connector namespaces plus the authoritative metaverse namespace.

▶ **Attributes**—Attributes are the fields of information that are exported from or imported to directory entries. Common directory entry attributes are name, alias, email address, phone number, employee ID, or other information.

MIIS 2003 can be used for many tasks, but is most commonly used for managing directory entry identity information. The intention here is to manage user accounts by synchronizing attributes, such as logon ID, first name, last name, telephone number, title, and department. For example, if a user named Jane Doe is promoted and her title is changed from manager to vice president, the title change could first be entered in the HR or Payroll databases; then through MIIS 2003 MAs, the change could be replicated to other directories within the organization. This ensures that when someone looks up the title attribute for Jane Doe, it is the same in all the directories synchronized with MIIS 2003. This is a common and basic use of MIIS 2003 referred to as *identity management.* Other common uses of MIIS 2003 include account provisioning and group management.

NOTE

MIIS 2003 is a versatile and powerful directory synchronization tool that can be used to simplify and automate some directory management tasks. Because of the nature of MIIS 2003, it can also be a very dangerous tool as MAs can have full access to the connected directories. Misconfiguration of MIIS 2003 MAs could result in data loss, so careful planning and extensive lab testing should be performed before MIIS 2003 is released to the production directories of any organization. In many cases, it might be prudent to contact Microsoft consulting services
and certified Microsoft solution provider/partners to help an organization decide whether MIIS 2003 is right for its environment, or even to design and facilitate the implementation.

Exploring MIIS 2003 Account Provisioning

MIIS enables administrators to easily provision and deprovision users' accounts and identity information, such as distribution, email and security groups across systems, and platforms. Administrators will be able to quickly create new accounts for employees based on events or changes in authoritative stores such as the human resources system. In addition, as employees leave a company, they can be immediately deprovisioned from those same systems.

Account provisioning in MIIS 2003 enables advanced configurations of directory MAs, along with special provisioning agents, to be used to automate account creation and deletion in several directories. For example, if a new user account is created in Active Directory, the Active Directory MA could tag this account. Then, when the respective MAs are run for other connected directories, a new user account could be automatically generated.

One enhancement of MIIS 2003 over MMS is that password synchronization is now supported for specific directories that manage passwords within the directory. MIIS 2003 provides an application programming interface (API) accessed through the Windows Management Instrumentation (WMI). For connected directories that manage passwords in the directory's store, password management is activated when a MA is configured in MA Designer. In addition to enabling password management for each MA, Management Agent Designer returns a system name attribute using the WMI interface for each connector space object.

Outlining the Role of Management Agents (MAs) in MIIS 2003

A MA links a specific connected data source to the metadirectory. The MA is responsible for moving data from the connected data source and the metadirectory. When data in the metadirectory is modified, the MA can also export the data to the connected data source to keep the connected data source synchronized with the metadirectory. Generally, there is at least one MA for each connected directory. MIIS 2003, Enterprise Edition, includes MAs for the following identity repositories:

- Active Directory

- Active Directory Application Mode (ADAM)

- Attribute-value pair text files

- Comma-separated value files

- Delimited text files

- Directory Services Markup Language (DSML) 2.0

- Exchange Server 5.5

- Exchange Server 2000/2003 and Exchange Server 2007 Global Address List (GAL) synchronization

- Fixed-width text files

- LDAP Directory Interchange Format (LDIF)

- Lotus Notes/Domino 4.6/5.0

- Novell NDS, eDirectory, DirXML

- Sun/iPlanet/Netscape directory 4.x/5.x (with "changelog" support)

- Microsoft SQL Server 2005/2000/7.0

- Microsoft Windows NT 4.0 domains

- Oracle 8i/9i

- Informix, dBase, ODBC, and OLE DB support via SQL Server Data Transformation Services

NOTE

Service Pack 2 for MIIS introduced integrated support for synchronization with additional directories such as Service Advertising Protocol (SAP). In addition, it also introduced the ability for end users to reset their own passwords via a web management interface.

MAs contain rules that govern how an object's attributes are mapped, how connected directory objects are found in the metaverse, and when connected directory objects should be created or deleted.

These agents are used to configure how MIIS 2003 will communicate and interact with the connected directories when the agent is run. When a MA is first created, all the configuration of that agent can be performed during that instance. The elements that can be configured include which type of directory objects will be replicated to the connector namespace, which attributes will be replicated, directory entry join and projection rules, attribute flow rules between the connector namespace and the metaverse namespace, plus more. If a necessary configuration is unknown during the MA creation, it can be revisited and modified later.

Defining MIIS 2003 and Group Management

Just as MIIS 2003 can perform identity management for user accounts, it also can perform management tasks for groups. When a group is projected into the metaverse namespace, the group membership attribute can be replicated to other connected directories through their MAs. This enables a group membership change to occur in one directory and be replicated to other directories automatically.

Installing MIIS 2003 with SQL 2000/2005

Both versions of MIIS 2003 require a licensed version of SQL Server 2000 with SP3 or greater or SQL Server 2005 to run, and an install of the product will prompt for the location of a SQL server, as illustrated in Figure 5.1.

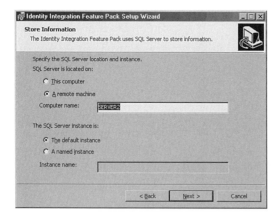

FIGURE 5.1   SQL install options with MIIS 2003.

It is not necessarily required to install a new instance of SQL because an existing SQL 2000 SP3 or greater system can be used as well. If an existing SQL 2000/2005 server is not available, SQL can be installed on the same system as MIIS 2003. This particular system must be running Windows Server 2003 as MIIS requires this version of the OS.

Synchronizing Exchange Server 2007 with Novell eDirectory

Novell eDirectory and Novell Directory Service (NDS) environments are relatively commonplace in business environments, and there is often a need to integrate them into deployed Exchange infrastructures. Several tools exist that can make this a reality, including the MIIS 2003 tools discussed. In addition, tools in the Microsoft-supplied Services for NetWare can be used to synchronize directory information between the two directory systems.

> **NOTE**
>
> Exchange 2000 Server and Exchange Server 2003 included a GroupWise connector component, to allow for the automatic synchronization of GroupWise address list information and calendaring data directly to Exchange. This connector is no longer supported in Exchange 2007, so the only effective way to synchronize a Novell directory with Exchange 2007 is either with a synchronization tool such as MIIS or Microsoft Directory Synchronization Services (MSDSS), or by keeping an Exchange 2003 server within the organization with the connector installed on it.

Understanding Novell eDirectory

Novell eDirectory is a distributed, hierarchical database of network information that is used to create a relationship between users and resources. It simplifies network management because network administrators can administer global networks from one location (or many) and manage all network resources as part of the eDirectory tree.

User administration is simplified because the users dynamically inherit access to network resources from their placement in the eDirectory tree. For example, eDirectory enables a user to dynamically inherit access to departmental resources, such as applications and printers, when that user is placed in the department's eDirectory container.

eDirectory information is typically stored on several servers, which are often at different locations. This enables information to be stored near the users who need it and provides efficient operation even if the users are geographically dispersed. Names are organized in a top-down hierarchy or tree structure. This helps users find resources in a structured manner. It also enables an administrator to administer a large network by delegating portions of the tree to local administrators.

The entries in an eDirectory database represent network resources available on the network and are referred to as objects. An object contains information that identifies, characterizes, and locates information pertaining to the resource it represents. eDirectory uses a single naming system that encompasses all servers, services, and users in an internetwork. In the past, names were administered separately on each server. Now, eDirectory enables information entered once to be accessible everywhere and lets a user log in once to access diverse, geographically separated resources.

An eDirectory database can be divided into logical partitions according to business needs, network use, geographical location, access time, and other factors. These partitions can be distributed to any server represented in the directory. When an eDirectory database is distributed to multiple servers, eDirectory maintains the equality of the distributed logical partitions by distributing object information changes to the appropriate servers.

Deploying MIIS 2003 for Identity Management with eDirectory

MIIS 2003 can be an effective tool for managing identities between Novell eDirectory environments and Active Directory. Identity information could include names, email and physical addresses, titles, department affiliations, and much more. Generally speaking, identity information is the type of data commonly found in corporate phone books or intranets. To use MIIS 2003 for identity management between Active Directory and Novell eDirectory, follow these high-level steps:

1. Install MIIS 2003 and the latest service packs and patches.

2. Create an MA for each of the directories, including an Active Directory MA and a Novell eDirectory MA.

3. Configure the MAs to import directory object types into their respective connector namespaces.

4. Configure one of the MAs—for example, the Active Directory MA—to project the connector space directory objects and directory hierarchy into the metaverse name-space.

5. Within each of the MAs, a function can be configured called attribute flow, which defines which directory object attributes from each directory will be projected into the respective metaverse directory objects. Configure the attribute flow rules for each MA.

6. Configure the account-joining properties for directory objects. This is the most crucial step because it determines how the objects in each directory are related to one another within the metaverse namespace. To configure the account join, certain criteria can be used, such as employee ID or first name and last name combination. The key is to find the most unique combination to avoid problems when two objects with similar names are located—for example, if two users named Tom Jones exist in Active Directory.

7. After completely configuring the MAs and account joins, configure MA run profiles to tell the MA what to perform with the connected directory and connector name-space. For example, perform a full import or export of data. The first time the MA is run, the connected directory information is imported to create the initial connector namespace.

8. After running the MAs once, you can run them a second time to propagate the authoritative metaverse data to the respective connector namespaces and out to the connected directories.

These steps outline the most common use of MIIS 2003; these steps can be used to simplify account maintenance tasks when several directories need to be managed simultaneously. When more sophisticated functionality using MIIS 2003 is needed, such as the automatic creation and deletion of directory entries, extensive scripting and customization of MIIS 2003 can be done to create a more complete enterprise account provisioning system.

Using Microsoft Directory Synchronization Services to Integrate Directories

MicrosoftDirectory Synchronization Services (MSDSS), part of the Services for NetWare Toolkit, is a tool used for synchronization of directory information stored in the Active Directory and NDS. MSDSS synchronizes directory information stored in Active Directory with all versions of NetWare; MSDSS supports a two-way synchronization with NDS and a one-way synchronization with Novell 3.x bindery services.

Because Active Directory does not support a container comparable to an NDS root organization and because Active Directory security differs from Novell, MSDSS, in Migration mode only, creates a corresponding domain local security group in Active Directory for each NDS organizational unit (OU) and organization. MSDSS then maps each Novell OU or organization to the corresponding Active Directory domain local security group.

MSDSS provides a single point of administration; with one-way synchronization, changes made to Active Directory will be propagated over to NDS during synchronization. Synchronization from Active Directory to NDS allows changes to object attributes, such as a user's middle name or address, to be propagated. In two-way synchronization mode, changes from NDS to Active Directory require a full synchronization of the object (all attributes of the user object).

One of the key benefits to MSDSS is password synchronization. Passwords can be administered in Active Directory and the changes propagated over to NDS during synchronization. Password synchronization allows users access to Windows Server 2003 and Novell NDS resources with the same logon credentials.

The MSDSS architecture is made up of the following three components. These components manage, map, read, and write changes that occur in Active Directory, NDS, and NetWare bindery services:

▶ The configuration of the synchronization parameters is handled by the session manager.

▶ An object mapper relates the objects to each other (class and attributes), namespace, rights, and permissions between the source and target directories.

▶ Changes to each directory are handled by a DirSync (read/write) provider. LDAP is used for Active Directory calls and NetWare Core Protocol (NCP) calls for NDS and NetWare binderies.

In addition to the core components of MSDSS, the session configuration settings (session database) are securely stored in Active Directory. Specific scenarios for MSDSS include the following:

▶ A company is migrating directly from Novell to a Windows Server 2003 network. All network services—such as domain name system (DNS), Dynamic Host Configuration Protocol (DHCP), and Internet Information Services (IIS)—are running on a single server. MSDSS can be used to migrate all users and files over to Windows Server 2003 after all services have been migrated.

▶ A company is gradually migrating from Novell to a Windows Server 2003 network. The network services—such as DNS, DHCP, and IIS—are installed on multiple servers and sites. MSDSS can be used to migrate and synchronize AD and NDS directories during the migration.

Installing the Microsoft Directory Synchronization Service

MSDSS needs to be installed on a Windows domain controller to properly synchronize directory information between the two different network environments. To install MSDSS on a Windows Server 2003 domain controller, follow these steps:

1. On the domain controller computer on which MSDSS will be installed, insert the CD into the CD-ROM drive.

2. Go into the MSDSS directory on the CD-ROM (such as d:\msdss) and run the msdss.msi script package. This launches the Microsoft Directory Synchronization Service Installation Wizard.

3. Choose to install the Microsoft Directory Synchronization Service.

> **NOTE**
>
> Installing MSDSS initiates an extension of the schema of the Active Directory forest. As with any schema update, the Active Directory should be backed up (see Chapter 32, "Backing Up the Exchange Server 2007 Environment," for details on doing a full backup of Active Directory). Also with a schema update, because the update will replicate directory changes to all global catalogs throughout the organization, the replication should be done at a time when a global catalog synchronization can take place without impact on the normal production environment.

Synchronizing eDirectory/NDS with Active Directory Using Services for NetWare

For organizations that have both a Windows Active Directory and a Novell eDirectory (or NDS) environment, two primary methods are available to perform directory synchronization between the two directories. One method is using the Novell DirXML product, and the other method is using the MSDSS utility. To set up directory synchronization with MSDSS, do the following:

1. Launch the MSDSS utility by selecting Start, Programs, Administrative Tools, Directory Synchronization.

2. Right-click on the MSDSS tool option, and select New Session.

3. Click Next at the New Session Wizard welcome screen.

4. At the Synchronization and Migration Tasks screen, choose either NDS or Bindery for the type of service.

> **NOTE**
>
> Use the NDS option if Novell NetWare 4.x or higher running NDS or eDirectory is used. Use the Bindery option if Novell NetWare 3.2 or lower bindery mode is running on the Novell network.

5. Depending on the synchronization option, choose either a one-way (from AD to NDS/Bindery), a two-way (AD to NDS/Bindery and back), or a migration from NDS/Bindery to AD. Click Next.

6. For the Active Directory container and domain controller, choose the AD container to which objects will be synchronized, as well as the name of the domain controller that will be used to extract and synchronize information, similar to the settings shown in Figure 5.2. Click Next.

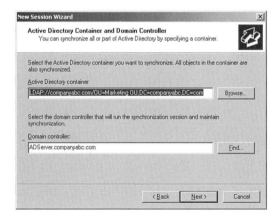

FIGURE 5.2   Setting server synchronization information settings.

7. For the NDS container and password, select the NDS container to and/or from which AD information will be synchronized. Enter a logon name and password for a supervisor account on Novell to access the Novell directory. Click Next.

8. On the initial reverse synchronization screen, select the password option to define passwords to be either blank, same as the username, set to a random value (that can be viewed in the log file), or set to an organizational default. Click OK after selecting the password option, and then click Next to continue.

9. Click Finish to begin the synchronization/migration process.

Implementing MSDSS

MSDSS runs on a Windows 2000 Server or Windows Server 2003 domain controller and replicates user account and password information between the Active Directory environment and a Novell eDirectory or NDS environment. MSDSS is a Windows service that synchronizes user account information between Active Directory and NetWare. The following are best practices determined in the implementation of MSDSS in an enterprise environment:

▶ Ensure that the Microsoft MSDSS server that is running on a Windows Active Directory domain controller and the Novell directory server are on the same network segment or have limited hops between each other.

▶ Because directory synchronization reads and writes information directly to the network directory, test the replication process between mirrored domain and directory services in a test lab environment before implementing MSDSS for the first time in a production environment.

▶ Monitor directory and password synchronization processing times to confirm the transactions are occurring fast enough for users to access network resources. If users get an authentication error, consider upgrading the MSDSS server to a faster system.

▶ Password characteristic policies (requiring upper- and lowercase letters, numbers, or extended characters in the password and password change times) should be similar on both the Microsoft and Novell environments to minimize inconsistencies in authorization and update processes.

Identifying Limitations on Directory Synchronization with MSDSS

Although directory synchronization can provide common logon names and passwords, MSDSS does not provide dual client support or any application-level linkage between multiple platform configurations. This means that if a Novell server is running IPX as a communication protocol and Windows is running TCP/IP, MSDSS does not do protocol conversion. Likewise, if an application is running on a Novell server requiring SAP, because Windows servers commonly use NetBIOS for device advertising, a dual client protocol stack must be enabled to provide common communications.

MSDSS merely links the logon names and passwords between multiple environments. The following are areas that need to be considered separate from the logon and password synchronization process:

▶ Protocols, such as TCP/IP and IPX/SPX, should be supported by servers and clients.

▶ Applications that require communication standards for logon authentication might require a client component to be installed on the workstations or servers in the mixed environment.

▶ Applications that were written for Novell servers (such as Network Loadable Modules [NLMs] or BTrieve databases) should be converted to support Windows.

▶ Logon scripts, drive mappings, or other access systems compatible with one networking environment might not work across multiple environments, so those components should be tested for full compatibility.

▶ Backup utilities, antivirus applications, network management components, or system monitoring tools that work on one system should be purchased or relicensed to support another network operating configuration.

Backing Up and Restoring MSDSS Information

MSDSS configuration, tables, and system configurations are critical to the operations of the MSDSS synchronization tool. Microsoft provides a backup and restore utility that enables the storage and recovery of MSDSS information. To back up MSDSS, do the following:

1. Select Start, Programs, Administrative Tools, MSDSS Backup & Restore Utility. A screen similar to the one shown in Figure 5.3 should appear.

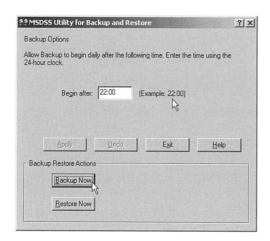

FIGURE 5.3   Backing up MSDSS information.

2. Either click Backup Now to back up the MSDSS session directory, or change the default time when the MSDSS information should be backed up.

3. If it is required to back up the session directory information, the process will notify that the MSDSS service will need to be stopped. Choose Yes to continue.

4. Upon completion of the backup, there will be a prompt that the MSDSS service will need to be restarted. Choose Yes to restart the MSDSS service.

At any time, if the MSDSS session directory information becomes corrupt or behaves erratically, the MSDSS information can be restored. To restore MSDSS, do the following:

1. Select Start, Programs, Administrative Tools, MSDSS Backup & Restore Utility.

2. Click Restore Now to restore the MSDSS session directory.

3. When notified that the MSDSS service will need to be stopped, choose Yes to continue.

4. Upon completion of the restore, a final prompt will appear to signify that the MSDSS service will need to be restarted. Choose Yes to restart the MSDSS service.

Managing Identity Information Between LDAP Directories and Exchange Server 2007

LDAP directories are commonplace today and can be found in many business environments. UNIX applications in particular make wide use of the LDAP standard for directories. Along with this proliferation of LDAP directory structures comes a need to synchronize the information contained within them to an Exchange 2007 environment. The Enterprise version of MIIS 2003 contains MAs that support synchronization to LDAP directories. Consequently, a good understanding of LDAP concepts is required before syncing between the environments.

Understanding LDAP from an Historical Perspective

To understand LDAP better, it is useful to consider the X.500 and Directory Access Protocol (DAP) from which it is derived. In X.500, the Directory System Agent (DSA) is the database in which directory information is stored. This database is hierarchical in form, designed to provide fast and efficient search and retrieval. The Directory User Agent (DUA) provides functionality that can be implemented in all sorts of user interfaces through dedicated DUA clients, web server gateways, or email applications. The DAP is a protocol used in X.500 directory services for controlling communications between the DUA and DSA agents. The agents represent the user or program and the directory, respectively.

The X.500 directory services are Application-layer processes. Directory services can be used to provide global, unified naming services for all elements in a network, translate between network names and addresses, provide descriptions of objects in a directory, and provide unique names for all objects in the directory. These X.500 objects are hierarchical with different levels for each category of information, such as country, state, city, and organization. These objects can be files (as in a file system directory listing), network entities (as in a network naming service such as NDS), or other types of entities.

Lightweight protocols combine routing and transport services in a more streamlined fashion than do traditional network and Transport-layer protocols. This makes it possible to transmit more efficiently over high-speed networks—such as Asynchronous Transfer Mode (ATM) or Fiber Distributed Data Interface (FDDI)—and media—such as fiber-optic cable.

Lightweight protocols also use various measures and refinements to streamline and speed up transmissions, such as using a fixed header and trailer size to save the overhead of transmitting a destination address with each packet.

LDAP is a subset of the X.500 protocol. LDAP clients are, therefore, smaller, faster, and easier to implement than X.500 clients. LDAP is vendor-independent and works with, but does not require, X.500. Contrary to X.500, LDAP supports TCP/IP, which is necessary for any type of Internet access. LDAP is an open protocol, and applications are independent of the server platform hosting the directory.

Active Directory is not a pure X.500 directory. Instead, it uses LDAP as the access protocol and supports the X.500 information model without requiring systems to host the entire X.500 overhead. The result is the high level of interoperability required for administering real-world, heterogeneous networks.

Active Directory supports access via LDAP from any LDAP-enabled client. LDAP names are less intuitive than Internet names, but the complexity of LDAP naming is usually hidden within an application. LDAP names use the X.500 naming convention called attributed naming.

An LDAP uniform resource locator (URL) names the server holding Active Directory services and the attributed name of the object—for example:

```
LDAP://Server1.companyabc.com/CN=JDoe,OU=Users,O=companyabc,C=US
```

By combining the best of the DNS and X.500 naming standards, LDAP, other key protocols, and a rich set of APIs, Active Directory enables a single point of administration for all resources, including files, peripheral devices, host connections, databases, web access, users, arbitrary other objects, services, and network resources.

Understanding How LDAP Works

LDAP directory service is based on a client/server model. One or more LDAP servers contain the data making up the LDAP directory tree. An LDAP client connects to an LDAP server and asks it a question. The server responds with the answer or with a pointer to where the client can get more information (typically, another LDAP server). No matter which LDAP server a client connects to, it sees the same view of the directory; a name presented to one LDAP server references the same entry it would at another LDAP server. This is an important feature of a global directory service such as LDAP.

Outlining the Differences Between LDAP2 and LDAP3 Implementations

LDAP3 defines a number of improvements that enable a more efficient implementation of the Internet directory user agent access model. These changes include the following:

▶ Use of UTF-8 for all text string attributes to support extended character sets

▶ Operational attributes that the directory maintains for its own use—for example, to log the date and time when another attribute has been modified

▶ Referrals enabling a server to direct a client to another server that might have the data that the client requested

▶ Schema publishing with the directory, enabling a client to discover the object classes and attributes that a server supports

▶ Extended searching operations to enable paging and sorting of results, and client-defined searching and sorting controls

▶ Stronger security through a Simple Authentication and Security Layer (SASL) based authentication mechanism

▶ Extended operations, providing additional features without changing the protocol version

LDAP3 is compatible with LDAP2. An LDAP2 client can connect to an LDAP3 server (this is a requirement of an LDAP3 server). However, an LDAP3 server can choose not to talk to an LDAP2 client if LDAP3 features are critical to its application.

NOTE

LDAP was built on Internet-defined standards and is composed of the following Request for Comments (RFCs):

▶ **RFC 2251**—Lightweight Directory Access Protocol (v3)

▶ **RFC 2255**—The LDAP URL format

▶ **RFC 2256**—A summary of the X.500(96) user schema for use with LDAP3

▶ **RFC 2253**—Lightweight Directory Access Protocol (v3): UTF-8 string representation of distinguished names

▶ **RFC 2254**—The string representation of LDAP search filters

---

Using Services for UNIX to Integrate UNIX Systems with an Active Directory/Exchange Server 2007 Environment

In many cases, it might be necessary to integrate many of the components of an existing UNIX implementation with the Exchange 2007 forest. In these cases, a tool most recently provided with Windows Server 2003 R2 Edition known as Services for UNIX (SFU) should be examined.

For many years, UNIX and Windows systems were viewed as separate, incompatible environments that were physically, technically, and ideologically different. Over the years, however, organizations found that supporting two completely separate topologies within their environments was inefficient and expensive; a great deal of redundant work was also required to maintain multiple sets of user accounts, passwords, environments, and so on.

Slowly, the means to interoperate between these environments was developed. At first, most of the interoperability tools were written to join UNIX with Windows, as evidenced by Samba, a method for Linux/UNIX platforms to be able to access Windows NT file shares. Microsoft tools always seemed a step behind that available elsewhere. With the release of the new Services for UNIX tools in Windows Server 2003 R2, Microsoft leapfrogs traditional solutions, like Samba, and becomes the leader for cross-platform integration. Long-awaited functionality such as password synchronization, the capability to run UNIX scripts on Windows, joint security credentials, and so on were presented as viable options and can be now be considered as part of a migration to or interoperability scenario with Windows Server 2003.

Understanding the Development of Services for UNIX

Services for UNIX has made large strides in its development. From initial skepticism, the product has developed into a formidable integration and migration utility that allows for a great deal of interenvironment flexibility. The first versions of the software, 1.x and 2.x, were limited in many ways, however. Subsequent updates to the software vastly improved its capabilities and further integrated it with the core operating system.

A watershed development in the development of Services for UNIX was the introduction of the 3.0 version of the software. This version enhanced support for UNIX through the addition or enhancement of nearly all components. Included with version 3.0 was the Interix product as well, an extension to the POSIX infrastructure of Windows to support UNIX scripting and applications natively on a Windows server.

Then, version 3.5 of SFU was released, which included several functionality improvements over SFU 3.0. The following components and improvements have been made in the 3.5 release:

- ▶ Greater support for Windows Server 2003 Active Directory authentication
- ▶ Improved utilities for international language support
- ▶ Threaded application support in Interix
- ▶ Significant Interix performance increases of up to 100%
- ▶ Support for the Volume Shadow Copy Service of Windows Server 2003

Finally, we come to the Windows Server 2003 R2-integrated version of SFU. Besides being slipstreamed directly into the operating system, some functional changes have been made as well. Most important, the structure of SFU has changed considerably. Here is the structure of major improvements for the R2 SFU offering:

▶ Network Information Service (NIS) and Active Directory integration with scripts for populating Active Directory from a NIS database

▶ Extended NIS interoperability, including allowing a Windows Server 2003 R2 system to act as a NIS master in a mixed environment

▶ Network File System (NFS) server functionality expanded to Mac OS X and higher clients

▶ Subsystem for UNIX Applications (SUA) allows POSIX-compliant UNIX application to be run on Windows Server 2003 R2, including many common UNIX tools and scripts

▶ Easier porting of native UNIX and Linux scripts to the SUA environment

Outlining the Components of Services for UNIX

Services for UNIX is composed of several key components, each of which provides a specific integration task with different UNIX environments. Any or all of these components can be used as part of Services for UNIX as the installation of the suite can be customized, depending on an organization's needs. The major components of SFU are as follows:

▶ Subsystem for UNIX-based applications

▶ Client for NFS

▶ Server for NFS

▶ Telnet server

▶ Telnet client

▶ Server for NIS

▶ Password synchronization

▶ NIS domains

Each component can be installed separately or multiple components can be installed on a single server as necessary. Components are all available from the Add/Remove Windows Components Wizard in Control Panel. Each component is described in more detail in the following sections.

Detailing the Prerequisites for Services for UNIX

Services for UNIX R2 interoperates with various flavors of UNIX, but was tested and specifically written for use with the following UNIX iterations:

- Sun Solaris 7.x, 8.x, 9.x, or 10

- Red Hat Linux 8.0 and later

- Hewlett-Packard HP-UX 11i

- IBM AIX 5L 5.2

- Apple Macintosh OS X

> **NOTE**
>
> SFU is not limited to these versions of Sun Solaris, Red Hat Linux, HP-UX, IBM AIX, and Apple OS X. It actually performs quite well in various other similar versions and implementations of UNIX, Linux, and Mac OS X.

Services for UNIX has some other important prerequisites and limitations that must be taken into account before considering it for use in an environment. These factors include the following:

- Server for NIS must be installed on an Active Directory domain controller. In addition, all domain controllers in the domain must be running Server for NIS.

- Password synchronization requires installation on domain controllers in each environment.

- Server for NIS must not be subservient to a UNIX NIS server—it can only be subservient to another Windows-based SFU server. This requirement can be a politically sensitive one and should be broached carefully, as some UNIX administrators will be hesitant to make the Windows-based NIS the primary NIS server.

- The Server for NIS authentication component must be installed on all domain controllers in the domain in which security credentials will be utilized.

Installing Services for UNIX R2

The installation of Services for UNIX for Windows Server 2003 R2 is as simple as adding another Windows component. From Control Panel, go to Add/Remove Programs and then Add/Remove Windows Components. The various parts that make up SFU are all available in their appropriate areas.

> **NOTE**
>
> You will need the Windows 2003 R2 installation CD to add each of the Services for UNIX components.

The installation of Services for UNIX is straightforward and uses the familiar Microsoft Add/Remove Windows Components Installation Wizard. After the prerequisites have been satisfied and the desired functionality has been identified, you can begin the SFU installation.

To install SFU R2, perform the following steps:

1. Click the Start menu and select Control Panel.

2. Choose Add/Remove Programs.

3. Choose Add/Remove Windows Components in the left column.

4. Select Subsystem for UNIX-based Applications, and then click Next.

5. You are prompted for the location of the CD or another location for the requested files.

6. The setup prompts you to download the Utilities and SDK for UNIX-based Applications. Click Yes to download the package, as illustrated in Figure 5.4.

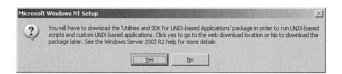

FIGURE 5.4   Download the Utilities and SDK for UNIX-based Applications.

NOTE

The Utilities and SDK for UNIX-based Applications is fairly large, approximately 180MB. You can download this package in advance if desired to speed the installation process. Different packages are available for x86 and AMD architectures.

---

7. Click Next through the first few screens, and then accept the license agreement.

8. Click the Enable Setuid Behavior for SUA Programs check box, as this is an important function for many UNIX applications. Click the Change the Default Behavior to Case Sensitive check box, as illustrated in Figure 5.5, if your UNIX environment is case sensitive.

9. Click Finish for both screens and the installation is complete. You will need to reboot for the components to become active.

10. To install the various Active Directory–related components, again go to the Add/Remove Windows Components menu.

11. Select Active Directory Services, and then click Details. Select Identity Management for UNIX, as shown in Figure 5.6, and then click Details again to drill down to the Identity Management for UNIX (IDMU) options. Select all three options for a full installation.

FIGURE 5.5   Reviewing the Utilities and SDK for UNIX-based Applications options.

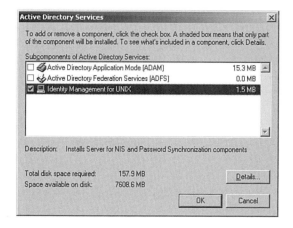

FIGURE 5.6   Active Directory Services details.

12. Click Next to begin the installation.

13. You are prompted to locate the request files on the CD. After installation, click Finish to finish the installation. Finally, reboot for the components to become active.

14. To install the NFS components, again go to the Add/Remove Windows Components menu.

15. The Microsoft Services for NFS are located under Other Network File and Print Services.

16. Select Details under Microsoft Services for NFS, and choose the appropriate options for your installation, as shown in Figure 5.7.

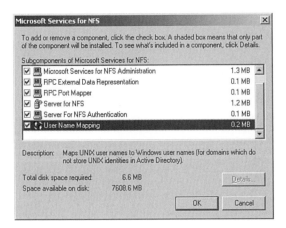

FIGURE 5.7   Microsoft Services for NFS options.

After being installed, the various functionalities can be tested in a lab environment or deployed into production.

Synchronizing User Information Between AD and UNIX

It might be necessary to maintain and support UNIX accounts and AD/Exchange 2007 mailboxes at the same time. SFU provides for synchronization between these accounts with the username mapping and password synchronization capabilities.

Username Mapping

Username mapping allows specific user accounts in Windows Server 2003 Active Directory to be associated with corresponding UNIX user accounts. In addition to mapping identically named user accounts, username mapping allows for the association of user accounts with different names in each organization. This factor is particularly useful considering the fact that UNIX user accounts are case sensitive, whereas Windows accounts are not.

Username mapping supports the capability to map multiple Windows user accounts to a single user account in UNIX. This capability allows, for example, multiple administrators to map Windows Server 2003 Active Directory accounts with the UNIX root administrator account.

Synchronizing Passwords with IDMU

Going hand in hand with the username mapping service, password synchronization allows for those user accounts that have been mapped to automatically update their passwords between the two environments. This functionality, accessible from the IDMU MMC administration menu, as illustrated in Figure 5.8, allows users on either side to change their passwords and have the changes reflected on the mapped user accounts in the opposite platform.

FIGURE 5.8   Adding a UNIX server to synchronize with and from.

As previously mentioned, password synchronization must be installed on all domain controllers on the Active Directory side because all the domain controllers must be able to understand the UNIX password requests forwarded to them. In addition, password synchronization is only supported out of the box in the following UNIX platforms:

▶ Solaris 7, 8, and 9

▶ Red Hat Linux 6.2, 7.0, and 8.0

▶ HP-UX 11

All other flavors of UNIX require a recompile of the platform, which is made easier by the inclusion of makefiles and SFU source code. SFU R2 also includes the encryption libraries, making it even easier to compile a customized solution.

Adding NIS Users to Active Directory

For users who want their existing NIS servers to continue to provide authentication for UNIX and Linux servers, the NIS Migration Wizard is not the best choice. There is a package of Korn shell scripts downloadable from Microsoft.com that makes this process simple. The getusers.ksh script gets a list of all users in a NIS database, including the comment field. This script must be run with an account with the permission to run ypcat passwd. The makeusers.ksh script imports these users to Active Directory. The makeusers. ksh script must be run by a user with domain admin privileges. The -e flag enables accounts, as by default the accounts are created in a disabled state. This is a perfect solution for migrations that will require the existing NIS servers to remain intact indefinitely.

Summary

Exchange 2007 running on Active Directory already goes far toward the goal of maintaining a single directory system for managing enterprise user accounts. The addition of advanced tools such as MIIS 2003, Services for NetWare, and Services for UNIX further extends the capabilities of an organization to achieve this goal by providing for single metadirectory functionality. Proper use of these tools can significantly reduce the overhead associated with maintaining separate Exchange, UNIX, NetWare, LDAP, and other directory implementations.

Best Practices

The following are best practices from this chapter:

- ▶ Keep an Exchange 2003 system in the organization if the functionality in the legacy GroupWise Connector or Lotus Notes Connector for Exchange is required. These connectors are not supported on an Exchange 2007 system.

- ▶ Use the Enterprise version of MIIS 2003 for synchronization between the Exchange 2007 directory service, Active Directory, and non-AD directories, such as Novell eDirectory, LDAP, and UNIX directories.

- ▶ Consider Services for NetWare when syncing directories or integrating a Novell NetWare environment with Exchange 2007.

- ▶ Deploy Services for UNIX to integrate UNIX directories and functionality into an Exchange 2007 environment.

- ▶ Use account provisioning in MIIS 2003 to reduce the overhead associated with creating and deleting user accounts.

CHAPTER 6

Understanding Network Services and Active Directory Domain Controller Placement for Exchange Server 2007

With Microsoft Exchange relying on Active Directory and domain name system (DNS) to function, it is important for an organization to make sure that critical networking services are configured and operating properly and that domain controllers have been deployed and configured to adequately support the environment. Exchange 2007 has removed its reliance on NetBios and WINS for its networking services and is now very dependent upon the successful operation of Active Directory and DNS. This chapter covers best practices for the design, implementation, and validation that Windows networking services and Active Directory are working properly in an Exchange 2007 environment.

Domain Name System and Its Role in Exchange Server 2007

For computer systems to communicate with each other, whether you are talking about a local area network (LAN), a wide area network (WAN), or the Internet, they must have the ability to identify one another using some type of name resolution. Several strategies have been developed over the years, but the most reliable one to date (and the current industry standard) is the use of a DNS.

Accurate name resolution is critical in a mail environment as well. For a message to reach its destination, it might pass through several systems that need to know where it came from and where it is going.

In the past, Microsoft has continued to support the Windows Internet Naming Service, commonly known as WINS, as an alternative way of performing name resolution within an environment. WINS provided a distributed database for registering and querying dynamic mappings of NetBIOS names for computers and groups. WINS mapped these NetBIOS names to IP addresses, and was originally designed to resolve problems that surrounded NetBIOS name resolution in routed networks.

However, in Microsoft Exchange Server 2007, support for WINS/NetBIOS broadcasts has been done away with. This makes the importance of DNS in Exchange 2007 greater than ever because if DNS is not configured and working properly, Exchange 2007 will not work at all.

Even Lightweight Directory Access Protocol (LDAP) queries for local mailbox users require the DNS client to be properly configured and functioning on your Exchange 2007 servers.

This first half of this chapter details how DNS interacts with Exchange 2007 and offers troubleshooting techniques and best practices to ensure the system functions properly. The second half of this chapter covers the proper placement and optimized configuration of Active Directory services for the successful operation of Exchange 2007.

Domain Name System Defined

The Internet, as well as most home and business networks, rely on Internet Protocol (IP) addresses to allow computers to connect to one another. If we had to remember the IP addresses of every website, server, workstation, and printer that we connect to on a daily basis, it would be very difficult to accomplish anything!

The domain name system, commonly abbreviated as DNS, is a hierarchical, distributed database used to resolve, or translate, domain and host names to IP addresses. Using DNS, users, computers, and applications that query DNS can specify remote systems by fully qualified domain names (FQDNs).

DNS is the primary method for name resolution for the Microsoft Windows Server platforms. DNS is also a requirement for deploying Active Directory (AD), though Active Directory is not a requirement for deploying DNS. That being said, in a Microsoft Windows environment, integrating DNS and Active Directory enables DNS servers to take advantage of the security, performance, and fault-tolerance capabilities designed into Active Directory.

Using DNS

DNS is composed of two components: clients and servers. Servers store information about specific components.

When a DNS client needs to contact a host system, it first attempts to do so by using local resources. The client first checks its local cache, which is created by saving the results of previous queries. Items in the local cache remain until one of three things occurs:

1. The Time-to-Live (TTL) period, which is set on each item, expires.

2. The client runs the `ipconfig /flushdns` command.

3. The DNS client is shut down.

Next, the client attempts to resolve the query using the local HOSTS file, which, on Windows systems, is located in the `%systemroot%\system32\drivers\etc` directory. This file is used to manually map host names to IP addresses, and remains in place even if the system is rebooted.

Finally, if the client is unable to resolve the query locally, it forwards the request to a DNS server for resolution. The DNS server attempts to resolve the client's query as detailed next:

▶ If the query result is found in any of the zones for which the DNS server is authoritative, the server responds to the host with an authoritative answer.

▶ If the result is in the zone entries of the DNS server, the server checks its own local cache for the information.

If the DNS server is unable to resolve the query, it forwards the request to other DNS servers, sending what is known as a recursive query. The server forwards to other servers that are listed as "forwarders," or to a set of servers configured in the DNS server's "Root Hints" file.

The DNS query is forwarded through communications channels on the Internet until it reaches a DNS server that is listed as being authoritative for the zone listed in the query. That DNS server then sends back a reply—either an "affirmative," with the IP address requested, or a "negative" stating that the host in question could not be resolved.

Understanding Who Needs DNS

Not all situations require the use of DNS. There are other name resolution mechanisms that exist besides DNS, some of which come standard with the operating system (OS) that companies deploy. While not all scenarios have the requirement of a complex name resolution structure, DNS makes life easier by managing name servers in a domain sometimes with little overhead.

In the past, an organization with a standalone, noninterconnected network could get away with using only host files or WINS to provide NetBIOS-to-IP address name translation. Some very small environments could also use broadcast protocols such as NetBEUI to provide name resolution. In modern networks, however, DNS becomes a necessity, especially in Active Directory environments.

As stated before, WINS is no longer used by Exchange with the release of Exchange 2007. The proper installation and configuration of DNS is critical to the successful deployment of Exchange 2007.

Outlining the Types of DNS Servers

DNS is an integral and necessary part of any Windows Active Directory implementation. In addition, it has evolved to be the primary naming service for UNIX operating systems and the Internet. Because of Microsoft's decision to make Windows 2000 Server and Windows Server 2003 Internet-compatible, DNS has replaced WINS as the default name resolution technology. Microsoft followed Internet Engineering Task Force (IETF) standards and made its DNS server compatible with other DNS implementations.

Examining UNIX BIND DNS

Many organizations have significant investment in UNIX DNS implementations. Microsoft Exchange heavily relies on Active Directory, and Active Directory heavily relies on DNS. Microsoft Active Directory can coexist and use third-party DNS implementations as long as they support active updates and SRV records. In some cases, organizations choose not to migrate away from the already implemented UNIX DNS environment; instead, they coexist with Microsoft DNS. Companies using UNIX DNS for Microsoft AD clients should consider the following:

▶ The UNIX DNS installation should be at least 8.1.2.

▶ For incremental zone transfers, the UNIX DNS implementation should be at least 8.2.1.

Exploring Third-Party (Checkpoint-Meta IP or Lucent Vital QIP) DNS

Third-party DNS implementations can provide significant enhancements in enterprise class IP management. They either provide integrated management of UNIX, Linux, and Microsoft DNS and Dynamic Host Configuration Protocol (DHCP) servers from a central location or can be used in place of the previously mentioned implementations. The most recent versions fully support Dynamic DNS updates, SRV records, and incremental zone transfer, which should be considered a necessity if Active Directory uses the third-party DNS servers.

Examining DNS Compatibility Between DNS Platforms

In theory, DNS clients should be able to query any DNS server. Active Directory, however, has some unique requirements. Clients that authenticate to Active Directory look specifically for server resources, which means that the DNS server has to support SRV records. In Active Directory, DNS clients can dynamically update the DNS server with their IP address using Dynamic DNS. It is important to note that Dynamic DNS is not supported by all DNS implementations.

Examining DNS Components

As previously mentioned, name servers, or DNS servers, are systems that store information about the domain namespace. Name servers can have either the entire domain namespace or just a portion of the namespace. When a name server only has a part of the domain namespace, the portion of the namespace is called a zone.

DNS Zones

There is a subtle difference between zones and domains. All top-level domains, and many domains at the second and lower levels, are broken into zones—smaller, more manageable units by delegation. A zone is the primary delegation mechanism in DNS over which a particular server can resolve requests. Any server that hosts a zone is said to be authoritative for that zone, with the exception of stub zones, defined later in the chapter.

A name server can have *authority* over more than one zone. Different portions of the DNS namespace can be divided into zones, each of which can be hosted on a DNS server or group of servers.

Forward Lookup Zones

A forward lookup zone is created to do forward lookups on the DNS database, resolving names to IP addresses and resource information.

Reverse Lookup Zones

A reverse lookup zone performs the opposite operation as the forward lookup zone. IP addresses are matched up with a common name in a reverse lookup zone. This is similar to knowing the phone number but not knowing the name associated with it. Reverse lookup zones must be manually created, and do not exist in every implementation. Reverse lookup zones are primarily populated with PTR records, which serve to point the reverse lookup query to the appropriate name.

Active Directory–Integrated Zones

A Windows 2003 DNS server can store zone information in two distinct formats: Active Directory–integrated or standard text file. An Active Directory–integrated zone is an available option when the DNS server is installed on an Active Directory domain controller. When a DNS zone is installed as an Active Directory zone, the DNS information is automatically updated on other server AD domain controllers with DNS by using Active Directory's multimaster update techniques. Zone information stored in the Active Directory allows DNS zone transfers to be part of the Active Directory replication process secured by Kerberos authentication.

Primary Zones

In traditional (non–Active Directory–integrated) DNS, a single server serves as the master DNS server for a zone, and all changes made to that particular zone are done on that particular server. A single DNS server can host multiple zones, and can be primary for one and secondary for another. If a zone is primary, however, all requested changes for that particular zone must be done on the server that holds the master copy of the zone. As illustrated in Figure 6.1, companyabc.com is set up on VMW-DC1 as an Active Directory-Integrated Primary zone. However, VMW-DC1 also holds a secondary zone copy of the HQ.COMPANYABC.COM zone.

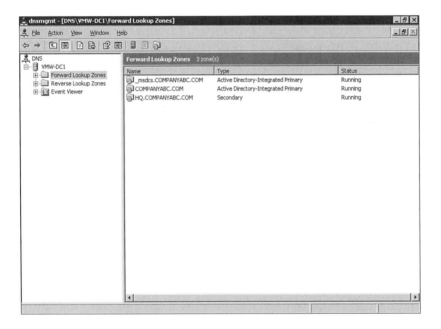

FIGURE 6.1   DNS primary and secondary zones.

Creating a new primary zone manually is a fairly straightforward process. The following procedure outlines the creation of a standard zone for the companyabc.com DNS namespace:

1. Open the DNS MMC snap-in (Start, Administrative Tools, DNS).

2. Navigate to DNS\<Servername>\Forward Lookup Zones.

3. Right-click Forward Lookup Zones, and choose New Zone.

4. Click Next on the welcome screen.

5. Select Primary Zone from the list of zone types available. Also, determine if the zone will be stored in Active Directory. If not, uncheck the Store the Zone in Active Directory check box. Click Next to continue.

6. Type the name of the primary zone to be created, and click Next.

7. Because a new zone file will be created, as opposed to importing an existing zone file, select Create a New File with This File Name, and click Next.

8. Determine whether dynamic updates will be allowed in this zone. By default, Do Not Allow Dynamic Updates is selected. Click Next to continue.

9. Click Finish on the Summary page to create the zone.

Secondary Zones

A secondary zone is established to provide redundancy and load balancing for the primary zone. Secondary zones are not necessary if the zone has been set up as the Active Directory Integrated Zone because the zone will be replicated to all domain controllers in the domain. With secondary zones, each copy of the DNS zone database is read-only, however, because all recordkeeping is done on the primary zone copy. A single DNS server can contain several zones that are primary and several that are secondary. The zone creation process is similar to the one outlined in the preceding section on primary zones, but with the difference being that the zone is transferred from an existing primary server.

Stub Zones (Delegated Zones)

A stub zone is a zone that contains no information about the members in a domain but simply serves to forward queries to a list of designated name servers for different domains. A stub zone contains only NS, SOA, and glue records. Glue records are A records that work in conjunction with a particular NS record to resolve the IP address of a particular name server. A server that hosts a stub zone for a namespace is not authoritative for that zone.

A stub zone effectively serves as a placeholder for a zone that is authoritative on another server. It allows a server to forward queries that are made to a specific zone to the list of name servers in that zone.

DNS Queries

The primary function of DNS is to provide name resolution for requesting clients, so the query mechanism is one of the most important elements in the system. Two types of queries are commonly made to a DNS database: recursive and iterative.

Recursive Queries

Recursive queries are most often performed by resolvers, or clients that need to have a specific name resolved by a DNS server. Recursive queries are also accomplished by a DNS server if forwarders are configured to be used on a particular name server. A recursive query asks whether a particular record can be resolved by a particular name server. The response to a recursive query is either negative or positive.

Iterative Queries

Iterative queries ask a DNS server to either resolve the query or make a best-guess referral to a DNS server that might contain more accurate information about where the query can be resolved. Another iterative query is then performed to the referred server and so on until a result, positive or negative, is obtained.

DNS Replication or Zone Transfer

Copying the DNS database from one server to another is accomplished through a process known as a zone transfer. Zone transfers are required for any zone that has more than one name server responsible for the contents of that zone. The mechanism for zone transfer varies, however, depending on the version of DNS and whether the zone is Active Directory–integrated.

Primary-Secondary (Master-Slave) (RW-RO)

The primary name server holds the authoritative copy of the zone. For redundancy and load sharing, a secondary or slave name server should be set up. The DNS name resolution does not care if it is dealing with a primary or secondary server.

The main difference between the primary and secondary server is where the data comes from. Primary servers read it from a text file, and the secondary server loads it from another name server over the network via the zone transfer process. A slave name server is not limited to loading its data from a primary master name server; a slave server can load a zone from another slave server.

A big advantage of using a secondary name server is that only one set of DNS databases needs to be maintained because all secondary name servers are read-only (RO) databases. All updates to the zone file have to be done at the server holding the primary zone file.

AD-Integrated Replication

One of the most significant changes from Windows Server 2000 to Windows Server 2003 is the location where the zone file is stored in Active Directory. Windows Server 2003 Active Directory–integrated zones are stored in the application partition, whereas in Windows 2000 Server the zones were part of the global catalog (GC). This change in the location of the zone file reduces cross-forest replication traffic because the application partition is unique to each domain.

DNS Resource Records

In the DNS hierarchy, objects are identified through the use of resource records (RRs). These records are used for basic lookups of users and resources within the specified domain and are unique for the domain in which they are located. Because DNS is not a flat namespace, multiple identical RRs can exist at different levels in a DNS hierarchy.

Start of Authority Record

The Start of Authority (SOA) record indicates that this name server is the best source for information within the zone. An SOA record is required for each zone. The server referenced by the SOA record maintains and updates the zone file.

The SOA record also contains other useful information, such as the latest serial number for the zone file, the email address of the responsible person for the zone and Time to Live (TTL).

Host Records

A host (A) record is the most common form of DNS records; its data is an Internet address in a dotted decimal form (for example, `10.32.1.132`). There should be only one A record for each address of a host.

Name Server Records

Name server (NS) records indicate which servers are available for name resolution for that zone. All DNS servers are listed as NS records within a particular zone. When slave servers are configured for the zone, they will have an NS record as well.

Mail Exchange Record

A mail exchange (MX) specifies a mail forwarder or delivery server for SMTP servers. MX records are the cornerstone of a successful Internet mail routing strategy.

One of the advantages of a DNS over HOSTS files is its support for advanced mail routing. LMHOST files allowed only attempts to deliver mail to the host's IP address. If that failed, they could either defer the delivery of the message and try again later or bounce the message back to the sender. DNS offers a solution to this problem, by allowing the setup of backup mail server records.

Mail server records are also MX records, but with a higher priority number as the primary MX record for the domain. In Figure 6.2, `microsoft.com` has three mail servers, all set with the same priority of `10`.

The preference value associated with an MX record determines the order in which a mailer uses a record. The preference value of an MX record is important only in relation to the other servers for the same domain. Mail servers attempt to use the MX record with the lower number first; if that server is not available, they try to contact the server with a higher number, and so on.

As shown in the example, MX record preferences can also be used for load sharing. When several mail hosts have the same preference number associated with them, a sender can choose which mail server to contact first.

Mail routing based on preference numbers sounds simple enough, but there are major caveats that mail administrators have to understand. When troubleshooting mail routing problems, administrators use the following concepts to pinpoint the problem.

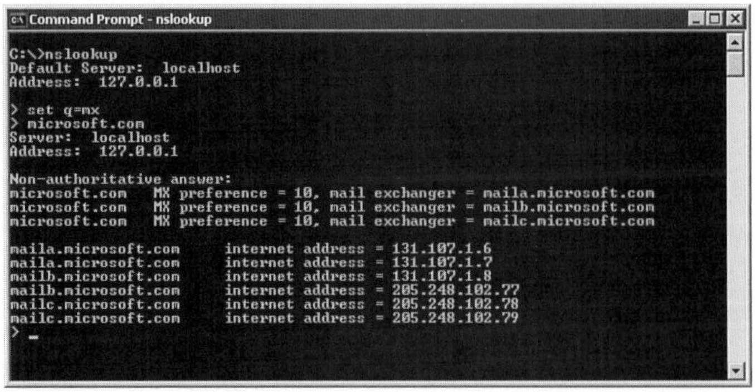

FIGURE 6.2   `Microsoft.com` mail server entries.

Mail routing algorithms based on preference numbers can create routing loops in some situations. The logic in mail servers helps circumvent this problem:

```
Companyabc.com  IN      MX      10      m1.companyabc.com
Companyabc.com  IN      MX      20      m2.companyabc.com
Companyabc.com  IN      MX      30      m3.companyabc.com
```

Using this example, if a message is sent from a client to Bob@companyabc.com from an email address outside of companyabc.com, the sending mail server looks up the receiving mail server for companyabc.com based on the MX records set up for that domain. If the first mail server with the lowest priority is down (m1.companyabc.com), the mail server attempts to contact the second server (m2.companyabc.com). m2 tries to forward the message to m1.companyabc.com because that server is on the top of the list based on preferences. When m2 notices that m1 is down, it tries to contact the second server on the list, (itself), creating a routing loop. If m2 tries to send the message to m3, m3 tries to contact m1, then m2, and then itself, creating a routing loop. To prevent these loops from happening, mail servers discard certain addresses from the list before they decide where to send a message. A mailer sorts the available mail host based on preference number first, and then checks the canonical name of the domain name on which it's running. If the local host appears as a mail exchange, the mailer discards that MX record and all MX records with the same or higher preference value. In this example, m2 does not try to send mail to m1 and m3 for final delivery.

The second common mistake administrators have to look out for with an MX record is the alias name. Most mailers do not check for alias names; they check for canonical names. Unless an administrator uses canonical names for MX records, there is no guarantee that the mailer will find itself, which could result in a mail loop.

Hosts listed as mail exchangers must have A records listed in the zone so that mailers can find address records for each MX record and attempt mail delivery.

Another common mistake when configuring mail hosts is the configuration of the hosted domain local to the server. Internet service providers (ISPs) and organizations commonly host mail for several domains on the same mail server. As mergers and acquisitions happen, this situation becomes more common. The following MX record illustrates that the mail server for `companyabc.com` is really the server `mail.companyisp.com`:

```
companyabc.com IN MX 10 mail.companyisp.com
```

Unless `mail.companyisp.com` is set up to recognize `companyabc.com` as a local domain, it tries to relay the message to itself, creating a routing loop and resulting in the following error message:

```
554 MX list for companyabc.com points back to mail.companyisp.com
```

In this situation, if `mail.companyisp.com` was configured not to relay messages to unknown domains, it would refuse delivery of the mail.

Service (SRV) Record

Service (SRV) records are RRs that indicate which resources perform a particular service. Domain controllers in Active Directory are referenced by SRV records that define specific services, such as the global catalog, LDAP, and Kerberos. SRV records are relatively new additions to DNS and did not exist in the original implementation of the standard. Each SRV record contains information about a particular functionality that a resource provides. For example, an LDAP server can add an SRV record indicating that it can handle LDAP requests for a particular zone. SRV records can be very useful for Active Directory because domain controllers can advertise that they can handle GC requests.

NOTE

Because SRV records are a relatively new addition to DNS, they are not supported by several down-level DNS implementations, such as UNIX BIND 4.1 and NT 4.0 DNS. It is, therefore, critical that the DNS environment that is used for Windows Server 2003 Active Directory has the capability to create SRV records. For UNIX BIND servers, version 8.1.2 or higher is required.

Canonical Name Record

A canonical name (CNAME) record represents a server alias or allows any one of the member servers to be referred to by multiple names in DNS. The record redirects queries made to the A record for the particular host. CNAME records are useful when migrating servers, and for situations in which friendly names, such as `mail.companyabc.com`, are required to point to more complex, server-naming conventions, such as `sfoexch01.companyabc.com`.

CAUTION

Though DNS entries for MX records can be pointed to canonical (CNAME) host records, doing so is not advised, and is not a Microsoft recommended best practice. Increased administrative overhead and the possibility of misrouted messages can result. Microsoft recommends that mail/DNS administrators always link MX records to fully qualified principal names or domain literals. For further details, see Microsoft Knowledge Base Article #153001 at http://support.microsoft.com/kb/153001/.

Other Records

Other, less common forms of records that might exist in DNS have specific purposes, and there might be cause to create them. The following is a sample list, but it is by no means exhaustive:

- ▶ **AAAA**—Maps a standard IP address into a 128-bit IPv6 address. This type of record becomes more prevalent as IPv6 is adopted.

- ▶ **ISDN**—Maps a specific DNS name to an ISDN telephone number.

- ▶ **KEY**—Stores a public key used for encryption for a particular domain.

- ▶ **RP**—Specifies the responsible person for a domain.

- ▶ **WKS**—Designates a particular well-known service.

- ▶ **MB**—Indicates which host contains a specific mailbox.

Multihomed DNS Servers

For multihomed DNS servers, an administrator can configure the DNS service to selectively enable and bind only to IP addresses that are specified using the DNS console. By default, however, the DNS service binds to all IP interfaces configured for the computer.

This can include the following:

- ▶ Any additional IP addresses configured for a single network connection.

- ▶ Individual IP addresses configured for each separate connection where more than one network connection is installed on the server computer.

- ▶ For multihomed DNS servers, an administrator can restrict DNS service for selected IP addresses. When this feature is used, the DNS service listens for and answers only DNS requests that are sent to the IP addresses specified on the Interface tab in the Server properties.

By default, the DNS service listens on all IP addresses and accepts all client requests sent to its default service port (UDP 53 or TCP 53 for zone transfer requests). Some DNS resolvers require that the source address of a DNS response be the same as the destination address that was used in the query. If these addresses differ, clients could reject the response. To accommodate these resolvers, you can specify the list of allowed interfaces for the DNS server. When a list is set, the DNS service binds sockets only to allowed IP addresses used on the computer.

In addition to providing support for clients that require explicit bindings to be used, specifying interfaces can be useful for other reasons:

- ▶ If an administrator does not want to use some of the IP addresses or interfaces on a multihomed server computer

- ▶ If the server computer is configured to use a large number of IP addresses and the administrator does not want the added expense of binding to all of them

When configuring additional IP addresses and enabling them for use with the Windows Server 2003 DNS server, consider the following additional system resources that are consumed at the server computer:

▶ DNS server performance overhead increases slightly, which can affect DNS query reception for the server.

▶ Although Windows Server 2003 provides the means to configure multiple IP addresses for use with any of the installed network adapters, there is no performance benefit for doing so.

▶ Even if the DNS server is handling multiple zones registered for Internet use, it is not necessary or required by the Internet registration process to have different IP addresses registered for each zone.

▶ Each additional address might only slightly increase server performance. In instances when a large overall number of IP addresses are enabled for use, server performance can be degraded noticeably.

▶ In general, when adding network adapter hardware to the server computer, assign only a single primary IP address for each network connection.

▶ Whenever possible, remove nonessential IP addresses from existing server TCP/IP configurations.

Using DNS to Route SMTP Mail in Exchange Server 2007

The primary protocol for sending email on the Internet today is known as Simple Mail Transfer Protocol, or SMTP. SMTP has been used for quite some time in UNIX and Linux environments, and has been incorporated into Active Directory as an alternative transport mechanism for site traffic.

Domains that want to participate in electronic mail exchange need to set up MX record(s) for their published zone. This advertises the system that will handle mail for the particular domain, so that SMTP mail will find the way to its destination.

Understanding SMTP Mail Routing

Email is arguably the most widely used TCP/IP and Internet application today. SMTP defines a set of rules for addressing, sending, and receiving mail between systems. As a result of a user mail request, the SMTP sender establishes a two-way connection with the SMTP receiver. The SMTP receiver can be either the ultimate destination or an intermediate (mail gateway). The SMTP sender generates commands that are replied to by the receiver. All this communication takes place over TCP port 25. When the connection is established, a series of commands and replies are exchanged between the client and server. This connection is similar to a phone conversation, and the commands and responses are equivalent to verbal communication.

> **NOTE**
>
> In various implementations, there is a possibility of exchanging mail between the TCP/IP SMTP mailing system and the locally used mailing systems. These applications are called mail gateways or mail bridges. Sending mail through a mail gateway may alter the end-to-end delivery specification because SMTP guarantees delivery only to the mail gateway host, not to the real destination host, which is located beyond the TCP/IP network. When a mail gateway is used, the SMTP end-to-end transmission is host-to-gateway, gateway-to-host, or gateway-to-gateway; the behavior beyond the gateway is not defined by SMTP.

Examining Client DNS Use for Exchange

Before users can access their mailboxes on an Exchange server, they must be authenticated. Authentication requires a DNS lookup to locate a domain controller on which the users' accounts can be authenticated.

Clients normally cannot deliver messages directly to destination mail hosts. They typically use a mail server to relay messages to destinations. Using SMTP, clients connect to a mail server, which first verifies that the client is allowed to relay through this server, and then accepts the message destined for other domains.

A client uses DNS to resolve the name of a mail server. For example, when configuring an Outlook mail client to connect to an Exchange server, only the short name and not the FQDN is used to connect to the server. The short name is resolved by DNS to the FQDN of the Exchange server to which the client is connected.

Understanding DNS Requirements for Exchange Server 2007

In Active Directory, all client logons and lookups are directed to local domain controllers and GC servers through references to the SRV records in DNS. Each configuration has its DNS and resource requirements. Exchange relies on other servers for client authentication and uses DNS to find those servers. In an Active Directory domain controller configuration, on the other hand, the Exchange server also participates in the authentication process for Active Directory.

Using DNS in Exchange Server 2007

As has been stated, Active Directory and DNS access are vital to an Exchange implementation. It is critical that the host records for all Exchange 2007 servers be properly registered and configured in the domain name system (DNS) server for the Active Directory forest. Clients, as well as other servers, will use DNS to locate and communicate with Exchange 2007 servers.

Any computer acting in one of the Exchange 2007 organizational server roles must be domain members and registered in DNS. The five server roles are as follows:

- ▶ Edge Transport

- ▶ Hub Transport

- ▶ Mailbox

- ▶ Client Access

- ▶ Unified Messaging

All server roles, with the exception of the Edge Transport, can be deployed on a single server. Although there are five roles listed, only the Hub Transport and Mailbox server roles are required for a minimal Exchange 2007 installation.

Configuring Edge Transport Server DNS Settings

For the Edge Transport server(s), which reside in the perimeter network, to communicate with the Hub Transport servers in your Exchange environment, they must be able to locate each other using host name resolution. This is accomplished by creating host records in a forward lookup zone on the internal DNS server that each server is config-ured to query, or by editing the local Hosts file for each server.

Before installing the Edge Transport server role, you have to configure a DNS suffix for the server name. After you have installed the Edge Transport server role, the server name cannot be changed.

To complete this task, you must log on to the Edge Transport server as a user who is a member of the local Administrators group.

To use Windows Control Panel to configure the DNS suffix, complete the following steps:

1. Open Windows Control Panel

2. Double-click on System to open the System Properties dialog box.

3. Click the Computer Name tab.

4. Click Change.

5. On the Computer Name Changes page, click More.

6. In the Primary DNS Suffix of This Computer field, type a DNS domain name and suffix for the Edge Transport server.

DNS and SMTP RFC Standards

In 1984, the first DNS architecture was designed. The result was released as RFC 882 and 883. These were superseded by RFC 1034 (Domain Names—concepts and facilities) and 1035 (Domain Names—implementation and specification), the current specifications of the DNS. RFCs 1034 and 1035 have been improved by many other RFCs, which describe fixes for potential DNS security problems, implementation problems, best practices, and performance improvements to the current standard.

RFC 2821 defines the SMTP, which replaced the earlier versions of RFC 821 and 822.

Interoperability with Older Versions of Exchange

Exchange 2007 can be deployed in an existing Exchange 2000 Server or Exchange Server 2003 organization, as long as the organization is operating in Native mode. This interoperability is supported; however, there are many differences between the older systems and the newer, especially in how the servers are administered and how server-to-server communication occurs.

Understanding Mixed Exchange Environments

For Exchange 2007 to communicate properly with Exchange 2000 or Exchange 2003, the routing group connectors between the Exchange 2007 Hub Transport servers and the older bridgehead servers must be configured correctly. When you install an Exchange 2007 server into an existing organization, the server is recognized by the Exchange 2000 Server or Exchange Server 2003 organization. However, because server-to-server communications differ greatly, you must configure routing group connectors to let the different versions communicate and transfer messages. This is because of the fact that Exchange 2000 Server and Exchange Server 2003 used SMTP as the primary communication protocol between Exchange servers, but in Exchange 2007, the server roles use remote procedure calls (RPCs) for server-to-server communication and allow the Hub Transport server to manage the transport of SMTP traffic.

Routing in Exchange Server 2007

Although Exchange 2000 Server and Exchange Server 2003 use routing groups to define the Exchange routing topology, Exchange 2007 uses Active Directory sites to do so, so an Exchange-specific routing configuration is no longer needed in a pure Exchange 2007 organization.

For the two routing topologies to coexist, all Exchange 2007 servers are automatically added to a routing group when the server is installed. This Exchange 2007 routing group is recognized in the Exchange System Manager for Exchange 2000 and 2003 as an Exchange Routing Group within Exchange Administrative Group.

For Exchange 2007 to coexist with Exchange 2000 Server or Exchange Server 2003, you need to perform the following tasks:

▶ A two-way routing group connector must be created from the Exchange routing group to each Exchange 2000 Server and Exchange Server 2003 routing group that Exchange 2007 will communicate with directly.

NOTE

The first routing group connector is created during installation of the first Hub Transport server when installed in an existing Exchange organization.

These connectors allow mail to be routed from Exchange 2000 Server or Exchange Server 2003 to Exchange 2007.

SMTP Mail Security, Virus Checking, and Proxies

Spamming and security issues are daily concerns for email administrators. As the Internet grows, so too does the amount of spam that mail servers have to confront. Unwanted messages not only can take up a lot of space on mail servers, but can also carry dangerous payloads or viruses. Administrators have to maintain a multilayered defense against spam and viruses.

There are several security areas that have to be addressed:

► Gateway security to control access to the mail server delivering messages to/from the Internet

► Mail database security where messages are stored

► Client mail security where messages are opened and processed

Gateway security is a primary concern for administrators because a misconfigured gateway can become a gateway used by spammers to relay messages. Unauthenticated message relay is the mechanism spammers rely on to deliver their messages. When a server is used for unauthenticated message relay, it not only puts a huge load on server resources, but also might get the server placed on a spam list. Companies relying on spam lists to control their incoming mail traffic refuse mail delivered from servers listed in the database; therefore, controlling who can relay messages through the mail relay gateway is a major concern.

Application-level firewalls such as Microsoft Internet Security and Acceleration (ISA) Server 2006 allow mail proxying on behalf of the internal mail server. Essentially, mail hosts trying to connect to the local mail server have to talk to the proxy gateway, which is responsible for relaying those messages to the internal server. Going one step further, these proxy gateways can also perform additional functions to check the message they are relaying to the internal host or to control the payload passed along to the internal server.

This configuration is also helpful in stopping dangerous viruses from being spread through email. For example, dangerous scripts could potentially be attached to email, which could execute as soon as the user opens the mail. A safe configuration allows only permitted attachment types to pass through. Even those attachments have to pass virus checking before they are passed to an internal mail server.

The following process describes how one server contacts another server to send email messages that include virus checking:

1. The sender contacts its SMTP gateway for message delivery.

2. The SMTP gateway looks up the MX record for the recipient domain and establishes communication with it. The application proxy acting as the SMTP server for the recipient's domain receives the message. Before the recipient gateway establishes

communication with the sender gateway, it can check whether the sender SMTP gateway is listed on any known spam lists. If the server is not located on any spam lists, communication can resume and the message can be accepted by the proxy server.

3. The application proxy forwards the message for virus checking.

4. After virus checking, the mail is routed back to the application proxy.

5. Mail is delivered to the internal SMTP gateway.

6. The recipient picks up the mail message.

> **NOTE**
>
> Application proxy and virus or spam checking might be done within the same host. In that case, steps 2–5 are done in one step without having to transfer a message to a separate host.

Third-party products can be used for virus checking not only at the gateway level, but also directly on an Exchange email database. Database-level scans can be scheduled to run at night when the load is lower on the server; real-time scans can perform virus checking in real time before any message is written to the database.

The final checkpoint for any multilayered virus protection is on the workstation. The file system and the email system can be protected by the same antivirus product. Messages can be scanned before a user is able to open the message or before a message is sent.

Protecting email communications and message integrity puts a large load on administrators. Threats are best dealt with using a multilayered approach from the client to the server to the gateway. When each step along the way is protected against malicious attacks, the global result is a secure, well-balanced email system.

The Edge Transport Servers Role in Antivirus and Antispam Protection

In Exchange 2007, the introduction of the Edge Transport server role was brought about by the increased need to protect organizations from unwanted message traffic. The Edge Transport server is designed to provide improved antivirus and antispam protection for the Exchange environment. This server role also applies policies to messages in transport between organizations. The Edge Transport server role is deployed outside the Active Directory forest in the perimeter network and can be deployed as a smarthost and SMTP relay server for an existing Exchange Server 2007 organization.

Actually, you can add an Edge Transport server to any existing Exchange environment without making any other organizational changes or upgrading the internal Exchange servers. There are no preparation steps needed in Active Directory to install the Edge Transport server. If you are currently using the antispam capabilities of the Intelligent

Message Filter in Exchange Server 2007, you can still use the Edge Transport server as an additional layer of antispam protection.

SMTP Server Scalability and Load Balancing

In a larger environment, administrators might set up more than one SMTP server for inbound and/or outbound mail processing. Windows Server 2003 and Exchange Server 2007 provide a very flexible platform to scale and balance the load of SMTP mail services. DNS and Network Load Balancing (NLB) are key components for these tasks.

Administrators should not forget about hardware failover and scalability. Multinetwork interface cards are highly recommended. Two network cards can be teamed together for higher throughput, can be used in failover configuration, or can be load-balanced by using one network card for front-end communication and another for back-end services, such as backup.

Network design can also incorporate fault tolerance by creating redundant network routes and by using technologies that can group devices together for the purpose of load balancing and delivery failover. Load balancing is the process where requests can be spread across multiple devices to keep individual service load at an acceptable level.

Using NLB, Exchange Server SMTP processes can be handed off to a group of servers for processing, or incoming traffic can be handled by a group of servers before it gets routed to an Exchange server. The following example outlines a possible configuration for using NLB in conjunction with Exchange.

DNS, in this example, has been set up to point to the name of the NLB cluster IP address. Externally, the DNS MX record points to a single mail relay gateway for companyabc.com. Exchange server uses smarthost configuration to send all SMTP messages to the NLB cluster. The NLB cluster is configured in balanced mode where the servers share equal load. Only port 25 traffic is allowed on the cluster servers. This configuration would off-load SMTP mail processing from the Exchange servers because all they have to do is to pass the message along to the cluster for delivery. They do not need to contact any outside SMTP gateway to transfer the message. This configuration allows scalability because when the load increases, administrators can add more SMTP gateways to the cluster. This setup also addresses load balancing because the NLB cluster is smart enough to notice whether one of the cluster nodes has failed or is down for maintenance. An additional ramification of this configuration is that message tracking will not work beyond the Exchange servers.

NOTE

Administrators should not forget about the ramifications of antivirus and spam checking software with NLB. These packages in Gateway mode can also be used as the SMTP gateway for an organization. In an NLB clustered mode, an organization would need to purchase three sets of licenses to cover each NLB node.

A less used but possible configuration for SMTP mail load balancing uses DNS to distribute the load between multiple SMTP servers. This configuration, known as DNS round-robin, does not provide as robust a message routing environment as the NLB solution.

Configuring DNS to Support Exchange Servers

Because DNS is already required and integrated with Active Directory before Exchange Server is installed, most companies already have a robust DNS environment in place. Exchange by itself accesses DNS servers to find resources on the local network, such as global catalog servers and domain controllers. It also uses DNS to search for MX records of other domains.

External DNS Servers for the Internet

The external DNS server for Exchange (or any other mail system) is responsible for giving out the correct MX and A records for the domain for which it is authoritative. Administrators should take security precautions regarding who can change these records—and how. Intentionally or accidentally changing these records can result in undelivered mail.

Most companies let their ISP host the external DNS entries for their domain. ISPs provide internal administrators with methods of managing DNS entries for their domain. In some cases, it has to be done over the phone, but normally a secure web interface is provided for management. Although this setup is convenient and ISPs usually take care of load balancing and redundancy, some companies opt to host their own zone records for the Internet. In this case, companies have to host their own DNS server in-house with the ISP responsible only for forwarding all requests to their DNS server. When hosting an external DNS server, in-house administrators have to think about security issues and DNS configuration issues.

Internal DNS Servers for Outbound Mail Routing

Exchange SMTP gateways are responsible for delivering mail to external hosts. As with any name process involving resolving names to IP addresses, DNS plays a major part in successful mail delivery.

Exchange can route mail to outbound destinations two ways. One is by using smarthosts to off-load all processing of messages destined to other domains. As seen in the previous section, an NLB cluster can be used to route Internet mail to its final destination.

The second way is the default, with Exchange Server 2007 taking care of delivering messages to other domains. In this scenario, Exchange queries DNS servers for other domains' MX records and A records for address resolution.

Troubleshooting DNS Problems

Troubleshooting is part of everyday life for administrators. DNS is no exception to this rule. Therefore, understanding how to use the following tools to troubleshoot DNS not only helps avoid mistakes when configuring DNS-related services, but also provides administrators with a useful toolbox to resolve issues.

Using Event Viewer to Troubleshoot

The first place to look for help when something is not working, or appears to not be working, is the system logs. With Windows Server 2003, the DNS logs are conveniently located directly in the DNS MMC console. Parsing this set of logs can help the administrator troubleshooting DNS replication issues, query problems, and other issues.

For more advanced event log diagnosis, administrators can turn on Debug Logging on a per-server basis. Debugging should be turned on only for troubleshooting because log files can fill up fast. To enable Debug Logging, follow these steps:

1. Open the DNS MMC snap-in (Start, Administrative Tools, DNS).

2. Right-click on the server name, and choose Properties.

3. Select the Debug Logging tab.

4. Check the Log Packets for Debugging check box.

5. Configure any additional settings as required, and click OK.

Turn off these settings after the troubleshooting is complete.

Troubleshooting Using the `ipconfig` Utility

The `ipconfig` utility is used not only for basic TCP/IP troubleshooting, but can also be used to directly resolve DNS issues. These functions can be invoked from the command prompt with the correct flag, detailed as follows:

- `ipconfig /displaydns`—This command displays all locally cached DNS entries. This is also known as the DNS resolver cache.

- `ipconfig /flushdns`—This switch can be used to save administrators from a lot of headaches when troubleshooting DNS problems. This command flushes the local DNS cache. The default cache time for positive replies is 1 day; for negative replies, it is 15 minutes.

- `ipconfig /registerdns`—This flag informs the client to automatically reregister itself in DNS, if the particular zone supports dynamic zone updates.

> **NOTE**
>
> Client-side DNS caching is configurable in the Registry via the following key:
>
> ```
> \\HKLM\System\CurrentControlSet\Services\DNSCach\Parameters
> Set MaxCacheEnrtyTtlLimit = 1 (default = 86400)
> Set NegativeCacheTim = 0 (default = 300)
> ```

The first entry overwrites the TTL number in the cached address to 1 second, essentially disabling the local cache. The second entry changes the negative cache from 15 minutes to 0, essentially disabling the negative cache facility.

Monitoring Exchange Using Performance Monitor

Performance Monitor is a built-in, often overlooked utility that enables a great deal of insight into issues in a network. Many critical DNS counters can be monitored relating to queries, zone transfers, memory use, and other important factors.

Using nslookup for DNS Exchange Lookup

In both Windows and UNIX environments, nslookup is a command-line administrative tool for testing and troubleshooting DNS servers. Simple query structure can provide powerful results for troubleshooting. A simple query contacts the default DNS server for the system and looks up the inputted name.

To test a lookup for www.companyabc.com, type

nslookup www.companyabc.com

at the command prompt. nslookup can also be used to look up other DNS resource types—for example, an MX or SOA record for a company. To look up an MX record for a company type, use the following steps, as illustrated in Figure 6.3:

1. Open a command prompt instance.

2. Type nslookup and press Enter.

3. Type set query=mx (or simply set q=mx), and press Enter.

4. Type microsoft.com and press Enter.

FIGURE 6.3   nslookup MX query.

An MX record output not only shows all the MX records that are used for that domain, their preference number, and the IP address they are associated with, but it also shows the name server for the domain.

By default, `nslookup` queries the local DNS server the system is set up to query. Another powerful feature of `nslookup` is that it can switch between servers to query. This feature enables administrators to verify that all servers answer with the same record as expected. For example, if an organization is moving from one ISP to another, it might use this technique because the IP addresses for its servers might change during the move. The DNS change takes an administrator only a few minutes to do, but replication of the changes through the Internet might take 24 to 72 hours. During this time, some servers might still use the old IP address for the mail server. To verify that the DNS records are replicated to other DNS servers, an administrator can query several DNS servers for the answer through the following technique:

1. Open a command prompt instance.

2. Type `nslookup` and press Enter.

3. Type `server <server IP address>` for the DNS server you want to query.

4. Type `set query=mx` (or simply `set q=mx`), and press Enter.

5. Type `microsoft.com` and press Enter.

Repeat from step 3 for other DNS servers.

`nslookup` can also help find out the version of BIND used on a remote UNIX DNS server. An administrator might find it useful to determine which version of BIND each server is running for troubleshooting purposes. To determine this, the following steps must be performed:

1. From the command line, type `nslookup`, and then press Enter.

2. Type `server <server IP address>` for the IP address of the DNS server queried.

3. Type `set class=chaos` and then press Enter.

4. Type `set type=txt` and then press Enter.

5. Type `version.bind` and then press Enter.

If the administrator of the BIND DNS server has configured the server to accept this query, the BIND version that the server is running is returned. As previously mentioned, the BIND version must be 8.1.2 or later to support SRV records.

Troubleshooting with `DNSLINT`

`DNSLINT` is a Microsoft Windows utility that helps administrators diagnose common DNS name resolution issues. The utility is not installed by default on Windows servers and has to be downloaded from Microsoft. Microsoft Knowledge Base Article #321046 found at http://support.microsoft.com/kb/321046 contains the link to download this utility.

When this command-line utility runs, it generates a Hypertext Markup Language (HTML) file in the directory it runs from. It can help administrators with Active Directory troubleshooting and also with mail-related name resolution and verification. Running `DNSLINT /d <domain_name> /c` tests DNS information as known on authoritative DNS servers for the domain being tested; it also checks SMTP, Post Office Protocol version 3 (POP3), and Internet Message Access Protocol (IMAP) connectivity on the server. For the complete options for this utility, run `DNSLINT /?`.

Using `dnscmd` for Advanced DNS Troubleshooting

The `dnscmd` utility is essentially a command-line version of the MMC DNS console. Installed as part of the Windows Server 2003 support tools, this utility enables administrators to create zones, modify zone records, and perform other vital administrative functions. To install the support tools, run the support tools setup from the Windows Server 2003 CD (located in the `\support\tools` directory). You can view the full functionality of this utility by typing `DNSCMD /?` at the command line.

Global Catalog and Domain Controller Placement

When deploying Exchange 2007 in your environment, Active Directory is a critical component. Exchange 2007 uses the Active Directory directory service to store and share directory information with Microsoft Windows.

If you have already deployed Active Directory into your environment, it is important that you have a solid understanding of your existing implementation and how Exchange will fit into your structure. If you have not deployed AD, you need to design the environment with your Exchange environment in mind.

In addition, you need to evaluate your organization's administrative model, as the marriage of Exchange 2007 and AD allows you to administer Exchange along with the operating system.

When integrating Exchange 2007 and Active Directory, the placement domain controllers and global catalog servers is paramount; without proper placement of these key items, your Exchange environment will not be able to perform optimally.

The remainder of this chapter discusses these items and offers troubleshooting techniques for directory access problems. In addition, best-practice recommendations are offered for the placement of domain controllers and global catalog servers.

Understanding Active Directory Structure

Active Directory (AD) is a standards-based LDAP directory service developed by Microsoft that stores information about network resources and makes it accessible to users and applications, such as Exchange 2007. Directory services are vital in any network infrastructure because they provide a way to name, locate, manage, and secure information about the resources contained.

The Active Directory directory service provides single-logon capability and a central repository for the information for your entire organization. User and computer management are greatly simplified and network resources are easier than ever to access.

In addition, Active Directory is heavily utilized by Exchange, and stores all of your Exchange attributes: email addresses, mailbox locations, home servers, and a variety of other information.

Exploring AD Domains
An Active Directory domain is the main logical boundary of Active Directory. In a standalone sense, an AD domain looks very much like a Windows NT domain. Users and computers are all stored and managed from within the boundaries of the domain. However, several major changes have been made to the structure of the domain and how it relates to other domains within the Active Directory structure.

Domains in Active Directory serve as a security boundary for objects and contain their own security policies. For example, different domains can contain different password policies for users. Keep in mind that domains are a logical organization of objects and can easily span multiple physical locations. Consequently, it is no longer necessary to set up multiple domains for different remote offices or sites because replication concerns can be addressed with the proper use of Active Directory sites, which are described in greater detail later in this chapter.

Exploring AD Trees

An Active Directory tree is composed of multiple domains connected by two-way transitive trusts. Each domain in an Active Directory tree shares a common schema and global catalog. The transitive trust relationship between domains is automatic, which is a change from the domain structure of NT 4.0, wherein all trusts had to be manually set up. The transitive trust relationship means that because the asia domain trusts the root companyabc domain, and the europe domain trusts the companyabc domain, the asia domain also trusts the europe domain. The trusts flow through the domain structure.

Exploring AD Forests

Forests are a group of interconnected domain trees. Implicit trusts connect the roots of each tree into a common forest.

The overlying characteristics that tie together all domains and domain trees into a common forest are the existence of a common schema and a common global catalog. However, domains and domain trees in a forest do not need to share a common namespace. For example, the domains microsoft.com and msnbc.com could theoretically be part of the same forest, but maintain their own separate namespaces (for obvious reasons).

NOTE

Each separate instance of Exchange Server 2007 requires a completely separate AD forest. In other words, AD cannot support more than one Exchange organization in a single forest. This is an important factor to bear in mind when examining AD integration concepts.

Understanding AD Replication with Exchange Server 2007

An understanding of the relationship between Exchange and Active Directory is not complete without an understanding of the replication engine within AD itself. This is especially true because any changes made to the structure of Exchange must be replicated across the AD infrastructure.

Active Directory replaced the concept of Primary Domain Controllers (PDCs) and Backup Domain Controllers (BDCs) with the concept of multiple domain controllers that each contains a master read/write copy of domain information. Changes that are made on any domain controller within the environment are replicated to all other domain controllers in what is known as multimaster replication.

Active Directory differs from most directory service implementations in that the replication of directory information is accomplished independently from the actual logical directory design. The concept of Active Directory sites is completely independent from the logical structure of Active Directory forests, trees, and domains. In fact, a single site in Active Directory can actually host domain controllers from different domains or different trees within the same forest. This enables the creation of a replication topology based on your WAN structure, and your directory topology can mirror your organizational structure.

From an Exchange point of view, the most important concept to keep in mind is the delay that replication causes between when a change is made in Exchange and when that change is replicated throughout the entire AD structure. The reason for these types of discrepancies lies in the fact that not all AD changes are replicated immediately. This concept is known as replication latency. Because the overhead required in immediately replicating change information to all domain controllers is large, the default schedule for replication is not as often as you might want. To immediately replicate changes made to Exchange or any AD changes, use the following procedure:

1. Open Active Directory Sites and Services.

2. Drill down to Sites, *sitename*, Servers, *servername*, NTDS Settings. The server name chosen should be the server you are connected to, and from which the desired change should be replicated.

3. Right-click each connection object and choose Replicate Now, as illustrated in Figure 6.4.

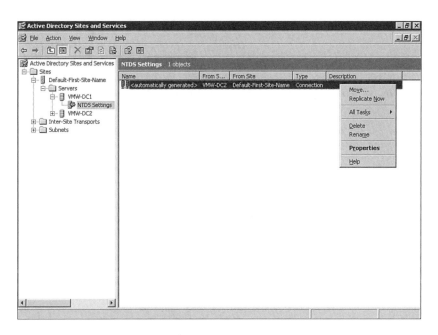

FIGURE 6.4   Forcing AD replication.

Examining the Role of Domain Controllers in AD

Even before the existence of Active Directory, Exchange has relied on domain controllers to authenticate user accounts. With the advent of Active Directory, this has not changed. Exchange still relies on domain controllers to provide all authentication services. To provide optimal logon authentication response times, the proper placement of domain controllers is crucial.

Examining Domain Controller Authentication in Active Directory

To understand how Exchange manages security, an analysis of Active Directory authentication is required. This information aids in troubleshooting the environment, as well as in gaining a better understanding of Exchange Server 2007 as a whole.

Each object in Exchange, including all mailboxes, can have security directly applied for the purposes of limiting and controlling access to those resources. For example, a particular administrator might be granted access to control a certain set of Exchange servers, and users can be granted access to mailboxes. What makes Exchange particularly useful is that security rights can be assigned not only at the object level, but also at the attribute level. This enables granular administration, by allowing tasks such as a Telecom group being able to modify only the phone number field of a user, for example.

When a user logs on to a domain, the domain controller performs a lookup to ensure a match between the username and password. If a match is made, the client is then authenticated and given the rights to gain access to resources.

Because the domain controllers provide users with the permission to access the resources, it is important to provide local access to domain controllers for all Exchange servers. If a local domain controller became unavailable, for example, users would be unable to authenticate to their mailboxes in Exchange, effectively locking them out.

Determining Domain Controller Placement with Exchange Server 2007

Because Exchange relies on the security authentication performed by Active Directory domain controllers, the placement of these domain controllers becomes critical to the overall performance of your messaging environment. If a domain controller cannot be reached in a reasonable amount of time, access to messages and network resources is delayed.

At a minimum, at least one Active Directory domain controller must be within close proximity to any Exchange server to ensure speedy authentication for local users and mailboxes. Additional Active Directory domain controllers can be implemented to provide increased performance in heavily utilized sites or to provide redundancy in the event of a domain controller failure.

For organizations with a high concentration of Exchange server and clients, a significant demand for directory services can negatively impact all aspects of network performance. The presence of other applications and services that require authentication, directory services, or directory replication can cause your Exchange performance to suffer. A current best practice to avoid these pitfalls is to create a dedicated Active Directory site, with dedicated domain controllers and global catalog servers. By segmenting a Service Delivery Location (SDL) into multiple Active Directory sites, you can separate the directory traffic generated by Exchange servers and Microsoft Outlook clients from other directory service traffic.

NOTE

When reading the preceding information, you might be tempted to place the domain controller role directly on the Exchange 2007 server to ensure fast authentication. However, this configuration rarely has the desired effect because both roles are resource intensive and can slow down the performance of both the Active Directory and Exchange services. Placement of the Active Directory and Exchange roles on different servers in close proximity and with a fast network connection will give the greatest performance.

In addition, you can deploy more than one Active Directory domain controller in close proximity to users for user authentication. This enables the distribution of domain controller tasks and builds redundancy into the design. Because each Microsoft Windows Server 2003 domain controller is a multimaster, in the event of a failure of one domain controller, others are able to continue to function and allow uninterrupted authentication.

Defining the Global Catalog

The global catalog is an index of the Active Directory database that stores a full replica of all objects in the directory for its host domain, and a partial replica of all objects contained in the directory of every domain in the forest. In other words, a global catalog contains a replica of every object in Active Directory, but with a limited number of each object's attributes.

Global catalog servers, often referred to as GCs, are Active Directory domain controllers that house a copy of the global catalog. A global catalog server performs two key roles:

- ▶ Provides universal group membership information to a domain controller when a logon process is initiated

- ▶ Enables finding directory information regardless of which domain in the forest contains the data

Access to a global catalog server is necessary for a user to authenticate to the domain. If a global catalog is not available when a user initiates a network logon process, the user is only able to log on to the local computer, and cannot access network resources.

With such an important role to play, it is a common practice to locate at least one global catalog server in each physical location, as it is referenced often by clients and by applications such as Exchange.

Understanding the Relationship Between Exchange Server 2007 and the AD Global Catalog

In the past, an Exchange server could continue to operate by itself with few dependencies on other system components. Because all components of the mail system were locally confined to the same server, downtime was an all-or-nothing prospect. The segregation of the directory into Active Directory has changed the playing field somewhat. In many cases, down-level clients no longer operate independently in the event of a global catalog server failure. Keep this in mind, especially when designing and deploying a domain controller and global catalog infrastructure.

> **NOTE**
>
> Because Outlook clients and Exchange can behave erratically if the global catalog they have been using goes down, it is important to scrutinize which systems receive a copy of the global catalog. In other words, it is not wise to set up a GC/DC on a workstation or substandard hardware, simply to off-load some work from the production domain controllers. If that server fails, the effect on the clients is the same as if their Exchange server failed.

Understanding Global Catalog Structure

The global catalog is an oft-misunderstood concept with Active Directory. In addition, design mistakes with global catalog placement can potentially cripple a network, so a full understanding of what the global catalog is and how it works is warranted.

As mentioned earlier, Active Directory was developed as a standards-based LDAP implementation, and the AD structure acts as an X.500 tree. Queries against the Active Directory must, therefore, have some method of traversing the directory tree to find objects. This means that queries that are sent to a domain controller in a subdomain need to be referred to other domain controllers in other domains in the forest. In large forests, this can significantly increase the time it takes to perform queries.

In Active Directory, the global catalog serves as a mechanism for improving query response time. The global catalog contains a partial set of all objects (users, computers, and other AD objects) in the entire AD forest. The most commonly searched attributes are stored and replicated in the global catalog (that is, first name, username, email address). By storing a read-only copy of objects from other domains locally, full tree searches across the entire forest are accomplished significantly faster. So, in a large forest, a server that holds a copy of the global catalog contains information replicated from all domains in the forest.

Using Best Practices for Global Catalog Placement

All users accessing Exchange resources should have fast access to a global catalog server. At least one global catalog server must be installed on each domain that contains an Exchange server; however, to achieve the best performance in larger organizations, additional global catalog servers should definitely be considered.

As a starting point, per site, there should be a 4:1 ratio of Exchange processors to global catalog server processors, assuming, of course, the processors are of comparable models and speeds. So, if you have four Exchange servers, each with four processors, you should have four processors running your global catalog servers.

Bear in mind, however, that increased global catalog server usage, very large Active Directory implementations, or the use of extremely large distribution lists might necessitate more global catalog servers.

NOTE

With respect to the global catalog processor ratio rule, the 4:1 processor ratio rule from prior versions of Exchange, which assumes a result of one global catalog server being deployed for every two mailbox servers, applies to any environment where the database file (the .dit file) for Active Directory is larger than 1GB, and, therefore, cannot fit into memory. Exchange 2007 is undergoing a variety of performance tests, and more prescriptive guidance is expected in the RTM version of Exchange 2007.

Promoting a Domain Controller to a Global Catalog

Although any domain controller can easily be promoted to a global catalog server, the promotion can have a significant impact on network operations and performance while the topology is updated and the copy of the catalog is passed to the server.

During the promotion, the server immediately notifies DNS if it's new status. In the early days of Active Directory, this often caused problems, as the Exchange servers would immediately begin utilizing the global catalog server before it had finished building the catalog. This problem was rectified in Exchange 2000, Service Pack 2, with the addition of a mechanism that detects the readiness of a global catalog server and prevents Exchange from querying new servers until a full copy of the catalog has been received.

The procedure to promote a domain controller to a global catalog server is as follows:

1. On the domain controller, click Start, point to Programs, click Administrative Tools, and then click Active Directory Sites and Service.

2. In the console tree, double-click Sites, double-click the name of the site, and then double-click Servers.

3. Double-click the target domain controller.

4. In the details pane, right-click NTDS Settings, and then click Properties.

5. On the General tab, click to select the Global Catalog check box, as shown in Figure 6.5.

6. Click OK to finalize the operation.

FIGURE 6.5   Making a domain controller a Global Catalog server.

In older versions of the Windows Server operating system, it was necessary to restart the domain controller after a promotion to a global catalog; however, as of Windows Server 2003, this step is no longer necessary.

Verifying Global Catalog Creation

When a domain controller receives the orders to become a global catalog server, there is a period of time when the GC information will replicate to that domain controller. Depending on the size of the global catalog, this could take a significant period of time. To determine when a domain controller has received the full subset of information, use the replmon (replication monitor) utility from the Windows Server 2003 support tools. The replmon utility indicates which portions of the AD database are replicated to different domain controllers in a forest, and how recently they have been updated.

Replmon enables an administrator to determine the replication status of each domain naming context in the forest. Because a global catalog server should have a copy of each domain naming context in the forest, determine the replication status of the new GC with replmon. For example, the fully replicated global catalog server in Figure 6.6 contains the default naming contexts, such as Schema, Configuration, and DnsZones, in addition to domain naming contexts for all domains. In this example, the companyabc.com domain has been replicated successfully to the VMW-DC2 domain controller.

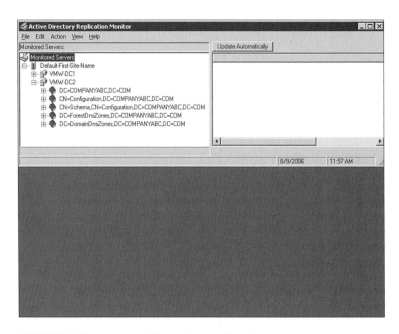

FIGURE 6.6   Replmon GC creation verification.

Exploring Global Catalog Demotion

Removing a global catalog server from production can also have a detrimental effect in certain cases. Outlook 2000 and older clients, for example, experience lockup issues if the global catalog server they have been using is shut down or removed from GC service. The loss of a GC server is the equivalent of the loss of an Exchange server, and should, therefore, not be taken lightly. Outlook 2002 and greater clients, however, automatically detect the failure of their global catalog server and reroute themselves within 30 seconds. Scheduling global catalog or domain controller demotions for the off-hours, therefore, is important.

> **NOTE**
>
> If a production global catalog server goes down, down-level (pre-2002) versions of Outlook can regain connectivity via a restart of the Outlook client. In some cases, this means forcing the closure of OUTLOOK.EXE and MAPISP32.EXE from the Task Manager or rebooting the system.

Deploying Domain Controllers Using the Install from Media Option

When deploying a remote site infrastructure to support Exchange Server 2007, take care to examine best-practice deployment techniques for domain controllers to optimize the procedure. In the past, deploying domain controller and/or global catalog servers to remote sites was a rather strenuous affair. Because each new domain controller would need to replicate a local copy of the Active Directory for itself, careful consideration into replication bandwidth was taken into account. In many cases, this required one of these options:

▶ The domain controller was set up remotely at the start of a weekend or other period of low bandwidth.

▶ The domain controller hardware was physically set up in the home office of an organization and then shipped to the remote location.

This procedure was unwieldy and time-consuming with Windows 2000 Active Directory. Fortunately, Windows Server 2003 addressed this issue through use of the Install from Media option for Active Directory domain controllers.

The concept behind the media-based GC/DC replication is straightforward. A current, running domain controller backs up the directory through a normal backup process. The backup files are then copied to a backup media, such as a CD or tape, and shipped to the remote GC destination. Upon arrival, the dcpromo command can be run with the /adv switch (dcpromo /adv), which activates the option to install from media, as illustrated in Figure 6.7.

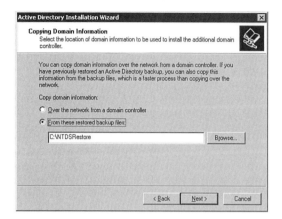

FIGURE 6.7   Install from media option.

After the dcpromo command restores the directory information from the backup, an incremental update of the changes made since the media was created is performed. Because of this, you still need network connectivity throughout the dcpromo process, although the amount of replication required is significantly less. Because some dcpromo operations have been known to take days and even weeks, this concept can dramatically help deploy remote domain controllers.

NOTE

If the copy of the global catalog that has been backed up is older than the tombstone date for objects in the Active Directory (which by default is 60 days), this type of dcpromo will fail. This built-in safety mechanism prevents the introduction of lingering objects and also assures that the information is relatively up to date and no significant incremental replication is required.

Understanding Universal Group Caching for AD Sites

Windows Server 2003 Active Directory enables the creation of AD sites that cache universal group membership. Any time a user uses a universal group, the membership of that group is cached on the local domain controller and is used when the next request comes for that group's membership. This also lessens the replication traffic that would occur if a global catalog was placed in remote sites.

One of the main sources of replication traffic is group membership queries. In Windows 2000 Server Active Directory, every time clients logged on, their universal group membership was queried, requiring a global catalog to be contacted. This significantly increased logon and query time for clients that did not have local global catalog servers. Consequently, many organizations had stipulated that every site, no matter the size, have a local global catalog server to ensure quick authentication and directory lookups. The downside of this was that replication across the directory was increased because every site would receive a copy of every item in the entire AD, even though only a small portion of those items would be referenced by an average site.

Universal group caching solved this problem because only those groups that are commonly referenced by a site are stored locally, and requests for group replication are limited to the items in the cache. This helps limit replication and keep domain logons speedy.

Universal group caching capability is established on a per-site basis, through the following technique:

1. Open Active Directory Sites and Services.

2. Navigate to Sites, *sitename*.

3. Right-click NTDS Site Settings, and choose Properties.

4. Check the Enable Universal Group Membership Caching check box, as shown in Figure 6.8.

5. Click OK to save the changes.

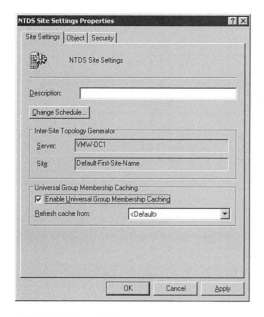

FIGURE 6.8   Universal group caching.

Universal group (UG) caching is useful for minimizing remote-site replication traffic and optimizing user logons. Universal group caching does not replace the need for local global catalog servers in sites with Exchange servers, however, because it does not replace the use of the GC port (3268), which is required by Exchange. UG caching can still be used in remote sites without Exchange servers that use the site consolidation strategies of Exchange Server previously mentioned.

Exploring DSAccess, DSProxy, and the Categorizer

The relationship that Exchange Server 2007 has with Active Directory is complex and often misunderstood. Because the directory is no longer local, special services were written for Exchange to access and process information in AD. Understanding how these systems work is critical for understanding how Exchange interacts with AD.

Understanding DSAccess

DSAccess is one of the most critical services for Exchange Server 2007. DSAccess, via the dsacccess.dll file, is used to discover current Active Directory topology and direct Exchange to various AD components. DSAccess dynamically produces a list of published AD domain controllers and global catalog servers and directs Exchange resources to the appropriate AD resources.

In addition to simple referrals from Exchange to AD, DSAccess intelligently detects global catalog and domain controller failures, and directs Exchange to failover systems dynamically, reducing the potential for downtime caused by a failed global catalog server. DSAccess also caches LDAP queries made from Exchange to AD, speeding up query response time in the process.

DSAccess polls the Active Directory every 15 minutes to identify changes to site structure, domain controller placement, or other structural changes to Active Directory. By making effective use of LDAP searches and global catalog port queries, domain controller and global catalog server suitability is determined. Through this mechanism, a single point of contact for the Active Directory is chosen, which is known as the configuration domain controller.

Determining the DSAccess Roles

DSAccess lists identified domain controllers on the Exchange server properties page and identifies servers belonging to either of two groups, as shown in Figure 6.9.

- ▶ **Domain Controller Servers Being Used by Exchange**—Domain controllers that have been identified by DSAccess to be fully operational are shown here.

- ▶ **Global Catalog Servers Being Used by Exchange**—Global catalog servers are shown here.

A third role, known as the configuration domain controller, was visible on the properties page in Exchange 2003, however, it is not in the same location in Exchange 2007.

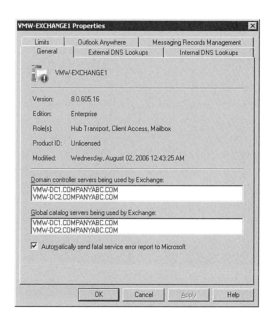

FIGURE 6.9   Viewing domain controllers and global catalog servers used by Exchange.

▶ **Configuration domain controller**—A single AD domain controller is chosen as the configuration domain controller to reduce the problems associated with replication latency among AD domain controllers. In other words, if multiple domain controllers were chosen to act as the configuration domain controller, changes Exchange makes to the directory could conflict with each other. The configuration domain controller role is transferred to other local domain controllers in a site every 8 hours.

To determine the default configuration domain controller, view the Event Viewer application log and search for Event ID 2150. The results of the dsaccess query are listed here as well, as shown in Figure 6.10.

In addition, the default configuration domain controller can be changed to one of your choice by performing the following steps:

1. In the Exchange Management Console, select Server Configuration.

2. In the action pane on the right side, click Modify Configuration Domain Controller.

3. You can click Browse to select the appropriate domain, and then place a check in the Configuration Domain Controller check box. Then, you can then click Browse, shown in Figure 6.11, to manually select the configuration domain controller.

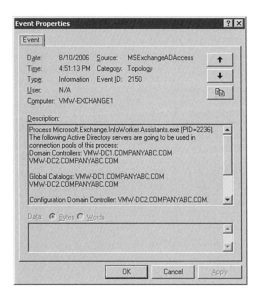

FIGURE 6.10   Identifying the default configuration domain controller.

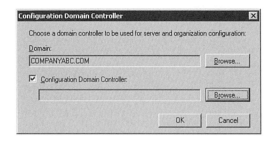

FIGURE 6.11   Manually setting the configuration domain controller.

Understanding DSProxy

DSProxy is a component of Exchange that parses Active Directory and creates an address book for down-level Outlook (pre–Outlook 2000 SR2) clients. These clients assume that Exchange uses its own directory, as opposed to directly using the Active Directory by itself, as Outlook 2000 SR2 and greater clients do. The DSProxy service provides these higher-level clients with a referral to an Active Directory global catalog server, which they then use without accessing the Exchange servers directly. The newer Outlook clients do not refresh this information unless a server failure has occurred or the client is restarted.

NOTE

DSProxy uses Name Service Provider Interface (NSPI) instead of LDAP for address list lookups, because NSPI is a more efficient interface for that type of lookup. Only global catalog servers support NSPI, so they are necessary for all client address list lookups.

Outlining the Role of the Categorizer

The SMTP Categorizer is a component of Exchange that is used to submit mail messages to their proper destination. When a mail message is sent, the Categorizer queries the DSAccess component to locate an Active Directory server list, which is then directly queried for information that can be used to deliver the message.

Although the Categorizer in Exchange gets a list of all global catalog servers from DSAccess, it normally opens only a single LDAP connection to a GC server to send mail, unless a large number of messages are queued for delivery.

> **TIP**
>
> Problems with the Categorizer are often the cause of DNS or AD lookup issues. When troubleshooting mail-flow problems, use message tracking in Exchange Server 2007 to follow the course of a message. If the message stops at the Categorizer, it is often wise to start troubleshooting the issue from a directory access perspective.

Understanding AD Functionality Modes and Their Relationship to Exchange Groups

The most recent versions of Exchange Server, as well as Active Directory, were designed to break through the constraints that had limited previous Exchange implementations. However, realistically, it was understood that the products would have to maintain a certain level of compatibility with previous NT domains and Exchange 5.5 organizations. After all, not all companies have the resources to completely replace their entire network and messaging infrastructure at once. This requirement stipulated the creation of several functional modes for AD and Exchange that allow backward compatibility, while necessarily limiting some of the enhanced functionality—at least for the duration of the migration/upgrade process. Several of the limitations of the AD functional modes in particular impact Exchange Server 2007, specifically Active Directory group functionality. Consequently, a firm grasp of these concepts is warranted.

Understanding Windows Group Types

Groups in Windows Server 2003 come in two flavors: security and distribution. In addition, groups can be organized into different scopes: machine local, domain local, global, and universal. It might seem complex, but the concept, once defined, is simple.

Defining Security Groups

The type of group that most administrators are most familiar with is the security group. A security group is primarily used to apply permissions to resources, enabling multiple users to be administered more easily. For example, users in the Sales department can be added as members to the Sales Department security group, which would then be given permission to specific resources in the environment. When a new member is added to the Sales department, instead of modifying every resource that the department relies on, you can simply add the new member to the security group and the appropriate permissions would be inherited by the new user. This concept should be familiar to anyone who has administered down-level Windows networks, such as NT or Windows 2000.

Defining Distribution Groups

The concept of distribution groups as it exists in Windows Server 2003 was first introduced in Windows 2000 with the deployment of Active Directory. Essentially, a distribution group is a group whose members are able to receive mail messages that are sent to the group. Any application that has the capability of using Active Directory for address book lookups can use this functionality in Windows Server 2003.

> **NOTE**
>
> Distribution groups can be used to create email distribution lists that cannot be used to apply security. However, if separation of security and email functionality is not required, you can make security groups mail-enabled instead of using distribution groups.

Outlining Mail-Enabled Security Groups in Exchange Server 2007

With the introduction of Exchange into an Active Directory environment came a new concept: mail-enabled groups. These groups are essentially security groups that are referenced by an email address, and can be used to send SMTP messages to the members of the group. This type of functionality becomes possible only with the inclusion of Exchange 2000 or greater, and Exchange actually extends the forest schema to enable Exchange-related information, such as SMTP addresses, to be associated with each group.

Most organizations will find that the use of mail-enabled security groups will satisfy the majority of their group requirements. For example, a single group called Marketing, which contains all users in that department, could also be mail-enabled to allow users in Exchange to send emails to everyone in the department.

Explaining Group Scope

Groups in Active Directory work the way that previous group structures, particularly in Windows NT, have worked, but with a few modifications to their design. As mentioned earlier, group scope in Active Directory is divided into several groups:

- ▶ **Machine local groups**—Machine local groups, also known as local groups, previously existed in Windows NT 4.0 and can theoretically contain members from any trusted location. Users and groups in the local domain, as well as in other trusted domains and forests can be included in this type of group. However, local groups allow resources only on the machine they are located on to be accessed, which greatly reduces their usability.

- ▶ **Domain local groups**—Domain local groups are essentially the same as local groups in Windows NT, and are used to administer resources located only on their own domain. They can contain users and groups from any other trusted domain and are typically used to grant access to resources for groups in different domains.

▶ **Global groups**—Global groups are on the opposite side of domain local groups. They can contain only users in the domain in which they exist, but are used to grant access to resources in other trusted domains. These types of groups are best used to supply security membership to user accounts who share a similar function, such as the sales global group.

▶ **Universal groups**—Universal groups can contain users and groups from any domain in the forest, and can grant access to any resource in the forest. With this added power comes a few caveats: First, universal groups are available only in Windows 2000 or 2003 AD Native mode domains. Second, all members of each universal group are stored in the global catalog, increasing the replication load. Universal group membership replication has been noticeably streamlined and optimized in Windows Server 2003, however, because the membership of each group is incrementally replicated.

Universal groups are particularly important for Exchange environments. For example, when migrating from Exchange 5.5 to later versions of Exchange, the Exchange 5.5 distribution lists were converted into universal groups for the proper application of public folder and calendaring permissions. An AD domain that contains accounts that have security access to Exchange 5.5 mailboxes must be in AD Native mode before performing the migration. This is because the universal groups are made as Universal Security groups, which are only available in AD Native mode.

Functional Levels in Windows Server 2003 Active Directory

Active Directory was designed to be backward-compatible. This helps to maintain backward compatibility with Windows NT domain controllers. Four separate functional levels exist at the domain level in Windows Server 2003, and three separate functional levels exist at the forest level:

▶ **Windows 2000 Mixed**—When Windows Server 2003 is installed in a Windows 2000 Active Directory forest that is running in Mixed mode, Windows Server 2003 domain controllers will be able to communicate with Windows NT and Windows 2000 domain controllers throughout the forest. This is the most limiting of the functional levels, however, because certain functionality—such as universal groups, group nesting, and enhanced security—is absent from the domain. This is typically a temporary level to run in because it is seen more as a path toward eventual upgrade.

▶ **Windows 2000 Native**—Installed into a Windows 2000 Active Directory that is running in Windows 2000 Native mode, Windows Server 2003 runs itself at a Windows 2000/2003 functional level. Only Windows 2000 and Windows Server 2003 domain controllers can exist in this environment.

▶ **Windows Server 2003 Interim**—Windows Server 2003 Interim mode gives Active Directory the capability of interoperating with a domain composed of Windows NT 4.0 domain controllers only. Although a confusing concept at first, the Windows Server 2003 interim functional level does serve a purpose. In environments that seek to upgrade directly from NT 4.0 to Windows Server 2003 Active Directory, Interim mode enables Windows Server 2003 to manage large groups more efficiently than if an existing Windows 2000 Active Directory exists. After all NT domain controllers have been removed or upgraded, the functional levels can be raised.

▶ **Windows Server 2003**—The most functional of all the various levels, Windows Server 2003 functionality is the eventual goal of all Windows Server 2003 Active Directory implementations. Functionality on this level opens the environment to features such as schema deactivation, domain rename, domain controller rename, and cross-forest trusts. To get to this level, first all domain controllers must be updated to Windows Server 2003. Only after this can the domains, and then the forest, be updated to Windows Server 2003 functionality.

NOTE

Beginning with Exchange Server 2003 Service Pack 1, Microsoft extended the ability to perform domain rename on an Active Directory forest that was previously extended for Exchange. Before SP1, it was not possible to rename an AD domain within a forest that contained Exchange.

As previously mentioned, it is preferable to convert AD domains into Windows 2000 Native mode, or Windows Server 2003 Functional mode before migrating Exchange 5.5 servers that use those domains. The universal group capabilities that these modes provide for make this necessary.

To change domain and forest functional levels in Active Directory to the highest level for Windows Server 2003, follow these steps:

1. Open Active Directory Domains and Trusts from Administrative Tools.

2. In the left scope pane, right-click your domain name, and select Raise Domain Functional Level.

3. Click on the Available Domain Functional Level option, select Windows Server 2003, and then choose Raise.

4. At the warning screen, click OK, and then click OK again to complete the task.

5. Repeat the steps for all domains in the forest.

6. Perform the same steps on the forest root, except this time click Raise Forest Functional Level, and follow the prompts.

After the domains and the forest have been upgraded, the Functional mode will indicate Windows Server 2003, as shown in Figure 6.12.

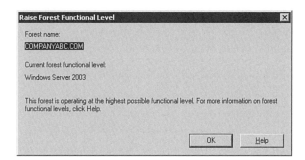

FIGURE 6.12   Windows Server 2003 forest functional level.

Summary

Exchange Server 2007 is a complicated, but extremely powerful messaging tool. With the scalability and performance enhancements comes an increased degree of interdependence with other system components, most notably the DNS and the global catalog. Access to the global catalog and AD domain controllers is critical and cannot be overlooked. A good Exchange deployment plan takes these factors into account.

Best Practices

The following are best practices from this chapter:

- ▶ Use Windows 2000/2003 DNS for client AD name resolution whenever possible. If not possible, ensure that the UNIX BIND version is 8.1.2 or higher to support SRV records.

- ▶ Administrators should set up redundant name resolution servers in the event that one server fails.

- ▶ Use caching-only DNS servers to help leverage load and minimize zone transfer traffic across WAN links.

- ▶ Make any DNS implementations compliant with the standard DNS character set so that zone transfers are supported to and from non–Unicode-compliant DNS implementations, such as UNIX BIND servers. This includes a–z, A–Z, 0–9, and the hyphen (-) character.

- ▶ Set up multiple MX records for all mail servers for redundancy. ISPs usually function as a secondary mail relay gateway for the hosted domain.

- ▶ It is wise to segregate inbound and outbound SMTP traffic from direct exposure to the Internet by deploying an SMTP smarthost in the demilitarized zone (DMZ) of the firewall.

▶ Deploy at least one domain controller in each physical location with more than 10 users.

▶ When possible, create a dedicated Active Directory site for Exchange, with dedicated domain controllers and global catalog servers.

▶ Promote or demote global catalog servers and domain controllers during off-hours.

▶ Use Exchange Server 2007 site consolidation concepts to reduce the total number of deployed Exchange servers and global catalog servers.

▶ Place at least one GC in close network proximity to any major service (such as Exchange Server 2007) that requires use of the global catalog (3268) port.

▶ Ensure that the AD domain is in Windows Server 2003 Functional mode before migrating to Exchange Server 2007.

▶ Do not use substandard hardware for global catalog servers, as a simple hardware failure can affect Outlook clients.

▶ Consider the use of universal group caching for domain controllers in sites without local Exchange servers.

PART III

Implementing Exchange Server 2007 Services

IN THIS PART

Installing Exchange Server 2007

In the latest version of Exchange, Microsoft has taken a big step in improving the installation process with a release of a new Exchange Installation Wizard, the flexibility to install specific roles, and a myriad of other new features. This chapter explains the prerequisites and installation process for a new Microsoft Exchange Server 2007 server in a typical configuration. A typical configuration consists of installing the following roles by default, Client Access server, Hub Transport server, and Mailbox server. In addition, this chapter assumes that the supporting infrastructure and server do not exist; therefore, it includes step-by-step instructions on how to install Windows Server 2003, Active Directory, and the Exchange prerequisites from scratch.

Understanding the Prerequisites for Exchange Server 2007

Before installing Exchange Server 2007, it is important to get acquainted with the prerequisites as many of these prerequisites outline best practices. As such, you should take the time to review the prerequisites before implementation to ensure success.

The Importance of .NET Framework 2.0 in Exchange Server 2007

The .NET Framework is a Microsoft Windows component that allows the ability to build, deploy, and run Web Services and other applications. Currently, .NET Framework 2.0 is the latest version. Exchange Server 2007 requires Microsoft .NET Framework, version 2.0, to be installed prior to implementation. The .NET Framework 2.0 code can be downloaded from the Microsoft website or it is included as an optional download via Windows Update or Microsoft Update. For those running the latest operating systems such as Windows Server 2003 R2, .NET Framework 2.0 is one of the optional components available by default.

Managing Exchange Server 2007 with the Microsoft Management Console 3.0

The Microsoft Management Console (MMC) was originally released back in 1996 with the Windows NT 4.0 Option Pack. This was the first time Microsoft released a consistent and integrated management tool that aimed at standardizing the way administrators conducted administrative and operational tasks on Microsoft software. Since 1996, Microsoft has been updating and improving its management console and releasing new versions. Currently, version 3.0 is the latest version of the Microsoft Management Console.

Some of these new features include an action pane, which resides on the right side of the console, that allows administrators to easily conduct tasks and a redesigned Add or Remove snap-in that makes it easier to add or remove components into the console.

Exchange Server 2007 requires the Microsoft Management Console 3.0 to be installed prior to the implementation of Exchange.

Scripting Exchange Server 2007 with the Exchange Management Shell

The Exchange Management Shell (EMS) is a new, powerful, and flexible command-line interface that allows administrators the potential to script Exchange Server 2007 tasks, such as automation, batching, and reporting.

Exchange Server 2007 requires the Exchange Management Shell to be installed prior to the implementation of Exchange.

Running Exchange Server 2007 on Windows Server 2003 Operating System

Exchange Server 2007 is designed to run on servers running the Windows Server 2003 operating systems. The minimum prerequisite required to install Exchange Server 2007 is Windows Server 2003 with at least Service Pack 1 or Windows Server 2003 R2, Standard or Enterprise x64-bit Editions. Windows Server 2003 Service Pack 1 and Windows Server 2003 R2 work to enhance security, increase reliability, and simplify administration for Windows Server 2003.

Internet Information Services (IIS) 6.0 as a Critical Component for Exchange Server 2007

Like earlier versions of Exchange, components such as Internet Information Services 6.0 (IIS) and ASP remain critical components. Because of their importance, they are prerequisites for the installation and function of Exchange Server 2007.

The following IIS components (ASP.NET and World Wide Web Service) must be installed prior to installing Exchange Server 2007. SMTP and Network News Transfer Protocol (NNTP) are no longer required as it was in Exchange Server 2000 or Exchange Server 2003.

Exchange Server 2007 Hardware Requirements

Microsoft maintains a list of minimum hardware requirements to install Exchange Server 2007. Microsoft recommends the following minimum hardware requirements, which are listed in Table 7.1.

TABLE 7.1   Minimum Hardware Requirements

Hardware	Minimum Requirements
Processor	▶ Intel Extended Memory 64 Technology (Intel EM64T) or ▶ AMD Opteron or AMD Athlon 64 processor, which supports AMD64 platform
Memory	▶ 2GB of RAM per server plus 5MB per user minimum
Disk space	▶ At least 1.2GB on the hard disk where Exchange Server 2007 will be installed ▶ 200MB on the system drive

> **NOTE**
>
> These hardware requirements from Microsoft are the bare minimum and should not be used in best-practice scenarios. In addition, hardware requirements can change because of features and functionality required by the company, for example, the implementation of Unified Messaging voice mail services or clustering on an Exchange 2007 server can require more memory. See Chapter 34, "Optimizing an Exchange Server 2007 Environment," for more tips and best practices on sizing the server for your environment.

Exchange Server 2007 Now Requires 64-bit Architecture

Microsoft Exchange has been a 32-bit application running in many organizations since its inception. The 32-bit architecture could handle the needs of organizations in the past; today, however, organizations have more demanding messaging requirements than before, such as higher productivity, high availability, increased mail traffic, continuous replication synchronization with wireless devices, access via the Web, and much more. To address these growing needs, Microsoft will only deliver an x64-bit edition of Exchange Server 2007; therefore, Exchange can access more processor and memory ensuring higher performance gains, larger volumes of messages, increased email message size, increased size of attachments, more users per server, and, finally, more connected mail clients, such as Outlook Web Access (OWA), remote procedure calls (RPC), and ActiveSync.

Many organizations and administrators were originally upset with this decision; however, as x64-bit systems have become standard server models shipped by most of the major hardware vendors, the availability and similar cost of x64-bit systems relative to 32-bit machines as well as the functionality and scalability benefits of x64-bit has made the migration to x64-bit a significant benefit for organizations. In almost every migration from 32-bit Exchange to Exchange 2007 64-bit, the authors of this book have found consolidation capabilities on average of 2–3 to 1, therefore eliminating the need for as many x64-bit servers as there were 32-bit servers in an earlier version of Exchange.

In any case, since Microsoft has standardized on a minimum x64-bit configuration for Exchange 2007, going forward organizations will require 64-bit hardware to support Exchange Server 2007. An x64-bit edition of the Windows operating system is also necessary.

NOTE

If a company is purchasing new hardware for Exchange 2000 or 2003, it is beneficial to take forward compatibility into consideration. Companies should purchase x64-bit servers now so that it is possible to reuse these servers when moving toward Exchange Server 2007 in the future. In the interim, the 32-bit versions of Windows Server 2003 and Exchange Server 2003 would be installed. Companies should contact their hardware vendor to verify compatibility before making purchases.

Understanding Active Directory Requirements for Exchange Server 2007

An Active Directory (AD) infrastructure running on Windows Server 2003 needs to be deployed before an organization can implement Exchange Server 2007. Exchange depends on the AD services, including domain name system (DNS) to successfully function. This integrated relationship between Exchange and AD means the design of AD can have an enormous impact on the success of Exchange. Mistakes made in the planning portion of AD and Exchange can prove to be costly and difficult to correct later.

If AD is already deployed, it is important that the team designing the Exchange infrastructure have a solid understanding of the AD environment as their knowledge of AD can influence the success of the Exchange implementation. Organizations with an AD infrastructure already in place need to evaluate how Exchange can fit into their existing environment. If AD has not been deployed, the organization or team designing Exchange needs to plan their implementation while keeping in mind their future Exchange installation.

Some of the AD factors that should be considered when deploying Exchange Server 2007 include the following:

▶ Global catalog server placement

▶ AD Sites and Services

▶ Domain and forest functional levels

- ▶ Flexible Single Master Operations role placement

- ▶ Permissions needed to install Exchange

- ▶ Bandwidth and latency

The Importance of Global Catalog Servers in Exchange Server 2007

Similar to Exchange 2000 Server and Exchange Server 2003, Exchange Server 2007 requires a global catalog server to function. The global catalog maintains an index of the AD database for objects within its domain and stores partial copies of data for all other domains within a forest. Exchange queries a global catalog to resolve email addresses for users within the organization. Therefore, failure to contact a global catalog causes emails to bounce as the recipient's name does not resolve. Global catalog server placement is discussed in the section "Establishing a Proper Global Catalog Placement Strategy."

The Importance of Active Directory Sites and Services in Exchange Server 2007

Unlike the previous versions of Exchange, Exchange Server 2007 no longer utilizes a separate routing topology for transporting email throughout the organization. Exchange Server 2007 is AD site aware and leverages AD Sites and Services topology for routing email between Exchange server roles and does away with Exchange routing groups and routing group connectors.

Because Exchange Server 2007 does away with Exchange routing groups and routing group connectors, it is important that the implementation of AD Site and Services is set up correctly within the infrastructure. In addition, the use of AD sites increases efficiency during new server discovery and configuration as this process is now automated.

Understanding Domain and Forest Functional Levels Relative to Exchange Server 2007

Domain and forest functional levels provide a way to enable specific new functionality for an AD domain and forest. In addition, the functional levels also allow for interoperability with legacy domain controllers such as Windows NT 4.0 and Windows 2000 Server.

Windows Server 2003 supports three forest functional levels:

- ▶ Windows 2000 Native

- ▶ Windows Server 2003 Interim

- ▶ Windows Server 2003

Windows 2000 forest functional level supports domain controllers running Windows NT 4.0, Windows 2000 Server, and Windows Server 2003. Windows Server 2003 Interim forest functional level is a special functional level used to support domain environments that will be upgraded from Windows NT 4.0. Finally, Windows Server 2003 forest functional level enables all the new forestwide features of Windows Server 2003 and no longer supports down-level domain controllers.

Similar to the forest concepts, Windows Server 2003 domains can operate in four different domain modes. Each functional domain level permits for a different set of domain controllers to coexist. Windows Server 2003 AD supports four domain functional levels:

- Windows 2000 Mixed Domain
- Windows 2000 Native
- Windows Server 2003 Interim
- Windows Server 2003 Native

The Windows 2000 Mixed Domain functional level allows Windows Server 2003 domain controllers to interoperate with other domain controllers running Windows Server 2003, Windows 2000 Server, and Windows NT 4.0. The Windows 2000 Native domain functionality allows domain controllers running Windows Server 2003 to interact with domain controllers running Windows Server 2003 and Windows 2000 Server. The Windows Server 2003 Interim domain functional level supports only domain controllers running Windows Server 2003 and Windows NT 4.0. Finally, when there are no longer any Windows 2000 Server or Windows NT 4.0 domain controllers, the functional level can be switched to Windows 2003 Native mode.

NOTE

To install Exchange Server 2007, the Windows Server 2003 Active Directory domain functional level must be Windows 2000 Server Native or higher for all domains in the Active Directory forest where Exchange will exist.

Using Flexible Single Master Operations Roles

Active Directory uses a multimaster replication scheme for replicating directory information between domain controllers. Certain domain and enterprisewide operations are not well suited for a multimaster model. Some services are better suited to a single master operation to prevent the introduction of conflicts while an Operations Master is offline. These services are referred to as Operations Master or Flexible Single Master Operations (FSMO) roles. These roles are either forest- or domainwide. The forestwide roles include Schema Master and Domain Naming Master, whereas the domainwide roles include RID Master, PDC Emulator, and Infrastructure Master.

Best practices for FSMO role placement when designing an Active Directory environment include the following: In a multidomain model, the Schema Master and Domain Naming

Master should be placed on the same domain controller in the root or placeholder domain. This server can also host the global catalog service. For the domain-based FSMO roles, the PDC Emulator and RID Master should reside on the same server and the Infrastructure Master should be distributed on a separate domain controller. The Infrastructure Master should never be placed on a domain controller that is also configured as a global catalog server. Keeping all FMSO roles on one server is an option for smaller, single-domain environments, but provides a single point of failure for key AD components.

The placement of FSMO roles does not have a direct impact on Exchange Server 2007; however, Exchange does require the domain controller that is the Schema Master to have Windows Server 2003 Service Pack 1 installed.

Permissions Considerations for Exchange Server 2007

Roles provide a consistent, yet flexible model for security administration. Roles are similar to the groups used in Exchange Server 2003. Permissions are applied to the role, and then members are added to the role. Any member of the role inherits the permissions that are permitted by that role.

The use of roles simplifies the administrative work related to security. Additional roles can be created based on job function, application, or any other logical group of users. With roles, it is not necessary for an administrator to apply security to each individual or AD object. Any required changes to permissions for the role can be made to the role security and the members of the role will receive those changes.

Exchange Server 2007 has the following four types of roles:

- ▶ Exchange Organization Administrators
- ▶ Exchange Recipient Administrators
- ▶ Exchange Server Administrators
- ▶ Exchange View-Only Administrators

Table 7.2 lists these Exchange Server roles and their related high-level permissions.

TABLE 7.2   Exchange Server Roles and Permissions

Role	Permission
Exchange Organization Administrators	Full Control to the Exchange Server organization, including all Exchange properties
Exchange Recipient Administrators	Modify Recipient Objects, such as AD users, contacts, groups, DLs, and public folders
Exchange Server Administrators	Full Control on local Exchange server, but not the organization, and View Only permissions on the Exchange organization
Exchange View-Only Administrators	Read Only Access on the full Exchange organization and domain controllers that have Exchange tools installed

> **NOTE**
>
> Members of the Exchange Organization Administrators role should be controlled very tightly, similar to domain administrators in AD. Only a limited amount of administrators who fully understand Exchange Server should be placed in this group.

Planning an Active Directory Infrastructure

The following section focuses on the AD infrastructure required to support an Exchange Server 2007 implementation. Many facets are involved when planning an AD infrastructure—for example, forest model, domain model, group policies, delegation of administration—but details for designing an AD infrastructure from end to end is beyond the scope of this book. For more information about designing an AD infrastructure, refer to *Windows Server 2003 Unleashed, R2 Edition*, by Sams Publishing (ISBN: 0-672-32898-4). These sections strictly focus on the AD components required for implementing Exchange Server 2007.

Impact Forests Have on an Exchange Server 2007 Design

An AD forest and an Exchange organization are tightly integrated as Exchange utilizes AD as its directory repository for mailboxes, mail-enabled objects, Exchange servers, and much more. There is a one-to-one relationship between AD and Exchange. An AD forest can only host a single Exchange organization and an Exchange organization can only span one AD forest.

It is recommended that a single AD forest should be utilized to minimize complexity and administration when designing and implementing a company's Exchange implementation. However, there will be times when a single AD forest will not meet the company's business, security, or political requirements.

If multiple AD forests are necessary to satisfy the company's requirements, it must be decided on which forest the Exchange organization will be hosted. It is possible to have Exchange reside in a single forest, a dedicated resource forest, or in multiple forests.

The Role of a Domain in Exchange Server 2007

After the AD forest structure has been laid out, the domain structure can be contemplated. Unlike the forest structure, an Exchange Server 2007 organization can span multiple domains within the forest if needed. Therefore, a user mailbox, Exchange server, or other Exchange object can reside in any domain within the forest where Exchange Server 2007 has been deployed. A company can plan its domain model structure (single domain model or multiple domain model) based on their business and security requirements without a direct negative impact to the Exchange Server 2007 design.

There is one major exception to the single domain model: the placeholder domain model. The placeholder domain model has an isolated domain serving as the root domain in the forest. The user domain, which contains all production user accounts, would be located in a separate domain in the forest, as illustrated in Figure 7.1.

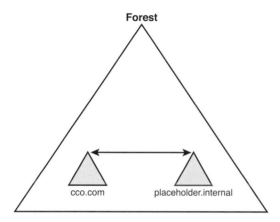

FIGURE 7.1   The placeholder domain model.

The placeholder domain structure increases security in the forest by segregating high-level schema-access accounts into a completely separate domain from the regular user domain. Access to the placeholder domain can be audited and restricted to maintain tighter control on the critical schema. The downside to this model, however, is the fact that the additional domain requires a separate set of domain controllers, which increases the infra-structure costs of the environment. In general, this makes this domain model less desir-able for smaller organizations because the trade-off between increased cost and less security is too great. Larger organizations can consider the increased security provided by this model, however.

Understanding How DNS and AD Namespace Are Used in Exchange Server 2007

The first step in the actual design of the AD structure is the decision on a common domain name system (DNS) namespace that AD will occupy. AD revolves around, and is inseparable from, DNS, and this decision is one of the most important ones to make. The namespace chosen can be as straightforward as companyabc.com, for example, or it can be more complex. Multiple factors must be considered, however, before this decision can be made. Is it better to register an AD namespace on the Internet and potentially expose it to intruders, or is it better to choose an unregistered, internal namespace? Is it neces-sary to tie in multiple namespaces into the same forest? These and other questions must be answered before the design process can proceed.

Planning a Proper Sites and Services Architecture

As stated earlier, one of the major changes in Exchange Server 2007 is that it no longer has an independent routing topology for sending email throughout the Exchange organization. In pure Exchange Server 2007 mode, Exchange Server 2007 piggybacks off AD Sites and Services for routing email.

If Exchange Server 2007 will be installed into an existing Exchange 2000 or 2003 organization, the administrators must take coexistence into consideration. It is necessary to configure routing group connectors to ensure that the Exchange Server 2007 servers are communicating to legacy servers.

For more information on coexistence of Exchange 2007 with legacy versions, review Chapter 15, "Migrating from Windows Server 2000 to Windows Server 2003."

Therefore, Exchange administrators must fully understand best practices around designing a proper Sites and Services architecture to support Exchange Server 2007. The AD Sites and Services concepts are fairly similar to Exchange routing topology. From a high-level perspective, within AD it is necessary for administrators to create sites, allocate subnets to sites, and then create site links between sites for communication to occur. Similar to Exchange 2000 and 2003, it is possible to set up redundant links between sites and allocate costs to control communication priorities.

Active Directory Sites

The basic unit of AD replication is known as the site. Not to be confused with physical sites or Exchange Server 5.5 sites, the AD site is simply a group of highly connected domain controllers. Each site is established to more effectively replicate directory information across the network. In a nutshell, domain controllers within a single site will, by default, replicate more often than those that exist in other sites. The concept of the site constitutes the centerpiece of replication design in AD.

Associating Subnets with Sites

In most cases, a separate instance of a site in AD physically resides in a separate subnet for other sites. This idea stems from the fact that the site topology most often mimics, or should mimic, the physical network infrastructure of an environment.

In AD, sites are associated with their respective subnets to allow for the intelligent assignment of users to their respective domain controllers. For example, consider the design shown in Figure 7.2.

In this example, Server-EX01 is a physical member of the 192.168.115.0/24 subnet. Server-EX02 and Client01 are both members of the 192.168.116.0/24 subnet. Based on the subnets, Server-EX01 will automatically be assigned to the domain controller Server01 in site01 and Server-EX02 and Client01 will be assigned to the domain controller in the second site, site02.

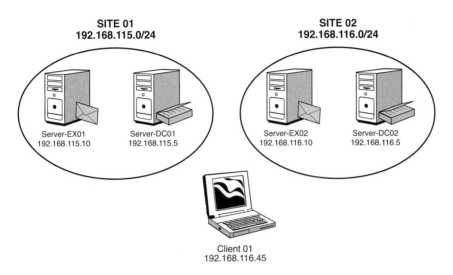

FIGURE 7.2   Sample Exchange and client site assignment.

Using Site Links

By default, the creation of two sites in AD does not automatically create a connection linking the two sites. This type of functionality must be manually created, in the form of a site link.

A site link is essentially a type of connection that joins together two sites and allows for replication traffic to flow from one site to another. Multiple site links can be set up and should normally follow the wide area network (WAN) lines that your organization follows. Multiple site links also assure redundancy so that if one link goes down, replication traffic follows the second link.

Site link replication schedules can be modified to fit the existing requirements of your organization. If, for example, the WAN link is saturated during the day, a schedule can be established to replicate information at night. This functionality allows you to easily adjust site links to the needs of any WAN link.

Exchange Server 2007 and Site Membership

After the AD site topology has been created, including adding the appropriate subnets to sites and creating site links between sites, an administrator can now take Exchange Server placement into consideration.

Similar to AD domain controllers, Exchange 2007 will automatically be associated with a site in AD based on their IP address and subnet mask. As stated earlier, it is beneficial to have a domain controller residing in the site that the Exchange 2007 server will be in.

For more information on creating an Exchange routing topology, refer to Chapter 4, "Architecting an Enterprise-Level Exchange Environment."

> **NOTE**
>
> If AD already exists prior to the implementation of Exchange Server 2007, there might be a need to make changes to the AD routing topology to support special Exchange routing requirements.

Establishing a Proper Global Catalog Placement Strategy

One item to review is the placement of global catalog servers within the AD site configuration. The importance of the global catalog server cannot be overstated. The global catalog is used for the address list that users see when they are addressing a message. If the global catalog server is not available, the recipient's address will not resolve when users address a message, and the message will immediately be returned to the sender.

One well-equipped global catalog server can support several Exchange 2007 servers on the same local area network (LAN) segment. There should be at least one global catalog server in every AD site that contains an Exchange 2007 server. For large sites, two global catalogs are much better and provide redundancy in the event the first global catalog server is unavailable.

For optimization, plan on having a global catalog server close to the clients to provide efficient address list access. Making all domain controller servers global catalog servers is recommended for an organization that has a single AD domain model and a single site. Otherwise, for multidomain models, all domain controllers can be configured as global catalog servers except for the domain controllers hosting the Infrastructure Master FSMO role. A good AD site design helps make efficient use of bandwidth in this design. This design helps reduce some of the overhead with multiple global catalogs in every AD site.

> **NOTE**
>
> It is a best practice to have a minimum of at least two global catalog servers within an AD infrastructure.

Upgrading from Previous Versions of Microsoft Windows

Many organizations already have an existing directory structure in place such as Windows NT 4.0 domain or Windows 2000 Server AD domain in their environment. It is great if a company has the opportunity to implement a new Windows Server 2003 AD environment from scratch; however, this is not always possible or practical because of costs, company politics, hardware limitations, or a business goal of minimizing end-user disruption during the migration. That being said, organizations typically upgrade their environment from a Windows NT 4.0 or Windows 2000 domain to the Windows Server 2003 AD to implement Exchange Server 2007.

Upgrading from a Windows NT 4.0 Domain

The first decision to be made when migrating from a Windows NT 4.0 domain is to determine which type of migration strategy best fits your requirements and AD design. Of the three migration paths described in the following list, each one is unique in characteristics and requires different tasks to complete. Therefore, each migration path should be planned in detail, scripted, and tested before you actually perform any migration tasks.

- ▶ The first migration option is an in-place upgrade. This migration path is a direct upgrade of the Windows NT 4.0 operating system and domain to Windows Server 2003 and AD.

- ▶ The second option is to migrate the NT 4.0 objects from an existing NT 4.0 domain to a brand-new Windows Server 2003 forest and AD.

- ▶ The third option is to consolidate multiple existing Windows NT 4.0 domains into a single AD domain configuration.

Each domain migration path offers different characteristics and functionality. Before you continue, review each migration path and perform all preparation tasks to prepare your Windows NT 4.0 environment to be migrated to AD. Begin by determining the specific criteria for your migration, such as the time frame in which to complete the migration and your final AD design. Understanding these key areas will assist you in determining which migration path is best for your organization.

NOTE

The Windows NT 4.0 upgrade is supported by Service Pack 5 (SP5) or later. If an earlier version of service pack is installed, the upgrade is not possible.

For more information on upgrading a Windows NT 4.0 domain to Windows Server 2003 AD, it is recommended to reference *Windows Server 2003 Unleashed, R2 Edition*, by Sams Publishing (ISBN: 0-672-32898-4).

Upgrading from Windows Server 2000 Active Directory

Because it is required to run Exchange Server 2007 on AD using Windows Server 2003, organizations need to upgrade their Windows 2000 domain controllers to Windows Server 2003.

In many ways, a migration from Windows 2000 Server domain to Windows Server 2003 is more of a service pack upgrade than a major migration scenario. The differences between the operating systems are more evolutionary than revolutionary; consequently, there are fewer design considerations than in upgrades from the NT 4.0 operating system.

Because the fundamental differences between Windows 2000 Server and Windows Server 2003 are not significant, the possibility of simply upgrading an existing Windows 2000 domain controller to Windows Server 2003 is an option. Depending on the type of hardware currently in use in a Windows 2000 AD environment, this type of migration strategy becomes an option. Often, however, it is more appealing to simply introduce new domain controllers running Windows Server 2003 into an existing environment and retire the domain controllers running Windows 2000 Server from production. This technique normally has less impact on current environments and can also support fallback more easily.

For more information on upgrading a Windows 2000 Server domain to Windows Server 2003 AD, see Chapter 15.

Implementing Active Directory from Scratch

The following sections focus on installing Windows Server 2003 AD to support an Exchange Server 2007 installation. This AD example consists of a single site and single domain controller representing a small organization. The order of operations of this installation includes the following:

- ▶ Installing Windows Server 2003
- ▶ Installing Windows Server 2003 Service Pack 1 or higher
- ▶ Installing the first domain controller
- ▶ Configuring AD Sites and Services
- ▶ Configuring a global catalog server

Installing Windows Server 2003

The mechanism that lies at the base of Exchange Server 2007 functionality is the operating system. Exchange draws from Windows its base functionality, and it cannot be installed without it. Consequently, the operating system installation is the first step in the creation of a new Exchange server.

As previously mentioned, Exchange Server 2007 requires an operating system to supply needed core functionality. The operating system of choice for Exchange Server 2007 is Windows Server 2003, Standard or Enterprise Edition with the latest Windows service pack or at least Windows Server 2003 Service Pack 1. The Windows Server 2003 operating system encompasses a myriad of new technologies and functionality, more than can be covered in this book. For more information on the capabilities of the operating system and migrating to Windows Server 2003, see Chapter 15.

NOTE

It is highly recommended to install Exchange Server 2007 on a clean, freshly built operating system on a reformatted drive. If the server that will be used for Exchange Server 2007 was previously running in a different capacity, the most secure and robust solution is to completely reinstall the operating system using the procedure outlined in the next passages.

Installation of Windows Server 2003 is straightforward, and takes approximately 30 minutes to an hour to complete. The following step-by-step installation procedure described in this book illustrates the procedure for installation of standard Windows Server 2003 media. Many hardware manufacturers include special installation instructions and procedures, which might vary from the procedure outlined here, but the concepts are roughly the same. To install Windows Server 2003, Standard or Enterprise Edition, perform the following steps:

1. Insert the Windows Server 2003 Standard CD into the CD drive.

2. Power up the server and let it boot to the CD-ROM drive. If there is currently no operating system on the hard drive, it automatically boots into the CD-ROM–based setup, as shown in Figure 7.3.

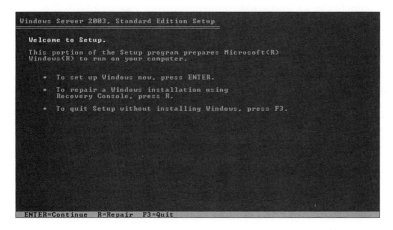

FIGURE 7.3   Running the CD-ROM–based Windows Server 2003 setup.

3. When prompted, press Enter to start setting up Windows.

4. At the licensing agreement screen, read the license, and then press F8 if you agree to the license agreement.

5. Select the physical disk on which Windows will be installed. Choose between the available disks shown by using the up and down arrows. When selected, press Enter to install.

6. At the next screen, choose Format the Partition Using the NTFS File System by selecting it, and press Enter to continue.

Following this step, Windows Server 2003 setup begins formatting the hard drive and copying files to it. After a reboot and more automatic installation routines, the setup process continues with the Regional and Language Options screen as follows:

1. Review the Regional and Language Options, and click Next to continue.

2. Enter a name and organization into the Personalization screen, and click Next to continue.

3. Enter the product key for Windows. This is typically on the CD case or part of the license agreement purchased from Microsoft. Click Next after the key is entered.

4. Select which licensing mode will be used on the server, either Per Server or Per Device, and click Next to continue.

5. At the Computer Name and Administrator Password screen, enter a unique name for the server, and type a cryptic password into the Password fields.

6. Check the Date and Time Zone settings, and click Next to continue.

The next screen to be displayed is where networking settings can be configured. Setup allows for automatic configuration (Typical Settings) or manual configuration (Custom Settings) options. Selecting Custom Settings allows for each installed network interface card (NIC) to be configured with various options, such as static IP addresses and custom protocols. Selecting Typical Settings bypasses these steps; however, they can easily be set later. Proceed with the following steps:

1. To simplify the setup, select Typical Settings, and click Next. Network settings should then be configured after the OS is installed.

2. Select whether the server will be a member of a domain, or whether it will be a workgroup member. For this demonstration, choose WORKGROUP because the server will be promoted to a domain controller in the upcoming steps.

3. Click Next to continue.

After more installation routines and reboots, setup will complete and the operating system can be logged on to as the local Administrator and configured for Exchange Server 2007.

Installing and Configuring Windows Server 2003 Service Pack 1

Windows Server 2003, like with all other Microsoft applications, has periodic updates that become available for the software. Interim updates can be downloaded and installed via the Windows Update option on the system, or a visit to the Windows Update website (http://update.microsoft.com) initiates the installer to check for the latest updates for Windows.

Major updates come in service packs that roll up patches and updates into a single installation. Installing a service pack brings a server up to date with all of the updates to the point in time when the service pack was issued. The service packs for Windows Server 2003 are cumulative, so the installation of Service Pack 2 includes all of the updates released prior to Service Pack 2, including the Service Pack 1 update.

You can install a service pack update in two ways:

- ▶ **Windows Update**—The service pack can be downloaded and automatically installed as part of the normal update process.

- ▶ **Download and install**—The service pack can be downloaded as a file and then the file can be launched to install the update. This is frequently done when a system is not connected to the Internet, or when a scheduled installation is desired as opposed to an immediate installation after a download from the Internet.

Installing the Service Pack

To update Windows Server 2003 with a service pack, obtain or download the service pack binaries from http://www.microsoft.com/downloads, and perform the following steps:

1. Start the installation by either double-clicking on the downloaded file or finding the `update.exe` file located with the Windows Server 2003 Service Pack 1 media.

2. At the welcome screen, shown in Figure 7.4, click Next to continue.

FIGURE 7.4   Updating Windows Server 2003 with Service Pack 1.

3. Read the licensing agreement, and select I Agree if you agree with the terms. Click Next to continue.

4. Accept the defaults for the Uninstall directory, and click Next to continue.

5. The service pack then begins the installation process, which takes 10 to 20 minutes to complete. Click Finish to end the service pack installation and reboot the server.

NOTE

It is also possible to obtain and install the latest service pack via Microsoft Update or Windows Update. The URL is http://update.microsoft.com/microsoftupdate/v6/default.aspx?ln=en-us.

Updating and Patching the Operating System

In addition to the patches that were installed as part of the service pack, security updates and patches are constantly being released by Microsoft. It is highly advantageous to install the critical updates made available by Microsoft for the operating system, particularly when it is first being built. These patches can be manually downloaded and installed, or they can be automatically applied by using Windows Update or Microsoft Update.

Installing the First Domain Controller for a New Domain

Installing a new domain requires the installation of a new domain controller and Microsoft AD. After the previous steps for installing Windows Server 2003 are complete, it is possible to run the dcpromo command to begin installing AD. To begin the AD Installation Wizard, do the following:

1. Choose Start, Run, type dcpromo in the Open text box, and then click OK. This opens the Welcome to the AD Installation Wizard screen and guides you through the installation of a new Windows Server 2003 forest.

NOTE

An administrator can use the AD Installation Wizard to install the first domain controller in the new AD forest. The wizard can also use it to install additional domain controllers and child domains after the first domain controller installation is complete.

2. On the Operating System Compatibility screen, read the information and then click Next.

3. At the welcome screen, click Next to begin installing the new AD domain. Because this installation is a new domain and it is the first server in the domain, on the Domain Controller Type page, select Domain Controller for a New Domain. This option creates a new AD forest and configure the first domain controller in the new domain, as illustrated in Figure 7.5.

4. To create the new domain in a new forest, on the Create New Domain page, select Domain in a New Forest, and click Next to continue.

5. Enter the fully qualified DNS name of the new AD domain. This DNS name is not the same as the existing Windows NT domain name and must be unique to any domain names on your network. For this example, companyabc was used, as illustrated in Figure 7.6. Click Next to continue.

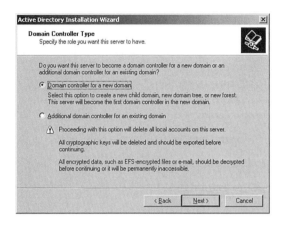

FIGURE 7.5   Domain controller for a new domain.

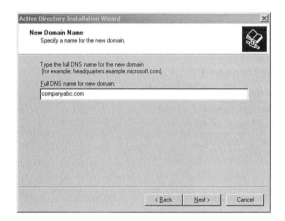

FIGURE 7.6   Full DNS name for a new domain.

6. Enter the NetBIOS name information, and then click Next. The NetBIOS domain name is the name you want Windows NT 4.0 domains to use when identifying your new AD domain. It is usually the same name as your new domain.

7. Depending on your server configuration design, select the location where the AD databases will be located.

NOTE

When configuring AD database locations, make sure that your server hardware configuration plan takes recoverability and performance into account.

For best performance, install the AD databases on a separate hard disk than the server operating system and server page file. Use the Browse buttons to select the disks where you want to store the AD databases.

For best recoverability, use disk fault tolerance such as RAID or disk mirroring for the AD databases.

8. Use the Browse button to select the location where the SYSVOL folder will be installed or use the default location, and click Next. The SYSVOL folder contains the new AD domain's data files. This information is replicated to all domain controllers in the domain and can be installed only on an NTFS volume. Your server design should account for the placement of the domain controller's SYSVOL folder.

9. On the Install and Configure DNS page, you can determine how DNS will be installed within the new AD domain. This page can be used to install DNS on the server or configure the upgrade to use a different DNS server on the network. Because this is the first domain controller in the new forest, select Install and Configure the DNS Server on This Computer. Choosing this option installs Microsoft DNS on the new domain controller and modifies the server's TCP/IP properties to use the new DNS installation for name resolution, as illustrated in Figure 7.7.

FIGURE 7.7   Install and configure DNS for AD.

When you configure AD permissions, the forest functionality must be configured for compatibility with other Windows Server family operating systems.

10. If the new domain installation will contain only Windows Server 2003 domain controllers, select permissions compatible with Windows 2000 or Windows Server 2003 operating systems. This option is applicable only when you're adding new domain controllers to your domain. This does not affect backward compatibility when migrating existing Windows NT 4.0 domains to AD. For this example, select Permissions Compatible Only with Windows 2000 or Windows Server 2003 Operating Systems, and click Next to continue.

11. Assign a password to the Directory Services Restore mode account. The Directory Services Restore mode password is used to recover a server in case of server failure. This password should be documented in a secure location in case a recovery of the server is required. When you're configuring the password, keep in mind that each

Windows Server 2003 server with AD in the domain has its own unique Directory Services Restore mode account. This account is not associated with the Domain Administrator account or any other Enterprise Administrator accounts in AD. Enter the Directory Services Restore password, and click Next.

12. Review the server configuration, and click Finish. This step completes the installation of AD.

Restart the domain controller by selecting Restart Now. Log on after the server restarts and review the server's Event Viewer application and system logs to identify any errors or potential problems with your installation before continuing.

Configuring Active Directory Sites and Services

After the AD domain controller has been installed, it is necessary to configure Sites and Services to support the Exchange Server deployment. To configure AD Sites and Services to support Exchange Server 2007 residing in two sites, the site properties need to be changed. Changing site properties is covered in the next section.

Changing Site Properties

To change the AD Default-First-Site-Name, follow these steps:

1. On the first domain controller, open AD Sites and Services, and then click Next.

2. Click the plus sign (+) to expand the Sites tree.

3. Right-click Default-First-Site-Name in the left pane of the console, and then click Rename.

4. Enter a name, and then press Enter, which changes the default site name to your custom site name, as illustrated in Figure 7.8 where the site was renamed to Site01.

Creating a New Active Directory Site

To create a new site in AD, follow these steps:

1. On the first domain controller, open AD Sites and Services, and then click Next.

2. Click the plus sign (+) to expand the Sites tree.

3. Right-click Sites in the left pane of the console, and then click New Site.

4. Enter the new site name in the New Object-Site dialog box. In this example, Site02 was used for the new site name, as shown in Figure 7.9.

5. Click to highlight DEFAULTIPSITELINK, and then click OK.

6. Review the AD message box information, and then click OK

FIGURE 7.8   Rename the first AD default site name.

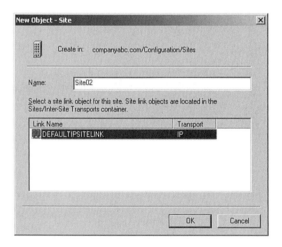

FIGURE 7.9   Create a new AD site.

Associating Subnets with Sites

In most cases, a separate instance of a site in AD physically resides in a separate subnet for other sites. This idea stems from the fact that the site topology most often mimics, or should mimic, the physical network infrastructure of an environment.

In AD, sites are associated with their respective subnets to allow for the intelligent assignment of users to their respective domain controllers.

To associate a subnet to the first site, follow these steps:

1. Open AD Sites and Services.

2. Click the plus sign (+) to expand the Sites tree.

3. Right-click Subnets and choose New Subnet.

4. Enter the network portion of the IP range that the site will encompass. The example uses the 192.168.115.0 subnet with a Class C (255.255.255.0) subnet mask.

5. Select a site to associate with the subnet. In the example, Site01 was selected, as illustrated in Figure 7.10, and then click OK.

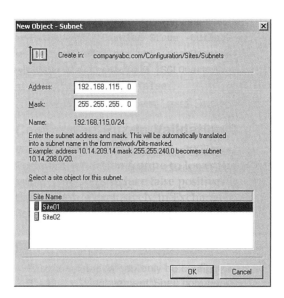

FIGURE 7.10   Associate a subnet to a site.

To associate a subnet to the second site, follow these steps:

1. Open AD Sites and Services.

2. Click the plus sign (+) to expand the Sites tree.

3. Right-click Subnets and choose New Subnet.

4. Enter the network portion of the IP range that the site will encompass. The example uses the 192.168.116.0 subnet with a Class C (255.255.255.0) subnet mask.

5. Select a site to associate with the subnet. In the example, Site02 was selected, and then click OK.

Configuring a Global Catalog Server

By default, the first domain controller in a domain is automatically configured as a global catalog server. Any additional domain controllers need to be configured manually.

To configure or verify that a domain controller is a global catalog server, follow these steps:

1. Open AD Sites and Services.

2. Click the plus sign (+) to expand the Sites tree.

3. Expand the desired site name, the Servers folder, and then the server object.

4. Right-click the NTDS Settings object, and then click Properties.

5. On the General Tab, either select or clear the Global Catalog check box, as illustrated in Figure 7.11, and then click OK.

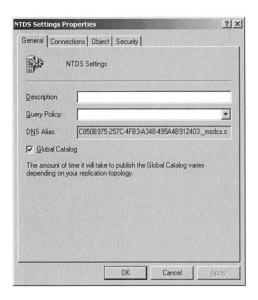

FIGURE 7.11   Configuring a global catalog server.

Preparing to Install Exchange Server 2007

After the AD infrastructure has been implemented, Exchange 2007 can be planned for implementation. The installation process should follow standard project methodology, which includes planning, prototype testing, implementing, and ongoing support.

Planning Your Exchange Server 2007 Installation

Chapter 1, "Exchange Server 2007 Technology Primer," covers what is new in Exchange 2007 and differences between the available versions. Chapter 2, "Best Practices at Planning, Prototyping, Migrating, and Deploying Exchange Server 2007," Chapter 3, "Understanding Core Exchange Server 2007 Design Plans," and Chapter 4, "Architecting an Enterprise-Level Exchange Environment," of this book address the planning and design of an Exchange Server 2007 implementation for a small, medium, or large enterprise organization. In addition, these chapters focus best practices on planning and deploying Exchange 2007.

Choosing to Install Exchange in Either a Test or Production Environment

When installing Exchange 2007 for the first time, the organization should make the decision whether the implementation should be exclusively in an isolated test environment, or whether the test will be simply a preinstallation of a future production environment.

To reduce risks, end-user downtime, and negative ramifications to the production environment, it is typically recommended that the first implementation of Exchange 2007 be conducted in an isolated test lab rather than being installed into a production environment.

Having a test environment isolates test functional errors so that if there are any problems in the testing phase, they will not be injected into the existing production environment. In addition, the test environment acts as a "Proof of Concept" for the new Exchange Server 2007 design and it is possible to move forward or roll back the implementation, whereas in production it is not.

Many times, when an organization begins to install Exchange as if it is a test environment, it loads an evaluation copy of the Windows or Exchange license on a low-end hardware system. Then, because it has so much success from the initial tests, the organization puts the system into a production environment. This creates a problem because the system is built on expiring licenses and substandard hardware. When committed to being solely a test environment, the results should be to rebuild from scratch, and not put the test environment into position as a full production configuration.

Prototyping an Exchange Server 2007 Installation

When the decision is made to build in a test or production environment, build Exchange 2007 in the expected environment. If the system will be solely a test configuration, the implementation of Exchange 2007 should be in an isolated lab. If the system will be used in production, the implementation of Exchange 2007 should be focused on building the appropriate best-practice server configuration, which will give the organization a better likelihood of full production implementation success.

Some of the steps an organization should go through when considering to build a test Exchange environment include the following:

▶ Building Exchange 2007 in a lab

▶ Testing email features and functions

▶ Reviewing Exchange Server 2007 server roles

▶ Verifying design configuration

▶ Testing failover and recovery

▶ Using physical hardware versus virtualization

Much of the validation and testing should occur during the test process. It's a lot easier testing a disaster recovery rebuild of Exchange in an exclusive test environment than to test the recovery of an Exchange server for the first time during a very tense server rebuild and recovery process after a production system crash. In addition, this is a good time to test application compatibility, before migrating to a full messaging environment and then testing to see whether a third-party fax, voice mail, or paging software will work with Exchange 2007.

Another item to test during the testing phase is directory replication in a large multisite environment to ensure that the global catalog is being updated fast enough between sites. In addition, because Sites and Services is the main transport mechanism for Exchange Server 2007, testing should be conducted to ensure replication is occurring properly. In addition, security is of concern for many organizations these days, and the appropriate level of security for the organization should be tested and validated. Many times, the plan for securing Mailbox servers or Client Access servers sounds great on paper, but when implemented, is too limiting for the average user to get functionality from the service. Slight adjustments in security levels help minimize user impact while strengthening existing security in the organization.

Another "hot" item to test is the new Exchange server roles. The new roles introduced in Exchange Server 2007 are a new concept that requires a great deal of understanding and planning to implement them efficiently in production.

Building an Exchange Server 2007 prototype test lab can be a costly affair for companies that want to simulate a large, global implementation. For example, many companies have a global presence where it is necessary to provide messaging services for 20,000 to 100,000 employees located in offices all over the world. When upgrading from a legacy version of Exchange, it is very common that these companies will have a requirement to prototype the installation, upgrade strategy, and application compatibility before they move forward in production.

For these organizations, the cost of building a test lab can be phenomenal because there is a need to duplicate the production environment consisting of AD domain controllers, Exchange 5.5 servers, Exchange 2000 servers, and/or Exchange 2003 servers and application servers. Therefore, the project could come to a halt because the hardware cost associated with the prototype phase could exceed the amount of the allocated budget for the project.

Therefore, virtualization is a great method of lowering costs within a prototype phase. Server virtualization enables multiple virtual operating systems to run on a single physical machine, yet remain logically distinct with consistent hardware profiles. The "host" operating system creates an illusion of partitioned hardware by executing multiple "guest" operating systems.

> **NOTE**
>
> It is an option to virtualize servers in the prototype phase to decrease the costs associated with procuring server hardware. However, virtualization should not be used if organizations are trying to performance test Exchange Server 2007 servers within the test lab if Exchange 2007 will ultimately be installed on a full server system (not virtualized).

Conducting Preinstallation Checks on Exchange Server 2007

When it comes to the actual installation of Exchange 2007, an administrator can run setup manually or create an unattended file so that the install can be automated for a branch office with no onsite technical staff. There are also different configurations of Exchange based on server roles such as Mailbox, Client Access, Bridgehead, Unified Messaging, and Gateway. This section covers the preinstallation tasks prior to installing the first typical Exchange server in the environment.

There are many changes in the Exchange 2007 setup program when compared to Exchange 2003. These changes include the flexibility to install a specific Exchange server role, prepare the AD schema and forest automatically during the installation process as a single process, and complete a more thorough health check on prerequisites such as AD.

Performing an Active Directory Health Check

If AD is not being set up from scratch, it is beneficial to validate that the existing AD environment is functioning correctly. Because Exchange requires AD as a prerequisite, an administrator should conduct an extensive health check on the directory structure with tools such as DCDIAG, NETDIAG, and Replication Monitor to identify any anomalies that will impact the installation of Exchange Server 2007. The Windows Server 2003 support tools are required to conduct these tasks.

Alternatively, the Exchange Server 2007 Installation Wizard also conducts a minor health check automatically as a prerequisite task when installing Exchange Server 2007. If an extensive AD health check is required, this must be conducted manually as a separate task. For detailed instructions on performing an AD health check, see the ShortCut titled "Performing an AD Health Check" (Sams Publishing, ISBN: 0-7686-6842-5), which can be

purchased and downloaded from http://www.samspublishing.com/bookstore/
product.asp?isbn=0768668425.

Preparing the Active Directory Domain and Forest

In Exchange 2000 Server and Exchange Server 2003, it was necessary to run two separate
processes to prepare the forest and the domain before the installation of Exchange. The
first process was extending the AD schema with ForestPrep and the second process was
preparing all the domains with DomainPrep.

With Exchange Server 2007, these prerequisite processes are eliminated and it is possible
to prepare both the forest and domain as part of the Exchange Server 2007 installation.
During the installation, a new process, ADprep, executes to prepare both the forest and
domain with the appropriate changes. Alternatively, the AD preparation can be conducted
manually, before the installation of Exchange similar to Exchange 2000 or 2003.
Preparing AD includes the following tasks:

▶ Extending the AD schema

▶ Creating the Exchange organization in AD

▶ Creating the Microsoft Exchange System Objects container for the domain

▶ Creating the following Universal Security groups (USGs) for Exchange; Exchange
Organization Administrators, Exchange Mailbox Administrators, Exchange
ReadOnly Administrators, and Exchange Servers Group

▶ Setting the appropriate permissions on the global Exchange configuration container,
the Microsoft Exchange System Objects container, and the Universal Security groups

To prepare AD for Exchange Server 2007 manually, use the following steps preferably on
the Schema Master:

1. Insert the Exchange Server 2007 CD or DVD (Standard or Enterprise).

2. From the Start menu, select Run. Then type [CDDrive]:\setup.exe /prepareAD,
and click OK.

> **NOTE**
>
> It is easier to allow the Exchange Server Installation Wizard to prepare the AD environment automatically. However, there might be a need to conduct this task separately as a manual process. In addition, it is common that a different AD administrator might conduct this task because the Exchange administrator might not be a member of the Enterprise and Schema Admins group, and a member of the local Administrators group of that server.

Raising the Domain Functional Levels

To bring a Windows Server 2003 domain to Windows Server 2003 functional levels, perform the following steps:

1. Ensure that all domain controllers in the forest are upgraded to Windows 2000 Server or Windows Server 2003.

2. From the first domain controller, open AD Domains and Trusts from the Administrative Tools menu.

3. In the left scope pane, right-click on the domain name, and then click Raise Domain Functional Level.

4. On the Raise Domain Functional Level screen, shown in Figure 7.12, select Windows Server 2003, and then click Raise.

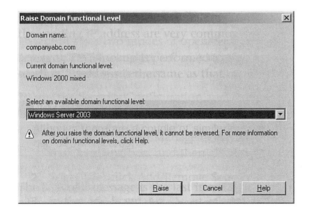

FIGURE 7.12   Raising the domain functional levels.

5. Click OK and then click OK again to complete the task.

Reviewing All Log Files Before Proceeding

Each of the utilities that have been executed has some form of output in its respective log files. Review the log file after running each utility to ensure no errors are encountered.

Installing the Prerequisites for Exchange Server 2007

This section of the chapter focuses on the step-by-step installation of the prerequisites required to install Exchange Server 2007.

Installing the .NET Framework 2.0 Component

To install the .NET Framework 2.0 component, complete the following steps:

1. Insert the Exchange Server 2007 CD or DVD (Standard or Enterprise).

2. AutoRun should launch a splash screen with options for Resources and Deployment Tools. (If AutoRun does not execute, select Start, Run. Then type [CDDrive]:\setup.exe, and click OK.)

3. On the Start page, click Install .NET Framework 2.0.

4. On the Welcome to the Microsoft .NET Framework 2.0 page, click Next.

5. On the Microsoft .NET Framework 2.0 Setup End-User License Agreement page, click I Accept the Terms of the License Agreement, and then click Install.

6. Click Finish to complete the installation.

> **NOTE**
>
> The .NET Framework 2.0 is included and installed by default with Windows Server 2003 R2; therefore, there isn't a need to conduct the preceding steps. However, .NET Framework 2.0 is not installed by default with Windows Server 2003 SP1 and needs to be installed as noted in the preceding steps.

Verifying That Microsoft Management Console 3.0 Is Installed

To install the Microsoft Management Console 3.0, use the following steps:

1. Insert the Exchange Server 2007 CD or DVD (Standard or Enterprise).

2. AutoRun should launch a splash screen with options for Resources and Deployment Tools. (If AutoRun does not execute, select Start, Run. Then type [CDDrive]:\setup.exe, and click OK.)

3. On the Start page, click Install MMC 3.0.

4. On the Software Update Installation Wizard page, click Next.

5. On the Software Update Installation Wizard License Agreement page, click I Agree, and then click Next.

6. On the Completing the Microsoft Management Console 3.0 Pre-Release Installation Wizard page, click Finish.

NOTE

The Microsoft Management Console 3.0 is included and installed by default with Windows Server 2003 R2; therefore, there isn't a need to conduct the preceding steps. However, the Microsoft Management Console 3.0 component is not installed by default with Windows Server 2003 SP1 and needs to be installed as noted in the preceding steps.

Installing the Exchange Management Shell (EMS)

To install the Exchange Management Shell prerequisite, use the following steps:

1. Insert the Exchange Server 2007 CD or DVD (Standard or Enterprise).

2. AutoRun should launch a splash screen with options for Resources and Deployment Tools. (If AutoRun does not execute, select Start, Run. Then type [CDDrive]:\setup.exe, and click OK.)

3. On the Start page, click Install Exchange Management Shell.

4. Double-click on the Msh_Setup.msi file to initiate the installation.

5. On the Welcome to the Exchange Management Shell Wizard page, click Next.

6. On the License Agreement page, click I Accept the Terms in the License Agreement, and click Next.

7. On the Destination Folder page, select the folder where the application will be installed, and then click Next.

8. On the Start Installation page, click Install to commence the installation.

9. Click Finish to complete the installation.

Configuring Internet Information Services (IIS) 6.0

To install IIS using Add or Remove Programs in Control Panel, follow these steps:

1. Click Start, Control Panel, Add or Remove Programs.

2. Click Add/Remove Windows Components in the Add or Remove Programs dialog box.

3. In the Windows Components Wizard, scroll down until you see Application Server. Highlight this entry, click the check box, and then click the Details button.

4. In the Application Server dialog box, illustrated in Figure 7.13, check the ASP.NET, Enable Network COM+ Access, and Internet Information Services check boxes, highlight Internet Information Services (IIS), and then click Details.

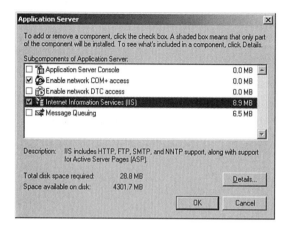

FIGURE 7.13   Installing Internet Information Services (IIS).

5. In the Internet Information Services (IIS) dialog box, select the Internet Information Services Manager, Common Files, World Wide Web Services, ASP.NET, Enable Network COM+ Access, and Internet Information Services check boxes, and then click OK.

6. Click OK on the Application Server dialog box, and then click Next in the Windows Components Wizard to begin installing IIS.

7. Click Finish when the installation is complete.

NOTE

Unlike the previous versions of Exchange, Exchange Server 2007 does not require the NNTP service component to be installed as a prerequisite.

Installing the First Exchange Server 2007 Server

Before installing Exchange Server 2007, it is beneficial to focus on the previous chapters to understand the new technologies included in Exchange Server 2007 such as server roles, planning, and deployment strategies. It will then be possible to plan an appropriate installation that is tailored toward the company's goals and requirements.

Compared to previous versions, the Exchange Server 2007 Installation Wizard offers administrators significant improvements to the installation process. For example, administrators have the flexibility to deploy a Typical or Custom installation. The Typical

Exchange Server installation option is best used for a single-server deployment and installs the following roles: Bridgehead role, Client Access role, Mailbox role, and Exchange Management Console. With the Custom Exchange Server Installation, the administrator has the flexibility to install desired Exchange roles.

The following example focuses on a Typical Exchange Server installation, whereas the upcoming chapters cover custom installation and configuration of all the Exchange 2007 server roles in its entirety.

To install the first Exchange server in an organization using the interactive installation process of Exchange Server 2007, use the following steps:

1. Insert the Exchange Server 2007 CD or DVD (Standard or Enterprise).

2. AutoRun should launch a splash screen with options for installing the prerequisites and application. (If AutoRun does not execute, select Start, Run. Then type [CDDrive]:\setup.exe, and click OK.)

3. On the Start page, click Install Microsoft Exchange.

> **NOTE**
>
> Before Microsoft Exchange Server 2007 can be installed, the Setup Installation Wizard verifies if the necessary prerequisites have been fulfilled. If the prerequisites have not been met, configure the prerequisites manually based on the previous steps, and then proceed with the installation again.

4. Setup.exe copies the setup files locally to the server on which Exchange Server 2007 is being installed.

5. In the Microsoft Exchange Server Installation Wizard dialog box, on the Introduction page, click Next.

6. At the License Agreement page, click I Accept the Terms in the License Agreement, and click Next.

7. At the Customer Feedback page, select whether to participate in the Customer Experience Improvement Program by sending feedback automatically to Microsoft, and then click Next.

8. At the Installation Type page, select the type of Exchange Server 2007 installation, and then click Next. For this example, a Typical Exchange Server Installation is being utilized, as shown in Figure 7.14.

> **NOTE**
>
> If there is a need to change the installation folder, click Browse before proceeding and specify a path for the Exchange Server installation.

FIGURE 7.14   Selecting the type of Exchange installation.

9. At the Exchange Organization page, type the name of the desired organization name, as illustrated in Figure 7.15, and then click Next.

FIGURE 7.15   Enter the Exchange organization name.

10. At the Client Settings page, indicate whether there are Outlook 2003 clients or earlier within the infrastructure, and then click Next.

NOTE

In the redesign of both Exchange Server 2007 and Outlook 2007, Microsoft has tightly integrated the two products together. Therefore, Outlook 2007 is the preferred client for Exchange 2007.

Another benefit of implementing just Outlook 2007 is that backward compatibility components in Exchange 2007 do not need to be installed if the organization does not need to support previous versions of Outlook. As an example, if client systems are running Outlook 2003 and earlier, objects such as public folders need to be installed to support free/busy information.

---

11. On the Readiness Checks page, the Installation Wizard is verifying that the appropriate Exchange Server prerequisites have been installed. View the status to determine if the organization and server role prerequisite checks completed successfully, and then click Install to implement the first Exchange Server 2007 in the organization.

NOTE

If errors are returned or prerequites are not met on the Readiness Checks page, it is necessary to address these issues and retry the setup.

---

12. To complete the Exchange Server 2007 installation, click Finish on the Completion page.

Completing the Installation of Exchange Server 2007

Postinstallation tasks should be conducted after the first Exchange 2007 server has been installed. Some of these postinstallation tasks will validate whether the installation was successful, whereas other tasks are required to ensure that the server is secure and operational. The postinstallation tasks include the following:

▶ Review installation logs

▶ Review event logs

▶ Obtain the latest Exchange critical updates

▶ Verify server roles are installed

▶ Run Microsoft Exchange Best Practice Analyzer

Reviewing Installation Logs

After the first Exchange 2007 server installation is complete, administrators should review the installation logs located on the root drive of the installation path selected. The typical location of the installation log file is `C:\Program Files\Microsoft\Exchange Server\logging\SetupLogs`.

The log files contain all the details pertaining to the installation of the Exchange server throughout the process.

Reviewing Event Logs

After an administrator has verified the installation logs for any anomalies and determined the implementation is a success, it is beneficial to review the Windows event logs.

The Application Event Log can contain both positive and negative Exchange information about the installation. The Exchange events can consist of information, warning, and critical errors. The Application Event Log can be found by launching the Event Viewer included with Windows Server 2003.

Performing Postinstallation Exchange Server Updates

Exchange Server 2007 is a constantly evolving set of technologies that occasionally needs patching and updating to keep it ahead of the constantly evolving threats and exploits on the Internet. Therefore, it is key to update Exchange Server 2007 with the latest service packs and security patches available for the system, and to check for new updates as part of a regular maintenance plan. These updates can always be found at http://www.microsoft.com\downloads or by selecting Step 5 Get Critical Updates for Exchange on the Exchange Server 2007 Installation dialog box.

Verify Server Roles Installed

Another recommended postinstallation task is to verify that the appropriate server roles were installed. This can be conducted by running the `get-ExchangeServer` command from within the Exchange Management Shell.

Microsoft Exchange Best Practice Analyzer

The final recommended postinstallation task is to run the Exchange Best Practice Analyzer tool included with Exchange Server 2007. The Microsoft Exchange Best Practice Analyzer tool is designed for administrators to determine the overall health of the Exchange topology. The tool analyzes Exchange servers and verifies items that do not adhere to Microsoft best practices against a local repository.

The Exchange Best Practice Analyzer tool is no longer a separate download. It can be found by expanding the Toolbox node in the Exchange Management Console.

Performing a Scripted Installation of Exchange Server 2007

In many enterprise situations, there is a need to automate the installation of an Exchange server. Exchange Server 2007 has the capability to automate the installation process with the assistance via a command prompt and the Exchange Management Shell. The unattended install file stores all the answers and configuration settings required for installing Exchange Server 2007 based on an administrator's input. The automated process definitely speeds up the installation and is great in environments where there is a need to install many Exchange servers seamlessly.

Install Exchange Server 2007 in Unattended Mode via the Command Prompt

To install the first Exchange 2007 server in Unattended mode, enter the following parameters and run this procedure from the command prompt. The predefined installation process consists of the following commands, as illustrated in Listing 7.1.

LISTING 7.1   Unattended Mode Setup Parameters

```
Setup /mode:<setup mode> /roles:<server roles to install>
[/TargetDir:<destination folder>] [SourceDir:<source folder>]
[/DomainController <FQDN of domain controller>] [/AnswerFile <file>]
[/DisableErrorReporting] [/NoSelfSignedCertificates]
[/AdamLdapPort <port>] [/AdamSslPort <port>] [/NewProvisionedServer]
[/RemoveProvisionedServer] [/ForeignForestFQDN]
[/ServerAdmin <user or group>] [/?]
```

The following bullets explain the parameters and information that can be inputted for installing Exchange Server 2007 in Unattended mode:

▶ The /mode parameter must be used to indicate the type of Exchange Server 2007 installation. The modes consist of Install, Upgrade, Uninstall, and RecoverServer. The default Install mode occurs if a mode is not indicated in the script.

▶ The /roles parameter must be used to indicate the type of server role that will be installed. The server roles that can be used are Client Access, Edge Transport, Hub Transport, Mailbox, and Unified Messaging as well as the option to install the Exchange 2007 Management Tools. More than one role can be selected. They must be separated by a comma.

▶ The /TargetDir parameter represents the destination location for the Exchange Server 2007 installation files.

▶ The /SourceDir parameter represents the location of the source Exchange Server 2007 installation files. For example, this could be the DVD drive or a location on a file server.

▶ The /DomainController parameter is used to indicate which domain controller will be used in the forest to read and write information to and from AD.

▶ The /Answerfile parameter is used to indicate the location of the file that contains advanced installation settings for Exchange Server 2007.

▶ The /DisableErrorReporting parameter is used to disable error reporting during the installation of Exchange 2007.

▶ The /NoSelfSignedCertificates parameter is required if there isn't a certificate authority present within the infrastructure and there is a need to create self-signed certificates for Secure Sockets Layer (SSL) or Transport Layer Security (TLS) sessions. This option is only available when installing the Client Access server role or the Unified Messaging server role.

▶ The /AdamLdapPort <port> and /AdamSslPort <port> parameters are used to indicate the Lightweight Directory Access Protocol (LDAP) port and the SSL port used when defining connectivity for an Edge Transport server role.

▶ The /NewProvisionedServer parameter should be used if there is a need to create a placeholder object in AD for an Exchange 2007 server. The installation permissions will be delegated, therefore, so that an administrator can conduct the installation at a later point of time.

▶ The /RemoveProvisionedServer parameter is similar to the /NewProvisionedServer parameter; however, instead of delegating permissions for installing Exchange, it removes the permissions.

▶ The /ForeignForestFQDN parameter is used when there is a need to configure Exchange Universal Security groups in another forest. This is common in an Exchange Federated Forest environment.

▶ The /ServerAdmin parameter is used when there is a need to provide an account with the appropriate Exchange privileges when installing Exchange Server 2007.

Installing Other Exchange Server 2007 Server Roles into the Infrastructure

In the past, there were typically two Exchange server roles: back-end servers, which hosted mailboxes and public folders, and front-end servers, which acted as a proxy gateway for clients. In Exchange 2007, Microsoft has expanded the range of supported server roles. There are now five major server roles, which are modular and can reside on a single system or on many. The roles are as follows:

▶ Client Access server role

▶ Edge server role

- ▸ Hub Transport server role

- ▸ Unified Messaging server role

- ▸ Mailbox server role

Installation of the Client Access Server Role

A Client Access server role is similar to an Exchange 2003 front-end server. It manages client access to connect to their Exchange mailbox via services such as Outlook Web Access, Exchange Active Sync, and Post Office Protocol version 3 (POP3).

It is necessary to install a Client Access server if users access their mailbox by using any client other than Microsoft Outlook.

For more information on Client Access servers and detailed steps on how to install and configure the role, review Chapter 8, "Implementing Edge Services for an Exchange Server 2007 Environment."

Establishing Perimeter Security with the Edge Server Role

The Edge Transport server role provides antivirus and antispam message protection for the Exchange infrastructure. The Edge server role acts as a message hygiene gateway and typically resides in a perimeter network or demilitarized zone (DMZ). It is typically the SMTP gateway for sending and receiving mail to and from the Internet.

For more information on the Edge Transport server role and details on how to install and configure the role, review Chapter 10, "Client-Level Secured Messaging."

Configuring Hub Transport Servers in an Exchange Server 2007 Environment

The Hub Transport server role is responsible for moving mail between Exchange Mailbox servers, similar to how bridgehead servers worked in the past. This role can be configured on a dedicated server or can be configured on a Mailbox server. A dedicated Hub Transport server is typical for large organizations that have many Exchange servers within a site or the company.

For more information on the Edge Transport server role and detailed steps on how to install and configure the role, see Chapter 8.

Installing a Unified Messaging Server System

The Unified Messaging server role is new to Exchange. It acts as a gateway for combining email, voice, and fax data into a single mailbox. All this data can be accessed via the mailbox or a telephone.

For more information on the Unified Messaging server and detailed steps on installing and configuring the role, refer to Chapter 24, "Designing and Configuring Unified Messaging in Exchange Server 2007."

Installing the Mailbox Server Role

The Mailbox server role is the core role within Exchange Server 2007. Regardless of the planned architecture, it is required to install at least a Mailbox server role and Hub Transport server role for Exchange 2007 to function properly. The Mailbox server role hosts mailboxes and mail enabled objects such as contacts and distribution lists.

For more information on the Mailbox server role and detailed steps on installing and configuring the role, refer to Chapter 4.

Summary

Microsoft has simplified the process for installing the Exchange Server 2007 product. Exchange Server 2007 is the easiest Exchange product to install to date. The new Exchange Server 2007 Installation Wizard makes deploying a typical installation and making changes to the AD environment very straightforward.

As with any simplified installation process, however, it is important to understand the steps leading to a successful implementation so that the appropriate planning, testing, and preparation is done prior to the live installation. In addition, because Exchange Server 2007 introduces new functionality beyond simple email, such as new server roles, unified messaging, and mobile messaging, getting the first Exchange 2007 server installed properly sets the foundation for a successful enterprise rollout of the Exchange messaging system.

Best Practices

The following are best practices from this chapter:

- ▶ Review Chapter 1 to understand what's new in Exchange Server 2007.
- ▶ Leverage Chapters 2, 3, and 4 for planning and designing an Exchange Server messaging infrastructure for a small, medium, or large enterprise organization.
- ▶ Before installing Exchange Server 2007 into a production environment, it is beneficial to prototype the design in a test environment.
- ▶ Use virtual servers when creating a test lab to simulate large production implementations and to minimize hardware costs.
- ▶ If there is a need to purchase new Exchange 2003 servers now, purchase x64-bit hardware with the intent of reusing the hardware for Exchange Server 2007 in the future.
- ▶ For small organizations, it is possible to install the Mailbox, Client Access, and Hub Transport roles all on the same server.
- ▶ For an organization that will be installing many Exchange servers and wants to ensure an identical build between servers, creating an unattended installation script can ensure that a common installation process is followed.

CHAPTER 8

Implementing Edge Services for an Exchange Server 2007 Environment

The Edge Transport server role provides an important layer of security between the Internet and an organization's messaging environment. Rather than having messages go straight from the Internet directly into an Exchange server, messages first go to an Edge server and are assessed and filtered based on certain policies or rules. The Edge server can identify spam and delete, quarantine, or simply tag potentially undesired messages to ultimately create rules that delete the messages that are not valid messages.

By default, Edge Services are not installed on an Exchange server in the organization, and an organization can choose to not have an Edge server and still have a fully operational Exchange messaging environment. However, by placing an Edge server in the network, the organization substantially improves its ability to eliminate unwanted messages.

This chapter focuses on the planning and implementation of Edge Services in an organization, along with critical configuration and tuning of Edge Services rules to further enhance the effectiveness of the Edge server in filtering messaging content.

Installing and Configuring the Edge Transport Server Components

The first thing that needs to be done is to determine how the Edge Transport server role will be implemented and configured in the Exchange environment. This involves planning and designing the placement of the Exchange Edge Transport server location, considering configuration options, and then actually installing the Edge Transport Services onto a server in the network. This section defines the configurable items for the components available on an Exchange 2007 server when the Edge Transport server role is selected during installation. Several items are identified in this section specific to the appropriate configuration options to properly achieve a secure, effective, and stable Edge Transport server environment.

Planning the Implementation of the Edge Transport Servers in Exchange

The first item to consider when installing and configuring the Edge Transport Services is the desired end result of the email message or connection being processed by the Edge Transport server. Determining what type of email should always be rejected, quarantined, or tagged for end-user review or which connections should be blocked and for how long will help reduce the amount of false positives and allow for a moderately aggressive spam filtering policy the first time Edge Transport servers begin monitoring email for an organization.

Planning for the Message Processing Order of Edge Services

To assist with the planning for your Edge Transport server deployment, take a moment to become familiar with the order in which filtering agents analyze messages. Understanding the order in which messages are processed will help you determine where you should place filters and assign settings for messages you do or don't want to receive. The Edge Transport Antispam filtering order is as follows:

1. An email message is received from the Internet.

2. The IP Block and Allow Lists are checked for a match to the sending IP address.

3. The IP Block List Providers and IP Allow List Providers are checked for a match to the sending IP address.

4. The Sender Filtering Agent checks the Blocked Senders list for a match.

5. The SenderID Agent performs a Sender Policy Framework (SPF) record lookup against the sending IP address.

6. The Recipient Filtering Agent checks the Blocked Recipients list for a match. This is also where messages addressed to nonexistent recipients get identified.

7. The Content Filtering Agent analyzes the content contained inside the message. Using Safelist Aggregation, the Content Filtering Agent also recognizes block and allow entries obtained from users' Outlook clients.

8. Attachments are analyzed by the Attachment Filter Agent. Edge transport rules run against the message.

9. The message is either delivered to the Hub Transport server, rejected, deleted, sent to the spam quarantine mailbox, or placed in the user's Junk E-Mail folder in the Outlook client.

> **NOTE**
>
> Messages can be identified for delivery or one of the blocking actions at any point in this process, depending on how the Edge Transport server agents have been configured.

> **TIP**
>
> Because the majority of unwanted email delivered today is spam, it is recommended to scan for spam messages before performing virus scanning. This reduces the load placed on the server when it performs virus scanning because virus scanning requires more processing power. This best practice assumes other antivirus mechanisms are in place throughout the network.

The Microsoft Exchange Server TechCenter located at http://www.microsoft.com/technet/prodtechnol/exchange/default.mspx contains a wealth of information, tools, tips, and virtual labs for Exchange administrators.

The Microsoft Exchange Team Blog located at http://www.msexchangeteam.com/ is a great place to stay current on Exchange news and communicate with other Exchange experts in the industry.

Installing Edge Transport Services on an Exchange Server

With a general concept of what the Edge Transport Services does, the next step is to install Edge Services on a system and begin configuring filters to test the results in your environment.

> **Testing Edge Services**
>
> Unlike some server functions where you can test functionality in a lab environment, such as performance, features, and functions, testing Edge Services filtering is a little harder to do in an isolated environment. You need to have incoming messages, including spam and good messages, to filter to determine the effective results of the filters you create.
>
> Many organizations insert an Edge Services system into their network and set the filter settings low enough that no good messages are accidentally filtered. Then, the organization tunes up the filters to be more and more restrictive, effectively increasing the filter catch rate. While the filtering is expanded, quarantine areas are monitored to look for false positive messages ensuring that good messages are not being filtered unnecessarily. This can take an organization several weeks to work through the tuning; however, it provides tight control on the processing of filtered messages.

Another option that is frequently used is where an organization sets up a test network with a live connection to the Internet and creates a "honeypot." A honeypot is an Internet-connected system that attracts messages, including spam and other content. The process involves establishing a domain on the Internet, setting up an email server to the domain, and then signing up to be on mailing lists with an email account from this test domain. This might include going to the websites of established businesses such as retail stores, mail-order houses, and so on and signing up to receive emails about their promotions and regular newsletters. To get less desirable content, you could sign up to receive notification of events on sites with questionable reputations such as triple-X sites. Do note that it could take several weeks before your honeypot attracts enough messages to make the filtering effective.

As a caution, make sure that if you sign up on sites for the purpose of attracting spam that you are connected to an Internet connection, that you clearly understand that the incoming content might be inappropriate for professional organizations, and that you expose the external IP address and incoming ports to questionable content.

Preparing an Exchange Server 2007 System

As covered in Chapter 7, "Installing Exchange Server 2007," for installing core Exchange Server 2007 systems, the Exchange Edge Transport server role also needs to be installed on a system running the Windows Server 2003 operating systems. The minimum prerequisite required to install Exchange Server 2007 is Windows Server 2003 with at least Service Pack 1 or Windows Server 2003 R2, Standard or Enterprise 64-bit Editions. Because this server will be connected to the Internet, hardening the server for security is extremely important; therefore, it is even more important that the server system has the latest service pack and patches installed on the system. For more details on installing Windows Server 2003, see Chapter 7.

Installing the Exchange Server 2007 Application on the Server

After the server has Windows Server 2003 installed and is properly patched and updated, you can begin the installation of Exchange Server 2007. To install Exchange Server using the interactive installation process of Exchange, use the following steps:

1. Insert the Exchange Server 2007 CD or DVD (Standard or Enterprise).

2. AutoRun should launch a splash screen with options for installing the prerequisites and application. (If AutoRun does not execute, select Start, Run. Then type `[CDDrive]:\setup.exe` and click OK.)

3. On the Start page, click Install Microsoft Exchange.

NOTE

Before Microsoft Exchange Server 2007 can be installed, the Setup Installation Wizard will verify if the necessary prerequisites have been fulfilled. If the prerequisites have not been met, configure the prerequisites as recommended by the Configuration Wizard. For more details, see Chapter 7.

---

4. Setup.exe copies the setup files locally to the server on which Exchange Server 2007 is being installed.

5. In the Microsoft Exchange Server Installation Wizard dialog box, on the Introduction page, click Next.

6. At the License Agreement page, click I Accept the Terms in the License Agreement, and click Next.

7. At the Customer Feedback page, select whether to participate in the Customer Experience Improvement Program by sending feedback automatically to Microsoft, and then click Next.

8. At the Installation Type page, select the type of Exchange Server 2007 installation, and then click Next. Because this will be an Edge Transport server, select Edge Transport for installation.

NOTE

If there is a need to change the installation folder, click Browse before proceeding and specify a path for the Exchange Server installation.

9. On the Readiness Checks page, the Installation Wizard is verifying that the appropriate Exchange Server prerequisites have been installed. View the status to determine if the organization and server role prerequisite checks completed successfully, and then click Install to implement the first Exchange Server 2007 server in the organization.

NOTE

If there are any errors returned or prerequisites not met on the Readiness Checks page, it is necessary to address these issues and retry the setup.

10. To complete the Exchange Server 2007 installation, on the Completion page, click Finish.

NOTE

The Verify Deployment and Secure the Edge Transport Server by Using the Security Configuration Wizard tasks should be completed after you have finished configuring the Edge Transport server filters and services.

To the right of the Finalize Deployment tab is the End-to-End Scenario tab, outlining the recommended tasks for end-to-end email routing scenarios along with other help topics. For example, the Configure the Spam Confidence Level (SCL) Junk E-Mail Folder Threshold link provides steps for setting the SCL thresholds for delivery to the end user's

Junk E-Mail folder in Outlook. Details for configuring these options are covered throughout the balance of this chapter.

Understanding the Edge Transport Components in the Exchange Management Console

After the Exchange Server software has been installed on the server system that will become the Edge Transport server, launch the Exchange Management Console to begin the process of configuring filters and parameters. The Exchange Management Console can be launched by doing the following:

1. Click Start, Program Files, Exchange Server 2007.

2. Choose the Exchange Management Console program.

If the Edge Transport server role was selected during the Exchange Server 2007 setup process, the Edge Transport object and Toolbox are the only items that will be available in the console tree of the Exchange Management Console. Selecting the Edge Transport object in the console tree of the Exchange Management Console populates the work pane similar to what is shown in Figure 8.1 with the configurable options for the Edge Transport server.

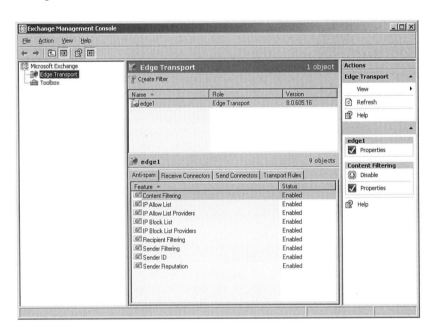

FIGURE 8.1   View of the Exchange Management Console configuration options for the Edge Transport server.

NOTE

All filters, lists, and connector settings are enabled by default. As changes are made and applied, they will be in effect on the Edge Transport server. Careful attention to changes is necessary, especially in a live environment. It is recommended to design and configure the first Edge Transport server offline with the minimal configuration needed for email routing and moderate antispam filtering. In the future, the aggressiveness of the antispam filters can be increased and additional filters can be added or modified. This makes troubleshooting easier and helps ensure delivery of legitimate email, while retaining the benefit of blocking known spam or obvious malicious email.

Several tabs are displayed within the action pane, including the following:

- ▶ Anti-Spam
- ▶ Receive Connectors
- ▶ Send Connectors
- ▶ Transport Rules

The Anti-Spam tab is selected by default and includes all of the configurable filters, lists, and agents for effective spam filtering. Listed alphabetically, the following nine items are available under the Anti-Spam tab in the work pane:

- ▶ Content Filtering
- ▶ IP Allow List
- ▶ IP Allow List Providers
- ▶ IP Block List
- ▶ IP Block List Providers
- ▶ Recipient Filtering
- ▶ Sender Filtering
- ▶ Sender ID
- ▶ Sender Reputation

To the right of the Anti-Spam tab is the Receive Connectors tab. The Receive Connectors tab is used to configure email routing for messages sent from internal users to recipients who reside outside of the organization. From here, you can either create a new Receive Connector or modify the default Receive Connector labeled "Default internal receive connector <SERVERNAME>." This connector is enabled by default.

The tab to the right of the Receive Connectors tab is the Send Connectors tab. The Send Connectors tab is used to configure email routing for messages sent to internal users received from recipients who reside outside of the organization. From here, you can either create a new Send Connector or modify the default Send Connector labeled "Default internal send connector <SERVERNAME>."

> **NOTE**
>
> The Send Connector does not need to be configured if the Edge Transport server is subscribed to the Exchange 2007 organization and is receiving data from Active Directory through EdgeSync. See the "Using EdgeSync to Synchronize Active Directory Information to the Edge Transport Server" section later in this chapter for details on how to set up and configure EdgeSync.

The last tab in the action pane of the Exchange Management Console for Edge Transport servers is the Transport Rules tab. The Transport Rules tab allows for the creation of rules that should be applied to email messages passing through the Edge Transport server. Different conditions to check in email messages can be set for a rule.

Take a few minutes to navigate through the different items in the Exchange Management Console to become familiar with the location and options for each Edge Transport server component and service.

Utilizing the Basic Sender and Recipient Connection Filters

Connection filtering combats spam by blocking and/or allowing email messages from specific networks, IP addresses, and IP ranges. Email that is routed through Receive Connectors is processed by the Connection Filtering Agent. These messages are received from the Internet and travel inbound to the Edge Transport server for delivery to the recipient. The connection filtering agents (IP Block List, IP Allow List, IP Block List Providers, and IP Allow List Providers) are all enabled by default and can be configured using the Exchange Management Console or Exchange Management Shell.

An IP Allow List is a manual list of servers you trust to send email to your organization, more specifically those for which email communication cannot be disrupted. An IP Block List works in reverse, blocking email from specific email servers without further processing or retaining copies of the message. IP Block and Allow List Providers make it easier to stop email from known malicious entities or ensure communication continues for others. This is usually a free service and allows administrators to easily subscribe to these lists and benefit from them.

One example of a real-time block list providers is The Spamhaus Project at http://www.spamhaus.org. Spamhaus maintains the Spamhaus Block List (SBL) and provides it as a free service for anyone to use. Spamhaus records their block entries in the SBL domain name system (DNS) zone and that list is updated every 30 minutes and then mirrored to more than 40 servers around the world with direct hourly feeds to major Internet service providers (ISPs).

NOTE

If the message matches an entry from the IP Allow List, the message is assigned a Spam Confidence Level (SCL) rating of 0 regardless of any matches from the IP Block List. SCLs are covered in more detail later in this chapter in the section, "Using Content Filtering to Isolate Inappropriate Content."

NOTE

Changes described in this section are applied only to the local system. This is important to know if you have more than one Edge Transport server in your environment because the change will need to be made locally on all other Edge Transport servers.

To disable the IP Block List, IP Allow List, IP Block List Providers, and IP Allow List Providers agents using the Exchange Management Console, right-click the appropriate agent icon in the action pane and select Disable.

To disable these same agents using the Exchange Management Shell, run the set-< IPAllowListConfig, IPAllowListProvider, IPAllowListProvidersConfig, IPBlockListConfig, IPBlockListProvider, or IPBlockListProvidersConfig> command with the -Enabled $false parameter. For example:

"set-IPBlockListConfig -Enabled $false".

When configuring an IP Block List or IP Allow List, entities to block must be entered manually by the administrator because these lists are created and maintained locally on the server. Unless specified otherwise by the organization, reject email messages received from addresses on IP Block Lists to avoid further processing, increased system overhead, and consumed disk space.

TIP

The IP Block List can be used to define IP addresses that consistently send virus-infected messages or unacceptable content to the organization, whereas an IP Block List Provider might not identify these messages, which can be for several reasons.

Configuring an IP Allow List Using the Exchange Management Console

Email administrators can configure Allow Lists on an Edge Transport server to ensure messages from desired source mail senders or organizations are not filtered and blocked at the Edge server. Administrators can define single IP addresses, IP addresses and subnet masks, and/or IP ranges from which to allow email messages.

> **NOTE**
>
> In some organizations, the Edge Transport server might sit behind another Simple Mail Transfer Protocol (SMTP) server that receives email from the Internet. In scenarios like this, the SMTP address of each upstream email server must be added to the Transport Configuration object in an Active Directory forest before connection filtering can be used. The SMTP addresses listed in the Transport Configuration object in Active Directory are replicated to the Edge Transport servers via EdgeSync. See the "Using EdgeSync to Synchronize Active Directory Information to the Edge Transport Server" section on how to configure EdgeSync.

To configure an IP Allow List using the Exchange Management Console, do the following:

1. Launch the Exchange Management Console.

2. Select Edge Transport in the console tree.

3. Double-click the IP Allow List item in the action pane.

4. In the IP Allow List Properties window, select the Allowed Addresses tab.

5. Click the Add button or the down arrow IP address button to add a Classless Internet Domain Routing (CIDR) IP address or range (for example, 192.168.1.10 or 192.168.1.10/24).

6. Click OK to add the IP address or address range.

7. The IP addresses or address ranges are shown in the Remote IP Address(es) section of the Allowed Addresses tab in the IP Allow List Properties window.

> **NOTE**
>
> You must first obtain the IP address or address ranges of the email server or servers for those you want included in the IP Allow List.

8. Click Apply to save changes or click OK to save changes and close the window.

> **NOTE**
>
> Entries in an IP Allow List cannot be scheduled to expire.

Alternatively, an IP address and subnet mask, or IP address range can be defined for filtering. To define an allowed IP address and subnet mask, do the following:

1. In the IP Allow List Properties window, select the Allowed Addresses tab.

2. Click the down arrow and select IP and Mask.

3. In the Add Allowed IP Address – IP and Mask window, enter the IP address in the IP Address field (for example, 192.168.1.10).

4. Enter the subnet mask of the IP address in the IP Mask field (for example, 255.255.255.0).

5. Click OK to add the IP address and IP mask.

To define an allowed IP address range, do the following:

1. In the IP Allow List Properties window, select the Allowed Addresses tab.

2. Click the down arrow and select IP Range.

3. In the Add Allowed IP Address – IP Range window, enter the first IP address in the Start Address field (for example, 192.168.1.1).

4. Enter the last IP address in the address range in the End Address field (for example, 192.168.255.255).

5. Click OK to add the IP address range.

Any defined IP addresses, IP addresses and subnet masks, and/or IP address ranges are shown in the Remote IP Address(es) section of the Allowed Addresses tab of the IP Allow List Properties window.

Several list providers are available; the criteria for being added to or removed from their databases along with how often those databases are updated is different. For example, Microsoft provides updates twice per week for their Intelligent Message Filter, which is used with content filtering and the heuristics rules specific to phishing attempts. To configure an IP Allow List Providers using the Exchange Management Console, complete the following steps:

1. Launch the Exchange Management Console.

2. Select Edge Transport in the console tree.

3. Double-click the IP Allow List Providers item in the action pane.

4. In the IP Allow List Providers Properties window, select the Providers tab.

5. Click the Add button to define an IP Allow List Provider.

6. Enter the name of the provider in the Provider Name field.

7. Enter the IP address or fully qualified domain name (FQDN) in the Lookup Domain field.

8. Check Match to Any Return Code to identify all delivery status notifications (DSN) and respond to them accordingly.

9. Check Match to the Following Mask to specify an IP address or subnet mask and respond accordingly.

10. Check Match to any of the Following Responses to list multiple IP addresses or subnet masks and respond accordingly.

11. Click OK when you are finished; the newly created provider entry will be displayed in the IP Allow List Providers Properties window.

Configuring an IP Block List Using the Exchange Management Console

The IP Block List is configured using the same procedures as the IP Allow List; however, an entry made in the IP Block List can be scheduled to expire, whereas an entry in the IP Allow List cannot. By default, new entries are set to never expire.

> **NOTE**
>
> You must first obtain the IP address or address ranges of the email server or servers that you want included in the IP Block List.

To configure an IP Block List using the Exchange Management Console, do the following:

1. Launch the Exchange Management Console.

2. Select Edge Transport in the console tree.

3. Double-click the IP Allow List item in the action pane.

4. In the IP Allow List Properties window, select the Allowed Addresses tab.

5. Click Add to make a new entry.

6. In the Add Blocked IP Address window, select Block Until Date and Time.

7. Specify a date and time to expire the entry, and click OK.

Known spam servers and IP addresses sending malicious email should be double-checked for compliance before the expiration date comes due. Consider keeping maintenance logs or check entries frequently to avoid letting unwanted and previously blocked email messages (back) into your organization.

Configuring an IP Block List Providers Using the Exchange Management Console

The IP Block List Providers is configured in the same manner as the IP Allow List Providers filter; however, two different options are available in the IP Block List Providers properties that are not available when configuring an IP Allow List Provider.

The first difference can be found in the Add IP Block List Providers window when adding an IP Block List Providers on the Providers tab. A custom message can be specified or the default can be used for the Determine Error Message Returned when a Sender Is Blocked by a Provider option in the Return Status Codes section. To configure a custom error message, click the Error Messages button at the bottom of the window and select Custom Error Message in the IP Block List Providers Error Message window.

NOTE

A maximum of 240 characters can be entered into the Custom Error Message field.

The second difference between the IP Allow List Providers and IP Block List Providers filters is the ability to add exceptions. Exceptions to the IP Block List Provider's database can be configured on the Exceptions tab of the IP Block List Providers Properties window. On the Exceptions tab, you can add email addresses of senders that should not be blocked in the Do Not Block Messages Sent to the Following E-Mail Addresses, Regardless of Provider Feedback field. Messages sent to addresses in this list will not be blocked if they trigger a match in the IP Block List Providers' database.

NOTE

You must first obtain the necessary DNS zone(s) or IP address(es) to query from the provider hosting the IP Block List being added.

Configuring IP Block and Allow Lists Using the Exchange Management Shell

Connection filtering can also be configured through the Exchange Management Shell. Each shell command has its own parameters you can set based on the action(s) performed by the command. There are four commands: Get, Add, Remove, and Set. Each command works with one or more IP Block and Allow List components.

The Get- command is used to retrieve the configuration of a component. For example, entering Get-IPBlockListConfig displays the IP Block List Configuration on the local system.

The Add- command can be used to add an IP Block or Allow List entry or list provider and to assign an expiration time to the entry. The following example adds an IP range to the block list with an expiration date and time (24-hour format).

Add-IPBlockListEntry -IPRange 192.168.1.1/16 -ExpirationTime 12/15/2007 11:30:00

The Remove- command can be used to remove an IP Block or Allow List entry, list provider, or list entry. The following example removes a list provider using the name.

Remove-IPAllowListProvider -Identity Spamhaus

NOTE

Only static list entries can be removed using this command.

8

The Set- command allows an administrator to enable or disable the agent or modify the configuration of an IP Block or Allow List or list provider's configuration. The following example enables the Connection Filtering Agent on email distributed internally.

```
Set-IPBlockListConfig -InternalMailEnabled $true
```

> **NOTE**
>
> The status of an IP Allow or Block List Providers can be tested using the Test-IPAllowListProvider or Test-IPBlockListProvider commands, respectively.

You can test the configuration of a Block or Allow List Providers using the Test-BlockListProvider and Test-AllowListProvider Exchange shell commands, respectively. The following example tests a Block List Provider on a remote server using the provider name.

```
Test-IPBlockListProvider -Identity Spamhaus -Server EDGE2
```

The Exchange Management Shell is covered in more detail in Chapter 9, "Using the Windows PowerShell in an Exchange Server 2007 Environment."

Configuring Sender Filtering

Sender filtering allows an administrator to block email messages received from specific email addresses, domains, and subdomains. Email that is routed through Receive Connectors is processed by the Sender Filtering Agent. These messages are received from the Internet and travel inbound to the Edge Transport server for delivery to the recipient. Sender filtering, for example, can be a very useful tool when someone in an organization is being harassed by an external person or ex-employee, receiving consistent nondeliverable receipts (NDRs) or strange messages from the same source because of a virus or spam.

> **NOTE**
>
> Changes described in this section are applied only to the local system. This is important if you have more than one Edge Transport server in your environment.

The Sender Filtering Agent is enabled by default and can be configured using the Exchange Management Console or Exchange Management Shell.

To disable the Sender Filtering Agent using the Exchange Management Console, right-click the agent icon in the action pane and select Disable. To disable the Sender Filtering Agent using the Exchange Management Shell, run the setSenderFilterConfig command with the -Enabled $false parameter, for example set-SenderFilterConfig -Enabled $false.

The General tab of the Agent Properties window displays a brief description of the agent and its capabilities, its current status, and the last time the agent's settings were modified.

To add email addresses to the Sender Filtering list, double-click the Sender Filtering Agent in the action pane and select the Blocked Senders tab. From here, you can add, edit, or delete entries in the list. Checking the box at the bottom of the window enables the Block Messages from Blank Senders option. If an email address isn't specified in the message received, it will be blocked. This is a fairly common trick used in spamming messages.

Click Add in the Add Blocked Senders window to do the following:

1. Add an individual email address to block.

2. Add a domain and subdomains (if applicable) to block.

> **NOTE**
>
> Limited wildcard usage is supported in these fields, specifically the asterisk (*). For example, you can add *@companyabc.com to the Individual E-Mail Address to Block field; however, it accomplishes the same result as adding companyabc.com to the Domain field. It is recommended to add the full email address to block.

The Action tab allows you to specify whether to reject or stamp messages with Block Sender and continue processing them if the address matches an entry in the list. Stamping the message updates the metadata to indicate the sender was on the block list. This is taken into account by the content filter when it tabulates an SCL. The Sender Reputation filter agent uses the SCL rating when developing a sender reputation level.

Using the Exchange Management Shell to Add Blocked Senders

Sender filtering can also be configured through the Exchange Management Shell. Each shell command has its own parameters you can set based on the action(s) performed by the command. There are two commands: Get and Set.

The Get- command is used to retrieve the configuration of the Sender Filtering Agent. For example, entering Get-SenderFilterConfig displays the Sender Filtering configuration on the local system.

The Set- command allows an administrator to enable or disable the agent and modify the configuration of the agent. The following example enables the Sender Filtering Agent and rejects messages from blank senders on external SMTP connections.

```
Set-SenderFilterConfig -Enabled $true -Action Reject
-BlankSenderBlockingEnabled $true -ExternalMailEnabled $true -Enabled $true
```

Configuring Recipient Filtering

Recipient filtering allows an administrator to block email delivery from the Internet to a specific email address. Email that is routed through Receive Connectors is processed by the Recipient Filtering Agent. In addition, recipient filtering can prevent delivery of email messages to nonexistent accounts in Active Directory. This is extremely effective in stopping spam and virus-laden email to abused or commonly named email accounts (for example, support@companyabc.com or domain@domain.com).

> **NOTE**
>
> A maximum of 800 email addresses can be placed in this list.

The Recipient Filtering Agent is enabled by default and can be configured using the Exchange Management Console or Exchange Management Shell.

> **NOTE**
>
> Changes described in this section are applied only to the local system. This is important if you have more than one Edge Transport server in your environment.

To disable the Recipient Filtering Agent using the Exchange Management Console, right-click the agent icon in the action pane and select Disable. To disable the Recipient Filtering Agent using the Exchange Management Shell, run the set-RecipientFilterConfig command with the -Enabled $false parameter.

Example: set-RecipientFilterConfig -Enabled $false

The General tab of the Agent Properties window displays a brief description of the agent and its capabilities, its current status, and the last time the agent's settings were modified.

To add email addresses to the Recipient Filtering list, double-click the recipient Filtering Agent in the action pane and select the Blocked Recipients tab, as shown in Figure 8.2. From here, you can add, edit, or delete entries in the list. You can also enable the Block Messages Sent to Recipients Not Listed in the Recipient List field. Enabling this feature prevents delivery of email messages to nonexistent accounts in Active Directory.

> **NOTE**
>
> For the Block Messages Sent to Recipients Not Listed in the Recipient List feature to work, you must first configure the EdgeSync process and Active Directory Application Mode (ADAM) for recipient lookup. See the "Using EdgeSync to Synchronize Active Directory Information to the Edge Transport Server" section of this chapter for more information.

> **TIP**
>
> Using the Block Messages Sent to Nonexistent Senders can help drastically reduce the amount of email sent to commonly targeted addresses like webmaster@companyabc.com, support@companyabc.com, and john@companyabc.com. This also reduces the spammer's ability to identify which email addresses are valid when no response or a response other than "nonexistent user" is returned in a nondelivery report (NDR).

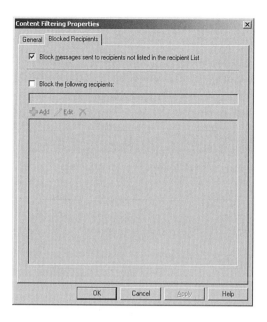

FIGURE 8.2   Blocked Recipients tab in the Exchange Management Console.

Using the Exchange Management Shell to Add Blocked Recipients

Recipient filtering can also be configured through the Exchange Management Shell. Each shell command has its own parameters you can set based on the action(s) performed by the command. There are two commands: Get and Set.

The Get- command is used to retrieve the configuration of the Sender Filtering Agent. For example, entering Get-RecipientFilterConfig displays the Recipient Filtering configuration on the local system.

The Set- command allows an administrator to enable or disable the agent or modify the configuration of the agent. The following example enables the Recipient Filtering Agent and rejects messages to nonexistent recipients on external SMTP connections.

```
Set-RecipientFilterConfig -Enabled $true -ExternalMailEnabled $true -
RecipientValidationEnabled $true
```

Utilizing SenderID on an Edge Transport Server

SenderID is a very effective defense mechanism against spam, phishing schemes, and mass-mailing computer viruses when an organization has their SenderID information properly registered. One of, if not the most common trick used by malicious email authors is the forging of fields in an email message's header information, specifically, the From address. This is often referred to as spoofing a sender's email address. SenderID processes inbound email from the Internet. These are the messages that are routed through the Receive Connector on the Edge Transport server.

Configuring SenderID

The SenderID Agent is installed and enabled by default when the Exchange Edge Transport server is installed on a Windows Server system. Because it is installed and enabled, the focus of this section is to identify the specific configuration tasks needed in configuring SenderID using the Exchange Management Console or Exchange Management Shell.

> **NOTE**
>
> Changes described in this section are applied only to the local system. This is impor-
> tant if you have more than one Edge Transport server in your environment.

To disable the SenderID Agent using the Exchange Management Console, right-click the agent icon in the action pane and select Disable. To disable the SenderID Agent using the Exchange Management Shell, run the set-SenderIDConfig command with the -Enabled $false parameter, for example:

```
"set-SenderIDConfig -Enabled $false"
```

The General tab of the Agent Properties window displays a brief description of the agent and its capabilities, its current status, and the last time the agent's settings were modified.

Malicious email crafters forge this field to hide their identity to avoid being discovered or direct any reply traffic to a specific or random domain, purposefully or not. Another reason this field is commonly forged is to trick the recipient into believing the message is from someone they know, thus increasing the likelihood it will be read and actions such as opening an attachment or web page will be carried out.

SenderID's primary purpose is validating that the server sending the message to your email server was authorized to do so for the domain specified in the From field of the message headers. When configured and maintained correctly, SenderID can accurately eliminate malicious email without extensive analysis of the content contained inside. In this section, you learn how to create and look up SPF records, how to configure SenderID, and how SenderID Framework (SIDF) has merged these technologies together.

When configuring SenderID, take into consideration which sending entities should always be allowed to deliver email messages to your organization, regardless of having a published SPF record. For example, in medium to large organizations a coordinated outreach to the other companies the organization does business with might be necessary to inform them of the impact SenderID could have on email they send to your organiza-tion and how to mitigate that impact. Administrators should avoid automatically reject-ing or deleting messages initially to help identify any senders that should be "white listed." Following this recommendation drastically reduces the impact the loss of legiti-mate email can have on an organization.

There are two components to getting SenderID functional on an Edge Transport server; the SenderID Agent and SPF records. SPF records aren't something that is configured on the Edge Transport server, but rather a piece of information SenderID is required to determine how to handle the message.

> **NOTE**
>
> SenderID also works with the Sender Reputation Agent to help the Sender Reputation Agent compute a Sender Reputation Level (SRL) for the sending entity. The Sender Reputation Agent is covered in the section "Configuring the Sender Reputation Agent Using the Exchange Management Console" later in this chapter.

SenderID validates the sending email server by querying the DNS server providing name resolution for the Internet for the sending server's Sender Policy Framework (SPF) record, provided the administrator of the sending system created and published one correctly. SPF is the "part" that makes SenderID work. SPF is an open standard added to the SMTP protocol and was designed by Meng Weng Wong and Mark Lentczner to help combat unwanted email without the use of antispam engines or extensive content filtering. Extensive SPF record creation, supporting different SPF configurations and/or multiple domains, and advanced syntax use is beyond the scope of this text. This section outlines what SPF is, how it works, how it integrates with SenderID, and how to create and activate a basic SPF record.

An SPF record, put simply, is a listing in DNS of what systems are authorized to send email for a specific domain or set of domains. Publishing an SPF record allows others to cross-reference the IP addresses of the mail servers in an organization against that organization's DNS entry for their domain, specifically a mail exchange (MX) record. This is also sometimes referred to as a reverse MX lookup.

The following is a sample SPF record for `CompanyABC.com`:

```
v=spf1 mx ip4:192.168.1.150 -all
```

The following is a sample SPF record for `CompanyABC.com` using multiple identifiers to include MX and A record lookup in DNS, and to allow email from another domain: `Company123.org`:

```
v=spf1 mx a:mail.companyabc.com include:company123.org -all
```

An SPF record can contain multiple domain mechanisms and domain modifiers to provide the correct identification and email handling or policy information when queried by other email systems running a SenderID or SPF filtering configuration. Although SenderID supports both SPF 1.0 and 2.0, this section focuses on SPF 1.0 because it is presently the de facto version.

> **NOTE**
>
> At the time of writing, SPF 2.0 was currently being reviewed by the Internet Engineering Task Force's (IETF; http://www.ietf.org) Internet Engineering Steering (IESG; http://www.ietf.org/iesg.html) unit for publication as a new Request for Comments (RFC). SPF

2.0 includes new mechanisms and modifiers for SPF records offering greater flexibility for antispam filters. The review focuses around whether the SPF 2.0 record should distinguish between a SPF record lookup and SenderID record lookup. The Microsoft SenderID supports both SPF 1.0 and 2.0.

SPF only needs three pieces of information to work:

▶ The domain of the From address in the message headers

▶ The purported IP address of the email server that sent the message

▶ The HELO or EHLO parameter of the server that sent the message

Using this information, SenderID can determine if the IP address was authorized to send email for the domain listed in the sender's email address.

SenderID Framework (SIDF) is a combination of two similar technologies: Sender Policy Framework (SPF) and Microsoft's CallerID for email. The SenderID Framework has been finalized and submitted to the IETF (http://www.ietf.org/) for final review in hopes it will soon become an Internet standard.

Creating a Sender Policy Framework Record

This section walks you through setting up an SPF record using the Microsoft Sender ID Framework SPF Record Wizard located at http://www.microsoft.com/mscorp/safety/content/technologies/senderid/wizard/.

On the Microsoft Sender ID Framework SPF Record Wizard web page, first enter the domain for which you want to create a record (for example, companyabc.com) in Step 1 of 4: Identify Your Domain field on the website, and click Next. The website checks DNS information about the domain to see what records, including SPF, exist. If no records exist, you are taken to the next step, Step 2 of 4: Display Published DNS Records. Review the information provided to ensure its accuracy, and click Next when you are ready to proceed to Step 3: Create SPF Record.

In Step 3 of 4: Create SPF Record of the Microsoft Sender ID Framework SPF Record Wizard, seven sections can be configured to support the organization's email structure. On this page, you can create an SPF record to reflect the following:

▶ That the domain does not send email.

▶ That inbound email servers also send email for the domain.

▶ That outbound email servers are different from the domain's inbound email servers.

▶ That all reverse DNS records (PTR) resolve to the domain's outbound email servers.

▶ That a domain's outbound email is routed through another domain (outsourced).

▶ That the domain will send email from an IP address not listed in the SPF record being created.

▶ That the SPF record can be used to validate either the Purported Responsible Address (PRA) derived from the message headers, or from the MAIL FROM (or reverse-path) address derived from the SMTP protocol's MAIL command, or both. The PRA is the [nonforged] IP address of the system responsible for sending the email message and the MAIL FROM tag (often forged) designates the email address the message is being delivered as.

NOTE

Some fields in the form might already contain data when the wizard queried DNS for information about the domain entered in Step 1.

For this example, you will create an SPF record in which companyabc.com's SMTP server is running the Edge Transport server role and handles both incoming and outgoing email. No other domains or IP addresses should be allowed to route email for companyabc.com.

In the form, specify that the domain's inbound email servers can send email by selecting the check box of the same name in the Inbound Mail Servers Send Outbound Mail section of the form. Next, specify that the IP address of the outbound email server for companyabc.com is 192.168.2.150 by adding that IP address to the Outbound Mail Server Addresses field in the form. Accept the default of Discouraged to the question regarding whether legitimate email can or will originate from an IP address not included in this record, and allow the record to be used to validate both the Purported Responsible IP address (PRA) and MAIL FROM address in the message headers. Now that the information has been entered, you can proceed to Step 4 of 4: Generate SPF Record, where the record can be created so it can be reviewed and saved for later use.

The record example for companyabc.com looks like this:

```
v=spf1 mx ip4:192.168.1.150 -all <or> ~all
```

The *v=spf1* designates that this is an SPF record and it is version 1. The portion *mx IP4:192.168.2.150* signifies the email server at 192.168.2.150 is authorized to send and receive email for company abc.com. The *-all* closes the record by stating that no one besides the IP addresses in companyabc.com's MX records are authorized to send email using a companyabc.com and can be rejected. From here, you can copy the syntax, paste it into a Notepad or WordPad document, save the file in standard ASCII text (TXT) format, and add it to DNS so other organizations using Edge Transport servers or an implementation of SPF can look up companyabc.com's SPF record.

NOTE

The SPF record must be published in DNS as a text file to be properly recognized. Beyond formatting of input on the form, the Sender ID Framework SPF Record Wizard does not test or validate the settings entered. After the wizard has finished creating your SPF record, take a moment to view it for accuracy before exporting it for use on the DNS servers.

More information about SPF—extensive SPF record creation, supporting different SPF configurations, multiple domains, and advanced syntax use—is beyond the scope of this text. More information can be obtained at the Microsoft website (http://www.microsoft. com/mscorp/safety/technologies/senderid/resources.mspx) or Sender Policy Framework (http://www.openspf.org).

So far, we've covered how SenderID works, how to create and manage simple SPF records, and considered the impact SenderID can have on legitimate email. At this point, the SenderID Agent on the Edge Transport server(s) can be configured.

Configuring the SenderID Agent on the Exchange Edge Transport Server

The SenderID Agent is enabled by default on Exchange 2007 Edge Transport servers. Configuration is quick and straightforward because SenderID only relies on a couple of items to function properly. SenderID like other spam-filtering technologies can impact legitimate email but, as discussed earlier, there are ways to mitigate this impact while still identifying messages that don't have an SPF record.

To begin configuring SenderID, do the following:

1. Launch the Exchange Management Console by doing the following on the Exchange server. Click Start, Programs, Microsoft Exchange Server 2007.

2. Choose Exchange Management Console.

3. Double-click the SenderID Agent in the action pane.

4. Select the Action tab.

From here, you can change the action taken on messages if the SenderID check fails. There are different actions to choose from. One action is to Stamp Message with Sender ID Result and Continue Processing. This is the default action and appends certain information to the message headers for further processing by the Content Filtering Agent. The Content Filtering Agent then takes this information into account when tabulating the overall spam score assigned to the message, also known as the Spam Confidence Level (SCL).

TIP

When you first implement SenderID filtering, it is a recommended to "stamp" messages to assist in filtering out false positives and generate a white list of legitimate senders and domains. After the organization is comfortable with the established white list, messages can be rejected.

Another option is to use the "exp" modifier in your SPF record and include a uniform resource locator (URL) to an Internet web page where others can retrieve information about your email policy, SPF records, and contact information. This helps offset false positives when rejecting email messages that fail to comply with SPF.

The actions available if a SenderID check fails include the following:

▶ Reject the message.

▶ Delete the message.

Choosing to reject the message sends an error response to the sending server. The text contained in this error message corresponds to the Sender ID status derived from processing the SPF record of the message.

Choosing to delete the message sends a fake OK SMTP command to the sending server. The message is deleted and the sender is not notified.

Accepting the default action of Stamp Message with Sender ID Result and Continue Processing appends the Sender ID status derived from the SPF record lookup into the message headers for further processing by the Content/IMF filter. This information, often called metadata, is used by the Content/IMF filter to create the SCL.

Using the Exchange Management Shell to Configure SenderID

One limitation of SenderID is the inability to exclude recipients and domains from SenderID filtering through the Exchange Management Console. Exclusion of recipients and domains from SenderID filtering can only be accomplished using the Exchange Management Shell's `Set-SenderIdConfig` command. The following example enables the SenderID Agent on external SMTP connections, bypasses checking one external domain, and sets the action on spoofed messages.

```
Set-SenderIdConfig -BypassedSenderDomains Microsoft.com -Enabled $true
➡-ExternalMailEnabled $true -SpoofedDomainAction Delete
```

The `Get-` command is used to retrieve the configuration of the Sender Filtering Agent. For example, entering `Get-SenderIDConfig` displays the Sender Filtering configuration on the local system.

You can test the configuration of SenderID using the `Test-SenderID` Exchange shell command. The following example tests to see if the SPF record resolves correctly.

```
Test-SenderId -IPAddress 192.168.1.150 -PurportedResponsibleDomain
➡mail.companyabc.com
```

The Exchange Management Shell is covered in more detail in Chapter 9, "Using the Windows PowerShell in an Exchange 2007 Environment."

Using Content Filtering to Isolate Inappropriate Content

Content filtering is not only effective for eliminating spam, but it can also be beneficial for identifying messages containing content deemed unacceptable to the organization, such as sexually derogatory remarks or racial slurs. The content filter processes messages that are routed through the Receive Connector on the Edge Transport server. The Content Filtering Agent is enabled by default and can be configured using the Exchange Management Console or Exchange Management Shell.

> **NOTE**
>
> Changes described in this section are applied only to the local system. This is important if you have more than one Edge Transport server in your environment.

To disable the Content Filtering Agent using the Exchange Management Console, right-click the agent icon in the action pane and select Disable. To disable the Content Filtering Agent using the Exchange Management Shell, run the `set-ContentFilterConfig` command with the `-Enabled $false` parameter.

For example `"set-ContentFilterConfig -Enabled $false"`

The General tab of the Agent Properties window displays a brief description of the agent and its capabilities, its current status, and the last time the agent's settings were modified.

The content filter in Exchange 2007 builds on the Intelligent Message Filter technology that Microsoft developed and included in Exchange 2003. The Intelligent Message filtering technology, a proprietary message–analyzing filter developed by Microsoft, "learns" which messages are spam and legitimate by analyzing the characteristics contained in both. This filter is updated periodically through Microsoft Software Update Services.

After message analysis has occurred, the content filter assigns an overall score to the message that corresponds with an action you choose based on the needs of the organization. For example, all messages scoring an 8 or higher might be deleted while any message scoring a 3 or lower might be delivered. This message score is often referred to as the SCL. Messages are assigned a score ranging from 0–9, with 9 being the "most confident" score that the message is spam.

The content filter can leverage the end user's Safe Recipients List, Safe Senders List, or trusted contacts list in Outlook (2003 or later) by enabling Safelist Aggregation. Safelist Aggregation uses the entries inside of Outlook to help populate the list of legitimate senders so they can be safely bypassed by the Content Filtering Agent. Configuring Safelist Aggregation is covered in the section "Implementing Safelist Aggregation for Outlook 2003 and Outlook 2007" later in this chapter.

To begin configuring content filtering, launch the Exchange Management Console, and double-click the Content Filtering Agent in the action pane. From here, you can customize the Custom Words list to block and allow certain words or phrases, add recipients to the exclusions list to exempt them from content filtering, and configure the actions to take on messages based on the messages' SCL. Some of these items are not available through the Exchange Management Console and can only be configured through the Exchange Management Shell.

The basic function of configuring the content filter on an Edge Transport server is performed as follows:

1. Enable the Content Filtering Agent (default is enabled).

2. Designate and specify a quarantine mailbox for captured messages.

3. Enable and configure SCL thresholds and actions.

4. Enable or disable puzzle validation.

5. Specify recipient and sender exceptions.

6. Configure Allow phrases and Block phrases.

7. Set the rejection response.

These functions are covered in the balance of this section.

Configuring the Quarantine Mailbox for Captured Messages

Before configuring other content filtering components, it is advised that you first configure the mailbox that will store messages on which an action of "quarantine" was taken. This action is based on the corresponding SCL for the Quarantine Messages That Have an SCL Rating Larger or Equal To setting in the Exchange Management Console, or the SCLQuarantineEnabled and SCLQuarantineThreshold parameters of the Set-ContentFilterConfig Exchange Management Shell command.

> **NOTE**
>
> The quarantine mailbox can only be assigned to content filtering through the Exchange Management Shell.

To configure a mailbox for content filtering, complete the following steps:

1. Create a user account with a mailbox in Active Directory if the quarantine mailbox will reside on your internal Exchange servers. Creating mailboxes is covered in Chapter 18, "Administering an Exchange Server 2007 Environment."

2. Run the Set-ContentFilterConfig with the –QuarantineMailbox parameter.

3. Then run the Exchange Management Console.

4. Select the Custom Words tab.

5. Enter the word or phrase you want to allow in the Messages Containing These Words or Phrases Will Not Be Blocked field. Email messages containing these entries will always be allowed to bypass content filtering.

6. Click Add to include the new entry.

7. To remove an entry, highlight it, and click the Delete button.

8. Click Apply to save your changes or OK to save changes and close the Content Filter dialog box.

Configuring Spam Quarantine

The spam quarantine holds messages that meet or exceed the SCL threshold set in the Content Filtering Agent on the Edge Transport server. Messages marked for quarantine are sent to a quarantine mailbox where they can be reviewed and delivered, if necessary. Administrators who need to resend a quarantined message can use the Send Again feature of Outlook. For more information regarding Microsoft Outlook, refer to Part VIII, "Client Access to Exchange Server 2007."

For messages to be quarantined, an Active Directory user and corresponding mailbox must exist, solely for this purpose. If you are running multiple Edge Transport servers, you might consider having one spam quarantine mailbox per server. Although this might increase the amount of effort needed to find captured messages, it decreases the load expected of one Mailbox server. This can also help with troubleshooting configuration differences between Edge Transport servers. Depending on the size of the organization and the amount of Internet email received, the spam quarantine can grow substantially. For more information on creating mailboxes, refer to Part VI, "Exchange Server 2007 Administration and Management."

TIP
It is recommended to dedicate an Exchange database to the spam quarantine mailbox, configure an email retention policy or recipient policy to restrict the mailbox size, and set the duration for how long quarantined messages should be retained.

After a mailbox has been created for the use of quarantining spam messages, the spam quarantine mailbox must be specified on the Edge Transport server. The spam quarantine mailbox can only be specified on an Edge Transport server using the Set-ContentFilterConfig command with the QuarantineMailbox parameter.

```
Set-ContentFilterConfig –QuarantineMailbox anti-spam@companyabc.com
```

The Set-ContentFilterConfig command is covered in more detail in the section "Using the Exchange Management Shell to Configure Content Filtering" later in this chapter.

Configuring the Allowed Keyword or Phrases List

Content filtering varies from organization to organization, so Exchange 2007 Edge Services has exceptions to allow for keywords or phrases to not cause a message to be filtered or blocked. This is commonly used in the medical profession where the reference to certain drugs, body parts, or human activities is part of the field of business, whereas in other organizations, those references are commonly used in unwanted or unsolicited email messages.

To configure the Exchange 2007 Edge Transport server to allow keywords or key phrases, do the following from within the Exchange Management Console:

1. Select the Custom Words tab.

2. Enter the word or phrase you want to allow in the Messages Containing These Words or Phrases Will Not Be Blocked field. Email messages containing these entries will always be allowed to bypass content filtering.

3. Click Add to include the new entry.

4. To remove an entry, highlight it, and click the Delete button.

5. Click Apply to save your changes or OK to save changes and close the Content Filter dialog box.

> **NOTE**
>
> Messages containing an allowed word or phrase are given an SCL score of 0.

Configuring Keyword or Phrases List to Block Messages

The second section of the Custom Words tab allows you to define words or phrases in messages that should be blocked. There are two exceptions to this: use of the allowed word or phrase list and the exclusions list. Entries in this section result in the message being blocked, unless the word or phrase appears in the Messages Containing These Words or Phrases Will Not Be Blocked section or the recipient's email address is listed in the exclusions list.

For example, your organization might have an email policy that states any message containing racial slurs or derogatory terms should be blocked unless the message is sent to or from the organization's attorneys and senior management. To accomplish this, you would use the Messages Containing These Words or Phrases Will Be Blocked, Unless section to include the racially discriminatory language, the Messages Containing These Words or Phrases Will Not Be Blocked section could contain the lawyers' names, office names, addresses, and so forth of the law firm the attorneys work for, and the exclusion list would hold the email addresses of the company's executive staff. This would ensure any message not deemed appropriate would be blocked unless it contained information about the company's lawyers or were sent or copied to one of the organization's executives.

To configure blocked keywords or phrases, from within the Exchange Management Console, do the following:

1. Select the Custom Words tab.

2. Enter the word or phrase you want to block in the Messages Containing These Words or Phrases Will Be Blocked, Unless field. Email messages containing these

entries will always be blocked unless they contain a word or phrase that is included in the allow list.

3. Click Add button to include the new entry.

4. To remove an entry, highlight it, and click the Delete button.

5. Click Apply to save your changes or OK to save changes and close the Content Filter dialog box.

NOTE

Messages containing a blocked word or phrase are given an SCL score of 9.

As a recommendation from experience, get creative but, be precise! In the previous example scenario, you could request the law firm to insert a particular code or phrase in messages sent to your company. This makes the message easier for your company to identify and entries in your content filter lists easier to manage, and increases the reliability of content filtering overall. Avoid entering words and phrases that are arbitrary. Instead choose keywords and phrases specific to why you are blocking the message and that won't be mistakenly identified in legitimate messages. This reduces the amount of false positives and processing power needed by the content filter.

Configuring the Exceptions List

The next item in the Content Filter Properties window is the Exceptions tab. The Exceptions tab is used to define email addresses for those you do not want to filter their messages by content. For example, a company might include the human resources', attorneys', or system administrator's mailbox because they might need to view these messages to fulfill the duties of their jobs, whereas the same is not true for the rest of the organization's employees. To configure exceptions, within the Exchange Management Console, do the following:

1. In the Content Filter Properties window, select the Exceptions tab.

2. In the Do Not Filter Content in Messages Addressed to the Following Recipients field, enter the full email address of the account.

3. Click Add to include the entry in the list.

4. To remove an entry, highlight it, and click the Delete button.

5. To edit the email address of an entry, highlight it, and click the Edit button.

6. Click Apply to save your changes or OK to save changes and close the Content Filter.

> **NOTE**
>
> The exception list is restricted to a maximum of 100 entries.

Setting the Action Tab of the Content Filtering Agent

The last tab of the Content Filtering Agent is the Action tab. The Action tab stores the configuration for what actions should be taken on a message based on the calculated SCL. The SCL can range from 0 to 9; 9 designating a high confidence level the message is spam or contains a match to a block list and 0 designating a high confidence level the message is valid or contains a match to an allowed list.

In the Content Filtering Agent, an action of Delete takes priority over the action of Reject, which takes priority over the action of Quarantine. For example, when all three actions are enabled with a threshold of Delete if SCL is 8 or higher, Reject if SCL is 6 or higher, and Quarantine if 4 or higher, a message with an SCL of 9 would get deleted even though it technically is higher than the other thresholds, and a message with an SCL of 5 would get quarantined. This hierarchy is by design. At least one but not all actions need to be enabled to use content filtering.

> **TIP**
>
> To avoid an impact on legitimate email (false positives), start with a more conservative approach leveraging either low SCL numbers as the threshold or quarantining most spam first. In addition, IP and sender blocking previously defined in this chapter also reduces the amount of false positives. The aggressiveness of the content filter can always be increased and messages that are quarantined can easily be delivered or retrieved.

Fine-Tuning Content Filtering

8

Content filtering can be used for more than just identifying the content of messages in reviewing whether content is considered spam or whether the content is appropriate for the users of an organization. The content filtering function can be used to delete, reject, or quarantine messages based on an SCL rating where the fine-tuning of the SCL helps keep unwanted messages out of the organization's email system, yet minimizes the potential of false positives where messages are deleted or quarantined even when they are being sent by legitimate senders. This section covers the fine-tuning of content filtering on an Edge Transport server.

Configuring Content Filtering Actions

Several options are available in the Content Filter properties that can be configured. The following goes through the configuration options and notes what the various settings do. To configure content filtering, do the following:

1. In the Content Filter Properties window, select the Action tab.

2. Check the Delete Messages That Have an SCL Rating Larger or Equal To option, and set the threshold appropriately. All messages with the respective SCL are deleted.

3. Check the Reject Messages That Have an SCL Rating Larger or Equal To option, and set the threshold appropriately. All messages with the respective SCL are rejected.

4. Check the Quarantine Messages That Have an SCL Rating Larger or Equal To option, and set the threshold appropriately. All messages with the respective SCL are quarantined.

NOTE

A quarantine mailbox must first be defined. A prompt appears if it is not and the action cannot be enabled. See the section "Configuring the Quarantine Mailbox for Captured Messages" of this chapter for more information.

---

5. To disable an action, uncheck the box next to it.

6. To change the corresponding SCL threshold of an action, either enter a new number in the box or use the up/down arrows to change the value.

7. Click Apply to save your changes or OK to save changes and close the Content Filter.

Using the Exchange Management Shell to Configure Content Filtering

Content filtering can also be configured through the Exchange Management Shell. Each shell command has its own parameters you can set based on the action(s) performed by the command. There are four commands: Get, Add, Remove, and Set. Each command works with one or more content filtering components.

The Get- command is used to retrieve the configuration of a component. For example, entering Get-ContentFilterConfig displays the Content Filter configuration on the local system.

The Add-ContentFilterPhrase command can be used to add an acceptable or unacceptable word or phrase to the filter. The following example adds an unacceptable phrase.

```
Add-ContentFilterPhrase -Phrase "this is unacceptable" -Influence BadWord
```

The Remove-ContentFilterPhrase command can be used to remove a blocked or allowed keyword or phrase. The following example removes an unacceptable phrase.

```
Remove-ContentFilterPhrase -Identity "this is unacceptable"
```

> **NOTE**
>
> When replacing the `<String>` option with a phrase, the phrase must be enclosed with quotation marks and the phrase must be "influenced" so it gets added to the correct list.

The Set command allows an administrator to enable or disable the agent and modify the configuration of the content filter components. The following example enables the Content Filtering Agent on email received on External SMTP connections, bypasses scanning of one domain, enables Outlook 2007 postmark validation, sets the spam quarantine mailbox, and assigns the thresholds for the different actions.

```
Set-ContentFilterConfig -BypassedSenderDomains Microsoft.com -Enabled $true
➥-ExternalMailEnabled $true -OutlookEmailPostmarkValidationEnabled $true
➥-QuarantineMailbox anti-spam@companyabc.com -SCLDeleteEnabled $true
➥-SCLDeleteThreshold 7 -SCLQuarantineEnabled $true -SCLQuarantineThreshold 4]
➥-SCLRejectEnabled $false
```

Configuring Puzzle Validation for Content Filtering

Puzzle validation in Exchange 2007 works in conjunction with the Outlook 2007 Email Postmark validation feature to lower the SCL of a message—if the message was detected as spam. This helps reduce false positives in email messages exchanged between organizations running exclusively in Exchange 2007 and Outlook 2007 messaging environments. Postmark validation is disabled by default.

> **NOTE**
>
> Puzzle validation can only be configured using the `Set-ContentFilterConfig` Exchange Management Shell command.

When Email Postmark validation is configured for Outlook 2007 clients, and those clients send an email message, a presolved computational puzzle that an Exchange 2007 server running the Content Filtering Agent with Puzzle Validation enabled will be able to "solve." If the message was marked as spam, but contains an Outlook 2007 Postmark Validation stamp and the Content Filtering Agent was able to successfully resolve the inserted "puzzle," then the SCL of the message will be lowered because the sender has technically been validated making the message unlikely to be spam. If the message contains an invalid Email Postmark validation header or no Email Postmark validation at all, the SCL will remain unchanged.

To enable or disable Puzzle Validation and Outlook 2007 Email Postmark validation, run the following command in the Exchange Management Shell:

```
Set-ContentFilterConfig [-OutlookEmailPostmarkValidationEnabled <$true | $false>
```

where *$true* enables puzzle validation and *$false* disables puzzle validation.

Using Content Filtering to Allow and Reject Domain-Level Content

At times, you might want to identify a specific email address or an entire domain on the Internet that is sending you messages that you either want to completely allow or specifically deny the receipt of messages from that source location. The content filtering function of Edge Transport Services enables you to create a white list that always allows content to be received from a user or domain, or specifically allows for the denial of messages from a user or domain.

Do note that each user can also allow and deny message communications, so the choice to allow or deny content at the server level should take into consideration that the communications is organizationwide and that making a setting at the Edge Transport server level will have a positive impact on the appropriate receipt of content to all users in the organization.

An example of a deny filter on a user address or entire domain would include a situation where a user or domain is sending inappropriate content to several users in the organization. Rather than having each user make a configuration to block content from a user or domain, it can be set at the server level.

Conversely, if users in an organization want to receive all messages from a user or domain, those names can be added to a white list that will always allow messages to be received by users or the entire domain in the organization.

Configuring the Content Filter Agent to Allow (White List) Specific Recipients, Senders, and Sending Domains

The Exchange Management Console allows you to exclude specific keywords, phrases, and recipients within your organization from content filtering checks; however, you can only exclude specific senders and sending domains from content filtering through the use of the Exchange Management Shell's Set-ContentFilterConfig command, using the BypassedSenders and BypassedSenderDomains parameters, respectively.

The BypassedSenders parameter allows you to specify up to 100 external email addresses to exclude from content filtering, with each entry separated by a comma.

```
Set-ContentFilterConfig –BypassedSenders fred@companyabc.com,
➥heather@company123.org
```

> **NOTE**
>
> The entry must be the full SMTP address; wildcard (*) use is not supported. For example, you cannot exclude john*@companyabc.com, or john@companyabc.*.

When excluding a specific email address (for example, user@companyabc.com), consider whether it is safe to exclude the domain using the BypassSenderDomains parameter instead (for example, companyabc.com). Not only does this save you time and message retrieval because of false positives, it also consumes fewer entries in your list, leveraging both lists and the allowed maximum of 100 more efficiently.

The `BypassedSenderDomains` parameter works similarly to the `BypassedSenders` parameter, allowing you to specify up to 100 external domains to exclude from content filtering, with each entry separated by a comma.

```
Set-ContentFilterConfig –BypassedSenderDomains *.companyabc.com, company123.org
```

> **NOTE**
>
> Wildcard use is supported to designate the exclusion of subdomains under the excluded domain, for example, `*.companyabc.com`.

Configuring the Content Filter's SMTP Rejection Response

The SMTP Rejection Response is inserted into a SMTP nondelivery report (NDR) that is sent in reply to a rejected message. The default message is Message Rejected Due to Content Restriction. This message can be changed using the `Set-ContentFilterConfig` command with the `-RejectionResponse` parameter. The SMTP Rejection Response cannot exceed 240 characters and must be enclosed in quotation marks.

> **NOTE**
>
> Configuring this feature is required if you have enabled message rejection for a specific SCL threshold through the Exchange Management Console or the `SCLRejectEnabled` parameter of the `Set-ContentFilterConfig` command.

The SMTP Rejection Response cannot exceed 240 characters and must be enclosed in quotation marks.

```
Set-ContentFilterConfig -RejectionResponse "Message rejected, an error has
occurred. Contact your HelpDesk"
```

8

Filtering Content in a Message Attachment

The Microsoft Exchange Edge Transport server can also filter content within attachments of a message. There are times when an organization wants to prevent offensive or malicious content being stored in a Word document, Hypertext Markup Language (HTML) attachment, and so on from being transmitted to users in a network, so a filter can be configured to identify and handle incoming attachment messages.

Understanding Attachment Filtering Processing

A powerful tool in the fight against computer viruses and other malicious email attachments is the use of attachment filtering. Attachment filtering allows you to identify a specific filename or all files of a particular type using Multipurpose Internet Mail Extensions (MIME) recognition. Attachment filtering can be applied to both incoming and outgoing email. This allows you the flexibility of implementing attachment distribution that complies with business requirements or policy. For example, you can choose to block all executable file types (for example, .bat, .exe, .scr) on inbound email to help prevent the spread of new computer viruses or distribution of unacceptable content. On outbound connections, you could elect to block distribution of particular files by name (for example, tradesecrets.doc, salaryinfo.xls), which can help prevent proprietary information from being accidentally or purposefully distributed. SMTP Send and Receive Connectors can be included or excluded from attachment filtering.

> **NOTE**
>
> Changes described in this section are applied only to the local system. This is important if you have more than one Edge Transport server in your environment.

Planning Attachment Filtering Processing

One limitation to attachment filtering is that it can only be configured using the Exchange Management Shell. No attachment filtering options are available in the Exchange Management Console.

Exchange 2007, Outlook 2007, and Active Directory's Group Policy can work together to orchestrate implementation of an organization's policy on email attachments. Outlook 2007 includes an enabled default list of Level 1 attachments—attachments that will not be allowed. The Level 1 attachment list was derived from their known or potential ability to carry malicious code. Level 2 attachments are attachments that will initiate a prompt suggesting the user first download the attachment prior to running it. This allows any locally installed antivirus product the opportunity to scan the attachment for viral code that might have bypassed email virus scanning, albeit a rare circumstance, but not impossible. By default, there are no Level 2 file types defined in Outlook 2007.

There are over 70 Level 1 files included in Outlook 2007. Some examples of Level 1 file types are shown in the following list. For a complete list, refer to the Microsoft Outlook 2007 documentation.

- .asp—Active Server Page
- .crt—Certificate file
- .hta—Hypertext application
- .msc—Microsoft Management Console snap-in
- .msh—Microsoft Shell

Using Group Policy, an administrator can "open up" Level 1 attachments to users so they can choose whether to accept the attachment and/or make modifications to the Level 1 and Level 2 attachment lists. Alternatively, administrators can take full control of this functionality. This flexibility, unfortunately, can pose a security risk. To offset this risk, administrators can use the attachment filtering component on an Edge Transport server to block specific attachments, regardless of the configuration in place on internal email systems.

First, you need to determine what attachments and/or types of attachments you want blocked and in what direction(s) attachment filtering should take place: inbound, outbound, or both. If you will be blocking a specific attachment, implement the block using the filename. If you want to block all email attachments of a specific type, add the file extension so it can be identified by its MIME type, regardless of the filename.

After you have decided on which attached files or file types you want to identify in email messages, you also need to determine what you want to do with messages containing those attachments. The default action is to block the attachment and the message (Reject). The available actions you can take on messages and attachments defined in the attachment filter include the following:

▶ **Reject**—Stops delivery of the message and attachments to the recipient and sends an undeliverable response to the sender.

▶ **Strip**—Delivers the message to the recipient, replacing the attachment in the message with a notification it has been removed. Any attachment not listed in the attachment filter will still be available to the recipient.

▶ **SilentDelete**—Similar to the Reject action in that the message and attachment aren't delivered; however, the SilentDelete action does not send an undeliverable notification to the sender.

Using the Exchange Management Shell to Configure Attachment Filtering

Attachment filtering, as previously mentioned, can only be configured through the Exchange Management Shell. Each shell command has its own parameters you can set based on the action(s) performed by the command. There are four commands: `Get`, `Add`, `Remove`, and `Set`. Each command works with one or more IP Block and Allow List components.

The `Get-` command is used to retrieve the configuration of a component. For example, entering `Get-AttachmentFilterEntry filename` displays the result of whether that file is being identified in messages.

The `Add-` command can be used to add an entry to the Attachment Filter Agent. The following example adds a filename to be blocked.

```
add-AttachmentFilterEntry -name virus.exe -type FileName
```

The `Remove-` command can be used to remove an attachment filter entry. The following example removes an entry by filename.

```
remove-AttachmentFilterEntry -Identity filename:virus.exe
```

The `Set-` command allows an administrator to modify the configuration of the attachment filter. In attachment filtering, it is primarily used to set the action. The following example configures the action and response options.

```
Set-AttachmentFilterListConfig -Action Reject -RejectResponse "Attachment type not
➥allowed."
```

Using Sender/IP Reputation to Filter Content

Sender Reputation when combined with the other antispam technologies in Edge Services can help reduce unwanted email very efficiently and effectively. Sender Reputation, simply put, allows administrators to answer the question, "Can I trust who sends us email and if I can't, why should I process it?" The Sender Reputation Agent answers this question for you by learning from values obtained in email messages to determine whether the source of the messages is legitimate or if it is sending junk.

Configuring Sender/IP Reputation

Email that is routed through Receive Connectors is processed by the Sender Reputation Agent. These messages are received from the Internet and travel inbound to the Edge Transport server for delivery to the recipient. The Sender Reputation Agent is enabled by default and can be configured using the Exchange Management Console or Exchange Management Shell.

> **NOTE**
>
> Changes described in this section are applied only to the local system. This is important if you have more than one Edge Transport server in your environment.

To disable the Sender Reputation Agent using the Exchange Management Console, right-click the agent icon in the action pane, and select Disable. To disable the Sender Reputation Agent using the Exchange Management Shell, run the `set-SenderReputationConfig` command with the `-Enabled $false` parameter.

```
"set-SenderReputationConfig -Enabled $false"
```

The General tab of the Agent Properties window displays a brief description of the agent and its capabilities, its current status, and the last time the agent's settings were modified.

The Sender Reputation Agent works by evaluating several items in an email message(s) and then assigns a score, known as the Sender Reputation Level (SRL). The SRL works very similarly to the SCL assigned to messages themselves. The SRL gets assigned to the IP address from which the email message(s) are originating. The Sender Reputation Agent adds the IP address to the IP Block List when the SRL corresponds with the tolerance threshold you have set for this action. The SRL can be adjusted from 0 to 9. You can also configure the amount of time (in hours, 0 to 48) the flagged IP address should remain on your IP Block List.

The SRL for an IP address is derived from the following four items: an open proxy test, HELO/EHLO validation check, reverse DNS lookup, and SCL ratings derived from messages received from the sending IP address. The Sender Reputation Agent takes the cumulative results of these items into account when composing the SRL.

An open proxy test determines whether the receiving Edge Transport server can communicate back to itself through the network on which the sending IP address resides. Open proxies are easy to establish and are commonly used by spammers to conceal the true identity of the server sending email. When email messages are routed through an open proxy, the information contained in the message changes to reflect that of the local host, that is, the network on the "other side" of the proxy server.

NOTE

Performing an open proxy test is enabled by default. This setting can be changed on the Sender Confidence tab of the Sender Reputation Properties window.

The HELO/EHLO SMTP commands are another item often forged by spammers. Their purpose is to provide the domain name or IP address from which the message originated. Spoofing the From address, using the same domain in the To and From fields, and forging the sending IP address are very common spam tricks.

A reverse DNS lookup is performed to determine if the domain name registered with the sending IP address is the same as that provided with the HELO/EHLO commands.

NOTE

Although there are a couple of similarities, this is not the same as SenderID and the use of SPF records.

The SCL of a message is the last item taken into account by the Sender Reputation Agent when calculating a SRL for a particular IP address. The Sender Reputation Agent tabulates SCL scores obtained from messages previously received from the same IP address.

Configuring the Sender Reputation Agent Using the Exchange Management Console

The Sender Reputation Agent can be configured using the Exchange Management Console interface. To configure the sender reputation from EMC, do the following:

1. Launch the Exchange Management Console.

2. Select Edge Transport in the console tree.

3. The General tab provides a quick overview of the Sender Reputation Agent along with the last time the agent's settings were modified. Typically, you would not make changes to items on this tab.

4. The Sender Confidence tab allows you to enable (default) or disable the open proxy test. This typically remains enabled.

5. The Action tab allows you to set the block threshold for SRL on a scale of 0 to 9. (The default setting is 9, the maximum.)

6. The Action tab also allows you to configure how long (0 to 48 hours) the IP address should remain on the Edge Transport server's IP Block List. (The default setting is 24 hours.)

7. Click Apply to save changes or click OK to save changes and close the window.

Configuring Sender Reputation Using the Exchange Management Shell

Sender Reputation can also be configured through the Exchange Management Shell. Each shell command has its own parameters you can set based on the action(s) performed by the command. There are two commands: `Get-` and `Set-`.

The `Get-` command is used to retrieve the configuration of Sender Reputation. For example, entering `Get-SenderReputationConfig` displays the Sender Reputation configuration on the local system.

The `Set-` command allows an administrator to enable or disable the agent and modify the configuration of the agent. The following example enables sender reputation on email received on external SMTP connections, activates the open proxy detection test, and configures the blocking options.

```
Set-SenderReputationConfig -Enabled $true -ExternalMailEnabled $true
➡-OpenProxyDetectionEnabled $true   -ProxyServerName proxy1.companyabc.com
➡-ProxyServerPort  8080 -SenderBlockingEnabled $true -SenderBlockingPeriod 48
➡-SRLBlockThreshold 8
```

Using Address Rewriting to Standardize on Domain Address Naming for an Organization

Address rewriting was created by Microsoft to allow an organization to have all outbound or inbound email appear to be delivered from one domain when several mail-enabled domains could be sending messages through the same systems. This allows a company to provide a consistent appearance when communicating via email. Address rewriting is commonly used on outbound email when companies merge with or acquire other organizations. Address rewriting is also used on outbound email when an organization's network contains several other domains. Using address rewriting in these scenarios results in external recipients seeing email as originating from one domain name even if it is coming from a domain with a completely different name.

> **NOTE**
>
> If you enable address rewriting on external messages, ensure you have enabled address rewriting on inbound messages as well, so that inbound messages will be delivered to the appropriate recipients.

Configuring Address Rewriting

As with many of the components for the Edge Transport server, address rewriting is enabled on inbound email messages so messages that were rewritten when sent externally can be routed back to the appropriate person. Address rewriting can also be beneficial when sending email between internal systems. For example, if an IT department has multiple domains and the organization wants all email communication from the IT department to internal departments (other than IT) to come from *@it.companyabc.com, then address rewriting would be used to accomplish this.

> **NOTE**
>
> Using address rewriting on your outbound email messages eases white-listing of your organization's email for external recipients and business partners by simplifying the answer to their question "What domain and systems can we expect to receive email from?"

> **NOTE**
>
> Changes described in this section are applied only to the local system. This is important if you have more than one Edge Transport server in your environment.

Some considerations to take into account when using address rewriting are items that will not be rewritten, end result of email addresses being combined, messages that have been secured, and rewriting in both directions.

Address rewriting will not modify messages that are attached to the message being rewritten and also will not modify the SMTP Return-Path, Received, Message-ID, X-MS-TNEF-Correlator, Content-Type Boundary=string headers, and headers located inside of MIME body parts. Message-ID, X-MS-TNEF-Correlator, Content-Type Boundary=string headers, and headers located inside of MIME body parts are used when securing email messages such as with encryption or Microsoft Rights Management and are, therefore, not rewritten purposely to ensure the message isn't modified to ensure delivery and integrity of the content.

To ensure messages (mainly responses to rewritten messages) get routed to the appropriate person, a few items need to be addressed. First, the end result of the email address must be unique between users so conflicts and incorrect delivery of messages does not occur; second, a proxy address must be configured on the mailbox that matches the rewritten address; and third, address rewriting must be configured on both the Send and Receive Connectors of the Edge Transport server.

To ensure the rewritten email address between domains will remain unique to the user, take into account how each domain creates their usernames. For example, domains that allow simple usernames like `Heather@`, `Reese@`, or `support@` will have more conflicts when using address rewriting than organizations that use more unique or defined usernames like `Heather_Loso@`, `RMChimner@`, or `online-sales-support@`. If two domains used simple usernames in their email addresses and the organization wanted to use address rewriting, the end result could contain too many conflicts presenting the need to change email addresses at least in one domain. This could end up being quite an involved task depending on the number of users in each domain. For example, `CompanyABC.com` wants to have all email from domains like `infosec.companyabc.com`, `it.companyabc.com`, and `development.companyabc.com` leave the organization as `companyabc.com`. If two different users named Mike have the same email prefix (mike) in `it.companyabc.com` and `infosec.companyabc.com`, there will be a conflict as they would both be rewritten to `mike@companyabc.com`. This has more of an impact on replies to rewritten messages than it does to new outbound messages.

For information on configuring a proxy address for a mailbox or multiple mailboxes, see Chapter 18.

> **NOTE**
>
> The use of wildcards is supported in limited usage when rewriting addresses. For example, wildcards can only be used on internal domains. Partial wildcard use such as `john*@finance.companyabc.com` or `username@sales*.companyabc.com` is not supported, whereas `username @*.companyabc.com` is. One example of wildcard usage is rewriting `*@development.companyabc.com` and `*@software.companyabc.com` to `*@support.companyabc.com`.

Address rewriting can only be configured through the Exchange Management Shell. No attachment rewriting options are available in the Exchange Management Console. Each shell command has its own parameters you can set based on the action(s) performed by the command. There are four commands: `Get-AddressRewriteEntry`, `New-AddressRewriteEntry`, `Set-AddressRewriteEntry`, and `Remove-AddressRewriteEntry`. An example of each is shown later in this chapter.

The `Get-` command is used to retrieve the configuration of address rewriting. For example, entering `Get-AddressRewriteEntry` displays the configuration settings on the local system.

The `New-AddressRewriteEntry` command can be used to add a new rewriting entry. Use of this command requires three parameters: `ExternalAddress`, `InternalAddress`, and `Name`. The following example rewrites all email addresses in both directions for `companyabc.com`.

```
New-AddressRewriteEntry -Name "Two-way Rewrite entry for companyabc.com"
➥-InternalAddress companyabc.com -ExternalAddress companydef.com
```

The `Set-` command allows an administrator to activate address rewriting or modify the existing configuration. The following example switches the internal and external domains given in our previous example and updates the description to reflect the change.

```
Set-AddressRewriteEntry -Identity "Two-way Rewrite entry for companyabc.com"
➥-ExternalAddress companydef.com -InternalAddress companyabc.com
➥-Name "Two-way Rewrite entry for companydef.com"
```

The `Remove-` command can be used to delete an address rewriting entry. The following example removes the entry created in the previous examples.

```
Remove-AddressRewriteEntry -Identity "Two-way Rewrite entry for companydef.com"
```

Using EdgeSync to Synchronize Active Directory Information to the Edge Transport Server

EdgeSync is a component of the Edge Transport server that allows replication of certain data from Active Directory to the Edge Transport server to support specific antispam and email filtering components. As an example, an organization might want a copy of their recipient email address list at the Edge Transport layer of their security system so that if an email comes in for a user who does not exist in the organization, the message can be purged immediately instead of taking up disk space to queue, route, or even manage unnecessary content.

Understanding the EdgeSync Process

The EdgeSync process runs on the Hub Transport server in an Active Directory forest and replicates data to the Edge Transport server(s). The EdgeSync communication between the Hub and Edge Transport server is secure. For example, EdgeSync is required if you plan on recognizing and taking action on email messages that are sent to nonexistent recipients. See the Recipient Filtering section of this chapter for more information on stopping email to nonexistent recipients. EdgeSync is also required if you intend to recognize entries in Outlook 2003 and 2007 clients, also known as Safelist Aggregation, which is covered later in this section.

> **NOTE**
>
> Active Directory Application Mode (ADAM) is installed on the Edge Transport server during the installation process because it is required to use EdgeSync. ADAM works in conjunction with EdgeSync as a directory in which EdgeSync collects directory information. ADAM can be used in conjunction with an organization's Active Directory in an extranet scenario where employees (in Active Directory) need mail routed through the Edge Transport server, but also nonemployees such as contractors or vendors would be populated in ADAM and EdgeSync'd into the Edge Transport server system filter tables.

Using EdgeSync to Subscribe the Server to the Exchange Server 2007 Organization

EdgeSync is also used to subscribe the Edge Transport server to the internal Exchange Server 2007 organization. Subscribing the Edge Transport server in this manner automatically defines the Send Connectors on the Edge Transport server after they have been replicated to ADAM on the Edge Transport server from a Hub Transport server. The Hub Transport server the Edge Transport server has subscribed with will now route all email from its domain addressed to Internet recipients through the subscribed Edge Transport server(s). Send Connectors must be configured manually if the Edge Transport server is not subscribed internally and utilizing EdgeSync. Send and Receive Connectors are covered in more detail in Chapter 17, "Implementing Client Access and Hub Transport Servers."

> **NOTE**
>
> Using EdgeSync overwrites previously defined Send Connector configurations and disables the Send Connector configuration on the Edge Transport server after replication to the Edge Transport server has occurred, unless you deselect having Send Connectors automatically defined when you import the Edge subscription file on the Hub Transport server.

Maintaining the EdgeSync Schedule of Replication

EdgeSync runs on a regularly scheduled basis with configuration data being replicated every hour and recipient information being replicated every 4 hours. This ensures the information needed by the Edge Transport server is up to date. EdgeSync replicates the following items from Active Directory to the ADAM instance on the Edge Transport server:

▶ Outlook 2003 and 2007 Safe Senders Lists (Blocked Senders are not replicated)

▶ Valid email recipients listed in AD (used by the Block E-Mail Sent to Non-Existent Recipients feature of the Recipient Filtering Agent)

▶ Accepted and remote domains

▶ Send Connector configuration

▶ List of Hub Transport servers

Configuring EdgeSync on an Edge Transport Server

Configuring EdgeSync begins with exporting the Edge Transport subscription file for importing on a Hub Transport server that communicates with Active Directory. The Edge Transport subscription file is in Extensible Markup Language (XML) format. This procedure must be repeated for each Edge Transport server.

1. Ensure communication through ports 50389 and 50636 is available between the Hub and Edge Transport servers.

> **NOTE**
>
> Ports 50389 (LDAP) and 50636 (Secure LDAP) were assigned at installation and cannot be changed on the Edge Transport server.

2. Use the Exchange Management Shell to export the Edge Transport subscription file.

3. Open the Exchange Management Shell.

4. Enter the following:

   ```
   New-EdgeSubscription -FileName "C:\temp\EdgeSubscriptionInfo.xml"
   ```

> **NOTE**
>
> You must include the full path to the file.

5. Copy the Edge subscription file to the Hub Transport server. (For security reasons, it is recommended to delete the Edge subscription file after it has been copied to the Hub Transport server and replication has been verified.)

6. Use the Exchange Management Console or Shell to import the Edge Transport subscription file on the Hub Transport server.

7. Place a copy of the EdgeSubscriptionInfo.xml file you created in the previous step onto the Hub Transport server (for example, C:\temp\EdgeSubscriptionInfo.xml) to import the Edge subscription file using the Exchange Management Console.

8. Open the Exchange Management Console. In the results pane for the Hub Transport role, click the Edge Subscriptions tab.

9. In the action pane, click New Edge Subscription to launch the New Edge Subscription Wizard.

10. Select an Active Directory site from the drop-down list.

11. Click Browse to browse to the location of the Edge subscription file you copied from the Edge Transport server (for example, `C:\temp\EdgeSubscriptionInfo.xml`), and click Next.

12. Click New.

13. Click Finish when the completion page appears.

14. Use the Microsoft Exchange Management Shell to import the Edge Transport subscription file.

```
New-EdgeSubscription -filename "C:\temp\EdgeSubscriptionInfo.xml"
➥-CreateInternetSendConnector $true -site "Default-First-Site-Name"
```

15. Verify synchronization to the Edge Transport server's ADAM instance.

16. Review the application log in Event Viewer for MsExchange EdgeSync events on the Hub and Edge Transport servers.

As noted earlier, EdgeSync is not configured through the Exchange Management Console. Four EdgeSync commands exist for use with the Exchange Management Shell:

▶ `Get-EdgeSubscription`

▶ `New-EdgeSubscription`

▶ `Remove-EdgeSubscription`

▶ `Start-EdgeSynchronization`

Each shell command has its own parameters you can set based on the action(s) performed by the command. Each command performs a specific task or set of tasks.

The `Get-` command is used to retrieve the current configuration for EdgeSync. For example, entering `Get- EdgeSubscription -Identity EDGE1` displays EdgeSync configuration on a server named EDGE1. This command can be run on any Exchange 2007 server on the network.

Running the `Get-EdgeSubscription` command on an Edge Transport server displays that server's EdgeSync subscription, whereas running the `Get-EdgeSubscription` on a Hub Transport server can also display EdgeSync subscriptions on Edge Transport servers. Use the `–Identity` parameter to specify the name of the Edge Transport server.

Creating a New EdgeSync Subscription File

The `New-EdgeSubscription` command is used to add a new Edge subscription to a Hub Transport server and configure the options for adding a new subscription, such as whether to automatically create the Send Connector or specify the Active Directory site. The following example imports a new Edge Transport subscription file, thus subscribing the Edge Transport server to the network. This command is run on the Hub Transport server.

```
New-EdgeSubscription -FileName "C:\temp\EdgeServerSubscription.xml"
```

Removing an EdgeSync Subscription

The `Remove-EdgeSubscription` command is used to unsubscribe an Edge Transport server from participating in EdgeSync. The following example removes an Edge subscription from Active Directory. This command is run on the Hub Transport server.

```
Remove-EdgeSubscription -Identity EDGE3 -DomainController dc1.companyabc.com
```

NOTE

This unsubscribes the Edge Transport server from the synchronization process on the Hub Transport server.

Starting EdgeSync Synchronization

Edge synchronization can be started by running the `Start-EdgeSynchronization` command on any Exchange 2007 server joined to the Active Directory domain. Starting Edge synchronization comes in handy when you have added a new Edge server, want to test synchronization, or replicate changes immediately. The `Start-EdgeSynchronization` command initializes EdgeSync to all Edge Transport servers.

```
Start-EdgeSynchronization
```

Implementing Safelist Aggregation for Outlook 2003 and Outlook 2007

8

The Safelist Aggregation component of an Edge Transport server allows an administrator to obtain copies of end users' Safe Senders lists from Outlook 2003 and 2007 clients. Safelist Aggregation essentially provides a mechanism to respect the entries users have made in their Safe Senders lists, which reduces false positives when filtering for spam. By moving the user's safelist to the Edge Transport server, a rule or spam filtering process set up at the Edge won't delete email that a user has deemed desired.

Configuring Safelist Aggregation for Outlook 2003/2007

As with all of the other Edge Transport rule processes, the Edge Transport server must be subscribed to the Exchange 2007 organization from which you want to retrieve Safe Senders list entries on Outlook 2003 and 2007 clients. Safe Senders are replicated to the

Edge Transport server using EdgeSync. Safelist entries created by users and imported using Safelist Aggregation are recognized when the Content Filtering Agent examines the message.

> **NOTE**
>
> You can only use Safelist Aggregation with the Content Filtering Agent enabled and on an Edge Transport server that has a subscription with the organization's Hub Transport server. Also, entries in the local Contacts list in Outlook and any external account the user sends email to is added to their safelist. These entries are replicated to the Edge Transport server and used with Safelist Aggregation. Outlook's safelist collection is composed of the Safe Senders, Recipients, Domains, and External Contacts. Each user can have a maximum of 1,024 entries in their safelist collection.

Safelist Aggregation can only be enabled with the Exchange Management Shell by running the `Update-SafeList` command against a user's mailbox on a server running under the Mailbox server role. That information must then be replicated to the Edge Transport server using EdgeSync. For more information about the Mailbox server role, see Part II, "Planning and Designing an Exchange Server 2007 Environment."

To configure Safelist Aggregation, complete the following steps:

1. Use the `Update-Safelist` Exchange shell command on a server running under the Mailbox server role to aggregate and copy the safelist collection data from the user's mailbox to the user object in Active Directory.

   ```
   Update-Safelist -Identity HeatherL –DomainController dc2.companyabc.com
   ➥-Type Both
   ```

> **NOTE**
>
> To run the `Update-SafeList` command against multiple mailboxes residing in a particular organizational unit, you must prepend its use with the `Get-Mailbox` command. This could also be useful when included inside of a script. At the end of the `Get-Mailbox` command statement, add the `update-safelist` command.

   ```
   Get-Mailbox -OrganizationalUnit CompanyABC.com\Sales\Users | update-safelist
   ```

2. Schedule the `Update-Safelist` command to run frequently.

   ```
   AT 19:00 /every:M,T,W,Th,F,S,Su  cmd /c "C:\Temp\Update-SafeList.vbs"
   ```

> **NOTE**
>
> You must use the AT command to schedule Safelist Aggregation. The AT command can call to a batch file or script that includes the commands to run Safelist Aggregation.

3. Verify that EdgeSync is properly replicating from the Hub Transport server to the Edge Transport server. See the section "Using EdgeSync to Synchronize Active Directory Information to the Edge Transport Server" on configuring EdgeSync in this chapter for more information regarding EdgeSync.

4. Ensure the Content Filtering Agent is enabled on the Edge Transport server on which you want to perform Safelist Aggregation. Content Filtering is covered in the section "Implementing Safelist Aggregation for Outlook 2003 and Outlook 2007."

Managing and Maintaining an Edge Transport Server

Managing and maintaining an Edge Transport server requires the same server hardware maintenance, Windows patching and updating, and ongoing system monitoring that is covered in Chapter 19, "Exchange Server 2007 Management and Maintenance Practices." However, there are a handful of things specific to the Edge Transport server, such as exporting the Edge Transport server configuration settings so that if the server needs to be recovered, you can more easily import in the settings after performing a server rebuild. In addition, you can view reports on messages and transport communications managed by the Edge Transport server. The details on how to perform these specific Edge Transport tasks are covered in this section.

Exporting and Importing Edge Transport Server Settings

Exporting the Edge Transport configuration from one server for use on another has two apparent benefits:

▶ Disaster recovery preparedness

▶ Cloning the configuration when multiple Edge Transport servers exist in an organization

This section focuses on exporting the Edge Transport configuration for use in these scenarios. For more information on disaster recovery for Exchange 2007, see Part IX, "Data Protection and Disaster Recovery of Exchange Server 2007."

Utilizing the process described in this section of the chapter can help ease deployment of Edge Transport servers when a network will have more than one Edge Transport server or changes are made frequently.

> **NOTE**
>
> Exporting and importing the Edge Transport server configuration does not include the Edge subscription file used by a Hub Transport server for EdgeSync replication. When importing the Edge configuration data to a new or restored server, ensure the Edge Transport server has a subscription on the Hub Transport server and that EdgeSync is properly replicating. More information regarding EdgeSync can be found in the "Configuring EdgeSync on an Edge Transport Server" section of this chapter.

Exporting the Edge Transport server configuration requires the use of a script included with Exchange 2007 when the Edge Transport server role is selected during installation. The script exports the configuration to an XML file, which can later be used to restore the configuration to the same system or another. The name of this script is `ExportEdgeConfig.ps1` and is located in the `C:\Program Files\Microsoft\Exchange Server\Scripts\` folder on the Edge Transport server. The `ExportEdgeConfig.ps1` script is executed through the Exchange Management Shell using the `ExportEdgeConfig` command.

Importing the Edge configuration data works in a similar manner, using the `ImportEdgeConfig` command. The name of this script is `ImportEdgeConfig.ps1` and is located in the `C:\Program Files\Microsoft\Exchange Server\Scripts\` folder on the Edge Transport server. The `ImportEdgeConfig.ps1` script is executed through the Exchange Management Shell using the `ImportEdgeConfig` command.

Exporting Edge Transport Server Configuration

Exporting the Edge Transport server configuration is a four-step process. The steps to export and import Edge Transport server configuration settings are shown next:

1. Copy the `ExportEdgeConfig.ps` file from the `C:\Program Files\Microsoft\Exchange Server\Scripts\` folder to the root of your user profile on the Edge Transport server (for example, `C:\Documents and Settings\Administrator\ExportEdgeConfig.ps`)

2. Open the Exchange Management Shell and run the following command:

   `./ExportEdgeConfig -cloneConfigData:"C:\temp\CloneConfigData.xml"`

3. If the export is successful, a confirmation message appears showing the location of the exported file.

4. Copy the file to a location where it can be imported by an Edge Transport server.

> **NOTE**
>
> The `CloneConfigData.xml` is intended for use on a server with a clean installation of Exchange Server 2007 under the Edge Transport role—with the same name as the server from which the file was exported.

The following items are exported to file:

▶ Log paths for receive and send protocols, pickup directory, and routing table

▶ Message tracking log path

▶ Status and priority of each transport agent

▶ Send and Receive Connector information

▶ Accepted and remote domain configurations

▶ IP Allow and IP Block List information (Provider Lists are not included)

▶ Content filtering configuration

▶ Recipient filtering configuration

▶ Address rewrite entries

▶ Attachment filtering entries

Importing Edge Transport Server Configuration

After you've export the Edge Transport server configuration information, you can store the information should you ever need to rebuild the Edge server again, or you might need to configure a secondary Edge server with the exact same configuration settings. The import process brings in the saved configuration settings to a freely installed ISA Server configuration.

To import the Edge Transport server configuration to a system, do the following:

1. Copy the `ExportEdgeConfig.ps` file from the `C:\Program Files\Microsoft\Exchange Server\Scripts\` folder to the root of your user profile on the Edge Transport server to which you are importing the `CloneConfigData.xml` file (for example, `C:\Documents and Settings\Administrator\ExportEdgeConfig.ps`).

2. Copy the `CloneConfigData.xml` file you created during the export process to a location on the server (for example, `C:\temp\CloneConfigData.xml`).

3. Launch the Exchange Management Shell.

4. Run the `ImportEdgeConfig` command to validate the configuration file and create an answer file (`CloneConfigAnswer.xml`).

   ```
   ./importedgeconfig -CloneConfigData:"C:\temp\CloneConfigData.xml" -IsImport
   $false -CloneConfigAnswer:"C:\temp\CloneConfigAnswer.xml"
   ```

5. A confirmation message is displayed if the answer file was properly exported.

6. Open the `CloneConfigAnswer.xml` file that was created in the previous step. If the file is blank, the configuration is correct and no modification is necessary. If any configuration items cause a discrepancy, they will be included in the answer file and must be modified for the correct configuration (for example, server name, invalid SMTP Connector IP address, log file path, and so on). Save your changes.

7. After you have reviewed and made any necessary modifications to the answer file, you must import both the `CloneConfigData.xml` file and the modified `CloneConfigAnswer.xml` file. The following syntax is for the `ImportEdgeConfig` command to accomplish this.

∞

> **NOTE**
>
> If the answer file is blank, the configuration is correct and can be used and there is no need to import the answer file.

```
./importedgeconfig -CloneConfigData:"C:\temp\CloneConfigData.xml" -IsImport
$true -CloneConfigAnswer:"C:\temp\CloneConfigAnswer.xml"
```

8. After the XML file(s) have been imported, a message stating "Importing Edge Configuration Information Succeeded" appears.

9. Configure and run EdgeSync and ensure replication is occurring successfully.

Export the Edge Transport server configuration file and test importing it on a regular basis, especially when multiple changes have been made to the Edge Transport server and to ensure the configuration will work in the event of a disaster or outage. Network Load Balancing and other mechanisms can also help offset the impact of a disaster or system outage. For more information on disaster recovery in an Exchange 2007 environment, see Part IX.

Viewing Antispam Reports Using Included PowerShell Scripts

The Edge Transport server includes several antispam reports that contain information about the top blocked items, such as IP addresses, domains, and senders, how frequently those items are blocked, how many times those items have been blocked, and who in the organization receives the most spam. The information contained in these reports can assist administrators in fine-tuning the spam filtering agents to achieve a higher level of spam detection while simultaneously reducing the number of false positives.

Antispam reports can only be generated using an Exchange Management Shell command. Each shell command will parse the logs files to create a report. The logs for each Antispam agent are stored in `C:\Program Files\Microsoft\Exchange Server\TransportRoles\Logs\`.

To run any of the following scripts to generate the respective Antispam report, perform the following steps:

1. Launch the Exchange Management Shell on the Edge Transport server.

2. Change to the `C:\Program Files\Microsoft\Exchange Server\Scripts\` folder.

3. Enter a `./` and the name of the script for the Antispam report you want to review.

```
./Get-AntispamTopBlockedSenderDomains
```

A handful of PowerShell scripts are included with Exchange 2007 to generate Antispam reports from the log files. Some of the default scripts are as follows:

▶ **Get-AntispamFilteringReport**—Generates a report displaying a summary of messages that have been rejected by connection, command, or filtering agent

▶ **Get-AntispamSCLHistogram**—Generates a report summarizing the amount of email identified with each SCL threshold (1 to 9 total)

▶ **Get-AntispamTopBlockedSenderDomains**—Generates a report summarizing how many times and how frequently a domain has been blocked

▶ **Get-AntispamTopBlockedSenderIPs**—Generates a report summarizing how many times and how frequently an IP address of a sending mail server has been blocked

▶ **Get-AntispamTopBlockedSenders**—Generates a report summarizing how many times and how frequently a sender's email address has been blocked

▶ **Get-AntispamTopRecipients**—Generates a report summarizing spam volume for recipients and the amount of spam messages received

Summary

The Edge Transport server provides an important layer of security between the general Internet and an organization's messaging environment. If set up properly, an Edge server can successfully filter unwanted content such as spam, viruses, or inappropriate content. If not set up properly, an Edge server can filter desired content and accidentally eliminate critical messages of communications. The focus of this chapter was to provide guidance on implementing, configuring, and fine-tuning an Edge server to improve its impact on the filtering and management of information into a network.

Best Practices

The following are best practices from this chapter:

▶ Filter for spam before processing messages because spam accounts for the majority of mail messages transported on the Internet.

▶ When configuring an Edge server, configure it with minimal configuration rules and then add rules, while testing a successful hit rate on filtration, and then fine-tune the filtering to be more restrictive.

▶ When first implementing filtration, consider stamping questionable messages with the word "Suspect" or something similar rather than deleting the message so you can track which messages might possibly be filtered when they otherwise shouldn't be.

▶ Configure allow lists to ensure messages from desired message senders or organizations are not filtered and that they are successfully received by the intended recipient.

▶ Configure custom block lists to ensure that messages from email senders or specific domains are not transmitted to users, but instead are blocked at the Edge server.

8

▶ Enable Safelist Aggregation that will collect users' safelists and add safelist users to the Edge server filters to allow content to be allowed instead of blocked by rule.

▶ Use message attachment filtering to assess the content of attachments as part of an appropriate content filtering process.

▶ Enable address rewriting to standardize on domain address names used by the organization.

▶ When an Edge-based application utilizes directory content such as username and email address lists, use EdgeSync to propagate the directory information to the Edge server.

▶ Export Edge Transport server configuration information and store the information along with other server build documentation. The exported Edge Transport configuration information can be imported to a new system in the event of a server replacement or server failure scenario.

CHAPTER 9

Using the Windows PowerShell in an Exchange Server 2007 Environment

For years, Microsoft Exchange has been administered through a graphical user interface (GUI) administrator tool; however, with Exchange 2007, Microsoft has included a command-line interface in addition to the graphical interface for management and administration tasks. The new command-line interface is called the Exchange Management Shell, or EMS. This chapter covers the core features, functions, as well as provides examples how the new Exchange Management Shell is used to help administrators manage their Exchange 2007 environment.

Understanding the Exchange Management Shell

The Exchange Management Shell in Exchange 2007 is a command-line interface that allows Exchange administrators to manage, check, and report on any Exchange objects. These objects include mailboxes, mailbox stores, storage groups, servers, connectors, and the Exchange organization itself—anything that can be managed in Exchange Server 2007 can be managed by the Exchange Management Shell.

The Exchange Management Console (EMC) is actually a graphical user interface (GUI) for the Exchange Management Shell, or EMS. Each task or operation that an administrator does using the Exchange System Console is actually calling an EMS command or series of commands.

The Exchange Management Shell is built on a Microsoft Windows technology called PowerShell. PowerShell, formally code-named Monad, is as powerful (or more powerful) than some programming languages. It plugs into the .NET runtime, also called the common language runtime. An administrator can sit at a PowerShell prompt and access almost everything in Windows.

The Exchange Management Shell and Windows PowerShell are extremely powerful, where virtually anything can be written and scripted from the shell. PowerShell is a fully featured command-line shell, similar to a Bash prompt. It is also an extremely powerful administrative scripting tool—think Perl or Ruby with AWK, SED, and Grep thrown in. And all of this is based on .NET—so administrators have direct access to the entire .NET common language runtime, plus the ability to script existing COM (ActiveX) and Windows Management Instrumentation (WMI) objects, similar to what can be done with VBScript.

Because EMS is based on PowerShell, administrators have access to the full set of features built in to PowerShell, plus extensions written by the Exchange 2007 team. These Exchange 2007 specific commands, or cmdlets, leverage the simplicity and power of PowerShell to perform common and some not-so-common Exchange tasks.

Administrators can now do almost every single administrative task with an interactive command line. EMS can be used to quickly check settings, create reports, check the health of the Exchange servers, or, best of all, automate all of the administrator's frequent operations.

The PowerShell team, led by the brilliant architect of PowerShell, Jeffrey Snover, realized that Windows needed a command-line interface that would allow administrators to do everything from the command line. GUIs can only do as much as they are written to do. Some changes are made in the Registry, some in Active Directory (AD) through Active Directory Services Interface (ADSI), and others in less often used or difficult to manage components like the Exchange metabase or Internet Information Services (IIS).

Scripting and automation are key to lowering total cost of ownership to Exchange administrators. By providing a simple platform that allows administrators to create, save, and distribute their own cmdlets, EMS allows administrators to easily extend Exchange functionality and administrative tasks that are appropriate for their support structure and line of business.

Since the beginning, Exchange administrators have requested ways to manage all the buttons and knobs that are built in to the server. The GUI only allows the administrator to do as much as the GUI was programmed to do. Now that all these objects and settings are available through EMS, administrators are free to develop, customize, save, and distribute their own cmdlets to Exchange support staff.

The power of EMS can be used to automate many different types of tasks. Imagine creating 10,000 test user accounts for a test lab with one line of code or setting a 200-MB mailbox quota on all mailboxes in the organization with one line. That's the power of the Exchange Management Shell.

The Exchange Management Shell and PowerShell replace VBScript, WMI, ADSI, LDP, and more—all within a single command-line interface. Tasks that used to require specialized scripting knowledge can now be easily learned using extensive help within the shell.

Cmdlets that administrators create can be modified to do other tasks. Administrators will quickly build a set of cmdlets that they will use and recycle into new and more complex sets of functions.

A common question asked by administrators is whether complex scripting is required in EMS to do simple tasks. Do administrators have to learn complex syntax and command switches to manage Exchange? Exchange Management Shell is extremely powerful, very easy to learn, and helps to simplify many tasks that previously had to be done by developers or programmers.

When the Exchange Server 2007 team started designing the Exchange cmdline and scripting interface, they made absolutely sure that 80% of Microsoft customers, who normally have little or no scripting experience, can still use the PowerShell/Exchange command line to automate or perform their tasks.

PowerShell comes in a dynamic link library (DLL) form as well so developers can include it in their own applications. Administrators, users, or developers can write their own cmdlets to extend the functionality of PowerShell. These cmdlets can either be written using PowerShell script or they can be compiled into a .NET assembly using any programming language that targets the common language runtime.

EMS makes it easier to administer Exchange 2007 by making administration more safe, easy, and fun. It improves the developer experience by making it easier to add command-line management capabilities using Microsoft .NET. It improves the administrative experience by enabling information technology (IT) professionals to write secure automation scripts that can run locally or remotely.

An abundance of resources are available to the administrator who uses EMS and PowerShell. Microsoft is committed to publishing dozens of example scripts and cmdlets highlighting some of the more common administrative tasks. Numerous other websites and utilities are also devoted to PowerShell. Some of these are covered in this chapter.

The book *Script the World Using PowerShell*, by Sams Publishing (ISBN: 0672329530), is an excellent resource. This book covers both basic and advanced concepts of PowerShell, the engine on which the Exchange Management Shell runs.

Understanding the Exchange Task Model

Four major groups of tasks are performed in Exchange 2007 administration. Each of these groups and tasks can be fully managed using EMS. The rich command-line interface in EMS provides more granularity than the Exchange Management Console.

▶ **Recipient management tasks**—These tasks include all facets of mailbox, contact, and distribution group management, including creation, moves, deletions, and modifications.

▸ **Organization management tasks**—These tasks include managing global rules, email life cycle policies, and unified messaging dial plans.

▸ **Server management tasks**—These tasks include managing and configuring all Exchange 2007 server roles, including Mailbox server, Client Access server, bridgehead server, gateway server, and Unified Messaging servers.

▸ **Diagnostic tasks**—These tasks include queue management, reporting, and analysis. Performance monitoring and alerts also fall into this group.

Tasks are further broken down into categories based on server role or features:

▸ **Edge server**—Managing Active Directory Application Mode (ADAM), receive, and send connectors

▸ **Bridgehead, CAS, Mailbox, and Unified Messaging roles**—Managing transport rules, Outlook Web Access configuration, storage group and mail store configuration, mailbox configuration, and unified messaging configuration

▸ **Antispam**—Managing content filtering, recipient filtering, IP Allow and Block filters, SenderID, and Sender Reputation settings

▸ **Email life cycle**—Creating, managing, and deleting Exchange 2007 Email Life Cycle folders

▸ **Transport**—Managing hub transport rules and policies

▸ **Rules**—Creating, managing, and deleting global rules, internal rules, external rules, and journal rules

Understanding EMS Is the Back End to the Exchange Management Console

The Exchange Management Console is simply a GUI to EMS. Whenever an operation is performed in EMC, it calls a set of cmdlets in EMS and presents the results back to the GUI.

Everything an administrator can do in EMC can be done in EMS, but not always vice versa. If the Exchange 2007 team were to add every configuration setting to the EMC, it would be much too complicated. Their goal was to put the most common administrative tasks in EMC.

When administrators perform most operations in EMC, the EMS command used to execute the task is presented in the GUI, similar to the screen shown in Figure 9.1.

The administrator can copy the code, edit it in a text editor if desired, and run it again (for example, against all servers in the organization).

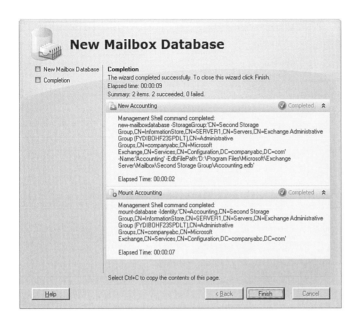

FIGURE 9.1   Sample EMC screen.

When any Exchange Server 2007 role is installed on a server or the administrative tools are installed on a management workstation, the .NET Framework, PowerShell, and Exchange Server 2007 cmdlets are installed automatically. The Exchange Management Shell is launched from the Microsoft Exchange menu after you install Exchange Server 2007 and looks similar to the screen shown in Figure 9.2.

```
Machine: server1 CWD: C:\
                  Welcome to the Exchange Management Shell!

Full list of cmdlets:          get-command
Only Exchange cmdlets:         get-excommand
Cmdlets for a specific role:   get-help -role *UM* or *Mailbox*
Get general help:              help
Get help for a cmdlet:         help <cmdlet-name> or <cmdlet-name> -?
Show quick reference guide:    quickref
Exchange team blog:            get-exblog
Show full output for a cmd:    <cmd> | format-list

Tip of the day #14:

To get a list of all users on an Exchange 2007 server who are Unified Messaging-
enabled type, use:

Get-UmMailbox | ForEach ( If($_.UmEnabled -Eq $True)($_.Name))

[PS] C:\>_
```

FIGURE 9.2   Sample EMS screen.

Understanding Cmdlets as the Core to EMS

A cmdlet is a lightweight command that is used in the PowerShell and Exchange Management Shell environments. Within that environment, the PowerShell command interpreter (PS.exe) executes these cmdlets within the context of automation scripts.

Cmdlets differ from commands in other shell environments in the following ways:

▶ Cmdlets are instances of .NET classes, not standalone executables.

▶ Cmdlets can be created with as few as a dozen lines of code.

▶ Cmdlets do not, in general, do their own parsing, error presentation, or output formatting. Parsing, error presentation, and output formatting are handled by a common engine that is provided by PowerShell.

▶ Cmdlets process input objects from the pipeline, rather than from streams of text, and deliver the objects as output to the pipeline.

▶ Cmdlets are record-oriented, processing a single object at a time.

As an example, the `get-mailbox` cmdlet returns all the mailbox objects on a server. It does this by binding to Active Directory, enumerating every user object in the domain, and returning all objects that have a valid populated `homeMDB` attribute.

Exchange cmdlets enforce strict rules and validation on configuration, unlike ADSIEdit, LDP, or VBScript. That means you cannot accidentally update a value for an object with an invalid value using the Exchange Management Shell. It also means that you can use the EMS to correct invalid values automatically. This can be done by simply getting and setting the current values for any object.

Common Uses of EMS

The Exchange Management Shell delivers powerful, single-line commands for scripting and robust reporting tools for administrators. EMS is commonly used to perform most all administrative and reporting functions. It is also used to make bulk changes to many objects at once.

Understanding Administrative Functions

The bulk of an Exchange administrator's duties in Exchange revolve around administrative functions. These functions include the following:

▶ **Mailbox management**—Adding, changing, and deleting mailboxes, contact, and distribution group membership in the Exchange organization

▶ **Setting limits on users**—Applying quota limits to some or all mailboxes in the organization

▶ **Moving mailboxes between servers**—Moving mailboxes between Exchange servers and mailbox stores within the organization

▶ **Configuring Exchange parameters**—Setting all configuration settings of the Exchange environment, including server, connector, policy, rules, and unified messaging configuration

Understanding Reporting Functions of EMS

Reporting is another function with which administrators are frequently tasked. The Exchange Management Shell makes robust reporting functions easy. Examples of some of the reports that can be generated are as follows:

▶ **Largest mail users**—A report listing the largest mailboxes in the Exchange organization

▶ **Messaging routing traffic**—A report displaying mail routing and transport statistics for servers or the entire organization

▶ **User distribution**—A report listing the mailbox distribution across all servers, storage groups, and mailbox stores in the organization

▶ **Mailbox size distribution**—A report showing the size of each mailbox in each mail store on one or more servers in the organization

Explaining the Difference Between PowerShell and EMS

The Exchange Management Shell is based on Microsoft PowerShell, which provides access to all .NET objects and classes. When the administrator installs Exchange Server 2007, the setup program automatically installs the .NET Framework and PowerShell. It also installs all the Exchange 2007 specific cmdlets.

The cmdlets were written by the Exchange 2007 team to perform Exchange-specific tasks. There are over 350 cmdlets unique to Exchange and each cmdlet has its own set of help.

Common PowerShell Functions in EMS

Because the Exchange Management Shell is based on PowerShell, it shares many functions with it.

EMS shares the same verb-noun syntax for all operations and cmdlets as PowerShell. This gives a consistent logical experience for the administrator while working in the EMS environment.

Comprehensive tab completion is also present in EMS and PowerShell. When the administrator presses the Tab key after typing some text, the function TabExpansion is called to generate the list of possible completion matches. Tab completion works on variables and parameters on cmdlets in addition to filename completion. Administrators can also define custom tab completions.

Both EMS and PowerShell offer a comprehensive help system with examples. Administrators can get both general and cmdlet-specific help within the command environment. The help systems support wildcards. Knowing the strong naming conventions used in the environment, administrators can leverage wildcards to guess at what they are looking for.

6

EMS and PowerShell cmdlets both offer an interactive completion process. The administrator can enter as many cmdlet parameters as he is comfortable with, and the command environment will prompt for the missing required parameters. This is very helpful for seldom-used cmdlets.

Unique EMS Functions Specific to Exchange

The Exchange Management Shell offers over 350 unique cmdlets that were written by the Exchange 2007 team specifically for Exchange. Each of these cmdlets has been optimized for performance, and they are the building blocks for all Exchange management functions.

Some Exchange operations and tasks take time to complete. Moving large mailboxes across a wide area network (WAN), for example, can take several minutes to complete. When operations like these take place, a textual status bar is presented at the top of the display indicating the progress of the task.

Understanding the EMS Syntax

The Exchange Management Shell shares the same verb-noun syntax as PowerShell. This provides a consistent set of commands to learn and understand within the command environment.

Understanding the Verb-Noun Construct

EMS uses a strict verb-noun naming constraint for all of its cmdlets. The verb is separated from the noun with a hyphen. For example, the cmdlet get-mailbox returns all of the mailbox objects in the organization.

Common verbs include add, clear, disable, enable, export, get, import, move, new, remove, set, test, update, and write. As in the English language, there are many more nouns than verbs. There is a very high level of verb reuse to provide a consistent, predictable user experience. Examples of nouns used in EMS are mailbox, mailboxserver, ExchangeServer, TransportSettings, GlobalRule, object, service, and so on.

Walking Through Cmdlets in EMS

Some cmdlets offer many different switches and parameters. If administrators are not comfortable entering all the parameters for a cmdlet in one line, they can enter as much as they want, press Enter, and EMS will prompt for the rest. This provides an easy way to run cmdlets that are not often used and that don't necessarily need to be saved for reuse.

For example, enter move-Mailbox and EMS prompts for the missing required parameters.

```
Cmdlet move-Mailbox at command pipeline position 1
Supply values for the following parameters:
TargetDatabase: Mailbox Store 2
Identity: Amy C. Guillet
```

This is the same as entering the following single line at the EMS command line:

```
Move-Mailbox "Amy C. Guillet" -Targetdatabase "Mailbox Store 2"
```

Getting Help with EMS

The Exchange Management Shell features a QuickStart guide that gives a quick tutorial on common commands and syntax. It provides common tasks and options, tips and tricks, recipient management examples, storage management examples, transport configuration examples, policy configuration, and server management examples. This is presented in a Hypertext Markup Language (HTML) page by simply typing Quickstart at the console.

The Exchange Management Shell includes two basic types of help—command help and conceptual help. Both types can be accessed from the console using the Get-Help cmdlet, which also uses the alias help.

To retrieve a list of all available help topics, simply type help *. To get help with a specific cmdlet, type help cmdlet-name. For example, help move-databasepath displays the purpose of the cmdlet, all required and optional parameters, return variables, and examples of its use.

By default, some information appears in the console window as one long, scrolling topic. To view the information a single page at a time, pipe the results to more. For example, Get-ExCommand | More displays all the Exchange-specific cmdlets in EMS, one page at a time.

Using Pipelining in EMS

Pipelining is the key to the power of EMS. It uses the output of one cmdlet to run through another cmdlet using the "|" (pipeline) operator. Pipelining provides bulk management changes. To understand this concept, examine this example:

```
Get-mailbox -server SERVER1 | move-mailbox -targetdatabase "UMSERVER\Mailbox
➥Database 1"
```

The first part of the line, the part before the "|" operator, tells EMS to get all the mailbox objects on server SERVER1. It then sends, or pipes, the resulting set of objects to the next command, which instructs it to move them to Mailbox Database 1 on the server UMSERVER.

Another way of saying it is that one process output is consumed by another and another. Consider another example:

```
get-mailbox | where-object { $_.name -like "amy*" } | set-Mailbox -MaxSendSize 10mb
```

In this example, the get-mailbox cmdlet returns all the mailbox objects on all servers in the organization. This collection is piped through the where-object filter cmdlet that filters out the mailbox objects to only include mailboxes with names beginning with "amy." The "$_" variable equates to "this object." These objects, in turn, are piped through the set-Mailbox cmdlet to pass the parameter –MaxSendSize and set the value to 10Mb.

Note that EMS is not case sensitive and that it understands that 10MB equates to 10,240,000 bytes. In this example, the get-mailbox cmdlet produces a result, the where-object consumes it and produces another result, and this result is consumed by the set-mailbox cmdlet to set the new value.

Using the WhatIf and Confirm Parameters

There are times when the administrator will write a simple or complicated script in EMS and wonder what results it will produce. Some cmdlets support the –WhatIf and –Confirm parameters. The –WhatIf parameter informs the administrator what action the script would take and the –Confirm parameter prompts for confirmation before taking action.

For example, suppose the administrator wants to retire Mailbox Store 5 on SERVER1, and move all the existing mailboxes from the the current database to Mailbox Store 2 on UMSERVER. The administrator could use the following command:

```
Get-mailbox –database "SERVER1\Mailbox Store 5" | move-mailbox –targetDatabase
➥"UMSERVER\Mailbox Store 2
```

By adding the –WhatIf parameter, the following result is output to the console for each mailbox:

```
What if: Performing operation "move-Mailbox" on Target "Move mailbox for:
Administrator (Administrator@companyabc.com) to Database: Mailbox Database
2,09014bc6-f977-4961-b4eb-8829fb13e5d6. The operation can take a long time and the
mailbox will be inaccessible until the move is complete".
```

This allows the administrator to easily see what operation would be performed by the script. If the results are as expected, the administrator presses the up arrow to recall the last typed line, and removes the –WhatIf parameter to execute the script.

If the administrator adds the –Confirm parameter, the following is output to the console:

```
Are you sure you want to perform this action?
Performing operation "move-Mailbox" on Target "Move mailbox for: Administrator
(Administrator@companyabc.com) to Database: Mailbox Database 1,09014bc6-f977-4961-
b4eb-8829fb13e5d6. The operation can take a long time and the mailbox will be
inaccessible until the move is complete".
[Y] Yes  [A] Yes to All  [N] No  [L] No to All  [S] Suspend  [?] Help
(default is "Y"):
```

Entering "Y" processes this move, "A" processes all moves, "N" skips this move, "L" cancels further processing, and "S" suspends processing and returns the administrator to the console. Typing "exit" resumes processing.

Creating Your Own Cmdlet

Exchange Management Console contains many built-in cmdlets. Administrators can create their own cmdlets using a common text editor. In this instance, the cmdlet is a series of commands, usually more than one line, stored in a text file with a `.ps1` extension.

The PowerShell common language runtime is an interpretive environment, meaning that cmdlets, functions, and scripts are loaded into random access memory (RAM) where they are validated and executed.

The Exchange Management Shell and PowerShell define several types of commands that administrators can use in development. These commands include functions, filters, scripts, aliases, and executables (applications). The main command type discussed in this chapter is a simple, small command called a cmdlet. Both EMS and PowerShell supply sets of cmdlets and fully support cmdlet customization to suit the organization's environment. The PowerShell/EMS runtime processes all cmdlets.

An EMS cmdlet is a simple set of commands bundled together to interact with any managed application, including the operating system. It is similar to a built-in command in any other shell, such as `Cmd.exe`, `Bash`, or `ksh`. A conventional shell processes most commands as separate executable programs. Each program must parse the input and parameters, bind values to the correct parameters, format the output, and display the output.

EMS, in contrast, processes commands as instances of .NET classes, concentrating on the simple cmdlet model. The administrator must provide the necessary parameters and validate the values, and then supply details of object types and formatting. EMS does the rest of the work: parsing the parameters and binding them to their values, formatting the output, and then displaying the output.

Demonstrating Cmdlet Examples

The administrator can run a cmdlet singly or as one of several cmdlets piped together on the command line. For example, the single cmdlet:

```
Get-AddressList
```

returns all attributes of an address list or set of address lists. The pipelined command:

```
Get-AddressList | export-csv "C:\AddressList.csv"
```

produces a collection of address lists and pipelines it to the export-csv cmdlet, which requires the file path and name parameter.

The following example is a custom cmdlet that connects to the WMI provider to display all public folders and their message counts in a table format:

```
get-wmiobject -class Exchange_PublicFolder -Namespace ROOT\MicrosoftExchangev2 -
ComputerName SERVER1 | select-object name,messagecount,totalmessagesize |
format-table
```

6

Although this is only a single-line command, it can be tedious to type every time it is needed. It can be typed into a text editor and saved as a `.ps1` file, `PFSize.ps1` for example, in the system path so that it can easily be run again and again.

A working knowledge of .NET is required to write more complex functions that access objects and classes that are not exposed using the built-in cmdlets. The following cmdlet example uses the `system.net.mail.smtpClient` class in the .NET 2.0 Framework to send Simple Mail Transfer Protocol (SMTP) email from the EMS command line:

```
$SmtpServer = "server1.companyabc.com"
$From = "EMStest@companyabc.com"
if ($args.Length -lt 1) {
        $To = "administrator@companyabc.com"
}
else {
        $To = $args[0]
}
$Subject = "Greetings from EMS!"
$Body = "Hello, this is a test from the Exchange Management Shell."
$SmtpClient = new-object system.net.mail.smtpClient
$SmtpClient.host = $SmtpServer
$SmtpClient.Send($From, $To, $Subject, $Body)
```

This cmdlet takes an argument, or parameter. If the cmdlet is saved as `TestMail.ps1`, the administrator can issue the following command to send a test SMTP email:

```
TestMail testuser@companyabc.com
```

Please refer to the book *Script the World Using PowerShell* for more detail on writing cmdlets.

Combining Functions to Create a Cmdlet Library

As the administrators become more familiar with EMS and using and writing cmdlets, they will begin to build a library of commonly used cmdlets and scripts. It is common to "recycle" similar cmdlets to use for different tasks. Over time, administrators will find useful scripts and concepts from many resources: colleagues, scripting blogs, newsgroups, and so on.

It is sometimes useful to put all the cmdlets in a common area where other administrators, users, and developers can peruse them and add to the knowledge base. Often, a fellow administrator will need to perform the same task that another administrator has already written. There is no reason to "reinvent the wheel."

A common practice is to create a network share where administrators and cmdlet developers have modify permissions and other users have read and execute access permissions. Arrange the folder structure based on business needs and technical requirements. It is also a best practice to include a folder with the Exchange Server 2007 setup bits, so that administrators can load the Exchange Management Shell components to run the cmdlets.

Modifying and Applying Server Cmdlets to Other Systems

After a cmdlet has been written and tested, it is often useful to run the same cmdlet against many or all servers in the organization. For example, consider the following cmdlet that sets the JournalRecipient value for Mailbox Store 3 on SERVER1 to use the CompanyJournal mailbox:

```
set-MailboxDatabase "SERVER1\Mailbox Store 3" -JournalRecipient companyabc\
➥CompanyJournal
```

It is very easy to convert this cmdlet so it will run against all databases in the Exchange organization using pipelining:

```
Get-MailboxDatabase | set-MailboxDatabase -JournalRecipient companyabc\
➥companyjournal
```

In this example, `Get-MailboxDatabase` returns a collection of all the mailbox databases in the organization and pipes them to the `Set-MailboxDatabase` cmdlet, where it assigns the value.

Managing Cmdlets

It is best practice to add the folder(s) that contain the custom cmdlets and scripts to the system path. This allows the administrator to run any one of the cmdlets from anywhere in the EMS console.

Cmdlets with the `.ps1` extension cannot be run directly from the `Cmd.exe` console; they must be run within the Exchange Management Shell. Administrators can run cmdlets from the `Cmd.exe` console by calling EMS and the cmdlet. For example,

```
C:\>powershell mycmdlet.ps1
```

invokes EMS because `powershell.exe` is in the path, runs the `mycmdlet.ps1` cmdlet, and exits back to the Cmd console.

The cmdlets that ship with Exchange Server 2007 and EMS cannot be modified. They have been optimized and compiled for maximum performance. These native cmdlets are contained in the DLL files in the `%SystemDrive%\Program Files\Microsoft\Exchange Server\bin` folder.

It is a best practice to create a folder to contain the custom `.ps1` files and add that folder to the system path. This facilitates the use of the `.ps1` files within the EMS command line.

6

Developing a Common Naming Scheme

When developing custom cmdlets, it is important to use functional names that denote the use of the cmdlet. It is a best practice to use the same verb-noun naming that is common in PowerShell and EMS. This provides consistency in the management environment.

A cmdlet to send SMTP email from the EMS command line might be called `send-email.ps1`, for example.

Distributing Cmdlets

Cmdlets can be distributed in a number of ways, similar to VBScripts or batch files. Because `.ps1` files cannot be executed from the `Cmd.exe` shell, they can be sent using Outlook without the security restrictions of executable code. Cmdlets can be emailed as attachments or their contents can be pasted into the body of a message.

The Microsoft distributed file system (DFS) offers another way to distribute cmdlets. By creating replicas in remote sites, the organization's cmdlet library can be fault tolerant and available locally to all administrators.

Another option for distributing cmdlets is via SharePoint. SharePoint's document management features allow administrators to check in and check out cmdlets as `.ps1` files. This makes managing `.ps1` files simple and provides full-text search capabilites. It also provides security so that only the appropriate administrators have access to certain cmdlets.

Enabling Logging in EMS

Logging can be enabled in the Exchange Management Shell. This is a great feature for Exchange administrators as every command executed in either the Exchange Management Console GUI or executed from the cmdline can be logged. Logging is not enabled by default; however, it is a function that can be enabled by configuration.

Using EMS to Do Administrative Mailbox Tasks

The Exchange Management Shell makes common mailbox management tasks such as adding, modifying, moving, and deleting mailboxes simple. The flexibility of EMS allows the administrator to easily perform tasks that would require much more time and labor if done from the Exchange Management Console.

Creating Mailboxes with EMS

Mailboxes can be created with EMS singly or in bulk. They can be created using the interactive command prompt or by specifying the required parameters from the command line. To enable a malbox using the interactive shell, simply enter:

```
Enable-mailbox
```

and answer the prompts for the missing parameters:

```
Supply values for the following parameters:
Database: mailbox store
Identity: companyabc\jason
```

The following example creates a mailbox for the existing user Jason in Mailbox Store 3 on SERVER1:

```
Enable-Mailbox "companyabc\jason" -database "SERVER1\mailbox store 3"
```

The next example demonstrates using EMS to create 1,000 users in Active Directory and create mailboxes for each user in the Test Mailbox Store on SERVER3. This single-line cmdlet is very useful in lab scenarios.

```
1..1000 | foreach {net user "user$_" MyPassword=01 /ADD /Domain; enable-mailbox
"user$_" -database "SERVER3\test mailbox store"}
```

Doing this same operation using VBScript would take many more lines of code and require much more development time.

Modifying Mailboxes with EMS

Mailbox attributes can easily be modified using EMS, as well. The following example modifies the mailbox for user Jason in the default domain to only accept emails from amy@companyabc.com:

```
set-Mailbox jason -AcceptMessagesOnlyFrom amy@companyabc.com
```

It is just as easy to make changes on many mailboxes at the same time using pipelining. Consider the following example that sets the mailbox quota for all user mailboxes at 250MB:

```
get-Mailbox | set-Mailbox -StorageQuota 250mb
```

In this example, we use the –OrganizationalUnit parameter of the Get-Mailbox cmdlet to set the maximum message size that users in the Accounting OU can send to 10MB:

```
get-Mailbox -OrganizationalUnit "Test Users" | set-Mailbox -MaxSendSize 10mb
```

Moving Mailboxes Using EMS

Moving mailboxes with the Exchange Management Shell is very easy and powerful. A simple move of a mailbox from one database to another on the same server is accomplished like this:

```
Move-Mailbox Claire –TargetDatabase "accounting database"
```

EMS knows the name of all the databases in the organization. If there is more than one database with the same name, EMS moves the database to the first alphabetic server with that database name. To target a specific server, explicitly name the server in the TargetDatabase parameter. For example:

```
Move-Mailbox Claire -TargetDatabase "SERVER2\accounting database"
```

More complex moves are achieved just as easily from the Exchange Management Shell command line. In the following example, the mailbox is moved from the companyabc.org forest to the companyabc.com forest.

```
Move-Mailbox -SourceForest company123.org -TargetForest companyabc.com
➥-targetDatabase "mailbox store 9" company123\lilly
```

Of course, a realm trust must be established prior to moving the mailbox.

Disabling Mailboxes with EMS

Administrators do not delete mailboxes in Exchange 2007—they disable them. Disabling a mailbox detaches the mailbox of an existing user or inetOrgPerson and removes all of that object's Exchange attributes from Active Directory. The mailbox is truly deleted by Exchange during the online maintenance cycle after exceeding the retention time.

The following example disables a mailbox of a user in the companyabc.com domain:

```
Disable-Mailbox companyabc\claire
```

The next example shows how to delete all the mailboxes in the "Test Database" mail store so that it can be decommissioned:

```
get-Mailbox -database "test database" | disable-Mailbox -whatif
```

The -WhatIf switch in the preceding example runs the task in Read-only mode, allowing the administrator to see what would happen by running this command.

Another related command is Remove-Mailbox. This command removes the user account that is associated with a particular mailbox in Active Directory and processes the associated, disconnected mailbox as directed by the specified parameters.

```
Remove-Mailbox -MailboxDatabase "Sales Database" "companyabc\storage group 2\jason"
```

Using EMS to Do Administrative Server Tasks

Thus far, most of the examples have been for managing mailbox resources. EMS can also be used to manage the Exchange servers in your environment. The following example shows how to disable a Unified Messaging server. This allows the administrator to start or stop call processing on a Unified Messaging server so that the Unified Messaging server can be brought online or taken offline in a controlled way.

```
Disable-UMServer UMserver3
```

This example uses the `Set-AttachmentFilterListConfig` command to modify the configuration of the Attachment Filter agent on the computer running the Edge server role.

```
Set-AttachmentFilterListConfig -action remove
```

And in this example, the `set-dsnmessage` command is used to modify the configuration for delivery status notification (DSN) messages on Hub Transport and Edge servers.

```
set-dsnmessage en\internal\5.2.2 -text "The message you attempted to send could not
be delivered because the recipient's mailbox is full."
```

These are just a few examples of what can be done with the Exchange Management Shell. Many, many more commands are available to the administrator.

Provisioning Storage Groups with EMS

Exchange 2007 storage groups can easily be provisioned, configured, and moved using the Exchange Management Shell. This first example creates a new storage group on SERVER3 called "Marketing Storage Group" with the logs on the L: drive.

```
New-StorageGroup -Server SERVER3 -name "Marketing Storage Group" -LogFileLocation
"L:\Marketing Storage Group Logs"
```

The next example configures the "Test Storage Group 2" in Active Directory to enable circular logging:

```
Set-StorageGroup "Test Storage_Group_2" -CircularLoggingEnabled $true
```

Use the `Move-StorageGroupPath` command to set a new path in Active Directory for the specified server object and then move the related files to the new location.

```
Move-StorageGroupPath "Sales Storage Group" -LogFolderPath
➡"L:\Sales Storage Group Logs" –SystemFolderPath "E:\Exchange Databases\Sales"
```

Managing Mailbox Stores with EMS

All facets of database administration can be handled with the Exchange Management Shell. Using the following examples, mailbox stores can be created, dismounted, and moved. The first example creates a new Sales Database in the First Storage Group on SERVER2:

```
New-MailboxDatabase -StorageGroup "SERVER2\First Storage Group" -name
➡"Sales Database"
```

The second example shows how to mount the same mailbox database after it has been created.

```
Mount-database "SERVER2\First Storage Group\Sales Database"
```

Use the `move-DatabasePath` command to set a new path location on a database object in Active Directory under the specified mailbox server and to move the related files to that location.

```
move-DatabasePath "SERVER2\Sales Database" -LogFolderPath
➥"E:\New Folder\Sales Database"
```

When the preceding command is run, EMS automatically takes the database offline, moves the database, and mounts it again.

The next example shows how to delete a mailbox database object in the storage group container under the specified server object.

```
Remove-MailboxDatabase "SERVER2\sales database"
```

When this command is run, Exchange Management Shell deletes the database and provides a warning, letting the administrator know that the database has been removed from Active Directory but the physical files remain. You will get a warning as follows:

```
WARNING: The specified database has been removed. You must remove the database file
from your computer manually. Specified database: Sales Database
```

Managing Connectors with EMS

All types of connectors can be managed with the Exchange Management Shell. Receive and Send connectors can be created, deleted, and configured. This example gets the existing credential object and creates a new secured Send connector on an Edge or Hub Transport server role and configures it to use that credential:

```
$CredentialObject = Get-Credential
New-SendConnector -Name "Secure E-Mail to Companyabc.org" -Type ToInternet
➥-AddressSpaces companyabc.com -AuthenticationCredential $CredentialObject
➥-AuthenticationMechanism Login
```

This example modifies an existing Receive connector. The Identity parameter is required when you are running the `Set-ReceiveConnector` command. This example sets the number of hops from the Edge server, sets the SMTP banner message, and configures the connection timeout value:

```
Set-ReceiveConnector -Identity "Internet Receive Connector" -NumberOfHopsFromEdge 1
➥-Banner "220 Authorized access only" -ConnectionTimeout 00:15:00
```

This command deletes the object and the configuration information for a Receive connector. After this task completes, the object and the configuration information for the Receive connector are deleted.

```
Remove-ReceiveConnector "Companyabc.com Receive Connector"
```

Using EMS to Do Reporting

EMS has built-in reporting features that use a variety of outputs. For example, the following cmdlet verifies server functionality by logging on to the specified user's mailbox and reporting the latency:

```
Test-MapiConnectivity amy@companyabc.com
```

The output is presented on the display similar to the one shown in Figure 9.3.

FIGURE 9.3   Output generated by EMS reporting.

Output is normally sent to the display, but it can also be sent to files using redirection. EMS has special cmdlets that also produce comma-separated values (CSV), Extensible Markup Language (XML), and HTML output. These types of output provide the flexibility that administrators need to manipulate the data using familiar tools, such as Microsoft Excel.

Generating Largest Mail User Reports

The following example uses PowerShell to list the top 25 largest mailboxes on the specified server, the total number of mail items, and the size of the mailbox. It sorts the list by descending size. The example uses the standard Exchange WMI provider to access this information.

```
Get-wmiobject -class Exchange_Mailbox -Namespace ROOT\MicrosoftExchangev2
➥-ComputerName  SERVER1 | select-object MailboxDisplayName,TotalItems,Size | sort
➥-descending "Size" | select-object -first 25
```

This data might be useful for administrators to know who might need data retention training. It might also be useful to demonstrate the need for email archiving.

To make this script more portable, the output can be converted to HTML and redirected to a file, like this:

```
Get-wmiobject -class Exchange_Mailbox -Namespace ROOT\MicrosoftExchangev2
➥-ComputerName  SERVER1 | select-object MailboxDisplayName,TotalItems,Size | sort
➥-descending "Size" | select-object -first 25 | ConvertTo-html -title
➥"Top 25 Largest Mailboxes on SERVER1" > "D:\Stats\25 Largest Mailboxes.html"
```

Improving it further, the output could be redirected to a unique filename, based on the system date:

```
Get-wmiobject -class Exchange_Mailbox -Namespace ROOT\MicrosoftExchangev2
➥-ComputerName  SERVER1 | select-object MailboxDisplayName,TotalItems,Size | sort
➥-descending "Size" | select-object -first 25 | ConvertTo-html -title
➥"Top 25 Largest Mailboxes on SERVER1" >
➥("D:\Stats" + (get-Date).ToString("yyyyMMdd") + ".html")
```

Now, the cmdlet can be scheduled to run once per day, maintaining a separate report for each day.

Save the cmdlet in a .ps1 file as Top25LargestMailboxes.ps1. Because .ps1 files cannot be run directly from the Cmd.exe prompt or by the Windows Task Scheduler, the administrator must run it within the EMS/PowerShell environment. This is accomplished by using the command PowerShell Top25LargestMailboxes.ps1. An alternative is to create a batch file containing the same command and run the batch file. The batch file can then be scheduled to run once per day.

TIP

The Top 25 Largest Mailboxes report could be published to the company's SharePoint "Wall of Shame." Users will take measures to not make the list.

Generating User Distribution Reports

Reports that list user mailbox distribution across all mailbox stores can be helpful to know if the user load is balanced in the organization. The following .ps1 example shows how to produce a report listing the total number of mailbox stores, the number of mailboxes in each store, and the total number of mailboxes.

This .ps1 script contains comments, variables, and error trapping. Comments begin with the "#" symbol and are useful for administrators to understand what the script or cmdlet is doing and are ignored by EMS/PowerShell. Variables always start with the "$" symbol and are used to assign values or collections. Error trapping handles exceptions or errors that can occur in the script so the script will continue to run.

```
#Get all mailbox stores in the organization and assign them to the $MailboxStores
➥array variable
$MailboxStores = get-mailboxdatabase
```

```
write-host "There are" $MailboxStores.Count "Mailbox Stores in the organization."
write-host ("-"*70)

#Get each database and assign it to the $Database array variable
foreach ($Database in $MailboxStores) {
        #Derive the Mailbox server name from the database
        $MailboxServer = $Database.server.name
        #Derive the database name from the database
        $Database = $Database.name
        #Assign the full database name to the $FullDatabaseName variable
        $FullDatabaseName = "$MailboxServer" + "\" + "$Database"
        #Get the mailboxes for this database
        $mailbox = get-mailbox -database $FullDatabaseName
        write-host "There are" $mailbox.Count.toString("#,#") "mailboxes in"
➥$FullDatabaseName

#The trap statement traps the NullException error which occurs when a database has
no mailboxes
trap{
        write-host "There are no mailboxes in" $FullDatabaseName;
        continue
}
}

write-host ("-"*70)
#Get all mailboxes in the organization
$mailboxes = get-Mailbox
write-host "The total number of mailboxes in the organization is"
$mailboxes.count.tostring("#,#")
```

Using This Data to Rebalance Mailbox Distribution

EMS can also be used to redistribute users equally across all mailbox stores in the organization. The script is based on the previous example and redistributes existing mailboxes evenly across all mailbox databases in the organization.

The script makes use of a dynamic array and operators that provide the addition and subtraction functions for building the array.

```
#Get all mailbox databases and assign them to the $MailboxDatabases array variable
$MailboxDatabases = get-mailboxdatabase
write-host ("There are " + $MailboxDatabases.Count + " Mailbox Databases.")

#Get all mailboxes in the organization and assign them to the $Mailboxes array
➥variable
```

```
$Mailboxes = get-mailbox
write-host ("There are " + $Mailboxes.Count + " mailboxes in total.")

#Derive the desired number of mailboxes per database by dividing the number of
mailboxes by the number of databases, less the remainder
$DesiredNumber = ($Mailboxes.Count - ($Mailboxes.Count % $MailboxDatabases.Count))
/ $MailboxDatabases.Count
write-host ("Desired number of mailboxes per database: " + $DesiredNumber +
➥" mailboxes.")
write-host ("="*70)

$MailboxesInDatabase
[int] $MailboxesToMove = 0

#Create a dynamically expanding ArrayList object to hold the mailboxes that can be
➥moved out
[System.Collections.ArrayList] $MailboxesOut = new-object
➥System.Collections.Araylist

#Loop through each database to build a list of excess mailboxes
foreach($mailboxDatabase in $MailboxDatabases){

        #Find out how many mailboxes are in each database by using a filter
        $MailboxesInDatabase = get-mailbox | where{$_.DataBase -like
➥$MailboxDatabase.ID}
        write-host $mailboxDatabase.Name "has"
➥$MailboxesInDatabase.Count.ToSTring("#,#") "mailboxes."

        #Calculate the number of mailboxes that need to be moved in or out
        $MailboxesToMove = $MailboxesInDatabase.Count - $DesiredNumber

        #If mailboxes need moving out of this database add them to the
➥$MailboxesOut ArrayList
        if($MailboxesToMove -gt 0 ){

                write-host $MailboxesToMove "mailboxes can be moved out."
                write-host ("-"*70)
                for($i=0;$i -ne $MailboxesToMove;$i++){
                  $count =  $MailboxesOut.Add($MailboxesInDatabase[$i])
                }

        }else{
                write-host ($MailboxesToMove*-1) "mailboxes can be moved in."
                write-host ("-"*70)
        }
```

```
#The trap statement traps the NullException error which occurs when a database has
no mailboxes
trap{
        write-host $mailboxdatabase.Name  "has no mailboxes.";
        continue
}
}


if($MailboxesOut.Count -gt $Mailboxes.Count % $MailboxDatabases.Count){
        write-host
        write-host "Moving" $MailboxesOut.Count "mailboxes."
        write-host
}else{
        write-host
        write-host "All mailboxes are balanced."
        write-host
}

#Loop through each database to locate databases that need more mailboxes and move
excess mailboxes into these databases
foreach($mailboxDatabase in $MailboxDatabases){

        #Find out how many mailboxes are in each database by using a filter
        $MailboxesInDatabase = (get-mailbox | where{$_.DataBase -like
➥$MailboxDatabase.ID})

        #Calculate the number of mailboxes that need to be moved in or out
        $MailboxesToMove = $MailboxesInDatabase.Count - $DesiredNumber

        #If this database needs more mailboxes move the required number from the
ArrayList holding excess mailboxes
        if($MailboxesToMove -lt 0 ){
        for($i=0;$i -ne $mailboxesToMove;$i--){
                write-host "Moving Mailbox" $MailboxesOut[$i].Alias "to"
➥$MailboxDatabase.Name
                move-mailbox -TargetDatabase ($MailboxDatabase.ID) -Identity
➥($MailboxesOut[$i].ID)
        }
        }
}
write-host ("="*70)
write-host "Script completed successfully!"
```

As demonstrated by this example, the Exchange Management Shell can easily do things that would be much more difficult from the Exchange Management Console GUI.

Working with Event Logs

Exchange administrators work often with Windows event logs to troubleshoot issues. Because EMS runs in the PowerShell environment, the administrator can take advantage of PowerShell's Get-Eventlog cmdlet to work with event logs.

This example displays all events in the Application Event Log where the source begins with the word "Exchange." The output is exported to a CSV file for easy manipulation in Microsoft Excel.

```
get-eventlog Application | where {$_.Source -ilike "Exchange*"} | export-csv
➥c:\events.csv
```

Finding Other Resources

Numerous resources are available for both PowerShell and the Exchange Management Shell. Microsoft has generated a lot of excitement about these technologies and is focused on delivering meaningful content and examples in a variety of ways.

Resources on the Web

The following are various PowerShell and Exchange Management Shell resources available on the Internet:

- ▶ **Microsoft Exchange Server 2007 tech center**—Exchange Management Shell product documentation. (http://www.microsoft.com/technet/prodtechnol/exchange/E2k7Help/925ad66f-2f05-4269-9923-c353d9c19312.mspx?mfr=true)

- ▶ **Beginner's Guide to Microsoft PowerShell**—Brings together resources for system administrators who are interested in learning about the Windows PowerShell command line and scripting environment. This section of the Script Center is under active development. (http://www.microsoft.com/technet/scriptcenter/hubs/msh.mspx)

- ▶ **TechNet Virtual Lab: Exchange**—Hosted by Microsoft, these virtual labs allow you to connect to an Exchange Server 2007 virtual environment to run various exercises and demos. (http://www.microsoft.com/technet/traincert/virtuallab/exchange.mspx)

- ▶ **Vivek Sharma's blog**—Vivek is a program manager for the Exchange Management Shell team. His blog includes many samples and explanations for working with EMS. (http://www.viveksharma.com/techlog/)

- ▶ **Scripting newsgroups**—These newsgroups provide a place for scripters of all types and abilities to ask questions and share information. (news://microsoft.public.windows.server.scripting), (news://microsoft.public.scripting)

Utilities and Tools

Several tools have been released or are in current development for working with Exchange Management Shell and PowerShell scripts. Most of these are editors that provide automatic formatting, cmdlet method and property exploration, and debugging:

▶ PowerShellIDE, ScriptInternals (http://powershell.com)

▶ Karl Prosser's PowerShell Analyzer (http://karlprosser.edify.us)

▶ PrimalScript, SAPIEN Technologies (http://www.primalscript.com)

Summary

PowerShell is required learning when it comes to Exchange Server 2007. Mastery of PowerShell and Exchange Management Shell sets the distinction between an Exchange administrator and an Exchange guru. Although having a deep understanding of both technologies will benefit both the administrator and the organization, the simple interface and easily understood syntax makes the administrator more productive from day one.

Both PowerShell and the Exchange Management Shell are continually being developed. Each Exchange service pack is expected to include additional optimized cmdlets to extend the use and functionality of EMS. The administrator is encouraged to check the Exchange Server 2007 website often for updates.

Best Practices

The following are best practices from this chapter:

▶ Leverage scripting to automate repetitive tasks.

▶ Use the Exchange Management Shell for tasks involving recipient management, organization management, server management, and diagnostics.

▶ Understand cmdlets because they are core to the Exchange Management Shell.

▶ Use cmdlets to enforce strict rules and to validate configurations.

▶ Take advantage of the Exchange Management Shell by automating tasks relative to mailbox management, setting user limits, moving mailboxes between servers, and configuring Exchange parameters.

▶ Use the Exchange Management Shell QuickStart guide to get a quick tutorial on common commands and shell syntax.

▶ Create a cmdlet library to reuse cmdlets and scripts in similar scripted functions.

▶ Develop a common naming scheme for cmdlets to make it easier to find and understand the function of cmdlets in your library.

6

▶ Use the Exchange Management Shell to perform basic administrative tasks, such as creating mailboxes, modifying mailbox settings, moving mailboxes, and disabling mailboxes.

▶ Create EMS scripts to perform server administration tasks, such as provisioning storage groups, managing mailboxes stores, and managing connectors.

▶ Take advantage of EMS for reporting by creating large mail user and user distribution reports.

PART IV

Securing an Exchange Server 2007 Environment

IN THIS PART

CHAPTER 10

Client-Level Secured Messaging

When discussing the broad topic of securing a messaging environment, it is best to break the subject down to three basic components: client-level, server-level, and transport-level security. You have likely heard the adage "A chain is only as strong as its weakest link"; this saying can easily be applied to an organization's security measures. If you have exceptionally good client-level security, and exceptionally strong server-level security, but your transport-level security is lacking—you are vulnerable to attack. Hackers thrive on researching environments, finding "the weakest link," and exploiting it.

This chapter focuses on client-level security, leaving "Server and Transport-Level Security" for Chapter 11. This book also addresses an additional component of messaging security, client-level encryption in Chapter 12, "Encrypting Email Communications with Exchange Server 2007."

Microsoft's Trustworthy Computing Initiative

In 2002, Microsoft Founder and Chairman Bill Gates sent a memo to all employees at Microsoft emphasizing the importance of making the company's software more "trustworthy." He labeled this new effort "Trustworthy Computing" and stated that the company focus needed to shift toward making software that was more secure and helping users become more comfortable with their electronic privacy.

This memo began a shift of focus for the entire organization that continues today. And it is working. Microsoft has recorded a significant reduction of publicly reported vulnerabilities in their products across the board.

However, no matter what security features are built in to a product, you still have to ensure that they are implemented and configured properly to be effective.

Microsoft Exchange Server 2007 was designed, built, and implemented with this new security effort in place. Microsoft has gone to great lengths to provide a rich array of security features at the client, server, and transport layers in Exchange Server 2007 to protect an organization's messaging environment investment.

By actively and aggressively securing each of these three layers, you can ensure your chain has no "weak links."

Securing Your Windows Environment

At its basic components, a Microsoft Exchange environment can be reduced to four main components:

- ▶ **Server operating system**—Microsoft's latest server operating system (OS), and the one that Exchange Server 2007 is designed to run on, is Microsoft Windows Server 2003 R2.

- ▶ **Server messaging system**—Exchange Server 2007 is the current messaging system from Microsoft. Exchange 2007 provides messaging, calendaring, mobile access, and unified communications for the enterprise.

- ▶ **Client operating system**—Microsoft's latest client operating systems are Microsoft Windows Vista and Microsoft Windows XP Service Pack 2 (SP2). Although Exchange Server 2007 can work with older versions of client software, this chapter focuses primarily on the security features available in the latest version of the client OS.

- ▶ **Client messaging application**—Microsoft's latest client messaging application is Microsoft Office Outlook 2007. Again, although Exchange can work with older versions of Outlook, this chapter focuses on the latest technologies.

Both the server messaging system and the client messaging application are only as secure as their underlying operating systems. Fortunately, Microsoft Windows Server 2003, Windows Vista, and Microsoft Windows XP are very secure by default, and with a little knowledge and experience can be made exceptionally secure.

NOTE

Implementing security measures in a computer network is an extremely complex process, and entire books have been devoted to the subject. This chapter endeavors to share best practices and tips and tricks for securing your mail client and the underlying OS, but it is recommended that additional resources focusing solely on security be referenced as well.

The concept of securing Windows Vista and Windows XP can best be grasped if it is broken down into smaller components. This chapter addresses the following primary areas:

▶ Authentication

▶ Access control

▶ Patch management

▶ Communications

This chapter addresses other areas as well, of course, but the recommendations in these key sections will get you off to a good start.

Windows Server 2003 Security Improvements

Although this chapter focuses on client-level security, we must discuss some server features as well because the two work hand in hand to create a secure network. Securing Windows Server 2003 is discussed in greater depth in Chapter 11.

Even from the default installation, Windows Server 2003 is significantly more secure than its predecessors. Previous versions installed with most features defaulting to an enabled state, counting on the administrator to disable them if they were not going to be used. This left a lot of openings for malicious intruders, especially in an environment where the administration staff was not well versed in hardening an underlying operating system.

In Windows Server 2003, many of the features and services are installed, but disabled by default, making it more difficult for unauthorized users to exploit vulnerabilities. This is one way of improving server security, known as "reducing the attack surface."

Some of the changes in Windows Server 2003 include the following:

▶ After a default installation, many services are disabled, rather than enabled.

▶ Internet Information Services (IIS), the built-in web server, has been completely overhauled and is no longer installed by default. In addition, group policies can be implemented that prevent the unauthorized installation of IIS in your environment.

▶ Access control lists (ACLs) have been redefined and are stronger by default.

▶ Security can be defined by server and user roles.

▶ Public Key Infrastructure (PKI) Certificate Services has been enhanced and includes advanced support for automatic smart card enrollment, certificate revocation list (CRL) deltas, and more.

▶ Wireless security features, such as IEEE 802.1X, are supported.

▶ The Security Configuration Wizard, included in Windows Server 2003 Service Pack 1 (SP1), can further lock down security based on server role and function.

10

Windows Vista Security Improvements

Windows Vista complements Windows Server 2003 from the client perspective by supporting the security features embedded in Windows Server 2003. The following are among the more notable security features in Window Vista:

▶ Core system files and kernel data structures are protected against corruption and deletion.

▶ Software policies can be used to identify and restrict which applications can run.

▶ Wireless security features, such as IEEE 802.1X, are supported.

▶ Sensitive or confidential files can be encrypted using Bitlocker encryption as well as Encrypting File System (EFS).

▶ Communications can be encrypted using IP Security (IPSec).

▶ Kerberos-based authentication is integrated in the core logon process.

▶ Enhanced security devices such as smart cards and biometric devices are supported.

All of the security improvements are supported with Group Policy enhancements to the Windows Vista operating system, providing centralized policy setting and management.

Windows Firewall Protection

In today's messaging environments, users often have to be able to access their emails from noncorporate locations. Gone are the days of accessing email only from the office computer; many users now access their mail from hotels, client sites, or wireless network "hot spots" such as the local coffee house.

Supporting this "anytime, anywhere" availability is important, but organizations must work to minimize potential security risks that can come with enhanced functionality.

Because remote users are often utilizing equipment that is not configured by their organization's security administrators, this equipment can be more susceptible to viruses and intrusions. To minimize security risks, client computers should have the Windows Firewall installed and operating.

Windows Firewall provides a protective boundary that monitors information traveling between a computer and a network (including the Internet). Windows Firewall blocks "unsolicited requests," which are often the result of external users located on a network trying to access your computer. Windows Firewall also helps protect you by blocking computer viruses and worms that try to reach your computer through a network connection.

The Windows Firewall uses stateful packet inspection to monitor all communications to and from the computer and records the outbound connections made from the protected system. Windows Firewall can also be customized to allow exceptions based on an application or port as well as to log security events.

Utilizing Security Templates

Security templates are a practical and effective means to apply standardized security policies and configurations to multiple systems in an environment. These security templates can be customized to meet the minimum security requirements of a particular organization, and can be applied to client computers as well as to servers using the Security Configuration and Analysis Microsoft Management Console (MMC) snap-in.

By utilizing the automatic deployment of security templates to client PCs, administrators can ensure that computers are identically configured and utilize available security measures, even if the system is not able to be managed by Group Policy Objects (GPOs).

TIP

Microsoft provides several security templates based on functional roles within a network environment. These can easily be applied to client computers and servers alike. However, organizations often have unique needs that are not met completely by these default templates so, as a best practice, administrators should always customize the security template to address particular application and access needs.

Using the Security Configuration and Analysis Tool

The Security Configuration and Analysis tool is a utility that can apply security templates to computers. It compares a computer's security configurations against an administrator-defined security template, and reports any differences found between the two. Furthermore, when the security configuration on the computer does *not* match the settings specified in the template, you can use the tool to update the system accordingly.

This utility has two modes of operation: analysis and configuration. An often-overlooked best practice is to analyze the system prior to making any changes so that you have a baseline frame of reference.

To run the Security Configuration and Analysis tool and analyze a computer, perform the following steps:

1. Start the Microsoft Management Console by selecting Start, Run, typing MMC in the Open text box, and then clicking OK.

2. Select File, click Add/Remove Snap-in, and then click Add.

3. In the Add Standalone Snap-in window, select Security Configuration and Analysis, click Add, and then click Close.

4. On the Add/Remove Snap-in page, click OK.

5. In the MMC, right-click the Security Configuration and Analysis snap-in, and select Open Database.

6. Type a database name, select a location to store the database, and then click Open.

10

7. Select a security template from those listed. If you want to implement a security template from another location, use the navigation tools to change to the directory where the .inf file is located. After you have selected the appropriate .inf file, click Open.

8. Back in the MMC, right-click the Security Configuration and Analysis snap-in, and choose Analyze Computer Now.

9. Enter a path to store the generated log file, and click OK to continue.

After the System Security Analysis has completed, the utility displays the security settings that are configured in the template you selected, and what is currently configured on the computer. Items for which the computer is not in compliance with the policy appear with a red "x" beside them, as shown in Figure 10.1.

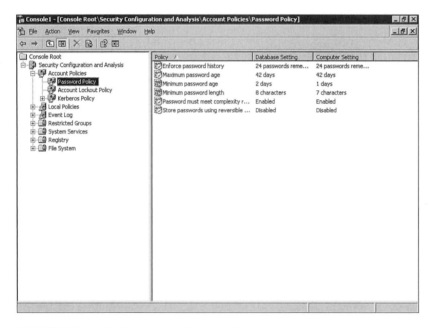

FIGURE 10.1   Reviewing security analysis.

If you want to configure the system with the security settings in the template, you can do so by performing a few extra steps:

1. In the MMC, right-click the Security Configuration and Analysis snap-in.

2. Select Configure Computer Now.

3. Enter a path for the error log to be written to, and then click OK.

Customizing Security Templates

An administrator might want to use custom security templates for several reasons. The organization might want a simple method of ensuring that attached computer systems meet with defined minimum security criteria. They might desire to ensure configured security settings that work for a particular application can be replicated to other servers of the same nature.

Larger organizations often have the need for customized security templates. For example, a member of the Internal Auditing department might need to regularly connect to employee hard drives, whereas the receptionist is only allowed basic Internet access. By applying different security settings to each of these machines, you can help the company ensure people have access to the data they need, and not to the resources they don't.

TIP

You can download and implement security templates provided by Microsoft, the National Security Agency (NSA), or the National Institute of Standards and Technology (NIST). These templates can be used as baselines, and can be customized to meet the needs of your particular environment. After being customized, you can distribute them to appropriate systems in your organization with minimal effort.

Windows Server 2003, Windows Vista, and Windows XP Professional are equipped with the Security Templates MMC snap-in that enables administrators to quickly and easily customize settings on individual systems. Loading this tool is similar to the Security Configuration and Analysis tool discussed previously. To add the snap-in, follow these steps:

1. Start the Microsoft Management Console by selecting Start, Run, typing MMC in the Open text box, and then clicking OK.

2. Select File, click Add/Remove Snap-in, and then click Add.

3. In the Add Standalone Snap-in window, select Security Templates, click Add, and then click Close.

4. On the Add/Remove Snap-in page, click OK.

When the Security Templates snap-in is expanded, it displays the default search path to where the built-in security templates are stored. By default, this is the c:\windows\ security\templates directory. Other paths can be opened to display other security templates that might reside on the system. Expand the default directory to see the available templates. Rather than editing these default templates, it is recommended that you select the one you are going to use as a baseline, right-click it, and save it as a new template.

After you have created the new template, expand it to display all of the modifiable security settings. From here, you can configure the template to apply the security settings you want.

10

After you have completed customizing the template, it is an easy process to save the file to an accessible network share, and then use the Security Configuration and Analysis tool to apply it to the appropriate systems.

Keeping Up with Security Patches and Updates

Applying service packs, updates, and hotfixes in a timely manner is critical to maintaining the security of an environment. Whether you are talking about a server operating system, an application such as Exchange Server 2007, a client operating system, or even client applications, keeping your systems up to date with the latest releases ensures that you are protected against known vulnerabilities.

Organizations often underestimate the importance of these updates, so let's look at them in a different light. These updates are released to protect against *known* vulnerabilities. That means that there is a good possibility that malicious users in the hacker community already know how to *exploit* them. So, there the system sits, not only does it have an unlocked door, but the criminals *know* it is unlocked.

In the past, updates often had to be manually implemented on a system-by-system basis and, for companies with hundreds (or thousands) of workstations, it proved to be a monumental task. These manual processes still exist, but rarely need to be used today.

With Windows Server 2003, Windows Vista, and Windows XP, utilities exist that allow you to automate this process and simplify the distribution of updates. Microsoft has provided several options: Windows Update, Microsoft Update, Microsoft Windows Server Update Services (WSUS), and Microsoft Systems Management Server (SMS). In addition, there are a variety of third-party applications that can assist you with this endeavor.

NOTE

In today's environments, distribution of updates is often considered the "easy" part. Automated methods of deployment have made the process fairly simple. However, one of the most important steps, and one of the most often overlooked, is the thorough and complete testing of updates in a lab environment before the release to a production environment. Strongly consider implementing a patch management system that includes adequate time and resources for testing.

Windows Update

Windows Update, located at http://www.microsoft.com/windowsupdate, is a website that scans a local system and determines whether it has the latest updates applicable to the operating system. Windows Update is a very useful tool when dealing with a small number of systems. One shortcoming of Windows Update is that it only addresses updates to the operating system—not to any applications installed on the computer. Windows Update was designed for Microsoft Windows 2000 SP2 and earlier. Those using later versions of the operating system (including Windows 2000 SP3 and higher, Windows 2003, Windows Vista, and Windows XP) can instead use the Microsoft Update discussed in the following section.

Microsoft Update

So, what are you to do for the other Microsoft applications on your system, including Microsoft Outlook? Enter Microsoft Update, located at http://update.microsoft.com. This website offers the same downloads available on the Windows Update site, plus the latest updates for Microsoft Office and other Microsoft applications.

When you visit the website, it scans your computer and allows you to review a list of available updates and select the ones you want to implement.

The site breaks down the available updates into categories, identifying those that are critical to the security and reliability of your computer as high-priority updates. Interestingly enough, updates to the antispam features of Microsoft Outlook are considered high-priority updates as well, showing that Microsoft has listened to the user community and no longer considers spam to be simply a "nuisance."

One other feature of the Microsoft Update website is the ability to review your update history. By selecting this link, you can see the update, the product it applied to, the status of the implementation, the date it was applied, and the method used to apply the patch—for example, Windows Update or Automatic Updates, which is discussed in the next section.

Like Windows Update, Microsoft Update is intended for managing one system at a time. As useful as it is for individual users and small environments, other alternatives should still be considered for larger organizations.

> **NOTE**
>
> You can remove an update by using the Add and Remove Programs applet in Control Panel. When this feature first appeared, it had the reputation of being somewhat unreliable. Sometimes, updates were removed and the system experienced problems afterward. However, this process has been greatly improved over the past several years and is significantly more stable and reliable now.

Automatic Updates

One of the most reliable, and least time consuming, methods of implementing updates from Microsoft is built in to Windows Server 2003, Windows Vista, and Windows XP. Known as *Automatic Updates*, this feature allows your system to automatically download and install high-priority updates, without manual intervention. Optional updates, however, still need to be implemented using other methods.

With Automatic Updates, shown in Figure 10.2, you can configure the utility to automatically download and install updates on a daily or weekly basis, at the time of day of your choice (for example, every Saturday at 2:00 a.m.).

Alternatively, you can select one of the following options:

- ▶ Download Updates for Me, But Let Me Choose When to Install Them.

- ▶ Notify Me But Don't Automatically Download or Install Them.

- ▶ Turn Off Automatic Updates.

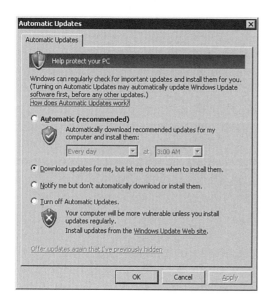

FIGURE 10.2   Configuration options for Automatic Updates.

When connecting to Microsoft Update or Windows Update, this method has a few draw-backs that must be mentioned. First, by automatically downloading and applying hotfixes, you are not afforded the opportunity to download and implement them in a test lab prior to deployment. Second, some high-priority updates require a reboot and might automatically restart your system without your prior approval.

To mitigate these shortcomings, you can configure Automatic Updates to *not* download and install updates directly from Microsoft, but can instead receive updates from a Microsoft Windows Server Update Services (WSUS) server, discussed next.

Windows Server Update Services (WSUS)

Realizing the increased administration and management efforts that challenge administrators of larger environments, Microsoft created the Microsoft Software Update Services (SUS), and the newer version called Windows Server Update Services (WSUS). This no-charge add-in component is designed to simplify the process of keeping computers in your organization up to date with the latest updates and service packs. WSUS communicates directly and securely with Microsoft to gather the latest security updates for a variety of Microsoft products, including Exchange Server, and enables administrators to manage the distribution of these updates to clients and servers in their environment. By utilizing WSUS, administrators can download updates, test them, and schedule the deployment to additional systems.

Utilizing Background Intelligent Transfer Service (BITS), the application allows administrators to download updates in the background, using available network bandwidth, to mini-mize the impact on their user community.

WSUS version 3.0 includes a new MMC-based user interface and has the following features:

- Advanced filtering and reporting

- Improved performance and reliability

- Branch office optimizations and reporting rollup

- Microsoft Operations Manager Management Pack

NOTE

You can find more information on WSUS and download the product from http://www.microsoft.com/windowsserversystem/updateservices/default.mspx.

Client-Based Virus Protection

One of the primary reasons why the installation of service packs and software updates in a timely manner is so important is the prevalence of computer viruses. Many viruses are written to exploit specific vulnerabilities that are found in computer operating systems and applications—both on clients and servers. Because Microsoft products are used so widely throughout the world, those who create viruses generally write them specifically to attack Microsoft products. This has resulted in the creation of an entire industry focused solely on protecting businesses and individuals from attack.

Companies truly concerned with protecting their environment from attack should use a multilayer approach to virus protection. By including antivirus applications on gateways, Exchange servers, and on the desktop, outbreaks can be prevented, or quickly detected and dealt with.

Gateway and Exchange server–level antivirus strategies are discussed in more depth in Chapter 11, so this section focuses for a moment on the client level.

There are many ways to distribute viruses, and one of the most effective is by installing unauthorized software on a workstation and turning it into a distribution point. This method might (or might not) utilize an existing messaging system. If it does not, gateway and Exchange-level antivirus methods might not be able to help at all. By implementing a separate antivirus solution on the desktop itself, you can minimize your exposure to attack.

An aggressive plan should be in place to keep antivirus signature files and engines up to date. Virus outbreaks that once took days (or weeks) to become widespread can now travel around the globe in a matter of hours. Antivirus updates (often referred to as "signature files") should be updated daily at a minimum and more often if your product supports it.

Windows Lockdown Guidelines and Standards

Microsoft has gone to great lengths to provide secure and reliable products. This endeavor was not accomplished in a vacuum—Microsoft has worked closely with companies, government agencies, security consultants, and others to identify and address security issues in the computer industry. Through this concerted effort and teamwork, security standards and guidelines have been developed that are applicable to not only Microsoft products, but also to the computing industry as a whole.

In addition to researching and implementing Microsoft recommended security standards and guidelines, responsible administrators can also use recommended best practices that have been compiled by the National Institute of Standards and Technologies (NIST) and the National Security Agency (NSA).

Both NIST and NSA provide security lockdown configuration standards and guidelines that can be downloaded from their websites (http://www.nist.gov and http://www.nsa.gov, respectively).

Exchange Server 2007 Client-Level Security Enhancements

As mentioned earlier, Exchange Server 2007 has several improved security features—especially when combined with Outlook 2007. Some of these features include the following:

▶ **Minimizing junk email**—The junk email folder, first introduced in Outlook 2003, helps protect users from junk email. Utilizing the Outlook 2007 junk email filter, Outlook 2007 can disable threatening links and warn you about possibly malicious content within an email message.

▶ **Antiphishing methods**—Exchange Server 2007 acts as the first scan on incoming email and works to determine the legitimacy of the message. If applicable, Exchange Server 2007 can disable links or uniform resource locators (URLs) present in the message to help protect users.

▶ **Information Rights Management (IRM)**—Exchange Server 2007 can help control the distribution of corporate data by preventing recipients from forwarding, copying, or printing confidential email messages. In addition, expiration dates can be applied to messages, after which they cannot be viewed or acted upon. IRM functionality is based on Microsoft Windows Rights Management Services (RMS) running on Windows Server 2003 servers.

▶ **Managed email folders**—Exchange Server 2007 helps organizations maintain compliance by applying a new approach to document retention. Utilizing managed email folders, users can see and interact with their messages in Outlook 2007 just as they would using regular mail folders, but the managed email folder applies retention, archive, and expiration policies defined by the administrator. Utilizing managed email folders, users and administrators can comply with regulations set by corporate policy or by external agencies.

In addition, Exchange Server 2007 continues to support several security technologies that were present in Exchange Server 2003, including the following:

- Support for MAPI (RPC) over HTTP or HTTPS, known as Outlook Anywhere, can be configured to use either Secure Sockets Layer (SSL) or NT LAN Manager (NTLM)–based authentication

- Support for authentication methods, such as Kerberos and NTLM

- Antispam features such as safe and block lists, as well as advanced filtering mechanisms to help minimize the number of unwanted emails that reach the end user

- Protection against web beaconing, which is used by advertisers and spammers to verify email addresses and determine whether emails have been read

- Attachment blocking by Exchange Server 2007 before it reaches the intended recipient

- Rights management support, which prevents unauthorized users from intercepting emails

Securing Outlook 2007

Exchange Server 2007 and Microsoft Outlook 2007 were designed to work together and, therefore, are tightly integrated. Utilizing these two products together can provide a formidable security front.

Outlook Anywhere

Prior to Exchange Server 2003, Outlook users who needed to connect to Exchange over the Internet had to establish a virtual private network (VPN) connection prior to using Outlook. The only alternatives were to open a myriad of remote procedure calls (RPC) ports to the Internet or make Registry modifications to statically map RPC ports. However, most companies felt that the benefits provided by these two "workarounds" were outweighed by the risks.

With Exchange Server 2003 and Outlook 2003, Microsoft provided an alternate (and very much improved) method for Outlook users to connect over the Internet. Known as RPC over HTTPS, this feature allowed Outlook 2003 users to access their mailboxes securely from remote locations utilizing the Internet and an HTTPS proxy connection. This feature reduced the need for VPN solutions, while still keeping the messaging environment secure.

In Exchange Server 2007, this functionality is known as Outlook Anywhere, and Microsoft has improved the functionality and greatly reduced the difficulty of deployment and management of the feature.

Outlook Anywhere can be used with both Outlook 2007 and Outlook 2003 clients. Outlook Anywhere provides the following benefits:

- Users can access Exchange servers remotely from the Internet.

- Organizations can use the same URL and namespace that is used for Exchange ActiveSync and Outlook Web Access.

▶ Organizations can use the same SSL server certificate that is used for Outlook Web Access and Exchange ActiveSync.

▶ Unauthenticated requests from Outlook are blocked and cannot access Exchange servers.

▶ Clients must trust server certificates, and certificates must be valid.

▶ No VPN is needed to access Exchange servers across the Internet.

NOTE

For a Windows client to use this feature, the system must be running Windows XP SP1 or higher or Windows Vista.

Preparing Your Environment for Outlook Anywhere

Enabling Outlook Anywhere in an Exchange Server 2007 environment is a very straightforward process, and can be done using either the Exchange Management Console or the Exchange Management Shell. However, prior to enabling the product, you must perform the following procedures:

1. Install a valid SSL certificate from a trusted certificate authority (CA).

NOTE

When you install Exchange Server 2007, you have the option of installing a default SSL certificate that is created during the Exchange setup process. However, this certificate is *not* a trusted SSL certificate. It is recommended that you either install your own trusted self-signed SSL certificate, or trust the default SSL certificate that is created during the Exchange setup process.

2. Install the RPC over HTTP Windows networking component. To do so, perform the following steps.

3. Log on to a server that has the Client Access server role installed. You must log on as an Exchange organization administrator and as a member of the local Administrators group on the server.

4. Select Start, Control Panel, and then double-click Add or Remove Programs.

5. Click Add/Remove Windows Components.

6. On the Windows Components page, select Networking Services, and click Details.

7. Select the RPC over HTTP Proxy check box, and then click OK.

8. Click Next and after the installation and configuration has completed, click Finish.

Enabling Outlook Anywhere from the Exchange Management Console

After the prerequisite steps have been met, you can enable Outlook Anywhere. To do so from the Exchange Management Console, perform the following steps:

1. Start the Exchange Management Console. In the console tree, expand the Server Configuration node, and then select the Client Access node.

2. In the action pane, click Enable Outlook Anywhere. This starts the Enable Outlook Anywhere Wizard.

3. In the External Host Name field, shown in Figure 10.3, type the appropriate external host name for your organization.

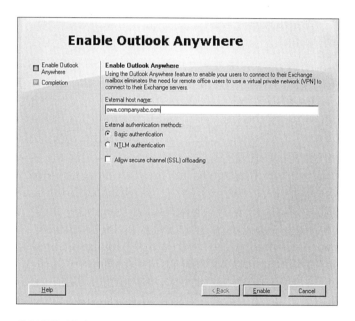

FIGURE 10.3   Configuring Outlook Anywhere.

4. Select the appropriate External Authentication Method, either Basic Authentication or NTLM Authentication.

5. If you are using an SSL accelerator and want to allow SSL offloading, select the Allow Secure Channel (SSL) Offloading check box.

CAUTION

Do *not* use the Allow Secure Channel (SSL) Offloading option unless you are sure you have an SSL accelerator that can handle SSL offloading. Selecting the option when you do not have this functionality prevents Outlook Anywhere from functioning properly.

10

6. Click Enable to apply the settings and enable Outlook Anywhere.

7. Review the completion summary to ensure there were no errors, and then click Finish to close the wizard.

Enabling Outlook Anywhere from the Exchange Management Shell

Alternatively, you can enable Outlook Anywhere from the Exchange Management Shell. To do so, run the following command from the shell:

```
enable-OutlookAnywhere -Server:'ServerName' -ExternalHostname:'ExternalHostName'
➥-ExternalAuthenticationMethod:'Basic' -SSLOffloading:$false
```

You can substitute "NTLM" for the ExternalAuthenticationMethod, and replace $false with $true if you are using SSL offloading.

Outlook Anywhere Best Practices

Consider the following best practices when deploying Outlook Anywhere:

▶ **Use at least one Client Access server per site**—In Exchange Server 2007, a site is considered to be a network location with excellent connectivity between all computers. You should have at least one Client Access server solely dedicated to providing client access to the Exchange Server 2007 server running the Mailbox server role. For increased performance and reliability, you can have multiple Client Access servers in each site.

▶ **Enable Outlook Anywhere on at least one Client Access server**—For each site, there should be at least one Client Access server with Outlook Anywhere enabled. This allows Outlook clients to connect to the Client Access server that resides closest to that user's Mailbox server. By configuring your environment in this manner, users connect to the Client Access server in the site with their Mailbox server utilizing HTTPS. This minimizes the risk of using RPC across the Internet, which can negatively impact overall performance.

Finally, you must configure your organization's firewall to allow traffic on port 443 because Outlook requests use HTTP over SSL. However, if you are already using either Outlook Web Access with SSL, or Exchange ActiveSync with SSL, you do not have to open any additional ports from the Internet.

TIP

Outlook users who will be using Outlook Anywhere as described in this section should be using Cached Exchange mode. Cached Exchange mode optimizes the communications between your Exchange servers and Outlook.

Encrypting Communications Between Outlook and Exchange

As a MAPI client, Outlook 2007 uses RPCs to communicate with Exchange Server 2007. RPCs are interprocess communications (IPC) mechanisms that can either use or not use encryption during the transfer of information. By default, Outlook 2007 encrypts data between Outlook and the Exchange server. However, Outlook 2003 does not have this security feature enabled by default.

To enable this feature in Outlook 2003, perform the following steps:

1. In Outlook 2003, select Tools, E-Mail Accounts.

2. Select View or Change Existing E-Mail Accounts, and then click Next.

3. Click Change and, on the next window, click More Settings.

4. Select the Security tab. Under the Security section, click the Encrypt Data Between Microsoft Office Outlook and Microsoft Exchange Server check box.

5. Click OK to close the window.

6. Click Next and then click Finish when you are done.

Authenticating Users

By default, both Outlook 2003 and Outlook 2007 use the credentials of the user who is currently logged on to the local computer to access the Outlook profile and mailbox. Both applications are also configured to first utilize Kerberos for the authentication process and, if this fails, utilize NT LAN Manager (NTLM). Administrators have the option of setting Outlook to only use Kerberos if they want to implement stronger security methods. The Kerberos/NTLM or NTLM Only options exist for backward compatibility with older systems. When using Kerberos, the user's credentials are encrypted when communicating with Active Directory for authentication.

To view or change the current authentication options in Outlook 2007, perform the following procedure:

1. In Outlook 2007, select Tools, Account Settings.

2. On the Account Settings page, select the email account, and click the Change icon.

3. On the Change E-Mail Account page, click More Settings.

4. Select the Security tab. Under Logon Network Security, select Kerberos Password Authentication from the drop-down box, and then click OK.

5. On the Change E-Mail Account page, click Next to complete the process, click Finish, and then click Close.

10

User Identification

An additional level of security can be applied to users accessing email through the Outlook client. In the event of a user closing Outlook, but not locking their computer or logging off the network, it is possible for an unauthorized user to access the system, start Outlook, and access the user's email.

It is possible to configure Outlook 2007 to require the user to input their username and password before accessing Outlook. To do so, follow the same steps detailed previously in the "Authenticating Users" section, and place a check mark in the Always Prompt for User Name and Password check box.

It should be noted that few organizations implement this security option, as most find that logging on and off the system properly provides adequate protection.

Blocking Attachments

A common and often effective way for viruses and malicious scripts to spread from user to user is through email. When a user receives a message with an attachment, simply opening the attachment can allow the virus to activate and, if proper security measures are not in place, the virus can do damage to the system or spread to other users.

To mitigate this threat, Microsoft has incorporated attachment blocking in Outlook and Outlook Web Access (OWA). By default, Outlook is configured to block attachments that contain file types that can run programs. Known as "executable" files, these blocked file types include those with .exe, .bat, .com, .vbs, and .js on the end of the filename.

It is important to note that this does not automatically protect you from being infected with a virus, as other file formats, including Microsoft Office files such as Word or Excel documents, can potentially contain viruses. However, implementing an antivirus solution on the client PC greatly reduces the possibility of such a file causing harm.

Users who are utilizing Outlook to send an attachment are notified when attaching an executable file that it is likely to be blocked by the recipient. An example of the warning message received is shown in Figure 10.4.

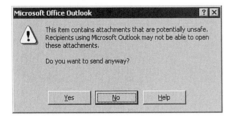

FIGURE 10.4   Outlook unsafe attachment warning.

If the user elects to send the message anyway, it might still be blocked on the receiving end.

Outlook does not provide any way for the end user to unblock these attachments. However, savvy users have found that, in many instances, they can rename the file to a nonexecutable extension (such as .txt) and send the file with instructions on how to rename the file back.

NOTE

File types can be categorized as Level 1 (the user cannot view the file) or Level 2 (the user can open the file only after saving it to disk). By default, Outlook classifies most executable file types as Level 1 and blocks the receipt of the file by users. There are no Level 2 file types by default. However, administrators can use Group Policy to manage how a file type is categorized. For example, if members of your organization regularly receive Visual Basic scripts (.vbs), you can change the categorization from Level 1 to Level 2 for that extension. Extreme caution should be used before changing this setting, as executable attachments are one of the most commonly used methods of distributing viruses.

Protecting Against Spam

Unsolicited email messages are often referred to as spam. These usually unwanted and often offensive messages are utilized as cheap advertising for unscrupulous organizations. In the past several years, the increase in spam traffic has surpassed even the most liberal estimates, and many studies have found that spam traffic accounts for up to 85%–90% of the messaging traffic on the Internet today.

Spam does not just affect your patience and productivity; it affects companies, Internet service providers, and anyone else who is hosting messaging services. The battle against spam is just beginning, and legal battles are well under way against both known spammers and companies that host the messaging services. In some cases, employees are suing employers on grounds that the employer has not taken adequate steps to protect them from offensive materials.

Exchange Server 2007 Antispam Features

Spammers are becoming increasingly more creative and cunning, frequently changing their email addresses, domain names, content, and more to get past a company's protective measures.

Microsoft has provided at least some basic form of antispam technologies in Exchange since version 5.5 and Outlook 98. For example, junk mail filters were provided to help identify messages that had either offensive material or other keywords indicating the message was spam. This form of spam prevention placed most, if not all, of the responsibility on the end user to block unwanted email messages.

10

Exchange Server 2007, when combined with Outlook 2007, provides several methods of reducing unwanted spam messages:

- ▶ Increase protection through integrated security technologies

- ▶ Improved email legitimacy assurance

- ▶ Distribution lists restricted to authenticated users

- ▶ Connection filtering

- ▶ Content filtering

- ▶ Frequent antispam updates

- ▶ Spam quarantine

- ▶ Recipient filtering

- ▶ SenderID

- ▶ Sender reputation

- ▶ IP reputation service

- ▶ Outlook junk email filter lists aggregation

Each of these methods is explained in Chapter 11.

Protecting Against Web Beaconing

A common and very popular format for email messages is Hypertext Markup Language, or HTML. This format is so popular because of the rich content that can be presented, including graphics, images, font formatting, and more. However, HTML-based messages can also present security problems and annoyances because of the ability to hide various codes and images within the message.

One such security problem is called web beaconing. *Web beaconing* is a term used to describe the method of retrieving valid email addresses and information on whether a recipient has opened a message. Advertisers, spammers, and the like utilize web beaconing to help them become more profitable and improve audience targeting. For instance, when an unsuspecting user opens an email message that contains a web beacon, the user's email address and possibly other information is sent to the solicitor, notifying them that they a) have reached a valid recipient and b) have reached a recipient who is willing to open their message before deleting it. The user is oblivious that their personal information has been given.

Outlook 2003 and 2007 can be used to block web beacons and, consequently, prevent the user's email address from ending up in the wrong hands. By default, if Outlook suspects that the content of a message could be used as a web beacon, it presents a pop-up window warning users that links to images, multimedia, or other external content have been blocked to help protect their privacy. The text content of the email message is viewable by the user, and the user is then presented with an option to unblock the content.

This enables the user to make a conscious decision of whether to display all the contents of the message.

This default setting is recommended because it is an excellent way to protect end users from unsolicited emails; however, it is possible to disable this option. To change the default settings in Outlook 2003, do the following:

1. In Outlook 2003, select Tools, Options.

2. Click the Security tab and then click Change Automatic Download Settings.

3. In the Automatic Picture Download Settings window, choose whether to download pictures or other content automatically. Outlook 2003 can also be customized to automatically download content from safe lists or from websites listed in the trusted Microsoft Internet Explorer security zones.

To change the default settings for automatic downloading of content in Outlook 2007, do the following:

1. Select Tools, Trust Center.

2. Click the Automatic Download tab, as shown in Figure 10.5. Select the desired settings from the available options. By default, all options are selected.

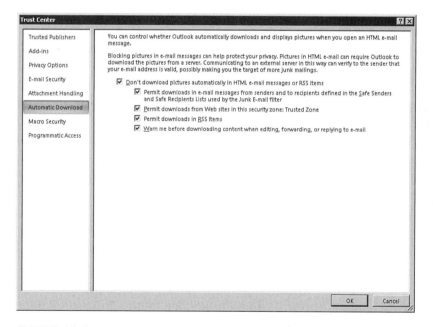

FIGURE 10.5   Configuring automatic picture downloads.

> **NOTE**
>
> If Automatic Picture Download is turned off, messages from or to email addresses or domain names on the Safe Senders and Safe Recipients lists are treated as exceptions and the blocked content is downloaded. Safe Senders and Safe Recipients lists are discussed in more depth later in this chapter.

Filtering Junk Mail

As mentioned earlier, junk mail filtering has been available in earlier versions of Exchange and Outlook. This feature has been improved with each new revision and is useful in minimizing the need for end users to configure junk mail filtering options. In fact, junk mail filtering is primarily controlled by Exchange administrators. However, some options can be configured by the users. With junk mail filtering, many unwanted messages can be segregated and set aside before they reach the user's Inbox.

Both Outlook 2003 and Outlook 2007 give you the ability to change the level of protection provided by your junk email filter. To do so, perform the following procedure:

1. Select Tools, Options.

2. On the Preferences tab, in the E-Mail section, click Junk E-Mail.

In addition, both Outlook 2003 and Outlook 2007 provide the following options:

- ▶ **No Protection (2003)** or **No Automatic Filtering (2007)**—Although the junk email filter does not perform any filtering on incoming mail, messages sent from the blocked senders list is still moved to the junk email folder.

- ▶ **Low** (the default setting)—Safe and block lists are consulted with this level of protection, but Outlook also searches for keywords and phrases in the message's subject and body.

- ▶ **High**—On this setting, the most aggressive filtering is performed. Although you can increase the amount of junk email captured by using this setting, there is the possibility of "false positives," which can result in valid messages being mistakenly filtered out.

- ▶ **Safe Lists Only**—This setting is the most restrictive because it allows only messages from preapproved senders to be delivered to the Inbox.

Both Outlook 2003 and Outlook 2007 offer you the additional option to Permanently Delete Suspected Junk E-Mail Instead of Moving It to the Junk E-Mail Folder. You should hesitate before using this option because you lose the ability to review the junk email folder to look for missing messages.

As illustrated in Figure 10.6, Outlook 2007 gives you the following options to battle email phishing attacks:

▶ **Disable Links and Other Functionality in Phishing Messages (Recommended)**—Using this option disables links, the "reply to" feature, and the "reply to all" feature on suspected phishing email messages.

▶ **Warn Me About Suspicious Domain Names in E-Mail Addresses (Recommended)**—Using this option warns you when a message comes from a domain name (for example, @mlcrosoft.com) that uses certain characters to make it appear to be a well-known domain.

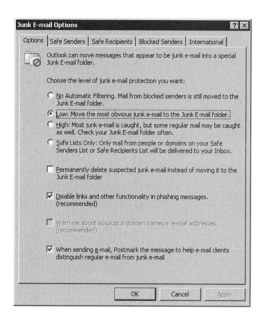

FIGURE 10.6   Outlook 2007 junk email options.

Filtering with Safe and Block Senders

Both Outlook 2003 and Outlook 2007 allow users to create and manage their own Safe Senders and Blocked Senders. As the name implies, the Safe Senders list is made up of user-defined addresses or domains, and messages from these addresses or domains will never be treated as junk email. Conversely, the Blocked Senders list is made up of user-defined email addresses or domain names, and all messages from them will automatically be treated as junk email.

In addition, both Outlook 2003 and 2007 provide the option to configure a Safe Recipients list. This option is useful when you are a member of an emailing list or group. By adding the list or group to your Safe Recipients list, any messages sent to the email addresses or domain names on that list will not be treated as junk email messages, regardless of the sender.

Both Outlook 2003 and Outlook 2007 allow you the option to automatically treat anyone in your Outlook Contacts list as a Safe Sender. This option is enabled on the Safe Senders tab by selecting the Also Trust E-Mail from My Contacts check box. By default, this feature is enabled.

In addition, with Outlook 2003 SP1 and later, there is an additional option. If there are people who are not in your Contacts list, but with whom you regularly correspond, you can select to Automatically Add People I E-Mail to the Safe Senders List. This option is also found on the Safe Senders tab.

To quickly add a sender, domain name, or mailing list to one of these lists, you can right-click the message, select Junk E-Mail, and choose the desired option.

Outlook Email Postmark

In Outlook 2007, the concept of the Outlook Email Postmark is introduced. This feature helps ensure that email placed in the client's Inbox is valid, and that email sent by Outlook 2007 will be trusted by the recipient's email client.

Microsoft has developed this new technology as part of their ongoing effort to minimize junk email. When using the Email Postmark, the sending computer performs a computation, and assigns the resulting work as a token that the email is valid. By making the computation and sending of the message time consuming and resource intensive, mass emailers will find the process detrimental to their productivity; however, the process does not change the user experience for normal email senders.

Exchange Server 2007, upon receiving a message with an Email Postmark, uses it as one method of verification of the reliability of the incoming message.

Blocking Read Receipts

Both Outlook 2003 and Outlook 2007 enable users to request read receipts for the messages that they send. Read receipts tell the sender that the intended recipient has at least opened the email. Automatically sending these read receipts can offer spammers (or others) more insight into your mail reading habits than you might want to share.

By default, both Outlook 2003 and Outlook 2007 block the automatic sending of read receipts. Instead, the recipient is prompted with a message that asks them if they want to send a response.

If you want, you can change this setting to Always Send a Response, or Never Send a Response. To change this behavior, do the following:

1. In Outlook, select Tools, Options.

2. On the Preferences tab, in the E-Mail section, click E-Mail Options.

3. Click the Tracking Options button.

4. Select your desired setting, and then click OK three times to exit the configuration.

Information Rights Management

Introduced in Microsoft Office 2003 products, Information Rights Management (IRM) helps organizations protect digital information from unauthorized use. By integrating with a Windows Server 2003 technology called Microsoft Windows Rights Management Services (RMS), IRM enables workers to define how a recipient can use the information contained in a Microsoft Office document.

Users can define exactly who can open, modify, print, forward, or take other actions with protected documents. In addition, users can specify an expiration date, after which the document cannot be viewed or acted upon.

> **NOTE**
>
> To create IRM-protected documents and email messages, the sending user must be using the Professional or Enterprise version of Office 2007. Users of Office Standard 2007 can still read and use IRM-protected documents, but cannot create them or apply policies to email messages.

IRM granularizes security for supported Microsoft Office applications such as Word, Excel, PowerPoint, and Outlook, as well as any other IRM-aware application. IRM is intended to complement other security technologies, such as Secure/Multipurpose Internet Mail Extensions (S/MIME) and Pretty Good Privacy (PGP) by securing the contents of information (contained in a document, for example), but it does not provide authentication to the information.

Securing Outlook Web Access

Outlook Web Access (OWA) provides the interface for users to access their mail across the Internet utilizing a web browser. With the implementation of OWA 2003, Microsoft improved the features and performance of the product until it was almost as powerful as the actual Microsoft Outlook client.

With OWA 2007, Microsoft has continued this trend, providing an improved user experience and enhanced security over previous versions.

Some of the security-related features that were included in OWA 2003, and remain in OWA 2007, include the following:

▶ Stripping of web beacons, referrals, and other potentially harmful content from messages

▶ Attachment blocking

▶ OWA forms-based (cookie) authentication

▶ Session inactivity timeout

10

► OWA infrastructure using IPSec and Kerberos

► Safe and block lists

In addition, Outlook Web Access 2007 provides features and improvements over OWA 2003. Some of these are listed here:

► **Improved logon screen**—In OWA 2003, there was the option to select a "private" logon, which increased the session timeout significantly. However, it was easy to forget to select this option when signing on. In OWA 2007, when you connect from a trusted machine, your previous "private" selection (and your username) is remembered on subsequent connections.

► **Junk email management**—OWA 2007 has improved the capabilities of the junk email filter by allowing users to manage their junk email settings from within OWA.

► **Protection from harmful content**—If an OWA 2007 user clicks a link that is embedded in an email message, and the link uses a protocol that is not recognized by OWA, the link is blocked, and the user receives a warning stating "Outlook Web Access has disabled this link for your protection."

Supported Authentication Methods

Client Access servers in Exchange Server 2007 support more authentication methods than Exchange Server 2003 front-end (OWA) servers did.

The following types of authentication are allowed:

► **Standard**—Standard authentication methods include Integrated Windows authentication, Digest authentication, and Basic authentication.

► **Forms-based authentication**—Using forms-based authentication creates a logon page for OWA. Forms-based authentication uses cookies to store user logon credentials and password information in an encrypted state.

► **Microsoft Internet Security and Acceleration (ISA) Server forms-based authentication**—By using ISA Server, administrators can securely publish OWA servers by using Mail server publishing rules. ISA Server also allows administrators to configure forms-based authentication and control email attachment availability.

► **Smart card and certificate authentication**—Certificates can reside on either a client computer or on a smart card. By utilizing certificate authentication, Extensible Authentication Protocol (EAP) and Transport Layer Security (TLS) protocols are used, providing a two-way authentication method where both the client and server prove their identities to each other.

Table 10.1 shows a comparison of authentication methods along with the security level provided relative to password transmission and client requirements.

TABLE 10.1   Authentication Methods for OWA Logon Options

Authentication Method	Security Level Provided	How Passwords Are Sent	Client Requirements
Basic authentication	Low (unless Secure Sockets Layer [SSL] is enabled)	Base 64-encoded clear text.	All browsers support Basic authentication.
Digest authentication	Medium	Hashed by using MD5.	Microsoft Internet Explorer 5 or later versions.
Integrated Windows authentication	Low (unless SSL is enabled)	Hashed when Integrated Windows authentication is used; Kerberos ticket when Kerberos is used. Integrated Windows authentication includes the Kerberos and NTLM authentication methods.	Internet Explorer 2.0 or later versions for Integrated Windows authentication. Microsoft Windows 2000 Server or later versions with Internet Explorer 5 or later versions for Kerberos.
Forms-based authentication	High	Encrypts user authentication information and stores it in a cookie. Requires SSL to keep the cookie secure.	Internet Explorer.

NOTE

When multiple methods of authentication are configured, Internet Information Services (IIS) uses the most restrictive method first. IIS then searches the list of available authentication protocols (starting with the most restrictive), until an authentication method that is supported by both the client and the server is found.

Disabling Web Beacons for Outlook Web Access

As previously mentioned in this chapter, web beaconing is a method used to retrieve valid email addresses and recipient information. Web beaconing is often used by unscrupulous advertisers and spammers to improve the accuracy and effectiveness of their spamming campaigns.

Exchange Server 2007 allows the disabling of web beacons for OWA users by utilizing one of two methods:

▶ Users can enable or disable web beacon content filtering from within OWA.

▶ Administrators can use the Exchange Management Shell to define the type of filtering that is used for web beacon content and enforce it for all users.

10

By default, web beacons are disabled for OWA users. To change the default setting in OWA:

1. Access OWA from a web browser.

2. Click Options.

3. Under Security, clear the Block External Content in HTML E-Mail Messages check box.

To use the Exchange Management Shell to configure web beacon filtering settings, perform the following command from the shell:

```
Set-OwaVirtualDirectory -identity "Owa (Default Web Site)"
➥-FilterWebBeaconsAndHtmlForms ForceFilter
```

This command configures the filtration of web beacon content in the Outlook virtual directory named OWA in the default IIS website. Possible values for the `FilterWebBeaconsandHtmlforms` setting are as follows:

▶ **UserFilterChoice**—Prompts the user to allow or block web beacons

▶ **ForceFilter**—Blocks all web beacons

▶ **DisableFilter**—Allows web beacons

Using Safe and Block Lists

OWA 2007 users can now manage their junk email settings from within OWA. Users can enable or disable junk email filtering, create and maintain Safe Senders, Blocked Senders, and Safe Recipient lists, enter email domains or Simple Mail Transfer Protocol (SMTP) addresses, and elect to trust email from their contacts.

> **NOTE**
>
> The option to "always trust contacts" does not function if the user has more than 1,024 contacts. Although this limitation will not be reached for most users, those with an exceptionally large number of contacts should be aware of the limitation.

To access the Junk E-Mail settings in OWA, select Options from the upper-right corner of the screen, and then select Junk E-Mail on the left side of the page.

Summary

As more and more organizations rely heavily on email as a primary communications tool, email security has become increasingly important. Some countries have even gone so far as to implement laws preventing the sending of unsecured email. The risk of an unauthorized or unintended third-party recipient capturing and reviewing corporate email messages is too great to be ignored, especially when there are preventative measures that can so easily and seamlessly be implemented.

Although client-level security is only one piece of the security puzzle, it is a very important one. Each of the three layers—client-level, server-level, and transport-level—must be addressed if you want to ensure your organization's messages are as safe as possible.

Fully implementing client-level security measures requires design and configuration of your operating systems (both client and server), your Exchange Server 2007 server, and your messaging client. In addition, strong antivirus and antispam measures must be implemented to protect your organization and users from malicious attacks.

Only by carefully addressing all of these areas can you ensure a secure messaging environment.

Best Practices

The following are best practices from this chapter:

- ▶ Use security templates provided by Microsoft, the National Security Agency (NSA), or the National Institute of Standards and Technology (NIST) as baselines for customizing the organization's security templates.

- ▶ Customize baseline security templates to reduce the attack surface of workstations and servers. However, implement adequate testing to ensure that required applications function as intended.

- ▶ Keep servers and client computers up to date with the latest service pack and security updates. Use automated processes whenever possible to ensure the timely application of updates.

- ▶ Consult Microsoft, NIST, and NSA security guidelines for securing the operating system.

- ▶ Implement antivirus software in a layered configuration, implementing gateway, server, and client-level antivirus solutions.

- ▶ Authenticate clients to the Exchange Server messaging infrastructure, using Kerberos whenever possible.

- ▶ Outlook Anywhere clients should use Cached Exchange mode to increase performance and minimize network impact whenever possible.

- ▶ Combat spam by utilizing the protective features included in both Exchange Server and Outlook. Fortify these features with additional or third-party measures when necessary.

- ▶ Configure Outlook to always prompt you before sending a read receipt.

- ▶ Review and implement Information Rights Management technologies.

CHAPTER 11

Server and Transport-Level Security

Securing your Microsoft Exchange Server 2007 organization is a complex process. Two primary components that must be addressed are server-level and transport-level security. In brief, server-level security refers to protecting data that is physically stored on an Exchange server. Transport-level security, on the other hand, refers to protecting data as it is passed into or out of the Exchange server along your network.

When server administrators think of "security," server-level security measures are often the first that come to mind. Because people share information and collaborate by sending messages and attachments that often contain proprietary data, a company's Exchange server can house information that could be potentially damaging if it were to fall into the wrong hands. Server-level security focuses on protecting the data that resides on the Exchange servers from being accessed by nonauthorized users.

As this chapter shows, transport-level security is just as important. Not only does the server need to be secured, the content of information being sent and received by a server also needs to remain protected.

Considering the Importance of Security in an Exchange Server 2007 Environment

Security in a networking environment first starts with considering the importance of a security model within the networking environment. Part of the security model involves internal security practices, and a portion of the security model depends on the level of security built in to the technology products being implemented.

When implementing Exchange 2007 with security in mind, a lot of the security infrastructure is dependent on the security built in to the Windows 2003 network operating system as well as the Exchange 2007 messaging system. Microsoft plays an important role in establishing a secured messaging environment from which an organization can build its security infrastructure.

An organization must then assess its risks and develop a security strategy that is customized to address the risks identified by the organization. Within Exchange 2007, the administration function of the Exchange messaging system is based on administrative roles in which an administrator allocates roles and levels of security access to other administrators and support personnel in the organization.

Microsoft's Trustworthy Computing Initiative

As the largest software company in the world, Microsoft has always been a target for people who thrive on hacking computer systems, whether they are doing so simply for the challenge, or with malicious intent.

On January 15, 2002, Bill Gates announced the "Trustworthy Computing Initiative" that focused the company in a new direction. The goal of this initiative was to create reliable, secure, and private technologies and committed the company to making products that protect user privacy.

Now, Trustworthy Computing is no longer an initiative; it is a corporatewide tenet that guides the development and maintenance of their products from the moment they are imagined until they are no longer supported. This new way of doing business has resulted in a significant reduction of publicly reported vulnerabilities in Microsoft products across the board.

Secure by Design

Under the Trustworthy Computing Initiative, a process has been implemented known as the Security Development Lifecycle, otherwise known as the SDL, which requires Microsoft developers to create formal threat models when they begin the design of a product. No longer are products envisioned and developed with potential security risks addressed as an afterthought, now all products, including Exchange 2007, are developed with an eye toward secure computing from the drawing board.

As an added measure, before a product ships, it is submitted to a final security review, or FSR, where a team of security experts review it to answer just one question—*From a security perspective, is this product ready to ship?*

Secure by Default

With older versions of Exchange (prior to Exchange Server 2003), the products were shipped with an "implement first, secure after" philosophy. Many services and functions were enabled by default, regardless of whether they would eventually be utilized in an environment.

With Exchange 2003, and now Exchange 2007, the opposite approach has been taken—by default, many services and functions are *disabled* at the time of installation, only to be enabled by an organization if the determination is made that the function is needed. Thanks to this mentality, organizations are less likely to have features unknowingly enabled that might present a security risk.

One such example is access to email via RPC over HTTP. To allow users to utilize this functionality, it must be enabled on each server where the user's mailbox resides. By default, this technology (now known as Outlook Anywhere) is disabled.

Secure by Deployment

Microsoft provides applications and documentation that enables information technology (IT) personnel to implement Exchange 2007 securely and successfully. These tools enable an administrator to ensure that all network prerequisites are met, and that the environment is properly configured and ready to accept the implementation of Exchange 2007.

Microsoft also provides training resources to ensure that administrators are adequately prepared to deploy Exchange 2007. These training resources should be reviewed by any organization implementing Exchange 2007, and should be made available to administrators prior to implementation of the product to ensure a successful deployment.

Assessing Your Risks

It has been said that "The only completely secure computer is one that is turned off—and even then, only if no one can find it."

As with most jokes, there is some underlying truth to the statement or it wouldn't be funny. Any computer that is accessible to authorized users is potentially accessible to malicious intruders. When designing security around particular subsets of data, you must strike a balance between security and usability—if you make the environment TOO secure, it is too difficult or time-consuming for valid employees to access the data.

In addition, an organization must consider the value of the data that they are trying to protect. For an email environment, this can be a particularly challenging task, as the actual value of the data contained can be difficult to assess. However, asking yourself "How much would it cost the organization if our email was destroyed, altered, or stolen?" and assigning an accurate monetary value to the data will help you determine how much you can feasibly spend to protect it.

The next step in assessing your risks is to analyze possible security vulnerabilities for the service or functionality with which you are working. The following is a list of some areas of security that you should take into consideration:

▶ **Viruses or Trojan horse messages**—Viruses have existed in the computer world long before the first email message was sent. However, just as email provides users with an easy method of communication, it also is an extremely efficient method of spreading malicious or troublesome code. Once considered the largest problem that email administrators had to face, viruses have been combated by an entire industry devoted to their prevention.

▶ **Spam**—The proliferation of unsolicited messages, often referred to as "spam" mail, has truly become the bane of the messaging world with recent estimates stating that spam accounts for 85%–90% of the messaging traffic on the Internet today. These unsolicited, usually unwanted, and often offensive advertisements cost companies and users billions of dollars annually in lost time and productivity. Unfortunately, because sending bulk messages to thousands (or millions) of recipients can be accomplished with very little expense, offending companies do not need a large response to maintain profitability. It is sad to note that as long as this method of advertising is profitable and effective, spam will be with us to stay. Fortunately, Exchange 2007 has several features to help alleviate the problem.

▶ **Address spoofing**—One tool that is commonly used by the distributors of both viruses and spam is known as *address spoofing*. By changing the From line in a Simple Mail Transfer Protocol (SMTP) message, users can often be fooled into opening a message that they think is from a friend or co-worker, only to find that the message originated somewhere else entirely. This method has been especially effective in the distribution of email worms. Because the message appears to come from a known associate, and often has an intriguing Subject line, the unwitting recipient opens the message and, if not properly protected, becomes a distributor of the virus to others.

▶ **Phishing**—Over the past several years, a relatively new type of fraudulent email has emerged. Known as *phishing*, this attack comes in the form of an official looking email message, often appearing to be from a reputable organization, such as a credit card company or a large electronics retailer. The message usually contains a link that, once clicked, brings up an official looking website—often an exact replica of the official site that is being mimicked. However, the fraudulent site has one purpose, to fool you into giving away personal information, such as passwords, credit card numbers, or Social Security numbers. With this information in hand, the offending party can steal your identity, make charges to your credit card, or otherwise profit from your loss.

Exchange Server 2007 Administrative Roles

In Exchange 2000 Server and Exchange Server 2003, there was not a clear separation between administrators of users in Active Directory (AD) and the administration of Exchange recipients. Utilizing the previous model, based on predefined security roles, administrators had to be granted high-level permissions to the Active Directory environment to perform even relatively simple Exchange recipient–related tasks. In addition, the majority of Exchange recipient management had to be accomplished utilizing the Active Directory Users and Computers utility.

Exchange 2007 has implemented much greater logical distinction between these two environements. Utilizing newly designed administrator roles, organizations can assign administrators permission to perform Exchange-related tasks, while minimizing their ability to directly modify the Active Directory itself. Furthermore, the majority of mail-related configuration items can be administered directly from the new Exchange Management Console and Exchange Management Shell.

This is important to Exchange security because you no longer have to grant administrative privileges over your Exchange environment to domain administrators (who might not have worked with Exchange at all). On the other side of the same coin, Exchange administrators can be granted permissions over the Exchange environment, yet remain restricted in Active Directory. This enables organizations to limit areas of responsibility based on proper administrator aptitude and abilities.

Table 11.1 lists the new Exchange 2007 administrator roles and the Exchange permissions associated with each.

TABLE 11.1   Exchange 2007 Administrative Roles

Administrator Role	Members	Member of	Exchange Permissions
Exchange Organization Administrators	Administrator, or the account that was used to install the first Exchange 2007 server	Exchange Recipient Administrators Administrators local group of <Server Name>	Full control of the Microsoft Exchange container in Active Directory
Exchange Recipient Administrators	Exchange Organization Administrators	Exchange View-Only Administrators	Full control of Exchange properties on Active Directory user object
Exchange Server Administrators	Exchange Organization Administrators	Exchange View-Only Administrators Administrators local group of <Server Name>	Full control of Exchange <Server Name>
Exchange View-Only Administrators	Exchange Recipient Administrators	Exchange Recipient Administrators	Read access to the Microsoft Exchange container in Active Directory.
	Exchange Server Administrators (<Server Name>)	Exchange Server Administrators	Read access to all the Windows domains that have Exchange recipients.

The Exchange administrator roles and the permissions associated with each are covered in greater detail in Chapter 18, "Administering an Exchange Server 2007 Environment."

Components of a Secure Messaging Environment

Although network administrators generally focus on server-level security, which protects data stored on the server itself, the administrators must keep in mind that the server they are attempting to protect is connected to a local area network (LAN), and usually the Internet, to allow it to function to its full potential.

To properly protect a server from attack, administrators should implement multiple layers of defense, each reinforcing the other, and each specializing in repelling certain types of attacks. Firewalls, network perimeters, accessibility options for users, security policies, and more are integral components that must be well designed and properly implemented to be effective.

A phrase coined by the military, "defense in depth," is used to describe this strategy. Defense in depth increases a server's security by creating multiple layers of protection between the server and potential attackers. An attacker who successfully maneuvers through the first line of defense finds himself faced with a second challenge, one requiring different skills and tools to bypass, and then a third, and so on.

Hardening Windows Server 2003

Exchange Server 2007 is designed to run on Windows Server 2003. No matter what steps you take to secure your Exchange Server 2007 servers, if the underlying operating system (OS) is not secure, the Exchange installation is vulnerable to attack. Therefore, it is critical that you secure Windows Server 2003 by utilizing a combination of your organization's security standards and industry best practices.

Layered Approach to Server Security

When discussing security measures, whether server-level or transport-level, protective measures work best when they are applied in layers. For example, if a thief were to attempt to steal your car, it might not be very challenging if all they had to do was break the window and hot-wire the vehicle. However, if you were to add a car alarm, or install an ignition block that requires a coded key, the level of difficulty is increased. Each of these obstacles takes additional time, as well as additional skill sets, to overcome.

This same principle applies to both server- and transport-level security methods. By applying multiple layers of security, you can effectively decrease the likelihood of a malicious user successfully tampering with your systems.

Many security features are already built in to Windows Server 2003. Among these are the following:

▶ **Kerberos authentication**—Windows Server 2003 uses the Kerberos version 5 authentication protocol to provide a mechanism for authentication between a client and a server, or between two servers.

▶ **NTFS file security**—Utilizing the NTFS file system provides improved performance and reliability over traditional file allocation table (FAT) file systems. NTFS has built-in security features, such as file and folder permissions and the Encrypting File System (EFS).

Windows Server 2003 also includes built-in security tools and features to help secure your environment. Among these are object-based access control, automated security policies, auditing, Public Key Infrastructure (PKI), and trusts between domains.

Physical Security Considerations

The first layer of security for any server, and one that is often overlooked, is preventing physical access to the computer. It takes very little skill or knowledge to simply unplug a computer or to remove it from the network; however, this could have a serious impact on your environment even if the intruder was not able to access your data. In addition, just as security professionals have tools and utilities to assist with the defense of computer systems, hackers have tools and utilities to assist them with their attacks. If a hacker can get physical access to a server, he can use a variety of methods to circumvent basic password security.

At a minimum, servers should be physically secured behind locked doors, preferably in an environmentally controlled area.

Some common physical security methods are the following:

▶ Configure the server BIOS so that it will not boot from a floppy disk drive or CD-ROM.

▶ Password protect the BIOS so that it cannot be reconfigured.

▶ Lock the server case to prevent access to the BIOS jumpers on the motherboard.

▶ Enclose the server in a locked cage or locked room that has limited access.

Restricting Logon Access

All servers should be configured so that only administrators can log on physically to the console. By default, Exchange Server 2003 does not allow any members of the domain users group local logon privileges. This prevents nonadministrators from logging on to the server even if they can gain physical access to the server.

Auditing Security Events

Auditing is a way to gather and keep track of activity on the network, devices, and entire systems. By default, Windows Server 2003 enables some auditing, but there are many additional auditing functions that must be manually turned on to be used. This control allows your system to easily be customized to monitor those features that you desire.

Although the primary use of auditing methods is to identify security breaches, this feature can also be used to monitor suspicious activity and to gain insight into who is accessing the servers and what they are doing. Windows Server 2003's auditing policies must first be enabled before activity can be monitored.

Auditing Policies

Audit policies are the basis for auditing events on a Windows Server 2003 system. Bear in mind that auditing can require a significant amount of server resources and can potentially slow server performance, especially if the server does not have adequate memory or CPU bandwidth available. Also, as more and more data is collected by auditing policies, it can require a significant amount of effort to evaluate. Administrators should be cautious, as gathering too much data can sometimes be overwhelming, effectively diminishing the desired benefits. As such, it is important to take the time to properly plan how your systems will be audited.

Audit policies can track successful or unsuccessful event activity in a Windows Server 2003 environment. These policies can audit the success and failure of events. The types of events that can be monitored include the following:

- **Account logon events**—Each time a user attempts to log on, the successful or unsuccessful event can be recorded. Failed logon attempts can include logon failures for unknown user accounts, time restriction violations, expired user accounts, insufficient rights for the user to log on locally, expired account passwords, and locked-out accounts.

- **Account management**—When an account is changed, an event can be logged and later examined. Although this pertains more to Windows Server 2003 than Exchange Server 2007, it is still very relevant because permissions granted in Active Directory can have an effect on what data or services an individual has access to in Exchange.

- **Directory service access**—Whenever a user attempts to access an Active Directory object that has its own system access control list (SACL), the event is logged.

- **Logon events**—Logons over the network or by services are logged.

- **Object access**—The object access policy logs an event when a user attempts to access a resource such as a printer or shared folder.

- **Policy change**—Each time an attempt to change a policy is made, the event is recorded. This can apply to changes made to user rights, account audit policies, and trust policies.

- **Privilege use**—Privileged use is a security setting and can include a user employing a user right, changing the system time, and more. Successful or unsuccessful attempts can be logged.

- **Process tracking**—An event can be logged for each program or process that a user launches while accessing a system. This information can be very detailed and take a significant amount of resources.

- **System events**—The system events policy logs specific system events, such as a computer restart or shutdown.

The audit policies can be enabled or disabled through either the local system policy or Group Policy Objects (GPOs).

To open the Group Policy Object Editor, which is a snap-in to the Microsoft Management Console (MMC), perform the following steps:

1. Click Start, Run, type MMC in the Open text box, and click OK.

2. In the MMC Console, click File, Add/Remove Snap-in.

3. On the Add/Remove Snap-in page, click Add.

4. Select the Group Policy Object Editor, and then click Add.

5. Under the Group Policy Object section, click Browse, and select the default domain policy. Click OK to continue, and then click Finish.

6. Close the Add Standalone Snap-in page by clicking Close, and then click OK to continue. On the Mail Flow Setting tab, select Message Delivery Restrictions and click Properties.

7. Check the Accept Messages: From Authenticated Users Only check box.

Audit policies are located within the `Computer Configuration\Windows Settings\Security Settings\Local Policies\Audit Policy` folder of the Group Policy Object Editor, as shown in Figure 11.1.

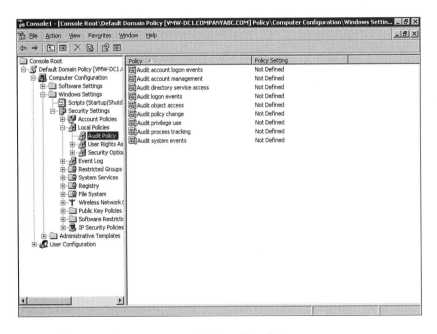

FIGURE 11.1   Windows Server 2003 audit policies.

Keeping Services to a Minimum

Depending on the role that an Exchange Server 2007 server will fulfill, not all services that are installed by default are necessary for the server to function. It is considered a best practice to limit the number of entry points (services) into a server to only those required. Any services that are not necessary for the system to operate properly should be disabled. Although this can be done manually on a server-by-server basis, it can also be performed using a customized security template to ensure all servers in your environment are configured properly.

Locking Down the File System

Files stored on a Windows Server 2003, including mail databases, are only as secure as the permissions that are assigned to protect them. As such, it is good to know that Windows Server 2003 (for the first time in a Microsoft operating system) does not grant the *Everyone* group full control over share-level and NTFS-level permissions by default. In addition, critical operating system files and directories are secured to disallow their unauthorized use.

Despite the overall improvements made, a complete understanding of file-level security is recommended to ensure that your files are properly protected.

> **NOTE**
>
> For increased file-level security, the Exchange Server 2007 installation process requires that partitions on the underlying operating system are formatted as NTFS.

Using the Microsoft Baseline Security Analyzer

The Microsoft Baseline Security Analyzer (MBSA) is a tool that identifies common security misconfigurations and missing hotfixes. This information is gathered via local or remote scans of Windows systems. MBSA allows administrators to have the ability to scan a single Windows system and obtain a security assessment, as well as a list of recommended corrective actions. In addition, administrators can use the MBSA tool to scan multiple functional roles of a Windows-based server on the network for vulnerabilities. This allows administrators to ensure systems are up to date with the latest security-related patches.

Figure 11.2 shows a sample output from the MBSA.

The MBSA can be downloaded from the Microsoft website at http://www.microsoft.com/mbsa.

Implementing Industry Standards and Guidelines

As discussed previously, Microsoft has gone to great lengths to provide secure and reliable products. Moreover, it has worked closely with companies, government agencies, security consultants, and others to address security issues in the computer industry.

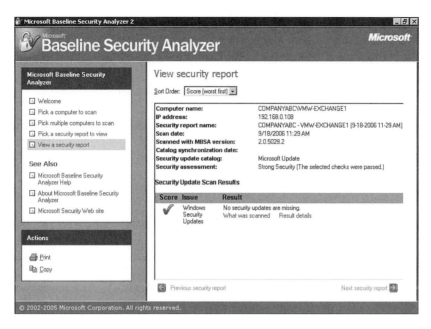

FIGURE 11.2   MBSA sample output.

In addition to Microsoft security standards and guidelines, it is advisable that organizations use recommended best practices compiled by the National Institute of Standards and Technologies (NIST) and the National Security Agency (NSA). Both NIST and NSA provide security lockdown configuration standards and guidelines that can be downloaded from their websites (http://www.nist.gov and http://www.nsa.gov, respectively).

Using the Security Configuration Wizard

The Security Configuration Wizard (SCW) is an attack-surface reduction tool for the Windows Server 2003 with Service Pack 1 or later. The SCW guides administrators in creating security policies based on the minimum functionality required for a server's role or roles.

SCW reviews the computer configuration, including but not limited to, the following:

- ▶ **Services**—SCW limits the number of services in use.

- ▶ **Packet filtering**—SCW can configure certain ports and protocols.

- ▶ **Auditing**—Auditing can be configured based on the computer's role and the organization's security requirements.

- ▶ **Internet Information Services (IIS)**—SCW can secure IIS, including web extensions and legacy virtual directories.

- ▶ **Server roles and tasks**—The role (file, database, messaging, web server, and so on), specific tasks (backup, content indexing, and so on), and placement in an environment of a computer is a critical component in any lockdown process or procedure.

Application services are also evaluated from products such as Exchange Server, SQL Server, ISA Server, SharePoint Portal Server, and Operations Manager.

CAUTION

The SCW is a very flexible and powerful security analysis and configuration tool. As a result, it is important to keep control over when and how the tool is used because system performance can be greatly degraded while the wizard is running. Equally important is testing possible configurations in a segmented lab environment prior to implementation. Without proper testing, environment functionality can be stricken or completely locked.

The SCW is used to assist in building specific security-related policies and to analyze computers against those policies to ensure compliance. SCW actually combines many of the security-related tasks performed by several other Microsoft security tools. For instance, SCW can take existing security templates created from the Security Configuration and Analysis tool and expand upon the restrictions to meet an organization's security policy requirements. In addition, SCW can analyze computers for any security updates that are needed, integrate with Group Policy, and provide a knowledge base repository.

Installing the Security Configuration Wizard

After you have installed Windows Server 2003 SP1 or higher, you are ready to install SCW. To install the wizard, do the following:

1. In Control Panel, double-click Add or Remove Programs.

2. Click Add/Remove Windows Components, and then select the Security Configuration Wizard check box.

3. Click Next to install the utility.

Running SCW

The SCW is installed in the Administrative Tools section of the Start menu. When you run the SCW, you will have an opportunity to select what roles the server plays. Note that the SCW has already selected the roles that it is aware of, as shown in Figure 11.3.

The SCW continues, giving you the opportunity to select client features (such as domain name system [DNS], Dynamic Host Configuration Protocol [DHCP], or the Automatic Update Client), and installed options (such as a global catalog, Windows Firewall, or time synchronization). Finally, there might be an additional screen for additional services. After you have selected all of the appropriate features, you must confirm service changes. A sample of the changed services can be seen in Figure 11.4.

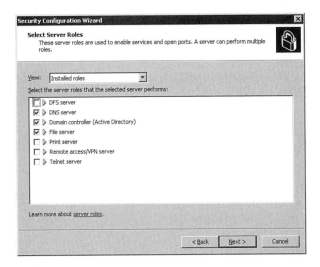

FIGURE 11.3   Selecting server roles.

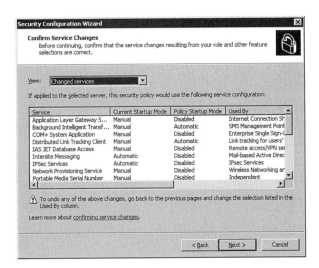

FIGURE 11.4   Confirming changed services.

The SCW continues through network security changes (locking down unused ports), Registry settings, and configuring policy auditing. After finishing, you have the option to apply the security policy to the computer immediately, or save it to apply to this server (or other servers) later.

Securing Servers with Security Templates

Security templates are a practical and effective means to apply security policies and configurations to Exchange servers. Although security templates are provided with

Windows Server 2003, it is recommended to customize them prior to applying them using the Security Configuration and Analysis Microsoft Management Console (MMC) snap-in.

This not only ensures that computers are identically configured with the same security configurations, but it also is an easy way to configure appropriate security measures for those computers that are not managed using GPOs.

> **NOTE**
>
> Microsoft creates Exchange-specific security templates and distributes them through their website. However, at the time of this writing, the security templates for Exchange Server 2007 have not yet been released.

Keeping Up with Security Patches and Updates

One of the least glamorous, but most important, security measures an organization can take is to ensure all of their products have the latest security patches implemented in a timely fashion. Applying service packs, security updates, and hotfixes for the operating system, as well as applications such as Exchange 2007, are crucial to maintaining a secure environment. As security shortcomings are identified, these service packs and hotfixes close the holes, often before they become publicly known, effectively protecting your environment from malicious users.

> **NOTE**
>
> Thoroughly test and evaluate service packs and hotfixes in a lab environment before installing them on production servers. Also, install the appropriate service packs and hotfixes on each production server to keep all systems consistent.

Windows Update

Windows Update is a web service, accessed in Microsoft Internet Explorer (Tools, Windows Update) that scans a local system and determines if the system has all current updates installed. This tool is extremely useful on individual systems, but can be time consuming when used to update multiple systems within an organization.

Windows Server Update Services

Windows Server Update Services (WSUS), an upgrade from its predecessor Software Update Services (SUS), minimizes administration, management, and maintenance of small- to midsized organizations by allowing them to communicate directly and securely with Microsoft to gather the latest security updates and service packs. WSUS is available for Windows Server 2003 and for Exchange servers.

The primary differences between WSUS and its predecessor are as follows:

▶ Support for a greater number of products, including service pack updates

▶ The ability to target computers using Group Policy or scripts

▶ Reports on update installation status

▶ Performs basic hardware inventory

With WSUS, the updates are downloaded from Microsoft to a local WSUS server. They can then be distributed to a lab environment for testing, or to targeted production servers. After being tested and approved, WSUS can be used to automatically distribute the updates thoughout your environment. By utilizing this service, updates can be downloaded from Microsoft once, and distributed locally, saving a significant amount of bandwidth when compared to hundreds (or thousands) of systems each downloading the updates themselves.

Establishing a Corporate Email Policy

Not all misuse of organizational email systems comes from external sources. Employees improperly utilizing a messaging system can put a company at risk as well, either by overloading the sytem, passing confidential data to nonauthorized personnel, or passing material that is offensive in nature, potentially exposing the organization to lawsuits from other personnel.

Established and documented corporate email policies are used to govern and enforce the appropriate use of the messaging environment. However, like most security policies, they cannot be effective if they are not created, approved, implemented, and communicated to the user community.

> **NOTE**
>
> Corporate email policies not only define how the system can and should be used; they also limit an organization's liability in the event of misuse.

The following are possible considerations and guidelines to include in the corporate email policy:

▶ **Personal usage**—The policy should state whether emails of a personal nature are accepted and, if so, to what extent. Some companies place a limit on the number of personal emails that can be sent each day. Others require personal emails to be stored in a separate folder within the email system. Most companies allow the sending and receiving of personal emails because this is often less time consuming than requiring employees to access external mail sources for personal communications.

▶ **Expectation of privacy**—A corporate email policy should plainly state that the messages contained within the system are the property of the organization, and that no expectation of privacy is implied. Email records can be subpoenaed, mailboxes can be reviewed for appropriate use, or data can be retrieved in the event of the termination of someone's employment. By setting the expectation up front, you can make it clear to your users that the email system is a tool for their use, but the messages contained do not belong to them.

▶ **Email monitoring**—If the organization monitors the content of its employees' emails, this should be stated in the email policy. Most countries and states allow the monitoring of corporate email by authorized individuals, as long as the employee has been made aware of the policy.

▶ **Prohibited content**—The policy should state that the email system is not to be used for the distribution of offensive or disruptive messages. This includes messages containing inappropriate content such as comments about race, religion, gender, or sexual orientation. The policy should also clearly state that pornographic pictures or emails with sexual content will not be tolerated, as these items are commonly the cause of offense between employees. The policy should mandate that employees receiving any such materials should report them to their supervisor or another appropriate entity for review immediately.

▶ **Confidential data**—Employees should not use the messaging system to discuss sensitive matter, such as potential acquisitions or mergers. Corporate secrets or other proprietary data should not be sent either, as an inadvertent forward could allow the sensitive data to pass to inappropriate personnel.

▶ **Email retention policies**—Many organizations, especially government, health-care, and financial institutions, are required by law to meet or exceed certain email retention policies. These policies should be clearly stated and meticulously enforced. Allowances should be made for employees to save messages of a critical nature—often companies allow them to be saved in separate folders to avoid automatic deletion.

▶ **Point of contact**—The email policy should clearly state where employees can go to have any questions about the corporate email policy answered.

Bear in mind, a corporate email policy that is unknown to the user community is not an effective one. The policy should be distributed to the users in a variety of ways, such as posting on an intranet site, in employee handbooks, on break room bulletin boards, or in company newsletters.

Securing Exchange Server 2007 Through Administrative Policies

Whereas a corporate email policy specifically governs the use of the messaging system for users, administrative policies govern the operation and usage of the messaging system in general. Many best practices have been worked out over the years, some of which are as follows:

▶ **Administrative and operator accounts should not have mailboxes**—Many viruses and email worms rely on the permissions of the authenticated user to perform. If the user opening the message has administrative access to the computer, there is a much greater potential for danger.

▶ **Grant permissions to groups rather than users**—By granting permissions to groups, rather than users, you can quickly grant or deny access to a wide range of resources with one change. For example, if your Human Resources department has hundreds of files, in dozens of directories throughout your network, you would have to add (or remove) an individual from the permissions from *each* of these folders when they join or depart the team. However, by granting the permissions instead to an HR group, and then giving the *group* permissions, you can now modify access simply by adding the user to, or removing them from, the group.

▶ **Require complex (strong) passwords for all users**—If left to their own devices, many users select passwords that are easy for them to remember. However, this behavior results in passwords that are also very easy for malicious users to crack. By requiring complex passwords, consisting of upper- and lowercase letters, numbers, and special characters, the likelihood of a breach of security is greatly reduced.

▶ **Require Secure Sockets Layer (SSL) for HTTP, POP3, IMAP4, NNTP, and LDAP clients**—The SSL encryption protects confidential or personal information sent between a client and a server. The SSL protocol uses a combination of public-key and symmetric-key encryption. Symmetric-key encryption is much faster than public-key encryption; however, public-key encryption provides better authentication techniques.

▶ **Set policies globally when possible**—Rather than setting policies for individual users or groups, companywide policies should be set, whenever possible, at a global level to ensure compliance.

Securing Groups

An important step in securing your messaging environment is to secure distribution and mail-enabled security groups. For instance, CompanyABC is a medium-sized company with 1,000 users. To facilitate companywide notifications, the HR department created a distribution group called "All Employees," which contains all 1,000 employees. By default, there are no message restrictions for new groups, meaning that anyone can send to this list. If CompanyABC has an Internet Mail SMTP Connector, this group will also have an SMTP address.

Consider what would happen if a new user sent an email to "All Employees" advertising a car for sale. Let's take it one step further and imagine that the user sent it with a read receipt and delivery notification requested. Thousands of messages can now be generated from this one mistake and could negatively impact server performance.

Often, intentions are not as innocent as the new user simply making a mistake. Sending repeated email messages to mail-enabled groups with large memberships is sometimes used in an attempted denial of service (DoS) attack. The attacker sends an SMTP message to the "All Employees" group with a delivery notification receipt requested and spoofs the "Return to" address with the same SMTP address used for the distribution group. So, 1,000 messages are sent, and 1,000 delivery notifications are returned—each of which is then sent to all 1,000 users in the group! From this one spoofed message, the net effect is $(1 + 1000) + (1000 * 1000)=1,001,001$ messages! By spoofing the distribution list and including a delivery notification receipt, this single email results in over 1 million messages processed by the system.

Fortunately, for this easy problem, there is an even easier solution. Exchange Server 2007 allows you to configure message restrictions on your distribution groups.

To secure distribution groups so that only authenticated users can use it, do the following:

1. Open the Exchange Management Console.

2. In the console tree, under Recipient Configuration, click Distribution Group.

3. In the results pane, select the distribution group you want to modify, and then click Properties.

4. On the Mail Flow Settings tab, highlight Message Delivery Restrictions, and click Properties.

5. Ensure there is a check in the Require That All Senders Are Authenticated check box.

6. Click OK when finished, and then click OK again to exit the configuration screen.

In addition, an administrator can further restrict the usage of this distribution group by allowing only a specific individual or security group to use it.

To restrict access to the distribution group to a specific user or group, do the following:

1. Open the Exchange Management Console.

2. In the console tree, under Recipient Configuration, click Distribution Group.

3. In the results pane, select the distribution group you want to modify, and then click Properties.

4. On the Mail Flow Settings tab, highlight Message Delivery Restrictions, and click Properties.

5. Under Accept Messages From, select the Only Senders in the Following List option button.

6. Click Add, and select the users or groups that are to have permission to send to the distribution group.

7. Click OK when finished, and then click OK again to exit the configuration screen.

An additional option allows you to configure the distribution list to reject messages from an individual or from members of a group. This setting is also configured using the Message Delivery Restrictions page.

Using Email Disclaimers

Email disclaimers are notices that are automatically appended to outgoing messages. These disclaimers are primarily intended to reduce liability, and to caution recipients not to misuse the information contained within. The following is a sample email disclaimer:

> The information contained in this message is intended solely for the individual to whom it is specifically and originally addressed. This message and its contents may contain confidential or privileged information. If you are not the intended recipient, you are hereby notified that any disclosure or distribution, or taking any action in reliance on the contents of this information, is strictly prohibited.

When implementing an email disclaimer, you should seek the review and approval of the disclaimer by the organization's legal department, if any.

Creating an Email Disclaimer in Exchange Server 2007

Email disclaimers are easily configured in the Exchange Management Console by performing the following actions:

1. Open the Exchange Management Console on the Hub Transport server.

2. In the console tree, click Organization Configuration, and then click Hub Transport.

3. In the results pane, click the Transport Rules tab, and then, in the action pane, click New Transport Rule.

4. In the Name field, enter the name of the disclaimer. If you have notes for this disclaimer, enter them in the Comments field.

5. If you want the disclaimer to be created in a disabled state, clear the Enabled check box. Otherwise, leave the Enabled check box selected. Click Next to continue.

6. In the Step 1. Select the Condition(s) dialog box, select all the conditions that you want to be applied to this disclaimer. If you want this disclaimer to be applied to all email messages, do not select any conditions in this step. However, if you want the disclaimer to only be applied to outgoing messages, select Sent to Users Inside or Outside the Corporation.

7. If you selected conditions in the previous step, in the Step 2. Edit the Rule Description (Click an Underlined Value) option, click each blue underlined word.

8. When you click a blue underlined word, a new window opens to prompt you for the values to apply to the condition. Select the values that you want to apply, or type the values manually. If the window requires that you manually add values to a list, type a value. Then click Add. Repeat this process until you have entered all the values, and then click OK to close the window.

9. Repeat the previous step for each condition that you selected. After you configure all the conditions, click Next.

10. In the Step 1. Select the Action(s) dialog box, click Append Disclaimer Text Using Font, Size, Color, and Fallback to Action if Unable to Apply.

11. In the Step 2. Edit the Rule Description (Click an Underlined Value) option, click each blue underlined word. Each word, except Disclaimer Text, is the default value for each field. The fields are Append (or Prepend), Disclaimer Text, Font, Font Size,

Font Color, and Fallback Action. Click Disclaimer Text and enter the text of your disclaimer.

12. When you click a blue underlined word, a new window opens to prompt you to select the items that you want to add or type values manually. When you are finished, click OK to close the window.

13. Repeat the previous step for each action that you selected. After you configure all the actions, click Next.

14. In the Step 1. Select the Exception(s) dialog box, select all the exceptions that you want to be applied to this rule. You are not required to select any exceptions.

15. If you selected exceptions in the previous step, in the Step 2. Edit the Rule Description (Click an Underlined Value) option, click each blue underlined word.

16. After you configure any exceptions, click Next.

17. Review the Configuration Summary. If you are happy with the configuration of the new rule, click New. The rule is tested and, if there are no errors, the Completion screen shows 1 item, 1 succeeded, 0 failed. Click Finish.

Standardizing Server Builds

One other easily overlooked component of a secure messaging environment is ensuring that all components are maintained regularly and consistently. Maintaining server builds that are as identical as possible allows an organization to save on administration, maintenance, and troubleshooting.

With standardized systems, all servers can be maintained, patched, and upgraded in similar or identical manners.

Understandably, most organizations cannot afford to standardize on a single hardware platform and replace all of their systems with each and every upgrade. Often, as servers are added to and removed from an environment, different hardware platforms require different server builds to function properly. However, keeping these systems as close as possible in configuration by using automated and/or scripted installations, automated update utilities, and regular monitoring can increase the likelihood that each server added to the environment meets the organization's security requirements.

Exchange Server-Level Security Features

As Exchange has adapted over the years, Microsoft has recognized the pitfalls encountered by companies overwhelmed by spam and email viruses. To combat this, they have consistently improved the features of their bundled tools to provide organizations with protection that would have had to be addressed with third-party applications in the past.

Exchange Server 2007 Antispam Measures

As previously mentioned, spam is a global problem that affects everyone with an Internet-accessible email address. The spam problem has grown beyond bothersome; it has become an issue that negatively impacts end-user productivity and places a significant burden on messaging systems.

Exchange 2007 has many antispam measures built in to the application. These methods are especially effective when coupled with Outlook 2007. A few of these features are as follows:

> ► **Increased protection through integrated security technologies**—Exchange Server 2007 acts as the first line of defense on incoming email messages. The Exchange server determines the legitimacy of the message, and is able to disable links or uniform resource locators (URLs) to help protect the user community. In addition, Exchange 2007 offers new antiphishing capabilities to help to prevent emails of this nature from reaching your users in the first place.

> ► **Improved email legitimacy assurance**—Email legitimacy is managed through Email Postmark technology when you combine Office Outlook 2007 and Exchange Server autoencryption. Outlook Email Postmark applies a token (actually a computational puzzle that acts as a spam deterrent) to email messages it sends. This token can be read by a receiving Exchange 2007 server to confirm the reliability of the incoming message.

> ► **Distribution lists restricted to authenticated users**—Using message delivery restrictions, you can configure a distribution list to accept mail from all senders, or specific senders or groups. In addition, you can require that all senders be authenticated before their message is accepted.

> ► **Connection filtering**—Improvements have been made in the configuration and management of IP Block lists, IP Allow lists, IP Block List providers, and IP Allow List providers. Each of these elements can now be reviewed and configured directly from the Exchange Management Console.

> ► **Content filtering**—Exchange 2007 includes the Exchange Intelligent Message Filter, or IMF, which uses the Microsoft SmartScreen patented "machine-learning" technology. This content filter evaluates inbound messages and determines the probability of whether the messages are legitimate, fraudulent, or spam.

> In addition, the IMF consolidates information that is collected from connection filtering, sender filtering, recipient filtering, sender reputation, SenderID verification, and Microsoft Office Outlook 2007 Email Postmark validation. The IMF then applies a Spam Confidence Level (SCL) rating to a given message. Based on this rating, an administrator can configure actions on the message based on this SCL rating. These actions might include the following:

>> ► Delivery to a user Inbox or Junk E-Mail folder.

>> ► Delivery to the spam quarantine mailbox.

> ▶ Rejection of the message and no delivery.

> ▶ Acceptance and deletion of the message. The server accepts the message and deletes it instead of forwarding it to the recipient mailbox.

▶ **Antispam updates**—Exchange 2007 now offers update services for their antispam components. The standard Exchange 2007 antispam filter updates every 2 weeks. The Forefront Security for Exchange Server antispam filter updates every 24 hours.

▶ **Spam quarantine**—The spam quarantine provides a temporary storage location for messages that have been identified as spam and that should not be delivered to a user mailbox. Messages that have been labeled as spam are enclosed in a nondelivery report (NDR) and are delivered to a spam quarantine mailbox. Exchange administrators can manage these messages and can perform several actions, such as rejecting the message, deleting it, or flagging it as a false positive and releasing it to the originally intended recipient. In addition, messages with an SCL rating that the administrator has defined as "borderline" can be released to the user's Junk E-Mail folder in Outlook. These borderline messages are converted to plain text to provide additional protection for the user.

▶ **Recipient filtering**—In the past, an email that was addressed to a specific domain would enter that domain's messaging service, regardless of whether it was addressed to a valid recipient. This not only utilized bandwidth, but also required Exchange servers to process the messages, create a nondelivery report (NDR), and send that message back out. Now, by using the EdgeSync process on your Hub Transport server, you can replicate recipient data from the enterprise Active Directory into the Exchange Active Directory Application Mode (ADAM) instance on the Edge Transport server. This enables the Recipient Filter agent to perform recipient lookups for inbound messages. Now, you can block messages that are sent to nonexistent users (or to internal use only distribution lists).

▶ **SenderID**—First implemented in Exchange Server 2003 SP2, Sender ID filtering technology primarily targets forgery of email addresses by verifying that each email message actually originates from the Internet domain that it claims to. Sender ID examines the sender's IP address, and compares it to the sending ID record in the originator's public DNS server. This is one way of eliminating spoofed email before it enters your organization and uses your company resources.

▶ **Sender reputation**—The Sender Reputation agent uses patented Microsoft technology to calculate the trustworthiness of unknown senders. This agent collects analytical data from Simple Mail Transfer Protocol (SMTP) sessions, message content, Sender ID verification, and general sender behavior and creates a history of sender characteristics. The agent then uses this knowledge to determine whether a sender should be temporarily added to the Blocked Senders list.

▶ **IP Reputation Service**—Provided by Microsoft exclusively for Exchange 2007 customers, this service is an IP Block list that allows administrators to implement and use IP Reputation Service in addition to other real-time Block list services.

▶ **Outlook junk email filter lists aggregation**—This feature helps reduce false positives in antispam filtering by propagating Outlook 2003 and Outlook 2007 Junk Email Filter lists to Mailbox servers and to Edge Transport servers.

Additional Antispam Measures

In the battle against spam, passive measures protect your organization, but more aggressive measures can help lessen the problem overall. The following sections cover some suggestions of ways that your organization can help fight back.

Utilizing Blacklists

Many companies are unknowingly serving as open relays. Many spammers take advantage of this lack of security and utilize the organization's messaging system to send their unsolicited email. When a company or domain is reported as an open relay, the domain can be placed on a blacklist. This blacklist, in turn, can be used by other companies to prevent incoming mail from a known open relay source.

You can find some organizations that maintain blacklists at the following addresses:

▶ Distributed Sender Blackhold List—http://www.dsbl.org

▶ SpamCop Website—http://www.spamcop.net

Report Spammers

Organizations and laws are getting tougher on spammers, but spam prevention requires users and organizations to report the abuse. Although this often is a difficult task because many times the source is undecipherable, it is nonetheless important to take a proactive stance and report abuses.

Users should contact the system administrator or help desk if they receive or continue to receive spam, virus hoaxes, and other such fraudulent offers. System administrators should report spammers and contact mail abuse organizations, such as those listed earlier in the "Utilizing Blacklists" section.

System administrators should use discretion before reporting or blocking an organization. For example, if your company were to receive spam messages that appeared to originate from Yahoo! or Hotmail, it wouldn't necessarily be in your best interest simply to block those domains. In that example, the cure might be worse than the disease, so to speak.

Third-Party Antispam Products

Although Microsoft has equipped users, system administrators, and third-party organizations with many tools necessary to combat spam, the additional use of a third-party product, or products, can provide additional protection. These third-party products can also provide a multitude of features that help with reporting, customization, and filtering mechanisms to maximize spam blocking, while minimizing false positives.

Do Not Use Open SMTP Relays

By default, Exchange Server 2007 is not configured to allow open relays. If an SMTP relay is necessary in the messaging environment, take the necessary precautions to ensure that only authorized users or systems have access to these SMTP relays.

> **NOTE**
>
> You can use the Exchange Best Practice Analyzer, or other tools such as Sam Spade (http://www.samspade.org/) to check your environment for open mail relays.

Protecting Exchange Server 2007 from Viruses

Exchange 2007 includes many improvements to assist organizations with their antivirus strategies. The product continues to support the Virus Scanning Application Programming Interface (VSAPI). In addition, Microsoft has made a significant investment in the creation of more effective, efficient, and programmable virus scanning at the transport level.

A few of the antivirus measures included in Exchange 2007 are listed as follows:

▶ **Transport agents**—Exchange 2007 introduces the concept of transport agents. *Agents* are managed software components that perform a task in response to an application event. These agents act on transport events, much like event sinks in earlier versions of Exchange. Third-party developers can write customized agents that are capable of utilizing the Exchange Multipurpose Internet Mail Extensions (MIME) parsing engine allowing extremely robust antivirus scanning. The Exchange 2007 MIME parsing engine has evolved over many years of Exchange development and is likely the most trusted and capable MIME engine in the industry.

▶ **Antivirus stamping**—Exchange 2007 provides antivirus stamping, a method of stamping messages that were scanned for viruses with the version of the antivirus software that performed the scan and the result of the scan. This feature helps reduce the volume of antivirus scanning across an organization because, as the message travels through the messaging system with the antivirus stamp attached, other systems can immediately determine whether additional scanning must be performed on the message.

▶ **Attachment filtering**—In Exchange 2007, Microsoft has implemented attachment filtering by a transport agent. By enabling attachment filtering on your organization's Edge Transport server, you can reduce the spread of malicious attachments before they enter the organization.

> **NOTE**
>
> Although Exchange Server 2007 provides features to help minimize an organization's exposure to viruses, it does not have true, built-in antivirus protection, as Exchange

does not actually scan messages or attachments to look for infection. However, continued support for the built-in Virus Scanning Application Program Interface (VSAPI) allows specialized antivirus programs to connect their applications to your Exchange environment to scan messages as they are handled by Exchange.

Forefront Security for Exchange Server

Designed by Microsoft specifically for Exchange Server 2007, Forefront Security for Exchange Server is the next generation of Microsoft Antigen for Exchange. Because these products were designed specifically to work together, Forefront integrates with Exchange Server 2007 to provide improved protection, performance, and centralized management.

Forefront Security for Exchange Server delivers the following:

▶ Advanced protection against viruses, worms, phishing, and other threats by utilizing up to five antivirus engines simultaneously at each layer of the messaging infrastructure

▶ Optimized performance through coordinated scanning across Edge, Hub, and Mail servers and features such as in-memory scanning, multithreaded scanning processes, and performance bias settings

▶ Centralized management of remote installation, engine and signature updating, reporting, and alerts through the Forefront Server Security Management Console

Although the client antivirus protection that is provided by Forefront Security for Exchange Server is language independent, the setup, administration of the product, and end-user notifications are currently available in 11 server languages. When Forefront Security for Exchange Server detects a message that appears to be infected with a virus, the system generates a notification message and sends it to the recipient's mailbox. This message is written in the language of the server running Forefront because the server is not able to detect the language of the destination mailbox.

Third-Party Antivirus Products for Exchange

In addition, there are many third-party antivirus vendors in the marketplace. At the time of this writing, there was little to no documentation on their websites about future integration with Exchange 2007; however, there is no doubt that most of these companies will have compatible products ready by the time the product is released.

Many mechanisms can be used to protect the messaging environment from viruses and other malicious code. Most third-party virus-scanning products scan for known virus signatures and provide some form of heuristics to scan for unknown viruses. Other antivirus products block suspicious or specific types of message attachments at the point of entry before a possible virus reaches the Information Store.

Antivirus products keep viruses from reaching the end user in two fundamental ways:

▶ **Gateway scanning**—Gateway scanning works by scanning all messages as they go through the SMTP gateway (typically connected to the Internet). If the message contains a virus or is suspected of carrying a virus, the antivirus product can clean, quarantine, or delete it before it enters your Exchange organization.

▶ **Mailbox scanning**—Mailbox scanning is useful to remove viruses that have entered the Information Store. For example, a new virus might make it into the Exchange environment before a signature file that can detect it is in place. These messages on the Information Store cannot be scanned by a gateway application; however, with an antivirus product that is capable of scanning the Information Store, these messages can be found and deleted.

Antivirus Outsourcing

Although an organization can put in place many gateway antivirus products to address antispam and antivirus issues, outsourcing these tasks has gained popularity in recent years. Companies specializing in antivirus and antispam are able to host your organization's MX records, scanning all messages bound for your company, and forwarding the clean messages to your organization. Although this removes a level of control from your administrators, many organizations are finding this outsourcing cost-effective, as they no longer have to maintain staff devoted strictly to these measures.

Transport-Level Security Defined

Whereas server-level security focuses on protecting the data stored on the server from internal or external attacks, transport-level security focuses on protecting the data while it is *in transit* from the sender to the recipient. When most people think of transport-level security, they think of protecting data that is leaving their company network, but protecting internal communications is equally important.

As mentioned earlier in the chapter, the concept of defense in depth is also critical to transport-level security. This concept is also sometimes called "The Onion Approach" because, like an onion, after you get past a single layer, you find another layer and, beneath that, another. By using a combination of authentication, encryption, and authorization, you can add extra layers to protect your more sensitive data.

Encrypting Email Communications

One of the most widespread and effective methods of transport-level security is the use of encrypting message traffic as it travels across the network. Encryption is important for both external and internal email communications. Securing external communications is important to ensure your messages are not intercepted and viewed by random entities on the Internet, and securing internal communications prevents the use of data capture utilities by personnel within your organization who are not authorized to view the messages.

Table 11.2 shows measures that are built in to Exchange Server 2007 to assist with the encryption of message traffic that is destined for both internal and external recipients.

TABLE 11.2   Confidential Messaging Improvements in Exchange Server 2007

Feature	Description
Intra-Org Encryption	New in Exchange 2007, all mail traveling within an Exchange Server 2007 organization is now encrypted by default. Transport Layer Security (TLS) is used for server-to-server traffic, remote procedure calls (RPC) is used for Outlook connections, and Secure Sockets Layer (SSL) is used for client access traffic (Outlook Web Access, Exchange ActiveSync, and Web Services). This prevents spoofing and provides confidentiality messages in transit.
SSL Certificates Automatically Installed	SSL certificates are installed by default in Exchange Server 2007, enabling broad use of SSL and TLS encryption from clients such as Outlook Web Access and other SMTP servers.
Opportunistic TLS Encryption	If the destination SMTP server supports TLS (via the STARTTLS SMTP command) when sending outbound email from Exchange Server 2007, Exchange Server will automatically encrypt the outbound content using TLS. In addition, inbound email sent to Exchange Server 2007 from the Internet will be encrypted if the sending server supports TLS (Exchange Server 2007 automatically installs SSL certificates). This is the first step in ensuring the default encryption of Internet-bound messaging traffic, and as more and more sites implement SMTP servers supporting this feature, the ability to encrypt Internet-bound messages by default will increase.
Information Rights Management (IRM)	Administrators can use transport rules on the Hub Transport server role to enforce IRM protection on messages based on subject, content, or sender/recipient. In addition, Exchange Server 2007 prelicenses IRM-protected messages to enable fast client retrieval for users.

Utilizing Public Key Infrastructure (PKI)

Because Microsoft Exchange Server 2007 is installed on Microsoft Windows Server 2003, it can take advantage of communications security features provided by the underlying operating system.

One of the most widely used security methods is the use of Public Key Infrastructure (PKI), which allows an administrator in an organization to secure traffic across both internal and external networks. Utilizing PKI provides certificate-based services by using a combination of digital certificates, registration authorities, and certificate authorities

(CAs) that can be used to provide authentication, authorization, nonrepudiation, confidentiality, and verification. A CA is a digital signature of the certificate issuer.

Chapter 12, "Encrypting Email Communications with Exchange Server 2007," goes into this technology in greater depth with instructions on how to install certificate services, information on the use of public and private keys, and the use of smart cards in a PKI environment.

Utilizing S/MIME

Another method of providing security to messages while in transit is the use of Secure/Multipurpose Internet Mail Extensions (S/MIME).

S/MIME allows the message traffic to be digitally signed and encrypted, and utilizes digital signatures to ensure message confidentiality. Chapter 12 goes into this technology in depth.

Utilizing TLS and SSL

Transport Layer Security (TLS) is an Internet standard protocol that is included in Microsoft Exchange Server 2007 that allows secure communications by utilizing encryption of traffic sent across a network. In a messaging environment, TLS is specifically utilized when securing server/server and/or client/server communications. Utilizing TLS can help ensure that messages sent across your network are not sent "in the clear," or in a format that is easily intercepted and deciphered.

Configuring your mail servers to utilize TLS and SSL to secure client access is addressed in depth in Chapter 10, "Client-Level Secured Messaging."

Exchange Server 2007 SMTP Connectors

SMTP is a protocol that is used for sending email messages between servers. Because most email systems that are connected to the Internet today utilize SMTP as their messaging standard, it is important to understand how it works with Exchange Server 2007.

Previous versions of Exchange supported SMTP, but they relied on a service provided by the underlying Windows operating system. Exchange Server 2007, on the other hand, has its own built-in SMTP server. As a matter of fact, the installation of Exchange Server 2007 requires that you do not have the SMTP service already installed on your underlying Windows platform.

In Exchange, for SMTP traffic to travel between computers, SMTP connectors are used. SMTP connectors are logical representations of connections between a source and destination server. These connectors dictate how Edge Transport servers and Hub Transport servers communicate with each other, with the Internet, and with previous versions of Exchange.

There are two types of SMTP connector in Exchange Server 2007, Send Connectors and Receive Connectors. Each of these types of connector represents a one-way connection, and the configuration of the connector mandates how messages will be transported.

To secure your Microsoft Exchange Server 2007 environment, you must have an understanding of these connectors and how to configure them properly.

Connector Topology

For messages to flow between servers in an Exchange organization, or between the organization and the Internet, several SMTP connectors must be in place and properly configured. These connectors are the minimum that are required for proper end-to-end mail flow. Table 11.3 lists these connectors.

TABLE 11.3   Exchange Server 2007 SMTP Connectors

Purpose	Type	How Created
Send messages between Hub Transport servers in the organization	Send	Implicit connector that is automatically computed based on the system topology.
Send messages from a Hub Transport server to an Edge Transport server	Send	Implicit connector that is automatically computed based on the system topology.
Send messages from an Edge Transport server to a Hub Transport server	Send	Implicit connector that is automatically created by the EdgeSync subscription process.
Send messages from a Hub Transport server to the Internet	Send	Explicit connector that is created by the administrator and is stored in Active Directory.
Send messages from an Edge Transport server to the Internet	Send	Explicit connector that is either created by the administrator on an Edge Transport server or automatically created using the EdgeSync subscription process.
Receive messages on a Hub Transport server from another Hub Transport server or from an Edge Transport server	Receive	Explicit Active Directory connector that is automatically created when the Hub Transport server role is installed. The connector is stored in Active Directory as a child object of the server.
Receive messages on the Edge Transport server from a Hub Tranport server or from the Internet	Receive	Explicit connector that is created automatically when the Edge Transport server role is installed. The connector is stored in ADAM. When the Edge Transport server is subscribed to an Active Directory site using EdgeSync, permissions to use this connector are granted to each Hub Transport server in the site.

NOTE

Send and Receive Connectors can be created implicitly, explicitly, or automatically. To say that a connector is created *implicitly* means that it is computed from the system topology and is not displayed in either the Exchange Management Console or the

Exchange Management Shell. A connector that is created *explicitly* is one that is
created when an administrator actively performs a task. Lastly, a connector can be
created *automatically* during the Edge Subscription process.

Understanding Receive Connectors

SMTP Receive Connectors serve the purpose of acting as incoming connection points for
SMTP traffic and dictates how incoming SMTP communications are managed on an
Exchange 2007 transport server. The Receive Connector actively listens for incoming
connections that match all settings configured on the connector, such as connections
utilizing a particular port or from a particular IP address range.

Receive Connectors have many configurable limits that can be set, such as the following:

▶ Number of active connections allowed

▶ Maximum incoming message size

▶ Maximum recipients per message

Receive Connectors are configured on a single server and determine what particular
message traffic that server will listen for. If the Receive Connector is created on a Hub
Transport server, it is stored in Active Directory as a child object of that server. However,
when it is created on an Edge Transport server, the connector is stored in Active Directory
Application Mode (ADAM).

Understanding Send Connectors

SMTP Send Connectors are used for relaying outgoing SMTP communications. Unlike
Receive Connectors; Send Connectors are not scoped to a single server. When an
Exchange 2007 server receives an SMTP message that is addressed to a remote destination,
the message is relayed to an appropriate Send Connector that is configured to handle
messages intended for that destination.

In Active Directory or in ADAM, a Send Connector is created as an object in a connectors
container. A connector can have more than one source server, which is defined as a Hub
Transport server that is associated with that connector.

For example, if a Send Connector is configured to handle message routing to a domain
that is external to the organization, whenever a Hub Transport server receives a message
destined for that remote domain, the message is routed to the Send Connector to be
relayed appropriately.

As with Receive Connectors, a variety of configuration settings can be defined by the
administrator. Send Connectors can be created and viewed in either the Exchange
Management Console or the Exchange Management Shell, but the majority of the configuration must be accomplished using the Exchange Management Shell. Send Connectors
are stored in Active Directory as a configuration object, and can be viewed from the
Exchange Management Console by going to the console tree, selecting Organization

Configuration, and then selecting Hub Transport. Next, in the results pane, select the Send Connectors tab.

How Connectors Are Created

As previously mentioned, connectors must exist between all messaging servers for SMTP traffic to be passed. However, inside the Active Directory forest, you do not have to create and configure the connectors between Hub Transport servers. These connections are created implicitly. This means that the connections are created by computing a path between AD sites that is based on Active Directory site link costs.

After you install an Edge Transport server and a Hub Transport server, the Edge Transport server must be subscribed to an Active Directory site by using the Edge Transport subscription process. This process enables the EdgeSync service to establish one-way replication of recipients and configuration details from the AD directory service to the Active Directory Application Mode (ADAM). This subscription process can be accomplished quickly and easily by following the steps listed on the Finalize Deployment tab on the Exchange Management Console. To get to the Finalize Deployment tab, open the Exchange Management Console and click on Microsoft Exchange in the console tree.

When you subscribe the Edge Transpor server, data that is stored in Active Directory gets replicated to the ADAM instance located on the Edge Transport server. Some examples of the data that gets replicated are as follows:

▶ Configuration of Send and Receive Connectors

▶ Domains to accept SMTP traffic from

▶ Remote domains

Connectors can be created using one of the following methods:

▶ **Explicit Active Directory Connector**—When an administratator creates a connector in the Exchange organization, an explicit connector is created. This object can be modified by the administrator and changes are replicated throughout the organization.

▶ **Explicit ADAM Connector**—When an administrator creates a connector on an Edge Transport server, it is stored in Active Directory Application Mode (ADAM). Connectors that are created on Edge Transport servers are scoped to a single server. An administrator can modify this object; however, the configuration applies only to that particular connector on that Edge Transport server only.

▶ **Implicit**—Implicit connectors are automatically computed using Active Directory site link information and existing explicit Active Directory connectors. This connector cannot be modified, and cannot be viewed either in Active Directory or ADAM. The only way to change an implicit connector is to make a change to the system topology. When a change to the topology is made, the connector is recomputed.

▶ **Automatic Explicit ADAM Connector**—When you subscribe an Edge Transport server, the EdgeSync subscription process creates an Automatic Explicit ADAM connector inside the Exchange organization. This connector is then replicated to the ADAM instance on the Edge Transport server. This connector cannot be modified on the Edge Transport server, but can be modified in Active Directory. Any changes made in Active Directory are replited to the Edge Transport server during routine synchronization.

▶ **Automatic Implicit ADAM Connector**—All implicit connectors are computed from the system topology as described previously. This applies to Automatic Implicit ADAM connectors as well. One or more Edge Transport servers must have access to the information contained in this connector. This connector cannot be modified in Active Directory; however, if a change is made to the system topology, the connector changes resulting from the topology change will be replicated to the Edge Transport server during routine synchronization.

> **NOTE**
>
> For the Edge Transport servers and the Hub Transport servers to communicate with each other, they must be able to find each other using host resolution in the domain name system (DNS).

Hub Transport Server Connectors

After the Hub Transport server role has been installed on an Exchange Server 2007 server in your environment, you must configure the appropriate Send and Receive Connectors. Until this has been accomplished, the server will be unable to send SMTP messages to, or receive them from, the Internet.

Send Connectors are configured in the Exchange Management Console in the Organization Configuration node, and are stored in AD as a configuration object. The Send Connectors must be configured so that the Hub Tranport server knows what source server to forward the message to. Bear in mind, there can be multiple source servers configured on the connector.

Receive Connectors, on the other hand, are configured in the Exchange Management Console in the Server Configuration node, and are stored in AD as a child object of the server. By default, when a Hub Transport server is brought online, it has two default Receive Connectors already configured.

Both Send and Receive Connectors can be viewed and modified using the Exchange Management Shell. As a matter of fact, many configuration settings can *only* be accomplished using the Exchange Management Shell.

So, SMTP Send Connectors handle outgoing messages; SMTP Receive Connectors handle incoming messages. For proper message flow, the Hub Transport server must have the appropriate connectors to allow mail flow to and from the Internet (by relaying through an Edge Transport server), as well as to and from other Hub Transport servers.

A Hub Transport server must have at least three required connectors to function properly. The first two, both of which are Receive Connectors, are created automatically during the installation of the Hub Transport server:

- A Receive Connector that is configured to accept SMTP messages on port 25 from all remote IP addresses. The usage type for this connector should be "Internal" as well. This connector is automatically generated during the installation of the Hub Transport server.

- A second Receive Connector that is configured to accept messages on port 587 from all remote IP addresses. This connector is needed to accept SMTP connections from non-MAPI clients who are connecting through a client access server. The usage type for this connector should be set to "Internal." This connector is automatically created during the installation of the Hub Transport server.

The third required connector is a Send Connector:

- By default, no explicit Send Connector exists on the Hub Transport server, so you must perform one of two actions to create it—either the connector is automatically generated when you create an Edge subscription, or you must manually configure it. After this process has been completed, your environment will be ready to route Internet-bound messages from the Hub Transport server to the Edge Transport server, and then out to the Internet.

Automatic Creation of Send Connectors

To automatically create the Send Connector, you must have a server with the Edge Transport server role and utilize an Edge subscription and the EdgeSync service. To do so, perform the following steps:

1. Install the Hub Transport server role.

2. On the Edge Transport server, export the Edge subscription file. If you have more than one Edge Transport server, each server requires a separate subscription file. The Edge subscription file can be exported in the Microsoft Exchange Shell utilizing the following command:

   ```
   new-edgesubscription - filename "c:\server1info.xml"
   ```

3. Next, you must import the Edge subscription. This file can be accomplished using either the Exchange Management Console or the Exchange Management Shell. To do so using the Exchange Management Shell, run the following command on the Hub Transport server:

   ```
   new-edgesubscription -filename "c:\server1info.xml" -site
   ➥"default-first-site-name"
   ```

4. Verify that synchronization was successful by viewing the Event Viewer application log and inspecting MsExchange EdgeSync events.

Data replicated to ADAM includes the Internet Send Connector. This connector is stored in AD and the settings for it are written on the Edge Transport server in the local ADAM instance. The connector has the Edge Transport server as the source server, and is configured to use DNS MX records to automatically route messages.

Manual Creation of Send Connectors

If you decide not to use an Edge subscription, you must manually create and configure the Send Connector. To do so, follow these steps:

1. Start the Exchange Management Console on the Hub Transport server.

2. In the console tree, expand the Organization Configuration node, and then select the Hub Transport node.

3. In the action pane, click New Send Connector. The New SMTP Send Connector Wizard starts.

4. On the Introduction page, type a name for the connector, and then select the intended usage from a drop-down box—the intended usage should be set to Internal.

5. On the Address Space page, click Add, and enter * (all domains) as the address space. Leave the Include All Subdomains check box checked, and click OK. Click Next to continue.

6. On the Network Settings page, ensure the Route All Mail Through the Following Smart Hosts option button is selected, and then click Add.

7. Enter the IP address or FQDN for the Edge Transport server, click OK, and then click Next to continue.

8. On the Smart Host Security Settings page, select the Exchange Server Authentication option button, and then click Next to continue.

9. Select one or more Hub Transport servers as the source for the connector, and then click Next.

10. Review the Configuration Summary, and then click New to create the connector.

11. From the Completion page, click Finish.

12. Now, you must perform manual configuration of the required connectors on the Edge Transport server. This information is covered in the next section.

Edge Transport Server Connectors

After the installation of the Microsoft Exchange Server 2007 Edge Transport server role, you must configure the appropriate Send and Receive Connectors. Until this has been accomplished, the server will be unable to send SMTP messages to, or receive them from, the Internet and your internal Hub Transport servers.

As discussed in the previous section, to complete the configuration of the Send Connector on an Edge Transport server, you subscribe the server to the organization using EdgeSync, which then replicates the appropriate connectors to the Edge Transport server. If you do not use EdgeSync, you must manually create and configure the connector.

This section covers additional information about Edge Transport server connectors that was not touched on in the previous section.

An Edge Transport server must have at least four required connectors to function properly. The first two, both Send Connectors, are created and configured for you automatically during the EdgeSync process:

▶ A Send Connector must exist that is configured to send messages to the Internet. Typically, the address space for this connector is set to * (all Internet domains). DNS routing is used to resolve destinations. The usage type for this connection is set to "Internet." This connector is created automatically when you use EdgeSync to subscribe the server to an Active Directory site.

▶ A Send Connector must exist that is configured to send messages to the Hub Transport servers in the Exchange organization. The address space for this connector can either be *, or you can manually list each of the domains for which you are processing mail. The smart hosts for the connector should be configured as your Hub Transport servers, and the usage type set to "Internal." This connector is also created automatically during the subscription process.

The next two required connectors are Receive Connectors:

▶ A Receive Connector must exist that is configured to accept messages from the Internet. Usually, this connector is configured to accept connections from any IP address range. Furthermore, it is normally configured to allow anonymous access. When configuring the local network bindings for this connection, they should be set to the external-facing IP address of the Edge Transport server, and the usage type should be set to "Internet."

▶ A second Receive Connector must exist that is configured to accept messages from Hub Transport servers in your organization. For security purposes, you can configure this connector to accept connections only from your Hub Transport servers by listing their IP address ranges. The local network bindings for this connector should be configured as the internal-facing IP address of the Edge Transport server, and the usage type should be set to "Internal."

Configuring Receive Connectors on the Edge Transport Server

When you install the Edge Transport server, one Receive Connector is automatically created. This connector is configured by default to accept SMTP traffic from all IP address ranges, and it is bound to all IP addresses associated with the local server. The usage type is set to "Internet," and the connection will accept anonymous connections. It is recommended that you modify the settings of this Receive Connector and create a second one for internal usage. To perform this procedure, follow these steps:

1. Start the Exchange Management Console on the Edge Transport server.

2. In the console tree, select Edge Transport.

3. In the results pane, select the appropriate Edge Transport server and then, on the bottom half of the pane, click the Receive Connectors tab.

4. Select the default connector and, in the action pane, click Properties.

5. Click the Network tab, and edit the existing Local IP Addresses (by default, set to All Available). Configure this address to be the IP address of the Internet-facing network adapter of the Edge Transport server. Save your changes and exit, as no other changes are needed on this connector.

6. Next, in the action pane, click New Receive Connector. On the Introduction page, enter a name for this connector, and select a usage type as Internal. Click Next to continue.

7. On the Remote Network Settings page, modify the Remote IP Addresses and configure them to accept mail from the IP addresses assigned to your Hub Transport servers. Save the settings and click New to create the connector.

8. After the connector has been created, you must make one more modification. Select the connector in the results pane and select Properties in the action pane. Click the Network tab, and double-click the Local IP Address(es) entry, currently set to (All Available). Click the Specify an IP Address option button, and enter the IP address of the internal-facing network adapter of the Edge Transport server. Save all settings and exit, as no other changes are needed on this connector.

Configuring Send Connectors on the Edge Transport Server

As discussed in the section on Hub Transport servers, the Send Connectors needed on your Edge Transport server are automatically generated by the EdgeSync service. If you elect to not create an Edge subscription, you must manually configure the Send Connectors.

Automatic Creation of Send Connectors

To automatically create the Send Connector on the Edge Transport server, follow the instructions in the previous section titled "Automatic Creation of Send Connectors" in the "Hub Transport Server Connectors" section.

Manual Completion of Send Connectors

To manually complete the configuration of the first Send Connector, do the following:

1. Start the Exchange Management Console on the Edge Transport server.

2. In the console tree, select Edge Transport.

3. In the results pane, select the appropriate Edge Transport server and then, on the bottom half of the pane, click the Send Connectors tab.

4. In the action pane, click New Send Connector.

5. On the Introduction page, type a name for the connector, and set the usage to Internet. Click Next to continue.

6. On the Address Space page, click Add. Set the Domain to * and ensure the Include All Subdomains option is selected. Click Next to continue.

7. On the Network Settings page, select Use Domain Name System (DNS) "MX" Records to Route Mail Automatically. Click Next to continue. Save all settings and exit, as no further configuration is needed on this connector.

To manually complete the configuration of the second Send Connector, do the following:

1. Start the Exchange Management Console on the Edge Transport server.

2. In the console tree, select Edge Transport.

3. In the results pane, select the appropriate Edge Transport server and then, on the bottom half of the pane, click the Send Connectors tab.

4. In the action pane, click New Send Connector.

5. On the Introduction page, type a name for the connector, and set the usage to Internal. Click Next to continue.

6. On the Address Space page, click Add. Set the domain to the domain(s) for which you accept mail. If you have more than one accepted domain, configure additional entries. Ensure the Include All Subdomains option is selected. Click Next to continue.

7. On the Network Settings page, select Route All Mail Through the Following Smart Hosts, and click Add.

8. Enter the IP address or FQDN of one of your Hub Transport servers as the smart host. Click OK to continue. To add additional Hub Transport servers, click Add again. When you are ready, click Next to continue.

9. On the Smart Host Security Settings page, ensure the None option button is selected, and click Next.

10. Review all entries and, after all entries are correct, click New to create the connector.

Setting Message Delivery Limits

One of the most important security measures you can implement on your SMTP connectors is setting message delivery limits. Message delivery limits prevent users from sending large messages through Exchange that can tie up Exchange resources (processing time, queue availability, disk storage, and more). When this occurs, the results can be just as bad as experiencing a DoS attack. Implementing these limits also encourages users to use alternative delivery methods, such as file shares, compression of attachments, and even document management portals.

In previous versions of Exchange, delivery limits were configured within the Exchange System Manager. Now, in Exchange 2007, these limits are set on specific Send and Receive Connectors using the Exchange Management Shell.

To determine the current maximum message size on a particular connector, perform the following procedure. For this example, you will work with a Receive Connector. To perform the same tasks on a Send Connector, replace the `receiveconnector` command with `sendconnector`.

1. Start the Exchange Management Shell.

2. Get a list of the existing connectors by using the following command:

   `get-receiveconnector`

   A list of existing Receive Connectors is returned. For this example, use a connector named "Default VMW-EXCHANGE1."

3. To view the configuration of a specific connector, use the following command:

   `get-receiveconnector "default vmw-exchange1" |format-list`

A detailed configuration of the connector is returned, and looks similar to what is shown in Figure 11.5.

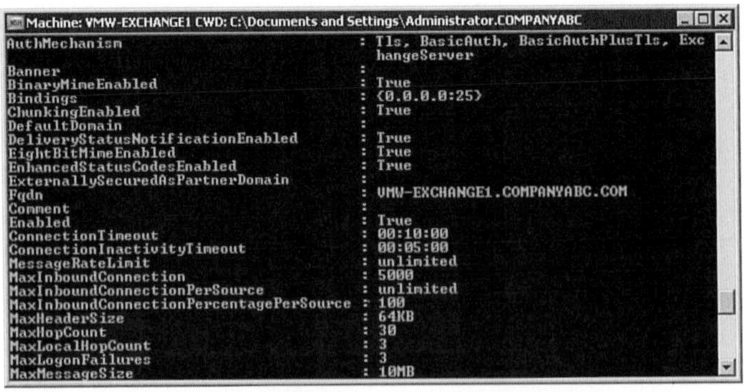

FIGURE 11.5   Sample Receive Connector configuration.

By default, the maximum message size is set to 10MB. To change this maximum message size, perform the following procedure:

1. In the Exchange Management Shell, type the following command:

```
set-receiveconnector "default vmw-exchange1" -MaxMessageSize 20MB
```

2. If you now view the configuration of the specific connector (as shown previously), you will see that the new `maxmessagesize` limit has been implemented.

NOTE

Configuring a different sending and receiving message size limit can cause potential problems. For example, if you configured a 5MB limit on sent messages, but a 10MB limit on received messages, a user might receive an email from an external source with a 9MB attachment. They would be able to receive the message, but any attempts to forward it to a co-worker would fail because of the sending restriction. A good best practice is to set these limits to the same size.

Another important message delivery limit that can be used to secure Exchange Server 2007 involves the number of recipients that a message can be sent to at any one time. Limiting the maximum number of recipients limits internal users' ability to essentially spam the enterprise with large numbers of emails.

Configuring the maximum number of recipients per message is done similiarly to the setting the maximum message size previously. The default setting is 5,000, but you can configure it to whatever number you desire. For this example, you will change this setting to 500 recipients. To do so, perform the following command in the Exchange Management Shell by typing the following command:

```
set-receiveconnector "default vmw-exchange1" -MaxRecipientsPerMessage 500
```

The majority of the configuration settings for the Send and Receive Connectors must be configured through the Exchange Management Shell. A complete list of available parameters can be found in the Microsoft Exchange Server 2007 Operations Guide found at http://www.microsoft.com/technet/prodtechnol/exchange/e2k7help on the Microsoft website.

Configuring Authoritative Domains

When an Exchange organization is responsible for handling message delivery to recipients in a particular domain, the organization is called *authoritative* for that domain. Configuring an authoritative domain in Exchange 2007 is a two-step process: First, you create an accepted domain, and second, you set the domain type as authoritative.

An accepted domain is any SMTP namespace that the Edge Transport server(s) in your organization sends messages to or receives messages from. Your organization might have one or more domains, so you might have more than one authoritative domain.

NOTE

If you have subscribed your Edge Transport server to the Exchange organization using the EdgeSync process, do not perform these procedures directly on the Edge Transport server. Instead, perform the steps on a Hub Transport server and allow it to replicate to the Edge Transport server during the next synchronization.

To create an authoritative domain, perform the following command in the Exchange Management Shell on your Hub Transport server:

```
New-AcceptedDomain -Name "CompanyABC" -DomainName companyabc.com -DomainType
➥Authoritative
```

NOTE

You must be logged on as an account that is a member of the Exchange Organization Administrators group and that is a member of the local Administrators group on the server. Also, replace this name with your own domain name in place of companyabc.com in the example.

Securing Windows for the Edge Transport Server Role

In Exchange Server 2007, your Edge Transport server roles are installed as standalone servers in your perimeter network (also referred to as the boundary network or screened subnet).

Because these servers exist in your perimeter network, they are more vulnerable to potential attacks than servers located on your internal network. To prepare a server for the Edge Transport server role, you should first utilize the Security Configuration Wizard (SCW) to minimize the attack service of the server by disabling functions that are not needed to perform the functions of an Edge Transport server.

Although it is possible to manually secure the server, the SCW automates the process and applies Microsoft recommended best practices to lock the server down by utilizing a role-based metaphor to determine what services are needed on a particular server. By utilizing the SCW, you can minimize your exposure to exploitation of security vulnerabilities.

One of the challenges to locking down ports and services on a particular server is ensuring you do not remove functionality that is necessary for the server to perform its functions. Often, mistakes can be made that are not immediately visible and that can cause problems in your environment that will require troubleshooting at a later date. However, within Exchange Server 2007, there is an SCW template that can be applied to a computer that has the Edge Transport server role installed that can automatically lock down services and ports that are not needed to perform Edge Transport functionality.

When you run the SCW, you can create a custom policy based on this template that can be applied to all Edge Transport servers in your environment.

Implementing Network Security

Edge Transport servers in a perimeter network are generally configured with two network adapters—one to communicate strictly with the Internet, and the other strictly for internal communications.

Each adapter must have a different level of security applied to it. It is recommended that the Internet-facing (or external) adapter be configured to only allow SMTP traffic on port 25.

The internal adapter, on the other hand, needs the following ports open to properly communicate with the server within your organization:

▶ Port 25/SMTP for SMTP traffic

▶ Ports 50389/TCP and 50636/UDP for Lightweight Directory Access Protocol (LDAP) communication

▶ Port 3389/TCP Remote Desktop Protocol

The LDAP ports are used during the EdgeSync process, and the RDP port is used to allow remote administration of the server.

Using the SCW Template

After the Edge Transport server role has been installed, you can follow this procedure to configure a security policy with the Security Configuration Wizard:

1. Install the Security Configuration Wizard. See "Installing the Security Configuration Wizard" earlier in this chapter for instructions on how to do so.

2. Register the Security Configuration Wizard extension by locating the file named Exchange2007.xml in the C:\Program Files\Microsoft\Exchange Server directory. If you installed Exchange in a different directory, you will have to go there to locate the file.

3. Copy the file to the C:\Windows\Security\Msscw\Kbs directory. If you installed Windows in a different directory, you will have to copy the file to that installation directory instead.

4. Open a command prompt window and register the Exchange 2007 extension with the local security configuration database by typing the following command:

```
scwcmd register /kbname:msexchangeedge /kbfile:%winddir%\security\msscw\kbs\
➥exchange2007.xml
```

5. Verify that the command has completed successfully by viewing the `SCWRegistrar_log.xml` file located in the `C:\Windows\Security\Msscw\Logs` directory.

6. Create the Edge Transport server SCW policy for your specific environment. For detailed steps, see the "Creating a New Edge Transport Server Security Policy" section later in this chapter.

7. If you have more than one Edge Transport server in your environment, you can apply this custom policy to each of them by performing the following steps:

   a. Log on to a server with the Edge Transport server role installed. You must be logged on as a user that is a member of the local Administrators group on that computer.

   b. Select Start, All Programs, Administrative Tools, Security Configuration Wizard to start the tool. Click Next on the welcome screen.

   c. On the Configuration Action page, select Apply an Existing Security Policy. Click Browse, select the XML file for your policy, and then click Open. Click Next.

   d. On the Select Server page, verify that the correct server name appears in the Server (use DNS name, NetBIOS name, or IP address) field. Click Next.

   e. On the Apply Security Policy page, click View Security Policy if you want to view the policy details, and then click Next.

   f. On the Applying Security Policy page, wait until the progress bar indicates Application Complete, and then click Next.

8. On the Completing the Security Configuration Wizard page, click Finish.

Creating a New Edge Transport Server Security Policy

When implementing network security through the implementation of an Edge Transport server, a security policy can be created on the Edge server. To create a new Edge Transport server security policy, do the following:

1. Click Start, point to All Programs, point to Administrative Tools, and then click Security Configuration Wizard to start the tool. Click Next on the welcome screen.

2. On the Configuration Action page, select Create a New Security Policy, and then click Next.

3. On the Select Server page, verify that the correct server name appears in the Server (use DNS name, NetBIOS name, or IP address) field. Click Next.

4. On the Processing Security Configuration Database page, wait for the progress bar to complete, and then click Next.

5. On the Role-Based Service Configuration page, click Next.

6. On the Select Server Roles page, select the Exchange 2007 Edge Server check box, and then click Next.

7. On the Select Client Features page, select each client feature that is required on your Edge Transport server, and then click Next.

8. On the Select Administration and Other Options page, select each administration feature that is required on your Edge Transport server, and then click Next.

9. On the Select Additional Services page, select each service that is required to be enabled on the Edge Transport server, and then click Next.

10. On the Handling Unspecified Services page, select the action to perform when a service that is not currently installed on the local server is found. You can select to take no action by selecting Do Not Change the Startup Mode of the Service, or you can select to automatically disable the service by selecting Disable the Service. Click Next.

11. On the Confirm Service Changes page, review the changes that this policy will make to the current service configuration. Click Next.

12. On the Network Security page, verify that Skip This Section is not selected, and then click Next.

13. On the Open Ports and Approve Applications page, you must add two ports for LDAP communication to Active Directory Application Mode (ADAM). To add the ports:

   a. Click Add. On the Add Port or Application page, in the Port Number field, enter 379. Select the TCP check box, and then click OK.

   b. Click Add. On the Add Port or Application page, in the Port Number field, enter 626. Select the UDP check box, and then click OK.

14. On the Open Ports and Approve Applications page, you must configure the ports for each network adapter. To do so:

   a. Select Port 25, and then click Advanced. On the Port Restrictions page, click the Local Interface Restrictions tab. Select Over the Following Local Interfaces, select both the Internal Network Adapter and External Network Adapter check boxes, and then click OK.

   b. Select Port 379, and then click Advanced. On the Port Restrictions page, click the Local Interface Restrictions tab. Select Over the Following Local Interfaces, select only the Internal Network Adapter check box, and then click OK.

   c. Select Port 626, and then click Advanced. On the Port Restrictions page, click the Local Interface Restrictions tab. Select Over the Following Local Interfaces, select only the Internal Network Adapter check box, and then click OK.

   d. Select Port 3389, and then click Advanced. On the Port Restrictions page, click the Local Interface Restrictions tab. Select Over the Following Local Interfaces, select only the Internal Network Adapter check box, and then click OK.

15. On the Open Ports and Approve Applications page, click Next.

16. On the Confirm Port Configuration page, verify that the incoming port configuration is correct, and then click Next.

17. On the Registry Settings page, select the Skip This Section check box, and then click Next.

18. On the Audit Policy page, select the Skip This Section check box, and then click Next.

19. On the Save Security Policy page, click Next.

20. On the Security Policy File Name page, enter a filename for the security policy and an optional description. Click Next. If a restart of the server is required after the policy is applied, a dialog box appears. Click OK to close the dialog box.

21. On the Apply Security Policy page, select Apply Now, and then click Next.

22. On the Completing the Security Configuration Wizard page, click Finish.

Administrator Permissions on an Edge Transport Server

By default, when you install an Edge Transport server role, the server is administered using local user accounts. This is because the server is configured as a standalone server in the perimeter network and has no domain membership.

The local Administrators group is granted full control over the Edge Transport server, including administration permissions over the instance of Active Directory Application Mode (ADAM) on the server. Logging on as an account with membership in the local Administrators group gives you permission to modify the server configuration, security configurations, ADAM data, and the status of queues and messages currently in transit on the server.

Generally, you would utilize Microsoft Windows Terminal server to administer an Edge Transport server, and the local Administrators group is granted remote logon permissions by default. Rather than allowing all of your administrators to use the default Administrator account, it is recommended that you create a separate local account for each administrator who will be administering your Edge servers, and adding these accounts to the local Administrators group on the server.

Table 11.4 below identifies administrative tasks that are commonly performed on an Edge Transport server, and the required group membership needed for each task.

TABLE 11.4   Edge Transport Server Administrative Tasks

Administative Task	Membership Needed
Backup and restore	Backup Operators
Enable and disable agents	Administrators
Configure connectors	Administrators
Configure antispam policies	Administrators

TABLE 11.4   Continued

Administative Task	Membership Needed
Configure IP Block lists and IP Allow lists	Administrators
View queues and messages	Users
Manage queues and messages	Administrators
Create an EdgeSync subscription file	Administrators

Summary

Securing Exchange Server 2007 requires a focus on both server-level and transport-level security measures. Utilizing a combination of techniques including proper planning and design, hardening the underlying operating system, and creating and implementing policies, as well as implementing other built-in security features, goes a long way toward assisting you with a more secure messaging environment.

Furthermore, the proper implementation and configuration of Send and Receive SMTP Connectors in your environment is necessary to allow mail flow in and out of your Exchange organization, while minimizing the risk of improper use by malicious users. Securing unneeded services and ports on the Internet-facing Edge Transport servers in your perimeter network is critical to this endeavor.

Best Practices

The following are best practices from this chapter:

- ▶ Accurately assess your messaging environment's risks before attempting to design your security infrastructure.

- ▶ Establish and implement a comprehensive corporate email policy.

- ▶ Establish and implement administrative policies.

- ▶ Create companywide email disclaimers and have them approved prior to implementation by your legal representative.

- ▶ Implement strong antispam and antivirus measures in your environment and devote resources to the maintenance and upkeep of these measures.

- ▶ Plan and implement Exchange Server 2007 security roles.

- ▶ Use a layered approach when hardening Windows Server 2003 and when applying transport-layer security methods.

- ▶ Perform periodic security assessments and include a review of your physical security methods with each.

- ▶ Keep updated with the latest service packs and hotfixes.

- ▶ Standardize Exchange Server 2007 security.

▶ Limit the size of incoming and outgoing emails in your environment. Not only does this helps save disk space on your Exchange Server 2007 servers, it also minimizes denial of service (DoS) vulnerabilities. By default, this feature is enabled with a maximum message size of 10MB.

▶ Only allow authenticated users to send email in your environment. This concept can be especially important when applied to sending messages to mail-enabled distribution lists.

▶ Properly configure your SMTP Send and Receive Connectors to control which IP addresses or domains can access them.

▶ Utilize the Security Configuration Wizard on all of your servers, especially any Internet-facing Edge Transport servers located in your perimeter network. Use the SCW template provided by Microsoft to configure a security policy for these servers.

CHAPTER 12

Encrypting Email Communications with Exchange Server 2007

As much as Chapter 11, "Server-Level and Transport-Level Security," covered securing a server and encrypting the transport of communications in an Exchange Server environment does not address the privacy of email communications of actual messages between email senders and recipients. This chapter covers email encryption where the actual email message from a sender is encrypted so that someone trying to intercept the message will not have the ability to read the message because of the encryption on the message itself.

A combination of Microsoft Exchange Server 2007, Outlook 2007, and Windows Server 2003 has several features in place to assist encrypting and securing the privacy of messaging communications between users:

▶ **Certificate-based encrypted messaging**—Encrypted messages based on certificates use Public Key Infrastructure (PKI), leveraging public keys and private keys to encrypt messages and exchange keys so that a sender and recipient can communicate privately over email.

▶ **Email Postmark**—Outlook 2007 has implemented this new technology as part of their ongoing effort to minimize junk email. Exchange Server 2007, upon receiving a message with an Email Postmark, uses it as one method of verification of the reliability of the incoming message. You can read more about email postmarks in Chapter 10, "Client-Level Secured Messaging."

▶ **Information Rights Management**—Administrators can use transport rules on the Hub Transport server role to enforce Information Rights Management (IRM) protection on messages based on subject, content, or sender/recipient. In addition, Exchange Server 2007 prelicenses messages protected with IRM to enable users to retrieve the messages quickly.

This chapter focuses on certificate-based encryption of messages, including the creation of a certificate server and the installation of certificates within the Microsoft Outlook client software.

Understanding Public Key Infrastructure

Because Microsoft Exchange Server 2007 resides on Microsoft Windows Server 2003, administrators can rely heavily on the technology of the underlying operating system in their effort to implement a secure messaging environment.

Microsoft Windows Server 2003 allows for the use of PKI, which enables an administrator to exchange information with strong security and easy administration across both internal and external networks. PKI is an extensible infrastructure used to provide certificate-based services by combining digital certificates, registration authorities, and certificate authorities that can be used to provide authentication, authorization, nonrepudiation, confidentiality, and verification. A certificate authority (CA) is a digital signature of the certificate issuer.

PKI implementations are widespread and are becoming a critical component of modern networks. Windows Server 2003 fully supports the deployment of various PKI configurations, ranging from very simplistic to extremely complex. Entire books have been written on the subject of implementing PKI, but this chapter endeavors to give administrators a basic understanding of the subject and show how PKI can be used to help secure your Exchange environment.

Certificate Services in Windows Server 2003

Windows Server 2003 includes a built-in CA known as Certificate Services. Certificate Services can be used to create certificates and subsequently manage them and is responsible for ensuring their validity. Certificate Services can also be used to trust external PKIs, such as a third-party PKI, to expand services and secure communication with other organizations.

The type of CA that you install and configure depends on the purpose or purposes of the Windows Server 2003 PKI. Certificate Services for Windows Server 2003 can be installed as one of the following CA types:

▶ **Enterprise root CA**—The enterprise root CA is the most trusted CA in an organization and, if utilized, should be installed before any other CA. All other CAs are subordinate to an enterprise root CA. Enterprise root CAs store certificates in Active Directory (AD) by default.

▶ **Enterprise subordinate CA**—An enterprise subordinate CA must get a CA certificate from an enterprise root CA and can then issue certificates to all users and computers in the enterprise. These types of CAs are often used for load balancing of an enterprise root CA. More important, using subordinates provides stronger security for the PKI.

▶ **Stand-alone root CA**—A stand-alone root CA is the root of a hierarchy that is not related to the enterprise domain information, and, therefore, certificates are not stored in AD. Multiple stand-alone CAs can be established for particular purposes.

▶ **Stand-alone subordinate CA**—A stand-alone subordinate CA receives its certificate from a stand-alone root CA and can then be used to distribute certificates to users and computers associated with that stand-alone CA.

Windows Server 2003 PKI can also be either online or offline based on the level of security that is required in the organization.

> **TIP**
>
> An enterprise root CA is the most versatile CA in Windows Server 2003 because it integrates tightly with AD and offers more certificate services. If you're unsure as to what CA to use, choose an enterprise root or subordinate CA for use with messaging. Most important, however, is that with any PKI there must be careful planning and design.

PKI Planning Considerations

Any PKI implementation requires thorough planning and design, as noted earlier. Possible planning and design considerations include the following:

▶ Multinational legal considerations, including creation and standardization of a formal Certificate Practice Statement (CPS)

▶ Policies and procedures for issuing, revoking, and suspending certificates

▶ PKI hardware identification and standardization, including employee badge integration

▶ Determination of CA hierarchy administration model

▶ Creation of a redundant CA infrastructure based on geographical location

▶ Policies and procedures for creation of CAs as subordinates and policy enforcers within a greater hierarchy, including qualified subordination and cross-certification

▶ Policies and procedures for creation of registration authorities (RAs) and their placement within the CA hierarchy

▶ CA trust strategies

▶ Policies and procedures for maintaining the CA as a 24x7x365 operation (24 hours a day, 7 days a week, 356 days a year)

▶ Policies and procedures for key and certificate management, including, but not limited to, key length, cryptographic algorithms, certificate lifetime, certificate renewal, storage requirements, and more

▶ Policies and procedures for securing the PKI

▶ Published plans for providing high availability and recoverability

▶ Policies and procedures for integrating the CA with Lightweight Directory Access Protocol (LDAP) and/or Active Directory

▶ Policies and procedures for integrating with existing applications

▶ Policies and procedures for security-related incidents (for example, bulk revocation of certificates)

▶ Policies and procedures for delegation of administrative tasks

▶ Standards for PKI auditing and reporting

▶ Policies and procedures for change control

▶ Standards for key length and expiration of certificates

▶ Policies and procedures for handling lost certificates (that is, smart card)

▶ Policies and procedures for safe distribution of the CA public key to end users

▶ Policies and procedures for enrollment (for example, autoenrollment, stations, and so forth)

▶ Policies and procedures for incorporating external users and companies

▶ Procedures for using certificate templates

As you can see from this list, implementing PKI is not to be taken lightly. Even if the organization is implementing PKI just for enhanced Exchange Server 2007 messaging functionality, the considerations should be planned and designed.

Fundamentals of Private and Public Keys

Encryption techniques can primarily be classified as either symmetrical or asymmetrical. Symmetrical encryption requires that each party in an encryption scheme hold a copy of a private key that is used to encrypt and decrypt information sent between the two parties. One shortcoming of the private key encryption method is that the private key must somehow be transmitted from one party to the other, without it being intercepted and used to decrypt the information.

Asymmetrical encryption uses a combination of two keys that are mathematically related to each other. The first key, known as the private key, is kept closely guarded and is used to encrypt the information. The second key, known as the public key, can be used to decrypt the information. The integrity of the public key is ensured through certificates. The asymmetric approach to encryption ensures that the private key does not fall into the wrong hands and only the intended recipient is able to decrypt the data.

Understanding Certificates

A certificate is essentially a digital document issued by a trusted central authority that is used by the authority to validate a user's identity. Central, trusted authorities such as VeriSign are widely used on the Internet to ensure that software that is being downloaded from Microsoft, for example, is actually originating from Microsoft, and is not in fact a virus in disguise.

Certificates can be used for multiple functions including, but not limited to, the following:

- ▸ Secure e-mail

- ▸ Web-based authentication

- ▸ IP Security (IPSec)

- ▸ Secure web-based communications

- ▸ Code signing

- ▸ Certification hierarchies

Certificates are signed using information from the subject's public key and the CA. Items such as the originator's name, email address, and others can be used.

Certificate Templates

Certificates have multiple functions, and, therefore, multiple types of certificates are available to meet the need. One certificate might be used to sign code, whereas another is used to provide support for secure email. In this one-to-one relationship, a certificate is used for a single purpose. Certificates can also have a one-to-many relationship in which one certificate is used for multiple purposes.

TIP

One of the best examples of a certificate that uses a one-to-many relationship is the user certificate. By default, a user certificate provides support for user authentication, secure email, and the Encrypting File System (EFS).

Windows Server 2003 contains a large number of certificates, each with an assigned set of settings and purposes. In essence, certificates can be categorized into six different functional areas:

- ▸ **Server authentication**—These certificates are used to authenticate servers to clients, as well as servers to other servers.

- ▸ **Client authentication**—These certificates are used to provide client authentication to servers or server-side services.

- ▸ **Secure email**—Utilizing these certificates, users can digitally sign and encrypt email messages.

- ▸ **Encrypting File System**—These certificates are used to encrypt and decrypt files using EFS.

▶ **File recovery**—These certificates are used for recovering encrypted EFS files.

▶ **Code signing**—These certificates can sign content and applications. Code signing certificates help users and services verify the validity of code.

Basic Encrypted Communications Using Outlook

Specific to this chapter, encryption is used for email communications to allow users to send and receive secured communications. An encryption system is built in to Exchange that allows users within an Exchange environment to send email messages to other users within their Exchange environment in an encrypted manner. The problem with the default encryption in Exchange is that it does not provide encryption outside of the company's Exchange environment. So, most organizations do not use the built-in email encryption in Exchange, but rather use a more standard method of encrypted communications built on the PKI standard.

You have several methods of providing encrypted communications between users within and external to a Microsoft Exchange and Outlook email system. Users can each get a certificate from an organization such as VeriSign and perform encrypted communications. Or, an organization can purchase an enterprise license of Pretty Good Privacy (PGP) that provides encryption between users and organizations also using PGP email security. In this example, the use of individual VeriSign certificates is noted.

In this case, a user who wants to encrypt messages between himself and someone else needs to get an individual email certificate and install that certificate in his Microsoft Outlook email client software. In this example using VeriSign, the user would go to http://www.verisign.com/products-services/security-services/pki/pki-application/email-digital-id/index.html and for approximately $20 per year, both individuals wanting to conduct secured communications can purchase a certificate. The individuals share the public portion of their certificates with the other individuals and they can now send encrypted messages back and forth.

To acquire a certificate, do the following:

1. Go to a certificate provider such as VeriSign, and sign up and purchase a digital ID: http://www.verisign.com/products-services/security-services/pki/pki-application/email-digital-id/index.html.

2. Follow the instructions to download and install the certificate in your Outlook client.

3. Have the individual you want to communicate with do the same.

This process of purchasing, downloading, and installing a certificate only needs to be done once per year.

NOTE

If you use multiple computers, you need to install the certificate on each machine on which you run the Outlook client to be able to send and receive encrypted email messages.

After you have downloaded and installed the certificate on your computer, you need to configure Outlook to support the certificate. To do so, do the following:

1. Launch Outlook.

2. For Outlook 2003 and earlier, choose Tools, Options, and then click the Security tab. For Outlook 2007, choose Tools, Trust Center, and then click Email Security.

3. Click the Settings button.

4. In the Security Settings Name text box, type Email Encryption. Using the Cryptographic Format list arrow, choose S/MIME. Check the Default Security Setting for This Cryptographic Message Format and the Default Security Settings for all Cryptographic Messages check boxes.

5. Next to the Signing Certificate box, click Choose.

6. From the Select Certificate page, select the certificate that was previously installed and click OK.

7. Using the Hash Algorithm list arrow, choose SHA1. Using the Encryption Algorithm list arrow, choose 3DES.

8. Check the Send These Certificates with Signed Messages check box.

9. The settings should look similar to the ones shown in Figure 12.1. Click OK to apply these settings, and then click OK again.

FIGURE 12.1   Configuring Microsoft Outlook to support encryption certificates.

Individual users, depending on how computer savvy they are, might have difficulties signing up, downloading, and installing the certificate, and then configuring Outlook to send emails. In addition, because the certificates are individual based, EACH individual user has to do this process themselves every year and for every system on which they conduct email communications. As you will see in the section "Implementing Secured Email Communications with Exchange Server 2007," the issuance of certificates and the configuration of the user's Outlook client can be completed automatically using autoenrollment of certificates as well as using Group Policy Objects in Windows Server 2003 Active Directory.

Installing a Windows Certificate of Authority Server

The manual processes noted in the previous section showed what is involved in manually enabling security in a Windows and Exchange environment. Beyond the complexity for users having to perform critical system tasks to enable and access secured information, the security provided by these manual methods is not even that good. A simple compromise of a shared key can invalidate the security of files, access systems, and secured communications. The better method is to use a certificate-based security system using encryption to provide a significantly higher level of security. In addition, by automating the process, users do not have to be involved in the encryption, transport, or communications between their laptop or desktop, and the network.

This section covers the creation of a certificate of authority server system that issues certificates and the process known as autoenrollment of certificates that automatically issues certificates to users and computers in a Windows Server 2003 Active Directory environment.

> **NOTE**
>
> This section assumes that you have a Windows Server 2003 system that has been fully patched with the latest Windows Server 2003 service pack and updates, and that the server is connected to a Windows Server 2003 Active Directory network. If you are creating this system in a limited lab environment, the certificate server can be added on the same server system as the global catalog server so that a single domain controller and certificate server can be used.

Adding Certificate Services to a Server

Certificate Services is the Windows service that allocates certificates to be issued to users and computers. It is nothing more than a service added to an existing Windows Server 2003 system.

To install Certificate Services on a system, do the following:

1. On the server that will become your certificate server, click Start, Settings, Control Panel.

2. Double-click on Add or Remove Programs, and then click on Add/Remove Windows Components.

3. Check the Certificate Services check box. The warning message that appears informs you that after you install Certificate Services on this system, you cannot change the server name or domain membership. Assuming you agree with this, click Yes to continue.

4. If you have not installed IIS Web Services on this system yet, on the Windows Components screen, highlight Application Server and click Details.

5. Check the Internet Information Services (IIS) check box, and then click OK. Click Next to begin the installation of Certificate Services and the IIS components.

6. Assuming this is the first certificate server in your environment, choose Enterprise Root CA for the type of certificate of authority server, and then click Next.

7. For the common name for this CA, enter in a name. Typically, the name of the server is selected; however, a distinguishable name such as "xyzCertServer" (where *xyz* is a short name of the company) can help identify the certificate server in the future.

8. Leave the distinguished name suffix and the validity period as is. The CA Identifying Information page should look similar to the one shown in Figure 12.2. Click Next.

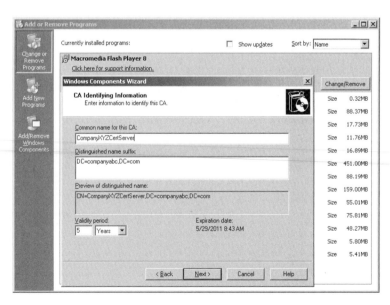

FIGURE 12.2   CA Identifying Information settings.

9. Click Next to accept the defaults on the Certificate Database Settings page (click Yes through the warning that IIS must be temporarily stopped). Click Finish after the installation of the component files has completed.

Implementing Secured Email Communications with Exchange Server 2007

Encrypted email communications can be sent by manually configuring certificates, or by enabling the autoenrollment of certificates for emails that are issued to users via Group Policy. Email encryption can be automated to the point where users are effectively issued certificates, the certificates are automatically installed, and the user can immediately begin to send and receive messages using encrypted communications.

If you have completed the steps at the very beginning of this text for the autoenrollment of certificates for a user, the certificate will automatically work for Exchange Outlook encryption.

To validate that the certificate has been installed, simply do the following:

1. Launch Microsoft Outlook.

2. For Outlook 2003 and earlier, choose Tools, Options, and then click the Security tab. For Outlook 2007, choose Tools, Trust Center, and then click Email Security.

3. Click the Settings button, and a My S/MIME Settings should automatically be configured for the user.

4. Click OK and then click OK again to exit the dialog boxes.

With a certificate already issued for Outlook, users can begin to send and receive encrypted emails with other users in the organization.

Configuring Exchange User Certificates Using Autoenrollment

After Certificate Services has been installed on the system, the administrator of the network can issue certificates to users and computers. However, rather than manually generating and issuing certificates, the best practice is to have the certificate server automatically issue certificates to users and computers in Active Directory. This is known as autoenrollment of certificates.

Autoenrollment of certificates requires the following processes to be followed:

1. A certificate template needs to be created.

2. The template needs to be added to the certificate of authority server.

3. A group policy needs to be created to automatically deploy the certificate to the user or computer.

With autoenrollment of certificates, rules are created that define which certificates should be issued to a user or computer. As an example, a rule can be created to create the autoenrollment of a certificate that allows a user to have his certificates automatically created for the encryption of data files. With autoenrollment of encrypted files, the user can simply save files to a shared location, and the files stored in the location will be encrypted.

To have certificates automatically installed for the Exchange users in Active Directory, do the following:

1. On the certificate server you just created, launch the Certificate Template Microsoft Management Console (MMC) by clicking Start, Run, typing mmc.exe in the Open text box, and then clicking OK.

2. Click File, Add/Remove Snap-in, and then click Add.

3. Select Certificate Templates and then click Add.

4. Click Close and then click OK.

5. Click the Certificate Templates folder.

6. Right-click on the Exchange User template, and select Duplicate Template.

7. In the Template Display Name text box, type AutoEnroll Exchange User.

8. Make sure the Publish Certificate in Active Directory and the Do Not Automatically Reenroll if a Duplicate Certificate Exists in Active Directory check boxes are both checked. The screen should look similar to Figure 12.3.

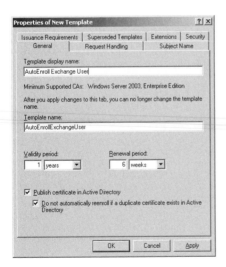

FIGURE 12.3   Creating an AutoEnroll Exchange User template.

9. Click the Security tab.

10. Highlight the Authenticated Users name and select the check boxes in the Allow column for the Read, Enroll, and the Autoenroll permissions for the Authenticated Users.

11. Click OK.

Adding the Template to the Certificate Server

After an autoenroll Exchange user template has been created, the template needs to be added to the certificate server and distributed to users. You can do this by completing the following steps:

1. Launch the Certification Authority Microsoft Management Console (MMC) by clicking Start, Run, typing `mmc.exe` in the Open text box, and then clicking OK.

2. Click File, Add/Remove Snap-in, and then click Add.

3. Select the Certification Authority snap-in, and then click Add. Assuming you are on the certificate server, select Local Computer, and then click Finish.

4. Click Close and then click OK.

5. Expand the Certification Authority folder.

6. Expand the folder for your certificate server.

7. Right-click on the Certificate Templates folder, and select New, Certificate Template to Issue.

8. Highlight the AutoEnroll Exchange User template, and then click OK.

> **NOTE**
>
> This step of adding the AutoEnroll Exchange User template you created earlier adds this new template to the certificate server. The AutoEnroll User template allows user certificates to be issued automatically through Group Policy.

Creating a Group Policy to Distribute User Certificates

The next step for autoenrollment is to create a group policy that can then distribute certificates to the users' laptops and desktops automatically. This is done by creating a group policy and having the group policy distribute the certificates created in the previous step. To create this group policy, do the following:

1. Launch the Active Directory Users and Computers tool by selecting Start, Programs, Administrative Tools, Active Directory Users and Computers.

2. Right-click the forest name of the network (such as companyabc.com), and choose Properties on the shortcut menu.

3. Click the Group Policy tab.

4. Highlight the Default Domain Policy, and then click Edit.

5. Under the User Configuration container, expand the Windows Settings folder.

6. Expand the Security Settings folder and then click to select the Public Key Policies folder. You will see an Object Type named Autoenrollment Settings, as shown in Figure 12.4.

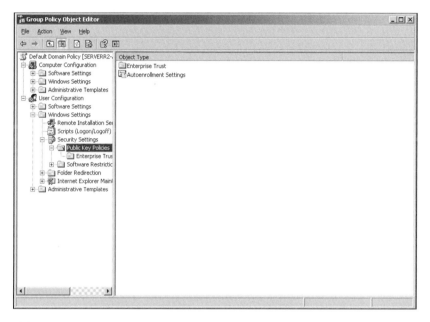

FIGURE 12.4   Expanding folders to access the Autoenrollment Settings object.

7. Right-click the Autoenrollment Settings object, and select Properties on the shortcut menu.

8. Check the Renew Expired Certificates, Update Pending Certificates, and Remove Revoked Certificates check boxes and check the Update Certificates That Use Certificate Templates check box. Then click OK.

Validating That Certificates Are Working Properly

The autoenrollment of user certificates has now been configured for all users who log on to the domain. To validate that certificates are working properly, do the following:

1. From a Windows XP workstation, log on to the domain.

2. Launch the Certificates Microsoft Management Console (MMC) by clicking Start, Run, typing mmc.exe in the Open text box, and then clicking OK.

3. Click File, Add/Remove Snap-in, and then click Add.

4. Select the Certificates snap-in, and then click Add. Assuming you logged on as the user for whom you want to verify that certificates are working, choose My User Account, and then click Finish.

5. Click Close and then click OK.

6. Expand the Certificates – Current User folder.

7. Expand the Personal folder and click to highlight the Certificates folder.

8. You should have a Client Authentication certificate created by the Autoenroll Exchange User certificate template, as shown in Figure 12.5.

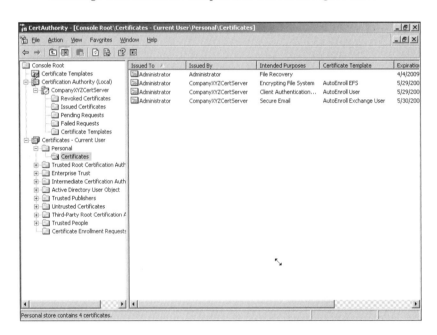

FIGURE 12.5 Exchange user certificate added to the user's Certificates folder.

If the Exchange user certificate has not pushed to the user's Certificates container, you can easily add the certificate by doing the following:

1. From a Windows XP or Vista workstation, log on to the domain.

2. Launch the Certificates Microsoft Management Console (MMC) by clicking Start, Run, typing mmc.exe in the Open text box, and then clicking OK.

3. Click File, Add/Remove Snap-in, and then click Add.

4. Select the Certificates snap-in, and then click Add. Assuming you logged on as the user for whom you want to verify that certificates are working, choose My User Account, and then click Finish.

5. Click Close and then click OK.

6. Expand the Certificates – Current User folder.

7. Expand the Personal folder, right-click the Certificates folder, choose All Tasks, Request New Certificate, and then click Next to begin the wizard.

8. Highlight AutoEnroll Exchange User, and then click Next.

9. Click Next to accept the defaults on the Friendly Name and Description page.

10. Click Finish.

Using Outlook to Send and Receive Digitally Signed and Encrypted Emails

After the Windows Server 2003 and Exchange 2007 environments have been set up to support a certificate-based infrastructure, the next step is to launch the Outlook client to confirm that certificates are working in the environment, and to then send and receive digitally signed and encrypted messages.

When discussing email security, you need to consider two primary questions:

▶ How do you know the message truly came from the suspected source?

▶ How do you know the message has not been intercepted or tampered with?

Both of these questions can be answered by the use of digital signatures and encryption. Digital signatures provide authentication, nonrepudiation, and data integrity, whereas encryption keeps message contents confidential.

In an Exchange environment, both of these solutions can be provided by using Secure/Multipurpose Internet Mail Extensions (S/MIME).

Utilizing S/MIME with Outlook 2003 or Outlook 2007 allows you to do the following:

▶ **Digitally sign a message to prove the identity of the sender**—S/MIME is the only option supported in Outlook 2007 to digitally sign a message. Although a message protected with Information Rights Management (IRM) can prevent a message from being tampered with, IRM protection is more limited because there is no authority to verify the identity of the sender. Furthermore, with IRM, the Outlook user interface does not show information about the identity of the sender like it does when using S/MIME.

▶ **Protect messages from unauthorized users**—By utilizing encryption, messages are not sent in "clear text." It is possible for attackers to monitor network traffic and intercept network traffic, but by encrypting the message, you can prevent them from gathering usable data. This protection is especially important for email sent over the Internet, as that is where point-to-point encryption is most valuable and where interoperability standards are most important.

Protecting your messages with S/MIME signatures and encryption is primarily used when users send or receive messages outside of your organization's boundaries, as they are no longer protected by the corporate firewall.

Fundamentals of Digital Signatures and Encryption

The primary purpose of S/MIME is to provide digital signatures and encryption. S/MIME is a small subset of PKI, which addresses a much wider array of security-related capabilities. For instance, PKI supports smart cards, Secure Sockets Layer (SSL), user certificates, and much more.

The International Telecommunication Union (ITU), based in Geneva, Switzerland, has a Telecommunication Standardization Sector (ITU-T) that coordinates standards for telecommunications. X.509 is an ITU-T standard for PKI that specifies (among other things) standard formats for public key certificates and a certification path validation algorithm. Originally issued in 1988, this standard has been revised twice over the years, and Version 3 (the current version) defines the format for certificate extensions used to store information regarding the certificate holder and to define certificate usage.

In short, X.509 is a digital certificate standard that defines the format of the actual certificate used by S/MIME.

The certificate identifies information about the certificate's owner and includes the owner's public key information. X.509 is the industry standard digital certificate and is, by far, the most widely used. PKI products such as Microsoft's Certificate Services (included in Windows Server 2003) adhere to this standard and generate X.509 digital certificates to be used with S/MIME-capable clients.

The Signing Process

When a message sender elects to sign a message, a process is completed where a numerical value is calculated based on the number of set bits in the message. Enclosing the numerical value, known as a *checksum*, with the original message allows the recipient to apply the same formula to the message.

The random checksum acts as the digital signature, sometimes called a digital ID. This signature is then encrypted using the user's private signing key. The user then sends the message to the recipient, and the message has three components: the message in plain text, the sender's X.509 digital certificate, and the digital certificate.

Upon receipt of the message, the recipient checks its certificate revocation list (CRL) to determine if the sender's certificate has been revoked. If it is found on the CRL, the recipient is warned that the sender's certificate has been revoked.

If the certificate is not on the revocation list, the digital signature is decrypted with the sender's public signing key (which is included in the digital certificate). The recipient's client then generates the checksum based on the plain text message and compares it to the digital signature.

If the checksum generated by the recipient does not match the one generated by the sender, the recipient knows that the message has been garbled or tampered with.

The Encryption Process

When a user elects to encrypt a message, the client generates a random bulk encryption key that is used to encrypt the contents of the message. The bulk encryption key is then encrypted using the *recipient's* public key. This is known as a *lockbox*. If the message has multiple recipients, individual lockboxes are created, one for each recipient, using his or her own public encryption key. However, the content of each is still the same bulk signing key. This process prevents the client from having to encrypt the message separately for each recipient, while ensuring the contents remain secure.

For this process to work, the sender must have a copy of the recipient's digital certificate. The certificate can be retrieved from either the Global Address List (GAL) or the sender's Contact list. The digital certificate contains the recipient's public encryption key, which is used to create the lockbox for the bulk encryption key.

When the message is received, the recipient uses his or her private encryption key to decrypt the lockbox, exposing the bulk encryption key that was used to encrypt the original message. The bulk encryption key is then used to decrypt the message.

This process sounds complicated, but it is actually very straightforward—the message is encrypted and needs a key to be decrypted. The key is sent with the message, but it is encrypted itself with the recipient's public key—so, only the intended recipient is able to unlock the key and, in turn, unlock the message.

> **NOTE**
>
> With Exchange 2003 SP1 and higher, antivirus software using the Virus Scanning API (VSAPI) 2.5 can scan digitally signed or encrypted messages.

Making Sure Outlook Acknowledges the Certificate

After autoenrollment has issued a certificate to the user and the user has confirmed the certificate has been successfully received, you can confirm that Microsoft Outlook recognizes the certificate for encrypted communications. To do so, do the following:

1. Launch Outlook.

2. For Outlook 2003, choose Tools, Options, and then click the Security tab. For Outlook 2007, choose Tools, Trust Center, and then click Email Security.

3. Click the Settings button.

   Under Security Settings Name is the email certificate that will allow you to send and receive encrypted communications.

4. Click OK and then click OK again to continue.

Sending a Digitally Signed Email

With the email certificate installed, you can now begin the process of sending and receiving encrypted emails. However, to complete the process, you need to communicate with someone who also has a certificate to send and receive encrypted emails. Email encryption requires both the sender and the receiver to have valid certificates.

The easiest process for setting up encrypted email communications is to send a user a digitally signed email with a copy of your public key certificate attached. With a digitally signed email and a copy of your public key, the recipient can then add your certificate to their address book, and then they can reply to the message sending you their public key. After you have exchanged public keys, you can send and receive encrypted emails.

The process for sending a person a digitally signed email with your public key is as follows:

1. Launch Outlook 2007.

2. Create a new email by selecting Actions, New Mail Message.

3. Enter in the recipient's email address that you want to communicate with in the To field, and enter in a subject such as "Initial Email for Secured Communications."

4. For the body of the message, you might want to enter in text such as "Here is an email message that will help us initiate secured communications. I am attaching a copy of my certificate for you to install; please reply to the message with a copy of your certificate."

> **NOTE**
>
> Writing a message in the body of the email might not be necessary; however, in this day and age of spam filters, if you just send a message with your digital signature and an attachment of your public key, the message will frequently be quarantined in the recipient's spam filter. So, it is best to write a few words describing what you are doing as part of the message.

5. On the Options tab at the top of the page, select Sign and ensure that it is highlighted. To see what settings this affects, you can click the arrow at the bottom of the Options box, and then click the Security Settings button.

6. The Add Digital Signature to This Message and Send This Message as Clear Text Signed check boxes should already be selected.

7. After selecting the Change Settings button, you should see that the Send These Certificates with Signed Messages check box is already be selected. If it is not, select the box so that your certificate is sent with the message, and then click OK.

8. Click OK and then click Close.

9. Click Send to send the message.

Your message will now be sent to the recipient with a copy of your key in a digitally signed email message. When the recipient opens the message, an error will likely appear that says "There are problems with the signature. Click the signature button for details," as shown in Figure 12.7. This message is because the certificate being received is from a domain with which they have not communicated in a secured or encrypted manner in the past.

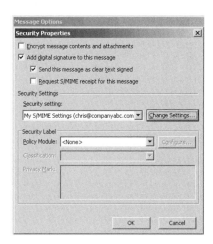

FIGURE 12.6   Security properties for sending an initial secured message.

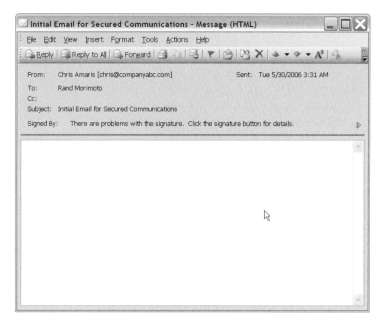

FIGURE 12.7   Initial receipt of a digitally signed, but not trusted message.

After confirming that you indeed sent the message and deciding to trust your certificate, the recipient should do the following:

1. Click on the yellow warning icon on the right side of the email message; a warning dialog box opens, as shown in Figure 12.8.

FIGURE 12.8   Certificate Authority Information warning dialog box.

2. Because you (the recipient) have confirmed the validity of the sender, click Trust.

3. A message box opens that warns and prompts that the recipient is trusting the sender. Click Yes to accept the trust.

4. Close and reopen the email. The error no longer appears, and the digital signature is confirmed.

Your certificate has now been installed on the recipient's system; they now need to send you their certificate so you can follow the exact same procedures to install their certificate on your system. They should follow the procedure described in "Sending a Digitally Signed Email" with you accepting their message and trusting their certificate.

Sending Encrypted Email Messages

After you have exchanged certificates, you can now send and receive fully encrypted email messages with another individual. To do so, complete the following steps:

1. Launch Outlook 2007.

2. Create a new email by selecting Actions, New Mail Message.

3. Enter in the recipient's email address in the To field, and enter in a subject such as "Encrypted Email Message."

4. For the body of the message, you might want to enter in text such as "Here is an email message that should now be encrypted. Please let me know if you successfully receive this message."

5. On the Options tab at the top of the page, select Encrypt and ensure that it is highlighted. To see what settings this affects, you can click the arrow at the bottom of the Options box, and then click the Security Settings button.

6. The Encrypt Message Contents and Attachments check box should be selected. Click OK, and then click Close.

7. Click Send to send the message.

The recipient will receive an encrypted copy of your message. This process not only works within Microsoft Outlook within an organization, but also works the same way when you want to send and receive encrypted messages to individuals outside of your organization. If the recipient is also running Outlook 2007 or Outlook 2003, the process to install your certificate into their address book is the same as described previously. If the recipient is using a different email system, they might need to detach the certificate, save it, and manually save the certificate into their address book.

Summary

The goal of this chapter was to provide step-by-step procedures that can be followed for the creation of a certificate server, creating the appropriate templates and certificates for users, and having certificates automatically issued to users and computers so that a certificate-based encryption system can be easily implemented in an environment.

When implementing security features in a network environment, it is important to look beyond the security of the computers alone. The data that travels between these computers is often more vulnerable than the data stored on the computers themselves. By implementing security methods such as certificate-based encryption to protect the information contained in the emails, administrators are taking one more step toward a well-rounded security solution.

Best Practices

The following are best practices from this chapter:

▶ Implement a Public Key Infrastructure solution within your environment that meets your organization's security needs.

▶ For environments requiring additional security measures, consider implementing smart cards to use in addition to ordinary network passwords.

▶ Set up autoenrollment of certificates on Windows Server 2003 to automatically generate certificates for users who have an Active Directory user account.

▶ Use group policies to push certificates to users to minimize the administrative overhead of having users manually download certificates and install the certificates in their Outlook application themselves.

▶ Utilize digital signatures and encryption in your messaging environment by implementing S/MIME for your Outlook 2003 and Outlook 2007 clients.

▶ Test to make sure certificates are working by sending a digital signature first, and then validate the complete successful exchange of keys by sending and receiving fully encrypted messages.

CHAPTER 13

Securing Exchange Server 2007 with ISA Server

In today's risk-fraught computing environment, any exposed service is subject to frequent attack from the Internet. This is particularly true for web services, including those offered by Outlook Web Access (OWA), Exchange ActiveSync, and Outlook Anywhere. Exploits using the Hypertext Transfer Protocol (HTTP) that these services use are becoming very commonplace, and it is not considered best practice to make an Exchange Client Access server (CAS) directly accessible via the Internet.

Fortunately, the productivity gains of OWA/ActiveSync can still be utilized and made more accessible by securing them behind a reverse-proxy server such as Microsoft Internet Security and Acceleration (ISA) Server 2006. ISA Server allows for advanced Application-layer filtering of network traffic, greatly securing the overall SharePoint environment. In addition, ISA Server supports deployment models in the demilitarized zone (DMZ) of existing firewalls, giving organizations the ability to deploy advanced Application-layer filtering for OWA without reconfiguring existing security infrastructure.

This chapter details the ways that Exchange services can be secured using the ISA Server 2006 product. Deployment scenarios for securing Exchange-related services with ISA are outlined, and specific step-by-step guides are illustrated.

Understanding the Internet Security and Acceleration (ISA) Server 2006

The rise in the prevalence of computer viruses, threats, and exploits on the Internet has made it necessary for organizations of all shapes and sizes to reevaluate their protection strategies for Edge Services such as SharePoint Portal Server. No longer is it possible to ignore or minimize these threats as the damage they can cause can cripple a company's business functions. A solution to the increased sophistication and pervasiveness of these viruses and exploits is becoming increasingly necessary.

Corresponding with the growth of these threats has been the development and maturation of the Internet Security and Acceleration (ISA) Server product from Microsoft. The latest release of the product, ISA Server 2006, is fast becoming a business-critical component of many organizations, which are finding that many of the traditional packet-filtering firewalls and technologies don't necessarily stand up to the modern threats of today. The ISA Server 2006 product provides for that higher level of application security required, particularly for common tools such as Exchange OWA and related services.

> **NOTE**
>
> Although it is possible to secure an Exchange 2007 server with the older version of ISA Server, ISA Server 2004, it is highly recommended to use the 2006 version because it is aware of the specific changes made to Exchange and can better protect the server. Therefore, this chapter only demonstrates the use of ISA Server 2006 for securing Exchange 2007.

Outlining the Need for ISA Server 2006 in Exchange Environments

A great deal of confusion exists about the role that ISA Server can play in an Exchange environment. Much of that confusion stems from the misconception that ISA Server is only a proxy server. ISA Server 2006 is, on the contrary, a fully functional firewall, virtual private network (VPN), web caching proxy, and application reverse-proxy solution. In addition, ISA Server 2006 addresses specific business needs to provide a secured infrastructure and improve productivity through the proper application of its built-in functionality. Determining how these features can help to improve the security and productivity of an Exchange environment is, therefore, of key importance.

In addition to the built-in functionality available within ISA Server 2006, a whole host of third-party integration solutions provide additional levels of security and functionality. Enhanced intrusion detection support, content filtering, web surfing restriction tools, and customized application filters all extend the capabilities of ISA Server and position it as a solution to a wide variety of security needs within organizations of many sizes.

Outlining the High Cost of Security Breaches

It is rare when a week goes by without a high-profile security breach, denial of service (DoS) attack, exploit, virus, or worm appearing in the news. The risks inherent in modern computing have been increasing exponentially, and effective countermeasures are required in any organization that expects to do business across the Internet.

It has become impossible to turn a blind eye toward these security threats. On the contrary, even organizations that would normally not be obvious candidates for attack from the Internet must secure their services as the vast majority of modern attacks do not focus on any one particular target, but sweep the Internet for any destination host, looking for vulnerabilities to exploit. Infection or exploitation of critical business infra-structure can be extremely costly for an organization. Many of the productivity gains in business recently have been attributed to advances in information technology (IT) func-tionality, including Exchange-related gains, and the loss of this functionality can severely impact the bottom line.

In addition to productivity losses, the legal environment for businesses has changed significantly in recent years. Regulations such as Sarbanes Oxley (SOX), HIPAA, and Gramm-Leach-Bliley have changed the playing field by requiring a certain level of secu-rity and validation of private customer data. Organizations can now be sued or fined for substantial sums if proper security precautions are not taken to protect client data. The atmosphere surrounding these concerns provides the backdrop for the evolution and acceptance of the ISA Server 2006 product.

Outlining the Critical Role of Firewall Technology in a Modern Connected Infrastructure

It is widely understood today that valuable corporate assets such as Exchange OWA cannot be exposed to direct access to the world's users on the Internet. In the beginning, however, the Internet was built on the concept that all connected networks could be trusted. It was not originally designed to provide robust security between networks, so security concepts needed to be developed to secure access between entities on the Internet. Special devices known as firewalls were created to block access to internal network resources for specific companies.

Originally, many organizations were not directly connected to the Internet. Often, even when a connection was created, there was no type of firewall put into place as the percep-tion was that only government or high-security organizations required protection.

With the explosion of viruses, hacking attempts, and worms that began to proliferate, organizations soon began to understand that some type of firewall solution was required to block access to specific, dangerous Transmission Control Protocol (TCP) or User Datagram Protocol (UDP) ports that were used by the Internet's TCP/IP protocol. This type of firewall technology would inspect each arriving packet and accept or reject it based on the TCP or UDP port specified in the packet of information received.

Some of these firewalls were ASIC-based firewalls, which employed the use of solid-state microchips, with built-in packet-filtering technology. These firewalls, many of which are still used and deployed today, provided organizations with a quick-and-dirty way to filter Internet traffic, but did not allow for a high degree of customization because of their static nature.

The development of software-based firewalls coincided with the need for simpler management interfaces and the ability to make software changes to firewalls quickly and easily. The most popular firewall in organizations today, CheckPoint, falls into this category, as do other popular firewalls such as SonicWall and Cisco PIX. ISA Server 2006 was built and developed as a software-based firewall, and provides the same degree of packet-filtering technology that has become a virtual necessity on the Internet today.

More recently, holes in the capabilities of simple packet-based filtering technology has made a more sophisticated approach to filtering traffic for malicious or spurious content a necessity. ISA Server 2006 responds to these needs with the capabilities to perform Application-layer filtering on Internet traffic.

Understanding the Growing Need for Application-Layer Filtering

Nearly all organizations with a presence on the Internet have put some type of packet-filtering firewall technology into place to protect the internal network resources from attack. These types of packet-filtering firewall technologies were useful in blocking specific types of network traffic, such as vulnerabilities that utilize the remote procedure calls (RPC) protocol, by simply blocking TCP and UDP ports that the RPC protocol would use. Other ports, on the other hand, were often left wide open to support certain functionality, such as the TCP 80 port, utilized for HTTP web browsing and for access to OWA/ActiveSync. As previously mentioned, a packet-filtering firewall is only able to inspect the header of a packet, simply understanding which port the data is meant to utilize, but is unable to actually read the content. A good analogy to this is if a border guard was instructed to only allow citizens with specific passports to enter the country, but had no way to inspect their luggage for contraband or illegal substances.

The problem that is becoming more evident, however, is that the viruses, exploits, and attacks have adjusted to conform to this new landscape, and have started to realize that they can conceal the true malicious nature of their payload within the identity of an allowed port. For example, they can "piggyback" their destructive payload over a known "good" port that is open on a packet-filtering firewall. Many modern exploits, viruses, and "scumware," such as illegal file-sharing applications, piggyback off the TCP 80 HTTP port, for example. Using the border guard analogy to illustrate, the smugglers realized that if they put their contraband in the luggage of a citizen from a country on the border guards' allowed list, they could smuggle it into the country without worrying that the guard would inspect the package. These types of exploits and attacks are not uncommon, and the list of known Application-layer attacks continues to grow.

In the past, when an organization realized that they had been compromised through their traditional packet-filtering firewall, the knee-jerk reaction was to lock down access from the Internet in response to threats. For example, an exploit that arrives over HTTP port 80 might prompt an organization to completely close access to that port on a temporary or semipermanent basis. This approach can greatly impact productivity as OWA access can be affected. This is especially true in a modern connected infrastructure that relies heavily on communications and collaboration with outside vendors and customers. Traditional security techniques involve a trade-off between security and productivity. The tighter a firewall is locked down, for example, the less functional and productive an end user can be.

In direct response to the need to maintain and increase levels of productivity without compromising security, Application-layer stateful inspection capabilities were built in to ISA Server that can intelligently determine if particular web traffic is legitimate. To illustrate, ISA Server inspects a packet using TCP port 80 to determine if it is a properly formatted HTTP request. Looking back to the border guard analogy, ISA Server is like a border guard who not only checks the passports, but is also given an X-ray machine to check the luggage of each person crossing the border.

The more sophisticated Application-layer attacks become, the greater the need becomes for a security solution that can allow for a greater degree of productivity while reducing the type of risks which can exist in an environment that relies on simple packet-based filtering techniques.

Outlining the Inherent Threat in Exchange HTTP Traffic

The Internet provides somewhat of a catch-22 when it comes to its goal and purpose. On one hand, the Internet is designed to allow anywhere, anytime access to information, linking systems around the world together and providing for that information to be freely exchanged. On the other hand, this type of transparency comes with a great deal of risk because it effectively means that any one system can be exposed to every connected computer, either friendly or malicious, in the world.

Often, this inherent risk of compromising systems or information through their exposure to the Internet has led to locking down access to that information with firewalls. Of course, this limits the capabilities and usefulness of a free-information exchange system such as what web traffic provides. Many of the web servers need to be made available to anonymous access by the general public, which causes the dilemma, as organizations need to place that information online without putting the servers it is placed on at undue risk.

Fortunately, ISA Server 2006 provides for robust and capable tools to secure web traffic, making it available for remote access but also securing it against attack and exploit. To understand how it does this, it is first necessary to examine how web traffic can be exploited.

Understanding Web (HTTP) Exploits

It is an understatement to say that the computing world was not adequately prepared for the release of the Code Red worm. The Microsoft Internet Information Services (IIS) exploit that Code Red took advantage of was already known, and a patch was made available from Microsoft for several weeks before the release of the worm. In those days, however, less emphasis was placed on patching and updating systems on a regular basis because it was generally believed that it was best to wait for the bugs to get worked out of the patches first.

So, what happened is that a large number of websites were completely unprepared for the huge onslaught of exploits that occurred with the Code Red worm, which sent specially formatted HTTP requests to a web server to attempt to take control of a system. For example, the following URL lists the type of exploits that were performed:

```
http://webmail.companyabc.com/scripts/..%5c../winnt/system32/cmd.exe?/c+dir+c:\
```

This one in particular attempts to launch the command prompt on a web or OWA server. Through the proper manipulation, worms such as Code Red found the method for taking over web servers and using them as drones to attack other web servers.

These types of HTTP attacks were a wake-up call to the broader security community as it became apparent that packet-layer filtering firewalls that could simply open or close a port were worthless against the threat of an exploit that packages its traffic over a legitimately allowed port such as HTTP.

HTTP filtering and securing, fortunately, is something that ISA Server does extremely well, and offers a large number of customization options that allow administrators to have control over the traffic and security of the web server.

Securing Encrypted (Secure Sockets Layer) Web Traffic

As the World Wide Web was maturing, organizations realized that if they encrypted the HTTP packets that were transmitted between a website and a client, it would make it virtually unreadable to anyone who would potentially intercept those packets. This led to the adoption of Secure Sockets Layer (SSL) encryption for HTTP traffic.

Of course, encrypted packets also create somewhat of a dilemma from an intrusion detection and analysis perspective because it is impossible to read the content of the packet to determine what it is trying to do. Indeed, many HTTP exploits in the wild today can be transmitted over secure SSL-encrypted channels. This poses a dangerous situation for organizations that must secure the traffic against interception, but must also proactively monitor and secure their web servers against attack.

ISA Server 2006 is uniquely positioned to solve this problem, fortunately, because it includes the ability to perform end-to-end SSL bridging. By installing the SSL certificate from the OWA server on the ISA server itself, along with a copy of the private key, ISA is able to decrypt the traffic, scan it for exploits, and then reencrypt it before sending it to the Exchange server. Very few products on the marketplace do this type of end-to-end encryption of the packets, and, fortunately, ISA allows for this level of security.

Outlining ISA Server 2006 Messaging Security Mechanisms

As a backdrop to these developments, ISA Server 2006 was designed with messaging security in mind. A great degree of functionality was developed to address email access and communications, with particularly tight integration with Microsoft Exchange Server built in. To illustrate, ISA Server 2006 supports securing the following messaging protocols and access methods:

- ▶ Simple Mail Transfer Protocol (SMTP)

- ▶ Messaging Application Programming Interface (MAPI)

- ▶ Post Office Protocol version 3 (POP3)

- ▶ Internet Message Access Protocol version 4 (IMAP4)

- ▶ Microsoft Exchange Outlook Web Access (OWA) with or without forms-based authentication (FBA)

- ▶ Exchange ActiveSync (EAS)

- ▶ Exchange Autodetection service

- ▶ Outlook Anywhere (formerly RPC over HTTP)

Securing each of these types of messaging access methods and protocols is detailed in subsequent sections of this chapter. For an understanding of how to initially set up web-related mail access with OWA/ActiveSync, and Outlook Anywhere, it might be wise to review Chapter 23, "Designing and Implementing Mobility in Exchange Server 2007," as this chapter only deals with securing existing OWA/ActiveSync deployments.

Securing Exchange Outlook Web Access with ISA Server 2006

As previously mentioned, OWA is one of the most commonly secured services that ISA servers protect. This stems from the critical need to provide remote email services while at the same time securing that access. The success of ISA deployments in this fashion gives tribute to the tight integration Microsoft built between its ISA product and Exchange product.

An ISA server used to secure an OWA implementation can be deployed in multiple scenarios, such as an edge firewall, an inline firewall, or a dedicated reverse-proxy server. In all these scenarios, ISA secures OWA traffic by "pretending" to be the CAS server itself, scanning the traffic that is destined for the CAS for exploits, and then repackaging that traffic and sending it on, such as that illustrated in Figure 13.1.

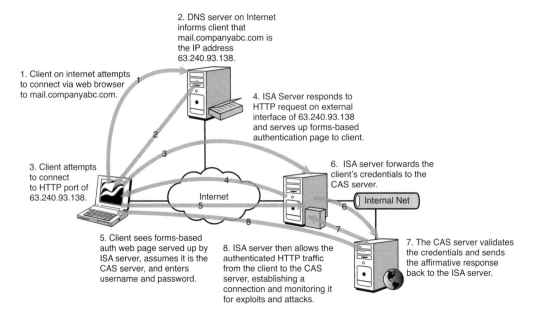

FIGURE 13.1   Explaining OWA publishing with ISA Server 2006.

ISA performs this type of OWA securing through an Exchange Web Client Access rule, which automatically sets up and configures a listener on the ISA server. A listener is an ISA component that listens to specifically defined IP traffic, and processes that traffic for the requesting client as if it were the actual server itself. For example, an OWA listener on an ISA server would respond to OWA requests made to it by scanning them for exploits and then repackaging them and forwarding them on to the OWA server itself. Using listeners, the client cannot tell the difference between the ISA server and the OWA server.

ISA Server is also one of the few products that has the capability to secure web traffic with SSL encryption from end to end. It does this by using the OWA server's own certificate to reencrypt the traffic before sending it on its way. This also allows for the "black box" of SSL traffic to be examined for exploits and viruses at the Application layer, and then be reencypted to reduce the chance of unauthorized viewing of OWA traffic. Without the capability to scan this SSL traffic, exploits bound for an OWA server could simply hide themselves in the encrypted traffic and pass right through traditional firewalls.

Exporting and Importing the OWA Certificate to the ISA Server

For ISA to be able to decrypt the SSL traffic bound for the Exchange OWA server, ISA needs to have a copy of the SSL certificate used on the OWA server. This certificate is used by ISA to decode the SSL packets, inspect them, and then reencrypt them and send them on to the OWA server. For this certificate to be installed on the ISA server, it must first be exported from the OWA server, as follows:

> **NOTE**
>
> The steps in Chapter 23 for setting up an OWA site and securing it with an SSL certificate must be run before performing these steps.

1. From the OWA server (not the ISA server), open IIS Manager (Start, All Programs, Administrative Tools, Internet Information Services [IIS] Manager).

2. Navigate to Internet Information Services, SERVERNAME (local computer), Web Sites.

3. Right-click on the OWA virtual server (typically named Default Web Site), and choose Properties.

4. Choose the Directory Security tab.

5. Click View Certificate.

6. Click the Details tab.

7. Click Copy to File.

8. At the wizard, click Next to begin the export process.

9. Select Yes, Export the Private Key, as shown in Figure 13.2, and click Next to continue.

FIGURE 13.2   Exporting the SSL private key.

10. Select Include All Certificates in the Certification Path option and also select the Enable Strong Protection option, then click Next to continue.

11. Type and confirm a password, and click Next to continue.

12. Enter a file location and name for the file, and click Next.

13. Click Finish.

After the .pfx file has been exported from the CAS server, it can then be imported to the ISA server via the following procedure:

> **CAUTION**
>
> It is important to securely transmit this .pfx file to the ISA server and to maintain high security over its location. The certificate's security could be compromised if it were to fall into the wrong hands.

1. From the ISA server, open the MMC console (Start, Run, mmc.exe, OK).

2. Click File, Add/Remove Snap-in.

3. Click Add.

4. From the list shown in Figure 13.3, choose the Certificates snap-in and then click Add.

FIGURE 13.3   Customizing an MMC Certificates snap-in console for import of the OWA certificate.

5. Choose Computer Account from the list when asked what certificates the snap-in will manage, and click Next to continue.

6. From the subsequent list in the Select Computer dialog box, choose Local Computer: (the computer this console is running on), and click Finish.

7. Click Close and then click OK.

After the custom MMC console has been created, the certificate that was exported from the OWA server can be imported directly from the console via the following procedure:

1. From the MMC Console root, navigate to Certificates (Local Computer), Personal.

2. Right-click the Personal folder, and choose All Tasks, Import.

3. When the wizard begins, click Next past the Welcome Screen to continue.

4. Browse for and locate the .pfx file that was exported from the OWA server. The location can also be typed into the File Name field. Click Next.

5. Enter the password that was created when the certificate was exported, as illustrated in Figure 13.4. Do not check to mark the key as exportable. Click Next to continue.

FIGURE 13.4   Installing the OWA certificate on the ISA server.

6. Choose Automatically Select the Certificate Store Based on the Type of Certificate, and click Next to continue.

7. Click Finish to complete the import.

After it is in the certificate store of the ISA server, the OWA SSL certificate can be used as part of publishing rules.

NOTE

If a rule that makes use of a specific SSL certificate is exported from an ISA server, either for backup purposes or to transfer it to another ISA server, the certificate must also be saved and imported to the destination server, or that particular rule will be broken.

Creating an Outlook Web Access Publishing Rule

After the OWA SSL has been installed onto the ISA server, the actual ISA mail publishing rule can be generated to secure OWA via the following procedure:

NOTE

The procedure outlined here illustrates an ISA OWA publishing rule that uses forms-based authentication (FBA) for the site, which allows for a landing page to be generated on the ISA server to preauthenticate user connections to Exchange. This FBA page can only be set on ISA, and must be turned off on the Exchange server to work properly.

1. From the ISA Management Console, click once on the Firewall Policy node from the console tree.

2. On the Tasks tab of the tasks pane, click the Publish Exchange Web Client Access link.

3. Enter a descriptive name for the publishing rule, such as "Outlook Web Access," and click Next to continue.

4. From the dialog box shown in Figure 13.5, choose the version of Exchange that will be secured, in this case Exchange Server 2007, and then click the Outlook Web Access check box. The other check boxes automatically dim. Click Next to continue.

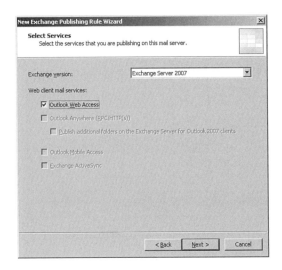

FIGURE 13.5   Creating an Exchange 2007 OWA publishing rule.

5. The subsequent dialog box allows an administrator to choose whether a single CAS server will be published, or whether a farm of load-balanced CAS servers will be published. In this scenario, a single CAS server will be used. Click Next to continue.

6. In the next dialog box, shown in Figure 13.6, the Use SSL to Connect to the Published Web Server or Server Farm option is illustrated. It is highly recommended to use SSL, and this scenario illustrates that concept. Click Next to continue.

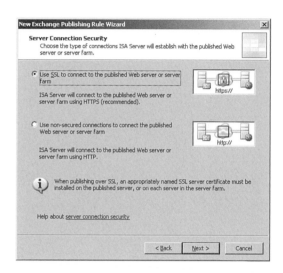

FIGURE 13.6   Choosing SSL publishing options.

7. On the Internal Publishing Details dialog box, enter the site name that internal users use to access the CAS server. It is recommended that the fully qualified domain name (FQDN), such as mail.companyabc.com, be entered, and that it is different from the physical name of the server itself. Examine the options to connect to an IP address or computer name; this gives additional flexibility to the rule. Click Next to continue.

8. In the subsequent dialog box, enter to accept requests for "This domain name (type below):" and enter the FQDN of the server, such as mail.companyabc.com. Click Next to continue.

9. Under Web Listener, click New.

10. At the start of the Web Listener Wizard, enter a descriptive name for the listener, such as Exchange HTTP/HTTPS Listener, and click Next to continue.

11. A prompt appears for you to choose between SSL and non-SSL. This prompt refers to the traffic between the client and ISA, which should always be SSL whenever possible. Click Next to continue.

12. Under Web Listener IP Addresses, select the External Network and leave it at All IP Addresses. Click Next to continue.

13. Under Listener SSL Certificates, click Select Certificate.

14. Select the previously installed certificate, as shown in Figure 13.7, and click the Select button.

15. Click Next to continue.

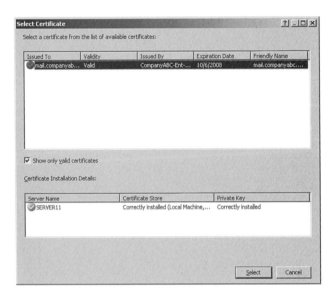

FIGURE 13.7   Choosing a certificate for the listener.

16. For the type of authentication, choose HTML Form Authentication, as shown in
    Figure 13.8. Leave the Windows (Active Directory) option selected, and click Next.

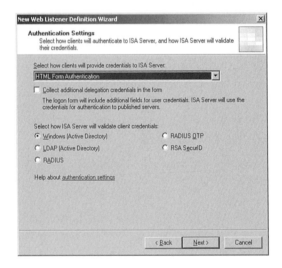

FIGURE 13.8   Choosing an authentication type.

17. The Single Sign On Settings dialog box is powerful; it allows all authentication
    traffic through a single listener to be processed only once. After the user has authen-
    ticated, he can access any other service, be it a SharePoint site, web server, or other
    web-based service that uses the same domain name for credentials. In this example,

enter .companyabc.com into the SSO domain name, as shown in Figure 13.9. Click Next to continue.

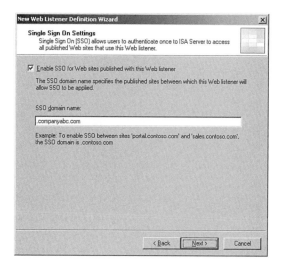

FIGURE 13.9   Enabling the Single Sign On settings.

18. Click Finish to end the Listener Wizard.

19. Click Next after the new listener is displayed in the Web Listener dialog box.

20. Under Authentication Delegation, choose Basic from the drop-down menu. Basic is used because SSL is the transport mechanism chosen. Click Next to continue.

21. Under User Sets, leave All Authenticated Users selected. In stricter scenarios, only specific Active Directory (AD) groups can be granted rights to OWA using this setting. In this case, the default is fine. Click Next to continue.

22. Click Finish to end the wizard.

23. Click Apply in the details pane, and then click OK when finished to commit the changes.

The rule will now appear in the details pane of the ISA server. Double-clicking on the rule brings up the settings, as shown in Figure 13.10. Tabs can be used to navigate around the different rule settings. The rule itself can be configured with additional settings based on the configuration desired. For example, the following rule information is used to configure our basic forms-based authentication web publishing rule for OWA:

▶ **General tab**—For Name, choose Outlook Web Access. Also make sure the Enabled option is checked.

▶ **Action tab**—For Action to take, choose Allow. Also make sure that the option Log Requests Matching This Rule is checked.

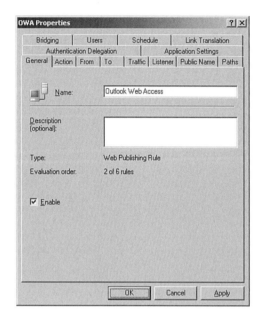

FIGURE 13.10   Viewing the OWA rule.

▶ **From tab**—Choose the option This Rule Applies to Traffic from These Sources and select Anywhere as the setting.

▶ **To tab**—For the option This Rule Applies to This Published Site, enter (for this example) `mail.companyabc.com`. Make sure the option Forward the Original Host Header Instead of the Actual One (which is specified in the Internal site name field) is checked. For the option Specify How the Firewall Proxies Requests to the Published Server, choose Requests Appear to Come from the ISA server.

▶ **Traffic tab**—For the option This Rule Applies to Traffic of the Following Protocols, choose HTTP and HTTPS. Also make sure the option Require 128-bit Encryption for HTTPS Traffic is checked.

▶ **Listener tab**—For Listener properties-Networks, choose External,Port(HTTP)=80, Port(HTTPS)=443, Certificate=`mail.companyabc.com`, Authentication methods=FBA with AD, and Always Authenticate-No,Domain for Authentication should be COMPANYABC.

▶ **Listener tab, Properties Button**—For the Networks tab, select External, All IP addresses. For the Connections tab–Enabled HTTP Connections on Port 80, set to Enable SSL Connections on Port 443. For HTTP to HTTPS Redirection select Redirect Authenticated Traffic from HTTP to HTTPS. For the Forms tab choose Allow Users to Change Their Passwords. Set the Remind Users That Their Password Will Expire in This Number of Days to 15. For the SSO tab, choose Enable Single Sign On. And for the SSO Domains, enter `companyabc.com` in this example.

▶ **Public Name tab**—For This Rule Applies to: Requests for the Following Web Sites, enter `mail.companyabc.com` in this example.

▶ **Paths tab**—For external paths, choose All Are Set to <same as internal>. For internal paths, enter `/public/*`, `/OWA/*`, `/Exchweb/*`, `/Exchange/*`, `/`.

▶ **Authentication Delegation tab**—For Method Used by ISA Server to Authenticate to the Published Web Server, choose Basic Authentication.

▶ **Application Settings tab**—For Use Customized HTML Forms Instead of the Default, make sure it is checked. For Type the Custom HTML Form Set Directory, choose Exchange. For Logon type, select As Selected by User. And for Exchange Publishing Attachment Blocking, make sure Public Computers is checked.

▶ **Bridging tab**—For Redirect Requests to SSL Port, enter 443.

▶ **Users tab**—For This Rule Applies to Requests from the Following User Sets, choose All Authenticated Users.

▶ **Schedule tab**—For Schedule, select Always.

▶ **Link Translation tab**—For Apply Link Translation to This Rule, make sure the option is checked.

Different rules require different settings, but the settings outlined in this example are some of the more common and secure ones used to set this scenario up.

NOTE

Exchange ActiveSync, Outlook Anywhere, and Exchange Web Services require their own rules to be set up. The process is very similar, with the only major difference being that a different option is chosen.

Securing Exchange MAPI Access

The Messaging Application Programming Interface (MAPI) has traditionally been used for communications between the client and an Exchange server. This type of traffic is highly functional, but can pose a security threat to an Exchange server because it requires the use of the dangerous remote procedure calls (RPC) protocol, which has become notorious through recent exploits that take advantage of the open nature of the RPC protocol to take over services on poorly coded applications.

In the past, organizations have been handcuffed by the fact that blocking RPC requires blocking a huge range of ports (all dynamic ports from 1024 to 65,536, plus others) because of the dynamic nature in which RPC works. Blocking RPC access to an Exchange server was not feasible either. This type of block would also block client access through MAPI, effectively crippling email access to an Exchange server.

ISA Server 2006 greatly simplifies and secures this process through its capability to filter RPC traffic for specific services, dynamically opening only those ports that are negotiated for use with MAPI access itself. This greatly limits the types of exploits that can take advantage of an Exchange server that is protected with MAPI filtering techniques.

Configuring MAPI RPC Filtering Rules

To configure an ISA server to filter and allow only MAPI access across particular network segments, use the following technique:

1. From the ISA console, navigate to the Firewall Policy node in the console tree.

2. On the Tasks tab, click the Publish Mail Servers link.

3. Enter a name for the rule, such as MAPI Access from Clients Network, and click Next.

4. Select Client Access from the list of access types, and click Next.

5. Check the Outlook (RPC) (Standard Port) check box, as shown in Figure 13.11, and click Next to continue.

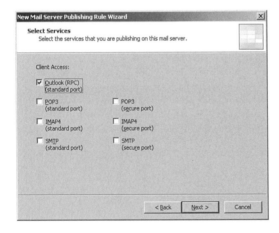

FIGURE 13.11   Enabling a MAPI filtering rule.

6. Enter the IP address of the Exchange server that is to be published, and click Next.

7. Select from which networks the rule will listen to requests, and click Next to continue.

8. Click Finish, click Apply, and then click OK.

To set up more advanced MAPI filtering, examine the Traffic tab of the rule that was created. Click on Filtering, Configure Exchange RPC and/or the Properties buttons, and, finally, choose the Interfaces tab. Advanced settings, such as which Unique User Identifiers (UUIDs) to allow, can be found here, as shown in Figure 13.12.

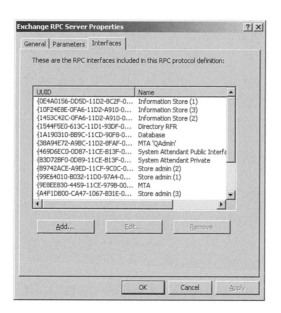

FIGURE 13.12   Examining advanced MAPI filtering.

Deploying MAPI Filtering Across Network Segments

Where MAPI filtering really shines is in scenarios where the ISA server is used to protect a server's network from the client's network in an organization.

In these scenarios, the ISA server acts as an Exchange firewall, providing secured mail, OWA, POP, and any other necessary services to the ISA server through a secured, Application-layer filtered environment. This type of deployment scenario is very useful for organizations that want to reduce the exposure to security threats faced from unruly or exploited clients. It allows for a great degree of control over which type of access to an Exchange environment can be set up.

Securing POP and IMAP Exchange Traffic

The ancillary mail services of the Post Office Protocol version 3 (POP3) and Internet Message Access Protocol version 4 (IMAP4) can be secured through an ISA server. This is particularly important for organizations that require support of these legacy protocols; they are less secure than the newer forms of mail access available.

Creating and Configuring a POP Mail Publishing Rule

POP3 servers are secured in ISA through the creation of a special rule that enables ISA to examine all traffic sent to the POP3 server and perform intrusion detection heuristics on it with an advanced POP intrusion detection filter. The POP server does not necessarily need to be a Microsoft server, such as Exchange, but can be run on any POP3-compliant messaging system.

CAUTION

Enable POP support in a messaging environment only if there is no other viable option. POP3 support is less secure than other access methods, and can cause mail delivery and security issues. For example, many POP clients are configured to pull all the mail off the POP server, making it difficult to do disaster recovery of mail data.

After a POP server has been enabled or established on the internal network, it can be secured via modification of an existing rule or creation of a new rule to secure POP traffic as follows:

1. From the ISA console, select the Firewall Policy node from the console tree.

2. In the tasks pane, click the Publish Mail Servers link.

3. Enter a descriptive name for the rule (for example, POP Access), and click Next.

4. Select the Client Access: RPC, IMAP, POP3, SMTP option, and click Next.

5. In the Select Services dialog box, select POP3 (Standard port), and click Next.

6. Enter the internal IP address of the POP server, and click Next.

7. Select to which networks the ISA server will listen by checking the boxes next to them, and click Next.

8. Click Finish, click Apply, and then click OK.

NOTE

By default, enabling a POP publishing rule turns on the POP intrusion detection filter, which can help protect a POP system from potential exploits. That said, POP3 is still an insecure protocol, and it is preferable not to deploy it on a server.

Creating and Configuring an IMAP Mail Publishing Rule

The Internet Message Access Protocol (IMAP) is often used as a mail access method for UNIX systems and even for clients such as Outlook Express. It also can be secured through an ISA server, using the same rule as a POP rule, or through the configuration of a unique IMAP publishing rule.

After the internal IMAP presence has been established, an ISA rule can be created to allow IMAP traffic to the IMAP server. The following procedure outlines this process:

1. From the ISA console, select the Firewall Policy node from the console tree.

2. In the tasks pane, click the Publish Mail Servers link.

3. Enter a descriptive name for the rule (for example, IMAP Access), and click Next.

4. Click the Client Access: RPC, IMAP, POP3, SMTP option button, as shown in Figure 13.13, and click Next.

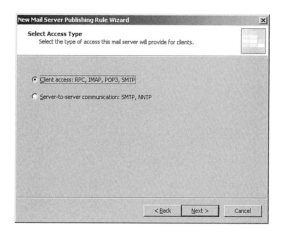

FIGURE 13.13   Setting up an ISA IMAP publishing rule.

5. In the Select Services dialog box, select Secure Ports for IMAP4, and click Next.

6. Enter the internal IP address of the POP server, and click Next.

7. Select to which networks the ISA server will listen by checking the boxes next to them, and click Next.

8. Click Finish.

Managing and Controlling Simple Mail Transfer Protocol (SMTP) Traffic

The Simple Mail Transfer Protocol (SMTP) is the second most commonly used protocol on the Internet, after the web HTTP protocol. It is ubiquitously used as an email transport mechanism on the Internet, and has become a critical tool for online collaboration.

Unfortunately, SMTP is also one of the most abused protocols on the Internet. Unsolicited email (spam), phishing attacks, and email-borne viruses all take advantage of the open, unauthenticated nature of SMTP, and it has become a necessity for organizations to control and monitor SMTP traffic entering and leaving the network.

ISA Server 2006's Application-layer inspection capabilities allow for a high degree of SMTP filtering and attack detection. By default, ISA supports the protocol as part of standard rules and policies.

ISA Server 2006 is an ideal candidate for deployment in an environment with an Exchange 2007 Edge Transport server, as it can scan the traffic bound for that server for irregularities and potential exploits before delivering messages to the Exchange environment.

Publishing the SMTP Server for Inbound Mail Access

The first step toward securing SMTP traffic is to create a server publishing rule that protects the internal SMTP server from direct external access. This can be done through an SMTP serverpublishing rule. In this scenario, an Exchange 2007 Edge Transport server in the DMZ of the ISA firewall is published.

1. From the ISA console, select the Firewall Policy node from the console tree.

2. In the tasks pane, click the Publish Mail Servers link.

3. Enter a descriptive name for the rule (for example, SMTP Inbound to Edge Transport Server), and click Next.

4. Select Server-to-Server Communication: SMTP, NTTP, and click Next.

5. In the dialog box shown in Figure 13.14, choose SMTP, and click Next.

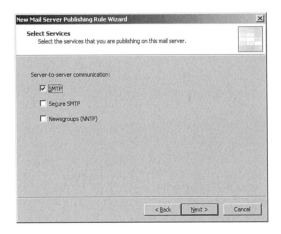

FIGURE 13.14   Setting up an inbound SMTP publishing rule.

6. Enter the internal IP address of the Edge Transport server, and click Next.

7. Select to which networks the ISA server will listen by checking the boxes next to them, and click Next. This is usually the external network. ISA then listens to this network for SMTP requests sent to it and relays them to the Edge Transport server.

8. Click Finish, click Apply, and then click OK.

Creating an SMTP Access Rule in ISA Server 2006

ISA can be easily configured to allow SMTP traffic and to scan that traffic as it passes through the ISA firewall. This can be configured with a simple access rule, set up as follows:

1. On the ISA server, open the ISA console, and choose the Firewall Policy node from the console tree.

2. In the tasks pane, click the Create Access Rule link.

3. Enter a descriptive name, such as Allow SMTP Outbound from Edge Transport Server, and click Next.

4. Select Allow from the rule action list, and click Next.

5. Under This Rule Applies To, select Specified Protocols.

6. Click Add under Protocols, then drill down and choose Common Protocols, SMTP. Click Add.

7. Click Close and then click Next.

8. Under Access Rule Sources, click Add.

9. Drill down to Networks, and select Perimeter (or the network where the Edge Transport server is), click Add, and then click Close. Note that it is often better practice to restrict this to the specific IP address of the Edge Transport server, rather than to a whole network.

10. Under Access Rule Destinations, click Add.

11. Under Networks, select External, click Add, and then click Close.

12. Click Next, click Next, and then click Finish.

13. Click Apply at the top of the details pane, and then click OK to confirm.

Customizing the SMTP Filter

After SMTP rules have been set up to allow the traffic to flow through the SMTP Screener, the ISA SMTP filter can be customized to block specific types of SMTP commands and content. To access the SMTP filter settings on the ISA server, do the following:

1. From the ISA console, click the Add-ins node in the console tree.

2. Under Application Filters in the details pane, double-click on SMTP Filter.

3. Examine and configure the settings in the SMTP Filter Properties dialog box, some of which are shown in Figure 13.15.

The SMTP Screener filter allows for the following default filtering functionality:

▶ Keyword filtering

▶ Email address/domain name filtering

▶ Attachment filtering

▶ SMTP command filtering

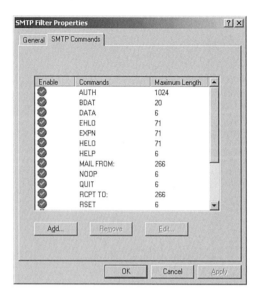

FIGURE 13.15   Configuring SMTP filter settings.

Logging ISA Traffic

One of the most powerful troubleshooting tools at the disposal of SharePoint and ISA administrators is the logging mechanism, which gives live or archived views of the logs on an ISA server, and allows for quick and easy searching and indexing of ISA Server log information, including every packet of data that hits the ISA server.

> **NOTE**
>
> Many of the advanced features of ISA logging are only available when using MSDE or SQL databases for the storage of the logs.

Examining ISA Logs

The ISA logs are accessible via the Logging tab in the details pane of the Monitoring node, as shown in Figure 13.16. They offer administrators the ability to watch, in real time, what is happening to the ISA server, whether it is denying connections, and what rule is being applied for each Allow or Deny statement.

The logs include pertinent information on each packet of data, including the following key characteristics:

- **Log Time**—The exact time the packet was processed.
- **Destination IP**—The destination IP address of the packet.
- **Destination Port**—The destination TCP/IP port, such as port 80 for HTTP traffic.

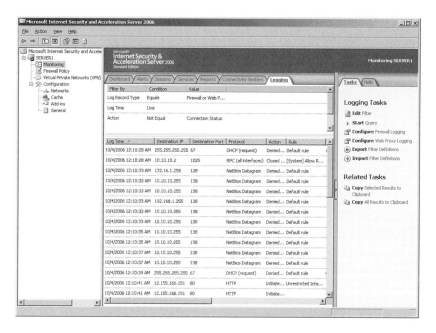

FIGURE 13.16   Examining ISA logging.

▶ **Protocol**—The specific protocol that the packet utilized, such as HTTP, LDAP, RPC, or others.

▶ **Action**—The type of action the ISA server took on the traffic, such as initiating the connection or denying it.

▶ **Rule**—The particular firewall policy rule applied to the traffic.

▶ **Client IP**—The IP address of the client that sent the packet.

▶ **Client Username**—The username of the requesting client. Note that this is only populated if using the Firewall Client.

▶ **Source Network**—The source network from which the packet came.

▶ **Destination Network**—The network where the destination of the packet is located.

▶ **HTTP Method**—If HTTP traffic, the type of HTTP method utilized, such as GET or POST.

▶ **URL**—If HTTP is used, the exact URL that was requested.

By searching through the logs for specific criteria in these columns, such as all packets sent by a specific IP address, or all URLs that match http://sharepoint.companyabc.com, advanced troubleshooting and monitoring is simplified.

Customizing Logging Filters

What is displayed in the details pane of the Logging tab is a reflection of only those logs that match certain criteria in the log filter. It is highly useful to use the filter to weed out the extraneous log entries, which just distract from the specific monitoring task. For example, on many networks, an abundance of NetBIOS broadcast traffic makes it difficult to read the logs. For this reason, a specific filter can be created to only show traffic that is not NetBIOS traffic. To set up this particular type of rule, do the following:

1. From the ISA Admin console, click the Monitoring node from the console tree, and select the Logging tab in the details pane.

2. On the Tasks tab in the tasks pane, click the Edit Filter link.

3. In the Edit Filter dialog box, change the Filter by, Condition, and Value fields to display Protocol, Not Equal, NetBios Datagram, and then click Add to List.

4. Repeat for the NetBios Name Service and the NetBios Session values, so that the dialog box looks like the one displayed in Figure 13.17.

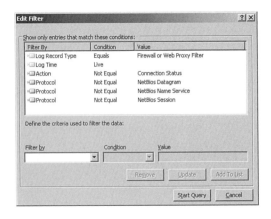

FIGURE 13.17   Creating a custom logging filter.

5. Click Start Query.

NOTE

It cannot be stressed enough that this logging mechanism is quite literally the best tool for troubleshooting ISA access. For example, it can be used to tell if traffic from clients is even hitting the ISA server, and if it is, what is happening to it (denied, accepted, and so on).

Monitoring ISA from the ISA Console

In addition to the robust logging mechanism, the ISA Monitoring node also contains various tabs that link to other extended troubleshooting and monitoring tools. Each of these tools performs unique functions, such as generating reports, alerting administrators, or verifying connectivity to critical services. It is, therefore, important to understand how each of these tools work.

Customizing the ISA Dashboard

The ISA Dashboard, shown in Figure 13.18, provides for quick and comprehensive monitoring of a multitude of ISA components from a single screen. The view is customizable, and individual components can be collapsed and/or expanded by clicking the arrow buttons in the upper-right corner of each of the components. All of the individual ISA Monitoring elements are summarized here.

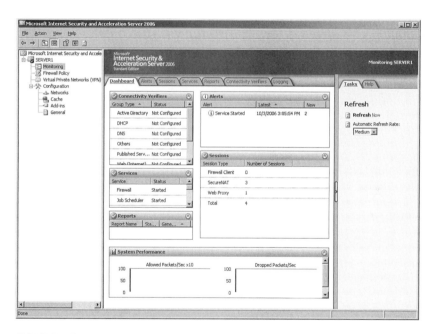

FIGURE 13.18   Viewing the ISA Dashboard.

> **TIP**
>
> The ISA Dashboard is the logical "parking" page for ISA administrators, who can leave the screen set at the Dashboard to allow for quick-glance views of ISA health.

Monitoring and Customizing Alerts

The Alerts tab, shown in Figure 13.19, lists all of the status alerts that ISA has generated while it is in operation. It is beneficial to look through these alerts on a regular basis, and acknowledge them when you no longer need to display them on the Dashboard. If alerts need to be permanently removed, they can be reset instead. Resetting or acknowledging alerts is as simple as right-clicking on them and choosing Reset or Acknowledge.

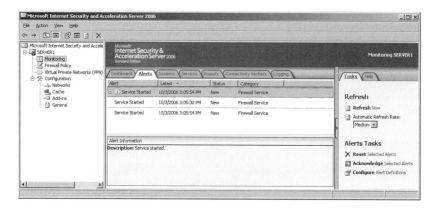

FIGURE 13.19   Viewing the ISA Alerts tab.

Alerts that show up in this list are listed because their default alert definition specified an action to display them in the console. This type of alert behavior is completely customizable, and alerts can be made to do the following actions:

- ▶ Send email
- ▶ Run a program
- ▶ Report to Windows event log
- ▶ Stop selected services
- ▶ Start selected services

For example, it might be necessary to force a stop of the firewall service if a specific type of attack is detected. Configuring alert definitions is relatively straightforward. For example, the following process illustrates how to create an alert that sends an email to an administrator when a SYN attack is detected:

1. From the Alerts tab of the ISA Monitoring node, select the Tasks tab in the tasks pane.

2. Click the Configure Alert Definitions link.

3. On the Alert Definitions tab of the Alert Properties dialog box, shown in Figure 13.20, choose SYN Attack, and click Edit.

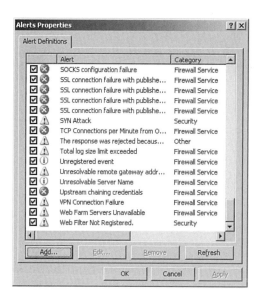

FIGURE 13.20   Creating a custom alert definition.

4. Choose the Actions tab in the SYN Attack Properties dialog box.

5. Check the Send E-mail check box.

6. Enter the SMTP server in the organization, and then complete the From, To, and CC fields, similar to what is shown in Figure 13.21.

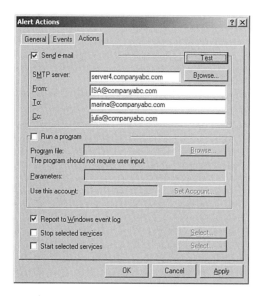

FIGURE 13.21   Setting an alert action for an event.

7. Click the Test button to try the settings, and then click OK to acknowledge a successful test.

8. Click OK, click OK, click Apply, and then click OK to save the settings.

As is evident from the list, a vast number of existing alert definitions can be configured, and a large number of thresholds can be set. In addition, more potential alerts can be configured by clicking Add on the Alerts Properties dialog box and following the wizard. This allows for an even greater degree of customization.

Monitoring Session and Services Activity

The Services tab, shown in Figure 13.22, allows for a quick-glance view of the ISA services, if they are running, and how long they have been up since last being restarted. The services can also be stopped and started from this tab.

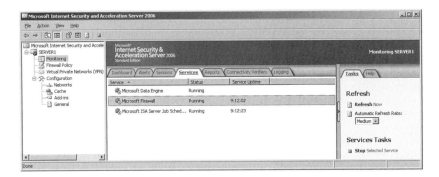

FIGURE 13.22   Monitoring ISA services.

The Sessions tab allows for more interaction, as individual unique sessions to the ISA server can be viewed and disconnected as necessary. For example, it might be necessary to disconnect any users who are on a VPN connection, if a change to the VPN policy has just been issued. This is because VPN clients that have already established a session with the ISA server are only subject to the laws of the VPN policy that was in effect when they originally logged on. To disconnect a session, right-click on the session, and choose Disconnect Session, as shown in Figure 13.23.

Creating Connectivity Verifiers

Connectivity verifiers can be a useful way of extending ISA's capabilities to include monitoring of critical services within an environment, such as domain name system (DNS), Dynamic Host Configuration Protocol (DHCP), HTTP, or other custom services. Connectivity verifiers are essentially a quick-and-dirty approach to monitoring an environment with very little cost, as they take advantage of ISA's alerting capabilities and the Dashboard to display the verifiers.

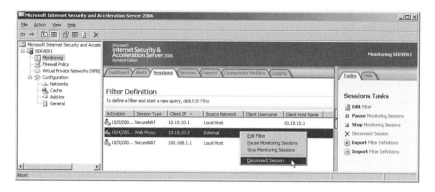

FIGURE 13.23   Disconnecting a session.

For example, the following step-by-step process illustrates setting up a connectivity verifier that checks the status of an internal SharePoint server:

1. On the Monitoring tab of the ISA console, click the Connectivity tab of the details pane.

2. On the Tasks tab of the tasks pane, click the Create New Connectivity Verifier link.

3. Enter a name for the connectivity verifier, such as Web Server Verifier, and click Next.

4. In the Connectivity Verification Details dialog box, enter the server FQDN, the group type (which simply determines how it is grouped on the Dashboard), and the type of verification method to use, in this case an HTTP GET request, as shown in Figure 13.24.

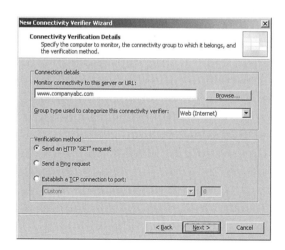

FIGURE 13.24   Configuring a SharePoint HTTP connectivity verifier.

5. Click Finish.

6. Click Yes when prompted to turn on the rule that allows ISA Server to connect via HTTP to selected servers.

7. Click Apply and then click OK.

After being created, connectivity verifiers that fit into the major group types are reflected on the Dashboard. Creating multiple connectivity verifiers in each of the common group types can make the Dashboard a more effective monitoring tool.

Summary

ISA Server 2006 has often been called the Exchange Server firewall, and for good reason. The capabilities of ISA Server 2006 to secure and protect Exchange services, whether through reverse-proxying HTTP traffic, filtering MAPI traffic, or screening SMTP messages, gives it capabilities not present in other firewall solutions. In addition, ISA's ability to be easily deployed in the DMZ of existing firewalls as a dedicated security appliance further extends its capabilities and allows it to be deployed in environments of all shapes and sizes.

Best Practices

The following are best practices from this chapter:

▶ Filter MAPI traffic destined for Exchange servers using ISA Server 2006's RPC filtering technology.

▶ Monitor ISA Server using the MSDE or SQL logging approaches to allow for the greatest level of monitoring functionality.

▶ Secure any edge-facing service such as OWA and Exchange ActiveSync with a reverse-proxy system such as ISA Server 2006.

▶ Deploy ISA reverse-proxy capability in the existing DMZ of a firewall if it is not feasible to replace existing firewall technologies.

CHAPTER 14

Understanding Enterprise Policy Enforcement Security

Microsoft Exchange Server 2007 evolved during a time when organizations became more and more aware of the need to gain greater control over the content that traversed through the system. In the past, these types of considerations were not given much thought, and email was pretty much open for all users to send whatever they needed, both internally and externally.

Over time, as specific high-profile lawsuits over email content took place and governmental regulations such as HIPAA and Sarbanes Oxley went into effect, organizations began to take note that they would have to establish policies to control their messaging environments.

Exchange Server 2007 provides for robust integrated support of enterprise policy enforcement, allowing organizations to apply restrictions to mail messages, limiting content that can be sent and creating a framework in which specific retention policies can be created.

This chapter focuses on the Exchange 2007 capabilities in this space. The role that governmental policies such as HIPAA and Sarbanes Oxley play in forming these policies is described. Specific information on policy enforcement using transport rules agents and Messaging Records Management are outlined and explained. In addition, best practices for organizations looking to use Exchange 2007 for policy management are defined.

What Is Enterprise Policy Management in Exchange Server 2007?

Exchange 2007 introduces the concept of Enterprise Policy Management as a built-in component of the application. Microsoft built this structure into Exchange as a direct result of the changes in the marketplace that required that certain types of communications such as email be controlled, managed, secured, and audited to levels previously unattainable without third-party products.

Enterprise Policy Management in Exchange 2007 is effectively composed of several components, each providing a different layer in the management space. These components are defined as follows:

- **Messaging Records Management (MRM)**—Messaging Records Management in Exchange 2007 defines retention settings for individual mail folders within mailboxes.

- **Journaling**—Exchange 2007 journaling allows for mailbox-specific archiving of all communications sent to or from specific users, allowing organizations to comply with strict retention policies stipulated by governmental regulations. The Exchange 2007 journaling feature is greatly improved over Exchange Server 2003, with premium journaling allowing for granular administration.

- **Edge Transport rules**—Exchange 2007 has the ability to apply policies and rules at the edge layer, protecting an organization from spam, spyware, undesired corporate information leakage, and other undesirable emails.

- **Hub Transport rules**—Exchange 2007 also allows for Hub Transport specific rules, which are run against all traffic sent through Hub Transport role servers.

- **Address rewriting**—Edge Transport servers in Exchange 2007 can implement a policy to rewrite all of the outgoing Simple Mail Transfer Protocol (SMTP) domain names within a company to a single domain name, thus ensuring consistency with corporate policies.

- **Disclaimers**—Disclaimer policies also run on Edge servers and are created to allow a corporate disclaimer to be appended to the end of every outgoing mail message.

- **Rights Management Services**—Exchange Server 2007 integrates directly with Rights Management Services, allowing rights-protected emails to be sent across forest boundaries encrypted.

Each of these components is described in more detail in later sections of this chapter. In addition, step-by-step guides for deploying best practice policies are defined.

Understanding Relevant Governmental Regulations for Policy Enforcement

Multiple governmental and industry regulations have direct consequences for messaging platforms within organizations. Security systems within an organization can be based on proprietary standards; however, as organizations have the need to securely exchange information with other entities, the need to have information systems built on standards becomes crucial. Security standards enable organizations to not only store and transmit information within the enterprise in a secure manner, but also securely exchange information with other entities.

A universal security standard requires the creation of common criteria for a secured environment, the adoption of the standard by an accepted standards organization, the acceptance of the standard by organizations, and the implementation of the standard in enterprise transactions.

There are many initiatives to create security standards. Some of these standards include ISO/IEC 17799, HIPAA, and provisions of the Gramm-Leach-Bliley Act. These initiatives, and how they relate to Exchange 2007 Policy Management, are detailed in the subsequent sections of this chapter.

Understanding the ISO/IEC 17799 Security Standard

ISO/IEC 17799 is "a comprehensive set of controls comprising best practices in information security." It is an internationally recognized generic information security standard. Its predecessor, titled BS7799-1, has existed in various forms for a number of years, although the standard only really gained widespread recognition following publication by ISO (the International Organization for Standardization) in December of 2000. Formal certification and accreditation were also introduced around the same time.

ISO/IEC 17799 is organized into 10 major sections, each covering a different topic or area:

- **Business Continuity Planning**—The objective of this section is to counteract interruptions to business activities and to critical business processes from the effects of major failures or disasters.

- **System Access Control**—The objectives of this section are a) to control access to information, b) to prevent unauthorized access to information systems, c) to ensure the protection of networked services, d) to prevent unauthorized computer access, e) to detect unauthorized activities, and f) to ensure information security when using mobile computing and telenetworking facilities.

- **System Development and Maintenance**—The objectives of this section are a) to ensure security is built in to operational systems; b) to prevent loss, modification, or misuse of user data in application systems; c) to protect the confidentiality, authenticity, and integrity of information; d) to ensure information technology (IT) projects and support activities are conducted in a secure manner; and e) to maintain the security of application system software and data.

▸ **Physical and Environmental Security**—The objectives of this section are a) to prevent unauthorized access, damage, and interference to business premises and information; b) to prevent loss, damage, or compromise of assets and interruption to business activities; and c) to prevent compromise or theft of information and information-processing facilities.

▸ **Compliance**—The objectives of this section are a) to avoid breaches of any criminal or civil law, statutory, regulatory, or contractual obligations, and of any security requirements; b) to ensure compliance of systems with organizational security policies and standards; and c) to maximize the effectiveness of and to minimize interference to/from the system audit process.

▸ **Personnel Security**—The objectives of this section are a) to reduce risks of human error, theft, fraud, or misuse of facilities; b) to ensure that users are aware of information security threats and concerns, and are equipped to support the corporate security policy in the course of their normal work; and c) to minimize the damage from security incidents and malfunctions and learn from such incidents.

▸ **Security Organization**—The objectives of this section are a) to manage information security within the company; b) to maintain the security of organizational information-processing facilities and information assets accessed by third parties; and c) to maintain the security of information when the responsibility for information processing has been outsourced to another organization.

▸ **Computer and Operations Management**—The objectives of this section are a) to ensure the correct and secure operation of information-processing facilities; b) to minimize the risk of systems failures; c) to protect the integrity of software and information; d) to maintain the integrity and availability of information processing and communication; e) to ensure the safeguarding of information in networks and the protection of the supporting infrastructure; f) to prevent damage to assets and interruptions to business activities; and g) to prevent loss, modification, or misuse of information exchanged between organizations.

▸ **Asset Classification and Control**—The objectives of this section are a) to maintain appropriate protection of corporate assets and b) to ensure that information assets receive an appropriate level of protection.

▸ **Security Policy**—The objectives of this section are a) to provide management direction and b) to provide support for information security.

The first step toward ISO/IEC 17799 certification is to comply with the standard itself. This is a good security practice in its own right, but it is also the longer-term status adopted by a number of organizations that require the assurance of an external measure, yet do not want to proceed with an external or formal process immediately.

In either case, the method and rigor enforced by the standard can be put to good use in terms of better management of risk. It is also being used in some sectors as a market differentiator, as organizations begin to quote their ISO/IEC 17799 status within their individual markets and to potential customers.

Understanding the Health Insurance Portability and Accountability Act of 1996 (HIPAA)

HIPAA is the acronym for the Health Insurance Portability and Accountability Act of 1996. When HIPAA was enacted in 1996, it had two major purposes. One was to allow employees to change jobs while maintaining health-care coverage. The second was to ensure that health-care providers maintain the confidentiality of patient information.

With respect to the portability of insurance, a few decades ago, people stayed in one or two jobs throughout a whole career. In those days, people had no need for HIPAA because their jobs were stable and their employee benefits were retained by a single or limited number of providers. However, today in a time when jobs and even careers are constantly changing, HIPAA provides the continuity of health insurance even through job changes and unemployment.

The original Act was unclear and led to much confusion in the health-care industry specifically how to comply with HIPAA, so several revisions to HIPAA were enacted along with clarification documents.

Early Provisions of HIPAA

The initial actions of HIPAA were clarified and implemented related to consumer rights to health-care coverage. HIPAA increased an individual's ability to get health coverage for themselves and their dependents. It also lowered an employee's chance of losing existing health-care coverage, through a job change or unemployment. HIPAA also helped employees buy health insurance coverage on their own if they lost coverage under an employer's group health plan and have no other health coverage available.

Among its specific protections, HIPAA limited the use of preexisting condition exclusions and prohibited group health plans from discriminating by denying coverage or charging employees extra for coverage based on their individual or family member's past or present poor health. HIPAA provided guarantees to employers or individuals who purchased health insurance so they could renew the coverage regardless of any health conditions of individuals covered under the insurance policy.

HIPAA, however, does not require employers to offer or pay for health coverage to their employees nor does it guarantee health coverage for all workers. HIPAA also does not control the amount that an insurer can charge for coverage nor require group health plans to offer specific benefits. Other provisions do not require an employer or insurer to offer the same level of health-care coverage as a previous provider nor eliminate all use of preexisting condition exclusions.

Later Provisions of HIPAA

After the early provisions for HIPAA relative to consumer rights to health care were defined and implemented, the focus of HIPAA turned to the accountability aspects of the Act. The focus areas were standards for transactions and code sets, privacy of patient information, and security of information.

HIPAA Transaction and Code Sets

The rules for Transactions and Code Sets (TCS) were published on August 17, 2000, and with modifications published in May 2002. The compliance date was October 16, 2002. On December 27, 2001, President Bush signed HR3323, which provided for a delay in the implementation of the TCS rules of HIPAA. This extended the compliance due date to October 16, 2003, if a compliance extension was requested.

Further modifications to the final rule were published in February 2003. This rule finalized provisions applicable to electronic data transaction standards from two related proposed rules published in the May 31, 2002, Federal Register. It adopted modifications to implement specifications for health-care entities and for several electronic transaction standards that were omitted from the May 31, 2002, proposed rules.

The purpose of those regulations was to standardize the electronic exchange of information (transactions) between trading partners. These transactions were mandated to be in the ANSI ASC X12 version 4010 format. The covered transactions include the following:

▶ 270 = Eligibility Inquiry

▶ 271 = Inquiry and Response

▶ 276 = Claim Status Inquiry

▶ 277 = Claim Status Inquiry and Response

▶ 278 = Authorization Request and Authorization Response

▶ 820 = Health Insurance Premium Payment

▶ 834 = Beneficiary Enrollment

▶ 835 = Remittance/Payment

▶ 837 = Claim or Encounter

The HIPAA Code Set Regulations establish a uniform standard of data elements used to document reasons why patients are seen and the procedures performed during health-care encounters. HIPAA specified code sets to be used as follows:

▶ Diagnoses - ICD 9

▶ Procedures - CPT 4, CDT

▶ Supplies/Devices – HCPCS

▶ Additional Clinical Data - Health Level Seven (HL7)

HIPAA specified administrative codes set for use in conjunction with certain transactions and HIPAA eliminated local codes.

HIPAA Privacy

As of April 14, 2003, health-care providers and health plans were required to be in compliance with the HIPAA Privacy Regulation. Both the 1996 Congress and the two subsequent administrations agreed that a privacy law was needed to ensure that sensitive personal health information can be shared for core health activities, with safeguards in place to limit the inappropriate use and sharing of patient data. The HIPAA privacy rule took critical steps in that direction to require that privacy and security be built in to the policies and practices of health-care providers, plans, and others involved in health care.

The U.S. Department of Health and Human Services (DHHS) had addressed the concerns with new privacy standards that set a national minimum of basic protections. Congress recognized that advances in electronic technology could erode the privacy of health information. Consequently, Congress incorporated into HIPAA provisions that mandate an adoption of federal privacy protections for certain individually identifiable health information.

The HIPAA Privacy Rule (Standards for Privacy of Individually Identifiable Health Information) provided the first national standards for protecting the privacy of health information. The Privacy Rule regulates how certain entities, called covered entities, use and disclose certain individually identifiable health information, called protected health information (PHI). PHI is individually identifiable health information that is transmitted or maintained in any form or medium (for example, electronic, paper, oral), but excludes certain educational records and employment records. Among other provisions, the Privacy Rule provides for the following:

- ▶ Gives patients more control over their health information

- ▶ Sets boundaries on the use and release of health records

- ▶ Establishes appropriate safeguards that the majority of health-care providers and others must achieve to protect the privacy of health information

- ▶ Holds violators accountable with civil and criminal penalties that can be imposed if they violate patients' privacy rights

- ▶ Strikes a balance when public health responsibilities support disclosure of certain forms of data

- ▶ Enables patients to make informed choices based on how individual health information can be used

- ▶ Enables patients to find out how their information can be used and what disclosures of their information have been made

- ▶ Generally limits release of information to the minimum reasonably needed for the purpose of the disclosure

- ▶ Generally gives patients the right to obtain a copy of their own health records and request corrections

14

▶ Empowers individuals to control certain uses and disclosures of their health information

The deadline to comply with the Privacy Rule was April 14, 2003, for the majority of the three types of covered entities specified by the rule [45 CFR § 160.102]. The covered entities are the following:

▶ Health plans

▶ Health-care clearinghouses

▶ Health-care providers who transmit health information in electronic form in connection with certain transactions

At DHHS, the Office for Civil Rights (OCR) has oversight and enforcement responsibilities for the Privacy Rule. Comprehensive guidance and OCR answers to hundreds of questions are available at http://www.hhs.gov/ocr/hipaa.

DHHS recognized the importance of sharing PHI to accomplish essential public health objectives and to meet certain other societal needs (for example, administration of justice and law enforcement). Therefore, the Privacy Rule expressly permits PHI to be shared for specified public health purposes. For example, covered entities can disclose PHI, without individual authorization, to a public health authority legally authorized to collect or receive the information for the purpose of preventing or controlling disease, injury, or disability [45 CFR § 164.512(b)]. Further, the Privacy Rule permits covered entities to make disclosures that are required by other laws, including laws that require disclosures for public health purposes. Thus, the Privacy Rule provides for the continued functioning of the U.S public health system.

HIPAA Security

The American public began to register serious concerns about the privacy and security of health records in the early 1990s. Breaches of health privacy, such as press disclosures of individuals' HIV status, network hacking incidents, and misdirected patient emails fueled this concern. At the same time, health-care industry and federal agencies working toward HIPAA "administrative simplification" and increased automation of health information realized that their initiatives would be unsuccessful without incorporating more effective information-security measures. When HIPAA was passed in 1996, it included a mandate for standards that would ensure the security and integrity of health information that is maintained or transmitted electronically. A Notice of Proposed Rulemaking (NPRM) on security was published by DHHS on August 12, 1998.

The Security Rule focuses on both external and internal security threats and vulnerabilities. Threats from "outsiders" include breaking through network firewalls, email attacks through interception or viruses, compromise of passwords, posing as organization "insiders," computer viruses, and modem number prefix scanning. These activities can result in denial of service, such as the disruption of information flow by "crashing" or overloading critical computer servers. The outsider might steal and misuse proprietary information, including individual health information. Attacks can also affect the integrity of information, by corrupting data that is being transmitted.

Internal threats are of equal concern, and are far more likely to occur according to many security experts. Organizations must protect against careless staff or others who are unaware of security issues, and curious or malicious insiders who deliberately take advantage of system vulnerabilities to access and misuse personal health information.

The rule is intended to set a minimum level or "floor" of security. Organizations can choose to implement safeguards that exceed the HIPAA standards—and, in fact, might find that their business strategies require stronger protections. Covered entities are required to

▶ Assess potential risks and vulnerabilities

▶ Protect against threats to information security or integrity, and against unauthorized use or disclosure

▶ Implement and maintain security measures that are appropriate to their needs, capabilities, and circumstances

▶ Ensure compliance with these safeguards by all staff

Central to HIPAA security is the tenet that information security must be comprehensive. No single policy, practice, or tool can ensure effective overall security. Cultural and organizational issues must be addressed, as well as technological and physical concerns. The safeguards that comprise HIPAA-mandated security focus on protecting "data integrity, confidentiality, and availability" of individually identifiable health information through the following:

▶ **Administrative procedures**—Documented, formal practices to manage the selection and execution of security measures

▶ **Physical safeguards**—Protection of computer systems and related buildings and equipment from hazards and intrusion

▶ **Technical security services**—Processes that protect and monitor information access

▶ **Technical security mechanisms**—Processes that prevent unauthorized access to data that is transmitted over a network

These regulations established standards for all health plans, clearinghouses, and storage of health-care information to ensure the integrity, confidentiality, and availability of electronic protected health information. Proposed rules were published on August 12, 1998. Final rules were published on February 20, 2003, and compliance had to occur by April 20, 2005.

HIPAA Implications for Exchange Server 2007 Environments

The most important implication that HIPAA requirements have on an Exchange 2007 environment is regarding data security. Organizations subject to HIPAA regulations must demonstrate that they are taking significant precautions against confidential patient data being compromised, lost, or stolen. This includes the transmission of this type of data across a medium such as email.

Exchange 2007 can help organizations become HIPAA compliant through the use of enterprise policies that define when email data is encrypted, thus securing the transmission of protected data. Information on how to set up these policies is presented in upcoming sections of this chapter.

Understanding the Gramm-Leach-Bliley Act

Information that many would consider private—including bank balances and account numbers—is regularly bought and sold by banks, credit card companies, and other financial institutions. The Gramm-Leach-Bliley Act (GLBA), which is also known as the Financial Services Modernization Act of 1999, provides limited privacy protections against the sale of the private financial information of consumers. In addition, the GLBA codifies protections against pretexting, the practice of obtaining personal information through false pretenses.

The GLBA primarily sought to "modernize" financial services—that is, end regulations that prevented the merger of banks, stock brokerage companies, and insurance companies. The removal of these regulations, however, raised significant risks that these new financial institutions would have access to an incredible amount of personal information, with no restrictions upon its use. Prior to GLBA, the insurance company that maintained health records was distinct from the bank that held the mortgage on a consumer's house or the stockbroker who traded a person's stock. After these companies merged, however, they had the ability to consolidate, analyze, and sell the personal details of their customers' lives. Because of these risks, the GLBA included three simple requirements to protect the personal data of individuals: First, banks, brokerage companies, and insurance companies must securely store personal financial information. Second, they must advise consumers of their policies on sharing of personal financial information. Third, they must give consumers the option to opt out of some sharing of personal financial information.

Privacy Protections Under the GLBA

The GLBA's privacy protections only regulate financial institutions—businesses that are engaged in banking, insuring, stocks and bonds, financial advice, and investing.

First, these financial institutions, regardless of whether they want to disclose the personal information of individuals, must develop precautions to ensure the security and confidentiality of customer records and information, to protect against any anticipated threats or hazards to the security or integrity of such records, and to protect against unauthorized access to or use of such records or information that could result in substantial harm or inconvenience to any customer.

Second, financial institutions are required to provide consumers with a notice of their information-sharing policies when the individual first becomes a customer, and annually thereafter. That notice must inform the consumer of the financial institutions' policies on disclosing nonpublic personal information (NPI) to affiliates and nonaffiliated third parties, disclosing NPI after the customer relationship is terminated, and protecting NPI. "Nonpublic personal information" means all information on applications to obtain financial services (credit card or loan applications), account histories (bank or credit card), and the fact that an individual is or was a customer. This interpretation of NPI makes names, addresses, telephone numbers, Social Security numbers, and other data subject to the GLBA's data-sharing restrictions.

Third, the GLBA gives consumers the right to opt out from a limited amount of NPI sharing. Specifically, a consumer can direct the financial institution to not share information with unaffiliated companies.

Consumers have no right under the GLBA to stop sharing of NPI among affiliates. An affiliate is any company that controls, is controlled by, or is under common control with another company. The individual consumer has absolutely no control over this kind of "corporate family" trading of personal information.

Several exemptions under the GLBA can permit information sharing over the consumer's objection. For instance, if a financial institution wants to engage the services of a separate company, they can transfer personal information to that company by arguing that the information is necessary to the services that the company will perform. A financial institution can transfer information to a marketing or sales company to sell new products (different stocks) or jointly offered products (cosponsored credit cards). After this unaffiliated third party has an individual's personal information, they can share it with their own "corporate family." However, they themselves cannot likewise transfer the information to further companies through this exemption.

In addition, financial institutions can disclose information to credit reporting agencies, to financial regulatory agencies, as part of the sale of a business, to comply with any other laws or regulations, or as necessary for a transaction requested by the consumer.

Fourth, financial institutions are prohibited from disclosing, other than to a consumer reporting agency, access codes or account numbers to any nonaffiliated third party for use in telemarketing, direct mail marketing, or other marketing through electronic mail. Thus, even if a consumer fails to "opt out" of a financial institution's transfers, the credit card numbers, PINs, or other access codes cannot be sold, as they had been in some previous cases.

Fifth, certain types of "pretexting" were prohibited by the GLBA. Pretexting is the practice of collecting personal information under false pretenses. Pretexters pose as authority figures (law enforcement agents, social workers, potential employers, and so on) and manufacture seductive stories (that the victim is about to receive a sweepstakes award or insurance payment) to elicit personal information about the victim. The GLBA prohibits the use of false, fictitious, or fraudulent statements or documents to get customer information from a financial institution or directly from a customer of a financial institution; the use of forged, counterfeit, lost, or stolen documents to get customer information from a financial institution or directly from a customer of a financial institution; and asking another person to get someone else's customer information using false, fictitious, or fraudulent documents or forged, counterfeit, lost, or stolen documents.

GLBA's Implications for Exchange Server 2007 Environments

GLBA strictly limits the disclosure of personal information outside of a company or its immediate corporate affiliates. Exchange policies in regard to email can be set up to monitor communications for specific types of personal data or key phrases, restricting where it can be sent.

Understanding Sarbanes-Oxley

Sarbanes-Oxley (often nicknamed SOX), named for the two congressmen who sponsored it, on the surface doesn't have much to do with IT security. The law was passed to restore the public's confidence in corporate governance by making chief executives of publicly traded companies personally validate financial statements and other information.

President Bush signed the law on July 30, 2002. Initially, companies had to be in compliance by the fall of 2003, but extensions were granted. Large corporations were given until June 15, 2004, to meet the requirements of Sarbanes-Oxley. Smaller companies had to comply by April 15, 2005.

Congress passed the law in quick response to accounting scandals surrounding Enron, Worldcom, and other companies. Sarbanes-Oxley deals with many corporate governance issues, including executive compensation and the use of independent directors. Section 404 mandates that each annual report contain an internal control report, which must state the responsibility of management for establishing and maintaining an adequate internal control structure and procedures for financial reporting. It must also contain an assessment, at the end of the issuer's most recent fiscal year, of the effectiveness of the internal control structure and procedures for financial reporting. The auditor must attest to, and report on, the assessment made by the management of the issuer. It's hard to sign off on the validity of data if the systems maintaining it aren't secure. It is the internal IT systems that keep the records of the organizations. If the IT systems aren't secure, internal controls can also be questioned.

Sarbanes-Oxley doesn't mandate specific internal controls such as strong authentication or the use of encryption. However, if someone can easily get in to an organization's IT system, the security hole can establish a condition of noncompliance. Sarbanes-Oxley creates a link between upper management and the security operation staff on what is needed to ensure that proper and auditable security measures are in place. The executives who have to sign off on the internal controls have to ensure the security in their organizations is well established; otherwise, the executive could face criminal penalties if a breach is detected.

Sarbanes-Oxley's Implications for Exchange Server 2007 Environments

SOX controls stipulate that data must be secured and audited to make sure that a third party cannot manipulate financial data. Exchange 2007 includes administrative controls that protect an organization from security breaches. In addition, SOX controls look to an organization to establish specific guidelines in regard to data retention and data transfer controls. These factors can be controlled using specific Exchange enterprise policies, such as mail retention policies, privacy policies, and confidentiality policies, as outlined in subsequent sections of this chapter.

Using Transport Agents in Exchange Server 2007

Transport agents are part of the core Exchange functionality provided to organizations that allow for policies to be enforced within the messaging platform. Microsoft designed these policies with built-in support for third-party add-ons. This allows other companies to build products that directly integrate with Exchange 2007 to scan mail and to run specific tasks on the mail that flows through the system.

At their core, Transport agents are just a programmatic method of performing tasks on mail based on a specified criterion. They can range in complexity from a simple "Forward a copy of all emails sent to this person to this particular email address" to "Apply this equation to this email message to determine whether or not it is spam."

Understanding the Role of Transport Agents in Policy Management

Transport agents are especially important for companies looking to bring their messaging platform into compliance with specific governmental regulations, as some of the default transport agents, such as journaling or mail retention policies, offer out-of-the-box functionality that is required by many of these regulations. For situations where built-in functionality might not suffice, the field of third-party add-ons to Exchange 2007 transport agents is increasing every day, so organizations can deploy a custom agent to perform a specific task.

Prioritizing Transport Agents

Exchange Server 2007 allows administrators to prioritize the order in which transport agents act on a message. As an SMTP message passes through the transport pipeline, different SMTP events are acted out. These events, with names such as OnHeloCommand and OnConnectEvent, happen in a specific order every time, and transport agents set to act upon a specific event will only fire when that event has occurred. After it occurs, however, the priority level can be set, determining which transport agent acts first at that particular juncture.

Changing priority on a specific transport rule is as simple as right-clicking on the rule in the details pane and choosing Change Priority.

Using Pipeline Tracing to Troubleshoot Transport Agents

Pipeline tracing with Exchange 2007 transport agents is a diagnostic tool that can be used to send a copy of the mail message as it existed before and after a transport rule went into effect. This copy is sent to a specific mailbox.

To enable Pipeline tracing on an Exchange server, run the following command from the Exchange Management Shell:

```
Set-TransportServer Server5 –PipelineTracingEnabled $True
```

where *Server5* is the name of the server. To set a specific mailbox to be the pipeline tracing mailbox, run the following command from the shell:

```
Set-TransportServer Server5 -PipelineTracingSenderAddress zack@companyabc.com
```

where *Server5* is the name of the server and *zack@companyabc.com* is the mailbox to send the files to.

Pipeline tracing must be enabled on all Hub Transport and/or Edge Transport servers in the topology for it to be useful as a troubleshooting mechanism.

Outlining the Built-in Transport Agents in Exchange Server 2007

Exchange 2007 contains built-in support for a wide variety of transport agents. Some of these agents run off of Hub Transport servers, and others run off of Edge Transport servers.

The Hub Transport server role transport agents are as follows:

▶ Journaling Agent

▶ AD RMS Prelicensing Agent

▶ Transport Rule Agent

▶ Disclaimers

The Edge Transport server role transport agents are as follows:

▶ Content Filter Agent

▶ Sender ID Agent

▶ Recipient Filter Agent

▶ Connection Filtering Agent

▶ Attachment Filtering Agent

▶ Address Rewriting Outbound Agent

▶ Edge Rule Agent

▶ Sender Filter Agent

▶ Protocol Analysis Agent

Understanding the Hub Role Transport Agents in Exchange Server 2007

As previously mentioned, a handful of the default transport agents in Exchange 2007 are designed to run on servers running the Hub Transport role in an Exchange organization.

These agents are designed to run against internal traffic as well as the external traffic that is being routed inside the organization. These agents are Transport Rule Agent, the AD RMS Prelicensing Agent, and the Journaling Agent, each of which is described further in the following sections.

Working with Transport Rule Agents

Transport Rule Agents is the generic term used to describe any server-side rule that is run on the Hub Transport servers. These rules are very similar in design to Outlook rules, but they are run against the entire organization.

To create a simple transport rule to test these chapter concepts, perform the following tasks in Exchange Management Console:

1. From Exchange Management Console, expand Organization Configuration and then click on Hub Transport in the console pane.

2. In the actions pane, click New Transport Rule.

3. From the New Transport Rule Wizard, enter a descriptive name for the rule and ensure that the Enable Rule check box is checked. Click Next to continue.

4. In the Conditions box, shown in Figure 14.1, select which conditions the rule will operate under. In this example, it will fire on messages received from all users outside the company. Click Next to continue.

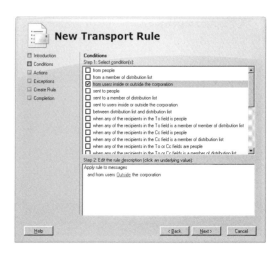

FIGURE 14.1   Creating a transport rule.

5. In the Actions box, select which action to take. In this example, an event will be written with a custom message. Click Next to continue.

6. In the Exceptions box, enter any potential exceptions to the rule, and click Next to continue.

7. Click New to finalize the transport rule creation.

8. Click Finish.

Transport rules use Active Directory (AD) replication to replicate any changes made to specific rules. Each Hub Transport server queries AD once every four hours for changes made to transport agents, and then processes all new messages based on the changes made to the rules.

Transport agents are highly customizable, and it is wise to go through the wizards several times to determine what type of rule functionality is available, and if your specific organization can take advantage of them.

Configuring Rights Management Services Prelicensing Agent

The Rights Management Services (RMS) Prelicensing Agent is a transport agent that runs on a Hub Transport server to allow for Rights Management processing of emails. It verifies the authenticity of an email message without prompting the user for authentication.

The RMS transport agent requires Windows Rights Management Services Service Pack 2 to function properly. Subsequently, adoption of this technology is still in its infancy stages.

Working with Journaling and Mail Retention Policies in Exchange Server 2007

Journaling in Exchange 2007 is a method by which all copies of emails sent to or from specific users is backed up and logged. Even if the original email is deleted, the journaling system has access to the original content in the email. Journaling is especially relevant to many organizations looking to comply with governmental regulations such as SEC Rule 17A-4, SOX, GLBA, HIPAA, the Patriot Act, and NASD 3110.

Exploring the Journaling Licensing Differences

Journaling in Exchange Server 2007 goes beyond the capabilities present in the older versions of Exchange. Exchange now allows for two types of journaling:

- ▸ **Standard journaling**—Standard journaling is essentially the same journaling mechanism used in Exchange Server 2003. This form of journaling requires that journaling be turned on to all users in a specific database.

- ▸ **Premium journaling**—Premium journaling offers new capabilities, such as per-recipient journaling, journal rule replication, and the ability to change the scope of the journaling rule.

Premium journaling allows for the scope of the journaling to be performed to be specified. Options are to limit the scope to Internal, External, or Global. If the scope is not changed from Internal to External, journaling is not performed if the user sending the message is not remote.

> **NOTE**
>
> Premium journaling requires an Exchange 2007 Enterprise Edition client access license (CAL) to be purchased for each user of the system. This should not be confused with server licenses for Exchange Enterprise, which are a completely different category.

Enabling per Mailbox Journaling

Standard journaling is turned on on a per-database basis. After being turned on, it is on for all mailboxes within that database. To configure a database for mailbox journaling, perform the following steps:

> **CAUTION**
>
> Per-database journaling is very intensive, and can increase the processing and memory needed by 25%. It is, therefore, important to understand the implications of turning on journaling, and to limit the functionality when possible.

1. Within the Exchange Management Console, navigate to Server Configuration and choose the Mailbox node in the console pane.

2. Select the server on which journaling will be turned on, then navigate to the specific storage group and database. Right-click on the database and choose Properties.

3. On the General tab, check the Journal Recipient check box, as shown in Figure 14.2. Click Browse to select the mailbox that will be used for journaling.

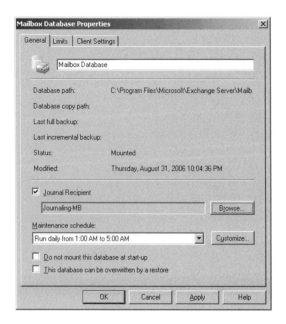

FIGURE 14.2   Enabling journaling on a database.

CAUTION

The mailbox that is used for journaling should be closely guarded and protected as all of the journaled messages from the databases will be stored there.

---

4. Click OK.

Creating Journal Rules

Journal rules can be created to activate the premium journaling options available in Exchange 2007 to those clients with Enterprise Edition Licensing CALs. To set up a journal rule, do the following:

1. From Exchange Management Console, click Organization Configuration, and then click the Hub Transport node.

2. In the actions pane, click New Journaling Rule.

3. Enter a descriptive name in the Rule Name field.

4. Click Browse to locate a journal email address where journal reports will be sent.

5. Change the scope to the desired level; this determines on which emails the rule will fire.

6. If you need to limit the journaling to a specific user or group of users, you can check the Journal E-mail for Recipient check box and click Browse to locate the group or user, as shown in Figure 14.3. When you are finished, click New.

FIGURE 14.3   Enabling a journaling rule on all e-mail messages.

7. Click Finish.

Setting Up Email Disclaimers

Email disclaimers have long been a desired feature in Exchange. In the past, complex SMTP event sinks or third-party products have provided this functionality, but Exchange 2007 now includes the built-in ability to apply a legal disclaimer to the end of all email messages. The transport rule topology is used for this mechanism.

To add a disclaimer to the Hub Transport role, do the following:

1. From Exchange Management Console, click on the Hub Transport node under the Organization Configuration.

2. Click New Transport Rule from the actions pane.

3. Under Name, enter a descriptive name for the disclaimer and click Next.

4. Leave the Conditions check boxes blank (so the rule will apply to all messages). Click Next.

5. Click Yes when prompted with the warning about the rule applying to all messages.

6. In the Actions box, check the "Append Disclaimer Text..." check box, as shown in Figure 14.4.

FIGURE 14.4   Creating a disclaimer.

7. Click the blue text shown in the diagram; this opens dialog boxes allowing for the disclaimer to be written. Click Next when you are finished.

8. Leave the Exceptions check boxes blank and click Next.

9. Click New.

10. ClickFinish.

Implementing Transport Agent Policies on the Edge

The Edge Transport server role is vital in today's risk-fraught messaging environment as it is responsible for intercepting the onslaught of viruses and spam before they reach the internal network. Special transport rules have been created specifically for Edge servers in Exchange 2007. These transport rules include address rewriting policies, content filtering policies, SenderID, and Sender Filtering.

Understanding the Role of EdgeSync in Exchange Policy Management

The EdgeSync service runs as a special synchronization component that keeps specific information from the internal AD forest in sync with an external AD in Application Mode (ADAM) forest. It uses this information to determine if policies have changed. For more information on EdgeSync, see Chapter 8, "Implementing Edge Services for an Exchange Server 2007 Environment."

Implementing Edge Rule Agents

Many of the transport rules in Exchange 2007 were designed to work on the Edge Transport role systems. This is especially true for services such as antivirus and antispam. Several other key pieces of functionality are run as policies on Edge Rule Agents, as described in this section.

Setting Up Address Rewriting Policies

One of the edge transport rules available by default is the address rewriting policy. This policy allows internal email domains to be rewritten to a common external domain, or any other combination of domain rewriting as necessary.

Address rewriting cannot currently be performed from the graphical user interface (GUI)—it must be scripted. The following illustrates a sample script to set up a rewriting policy:

```
New-AddressRewriteEntry -name "marina@abc.internal to marina@companyabc.com"
-InternalAddress marina@abc.internal -ExternalAddress marina@companyabc.com
```

This sample policy rewrites any instance of `marina@abc.internal` to `marina@companyabc.com`.

Configuring Content Filtering Policies

Edge Server role systems have a built-in Content filter running to provide for antispam and antivirus functionality. This agent serves as a direct replacement for the Exchange 2003 Intelligent Message Filter (IMF). The agent works by assigning a Spam Confidence Level of 1-9 for an email. The higher the number, the more likely it is to be spam. Removing the junk messages at the edge is the best way to reduce the load that this type of environment has on the current messaging environment.

Working with Sender Filtering Policies

Sender filtering on an Edge Transport role server allows for antispam functionality on the edge. It can be easily enabled or disabled for a server by following the command outlined as follows:

1. On the Edge server in Exchange Management Console, click Edge Transport.

2. In the work pane, click the Antispam link.

3. Click Sender Filtering.

4. Click either Disabled or Enabled, depending on how you want to set it up.

Understanding and Configuring SenderID

SenderID is an antispam framework that defines how organizations can create special domain name system (DNS) records, known as Sender Policy Framework (SPF) records, to easily verify that they really are who they purport to be.

SenderID can be disabled or enabled on an Edge Transport server via the following process:

1. On the Edge server in Exchange Management Console, click Edge Transport.

2. In the work pane, click the Antispam link.

3. Click SenderID.

4. Click either Disabled or Enabled, depending on the action desired.

Creating Messaging Records Management Policies

Messaging Records Management (MRM) in Exchange 2007 allows organizations to create and enforce mailbox retention policies for their messaging environment. It has a very granular administration model, so administrators can turn the process off for individual users.

Understanding the Scope of MRM

MRM is flexible in its approach, as it allows for different policies to be set up for different managed folders. MRM deployment takes place in several steps, as follows:

1. Create any custom managed folders, as necessary.

2. Create Managed Content Settings on specific managed folders.

3. Create any managed folder mailbox policies as necessary to group together specific Managed Content Settings.

4. Apply the managed folder mailbox policy to a mailbox or set of mailboxes.

5. Schedule the Managed Folder Assistant.

For example, an administrator might want to set up a data retention policy that allowed items stored in the Inbox to be stored for 60 days. That administrator could then create a new custom managed folder named "Data Retention Folder" that had a policy of not deleting items before 6 months. These two managed folders could have the specific Managed Content Settings set on them, and then they would be grouped together into a single managed folder mailbox policy. This policy would then be applied to all mailboxes in the organization. Finally, the administrator could schedule the Managed Folder Assistant to run on a regular basis to enforce these policies.

The step-by-step procedures for setting up this type of scenario are outlined in the following sections.

Creating Custom Managed Folders

The first step is to create a custom folder definition for the 6-month retention folder. This folder will be added as a subfolder in all mailboxes that are added to the policy. To create this custom managed folder, do the following:

1. From Exchange Management Console, expand Organization Configuration and choose the Mailbox node.

2. In the actions pane, click New Managed Custom Folder.

3. Type a descriptive name for the custom folder in the Name field. In addition, list a display name that will be shown when it is viewed in Outlook. As optional settings, you can configure a storage limit, comments, and force users to not be able to minimize the folder, as shown in Figure 14.5.

FIGURE 14.5   Creating a managed custom folder.

4. Click New and then click Finish.

Creating Managed Content Settings

The second step is to define the content settings that will be applied to the Inbox and to the custom folder that was created. The content settings define how long the data will be kept before it is deleted. To perform this task, complete the following steps:

1. From the Mailbox node under Organization Configuration, right-click on the newly created custom folder, and choose New Managed Content Settings.

2. Type a descriptive name for the content settings, and then enter in the type of retention policy. In this case, we are setting the policy at 6 months, or 180 days. Click Next when you are finished.

3. On the Journaling tab, shown in Figure 14.6, you have the option to forward a copy of the item to another location. Click Next to continue.

4. Click New and then click Finish.

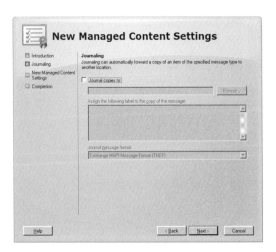

FIGURE 14.6   Creating Managed Content Settings.

5. Repeat the process for any other custom folders or the default folders. In this example, you would repeat the process for the default Inbox folder, and set the policy retention to 60 days for that folder.

Creating Managed Folder Mailbox Policies

Next, these folders must be added into a single overarching policy. To do so, perform the following tasks:

1. From Exchange Management Console, in the Mailbox node under Organization Configuration, choose the Managed Folder Mailbox Policies tab.

2. Click New Managed Folder Mailbox Policy from the actions pane.

3. Enter a descriptive name for the policy, and then click the Add button.

4. Select a managed folder from the list, in this case the Inbox and the Data Retention Folder (the custom one created; hold down the Ctrl key while selecting more than one option). Click OK and review the additions to the wizard, as shown in Figure 14.7.

5. Click New and then click Finish.

Applying Managed Folder Mailbox Policies to Mailboxes

Finally, the mailboxes themselves must be added into this policy. To do so, follow these steps:

1. In Exchange Management Console, select the Mailbox node under the Recipient Configuration node.

FIGURE 14.7   Creating a managed folder mailbox policy.

2. Right-click the user who will be added to the policy, and select Properties.

3. Select the Mailbox Settings tab.

4. Click Messaging Records Management, and then click the Properties button.

5. Check the Managed Folder Mailbox Policy check box, and click the Browse button and choose the Managed Folder Mailbox Policy you just created. Click OK. Review the settings, as shown in Figure 14.8.

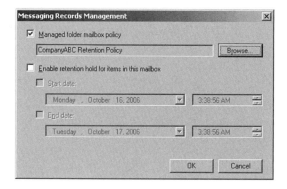

FIGURE 14.8   Applying a managed folder mailbox policy to a mailbox.

6. Click OK and then click OK again to save the changes.

An alternative method to using the GUI is to use the command-line shell. The syntax would be similar to the following example:

```
Set-Mailbox -Identity Carrie -ManagedFolderMailboxPolicy "CompanyABC Retention Policy"
```

Scheduling the Managed Folder Assistant

By default, the policies will never be enforced as the Managed Folder Assistant is not set to run cleanup at any time. It must be scheduled to do so through the following process:

1. From Exchange Management Console, click the Mailbox node under the Server Configuration node.

2. Select the server name from the list, right-click it, and choose Properties on the shortcut menu.

3. Select the Messaging Records Management tab, and change the drop-down box to say Use Custom Schedule.

4. Click the Customize button.

5. Select a time window for the management to occur, similar to what is shown in Figure 14.9.

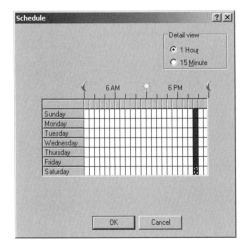

FIGURE 14.9   Scheduling the Managed Folder Assistant.

6. Click OK and then click OK again to save the settings.

The same process outlined in these step-by-step guides can be used to create any number of granular mailbox retention policies, as needed for governmental regulation and/or compliance.

Summary

Organizations today are subject to any number of strict governmental and industry regulations in regard to messaging retention, email security, and policy enforcement. Fortunately, Exchange Server 2007 has unprecedented levels of policy enforcement built in to the application, helping organizations to become compliant with these regulations and positioning them to better control their messaging environment going forward.

Best Practices

The following are best practices from this chapter:

- ▶ Establish Messaging Records Management policies to control mailbox retention in Exchange 2007.

- ▶ Fully understand the implications of the various governmental regulations, such as HIPAA, SOX, GLBA, and others.

- ▶ Use transport agents to control email traffic with well-defined policies. This includes Edge Transport server role transport agents and Hub Transport server role transport agents.

- ▶ Use Premium journaling when you are licensed with Enterprise Server client access licenses (CALs) and when the need for journaling on individual mailboxes is required.

14

PART V

Migrations and Coexistence with Exchange Server 2007

IN THIS PART

CHAPTER 15

Migrating from Windows 2000 Server to Windows Server 2003

As organizations plan their migration to Microsoft Exchange Server 2007, many organizations still have to complete their migration to Windows Server 2003 as a prerequisite. Although the entire organization does not need to be on Windows 2003 to be able to run Exchange 2007, the server that Exchange 2007 runs on must be Windows 2003, and the forest that Exchange 2007 will be a member of needs to be at a Windows 2003 functional level. This chapter focuses on the steps necessary to help an organization plan, prepare, and implement their migration to Windows Server 2003.

Understanding What Needs to Be Migrated to Windows Server 2003

As you plan your migration to Windows Server 2003, it would help if you knew exactly what needs to be on Windows 2003. There are many components in a network from the server on which Exchange 2007 is installed to the Active Directory to which the Exchange server is connected. Specifically, the various components of a network with which Exchange 2007 interacts include the following:

▶ Server operating system

▶ Domain functional level

▶ Flexible Single Master Operations roles

▶ Forest functional level

Exchange Server 2007 on a Windows Server 2003 Operating System

Exchange 2007 will only run on a Windows 2003 operating system (OS)—it won't run on Windows 2000 Server or any other version of Windows. More specifically, Exchange 2007 requires an x64-bit version of Windows 2003 to run on because Exchange 2007 is a 64-bit application. Therefore, the migration path from Exchange 2000 or 2003 to Exchange 2007 typically requires a migration between servers because most organizations run earlier versions of Exchange on a 32-bit server hardware platform and on a 32-bit version of Windows.

Beyond running on Windows 2003 x64-bit edition, Exchange 2007 requires Windows 2003 x64-bit Service Pack 1 or R2 edition as the core operating system.

> **NOTE**
>
> The reason the Exchange 2007 server must run on Windows 2003 SP1 or higher is because the service notifications in Exchange 2007, as well as the process for Outlook Web Access to browse the address book, require SP1 or higher.

Exchange Server 2007 in a Windows 2000 Server Native Functional Level Domain

In addition to running on a Windows 2003 x64-bit operating system, Exchange 2007 needs to be installed in a domain that is running at a functional level of Windows 2000 native or Windows Server 2003. This means that the domain can no longer have Windows NT 4.0 domain controllers. The domain controllers in the domain must be either Windows 2000 domain controllers or Windows 2003 domain controllers. This has confused many organizations as a Windows 2000 native functional level DOES NOT mean that all Windows NT 4.0 workstations or servers must be upgraded. A Windows 2000 native functional level domain can have Windows NT 4.0 servers and workstations as member servers and systems in the domain. The Windows NT 4.0 systems just cannot be domain controllers.

Importance of Windows Server 2003 Relative to Flexible Single Master Operation Roles

The Windows domain that Exchange 2007 is installed in needs to have specific Flexible Single Master Operations (FSMO) roles. The domain controller that is the Schema Master of the forest where Exchange 2007 will reside must be running on a system that has Windows 2003 SP1 or higher installed. This is because Exchange 2007 requires a version of the schema that is not supported by the attributes available on a Windows 2000 Schema Master domain controller. As with the domain functional level, this does not mean ALL servers must be running Windows 2003 in the environment. Simply the domain controller holding the master schema for the network, which is typically the first domain controller that was used to create the Active Directory (AD) forest, needs to be running Windows 2003 SP1 or higher.

In addition, at least one global catalog server in every Active Directory site that Exchange 2007 is installed in needs to run Windows 2003 SP1 or higher. This is a requirement because Exchange 2007 gets its directory information for routing of messages as well as user and resource lookup through Active Directory objects that can only be queried on a Windows 2003 SP1 or higher global catalog system. This does not mean that every single global catalog server needs to be running Windows 2003 SP1 or higher, nor does it mean that every site needs to have a global catalog server. What this means is that every Active Directory site that has an Exchange 2007 installed in it must have a Windows 2003 SP1 or higher global catalog server.

NOTE

Although an actual Exchange 2007 server needs to run on Windows 2003 x64-bit edition, the domain controllers, global catalog servers, Schema Master server, or other Windows 2003 systems in a network can run a 32-bit version of Windows 2003. Only the actual Exchange 2007 servers need to be on a 64-bit platform.

Forest Functional Level Requirements for Server Exchange 2007

Lastly, the forest in which Exchange 2007 will reside needs to be at a forest functional level of Windows Server 2003. Promoting a forest to a Windows Server 2003 forest functional level is covered in the section "Upgrading Domain and Forest Functional Levels" later in this chapter.

In many ways, a migration from Windows 2000 Server to Windows Server 2003 is more of a service pack upgrade than a major migration scenario. Different components can be upgraded to Windows 2003 whether it is the operating system or the functional level of the domain or forest. The differences between the operating systems are more evolutionary than revolutionary, and, consequently, there are fewer design considerations upgrading from Windows 2000 Server to Windows Server 2003 than with an upgrade from Windows NT 4.0.

This chapter focuses on the planning, strategy, and logistics of migration from Windows 2000 to Windows Server 2003. In addition, specialized procedures such as using Mixed-Mode Domain Redirect and migrating using the Active Directory Migration Tool (ADMT) are described, and step-by-step instructions complement these processes.

Beginning the Migration Process

Any migration procedure should identify what needs to be upgraded (server, domain, and/or forest functional level), steps involved, fallback precautions, and other important factors that can influence the migration process. After finalizing these items, the migration can begin.

Establishing Migration Project Phases

After it is determined what needs to be upgraded to Windows 2003, a detailed plan of the resources, timeline, scope, and objectives of the project should be outlined. Part of any migration plan requires establishing either an ad hoc project plan or a professionally drawn-up project plan. The migration plan assists the project managers of the migration project to accomplish the planned objectives in a timely manner with the correct application of resources.

The following is a condensed description of the standard phases for a migration project:

▶ **Discovery**—The first portion of a design project should be a discovery, or fact-finding, portion. This section focuses on the analysis of the current environment and documentation of the analysis results. Current network diagrams, server locations, wide area network (WAN) throughputs, server application dependencies, and all other networking components should be detailed as part of the discovery phase.

▶ **Design**—The design portion of a project is straightforward. All key components of the actual migration plan should be documented, and key data from the discovery phase should be used to draw up Design and Migration documents. The project plan itself would normally be drafted during this phase. Because Windows Server 2003 is not dramatically different from Windows 2000, significant reengineering of an existing Active Directory environment typically is not necessary. However, other issues such as server placement, new feature utilization, and changes in AD replication models should be outlined.

▶ **Prototype**—The prototype phase of a project involves the essential lab work to test the design assumptions made during the design phase. The ideal prototype would involve a mock production environment that is migrated from Windows 2000 to Windows Server 2003. For Active Directory, this means creating a production domain controller (DC) and then isolating it in the lab and promoting it to the Operations Master (OM) server in the lab. The Active Directory migration can then be performed without affecting the production environment. Step-by-step procedures for the migration can also be outlined and produced as deliverables for this phase.

▶ **Pilot**—The pilot phase, or proof-of-concept phase, involves a production "test" of the migration steps, on a limited scale. For example, a noncritical server could be upgraded to Windows Server 2003 in advance of the migration of all other critical network servers. In a slow, phased migration, the pilot phase would essentially spill into implementation, as upgrades are performed slowly, one by one.

▶ **Production Migration/Upgrade**—The production migration/upgrade portion of the project is the full-blown migration of network functionality or upgrades to the operating system. As previously mentioned, this process can be performed quickly or slowly over time, depending on an organization's needs. It is important to make the timeline decisions in the design phase and incorporate them into the project plan.

▶ **Training and support**—Learning the ins and outs of the new functionality that Windows Server 2003 can bring to an environment is essential in realizing the increased productivity and reduced administration that the operating system can bring to the environment. Consequently, it is important to include a training portion into a migration project so that the design objectives can be fully realized.

For more detailed information on the project plan phases of a migration, refer to Chapter 2, "Best Practices at Planning, Prototyping, Migrating, and Deploying Exchange Server 2007."

Comparing the In-Place Upgrade Versus New Hardware Migration Methods

Because the fundamental differences between Windows 2000 and Windows Server 2003 are not significant, the possibility of simply upgrading an existing Windows 2000 infrastructure is an option for the domain or forest. Depending on the type of hardware currently in use in a Windows 2000 network, this type of migration strategy becomes an option. Often, however, it is more appealing to simply introduce newer systems into an existing environment and retire the current servers from production. For example, migrating a server that will host Exchange 2007 as a 64-bit operating system typically requires the acquisition of new hardware. This technique normally has less impact on current environments and can also support fallback more easily.

Determining which migration strategy to use depends on one major factor: the condition of the current hardware environment. If Windows 2000 is taxing the limitations of the hardware in use, it might be preferable to introduce new servers into an environment and simply retire the old Windows 2000 servers. Or if the server being upgraded will be an Exchange 2007 server that requires an x64-bit platform, then an in-place upgrade is not feasible. If, however, the hardware in use for Windows 2000 is newer and more robust, and could conceivably last for another 2–3 years, it might be easier to simply perform in-place upgrades of the systems in an environment.

In most cases, organizations take a dual approach to migration. Older hardware is replaced by new hardware running Windows Server 2003. Newer Windows 2000 systems are instead upgraded in place to Windows Server 2003. And systems that will be Exchange 2007 servers requiring 64-bit hardware are replaced. Consequently, auditing all systems to be migrated and determining which ones will be upgraded and which ones will be retired are important steps in the migration process.

Identifying Migration Strategies: "Big Bang" Versus Slow Transition

As with most technology implementations, there are essentially two approaches in regard to deployment: a quick "Big Bang" approach or a slower, phased approach. The Big Bang option involves the entire Windows 2000 infrastructure being quickly replaced, often over the course of a weekend, with the new Windows Server 2003 environment; whereas the phased approach involves a slow, server-by-server replacement of Windows 2000.

Each approach has its particular advantages and disadvantages, and key factors to Windows Server 2003 should be taken into account before a decision is made. Few Windows Server 2003 components require a redesign of current Windows 2000 design elements. Because the arguments for the Big Bang approach largely revolve around not maintaining two conflicting systems for long periods of time, the similarities between Windows 2000 and Windows Server 2003 make many of these arguments moot. With this point in mind, it is more likely that most organizations will choose to ease into Windows Server 2003, opting instead for the phased migration approach to the upgrade. Because Windows Server 2003 readily fits into a Windows 2000 environment, and vice versa, this option is easily supported.

Exploring Migration Options

As previously mentioned, Windows Server 2003 and Windows 2000 "play" together very well. The added advantage to this fact is that there is greater flexibility for different migration options. Unlike migrations from NT 4.0 or non-Microsoft environments, the migration path between these two systems is not rigid, and different approaches can be used successfully to achieve the final objectives desired.

Upgrading a Single Member Server

The direct upgrade approach from Windows 2000 to Windows Server 2003 is the most straightforward approach to migration. An upgrade simply takes any and all settings on a single server and upgrades them to Windows Server 2003. If a Windows 2000 server handles Windows Internet Naming Service (WINS), domain name system (DNS), and Dynamic Host Configuration Protocol (DHCP), the upgrade process will upgrade all WINS, DNS, and DHCP components, as well as the base operating system. This makes this type of migration very tempting, and it can be extremely effective, as long as all prerequisites described in the following sections are satisfied.

Often, upgrading a single server can be a project in itself. The standalone member servers in an environment are often the workhorses of the network, loaded with a myriad of different applications and critical tools. Performing an upgrade on these servers would be simple if they were used only for file or print duties and if their hardware systems were all up to date. Because this is not always the case, it is important to detail the specifics of each server that is marked for migration.

Verifying Hardware Compatibility

It is critical to test the hardware compatibility of any server that will be directly upgraded to Windows Server 2003. In the middle of the installation process is not the most ideal time to be notified of problems with compatibility between older system components and the drivers required for Windows Server 2003. Therefore, the hardware in a server should be verified for Windows Server 2003 on the manufacturer's website or on the Microsoft Hardware Compatibility List (HCL), currently located at http://www.microsoft.com/whdc/hcl.

Microsoft suggests minimum hardware levels on which Windows Server 2003 will run, but it is highly recommended that you install the OS on systems of a much higher caliber because these recommendations do not take into account any application loads, domain controller duties, and so on. The following is a list of Microsoft recommended hardware levels for Windows Server 2003:

- Intel Pentium III 550MHz CPU or equivalent

- 256MB of RAM

- 1.5GB free disk space

That said, it cannot be stressed enough that it is almost always recommended that you exceed these levels to provide for a robust computing environment.

> **NOTE**
>
> One of the most important features that mission-critical servers can have is *redundancy*. Putting the operating system on a mirrored array of disks, for example, is a simple, yet effective way of increasing redundancy of individual servers in an environment.

Verifying Application Readiness

Nothing ruins a migration process like discovering a mission-critical application will not work in the new environment; therefore, it is very important to list all applications on a server that will be required in the new environment. Applications that will not be used or whose functionality is being replaced in Windows Server 2003 can be removed from consideration or retired altogether. Likewise, applications that have been verified for Windows Server 2003 can be designated as safe for upgrade. For any other applications that might not be compatible but are necessary, you either need to delegate them to another Windows 2000 server or delay the upgrade of that specific server.

In addition to the applications, the version of the operating system that will be upgraded is an important consideration in the process. A Windows 2000 server install can be upgraded to either Windows Server 2003, Standard Edition or Windows Server 2003, Enterprise Edition; however, Windows 2000 Advanced Server can be upgraded only to Windows Server 2003, Enterprise Edition. Finally, only Windows 2000 Datacenter Edition can be upgraded to Windows Server 2003, Datacenter Edition.

Backing Up and Creating a Recovery Process

It is critical that a migration does not cause more harm than good to an environment. It cannot be stressed enough that a good backup system is essential for quick recovery in the event of upgrade failure. Often, especially with the in-place upgrade scenario, a full system backup is the only way to recover; consequently, it is very important to detail fall-back steps in the event of problems.

Upgrading a Standalone Server

After all various considerations regarding applications, the hardware compatibility has been thoroughly validated and a full backup has been completed and tested, a standalone server can be upgraded. Follow these steps to upgrade:

1. Insert the Windows Server 2003 CD into the CD-ROM drive of the server to be upgraded.

2. The Welcome page should appear automatically. If not, choose Start, Run, type d:\Setup, where *d:* is the drive letter for the CD-ROM drive.

3. Click Install Windows Server 2003 (Enterprise Edition).

4. Select Upgrade from the drop-down box, as indicated in Figure 15.1, and click Next to continue.

5. Select I Accept This Agreement at the License screen, and click Next to continue.

6. The following screen prompts you to enter the 25-character product key. You can find this number on the CD case or in the license documentation from Microsoft. Enter the product key, and click Next to continue.

7. The following screen allows for the download of updated Windows Server 2003 files. They can be downloaded as part of the upgrade or installed later. For this example, select No, Skip This Step and Continue Installing Windows. Then click Next to continue.

FIGURE 15.1   Starting the Windows Server 2003 upgrade.

8. The next prompt is crucial. It indicates which system components are not compatible with Windows Server 2003. It also indicates, for example, that Internet Information Services (IIS) will be disabled as part of the install, as you can see in Figure 15.2. IIS can be reenabled in the new OS but is turned off for security reasons. Click Next after reviewing these factors.

FIGURE 15.2   Checking the System Compatibility report.

9. The system then copies files and reboots, continuing the upgrade process. After all files are copied, the system is then upgraded to a fully functional install of Windows Server 2003. If upgrading to Windows Server 2003 R2, setup then invokes the R2 upgrade process by asking to insert the second CD containing R2 information. After being inserted, the final R2 upgrade process can take place.

NOTE

Many previously enabled components such as IIS are turned off by default in Windows Server 2003. Ensure that one of the postupgrade tasks performed is an audit of all services so that those disabled components can be reenabled.

Upgrading a Windows 2000 Server Active Directory Forest

In many cases, the Windows 2000 environment that will be migrated includes one or many Active Directory domains and forests. Because Active Directory is one of the most important portions of a Microsoft network, it is also one of the most important areas to focus on in a migration process. In addition, many of the improvements made to Windows Server 2003 are directly related to Active Directory, making it even more appealing to migrate this portion of an environment.

Because Exchange 2007 requires the active forest to be at a Windows Server 2003 functional level, the organization needs to proceed with the steps to migrate to Windows 2003. As a benefit, in addition to getting a forest that is ready to support Exchange 2007, the following additional functionality is available with a Windows Server 2003 forest:

▶ **Domain Rename Capability**—Windows Server 2003 Active Directory supports the renaming of either the NetBIOS name or the Lightweight Directory Access Protocol

(LDAP)/DNS name of an Active Directory domain. The Active Directory rename tool can be used for this purpose, but only in domains that have completely upgraded to Windows Server 2003 domain controllers.

▸ **Cross-Forest Transitive Trusts**—Windows Server 2003 now supports the implementation of transitive trusts that can be established between separate Active Directory forests. Windows 2000 supported only explicit cross-forest trusts, and the trust structure did not allow for permissions to flow between separate domains in a forest. This limitation has been lifted in Windows Server 2003.

▸ **Universal Group Caching**—One of the main structural limitations of Active Directory was the need to establish very "chatty" global catalog servers in every site established in a replication topology, or run the risk of extremely slow client logon times and directory queries. Windows Server 2003 enables remote domain controllers to cache universal group memberships for users so that each logon request does not require the use of a local global catalog server.

▸ **Inter-Site Topology Generator (ISTG) Improvements**—The ISTG in Windows Server 2003 has been improved to support configurations with extremely large numbers of sites. In addition, the time required to determine site topology has been noticeably improved through the use of a more efficient ISTG algorithm.

▸ **Multivalued Attribute Replication Improvements**—In Windows 2000, if a universal group changed its membership from 5,000 users to 5,001 users, the entire group membership had to be rereplicated across the entire forest. Windows Server 2003 addresses this problem and allows incremental membership changes to be replicated.

▸ **Lingering Objects (Zombies) Detection**—Domain controllers that have been out of service for a longer period of time than the Time to Live (TTL) of a deleted object could theoretically "resurrect" those objects, forcing them to come back to life as zombies, or lingering objects. Windows Server 2003 properly identifies these zombies and prevents them from being replicated to other domain controllers.

▸ **AD-Integrated DNS Zones in Application Partition**—Replication of DNS zones has been improved in Windows Server 2003 by storing AD-integrated zones in the application partition of a forest, thus limiting their need to be replicated to all domain controllers and reducing network traffic.

Migrating Domain Controllers

When planning a migration of the Active Directory environment, it is considered wise to make a plan to upgrade all domain controllers in an environment to Windows Server 2003. Unlike with member servers, the full benefits of the Active Directory improvements in Windows Server 2003 and the ability to install Exchange 2007 in the forest are not fully realized until the entire environment is "Windows Server 2003 functional."

There are two approaches to migrating domain controllers, similar to the logic used in the "Upgrading a Standalone Server" section. The domain controllers can either be directly upgraded to Windows Server 2003 or replaced by newly introduced Windows Server 2003 domain controllers. The decision to upgrade an existing server largely depends on the hardware of the server in question. The rule of thumb is, if the hardware will support Windows Server 2003 now and for the next 2 to 3 years, a server can be directly upgraded. If this is not the case, using new hardware for the migration is preferable.

> **NOTE**
>
> A combined approach can be and is quite commonly used to support a scenario in which some hardware is current but other hardware is out-of-date and will be replaced. Either way, the decisions applied to a proper project plan can help to ensure the success of the migration.

Upgrading the AD Schema Using adprep

The introduction of Windows Server 2003 domain controllers into a Windows 2000 Active Directory requires that the core AD database component, the schema, be updated to support the increased functionality. In addition, several other security changes need to be made to prepare a forest for inclusion of Windows Server 2003. The Windows Server 2003 CD includes a command-line utility called adprep that will extend the schema to include the extensions required and modify security as needed. Adprep requires that both forestprep and domainprep be run before the first Windows Server 2003 domain controller can be added.

The Active Directory schema in Windows 2000 is composed of 1,006 attributes, by default, as shown in Figure 15.3. After running adprep forestprep, the schema will be extended to include additional attributes that support Windows Server 2003 functionality.

> **NOTE**
>
> Windows Server 2003 R2 contains additional schema updates, above and beyond the additions that the RTM version of Windows Server 2003 introduced. If adprep is run from a server running R2, the schema will be extended to include not only the 2003 enhancements, but the R2 ones as well.

The adprep utility must be run from the Windows Server 2003 CD or copied from its location in the \i386 folder. The adprep /forestprep operation can be run on the server that holds the Schema Master Operations Master (OM) role by following these steps:

1. On the Schema Master domain controller, choose Start, Run, type cmd in the Open text box, and click OK to open a command prompt.

2. Enter the Windows Server 2003 CD into the CD drive.

3. Where *D:* is the drive letter for the CD drive, type in D:\i386\adprep /forestprep, and press Enter.

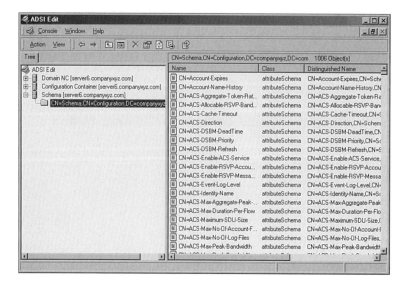

FIGURE 15.3   ADSI Edit before running `forestprep`.

4. Upon verification that all domain controllers in the AD forest are at Windows 2000 Server Service Pack 2 or greater, type C at the prompt and press Enter.

5. The `forestprep` procedure extends the Windows 2000 AD schema. After the schema is extended, it is replicated to all domain controllers in the forest. Finally, close the command prompt window.

After this step is accomplished, the `domainprep` procedure must be run.

The `adprep /domainprep` operation must be run once in every domain in a forest. It must be physically invoked on the server that holds the Operations Master (OM) role. The steps for executing the `domainprep` procedure are as follows:

1. On the Operations Master domain controller, open a command prompt (choose Start, Run, type `cmd`, and press Enter).

2. Enter the Windows Server 2003 CD into the CD drive.

3. Where *D:* is the CD drive, type `D:\i386\adprep/ domainprep` and press Enter.

4. Type exit to close the command prompt window.

After the `forestprep` and `domainprep` operations are run, the Active Directory forest will be ready for the introduction or upgrade of Windows Server 2003 domain controllers. The schema is extended and includes support for application partitions and other enhancements. The process of upgrading the domain controllers to Windows Server 2003 can then commence.

> **NOTE**
>
> Any previous extensions made to a Windows 2000 schema, such as those made with Exchange 2000/2003, are not affected by the adprep procedure. This procedure simply adds additional attributes and does not change those that currently exist.

Upgrading Existing Domain Controllers

If the decision has been made to upgrade all or some existing hardware in a Windows Server 2003 domain controller, the process for accomplishing this is straightforward. However, as with the standalone server, you need to ensure that the hardware and any additional software components are compatible with Windows Server 2003. After establishing this, the actual migration can occur.

The procedure for upgrading a domain controller to Windows Server 2003 is nearly identical to the procedure outlined in the previous section "Upgrading a Single Member Server." Essentially, simply insert the CD and upgrade, and an hour or so later the machine will be updated and functioning as a Windows Server 2003 domain controller.

Replacing Existing Domain Controllers

If you need to migrate specific domain controller functionality to the new Active Directory environment but plan to use new hardware, you need to bring new domain controllers into the environment before retiring the old servers. The process for installing a new server is similar to the process with Windows 2000 Server. The DCPromo utility is used to promote a server to domain controller status.

Windows Server 2003 supports an enhanced Configure Your Server Wizard, however, which allows an administrator to designate a server into multiple roles. This is the most thorough approach, and the following steps show how to accomplish this to establish a new domain controller in a Windows 2000 Active Directory domain:

1. Open the Configure Your Server Wizard (Start, All Programs, Administrative Tools, Configure Your Server Wizard).

2. Click Next at the welcome screen.

3. Verify the preliminary steps, and click Next.

4. Select Domain Controller from the list, and click Next.

5. Check the settings at the Summary page, and click Next.

6. After the AD Installation Wizard is invoked, click Next to continue.

7. At the Operating System Compatibility window, click Next to verify that old versions of Microsoft software such as Windows 95 will not be supported.

8. Select Additional Domain Controller for an Existing Domain, and click Next.

9. Type the password of an Administrator account in the AD domain, and click Next to continue.

10. Type the domain name into the dialog box of the target AD domain, and click Next to continue.

11. Enter a location for the AD database and logs. (You can achieve the best performance if they are stored on separate volumes.) Click Next to continue.

12. Enter a location for the SYSVOL folder. Click Next to continue.

13. Enter a password for Directory Services Restore mode, which can be used in the event of directory recovery. Click Next to continue.

14. Verify the tasks indicated, and click Next to continue. The server then contacts another domain controller in the domain and replicates domain information, as indicated in Figure 15.4.

15. Click Finish when the process is complete.

16. Click Restart Now when prompted to reboot the domain controller and establish it in its new role in AD.

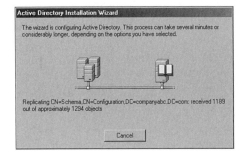

FIGURE 15.4   Configuring AD.

Moving Operation Master Roles

Active Directory sports a multimaster replication model, in which any one server can take over directory functionality, and each domain controller contains a read/write copy of directory objects. There are, however, a few key exceptions to this, in which certain forest-wide functionality must be held by a single domain controller. These exceptions are known as Operation Master (OM) roles, also known as Flexible Single Master Operations (FSMO) roles. There are five OM roles, as follows:

▶ Schema Master

▶ Domain Naming Master

▶ RID Master

▶ PDC Emulator

▶ Infrastructure Master

If the server or servers that hold the OM roles are not directly upgraded to Windows Server 2003 but will instead be retired, these OM roles will need to be moved to another server. The best tool for this type of move is the `ntdsutil` command-line utility. Follow these steps using `ntdsutil` to move all OM roles to a single Windows Server 2003 domain controller:

1. Open a command prompt (choose Start, Run, type `cmd`, and press Enter).

2. Type `ntdsutil` and press Enter.

3. Type `roles` and press Enter.

4. Type `connections` and press Enter.

5. Type `connect to server <Servername>`, where *<Servername>* is the name of the target Windows Server 2003 domain controller that will hold the OM roles, and press Enter.

6. Type `quit` and press Enter.

7. Type `transfer schema master`, as shown in Figure 15.5, and press Enter.

```
C:\WINDOWS\system32\cmd.exe - ntdsutil

C:\>ntdsutil
ntdsutil: roles
fsmo maintenance: connections
server connections: connect to server server1
Binding to server1 ...
Connected to server1 using credentials of locally logged on user.
server connections: quit
fsmo maintenance: transfer schema master
```

FIGURE 15.5   Using the `ntdsutil` utility to transfer OM roles.

8. Click Yes at the prompt asking to confirm the OM change.

9. Type `transfer domain naming master`, and press Enter.

10. Click Yes at the prompt asking to confirm the OM change.

11. Type `transfer pdc` and press Enter.

12. Click OK at the prompt asking to confirm the OM change.

13. Type `transfer rid master`, and press Enter.

14. Click OK at the prompt asking to confirm the OM change.

15. Type `transfer infrastructure master`, and press Enter.

16. Click OK at the prompt asking to confirm the OM change.

17. Type exit to close the command prompt window.

Retiring Existing Windows 2000 Domain Controllers

After the entire Windows 2000 domain controller infrastructure is replaced by Windows Server 2003 equivalents and the OM roles are migrated, the process of demoting and removing all down-level domain controllers can begin. The most straightforward and thorough way of removing a domain controller is by demoting them using the dcpromo utility, per the standard Windows 2000 demotion process. After you run the dcpromo command, the domain controller becomes a member server in the domain and can safely be disconnected from the network.

Retiring "Ghost" Windows 2000 Domain Controllers

As is often the case in Active Directory, domain controllers might have been removed from the forest without first being demoted. This can happen because of server failure or problems in the administrative process, but you must remove those servers from the directory before completing an upgrade to Windows Server 2003. Simply deleting the object from Active Directory Sites and Services does not work. Instead, you need to use a low-level directory tool, ADSIEdit, to remove these servers. The following steps outline how to use ADSIEdit to remove these "ghost" domain controllers:

1. Install ADSIEdit from the support tools on the Windows Server 2003 CD and open it.

2. Navigate to Configuration\CN=Configuration\CN=Sites\CN=<Sitename>\ CN=Servers\CN=<Servername>, where *Sitename* and *Servername* correspond to the location of the ghost domain controller.

3. Right-click CN=NTDS Settings, and click Delete, as shown in Figure 15.6.

4. At the prompt, click Yes to delete the object.

5. Close ADSIEdit.

At this point, after the NTDS settings are deleted, the server can be normally deleted from the Active Directory Sites and Services snap-in.

Upgrading Domain and Forest Functional Levels

Windows Server 2003 does not immediately begin functioning at a native level, even when all domain controllers have been migrated. In fact, a fresh installation of Windows Server 2003 supports domain controllers from Windows NT 4.0, Windows 2000, and Windows Server 2003. You first need to upgrade the functional level of the forest and the domain to Windows Server 2003 before you can realize the advantages of the upgrade.

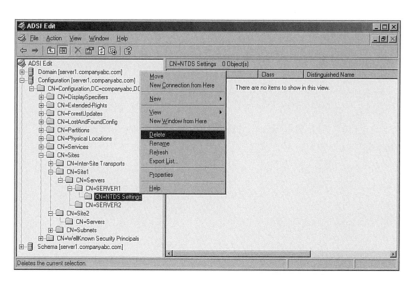

FIGURE 15.6   Deleting ghost domain controllers.

Windows Server 2003 supports four domain functional levels. The following levels allow Active Directory to include down-level domain controllers during an upgrade process:

▶ **Windows 2000 Mixed** —When Windows Server 2003 is installed into a Windows 2000 Active Directory forest that is running in Mixed mode, it essentially means that Windows Server 2003 domain controllers can communicate with Windows NT and Windows 2000 domain controllers throughout the forest. This is the most limiting of the functional levels, however, because functionality such as universal groups, group nesting, and enhanced security is absent from the domain. This is typically a temporary level to run in because it is seen more as a path toward eventual upgrade.

▶ **Windows 2000 Native** —Installed into a Windows 2000 Active Directory that is running in Windows 2000 Native mode, Windows Server 2003 runs itself at a Windows 2000 functional level. Only Windows 2000 and Windows Server 2003 domain controllers can exist in this environment.

▶ **Windows Server 2003 Interim** —Windows Server 2003 Interim mode enables the Windows Server 2003 Active Directory to interoperate with a domain composed of Windows NT 4.0 domain controllers only. Although this is a confusing concept at first, the Windows Server 2003 Interim functional level does serve a purpose. In environments that seek to upgrade directly from NT 4.0 to Windows Server 2003 Active Directory, Interim mode allows Windows Server 2003 to manage large groups more efficiently than if an existing Windows 2000 Active Directory exists. After all NT domain controllers are removed or upgraded, the functional levels can be raised.

▶ **Windows Server 2003** —The most functional of all the various levels, Windows Server 2003 functionality is the eventual goal of all Windows Server 2003 Active Directory implementations.

After all domain controllers are upgraded or replaced with Windows Server 2003, you can raise the domain and then the forest functional levels by following these steps:

1. Ensure that all domain controllers in the forest are upgraded to Windows Server 2003.

2. Open Active Directory Domains and Trusts from the Administrative Tools.

3. In the left pane, right-click Active Directory Domains and Trusts, and then click Raise Domain Functional Level.

4. In the Select an Available Domain Functional Level box, click Windows Server 2003, and then select Raise, as shown in Figure 15.7.

FIGURE 15.7   Raising the domain functional level.

5. Click OK and then click OK again to complete the task.

6. Repeat steps 1–5 for all domains in the forest.

7. Perform the same steps on the forest root, except this time click Raise Forest Functional Level in step 3 and follow the prompts, as indicated in Figure 15.8.

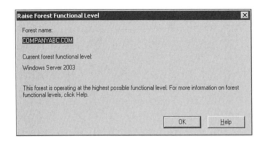

FIGURE 15.8   Raising the forest functional level.

> **NOTE**
>
> The decision to raise the forest or domain functional levels is final. Be sure that any Windows 2000 domain controllers do not need to be added anywhere in the forest before performing this procedure. When the forest is Windows Server 2003 functional, this also includes being unable to add any Windows 2000 Active Directory subdomains.

After each domain functional level is raised, as well as the forest functional level, the Active Directory environment is completely upgraded and all of the AD improvements introduced with Windows Server 2003 will be available. Functionality at this level opens the environment to features such as schema deactivation, domain rename, domain controller rename, and cross-forest trusts.

Moving AD-Integrated DNS Zones to Application Partitions

The final step in a Windows Server 2003 Active Directory upgrade is to move any AD-integrated DNS zones into the newly created application partitions that Windows Server 2003 uses to store DNS information. To accomplish this, follow these steps:

1. Open the DNS Microsoft Management Console snap-in (Start, All Programs, Administrative Tools, DNS).

2. Navigate to DNS*<Servername>*\\Forward Lookup Zones.

3. Right-click the zone to be moved, and click Properties.

4. Click the Change button to the right of the Replication description.

5. Select either To All DNS Servers in the Active Directory Forest or To All DNS Servers in the Active Directory Domain, depending on the level of replication you want, as shown in Figure 15.9. Click OK when you are finished.

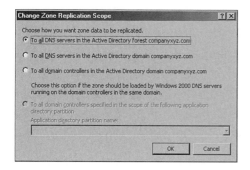

FIGURE 15.9   Moving AD-integrated zones.

6. Repeat the process for any other AD-integrated zones.

Upgrading Separate AD Forests to a Single Forest Using Mixed-Mode Domain Redirect

Active Directory domains that are running in Windows 2000 Mixed mode can be joined into a separate forest without the need for domain migration tools or workstation reboots. To accomplish this, however, you must run a previously unknown process known as Mixed-Mode Domain Redirect on the environment.

Mixed-Mode Domain Redirect is useful in situations in which branch offices have deployed their own separate Active Directory forests, and the need later surfaces to join these disparate forests into a single, common forest. It is also useful in corporate acquisitions and mergers, where separate forests are suddenly required to merge into a single, unified directory.

Prerequisites and Limitations of the Mixed-Mode Domain Redirect Procedure

The first prerequisite for Mixed-Mode Domain Redirect is that each Active Directory domain in a forest must be running in Windows 2000 Mixed mode. If an organization needs to merge forests but has already gone to Windows 2000 Native mode, other procedures such as using the Active Directory Migration Tool or synchronizing directories must be utilized instead.

A big caveat and limitation to this approach is that Windows 2000/XP/2003 clients might already view the domain as an Active Directory domain, requiring themselves to be rejoined to the domain or have their machine/domain password relationship reset using the netdom utility after the operation is complete. Unfortunately, there is no way around this as these client machines eventually discover that their NT domain has become an AD domain, and adjust themselves accordingly. Postoperation, it becomes necessary to identify these machines and rejoin them to the new domain structure. This caveat does not hold true for Windows NT 4.0 clients, however.

In addition, this procedure also requires several reboots of existing domain controller servers and is, therefore, best performed on a weekend or over a holiday.

Mixed-Mode Domain Redirect Procedure

The concept behind Mixed-Mode Domain Redirect is simple: Take an existing Active Directory domain, downgrade it to a Windows NT 4.0 domain, and upgrade it back into a different environment, as illustrated in Figure 15.10.

The example in the diagrams and in the following sections is based on a fictional scenario. You can modify this scenario, however, to include any environment that satisfies the prerequisites outlined previously.

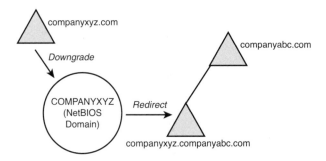

FIGURE 15.10   The Mixed-Mode Domain Redirect procedure.

In this scenario, CompanyXYZ has been acquired by CompanyABC, and the need has arisen to merge the CompanyXYZ Windows 2000 forest with the CompanyABC Windows Server 2003 forest. Because the CompanyXYZ domain is running in Windows 2000 Mixed mode, the staff determined that using the Mixed-Mode Domain Redirect procedure would be the most straightforward approach, and there would be no need to change any client settings.

Establishing a Temporary Windows 2000 Domain Controller
The first step in the Mixed-Mode Domain Redirect process is identifying two temporary servers that will be needed in the migration. These servers do not necessarily need to be very fast servers because they will be used only for temporary storage of domain information.

The first temporary server should be set up as a Windows 2000 domain controller in the current Active Directory domain. After the operating system is loaded (Windows 2000 Server or Advanced Server), you can run the dcpromo command to make it a domain controller in the current domain, per the standard Windows 2000 domain controller upgrade procedure. In addition, this domain controller does not need to be made into a global catalog server.

In the merger scenario, the temporary server SFDCTEMP01 is built with Windows 2000 and Service Pack 3 and added to the companyxyz.com Windows 2000 domain, where it becomes a domain controller, as illustrated in Figure 15.11. The current domain controllers—SFDC01, SFDC02, LADC01, and SDDC01—are illustrated as well. These four domain controllers will be migrated to the new environment.

Moving Operations Master Roles and Demoting Existing Domain Controllers
After the new server is introduced to an environment, the five OM roles must be moved from their existing locations and onto the temporary server. This can be done by using the ntdsutil utility. The steps to move OM roles were demonstrated previously in the "Moving Operation Master Roles" section of this chapter.

In the merger example, the Schema Master and Domain Naming Master OM roles were moved from SFDC01 to SFDCTEMP01, and the OM roles of PDC Emulator, RID Master, and Infrastructure Master were moved from SFDC02 to SFDCTEMP01.

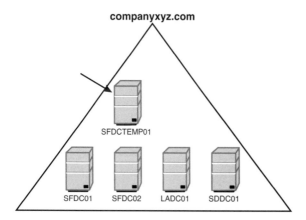

FIGURE 15.11   Establishing a temporary domain controller.

Demoting Production Domain Controllers

Because the old Active Directory forest will be retired, you need to run dcpromo on the remaining domain controller servers and demote them from domain controller duties. This effectively makes them member servers in the domain and leaves the only functional domain controller as the temporary server built in the preceding section.

In the merger example, as illustrated in Figure 15.12, SFDC01, SFDC02, LADC01, and SDDC01 are all demoted to member servers, and only SFDCTEMP01 remains as a domain controller.

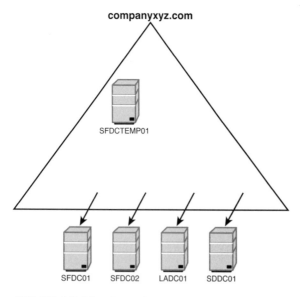

FIGURE 15.12   Demoting production domain controllers.

Building a Temporary NT 4.0 Domain Controller

An NT domain controller will need to be built to allow the procedure to work. It must be brought up as an NT Backup Domain Controller (BDC) for the domain. Because there are no more NT domain controllers, the DC account for the computer must be created on the first temporary domain controller established. The DC account can be created by typing the following at a command prompt:

```
netdom add SFDCTEMP02 /domain:companyxyz.com /DC
```

It is important to note that even though the domain is in Mixed mode, the account must be created in advance if the Primary Domain Controller (PDC) function in the domain runs on a Windows 2000 domain controller; otherwise, the BDC cannot be added to the domain. When the account is established in advance, the second temporary domain controller must be built with Windows NT 4.0 and configured as a BDC in the domain that will be migrated. Because the domain is still in Windows 2000 Mixed mode, NT BDCs are still supported.

In the merger example, the second temporary domain controller is established as SFDCTEMP02 after the computer account is created on SFDCTEMP01 using the netdom procedure just described. All existing computer and user accounts are copied into the SAM database on SFDCTEMP02.

Retiring the Existing Forest

The existing Windows 2000 forest can be safely retired by simply shutting down the temporary Windows 2000 domain controller. Because this machine controls the OM roles, the Active Directory is effectively shut down. The added advantage of this approach is that you can resurrect the old domain if there are problems with the migration by turning on the first temporary server.

As illustrated in Figure 15.13, the SFDCTEMP01 server is shut off, retiring the companyxyz.com Active Directory domain. However, the COMPANYXYZ NetBIOS domain still exists in the SAM database of SFDCTEMP02, the NT BDC.

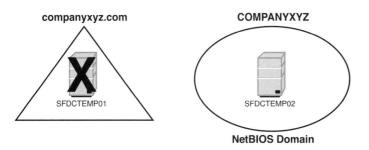

FIGURE 15.13   Retiring the old forest.

Promoting the Second Temporary Server to NT PDC

The NT BDC that you set up then needs to take over as the PDC for the domain, which effectively resurrects the old NetBIOS NT domain structure. This also leaves the domain in a position to be upgraded into an existing Active Directory structure.

In the merger example, the NT BDC SFDCTEMP02 is promoted to the PDC for the COMPANYXYZ NT domain, preparing it for integration with the companyabc.com Windows Server 2003 domain.

Promoting the NT PDC to Windows Server 2003 and Integrating with the Target Forest

Next, the NT PDC can be promoted to Windows Server 2003 Active Directory. This procedure upgrades all computer and user accounts to Active Directory, and the client settings will not need to be changed.

In the merger example, the Windows Server 2003 CD is inserted into the SCDCTEMP02 server, and a direct upgrade to Windows Server 2003 is performed. As part of the upgrade, the Active Directory Wizard allows the domain to be joined with an existing AD structure. In this case, the CompanyXYZ domain is added as a subdomain to the companyabc.com domain, effectively making it companyxyz.companyabc.com, as illustrated in Figure 15.14.

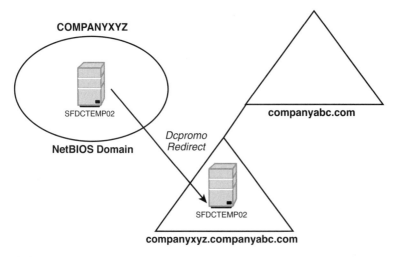

FIGURE 15.14   Redirecting the CompanyXYZ domain to the CompanyABC forest.

Reestablishing Prior Domain Controllers and Moving OM Roles

Another useful feature of this approach is that all the original servers that were domain controllers can be promoted back to their original functions without reloading the operating system. The DCPromo process can be run again on the servers, adding them as domain controllers for the domain in the new forest. In addition, the OM roles can be transferred as previously defined to move the original roles back to their old locations.

In the merger example, all the original domain controllers that are now member servers in the domain are repromoted using DCPromo. SFDC01, SFDC02, LADC01, and SDDC01 are all readded as domain controllers, and the proper OM roles are replaced.

Retiring the Temporary Domain Controller

The final step in the Mixed-Mode Domain Redirect is to retire the promoted NT BDC from the domain. The easiest way to accomplish this is to run DCPromo to demote it and then simply shut off the server. Both temporary servers can then be retired from duty and recycled into other uses.

In CompanyXYZ, the SCDCTEMP02 server is demoted using DCPromo and turned off. Overall, the procedure spares the company the need to change client logons, user settings, or server hardware and allows it to re-create the existing Windows 2000 domain within a different Windows Server 2003 Active Directory forest.

Consolidating and Migrating Domains Using the Active Directory Migration Tool

The development of Windows Server 2003 coincides with improvements in the Active Directory Migration Tool (ADMT), a fully functional domain migration utility included on the Windows Server 2003 CD. ADMT allows Active Directory and NT domain users, computers, and groups to be consolidated, collapsed, or restructured to fit the design needs of an organization. In regard to Windows 2000 migrations, ADMT provides for the flexibility to restructure existing domain environments into new Windows Server 2003 Active Directory environments, keeping security settings, user passwords, and other settings.

Understanding ADMT Functionality

ADMT is an effective way to migrate users, groups, and computers from one domain to another. It is robust enough to migrate security permissions and Exchange mailbox domain settings; plus, it supports a rollback procedure in the event of migration problems. ADMT is composed of the following components and functionality:

▶ **ADMT migration wizards**—ADMT includes a series of wizards, each specifically designed to migrate specific components. You can use different wizards to migrate users, groups, computers, service accounts, and trusts.

▶ **Low client impact**—ADMT automatically installs a service on source clients negating the need to manually install client software for the migration. In addition, after the migration is complete, these services are automatically uninstalled.

▶ **SID history and security migrated**—Users can continue to maintain network access to file shares, applications, and other secured network services through migration of the SID history attributes to the new domain. This preserves the extensive security structure of the source domain.

▶ **Test migrations and rollback functionality**—An extremely useful feature in ADMT is the capability to run a mock migration scenario with each migration wizard. This helps to identify any issues that might exist prior to the actual migration work. In addition to this functionality, the most recently performed user, computer, or group migration can be undone, providing for rollback in the event of migration problems.

Consolidating a Windows 2000 Domain to a Windows Server 2003 Domain Using ADMT

ADMT installs very easily but requires a thorough knowledge of the various wizards to be used properly. In addition, best-practice processes should be used when migrating from one domain to another.

The migration example in the following sections describes the most common use of the Active Directory Migration Tool: an interforest migration of domain users, groups, and computers into another domain. This procedure is by no means exclusive, and many other migration techniques can be used to achieve proper results. Thus, matching the capabilities of ADMT with the migration needs of an organization is important.

Using ADMT in a Lab Environment

ADMT comes with unprecedented rollback capabilities. Not only can each wizard be tested first, but the last wizard transaction can also be rolled back in the event of problems. In addition, it is highly recommended that you reproduce an environment in a lab setting and that the migration process is tested in advance to mitigate potential problems that might arise.

You can develop the most effective lab by creating new domain controllers in the source and target domains and then physically segregating them into a lab network, where they cannot contact the production domain environment. The Operations Master (OM) roles for each domain can then be seized for each domain using the `ntdsutil` utility, which effectively creates exact replicas of all user, group, and computer accounts that can be tested with the ADMT.

ADMT Installation Procedure

The ADMT component should be installed on a domain controller in the target domain, to which the accounts will be migrated. To install, follow these steps:

1. Insert the Windows Server 2003 CD into the CD-ROM drive of a domain controller in the target domain.

2. Choose Start, Run. Then type `d:\i386\admt\admigration.msi`, where *d:* is the drive letter for the CD-ROM drive, and press Enter.

3. At the welcome screen, click Next to continue.

4. Accept the end-user license agreement (EULA), and click Next to continue.

5. Accept the default installation path, and click Next to continue.

6. When ready to begin the installation, click Next.

7. After installation, click Finish to close the wizard.

ADMT Domain Migration Prerequisites

As previously mentioned, the most important prerequisite for migration with ADMT is lab verification. Testing as many aspects of a migration as possible can help to establish the procedures required and identify potential problems before they occur in the production environment.

That said, several functional prerequisites must be met before the ADMT can function properly. Many of these requirements revolve around the migration of passwords and security objects, and are critical for this functionality.

Creating Two-Way Trusts Between Source and Target Domains

The source and target domains must each be able to communicate with each other and share security credentials. Consequently, it is important to establish trusts between the two domains before running the ADMT.

Assigning Proper Permissions on Source Domain and Source Domain Workstations

The account that will run the ADMT in the target domain must be added into the Builtin\Administrators group in the source domain. In addition, each workstation must include this user as a member of the local Administrators group for the computer migration services to be able to function properly. Domain group changes can be easily accomplished, but a large workstation group change must be scripted, or manually accomplished, prior to migration.

Creating Target Organizational Unit (OU) Structure

The destination for user accounts from the source domain must be designated at several points during the ADMT migration process. Establishing an OU for the source domain accounts can help to simplify and logically organize the new objects. These objects can be moved to other OUs after the migration and this OU can be collapsed, if you want.

Modifying Default Domain Policy on the Target Domain

Unlike previous versions of Windows operating systems, Windows Server 2003 does not support anonymous users authenticating as the Everyone group. This functionality was designed in such a way as to increase security. However, for ADMT to be able to migrate the accounts, this functionality must be disabled. When the process is complete, the policies can be reset to the default levels. To change the policies, follow these steps:

1. Open the Domain Security Policy (Start, All Programs, Administrative Tools, Domain Security Policy).

2. Navigate to Security Settings\Local Policies\Security Options.

3. Double-click Network Access: Let Everyone Permissions Apply to Anonymous Users.

4. Check the Define This Policy Setting check box, and choose Enabled, as indicated in Figure 15.15. Click OK to finish.

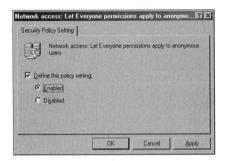

FIGURE 15.15   Modifying the domain security policy.

5. Repeat the procedure for the Domain Controller Security Policy snap-in.

Exporting Password Key Information

A 128-bit encrypted password key must be installed from the target domain on a server in the source domain. This key allows for the migration of password and SID history information from one domain to the next.

To create this key, follow these steps from the command prompt of a domain controller in the target domain where ADMT is installed:

1. Insert a floppy disk into the drive to store the key. (The key can be directed to the network but, for security reasons, directing to a floppy is better.)

2. Change to the ADMT directory by typing cd C:\program files\active directory migration tool, where *C:* is the OS drive. Then press Enter.

3. Type admt key <SourceDomainName> a: <password>, where <SourceDomainName> is the NetBIOS name of the source domain, a: is the destination drive for the key, and <password> is a password that is used to secure the key. Refer to Figure 15.16 for an example. Then press Enter.

4. Upon successful creation of the key, remove the floppy and keep it in a safe place.

Installing a Password Migration DLL on the Source Domain

A special password migration dynamic link library (DLL) must be installed on a domain controller in the source domain. This machine will become the Password Export Server for the source domain. The following procedure outlines this installation:

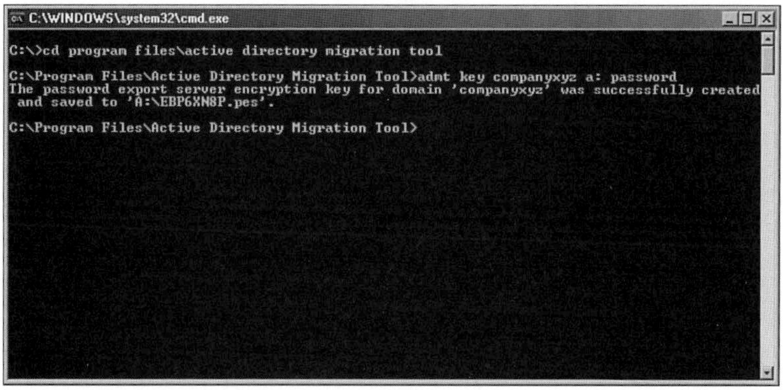

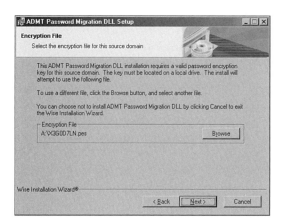

FIGURE 15.16   Exporting the password key.

1. Insert the floppy disk with the exported key from the target domain into the server's disk drive.

2. Insert the Windows Server 2003 CD into the CD-ROM drive of the domain controller in the source domain where the Registry change will be enacted.

3. Start the Password Migration Utility by choosing Start, Run, and typing d:\i386\ADMT\Pwdmig\Pwdmig.exe, where *d:* is the drive letter for the CD-ROM drive. Then click OK.

4. At the welcome screen, click Next.

5. Enter the location of the key that was created on the target domain; normally, this is the A: floppy drive, as indicated in Figure 15.17. Click Next to continue.

6. Enter the password twice that was set on the target domain, and click Next.

7. At the Verification page, click Next to continue.

FIGURE 15.17   Setting up the password migration DLL.

8. Click Finish after the installation is complete.

9. The system must be restarted, so click Yes when prompted to automatically restart. Upon restarting, the proper settings will be in place to make this server a Password Export Server.

Setting Proper Registry Permissions on the Source Domain

The installation of the proper components creates special Registry keys but leaves them disabled by default, for security reasons. You need to enable a specific Registry key to allow passwords to be exported from the Password Export Server. The following procedure outlines the use of the Registry Editor to perform this function:

1. On a domain controller in the source domain, open the Registry Editor (Start, Run, Regedit).

2. Navigate to HKEY_LOCAL_MACHINE\SYSTEM\CurrentControlSet\Control\Lsa.

3. Double-click the AllowPasswordExport DWORD value.

4. Change the properties from 0 to 1–Hexadecimal.

5. Click OK and close the Registry Editor.

6. Reboot the machine for the Registry changes to be enacted.

At this point in the ADMT process, all prerequisites have been satisfied, and both source and target domains are prepared for the migration.

Migrating Groups

In most cases, the first objects to be migrated into a new domain should be groups. If users are migrated first, their group membership will not transfer over. However, if the groups exist before the users are migrated, they will automatically find their place in the group structure. To migrate groups using ADMT, use the Group Account Migration Wizard, as follows:

1. Open the ADMT MMC snap-in (Start, All Programs, Administrative Tools, Active Directory Migration Tool).

2. Right-click Active Directory Migration Tool in the left pane and choose Group Account Migration Wizard.

3. Click Next to continue.

4. On the next screen, shown in Figure 15.18, you can choose to test the migration. As mentioned previously, the migration process should be thoroughly tested before actually being placed in production. In this example, however, you want to perform the migration. Choose Migrate Now and click Next to continue.

5. Select the source and destination domains, and click Next to continue.

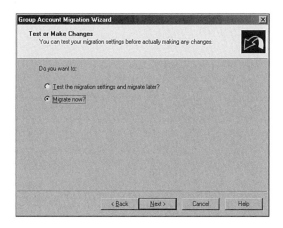

FIGURE 15.18   Choosing to migrate in the Group Account Migration Wizard.

6. On the subsequent screen, you can select the group accounts from the source domain. Select all the groups required by using the Add button and selecting the objects manually. After you select the groups, click Next to continue.

7. Enter the destination OU for the accounts from the source domain by clicking Browse and selecting the OU created in the steps outlined previously. Click Next to continue.

8. On the following screen, there are several options to choose from that determine the nature of the migrated groups. Clicking the Help button details the nature of each setting. In the sample migration, choose the settings shown in Figure 15.19. After choosing the appropriate settings, click Next to continue.

FIGURE 15.19   Setting group options.

15

9. If auditing is not enabled on the source domain, you will see the prompt shown in Figure 15.20. It gives you the option to enable auditing, which is required for migration of SID history. Click Yes to continue.

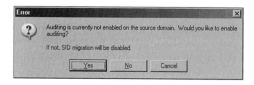

FIGURE 15.20   Enabling auditing.

10. Another prompt might appear if auditing is not enabled on the target domain. Auditing is required for migration of SID history and can be disabled after the migration. Click Yes to enable and continue.

11. A local group named SOURCEDOMAIN$$$ is required on the source domain for migration of SID history. A prompt asking to create this group is displayed at this point, as shown in Figure 15.21, if it was not created beforehand. Click Yes to continue.

12. Another prompt might appear asking to create a Registry key named TcpipClientSupport in the source domain. Once again, this is required for SID history migration. Click Yes to continue.

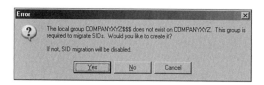

FIGURE 15.21   Creating a local group.

13. If you created the Registry key, an additional prompt then asks whether the PDC in the source domain will require a reboot. In most cases, it will, so click Yes to continue.

14. The next prompt exists solely to stall the process while the reboot of the Source PDC takes place. Wait until the PDC is back online, and then click OK to continue.

15. The subsequent screen allows for the exclusion of specific directory-level attributes from migration. If you need to exclude any attributes, they can be set here. In this example, no exclusions are set. Click Next to continue.

16. Enter a user account with proper administrative rights on the source domain on the following screen. Then click Next to continue.

17. Naming conflicts often arise during domain migrations. In addition, different naming conventions might apply in the new environment. The next screen allows

for these contingencies. In this example, any conflicting names will have the XYZ-prefix attached to the account names. After defining these settings, click Next to continue.

18. The verification screen is the last wizard screen you see before any changes are made. Once again, make sure that the procedure has been tested before running it because ADMT will henceforth write changes to the Target Windows Server 2003 Active Directory environment. Click Finish when you're ready to begin group migration.

19. The group migration process then commences. Changing the refresh rate, as shown in Figure 15.22, allows for a quicker analysis of the current process. When the procedure is complete, the log can be viewed by clicking View Log. After finishing these steps, click the Close button to end the procedure.

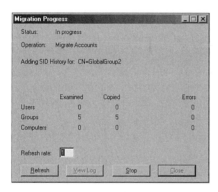

FIGURE 15.22   Altering the migration progress of group accounts.

Migrating User Accounts

User accounts are the "bread and butter" of domain objects and are among the most important components. The biggest shortcoming of ADMT v1.0 was its inability to migrate passwords of user objects, which effectively limited its use. However, ADMT does an excellent job of migrating users, their passwords, and the security associated with them. To migrate users, follow these steps:

1. Open the ADMT MMC snap-in (Start, All Programs, Administrative Tools, Active Directory Migration Tool).

2. Right-click Active Directory Migration Tool, and choose User Account Migration Wizard, as indicated in Figure 15.23.

3. Click Next at the welcome screen.

4. The next screen offers the option to test the migration before actually performing it. As previously mentioned, this process is recommended, so for this example, perform the full migration. Select Migrate Now and then click Next.

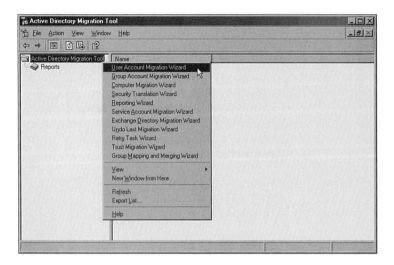

FIGURE 15.23   Starting the User Account Migration Wizard.

5. Select the source and target domains on the subsequent screen, and click Next to continue.

6. The following screen allows you to choose user accounts for migration. Just click the Add button and select the user accounts to be migrated. After you select all the user accounts, click Next to continue.

7. The next screen, shown in Figure 15.24, allows you to choose a target OU for all created users. Choose the OU by clicking the Browse button. After you select it, click Next to continue.

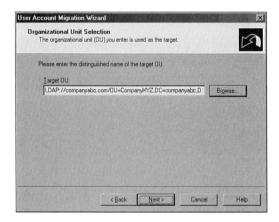

FIGURE 15.24   Selecting the target OU.

8. The new password migration functionality of ADMT is enacted through the following screen. Select Migrate Passwords and then select the server in the source domain in which the Password Migration DLL was installed, as covered in the "Installing a Password Migration DLL on the Source Domain" section. Click Next to continue.

> **NOTE**
>
> Depending on if other wizards have already been run, there might be additional steps at this point that happen one time only to set up proper Registry settings, reboot domain controllers, and create special groups. These steps and dialog boxes are documented in steps 9–14 of the "Migrating Groups" section that precedes this section.

9. The subsequent screen deals with security settings in relation to the migrated users. Click Help for an overview of each option. In this example, select the settings shown in Figure 15.25. Then click Next to continue.

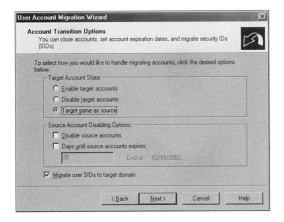

FIGURE 15.25   Setting the account transition options.

10. Enter the username, password, and domain of an account that has Domain Admin rights in the source domain. Click Next to continue.

11. Several migration options are presented as part of the next screen. As before, clicking Help elaborates on some of these features. In this example, select the options shown in Figure 15.26. Click Next to continue.

12. The next screen is for setting exclusions. Specify any property of the user object that should not be migrated here. In this example, no exclusions are set. Click Next to continue.

13. Naming conflicts for user accounts are common. Designate a procedure for dealing with duplicate accounts in advance and enter such information in the next wizard screen, as shown in Figure 15.27. Select the appropriate options for duplicate accounts, and click Next to continue.

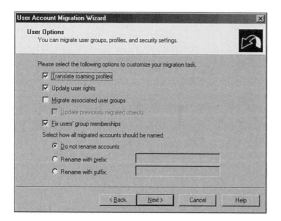

FIGURE 15.26   Setting user options for the User Account Migration Wizard.

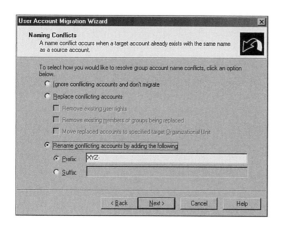

FIGURE 15.27   Setting naming conflict settings.

14. The following verification screen presents a summary of the procedure that will take place. This is the last screen before changes are written to the target domain. Verify the settings and click Next to continue.

15. The Migration Progress status box displays the migration process as it occurs, indicating the number of successful and unsuccessful accounts created. When the process is complete, review the log by clicking View Log and verify the integrity of the procedure. A sample log file from a user migration is shown in Figure 15.28. Click Close when you are finished.

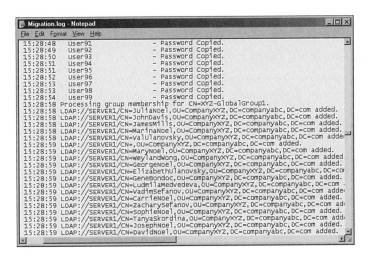

FIGURE 15.28   Viewing a sample user migration log.

Migrating Computer Accounts

Another important set of objects that must be migrated is also one of the trickier ones. Computer objects must not only be migrated in AD, but they must also be updated at the workstations themselves so that users will be able to log on effectively from their consoles. ADMT seamlessly installs agents on all migrated computer accounts and reboots them, forcing them into their new domain structures. Follow these steps to migrate computer accounts:

1. Open the ADMT MMC snap-in (Start, All Programs, Administrative Tools, Active Directory Migration Tool).

2. Right-click Active Directory Migration Tool, and choose Computer Migration Wizard.

3. Click Next at the welcome screen.

4. Just as in the previous wizards, the option for testing the migration is given at this point. It is highly recommended that you test the process before migrating computer accounts. In this case, because a full migration will take place, choose Migrate Now. Click Next to continue.

5. Type the names of the source and destination domains in the drop-down boxes on the next screen, and click Next to continue.

6. On the following screen, select the computer accounts that will be migrated by clicking the Add button and choosing the appropriate accounts. Click Next to continue.

7. Select the OU to which the computer accounts will be migrated, and click Next to continue.

8. The next screen allows for the option to specify which settings on the local clients will be migrated. Click the Help button for a detailed description of each item. In this example, select all items, and then click Next to continue.

9. The subsequent screen prompts to choose whether existing security will be replaced, removed, or added to. In this example, replace the security. Click Next to continue.

10. A prompt then informs you that the user rights translation will be performed in Add mode only. Click OK to continue.

11. The next screen is important. It allows an administrator to specify how many minutes a computer will wait before restarting itself. In addition, you can define the naming convention for the computers. After choosing options, click Next to continue.

12. Just as in the previous wizards, exclusions can be set for specific attributes in the following wizard screen. Select any exclusions needed, and click Next to continue.

13. Naming conflicts are addressed in the subsequent screen. If any specific naming conventions or conflict resolution settings are required, enter them here. Click Next to continue.

14. The Completion screen lists a summary of the changes that will be made. Review the list and click Finish when you are ready. All clients that will be upgraded are subsequently rebooted.

15. When the migration process is complete, you can view the Migration log by clicking the View Log button. After verifying all settings, click Close.

16. The client agents are subsequently distributed to all clients that have been migrated. Each agent is installed automatically and counts down until the designated time limit set during the configuration of the Computer Migration Wizard. At that point, a dialog box opens on each workstation.

17. Click Close on the ADMT MMC snap-in to end the wizard.

Migrating Other Domain Functionality

In addition to the Group, User, and Computer Migration Wizards, several other wizards can be used to migrate specific domain-critical components. These wizards operate using the same principles as those described in the preceding sections, and are as straightforward in their operation. The following is a list of the additional wizards included in ADMT:

- ▶ Security Translation Wizard

- ▶ Reporting Wizard

- ▶ Service Account Migration Wizard

- ▶ Exchange Directory Migration Wizard

- ▶ Retry Task Wizard

- ▶ Trust Migration Wizard

- ▶ Group Mapping and Merging Wizard

Virtually all necessary functionality that needs replacing when migrating from one domain to another can be transferred by using ADMT. It has proven to be a valuable tool that gives administrators an additional option to consider when migrating and restructuring Active Directory environments.

Summary

Although Windows 2000 and Windows Server 2003 are close cousins in the operating system family tree, there are some compelling reasons to upgrade some, if not all, network components. At a minimum, in planning a migration to Exchange 2007, the organization needs to ensure that the server running Exchange 2007 is running an x64-bit version of Windows 2003 SP1 or higher, and that the forest functional level is set to Windows 2003.

Fortunately, many tools come with Windows Server 2003, which make performing the migration process more straightforward. In addition, advanced procedures and tools such as Mixed-Mode Domain Redirect and ADMT provide for a broad range of options to bring organizations to Windows Server 2003 functionality and ready to migrate the organization to Exchange 2007.

Best Practices

The following are best practices from this chapter:

- ▶ Ensure that one of the postupgrade tasks performed is an audit of all services so that servers that need IIS have the service reenabled after migration.

- ▶ Because prototype phases of a project are essential to test the design assumptions for a migration or implementation, create a production domain controller and then isolate it in the lab for testing.

- ▶ Test the hardware compatibility of any server that will be directly upgraded to Windows Server 2003 against the published Hardware Compatibility List from Microsoft.

- ▶ Because the decision to raise the forest or domain functional levels is final, ensure that there is no additional need to add Windows 2000 domain controllers anywhere in the forest before performing this procedure.

- ▶ If the server or servers that hold the OM roles are not directly upgraded to Windows Server 2003 but will instead be retired, move these OM roles to another server.

- ▶ When using ADMT, migrate groups into a new domain first to keep users' group membership intact.

CHAPTER 16

Migrating to Exchange Server 2007

In this day and age, most organizations already have some form of email in their environment; therefore, it is important to consider that when implementing Microsoft Exchange Server 2007 in an organization, it might not be the organization's first messaging system. That said, it is likely the organization will be migrating from an existing messaging system to Exchange 2007, whether it be from a previous version of Microsoft Exchange, or from a completely different messaging system.

This chapter covers "migrations," which means this chapter addresses the migration process that takes an organization from one messaging environment into Exchange Server 2007. The strategy to migrate to Exchange 2007 as well as the tools available for the migration process are pretty contained. Regardless of the source messaging environment being migrated, the core process and tools available from Microsoft are relatively contained.

The question many organizations ask as they plan their migration to Exchange 2007 is whether they need to purchase a third-party migration tool for the migration to be successful. There are always pros and cons to buying a third-party tool for a migration; however, the end result is if the free tools from Microsoft provide all of the necessary components required to successfully complete the migration, then the free tools might as well be used. The best way to find out whether Microsoft's out-of-the-box migration tools do the job is to test the migration in a test lab. If it works, the free tool is all that is needed.

The focus of this chapter is on the free tools available from Microsoft, and the process involved in using the tools based on tips, tricks, and lessons learned from previous migrations leveraging the built-in tools from Microsoft.

Understanding How to Migrate to Exchange Server 2007

Before getting too far into the tools and process of migrating to Exchange 2007, it is important to understand, from a high level, the strategy on how to migrate to Exchange 2007. The migration strategy could be as simple as effectively moving everything from Exchange 2000 Server or Exchange Server 2003 straight in to Exchange 2007 without making drastic modifications. Or, it could mean a very complex Exchange environment restructuring is performed as part of the migration process.

It is not required to completely restructure Exchange as part of the migration. In fact, if Exchange 2000 or 2003 is working fine today, then just a simple migration is all that is required. The reason this book even addresses organizational restructuring as a potential option is that over the years with mergers, acquisitions, downsizing, or business changes, many organizations have Exchange structures that are not appropriate for the ongoing needs of an organization. Possibly, the organizational structure worked fine for years for the organization; however, a redesign is now needed because of a change in how the organization does business. These types of changes can make the migration process more complex as are migrations that take place from a messaging system other than Exchange 2000 or Exchange 2003. Some of the migration changes are things that could take place before or after the migration to Exchange 2007. This chapter covers the general process of migrating to Exchange 2007.

Simple Migration from Exchange 2000 Server and Exchange Server 2003 to Exchange Server 2007

For organizations that have a working Exchange 2000 or Exchange 2003 environment that is happy with the architecture and operation of their Exchange environment and simply want to move to Exchange 2007, the migration process is a relatively simple and methodical process. In a condensed format, the process involves replacing Exchange 2000 or Exchange 2003 front-end servers with Client Access servers, replacing bridgehead servers with Hub Transport servers, adding new Exchange 2007 Mailbox servers, and "dragging and dropping" the data from the old server, or servers, to the new server, or servers. It's not quite that simple because there are several preparation steps that need to be conducted, a handful of test procedures that can assist the organization in the event of a migration failure that requires rolling back during the migration process. However, to migrate to Exchange 2007 from an already operational Exchange 2000 or Exchange 2003 environment just requires following the step-by-step procedure outlined in the "Migrating from Exchange 2000 Server and Exchange Server 2003 to Exchange Server 2007" portion of this chapter.

Restructuring Exchange as Part of the Migration to Exchange Server 2007

For organizations that have undergone business changes since the installation of Exchange 2000 or 2003, or that have an Exchange environment that is not architected properly for the current and near future business environment of the organization, they might choose to restructure Exchange as part of their migration to Exchange 2007. The restructuring can occur with Exchange 2000 or 2003 prior to the migration, the restructuring can occur during the Exchange 2007 migration, or the restructuring can occur after Exchange 2007 has been put in place.

The deciding factor on when the restructure occurs depends on the effort involved to perform the restructuring. Some organizations will consolidate servers as part of their restructuring process. This is a simple process that can usually be done during the migration where, for example, several Exchange 2000 or 2003 back-end servers are consolidated into a single Exchange 2007 Mailbox server. As mailboxes are moved from the old Exchange to the new Exchange, they can be moved from multiple systems to a single system. This restructuring is easy to do as part of the migration process.

Some migration processes are more complex, for example, if the organization wants to completely collapse remote site servers and bring all of the servers into a centralized Exchange environment model. From an Exchange perspective, collapsing sites is one of the restructuring options that can be done as part of the migration; however, the challenge is typically trying to move large amounts of email over a wide area network (WAN) connection. If a remote site has several gigabytes or even tens or hundreds of gigabytes, it is unrealistic to migrate that amount of mail over a WAN connection as part of a migration process. In many cases, the actual server, hard drives of the server, or backup of the databases are physically brought into the centralized data center, and the data is migrated in the data center. Although a logistical shuffle to physically move servers or data during the migration process, this is not an insurmountable process than trying to move large sets of data across a slow WAN link connection.

The more complex restructuring model is required when an organization wants to add some sites, remove some sites, consolidate other sites, and completely redo sites that already exist. The choice of when to do the changes depends on the length and scope of the Exchange migration. If the scope and goal of the migration is to do the restructuring in the Exchange migration project, plan the process and proceed with a restructuring of Exchange as part of the migration to Exchange 2007. However, if the restructuring would be nice to have, but not significant to the scope of the project, you might choose to consolidate servers and migrate to Exchange, and then perform the restructuring after Exchange 2007 has been installed.

Migrating to a Brand-New Exchange Server 2007 Organization

Another method for migrating to Exchange 2007 is one where a brand-new Exchange 2007 server is built from scratch, and then data is moved into the new Exchange environment. An organization might choose to use this method if there are significant problems with their existing Exchange 2000 or 2003 environment, or if the configuration of their existing Exchange environment is not ideally suited for Exchange Server 2007. This is a significant migration task and requires serious consideration regarding whether this is the best option. Instead, perhaps the Exchange 2000 or 2003 environment can be cleaned up to a state where a simpler migration could take place.

16

When building a new Exchange 2007 environment, data can be exported and imported from an old Exchange environment to a new one; however, there will be many user interruptions and impacts. At a minimum, the Outlook profiles on user systems will need to be changed to point the user to a completely new Exchange server. Anyone with offline stores or cached-mode Exchange configurations will need to completely rebuild their offline Outlook databases. Furthermore, in cases where the new Exchange has a completely new organizational structure, links such as appointments or meeting requests will be disconnected from the person who invited them to the appointment because the new calendar might have different usernames, site configurations, and so on.

In addition, with a clean installation of Exchange 2007, the organization will not be able to add back in an Exchange 2000 or Exchange 2003 server. Old Exchange server versions are only supported in an Exchange 2007 environment that was migrated from the old version to the new version of Exchange. When Exchange 2007 is installed from scratch, none of the legacy backward-compatibility tools are installed or configured to work.

So, a brand-new Exchange 2007 installation is a drastic move for an organization that already has Exchange 2000 or 2003. If the organization can do one of the migration methods and then clean up the model after migration, it would be easier to perform the migration.

Migrating from Exchange Server 5.5

A migration from Exchange 5.5 to Exchange 2007 is not directly supported and requires a migration first from Exchange 5.5 to Exchange 2000 or from Exchange 5.5 to Exchange 2003. After successfully migrating to Exchange 2000 or Exchange 2003, the organization can then execute the migration to Exchange 2007. This migration process from Exchange 5.5 is covered later in this chapter in the section "Migrating from Exchange Server 5.5 to Exchange Server 2003."

Migrating from Lotus Notes, Novell GroupWise, and Sendmail

Yet another migration scenario is when an organization has an existing non-Exchange environment, such as Lotus Notes, Novell GroupWise, or sendmail. A migration from a non-Microsoft Exchange messaging platform is not covered in this chapter. The process of migrating from a non-Exchange environment is one that requires tools to migrate user email, calendars, contacts, shared folders, and other information stored in the old email system to Exchange 2007. This type of migration usually starts with the installation of a completely clean Exchange 2007 environment in which user data is then migrated into the new environment.

Migrations Involving a Limited Number of Servers

Beyond just migrating from one version of messaging to Exchange 2007, the destination environment of Exchange 2007 can depend on the size and architectural structure of the resulting Exchange 2007 environment. For a small organization, the destination Exchange environment could be a single server where the various Exchange 2007 roles are all on a single system. If there is no need to add additional server systems to the environment, then having a limited number of servers and placing server roles on a single system is easy to do.

The Hub Transport, Client Access, and Mailbox server roles of Exchange 2007 can all be placed on a single server; however, if the organization wants to add an Edge Transport server role to the organization, the Edge Transport server needs to be on a separate server. This is done for security purposes to isolate the Edge Transport server from other servers in the Exchange 2007 organization that host production data.

Migrations Involving a Distributed Server Strategy

For larger organizations, the various server roles will likely be applied to systems dedicated to a particular server role for purposes of performance and scalability. In many cases, a larger organization will already have existing roles for front-end and back-end servers, as well as bridgehead servers. In these larger environments, assuming that separate servers will be retained, the Exchange 2007 server roles will replace the existing Exchange 2000 and Exchange 2003 server systems with a similar distribution of server systems.

When migrating to an Exchange 2007 environment with individual servers, the process of migrating involves the following:

1. Migration of the Client Access server roles first

2. Followed by the migration of Hub Transport server roles

3. Then the installation of Mailbox server roles

4. And finally the installation of servers such as Edge Transport servers and Unified Messaging servers, if desired

Understanding What's New and What's Different with Exchange Server 2007

This section covers what is new and what is different with Exchange 2007, not from a product function and feature basis, which is covered in Chapter 1, "Exchange Server 2007 Technology Primer," but rather how certain changes in Exchange 2007 impact the migration process to Exchange 2007. This includes things such as the support for only 64-bit hardware, changes in the Exchange database structure, routing groups and administrative groups, elimination of the use of link states, and the removal of support for specific Exchange 2000 and Exchange 2003 components.

Exchange Server 2007 on x64-bit

One of the first things most organizations become aware of about Exchange 2007 is that it only supports x64-bit hardware running the Windows Server 2003 x64-bit edition operating system. There are many reasons why Microsoft shifted to a 64-bit only platform that were covered in Chapter 1. At the bottom line, this means that, during a migration from

Exchange 2000 or Exchange 2003 to Exchange 2007, in-place upgrades are not supported, and that, in many cases new hardware is required for the migration to Exchange 2007.

Most organizations migrating to Exchange 2007 have found that the migration process between servers is relatively simple, so there hasn't been any major concerns migrating from Exchange 2000 and Exchange 2003 to Exchange 2007 from one server to another. And because 64-bit Exchange 2007 is significantly more reliable and has better performance and scalability benefits, the requirement to forego in-place upgrades has been far outweighed by the enhancements 64-bit has brought to Exchange 2007.

Back to Just the EDB Database (STM Is Gone)

Another thing you will notice in a migration from Exchange 2003 to Exchange 2007 is that the STM database disappears. Not to worry, Exchange 2007 no longer has an STM database. Microsoft has gone back to a sole EDB database for Exchange and has incorporated the benefits that the streaming STM database brought to Exchange 2003 into the new Exchange 2007 EDB format. Because the EDB database is new and improved, you cannot mount an Exchange 2000 or 2003 database on Exchange 2007, and during the migration process if you find that there is no STM database on your server, don't worry that you have lost any data during the migration process.

No Routing Groups in Exchange Server 2007

Exchange 2007 has also brought about the elimination of the concept of a routing group in Exchange. Routing groups were used in Exchange 2000 and Exchange 2003 to allow Exchange administrators to create groups of servers that communicated with each other and to identify common routes in which the servers in a group communicated with servers in another group. Exchange 2007 now uses Active Directory Sites and Services to identify subnets, where servers on the same subnet are, by default, part of the same routing communication group, but not as a formal group that requires specific administration or management. If an Exchange server is moved to a different subnet, the Exchange server acknowledges a new subnet from Active Directory Sites and Services, and associates itself with the servers on the same subnet if they exist.

The Hub Transport server role replaces the old Exchange 2000 and Exchange 2003 bridgehead server, and the Hub Transport server knows which Exchange servers it is servicing by the identification of the subnets that the Hub Transport server is configured to service. It's much easier to just set a table of servers and how they communicate with one another than to create specific groups and then move the servers within a group or between groups to meet the needs of the organization.

The elimination of the routing group requires that a temporary routing group connector be configured between Exchange 2007 and the old Exchange 2000 or 2003 environment. During the installation of Exchange 2007 as it is joined to an Exchange 2000 or Exchange 2003 organization, the installation process prompts for the name of the Exchange 2000 or 2003 server from which the new Exchange 2007 server will route its messages to and from. The purpose of this special routing group connector is to ensure proper mail flow between Exchange 2007 and the older Exchange 2000 or 2003 environment. This routing group connector shows up as "Exchange Routing Group (DWBGZMFD01QNBJR)."

NOTE

Some have asked how Microsoft came about naming the temporary routing group connector with DWBGZMFD01QNBJR attached to the connector name. If you advance each letter in that routing group by one letter (D becomes an E, W becomes an X, B becomes a C, and so on), DWBGZMFD01QNBJR becomes EXCHANGE12ROCKS.

No Administrative Groups in Exchange Server 2007

In addition to having routing groups removed in Exchange 2007, Microsoft has also removed administrative groups from Exchange 2007. As part of the administrative model in Exchange 2000 and 2003, the concept of having administrative groups was to have resources placed in the administrative groups for easier administration and management. This allowed certain Exchange administrators to manage the associated resources in their group. Rather than creating a special administrative role with resources associated with the administrative group, Exchange 2007 has done away with the administrative group and just has administration associated with user accounts or groups, and not as a special group to create, manage, and administer.

Just as with the elimination of the Exchange routing group needing a temporary routing group connector for Exchange 2000 and Exchange 2003 backward compatibility, you will find a temporary administrative group created with the designation "Exchange Administrative Group (FYDIBOHF23SPDLT)." For those with the magic decoder ring that advanced each letter in the routing group connector name to come up with EXCHANGE12ROCKS, subtract a letter for each letter in the name of the administrative group to come up with the same name.

No Link State Updates Required in Exchange Server 2007

Because Exchange 2007 no longer requires routing group connectors other than to communicate between Exchange 2007 and earlier Exchange 2000 or 2003 servers, the link state update process needs to be suppressed during the coexistence of Exchange 2007 with earlier versions of Exchange. Link state updates were needed in Exchange 2000 and Exchange 2003 to establish a rerouting process if a routing group connector was down and messages needed to be rerouted in the Exchange organization.

Exchange 2007 uses Active Directory Sites and Services site links and site link bridge information to determine the best routing communications of messages, and it leverages Active Directory (AD) to determine the best way to reroute messages should a link be unavailable.

During the migration process to Exchange 2007, because the temporary routing group connector will be established as part of the installation process of an Exchange 2007 server, a Registry hack needs to be performed on EVERY Exchange 2000 and Exchange

16

2003 server prior to migrating to Exchange 2007 to suppress link state updates. This prevents Exchange 2000 or 2003 servers from marking the connectors as being down, and forces Exchange 2000 and Exchange 2003 servers to use least-cost routing in the calculation of alternate routes in message communications.

Elimination of the Recipient Update Service (RUS) in Exchange Server 2007

Exchange 2007 also eliminated the Recipient Update Service (RUS), which requires a temporary workaround in a coexistence environment. The RUS was the function that took a user account created in Active Directory Users and Computers and completed the provisioning process by autogenerating the user's email objects such as the user's email address. Many Exchange 2000 and 2003 administrators never understood why after creating a user in Active Directory that many times the user's email address wasn't created and sometimes it would be created. It was because Active Directory Users and Computers was not the tool that generated the address information—the RUS created it. Depending on how busy the RUS was on a system, it could take a while for the email address information to show up for a newly created user.

In Exchange 2007, email recipients are now fully provisioned at the time a user is created in the Exchange Management Console or from the Exchange Management Shell. During the coexistence of an Exchange 2007 and Exchange 2000 or 2003 environment, the RUS still needs to be created and present for each domain that has Exchange servers and users; however, you must use the Exchange System Manager from Exchange 2000/2003 to provision the RUS because the provisioning service cannot be configured from within the Exchange Management Console or Exchange Management Shell tools of Exchange 2007.

> **NOTE**
>
> Although the Recipient Update Service (RUS) needs to be created from the Exchange System Manager utility (found in Exchange 2000/2003) for each domain that an Exchange server or user resides, you cannot make an Exchange 2007 server the RUS. RUS will only work on an Exchange 2000 or 2003 server system. If you create the RUS on an Exchange 2007 system, RUS will stop working altogether for the domain in which RUS on the Exchange 2007 server was created. As a rule of thumb, RUS is already configured and working in the existing Exchange 2000 or 2003 environment. During the migration to Exchange 2007, keep the RUS server(s) in each domain operating and only remove those servers in each domain as the cleanup process to go to a native Exchange 2007 environment.

Managing a Coexisting Environment

During the coexistence between Exchange 2000 or 2003 and Exchange 2007, an administrator needs to be mindful which administration tool to use for which function. This is a confusing task because many functions that no longer exist in Exchange 2007 require the administrator to go back to the Exchange System Manager tool in Exchange 2000 or 2003 to perform tasks. This is why the shorter the coexistence between Exchange 2000 or 2003 and Exchange 2007, the better.

The following list discusses some of the administrative tasks that need consideration for environments where Exchange 2000, 2003, and 2007 are coexisting:

▶ Exchange 2007 mailboxes must be managed with the Exchange Management Console found in Exchange 2007. Many objects in Exchange 2007 are not exposed in Exchange 2003, and if mailboxes are created in Exchange 2003 for an Exchange 2007 user, certain objects will not be provisioned.

▶ Mailboxes on Exchange 2003 must be created using the Exchange System Manager found in Exchange 2003. Just as the Exchange System Manager doesn't fully support Exchange 2007 object creation, the creation of Exchange 2003 mailboxes needs the RUS process to fully provision an Exchange 2003 mailbox from the Exchange System Manager tool.

▶ The Exchange Management Console will successfully manage an Exchange 2003 mailbox. So, as long as the mailbox has been created with the Exchange System Manager tool, thereafter the mailbox can be managed or administered from either tool.

▶ Moving mailboxes between Exchange 2003 and 2007 (either way) must be done with the Exchange Management Console tool. Do not use the Exchange System Manager tool to move mailboxes to or from Exchange 2007 because certain components are not in the Exchange System Manager tool to successfully complete the mailbox move process.

No Support for Certain Exchange 2000 Server Components

Several components in Exchange 2000 are no longer supported in Exchange 2007. Most of these components weren't supported in a native Exchange 2003 environment either, and an organization needs to take this into consideration when migrating to Exchange 2007. The following Exchange 2000 components are no longer supported in Exchange 2007:

▶ Key Management Service (KMS)

▶ Microsoft Mobile Information Service

▶ Exchange Instant Messaging Service

▶ Exchange Chat Service

▶ Exchange 2000 Conferencing Service

▶ MS-Mail Connector

▶ cc:Mail Connector

These services do not exist in Exchange 2007 and an organization requiring functionality of these services needs to keep Exchange 2000 servers in the organization long enough to retain the service or replace the service with an Exchange 2007–supported equivalent service.

For services such as the MS-Mail Connector and cc:Mail Connector, those services can run for a while on an Exchange 2000 server even if all of the users' mailboxes have been migrated to Exchange 2007. However, services keyed to user mailboxes, such as the Exchange 2000 Conferencing Service, Chat, Instant Messaging, Mobile Information Service, or Key Management Service, will cease to work for each user as their mailboxes are migrated to Exchange 2007.

The following are current services that are not supported by Microsoft Exchange 2007:

- **Key Management Service (KMS)**—Use Active Directory autoenrollment of certificates and issue certificates to users for encrypted email communications.

- **Microsoft Mobile Information Service**—Exchange 2003 and Exchange 2007 support mobile devices directly within the Exchange environment and no longer require the separate Microsoft Mobile Information Service to support mobile users.

- **Exchange Instant Messaging Service**—Instant messaging moved to Microsoft Live Communications Server 2003 and 2005 with Exchange 2003, and is now Office Communications Server 2007 that is compatible with Exchange 2007.

- **Exchange Chat Service**—Chat has also been integrated into Office Communications Server 2007.

- **Exchange 2000 Conferencing Service**—Conferencing is also a core component of Office Communications Server 2007.

- **MS-Mail Connector**—There is no equivalent support for a connector to MS-Mail in Exchange 2007.

- **cc:Mail Connector**—There is no equivalent support for a connector to cc:Mail in Exchange 2007.

No Support for Certain Exchange Server 2003 Components

Those migrating from Exchange 2003 to Exchange 2007 will notice that the Novell GroupWise Connector is no longer supported in Exchange 2007. If the organization requires continued support of Exchange-to-GroupWise connectivity, the organization should keep at least one Exchange 2003 server in the organization running the Novell GroupWise Connector for Exchange. This will keep mail flow and synchronization operating between the environments.

In addition, the organization should ensure there are no Exchange 2000 servers still running any of the Exchange 2000 components noted in the previous section titled "No Support for Certain Exchange 2000 Server Components" so that as the organization shifts to a completely native Exchange 2007 environment, connectivity or support of certain functionality is not missed or forgotten.

Moving to Native Mode in Exchange

For an organization that previously had Exchange Server 5.5 in their environment, or possibly still has Exchange 5.5 servers in the environment, before the migration to Exchange 2007 can begin, the organization must remove all Exchange 5.5 servers. In addition, the organization must decommission all remnants of Exchange 5.5, such as site connectors and Active Directory Connectors (ADCs), and switch the Exchange organization into Native mode before proceeding with the migration to Exchange 2007.

This section covers the steps that need to be accomplished before the conversion to Native mode can be completed. This section also covers some of the postmigration cleanup processes that need to be run in the existing Exchange 2000 or Exchange 2003 organization structure prior to migrating to Exchange 2007. Not all of the cleanup processes need to be run in all environments; this depends on the method the organization used to populate Active Directory.

> **NOTE**
>
> When referring to Native mode in Exchange, sometimes people confuse it with Native mode in Windows, but they are two completely different things. Native mode in Exchange, which is referred to here in this chapter, addresses the removal of Exchange 5.5 in the Exchange organization so that the Exchange environment is natively Exchange 2000 and Exchange 2003 servers. This is completely different than Windows Native mode, which means that no Windows NT 4.0 domain controllers can exist in a Windows Active Directory environment. Windows Mixed mode allows Windows NT 4.0 Backup Domain Controllers (BDCs) to exist in a Windows 2000 or Windows 2003 Active Directory. For reference to Native mode in Exchange in this chapter, we are referring solely to the removal of support for Exchange 5.5 in an Exchange organization.

Converting to Native Mode

Converting to Native mode changed the way that Exchange 2000 and Exchange 2003 operated that was slightly different from the way Exchange 5.5 worked. The functions in Native mode Exchange are similar to the way Exchange 2007 operates, so rather than having backward support to Exchange 5.5 functionality that is not supported in Exchange 2007, Microsoft requires Native mode as a prerequisite before the organization can migrate to Exchange 2007. The functions in Exchange Native mode are as follows:

▶ Multiple routing groups are supported.

▶ Routing groups can contain servers from different administrative groups.

▶ Servers can move between routing groups.

▶ Mailboxes can be moved between administrative groups.

▶ Simple Mail Transfer Protocol (SMTP) becomes the default routing protocol.

To shift the organization to Native mode, the following conditions must be met:

▶ No more Exchange 5.5 servers exist in the organization.

▶ No plans exist to add Exchange Server 5.5 servers to the organization in the future—the likelihood for a merger or acquisition is low.

▶ No need exists for connectors or gateways that run only on Exchange 5.5.

To convert to Native mode Exchange, the following steps must be accomplished in the following order:

1. Remove all directory replication connectors.

2. Remove all Exchange 5.5 servers from each remaining site.

3. Remove the recipient connection agreements and all other connection agreements for each Exchange 5.5 site.

4. Remove the Site Replication Service (SRS) from all Exchange Server 2003 systems.

5. Switch to Native mode using the Change Mode button on the organization's properties.

Deleting All Directory Replication Connectors

For any remaining Exchange 5.5 site that will not be migrated to Exchange Server 2003, the directory replication connectors must be deleted.

Use the Exchange System Manager to delete all directory replication connectors. To delete the directory replication connectors, click to expand the Tools view to display the Site Replication Service objects in the Exchange organization. Click the View menu and select Directory Replication Connector View. Click each directory replication connector and press Delete.

Next force replication to propagate the deletion of the directory replication connectors in the Active Directory Connector Manager by using the Replicate Now option on the connection agreements for the site. Verify the deletion of the directory replication connectors by opening the Exchange System Manager on another Exchange Server 2003 system and viewing the Site Replication Service with the Directory Replication Connector view. When the directory replication connector no longer appears, the deletion has been replicated .

Removing All Exchange Server 5.5 Servers from the Organization

When all the Exchange 5.5 servers are no longer needed, they should be uninstalled through the Exchange 5.5 setup program. The last server to be uninstalled should be the server that was the first server in the site or that contains the first server in the site components.

After all the servers have been uninstalled, the last server must be deleted manually from the Exchange hierarchy. To delete the server from the hierarchy, use the Exchange 5.5 Administrator program to connect to the Exchange Server 2003 system running the Site Replication Service and locate the list of servers in the site. Click the server to be removed and then click Edit, Delete. A warning appears if the server still contains mailboxes or connectors. Click Yes to continue the deletion. Another warning appears if there are still public folder replicas on the server. Click Yes to continue the deletion.

The next step is to force replication through the ADC for all connection agreements for the site by using the Replicate Now option. Verify that the server has been removed from Active Directory through the ADC before deleting the connection agreements and uninstalling the ADC. The server should no longer appear in the Exchange System Manager.

Removing Active Director Connectors

Open the Active Directory Connector Manager and delete all connection agreements. If the connection agreements are not deleted, the membership of distribution groups could be lost.

If the Active Directory Connector is no longer needed and all connection agreements have been removed, uninstall the Active Directory Connector through Control Panel, Add/Remove Programs. Also remember to disable or delete the service account used for the ADC if it's not used for any other services.

Deleting the Site Replication Service

The Site Replication Service is the last service to be deleted before the conversion to Native mode can take place. To delete the Site Replication Service, open the Exchange System Manager, and expand the Tools icon. Next expand the Site Replication Service icon, and then right-click each Site Replication Service and click Delete.

Throwing the Native Mode Switch

After the conversion to Native mode, there is no way to return to Mixed mode. The organization should be completely confident about the transition. When all the prerequisite steps have been accomplished, the Change Mode button on the organization properties in the Exchange System Manager should be available. Use the following steps to convert to Native mode Exchange Server 2003:

1. Open the Exchange System Manager.

2. Right-click the organization and click Properties.

3. Click the General tab, and then click Change Mode under Change Operations Mode. You will be warned that after you make the switch to Native mode, you cannot go back, as shown in Figure 16.1. Click Yes to permanently switch the organization's mode to Native mode.

FIGURE 16.1   Warning on moving to Native mode Exchange.

After the conversion to Exchange Server 2003 Native mode, administrative groups are always displayed in the organization. Administrators have the choice of disabling the display of routing groups .

Performing Postmigration Cleanup

Depending on the method that was used to populate the Active Directory, the organization might have to use a utility called ADClean that merges duplicate Active Directory accounts created during the migration process to Exchange Server 2003. If the Active Directory Connector was used to populate the Active Directory from the Exchange 5.5 directory before the Windows NT 4.0 domain accounts were migrated to Active Directory, two entries will exist for each user. The two user account entries should be merged through ADClean to complete the migration and clean up Active Directory.

Duplicate accounts in Active Directory can also occur if two ADC recipient connection agreements were created and marked as primary on a particular container. One account displays as disabled with a red x in the user icon and with a –1 appended to the display name. The other account displays normally. ADClean can also be used to merge these accounts. To merge accounts created because of duplicate connection agreements, run ADClean and select the container to search. On the next screen, verify the accounts to merge and then choose the option to begin the merge or export the merge to a file for import through ADClean later.

> **TIP**
>
> The Search Based on Exchange Mailboxes Only option allows ADClean to search for only duplicate accounts created by the ADC.

The ADClean utility is installed during setup in the \exchsrvr\bin directory. ADClean gives administrators the capability to manually select accounts to be merged or run the wizard to search for and suggest accounts to be merged. The merge can be executed immediately or exported to a .csv file to be reviewed by the administrator and then executed later through ADClean.

Deploying a Prototype Lab for the Exchange Server 2007 Migration Process

Regardless of the method that is chosen to migrate Exchange, care should be taken to test design assumptions as part of a comprehensive prototype lab. A prototype environment can help simulate the conditions that will be experienced as part of the migration process. Establishing a functional prototype environment also can help reduce the risk associated with migrations. In addition to traditional approaches for creating a prototype lab, which involves restoring from backups, several techniques exist to replicate the current production environment to simulate migration.

Creating Temporary Prototype Domain Controllers to Simulate Migration

Construction of a prototype lab to simulate an existing Exchange infrastructure is not particularly complicated, but requires thought in its implementation. Because an exact copy of the Active Directory is required, the most straightforward way of accomplishing this is by building a new domain controller in the production domain and then isolating that domain controller in the lab to create a mirror copy of the existing domain data. DNS and global catalog information should be transferred to the server when in production, to enable continuation of these services in the testing environment.

NOTE

You should keep several considerations in mind if planning this type of duplication of the production environment. First, when the temporary domain controller is made into a global catalog server, the potential exists for the current network environment to identify it as a working global catalog server and refer clients to it for directory lookups. When the server is brought offline, the clients would experience connectivity issues. For these reasons, it is good practice to create a temporary domain controller during off-hours.

A major caveat to this approach is that the system must be completely separate, with no way to communicate with the production environment. This is especially the case because the domain controllers in the prototype lab respond to requests made to the production domain, authenticating user and computer accounts and replicating information. Prototype domain controllers should never be added back into a production environment.

Seizing Operations Master (OM) Roles in the Lab Environment

Because Active Directory is a multimaster directory, any one of the domain controllers can authenticate and replicate information. This factor is what makes it possible to segregate the domain controllers into a prototype environment easily. There are several different procedures that can be used to seize the OM (also referred to as Flexible Single Master Operations [FSMO]) roles. One approach uses the `ntdsutil` utility, as follows:

1. Open a command prompt by selecting Start, Run, typing `cmd` in the Open text box, and then clicking OK.

16

> **CAUTION**
>
> Remember, this procedure should only be performed in a lab environment or in disaster recovery situations. Never perform it against a running production domain controller unless the intent is to forcibly move OM roles.

2. Type ntdsutil and press Enter.

3. Type roles and press Enter.

4. Type connections and press Enter.

5. Type connect to server *SERVERNAME* (where *SERVERNAME* is the name of the target Windows Server 2003 domain controller that will hold the OM roles), and press Enter.

6. Type quit and press Enter.

7. Type seize schema master and press Enter.

8. Click Yes at the prompt asking to confirm the OM change.

9. Type seize domain naming master and press Enter.

10. Click Yes at the prompt asking to confirm the OM change.

11. Type seize pdc and press Enter.

12. Click OK at the prompt asking to confirm the OM change.

13. Type seize rid master and press Enter.

14. Click OK at the prompt asking to confirm the OM change.

15. Type seize infrastructure master and press Enter.

16. Click OK at the prompt asking to confirm the OM change.

17. Exit the command prompt window.

After these procedures have been run, the domain controllers in the prototype lab environment will control the OM roles for the forest and domain, which is necessary for additional migration testing.

> **NOTE**
>
> Although the temporary domain controller procedure just described can be very useful toward producing a copy of the AD environment for a prototype lab, it is not the only method that can accomplish this. The AD domain controllers can also be restored via the backup software's restore procedure. A third option—which is often easier to accomplish but is somewhat riskier—is to break the mirror on a production domain controller, take that hard drive into the prototype lab, and install it in an identical

server. This procedure requires the production server to lose redundancy for a period of time while the mirror is rebuilt, but is a "quick-and-dirty" way to make a copy of the production environment.

Restoring the Exchange Environment for Prototype Purposes

After all forest and domain roles have been seized in the lab, the Exchange server or servers must be duplicated in the lab environment. Typically, this involves running a restore of the Exchange server on an equivalent piece of hardware. All of the major backup software implementations contain specific procedures for restoring an Exchange 2000 environment. Using these procedures is the most ideal way of duplicating the environment for the migration testing.

Validating and Documenting Design Decisions and Migration Procedures

The actual migration process in a prototype lab should follow, as closely as possible, any design decisions made regarding an Exchange Server 2003 implementation. It is ideal to document the steps involved in the process so that they can be used during the actual implementation to validate the process. The prototype lab is not only an extremely useful tool for validating the upgrade process, but it can also be useful for testing new software and procedures for production servers.

The chosen migration strategy—whether it be an in-place upgrade, a move mailbox method, or another approach—can be effectively tested in the prototype lab at this point. Follow all migration steps as if they were happening in production.

Migrating to a Brand-New Exchange Server 2007 Environment

One of the migration options to get to Exchange 2007 is to build a brand-new Exchange 2007 environment, and then import any existing data into the new Exchange environment. This scenario is not much of a migration being that a brand-new environment is created. The only migration addressed by this scenario is potentially that of having user data such as email messages, calendar appointments, and contacts imported into the new environment.

This scenario is typically limited to organizations that might have one of the following environments:

▶ An organization that has never had email, such as a brand-new organization

▶ An organization that is migrating from a completely non-Microsoft environment where a brand-new Exchange 2007 is installed, and then data from the old non-Microsoft messaging system is migrated to the new Exchange 2007 environment

▶ An organization that is undergoing a drastic business change that dictates the need to start from scratch with a new Exchange 2007 configuration such as a merger of two companies with a third company emerging that has a completely different business name and organizational structure

This scenario is not expanded on further in this chapter as the migration process really mirrors that of a brand-new installation of Exchange 2007 (covered in Chapter 7, "Installing Exchange Server 2007") with the process of importing old data, if desired, into the new environment.

The new Exchange 2007 environment should be designed and implemented to meet the needs of the new organization, through the use of third-party migration tools, or even tools made available from Microsoft on the downloads page http://www.microsoft.com/technet/prodtechnol/exchange/downloads/2003/default.mspx can be used to assist with the import of data to the new environment.

Migrating from Exchange 2000 Server or Exchange Server 2003 to Exchange Server 2007

For organizations that currently have Exchange 2000 or Exchange 2003 looking to migrate to Exchange 2007, the migration strategy pretty much involves replacing front-end servers with Client Access servers, bridgehead servers with Hub Transport servers, back-end servers with Mailbox servers, and adding in Edge Transport and Unified Messaging servers as desired. There is a very specific order that works best in the migration process as well as tips and tricks that help you navigate around known migration challenges. These tips, tricks, and best practices for migrating from Exchange 2000 and Exchange 2003 to Exchange 2007 have been documented in this section of the chapter.

> **NOTE**
>
> There can be several variations of an existing Exchange 2000 or 2003 environment where the organization has clustered back-end servers, or has an SMTP relay server ahead of the Exchange environment, or has servers residing in different physical sites that can still use this migration process. There are no migration limitations that prevent an organization from using this migration strategy and making variations to it, including migrating onto a clustered Mailbox server, adding Hub Transport or Client Access servers, or consolidating servers as part of the migration process.

Planning Your Migration

The planning process in migrating from an environment that has Exchange 2000 or 2003 to Exchange 2007 involves ensuring that the existing environment is ready for a migration, and that the hardware necessary to accept the migrated server roles is compatible with Exchange 2007. The planning process to Exchange 2007 proceeds using the following path:

1. Review Chapter 3, "Understanding Core Exchange Server 2007 Design Plans," to become familiar with terminology used in Exchange 2007 design architecture.

2. Confirm that you want to do a one-to-one migration of servers from Exchange 2000 or 2003 to Exchange 2007 (that is, Exchange 2000 or 2003 front-end servers become Exchange 2007 Client Access servers, and Exchange 2000 or 2003 back-end servers become Exchange 2007 Mailbox servers).

NOTE

As part of this migration, you can do server consolidation by moving mailboxes from multiple servers to fewer servers, migrate from basic Exchange 2000 or 2003 servers to clustered 2007 servers, or add in Edge Transport or Unified Messaging server role systems as part of the migration process. These variations just need to be slipped in to the migration plan. For implementation of Hub Transport servers, see Chapter 17, "Implementing Client Access and Hub Transport Servers." For implementation of Edge Transport servers, see Chapter 8, "Implementing Edge Services for an Exchange Server 2007 Environment." And for implementation of clustered servers, see Chapter 31, "Continuous Backups, Clustering, and Network Load Balancing in Exchange Server 2007."

---

3. Select the proper version of Exchange Server 2007 in which you will be implementing Exchange 2007 on, whether it is the Standard Edition or the Enterprise Edition of the server software.

16

Choosing Between Standard and Enterprise Editions

The Exchange Server 2007, Standard Edition is the basic messaging server version of the software. The Standard Edition supports five data stores and has full support for web access, mobile access, and server recovery functionality. The Standard Edition is a good version of Exchange to support a messaging system for a small organization, or as a dedicated Edge Transport, Hub Transport, or Client Access server for a larger environment. Many small and medium-sized organizations find the capabilities of the Standard Edition sufficient for most messaging server services, and even large organizations use the Standard Edition for message routing servers or as the primary server in a remote office. The Standard Edition meets the needs of effectively any environment wherein a server with a limited database storage capacity is sufficient.

The Exchange Server 2007, Enterprise Edition is focused at server systems that require more Exchange messaging databases and support for clustering for higher availability. With support for up to 50 databases per server, the Enterprise Edition of Exchange 2007 is the appropriate version of messaging system for organizations that have a lot of mailboxes or a lot of mail storage, and for an organization that wants to set up clustering for higher reliability and redundancy of the Exchange environment. Although clustering used to be considered something that only large enterprises implemented, Exchange 2007 supports Cluster Continuous Replication (CCR) that provides mailbox redundancy as part of a disaster recovery process. CCR clusters Exchange and associated mailboxes across a local area network (LAN) or wide area network (WAN) segment, thus providing remote site failover in the event of a primary server failure. If the organization is considering using Exchange 2007's CCR capability, the Enterprise Edition is required for the Mailbox server roles in the organization.

4. The next step is to acquire the appropriate hardware necessary to implement the new Exchange 2007 environment. Remember that Exchange 2007 now requires x64-bit hardware and Windows 2003 x64-bit edition operating system software. Table 16.1 highlights the minimum hardware requirements.

TABLE 16.1   Minimum Hardware Requirements

Hardware	Minimum Requirements
Processor	▶ Intel Extended Memory 64 Technology (Intel EM64T) or ▶ AMD Opteron or AMD Athlon 64 processor, which supports AMD64 platform
Memory	▶ 1GB of RAM per server plus 7MB per user minimum
Disk Space	▶ At least 1.2GB on the hard disk where Exchange Server 2007 will be installed ▶ 200MB on the system drive

NOTE

The variables to an Exchange Server 2007 environment are random access memory (RAM) and disk storage. Because 64-bit systems now support more than 4GB of RAM and actually require 1GB of RAM plus 7MB per user, it has been found that most Exchange 2007 servers have 16GB to 32GB of RAM in the system as the base configuration (more memory for servers hosting thousands of users). Instead of spooling or caching transactions primarily to disk, Exchange 2007 takes advantage of memory for caching transactions. For disk storage, Exchange 2007 does not require more disk storage than previous versions of Exchange. Therefore, as a rule of thumb, choose Exchange 2007 server hardware that has enough storage space to hold the current Exchange database plus plenty of additional storage space for the growth needs of the organization. For more details on Exchange 2007 server sizing and optimization, see Chapter 34, "Optimizing an Exchange Server 2007 Environment."

5. Confirm that the current Exchange 2000 or 2003 environment server components are compatible with Exchange 2007. This means checking to see if there are Exchange 2000 or 2003 components referenced in the sections "No Support for Certain Exchange 2000 Server Components" and "No Support for Certain Exchange Server 2003 Components" earlier in this chapter running in the current Exchange environment. If there are components such as the GroupWise Connector for Exchange, Key Management Server, or Exchange 2000 Conference Service, those services need to be migrated to current technologies that are supported in Exchange 2007. In the two sections referenced in this paragraph, workarounds are noted to address these issues.

6. Validate that add-ons and utilities used in the existing Exchange 2000 or 2003 environment are compatible with Exchange 2007 or upgraded to support Exchange 2007. This includes products like BlackBerry services, Cisco Unity voice mail services, tape backup software, and so on.

> **NOTE**
>
> If a software program is not compatible with Exchange 2007, many times you can keep the software operating on an older Exchange 2000 or 2003 server, and migrate the rest of the environment to Exchange 2007. This can typically be done for gateway tools that route information in to or out of an Exchange environment.

7. Make sure to bring the Exchange 2000 or 2003 environment into a Native mode (as covered in section "Moving to Native Mode in Exchange" earlier in this chapter) effectively eliminating any Active Directory Connectors (ADCs), site connectors, Site Replication Service (SRS) connections, and so on.

8. Test the migration process in a lab environment to confirm all of the steps necessary in migrating to Exchange 2007. The test migration is covered in the next section.

Testing the Migration Process

Part of any migration best practice is to perform the migration in a test lab prior to performing the migration in a real production environment. The test lab allows the person performing the migration to test and validate assumptions. Effectively, if it works in the lab, you have a higher level of confidence that it will work in the production environment. At a minimum, after walking through the migration process, you will understand the steps necessary to perform the migration, become familiar with the steps, work through problems if they arise, and correct problems so that if or when they happen in the production migration you will already be prepared for the necessary action. In addition, testing the migration process provides you with a timeline to know how long it will likely take to migrate the databases into the Exchange 2007 environment.

The test lab creation process is covered in detail earlier in this chapter in the section "Deploying a Prototype Lab for the Exchange Server 2007 Migration Process." This section addresses getting a copy of an Active Directory global catalog (GC) server and seizing the roles to make this GC replica the master global catalog for the lab environment. This section also addresses getting a copy of the current Exchange 2000 or 2003 server data into the lab.

Key to the test lab process is to validate the operation of your third-party add-ons, utilities, backup software, and so on to confirm that all of the components in your current Exchange environment will successfully migrate to Exchange 2007. Take this chance to confirm whether you need to download any patches or hotfixes from the third-party product vendors, and whether you can simply reinstall the third-party products on an Exchange 2007 server, or whether you need to keep a legacy Exchange 2000 or Exchange 2003 server in your environment to maintain backward compatibility for a while.

When the lab is ready, you can run through the processes outlined in the following step-by-step sections to confirm that the processes outlined work as planned in your migration environment. Again, make note of all problems you run in to and document the workarounds you come up with in the lab so that when you get into the production

16

migration, you will have step-by-step notes on how to work through problems that come up. And also keep track of how long it takes processes to complete so you are prepared for how long the production migration process will take to complete.

Backing Up Your Production Environment

When you are ready to perform the migration in your production environment, you need to have a complete backup of the critical components that you will be working on just in case you need to roll back your environment. The expectation is that if your test lab replicated as much of your production environment as possible, then there should be no surprises in your production migration. However, as a best practice, make a backup of your Active Directory global catalog server, all of your Exchange servers, and all of the servers that interoperate with Exchange, such as gateway systems or replicated directory servers.

It is also a best practice to turn off any replication to other environments during the migration process, such as Microsoft Identity and Integration Server (MIIS), Identity and Integration Feature Pack (IIFP), Services for UNIX or Services for NetWare synchronization, or other directory synchronization tools.

Preparing the Exchange Server 2007 Server with Windows

Each Exchange 2007 server in the new environment needs to have Windows Server 2003 SP1 or higher installed on the system. There are components in the R2 edition of Windows Server 2003 that are used in Exchange 2007, such as the .NET Framework 2.0 component; however, it is not necessary to actually install the R2 updates to the Windows installation. You can add the appropriate R2 update components or even download the necessary components at the time of installation. The Exchange 2007 should have a basic installation of Windows 2003 SP1 or higher on a 64-bit server system that has been joined to the expected Active Directory domain.

Preparing Exchange 2000 Server or Exchange Server 2003 Permissions

Whether you are performing this migration in a lab environment or in production, after performing a backup of your production environment, the first step in the migration process is to prepare the permissions in Exchange 2000 or 2003. This readies Active Directory and Exchange 2000 or 2003 to integrate Exchange 2007 in the existing Exchange environment. This is necessary because during the migration process, or potentially in a long-term coexistence between Exchange 2000 or 2003 with Exchange 2007, the old and new environments need to support each other.

The process for preparing Exchange 2000 or 2003 permissions is as follows:

1. Insert the Exchange 2007 disc in the DVD/CD drive of the new Windows Server system.

2. From a command prompt from the setup directory of the Exchange 2007 disc (click Start, click Run, type CMD in the Open text box, and then click OK), type:

```
Setup /PrepareLegacyExchangePermissions
```

This setup command does the following:

- ▶ Copies setup files
- ▶ Performs Microsoft Exchange Server prerequisite check
- ▶ Updates legacy permissions

This process takes a couple of minutes and prepares the necessary basic environment permissions.

Extending the Active Directory Schema

The next step is to extend the Active Directory schema. This is performed as follows:

1. Insert the Exchange 2007 disc in the DVD/CD drive of the new Windows Server system.

2. From a command prompt from the setup directory of the Exchange 2007 disc (click Start, click Run, type CMD in the Open text box, and then click OK), type:

```
Setup /PrepareAD
```

This setup command does the following:

- ▶ Copies setup files
- ▶ Performs organizational checks
- ▶ Conducts the organizational preparation

This process can take several minutes depending on the size of the organization's existing Active Directory as the changes modify the Active Directory database.

Installing Exchange Server 2007 Prerequisites

The next step is to install the prerequisites necessary to run Exchange 2007 on a server system. The prerequisites for each Exchange 2007 server include the following:

- ▶ .NET Framework 2.0
- ▶ Microsoft Management Console (MMC) 3.0
- ▶ Exchange Management Shell

16

Installing the .NET Framework 2.0 Component

To install the .NET Framework 2.0 component, use the following steps:

1. Insert the Exchange Server 2007 CD or DVD (Standard or Enterprise).

2. AutoRun should launch a splash screen with options to plan and install Exchange 2007, similar to the screen shown in Figure 16.2. (If AutoRun does not execute, select Start, Run, type [CDDrive]:\setup.exe, and then click OK.)

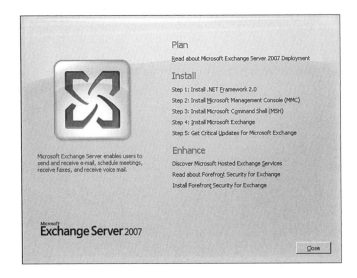

Plan
Read about Microsoft Exchange Server 2007 Deployment

Install
Step 1: Install .NET Framework 2.0
Step 2: Install Microsoft Management Console (MMC)
Step 3: Install Microsoft Command Shell (MSH)
Step 4: Install Microsoft Exchange
Step 5: Get Critical Updates for Microsoft Exchange

Microsoft Exchange Server enables users to send and receive e-mail, schedule meetings, receive faxes, and receive voice mail.

Enhance
Discover Microsoft Hosted Exchange Services
Read about Forefront Security for Exchange
Install Forefront Security for Exchange

Microsoft
Exchange Server 2007

Close

FIGURE 16.2   Exchange 2007 setup and installation menu.

3. On the Start page, click Step 1: Install .NET Framework 2.0.

4. On the Welcome to the Microsoft .NET Framework 2.0 page, click Next.

5. On the Microsoft .NET Framework 2.0 Setup End-User License Agreement page, click I Accept the Terms of the License Agreement, and then click Install.

6. Click Finish to complete the installation.

Installing Microsoft Management Console 3.0

To install the Microsoft Management Console 3.0, with the Exchange 2007 CD or DVD Setup Wizard already active, choose the second option, which is to install the Microsoft Management Console 3.0 on the system. To do so, do the following:

1. Click Step 2: Install Microsoft Management Console (MMC).

2. On the Software Update Installation Wizard page, click Next.

3. On the Software Update Installation Wizard License Agreement page, click I Agree, and then click Next.

4. On the Completing the Microsoft Management Console 3.0 Pre-Release Installation Wizard page, click Finish.

Installing the Exchange Management Shell (EMS)

To install the Exchange Management Shell prerequisite, with the Exchange 2007 CD or DVD Setup Wizard already active, choose the third option, which is to install the Exchange Management Shell on the system. To do so, do the following:

1. Click Step 3: Microsoft Command Shell (MSH).

2. Double-click on the `Msh_Setup.msi` file to initiate the installation.

3. On the Welcome to the Exchange Management Shell Wizard page, click Next.

4. On the License Agreement page, click I Accept the Terms in the License Agreement, and click Next.

5. On the Destination Folder page, select the folder where the application will be installed, and then click Next.

6. On the Start Installation page, click Install to commence the installation.

7. Click Finish to complete the installation.

Installing Exchange Server 2007 on a Server System

After the Exchange 2007 prerequisites have been installed on the server that will become the Exchange 2007 system, the next step is to install the Exchange 2007 application.

> **NOTE**
>
> In an environment where you have front-end and back-end servers, choose to migrate all of the front-end server(s) first before you install the back-end servers. With Exchange 2007, Client Access servers (CAS) can serve as both an Exchange 2007 CAS server and are fully functional as Exchange 2000 or 2003 front-end servers. This allows you to install a new Exchange 2007 CAS server and remove Exchange 2000 or 2003 front-end servers to complete the total replacement of all Exchange 2000 or 2003 front-end servers from the Exchange organization.

With the Setup Wizard still active, similar to what is now shown in Figure 16.3, do the following:

1. Click Step 4: Install Microsoft Exchange.

2. In the Microsoft Exchange Server Installation Wizard dialog box, on the Introduction page, click Next.

3. At the License Agreement page, after reviewing the license agreement, click I Accept the Terms in the License Agreement, and then click Next.

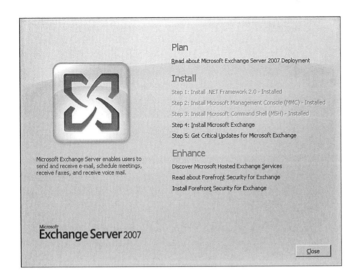

FIGURE 16.3   Exchange Server 2007 Setup Wizard with prerequisites completed.

4. At the Customer Feedback page, select whether to participate in the Customer Experience Improvement Program by sending feedback automatically to Microsoft, and then click Next.

5. At the Installation Type page, select the type of Exchange Server 2007 installation (Typical or Custom).

Server Migration Sequencing

If you have various existing Exchange 2000 or 2003 server roles, such as bridgehead servers, front-end servers, and back-end servers, the process is to migrate each server role in a logical sequence. The proper sequence is as follows:

1. Migrate all front-end servers to Exchange 2007 Client Access servers first.

2. Then migrate all bridgehead servers to Exchange 2007 Hub Transport servers second.

3. Finally, migrate back-end servers to Exchange 2007 Mailbox servers.

The reason you need to migrate Exchange 2000 or 2003 front-end servers to Exchange 2007 Client Access servers first is because an Exchange 2007 Client Access server can fully host Exchange 2000 or 2003 front-end services as well as Exchange 2007 Client Access server functions. In contrast, an Exchange 2003 front-end server can only host the front-end process of an Exchange 2003 back-end server. Before you can migrate mailboxes from Exchange 2003 to Exchange 2007, the front-end server supporting the back-end server needs to be replaced with an Exchange 2007 Client Access server.

After the front-end servers have been replaced, proceed with the installation of bridge-head servers being replaced one for one with Hub Transport servers. Hub Transport servers will service all Exchange 2000, 2003, and 2007 routing functions. Unlike the requirement for front-end servers to be replaced by Exchange Client Access servers before mailboxes are moved to Exchange 2007, all bridgehead servers do not necessarily need to be replaced by Hub Transport servers before the migration of mailboxes. Bridgehead servers will continue to successfully route information for both the Exchange 2003 and Exchange 2007 environment as long as at least one routing group connector exists between each Exchange routing group in the organization.

After the front-end and bridgehead servers are replaced by CAS and Hub Transport servers, install Exchange 2007 Mailbox server systems and move mailbox data to the new servers.

6. On the Installation page, if there is a need to change the installation folder, click Browse before proceeding and specify a path for the Exchange Server installation. Click Next to continue.

7. In an Active Directory where Exchange 2000 or 2003 already exists, the next page will be the Mail Flow Server page. If you end up with an Exchange Organization Page prompting you to enter the name of the new Exchange organization, STOP! For some reason, the Exchange 2007 installation is not recognizing your existing Exchange 2000 or 2003 environment. You need the Mail Flow Server page for interoperability with an existing Exchange environment. Assuming you have the Exchange Mail Flow Server page, enter in the name of an Exchange server to which you want this new Exchange 2007 server to route messages, similar to what is shown in Figure 16.4. This mail flow creates a routing group connector between this new Exchange 2007 server and the Exchange 2000 or 2003 server. The Exchange 2000 or 2003 server you choose would be a bridgehead server in an environment with bridgehead servers; however, in an environment without a bridgehead server, the rule of thumb is to choose the Exchange 2000 or 2003 server that will be the last Exchange 2000 or 2003 server to be removed in your environment so that communications will remain operating as long as Exchange 2000 or 2003 exists in your environment.

NOTE

To create a new routing group connector between Exchange 2007 and the old Exchange 2000 or 2003 environment, you can use something similar to the following syntax:

```
New-RoutingGroupConnector -Name "E2003 to E2007 RGC" -SourceTransportServers
➥"E2007Hub1.companyabc.com" -TargetTransportServers "E2003BH1.companyabc.com"
➥-Cost 10 -Bidirectional $true -PublicFoldersEnabled $True
```

8. On the Readiness Checks page, the Installation Wizard is verifying that the appropriate Exchange Server prerequisites have been installed. View the status to determine if the organization and server role prerequisite checks completed successfully, and then click Install to implement the first Exchange Server 2007 server in the organization. This process might take a while as the Exchange software is installed on the system. During this process, you will see a screen similar to the one shown in Figure 16.5.

FIGURE 16.4   Setting mail flow server settings.

FIGURE 16.5   Exchange 2007 setup in progress.

> **NOTE**
>
> If there are any errors returned or prerequisites not met on the Readiness Checks page, it is necessary to address these issues and retry the setup.

9. After the installation has been completed, click Finish.

> **NOTE**
>
> To perform an unattended installation of Exchange 2007, you can use something similar to the following syntax:
>
> ```
> Setup /mode:install /roles:ClientAccess,HubTransport,Mailbox
> ➥/LegacyRoutingServer:Exch2000.companyabc.com
> ```

After replacing an old Exchange 2000 or 2003 front-end server with an Exchange 2007 Client Access server, confirm you can render an Outlook Web Access page on the new Client Access server to mailboxes on the old Exchange 2000 or 2003 Mailbox server. After you confirm that all functions of the new Client Access server seem to operate, you can remove the old Exchange 2000 or 2003 front-end server for Exchange. To remove the server, see the section "Uninstalling Exchange from Old Exchange 2000 Server or Exchange Server 2003 Servers."

Continue to install new Exchange 2007 Client Access servers to replace all Exchange 2000 or 2003 front-end servers, and then proceed with the same steps to install new Exchange 2007 Mailbox servers, this time choosing a custom installation of a Mailbox server. When a new Exchange 2007 Mailbox server has been added to the organization and you are ready to move mailboxes from Exchange 2000 or 2003 to Exchange 2007, proceed to the next section.

Moving Mailboxes

After a new Exchange 2007 server has been inserted into an existing Exchange 2000 or 2003 organization, the movement of mailboxes from an old Exchange back-end server to a new Exchange 2007 Mailbox server is as simple as selecting the mailbox or mailboxes, and through a few mouse clicks, selecting the new destination server. The specific process is as follows:

1. Launch the Exchange Management Console (EMC) on an Exchange 2007 server.

2. Expand the recipient configuration, and click on the mailbox container. You will see a list of mailboxes similar to the one shown in Figure 16.6. In the Recipient Type Details column, you will notice some of the mailboxes are flagged as Legacy Mailbox and some of the mailboxes are flagged as Mailbox User. Those flagged as Legacy Mailbox are still on Exchange 2000 or 2003 and need to be migrated to Exchange 2007. Those mailboxes already on Exchange 2007 are flagged as Mailbox User.

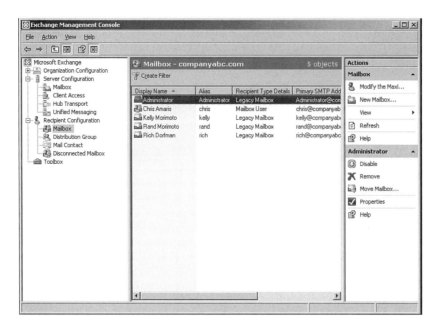

FIGURE 16.6   Mailboxes in Exchange—some are legacy mailboxes, and some are already migrated.

3. Click on a mailbox, or alternately hold down the Shift key and select a group of mailboxes, or hold down the Ctrl key and click on specific mailboxes that you want to migrate.

4. Click on the Move Mailbox action in the right column.

5. A Move Mailbox Wizard appears and you are prompted with the option of choosing which server, storage group, and mailbox database you want to move the mailbox to, as shown in Figure 16.7. Choose the destination of the mailbox(es), and then click Next.

6. You are prompted with a Move Options screen to choose to Skip the Mailbox or to Skip the Corrupted Messages if corrupted messages are found during the move process. Usually, you would want to choose to skip the corrupt messages so you can complete the migration; however, if you want to problem-solve the corrupt messages, you can skip the migration of the mailbox, and then debug the mailbox problem and try the migration of the mailbox later. Click Next to continue.

7. The next screen is to choose to select a Move Schedule. You can choose to move the mailboxes immediately, or choose to launch the migration of the mailboxes at a later time. Some administrators set up the movement of mailboxes during the day, and then choose a time later in the evening for the mailbox migration to automatically kick off when everyone is off the network. Click Next to continue.

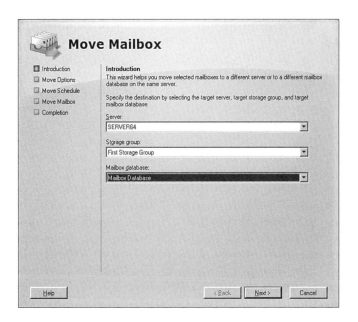

FIGURE 16.7   Choosing the Exchange Server 2007 destination server for mailbox moves.

8. A summary screen is shown that summarizes the choices made. Review the source and destination of the mailboxes that will be moved, and either click Back and make any desired changes, or click Move to begin the movement of mailboxes to the Exchange 2007 environment.

9. The move time will vary based on the amount of data to be moved, and the bandwidth between the source and destination server. This is something that should be tested in the lab to determine whether all of the mailboxes desired to be moved at any one time can be accomplished in the time available. Organizations with a lot of data to move choose to install gigabit Ethernet adapters in servers and place systems on the same subnet to efficiently move large sets of data. This is also something to ensure if mirrored in the test environment as some organizations test the movement of mail on an isolated gigabit test lab switch with fast results, and then when performing the real migration, are working across a slower WAN backbone with very slow performance speeds. After the Move Mailbox Wizard opens the source, opens the destination, and successfully moves the chosen mailboxes, a summary screen of the completed actions appears, as shown in Figure 16.8. Click Finish.

16

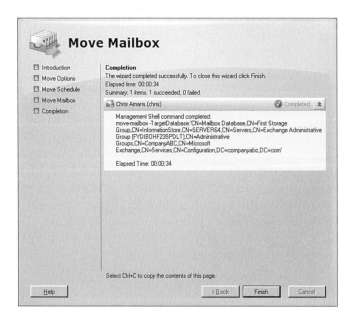

FIGURE 16.8   Summary of completed Exchange mailbox move.

Changing User Profile Configuration

Even after the Exchange mailboxes have been successfully moved from the old Exchange 2000 or 2003 server(s) to the new Exchange 2007 server(s), keep the old Exchange 2000 or 2003 servers running on the network for typically 2 weeks. The reason is that in Outlook 97, 2000, XP, and 2003, the Outlook profile on each user's system is keyed to a server, in this case the old Exchange 2000 or 2003 server. If you remove the old server immediately after the mailboxes are moved, the next time the users launch Outlook, their profiles will look for the old server, not find the server, and the users will not have access to email. You will need to go to each user's Outlook profile and enter in the name of the new server so that the Outlook client will be able to find the new Mailbox server where the user's mailbox contents are stored.

However, if you leave the old server running, when the user launches Outlook, the Outlook profile connects the user to the old Exchange 2000 or 2003 server. The old server tells the Outlook client that the user's mailbox has been moved to a new server and the user's profile is automatically updated on each user's client system to now find the user's mailbox on the new server. When this is done once for each user, it never needs to be done again. The user's Outlook client profile is set to find the user's mailbox on the new server. The idea of leaving the old server running for 2 weeks is usually within a couple of weeks, all users will have launched Outlook once and their profile will automatically change. After 2 weeks, you can remove the old Exchange 2000 or 2003 server. See the section on "Cleaning Up the Exchange 2000 Server and Exchange Server 2003 Environments" for the process to properly remove an Exchange server from the network.

If a user had not launched Outlook in the 2-week timeframe that you had the old server running, such as the individual on maternity leave, on a sabbatical, or on an extended leave of absence, you will need to go back to the user's system and manually change the user's Outlook profile to connect the user to the new Exchange 2007 server. This will likely be done for a very limited number of users. Obviously, the old Exchange 2000 or 2003 server can remain on for a very long time with no mailboxes on the system, but merely be there to redirect users to the new system. However, it is usually recommended to remove the old server just so that objects can be removed from Exchange and the organization doesn't have to patch, maintain, and manage a server in the environment beyond a reasonable operating timeframe.

Adding Unified Messaging and Edge Transport Servers and Enterprise Policies

After the core Exchange 2000 or 2003 front-end and back-end servers have been migrated to applicable Exchange 2007 Client Access and Mailbox servers, additional server roles such as Unified Messaging servers, Edge Transport servers, or Hub Transport servers, including servers managing enterprise policies can be added to the new Exchange 2007 organization. Because the addition of these additional server roles are not directly related to the migration of mail from Exchange 2000 or 2003 to Exchange 2007, usually it is recommended to wait a few days and make sure that Exchange 2007 is operating smoothly in its new environment before adding more to the network.

The addition of enterprise policies on a Hub Transport server or security policies on a Edge Transport server in Exchange 2007 environment might cause mail to be filtered, blocked, or altered as part of a spam filtering or policy management rule. This might appear to be a problem with basic Exchange 2007 functionality, whereas it is a function of a change in content filtering added to the new Exchange environment. Allowing Exchange 2007 to operate for a week or two as a basic Exchange 2007 environment provides the Exchange administrators as well as Exchange users time to become familiar with the operation of the new Exchange 2007 environment before changes are made in applying filters, new routes, or new operational structure changes.

Replicating Public Folders from Exchange 2000 Server or Exchange Server 2003 to Exchange Server 2007

Just as mailboxes are migrated from Exchange 2000 or 2003 servers to Exchange 2007 systems, public folders need to be replicated before retiring the old Exchange 2000 or 2003 servers. Previously, this procedure involved a manual replication of folder hierarchy, which could prove to be a tedious process. Microsoft addressed this drawback with a new utility called PFMigrate, which is accessible via the Exchange Deployment Tools. PFMigrate can create public and system folder replicas on new systems, and remove them from old servers. The following procedure outlines how to use PFMigrate to migrate from an Exchange 2000 or 2003 server to an Exchange 2007 system:

1. Open a command prompt (select Start, Run, type cmd, and click OK).

2. Type cd D:\support\Exdeploy and press Enter.

3. To create a report of current public folder replication, type the following:

```
pfmigrate.wsf /S:OLDSERVERNAME /T:NEWSERVERNAME /R /F:c:\LOGNAME.log
```

This generates a report named LOGNAME.log on the C: drive. OLDSERVERNAME should be the name of the old Exchange 2000 or 2003 system, and NEWSERVERNAME should be the new Exchange 2007 system.

4. To replicate system folders from the Exchange 2000 or 2003 server to the Exchange 2007 server, type the following:

```
pfmigrate.wsf /S:OLDSERVERNAME /T:NEWSERVERNAME /SF /A /N:10000
➥/F:c:\LOGNAME.log
```

5. To replicate public folders from Exchange 2000 or 2003 to Exchange Server 2007, type the following:

```
pfmigrate.wsf /S:OLDSERVERNAME /T:NEWSERVERNAME /A /N:10000 /F:c:\LOGNAME.log
```

NOTE

The /N:#### field determines how many public folders should be addressed by the tool. If a larger number of public folders than 10,000 exists, the parameter should be increased to match.

---

6. After all public folders have replicated, the old replicas can be removed from the Exchange 2000 or 2003 servers by typing the following, as illustrated in Figure 16.9:

```
pfmigrate.wsf /S:OLDSERVERNAME /T:NEWSERVERNAME /D
```

FIGURE 16.9   Command-line PFMigrate functionality.

7. The LOGNAME.log file can be reviewed to ensure that replication has occurred successfully and that a copy of each public folder exists on the new server.

> **TIP**
>
> Become familiar with the command-line options that are available with the PFMigrate tool because they can be useful for managing the replication of public folders across a newly deployed Exchange Server 2007 environment.

Cleaning Up the Exchange 2000 Server and Exchange Server 2003 Environments

After a new Exchange 2007 server is added to the network to functionally replace an old Exchange 2000 or 2003 server, there comes a time when the old server should be removed. As noted in the sidebar "Changing User Profile Configuration," the Exchange 2000 or 2003 Mailbox servers should remain on the network for 2 weeks after the migration of mailboxes to ensure that users connect to the new Exchange 2007 Mailbox server at least once to automatically change the users' Outlook profiles on their client system.

For front-end servers, however, they can be removed as soon as a new Exchange 2007 Client Access server is added to the network because the new Exchange 2007 Client Access servers will host both Exchange 2000 or 2003 back-end servers as well as Exchange 2007 Mailbox servers.

The removal process is more than just powering off the system and disconnecting it from the network. It is very important that the old Exchange servers are properly removed from the Exchange organization; otherwise, Exchange does not know that a server has been removed, and the server remains in the Exchange organization configuration tables. As an example, if you have a bridgehead server that used to route mail messages between sites and you just unplugged the server without properly removing it, Exchange servers in the organization will not know that the server has been removed, and will continue to try to route messages to the server. This could cause messages to pile up in a queue and unless the Exchange servers can recalculate a new message route for messages, the lack of removing a specific server can prevent messages from ever routing within the organization until the server is properly removed. So, remove servers properly.

The proper process of removing an old Exchange 2000 or 2003 server is a three-step process:

1. Remove all routing connectors to the server.

2. Uninstall Exchange from the server.

3. Remove routing groups.

Removing Routing Group Connectors to Servers

The removal process of an Exchange 2000 or 2003 server starts with the removal of routing group connectors from the server being removed. It is important to confirm that the routing group connector that is being removed is not serving a key communication route for a site or for the organization. As an example, if the routing group connector is the only link for a server to another site in the organization, the removal of the routing group connector will have messages cease being sent or received to the remote site. Alternatively, if the routing group connector is the link between Exchange 2000 or 2003 and Exchange 2007 and if there are no other routing group connectors between Exchange 2000 or 2003 and Exchange 2007, the removal of the routing group connector will effectively drop any communications between the old and new Exchange environment.

If you are certain that the routing group connector serves no purpose, remove the routing group connector so that you can remove the Exchange server from the organization.

> **TIP**
>
> If you aren't sure whether a routing group connector serves an important function in the network, and cannot figure out through looking at architectural or mail flow diagrams of the organization whether the RGC is of value, just stop the Routing Group Connector (RGC) service. On the Exchange 2000 or 2003 server, click on Start, Programs, Administrative Tools, Service. Right-click on the Microsoft Exchange Routing Engine, and choose Stop. Wait a few hours or days to see if anybody complains that their messages aren't being transmitted properly. If after a few days no one has complained, you can probably assume the RGC is not serving any valuable function.

To remove a routing group connector, do the following:

1. On the Exchange 2000 or 2003 server on which you plan to remove the routing group connector, launch the Exchange 2000 or 2003 System Manager program.

2. Expand the Administrative Groups container.

3. Choose and expand the administrative group where the server that you are on resides.

4. Choose and expand the Routing Groups container.

5. Choose and expand the routing group that holds the routing group connector you want to remove.

6. Choose and expand the Connectors container.

7. Right-click on the routing group you want to remove, and choose Delete. Confirm Yes that you want to remove the routing group connector.

This process removes the routing group connector and you can now proceed with removing the server itself from Exchange.

Uninstalling Exchange from Old Exchange 2000 Server or Exchange Server 2003 Servers

Rather than simply removing or disconnecting an old Exchange server from the network, it is important to uninstall Exchange from the old server system. The uninstall process doesn't just remove the Exchange software off the hard drive of the system; it performs a very important task of properly removing that Exchange server from the Exchange directory.

After all mailboxes, public folder replicas, and connectors have been moved off an old Exchange 2000 or 2003 server, the server can be retired and removed from service. The easiest and most straightforward approach to this is to uninstall the Exchange 2000 or 2003 component via the Add/Remove Programs applet in Windows. To perform this operation, do the following:

1. On the Exchange server, select Start, Control Panel.

2. Double-click Add/Remove Programs.

3. Select Microsoft Exchange (2000 or 2003) and click Change/Remove.

4. Click Next at the welcome screen.

5. Under Action, select Remove from the drop-down box, and click Next to continue.

6. At the summary screen, click Next to continue. The Exchange server will then be uninstalled.

7. Repeat the process for any additional Exchange 2000 or 2003 servers.

As Exchange 2000 or 2003 servers are removed from Exchange 2000 or 2003 routing groups, upon the removal of the last Exchange 2000 or 2003 system from a routing group, the routing group itself can be removed.

Removing an Exchange 2000 Server or Exchange Server 2003 Routing Group
In Exchange 2000 or 2003, routing groups are containers that hold groups of Exchange servers that frequently communicate with each other, typically servers within a site, or servers within a region. Because the concept of a routing group does not exist in Exchange 2007, as Exchange 2000 or 2003 servers are removed from the network, when the last Exchange server in a routing group has been removed, the routing group itself can be deleted, thus cleaning up the Exchange environment of remnants of Exchange 2000 or 2003.

To remove a routing group, do the following:

1. Remove routing group connectors to servers that are being removed per the instructions covered in the "Removing Routing Group Connectors to Servers" section.

2. Remove old Exchange 2000 or 2003 servers as they are no longer needed.

3. When all of the servers in a routing group have been removed, go into the Exchange 2000 or 2003 System Manager utility by selecting Start, All Programs, Microsoft Exchange, Exchange System Manager.

4. Expand the Administrative Groups container.

5. Choose and expand the administrative group where the routing group that you want to remove resides.

6. Choose and expand the Routing Groups container.

16

7. Choose and expand the routing group that you want to remove and confirm that no member servers exist in the routing group anymore by choosing the Members container to see if any servers exist. If servers are still in the Members container, go back to the section "Uninstalling Exchange from Old Exchange 2000 Server or Exchange Server 2003 Servers" and remove the remaining server(s).

8. If no servers are in the Members container, right-click on the routing group that you want to remove, and select Delete. Confirm Yes that you want to remove the routing group.

Upon removal of the last Exchange 2000 or 2003 routing group, the environment should be completely void of any Exchange 2000 or 2003 servers. There is no Native Exchange 2007 mode. The removal of the last Exchange 2000 or 2003 routing group clears legacy mail routing that is no longer needed in Exchange 2007.

Migrating from Exchange Server 5.5 to Exchange Server 2003

The balance of this chapter is dedicated to the migration from Exchange 5.5 to Exchange 2003 for organizations needing to get to Exchange 2003 before they can even begin their migration from Exchange 2003 into Exchange 2007. If you are not migrating from Exchange 5.5 to Exchange 2007, you can disregard the balance of this chapter.

Because Exchange 2007 does not support a direct migration from Exchange 5.5 to Exchange 2007, some organizations might need to migrate from Exchange 5.5 to Exchange 2003 as an interim migration step, and then migrate from Exchange 2003 to Exchange 2007. It is not recommended to make the migration from Exchange 5.5 to Exchange 2003, and then to Exchange 2007 in a short-order process. Rather, it is best to migrate from Exchange 5.5 to Exchange 2003, wait a while to make sure that Exchange 2003 is operating in a stable manner, and then make the migration from Exchange 2003 to Exchange 2007. The migration from Exchange 2003 to Exchange 2007 is not a complicated process as detailed earlier in this chapter, so after Exchange 2003 is operational and stable, the final migration step to Exchange 2007 is not that complicated. However, the migration from Exchange 5.5 to Exchange 2003 is a relatively complex process and care needs to be taken to ensure the migration to the interim Exchange 2003 environment is successful and stable before proceeding on to Exchange 2007.

This chapter focuses on best-practice migration from Exchange 5.5 to Exchange Server 2003. It discusses the differences between Exchange 5.5 and Exchange Server 2003, and it then details specific steps required to migrate an environment. Close attention is given to new migration techniques made available with the Exchange Deployment Tools, in addition to the more "manual" approaches to migration.

How Exchange Server 2003 Differed from Exchange Server 5.5

Exchange Server 2003 provided the features necessary to build a more robust messaging environment. It removed many of the boundaries that tied the hands of architects and administrators in Exchange Server 5.5. As Exchange Server 2003 matured, the messaging designs continued to centralize, with only a portion of the services still being distributed. Exchange Server 2003 improved upon the shortcomings of Exchange 5.5 in the following ways:

- **Separate administration and routing**—In Exchange Server 2003, separate routing and administration can be achieved through the creation of routing and administrative groups. To fully use these containers, the organization must be converted to Native mode Exchange Server 2003. This requires all Exchange 5.5 servers to be converted to Exchange Server 2003 or be uninstalled from the organization. The combination of administrative and routing groups with the granular permission of Active Directory helps messaging administrators better control access to the messaging services in the organization.

- **Increased degree of scalability**—Scalability is provided in multiple mail and public folder databases that can be used to keep the database performance high while keeping backup and restore times low. This means that the number of users supported per server can be increased, reducing the number of servers on the network. Each database can be mounted and dismounted individually, allowing the server to continue to function even when some databases are offline.

- **Improved redundancy**—Redundancy in Exchange Server 2003 is provided through full support of the Microsoft Cluster Service (MCS). Connectors in Exchange Server 2003 can also be redundant. By using SMTP for message delivery and a link state routing algorithm, message-routing designs can be built to route messages efficiently and to take advantage of redundant links on the WAN.

- **Enhanced stability**—Stability is provided within the Windows Server 2003 operating system and at the core of Exchange Server 2003 in the Extensible Storage Engine (ESE) database. Small efficient databases, redundant connector designs, and clustering technology all increase the stability of Exchange Server 2003, improving the end-user experience and letting information technology groups create service level agreements that they can stand by.

Reviewing the Prerequisites for Migrating from Exchange Server 5.5 to Exchange Server 2003

Before moving the Exchange 5.5 organization to Exchange Server 2003, several items need to be addressed from a technical implementation and design standpoint. Some of these prerequisites include preparing the Exchange 5.5 organization prior to migration and making sure the existing Exchange 5.5 environment is ready for the migration.

Checking the Exchange 5.5 Environment with the Exchange Server 2003 Deployment Tools

The Exchange Deployment Tools in Exchange 2003 are an invaluable asset to any deployment team. They are straightforward and robust, and they cover a multitude of migration scenarios. Even die-hard Exchange upgrade enthusiasts with years of Exchange 2000 migration experience under their belt can benefit from the tactical advice and safeguards built in to the tools.

The Exchange Deployment Tools guide administrators through the Exchange Server 2003 migration process in a step-by-step fashion. The tools themselves can be invoked by simply inserting the Exchange Server 2003 CD (or clicking Setup.exe if AutoRun is disabled) and then clicking on the Exchange Deployment Tools link. The tools, illustrated in Figure 16.10, initially lead the migration team through a series of prerequisite steps.

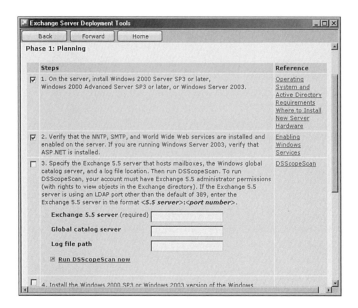

FIGURE 16.10   Using the Exchange Deployment Tools.

These prerequisite steps should be followed exactly as described in the tool. In fact, the entire migration process outlined in this chapter can be followed via the Exchange Deployment Tools. In addition to running through the prerequisite steps listed in the tools, several key factors must be taken into account before deploying Exchange Server 2003.

Preparing the Exchange Server 5.5 Organization for the Migration

When moving to Exchange Server 2003, one of the biggest items that organizations should be concerned about is that Exchange Server 2003 is a one-to-one Exchange organization to Active Directory forest environment. This means that there can only be one Exchange Server 2003 organization per Active Directory forest. Some organizations have one or more Exchange organizations in their environment. This type of installation can result from mergers and acquisitions that were never fully meshed or breakaway lines of business that established their own organization or it could be done by design to create an SMTP relay routing hub. In any case, only one organization can remain in Exchange Server 2003, and this organization must be chosen before the start of the migration.

> **TIP**
>
> For organizations designed to support SMTP relay functions, continue to use them through the migration process and then replace them with routing groups. If the Exchange 5.5 relay servers are under the control of another group in the organization, place the routing group with the relay server in its own administrative group.

The second piece of the one-to-one environment that must be one-to-one is the number of mailboxes per Active Directory account. In Exchange 5.5, a Windows NT account could have an unlimited number of mailboxes associated with it. In Active Directory, the messaging components of the user account are just additional attributes of the user, so the mailbox is really part of the user account. It was quite common for Exchange 5.5 administrators to use a single account for multiple mailboxes, especially for administrative functions such as backup and virus-scanning products, and also for resources such as conference rooms. Linking the Active Directory accounts to the Exchange 5.5 mailboxes can be done either manually for a few mailboxes or for a large number of mailboxes by using the NTDSNoMatch utility, or by using the Resource Mailbox Wizard in the ADC Tools, described in more detail later in this chapter.

> **TIP**
>
> To view the Windows NT accounts with multiple mailboxes, use the Exchange 5.5 Administrator program and run a directory export to a CSV file. In the Exchange Administrator program, select Tools, Directory Export and export all mailboxes from the Global Address List container. Open the export file in Excel and sort the spreadsheet by the Primary Windows NT account column. Scrolling through the Excel sheet or running a duplicates query in Microsoft Access reveals all of the Windows NT 4.0 accounts that were used on more than one mailbox.

Compacting the Exchange Server 5.5 Organization

The more items that exist in Exchange 5.5, the more items must be migrated to Exchange Server 2003. It's a given that mail database and public folder servers need to be migrated, but all the connector servers might not be necessary in the Exchange Server 2003 environment. Now is the time to rethink the Exchange design. By consolidating servers and using features such as clustering, it is now possible to locate all the Exchange installations at a few central hubs on the WAN where the administrators with the best Exchange skills reside. In addition, the enhanced remote client access capabilities introduced in Exchange Server 2003 allow for site consolidation, further reducing the number of servers that must be supported. Of course, the migrated Exchange Server 2003 environment can mirror the exact same configuration as Exchange 5.5. It's just an option (and opportunity) to rethink the best configuration for the organization.

Later revisions of Exchange 5.5 introduced a utility called the Move Server Wizard that allows for the consolidation of Exchange 5.5 organizations and sites. This tool allowed an organization to consolidate servers into a single site. Service Pack 1 for Exchange Server 2003 introduced the ability to move mailboxes between administrative groups while in Mixed mode, which greatly improved the migration options available.

Connecting with Foreign Mail Systems

One of the changes that might affect organizations moving from Exchange 5.5 to Exchange Server 2003 regarding foreign mail connectivity is that there is no Exchange Server 2003 version of the PROFS/SNADS connector. The easiest solution to this problem is to leave a single Exchange 5.5 site behind to handle the PROFS/SNADS connectivity. The downside to this solution is that it delays the organization's move to Exchange Server 2003 Native mode until another solution is put into place. For a long-term solution, investigate using SMTP to connect the systems, or migrate the PROFS user to Exchange Server 2003.

A second issue regarding foreign mail connectivity is that organizations might have put so much effort into getting their connectors stable and configured properly that they might not want to move their foreign mail connectors to Exchange Server 2003. As long as the organization can remain in Mixed mode, it's okay to leave the connectors in Exchange 5.5. As with the PROFS/SNADS connector, it's better to leave all Exchange 5.5 connectors in a single Exchange 5.5 site than in multiple sites. If this means moving the connector anyway to consolidate to a single Exchange 5.5 site, or if a single Exchange site doesn't make sense because of geography or WAN issues, consider moving the connectors sooner rather than later to Exchange Server 2003.

Upgrading Service Pack Levels

To migrate from Exchange 5.5 to Exchange Server 2003, some or all of the Exchange 5.5 servers must be running at least Service Pack 3, and preferably Service Pack 4. Most organizations are already at that level, but those that are not should plan to perform the Service Pack 3 upgrade before starting the Exchange migration. Although it is wise to upgrade all, only one Exchange 5.5 server in the organization technically must run SP3— the one in each site that the ADC replicates to.

If the organization is planning to consolidate services before migrating to Exchange Server 2003, it makes sense to postpone the Service Pack 3 upgrade until the consolidation through the Move Server Wizard is completed.

Structuring the Migration for Best Results

When structuring the migration, the end goal is to move to the new platform without disrupting current services or losing functionality. The only way to be sure that service and functionality will not be lost during the migration is to perform lab testing. Having a fallback plan and solid disaster recovery processes are also essential when planning the Exchange Server 2003 deployment. By breaking the migration into sections, the organization can move cautiously through the migration without making too many changes at one time. The following best practices deploy Exchange Server 2003 by migrating each service one type at a time. For many smaller remote locations, this might not be feasible and all services might have to be migrated at the same time. Migrating by service type is usually the best solution for corporate sites and large remote offices.

Performing Single-Site Exchange Server 5.5 Migrations

Within the same Exchange 5.5 site, administrators have the flexibility of moving users between servers. Single-site Exchange 5.5 installations become a single administrative group with a single routing group when converted to Exchange Server 2003. If granular message routing is needed, additional routing groups can be added and servers within the administrative group can be moved to new routing groups after the conversion to Native mode.

Because servers cannot be moved between administrative groups even after the conversion to Native mode, administrators need to examine whether a single administrative group will fulfill the organization's administrative needs. Additional administrative groups can be added to the organization, but only by installing new Exchange Server 2003 systems. Users can be moved between administrative groups by moving the mailbox from administrative group to administrative group, either before the switch to Native mode by using the cross-site migration tool introduced in Service Pack 1 or normally when in Native mode.

Performing Multisite Exchange Server 5.5 Migrations

Multisite migrations are a bit more complex than single-site migrations. After the first Exchange server is installed, administrators can use the *Move Mailbox method* covered in the "Migrating Using the Move Mailbox Approach" section later in this chapter to migrate users to Exchange Server 2003.

Understanding why the multiple sites were established might help in deciding how to handle the multiple sites. If the decision to have multiple sites was to originally delegate control of administration, then multiple administrative groups might still be needed. If multiple sites were implemented to control message flow and directory replication, consolidating many of the administrative groups might be desired.

Performing Multiorganization Exchange Server 5.5 Migrations

Multiorganization environments must consolidate to a single Exchange Server 2003 organization in order to migrate to Exchange Server 2003 unless the organization plans to support multiple Active Directory forests. Multiple organization environments have the following choices when moving to Exchange Server 2003:

▶ **Select one organization to be migrated to Exchange Server 2003**—Use the most heavily populated organization if it fits the company's standards. Create new Exchange Server 2003 mailboxes for users in the other organization. Use ExMerge or the Exchange Migration Wizard to move user data from the abandoned organization to Exchange Server 2003.

▶ **Start with a clean Exchange Server 2003 organization and do not migrate either organization**—Both organizations feel equal pain that might be politically acceptable. Look at the ExMerge utility or the Exchange Migration Wizard to migrate user data, or run both Exchange 5.5 organizations for a short period of time and allow users to forward mail to their Exchange Server 2003 mailbox.

Preparing the Active Directory Forest and Domain for Exchange Server 2003

After the prerequisite steps have been satisfied, the Exchange Deployment Tools prompt the administrator to run the ForestPrep and DomainPrep processes. These processes can be invoked manually via setup.exe switches (/forestprep and /domainprep), or they can simply be launched via the Exchange Server Deployment Tools, as illustrated in Figure 16.11.

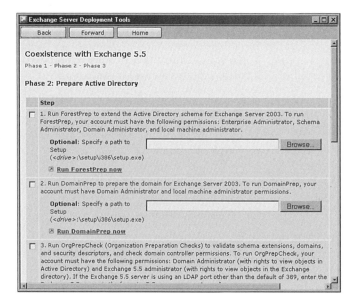

FIGURE 16.11   Launching ForestPrep and DomainPrep from the Exchange Deployment Tools.

A greater understanding of what tasks these two utilities perform is crucial to understanding the Exchange deployment process as a whole.

Extending the Active Directory Schema

To extend the Active Directory schema, Exchange setup relies on the capabilities of the /forestprep switch, which can be invoked via the Exchange Deployment Tools. Running the ForestPrep procedure requires that the account invoking the command have Schema Admin privileges in the schema root domain because the command extends the Active Directory schema to support the attributes that Exchange Server 2003 requires. The schema extension is quite extensive, and the changes are replicated to all domain controllers in the Active Directory forest. This might require special consideration into replication issues if the AD forest is large and spread out across slow replication links.

> **NOTE**
>
> The ForestPrep performed by the Exchange Deployment Tools is different from the ForestPrep procedure that is performed during a Windows Server 2003 schema extension. Indeed, Exchange Server 2003 does not require the schema extensions for Windows Server 2003 to function, as the Windows 2000 Server schema is sufficient.

Preparing the Windows Server 2003 Domains to Support Exchange Server 2003

The Active Directory domains that will host Exchange servers or mailbox-enabled users must be prepared before installing the first Exchange Server 2003 system. Prepare the Windows Server 2003 domains using the /domainprep switch, also invoked via the Exchange Deployment Tools. The /domainprep process configures the Recipient Update Service parameters, which are responsible for keeping Exchange address lists up to date and for creating proxy addresses for users based on recipient policy addressing configuration. In addition, it creates the Exchange Server 2003–specific groups that allow Exchange services to run without a service account.

Verifying the Organization Settings with OrgPrepCheck

Exchange Server 2003 introduces a new utility named OrgPrepCheck to validate that the ForestPrep and DomainPrep utilities were functionally successful. The OrgPrepCheck utility is invoked via the Exchange Server Deployment Tools and is a recommended way of determining whether it is safe to proceed with the migration process.

Installing and Configuring the Active Directory Connector

Unlike in Exchange 2000 Server, the Active Directory Connector (ADC) does not need to be installed until after the /forestprep command has run. This was designed so that only a single schema extension is required for upgrading to Exchange Server 2003, as opposed to the dual-extension that was performed with Exchange 2000 Server.

After the Exchange Deployment Tools have run through the ForestPrep and DomainPrep processes, the ADC can be installed. The connection agreements in ADC are necessary to synchronize directory entries between the Exchange 5.5 and Exchange Server 2003 systems. Unlike in Exchange 2000, the Exchange Server 2003 ADC can be installed on a member server and is often installed on the first Exchange Server 2003 system in a site.

Organizations can choose to implement one or more ADCs in the organization. Implementing additional ADC connectors and connection agreements should not be seen as a fault-tolerant solution for the ADC. The ADC should be seen as a temporary coexistence solution, with migration being the intended end goal.

ADC installations are better off being left as simple as possible. A single ADC installed with one connection agreement to each Exchange 5.5 site is much easier to manage than multiple ADCs, all with their own connection agreements. This might or might not be possible based on the Exchange 5.5 site design and WAN layout. The ADC and its connection agreements should communicate with servers on the same network segment that will require multiple ADC installations.

Installing the ADC

Both the Active Directory domain controller and the Exchange 5.5 server that will be joined through the Active Directory Connector should be on the same physical network segment. Schema Admin and Enterprise Administrator rights are required to install the ADC.

Plan a few days to install and configure the ADC and the connection agreements. The initial installation and configuration take only a few hours, but it generally takes a few days to work out the kinks and resolve the errors in the Application Event Log. Problems in the ADC will show up later and complicate the migration, so don't rush the ADC installation. Microsoft recommends allocating 2 hours for replicating about 5,000 objects in a single direction, but the length of time for replication really varies on the number of connection agreements, recipient containers, and populated attributes on the actual directory objects.

The ADC has the capability to delete objects in both directories, so check whether the backup media and procedures have been recently verified before configuring the ADC. The organization should be familiar with how to perform an authoritative restore through NTDSUTIL for the Active Directory database.

The first step in installing the ADC is to create or choose a user account that will be used to run the ADC service and manage the connection agreements. This account does not have to be the same account that is used in each of the connection agreements configured later in the chapter. This account needs to be added to the Administrators group in the domain if the ADC is installed on a domain controller or to the local Administrators group if the ADC is installed on a member server.

To manually start the ADC installation, insert the Exchange Server 2003 CD and select ADC Setup from the AutoRun menu, or simply invoke the setup from the Exchange Deployment Tools. The ADC prompts for the component selection and allows just the MMC administration snap-in to be installed or the ADC service. Select both components when installing the ADC on the server. If the ADC will need to be remotely managed, the administration component can be installed later on the administrator's workstation.

Next, the installation prompts for the path to install the ADC and the ADC service account credentials. When the installation is complete, the next step is to configure the connection agreements to begin synchronizing the Active Directory and Exchange 5.5 directories.

Creating Connection Agreements

Configuring connection agreements (CAs) has been the bane of many an Exchange 2000 administrator. Improperly configured connection agreements can seriously corrupt an Active Directory or Exchange 5.5 database, so it is extremely important to properly configure CAs for the migration process. Luckily, Exchange Server 2003 includes a series of ADC Tools that streamline the process of creating CAs for migration, as illustrated in Figure 16.12. After installation, it is highly recommended that you use these wizards to install and configure the CAs.

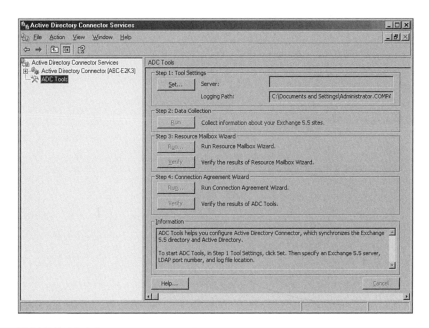

FIGURE 16.12   Using the ADC Tools.

Two tools in particular are extremely helpful in the migration process. The first tool, the Resource Mailbox Wizard, illustrated in Figure 16.13, can help to identify users with multiple mailboxes and fix them in advance of the migration. This tool streamlines the process that the ntdsutil utility previously utilized.

The second tool, the Connection Agreement Wizard, walks an administrator through the tricky process of creating the connection agreements required to migrate from Exchange 5.5. The wizard helps to identify "gotchas" such as the AD domain being in Mixed mode (it should be changed to Native mode in advance of the migration) and other important factors. As illustrated in Figure 16.14, it automatically creates a recipient CA and a public folder CA, which can then be manually tweaked as necessary.

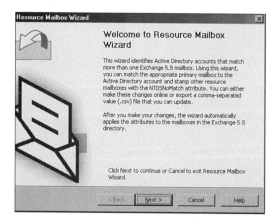

FIGURE 16.13   Viewing the Resource Mailbox Wizard.

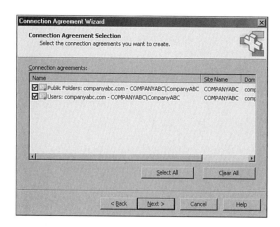

FIGURE 16.14   Connection Agreement Wizard.

After initial setup, several properties can be configured on the ADC to give the administrator more information and control over the ADC and its connection agreements. Attribute replication, account-matching rules, and diagnostic logging properties should all be configured before building the connection agreements and replicating directory entries. Even when using the default settings on the ADC, it is a best practice to prototype the ADC replication processes in a lab before attempting the synchronization on production systems.

Connection agreements are configured by an administrator who controls the type of objects that are replicated between Active Directory and Exchange 5.5. They also contain the credentials and connection information needed to connect to both systems and other attributes, such as handling deletion and what to do when there is no matching account for the mailbox in the destination directory. Connection agreements operate using two different approaches:

▶ **One way**—Information is synchronized only one way. The connection agreement can be from Windows or from Exchange, but not from both. After the direction is selected, the opposite system's tabs and controls are grayed out.

▶ **Two way**—Information is synchronized in both directions. This is generally the preferred method and keeps the configuration simple.

Connection agreements also need to be designated as primary or not. A primary connection agreement has the capability to create objects in the directory. A connection agreement that is not marked as primary cannot create new objects and can only update the attributes of existing objects. To ensure that objects are created, the ADC marks all connection agreements as primary by default.

Understanding Configuration Connection Agreements

Configuration connection agreements are used for coexistence between the Exchange 5.5 and Exchange 2003 servers, and they transfer information such as site addressing and routing information between the Exchange platforms. The configuration connection agreement cannot be created manually and is created by the Exchange Server 2003 setup program when the first Exchange Server 2003 system is installed. After the replication of the configuration information, Exchange 5.5 sites are visible in the Exchange System Manager program and are represented as administrative groups. Exchange Server 2003 systems are also visible in the Exchange 5.5 Administrator program.

Defining Recipient Connection Agreements

Recipient connection agreements are responsible for replicating mailbox, distribution list, and custom recipient information from the Exchange 5.5 directory to Active Directory. They are also used to send users, groups, and contacts from Active Directory to Exchange 5.5. Recipient connection agreements can be configured as one-way or two-way connection agreements. Most often a two-way connection agreement is used. Each connection agreement has its own schedule, so using one-way connection agreements might be preferred if the organization has specific requirements on when each side should be updated.

Using Public Folder Connection Agreements

Public folder connection agreements are responsible for replicating mail-enabled public folder information from and to Exchange 5.5 and Active Directory. Public folder connection agreements can be configured only as two-way connection agreements. It is a best practice to create one public folder connection agreement per Exchange 5.5 site. This is true even if the organization does not mail-enable public folders. Administrators might not be aware of some folders that are mail-enabled, and it is best to create the connection agreement for each Exchange 5.5 site, to reduce the likelihood of problems with the folders during the migration.

Configuring Connection Agreements

As previously mentioned, it is wise to allow the ADC Tools to create the necessary CAs for the migration process. If a manual CA will need to be configured, however, it can be

16

done in the following fashion. Open the ADC MMC snap-in on the domain controller running the ADC by selecting Start, All Programs, Microsoft Exchange, Active Directory Connector. Right-click the Active Directory Connector service icon for the server, and then select New, Recipient Connection Agreement.

The following tabs must be populated:

▶ **General**—Select the direction and the ADC server responsible for the connection agreement. It's usually best to select a two-way connection agreement for the primary connection agreement.

▶ **Connections**—Enter the username and password combination that will be used to read and write to Active Directory. Next enter the server name and Lightweight Directory Access Protocol (LDAP) port number for the Exchange 5.5 server, and the username and password that will be used to read and write to the Exchange 5.5 directory. When entering the user credentials, use the format domain\user—such as, companyabc.com\administrator.

> **TIP**
>
> To locate the LDAP port number on the Exchange 5.5 server, open Exchange Administrator and access the LDAP protocol properties under the Protocols container beneath the server object.

▶ **Schedule**—The directory synchronization process takes place between midnight and 6:00 a.m. daily under the default schedule. Use the grid to modify the schedule, or select Always, which replicates every five minutes.

▶ **From Exchange**—Select all the recipient containers in the Exchange 5.5 site to synchronize with Active Directory. Remember to select any containers that might be used as import containers for foreign mail connectors. Next select the destination container in Active Directory where the ADC will search for matching accounts and create new accounts. Select the object types to replicate, such as mailboxes, distribution lists, and custom recipients.

▶ **From Windows**—Select the organizational units in Active Directory to take updates from and the Exchange 5.5 container to place the updates in. The object types to replicate are selectable for users, groups, and contacts. The check boxes for Replicate Secured Active Directory Objects to the Exchange Directory and Create Objects in Location Specified by Exchange 5.5 DN are best left blank in most instances. Click Help while in the From Windows tab for more information on these options.

▶ **Deletion**—The Deletion option controls whether deletions are processed or stored in a CSV or LDF file, depending on the platform. If this is a short-term connection for migration, it's usually best to mark these options to not process the deletions and store the change in a file. The CSV and LDF files get created in the path that the ADC was installed into. Each connection agreement has its own subdirectory, and the output CSV and LDF files get created there.

> ▶ **Advanced**—The Advanced tab is set correctly for the first primary connection agreement and does not need to be modified. The settings on this tab should be modified when multiple connection agreements exist or when configuring the ADC to replicate between Exchange organizations. Leaving the Primary Connection Agreement check box selected on multiple connection agreements for the same containers creates duplicate directory entries. Never have the ADC create contacts unless the ADC is being used to link two Exchange organizations for collaboration purposes.

To configure a public folder connection agreement, right-click the Active Directory Connector service icon for the server, and select New, Public Folder Connection Agreement.

The following tabs must be populated:

> ▶ **General**—Select the ADC server responsible for the connection agreement. The direction can be only two-way on public folder connection agreements.
>
> ▶ **Connections**—Enter the username and password combination that will be used to read and write to Active Directory. Next enter the server name and LDAP port number for the Exchange 5.5 server, and the username and password that will be used to read and write to the Exchange 5.5 directory. When entering the user credentials, use the format domain\user—in this case, companyabc\administrator.
>
> ▶ **Schedule**—The directory-synchronization process takes place between midnight and 6:00 a.m. daily under the default schedule. Use the grid to modify the schedule. Select the check box for Replicate the Entire Directory the Next Time the Agreement Is Run to perform a full synchronization on the first run.
>
> ▶ **From Windows**—The only option available here is the check box for Replicate Secured Active Directory Objects to the Exchange Directory. This replicates objects that contain an explicit deny in the access control list to Exchange 5.5. Exchange 5.5 does not support explicit deny entries, so the objects are not replicated by default.

The final step is to force the connection agreement to replicate immediately. To force the replication, right-click the connection agreement and select Replicate Now. Be sure to check the Application Event Log in Event Viewer for errors during the replication process.

Installing the First Exchange Server 2003 System in an Exchange Server 5.5 Site

Because there are many prerequisite tasks and processes to run, getting to the point of the actual Exchange Server setup is a watershed event. The following section double-checks that the prerequisites have been fulfilled. When installing the first Exchange Server 2003 system, it is recommended that you use a server that has been wiped clean and has a fresh installation of Windows Server 2003. This is because the first server in Exchange holds many critical Exchange organizational management and routing master tables, and having a new, clean server ensures that the masters are created and stored on a solidly configured system.

Installing the First Exchange Server 2003 System

The actual Exchange Server 2003 installation of the first server is quite easy after the prerequisite conditions are met. The installation takes about 30 minutes on average.

TIP

The first Exchange 2003 server in a site runs the Site Replication Service, which is used to synchronize site topology information between Exchange 5.5 and Exchange Server 2003. Because of this special role, larger organizations might want to install this role onto a dedicated server, rather than a production Mailbox server. This is also highly recommended if the Mailbox servers are to be set up as cluster nodes.

One final step before running the Exchange Server 2003 setup is to run a tool called SetupPrep, shown in Figure 16.15. This tool validates that all necessary prerequisites are in place for the installation of the first Exchange Server 2003 in the site.

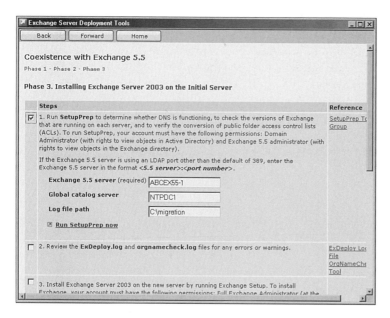

FIGURE 16.15   Running SetupPrep.

After SetupPrep has been run, the actual setup of the server can be invoked via the tools or simply by running the Setup.exe in the \setup\i386 folder. The following steps properly install Exchange Server 2003 on the system on which they are run:

1. Click Next at the welcome screen.

2. Agree to the end-user licensing agreement, and click Next.

3. Choose the installation path and ensure that Typical Installation is chosen. Click Next.

4. Select Join or Upgrade an Existing Exchange 5.5 Organization, as illustrated in Figure 16.16, and click Next.

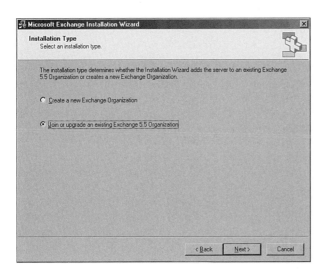

FIGURE 16.16   Joining an Exchange 5.5 organization.

NOTE

It is imperative that Join or Upgrade an Existing Exchange 5.5 Organization is chosen at this point. If Create a New Exchange Organization is chosen, connectivity will be lost to the Exchange 5.5 organization, and the organization will have to be removed completely by using the `setup /removeorg` option.

---

5. Enter the name of an Exchange 5.5 server in a site the Exchange Server 2003 system will join.

6. Click OK at the prompt to test prerequisite conditions.

7. Select I Agree to agree to the license agreement.

8. Enter the password of the Exchange 5.5 service account.

9. Verify the installation options, and click Next to start the installation.

10. When the installation is complete, click Finish.

16

To install additional Exchange Server 2003 systems, the installation process is almost identical, and the same procedure can be followed.

Understanding What Happens Behind the Graphical User Interface (GUI) During the Installation

Quite a few items are installed and configured during the installation. The following items describe some of the major components that are installed and configured during setup. The new terms and features are discussed more in depth in the next few sections.

- ► **Exchange Server 2003 binaries and services installed**—All the basic services for Exchange Server 2003 are installed and started. The SMTP and NNTP services from Internet Information Services (IIS) are modified for Exchange Server 2003.

- ► **Changes to Active Directory Configuration container**—Information about the Exchange installation, such as administrative and routing group configurations, are in the Services container.

- ► **Exchange Server added to Exchange Domain Servers security group**—The machine account for the server is added to the Exchange Domain Servers security group to let Exchange Server 2003 run under the local system account.

- ► **Configuration connection agreement created**—A new connection agreement is added to the ADC to replicate configuration and routing information between Exchange 5.5 and Exchange Server 2003.

- ► **Recipient Update Service created**—The RUS is created to update address lists and recipient policies in Active Directory.

- ► **Site Replication Service (SRS) installed**—The SRS is installed and synchronizes the directory with the Exchange 5.5 server in the site.

Understanding the Configuration Connection Agreement

During the installation, a new connection agreement called the ConfigCA is added to the Active Directory Connector. The ConfigCA is responsible for replicating the configuration information between the Exchange platforms. The ConfigCA replicates items such as the site addressing policies and the routing information in the Gateway Address Routing Table (GWART).

Examining the Site Replication Service (SRS)

The Site Replication Service (SRS) provides directory interoperability between the Exchange 5.5 and Exchange 2003 servers. The SRS runs as a service and is needed only during the migration period. SRS uses LDAP to communicate between directories, and to Exchange 5.5 servers it looks just like another Exchange 5.5 server. The SRS works in conjunction with the Active Directory Connector for directory synchronization.

Only one SRS is allowed per Exchange Server 2003 system. Additional SRSs can be added, as long as there are additional Exchange Server 2003 systems available to run the service. The SRS has no configuration parameters in the Exchange System Manager. Synchronization can be forced through the SRS by accessing the SRS from the Exchange 5.5 Administrator program.

SRSs are created on all servers that house Exchange 5.5 Directory Replication Connectors. The Directory Replication Connector is replaced by the SRS to perform intersite replication with the remote Exchange 5.5 site; if an Exchange Server 2003 is configured to communicate with an Exchange 5.5 server, the SRS automatically is installed and configured at the time of Exchange Server 2003 installation.

> **TIP**
>
> To view the Directory Replication Connector endpoints in the SRS, open Exchange System Manger and expand the Tools icon. Next click the Site Replication Service icon and then select Directory Replication Connector View from the View menu. Each Exchange 5.5 site's Directory Replication Connector is now displayed under the SRS.

No Service Account in Exchange Server 2003

Exchange Server 2003 runs under the Local System account. This is a major change from Exchange 5.5, where the Exchange Service account was used on all servers. The benefit of the new architecture is that the service account was a single point of failure in case of a password change or if the account was deleted. When Exchange Server 2003 systems communicate between servers, they are authenticated by the server's machine account in Active Directory.

When the /domainprep option is run, it creates two groups called Exchange Domain Servers and Exchange Enterprise Servers. During Exchange setup, the Exchange server's machine account is added to a Global Security group called Exchange Domain Servers. The Exchange Domain Servers group is granted permissions on all Exchange objects to allow the Exchange Server 2003 services to access and update Active Directory. The Exchange Enterprise Servers group contains the Exchange Domain Servers groups from all domains in the forest and provides cross-domain access between all Exchange Server 2003 systems.

Using the Recipient Update Service (RUS)

The Recipient Update Service (RUS) is responsible for updating address lists and email addresses in Active Directory. Two objects are contained in the RUS container by default. The RUS (with "Enterprise Configuration" in brackets) is responsible for updating the Enterprise Configuration information in Active Directory, such as administrative and routing group information. The domain specified is responsible for updating the address lists and email addresses configured on objects in the Active Directory domain in which

16

the Exchange server resides. The address list and email addresses are configured under the Recipient Policies and Address List icon, discussed previously in this section.

Understanding Exchange Server 2003 Mailbox-Migration Methods

Two methods exist for moving mailboxes to Exchange Server 2003, and each differs in hardware requirements and the amount of risk and interoperability during and after the migration. The following migration methods for mailboxes are covered in this section:

▶ Move Mailboxes

▶ ExMerge

Migrating Using the Move Mailbox Approach

Moving user mailboxes between servers is the safest migration method because the servers' databases are not in jeopardy if the migration fails. Moving the users also provides the opportunity to use new hardware with little or no downtime. In addition, moving users allows the organization to migrate users in sizable chunks over time. Outlook profiles automatically are updated on the desktop, and users are redirected to the new Exchange Server 2003 systems when they log on. The limitation of moving users to a new server is that they can be moved only to an Exchange Server 2003 system in the same administrative group. Moving users can also slow the speed of the migration, which can be seen as a positive or negative, depending on the organization's goals.

The Exchange Server 2003 database is much more efficient than Exchange 5.5 was at storing messages. Even with full copies of all messages created by moving the users, administrators might actually see the database size shrink when comparing the size of the Exchange 5.5 and Exchange Server 2003 databases before and after migration. Quite a bit of empty space in the Exchange 5.5 database might also account for a portion of the reduced database size.

To move user mailboxes, open the Active Directory Users and Computers administrative tool, right-click the user to move, and then select Exchange Tasks, as illustrated in Figure 16.17.

Once the Mailbox Move Wizard begins, do the following:

1. Click Next at the welcome screen.

2. Choose the option for Move Mailbox, and click Next.

3. When prompted for the type of move, select Same Administrative Group Move, and click Next.

4. Select the destination server and mailbox store, and click Next.

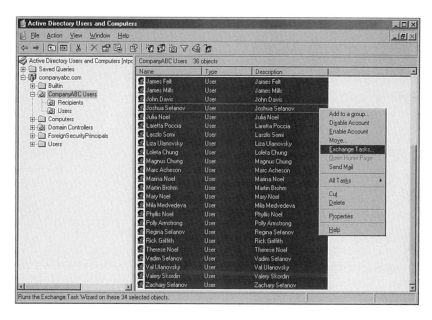

FIGURE 16.17   Selecting mailbox-enabled users to move.

5. At the next screen, choose either to create a failure report if corruption is detected or to skip corrupted items and continue the mailbox move. Click Next to continue.

6. At the next prompt, you can specify what time the Move Mailbox command should start and finish by. This is very useful when scheduling mailbox moves for off-hour periods. Click Next to continue.

Connections are then made to the source and destination server, and the mailbox contents are moved four at a time, as illustrated in Figure 16.18. If the move is unsuccessful, the user's mailbox is still available on the source Exchange 5.5 server.

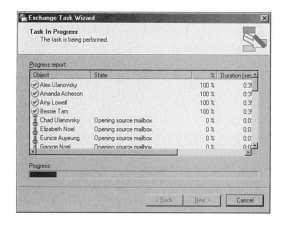

FIGURE 16.18   Moving mailboxes to Exchange Server 2003.

Leapfrogging Server Migrations to Reduce Costs

If server hardware or budget is a limiting factor in the project, the organization might want to consider using a leapfrog method (also called the swing upgrade method) to migrate the users to Exchange Server 2003. Using the leapfrog method, fewer servers need to be purchased to perform the migration through the Move Users method.

One server still needs to be installed into the Exchange 5.5 site to house the SRS. Users can then be moved to that server or a second Exchange Server 2003 system installed into the site. After all users, connectors, and public folders are moved off the Exchange 5.5 server, that server can be formatted and reinstalled as an Exchange Server 2003 system, allowing the next Exchange 5.5 server's users to be migrated to Exchange Server 2003.

This greatly reduces the speed of the migration process and also requires a Native mode Windows Server 2003 domain to support the public folders if they are scattered across the Exchange 5.5 servers. Another option for public folders in this scenario is to consolidate the public folders by replicating all the folders to a single Exchange 5.5 server in the site if a Native mode Windows Server 2003 domain is not available. Connectors could also pose a problem with this method and require a solution before starting the leapfrog process.

One problem with this leapfrog method to be aware of is to not remove the first Exchange 5.5 server in a site until it's the last remaining 5.5 system in that site. The first Exchange server in the site hosts folders and other functions that are required by the Exchange 5.5 organization.

Using ExMerge to Migrate Mailboxes

Exmerge.exe is a Microsoft utility that can extract the contents of a user's mailbox to a personal folder (PST) file. The PST file created by ExMerge can be added to a user's Outlook profile so the user can access the contents of his old mailbox. ExMerge can also import the PST file to a destination mailbox to another server, site, or organization. On the destination server, ExMerge can merge the imported PST file or overwrite data in the target mailbox.

ExMerge can be used in disaster recovery and in migration scenarios to move user data from point A to point B by selecting the source and destination Exchange servers. ExMerge can be used when an organization wants to simply export their data out of Exchange 5.5 and wants to be able to move mailbox contents to a new Exchange environment or archive the contents of the Exchange 5.5 mailbox in case a user needs access to his old information. ExMerge can also be used to move mailbox contents in organization-naming hierarchies that are the same or different. This is beneficial to organizations that want to build a new naming context when converting to Active Directory and Exchange Server 2007.

A few issues should be considered when using ExMerge to move mailbox contents to a new organization. The biggest one is that the capability to reply to all recipients on old messages could be lost. At a minimum, end users need to force the names on old messages to be resolved against the new directory by using Alt+K or the Check Name button on the toolbar. End users might be confused and frustrated if the new system cannot locate all of the users. This can occur if all users have not been migrated from the old organization or if mail connectivity to foreign mail systems has not been reestablished in the new Exchange organization.

The second-biggest issue is that appointments on the user's calendar that contain other attendees are severed. The original appointments were resolved to the attendee's old addresses when they were created. This means that if the user deletes the appointment or makes a change to the time or location of the meeting, the other attendees will not be notified.

Even with these issues, ExMerge can be just the thing organizations are looking for, especially when they have survived multiple mergers and acquisitions and are looking to start over with a new Exchange organizational design. If the organization plans to use ExMerge for the entire migration process, spend extensive time prototyping the merge process to catch other issues the organization might encounter.

ExMerge merges the following information:

▶ User folders

▶ User messages

▶ Outlook calendars

▶ Contacts

▶ Journal

▶ Notes

▶ Tasks

▶ Folder rules that were created in Exchange 5.0 or later

ExMerge does not support the following:

▶ Forms

▶ Views

▶ Schedule+ data

▶ Folder rules that were created in Exchange 4.0

ExMerge also supports advanced options such as extracting folder permissions. It can filter the messages for extraction from the source store by attachment name or subject that are accessible under the Options button on the source server selection screen.

ExMerge can be configured in either a one- or a two-step merge process. One-step merge processes copy the data from the source mailbox to a PST and then merge the data into the same mailbox on the destination server. The distinguished name of the mailbox and container path of the source and destination servers must be identical to perform a one-step merge.

When using ExMerge to move mailbox data from different organizations and sites, administrators need to be aware that ExMerge cannot create a mailbox on a destination server or set alternative recipient and forwarding rules on the source server. Another item that administrators should be aware of is that ExMerge runs only on Windows Server 2003. ExMerge needs to be able to access several Exchange DLL files. To run ExMerge, copy the `Exmerge.exe` and `Exmerge.ini` files to the Exchange \bin directory, or update the system path to include the Exchange \bin directory if ExMerge will run from another file location.

To run ExMerge using Exchange 5.5 as the source and Exchange Server 2007 as the destination, the credentials used for ExMerge must have Service Account Administrator privileges in Exchange 5.5 at the Organization, Site, and Configuration container levels. The credentials must also have at least Receive As permission on the destination Exchange 2007 mailbox.

> **NOTE**
>
> For inter-org migrations, Exmerge can be useful, but administrators should also look into using the built-in Exchange Migration Wizard, as it will preserve legacy directory information on mail items and can be a useful tool in the migration process.

Migrating Exchange Server 5.5 Public Folders to Exchange Server 2003

Exchange mailboxes on the new Exchange Server 2003 systems must be able to access system and public folders, and, subsequently, require copies of the information that existed in those folders. Previously, in Exchange 2000, this required a fairly manual process of marking top-level public folders for replication and then propagating those changes down to subfolders. With Exchange Server 2003, however, a utility called pfmigrate automates this functionality. The options for pfmigrate are illustrated in Figure 16.19.

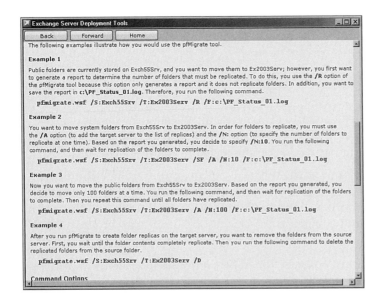

FIGURE 16.19   PFMigrate options.

The PFMigrate utility can be used in advance of a migration to make copies of public folders on the new servers; it then can be used later to remove the public folder copies from the old Exchange 5.5 servers.

Migrating Exchange 5.5 Connectors and Services to Exchange Server 2003

With connectors in general, the best migration path is to build parallel connectors on Exchange Server 2003 systems. This way, the Exchange 5.5 connectors can remain intact and continue to route mail and perform directory synchronization with the foreign mail system.

The benefits of running connectors on both systems are as follows:

▶ Involves less risk when migrating the connectors

▶ Enables administrators to view Exchange 5.5 connector configuration when configuring and administering the Exchange Server 2003 connector

▶ Allows for controlled mail flow testing

▶ Provides a fallback plan if software defects or configuration issues are encountered with the Exchange Server 2003 connector

While testing the Exchange Server 2003 connectors, configure the Exchange Server 2003 connector with a higher cost and limited address space. This enables administrators to perform controlled tests of mail flow. When the organization is comfortable with the test results, the address space can be configured to match that of the Exchange 5.5 connectors. Also, the cost parameter on the connector can be dropped below that of the Exchange 5.5 connector, and the Exchange Server 2003 connector can begin routing all mail to the foreign system. The Exchange 5.5 connectors can remain in place until the organization is comfortable shutting them down.

Many Exchange 5.5 connectors also provide directory synchronization with foreign mail systems. Directory synchronization on the Exchange Server 2003 version of the connector should not be enabled until the mail flow through the connector works properly and the organization is ready to use the Exchange Server 2003 connector full-time. Most connectors such as GroupWise and Lotus Notes provide filtering options for directory synchronization. Marking the option Do Not Import Address Entries of This Type and using an asterisk (*) as a wildcard means that no entries will be imported and directory synchronization will remain on the Exchange 5.5 server. Also, do not export address entries to the foreign mail system in order to avoid duplicate address entries in the foreign mail system's address list.

16

> **TIP**
>
> Take screenshots of all connector configuration property pages before attempting to migrate any connector. A lost setting such as an address space entry that is not transferred to the Exchange Server 2003 connector can cause a major routing or directory synchronization disaster on both mail platforms.

Migrating the Internet Mail Service

The Internet Mail Service (IMS) has been replaced by several components in Exchange Server 2003:

- ▶ SMTP Connector
- ▶ Internet Message Format
- ▶ Message Delivery Properties

The Internet Mail Service needs to be replaced by an equivalent SMTP Connector in Exchange Server 2003. After the migration, the new connector must be reconfigured to match the settings of the old IMS.

Migrating Site Connectors

Site connectors in Exchange 5.5 are replaced by routing group connectors in Exchange Server 2003. Routing group connectors that communicate with Exchange 5.5 servers communicate over RPC. When routing group connectors communicate between Exchange Server 2003 systems, they communicate over SMTP.

To buildparallel connectors to Exchange 5.5 sites, create a routing group connector to the remote Exchange 5.5 site and configure the local bridgehead server as the new Exchange Server 2003 connector server.

Migrating Foreign Mail Connectors

Exchange Server 2003 includes support for the following foreign mail connectors:

- ▶ GroupWise Connector
- ▶ Lotus Notes Connector
- ▶ X.400 Connector

The best strategy to migrate these connectors is to use a parallel connector strategy. The following configuration settings must be reconfigured after an upgrade is in place on the foreign mail connectors:

- ▶ Directory synchronization schedule
- ▶ Address spaces

- ▶ Import container and export container configurations

- ▶ Delivery restriction options, such as message size

Always prototype the configuration, mail transfer, and directory synchronization for foreign mail connectors in a lab environment before implementing them in production. Mistakes in foreign mail connector configuration are usually quite costly and require extensive cleanup on both sides of the connection.

Creating Support for Unsupported Connectors

To support unsupported connectors, such as the PROFS/SNADS, cc:Mail, and MS-Mail connectors, remain in Mixed mode Exchange Server 2003 and leave an Exchange 5.5 site to handle the unsupported connector. For a long-term solution, consider an SMTP solution for mail transfer and LDAP for directory synchronization. Another solution is to locate a third-party replacement connector.

Completing the Migration to Exchange Native Mode

After the organization has successfully migrated from Exchange 5.5 to Exchange 2003, the Exchange 2003 environment needs to be switched to Native mode so that it is ready to migrate to Exchange Server 2007. For details on switching to an Exchange Native mode, see the section earlier on "Moving to Native Mode in Exchange." After running Exchange 2003 for a few weeks to confirm that the migration was successful and any hiccups are worked out, the organization can now begin its migration plan from Exchange 2003 to Exchange 2007.

Summary

A migration to Exchange 2007 is relatively straightforward being that Microsoft does not provide a lot of options when making the transition. Effectively, the process merely involves adding Exchange 2007 servers to an existing Exchange 2000 or Exchange 2003 environment, and migrating server roles and mailbox data to the new servers. This chapter covered several other prerequisite processes along with tips and tricks needed to have a higher success factor in the migration process; however, in the end, a migration from Exchange 2000 and 2003 to Exchange 2007 is relatively prescriptive.

What does vary in a migration process are the steps when an organization wants to consolidate multiple Exchange organizations into a new Exchange 2007 environment, or if the organization is migrating from a non-Exchange 2000 or Exchange 2003 environment into Exchange 2007. Again, there are prescriptive steps to perform the migrations— they are just more extensive in the process of converting data as part of the migration procedure.

It is most critical to follow the steps outlined in this chapter to ensure that the necessary procedures are followed that help an organization properly plan the migration, meet the prerequisites, and then proceed with getting data into Exchange and users connected to the new Exchange 2007 environment.

Best Practices

The following are best practices from this chapter:

▶ Key to a successful migration to Exchange 2007 is to properly plan and test the migration process to ensure all data as well as server role functions have a successful transition to the new environment. See Chapters 3 and 4 of this book on design and architecture best practices prior to performing a migration to Exchange 2007.

▶ Because Exchange 2007 does not support certain Exchange 2000 Server functions such as Mobile Information Server or Exchange Messenger, those functions need to be migrated off to new services before Exchange 2007 can be installed.

▶ For an organization that depends on certain Exchange 2000 or Exchange 2003 functions that are not supported in Exchange 2007, or even third-party add-ins that aren't supported in Exchange 2007, the organization should consider keeping an Exchange 2000 or Exchange 2003 server connected to the Exchange environment as a host for non-Exchange 2007–compatible applications.

▶ Before migrating to Exchange 2007, the Active Directory schema needs to be updated. This should be done as a separate step of the migration process because it relates to Active Directory.

▶ Before migrating to Exchange 2007, the Exchange organization must be in Exchange Native mode.

▶ To get an Exchange organization into Native mode, all Exchange 5.5 servers as well as remnants from the Exchange 5.5 organization such as site connectors and Active Directory Connectors (ADCs) need to be removed.

▶ Being that Microsoft does not provide a direct migration from Exchange 5.5 to Exchange 2007, the organization should plan their migration from Exchange 5.5 to Exchange 2003 as a separate step before migrating to Exchange 2007.

▶ A replica of a public folder must be created using the Exchange 2000 or Exchange 2003 Exchange System Manager tool or PFMigrate tool because there is no equivalent public folder replica creation tool in Exchange 2007.

▶ Test the migration process in a lab environment before implementing the migration in production. A test migration confirms that all data successfully migrates to the new environment (that is, there is no mailbox corruption that can halt the migration process). In addition, by running through the process in a lab, you gain experience on the migration process and gain a good sense of how long it will take to complete the migration at the time of the live migration.

▶ When migrating to an Exchange 2007 environment that will have distributed server roles (that is, not all server roles will reside on a single server), the proper order of implementation is Client Access server, Hub Transport server, and then Mailbox server.

▶ Because Exchange 2007 Client Access servers can serve as Exchange 2000 or 2003 front-end servers, migrate all front-end servers to CAS servers, and remove all front-end servers as one of the first server migration steps in the migration process.

▶ If a brand-new Exchange 2007 environment is implemented as a clean installation of Exchange, it must be noted that a clean Exchange 2007 environment cannot have Exchange 2003, Exchange 2000, or earlier versions of Exchange added in to the new Exchange 2007 environment.

▶ After the organization has completed its migration to Exchange 2007, all remnants of previous interoperability to Exchange 2000 or Exchange 2003 should be removed, such as legacy routing group connectors, routing groups, and administrative groups.

16

CHAPTER 17

Implementing Client Access and Hub Transport Servers

Two new roles within the Microsoft Exchange Server 2007 family are the Client Access server (CAS) and the Hub Transport server. In reality, these two roles are really specializations and evolutions of the original Exchange front-end and bridgehead server concepts, along with the Edge Transport server.

To see the place that the CAS and the Hub Transport server role hold in the constellation of Exchange 2007 roles, refer to Figure 17.1.

In this chapter, the discussion focuses on the CAS and Hub Transport server features. These two servers play pivotal roles in client access and routing within the Exchange 2007 infrastructure. The Edge Transport server is discussed at length in Chapter 8, "Implementing Edge Services for an Exchange Server 2007 Environment."

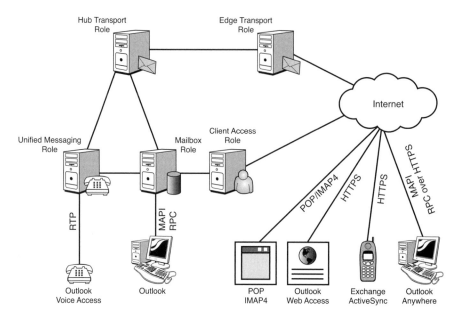

FIGURE 17.1   Exchange 2007 server roles and relationships.

Understanding the Client Access Server

In many ways, the Exchange 2007 CAS is fundamentally the equivalent of the front-end server in Exchange Server 2003. It provides client access services for clients that don't directly access the Mailbox server (for example, Outlook 2007) as well as some interesting new client-oriented services such as the Autodiscover service.

Clients can access their mailboxes using Messaging Application Programming Interface (MAPI), voice access, Hypertext Transfer Protocol (HTTP), RPC over HTTP, ActiveSync, Post Office Protocol (POP), or Internet Message Access Protocol version 4 (IMAP4). Of these, all but MAPI and voice access use the CAS role. Even MAPI uses the CAS for the Autodiscover service and when using the RPC over HTTP feature of Outlook Anywhere.

NOTE

The Messaging Application Programming Interface (MAPI) is technically not a protocol, but is rather a general framework. This is implemented as the Exchange remote procedure calls (RPC) protocol in Exchange 2003 and 2007. So, technically, the protocol used by Outlook clients is called Exchange RPC.

However, the term MAPI is used synonymously and more commonly in place of Exchange RPC.

There are seven client types, shown in Table 17.1.

TABLE 17.1   Client Types

Client	Protocol
Outlook	MAPI over RPC
Outlook Voice Access	RTP
Outlook Web Access	HTTP/HTTPS
Exchange ActiveSync	HTTP/HTTPS
Outlook Anywhere	MAPI over RPC over HTTP/HTTPS
POP Client	POP/SMTP
IMAP Client	IMAP4/SMTP

These seven client types connect to the CAS in various ways, as shown in Figure 17.2.

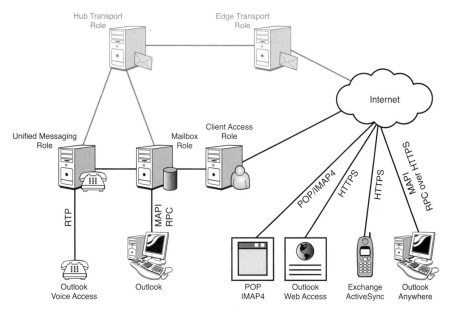

FIGURE 17.2   Client type connections to the CAS.

A CAS must exist in every Exchange 2007 organization. A best practice is to have a CAS in every Active Directory (AD) site, where AD sites represent contiguous areas of high bandwidth. There should be a minimum of one CAS in every site that has a Mailbox server. Additional CASs can be deployed for performance and fault tolerance.

As indicated before, the CAS is used for the following clients and services:

- Outlook Web Access (OWA)
- ActiveSync
- Outlook Anywhere
- Availability service
- Autodiscover service
- POP3 and IMAP

Each of these is discussed individually in the following sections. For a detailed discussion of the design and implementation of client mobility features, see Chapter 23, "Designing and Implementing Mobility in Exchange Server 2007."

OWA

The Premium version of OWA includes many features, such as telephony integration and mobile device support. The Light version is designed for use on mobile devices, slow connections, or non-Microsoft browsers. The differences between the two versions are shown in Table 17.2.

TABLE 17.2   OWA Light Versus Premium

Feature	Light Version	Premium Version
Spelling Checker	Not available	Available
Reading Pane	Not available	Available
Accessibility for Blind and Low Vision Users	Available	Not available
Notifications and Reminders	Not available	Available
Weekly Calendar Views	Not available	Available
Windows SharePoint Services and UNC File Shares Integration	Not available	Available
Compose Messages by Using HTML	Only plain text is available in Outlook Web Access Light	Available
Calendar Options	Limited to the following features: Show Week Numbers, Set the First Day of the Week, Select Days of the Week, Set Day Start and End Times	Available
Appearance (color scheme)	Not available	Available
Voice Mail Options	Not available	Available

NOTE

Switching to the Accessibility for Blind and Low Vision Users option in Outlook Web Access Premium or selecting it at the initial logon window forces the client into Outlook Web Access Light. The can be undone using the Outlook Web Access Light Accessibility option to switch back to the Premium version.

ActiveSync

ActiveSync is a synchronization protocol that allows mobile devices to synchronize the user's Exchange mailbox, including email, calendar, contacts, and tasks. It is based on HTTP and Extensible Markup Language (XML). ActiveSync supports the following devices:

▶ Windows Mobile 5.0

▶ Pocket PC 2003

▶ Pocket PC 2002

Unlike Exchange Server 2003, in Exchange 2007 the ActiveSync feature is enabled by default. The Exchange 2007 ActiveSync has a number of new features and improved features, including the following:

▶ Support for HTML messages

▶ Support for follow-up flags

▶ Support for fast message retrieval

▶ Meeting attendee information

▶ Enhanced Exchange Search

▶ Windows SharePoint Services and Universal Naming Convention (UNC) document access

▶ PIN reset

▶ Autodiscover for over-the-air provisioning

▶ Support for Out of Office configuration

▶ Support for tasks synchronization

▶ Support for Direct Push

Some of the new features, such as Direct Push and Autodiscover, require Windows Mobile 5.0 with the Messaging and Security Feature Pack (MSFP) installed on the device to function.

17

Exchange 2007 ActiveSync also has a number of new security features, including the following:

▸ Exchange ActiveSync mailbox policies

▸ Device password policies

▸ Remote Device Wipe

These new security features allow Exchange 2007 administrators to effectively manage the security of their mobile devices. Table 17.3 lists the settings available in the ActiveSync mailbox policy.

TABLE 17.3   List of ActiveSync Mailbox Policy Settings

Setting	Default Value	Description
Allow nonprovisionable devices	True	Allows older devices (those that do not support the Autodiscover service) to connect to Exchange 2007 by using Exchange ActiveSync
Allow simple password	False	Enables or disables the ability to use a simple password such as 1234
Alphanumeric password required	False	Requires that a password contains numeric and nonnumeric characters
Attachments enabled	True	Enables attachments to be downloaded to the mobile device
Device encryption enabled	False	Enables encryption on the device
Password enabled	False	Enables the device password
Password expiration	Not Set	Enables the administrator to configure a length of time after which a device password must be changed
Password history	0	Defines the number of past passwords stored in the user's mailbox; previously stored passwords cannot be reused
Policy refresh interval	Not Set	Defines how frequently the device updates the Exchange ActiveSync policy from the server
Maximum attachment size	Not Set	Specifies the maximum size of attachments that are automatically downloaded to the device
Maximum failed password attempts	4	Specifies how many times an incorrect password can be entered before the device performs a wipe of all data
Maximum inactivity time lock	15 minutes	Specifies the length of time a device can go without user input before it locks
Minimum password length	4	Specifies the minimum password length

TABLE 17.3   Continued

Setting	Default Value	Description
Password recovery	Disabled	Enables the device password to be recovered from the server
UNC file access	Enabled	Enables access to files stored on UNC shares
WSS file access	Enabled	Enables access to files stored on Microsoft Windows SharePoint Services sites

To use the password policy features and the Remote Device Wipe, you need to create and associate the user with an Exchange ActiveSync mailbox policy.

Different policies can be created to meet the needs of different user communities. For example, an organization might have one general user ActiveSync mailbox policy with default password settings that require a minimum of 4 characters. A second ActiveSync mailbox policy for executives with higher security requirements and more secure password settings might require a minimum of 10-character passwords. These policies would be assigned to the appropriate mailboxes.

By default, no ActiveSync mailbox policies are created. To create a new ActiveSync mailbox policy, execute the following steps:

1. Expand the Organization Configuration folder.

2. Select the Client Access folder.

3. In the actions pane, select New Exchange ActiveSync Mailbox Policy.

4. Enter the policy name, such as Default Exchange ActiveSync Mailbox Policy.

5. Click New to create the policy.

6. Click Finish to close the wizard.

To associate a user with an Exchange ActiveSync mailbox policy, execute the following steps:

1. Expand the Recipient Configuration folder.

2. Select the Mailbox folder.

3. Select the mailbox.

4. Select Properties in the actions pane.

5. Select the Mailbox Features tab.

6. Select Activesync and click Properties.

17

7. Click Browse and select a policy, such as the Default Exchange ActiveSync Mailbox Policy created earlier.

8. Click OK three times to save the settings.

Now, the user's mobile device will have the policies applied and can be managed remotely, as is evidenced by the Manage Mobile Device selection in the mailbox actions pane.

ActiveSync Remote Wipe

The ActiveSync Remote Wipe function deletes the data off the device. Applications and other program data remain on the system, only the data is removed. To administratively remote wipe a device:

1. Expand the Recipient Configuration folder.

2. Select the Mailbox folder.

3. Select the mailbox.

4. In the mailbox actions pane, click Manage Mobile Device.

5. Select the appropriate device from the list of user devices.

6. Select the Clear option button in the Action pane.

7. Click Clear.

8. Click Yes in the pop-up message box to confirm the remote wipe.

9. Click Finish to close the window.

The device will be wiped the next time it synchronizes. There might be an ActiveSync warning dialog box on the mobile device saying "Exchange Server must enforce security policies on your device to continue synchronizing. Do you want to continue?" The user must select OK or Cancel. If the user selects OK, the device restarts and comes up in a clean default Windows Mobile 5.0 state. If the user selects Cancel, the device does not synchronize any new data. However, the user can still continue to look at the information already there.

NOTE

After the wipe is successful, the device needs to be removed from the list of user devices. If this is not done, the device continues to wipe every time it synchronizes.

The user can also wipe their device remotely, using OWA. To wipe the device from OWA, complete the following steps:

1. In OWA, select Options.

2. From the Options menu, select Mobile Devices.

3. Select the device, and then click Wipe All Data from Device.

4. Click OK to wipe.

Note that the status changes to pending wipe. After the device synchronizes, the status changes to wipe successful. Once again, the device needs to be removed from the users list if it will be used again.

> **NOTE**
>
> It can be hard to find a free Windows Mobile Device 5.0 device to test with because it requires the purchase of hardware and a connection plan. An alternative is the Standalone Device Emulator 1.0 with Windows Mobile OS Images. This emulates both the Pocket PC and Smartphone devices for ActiveSync, remote wipe, and other functions.
>
> The emulator can be downloaded from http://www.microsoft.com/downloads/details. aspx?FamilyId=C62D54A5-183A-4A1E-A7E2-CC500ED1F19A&displaylang=en. The emulator also requires the Virtual Machine Network Driver (VMNet), which can be downloaded from http://www.microsoft.com/downloads/details.aspx?FamilyID=dc8332d6-565f-4a57-be8c-1d4718d3af65&displaylang=en.

Outlook Anywhere

Outlook Anywhere is the new Exchange 2007 name for the original RPC over HTTP feature in Exchange Server 2003. It essentially allows remote procedure calls (RPC) clients such as Outlook 2003 and Outlook 2007 to traverse firewalls by wrapping the RPC traffic in HTTP. This allows traveling or home users to use the full Outlook client without the need for a dedicated virtual private network (VPN) connection, which is frequently blocked by firewalls.

For security, the Outlook Anywhere protocol is always implemented with Secure Sockets Layer (SSL) to secure the transport, so it is really RPC over HTTPS. This ensures that the confidentiality and integrity of the Outlook Anywhere traffic is protected.

> **NOTE**
>
> The idea of allowing RPC over the Internet is anathema to many organization's security groups. In the past decade, a number of well-publicized vulnerabilities have occurred in the native RPC protocol, which gave it a bad reputation.
>
> With the evolution of the RPC protocol and the securing of the transport with SSL, the Outlook Anywhere feature provides as much security as Outlook Web Access (OWA) or ActiveSync. Outdated security concerns should not prevent an organization from deploying Outlook Anywhere.

Outlook Anywhere is not enabled by default. Two tasks need to be accomplished to enable Outlook Anywhere on the CAS: Install the RPC over HTTP networking component and enable Outlook Anywhere in the Exchange Management Console.

17

To install the networking component:

1. Launch Control Panel and select Add or Remove Programs.

2. Click Add/Remove Windows Components.

3. Select Networking Services and click Details.

4. Check the RPC over HTTP Proxy check box.

5. Click OK.

6. Click Next.

7. Click Finish to close the wizard.

To enable Outlook Anywhere in the Exchange Management Console:

1. Expand the Server Configuration tree.

2. Select the Client Access folder.

3. Select the CAS on which you want to enable Outlook Anywhere.

4. Click Enable Outlook Anywhere in the actions pane.

5. Enter the External Host Name and the appropriate authentication options.

6. Click Next to enable Outlook Anywhere on the CAS.

7. Click Finish to close the wizard.

Outlook Anywhere will now be enabled on the CAS. This must be repeated for each CAS and the additional steps to provide external access through the firewall must be completed.

Availability Service

The Availability service is the name of the service that provides free/busy information to Outlook 2007 clients. It is integrated with the Autodiscover service (discussed in the following section) and improves on the Exchange 2003 version.

In Exchange 2003, the free/busy information was published in local public folders. In Exchange 2007, the Availability service is web-based and is accessed via a uniform resource locator (URL). The service can be load-balanced with Network Load Balancing (NLB) and can provide free/busy information in trusted cross-forest topologies.

The Autodiscover service provides the closest availability service URL to the client in the XML file.

The Availability service is installed by default on each CAS. Interestingly, there are no Exchange Management Console options for the Availability service. All interaction with the service is through the Exchange Management Shell.

Autodiscover Service

In previous versions of Exchange, profiles were a frequent source of headaches for administrators. The new Exchange 2007 Autodiscover feature automatically generates a profile from the user's email address and password. The service works with the clients and protocols listed in Table 17.4.

TABLE 17.4   Autodiscover Supported Clients and Protocols

Client	Protocol
Outlook 2007	MAPI (Exchange RPC)
	Outlook Anywhere (RPC over HTTP)
ActiveSync	ActiveSync

Autodiscover is an evolution of the Exchange 2003 MAPI referral feature, which would redirect the user to the appropriate Exchange back-end server and modify the user's profile. All that the user needed to provide was their alias and the name of any Exchange server. This was a very useful feature if the location of a user's mailbox would change from one server to another, as it would automatically redirect the user and permanently change the profile. This was a marked improvement over the Exchange 2000 profile generation, which would simply fail if the server or alias were not specified correctly. Any Exchange server would do and the user could type their full name, the account name, or even their email address. However, in Exchange 2003 the user still had to enter the information to get access.

With Outlook 2007 and Exchange 2007, it gets even better. The user simply provides authentication credentials and the Autodiscover service determines the user's profile settings. Then, the Autodiscover function of Outlook 2007 configures the user's profile automatically, basically filling in the information automatically. No manual entry of the server name or username is needed.

When the CAS is created, a virtual directory is created in the default website on the CAS server. The CAS role also creates Service Connection Point (SCP) objects in Active Directory.

When a client is domain joined and domain connected, the Outlook 2007 client looks up the SCP records in AD. The client picks the one in its site or a random one if there is none in its site. It then communicates with the CAS and gets an XML file with profile information. The Outlook client consumes this XML file to generate or update its profile.

The Autodiscover service can also be used by Outlook Anywhere and ActiveSync clients over the Internet, which requires SSL for security. The Outlook 2007 client uses the domain portion of the Simple Mail Transfer Protocol (SMTP) address of the user to locate the Autodiscover service. When the client communicates with the Autodiscover service over the Internet, the Outlook 2007 client expects that the URL for the service will be https://domain/autodiscover or https://autodiscover.domain/autodiscover/. For example, for the user chrisa@companyabc.com, the Autodiscover service URL will be https://www.companyabc.com/autodiscover/ or https://autodiscover.companyabc.com/autodiscover/.

17

The Autodiscover service requires the CAS. The Autodiscover service also requires that the forest in which it resides has the Exchange 2007 AD schema changes applied.

The functionality of the Autodiscover service and the Autodiscover feature can be tested using the Outlook 2007 client. The steps are as follows:

1. Launch Outlook 2007.

2. Press and hold the Ctrl key, and then select the Outlook icon in the system tray.

3. Select Test E-Mail AutoConfiguration in the menu.

4. The email address should already be populated, so enter the user's password.

5. Uncheck the Use Guessmart check box.

6. Click the AutoConfigure button.

7. Review the Results, Log, and XML tabs.

The log should show a series of three lines in the log with the text:

```
Attempting URL https://ex1.companyabc.com/Autodiscover/Autodiscover.xml found
➥though SCP
Autodiscover to https://ex1.companyabc.com/Autodiscover/Autodiscover.xml starting
Autodiscover to https://ex1.companyabc.com/Autodiscover/Autodiscover.xml succeeded
➥(0x00000000)
```

This shows that the Autodiscover URL was identified from the SCP record in AD. The client then attempts the autodiscovery and is finally successful in the last line.

The XML tab shows (data shown next) the actual file that is returned by the Autodiscover service. This not only includes information such as the user's server and alias, but also information such as the URLs for the Availability service, Unified Messaging server, and OWA.

```
<?xml version="1.0" encoding="utf-8"?>
<Autodiscover xmlns=
➥"http://schemas.microsoft.com/exchange/autodiscover/responseschema/2006">
➥<Response xmlns="http://schemas.microsoft.com/exchange/autodiscover/
➥outlook/responseschema/2006a">
  <User>
    <DisplayName>Chris Amaris</DisplayName>
    <LegacyDN>/o=CompanyABC/ou=Exchange Administrative Group
➥(FYDIBOHF23SPDLT)/cn=Recipients/cn=chrisa</LegacyDN>
    <DeploymentId>26902be6-4e19-4e1b-a758-a174748122a1</DeploymentId>
  </User>
  <Account>
    <AccountType>email</AccountType>
    <Action>settings</Action>
```

```
    <Protocol>
      <Type>EXCH</Type>
      <Server>ex1.companyabc.com</Server>
      <ServerDN>/o=CompanyABC/ou=Exchange Administrative Group
➡(FYDIBOHF23SPDLT)/cn=Configuration/cn=Servers/cn=EX1</ServerDN>
      <ServerVersion>7200825D</ServerVersion>
      <MdbDN>/o=CompanyABC/ou=Exchange Administrative Group
➡(FYDIBOHF23SPDLT)/cn=Configuration/cn=Servers/cn=EX1/
➡cn=Microsoft Private MDB</MdbDN>
      <ASUrl>https://ex1.companyabc.com/EWS/Exchange.asmx</ASUrl>
      <OOFUrl>https://ex1.companyabc.com/EWS/Exchange.asmx</OOFUrl>
      <UMUrl>https://ex1.companyabc.com/unifiedmessaging/service.asmx</UMUrl>
      <OABUrl>Public Folder</OABUrl>
    </Protocol>
    <Protocol>
      <Type>EXPR</Type>
      <Server>ex1.companyabc.com</Server>
      <ASUrl>https://ex1.companyabc.com/EWS/Exchange.asmx</ASUrl>
      <OOFUrl>https://ex1.companyabc.com/EWS/Exchange.asmx</OOFUrl>
      <UMUrl>https://ex1.companyabc.com/unifiedmessaging/service.asmx</UMUrl>
      <OABUrl>Public Folder</OABUrl>
      <AuthPackage>Basic</AuthPackage>
    </Protocol>
    <Protocol>
      <Type>WEB</Type>
      <Internal>
        <OWAUrl AuthenticationMethod="Basic">
➡https://ex1.companyabc.com/owa</OWAUrl>
      </Internal>
    </Protocol>
  </Account>
</Response></Autodiscover>
```

This information is presented in a neater form on the Results tab.

POP and IMAP

Post Office Protocol (POP) and Internet Message Access Protocol (IMAP) are legacy messaging protocols that are used mostly by home users and some third-party applications.

Exchange 2007 supports them for backward compatibility and the services are disabled by default. To use these protocols, the services must be started on the CAS.

Installing the Client Access Server

The installation of the Exchange 2007 CAS role is a straightforward task. This section covers the installation and configuration of a basic system to illustrate the concepts.

The installation of the CAS role assumes that Exchange 2007 is already installed on the target server. For detailed instructions on installing Exchange Server 2007, see Chapter 7, "Installing Exchange Server 2007."

Memory and CPU maximum recommendations for the CAS role are shown in Table 17.5. Beyond these capacities, there will be diminishing returns. These are based on the Exchange product group testing.

TABLE 17.5   CAS Role Server Maximums

Role	Maximum Processor	Maximum Memory
CAS	2 Dual Core	8GB

Installation of the CAS role modifies the base installation of Exchange 2007 and is done in what is termed Exchange Maintenance mode. The procedures in this section step through the build of a basic Exchange 2007 CAS system.

Installing the Client Access Server Role

This procedure assumes that the Exchange 2007 server has already been installed. The steps to add the CAS role are as follows:

1. In Control Panel, double click Add or Remove Programs.

2. Select Microsoft Exchange Server 2007.

3. Click Change to enter Exchange Maintenance mode.

4. Click Next.

5. Select the Client Access Role check box (shown in Figure 17.3), and click Next.

6. The installer will conduct readiness checks.

7. Click Install to install the CAS role.

8. After the installation has successfully completed, click Finish.

> **NOTE**
>
> The CAS role installation sets the default ASP.NET version, and the version for all ASP.NET scripts is revision level v2.0.5027. This setting might cause applications that require a different version. To fix this issue, the ASP.NET version needs to be changed for each affected virtual directory. Run the following command: `aspnet_regiis.exe -s <Metabase_Path_to_ virtual_directory>` from the appropriate version of ASP.NET for each affected virtual directory. The `aspnet_regiis.exe` for each of the installed versions of ASP.NET is in the `c:\windows\microsoft.net\framework\` in the appropriate version folder.

FIGURE 17.3   Client Access role installation.

Understanding the Hub Transport Server

The Hub Transport server is part of the internal Exchange infrastructure. It is the evolved form of the bridgehead server in Exchange 2003, which was really the name of a configuration rather than a specific server component. The Hub Transport server has been developed to provide a number of key features that Exchange customers have long been clamoring for, such as disclaimers and transport rules.

The Hub Transport server provides four major services:

▶ Mail flow

▶ Categorization

▶ Routing

▶ Delivery

These services can collectively check mail for any problems such as spam or viruses, check mail for appropriateness, append any information that the organization needs, and finally route mail to the correct destination.

There should be a Hub Transport server in every AD site where there is a Mailbox server for mail to flow and route correctly. Additional Hub Transport servers can be deployed for fault tolerance and load balancing, especially when paired with an Edge Transport server.

17

Mail Flow

The Hub Transport server is responsible for processing all mail that is sent within an Exchange 2007 organization. There is no exception to this. This allows the Hub Transport server to accomplish its other functions, such as categorization and routing.

It is important to understand that there are no exceptions to this rule. Thus, all mail flows through the Hub Transport servers. This ensures that the features that Hub Transport servers provide, such as transport rules, disclaimers, and journaling, are applied uniformly across the entire Exchange 2007 infrastructure.

Categorization

The categorizer does all the address lookups, route determination, and conversion of the content of messages. It determines where the messages are destined to and what rules apply to the messages (see the "Transport Rules" section later in the chapter).

It is at this stage that the various agents, such as the transport rules agent and the journaling agent, process mail as well.

Routing

Ther Hub Transport server determines the path to route mail to. This applies to all messages that are not destined for Mailbox servers in the local site. Messages that are destined for a Mailbox server that is in another AD site are routed to a Hub Transport server in that site, whereas messages destined for external recipients are routed to Edge Transport servers.

Microsoft Exchange 2007 is AD site aware and uses the AD site topology for routing internally. It computes the most efficient—that is lowest cost—route based on the sites and site links that it reads from Active Directory.

> **NOTE**
>
> It is critical to define the sites and the subnets that are associated with the sites for Exchange 2007 to route mail properly. These are fundamentally Active Directory design and deployment tasks, but not having it done properly can result in incorrect routing of email.
>
> This is true for all Active Directory–aware applications, such as Exchange 2007, Systems Management Server (SMS), distributed file system (DFS), and even Active Directory itself. Without a properly designed and deployed site and subnet infrastructure, they will fail or perform inefficiently.

The Hub Transport servers are intelligent and understand the architecture of the network based on the information in the sites and IP site links. If a message is destined for two different recipients, the Hub Transport servers will delay bifurcation of the message until the last possible hop.

This is illustrated in Figure 17.4. The user Chris in San Francisco sends a message to Sophia and Mike, who are in different locations (London and Frankfurt) and, thus, in different AD sites. A single message is routed through the transport from San Francisco to New York until it reaches Paris, which is the last possible hop for the message to split. The Paris Hub Transport server then bifurcates the message and sends one to London and one to Frankfurt.

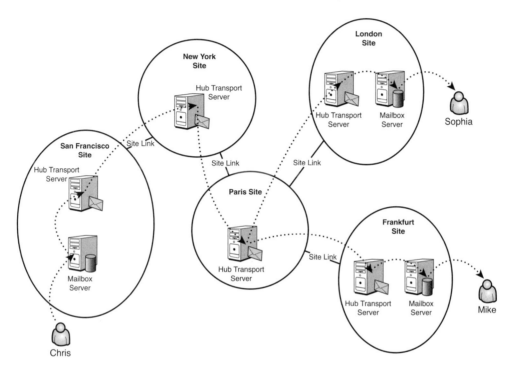

FIGURE 17.4   Message bifurcation.

Delivery

If the categorizer determines that the recipient of the messages is on a Mailbox server in the local AD site, the message is delivered directly to the Mailbox server.

Hub Transport Server Policy Compliance Features

Regulatory and best practices are driving organizations to create an increasing number of policies with regard to electronic messaging traffic. Organizations are required to enforce policies and ensure that all email complies with those policies. The Exchange 2007 Hub Transport server aids organizations in instantiating and enforcing those policies.

Some of the questions that organizations ask include the following:

▶ Is there a way to enforce corporate or regulatory email mandates?

▶ Can messages be identified for long-term document retention?

▶ Can the organization transmit confidential messages?

▶ Can the organization journal communications between individuals and groups?

▶ Can the organization add disclaimers to particular messages?

▶ Can the organization restrict messages by attachment size or type?

▶ Can certain messages be rejected by content or attachment name?

The Hub Transport server provides the answers to all of these questions.

Three transport agents built in to the Hub Transport role help provide this functionality: the transport rule agent, journaling agent, and AD RMS Prelicensing agent.

Transport Rules

This is a powerful tool for controlling message flow in the Exchange 2007 organization. Rules contain conditions, exceptions, and actions. They are stored in AD and are applied by the transport rule agent on all Hub Transport servers in the Exchange 2007 organization. This is different than for the Edge Transport servers, which each store their own transport rules. The Hub Transport rule conditions, exceptions, and action options are targeted at organizational policy and compliance.

NOTE

Transport rules allow the construction of what is termed ethical walls. This is a zone of noncommunication or restricted communication between distinct departments of a business or organization to prevent conflicts of interest that might result in the inappropriate release of sensitive information. For example, a large real estate organization might build an ethical wall between two business units that compete for the same clients.

For example, suppose an organization has a security policy that prohibits the users from sending passwords over email. So, the rule will key on the word "password" in various spellings (the condition). The rule does not interfere with the transmission, but does blind carbon copy (BCC) a security administrator to review the message (the action) and allow him to decide if there has been a violation of security policy.

To create the new transport rule, execute the following steps:

1. From the Exchange Management Console, expand the Organization folder and select the Hub Transport folder.

2. In the actions pane, select New Transport Rule.

3. Enter in a name for the rule, such as Password Email Capture Transport Rule.

4. Click Next.

5. Select the condition, in this case When the Subject Field or the Body of the Message Contains Specific Words.

6. Specify the values by clicking on the blue, hypertext "Specific Words" text.

7. Add "Password", "password", and "PASSWORD" into the word list, and click OK.

8. The words are displayed in the rule description.

9. Click Next.

10. Select the action to take by checking the appropriate box, in this case Blind Carbon Copy (Bcc) the Message to Address.

11. In the rule description pane, click the blue hypertext to select a recipient.

12. Select a recipient and click OK.

13. Click Next.

14. Leave the exceptions blank and click Next.

15. Click New to create the transport rule.

16. Click Finish to exit the wizard.

The rule will now BCC any message sent anywhere in the Exchange organization that contains the word "password" to the selected recipient.

After creation, rules take effect immediately. Rules can be disabled, edited, or removed after creation as well.

> **NOTE**
>
> Even though transport rules take effect immediately, the Hub Transport server relies on the recipient cache for recipient and distribution list information. This is updated every 4 hours, by default. Thus, changes to the distribution lists referenced in the transport rules might not be reflected for up to 4 hours.

Transport rules are stored in Active Directory. They are also replicated via Active Directory to all Hub Transport servers in the organization for consistency. The rules are stored in the Configuration partition under Service, Microsoft Exchange, <Organization Name> Transport Settings, Rules, Transport. Each rule is stored as a separate object in AD, which has the same name as the rule.

Disclaimers

Disclaimers are important to limit liability and comply with security and legal policies, as they make the position of the organization clear on each and every message that is sent by the organization. Disclaimers can take different legal aspects, such as:

- ▶ Breach of confidentiality and accidental breach of confidentiality

- ▶ Transmission of viruses

- ▶ Entering into contracts

- ▶ Negligent misstatement

- ▶ Employer's liability

They can also be used in interdepartmental email, provide helpful contact information, or simply ensure that the corporate address is on every email.

> **NOTE**
>
> A sample disclaimer covering breach of confidentiality and accidental breach of confidentiality:
>
> "This email and any files transmitted with it are confidential and intended solely for the use of the individual or entity to whom they are addressed. If you have received this email in error, please notify the system manager. This message contains confidential information and is intended only for the individual named. If you are not the named addressee, you should not disseminate, distribute, or copy this email. Please notify the sender immediately by email if you have received this email by mistake and delete this email from your system. If you are not the intended recipient, you are notified that disclosing, copying, distributing, or taking any action in reliance on the contents of this information is strictly prohibited."

In a welcome change from Exchange 2003, Exchange 2007 offers an easy and effective way to add disclaimers to messages traversing the messaging infrastructure. Historically, this was very difficult to do in the Exchange family.

The position of the disclaimer can be specified by the rule. Disclaimers can be either appended (the default and customary option) or prepended. Prepending the disclaimer is a way to ensure that it is read, but can interfere with the readability of the email.

The font of the disclaimer can be specified, although the font types, sizes, and colors are somewhat limited. Table 17.6 shows the different settings and values.

TABLE 17.6   Disclaimer Font Settings

Setting	Values
Font type	Arial, Courier New, or Verdana
Font size	Smallest, Smaller, Normal, Larger, or Largest
Font color	Black, Blue, Fuchsia, Gray, Green, Lime, Maroon, Navy, Olive, Purple, Red, Silver, Teal, White, or Yellow

An interesting option is the fallback action. Encrypted and other protected email cannot be modified, which interferes with the process of adding disclaimers. To deal with this, the disclaimer rule has three options to choose from when a disclaimer cannot be added directly:

▶ **Wrap (the default)**—The original message is wrapped in a new message and the disclaimer is appended to the new message.

▶ **Ignore**—The disclaimer is not added to the message and the message is delivered as normal.

▶ **Reject**—The message is not delivered. A nondelivery report (NDR) message is sent to the sender notifying them why it was not delivered.

Another useful option is the ability to create a separator line between the disclaimer text and the message. This helps the readability. If specified, the agent is smart enough to put the line in the appropriate position depending on if the disclaimer is appended or prepended.

Exchange does not check if disclaimers have been added to earlier messages, so the transport rule could wind up adding multiple disclaimers if not configured properly or if messages are forwarded or replied to. This tends to be more of a problem with internal disclaimers, rather than external disclaimers.

Disclaimers are basically a form of the transport rule and are implemented using them. See the previous section, "Transport Rules," for a discussion of the various transport rule options.

As an example of implementing a disclaimer, suppose an organization wants to add a disclaimer to all email that is destined for external recipients. To do this, complete the following steps:

1. From the Exchange Management Console, expand the Organization folder, and select the Hub Transport folder.

2. In the actions pane, select New Transport Rule.

3. Enter in a name for the rule, such as Corporate Disclaimer on All Outbound Email.

4. Click Next.

5. Select the condition, in this case Sent to Users Inside or Outside the Corporation.

6. Specify outside the corporation by clicking the blue, hypertext "Inside" text.

7. Select Outside from the Scope drop-down, and click OK.

8. The word *Outside* will be displayed in the rule description.

9. Click Next.

10. Select the action to take by checking the appropriate box, in this case Append Disclaimer Text Using Font, Color, and Fallback to Action if Unable to Apply.

17

11. In the rule description pane, click the blue, hypertext "text" to enter the disclaimer text, and click OK.

12. Leave the position as "prepend," and the fallback action as "wrap."

13. Click Next.

14. Leave the exceptions blank, and click Next.

15. Click New to create the disclaimer transport rule.

16. Click Finish to exit the wizard.

Now, the disclaimer text will be appended to all outgoing messages.

Journaling

In the new regulatory climate, there are numerous requirements for record retention and monitoring. This can include the requirement to journal some or all messages that traverse the messaging system. Some regulations that might be interpreted as requiring journaling include the following:

▶ Sarbanes-Oxley Act of 2002 (SOX)

▶ Gramm-Leach-Bliley Act (Financial Modernization Act)

▶ Health Insurance Portability and Accountability Act of 1996 (HIPAA)

▶ European Union Data Protection Directive (EUDPD)

▶ Japan's Personal Information Protection Act

The journaling agent on the Hub Transport server allows organizations to comply with these regulatory requirements by using journaling rules. This is a feature that is called premium journaling to distinguish it from the still available Exchange 2003 form of journaling called standard journaling.

NOTE

Within Exchange 2007, journaling comes in two flavors: standard and premium.

Premium journaling is a Hub Transport server function with journaling rules that is discussed in this section.

Standard journaling is really a Mailbox role feature and is configured in the properties of each database on the Mailbox server. It allows you to specify a journal recipient and all messages into and out of the database are journaled to that mailbox on the server. However, it does not allow you to control the journaling nor is it replicated throughout the organization.

Standard journaling was available as a feature in Exchange 2003 and continues to be available in Exchange 2007.

Journaling allows the Exchange 2007 to journal messages to a mailbox based on rules. This is a Hub Transport server role feature.

The scope of journaling can be:

▶ **Internal**—This applies to messages sent and received by recipients within the Exchange 2007 organization.

▶ **External**—This applies to messages sent to and from recipients outside of the Exchange 2007 organization.

▶ **Global**—This applies to all messages regardless of destination.

For example, suppose an organization is required by statute to retain records of all email that is sent or received by the organization. The organization will store it in a mailbox named "journal." To create the journal rule, execute the following steps:

1. From the Exchange Management Console, expand the Organization folder, and select the Hub Transport folder.

2. In the actions pane, select New Journaling Rule.

3. Enter the rule name, such as Journal All Email.

4. Click the Browse button to specify the journal email address (this is the mailbox that will hold the journal).

5. Select the journal mailbox, in this case Journal, and click OK.

6. Make sure Global is selected as the scope, which is the default.

7. Click New to create the rule.

8. Click Finish to close the wizard.

Now, all messages through the organization will be copied to the journal mailbox, allowing all messages to be retained and enabling the organization to meet its statutory requirements.

After creation, journal rules take effect immediately. Rules can be disabled, edited, or removed after creation as well.

> **NOTE**
>
> Even though journal rules take effect immediately, the Hub Transport server relies on the recipient cache for recipient and distribution list information. This is updated every 4 hours, by default. Thus, changes to the distribution lists referenced in the transport rules might not be reflected for up to 4 hours.

Similar to transport rules, journal rules are stored in Active Directory. They are also replicated via Active Directory to all Hub Transport servers in the organization for consistency.

17

The rules are stored in the Configuration partition under Service, Microsoft Exchange, <Organization Name> Transport Settings, Rules, Journal. Each rule is stored in AD as a separate object, which has the same name as the rule.

Interestingly, the messages are not simply transferred to the journaling mailbox by the journaling agent on the Hub Transport server. Rather, they are converted by the journaling agent into a journal report format and then sent to the journaling mailbox. Each message creates a corresponding journal report message. In the message, key fields, such as Sender, Subject, Message ID, and To fields, are placed into the body of the report in a separate line preceded by the field name (for example, Sender: chrisa@companyabc.com or Subject: Vacation). This format allows for easy parsing of the reports by automated tools. The actual message is attached to the journal report message.

Message Classification

Message classification applies a designation that helps guide the intended usage of the information contained in the email. This differs from Rights Management Services (RMS), which enforces the restrictions. An example of a classification is the built in Attorney/ Client Privileged (A/C) classification shown in Figure 17.5. On selecting the A/C Privileged classification, recipients would see the informational header advising them of the message class.

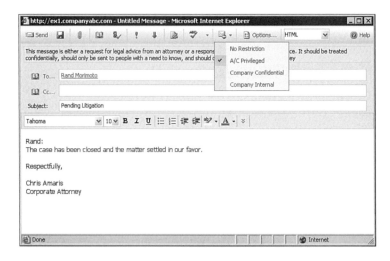

FIGURE 17.5   Message classification.

The classification is retained by the email until it leaves the organization. This applies even if the message is forwarded to a third party within the organization.

Although classification is informational by default, transport rules can be created that control and enforce the classification. For example, a transport rule could be created that would prevent a message with the A/C designation from being sent external to the company. See the "Transport Rules" section earlier in this chapter.

Message classification requires Outlook 2007 or Exchange 2007 OWA. This feature needs to be enabled in Outlook 2007 by changing the Registry, generating a classifications definition file on the Exchange 2007 server, and finally copying the file to each client.

First, modify the Registry by adding a key and three values. The key and values to create are as follows:

```
[HKEY_CURRENT_USER\Software\Microsoft\Office\12.0\Common\Policy]
"AdminClassificationPath"="c:\\Class\Classifications.xml"
"EnableClassifications"=dword:00000001
"TrustClassifications"=dword:00000001
```

This needs to be done on each client.

> **CAUTION**
>
> Incorrectly editing the Registry can cause serious problems that might require you to reinstall your operating system. Problems resulting from editing the Registry incorrectly might not be able to be resolved. Before editing the Registry, back up any valuable data.

Next, create a directory `c:\class\` on the Exchange server to receive the XML file with the classification definition. The following command generates the XML file referenced in the Registry value. This needs to be run in the Exchange Management Shell and the directory needs to be changed to `c:\program files\microsoft\exchange server\scripts\` before running the command:

```
"ExACPrivileged"|Get-MessageClassification | ./Export-OutlookClassification.msh >
c:\Class\Classifications.xml
```

Finally, copy the resulting `Classifications.XML` file to each of the clients. After launching Outlook 2007, the classifications will be available.

Interestingly, the classifications come preenabled in Outlook Web Access without having to go through the gyrations needed for Outlook 2007.

The message classifications can be modified and extended using the `Set-MessageClassification` and the `New-MessageClassification` cmdlets in the Exchange Management Shell. There are no message classification options in the Exchange Management Console.

Rights Management and the Hub Transport Server

The Hub Transport server has an agent, the AD RMS Prelicensing agent, which facilitates the use of RMS in Exchange 2007. It essentially acquires an RMS license before delivering the email to the user's desktop. This allows the user to open the email while disconnected or open messages sent across forest boundaries. It also provides access to rights-protected email through Outlook Anywhere or Outlook Web Access.

The agent is not enabled by default. The high-level steps to configure the AD RMS Prelicensing agent are as follows:

1. Install the RMS Client with SP2 on the Hub Transport server.

2. Register the `Rightsmanagementwrapper.dll` in the Exchange Management Shell.

3. Enable the agent in the Exchange Management Shell using the command `Enable-TransportAgent "AD RMS Prelicensing Agent"`.

4. Restart the MSExchangeTransport service.

Proper authentication and access control configurations are required to enable the AD RMS Prelicensing agent running as a network service to access the precertified URL found in the Active Directory of the other forest.

In addition, it is a requirement that the RMS server clusters are upgraded to Microsoft Windows Rights Management Services (RMS) Service Pack 2 and the RMS Client on the Hub Transport server be upgraded to RMS Client with SP2 Beta – x64.

Prioritization of Agents

Each of the agents in the Hub Transport server has a different priority and trigger events, although the latter overlap in some respects. Understanding these helps determine the net effect of the agents' activities in complex situations.

The hub transport agents' priority and trigger events are listed in Table 17.7.

TABLE 17.7   Hub Transport Agents Priority and Triggers

Agent Name	Priority	SMTP Trigger Events
Transport rule agent	1	OnRoutedMessage
Journaling agent	2	OnSubmittedMessage, OnRoutedMessage
AD RMS Prelicensing agent	4	OnRoutedMessage

For example, assume an organization was journaling and adding disclaimers to outbound messages. Based on the priority of the agents in the table, the messages should be journaled with the disclaimer text appended to them.

This is because the disclaimers are implemented by the transport rule agent, which has a higher priority than the journaling agent. Thus, the disclaimer rule is applied prior to the journaling rule. A quick inspection of the journal report and its attached message confirms this.

> **NOTE**
>
> Transport agents have full access to all emails that travel through the Hub Transport server, which can impact the security and stability of the message flow.

Transport Pipeline

The transport pipeline reflects the internal routing of messages within the Hub Transport server. The elements of this are shown in Figure 17.6. These consist of the following:

▶ SMTP Receive

▶ Submission queue

▶ Categorizer

▶ Mailbox delivery queue

▶ Remote delivery queue

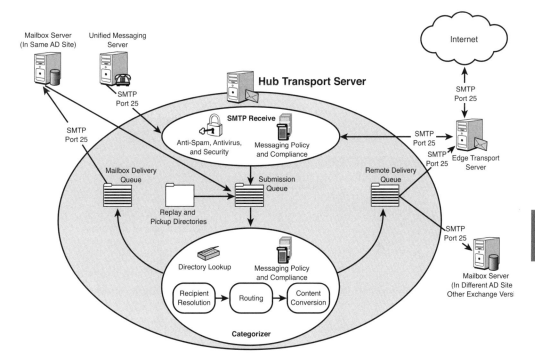

FIGURE 17.6   Transport pipeline.

The figure also illustrates the relationships that the Hub Transport server role has with the other Exchange 2007 roles.

Messages get into the transport pipeline onto a Hub Transport server through one of four ways, as shown in Figure 17.6:

▶ Through the SMTP Receive connector

▶ Through files being placed in the pickup or replay directories

▶ Through the submission queue by the mailbox store driver

▶ Through submission from an agent (not shown)

After the messages have gotten into the pipeline, they flow through the pipeline. The various segments of that pipeline are discussed in the following sections.

SMTP Receive Connector

In the Hub Transport server, the SMTP Receive Connector accepts SMTP (port 25) messages. Basic server-level policies are applied, such as the authorization of the remote IP address of the server and authentication of the server.

If installed on the Hub Transport server, the messages coming into the SMTP Receive Connector are also processed by antivirus and antispam services.

If they pass the SMTP Receive Connector, the messages flow down the transport pipeline to the submission queue.

Submission Queue

The submission queue takes messages from the SMTP Receive Connector, as well as from the mailbox store driver, the pickup and replay directories, and from agents such as the transport rules agent.

When messages enter the submission queue, the `OnSubmittedMessage` event activates. This triggers the journaling agent.

The messages are held in the submission queue until they are pulled out one at a time (first in, first out) by the categorizer.

Categorizer

The categorizer processes each message that it retrieves from the submission queue. The categorizer does four main steps:

▶ Resolving recipient addressing

▶ Determining routes to recipients

▶ Converting message content

▶ Rules processing

The last step, rule processing, is where the agents that trigger on the `OnRoutedMessage` event activate. On the Hub Transport server, that is all the default agents, including the rules transport agent, the journaling agent, and the AD RMS Prelicensing agent.

Mailbox Delivery Queue

The mailbox delivery queue handles messages that are destined for local delivery, that is, messages for recipients in Mailbox servers in the same site as the Hub Transport server.

These messages are pulled off the queue one by one and delivered to the user's mailbox by the store driver.

Remote Delivery Queue

The remote delivery queue handles messages to be routed to other Hub Transport servers within the forest for messages destined for other Mailbox servers within the organization but in a different AD site. The remote delivery queue also handles messages destined for external mail systems in other forests and for the Edge Transport servers.

Messages in the remote delivery queue are sent out via the SMTP Send Connector.

Installing the Hub Transport Server

The installation of the Exchange 2007 Hub Transport server role is a straightforward task. This section covers the installation and configuration of a basic system to illustrate the concepts.

The installation of the Hub Transport role assumes that Exchange 2007 is already installed on the target server. For detailed instructions on installing Exchange Server 2007, see Chapter 7.

Memory and CPU maximum recommendations for the Hub Transport server role are shown in Table 17.8.

TABLE 17.8   Hub Transport Server Role Server Maximums

Role	Maximum Processor	Maximum Memory
Hub Transport server	2 Dual Core	8GB

Beyond these capacities, there will be diminishing returns. These are based on the Exchange product group testing.

> **NOTE**
>
> The Hub Transport role cannot be installed on an Exchange server that is a node in a cluster.

The first step is to install the Hub Transport server role. The following procedure assumes that the Exchange 2007 server has already been installed. The steps to add the Hub Transport server role are as follows:

1. In Control Panel, double click on Add or Remove Programs.

2. Select Microsoft Exchange Server 2007.

3. Click Change to enter Exchange Maintenance mode.

4. Click Next.

5. Select the Hub Transport Role check box (shown in Figure 17.7), and click Next.

FIGURE 17.7   Hub Transport role installation.

6. The installer will conduct readiness checks.

7. Click Install to install the Hub Transport server role.

8. After the installation has successfully completed, click Finish.

Configure SMTP Send Connectors

When a Hub Transport server is installed, there is no SMTP Send Connector installed. Without an SMTP Send Connector, the Hub Transport server can receive mail but not send mail.

The SMTP Send Connector can be configured as follows:

▶ **Internal**—For routing to other Hub Transport servers and Edge Transport servers

▶ **Legacy**—For routing to Exchange 2003 and previous versions

▶ **Custom**—For routing to non-Exchange servers

The steps to configure the SMTP Send Connector are as follows:

1. Launch the Exchange Management Console.

2. Expand the Organization Configuration branch, and select the Hub Transport folder.

3. In the actions pane, select New Send Connector.

4. Enter in a name for the connector.

5. Enter in the intended use of the connector, such as Custom.

6. Add the address space for which the SMTP connector will send mail to, typically "*".

7. Click Next.

8. Click Next to route using the domain name system (DNS).

9. Click Next to use the current server as the source server.

10. Click New to create the SMTP Send Connector.

11. Click Finish to close the wizard.

Summary

The new and improved roles in Exchange 2007 are the CAS and Hub Transport server roles. In reality, these two roles are really specializations and evolutions of the original Exchange front-end and bridgehead server concepts, along with the Edge Transport server. The CAS and the Hub Transport server provide both sophisticated external client access and controlled routing and delivery throughout the organization.

The two new roles within the Exchange 2007 family offer a wealth of features and functions that Exchange administrators have been clamoring for. Ranging from the transport rules and journaling on the Hub Transport servers to Remote Wipe on the CASs, these features make Exchange 2007 the premier messaging system.

Best Practices

The following are best practices from this chapter:

▶ Have a CAS in every AD site to ensure that users connect to the CAS closest to their mailbox.

▶ For client access to work correctly, you must install a CAS in each AD site that has a Mailbox server.

▶ Deploy Exchange ActiveSync mailbox policies to ensure remote management of mobile devices.

▶ For email messages to flow correctly, you must install the Hub Transport server role in each AD site.

17

▶ Given the dependence of the Hub Transport server on AD sites for routing email, it is critical to correctly design and deploy the AD site architecture.

▶ Be careful with the order of disclaimers and the number of disclaimers to avoid cluttering emails.

▶ Create ActiveSync mailbox policies to ensure the manageability of the users' mobile devices.

▶ Always append disclaimers, rather than prepend disclaimers.

PART VI

Exchange Server 2007 Administration and Management

IN THIS PART

CHAPTER 18

Administering an Exchange Server 2007 Environment

Exchange Administrator Roles in Exchange Server 2007

As with previous versions of Exchange, the ability to administer an Exchange Server 2007 environment is based on permissions. Earlier versions like Exchange Server 2003 based its security around the concept of Exchange roles. These three Exchange roles were basically security groups that were granted specific administrative permissions in the Exchange environment, and were easily configured using the Delegation Wizard:

▶ Exchange Full Administrator

▶ Exchange Administrator

▶ Exchange View Only Administrator

However, this model had some limitations. The Exchange Administrator group was too large, and many organizations wanted the ability to manage their security and permissions model at the individual server level.

In addition, there was no clear differentiation between administrators of users and groups by the Active Directory administrators and the Exchange recipient administrators. Exchange administrators had to be granted a very high level of permissions in Active Directory to perform Exchange recipient–related tasks.

In Microsoft Exchange Server 2007, these Exchange roles have been renamed "Exchange administrator roles," and have been completely redesigned. The Exchange security and permissions model has been improved by the following changes:

▶ Exchange has several new/redefined administrator roles that are similar to the built-in Windows Server security groups.

▶ The Exchange Management Console (formerly known as the Exchange System Manager) and the Exchange Management Shell can be used to administer security groups. You can now view, add, or remove members from any administrator role directly in the Exchange Management interface.

▶ When modifying an administrator role membership, no access control list (ACL) setting is required. The administrator roles are statically added to the appropriate object ACLs during setup.

The new predefined groups for Exchange configuration are as follows:

▶ Exchange Organization Administrators

▶ Exchange Recipient Administrators

▶ Exchange Server Administrators

▶ Exchange View-Only Administrators

During the Exchange setup process, when the Active Directory environment is being prepared, all of the administrator roles, with the exception of the Exchange Server Administrators, are created in the new Microsoft Exchange Security Groups container in Active Directory.

By granting a user membership in one of these groups, you allow them to manage Exchange data in Active Directory. These groups can manage three types of Exchange data:

▶ **Global data**—Data stored in an Active Directory configuration container that is not associated with a particular server is known as global data. This includes mailbox policies, address lists, and the configuration of Exchange unified messaging. Global data generally impacts the entire organization, rather than individual users or groups. Potentially, it can affect all users in your company. Membership in this group should be kept to a limited number of skilled, trusted administrators.

▶ **Recipient data**—Exchange 2007 recipients are Active Directory user objects that are mail-enabled. Recipient data includes mail-enabled contacts, distribution groups, and mailboxes.

▶ **Server data**—Exchange server data is stored in Active Directory under the node for that specific server. Server data includes receive connectors, virtual directories, and server-specific configuration settings, as well as mailbox and storage group data.

Exchange Organization Administrators Role

The Exchange Organization Administrators role provides members with full access to all Exchange objects and properties throughout the organization. During the Exchange setup procedure, ForestPrep creates this group in the Microsoft Exchange Security Groups container within Active Directory Users and Computers.

Exchange Organization Administrators have the highest level of permissions in the Exchange environment. Performing any task that affects the entire organization requires this level of administrative rights. For example, membership in this group is required to create or delete connectors, change server policies, or change any global configuration settings.

By adding a user to this group, you grant the following permissions to that user:

▶ Owner permission on the Exchange organization in the Configuration container of Active Directory. As an owner, the user has full control over the Exchange organization data located in the configuration container. Furthermore, the user has full control over the local Exchange server administrator group.

▶ Read access to all domain user containers in AD. When the first Exchange 2007 server is installed in a domain, Exchange grants this permission for that domain.

▶ Write access to all Exchange-specific attributes in all domain user containers in Active Directory. This access is set during the setup of the first Exchange 2007 server in the domain.

▶ Owner of all local server configuration data. This permission gives members full control over the local Exchange server. This access is granted during the setup of each Exchange server.

Exchange Recipient Administrators Role

Exchange Recipient Administrators have permissions to modify Exchange properties on any object in Active Directory, including users, contacts, groups, public folder objects, or dynamic distribution lists. Like the previous role, this role is created during ForestPrep in the Exchange setup procedure in the Microsoft Exchange Security Groups container in Active Directory. In addition, this role also allows you to manage Unified Messaging mailbox settings and Client Access mailbox settings.

Members of this role have the following permissions:

▶ Read access to all the domain user containers in Active Directory (providing the domain has had DomainPrep run)

▶ Write access to all the Exchange-specific attributes on the domain user containers in Active Directory (again, the domain must have had DomainPrep run)

18

> **NOTE**
>
> If a domain has not had DomainPrep completed, members of this group will *not* have permission to that domain. So, it is important to remember, when adding a new Exchange domain, make sure you run DomainPrep in that domain to grant the Exchange administrator role groups the appropriate permissions.

Exchange Server Administrators Role

The Exchange Server Administrators role only has access to the local server Exchange configuration data. This data might be stored either in Active Directory, or on the actual Exchange 2007 server. This role is designed to give limited access to administrators who are authorized to administer a particular server, but who are not authorized to perform tasks that have a global impact in the Exchange environment.

A common use for this role might be an Exchange administrator in a remote site, who is able to administer the Exchange server(s) in their location, but who cannot add or delete users to the organization.

After a user is added to the Exchange Server Administrators role, they become a member of the Exchange Server Administrator (<Server Name>) group, which is created by Exchange 2007 during setup. Members of this role have the following permissions:

- ▶ "Owner" access to all local server configuration data. Members of this group have full control over the configuration data of the local server itself.

- ▶ Local administrator on the computer on which Exchange is installed.

- ▶ Member of the Exchange View-Only Administrators role.

Exchange View-Only Administrators Role

The final (and least powerful) of the administrator roles is the Exchange View-Only Administrators role. Administrators assigned to this role have read-only access to the entire Exchange organization tree in the Active Directory Configuration container and read-only access to all the Windows domain containers that have Exchange recipients.

The View-Only Administrators role is created in the Microsoft Exchange Security Groups container in Active Directory during the Exchange ForestPrep process.

Required Roles to Install Exchange Server 2007

If you are installing the first Exchange Server 2007 into an environment that has an existing Exchange presence, you must prepare the Active Directory schema. To accomplish this, you must be logged on as a user who is a member of the Exchange Schema Administrators group.

If the schema has already been prepped, and you are installing the first Exchange 2007 server in your environment, you must log on as a member of the Enterprise Administrators group.

Finally, if you are installing an additional Exchange 2007 server into an environment where one already exists, you must log on to an account that is a member of the Exchange Organization Administrators group. In addition, the account must be a member of the local Administrators group on that computer.

Administrative Tools

In Exchange 2000 Server and Exchange Server 2003, administrators had to use a combination of the Active Directory Users and Computers utility and the Exchange System Manager to manage and configure mail-enabled user accounts. This has changed in Exchange Server 2007. With Exchange 2007, much of the administration process can be performed within the new Exchange 2007 Exchange Management Console (EMC) tool or from an included scripting language called Exchange Management Shell (EMS).

Exchange Management Console

In Exchange 2007, the primary management utility is now called the Exchange Management Console. The Exchange Management Console is a Microsoft Management Console (MMC) 3.0–based utility that allows administrators to view and modify the configuration of Exchange Server 2007 organizations utilizing a graphical user interface (GUI). In addition, the Exchange Management Console snap-in can be added to custom MMC-based tools.

The Exchange Management Console is supported and can be installed on any Exchange 2007 server. When utilized on Exchange 2007 servers housing the Exchange 2007 Hub Transport, Client Access, Unified Messaging, and/or Mailbox server roles, the console displays all servers in the organization and includes all console tree nodes. However, if the Exchange server has the Edge Transport server role installed, the console only displays the Edge Transport server role.

Improvements to the Exchange Management Console

In Exchange 2000/2003, the GUI interface was known as the Exchange System Manager (ESM). In Exchange Server 2007, Microsoft has completely redesigned the interface, so it is only fitting that they offer the utility a new name as well. The Exchange Management Console is more intuitive and organized than previous versions, which were somewhat tedious to utilize.

One other significant change is the integration of recipient management directly into the Exchange Management Console. With previous versions of Exchange, the configuration of recipients was accomplished in the Active Directory Users and Computers application.

The new interface consists of three sections, the console tree, the results pane, and the action pane, as shown in Figure 18.1.

18

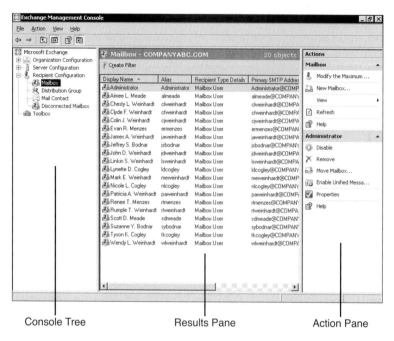

Console Tree   Results Pane   Action Pane

FIGURE 18.1   Exchange Management Console components.

The console tree is on the left side of the management console and consists of four nodes:

▶ **Organization Configuration**—This section is used to configure Exchange global data. Data residing here applies to all servers in your organization that hold a particular role. For example, email address policies and the Offline Address Book (OAB) can be managed from this node.

▶ **Server Configuration**—This section is used to manage the configuration of all Exchange servers and the server's child objects. Examples of these child objects are server databases and protocols.

▶ **Recipient Configuration**—This section is used to manage settings for email recipients throughout your organization. Exchange mailboxes, distribution groups, contacts, and disabled mailboxes can be managed from this node.

▶ **Toolbox**—Finally, the Toolbox includes additional tools that are useful when managing an Exchange 2007 organization. The Toolbox consists of the Exchange Best Practices Analyzer, Database Troubleshooting and Recovery Management utilities, Message Tracking and Mail Flow utilities, and several other troubleshooting and performance utilities.

NOTE

Additional tools can be added to the Exchange Toolbox and can be downloaded from the Microsoft Exchange website located at http://www.microsoft.com/exchange.

The console tree can be shown or hidden by clicking Show/Hide Console Tree on the Exchange Management Console toolbar.

The results pane, located in the center of the console, displays a collection of objects that an administrator can select, based on the object that is selected in the console tree.

Finally, the action pane is located on the right side of the console. This pane lists all actions that are available to administrators based on the items selected in the console tree or results pane. Like the console tree, the action pane can be shown or hidden by clicking Show/Hide on the console toolbar. Bear in mind, even with the action pane hidden, you can still access the relevant actions through context menus available by right-clicking the object.

Exchange Server 2007 Final Deployment Guides

After Exchange 2007 has been installed, the first time the Exchange Management Console is launched, a new screen appears, the Exchange Server 2007 Finalize Deployment page. This page details a series of tasks that are recommended by Microsoft to ensure the server performs properly. This page can be reviewed at a later date by selecting Microsoft Exchange at the top of the console tree.

The Finalize Deployment page might show tasks such as the following:

▶ Configure domains for which you will accept email

▶ Subscribe the Edge Transport server

▶ Create a postmaster mailbox

It is strongly recommended that you review this page to finalize the server configuration.

In addition, there is another tab on the page labeled End-to-End Scenario. This page contains additional tasks and instructional guides that will assist you with items such as the following:

▶ Managing Outlook Anywhere

▶ Securing your Exchange server from viruses, worms, and other malware

▶ Configure your system for the Rights Management Services (RMS) Policy Application Agent

As with the Finalize Deployment page, these items should be reviewed for applicability in your environment.

The Exchange Management Console

Unlike the Exchange System Manager of the past, an administrator no longer selects a specific server from the console tree to view its resources; instead a server role is selected in the console tree and a list of the servers in your organization that hold that role are shown in the results pane. From there, you can select a specific service and see the available options in the action pane.

Items in the results pane can be filtered based on several expressions. This allows an administrator to filter, or focus on, a subset of items that meet specific criteria. Filters can be made up of one or more expressions and allow minute control over which items are displayed in the results pane.

To create a filter, click Create Filter located in the upper-left corner of the results pane. A filter is made up of one or more administrator-defined expressions. Each expression contains three parts: an attribute, an operator, and a value.

The attributes that are available are determined by the object for which you are creating a filter. For example, when selecting a Mailbox server, the available attributes are Cluster, Edition, Name, Product ID, Role, Site, and Version.

The operators that are available are based on the attribute you selected. Some of the possible operators are Equals, Does Not Equal, Is Present, or Starts With.

Finally, the list of values is also based on the attribute selected. Some values, such as Name or Site, can be typed in to match the name or site of an object in your organization. Others, such as when selecting the attribute of Edition or Role, are selected from a drop-down list.

To add additional expressions (and make the filter more restrictive), click the Add Expression box and input another attribute, operator, and value.

After you have set the expressions that you want, you can click Apply Filter. The expressions you configured are applied to the results pane, effectively filtering the results so that only the objects that match the expression are shown.

Applied expressions can be modified on the fly—simply click on the attribute, operator, or value, make the changes you desire, and click Apply Filter. This feature can be extremely useful when you make a mistake and find that you have "filtered" yourself into an empty results pane.

To remove any of the created expressions, simply click Remove Expression located to the right of it. This button resembles a red X. However, after you have removed an expression, you must click Apply Filter again to implement the change.

The Exchange Management Shell

New in Exchange 2007, the Exchange Management Shell (EMS) is a command-line management interface that can be utilized to perform server administration in an Exchange 2007 organization. Tasks that have had to be done manually within the confines of the management application in previous versions can now be scripted, allowing administrators increased flexibility for repetitive tasks. The Exchange Management Shell, shown in Figure 18.2, looks similar to the command prompt (cmd.exe), in that it opens a window with a black background and a text interface. However, you will notice immediately that certain commands and pointers are highlighted in yellow text, rather than the traditional monochromatic command prompt.

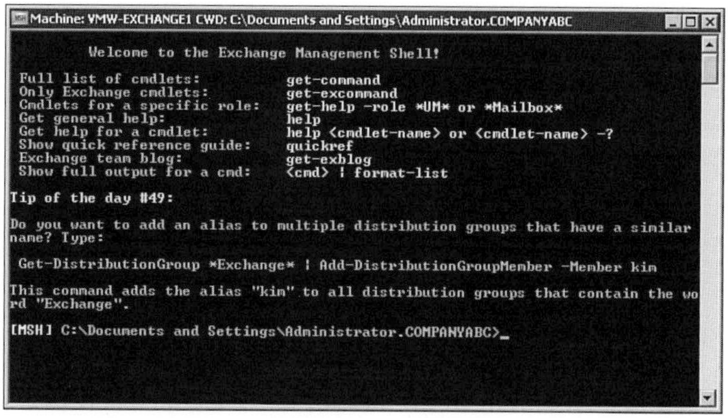

```
Machine: VMW-EXCHANGE1 CWD: C:\Documents and Settings\Administrator.COMPANYABC

       Welcome to the Exchange Management Shell!

Full list of cmdlets:            get-command
Only Exchange cmdlets:           get-excommand
Cmdlets for a specific role:     get-help -role *UM* or *Mailbox*
Get general help:                help
Get help for a cmdlet:           help <cmdlet-name> or <cmdlet-name> -?
Show quick reference guide:      quickref
Exchange team blog:              get-exblog
Show full output for a cmd:      <cmd> | format-list

Tip of the day #49:

Do you want to add an alias to multiple distribution groups that have a similar
name? Type:

 Get-DistributionGroup *Exchange* | Add-DistributionGroupMember -Member kim

This command adds the alias "kim" to all distribution groups that contain the wo
rd "Exchange".

[MSH] C:\Documents and Settings\Administrator.COMPANYABC>_
```

FIGURE 18.2   Exchange Management Shell.

With the Exchange Management Shell, administrators can manage every aspect of Exchange 2007, including the creation and management of new email accounts, the configuration of Simple Mail Transfer Protocol (SMTP) connectors and transport agents, or properties of database stores. Every task that can be accomplished within the Exchange Management Console can now be accomplished from a command line. More so, there are tasks that can be accomplished in the shell that can *not* be performed in the console.

With the new Exchange Management Shell, administrators now have a flexible scripting platform that is much easier to take advantage of than using Microsoft Visual Basic scripts in previous revisions. According to Microsoft, "What once took hundreds of lines in Visual Basic scripts can now be accomplished easily with as little as one line of code."

The Exchange Management Shell does not use text as the basis for communicating with Exchange 2007, instead using an object model that is based on the Microsoft .NET platform. This allows the shell commands to apply the output from one command to subsequent commands when they are run.

Exchange Management Shell Key Features

The Exchange Management Shell has a number of command functions, support options, and customization features. The following is a list key features of the Exchange Management Shell:

- ▶ **Command-line interface**—Unlike the GUI interface of the Exchange Management Console (and the Exchange System Manager before it), the command-line interface allows you to access and modify Exchange 2007 features and their values. In addition, it allows you to perform repetitive tasks that would be time consuming and tedious through the GUI interface of the Exchange Management Console and the Exchange System Manager before it.

- ▶ **Piping of data between commands**—One of the shortcomings of scripting Exchange tasks prior to Exchange Server 2007, was that there was no way to take the output of one command and utilize it directly as the input for other commands.

18

Output data had to be stored and recalled utilizing many lines of code. With the Exchange Management Shell, the ability to "pipeline" can help you increase your productivity with programmatic changes. Pipelining allows you to utilize the output from one command as input in other commands, so you can now easily perform complex operations utilizing criteria applied to filtering commands that then supply the objects to be modified to commands down the "pipe."

▶ **Object-oriented data handling**—Because the resulting output from any command in the Exchange Management Shell is an object, all output can be acted upon and processed by other commands with little to no changes. Commands that are intended to work together on particular feature sets accept the output from other commands in the same feature set.

▶ **Extensive support for scripting**—Whether you are performing multiple mailbox creations or modifications, monitoring the performance of several servers, or any other automated administrative task, the Exchange Management Shell provides a powerful object model environment based on the .NET platform.

▶ **Access `cmd.exe` commands**—Although the Exchange Management Shell has a similar look and feel to the command prompt (`cmd.exe`), it is much more powerful. Through the shell, not only can you utilize any and all commands that are available through the command prompt, but you also can take the output from those commands and perform actions based on that output. In addition, you can integrate the output into data that you can then provide to another command.

▶ **Trusted scripts**—Administrators have long been concerned that the ability to run scripts in an organization could be dangerous. Now, to improve security, the Exchange Management Shell requires that all scripts are digitally signed before they are allowed to run. This feature is intended to prevent malicious users from inserting a dangerous or harmful script in the Exchange Management Shell. Before a script can be run, the administrator must specifically "trust" it, helping to protect the entire organization.

▶ **Profile customization**—The Exchange Management Shell provides a powerful, easy-to-use interface with the default installation. However, administrators might want to customize the interface by adding shortcuts to frequently used commands. In addition, an administrator can adjust the interface to suit his or her tasks. This can be accomplished by editing the personal Exchange Management Shell profile. With this, you can control how your interface is configured or even specify commands to automatically run when the Exchange Management Shell starts. Furthermore, profile customization allows you to assign scripts to different aliases that you use frequently in the daily administration of your Exchange 2007 organization.

▶ **Extensible shell support**—An administrator can change the way data is displayed within the Exchange Management Shell because the application uses Extensible Markup Language (XML) to let you modify many aspects of its behavior. Programmers can even create new commands that integrate with the built-in Exchange Management Shell commands. This open platform gives administrators more control over their Exchange environment than ever before.

▶ **Tip of the day**—Although perhaps not as impressive as the preceding features, the author was pleased to see a "tip of the day" appear each time the Exchange Management Shell is opened. The tip of the day offers advice on how to perform specific tasks within the shell, and lists the command and proper syntax for its use.

Managing Exchange Server 2007 Remotely

Because Exchange Server 2007 sits on top of Microsoft Windows Server 2003, there are several inherent options for remotely managing your Exchange environment. This can allow you to reduce costs by allowing administrators to manage systems from remote locations, rather than having the need to physically sit in front of each system.

Commonly used remote management tools include the following:

▶ **Microsoft Management Console**—Otherwise known as the MMC, this console provides a unified interface for most graphical management utilities provided by Microsoft. The latest revision of the Microsoft Management Console, MMC 3.0, has improved functionality for snap-ins that were created specifically to interact with it. The Exchange Management Console is such a snap-in. It was designed specifically to take advantage of the MMC 3.0 infrastructure.

▶ **Remote Desktop for Administration**—Formerly known as Terminal Services in Remote Administration mode, Remote Desktop for Administration allows administrators to access the desktop of any computer running Microsoft Windows Server 2003 and administer the server as if they were logged on to the system locally. However, it is important to note, Remote Administration is NOT "application serving," meaning that certain applications might require special installation scripts or environment management to perform properly in a remote session. These are provided when you use Terminal Services through a terminal server, but are not available for Remote Desktop for Administration. In short, although Remote Desktop for Administration is an adequate substitute for Terminal Services under most circumstances, it is not a complete replacement.

▶ **Telnet**—Although not the strongest or flashiest of tools, Telnet still comes in handy for administrators who want to test basic SMTP connectivity on Exchange servers. To determine if a server is responding to SMTP requests, enter the following command from a command prompt:

telnet *servername portnumber* <enter>, where *servername* is either the fully qualified domain name (FQDN) or the IP address of the server you are connecting to, and *portnumber* is the port the server is using for SMTP messages. For example, by typing:

telnet server1 25 <enter>, you would be contacting the server named *server1* on port 25. If the command works properly, and the server is responding to SMTP requests, you should receive a response that reads something like:

220 server1 Microsoft ESMTP Mail Service ready at ...

Although several versions of SMTP servers are in existence, and you might receive different responses from the server in question, the important part is that you receive the 220 response with the name of the server and the version of SMTP.

Exchange Server 2007 and 2000/2003 Co-existence

Exchange Server 2007 can be installed into an existing Exchange 2000/2003 organization. This method of introduction will generally be done as one step in the migration process.

Once Exchange 2007 has been introduced into the 2000/2003 environment, the organization is considered to be in a state of coexistence known as "interop" mode (short for interoperability). The environment will remain in this mode as long as any Exchange Server 2000/2003 server remains.

While the organization is in interop mode, there are some management best practices to keep in mind. These are detailed in the following section.

Managing Mailboxes

Exchange Server 2007 mailbox management is accomplished through the Exchange Management Console and the Exchange Management Shell. On the other hand, Exchange 2000/2003 is managed through the Active Directory Users and Computers (ADUC) snap-in for Exchange. When an organization is in a state of coexistence, both management tools will be present and necessary for particular tasks.

To determine which tool to use for which task, refer to the following list:

▶ Exchange 2007 mailboxes must be managed with Exchange 2007 management console or shell only. While it is physically possible to manage an Exchange 2007 mailbox with the Exchange 2000/2003 tools, any Exchange 2007 mailboxes managed from the ADUC will not have full functionality.

▶ Exchange 2000/2003 mailboxes can be edited or deleted using the Exchange 2007 tools, but they cannot be created by Exchange 2007 tools.

▶ Exchange 2000/2003 mailboxes can be created, edited, or deleted with Exchange 2000/2003 tools.

▶ The Exchange 2007 move mailbox utility can be used to move both Exchange 2000/2003 and Exchange 2007 mailboxes (in either direction); however, the Exchange 2000/2003 move mailbox utility cannot be used to move mailboxes to or from Exchange 2007 mailbox server.

Managing Recipients

Unlike mailboxes, recipient objects (including contacts, groups, and so on) are not tied to a specific version of Exchange. These objects can be successfully managed using either Exchange 2007 or Exchange 2000/2003 tools.

That being said, Exchange 2007 tools have knowledge of the full set of Exchange 2007 properties and validation rules, so consistent use of the Exchange 2007 tools is recommended for recipient management.

The one exception to this rule is Dynamic Distribution Groups (DDGs). When created in Exchange 2007, these groups store their `RecipientFilter` in an OPATH format. When created in Exchange 2000/2003, the filter is stored as LDAP. This difference makes these edits incompatible.

If a Dynamic Distribution Group was created in Exchange 2007, it should only be managed with Exchange 2007 tools.

Global Objects

Global configuration objects (Address Lists, Email Address Policies, Offline Address Books, and so on) are shared between the Exchange 2007 and Exchange 2000/2003 environments.

The general rule for these objects is

- ▶ If created in Exchange 2000/2003, they can only be fully managed by Exchange 2000/2003 tools until they are upgraded to an Exchange 2007 version.

- ▶ If created in Exchange 2007 or upgraded to an Exchange 2007 version, they can only be edited by Exchange 2007 tools.

Unlike some of the other objects mentioned, objects of this type that are created in, or upgraded to, Exchange 2007 will be actively blocked by the Exchange 2000/2003 System Manager.

Miscellaneous Objects

Other best practices to keep in mind include the following:

- ▶ Exchange 2000/2003 Recipient Update Service—Never configure an Exchange 2007 server to act as the "Exchange Server" for a Recipient Update Service (RUS). Doing so will break the RUS.

- ▶ Exchange 2003 Administrative and Routing Groups—These objects can be managed using Exchange 2003 tools only, as they are not visible utilizing Exchange 2007 tools.

18

Performing Common Tasks

As previously discussed in this chapter, Exchange maintenance and configuration tasks can be accomplished utilizing either the Exchange Management Console or the Exchange Management Shell. For simple, infrequent tasks, the GUI interface of the Exchange Management Console will likely be the easiest and most convenient interface to use. But for repetitive or frequently occurring tasks, the command-line interface of the Exchange Management Shell will prove very useful.

However, you should keep in mind that although every task that can be accomplished in the console can be accomplished in the shell, this does not go both ways. Many configurations and settings cannot be accessed from the console and can only be implemented utilizing the Exchange Management Shell.

Creating User Mailboxes

The creation of a new user mailbox, either for an existing user or in conjunction with the creation of a new user, is one task that can be accomplished either from the Exchange Management Console or from the Exchange Management Shell.

Creating a New Mailbox in the Exchange Management Console

Using the GUI interface is easy and familiar to those who have worked with previous versions of Exchange. To do so:

1. Start the Exchange Management Console.

2. In the console tree, click the Recipient Configuration node.

3. In the action pane, click New Mailbox. The New Mailbox Wizard appears.

4. On the Introduction page shown in Figure 18.3, click User Mailbox, and then click Next.

> **NOTE**
>
> Exchange Server 2007 addresses several shortcomings of previous versions in the area of resource management. When creating a Room or Equipment mailboxes, the mailbox no longer needs to be owned by a user. There is an associated user account with these resources, but the account is disabled automatically when the resource mailbox is created.

5. On the User Type page, click New User, and then click Next.

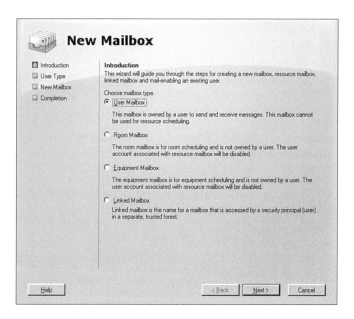

FIGURE 18.3   Types of mailboxes.

6. On the Mailbox Information page, complete the following fields:

  ▸ **Organizational Unit**—By default, the New Mailbox Wizard displays the Users container in Active Directory. To change the default organizational unit (OU), click Browse, and then select the OU you want.

  ▸ **First Name**—Type the first name of the user. This field is optional.

  ▸ **Initials**—Type the initials of the user. This field is optional.

  ▸ **Last Name**—Type the last name of the user. This field is optional.

  ▸ **User Name**—By default, this field is populated with the user's first name, initials, and last name. You can modify the name in this field.

  ▸ **User Logon Name (pre-Windows 2000)**—Also known as the Security Account Manager Account Name (SAMAccountName), this name is used for Windows Internet Naming Service (WINS) name resolution and must be unique within the domain. Typically, the pre-Windows 2000 user logon name is the same as the user principal name (UPN). This field is required.

  ▸ **User Logon Name (User Principal Name)**—The name that the user will use to log on to the mailbox. The user logon name consists of a username and a suffix. Typically, the suffix is the domain name in which the user account resides.

  ▸ **Display Name**—By default, this field is populated with the user's first name, initials, and last name. You can modify the name in this field.

18

▸ **Password**—Type the password that the user must use to log on to his mailbox.

▸ **Confirm Password**—Retype the password that you entered in the Password field.

▸ **User Must Change Password at Next Logon**—Select this check box if you want the user to reset the password.

7. Click Next.

8. On the Mailbox Settings page, complete the following fields:

▸ **Alias**—By default, this field is populated with the user's first and last name, with no space between the names. You can modify the alias in this field.

▸ **Server**—To change the default server, select the server you want from this list.

▸ **Storage Group**—To change the default storage group, select the storage group you want from this list.

▸ **Mailbox Database**—To change the default mailbox database, select the mailbox database you want from this list.

▸ **ELC Mailbox Policy**—To specify an email life cycle (ELC) policy, select this check box, and then click Browse to select the ELC mailbox policy to be associated with this mailbox. For example, use this option if you want this mailbox to adhere to an ELC policy such as the retention period for the mailbox data. This is an optional field.

▸ **Exchange ActiveSync Mailbox Policy**—To specify an Exchange ActiveSync mailbox policy, select this check box, and then click Browse to select the Exchange ActiveSync mailbox policy to be associated with this mailbox. This is an optional field.

9. Click Next.

10. On the New Mailbox page, review the Configuration Summary. To make any configuration changes, click Back. To create the new mailbox, click New.

11. On the Completion page, the summary states whether the mailbox was successfully created. The summary also displays the Exchange Management Shell command that was used to create the mailbox.

12. Click Finish.

Creating a New Mailbox in the Exchange Management Shell

Although there is no GUI interface in the Exchange Management Shell, tasks like the creation of a new user mailbox can be quickly accomplished with a single command line. However, bear in mind that there are many options when creating a new user account and mailbox, and the command necessary can be extremely complex.

The following is a sample Exchange Management Shell command that was automatically generated by the Exchange Management Console during a routine user and mailbox creation:

```
New-Mailbox -Name:'Jack Y. Reddy' -Alias:'jyreddy' -OrganizationalUnit:
➡'COMPANYABC.COM/Users' -Database:'CN=Mailbox Database,CN=
➡First Storage Group,CN=InformationStore, CN=VMW-EXCHANGE1,
➡CN=Servers,CN=Exchange Administrative Group (FYDIBOHF23SPDLT),
➡CN=Administrative Groups,CN=335A1087-5131-4D45-BE3E-3C6C7F76F5EC,
➡CN=Microsoft Exchange,CN=Services,CN=Configuration,
➡DC=COMPANYABC,DC=COM' -UserPrincipalName:'jyreddy@COMPANYABC.COM'
➡-SamAccountName:'jyreddy' -FirstName:'Jack' -Initials:'Y' -LastName:'Reddy'
➡-Password:'System.Security.SecureString' -ResetPasswordOnNextLogon:
➡$false
```

As you can see, every option configured during the creation of the account in the GUI interface can be replicated using the Exchange Management Shell.

Managing User Mailboxes

Administrators can utilize the Exchange Management Console to perform a wide variety of user-specific configurations on an individual mailbox. Each mail-enabled object in an Exchange environment has specific settings that can be configured for that individual mailbox. This can come in handy when an individual user has different requirements than other users located in the same database. Settings on the database that apply to the majority of users can be overwritten using these individual settings.

Several mailbox configurable properties are available on individual user mailboxes, including mailbox settings, mail flow settings, and mailbox features.

Mailbox Settings

Mailbox settings address storage quotas and records management functionality. Some of the detailed functions covered in mailbox settings are as follows:

▶ **Storage Quotas**——By default, individual mailboxes are configured to use the mailbox database defaults for storage quotas. However, you can select the Storage Quotas tab in the individual mailbox properties to override this setting. By removing the checkmark from Use Mailbox Database Defaults, you can configure custom Warning, Prohibit Send, and Prohibit Send and Receive quotas for the mailbox. In addition, you can specify a deleted item retention time that differs from the database default.

▶ **Messaging Records Management**—On this tab within the mailbox properties, you can configure a Managed folder mailbox policy that differs from the database default. This setting can be turned on for all messages, or can be turned on for a particular time period using the Start and End date feature located here.

Mail Flow Settings

Mail flow settings can be modified to allow for changes in delivery options, message size restrictions, and message delivery restrictions. Some specifics on the mail flow settings are as follows:

> ▶ **Delivery Options**—Utilizing this tab, you can enable other user accounts to "Send on Behalf" of this user. You can also configure the mailbox to forward messages to another mailbox and can dictate whether the original recipient should receive a copy, or if the message should only go to the forwarded mailbox. You can also use this tab to set recipient limits on the mailbox, stating the maximum number of recipients that user can send to at a time.

> ▶ **Message Size Restrictions**—Utilizing this option, you can mandate the maximum message size that a user can send or receive. Bear in mind, by setting different sizes for these two settings, you can run into a situation where a user is able to receive a message, but cannot forward it (or reply with the original message attached) because he has a lower Sending Message Size restriction. Likewise, if the Receive limits are lower than the Send limits, he might be able to send a message to a fellow employee, but not receive a reply that includes the original message. Set these settings carefully.

> ▶ **Message Delivery Restrictions**—With this feature, you can dictate whether an individual mailbox can receive messages from all senders, or only specified senders. You can require that all senders are authenticated, or configure the mailbox to reject messages from particular senders.

Mailbox Features

Several property options for mailbox features allow for changes in settings for Outlook Web Access (OWA), Exchange ActiveSync, unified messaging, and the Messaging Application Programming Interface (MAPI) communications protocol. Specific details on these mailbox feature properties are as follows:

> ▶ **Outlook Web Access**—Although there are no properties to be configured on this option, you can elect whether to allow the user to access his mailbox utilizing OWA. This setting can be set to Enable or Disable. By default, OWA access is enabled for all user mailboxes in an organization.

> ▶ **Exchange ActiveSync**—This feature can be enabled or disabled for an individual mailbox. If enabled, you have the option in the properties to apply an Exchange ActiveSync mailbox policy for the mailbox. By default, Exchange ActiveSync is enabled for all user mailboxes in an organization.

> ▶ **Unified Messaging**—You have the option to enable or disable unified messaging for the mailbox using this feature setting.

> ▶ **MAPI**—With this setting, you can dictate whether the user can access his mailbox from a MAPI-enabled client. You have the option to enable or disable MAPI access. By default, MAPI access is enabled for all user mailboxes in an organization.

Managing Mailbox Locations

Because Exchange 2007 is designed to be implemented on 64-bit systems, there is improved performance and capacity for individual servers. The Enterprise Edition of Exchange Server 2007 now supports as many as 50 storage groups per server. Although a storage group can contain as many as five databases, there is a limit of 50 databases per server.

When designing your organization's mail storage solution, you should keep the following in mind:

▶ **Decreased database restoration time**—Whether because of catastrophic server failure or severe database corruption, there is always the possibility of the loss of a server or a mail database. This possibility is the driving force behind the need for comprehensive server backup policies and procedures. If the need to recover a server or database from your backups ever comes to pass, smaller databases can be recovered faster than larger ones simply because of the amount of data to be transferred. Whether your company prioritizes management, customer service, or sales departments, by breaking key users apart from the pack and placing their mailboxes into separate, smaller databases, there is the potential to recover these users quickly, get them online, and then move on to recovering the remaining users.

▶ **Distribution of user load**—Users can be broken up into separate mailbox storage groups or databases. The benefit of this is to mitigate risk by distributing your user load. You have probably heard the phrase "Don't put all of your eggs in one basket." This concept follows that principle: If all of your users have their mailboxes stored on a single server, something as simple as an unplanned server reboot, or a disconnected network cable, can bring your entire organization down. By distributing your user load across multiple databases, storage groups, servers, or even sites, you can increasingly mitigate the possibility of a single point of failure negatively impacting your entire organization.

▶ **User mailbox policies and restrictions**—Users can also be broken out into separate mailbox databases to ease user interruption caused by the implementation of storage limits and mailbox deletion policies. For example, if users in your Customer Service department are allowed 100MB of mail storage, but users in your Sales department are allowed 500MB, this can easily be implemented by maintaining the users in separate databases and setting the policies on the database, rather than on individual users. You can see the options for setting message size restrictions on a database in Figure 18.4.

Managing Email Addresses

When a new mail-enabled user is created in your Exchange environment, the creation of their primary SMTP address is controlled by a recipient policy. By default, the recipient policy creates two email addresses: an X400 address and a primary SMTP address that is formatted as First Initial, Middle Initial, Last Name at your default organization. For example, user James A. Weinhardt at companyabc.com would have a default SMTP address of `jaweinhardt@companyabc.com`.

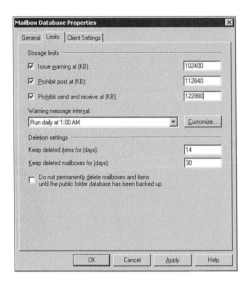

FIGURE 18.4   Mailbox Database Properties dialog box.

However, the default behavior of this recipient policy can easily be modified to create primary SMTP addresses that conform to your organization's standard. For example, if your organization uses FirstName.LastName@companyname.com as their standard SMTP address, you can configure the recipient policy to generate this address for you when the user mailbox is created. To do so, perform the following procedure:

1. Start the Exchange Management Console.

2. In the console tree, select Organization Configuration, then select Hub Transport.

3. In the results pane, select the E-Mail Address Policies tab, and then highlight the default policy.

4. In the action pane, click Edit.

5. On the Introduction page, when modifying the Default Policy, all of the options are hard-coded and cannot be changed. If you are creating an additional policy, these settings can be modified. Click Next to continue.

6. On the Conditions page, leave the default settings and click Next to continue.

7. On the E-Mail Addresses page, you can see the two default addresses that are generated. To modify the SMTP address, under SMTP, select the policy and click Edit.

8. By default, this is set to Use Alias. To modify the policy, click the E-Mail Address Local Part check box, and then select the appropriate SMTP naming standard for your organization. For available options, see Figure 18.5. In the example, First Name.last name is selected. Select the appropriate entry, and then, under E-Mail Address Domain, use the drop-down box to select from the available email domains. After you are ready, click OK to continue.

FIGURE 18.5   SMTP email address selections.

9. You should now be back at the E-Mail Addresses page. Click Next to continue.

10. On the Schedule page, specify when the email address policy will be applied. Note that if you select a time and date in the future, the wizard will remain open until the countdown has completed. Select the appropriate option, and click Next to continue.

11. On the Edit E-Mail Address Policy page, the Configuration Summary is shown. Review the policy to ensure all is correct, and then click Edit to continue.

12. On the Completion page, a summary is shown informing you how many items were modified, how many succeeded, and how many failed. Click Finish to continue.

After this policy has been applied, existing users will have a new SMTP email address generated that conforms to the policy and it will be set as their primary (reply-to) address. Previously assigned addresses will remain in place as secondary addresses. Users created from this point on, however, will have only the new address, and it will be set as their primary SMTP address.

Note the difference in the two users shown in Figures 18.6 and 18.7. The first, James Weinhardt, shown in Figure 18.6, was created prior to the modification of the policy. The second, John Weinhardt, shown in Figure 18.7, was created after the policy was modified.

Creating Distribution Groups

In Exchange Server 2007, distribution groups serve two primary purposes. They can be used as email distribution lists that allow messages to be sent to multiple users with a single address entry, or as security groups to assign permissions for a shared resource.

To manage distribution groups on a computer that has the Mailbox server role installed, you must be logged on as a member of the Exchange Recipient Administrators group. You must also be a member of the local Administrators group on that computer.

When a new distribution group is created, a new mail-enabled group object is created within Active Directory.

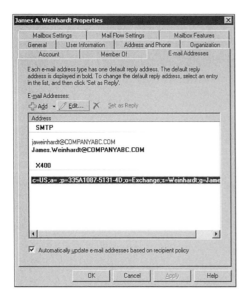

FIGURE 18.6   SMTP email address before policy change.

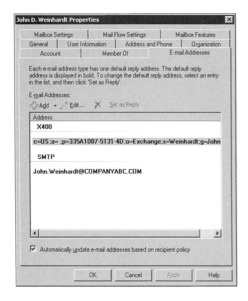

FIGURE 18.7   SMTP email address after policy change.

> **NOTE**
>
> Whether you are creating a distribution group solely for the purpose of email distribu-
> tion or a security group that is capable of being used both for email distribution and
> for assigning permissions, the creation process is the same and both types are

created as mail-enabled objects. When possible, create a single, mail-enabled security group to provide both security and distribution group functionality, rather than two separate groups for the same list of users.

When creating a distribution group, the naming convention can be somewhat confusing; it doesn't matter if you are creating a Universal Distribution group or a Universal Security group—you still click the New Distribution Group button. To create a new distribution group:

1. Start the Exchange Management Console.

2. In the console tree, select Recipient Configuration.

3. In the action pane, click New Distribution Group. The New Distribution Group Wizard appears.

4. On the Introduction page, click New Group, and then click Next.

5. On the Group Information page, complete the following fields:

    ▶ **Group Type**—To create a distribution group, select Distribution. To create a security group, click Security. The remaining steps are identical, regardless of which type of group you create.

    ▶ **Organizational Unit**—By default, the New Distribution Group Wizard displays the Users container in the Active Directory service. To change the default organizational unit (OU), click Browse, and then select the OU you want.

    ▶ **Group Name**—Type the group name you want.

    ▶ **Group Name (pre-Windows 2000)**—By default, the group name for pre-Windows 2000 operating systems is automatically generated to be the same as the group name. You can modify the name in this field.

    ▶ **Display Name**—By default, the display name is the same as the group name. You can modify the name in this field.

    ▶ **Alias**—By default, the alias is the same as the group name. You can modify the name in this field.

6. Click Next.

7. On the New Distribution Group page, review the Configuration Summary. To make any configuration changes, click Back. To create the new distribution group, click New.

8. On the Completion page, the summary states whether the distribution group was successfully created. The summary also displays the Exchange Management Shell command that was used to create the distribution group.

9. Click Finish.

18

NOTE

On the Completion page, although it is not possible to highlight and copy the Exchange Management Shell command that was utilized to create the object, you CAN click Ctrl+C to copy the contents of the page. These contents can then be pasted into a text file, allowing you to save the EMS command for future use without the GUI interface. This can be extremely helpful when you need to perform repetitive tasks because you can perform the task once in the GUI interface, and then copy and modify the shell command to perform the task repeatedly for your other items.

Dynamic Distribution Groups

Distribution groups can also be dynamic in nature. These groups provide the same functionality as a standard distribution group, but the membership of the group is built based on a Lightweight Directory Access Protocol (LDAP) query that you have defined. For example, you could build a dynamic distribution group that is intended to include all recipients in a particular state. Each time the list is accessed, the membership would be built based on information gathered from the Active Directory.

Dynamic distribution groups require less maintenance than standard groups, as the query is defined once, and the membership is built automatically every time the group is called. However, there is a performance cost associated with their use, especially if the query produces a large number of results. Every time an email is sent to a query-based distribution group, server and domain resources are utilized to determine its membership. Dynamic distribution groups are an extremely functional tool, but should be used with discretion. To create a new dynamic distribution group:

1. Start the Exchange Management Console.

2. In the console tree, select Recipient Configuration.

3. In the action pane, click New Dynamic Distribution Group. The New Dynamic Distribution Group Wizard appears.

4. On the Introduction page, click Next to continue.

5. On the Group Information page, complete the following fields:

    ▶ **Organizational Unit**—By default, the New Distribution Group Wizard displays the Users container in the Active Directory service. To change the default organizational unit (OU), click Browse, and then select the OU you want.

    ▶ **Group Name**—Type the group name you want.

    ▶ **Display Name**—By default, the display name is the same as the group name. You can modify the name in this field.

    ▶ **Alias**—By default, the alias is the same as the group name. You can modify the name in this field.

6. Click Next.

7. On the Filter Settings page, you will configure the filter that is used to select the recipients for the dynamic group. If you want to limit the membership to only users, resources, mail-enabled groups, or contacts, you can select any combination of them on this screen. When you are ready, click Next to continue.

8. On the Conditions page, you can select the conditions that will build the LDAP query that will identify the recipients to be included in the list. When you are ready, click Next to continue.

9. On the New Dynamic Distribution Group page, review the Configuration Summary. To make any configuration changes, click Back. To create the new dynamic distribution group, click New.

10. On the Completion page, the summary states whether the distribution group was successfully created. The summary also displays the Exchange Management Shell command that was used to create the distribution group.

11. Click Finish.

Managing Distribution Groups

As organizations grow, they might find that the number of distribution groups that are maintained can get extremely large. As the membership of these groups can change often, the maintenance of them can take a significant amount of administrative resources. Because of this, Exchange allows administrators to delegate the management of distribution groups to users who they designate.

Delegating Management of Distribution Groups

Often, after a distribution group has been created, an administrator can delegate the maintenance of the group membership to another user. For example, if the manager of a project team has constantly shifting resources reporting to her, the management of the distribution group might be relinquished so that she can update it as necessary. To delegate the management of a distribution group:

1. Start the Exchange Management Console.

2. In the console tree, click the Recipient Configuration node, and then select Distribution Group.

3. From the results pane, select the distribution group you want to manage.

4. In the action pane, click Properties.

5. Select the Group Information tab, and place a check mark in the Managed By check box.

6. Click Browse, and select the appropriate recipient to manage the distribution list.

7. Click OK to save the changes and exit.

18

Distribution List Mail Flow Settings

Often, distribution lists are created with a specific user base in mind. For example, although you might want any employee in the company to be able to send to your "Employee Suggestions" mailbox, you probably would want to restrict who can send to "All Employees," or "All District Managers."

To restrict who can send to a particular distribution group, perform the following actions:

1. Start the Exchange Management Console.

2. In the console tree, click the Recipient Configuration node, and then select Distribution Group.

3. From the results pane, select the distribution group you want to manage.

4. In the action pane, click Properties.

5. Select the Mail Flow Settings tab, and then double-click the Message Delivery Restrictions option.

6. Click the Browse button, and select the appropriate recipient to manage the distribution list.

7. Click OK to save the changes and exit.

When an unauthorized sender creates and sends an email to a restricted distribution group, a message similar to the one shown in Figure 18.8 will be seen by the sender.

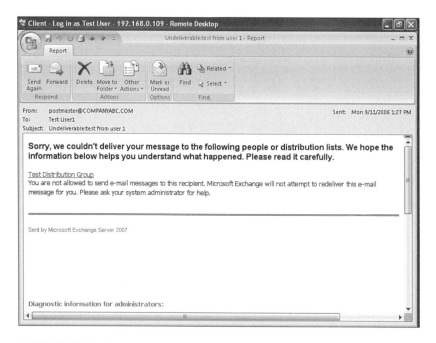

FIGURE 18.8   Undeliverable message notification.

As you can see, the message generated by Exchange Server 2007 is much more friendly and informative than the nondelivery reports (NDRs) sent by previous versions of Exchange.

Other delivery restriction options include Require That All Senders Are Authenticated, which prevents anonymous users from sending messages to the distribution group, and Reject Messages From, which allows you to configure specific users or groups that are restricted from sending messages to the group. In addition, message size restrictions can be placed on the distribution group, only allowing messages smaller than the mandated size to be delivered.

Creating Mail Contacts

There are many times when an organization has the desire or need to communicate with nonnative Microsoft messaging systems or external SMTP addresses. When this situation occurs, it is an ideal opportunity to utilize a mail contact.

For example, your organization might regularly communicate with a client who has an email account outside of your organization. So many of your users have a need to communicate regularly with this user that you want to have them included in your corporate email address book, but any messages sent to them should go directly to their account outside of your organization.

Known as a custom recipient in some older versions of Exchange, this functionality has existed for some time, but the creation and management process has changed slightly from revision to revision.

To create a mail contact in the Exchange Management Console, perform the following steps:

1. Start the Exchange Management Console.

2. In the console tree, expand Recipient Configuration, and then select Mail Contact.

3. In the action pane, click New Mail Contact; this starts the New Mail Contact Wizard.

4. On the Introduction page, you can select whether you are creating a new contact, or choosing to mail-enable a contact that exists in your organization but was previously not mail-enabled. For this instruction, select New Contact, and then click Next to continue.

5. On the Contact Information page, fill out the following fields:

    ▶ **Organizational Unit**—Use the Browse button to select the organizational unit where the contact will reside. The default location is in the Users container.

    ▶ **First Name, Initials, Last Name**—Enter the appropriate information in these fields.

18

> ▶ **Contact Name, Display Name, Alias**—These fields will be filled out by default based on the information entered in the Name fields. You can change these settings to match your company policies if needed.

> ▶ **External E-Mail Address**—This is where you will enter the SMTP address for your mail-enabled contact. Click Edit and enter the email address in the following format: username@domain (example, remote.user@yahoo.com). Click OK to continue.

6. Click Next to continue.

7. Review the Configuration Summary, and click New to accept the current configuration and create the mail contact.

8. On the Completion page, review the summary and ensure the item was created without error. Click Finish to continue.

Mail contacts can be created using the Exchange Management Shell by utilizing the new-mailcontact command. The following is s sample EMS command:

```
New-MailContact -ExternalEmailAddress:'SMTP:Test.Mailcontact@yahoo.com'
➥-Name:'Test MailContact' -Alias:'Test_MailContact' -OrganizationalUnit:
➥'COMPANYABC.COM/Users' -DisplayName:'Test MailContact' -FirstName:'Test'
➥-Initials:'' -LastName:'MailContact'
```

> **NOTE**
>
> It is challenging to show the command in print with the proper formatting. For example, there is a space before –ExternalEmailAddress, -Name, -Alias, and other arguments in the command. One easy way to get the proper formatting is to create a new mail contact in the Exchange System Manager, and then copy the Exchange Management Shell command that is automatically generated and shown on the Completion page of the wizard. Remember, you can select Ctrl+C to copy the contents of that page.

Managing Mail Contacts

After a mail contact has been created, you can view the properties of the object in the Exchange Management Console. Several settings are available that you might want to configure for the contact. The most commonly accessed settings are as follows:

> ▶ **General tab**—You will find two options on the General tab that address display name and inclusion of the name in the address book.

> > ▶ **Display Name**—Located at the top of the General tab, the display name is how the contact appears in the Exchange Management Console and in the organization's address book. Changes made here are *not* reflected in the user-name in other fields of the contact.

▶ **Hide from Exchange Address Book**—If you want to hide the contact from your organization's address book, place a check mark here.

▶ **Contact Information tab**—You can update the name of the user here, however, any changes are *not* reflected in the display name. However, much of the information contained on the Contact Information tab can be accessed by your user community in Outlook.

▶ **Address and Phone tab**—Like the Contact Information tab, information in this section can be accessed by your user community in Outlook. By selecting the contact from the address book, users can view the contact's address and phone numbers if they are filled out on this page.

▶ **Organization tab** —The Organization tab enables you to document the contact's title, company, department, office, manager, and direct reports, if applicable.

▶ **Mail Flow Settings tab**—Arguably the most important of the configuration settings (next to the SMTP address), the Mail Flow Settings tab allows you to configure message size restrictions (a configurable receiving message size) and message delivery restrictions (who the contact can receive mail from and who it will reject messages from).

Managing Disconnected Mailboxes

Exchange Server 2003 introduced an exciting concept in mailbox administration—the Mailbox Recovery Center. Utilizing this feature, administrators could identify disconnected mailboxes (those no longer associated with a user account) and perform a variety of actions—including recovering the mailbox by connecting it to a new or existing user.

In Exchange 2007, this process has been greatly simplified by the addition of a Disconnected Mailbox node located in the console tree of the Exchange Management Console.

With this utility, you can quickly and easily recover a mailbox that has been disassociated from a corresponding user mailbox. To reconnect a disconnected mailbox, perform the following procedure:

1. Start the Exchange Management Console.

2. In the console tree, select Disconnected Mailbox.

3. In the action pane, click Connect to Server, and then click Browse. Select the Exchange server where the mailbox resides, click OK, and then click Connect.

4. In the results pane, select the disconnected mailbox that you want to reconnect; then, in the action pane, click Connect. This starts the Connect Mailbox Wizard.

5. On the Introduction page, select the type of mailbox you are reconnecting. By default, User Mailbox is selected, regardless of the mailbox type of the original mailbox. Click Next to continue.

18

6. On the Mailbox Settings page, fill out the following fields:

    ▶ **Matching User**—If the Exchange server was able to locate a matching user object in Active Directory, this field will be prepopulated. There are times that a matching user exists, but Exchange does not locate it—in those instances, you can click Browse and, if found, you can insert the user by selecting it and clicking OK.

    ▶ **Existing User**—If you want to connect the mailbox to another existing user (but not a "matching" user), select this option button. Click Browse and select the user from those shown. After selecting the option, click OK to continue.

    ▶ **Alias**—The Alias is automatically filled in based on the alias of the account you have selected previously.

    ▶ **Managed Folder Mailbox Policy and Exchange ActiveSync Mailbox Policy**—Select the associated check boxes for these items if you want to associate the mailbox with an existing policy. The policy can be selected by clicking the Browse button.

7. Click Next to continue.

8. View the Configuration Summary and ensure all is correct. If you need to make any changes, use the Back button. After all of the information is correct, click Connect.

9. From the Completion page, review the Completion Summary and ensure the reconnection was successful. Click Finish to close the wizard.

Moving Mailboxes

Starting with Exchange Server 2003, the utility used to move user mailboxes was removed from Active Directory Users and Computers and was relocated to the Exchange System Manager. This allowed administrators to move user mailboxes more easily and effectively because they could move multiple mailboxes simultaneously.

Administrators might want to move an individual mailbox from the database, storage group, or server on which it currently resides. The desire to accomplish this might result from a variety of situations, such as a user being transferred to a different department or location or receiving a promotion (or demotion), and the mailbox needing to be stored with others in that position.

In addition, the ability to move several mailboxes from their existing location can be helpful when performing load balancing across multiple Exchange servers (moving mailboxes from an overutilized location to an underutilized one).

Mailbox moves can also be extremely useful when implanting new Exchange hardware. The new server can be built in the existing environment, mailboxes can be moved to the new location, and the old server hardware can be decommissioned, all with minimal impact on the user community.

One other situation when the ability to move multiple mailboxes is helpful is during an upgrade to a newer version of Exchange, for example, when migrating your organization from an older version of Exchange to a new Exchange 2007 environment. You are able to install your new Exchange Server 2007 servers, move all user mailboxes from your old environment to your new one, and then decommission your older Exchange servers when they are no longer needed.

In Exchange 2007, the Move Mailbox feature is located in the Exchange Management Console, and it is more functional than ever before. Administrators now have the option to perform a mailbox move immediately or to schedule the move at a future time and date when the mailbox will be unused, or when the mailbox moves will have less impact on the Exchange infrastructure.

Preparing for Mailbox Moves

Before moving mailboxes, some standard tasks need to be completed in advance to minimize the potential for data loss and to streamline the process. These two primary tasks are as follows:

▶ **Backing Up Exchange Mailboxes**—Before performing any major work on a messaging system, it is a good practice to back up the message store. In the event of serious problems, you can always recover to your last known good backup.

▶ **Performing Mailbox Cleanup**—User mailboxes can grow rather large in size over time. Storing important messages, especially when there are attachments included, can take up a significant amount of disk space. Because moving larger mailboxes takes longer than smaller ones, it is always a good idea to have users clean up their mailboxes prior to moving them. One easy way to accomplish this is with the Mailbox Cleanup utility in Outlook. With this tool, users can view their current mailbox size, search for items older than, or larger than, a specified date and size, or run the autoarchive utility. Users can also empty their deleted items permanently, as there is no need to waste time and bandwidth to move unwanted messages with the mailbox. Lastly, the utility allows users to delete all alternate versions of items in their mailbox. By cleaning up user mailboxes prior to moving them, you can significantly decrease the amount of time and resources needed to accomplish the task.

Performing the Mailbox Move

Microsoft Exchange Server mailboxes are easily moved between servers that are running the same version of Exchange and are in the same administrative group. Mailbox databases created on one server can be renamed or copied to a different storage group, either on the same server or on a different server in the same administrative group.

During a move mailbox operation, all end users are able to access their mailboxes throughout the operation, except for the mailbox currently being moved.

Moving a mailbox (or mailboxes) in Exchange Server 2007 is a very simple process. To move a mailbox:

1. Start the Exchange Management Console.

2. In the console tree, select Recipient Configuration, and then select Mailbox.

3. In the results pane, locate the mailbox(es) that you want to move and select them.

4. In the action pane, click Move Mailbox. This starts the Move Mailbox Wizard.

5. On the Introduction page, select the server, storage group, and mailbox database where you want to move the mailboxes to, and then click Next to continue.

6. On the Move Options page, select how you want the wizard to handle mailboxes that contain corrupted messages. You have the following options:

   ▶ **Skip the Mailbox**—By selecting this option, you are instructing the wizard to skip moving the mailbox completely if it detects corrupted messages within.

   ▶ **Skip the Corrupted Messages**—By selecting this option, you instruct the wizard to skip any corrupted messages found and attempt to move the mailbox anyway.

   ▶ **Maximum Number of Messages to Skip**—If you select Skip the Corrupted Messages, you have the option to specify the maximum number of corrupted messages that can be skipped. If this number is reached, the wizard stops trying to move the mailbox and skips it completely.

7. Click Next to continue.

8. On the Move Schedule page, you are able to specify when you want the mailbox move to occur. You have the following options

   ▶ **Immediately**—Use this option when you want the wizard to perform the Move Mailbox task as soon as you click the Next button.

   ▶ **At the following time**—With this option, you can postpone the mailbox moves to a specific date and time in the future. This option can be helpful in several instances; for example, you can move mailboxes after the workday has completed and the users are no longer utilizing the system, or you can schedule the move for a future weekend or prescheduled maintenance window. Use the drop-down boxes to select the date and time that you want the wizard to perform the move.

   ▶ You can also specify the maximum length of time that the Move Mailbox task is allowed to run before canceling the task. To specify a maximum time, click the Cancel Tasks That Are Still Running After check box and select how long you want the wizard to try to move the mailbox before it cancels. By default, when the Cancel Tasks option is selected, the timeout is set to 8 hours.

9. When you have made your selections on the Move Schedule page, click Next to continue.

10. On the Move Mailbox page, the summary is displayed, detailing what mailboxes are going to be moved. After you have reviewed the summary, click Move to continue.

If you elected to move the mailboxes immediately, the move begins at this time. If you elected to move the mailboxes at a future date, the Move Mailbox screen begins counting down the time until the mailbox move will take place.

> **NOTE**
>
> When moving mailboxes at a future date and time, the Move Mailbox Wizard, shown in Figure 18.9, continues to run until the scheduled move date and time is reached. This means that you will not be able to close the wizard, or log off the session, until the mailbox move has completed.

FIGURE 18.9   Future mailbox move scheduled.

Server Administration

In Exchange, a storage group is a logical grouping of mail databases that share a single set of logs. As previously mentioned, each Exchange 2007 server can have up to 50 storage groups, a significant increase from Exchange 2003, which allowed a maximum of 4.

Each storage group can have up to 5 databases. However, Exchange Server 2007 servers are limited to 50 databases total.

Each instance of a storage group can use a significant amount of server resources, so you should plan your storage group and database design carefully.

Creating a New Storage Group

Creating a new storage group in Exchange 2007 is an extremely simple process. To do so:

1. Start the Exchange Management Console.

2. In the console tree, expand Server Configuration, and select Mailbox.

3. In the results pane, select the server where your new storage group will reside.

4. In the action pane, click New Storage Group. This starts the New Storage Group Wizard.

5. The server name is automatically filled in for you. Continue on the page, filling out the following fields:

   ▶ **Storage Group Name**—The storage group name will be displayed in the Exchange Management Console. Select a name that meets your organization's naming conventions.

   ▶ **Log Files Location**—You can click Browse to relocate the log files associated with this storage group. The default location is `C:\Program Files\Microsoft\Exchange Server\Mailbox\`*storage group name*.

   ▶ **System Files Location**—By default, these are stored in the same directory as the log files.

   ▶ **Local Continuous Replication System Files Location**—This option is only enabled if the Enable Local Continuous Replication for this Storage Group option at the bottom of the page is enabled. The default location is `C:\Program Files\Microsoft\Exchange Server\Mailbox\LocalCopies\`*storage group name*.

NOTE

New in Exchange Server 2007, Local Continuous Replication (LCR) is a single-server solution that utilizes built-in asynchronous log shipping technology to create and maintain a copy of a storage group. This copy is stored on a second set of disks that are connected to the same server as the production storage group. LCR allows for a quick manual switch to a secondary copy of the data in the event of a failure. More information on LCR and how it relates to backup strategies can be found in Chapters 31 and 32.

   ▶ **Local Continuous Replication Log Files Location**—Like the system files, this option is only enabled if Local Continuous Replication is enabled on the storage group. The default location for the log files is in the same directory as the Local Continuous Replication system files.

6. Click New to continue and create the storage group.

7. On the Completion page, you can review the summary to ensure the storage group was successfully created. Click Finish to close the wizard.

Creating a New Database

Like the storage groups, creating a new database is a straightforward process in the Exchange Management Console using the wizard. To do so:

1. Start the Exchange Management Console.

2. In the console tree, expand Server Configuration, and then select Mailbox.

3. In the results pane, select the server, and then the storage group where your new database will reside.

4. In the action pane, click either New Mailbox Database or New Public Folder Database, depending on the type you want to create. This launches the New Database Wizard.

5. The storage group name is automatically filled in for you with the selected server and storage group. Continue on the page, filling out the following fields:

   ▶ **Mailbox Database Name**—The database name will be displayed in the Exchange Management Console and used whenever new mailboxes are added. Select a name that meets your organization's naming conventions.

   ▶ **Exchange Database File Path**—You can click Browse to relocate the database you are creating. The default location is `C:\Program Files\Microsoft\Exchange Server\Mailbox\`*`storage group name`*.

   ▶ **Local Continuous Replication Exchange Database File Path**—If you have created the storage group with Local Continuous Replication enabled, this option is available. If LCR was not enabled on the storage group, you won't see this option now.

   ▶ **Mount This Database**—By default, this box is checked, instructing Exchange to mount the database upon creation. If you do not want the database mounted automatically, uncheck this selection.

6. Click New to continue and create the new database.

7. On the Completion page, you can review the summary to ensure the database was completed and mounted successfully (if the mounting option was selected). Click Finish to close the wizard..

Setting Limits on Databases

After you have created a database, it can be configured to mandate storage limits and deletion settings. These settings apply to all user mailboxes stored on that database. However, user settings on individual mailboxes can be configured to override these settings. This can be useful when you want to set a limit for all users on a particular database, but you have one user who needs more (or less) restrictive settings. To configure these options, perform the following tasks:

18

1. Start the Exchange Management Console.

2. In the console tree, expand Server Configuration, and then select Mailbox.

3. In the results pane, select the server, storage group, and database you want to modify.

4. In the action pane, click Properties to open the database properties sheet. Select the Limits tab.

Several limits can be set regarding server configurations. You can configure the following settings on the database:

▶ **Storage Limits**—The. storage limits allows you to configure restrictions on all mailboxes located within that database. The available storage limits options are as follows:

  ▶ **Issue Warning At (KB)**—This option allows the Exchange system to automatically send a warning message to users whose mailbox size exceeds the size limits set. It is important to note that this size includes all data stored in the mailbox. Users often overlook their Deleted Items and Sent Items folders and wonder why their mailboxes are still over the limits. In addition, outdated calendar items (often with large attachments) can be forgotten when users are cleaning their mailboxes.

  ▶ **Prohibit Post At (KB)**—This option allows administrators to enforce storage limits by restricting the ability of offending users to send messages until their mailbox size has fallen below the prescribed limits. This is often used in conjunction with the Issue Warning At setting, and is usually set to a higher limit to allow users adequate time between receiving a warning and having their ability to send messages restricted.

  ▶ **Prohibit Send and Receive At (KB)**—The most restrictive of the storage limits, this setting blocks both the sending and receiving of messages after the limit has been reached. This setting is not normally enforced, except in the strictest of environments, because the overwhelming need for uninterrupted business communications often outweighs the unyielding enforcement of size limitations. Use this option with caution, and ensure there is full executive approval before implementing.

  ▶ **Warning Message Interval**—By default, storage limit warning messages are sent daily at 1:00 a.m. This selection can be customized to perform the warning at a different time of the day, or even to send multiple messages at various times of the day. Click Customize to change the default setting.

▶ **Deletion Settings**—The deletion settings dictate how deleted items and mailboxes in the database will be dealt with. The available deletion settings options are as follows:

▶ **Keep Deleted Items for (Days)**—By default, mailbox databases are configured to keep deleted items for 14 days. This default setting is increased from Exchange Server 2003, which defaulted to 7 days.

NOTE

There is often some user confusion as to what messages can be recovered using the Tools, Recover Deleted Items option in Outlook. There are two types of deletion—Hard (or physical) deletion and Soft (or logical) deletion. When a user deletes an item, it goes to their Deleted Items folder and can be recovered simply by dragging and dropping it back into their Inbox. If the user goes to the Deleted Items folder, and again deletes the message, or if they select Tools, Empty Deleted Items Folder, the item has been soft deleted and can be recovered using the Tools, Recover Deleted Items option. This recovery can be accomplished as long as it is initiated within the window set in the Keep Deleted Items for (Days) section field. However, if a user enters the Recover Deleted Items utility, and selects to purge a message, or if the Keep Deleted Items for (Days) period has expired, the item is hard deleted and cannot be recovered without resorting to backup/restore methods.

▶ **Keep Deleted Mailboxes for (Days)**—In Exchange 2007, deleting a mailbox does not mean that it is permanently purged from the database immediately. The mailbox is flagged for deletion and can no longer be accessed by users. After the mailbox retention period controlled by this setting has been reached, the mailbox is then purged from the system. This option is extremely useful in the event of a user deletion that is the result of a mistake, and allows the administrator to re-create the user object and reconnect the deleted mailbox. By default, this setting is set to 30 days. It can be configured anywhere from 0 (immediate purge upon deletion) to 24,855 days. It is unlikely you will ever need the upper limit (equivalent to a little over 68 years), but this setting can be adjusted to meet your organization's needs. Unless disk space becomes an issue, it is recommended that you do *not* disable the deleted mailbox retention feature.

▶ **Do Not Permanently Delete Mailboxes and Items Until the Public Folder Database Has Been Backed Up**—This final setting is not enabled by default. By checking this option, you instruct Exchange to *not* delete items or mailboxes, even after the retention period has expired, until the database has been successfully backed up. By selecting this option, you ensure that you are able to recover critical items or mailboxes from backup tape, even after the purge has been completed.

Journaling and Archiving

Journaling and archiving are two concepts that are sometimes confused with one another. *Journaling* is the recording of all email communications in an organization. *Archiving* is a method of backing up and storing data and removing it from its native environment.

Both of these strategies can be used for meeting certain regulatory requirements, and journaling can often be used as a tool in an organization's archiving strategy.

In the past several years, there has been a significant increase in regulations requiring organizations to maintain records of communication. Although the financial services, insurance, and health-care industries have faced many more requirements than most other lines of business, many companies have found that maintaining accurate and complete records of employee communications can assist them in the legal arena, whether they are defending against or initiating lawsuits.

For example, a disgruntled former employee might file a lawsuit against a company for wrongful termination stating that he had never been notified that the employee's behavior was unsatisfactory. If the organization has an email journaling solution in place, they could go through the historical data and show specific examples where the behavior problems were discussed with the employee. More and more courts are accepting, and often insisting on, historical corporate messaging data in the effort to determine culpability.

Some of the more well-known U.S. regulations that, in recent years, have specified requirements that may rely on journaling technology are as follows:

▶ **Sarbanes-Oxley Act of 2002 (SOX)**—One of the most widely known regulatory acts, the Sarbanes-Oxley act is a U.S. federal law that requires the preservation of records by certain Exchange members, brokers, and dealers. This act was passed into law in response to a number of major corporate and accounting scandals that resulted in a decline of public trust in corporate accounting and reporting practices.

▶ **Security Exchange Commission Rule 17a-4 (SEC Rule 17a-4)**—A U.S. Security and Exchange Rule that provides rules regarding the retention of electronic correspondence and records.

▶ **National Association of Securities Dealers 3010 & 3110 (NASD 3010 & 3110)**—The NASD details requirements for member firms that include the supervision of registered representatives, including inbound and outbound electronic correspondence with the public. In addition, the NASD details how long this information must be maintained, and what conditions must be met.

▶ **Health Insurance Portability and Accountability Act of 1996**—More commonly known as HIPAA, this U.S. federal law provides rights and protections for participants and beneficiaries in group health plans.

▶ **Uniting and Strengthening America by Providing Appropriate Tools Required to Intercept and Obstruct Terrorism Act of 2001**—Better known as the Patriot Act, this U.S. federal law expands the authority of U.S. law enforcement for the stated purpose of fighting terrorist acts in the United States and abroad.

The Journaling Agent

Exchange 2007 contains a journaling agent that can be configured to capture email messages that meet the following criteria:

- ▶ Sent or received by mailboxes in your Exchange 2007 organization

- ▶ Sent to and from recipients outside of your organization

- ▶ Or both of the above

Previous revisions of Exchange Server allowed the administrator to configure journaling at a message store level—either all recipients were journaled, or none of them. However, Exchange Server 2007 allows you to configure and implement rules that give you more granular control over what messages will be journaled.

The Scope of a Journal Rule

When configuring a journal rule, the *scope* of the rule defines what type of messages will be journaled. You can choose from the following three scopes:

- ▶ **Internal**—When journaling entries are based on the Internal scope, messages that are sent and received by mailboxes within the Exchange organization are journaled.

- ▶ **External**—When journaling entries are based on the External scope, messages that are sent to recipients outside the Exchange organization, or that are received from senders outside of the Exchange organization, are journaled.

- ▶ **Global**—When journaling entries are based on the Global scope, all messages that pass through a server with the Hub Transport server role are journaled.

> **NOTE**
>
> When the Global scope is selected, the Hub Transport servers journal ALL messages that pass through. This includes messages that might or might not have been journaled already by rules in the Internal and External scopes.

In addition to defining the scope of the rule, you must decide if you want to journal any voice mail or missed call notifications that are processed by your Exchange 2007 Unified Messaging servers. These messages can be significant in size, so if your organization is not required to store this historical data, significant disk space savings can be realized. However, messages that contain faxes and that are generated by a Unified Messaging server are *always* journaled, even if you disable journaling of unified messaging voice mail and missed call notifications.

18

Journal Recipients

In addition to the journaling scopes just discussed, the journaling agent also allows you to create additional rules that can target specific SMTP addresses that exist in your organization. This can be helpful when your organization has specific individuals or positions that are subject to regulatory requirements that are more stringent than other personnel in your organization. In addition, this feature can be extremely useful when an individual is being investigated for a legal proceeding and your organization wants to track his or her messages to be used as evidence.

Journaling Mailboxes

All of these journaled messages must reside somewhere if they are ever to be utilized. A journaling mailbox is one that is used only for collecting journal reports. In Exchange Server 2007, you have the flexibility to create a single journaling mailbox to store all journal reports, or you can create separate journaling mailboxes for each journal rule that you configure. This flexibility even allows you to configure multiple journal rules to use one specific journaling mailbox, and then configure other rules to each use their own specific one.

It is important to note that journaling mailboxes contain sensitive information, and should be handled with the utmost security. There are various laws in place that mandate who should be able to access these message stores, and other laws that require these stored messages to be tamper-free if they are going to be used in any type of investigation. You should work with the legal department in your organization (if one exists) to develop policies that mandate who can access this data, and put security measures in place to ensure no unauthorized access.

Creating a New Journal Rule

To create a journal rule on a Hub Transport server, you must log on as a member of the Exchange Organization Administrators group. You must also be a local Administrator of the server you are working on.

For journaling to function, the journaling agent must be enabled. If individual rules are enabled, but the agent is not, Exchange Server 2007 *will not* apply the rules.

To determine if the journaling agent is enabled on a server, run the following command from the Exchange Management Shell:

```
get-transportagent <enter>
```

A report will be generated on the screen showing the current status of several agents. Look for the journaling agent, and check the Enabled column. If this reads True, the agent is enabled. If this reads False, use the following command to enable the agent:

```
enable-transportagent <enter>
```

You will then have to supply a value telling the shell *which* agent you want to enable. Next to the *Identity:* prompt, type:

```
journaling agent <enter>
```

After doing this, you can run the `get-transportagent` command again to ensure the journaling agent is now enabled.

Now that the agent is enabled, you can create a journal rule in the Exchange Management Console. To do so, follow these steps:

1. Open the Exchange Management Console on the Hub Transport server.

2. In the console tree, expand Organization Configuration, and then select Hub Transport.

3. In the results pane, select the Journaling tab, and then in the action pane, click New Journaling Rule.

4. In the New Journaling Rule dialog box, enter a name for your journaling rule.

5. In the Journal E-Mail Address field, click Select. In the Journal Mailbox window, select the recipient who will receive the journal reports.

6. Under Scope, select the scope to which the journal rule should be applied. See the previous section titled "The Scope of a Journal Rule" if you are unsure which scope to select.

7. If you want to target a specific recipient, in the Recipient Text field, click Select. In the Select Recipient window, select the mailbox, contact, or distribution group that you want to journal, and then click OK.

8. By default, the rule will be enabled upon completion. If you do not want the rule enabled, remove the check mark from the Enable Rule check box.

9. Click New to create the new journal rule, and then click Finish.

You can also create a new journaling rule using the Exchange Management Shell. You must have the following parameters:

▶ **Name**—The name of the new journaling rule

▶ **JournalEmailAddress**—The name of the mailbox that the messages will be journaled to

▶ **Scope**—The scope of the journaling rule that is either global, internal, or external

▶ **Enabled**—The state of rule whether it is enabled or disabled

▶ **Recipient**—The association of the journal rule whether it is for a specific recipient or group

18

The following is a sample Microsoft shell command:

```
new-journalRule -Name:'TestRule'
➥-JournalEmailAddress:'COMPANYABC.COM/Users/TestJournalingMailbox1'
➥-Scope:'Global' -Enabled:$true -Recipient:'testuser1@COMPANYABC.COM'
```

Although the preceding command is spread across several lines, it is entered in the shell command as one continuous command. As mentioned previously, you can create a journal rule within the Exchange Management Console, allow the wizard to generate the Exchange Management Shell command for you, and then copy the command and save it to a text file for later use.

Using the Exchange Server 2007 Toolbox

The Exchange Server 2007 Management Console includes a Toolbox with several tools that can assist you in the identification and resolution of common Exchange problems.

The Toolbox can be accessed from the Exchange Management Console, in the console tree.

Included in the Toolbox are a series of configuration management tools, disaster recovery tools, mail flow tools, and performance tools. Each of these is covered in the following sections, with some information about their use.

As previously mentioned, the Toolbox is extensible, meaning that additional tools can be added to it from the Microsoft Exchange website, located at http://www.microsoft.com/exchange. However, third-party tools cannot be added to the Toolbox.

Another feature of the Toolbox, and one that is extremely forward thinking, is that each time you launch one of the utilities, a connection is made back to Microsoft to determine if you are running the most recent iteration of the tool. If not, an update is downloaded and installed, ensuring that you have access to the most current updates.

Configuration Management Tools

Utilities in the Configuration Management Tools section are intended to review an existing Exchange environment and make recommendations that will help organizations with improperly configured settings. The findings are compared against best practices and recommendations developed by the Microsoft Exchange Server Team and reports are generated that offer recommended changes.

Exchange Best Practices Analyzer (ExBPA)

At Microsoft, when a customer needs urgent assistance with problems that affect their business and end users, they refer to the issue as a "critical situation," or CritSit. In 2003, the Microsoft Exchange Server Team noticed that, in over 60% of these situations, the issue was because of a configuration error, not a bug in the software.

From this discovery, the decision was made to design and implement a utility that would gather information about an organization's Exchange and Active Directory implementation and compare what was found against Microsoft recommended best practices.

Included with Exchange Server 2007, the Exchange Best Practices Analyzer, or ExBPA, does exactly that.

When running the ExBPA, the scope of the scan determines how in depth the analysis will be. You can choose from three options:

- ▶ The entire Exchange organization

- ▶ One or more administrative groups

- ▶ One or more servers from any administrative group within the organization

After the scope of the scan has been determined, you can choose from several types of scans:

- ▶ **Health Check**—This check performs a full scan, checking the environment for errors, warnings, recent changes, and configuration settings that are not at the default settings. As the name implies, Health Check scans are useful to assess the overall health of your organization, and can also be extremely useful when troubleshooting particular problems.

  By adding the Performance Check option, the analyzer completes the health check and then gathers information by sampling various Exchange Server performance counters for a period of 2 hours.

- ▶ **Permission Check**—The permission check reviews administrative groups and permissions on the Exchange servers in your environment and reports on critical issues, noncritical issues, nondefault settings, and recent changes in the environment.

- ▶ **Connectivity Test**—This type of scan tests network connections and permissions on all Exchange servers identified in the selected scope. A connectivity test can be helpful to evaluate the configuration of firewalls in your environment to ensure they do not hamper necessary Exchange server communications. You can also use this test if you suspect a problem that is caused by permissions access.

- ▶ **Baseline**—The baseline scan compares findings on servers to baseline values that you configure. The report then identifies any findings that differ from the values you configured.

- ▶ **Exchange 2007 Readiness Check**—It is recommended to run this check early in your planning phase for Exchange 2007. This check is intended to identify potential problems in your environment that will hamper your deployment.

18

It is recommended to use ExBPA after you install a new Exchange server, upgrade an exist-ing server, or make configuration changes to your environment.

Disaster Recovery Tools

Utilities in the Disaster Recovery Tools section are intended to review the health and stability of mail databases in your Exchange organization.

Database Recovery Management

The Database Recovery Management tool is intended to help administrators restore Exchange messaging services in the event of a disaster. This utility examines an Exchange Server deployment when a database is unable to mount. Based on the information gath-ered, the tool automatically generates recommended step-by-step instructions to bring the database back online.

To use the Database Recovery Management tool, double-click the appropriate icon in the Toolbox. A wizard walks you through the steps for performing an analysis and viewing the results.

Database Troubleshooter

The Database Troubleshooter analyzes the databases and any available transactions logs on a particular Exchange server. The utility reports any issues found that might affect the ability to recover the database in the event of a failure. By scanning the log files, the tool is able to report on missing or corrupted files and offers recommended steps to perform to ensure the database is brought to a clean, mountable condition.

To use the Database Troubleshooter, double-click the Database Troubleshooter icon to launch the tool. A wizard walks you through the steps for performing an analysis and viewing the results.

Mail Flow Tools

Utilities in the Mail Flow Tools section are designed to assist in monitoring your Exchange environment to see where bottlenecks or complete mail flow blockages might be occurring.

Mail Flow Troubleshooter

The Mail Flow Troubleshooter provides easy access to various data sources that are neces-sary to troubleshoot common problems with mail flow, such as messages backed up in mail queues, slow delivery of messages, or unexplained nondelivery reports.

When you run the Mail Flow Troubleshooter, you begin by selecting the problem you are experiencing from a drop-down box.

NOTE

Although this tool can be run against servers running Exchange 2000 Server, Exchange Server 2003, and Exchange Server 2007, some of the options (such as Find a Lost Message) are restricted to only run against Exchange Server 2007 servers. These restricted options are labeled with For Exchange Server 2007 Only.

Based on the symptoms selected, the utility guides administrators through a recommended troubleshooting path.

Administrators start by selecting the symptoms observed. The utility then automatically diagnoses the data gathered and presents a report that contains possible root causes. The utility also suggests corrective actions and guides administrators through the correct troubleshooting path.

To launch the Mail Flow Troubleshooter, double-click the appropriate icon. A wizard walks you through the troubleshooting steps.

Message Tracking

The message tracking utility has been around in one form or another since Exchange 5.5. This utility allows administrators to search for messages and determine the path they took through the Exchange environment. In Exchange 2007, message tracking records the SMTP transport activity of all messages entering or leaving an Exchange 2007 Server with the Hub Transport, Mailbox, or Edge Transport server roles. By default, message tracking is enabled on all Exchange 2007 servers running one of these roles.

The message tracking logs cannot be configured utilizing the Microsoft Management Console. To make any changes to the default configuration log settings, you must use the Exchange Management Shell.

The message tracking utility is intended primarily for mail flow analysis, reporting, and (of course) determining the status of a message that has been reported as undelivered.

Administrators can search for messages based on any combination of the following fields:

▶ Server

▶ Event ID

▶ Sender

▶ Message ID

▶ Subject Line

In addition, the administrator can specify a Start and End date and time to search for the message. In organizations with large message stores, it can be extremely beneficial to narrow the scope of the search as much as possible, as sorting through all messages in the environment to look for a particular one can take a significant amount of time.

Double-click the Message Tracking icon to launch the tool. A wizard walks you through the steps for tracking messages.

Queue Viewer

The Exchange Queue Viewer is an Exchange Management Console snap-in that is added to the Toolbox when an Exchange Server 2007 Hub Transport or Edge Transport server is installed.

The Queue Viewer is a graphical interface that allows administrators to view information about mail queues and mail items on a transport server. In addition, administrators can perform management actions on these items. Often used for troubleshooting mail flow and identifying spam messages, administrators can also use the viewer to easily perform intrusive actions against the queuing databases, such as suspending or resuming a queue, or removing messages.

Using the Queue Viewer requires certain administrative permissions. To use Queue Viewer on a computer that has the Edge Transport server role, you must use an account that is a member of the local Administrators group on that computer. To use Queue Viewer on a computer that has the Hub Transport server role, the account you use must also be a domain account that has the permissions assigned to the Exchange View-Only Administrators Universal Security group. Double-click the Queue Viewer icon to launch the tool.

Performance Tools

The Toolbox also contains tools that are intended to assist with improving and maintaining the overall health of the Exchange servers and environment.

Exchange Server Performance Monitor

One of the most powerful, yet often overlooked, utilities is the Exchange Server Performance Monitor. This tool is essentially the same as the Windows Performance Monitor, but it has a series of predefined counters that are related specifically to Exchange, including message traffic sent or received per second, Average Disk Queue Length, and several counters to monitor remote procedure calls (RPC) traffic. Of course, the old favorites are still there, including memory, processor, hard drive, and network utilization.

This utility might be considered less intuitive because there is no built-in wizard to assist with its configuration, but a great deal of information can be gathered about your Exchange environment, virtually every measurable aspect of an Exchange server can be monitored using this tool. The data collected can be presented in a variety of forms, including reports, real-time charts, or logs. Using the Performance Monitor, administrators can take baseline readings on server and network performance, and compare them over time to spot trends and plan accordingly, but it is most commonly used to view parameters while troubleshooting performance problems.

Double-click the Performance Monitor icon to launch the tool. It automatically starts displaying a live graph of the key performance indicators for the machine on which tool is launched. More information on the usage of the tool can be found in the System Monitor Help files within the tool, and from the Microsoft website.

Performance Troubleshooter

With an interface that looks very similar to the Exchange Mail Flow Troubleshooter, the Performance Troubleshooter is designed to help administrators identify and locate performance issues that are having a negative impact on an Exchange environment.

Like the Mail Flow Troubleshooter, administrators begin by selecting the symptoms they are experiencing. Based on these systems, the utility identifies potential bottlenecks in the messaging system and outlines a troubleshooting path for the administrators to follow.

Double-click the Performance Troubleshooter icon to launch the utility, bringing up a wizard that walks you through the steps necessary to perform an analysis and view the results.

Summary

As the Microsoft Exchange platform has evolved over the past several revisions, the processes and utilities used to administer and monitor the environment have improved tremendously with each new platform. Exchange Server 2007 is no exception. The ability to separate the administration of the Exchange and Active Directory environments is huge—no longer do you need to grant domain administrators (who might have *no* Exchange experience) full permissions to your Exchange organization. And, conversely, permission can be granted to the Exchange environment while protecting your Active Directory from unauthorized users.

Furthermore, the ability to delegate the level of control over the Exchange environment based on the new Exchange administrator roles gives an organization much greater control over *who* gets access to *what*.

The Exchange Management Console and Exchange Management Shell are extremely powerful interfaces, enabling an administrator to perform tasks quickly and easily, whether from a familiar GUI interface of the Exchange Management Console, or from the versatile command-line interface of the Exchange Management Shell.

Whether dealing with users and mailboxes, distribution groups, journaling of messages for regulatory compliance, or monitoring and analyzing the environment for performance bottlenecks, Exchange 2007 has tools and utilities that give administrators more control over their Exchange environments than ever before.

Best Practices

The following are best practices from this chapter:

▶ Review the Finalize Deployment and End-to-End Scenario Guides tabs in the Exchange Management Console carefully. The tasks and documentation there might prove to be invaluable when verifying your Exchange 2007 implementation.

▶ Minimize membership in the Exchange Organization Administrators role. This, the most powerful of Exchange roles, gives members full access to all Exchange objects and properties throughout the organization. Membership should be restricted solely to high-level administrators, who can then grant appropriate permissions to subordinate administrators.

▶ Grant the Exchange Recipient and Exchange Server Administrators roles appropriately, giving permissions to those properly trained and approved to modify and maintain users in Active Directory and mailboxes in Exchange.

▶ Grant the Exchange View-Only Administrators role to operations staff, network infrastructure staff, or other administrators who might have a need to *view* the status of Exchange functions, but who do not need the ability to modify or configure these functions.

▶ For scripting routine or repetitive tasks, consider performing the task once in the Exchange Management Console and, when possible, copy the associated Exchange Management Shell command that is automatically generated by the wizard. This can give you a starting point for creating your scripts.

▶ Keep database sizes small to ensure backup, restore, and maintenance times are short enough to meet service level agreements (SLAs). If the backup and restore times for your databases have grown beyond reasonable expectations, you can lighten the load by moving mailboxes from the server. The alternative is to either improve the performance of the existing hardware by increasing system resources or migrate the data to a more powerful server.

▶ When possible, create a single mail-enabled security group to provide both security and distribution group functionality, rather than two separate groups for the same list of users.

▶ Restrict access to large distribution groups to those who truly need it. Require that all senders are authenticated whenever possible.

▶ Use dynamic distribution lists with caution if they will be frequently used. The list is re-created every time it is accessed, requiring both server and domain resources to determine the membership.

▶ When possible, create additional databases rather than additional storage groups. The log file management associated with new storage groups can add a significant amount of overhead on a server.

▶ Implement storage limits on user mailboxes. Use the Issue Warning option to warn the users and the Prohibit Send option to enforce the limits; however, use the Prohibit Send and Receive option with discretion.

▶ Do not use circular logging. Circular logging was sometimes necessary in older versions of Exchange because log files could quickly grow to a size that would fill up the Exchange server hard drives. With today's technology, and with hard drive space relatively inexpensive, there are rarely situations where circular logging is needed.

- Use either automated or manual processes to ensure successful backups are completed daily and that log files are purged.

- Stagger database maintenance so that all storage groups are not attempting to run maintenance at the same time.

- Keep deleted items for at least 14 days, and deleted mailboxes for at least 30 days. Use the option to not remove the items permanently until the store has been backed up.

- Use the Exchange Best Practices Analyzer tool whenever you install a new Exchange server, upgrade an existing server, or make configuration changes to your environment.

- Periodically, run the Exchange Best Practices Analyzer tool against your Exchange environment, simply to look for anything out of place.

- Regularly launch the tools in the Exchange Management Console Toolbox, allowing them to check for updates from the Microsoft website. Whenever the Exchange Best Practices Analyzer is updated, run it against your Exchange environment to check if there are any new/updated recommendations that you can implement that will improve performance and reliability for your organization.

18

CHAPTER 19

Exchange Server 2007 Management and Maintenance Practices

Organizations have become increasingly reliant on email as a primary method of communication and, as such, the messaging system in most environments has come to be considered a mission-critical application. Any messaging downtime results in frustrated calls to the help desk. For most organizations, gone are the days where the email system can be taken offline during business hours for configuration changes.

To ensure the dependability and reliability of any application, proper maintenance and upkeep is vital, and Exchange Server 2007 is no exception. By implementing and performing proper management and maintenance procedures, administrators can minimize downtime and keep the system well tuned. If proper management, maintenance, and procedures are neglected, overall system performance can be negatively impacted, databases can become corrupt, and messaging outages are the likely result.

This chapter focuses on recommended best practices for an administrator to properly maintain an Exchange Server 2007 messaging environment.

Proper Care and Feeding of Exchange Server 2007

This section is not about how to perform common, albeit necessary, management tasks such as using the interface to add a database. Instead, it focuses on concepts such as identifying and working with the server's functional roles in the network environment, auditing network activity and usage, and monitoring the health and performance of your messaging system.

With each new iteration of Exchange, Microsoft has greatly improved the tools and utilities used to manage the environment. Exchange 2007 is no exception. Exchange Server 2007 management can be done locally or remotely. There are new primary management interfaces, the Exchange Management Console and the Exchange Management Shell, and new tools and utilities to assist administrators in the upkeep of their environment.

Managing by Server Roles and Responsibilities

New in Exchange Server 2007 is the concept of role-based deployment, allowing administrators to deploy specific server roles to meet the requirements of their environment. Exchange 2007 provides five distinct server roles: Edge Transport, Hub Transport, Client Access, Mailbox, and Unified Messaging.

The Edge Transport Server Role

The Edge Transport server role is responsible for all email entering or leaving the Exchange organization. To provide redundancy and load balancing, multiple Edge Transport servers can be configured for an organization.

The Edge Transport role is designed to be installed on a standalone server that resides in the perimeter network. As such, it is the only Exchange server designed to NOT be a member of the Active Directory (AD) domain. Synchronization with Active Directory is provided through the use of Active Directory Application Mode (ADAM) and a component called EdgeSync.

Edge Transport servers can provide antispam and antivirus protection, as well as the enforcement of Edge Transport rules based on Simple Mail Transfer Protocol (SMTP) and Multipurpose Internet Mail Extensions (MIME) addresses, particular words in the subject or message body, and a Spam Confidence Level (SCL) rating. In addition, Edge Transport servers can provide address rewriting—an administrator can modify the SMTP address on incoming and outgoing messages.

It is possible for an organization to avoid the use of an Edge Transport server completely and simply configure a Hub Transport server to communicate directly with the Internet. However, this scenario is not recommended because it exposes your Hub Transport server to potential attack. The Edge Transport server has a reduced attack surface to protect against these external threats.

The Hub Transport Server Role

The Hub Transport role is responsible for managing internal mail flow in an Exchange organization and is installed on a member server in the AD domain.

The Hub Transport role handles all mail flow within the organization, as well as applying transport rules, journaling policies, and delivery of messages to recipient mailboxes. In addition, Hub Transport agents can be deployed to enforce corporate messaging policies such as message retention and the implementation of email disclaimers.

Hub Transport servers accept inbound mail from the Edge Transport server(s) and route them to user mailboxes. Outbound mail is relayed from the Hub Transport server to the Edge Transport server and out to the Internet.

The Hub Transport role can be installed on the same hardware with any other nonclustered internal server role or as a dedicated Hub Transport server. It can *not* be installed on the same hardware as an Edge Transport server role.

Each AD site that contains a Mailbox server role must contain at least one Hub Transport server role.

The Client Access Server Role

The Client Access role is similar to the front-end server in Exchange 2000/2003. Users who are accessing mailboxes via Outlook Web Access (OWA), Microsoft ActiveSync, Post Office Protocol version 3 (POP3), or Internet Message Access Protocol version 4 (IMAP4) must connect to the Client Access server to gain entry. As a matter of fact, for a user to access an Inbox with any client other than Microsoft Outlook, a Client Access server must be installed in the Exchange organization.

The Mailbox Server Role

The Mailbox role will be the most familiar to administrators with previous Exchange experience. As the name implies, the Mailbox role is responsible for housing mailbox databases which, in turn, contain user mailboxes. The Mailbox server role also houses public folder databases if they are implemented in the environment.

The Mailbox server role integrates with the directory in the Active Directory service much more effectively than previous versions of Exchange allowed, making deployment and day-to-day operational tasks much easier to complete. The Mailbox server role also provides users with improved calendaring functionality, resource management, and Offline Address Book downloads.

The Unified Messaging Server Role

The Unified Messaging server role is responsible for the integration of Voice over IP (VoIP) technology into the Exchange messaging system. When implementing Unified Messaging with Exchange 2007, users can have access to voice, fax, and email messages all in the same mailbox, and these messages can be accessed through multiple client interfaces.

Maintenance Tools for Exchange Server 2007

Several new and improved tools are available to administer and manage an Exchange Server 2007 environment. There are Microsoft Management Console snap-ins, an automation and scripting shell, and several tools native to the Windows Server 2003 operating system and the Exchange Server 2007 application.

The Exchange Management Console

The Exchange Management Console shown in Figure 19.1 is one of the primary tools provided with Exchange Server 2007. This utility replaces the Exchange System Manager

from Exchange 2000/2003 and can be used to manage Exchange Server 2007 and
Exchange Server 2003 servers in the organization.

FIGURE 19.1   Exchange Server 2007 Exchange Management Console.

The Exchange Management Console is a snap-in that is designed to work with the new
Microsoft Management Console (MMC) 3.0, a new and improved version of the MMC. To
install MMC 3.0 on a system, the system must be running Microsoft Windows Server
2003 (SP1) or higher, or Microsoft Windows XP (SP2) or higher. MMC 3.0 is included by
default with Microsoft Windows Server 2003 R2 and Microsoft Windows Vista.

Unlike the Exchange System Manager, which allowed administrators to access all configuration settings of their Exchange 2003 environment, the Exchange Management Console
is designed to allow administrators access to common configuration settings from the
familiar graphical user interface (GUI). However, many aspects of the environment cannot
be viewed or modified with this utility. For such configuration settings, the Exchange
Management Shell, which is discussed next, must be used.

For more in-depth information on the Exchange Management Console, refer to Chapter
18, "Administering an Exchange Server 2007 Environment."

The Exchange Management Shell

The second utility for managing an Exchange 2007 environment is a new automation and
scripting tool called the Exchange Management Shell, shown in Figure 19.2. This shell is a
command-line management interface that can be used to administer servers in an

Exchange 2007 organization. Built on Microsoft Windows PowerShell technology (formerly code-named "Monad"), the Exchange Management Shell can perform any task that can be accomplished in the Exchange Management Console, and a lot more. In fact, many configuration settings in an Exchange 2007 environment can only be accomplished using the Exchange Management Shell.

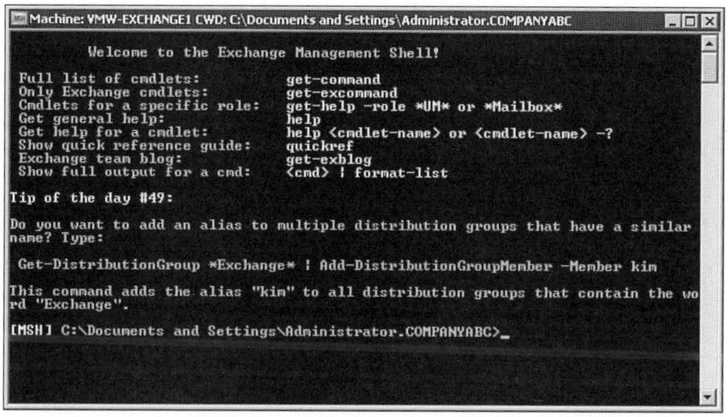

FIGURE 19.2   Exchange Server 2007 Exchange Management Shell.

The Exchange Management Shell can be installed on computers with a 32-bit processor running Windows 2000, Windows Server 2003, Windows XP, and Windows Vista.

For more in-depth information on the Exchange Management Shell, refer to Chapter 9, "Using the Windows PowerShell in an Exchange Server 2007 Environment."

Exchange Best Practices Analyzer

The Exchange Best Practices Analyzer (ExBPA) is included in Exchange Server 2007 and can be found in the Exchange Management Console toolbox.

The ExBPA can be used to run health checks on an Exchange environment, and can also run performance checks, permissions checks, and connectivity tests to assist when troubleshooting problems.

The ExBPA should be run whenever a new server is added to an Exchange 2007 environment, or whenever configuration changes are made. More information on this utility can be found in Chapter 18.

Disaster Recovery Tools

Also included in the Exchange Management Console toolbox are two utilities designed to analyze and maintain Exchange databases. The Database Troubleshooter can inspect existing databases and available transaction logs and report on any problems found. The tool also offers recommended steps that should be taken to ensure the database is healthy.

19

The Database Recovery Management utility is intended to assist administrators when a database is unable to mount. This tool also generates recommended step-by-step instructions to follow to bring the database back online.

Mail Flow Tools

The Mail Flow Troubleshooter is a utility that assists with troubleshooting common mail flow issues in an Exchange environment. Administrators can input the issues they are encountering, and the utility gathers information, diagnoses the environment, and presents a recommended plan of action.

The Message Tracking utility allows administrators to search for messages and track them through the Exchange environment. Message tracking can be extremely useful for determining where a message was delayed or "stuck" in the messaging environment.

The Mail Flow Troubleshooter and the Message Tracking utility are both included in the Exchange Server 2007 Exchange Management Console toolbox. For more information on these two utilities, refer to Chapter 18. For information on configuring message tracking logs, refer to the "Message Tracking" section later in this chapter.

Exchange Queue Viewer

The Exchange Queue Viewer is another utility included in the Exchange Management Console toolbox that is added to an Exchange server when the Hub Transport or Edge Transport role is installed. The Exchange Queue Viewer is used to view the contents of the queues for each particular protocol on a server. Although this tool is more of a troubleshooting tool, it is important to periodically check protocol queues (for example, SMTP or X.400 queues) to ensure that no delivery problems exist.

Performance Tools

The Exchange Management Console toolbox includes two tools that are designed to monitor and troubleshoot performance issues in an Exchange environment.

The Exchange Server Performance Monitor is based on the Windows Performance Monitor, but includes a series of predefined counters that are specifically related to an Exchange environment.

The Performance Troubleshooter is designed to help administrators identify and locate performance issues that are impacting the Exchange environment.

More information on these tools can be found in Chapter 18.

Windows Server 2003 Backup

The Windows Server 2003 backup utility (`ntbackup.exe`) is a utility that exists on all Windows Server 2003 systems and is located under the Start, All Programs, Accessories, System Tools menu. Out of the box, this utility can back up and restore an entire system, including the System State and data.

To properly back up Exchange Server 2007 databases and log files, and the Windows Server 2003 System State using ntbackup, administrators should perform two separate backup jobs. Errors can occur when an attempt is made to back up the Exchange databases and the server System State. In addition, if the need to restore the System State should arise, it can be accomplished much faster if it was backed up using a separate job.

Local and remote Exchange storage groups and databases can be backed up and restored from any Exchange 2007 server, but not from any other server.

Third-party software vendors, such as EMC Legato and Symantec, produce Exchange Server backup and restore agents for the purpose of Exchange database backup and recovery.

For more detailed information on Exchange Server 2007 backup and recovery, refer to Chapters 31, 32, and 33 ("Continuous Backups, Clustering, and Network Load Balancing in Exchange Server 2007," "Backing Up the Exchange Server 2007 Environment," and "Recovering from a Disaster in an Exchange Server 2007 Environment," respectively).

Active Directory Database Maintenance Using ntdsutil

Exchange Server 2007 uses Windows Server 2003 AD to store all its directory information. As a result, it is important to keep AD as healthy as possible to ensure that Exchange Server 2007 remains reliable and stable.

Windows Server 2003 automatically performs maintenance on Active Directory by cleaning up the AD database on a daily basis. The process occurs on domain controllers approximately every 12 hours. One example of the results of this process is the removal of tombstones, which are the "markers" for previously deleted objects. In addition, the process deletes unnecessary log files and reclaims free space.

The automatic daily process does not, however, perform all maintenance necessary for a clean and healthy database. For example, the maintenance process does not compress and defragment the Active Directory database. To perform this function, the ntdsutil command-line utility is needed.

CAUTION

To avoid possible adverse affects with the AD database, run ntdsutil in Directory Service Restore mode. Reboot the server, press the F8 key, and then select this mode of operation.

To use ntdsutil to defragment the AD database, perform the following steps:

1. Restart the domain controller.

2. When the initial screen appears, press the F8 key.

3. From the Windows Advanced Options menu, select Directory Services Restore Mode.

4. Select the Windows Server 2003 operating system being used.

19

5. Log on to the Windows Server 2003 system.

6. Click OK when the informational message appears.

7. At a command prompt, create a directory where the utility can store the defragmented file. For example, `C:\NTDS`.

8. At a command prompt, type `ntdsutil` files, and then press Enter.

9. At the file maintenance prompt, type compact to <TargetDirectory>, where <TargetDirectory> identifies the empty directory created in step 7. For example:

   ```
   compact to c:\ntds
   ```

This invokes the `esentutl.exe` utility to compact the existing database and write the results to the specified directory. The compaction process is shown in Figure 19.3.

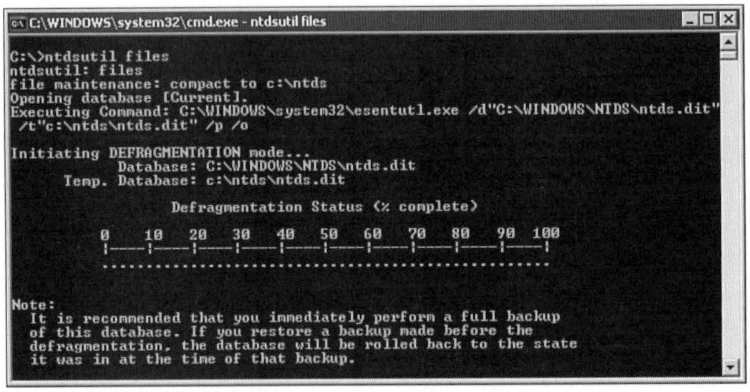

FIGURE 19.3   Using `ntdsutil` to defragment the AD database.

10. If compaction was successful, copy the new `ntds.dit` file to `%systemroot%\NTDS`, and delete the old log files located in that directory.

11. Type quit twice to exit the utility.

12. Restart the domain controller.

Integrity Checking with the `isinteg` Utility

The Information Store Integrity Checker (`isinteg.exe`) is a command-based utility that finds and eliminates errors from mailbox and public folder databases at the application level. Although this tool is not intended for use as a part of routine Information Store maintenance, it is mentioned here because it can assist in disaster recovery situations.

`isinteg` is most often used in conjunction with the `eseutil` repair operation, and can recover data that the `eseutil` tool cannot.

Using this utility in any mode other than Test mode results in irreversible changes to the database.

It is best to restore a copy of a suspected corrupt database in a lab environment, and then run `isinteg` against that copy prior to any attempts to use it in a production environment.

Dismount the Exchange databases that you plan to perform maintenance on and stop the Microsoft Exchange Information Store service prior to running this utility. Keep in mind that this makes the databases unavailable to users until after the maintenance has been completed.

Database table integrity problems are caused by corruption, which can occur if the server is shut down improperly, if the drive or controller fails, and so forth.

To view the command-line help about usage of the `isinteg` utility, type the following command from a command prompt: `isinteg /?`

For more information on using `isinteg`, refer to the "Performing Offline Database Maintenance" section later in this chapter, and to Chapter 33.

Database Maintenance with the `eseutil` Utility

The `eseutil` utility is a database-level utility that is not application-specific. It can, for example, be used to maintain, test, and repair both AD and Exchange databases. More specifically, `eseutil` is used to maintain database-level integrity, perform defragmentation and compaction, and repair even the most severely corrupt databases. It is also the utility to use when maintaining Exchange Server 2007 transaction log files to determine which transaction logs need to be replayed or which log file the `Edb.chk` file points to.

CAUTION

Using the `eseutil` utility on an AD or Exchange database can produce irreversible changes.

As with the `isinteg` utility, it is best to restore a copy of a suspected corrupt database in a lab environment, and then run `eseutil` against that copy prior to any attempts to use it in a production environment.

NOTE

`eseutil` investigates the data that resides in the database table for any corruption or errors, which is why it is called a database-level utility. The `eseutil` options are shown in Table 19.1.

TABLE 19.1   `eseutil` Syntax

Mode of Operation	Syntax
Defragmentation	ESEUTIL /d <database name> [options]
Recovery	ESEUTIL /r <logfile base name> [options]
Integrity	ESEUTIL /g <database name> [options]
Checksum	ESEUTIL /k <filename> [options]
Repair	ESEUTIL /p <database name> [options]
File dump	ESEUTIL /m[mode-modifier] <filename>
Copy file	ESEUTIL /y <source file> [options]
Restore	ESEUTIL /c[mode-modifier] <pathname> [options]

For more information on using `eseutil`, refer to the "Performing Offline Database Maintenance" section later in this chapter, and to Chapter 33.

Auditing the Environment

Various methods of auditing the Exchange environment exist to gather and store records of network and Exchange access and to assist with the monitoring and tracking of SMTP connections and message routing.

Typically used for identifying security breaches or suspicious activity, auditing has the added benefit of allowing administrators to gain insight into how the Exchange Server 2007 systems are accessed and, in some cases, how they are performing.

This chapter focuses on three types of auditing:

▶ **Audit logging**—For security and tracking user access

▶ **SMTP logging**—For capturing SMTP conversations between messaging servers

▶ **Message tracking**—For tracking emails through the messaging environment

Audit Logging

In a Windows environment, auditing is primarily considered to be an identity and access control security technology that can be implemented as part of an organization's network security strategy. By collecting and monitoring security-related events, administrators can track user authentication and authorization, as well as access to various directory services (including Exchange Server 2007 services).

Exchange Server 2007 relies on the audit policies of the underlying operating system for capturing information on user access and authorization. Administrators can utilize the built-in Windows Server event auditing to capture data that is written to the security log for review.

Enabling Event Auditing

Audit policies are the basis for auditing events on Windows Server 2003 systems. Administrators must be aware that, depending on the policies configured, auditing might require a substantial amount of server resources in addition to those supporting the primary function of the server. On servers without adequate memory, processing power or hard drive space, auditing can potentially result in decreased server performance. After enabling auditing, administrators should monitor server performance to ensure the server can handle the additional load.

To enable audit policies on a Windows Server 2003 server, perform the following steps:

1. On the server to be audited, log on as a member of the local Administrators group. From the Start Menu, select Run, type MMC in the Open text box, and then click OK to start the Microsoft Management Console.

2. Select File, Add/Remove Snap-in.

3. On the Add/Remove Snap-in page, click Add.

4. On the Add Standalone Snap-in page, scroll down to Group Policy Object Editor, select it, and click Add.

5. On the Select Group Policy Object page, click Finish. Then click Close on the Add Standalone Snap-in page.

6. On the Add/Remove Snap-in page, click OK.

7. Expand each level, drilling down to Local Computer Policy, Computer Configuration, Windows Settings, Security Settings, Local Policies, Audit Policy.

8. In the right pane, double-click the policy to be modified.

9. Select to audit Success, Failure, or both.

10. Click OK to exit the configuration screen, and then close the MMC.

Figure 19.4 shows an example of typical auditing policies that might be configured in an Exchange environment.

These audit policies can be turned on manually by following the preceding procedure or by the implementation of security templates.

19

> **NOTE**
>
> After enabling audit policies, Windows event logs (specifically the security log) will capture a significant amount of data. Be sure to increase the "maximum log size" in the security log properties page. A best practice is to make the log size large enough to contain at least a week's worth of data, and configure it to overwrite as necessary so that newer data is not sacrificed at the expense of older data.

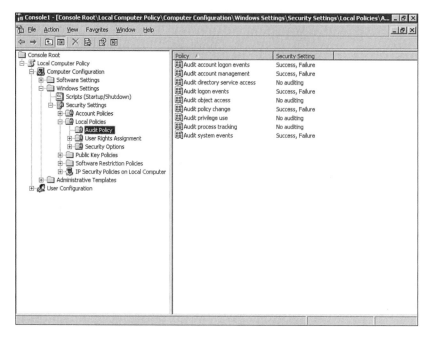

FIGURE 19.4   Windows Server 2003 audit policies.

Viewing the Security Logs

The events generated by the Windows Server 2003 auditing policies can be viewed in the security log in the Event Viewer.

Understanding the information presented in the security log events can be a challenge. The event often contains error codes, with no explanation on their meaning. Microsoft has taken strides to make this easier by providing a link to the Microsoft Help and Support Center within the event.

When an administrator clicks on the link, the Event Viewer asks for permission to send information about the event to Microsoft. Administrators can select the option to always send information if they want, and can then click Yes to authorize the sending of the data. A connection is made to the Help and Support Center, and information about the Event ID is displayed. This information can be invaluable when trying to decipher the sometimes cryptic events in the security log.

Administrators can use the Filter feature (from the View menu) to filter the events based on various fields. In addition, when searching for a specific event within a specific time frame, administrators can select a specific window of time to filter on. Some of the common events that administrators might be interested in monitoring are listed in Table 19.2.

TABLE 19.2   Windows Security Events

Event ID	Category	Explanation
675	Account Logon	A failed logon attempt via Kerberos from a workstation with a domain account has occurred. This is usually because of a bad password. The failure code indicates the reason for the failure. See Table 19.3 for a list of common failure codes.
672	Account Logon	An account logon was attempted. The type shows either Success or Failure. Failed logon attempts with this Event ID are often due to an invalid username.
680	Account Logon	A set of credentials was passed to the authentication system. If success is displayed, the credentials presented were valid and an error code of 0x0 is displayed. For failure messages, an NTStatus code is displayed. See Table 19.4 for a list of NTStatus codes.
642	Account Management	A change to the specified user account has occurred, such as a reset password or the enabling of a disabled account. The description details which attribute was changed.
632. 636, 660	Account Management	These three events signify that a user was added to a group. The user and group modified are shown in the description. Event ID 632 is for a global group, Event ID 636 is for a local group, and Event ID 660 is for a universal group.
624	Account Management	A new user account was created.
644	Account Management	The specified user account was locked out after repeated logon failures.
538	Logon/Logoff	The user identified in the description has logged off.
517	System Event	The specified user cleared the security log.

NOTE

For a more complete list of Windows 2003 security log Event IDs and their descriptions, refer to: http://www.eventid.net/downloads/w2k3security.txt.

Table 19.3 contains some common Kerberos failure codes that can be helpful when reviewing some of the events in the security log. This table only contains a few of the many possible codes, but a complete list of Kerberos failure codes can be seen in Request for Comments 1515 (RFC 1510) in the "error codes" section. A copy of RFC 1510 can be viewed at http://www.ietf.org/rfc/rfc1510.

TABLE 19.3   Common Kerberos Failure Codes

Kerberos Failure Code	Meaning
0x0	This code indicates there is no error.
0x6	The username does not exist.
0x12	The workstation or logon time restriction prevented authorization.
0x18	The account is disabled, expired, or locked out.
0x23	The user's password has expired.
0x32	The ticket expired, a common event logged by computer accounts.
0x37	The workstation clock is too far out of synchronization with the domain controller clock.

Table 19.4 is a list of NTStatus codes that are returned during user account logon attempts. These status codes are referenced in some of the security log Event IDs.

TABLE 19.4   NTStatus Codes

NTStatus Code	Meaning
0x0	This code indicates a successful logon.
0xC0000064	The specified user does not exist.
0xC000006A	The value provided as the current password is not correct.
0xC000006C	The password policy is not met.
0xC000006D	The attempted logon is invalid because of a bad username.
0xC000006E	A user account restriction has prevented successful logon.
0xC000006F	The user account has time restrictions and may not be logged on to at this time.
0xC0000070	The user is restricted and may not log on from the source workstation.
0xC0000071	The user account's password has expired.
0xC0000072	The user account is currently disabled.
0xC000009A	There are insufficient system resources.
0xC0000193	The user's account has expired.
0xC0000224	The user must change his password before he logs on the first time.
0xC0000234	The user account has been automatically locked.

The information supplied here on viewing security log Event IDs is intended to help administrators get a basic understanding of the topic. There is much more that can be learned on the subject of security auditing and event monitoring, and the Microsoft website is an excellent resource for doing so.

SMTP Logging

Logging SMTP protocol activity provides administrators with a powerful tool when troubleshooting issues with message delivery. By enabling SMTP logging, administrators can capture the SMTP conversations with email servers during message transport. Each Receive and Send Connector in an Exchange 2007 environment has the capability of logging SMTP activity, providing information regarding messaging commands that a user sends to the Exchange Server 2007 server. This includes, but is not limited to, such information as IP address, bytes sent, data, time, protocol, and domain name.

To enable SMTP protocol logging, administrators must enable the feature on each Send and Receive Connector on each 2007 Exchange server where logging is desired. By default, SMTP logging is disabled on all Send and Receive Connectors.

Configure SMTP Logging from the Exchange Management Console

The configuration of SMTP protocol logging utilizing the Exchange Management Console is limited to enabling or disabling the feature. To enable or disable SMTP protocol logging from the Exchange Management Console, perform the following tasks:

1. Start the Exchange Management Console by selecting Start, All Programs, Microsoft Exchange Server 2007, Exchange Management Console.

2. Locate the Send or Receive Connector on which you want to enable logging.

   ▶ **For Hub Transport Send Connectors**—In the console tree, select Organization Configuration, then Hub Transport. In the results pane, click the Send Connectors tab, and then select the appropriate Send Connector.

   ▶ **For Hub Transport Receive Connectors**—In the console tree, select Server Configuration, then Hub Transport. Select the appropriate server in the results pane, and then select the appropriate connector in the bottom half of the results pane.

   ▶ **For Edge Transport Connectors**—On the Edge Transport server, select Edge Transport in the console tree. Select the appropriate server in the results pane, and then select the Receive Connectors or Send Connectors tab in the bottom half of the results pane. Select the desired connector from those displayed.

3. After you have selected the appropriate connector, select Properties from the action pane.

4. On the General tab, configure the desired protocol logging level. By default, all connectors are set to None .

Configure SMTP Logging from the Exchange Management Shell

Most of the configuration settings for SMTP protocol logging must be accomplished from the Exchange Management Shell. All of the following commands must be performed from within the Exchange Management Shell.

For all following commands, arguments that contain a space must be in quotes. For example, where the command says <connector name>, an administrator might put "Default Receive Connector", or where the command says <LogPath>, the administrator might put "C:\Receive Log Files".

19

To enable SMTP protocol logging on a Receive Connector:

```
Set-ReceiveConnector <ConnectorName> -ProtocolLoggingLevel Basic
```

To disable SMTP protocol logging on a Receive Connector:

```
Set-ReceiveConnector <ConnectorName> -ProtocolLoggingLevel None
```

To enable or disable SMTP protocol logging on a Send Connector:

Use the same commands as previously shown, but replace `Set-ReceiveConnector` with `Set-SendConnector`.

Sample command: To enable SMTP protocol logging on a Receive Connector called Default Receive Connector, use the following command:

```
Set-ReceiveConnector "Default Receive Connector" –ProtocolLoggingLevel Basic
```

Changing the Protocol Log Path

Exchange Server 2007 allows administrators to specify the location of the Send and Receive log files. The log files for all Send Connectors on a particular server are in one location, and the log files for all Receive Connectors are in another.

By default, these files are located in the following locations:

- ▶ **Receive log**—`C:\Program Files\Microsoft\Exchange Server\TransportRoles\Logs\ProtocolLog\SmtpReceive`

- ▶ **Send log**—`C:\Program Files\Microsoft\Exchange Server\TransportRoles\Logs\ProtocolLog\SmtpSend`

To change the default location for these log files, use the following commands in the Exchange Management Shell:

Change log file location for the Receive Connectors:

```
Set-TransportServer <Identity> -ReceiveProtocolLogPath <LogPath>
```

Change log file location for the Send Connectors:

```
Set-TransportServer <Identity> -SendProtocolLogPath <LogPath>
```

Sample command: To set the Receive SMTP protocol log path for all Receive Connectors on Server1 to `C:\SMTP Receive Logs`, use the following command:

```
Set-TransportServer Server1 -ReceiveProtocolLogPath "C:\SMTP Receive Logs"
```

Configuring Log File and Log Directory Maximum Size

To prevent log files from growing so large that they deplete all available disk space, Exchange Server 2007 allows administrators to configure maximum log file and directory sizes. This configuration setting is a per-server setting and, by default, the maximum directory size is 250MB, whereas the maximum log file size is 10MB. When the maximum file size is reached, Exchange opens a new log file. When the maximum directory size is reached, Exchange overwrites the log files, starting with the oldest logs first.

To configure SMTP protocol log directory and file sizes, use the following commands in the Exchange Management Shell. Be aware, these commands must be performed for each server that you want to modify. The `<DirectorySize>` and `<FileSize>` arguments should be entered as a number followed by one of the following:

- ▶ B (bytes)
- ▶ KB (kilobytes)
- ▶ MB (megabytes)
- ▶ GB (gigabytes)
- ▶ TB (terabytes)

Change maximum size for Receive SMTP protocol log directory:

```
Set-TransportServer <Identity> -ReceiveProtocolMaxDirectorySize <DirectorySize>
```

Change maximum size for Send SMTP protocol log directory:

```
Set-TransportServer <Identity> -SendProtocolMaxDirectorySize <DirectorySize>
```

Change maximum size for Receive SMTP protocol log files:

```
Set-TransportServer <Identity> -ReceiveProtocolMaxFileSize <FileSize>
```

Change maximum size for Send SMTP protocol log files:

```
Set-TransportServer <Identity> -SendProtocolMaxFileSize <FileSize>
```

Sample command: To set the maximum size for the Receive SMTP protocol log directory on Server1 to 1 Gigabyte, use the following command:

```
Set-TransportServer Server1 -ReceiveProtocolMaxDirectorySize 1GB
```

19

Configuring the Maximum Age for the SMTP Protocol Log

In addition to having the ability to configure the maximum file and directory sizes for SMTP protocol logs, administrators can also configure a maximum age for each SMTP protocol log file. The default age for all log files is set to 30 days, and any log files that exceed this age are deleted by Exchange.

To change the maximum age of SMTP protocol log files, use the following commands in the Exchange Management Shell. The `<Age>` argument is entered in the following format: DD.HH:MM:SS, for Days, Hours, Minutes, Seconds.

Change maximum age for the Receive SMTP protocol log file:

```
Set-TransportServer <Identity> -ReceiveProtocolLogMaxAge <Age>
```

Change maximum age for the Send SMTP protocol log file:

```
Set-TransportServer <Identity> -SendProtocolLogMaxAge <Age>
```

Sample command: To set the maximum age of the Send SMTP protocol log file on Server1 to 60 days, use the following command:

```
Set-TransportServer Server1 –SendProtocolLogMaxAge 60.00:00:00
```

Message Tracking

Of the auditing techniques available in Exchange, message tracking is by far the least resource-intensive and will likely be the most commonly used by administrators. Because this feature has proven so valuable in previous versions of Exchange, Microsoft has enabled it by default in Exchange 2007. Previously, message tracking was disabled by default, and had to be enabled on a server-by-server basis.

Administrators can use message tracking logs for message forensics, reporting, and troubleshooting, as well as analyzing mail flow in an organization.

Message tracking records the SMTP transport activity of all messages sent to or from any Exchange 2007 Hub Transport, Edge Transport, or Mailbox server.

Message tracking logs cannot be configured by using the Exchange Management Console; all settings must be configured using the Exchange Management Shell.

To perform these procedures on a computer with the Hub Transport or Mailbox server role installed, administrators must be logged on using an account that is a member of the Exchange Administrators group. The account must also be a member of the local Administrators group on that computer. For a computer with the Edge Transport server role installed, administrators must be logged on using an account that is a member of the local Administrators group on that computer.

Enabling or Disabling Message Tracking

As previously stated, by default, message tracking is enabled on all Exchange 2007 computers that deal with message transport. This includes Hub Transport, Edge Transport, and Mailbox servers. Message tracking can prove to be extremely useful, and administrators should avoid disabling the feature unless there are overwhelming reasons. All commands must be run from the Exchange Management Shell.

As in other shell commands, the `<Identity>` argument is replaced by the server name. To enable the feature, use the `$true` argument, and to disable it use `$false`.

To enable or disable message tracking on a Hub Transport or Edge Transport server:

```
Set-TransportServer <Identity> -MessageTrackingLogEnabled:<$true or $false>
```

To enable or disable message tracking on a Mailbox server:

```
Set-MailboxServer <Identity> -MessageTrackingLogEnabled:<$true or $false>
```

Sample command: To disable message tracking on a Mailbox server named Server1, use the following command:

```
Set-MailboxServer Server1 –MessageTrackingLogEnabled:$false
```

> **NOTE**
>
> If a server has *both* the Mailbox server role and the Hub Transport server role installed, you can use either the `Set-MailboxServer` or `Set-TransportServer` cmdlet.

Changing the Location of Message Tracking Logs

Exchange Server 2007 allows administrators to specify the location of the message tracking logs. The new location becomes effective immediately upon the completion of the command; however, any existing log files are not copied to the new directory—they will remain in the old directory.

By default, these files are located in the `C:\Program Files\Microsoft\Exchange Server\TransportRoles\Logs\MessageTracking` directory.

When creating a new directory, the following permissions are required:

▶ **Administrator**—Full Control

▶ **System**—Full Control

▶ **Network Service**—Read, Write, and Delete Subfolders and Files

To change the default location for these log files, use the following commands in the Exchange Management Shell:

Change message tracking log file location for a Hub Transport server or an Edge Transport server:

```
Set-TransportServer <Identity> -MessageTrackingLogPath <LocalFilePath>
```

Change message tracking log file location for a Mailbox server:

```
Set-MailboxServer <Identity> -MessageTrackingLogPath <LocalFilePath>
```

Sample command: To change the location of the message tracking log to `D:\Message Tracking` on an Exchange 2007 Hub Transport server named Server1, use the following command:

```
Set-TransportServer Server1 –MessageTrackingLogPath "D:\Message Tracking"
```

19

Configuring Message Tracking Log File and Log Directory Maximum Size

To prevent log files from growing so large that they deplete all available disk space, Exchange Server 2007 allows administrators to configure maximum log file and directory sizes. This configuration setting is a per-server setting and, by default, the maximum directory size is 250MB, whereas the maximum log file size is 10MB. When the maximum file size is reached, Exchange opens a new log file. When the maximum directory size is reached, Exchange overwrites the log files, starting with the oldest logs first.

To configure message tracking log directory and file sizes, use the following commands in the Exchange Management Shell. Be aware, these commands must be performed for each server you want to modify. The `<DirectorySize>` and `<FileSize>` arguments should be entered as a number followed by one of the following:

- B (bytes)
- KB (kilobytes)
- MB (megabytes)
- GB (gigabytes)
- TB (terabytes)

Change maximum size for message tracking log directory on a Hub Transport or Edge Transport server:

```
Set-TransportServer <Identity> -MessageTrackingLogMaxDirectorySize <DirectorySize>
```

Change maximum size for message tracking log directory on a Mailbox server:

```
Set-MailboxServer <Identity> -MessageTrackingLogMaxDirectorySize <DirectorySize>
```

Change maximum size for individual message tracking log files on a Hub Transport or Edge Transport server:

```
Set-TransportServer <Identity> -MessageTrackingLogMaxFileSize <FileSize>
```

Change maximum size for individual message tracking log files on a Mailbox server:

```
Set-MailboxServer <Identity> -MessageTrackingLogMaxFileSize <FileSize>
```

Sample command: To set the maximum size for the message tracking log directory on a Hub Transport server named Server1 to 500MB, use the following command:

```
Set-TransportServer Server1 –MessageTrackingLogMaxDirectorySize 500MB
```

Configuring the Maximum Age for the Message Tracking Logs

In addition to having the ability to configure the maximum file and directory sizes for message tracking logs, administrators can also configure a maximum age for each message tracking log file. The default age is set to 30 days, and any log files that exceed this age are deleted by Exchange.

To change the maximum age of message tracking log files, use the following commands in the Exchange Management Shell. The <Age> argument is entered in the following format: DD.HH:MM:SS, for Days, Hours, Minutes, Seconds.

Change maximum age for the message tracking log files on a Hub Transport or Edge Transport server:

```
Set-TransportServer <Identity> -MessageTrackingLogMaxAge <Age>
```

Change maximum age for the message tracking log files on a Mailbox server:

```
Set-MailboxServer <Identity> -MessageTrackingLogMaxAge <Age>
```

Sample command: To set the maximum age of the message tracking log files on an Exchange 2007 Mailbox server named Server1 to 45 days, use the following command:

```
Set-MailboxServer Server1 -MessageTrackingLogMaxAge 45.00:00:00
```

Best Practices for Performing Database Maintenance

One of the most often avoided maintenance tasks in an Exchange environment is performing database maintenance. It is, however, also one of the most important steps an administrator can take to ensure a healthy environment.

By performing regular database maintenance, administrators can prevent downtime, maintain service level agreements (SLAs), minimize database corruption, and reduce the possibility of data loss.

As messaging environments have evolved from "nice to have" to "business critical," database maintenance has evolved from "should be done" to "must be done." Any database that is not regularly maintained will suffer from some level of corruption and, if left unchecked, might fail.

In addition to lack of routine maintenance, other potential causes of database corruption include the following:

▶ Improper shutting down of the system, including unexpected power outages

▶ A poorly maintained disk subsystem

▶ Hardware failures

▶ Failure to use or review systems or operational management tools

▶ Manual modification of Exchange databases

▶ Deletion of Exchange transaction logs

Automatic Database Maintenance

Exchange Server 2007 automatically performs database maintenance procedures on a nightly basis during the scheduled maintenance window. The following tasks are automatically performed by this process:

1. Purge the indexes on the mailbox and public folder stores.

2. Perform tombstone maintenance on mailboxes and public folders.

3. Remove expired messages from the dumpster for the mailbox and public folder stores.

4. Remove expired messages from public folders.

5. Remove deleted public folders with tombstones over 180 days old.

6. Clean up message conflicts within public folders.

7. Update server version information on public folders.

8. Check for and remove duplicate site folders on public folder stores.

9. Clean up deleted mailboxes on mailbox stores.

10. Check the message table for orphaned messages (messages with a reference count of 0).

11. Perform an online defragmentation of the store.

Exchange performs these tasks in order, completing as many as possible within the time allotted by the scheduled maintenance window. If the tasks are unable to complete, Exchange begins where it left off during the next scheduled maintenance opportunity. As long as at least one of the previously listed tasks has completed successfully, Exchange Server spends the last 15 minutes of the cycle performing an online defragmentation of the database. The defragmentation process continues for one hour after the end of the maintenance cycle.

By default, the maintenance schedule is set to run daily from 1:00 a.m. to 5:00 a.m. Because the maintenance cycle can be extremely resource intensive, this default schedule is intended to perform the maintenance during periods when most of an organization's mail users are not connected. However, organizations should also take their Exchange backup schedules into consideration. Backing up an Exchange database causes the online defragmentation to be suspended until after the backup has completed.

Configuring Database Maintenance Schedules

Administrators can stagger the maintenance schedules for different databases. For example, database 1 might have the maintenance cycle performed from 1:00 a.m. to 2:00 a.m., and the next store from 2:00 a.m. to 3:00 a.m., and so on. To view or change the default maintenance schedule on a database, perform the following steps:

1. Open the Exchange Management Console.

2. In the console tree, expand Server Configuration and select Mailbox.

3. In the action pane, select the server you want to view. In the work pane, expand the storage group that contains the database you want to view, and then select the appropriate database.

4. In the action pane, click Properties.

5. On the General tab, locate the Maintenance Schedule.

6. To change the default schedule, select one of the options from the drop-down box, or click Customize to create your own schedule.

Offline Database Maintenance

As the name implies, *offline* database maintenance is performed while the database is unavailable to the user community. As such, offline maintenance should be scheduled (whenever possible) during nonbusiness hours.

As discussed, Exchange Server 2007 performs an automated daily defragmentation as part of the scheduled database maintenance. This process, known as an *online* defragmentation, is intended to keep the databases healthy and free from corruption, but it does not shrink the physical size of the database.

In an Exchange environment, as more data is added to a database, the database grows in size. When messages or mailboxes are deleted, however, the database does not decrease in size, it simply frees up available "whitespace" that can be overwritten by new mail or mailboxes.

Although this is not normally a problem for an environment, there are scenarios in which it can create issues. For example, if a database was to grow extremely large and, in an effort to redistribute the load, an administrator was to move 50% of the mailboxes to another server, the database would still remain the same size. Even though the database contains 50% whitespace, it still must be backed up in its entirety and, in the event of a disaster, would have to be restored as such.

The only way to shrink a database is to perform an offline defragmentation, which is a manual process utilizing the `eseutil /d` command.

To determine the amount of whitespace contained within a database, view the application log of the Exchange server and filter on Event ID 1221. This event shows how much free space exists within each database.

Caution should be used before performing an offline defragmentation, and administrators should be sure to back up the database prior to the maintenance. Although Exchange databases have become more and more stable over the past several iterations of Exchange, there is still the possibility of an offline defragmentation corrupting a database. An additional protective measure is to make a copy of the database after it has been taken offline,

19

and then perform the maintenance procedures on the copy, rather than on the original. In the event of severe problems, the original database can be brought back online.

> **CAUTION**
>
> Exchange Server 2007 databases and transaction log files should never be manually modified. Although there are many database utilities in existence that are capable of modifying Exchange databases, only those utilities recommended by Microsoft for use with Exchange should be utilized.

Performing Offline Database Maintenance

To perform offline database maintenance, ensure a valid backup of the database exists. The following steps can be followed to utilize the `isinteg` and `eseutil` utilities to perform offline database maintenance:

1. Log on using an account that is an Exchange Server Administrator for the Exchange server housing the databases being maintained.

2. Open the Exchange Management Console.

3. In the console tree, expand Server Configuration and select Mailbox.

4. In the action pane, select the server you want to view. In the work pane, expand the storage group that contains the database you want to view, and then select the appropriate database.

5. Note the database file path for the database. This can be copied to the Clipboard by viewing the properties of the database, highlighting the *Database path,* and clicking Ctrl+C. You will need this information later when you use the `eseutil` utility.

6. In the action pane, click Dismount Database, and then click Yes to confirm.

7. Open a command prompt by selecting Start, Run, typing cmd in the Open text box, and clicking OK to continue.

8. Change to the drive and directory where `isinteg` resides. The default location is:

   ```
   C:\Program Files\Microsoft\Exchange Server\Bin
   ```

9. Type

   ```
   isinteg.exe -s <ServerName> -test allfoldertests
   ```

   and then press Enter. A list of available databases on the server will be presented, indicating which are online or offline, as shown in Figure 19.5.

10. Choose to run maintenance on the offline database by typing the appropriate number and pressing Enter. Confirm the appropriate database, press Y, and then press Enter to continue.

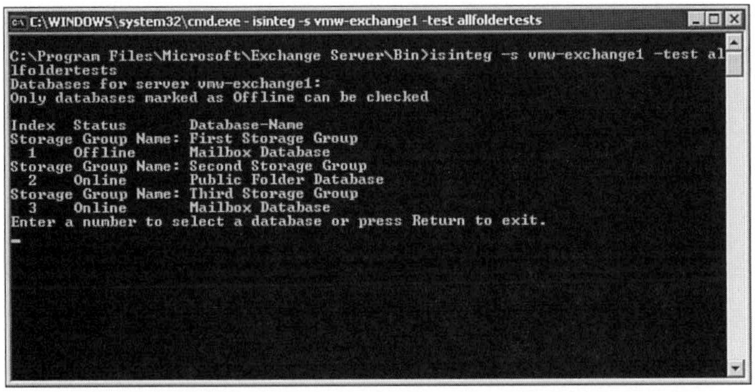

```
C:\WINDOWS\system32\cmd.exe - isinteg -s vmw-exchange1 -test allfoldertests    _ □ X

C:\Program Files\Microsoft\Exchange Server\Bin>isinteg -s vmw-exchange1 -test al
lfoldertests
Databases for server vmw-exchange1:
Only databases marked as Offline can be checked

Index  Status      Database-Name
Storage Group Name: First Storage Group
   1    Offline     Mailbox Database
Storage Group Name: Second Storage Group
   2    Online      Public Folder Database
Storage Group Name: Third Storage Group
   3    Online      Mailbox Database
Enter a number to select a database or press Return to exit.
_
```

FIGURE 19.5   Performing maintenance using `isinteg`.

If `isinteg` finds errors, run the appropriate fix as recommended and displayed within the command prompt. The same error and recommended fix is recorded in the Application Event Log. If necessary, repeat the `isinteg` integrity check until no errors are reported. When no errors are reported, continue to the next step.

11. At the command prompt, type the following command to perform a database-level integrity check:

    ```
    Eseutil.exe /g "database file path"
    ```

    Replace *database file path* with the database location and filename copied in step 5. If there is a space anywhere in the path or filename, be sure to enclose the entire path and filename in double quotes, as shown previously. A sample path and filename are as follows:

    ```
    "D:\Program Files\Microsoft\Exchange Server\Mailbox\First Storage Group\
    Mailbox Database.edb"
    ```

    When ready, press Enter to continue.

    If any errors are reported, refer to Chapter 33.

12. At the command prompt, type the following command to defragment the database:

    ```
    Eseutil.exe /d "database file path"
    ```

    and press Enter. Again, the double quotes are necessary for paths with spaces in the names.

19

TIP

Although it is always a good practice to perform offline database maintenance, including defragmentation, on a quarterly basis, it is necessary only when the amount of free space in the database is greater than 15% of the total database size.

To calculate the percentage of free space, take the total free space recorded in the application log (Event ID 1221) and divide that by the size of the EDB file.

13. When the database compaction has completed, use the Exchange Management Console to mount the database.

14. Using NTBackup or a third-party product, perform a full backup of the database. This step should be accomplished as soon as possible. If the database should fail prior to a backup being completed, the old database would have to be restored, and offline maintenance performed all over again.

Performing Database Maintenance Through Mailbox Moves

Online and offline database maintenance each have their purposes, with offline maintenance routines performing the most thorough maintenance. Offline maintenance can take a significant amount of time to perform based on the size of the database and its overall condition, as well as the performance capabilities of the server housing the database. Even on high-performance servers, offline database maintenance can sometimes progress at a rate of approximately 5GB per hour. So, performing offline maintenance on a large database (for example, 40GB) could take 8 hours or more to complete.

An alternative method that does not require nearly as much downtime is moving mailboxes to another mailbox store. An Exchange administrator can create a new mailbox store either on the same Exchange Server 2007 server or on a separate server altogether. After the new mailbox store is created, the administrator can move mailboxes over to the new mailbox store. By moving the mailboxes over to the new mailbox store, the database is in optimal condition. After all mailboxes have been moved, the old database can be deleted.

> **NOTE**
>
> As with any maintenance process, it is important to perform backups of Exchange prior to performing the maintenance tasks. Also, moving mailboxes for maintenance reasons should be performed during nonbusiness hours to avoid interrupting users.

In some cases where the database is experiencing many corruptions, not all mailboxes will be able to be moved. For instance, there might be roughly 5%–10% of the mailboxes still on the original mailbox store that generated errors and did not move over to the new mailbox store. In this scenario, the administrator can then perform offline database maintenance on the message store.

The benefit of this process is that, instead of performing long and arduous offline maintenance routines on the large database, the utilities are run against a much smaller database. This results in a significant savings in maintenance time needed.

Prioritizing and Scheduling Maintenance Best Practices

Exchange 2007 is a very efficient messaging system. However, as mailboxes and public folders are used, there is always the possibility of the logical corruption of data contained within the databases. It is important to implement a maintenance plan and schedule to minimize the impact that database corruption will have on the overall messaging system.

This section focuses on tasks that should be performed regularly—on a daily, weekly, monthly, and quarterly schedule. Besides ensuring optimum health for an organization, following these best practices will have the additional benefit of ensuring that administrators are well informed about the status of their messaging environment.

> **TIP**
>
> Administrators should thoroughly document the Exchange Server 2007 messaging environment configuration and keep it up to date. In addition, a change log should be implemented that is used to document changes and maintenance procedures for the environment. This change log should be meticulously maintained.

Daily Maintenance

Daily maintenance routines require the most frequent attention of an Exchange administrator. However, these tasks should not take a significant amount of time to perform.

Verify the Online Backup

One of the key differences between disaster and disaster recovery is the ability for an organization to resort to backups of their environment if the need arises. Considering the potential impact to an environment if the data backed up is not recoverable, it is amazing to see how often backup processes are ignored. Many organizations implement a "set it and forget it" attitude, often relying on nontechnical administrative personnel to simply "swap tapes" on a daily basis.

Whatever method is used to back up an Exchange environment, daily confirmation of the success of the task should be mandatory. Although the actual verification process will vary based on the backup solution being utilized, the general concept remains the same. Review the backup program's log file to determine whether the backup has successfully completed. If there are errors reported or the backup job set does not complete successfully, identify the cause of the error and take the appropriate action to resolve the problem.

Some best practices to keep in mind when backing up an Exchange environment are as follows:

- Include System State data to protect against system failure.

- Keep note of how long the backup process is taking to complete. This time should match any service level agreements that might be in place.

▶ Determine the start and finish times of the backup process. Attempt to configure the environment so that the backup process completes before the nightly mainte-nance schedule begins.

▶ Verify that transaction logs are successfully truncated upon completion of the backup.

Check Free Disk Space

All volumes that Exchange Server 2007 resides on (Exchange system files, databases, trans-action logs, and so forth) should be checked on a daily basis to ensure that ample free space is available. If the volume or partition runs out of disk space, no more information can be written to the disk, which causes Exchange to stop the Exchange services. This can also result in lost data and the corruption of messaging databases.

Although it is possible to perform this process manually, it is easily overlooked when "hot" issues arise. As a best practice, administrators can utilize Microsoft Operations Manager (MOM) or a third-party product to alert administrators if free space dips below a certain threshold.

For organizations without the resources to implement such products, the process can be accomplished utilizing scripting technologies, with an email or network alert being gener-ated when the free space falls below the designated threshold.

Review Message Queues

Message queues should be checked daily to ensure that the mail flow in the organization is not experiencing difficulties. The Queue Viewer in the Exchange Management Console toolbox can be accomplished for this task.

If messages are found stuck in the queue, administrators can utilize the Message Tracking and Mail Flow Troubleshooter to determine the cause.

Check Event Viewer Logs

On Exchange Server 2007 servers, the application log within the Event Viewer should be reviewed daily for any *Warning* or *Error* level messages. Although some error messages might lead directly to a problem on the server, some might be symptomatic of other issues in the environment. Either way, it is best to evaluate and resolve these errors as soon as possible.

Filtering for these event types can assist with determining if any have occurred within the last 24 hours.

Alternatively, if a systems or operational management solution (such as Microsoft Operations Manager) is utilized, this process can be automated, with email or network notifications sent as soon as the error is generated.

Weekly Maintenance

Tasks that do not require daily administrative input, but that still require frequent attention, are categorized as weekly maintenance routines. Recommended weekly maintenance routines are described in the following sections.

Document Database File Sizes

In an environment without mailbox storage limitations, the size of the mailbox databases can quickly become overwhelmingly large. If the volume housing the databases is not large enough to accommodate the database growth beyond a certain capacity, services can stop, databases can get corrupted, performance can get sluggish, or the system can halt.

Even with mailbox size limitations implemented, administrators should be aware of and document the size of databases so that they can determine the estimated growth rate.

By documenting the size of all mailbox databases on a weekly basis, administrators can have a more thorough understanding of the system usage and capacity requirements in their environment.

Verify Public Folders Replication

Many environments rely on public folders to share information, and the public folder configurations can vary widely from environment to environment.

With environments that replicate public folder information among different Exchange Server servers, administrators should inspect the replication to ensure all folders are kept up to date.

There are several ways to perform quick tests to determine if a public folder is replicating properly. Among these are manual testing and reviewing the `Ex00yymmdd.log` and `Ex01yymmdd.log` files. If problems exist, administrators can use these logs to troubleshoot.

Verify Online Maintenance Tasks

Exchange Server 2007 records information in the application log about scheduled online maintenance processes. Check this event log to verify that all the online maintenance tasks are being performed and that no problems are occurring.

Using the filtering capabilities of the Event Viewer (View, Filter), administrators can apply a filter to search for specific events, and can specify a date (and time) range to search for these events. For example, it is easy to filter the events to view all events with an ID of 1221 that have occurred in the past week.

Alternatively, in the right pane of the Event Viewer, click on the Event column to sort events by their ID number; however, this view is more challenging to read because you must then verify the dates of the events as well.

The following Event IDs should be regularly reviewed:

▶ **Event ID 1221**—This event reveals how much whitespace there is in a database. This information is also useful in determining when offline database defragmentation might be necessary.

▶ **Event ID 1206 and 1207**—These IDs give information about the start and stop times for the cleanup of items past the retention date in Item Recovery.

▶ **Event ID 700 and 701**—These IDs indicate the start and stop times of the online database defragmentation process. Administrators should ensure that the process does not conflict with Exchange database backups and make sure that the process completed without interruptions.

▶ **Event IDs 9531–9535**—These IDs indicate the start and end times of the cleanup of deleted mailboxes that are past the retention date.

Analyze Resource Utilization

To keep any environment healthy, overall system and network performance should be regularly evaluated. An Exchange Server 2007 environment is no exception.

At a minimum, administrators should monitor system resources at least once a week. Primary areas to focus on include the four common contributors to bottlenecks: memory, processor, disk subsystem, and network subsystem.

Ideally, utilizing a monitoring utility such as Microsoft Operations Manager to gather performance data at regular intervals is recommended because this data can be utilized to discover positive and negative trends in the environment.

Check Offline Address Book Generation

An Offline Address Book (OAB) is used by Outlook to provide offline access to directory information from the Global Address List (GAL) when users are working offline or in Cached Exchange mode. When a user starts Outlook in Cached Exchange mode for the first time, the user's Exchange mailbox is synchronized to a local file (an .ost file) and the offline address list from the Exchange server is synchronized to a collection of files (.oab files) on the user's computer.

By default, the OAB is updated daily at 5:00 a.m. if there are changes. Administrators can use the Exchange Management Console to determine the last time it was updated to ensure remote users have a valid copy to update from. To do so, follow these steps:

1. Open the Exchange Management Console.

2. In the console tree, expand Organization Configuration and select Mailbox.

3. In the results pane, select the Offline Address Book tab. Select the address book you want to view, and then, in the action pane, click Properties.

4. Check the Modified field to determine when the Offline Address Book was last updated.

5. If you want to modify the default update schedule, that can be accomplished on this page as well. Select one of the predefined schedules from the drop-down box, or click Customize to create your own schedule.

6. Click OK to exit the configuration.

> **NOTE**
>
> If you are experiencing problems with OAB generation, enable diagnostic logging and review the application log for any OAB generator category events.

Monthly Maintenance

Recommended monthly maintenance practices for Exchange Server 2007 do not require the frequency of daily or weekly tasks, but they are, nonetheless, important to maintaining the overall health of the environment. Some general monthly maintenance tasks can be quickly summarized; others are explained in more detail in the following sections.

General tasks include the following:

- Perform a reboot on the Exchange Server 2007 servers to free up memory resources and kick-start online maintenance routines. This procedure can usually coincide with the implementation of any necessary hotfixes and/or service packs.

- Install approved and tested service packs and updates.

- Schedule and perform, as necessary, any major server configuration changes, including hardware upgrades.

Run the Exchange Best Practices Analyzer

Administrators should run the Exchange Best Practices Analyzer (ExBPA) in their environments on a regular basis to determine if there are any configurations or settings that are not in line with Microsoft recommended best practices. This utility and its configuration files are updated often with new and improved settings, and available updates are installed every time the utility is run.

Administrators should perform a health check, permissions check, and connectivity test at regular intervals, and the quarterly maintenance period is an ideal time to do so.

During the health check, a 2-hour performance baseline can be gathered as well.

The results of these scans can be saved and compared from month to month to determine when particular issues might have occurred.

Analyze Database Free Space

As mentioned earlier in the "Performing Offline Database Maintenance" section, an approximation of a database's fragmentation can be made using the database size and the amount of free space. The amount of free space that can be recovered from a defragmentation and compaction is provided within Event ID 1221 entries.

Test Uninterruptible Power Supply

Uninterruptible Power Supply (UPS) equipment is commonly used to protect the server from sudden loss of power. Most UPS solutions include supporting management software to ensure that the server is gracefully shut down in the event of power failure, thus

19

preserving the integrity of the system. Each manufacturer has a specific recommendation for testing, and the recommended procedures should be followed carefully. However, it should occur no less than once per month, and it is advantageous to schedule the test for the same time as any required server reboots.

Quarterly Maintenance

Although quarterly maintenance tasks are infrequent, some might require downtime and are more likely to cause serious problems with Exchange Server 2007 if not properly planned or implemented. Administrators should proceed cautiously with these tasks.

General quarterly maintenance tasks include the following:

- ▶ Check the Property pages of mailbox and public folder stores to verify configuration parameters, review usage statistics, determine mailbox sizes, and more.

- ▶ Evaluate the current rate of growth on server hard drives to ensure there is adequate space available on all volumes. This evaluation is based on the information gathered during the weekly maintenance tasks.

Perform Offline Maintenance

As mentioned earlier, offline maintenance is an important maintenance task, but it can be time consuming and hazardous. Administrators should always put adequate time into the planning of offline maintenance tasks.

This work should be scheduled during periods of minimal user impact, and administrators should perform both an online and offline backup of the Information Stores prior to beginning the tasks.

By planning this process meticulously, administrators can save a lot of time and frustration. For more information on this process, refer to the earlier section, "Performing Offline Database Maintenance."

Validate Information Store Backups

As previously mentioned, the backing up of an environment's data is one of the most important steps an organization can take to ensure recoverability in the event of a disaster.

However, simply backing up the data, and *assuming* the ability to recover it is inadequate.

Backups should be regularly restored in a test environment to ensure the recoverability of systems. By performing regular restores in a test environment, administrators are providing several services:

- ▶ Confirmation that the data is truly being backed up successfully

- ▶ Verification of the actual restore procedures

- ▶ Training for new Exchange administrators, or practice for existing ones, in the steps needed to recover an Exchange environment

Organizations that do not implement regular testing of restore procedures often find that, in the time of actual need, restorations take significantly longer than necessary because of missing hardware, missing software, inadequate or inaccurate procedures, administrators unfamiliar with the process or, worst of all, backup sources that had been reported good, but are unable to be restored.

> **TIP**
>
> Backup and recovery procedures are one of the most critical documents in an Exchange organization. These procedures should be thoroughly tested and updated whenever changes to the process occur. And remember, it is not enough to store copies of this documentation electronically on network shares or (worse) within the messaging system. If these procedures can't be quickly accessed when they are most needed, they are practically useless.

Postmaintenance Procedures

Postmaintenance procedures are designed to quickly and efficiently restore Exchange operations to the environment following any offline maintenance. Devising a checklist for these procedures ensures that the systems are brought back online quickly and efficiently, without time wasted because of minor errors. The following is a sample checklist for maintenance procedures:

1. Start all the remaining Exchange services.

2. Test email connectivity from Outlook, Outlook Web Access, Outlook Anywhere, and ActiveSync.

3. Perform a full backup of the Exchange Server 2007 server(s).

4. Closely review backup and server event logs over the next few days to ensure that no errors are reported on the server.

Reducing Management and Maintenance Efforts

As you have seen throughout the chapter, numerous utilities are available with Exchange Server 2007 for managing, maintaining, and monitoring the messaging system. These utilities can often help administrators avoid problems, and can save time and energy addressing those that arise.

In any messaging environment, administrators should always attempt to develop processes and procedures that can reduce maintenance efforts while maximizing effectiveness and efficiency. Many management and maintenance procedures can be streamlined, or even automated, ensuring a maximum return for minimum time spent, resulting in a significant monetary savings for the organization. Equally important, proper upkeep of the Exchange environment ensures administrators are one step ahead of preventable issues, allowing more time for proactively managing the environment, and less time reacting to problems.

19

Using Microsoft Operations Manager

Microsoft Operations Manager (MOM) is one tool that can be used to streamline and automate many of an administrator's messaging responsibilities. More specifically, the MOM Exchange Server management pack provides the key features required to manage, maintain, and monitor the Exchange Server 2007 environment. More on MOM in Chapter 20, "Using Microsoft Operations Manager to Monitor Exchange Server 2007."

Key features to consider evaluating include, but are not limited to, the following:

▶ Provides rules and scripts to track Exchange performance, availability, and reliability of all Exchange-related components, including Internet-related services, Extensible Storage Engine, System Attendant, Microsoft Exchange Information Store service, and SMTP

▶ Sends test emails to verify operations and measures actual delivery times

▶ Gathers Exchange data and provides technical reports on Exchange service delivery, traffic, storage capacity, and usage

▶ Alerts administrators when various thresholds are met, such as resource utilization statistics or capacity

▶ Performance baselining and continuous monitoring of system resources and protocols

▶ Trend analysis of usage and performance

▶ A full knowledge base of Exchange-specific solutions tied directly to over 1,700 events

▶ Reporting on usage, problems, security-related events, and much more

Summary

Most organizations consider their email systems to be one of the most mission-critical applications in their environment. Message delays, nondeliveries, and unscheduled downtime are usually considered unacceptable, and administrators who cannot maintain their environments well enough to meet service level agreements and management expectations are often quickly out of a job.

For a messaging environment to perform well, remain reliable, and continue to provide full functionality, it must be properly managed and maintained. Exchange Server 2007 provides tools and utilities to assist in this endeavor, but they must be used properly and regularly to be effective.

With proper care and feeding, Exchange Server 2007 can meet and exceed the messaging needs for just about any organization.

Best Practices

The following are best practices from this chapter:

▶ Manage Exchange Server 2007 based on server roles and responsibilities.

▶ Utilize the Exchange Best Practices Analyzer on a monthly basis to evaluate the current environment and compare it to Microsoft recommended best practices.

▶ Audit the messaging environment using Windows Server 2003 auditing.

▶ Use Exchange Server 2007 protocol logging and diagnostic utilities for troubleshooting purposes.

▶ Install the Exchange Management Console and the Exchange Management Shell on a client computer to remotely administer Exchange Server 2007.

▶ Keep AD well tuned using ntdsutil because Exchange Server 2007 relies heavily on it.

▶ Avoid possible adverse affects with the AD database by running ntdsutil in Directory Service Restore mode.

▶ Perform an online and offline full backup of the Information Stores prior to running offline maintenance tasks.

▶ Use isinteg in Test mode unless there is a specific problem reported.

▶ Never manually modify Exchange Server 2007 databases or transaction log files.

▶ Thoroughly document the Exchange Server 2007 messaging environment and configuration. Create and maintain change logs to document changes and maintenance procedures.

▶ Document the process of restoring Exchange Server 2007 databases thoroughly and completely. If documentation already exists, verify that the existing process has not changed. If it has changed, update the documentation.

▶ Store printed copies of the Exchange Server 2007 restoration process in an easy-to-access location.

▶ Create postmaintenance procedures to minimize time needed for restoration.

▶ Include the System State data in daily backup routines. Be sure to back the System State up with a separate backup job if using the ntbackup utility.

▶ Implement Microsoft Operations Manager with the available Exchange management packs to minimize administrative overhead for daily routines.

19

CHAPTER 20

Using Microsoft Operations Manager to Monitor Exchange Server 2007

Microsoft Operations Manager (MOM) 2005 provides numerous advantages when implemented as part of an operational framework supporting Microsoft Exchange Server 2007. Some of the key features provided by MOM are proactive monitoring, capacity planning, and trend analysis across the entire Exchange 2007 infrastructure. To understand these advantages, these key features will be reviewed from an Exchange perspective.

Benefits of Using Microsoft Operations Manager

Exchange 2007 implements several different roles that operate as a system to provide a rich collaboration and communication infrastructure. Identifying and maintaining a best-practice configuration for each role, along with event and performance monitoring of each component found within each role can be a daunting task for any size environment. Fortunately, the Exchange 2007 development team has taken on the bulk of this work by identifying key Exchange 2007 components that should be monitored and providing a set of monitoring rules designed specifically for these key areas.

This prebuilt set of rules is contained within a single file referred to as the Exchange 2007 management pack and can be imported directly into an existing MOM infrastructure. Because the Exchange 2007 development team is closely involved with the creation of the Exchange 2007 Management Pack, very accurate monitoring can be quickly achieved across the entire Exchange environment, while significantly lowering the amount of customization and configuration needed.

Event Monitoring

The majority of the rules within the Exchange 2007 Management Pack are configured to look for specific events recorded in the Windows event log. As an event is generated on the Exchange server, the locally installed MOM agent detects and sends details of the event to the MOM management server. The management server receives the event details and performs one or more actions based on rule criteria defined within the management pack. These actions can include raising an alert or changing the State view of an Exchange 2007 component. The entire process of responding to Exchange 2007 conditions often occurs within seconds, providing timely notification when a problem occurs.

Detailed knowledge provided by Microsoft has been included in each of the alerts to help identify the cause of problems and, in many cases, provide an Exchange administrator with the steps necessary to correct and prevent the issue from reoccurring. Along with Microsoft-specific knowledge, each alert provides a form to create and save company knowledge, specific to the environment being monitored. For example, the first time an alert is generated, an Exchange team member might need to research the cause of the problem before it can be resolved. Custom research notes, links to patches, or other actions the Exchange administrator took to correct the problem can be recorded in the company knowledge section of the alert. If the problem happens to reoccur, the notes taken during the previous diagnostics are displayed as part of the new alert.

This detailed knowledge can be accessed by an operator through the MOM Operator console and through the MOM web interface. In addition, when an operator receives an alert notification, a link to the specific alert in the web console can be provided. This web link allows simple access to both Microsoft and company knowledge base information.

Performance Monitoring

Another strong point of MOM is performance monitoring. Two distinct types of performance monitoring rules have been provided in the Exchange 2007 Management Pack.

The first type of performance rule is known as a measuring rule. Performance measuring rules simply collect current value from the performance instance defined within the rule. The sampled value can be displayed as a chart within the MOM Operator console or in the various Exchange 2007 reports.

The second type of performance rule is known as a threshold rule. Performance threshold rules compare the sampled value to a predefined threshold criterion; if the sampled number is outside the boundary of the defined limit, a response can be generated, such as raising an alert and notifying an operator of a performance problem. The sampled value can be analyzed during each collection. The sampled value can also be averaged or differenced over a definable number of samples.

State Monitoring

The State view in the MOM Operator console provides an Exchange administrator with an up-to-date view of each role and component associated with the Exchange 2007 environment. Each component is presented to the administrator as a red, yellow, or green colored light. As data is collected through the various state-specific event rules, performance threshold rules, and custom scripts, the corresponding component is updated to reflect its current condition. For example, when the queues on an Exchange Edge server become backlogged, the State view of the Queues component found within the Ex. Edge Transport role is changed from a green light to a yellow or red light, depending on the severity of the backlog. If the queues return to normal levels, the light is then changed from red or yellow, back to green. A notification can also be generated when the state of these components is changed.

The Queues component found within the Ex. Hub Transport role, shown in Figure 20.1, has changed from a green colored check to a red colored X indicating that one of the queues on the server is currently experiencing a problem. When this occurs, the operator can double-click the degraded component to see additional details, such as what queue is experiencing the problem and knowledge from Microsoft on how to correct the problem.

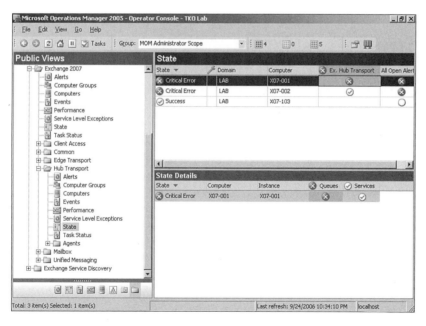

FIGURE 20.1   MOM Operator console State view.

Alert Notification

When an alert is raised, the Exchange group responsible for the environment or the specific Exchange role is often notified through an alert response. This feature provides freedom from the MOM Operator console as important information is delivered directly to the people responsible for the problem. Alert responses can be configured to perform the following actions:

▶ Launch a script

▶ Send a Simple Network Management Protocol (SNMP) trap

▶ Send a notification to a notification group

▶ Execute a command or batch file

▶ Update a state variable

▶ Transfer a file

▶ Call a method on a managed code assembly

The only response action used in the Exchange 2007 Management Pack is Send a Notification to a Notification Group. As a best practice when monitoring Exchange, email alert notifications should be delivered through an alternate method and not from the Exchange server. If the queues on the Exchange server are backlogged, the notification email might not reach the correct people fast enough.

Trend Analysis

All of the Exchange 2007 data collected with MOM can be stored in two databases. The first database, referred to as the Operations database, stores data for a limited number of days (four by default). Data is transferred on a predefined schedule (daily by default) to the second database for long-term archiving; this optional database is known as the Reporting database.

Data in the Operations database is very important to the Exchange team because it contains current environmental conditions that can be used for troubleshooting and the immediate detection of trend deviations over a short time frame. Data contained in the Operations database is viewable through the different MOM Operator console views. Data in the Reporting database is viewable through the MOM Reporting console. Because data is kept in this database for a much longer period (13 months by default), this database can be used for trend analysis, critical pattern analysis, and capacity planning purposes.

Reports are an important aspect of trend analysis because they help sort and display the vast amount of collected Exchange data. Many key reports are included with the Exchange 2007 Management Pack; these reports provide important Exchange information such as database performance and service availability. Reports can be scheduled and automatically delivered to an Exchange administrator through email or a file share.

Extensible Functionality

The functionality found within MOM can be extended in many different ways to accommodate custom monitoring scenarios. This extension of functionality is commonly done through script and managed code development. For example, the Exchange 2007 Management Pack contains several custom rules used to launch scripts during predefined intervals; these scripts are used for a range of activities, including information collection and health verification. The data collected through each of these scripts is sent to the MOM management server for analysis. Based on the data gathered or generated by the script, the appropriate alerts can be raised and responses executed.

Please refer to the MOM Software Development Kit (SDK) for additional details on script and managed code development. The MOM SDK can be obtained through the following link: http://www.microsoft.com/mom/downloads/sdk/default.mspx.

Obtaining the Management Pack

The Exchange 2007 Management Pack is included with the Exchange 2007 media, and is available for download from within the MOM 2005 online management pack catalog. The following link can be used to located the MOM online management pack catalog: http://www.microsoft.com/technet/prodtechnol/mom/mom2005/catalog.aspx.

> **NOTE**
>
> Always obtain the latest version of the management pack through the Microsoft website. Because the management pack can be regularly updated with new features and functionality, using the latest version is highly recommended. It is equally important to keep the management pack up to date after being deployed.

Installing the Management Pack

The management pack for Exchange 2007 is downloaded from the Microsoft website in the form of a Microsoft Installer (MSI) file. This MSI file cannot be imported directly into the MOM environment. The MSI file must be installed and then imported.

> **CAUTION**
>
> The Exchange 2007 Management Pack requires the MOM environment to be at the Service Pack 1 level. The MOM 2005 SP1 update can be obtained from the following link on the Microsoft website: http://www.microsoft.com/mom/downloads/2005/sp1.mspx.

The installation of the MSI file only needs to be performed once on a system where the MOM Administrator console has been installed because this console is used to import the management pack. After the MSI file has been downloaded, simply double-click the downloaded file to initiate the installation process. The installation process allows the selection of a directory where the management pack AKM files and Extensible Markup Language (XML) files will be placed.

20

Importing the Management Pack

After the management pack is installed, the folder selected during the installation wizard will contain the following types of files:

▶ **AKM files**—This file contains the business logic used to monitor the environment. This includes everything from events to monitor to the scripts used for custom Exchange diagnostics.

▶ **XML files**—This file contains all the reports that will be uploaded to the MOM reporting server.

The following procedure can be used to import the management pack into a MOM 2005 SP1 environment:

1. Open the MOM Administrator console.

2. Right-click Management Packs and select Import/Export Management Pack.

3. The Import/Export Wizard opens; click Next.

4. Choose Import Management Packs and/or reports, and click Next.

5. Browse to the location of the AKM and XML files.

6. Select Import Management Packs and Reports, and click Next.

7. Select the Exchange AKM file from the list, and click Next.

8. Select the Exchange XML file from the list, and click Next.

9. Click Finish; the management pack and report will install.

10. Click Close when the Import Wizard has completed.

Understanding Management Pack Components

Management packs developed for MOM 2005 are composed of several different components to create a highly functional monitoring solution. The Exchange 2007 Management Pack is no different as it spans the entire range of functionality provided by MOM.

Looking Inside the MOM Administrator Console

The following management pack components are divided into containers that can be accessed through the MOM Administrator console. Exchange 2007–specific items were added to each container when the management pack was imported:

▶ Computer attributes

▶ Computer groups

▶ Rules

▶ Scripts

▶ Notification groups

The MOM Administrators can make changes to all components found in this console, whereas the MOM Authors role can only make changes to rules found within the rule groups. The MOM Users role cannot make changes in this console.

Identifying Computer Attributes

When a MOM agent is deployed to an Exchange server, the agent scans the HKEY_LOCAL_MACHINE hive for a list of predefined Registry keys and their associated values. This list of Registry key/value pairs is known in MOM as computer attributes, and is imported with the management pack. Computer attributes can be viewed by navigating to the Microsoft Operations Manager, Management Packs, Computer Attributes container within the MOM Administrator console.

> **NOTE**
>
> By default, the MOM agent scans for new computer attribute values immediately after installation of the MOM agent and every 60 minutes thereafter.

Each of the following Exchange-specific computer attributes has been defined as part of the Exchange 2007 Management Pack. Each of the computer attributes helps identify a specific Exchange 2007 server role:

▶ Microsoft Exchange 2007—Client Access version

▶ Microsoft Exchange 2007—Edge Transport version

▶ Microsoft Exchange 2007—Hub Transport version

▶ Microsoft Exchange 2007—Mailbox version

▶ Microsoft Exchange 2007—Unified Messaging version

The value of these attributes is used in the formulas used to decide the membership of MOM-specific computer groups.

Identifying Computer Groups

When the attribute scan has completed, the value associated with each computer attribute is then sent to the MOM management server. The data collected through the different computer attributes is important because it is used to identify the various Exchange roles. MOM-specific computer groups can be dynamically calculated based on the attribute values associated with each computer. As MOM initiates group membership recalculations, the correct Exchange servers are automatically added to one or more of the Exchange computer groups.

20

Each of the following Exchange-specific computer groups has been defined as part of the Exchange 2007 Management Pack:

- ▶ Microsoft Exchange 2007 All Servers

- ▶ Microsoft Exchange 2007 Client Access Servers

- ▶ Microsoft Exchange 2007 Edge Transport Servers

- ▶ Microsoft Exchange 2007 Hub Transport and Edge Transport Servers

- ▶ Microsoft Exchange 2007 Hub Transport Servers

- ▶ Microsoft Exchange 2007 Mailbox Server Physical Machines

- ▶ Microsoft Exchange 2007 Mailbox Servers

- ▶ Microsoft Exchange 2007 Unified Messaging Servers

The search criteria and formula for each computer group can be viewed by navigating to the Microsoft Operations Manager, Management Packs, Computer Groups container, right-clicking one of the listed Exchange 2007 computers groups, and selecting Properties. The Search for Computers and Formula tabs in the Computer Group properties window are used to display the group criteria used for dynamic group population. The formula specified on the Formula tab is used in conjunction with the search criteria to limit the search results .

Figure 20.2 shows the formula used to identify Exchange 2007 Hub Transport servers; this formula uses values associated with the "Microsoft Exchange 2007 - Hub Transport version" computer attribute to identify Exchange 2007 Hub Transport servers. If the value associated with this attribute starts with an "8." the computer will be added to the Exchange Hub Transport server's computer group. The asterisk is used as a wildcard character, essentially allowing any build number after the period. If the server is not hosting the Exchange 2007 Hub Transport role, the local Registry key won't exist, the attribute won't contain any data, and the server won't be added to the group .

Identifying Rules

The Exchange 2007 Management Pack rules can be viewed by navigating to the Microsoft Operations Manager, Management Packs, Rule Groups, Microsoft Exchange Server, Microsoft Exchange 2007 rule group.

The Microsoft Exchange 2007 rule group doesn't contain any rules and is not associated with any computer groups. This rule group acts as a container to hold additional rule groups. Additional information on each of these lower-level rule groups is provided in the section, "Examining Management Pack Rules," found later in this chapter.

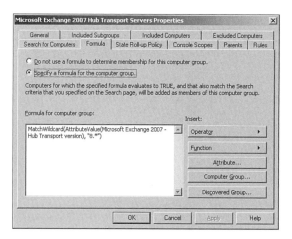

FIGURE 20.2   Computer group formula.

Identifying Scripts

Scripts included with the Exchange 2007 Management Pack have been designed to perform a variety of tasks. Each of these scripts is associated with one or more rules throughout the management pack; the rules that implement these scripts are related to discovery or diagnostics of the Exchange environment. To facilitate the monitoring of Exchange 2007, the following scripts have been included in the Exchange 2007 Management Pack:

▶ **Microsoft Exchange 2007 - Execute Diagnostic Cmdlet**—This script allows the execution an Exchange Management Shell (EMS) cmdlet against Exchange servers—the results of the command are sent to the MOM management server. This script is used by several rules to execute different types of EMS commands for a wide degree of functionality.

▶ **Microsoft Exchange 2007 - Get Mailbox Count**—This script is responsible for counting the number of mailboxes on each Mailbox server.

▶ **Microsoft Exchange 2007 - Get Site Name**—This script is responsible for generating an event with the Active Directory site name in which the Exchange server currently resides. The site name of the Exchange server is used in the different Exchange reports.

The Exchange 2007 Management Pack scripts can be viewed by navigating to the Microsoft Operations Manager, Management Packs, Scripts container. Additional information on the rules that use each of these scripts is provided in the section "Examining Management Pack Rules," found later in this chapter.

20

Identifying Notification Groups

Alert notification rules configured within the Alert Rules container of each rule group are designed to deliver messages to one or more of the following notification groups:

▶ Exchange Client Access Server Administrators

▶ Exchange Edge Transport Server Administrators

▶ Exchange Hub Transport Server Administrators

▶ Exchange Mailbox Server Administrators

▶ Exchange Unified Messaging Server Administrators

▶ Exchange Mail Administrators

The Exchange 2007 notification groups can be viewed by navigating to the Microsoft Operations Manager, Management Packs, Notification, Notification Groups container. To modify the notification group members, right-click the desired notification group, and select Properties. From within the notification group properties, operators can be added or removed. New operators can be easily created by clicking the New Operator button.

Looking Inside the MOM Operator Console

Operator console views are an important feature found within the MOM 2005 Operator console. Exchange 2007–specific Operator console views provide an effective method of sorting and displaying data relevant to the Exchange 2007 environment.

When configured correctly, the vast amounts of data can be easily handled instead of overwhelming the operator. Each of the following containers is located beneath the Exchange 2007 node of the Operator console navigation pane.

▶ Client Access view

▶ Common view

▶ Edge Transport view

▶ Hub Transport view

▶ Mailbox view

▶ Unified Messaging view

Each of the Exchange-specific containers holds several views that show information for that component.

Examining Management Pack Rules

To monitor Exchange more effectively, it is important to become familiar with how the rules are configured and applied to Exchange servers throughout the organization.

Some of the rules found within the management pack require additional tweaking as part of an ongoing tuning and update process. For example, it is common to deploy the management pack and adjust the performance thresholds for the various Exchange components to reflect changing environmental conditions within the organization more closely. This tuning process ensures Exchange operators receive the correct notification in a timely fashion while reducing the likelihood of false positives.

The Exchange 2007 Management Pack has many different rules across a number of different rule groups. The rules are arranged in a structured hierarchy to provide simplified navigation; the Exchange 2007 Management Pack rules can be viewed by navigating to the Microsoft Operations Manager, Management Packs, Rule Groups, Microsoft Exchange Server, Microsoft Exchange 2007 rule group. The Exchange 2007 rule group is not directly associated with any computer groups and does not contain rules—this rule group simply acts as a container housing additional rule groups.

Monitoring Common Components

The Common Components rules can be viewed by navigating to the Microsoft Operations Manager, Management Packs, Rule Groups, Microsoft Exchange Server, Microsoft Exchange 2007, Common Components rule group. This is one of the most important rule groups because this rule group contains many different lower-level rule groups that assist in the monitoring of common services found across the organization.

All Server Roles

The All Server Roles rules can be viewed by navigating to the Microsoft Operations Manager, Management Packs, Rule Groups, Microsoft Exchange Server, Microsoft Exchange 2007, Common Components, All Server Roles rule group.

The All Server Roles rule group is associated with the Microsoft Exchange 2007 All Servers computer group. Each of the event rules located within this rule group is designed to identify Windows events generated with MSExchange Common as the event source. Figure 20.3 shows the Criteria tab of the rule No DNS Servers Could Be Retrieved from Network Adapter. This rule is designed to identify events logged with the event ID 205 from the source MSExchange Common.

This rule group contains a single Alert rule, designed to send notifications to the Mail Administrators notification group for all alerts with a severity of Critical or higher.

Best Practice Analyzer

The Best Practice Analyzer rules can be viewed by navigating to the Microsoft Operations Manager, Management Packs, Rule Groups, Microsoft Exchange Server, Microsoft Exchange 2007, Common Components, Best Practice Analyzer rule group.

The Best Practice Analyzer rule group is associated with the Microsoft Exchange 2007 All Servers computer group. Each of the event rules located within this rule group is designed to identify Windows events generated with MSExchange ExBPA as the event source, or in other words all events generated when the Exchange Best Practice Analyzer cmdlet (Test-SystemHealth) are executed on Exchange servers across the organization.

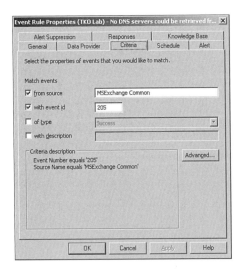

FIGURE 20.3   Exchange event monitoring rule.

The "Execute test-SystemHealth diagnostic cmdlet" rule located within this rule group is significant because it is designed to use the "Microsoft Exchange 2007 - Execute Diagnostic Cmdlet" script. This script is used to execute the Test-SystemHealth EMS cmdlet against all Exchange servers each day at 1:00 a.m. The Test-SystemHealth cmdlet essentially runs an Exchange Best Practice Analyzer (ExBPA) scan.

When the Test-SystemHealth cmdlet is executed, the latest best practice configuration file is downloaded from Microsoft and the server is scanned. The scan results are then sent to the MOM management server where the data is analyzed and alerts are raised for each component that falls outside the recommended best practice configuration. The ExBPA scan can be completely disabled or enabled through this rule, whereas specific ExBPA rules can be controlled by directly modifying the corresponding event rule found within this rule group. For example, to prevent open relay alerts from being raised during the scan process, disable the event rule called Open Relay Test Failed.

This rule group does not contain any Alert rules. If alerting is needed for any of the data returned by the ExBPA scan, an alert should be added to the Alert Rules container of the rule group or directly to the desired event rule.

Directory Service Access

The Directory Service Access rules can be viewed by navigating to the Microsoft Operations Manager, Management Packs, Rule Groups, Microsoft Exchange Server, Microsoft Exchange 2007, Common Components, Directory Service Access rule group.

The Directory Service Access rule group is associated with the Microsoft Exchange 2007 All Servers computer group. Each of the event rules located within this rule group is designed to identify Windows events generated with MSExchangeADAccess as the event source, or in other words, all events generated when Exchange 2007 problems associated with Active Directory occur.

This rule group contains two Alert rules designed to send notifications to the Exchange Mailbox Server Administrators and Mail Administrators notification groups for all alerts with a severity of Error or higher.

This rule group also contains both measuring and threshold rules for the following performance counters. The measuring rules simply store the data for trend analysis, whereas the threshold rules are responsible for controlling the AD Access component of the Ex. Common state role in the MOM Operator console:

▶ **LDAP Long Running Operations**—An average value greater than 50 changes the component to yellow, whereas an average value greater than 100 changes the component to red. The sampled value is averaged over a 5-minute period.

▶ **LDAP Search Time**—An average value greater than 50 milliseconds changes the component to yellow, whereas an average value greater than 100 milliseconds changes the component to red. The sampled value is averaged over a 5-minute period.

▶ **LDAP Search Timeouts**—An average value greater than 10 changes the component to yellow, whereas an average value greater than 20 changes the component to red. The sampled value is averaged over a 5-minute period.

Although these performance threshold settings provide an adequate starting point for most environments, additional tuning of these threshold rules might be necessary to compensate for environmental differences or until an ideal configuration is achieved.

Figure 20.4 shows the Threshold tab for the LDAP Search Time performance threshold rule. The properties of the Threshold tab show the value of the counter will be averaged over five samples. The number of samples used to calculate the average can be increased or decreased as necessary to allow a greater or lower amount of leniency. If the Threshold Value option is changed to The Sampled Value, then the value of the counter is evaluated every sample.

Extensible Storage Engine

The Extensible Storage Engine rules can be viewed by navigating to the Microsoft Operations Manager, Management Packs, Rule Groups, Microsoft Exchange Server, Microsoft Exchange 2007, Common Components, Extensible Storage Engine rule group.

The Extensible Storage Engine rule group is associated with the Microsoft Exchange 2007 Edge Transport Servers, the Microsoft Exchange 2007 Hub Transport Servers, and the Microsoft Exchange 2007 Mailbox Servers rule groups. Each of the event rules located within this rule group is designed to identify Windows events generated with Extensible Storage Engine (ESE) or ESE Backup as the event source.

This rule group contains a single Alert rule, designed to send notifications to the Mail Administrators notification group for all alerts with a severity of Error or higher.

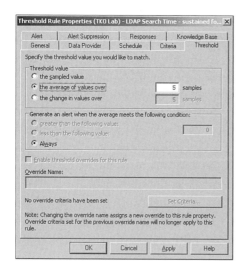

FIGURE 20.4   Threshold tab showing a performance threshold rule.

Hub Transport and Edge Transport

The Hub Transport and Edge Transport rules can be viewed by navigating to the Microsoft Operations Manager, Management Packs, Rule Groups, Microsoft Exchange Server, Microsoft Exchange 2007, Common Components, Hub Transport and Edge Transport rule group.

The Hub Transport and Edge Transport rule groups contains several lower-level rule groups; each is associated with the Microsoft Exchange 2007 Edge Transport Servers and the Microsoft Exchange 2007 Hub Transport Servers rule groups. Each of the event rules located within this rule group is designed to identify Windows events generated with MSExchange Messaging Policies or MSExchange Transport as the event source.

Each of the lower-level rule groups contain three Alert rules designed to send notifications to the Mail Administrators, Exchange Edge Transport Server Administrators, and the Exchange Hub Transport Server Administrators notification groups for all alerts with a severity of Error or higher.

Server

The Server rules can be viewed by navigating to the Microsoft Operations Manager, Management Packs, Rule Groups, Microsoft Exchange Server, Microsoft Exchange 2007, Common Components, Servers rule group.

The Server rule group is associated with the Microsoft Exchange 2007 All Servers computer group. Each of the event rules located within this rule group is designed to collect Exchange service and Exchange search start and stop events. These events are used by the various service availability reports described in the section "Using the Exchange Server 2007 Reports," found later in this chapter.

The Get Server Site Name rule located within this rule group is significant because it is designed to execute the "Microsoft Exchange 2007 – Get Site Name" script against all Exchange servers each day at 1:30 a.m. The script essentially generates an event with the Active Directory site name in which the target Exchange server is located.

This rule group also contains both measuring and threshold rules for the following performance counters. The measuring rules simply store the data for trend analysis, whereas the threshold rules are responsible for controlling the Disk Space component of the Ex. Common state role in the MOM Operator console.

▶ **Disk % Free Space Low**—A sampled value less than 15% changes the component to yellow, whereas a sampled value less than 10% changes the component to red. The value is sampled every minute.

▶ **Disk Free Megabytes Low**—An average value less than 40MB changes the component to yellow, whereas an average value less than 20MB changes the component to red. The sampled value is averaged over a 5-minute period.

This rule group contains a single Alert rule, designed to send notifications to the Mail Administrators notification group for all alerts with a severity of Error or higher.

Figure 20.5 shows the Alert tab of the Disk Free Megabytes Low Performance threshold rule. The properties of the Alert tab show this rule controls the Disk Space component of the Server role. Click Edit to change the percentage of free disk space that triggers the warning and critical alert thresholds.

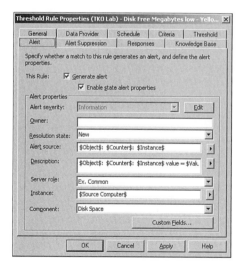

FIGURE 20.5   Alert tab showing a performance threshold rule.

20

Service Monitoring

The Service Monitoring rules can be viewed by navigating to the Microsoft Operations Manager, Management Packs, Rule Groups, Microsoft Exchange Server, Microsoft Exchange 2007, Common Components, Service Monitoring rule group.

The Service Monitoring rule group is associated with the Microsoft Exchange 2007 All Servers computer group. The "Execute test-ServiceHealth diagnostic cmdlet" rule located within this rule group is significant because it is designed to use the "Microsoft Exchange 2007 - Execute Diagnostic Cmdlet" script to execute the test-ServiceHealth cmdlet against all Exchange servers every 2 minutes.

The test-ServiceHealth cmdlet essentially detects if the appropriate services are running for each role hosted by each Exchange server. Data collected through this script is used in other parts of the Exchange 2007 Management Pack, allowing state control of different Exchange-related components.

The only other event rule in this rule group is designed to prevent successful events generated with the test-ServiceHealth cmdlet from being stored in the database. This rule (Filter Service Monitoring Success Events) is enabled by default because recording success events can unnecessarily exhaust database resources over time. However, during testing or diagnostics, this rule can be disabled to show successful events as they can provide verification that the script is functioning correctly.

Monitoring the Client Access Role

The Client Access rules can be viewed by navigating to the Microsoft Operations Manager, Management Packs, Rule Groups, Microsoft Exchange Server, Microsoft Exchange 2007, Client Access rule group.

The Client Access rule group acts as a container for additional rule groups. These lower-level rule groups are used to monitor the components associated with the Exchange Client Access server role. Each of these groups is associated with the Microsoft Exchange 2007 Client Access Servers computer group.

The following lower-level rule groups can be found within the Client Access rule group:

▶ **ActiveSync**—Each of the event rules located within this rule group is designed to identify Windows events generated with MSExchange ActiveSync as the event source.

▶ **Auto Discovery**—Each of the event rules located within this rule group is designed to identify Windows events generated with the MSExchange Autodiscover event source.

▶ **IMAP4**—Each of the event rules located within this rule group is designed to identify Windows events generated with Imap4Svc as the event source.

▶ **Information Worker**—Each of the event rules located within this rule group is designed to identify Windows events generated with MSExchange Availability as the event source.

- **Outlook Web Access**—Each of the event rules located within this rule group is designed to identify Windows events generated with MSExchange OWA as the event source.

- **POP3**—Each of the event rules located within this rule group is designed to identify Windows events generated with Pop3Svc as the event source.

- **Service Monitoring**—Each of the event rules located within this rule group is designed to report on the health of the Client Access–related services and diagnostics cmdlet. Event rules in this rule group are dependent on the timed event rule located in the Exchange Server 2007, Common Components, Service Monitoring rule group.

- **Web Services**—Each of the event rules located within this rule group is designed to identify Windows events generated with MSExchangeEPI as the event source.

Each rule group has two Alert rules defined; if the alert severity matches or exceeds a Critical level, a notification is delivered to the Mail Administrators and the Client Access notification groups.

ActiveSync Connectivity Monitoring

The ActiveSync Connectivity rules can be viewed by navigating to the Microsoft Operations Manager, Management Packs, Rule Groups, Microsoft Exchange Server, Microsoft Exchange 2007, Client Access, ActiveSync, ActiveSync Connectivity rule group.

The ActiveSync rule group is unique because it contains an additional lower-level rule group called ActiveSync Connectivity. The ActiveSync Connectivity rule group contains two rules that are used to validate internal and external ActiveSync connectivity. Each of these rules is designed to execute the Test-MobileSyncConnectivity cmdlet against all Exchange 2007 Client Access servers every 5 minutes.

Data collected through this script is used by the event rules found within this rule group to control the State view of the EASConnectivity component. This component is associated with the Ex. Client Access role.

Monitoring the Edge Transport Role

The Edge Transport rules can be viewed by navigating to the Microsoft Operations Manager, Management Packs, Rule Groups, Microsoft Exchange Server, Microsoft Exchange 2007, Edge Transport rule group.

The Edge Transport rule group acts as a container for additional rule groups. These lower-level rule groups are used to monitor the components associated with the Edge Transport role. Each of these groups is associated with the Microsoft Exchange 2007 Edge Transport Servers computer group.

The following lower-level rule groups can be found within the Edge Transport rule group:

▶ **Agents**—Each of the rule groups within the Agents rule group is designed to collect performance data. These performance rules are required for the Exchange 2007 Message Hygiene reports.

▶ **Service Monitoring**—Each of the event rules located within this rule group is designed to report on the health of the Edge Transport–related services and diagnostics cmdlet. Event rules in this rule group are dependent on the timed event rule located in the Exchange Server 2007, Common Components, Service Monitoring rule group.

▶ **Transport**—This rule group contains both measuring and threshold rules for the key queue lengths found on Exchange Edge Transport servers. The measuring rules simply store the data for trend analysis, whereas the threshold rules are responsible for controlling the Queues component of the Ex. Edge Transport state role in the MOM Operator console.

The following performance counters are monitored with both measuring and threshold rules located in the Transport rule group:

▶ **Active Remote Delivery Queue Length**—An average value greater than 2,000 changes the component to yellow, whereas an average value greater than 2,500 changes the component to red. The sampled value is averaged over a 5-minute period.

▶ **Retry Remote Delivery Queue Length**—An average value greater than 2,000 changes the component to yellow, whereas an average value greater than 2,500 changes the component to red. The sampled value is averaged over a 5-minute period.

▶ **Submission Queue Length**—An average value greater than 150 changes the component to yellow, whereas an average value greater than 250 changes the component to red. The sampled value is averaged over a 5-minute period.

▶ **Unreachable Queue Length**—An average value greater than 150 changes the component to yellow, whereas an average value greater than 250 changes the component to red. The sampled value is averaged over a 5-minute period.

Although these performance threshold settings provide an adequate starting point for most environments, additional tuning of these threshold rules might be necessary to compensate for environmental differences or until an ideal configuration is achieved.

Monitoring the Hub Transport Role

The Hub Transport rules can be viewed by navigating to the Microsoft Operations Manager, Management Packs, Rule Groups, Microsoft Exchange Server, Microsoft Exchange 2007, Hub Transport rule group.

The Hub Transport rule group acts as a container for additional rule groups. These lower-level rule groups are used to monitor the components associated with the Hub Transport role. Each of these groups is associated with the Microsoft Exchange 2007 Hub Transport Servers computer group.

The following lower-level rule groups can be found within the Hub Transport rule group:

- **Agents**—Each of the rule groups within the Agents rule group is designed to collect performance data. These performance rules are required for the Exchange 2007 Message Hygiene reports.

- **Service Monitoring**—Each of the event rules located within this rule group is designed to report on the health of the Hub Transport–related services and diagnostics cmdlet. Event rules in this rule group are dependent on the timed event rule located in the Exchange Server 2007, Common Components, Service Monitoring rule group.

- **Transport**—This rule group contains Event and Alert rules for a variety of conditions that can occur on Hub Transport servers. This rule group also contains measuring and threshold rules for the key queue lengths found on Exchange Hub Transport servers. The measuring rules simply store the data for trend analysis, whereas the threshold rules are responsible for controlling the Queues component of the Ex. Hub Transport state role in the Operator console.

The following performance counters are monitored with both measuring and threshold rules located in the Transport rule group:

- **Active Remote Delivery Queue Length**—An average value greater than 2,000 changes the component to yellow, whereas an average value greater than 2,500 changes the component to red. The sampled value is averaged over a 5-minute period.

- **ESE Log Generation Checkpoint Depth**—A sampled value greater than 500 changes the component to yellow, whereas a sampled value greater than 800 changes the component to red. The value is sampled every 15 minutes.

- **Retry Remote Delivery Queue Length**—An average value greater than 2,000 changes the component to yellow, whereas an average value greater than 2,500 changes the component to red. The sampled value is averaged over a 5-minute period.

- **Submission Queue Length**—An average value greater than 150 changes the component to yellow, whereas an average value greater than 250 changes the component to red. The sampled value is averaged over a 5-minute period.

- **Unreachable Queue Length**—An average value greater than 150 changes the component to yellow, whereas an average value greater than 250 changes the component to red. The sampled value is averaged over a 5-minute period.

20

Although these performance threshold settings provide an adequate starting point for most environments, additional tuning of these threshold rules might be necessary to compensate for environmental differences or until an ideal configuration is achieved. Figure 20.6 shows the Data Provider tab for the Unreachable Queue Length rule.

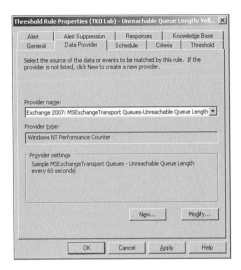

FIGURE 20.6   Data Provider tab showing threshold rule details.

The Data Provider tab shown in Figure 20.6 shows the counter will be sampled every 60 seconds. This value can be changed by clicking Modify, and changing the value found in the Sample Every field.

Monitoring the Mailbox Role

The Mailbox rules can be viewed by navigating to the Microsoft Operations Manager, Management Packs, Rule Groups, Microsoft Exchange Server, Microsoft Exchange 2007, Mailbox rule group.

The Mailbox rule group is more complex because it contains the different lower-level rule groups for each component related to mailbox health. These components include the following:

▶ **Assistants**—Each of the event rules located within this rule group is designed to identify Windows events generated with MSExchange Assistants as the event source. Performance rules are responsible for controlling the Performance component of the Ex. Mailbox state role in the Operator console.

▶ **Cluster**—Each of the event rules located within this rule group is designed to identify Windows events generated with MSExchangeRepl as the event source.

▶ **Continuous Replications**—Each of the event rules located within this rule group is designed to identify Windows events generated with MSExchangeRepl as the event source. Performance rules are responsible for controlling the Replication (CCR,LCR) component of the Ex. Mailbox state role in the MOM Operator console.

▶ **Exchange Search**—Each of the event rules located within this rule group is designed to report on the health of the Exchange Search–related services and Test-ExchangeSearch cmdlet. This cmdlet is designed to use the "Microsoft Exchange 2007 - Execute Diagnostic Cmdlet" script and is executed against all Mailbox servers every 20 minutes. During testing or diagnostics, the database filter rule can be disabled to allow collection of successful events as they can provide verification that the script is functioning correctly.

▶ **Information Store**—Each of the event rules located within this rule group is designed to identify Windows events generated with an event source description beginning with MSExchangeIS. This rule group contains a timed event that executes the "Microsoft Exchange 2007 - Get Mailbox Count" script; essentially this script counts the number of mailboxes on each server. Performance rules are responsible for controlling the Performance component of the Ex. Mailbox state role in the MOM Operator console and for the collection of database and Remote Procedure Call (RPC) statistics used in the Exchange 2007 Metrics reports.

▶ **Information Worker**—Each of the event rules located within this rule group is designed to identify Windows events generated with MSExchangeMailboxAssistants as the event source.

▶ **MAPI Connectivity**—Each of the event rules located within this rule group is designed to report on the health and availability of Exchange Messaging Application Programming Interface (MAPI)–related components and the Test-MAPIConnectivity cmdlet. This script is executed against all Mailbox servers every 1 minute. During testing or diagnostics, the database filter rule can be disabled to allow collection of successful events as they can provide verification that the script is functioning correctly.

▶ **Reset Connectivity Credentials**—Each of the event rules located within this rule group is designed to report on Windows events generated when connectivity credentials are reset. Connectivity credentials are typically reset when configuration changes are made.

▶ **Search**—Each of the event rules located within this rule group is designed to identify Windows events generated with MSExchange Search as the event source.

▶ **Service Monitoring**—Each of the event rules located within this rule group is designed to report on the health of the Mailbox-related services and diagnostics cmdlet. Event rules in this rule group are dependent on the timed event rule located in the Exchange Server 2007, Common Components, Service Monitoring rule group.

▶ **System Attendant**—Each of the event rules located within this rule group is designed to identify Windows events generated with MSExchangeSA as the event source. A database filter rule is used to prevent events related to "message tracking decode operations," with event ID 5007 from being recorded by MOM .

Monitoring the Unified Messaging Role

The Unified Messaging rules can be viewed by navigating to the Microsoft Operations Manager, Management Packs, Rule Groups, Microsoft Exchange Server, Microsoft Exchange 2007, Unified Messaging rule group.

The Unified Messaging rule group acts as a container for additional rule groups. These lower-level rule groups are used to monitor the components associated with the Unified Messaging role. Each of these groups is associated with the Microsoft Exchange 2007 Unified Messaging Servers computer group.

Each of the event rules located within the Unified Messaging rule group is designed to identify Windows events generated with MSExchange Unified Messaging as the event source. This rule group also contains the following lower-level rule groups:

- ▶ **Performance Reporting**—Performance rules are responsible for collecting Unified Messaging server statistics such as the total number of calls. This rule group is disabled by default and must be enabled to collect this data.

- ▶ **Service Monitoring**—Each of the event rules located within this rule group is designed to report on the health of the Unified Messaging–related services and diagnostics cmdlet. Event rules in this rule group are dependent on the script located in the Exchange Server 2007, Common Components, Service Monitoring rule group.

- ▶ **UM Connectivity**—Each of the event rules located within this rule group are designed to report on the status of the Local and Remote service for both voice and fax. The remote tests are disabled by default and must be enabled before these tests will be executed.

Tuning the Exchange Server 2007 Management Pack

To achieve the most effective monitoring of the Exchange 2007 environment, some of the rules found within the Exchange 2007 Management Pack might need tuning. Part of the tuning process involves using MOM to monitor and baseline the existing environment; rules can then be adjusted as needed or as the environment changes. Each of the various rule types can be easily located through the search functionality of the MOM Administrator console. For example, the following procedure can be used to locate all threshold rules:

1. Open the MOM Administrator console.

2. Expand Management Packs.

3. Expand Rule Groups.

4. Expand Microsoft Exchange Server.

5. Right-click Exchange 2007 and select Find Rules.

6. Step through the Search Wizard, and configure the search criteria to find performance rules with the type Compare Performance Data.

Adjusting Performance Rules

Performance collection rules are used to display data in MOM Operator console performance views. These rules can also be used in reports for long-term trend analysis and capacity planning. Performance threshold rules are responsible for generating alerts along with changing the color of Exchange 2007 roles and components associated with the State view.

Figure 20.7 shows the I/O Database Reads Average Performance view found in the MOM Operator console; it is clear from the chart that one of the servers experienced a sharp rise in activity between samples. The operator can compare this data to other views, such as the RPC Average Latency to determine if the change in database reads has affected user experience of the environment.

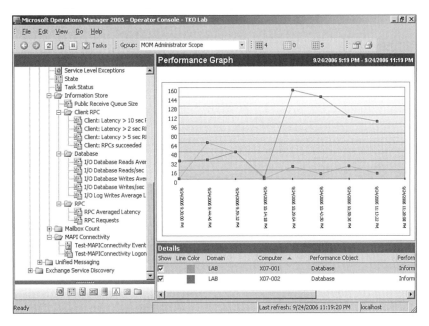

FIGURE 20.7   MOM Operator console performance view.

Performance rules are found throughout the management pack in many of the Exchange 2007 rule groups. These rules can be enabled or disabled to control the number of performance points collected throughout the environment. It is highly recommended to enable performance collection rules to achieve a much more in-depth analysis of the environment.

The frequency with which performance samples are collected can be adjusted on a per-rule basis by changing the properties found on the Data Provider tab of the performance rule. An example of the Data Provider tab was shown in Figure 20.6. In addition, the threshold criteria found in the properties of threshold performance rules can be adjusted to control the conditions in which the event is generated. The threshold criterion is defined on the Threshold tab of a performance threshold rule. An example of the Threshold tab was shown in Figure 20.4.

When monitoring an Exchange environment, additional performance collection rules can be created to monitor additional Exchange components or third-party Exchange add-ons that can play a factor in Exchange performance.

Changing Event Rules

Event rules found throughout the management pack can be modified by enabling or disabling the rule or by changing the severity level of the alert. The response actions for an event rule can also be changed as necessary.

Configuring Rule Overrides

Often, a scenario is encountered in which the single server or a subset of servers display slightly different characteristics from the baseline. Several different types of overrides exist to handle these situations. The first type of override is known as a rule-disable override and can be assigned to the rule to prevent a single server or a group of servers from having the specified rule applied. The second type of override is found on the Threshold tab of the performance threshold rules console option screen. This type of override allows the configuration of a new threshold value for a single server or a group of servers.

Using the Exchange Server 2007 Reports

Many reports are included with the Exchange 2007 Management Pack. These reports range in functionality from analysis of messages to server availability statistics.

Exchange Server 2007 Message Hygiene Analysis

Message hygiene reports show trends associated with each of the components found on Exchange servers hosting the Hub and/or Edge Transport server role:

▶ **Attached File Filter**—The Attached File Filter report shows the number of messages that have been blocked on Exchange servers hosting the Edge Transport role.

▶ **Connection Filter**—The Connection Filter report shows the number of connections that have been blocked on Exchange servers hosting the Hub or Edge Transport roles.

▶ **Content Filter**—The Content Filter report shows the statistics from the Intelligent Message Filter performance measuring rules associated with Exchange servers hosting the Hub or Edge Transport roles.

- ▶ **Protocol Analysis**—The Protocol Analysis report shows statistics based on information collected through the MSExchange Protocol Analysis Agent rules associated with Exchange servers hosting the Hub or Edge Transport roles.

- ▶ **Recipient Filter**—The Recipient Filter report shows statistics collected when a message is filtered with the recipient filter found on the Exchange servers hosting the Hub or Edge Transport roles.

- ▶ **Sender Filter**—The Sender Filter report shows statistics collected when a message is filtered with the sender filter components found on the Exchange servers hosting the Hub or Edge Transport role.

- ▶ **SenderID**—The SenderID report shows statistics collected from the SenderID component found on the Exchange servers hosting the Hub or Edge Transport role.

Exchange 2007 Metrics

The Exchange 2007 Metrics folder contains several reports designed to show the overall performance and scalability trends for the environment. These reports can be used for trend analysis, allowing mail architects to identify existing possible bottlenecks or future resource considerations. This data can also be extrapolated to show future environmental requirements.

- ▶ **Client Performance**—The Client Performance report shows how quickly the server can respond to client RPC requests. This report provides the ability to include a service level agreement (SLA) number during the report execution; servers that are outside the SLA are colored red for quick identification.

- ▶ **Mailbox Count**—The Mailbox Count report shows the distribution of mailboxes across all Exchange 2007 Mailbox servers in the environment.

- ▶ **RPC and Database Performance**—The RPC and Database Performance report shows several very useful capacity planning charts. These charts show user requests compared to database latency on an Exchange server.

Exchange 2007 Service Availability

The Exchange 2007 Service Availability folder contains several reports designed to show the availability of the Exchange 2007 environment or individual services provided by Exchange. These reports provide the ability to include an SLA number; during the report execution, servers that are outside the SLA are colored red for quick identification. Figure 20.8 shows an example of the Mailbox Service Availability report; the servers highlighted in red were outside the specified 99% SLA.

20

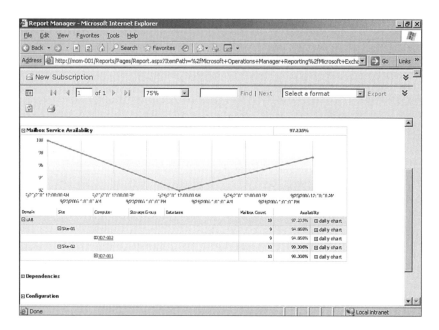

FIGURE 20.8   Mailbox Service Availability report.

The following reports are included in the Exchange 2007 Service Availability folder:

▶ **Service Availability Summary**—The Service Availability Summary report shows availability of all services across each Exchange server in the organization. This report combines all other availability reports in this folder into a single report.

▶ **ActiveSync External Service Availability**—The ActiveSync External Service Availability report shows external availability of ActiveSync on servers hosting the Client Access Exchange role. Data for this report is generated with the "Execute test-ActiveSyncConnectivity External diagnostic cmdlet" timed event rule.

▶ **ActiveSync Internal Service Availability**—The ActiveSync Internal Service Availability report shows external availability of ActiveSync on servers hosting the Client Access Exchange role. Data for this report is generated with the "Execute test-ActiveSyncConnectivity External diagnostic cmdlet" timed event rule.

▶ **Mailbox Service Availability**—The Mailbox Service Availability report shows successful MAPI requests made to the environment. Data for this report is generated with the "Execute test-MAPIConnectivity diagnostic cmdlet" timed event rule.

▶ **Unified Messaging Local Fax Service Availability**—The Unified Messaging Local Fax Service Availability report shows availability statistics for the fax service provided by Exchange Unified Messaging servers. Data for this report is generated with the "Execute test-UMConnectivity Local Fax diagnostic task" timed event rule.

▶ **Unified Messaging Local Voice Service Availability**—The Unified Messaging Local Voice Service Availability report shows availability statistics for the voice service provided by Exchange. Data for this report is generated with the "Execute test-UMConnectivity Local Voice diagnostic task" timed event rule.

▶ **Unified Messaging Remote Fax Service Availability**—The Unified Messaging Remote Fax Service Availability report shows availability statistics for the fax service provided by Exchange Unified Messaging servers. Data for this report is generated with the "Execute test-UMConnectivity Remote Fax diagnostic task" timed event rule.

▶ **Unified Messaging Remote Voice Service Availability**—The Unified Messaging Remote Voice Service Availability report shows availability statistics for the voice service provided by Exchange. Data for this report is generated with the "Execute test-UMConnectivity Remote Voice diagnostic task" timed event rule.

The following additional reports can be found within the supplemental reports folder. These reports are used within each of the availability reports; it is not necessary to run these reports individually:

▶ General Events

▶ Table-ActiveSync External Service Availability

▶ Table-ActiveSync Internal Service Availability

▶ Table-Mailbox Service Availability

▶ Table-Unified Messaging Local Fax Service Availability

▶ Table-Unified Messaging Local Voice Service Availability

▶ Table-Unified Messaging Remote Fax Service Availability

Summary

An integral part of ensuring any system is dependable or reliable is care and feeding. Monitoring Exchange 2007 with MOM helps ensure the organization is operating smoothly by proactively monitoring servers across the environment and notifying administrators when a problem is detected. This level of monitoring is quickly achieved with custom rules provided by Microsoft and designed specifically for Exchange 2007. MOM also facilitates trend analysis and capacity planning through customizable reports executed against data captured over a long period.

20

Best Practices

The following are best practices from this chapter:

▶ Leverage Microsoft Operations Manager to assist with proactive monitoring and trend analysis of the environment.

▶ Use the latest Exchange 2007 Management Pack as it provides the most accurate business logic and knowledge base information critical for monitoring Exchange.

▶ A well-tuned implementation of MOM can provide accurate Exchange monitoring and guidance when it's needed. Tune the alerts and performance rules found in the management pack for the environment being monitored. Perform ongoing tuning as the environment changes.

▶ Ensure the MOM environment has been updated with the latest service pack. The Exchange 2007 Management Pack requires MOM 2005 SP1 to operate correctly.

▶ Do not use the Exchange environment to send alert notifications to the Exchange team.

CHAPTER 21

Using Terminal Services to Manage Exchange Servers

To keep maintenance and administration costs down and promote efficiency in any Microsoft Exchange Server 2007 messaging environment, you must have a secure and reliable means of managing the servers remotely. Windows Server 2003 and Exchange Server 2007 have these capabilities built in so that you do not have to rely on third-party solutions.

You can manage Exchange systems remotely using Terminal Services in different ways, and it is important to understand not only what these options are, but also which one is best for your particular environment. This chapter complements Chapter 19, "Exchange Server 2007 Management and Maintenance Practices," and expands on the different remote management capabilities and when to use them.

There are two Terminal Services functions within Windows Server 2003: Remote Desktop for Administration and Terminal Services (formerly known as Terminal Services Application Mode). Remote Desktop for Administration mode is installed (but not enabled) by default; Terminal Services must be manually installed and configured.

Planning and Preparing Terminal Services for Exchange Administration

Terminal Services mode is available in all editions of Windows Server 2003 (that is, Standard, Enterprise, and

DataCenter) except the Web Edition. It enables any authorized user to connect to the server and run a single application or a complete desktop session from the client workstation. Because the applications are loaded and running on the Terminal Services server, client desktop resources are barely used; all the application processing is performed by the Terminal Services server. This enables companies to extend the life of old, less-powerful workstations by running applications only from a Terminal Services server session.

Terminal Services is generally not considered a viable technology to manage Exchange remotely. Although it is possible to use Terminal Services to manage Exchange 2007, several planning considerations must be addressed to determine whether Terminal Services is suitable in your environment.

The narrow use for Terminal Services is in the case of a centralized tool platform where multiple administrators (more than two at a time) log on and use the administration tools. Terminal Services in this case allows the organization to set up a central server or set of servers with all the tools that the administrators use.

Planning Considerations for Using Terminal Services

Terminal Services can require a lot of planning, especially when you're considering whether to use it to manage Exchange remotely. Because Terminal Services is intended to make applications available to end users rather than serve as a remote management service, security, server performance, and licensing are key components to consider before using it in a production environment.

Terminal Services Security

Terminal Services servers should be secured following standard security guidelines defined in company security policies and as recommended by hardware and software vendors. Some basic security configurations include removing all unnecessary services from the Terminal Services nodes and applying security patches for known vulnerabilities on services or applications that are running on the terminal server.

An administrator can use Group Policy to limit client functionality as needed to enhance server security, and if increased network security is a requirement, can consider requiring clients to run sessions in 128-bit high-encryption mode.

Windows Server 2003 Terminal Services can be run in either Full Security or Relaxed Security Permission compatibility mode to meet an organization's security policy and application requirements. Full Security mode was created to help lock down the terminal server environment to reduce the risk of users mistakenly installing software or inadvertently disabling the Terminal Services server by moving directories or deleting Registry keys. This mode can be used for most certified terminal server applications. Relaxed Security Permission compatibility mode was created to support legacy applications that require extended access into the server system directory and system Registry.

In addition to the more common security precautions that are recommended for Terminal Services, you must also consider how running Terminal Services on an Exchange Server 2007 server affects security. Using a server with both Terminal Services and Exchange

Server 2007 roles and responsibilities can be a dangerous combination and should be considered only in the smallest of environments with very relaxed security requirements. In any circumstance, the combination is not recommended.

Combining the two services and configuring Terminal Services to remotely manage Exchange can result in many security-related hazards, including the following:

▶ A single misconfiguration or setting can enable users to change specific Exchange settings or parameters.

▶ Users authorized to shut down or restart the system might inadvertently do so, causing messaging downtime.

▶ Application-specific security might conflict or, in some cases, unintentionally allow or restrict access to messaging components on the server.

Terminal Server Licensing

Terminal Services requires the purchase of client access licenses (CALs) for each client device or session. A Terminal Services License Server also must be available on the network to allocate and manage these CALs. When a Terminal Services server is establishing a session with a client, it checks with the Terminal Services License Server to verify whether this client has a license. A license is allocated if the client does not already have one.

NOTE

Using Terminal Services to connect to and remotely manage an Exchange Server 2007 server does not exempt you from needing a Terminal Services CAL. This adds to the overall cost of supporting Exchange Server 2007.

To install licenses on the Terminal Services License Server, the Terminal Services License Server must first be installed and then activated online. The Terminal Services License Server requires Internet access or dial-up modem access to activate the CALs added to the server.

When a Terminal Services server cannot locate a Terminal Services License Server on the network, it still allows unlicensed clients to connect. This can go on for 120 days without contacting a license server, and then the server stops serving Terminal Services sessions. It is imperative to get a license server installed on the network as soon as possible—before Terminal Services servers are deployed to production.

Installing Terminal Services for Remote Administration

To install Terminal Services, a network administrator can use the Configure Your Server Wizard as follows:

1. Log on to the desired server with Local Administrator privileges.

2. Insert the Windows Server 2003 CD in the CD-ROM drive and close any autorun pop-up windows that open.

3. Click Start, All Programs, Administrative Tools, Configure Your Server Wizard.

4. Click Next on the welcome screen to continue.

5. Verify that you have completed the steps as outlined on the Preliminary Steps page, and click Next to continue.

6. From the Server Role page, select Terminal Server from the list, and click Next to continue.

7. On the Summary of Selections page, Install Terminal Server should be listed in the summary. If this is correct, click Next to continue.

8. When a pop-up warning message states that the server will be restarted as part of the installation process, click OK to continue.

9. After the system restarts, log on with the same account used to install the terminal server.

10. After the logon process completes, Terminal Server Help appears with direct links to terminal server checklists. Close this window or minimize it to review information later.

11. When you see the Configure Your Server Wizard message stating This Server Is Now a Terminal Server, click Finish to complete the installation.

Accessing a Server Using the Remote Desktop Client

A Windows Server 2003 system with Terminal Services installed can be accessed from a variety of clients. These clients include 32-bit Windows-based clients and ActiveX web-based clients.

Accessing Terminal Services Using the 32-bit Windows Remote Desktop Protocol (RDP) Client

All Windows Server 2003 server versions and Windows XP Professional include a 32-bit terminal server client called Remote Desktop Connection. This full-featured client enables end users to tune their connections to run in Full-screen mode, utilizing advanced features, such as server audio redirection, true-color video, and local disk, COM port, and printer redirection. Remote Desktop Connection can also be optimized to run over a 28.8Kbps connection.

Down-level client workstations can get the RDP client as a free download from the Microsoft website.

Accessing Terminal Services Using the Web Client

Terminal Services provides a web-based client that can easily be distributed through a web browser. This client downloads as an ActiveX object and needs to be installed only once.

Connecting to a terminal server using this client requires a web port connection to the terminal server logon web page and also access to TCP port 3389 on the terminal server. The web-based client still uses the RDP native to Windows Server 2003 Terminal Services.

Contrary to many terminal server administrators' beliefs, the web server system hosting the web client pages does not need to be running on the terminal server. If there is no particular reason to run a web server on the terminal server, for security and performance reasons, place the terminal server web client on a separate web server.

To install the web server client on a web server system, do the following:

1. Click Start and select Control Panel.

2. Locate and double-click the Add/Remove Programs icon.

3. Select the Add/Remove Windows Components button.

4. Assuming this server does not already have the Application Server running, check the Application Server check box, and click the Details button.

5. Ensure that the Internet Information Services (IIS) check box is checked, highlight this option, and click the Details button.

6. Scroll down and check the World Wide Web Service check box, and click the Details button once again.

7. Check the Remote Desktop Web Connection check box, and click OK three times followed by clicking the Next button to begin the installation.

8. After the installation has completed, click Finish and close the Add/Remove Programs window. To access this page, open a web browser and type http://servername/tsweb.

Using the Remote Desktop MMC (Tsmmc.msc)

Remote Desktop is a utility that provides a way to manage several Terminal Services sessions from within one window. This utility still uses RDP to connect to servers and workstations, but it allows an administrator to switch between terminal sessions by clicking a button instead of having to switch windows. Also, because the console settings can be saved, a new terminal session can also be established with the click of a button.

Remotely Connecting to a Terminal Server Console

Administrators can connect to terminal server consoles remotely by using the Remote Desktop Connection client or the Remote Desktop MMC snap-in. With remote console access, administrators can use Terminal Services to log on to the server remotely as though they were logged on at the console.

Using the Remote Desktop MMC snap-in, administrators can configure remote desktop sessions that always connect to the terminal server console session. This enables administrators to successfully install and update the operating system and applications remotely.

> **CAUTION**
>
> You need to know whether to leave the console session logged on and/or locked. If a user logs off the session, the console will also be logged off. So, you need to be informed and be safe.

To connect to a terminal server console using Remote Desktop Connection, run `mstsc.exe` from the command prompt with the `/console` switch to gain console access.

Planning and Using Remote Desktop for Administration

As mentioned earlier, Remote Desktop for Administration is included and installed with the Windows Server 2003 operating system and needs only to be enabled. This eases automated and unattended server deployment by enabling an administrator to deploy servers that can be managed remotely after the operating systems have completed installation. This allows Exchange administrators in central offices to manage servers in branch offices or Exchange administrators in one region (such as the America region) to manage servers in another region (such as the Asian region). This can reduce the required headcount to manage Exchange infrastructure and facilitate a follow-the-sun model of global support.

This model can also be used to manage a headless server, which can reduce the amount of space needed in any server rack. More space can be dedicated to servers instead of switch boxes, monitors, keyboards, and mouse devices.

This also provides for an improved security model because Exchange administrators can administer the Exchange servers without having to get physical access to the servers. This is a very effective security strategy for large data centers with various application servers that might be collocated in the same racks as the Exchange servers. It allows the Exchange administrators to perform their job functions without needed access to the data center.

Remote Desktop for Administration limits the number of terminal sessions to two, with only one Remote Desktop Protocol (RDP) or Secure Sockets Layer (SSL) for remote administration connection per network interface. Only administrators can connect to these sessions. No additional licenses are needed to run a server in this Terminal Services mode, which enables an administrator to perform almost all the server management duties remotely.

Even though Remote Desktop for Administration is installed by default, this mode does not have to be enabled. Some organizations might see Remote Desktop for Administration as an unneeded security risk and choose to keep it disabled. This function can easily be disabled throughout the entire Active Directory (AD) forest by using a Group Policy setting to disable administrators from connecting through Remote Desktop for Administration.

Planning for Remote Desktop for Administration Mode

Unless Remote Desktop for Administration is viewed as a security risk, you should enable it on all internal servers to allow remote administration. For servers that are on the Internet or for demilitarized zone (DMZ) networks, Remote Desktop for Administration can be used, but access should be even more restricted. For example, consider limiting access to a predefined IP address or set of IP addresses, using firewall access control lists (ACLs) to eliminate unauthorized attempts to log on to the server. Another option is to limit connections to the server based on protocol.

> **NOTE**
>
> The level of encryption for remote sessions by default is 128-bit (bidirectional). It is also important to note that some older Terminal Services clients might not support that level of encryption. See the section "Securing Remote Desktop for Administration" for more details and how to increase the security.

Enabling Remote Desktop for Administration

Remote Desktop for Administration mode is installed on all Windows Server 2003 servers by default and needs only to be enabled. To manually enable this feature, follow these steps:

1. Log on to the desired server with Administrator privileges.

2. Click Start, right-click the My Computer shortcut, and then click Properties on the shortcut menu.

3. Select the Remote tab, and in the Remote Desktop section, check the Enable Remote Desktop on this Computer check box, as shown in Figure 21.1.

4. Click OK on the Systems Properties page to complete this process.

The connection can be tested by launching the Remote Desktop Client from Start, All Programs, Accessories, Communications and selecting the Remote Desktop Communications icon. Enter in the name of the Exchange server to connect to.

Enabling Remote Desktop for Administration After the Fact

Sometimes, an Exchange server is built and deployed, but the Remote Desktop option is not enabled. This is a problem when subsequently attempting to remotely administer the server. The Terminal Services Client will behave as if the server could not be found.

Even though Remote Desktop is not enabled, the Exchange server can still be accessed administratively. In particular, the Registry can still be modified remotely and the Remote Desktop setting can be enabled using the RegEdit tool.

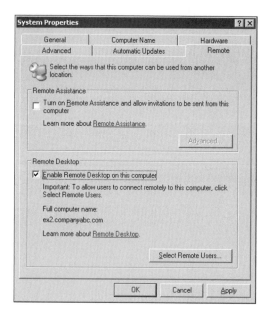

FIGURE 21.1   Enabling users to connect to the system remotely.

To enable Remote Desktop remotely, complete the following steps:

1. From a domain member computer, log on as a user with Administrator privileges on the server.

2. Launch `regedit.exe`.

3. Click File and then select Connect Remote Registry.

4. Enter the name of the server on which you want to enable Remote Desktop, and click OK.

5. Under the Exchange server tree, go to the key `HKLM\Software\Policies\Microsoft\Windows NT\Terminal Services\`.

6. Change the value `fDenyTSConnections` from "1" to "0".

7. Close `regedit.exe`.

8. The change will take effect immediately.

The server will now accept Terminal Services connections.

Remote Desktop Client Command-line Options

The Remote Desktop Connection client (`mstsc.exe`) can be launched from the command line for additional control.

The command line for the Remote Desktop Client is as follows:

```
mstsc.exe {ConnectionFile | /v:ServerName[:Port]} [/console] [/f]
[/w:Width/h:Height]
```

There are a handful of switch commands for the Remote Desktop Client that can be used to choose specific servers and options. The commands are as follows:

- **/v:ServerName[:Port]**—Specifies the remote computer and, optionally, the port number to which you want to connect

- **/console**—Connects to the console session of the specified Windows Server 2003 family operating system

- **/f** —Starts the Remote Desktop connection in full-screen mode

- **/w:Width/h:Height**—Specifies the dimensions of the Remote Desktop screen

In particular, the `/console` switch setting is very useful. It allows the Exchange administrator to connect directly to the console session on the Exchange server, which is the session used when logging on at the keyboard of the Exchange server. This, in effect, allows the Exchange administrator to assume control of the keyboard of the Exchange server.

Remote Desktop Administration Tips and Tricks

You should consider several key points before using either Remote Desktop for Administration or Remote Administration (HTML), including, but not limited to, the following:

- **Make sure resources are available**—What information technology (IT) personnel resources, if any, are available at the remote location or at the Exchange server's location? If a problem arises with the connection to the remote Exchange server or the server itself (for example, a disconnection), contingency plans should be available to recover and continue to remotely manage the system. Generally speaking, it is a good idea to have someone in the vicinity who can assist the administrator in some form or fashion.

- **Use care when modifying network configurations**—With any remote administration tool, you are dependent upon the connectivity between the client computer and the Exchange server that is being remotely managed. If network configuration settings must be modified remotely, consider having alternative methods of access. For instance, dial-up or a separate network connection might minimize downtime or other issues stemming from loss of connectivity.

- **Use disconnect and reset timeout values**—Anytime a connection is accidentally broken or an administrator disconnects, the remote session is placed into a disconnected state that can later be reconnected and used to manage a server remotely. Disconnect and reset timeouts are not configured by default for Remote Desktop administration tools. These values can be used to ensure that administrators are not unintentionally locked out (for example, when there are two remote sessions that are active but in a disconnected state). Generally speaking, using a 5-minute timeout value allows enough time for administrators to reconnect if they were accidentally disconnected. Moreover, it helps minimize the number of sessions that are disconnected and not being used.

▶ **Coordinate remote administration efforts**—The number of remote administration connections is limited to a precious two. Therefore, plan and coordinate efforts to reduce the number of attempts to access Exchange servers remotely. This also helps ensure that remote administration activities do not conflict with other administrators and sessions or, in the worst of cases, corrupt information or data on the server.

Remote Desktop Administration Keyboard Shortcuts

The keyboard shortcuts that work on the server have equivalents when running in Terminal Services. Table 21.1 lists the most common ones.

TABLE 21.1   Keyboard Shortcuts in a Remote Desktop Session

Windows Keyboard Shortcut	Terminal Services Keyboard Shortcut	Description
Alt+Tab	Alt+Page Up	Switches between programs from left to right
Alt+Shift+Tab	Alt+Page Down	Switches between programs from right to left
Alt+Esc	Alt+Insert	Cycles through the programs in the order they were started
	Ctrl+Esc	Switches the client between a window and full screen
Ctrl+Esc	Alt+Home	Displays the Start menu
	Alt+Delete	Displays the Windows menu
Prnt Scrn	Ctrl+Alt+Minus (–) symbol on the numeric keypad	Places a snapshot of the active window in the Remote Desktop session on the Clipboard
Ctrl+Alt+Del	Ctrl+Alt+End	Displays the Task Manager or Windows Security dialog box
Alt+Prnt Scrn	Ctrl+Alt+Plus (+) symbol on the numeric keypad	Places a snapshot of the entire Remote Desktop session window on the Clipboard

These keyboard shortcuts can be very handy when working within Terminal Services sessions, be it to capture a screen for documentation, check the performance in Task Manager, or quickly switch between windows in the session.

Securing Remote Desktop for Administration

The security of the Remote Desktop for Administration can be adjusted in a variety of ways to enhance the security of the sessions. All of these settings are configured in the

Terminal Services Configuration MMC snap-in, which is, by default, installed in the Administrative Tools. The security settings are properties of the RDP-Tcp connection under the Connections folder in the tool.

These settings ensure that the Remote Desktop for Administration is secure.

Encryption Level

The Terminal Services protocol supports high (128-bit), low (56-bit), and Federal Information Processing Standards (FIPS) compliant encryption settings. The settings are High, Low, Client Compatible, and FIPS Compliant, and can be found on the General tab, as shown in Figure 21.2. The default setting is Client Compatible, which means that the sessions default to 128-bit encryption but will drop down to 56-bit encryption if older clients connect or if the client setting is set for 56-bit.

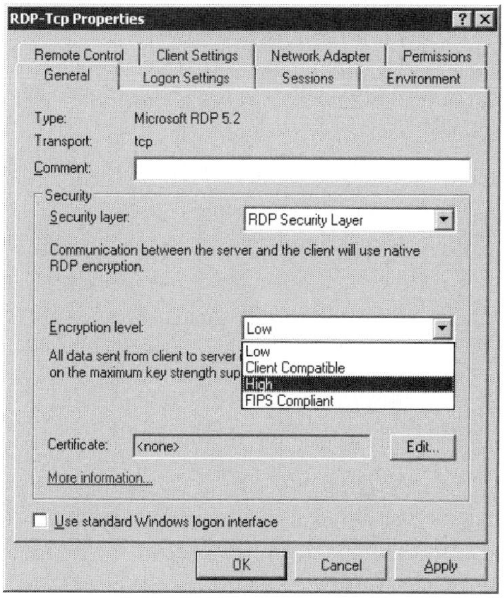

FIGURE 21.2   Encryption Level security setting.

The sessions can be made more secure by changing the setting to High, which ensures that the clients will always connect at 128-bit. Older clients that don't support 128-bit or clients that are hard-coded for 56-bit will fail.

Remote Control

The Terminal Services connection allows the sessions to be remotely controlled, meaning that a third party can view and possibly interact with the Terminal Services session. Although this can be useful for training and support by facilitating support, it can also present a security risk.

The ability to use remote control can be disabled by selecting the Do Not Allow Remote Control check box on the Remote Control tab.

Encryption Layer

The Encryption Level setting can be used to change the encryption from the RDP Security Layer to SSL. This supports the use of certificates. This is a little-used feature of Remote Desktop for Administration, but can be used to enhance or standardize security.

Disable Mappings

Another feature of the Terminal Services connection is to map local drives, printers, LPT ports, COM ports, the Clipboard, and the audio. These allow for a much richer experience by allowing the administrator to copy files from local drives, print to the local printer, and cut/paste from the Terminal Services session to the local system.

However, these features could also be security risks as they allow direct interaction between the client and the Terminal Services session. These mapping features can be disabled as needed on the Client Settings tab in the Connection Properties dialog box. By default, all are allowed except the Audio mapping.

Always Prompt for Password

The Terminal Services Client can be configured to save the logon password and allow for automatic logon to the Exchange server. This is very convenient for the Exchange administrator, who can just launch the Terminal Services client and get access to the Exchange server without being prompted to enter credentials.

However, this is a very bad security practice because any user can click on the icon and then have full access to the Exchange server. Unfortunately, the password is saved at the client level and not on the server side.

Fortunately, the Terminal Services connection can be configured to always prompt for a password regardless of whether one is supplied automatically. The Always Prompt for Password feature can be enabled on the Logon Settings tab of the Connection Properties dialog box.

Session Disconnect

If an Exchange administrator's Terminal Services session breaks, the session is normally left in a disconnected state. This allows the Exchange administrator to reconnect to the session and pick up where he left off. The Exchange administrator can also choose to disconnect rather than log off a session. This is frequently done when a long-running process is started on the Exchange server, such as a database repair or an Exmerge of a large mailbox.

Although the disconnected session is convenient, it might also be considered a security risk to have active sessions left unattended so to speak. If this is a security concern, the connection can be configured on the Sessions tab to end a disconnected session after a

period of time, as shown in Figure 21.3. The session is ended after being in a disconnected state for 5 minutes, which gives the Exchange administrator ample time to reconnect following connection problems.

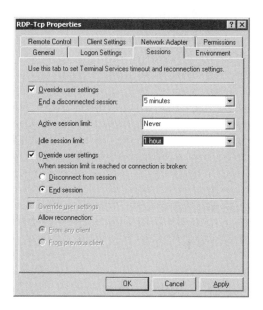

FIGURE 21.3   Idle session limit configuration.

Other session limits can be configured on this tab as well, such as ending or disconnecting a session that has been active too long (not recommended) or that has been idle too
long.

Permissions

By default, only members of the local Administrators group or the local Remote Desktop
Users group are able to access the server via the Remote Desktop for Administration.
These permissions can be customized to explicitly grant access or explicitly deny access.
The permissions for the connection can be accessed in the RDP-Tcp connection properties
on the Permissions tab.

Conducting Remote Administration Using HTML

Microsoft provides a tool called Remote Administration (HTML) that can be used to
remotely access and manage an Exchange 2007 server. The primary intention of this tool
is to provide basic remote administration capabilities for Internet Information Services 6.0
web servers, as shown in Figure 21.4. However, there are capabilities built in that enable
administrators to not only check server status, logs, and IIS functionality, but also to
manage server network configurations and email alerts, and use the Exchange System
Manager (ESM) through Remote Desktop, as shown in Figure 21.5.

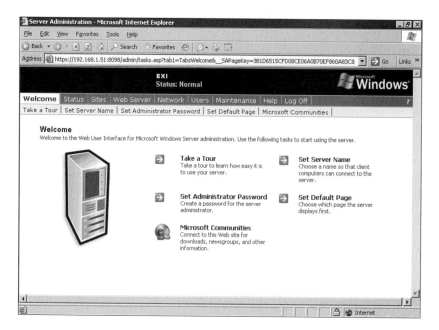

FIGURE 21.4   Remote Administration (HTML) tool options.

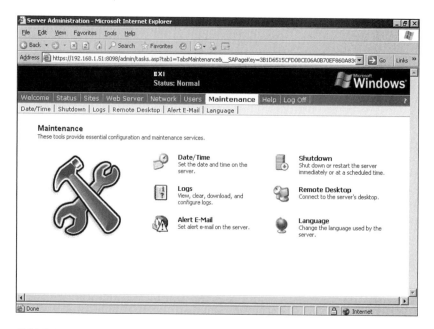

FIGURE 21.5   Remote Desktop access from the Remote Administration (HTML) tool.

The Remote Administration (HTML) tool is only available in the following operating systems that are supported by Exchange Server 2007:

▶ Windows Server 2003 x64, Standard Edition

▶ Windows Server 2003 x64, Enterprise Edition

Remote Administration (HTML) has been deprecated in Windows Server 2003 R2 and is not available in any of the following operating systems supported by Exchange Server 2007:

▶ Windows Server 2003 x64 R2, Standard Edition

▶ Windows Server 2003 x64 R2, Enterprise Edition

In addition, Remote Administration (HTML) cannot be installed on a domain controller. The option is not available in the list of choices to select.

Installing and Enabling Remote Administration (HTML)

As hinted at in the preceding section, Remote Administration (HTML) is a Windows Server 2003 IIS component, and it cannot be used to manage earlier versions of IIS. It is also not enabled by default. This does not mean that using this tool creates unnecessary security risks. Instead, it keeps Windows Server 2003 security in a more consistent, locked-down state, and you need to manually install and configure its settings to meet the security requirements of your company.

To install Remote Administration (HTML), do the following:

1. Select Add or Remove Programs from the Control Panel.

2. Choose Add/Remove Windows Components and then highlight Application Server in the Windows Components Wizard window.

3. Click Details and then highlight Internet Information Services (IIS) in the Application Server window.

4. Click Details again and highlight World Wide Web Services. Click Details one more time to view the Remote Administration (HTML) option, as shown in Figure 21.6.

5. Click OK three times to return to the Windows Components Wizard window, and then click Next.

6. When installation completes, click Finish.

To enable Remote Administration (HTML), perform the following steps:

1. Select the Internet Information Services Manager from the Administrative Tools menu by selecting Start, Programs, Administrative Tools.

2. Expand the server and also the Web Site folder to display a list of websites hosted on the Exchange Server 2007 server.

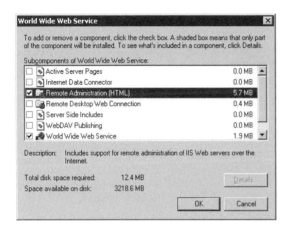

FIGURE 21.6   Installing the Remote Administration (HTML) tool.

3. Right-click the Administration website, and then select Properties.

4. Within the Web Site Identification section, record the port numbers that are displayed for the TCP and SSL ports. The defaults are 8099 and 8098.

5. Select the Directory Security tab and then click the Edit button in the IP Address and Domain Name Restrictions section. You can select restrictions either by IP address, a group of IP addresses, or by domain name.

CAUTION

Although you can grant access to all computers, all computers in an IP address subnet, or all computers in a domain, you should limit the number of computers that can have access using Remote Administration (HTML) to Exchange Server 2007. Otherwise, unnecessary security vulnerabilities can be introduced on the Exchange server.

6. In the IP Address and Domain Name Restrictions dialog box, select Denied Access, and then click the Add button. Note that you can optionally click DNS Lookup to verify the name of the server to which you are granting access.

7. In the Grant Access dialog box, click Single Computer, and then enter in the IP address of the computer to which you want to grant access.

8. Click OK twice and then close the IIS Manager.

To remotely administer the Exchange server from the computer that has been granted access, open Microsoft Internet Explorer and type https://servername:8098, where *servername* is the name of the server or the IP address. You will be prompted to provide username and password credentials to log on to the server.

> **NOTE**
>
> As mentioned earlier, Remote Administration (HTML) provides the necessary tools for managing essential IIS components and basic Windows Server 2003 features, but it also provides a link for the Remote Desktop. The Remote Desktop is the web-based equivalent of Remote Desktop for Administration. This link must be used if you are to manage an Exchange server.
>
> The Remote Administration (HTML) tool is useful on older or non-Windows computers that need access for remote Exchange Server 2007 management purposes. Otherwise, if the computer accessing Exchange Server 2007 remotely via the Remote Administration (HTML) tool also has the Remote Desktop Connection tool (for the client side), it begs the question of why the Remote Desktop for Administration tool is not being used in the first place. Unless a security policy dictates that the RDP port should not be open on the firewall, the Remote Desktop for Administration tool is recommended.

Using Terminal Services on Mobile Devices

Many mobile devices, such as Microsoft Windows Mobile 5 devices, have Terminal Services Client components built in to the device's operating system, as shown in Figure 21.7. The Terminal Services Client connects to the server as a client computer would connect, using Remote Desktop for Administration. After it's connected, as shown in Figure 21.8, administrators can manage the Exchange server from the mobile device the same way they would if they were logged on locally. The obvious downside to using a mobile device is the screen size. Although some mobile devices can resize the screen to accommodate the entire desktop on it, the screen size and resolution is limited.

Locking Down Mobile Devices Terminal Services

Securing mobile devices, such as the Windows Mobile 5.0 device illustrated in Figures 21.7 and 21.8, is often more challenging than securing a client computer or another server. Because the device is designed for mobility, it opens up the possibility of losing the device or having it stolen. Then, an unauthorized person could use it to gain access to the network environment.

One of the more important ways to mitigate the risk is to ensure that the Remote Desktop for Administration connection is configured to Always Prompt for Password, as described in the section "Securing Remote Desktop for Administration."

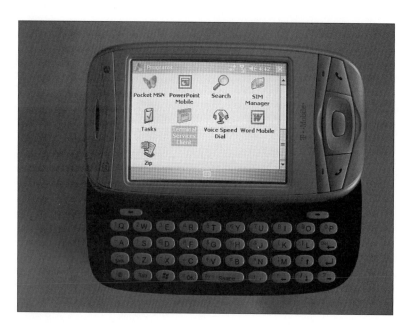

FIGURE 21.7   The Terminal Services Client component on a Windows Mobile 5.0 device.

FIGURE 21.8   Managing an Exchange Server 2007 server from a Windows Mobile 5.0 device.

An obvious deterrent is securing access to the mobile device's own security features. For instance, the device can be configured so that a person has to use a password to use the mobile device. If the mobile device were stolen or found, the person with the device would have to figure out the password before gaining access to the mobile device. Windows Mobile 5.0 supports four-digit personal identification numbers (PINs; similar to a bank ATM card) and strong, alphanumeric passwords. In addition, each time the incorrect password is entered, a timed delay increases before the person can attempt to reenter a PIN or password. The time delay increases exponentially after each unsuccessful logon attempt. The device can even be configured to completely wipe itself if too many password attempts are made. Other mobile devices complement password or PIN support with biometrics such as a fingerprint reader.

Another important aspect to secure is mobile device communications with the rest of the world. The type of security that can be used depends on how the mobile device is configured to communicate. Most devices, however, support using SSL or Wired Equivalent Protocol (WEP).

NOTE

Although viruses for mobile devices are rare, it is important to implement virus-protection software. Antivirus software can also help prevent tracing or monitoring applications from being installed that could record everything that is entered into the mobile device, including passwords.

Using the Remote Desktop Tool for Remote Exchange Management

The Remote Desktop tool comes standard with all Windows 2003 implementations and facilitates managing multiple Exchange servers. As shown in Figure 21.9, multiple console screens can be defined for each server in the tool as well as multiple connections can be established simultaneously to various servers in the environment. The left pane shows a list of servers that can be connected to and switched between.

The multiple connections can be toggled between quickly simply by clicking on their icon or even arranged in multiple panes on a single screen. A large display is very effective for this.

Another interesting Remote Desktop tool feature is that the tool has an option to connect to the console session rather than establish a new session. This allows the Exchange administrator to connect directly to the console session and interact with any applications that were started at the server keyboard.

The Remote Desktop tool is installed by default on Windows Server 2003 servers in the Administrative Tools folder. It is also installed with the Administration Tools Pack (`adminpack.msi`), which installs the Windows Server 2003 tools on a Windows XP workstation. The Administration Tools Pack is available on the Windows Server 2003 media or on the Microsoft website (see Knowledge Base Article 304718 at http://support.microsoft.com/default.aspx?scid=kb;en-us;304718).

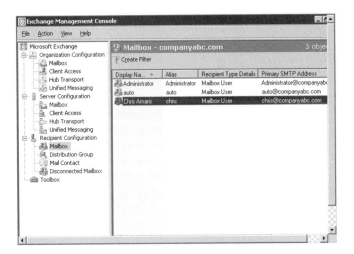

FIGURE 21.9   Managing Exchange Server 2007 servers using the Remote Desktop tool.

The Remote Desktop configuration can be saved in Microsoft Management Console files (*.msc) to be quickly launched. This allows the Exchange administrator to create different custom consoles with the appropriate Terminal Services sessions for the task at hand, such as when doing mailbox maintenance or troubleshooting front-end problems.

Summary

Many messaging environments today require an easy and effective way to remotely manage and maintain systems. Terminal Services provides an excellent mechanism to accomplish this. Windows Server 2003 has a variety of tools built-in that administrators can use to securely manage and maintain Exchange from any location using Terminal Services. This chapter examined the most common Terminal Services management tools and highlighted which ones are more appropriate in various real-world circumstances.

Best Practices

The following are best practices from this chapter:

- ▶ Carefully plan which Exchange servers should use Remote Desktop for Administration or Remote Administration (HTML) for remote management.

- ▶ Restrict Remote Desktop for Administration or Remote Administration (HTML) access on Exchange 2007 servers that are facing the Internet (for example, limiting access to a predefined IP address or set of IP addresses).

- ▶ Have a person in the vicinity of the server that is being managed remotely assist the administrator in case network connectivity is lost.

▶ Use care when modifying network configurations over a Remote Desktop for Administration connection.

▶ Use disconnect and reset timeout values for Remote Desktop for Administration connections.

▶ Plan and coordinate remote administration efforts to reduce the number of attempts to access Exchange servers remotely.

▶ Do not implement Terminal Services on an Exchange server solely to manage Exchange remotely.

CHAPTER 22

Documenting an Exchange Server 2007 Environment

Documentation is the cornerstone for building and maintaining a streamlined Microsoft Exchange Server 2007 environment. Documentation is not only an integral part of the installation or design of an Exchange Server 2007 environment, but it is also important for the maintenance, support, and recovery of new or existing environments.

Documentation serves several purposes throughout the life cycle of Exchange Server 2007 and is especially critical on a per-project basis. In the initial stages of a project, it serves to provide a historical record of the options and decisions made during the design process. During the testing and implementation phases, documents such as step-by-step procedures and checklists guide project team members and help ensure that all steps are completed. When the implementation portion of the project is complete, support documentation can play a key role in maintaining the health of the new environment. Support documents include administration and maintenance procedures, checklists, detailed configuration settings, and monitoring procedures.

In the discovery stages of the project, documentation serves to record the key elements of a successful implementation:

▶ Organizational goals and objectives

▶ Business requirements

▶ Technical specifications

It quickly becomes apparent how the documents become building blocks for the remaining documentation needs. By defining the organizational goals and objectives, the business requirements can be identified. After the business requirements are listed, the technical specifications are developed to support them.

This chapter is dedicated to providing the breadth and scope of documentation for an Exchange Server 2007 environment. Equally important, it provides considerations and best practices for keeping your messaging environment well documented, maintained, and manageable.

Benefits of Documentation

Although many of the benefits of Exchange Server 2007 documentation are obvious and tangible, others can be harder to identify. A key benefit to documentation is that the process of putting the information down on paper encourages a higher level of analysis and review of the topic at hand. The process also encourages teamwork and collaboration within an organization and interdepartmental exchange of ideas.

Documentation that is developed with specific goals, and goes through a review or approval process, is typically well organized and complete, and contributes to the overall professionalism of the organization and its knowledge base. The following sections examine some of the other benefits of professional documentation in the Exchange Server 2007 environment.

In today's world of doing more with less, the intangible benefits of good documentation can become a challenge to justify to upper management. Some key benefits of documentation include the following:

- ▶ **Collaboration**—Producing the documentation to support a good Exchange Server 2007 implementation requires input from departments across the organization. This teamwork encourages deeper analysis and more careful review of the project goals. With better base information, the project team can make more informed decisions and avoid having to go back to the drawing board to address missed objectives.

- ▶ **Historical records**—Implementation projects are composed of several different stages where goals are identified and key decisions are made to support them. It is important to make sure these decisions and their supporting arguments are recorded for future reference. As the project moves forward, it is not uncommon for details to get changed because of incomplete information being passed from the design stage onto the implementation stage.

- ▶ **Training**—Life is ever changing. That might sound a bit philosophical for a book on technology but when it comes to people, we know that some of them move on to other challenges. And that is when good documentation will become an invaluable tool to provide information to their replacement. This is equally true for the executive sponsor, the project manager, or the engineer building the Exchange server.

Knowledge Sharing and Knowledge Management

The right documentation enables an organization to organize and manage its data and intellectual property. Company policies and procedures are typically located throughout multiple locations that include individual files for various departments. Consolidating this information into logical groupings can be beneficial.

> **TIP**
>
> Place documentation in at least two different locations where it is easily accessible for authorized users, such as on the intranet, in a public folder, or in hard-copy format. Also consider using a document management system such as Microsoft Office SharePoint Services 2007.

A complete design document consolidates and summarizes key discussions and decisions, budgetary concerns, and timing issues. This consolidation provides a single source of information for questions that might emerge at a later date. In addition, a document that describes the specific configuration details of the Exchange server might prove very valuable to a manager in another company office when making a purchasing decision.

All of the documents should be readily available at all times. This is especially critical regarding disaster recovery documents. Centralizing the documentation and communicating the location helps reduce the use of out-of-date documentation and reduce confusion during a disaster recovery. It is also recommended that they be available in a number of formats, such as hard copy, the appropriate place on the network, and even via an intranet.

Financial Benefits of Documentation

Proper Exchange Server 2007 documentation can be time consuming and adds to the cost of the environment and project. In lean economic times for a company or organization, it is often difficult to justify the expense of project documentation. However, when looking at documents, such as in maintenance or disaster recovery scenarios, it is easy to determine that creating this documentation makes financial sense. For example, in an organization where downtime can cost thousands of dollars per minute, the return on investment (ROI) in disaster recovery and maintenance documentation is easy to calculate. In a company that is growing rapidly and adding staff and new servers on a regular basis, tested documentation on server builds and administration training can also have immediate and visible benefits.

Financial benefits are not limited to maintenance and disaster recovery documentation. Well-developed and professional design and planning documentation helps the organization avoid costly mistakes in the implementation or migration process, such as buying too many server licenses or purchasing too many servers.

Baselining Records for Documentation Comparisons

Baselining is a process of recording the state of an Exchange Server 2007 system so that any changes in its performance can be identified at a later date. Complete baselining also pertains to the overall network performance, including wide area network (WAN) links, but in those cases it might require special software and tools (such as sniffers) to record the information.

An Exchange Server 2007 system baseline document records the state of the server after it is implemented in a production environment and can include statistics such as memory use, paging, disk subsystem throughput, and more. This information then allows the administrator or appropriate IT resource to determine at a later date how the system is performing in comparison to initial operation.

Using Documentation for Troubleshooting Purposes

Troubleshooting documentation is a record of identified system issues and the associated resolution. This documentation is helpful both in terms of the processes that the company recommends for resolving technical issues and a documented record of the results of actual troubleshooting challenges. Researching and troubleshooting an issue is time consuming. Documenting the process followed and the results provides a valuable resource for other company administrators who might experience the same issue.

Exchange Server 2007 Project Documentation

An Exchange Server 2007 implementation is a complex endeavor that should be approached in phases. First and foremost, a decision should be made on how the project will be tracked. This can be done using a simple Microsoft Excel spreadsheet, but a tool like Microsoft Project makes mapping out the tasks much easier. Also, the first round of mapping out a project will most likely have at most 15-20 lines of tasks. Using a tool like Microsoft Project makes it easier to fill in more line items as you progress in the design and planning stages.

With the tracking method in place, you can move on to address the documents that are typically created for an Exchange Server 2007 implementation:

- Design and planning document
- Communication plan document
- Migration plan document
- Training plan document
- Prototype lab document
- Pilot test document
- Support and project completion document

This chapter examines each of these documents individually and focuses on their key elements.

Design and Planning Document

One of the concepts discussed earlier in the chapter was that of documents being used as building blocks. Continuing with that idea, the Exchange Server 2007 design and planning document is considered the foundation for all of the documentation created from this point forward. The design and planning document takes the original business requirements, matches them to the technical specifications, and then maps out how to produce the end product. It cannot be stressed enough the importance of a well-developed design and planning document.

The Exchange Server 2007 design and planning document is the outcome of the design sessions held with the subject matter expert (SME) and the technical staff within the organization. A standard Exchange Server 2007 design and planning document contains the following information:

Executive Summary

    Project Overview

Project Organization

    Resources

    Costs

    Risk Assessment

Existing Environment

    Network Infrastructure

    Active Directory Infrastructure

    Exchange Topology

    Backup and Restore

    Administrative Model

    Client Systems

Exchange Server 2007 Environment

    Goals and Objectives

Exchange Server 2007 Architecture

    Server Placement

    Exchange Version

    Storage Groups

    Databases

    Recipient Policies

    Connectors

22

Communication Plan Document

The detail of the communication plan depends on the size of the organization and management requirements. From the project management perspective, the more communication, the better! This is especially important when a project affects something as visible as the email system.

Mapping out the how, when, and who to communicate with allows the project team to prepare well-thought-out reports and plan productive meetings and presentations. This also provides the recipients of the reports the chance to review the plan and set their expectations. Once again, no surprises for the project team or the project sponsor.

A good communication plan should include the following topics:

- Audience
- Content
- Delivery method
- Timing and frequency

Table 22.1 gives an example of a communication plan. To make the plan more detailed, columns can be added to list who is responsible for the communication and specific dates for when the communication is delivered.

TABLE 22.1   Communication Plan

Audience	Content (Message)	Delivery Method	Timing Stage/Frequency
Executive sponsor	Project status	Written report	Weekly in email
Project team	Project status	Verbal updates	Weekly in meeting
IT department	Project overview	Presentation	Quarterly meeting

Migration Plan Document

After the design and planning document has been mapped out, the project team can begin planning the logistics of implementing Exchange Server 2007. This document is a guide that contains the technical steps needed to implement Exchange Server 2007 from the ground up. However, depending on how the migration team is set up, it can also include logistical instructions such as the following:

- Communication templates
- Location maps
- Team roles and responsibilities during the implementation

In a large organization, a session or sessions will be held to develop the migration plan. An agenda for the development of the plan might look similar to the following:

Goals and Objectives

Migration Planning - E2K7

    New Exchange Organization Versus Upgrade

    Exchange 2007 Directory Cleanup/One-to-One Mapping

    Migration Tools

    Migration Using the AD Connector (ADC)

    ForestPrep/DomainPrep

    Rolling Migration

    Gateway Migration

    Special Considerations: Third-Party Add-ins (fax, voicemail, apps)

Rollback Planning

    Backup and Restore

    Phased Migration Rollback

Training

    Users

    Administrators

Communications

    Status Meetings

    Open Issues Log

Administration and Maintenance

    Administration

    Maintenance

    Disaster Recovery

    Guides

    Periodic Schedules

    Daily/Weekly/Monthly

    Planned Downtime

    Checklists

    Test

Project Management

    Phased Approach

    Phase I - Design/Planning

Phase II - Prototype

Phase III - Pilot

Phase IV - Implement

Phase V - Support

Timelines

Resource Requirements

Risk Management

Interactive Refinement of Plan

Migration Planning - AD

In Place Versus Restructuring

Account Domains

Resource Domains

Active Directory Migration Tool (ADMT)

DNS Integration

Switching to Native Mode

Deployment Tools

Scripting

Built-in

Third-party

Building

Normalize Environment

Data Center First

Branch Offices Second

Deployment Strategies

Staged Versus Scripted Versus Manual

Documentation

Design

Plan

Build Guides

Migration Guides

Administration Guides

Maintenance Guides

As Builts

Disaster Recovery Guides

User Guides

Training

Users

Administrators

Migration Team

Technical Experts

Communications

Migration Team

Executives and Management

Administrators

Users

Methods

Frequency

Detail Level

Administration and Maintenance

Administration

Maintenance

Disaster Recovery

Guides

Periodic Schedules

Daily/Weekly/Monthly

Planned Downtime

Checklists

Testing

Note that many of the agenda topics are stated in a way that facilitates discussion. This is a great way to organize discussion points and at the same time keep them on track.

Training Plan Document

When creating a training plan for an Exchange Server 2007 implementation, the first thing that needs to be identified is the target audience. That determines what type of training needs to be developed. Some of the user groups that need to be targeted for training are as follows:

▶ **End users**—If the implementation is going to change the desktop client, the end user must receive some level of training.

▶ **Systems administrators**—The personnel involved in the administration of the messaging systems must be trained.

▶ **Help desk**—In organizations where the support is divided among different teams, each team must be trained on the tasks they will be carrying out.

▶ **Implementation team**—If the implementation is spread across multiple locations, some project teams choose to create implementation teams. These teams must be trained on the implementation process.

22

After the different groups have been identified, the training plan for each one can be created. The advantage of creating a training plan in-house is the ability to tailor the training to the organization's unique Exchange environment. The trainees will not have to go over configurations or settings that do not apply to their network.

As a special note, if the systems administrators and implementation team members can be identified ahead of time, it is wise to have them participate in the prototype stage.

The implementation team can assist by validating procedures and through the repetitive process can become more familiar with the procedures. After the prototype environment is set up, administrators and help desk resources can come in to do the same for the administrative procedures.

This provides the necessary validation process and also allows the systems groups to become more comfortable with the new tools and technology.

Prototype Lab Document

Going in to the prototype stage, experienced engineers and project managers are aware that the initial plan will probably have to be modified. This is because of a range of factors that can include application incompatibility, administrative requirements, or undocumented aspects of the current environment.

So, if it was important to start out this stage with a well-documented plan, the most important documentation goal for the prototype is to track these changes to ensure that the project still meets all goals and objectives of the implementation.

The document tool the project team will use to do this is the test plan. A well-developed test plan contains a master test plan and provides the ability to document the test results for reference at a later date. This is necessary because the implementation procedures might change from the first round of testing to the next and the project team will need to refer to the outcome to compare results.

A prototype lab test plan outline contains the following:

Summary of what is being tested and the overall technical goals of the implementation

Scope of what will be tested

Resources Needed

  Hardware

  Software

  Personnel

Documentation

  What will be recorded

  Test Plan Outline

Operating System

  Hardware Compatibility

  Install First Domain Controller

  Test Replication

  Install Additional Domain Controllers

  Client Access

  Role-Based Configuration

  DNS
  WINS

  DHCP

  IIS

  Domain Controller

  Exchange

  Group Policy

  New Settings

  GPMC

  RSoP

  Antivirus

  Password Policy

  Security Templates

  File Migration

  Print Migration

  DFS

  Volume Shadow Copy

  Remote Assistance

  UPS Software

  Applications Testing

Exchange Server 2007

    Exchange Install and Configuration

    Exchange Migration

    OWA

        Functionality

        Forms-Based Authentication

    Individual Mailbox/Message Restores

    Database Restore

    Antivirus

    Exchange Management Console

        Functionality

    Backup and Restore

    MOM Agents

    Administrative Rights

Each individual test should be documented in a test form listing the expected outcome and the actual outcome. This becomes part of the original test plan and is used to validate the implementation procedure or document a change.

A sample prototype lab test form is shown in Table 22.2.

TABLE 22.2   Sample Test Form

Test Name:
Hardware Requirements:
Software Requirements:
Other Requirements:
Expected Outcome:
Actual Outcome:

TABLE 22.2   Continued

Test Name:
Tester:
Date:

At the end of the stage, it should be clearly documented what, if anything, has changed. The documentation deliverables of this stage are as follows:

▶ Test plan

▶ Implementation plan

▶ Pilot implementation plan

▶ Rollback plan

Pilot Test Document

Documenting a pilot implementation has special requirements because it is the first time the implementation will touch the production environment. If the environment is a complex one where multiple applications are affected by the implementation, all details should be documented along with the outcome of the pilot.

This is done by having a document similar in content to the prototype lab test plan form and tracking any issues that come up.

In extreme cases, the project team must put the rollback plan into effect. Before starting the pilot implementation, the team should have an escalation process along with contact names and phone numbers of the personnel with the authority to make the go-no-go decision in a given situation.

Support and Project Completion Document

An Exchange implementation should include a plan for handing off administration to the personnel who will be supporting the messaging environment after the implementation is complete—especially if the SMEs are brought in to implement the Exchange messaging infrastructure and will not be remaining onsite to support it.

The handoff plan should be included in the original project plan and have a timeline for delivery of the administrative documentation as well as training sessions if needed.

Exchange Server 2007 Environment Documentation

As the business and network infrastructure changes, it is common for the messaging infrastructure to change as well. Keep track of these changes as they progress through baselines (how the Exchange Server 2007 environment was built) and other forms of documentation, such as the configuration settings and connectivity diagrams of the environment.

Documents that map out the Exchange Server 2007 environment will prove to be an invaluable tool for maintaining, expanding, or troubleshooting the messaging infrastructure.

These documents should provide information on the physical setup of the network, such as server configuration and location, and also go over the logical elements such as mail flow.

Some of the key documents that are used for this include the following:

▶ **Network diagrams**—To give a visual of the messaging infrastructure. This should show mail flow, location of front-end servers, site connectors, and WAN topology. A large or very complex organization might prefer to have this information mapped out in several different diagrams.

▶ **Server builds**—The server builds are guides that instruct on how to build the server from the ground up. These guides are key in ensuring standardized builds during an implementation as well as recovering from a major server crash or for use during a disaster recovery scenario.

Another document that is especially useful in larger organizations is the roles and responsibilities guide that outlines the administrative model used in the Exchange infrastructure.

> **NOTE**
>
> A great tool for examining the Exchange Server 2007 environment is the Exchange Best Practices Analyzer (ExBPA). This Microsoft tool can be run from the Exchange Management Console (EMC) and will produce reports on a variety of topics.

Server Build Procedures

The server build procedure is a detailed set of instructions for building the Exchange Server 2007 system. This document can be used for troubleshooting and adding new servers, and is a critical resource in the event of a disaster.

The following is an example of a table of contents from a server build procedure document:

Windows Server 2003 Build Procedures

System Configuration Parameters

Configure the Server Hardware

Install Vendor Drivers

Configure RAID

Install and Configure Windows Server 2003

Using Images

Scripted Installations

Applying Windows Server 2003 Security

Using a Security Template

Using GPOs

Configuring Antivirus

Installing Service Packs and Critical Updates

Backup Client Configuration

Exchange Server 2007 Build Procedures

System Configuration Parameters

Configuring Exchange as a Mailbox Server

Creating Storage Groups

Creating Databases

Configuring Exchange as an Edge, Client Access, or UM Server

Configuration (As-Built) Documentation

The configuration document, often referred to as an as-built, details a snapshot configuration of the Exchange Server 2007 system as it is built. This document contains essential information required to rebuild a server.

The following is an Exchange Server 2007 server as-built document template:

Introduction

The purpose of this Exchange Server 2007 as-built document is to assist an experienced network administrator or engineer in restoring the server in the event of a hardware failure. This document contains screenshots and configuration settings for the server at the time it was built. If settings are not implicitly defined in this document, they are assumed to be set to defaults. It is not intended to be a comprehensive disaster recovery with step-by-step procedures for rebuilding the server. For this document to remain useful as a recovery aid, it must be updated as configuration settings change.

System Configuration

    Hardware Summary

    Disk Configuration

        Logical Disk Configuration

    System Summary

    Device Manager

    RAID Configuration

    Windows Server 2003 TCP/IP Configuration

    Network Adapter Local Area Connections

Security Configuration

    Services

    Lockdown Procedures (Checklist)

    Antivirus Configuration

Share List

Applications and Configurations

Topology Diagrams

Network configuration diagrams and related documentation generally include local area network (LAN) connectivity, wide area network (WAN) infrastructure connectivity, IP subnet information, critical servers, network devices, and more. Having accurate diagrams of the new environment can be invaluable when troubleshooting connectivity issues. For topology diagrams that can be used for troubleshooting connectivity issues, consider documenting the following:

- Internet service provider contact names, including technical support contact information
- Connection type (such as frame relay, ISDN, OC-12)
- Link speed
- Committed Information Rate (CIR)
- Endpoint configurations, including routers used
- Message flow and routing

Exchange Server 2007 Administration and Maintenance Documents

The administrative documents are designed to provide information for the ongoing support and administration of the Exchange Server 2007 environment. Most of the diagrams and guides created to document the environment (discussed in the previous section) will also be used for reference in the day-to-day administration. These documents should address the basic administrative tasks, such as adding a user and troubleshooting documents.

It is a best practice to have one location where all of the documents are consolidated to make it easy to find any one of them. This also facilitates replication of the directory to a website or a share on another server for disaster recovery purposes.

Administration Manual

The administration manual is the main tool for the administrative group. All of the Exchange tasks are documented with the organization-specific details. A well-prepared administration manual can also be used for training new administrators.

Some of the documents that are typically consolidated into the enterprise Exchange Server 2007 administration manual are as follows:

Exchange User Administrative Tasks

   Creating a Mailbox

   Creating a Shared Mailbox

   Modifying Mailbox Permissions

   Moving an Exchange Mailbox

   Reconnecting a Deleted Exchange Mailbox

   Hiding and Unhiding a User

   Setting User-Specific Storage Limits

Contacts

   Creating a Contact

   Deleting a Contact

   Modifying a Contact

Group Distribution Lists

   Creating a Group Distribution List

   Deleting a Group Object

   Modifying Group Properties

Outlook Administration

   Recovering Deleted Items in Outlook

   Re-creating an Outlook Profile

   Creating a Resource Account

Message Tracking

Exchange Server Administration Tasks

    Creating a Mailbox Store in Exchange

    Configuring an Exchange Alert Notification

Exchange Server Troubleshooting Tasks

    Exchange Database Repair Procedures

Although the outline provided is a pretty complete example, some additional documents are outlined in more detail in the following sections.

Troubleshooting Guide

Troubleshooting documents are especially useful for larger organizations where multiple administrators are working together. Providing the information to all administrators can potentially shorten or avoid server downtime and user impact.

Procedural Documents

An important aspect of creating the administrative documentation is that it is mainly procedural. These are step-by-step guides that walk the administrator through any given task and it is imperative that the documents are validated. This is a collaborative effort in which one person writes the document and another validates the procedures noting any differences so that they can be corrected. These are living documents that change along with the environment and updates to the documents should be routinely included as a part of changes or updates to the infrastructure or administrative model.

Exchange Server Maintenance

In most organizations, email is one of the most visible, if not number one, business applications. How to keep email up and running is the topic of many technical and business discussions. To keep the Exchange Server 2007 infrastructure up and running, the main goal of an Exchange administrator should be to be proactive. This is achieved by setting up a well-thought-out maintenance plan that checks all of the components of the Exchange infrastructure and addresses issues before they affect the email system causing downtime.

The maintenance plan should include daily, weekly, monthly, and quarterly tasks. The execution and status or outcome of the tasks should be documented and archived for historical reference. The best way to do this is by using checklists that can be easily followed and signed off on when the tasks are completed.

A standard maintenance schedule includes, but is not limited to the following:

    Exchange Server Maintenance

    Exchange Status Monitor

        Monitoring Tool

        Monitoring Services with the Computer Management Console

Daily Tasks

    Examine Performance Counters

    Monitor Services and Links

    Check Server Mail Queues

    SMTP Log Files

    Check Daily Backup Logs

    Check Available Disk Space

    Verify the Alerter Service Is Running

    Physical Server Check

Weekly Tasks

    Check Event Logs for Errors and Warnings

    Check for Message Tracking Log File Buildups

Monthly Tasks

    Validate Exchange Backup

Quarterly Tasks

    IS Maintenance

    Check Mailbox Usage

Event Logs

    Checking Event Log Events

    Tools for Troubleshooting Event Log Messages

        Microsoft Online TechNet Website

Disaster Recovery Documentation

Creating and maintaining a disaster recovery plan for the Exchange Server 2007 infrastructure requires the commitment of IT managers as well as the systems administrators in charge of the messaging systems. This is because creating a disaster recovery plan is a complex process and after it is developed the only way of maintaining it is by practicing the procedures on a regular schedule. This, of course, involves the administrative personnel and should be worked into their scheduled tasks.

The initial steps of creating the disaster recovery plan involve determining the desired recovery times. Then, the team moves on to discuss possible disaster scenarios and maps out a plan for each one. The following table of contents outlines the different topics that are addressed when creating the disaster recovery plan:

    Executive Summary or Introduction

    Disaster Recovery Scenarios

22

Complete System Failure

NIC, RAID Controller Failures

Train Personnel and Practice Disaster Recovery

Disaster Recovery Planning

The first step of the disaster recovery process is to develop a formal disaster recovery plan. This plan, although time consuming to develop, serves as a guide for the entire organization in the event of an emergency. Disaster scenarios, such as power outages, hard drive failures, and even earthquakes, should be addressed. Although it is impossible to develop a scenario for every potential disaster, it is still helpful to develop a plan to recover from different levels of disaster. It is recommended that organizations encourage open discussions of possible scenarios and the steps required to recover from each one. Include representatives from each department because each department will have its own priorities in the event of a disaster. The disaster recovery plan should encompass the organization as a whole and focus on determining what it will take to resume normal business function after a disaster.

Backup and Recovery Development

Another important component of a disaster recovery development process is the evaluation of the organization's current backup policies and procedures. Without sound backup policies and procedures, a disaster recovery plan is useless. It is not possible to recover a system if the backup is not valid.

A backup plan does not just encompass backing up data to tape or another medium. It is an overarching plan that outlines other tasks, including advanced system recovery, offsite storage, testing procedures, and retention policies. These tasks should be carefully documented to accurately represent each backup methodology and how it's carried out. Full documentation of the backup process includes step-by-step procedures, guidelines, policies, and checklists.

Periodically, the backup systems should be reviewed and tested, especially after any configuration changes. Any changes to the system should be reflected in the documentation. Otherwise, backup documents can become stale and can add to the problems during recovery attempts.

Recovery documentation complements backup documentation. The primary purpose of the documented backup process is to provide the ability to recover that backup in the event of an emergency. Recovery documentation should outline where the backup data resides and how to recover from various types of failures, such as hard drive failure, system failure, and natural disasters. Just like backup documentation, recovery documentation takes the form of step-by-step procedures, guidelines, policies, and checklists.

Exchange System Failover Documentation

Many organizations use clustering in their Exchange environment to provide failover and redundancy capabilities for their messaging systems. When a system fails over, having fully tested and documented procedures helps get the system back up and running quickly. Because these procedures are not used often, they must be thoroughly tested and reviewed in a lab setting so that they accurately reflect the steps required to recover each system.

Performance Documentation

Performance documentation helps monitor the health and status of the Exchange environment. It is a continuous process that begins by aligning the goals, existing policies, and service-level agreements of the organization. When these areas are clearly defined and detailed, baseline performance values can be established, using tools such as the System Monitor, Microsoft Operations Manager (MOM), or other tools (such as PerfMon). These tools capture baseline performance-related metrics that can include indicators such as how much memory is being used, average processor use, and more. They also can illustrate how the Exchange Server 2007 environment is performing under various workloads.

After the baseline performance values are documented, performance-related information gathered by the monitoring solution should be analyzed periodically. Pattern and trend analysis reports need to be examined at least on a weekly basis. This analysis can uncover current and potential bottlenecks and proactively ensure that the system operates as efficiently and effectively as possible. These reports can range from routine reports generated by the monitoring solution to complex technical reports that provide detail to engineering staff.

Routine Reporting

Although built-in system monitoring tools log performance data that can be used in reports in conjunction with products such as Excel, it is recommended that administrators use products such as MOM for monitoring and reporting functionality. MOM can manage and monitor the Exchange systems and provide preconfigured graphical reports with customizable levels of detail. MOM also provides the framework to generate customized reports that meet the needs of the organization.

Management-Level Reporting

Routine reporting typically provides a significant amount of technical information. Although helpful for the administrator, it can be too much information for management. Management-level performance reporting should be concise and direct. Stakeholders do not require the specifics of performance data, but it's important to take those specifics and show trends, patterns, and any potential problem areas. This extremely useful and factual information provides insight to management so that decisions can be made to determine proactive solutions for keeping systems operating in top-notch condition.

For instance, during routine reporting, administrators identify and report to management that Exchange Server processor use is on the rise. What does this mean? This information by itself does not give management any specifics on what the problem is. However, if the administrator presents graphical reports that indicate that if the current trends on Exchange Server processor use continue at the rate of a 5% increase per month, an additional processor will be required in 10 months or less. Management can then take this report, follow the issue more closely over the next few months, and determine whether to allocate funds to purchase additional processors. If the decision is made to buy more processors, management has more time to negotiate quantity, processing power, and cost instead of having to pay higher costs for the processors on short notice.

Technical Reporting

Technical performance information reporting is much more detailed than management-level reporting. It goes beyond the routine reporting to provide specific details on many different components and facets of the system. For example, specific counter values might be given to determine disk subsystem use. This type of information is useful in monitoring the health of the entire Exchange environment. Trend and pattern analysis should also be included in the technical reporting process to not only reflect the current status, but to allow comparison to historical information and determine how to plan for future requirements.

Security Documentation

Just as with any other aspect of the Exchange environment, security documentation also includes policies, configurations and settings, and procedures. Administrators can easily feel that although documenting security settings and other configurations are important, it might lessen security mechanisms established in the Exchange Server 2007 environment. However, documenting security mechanisms and corresponding configurations are vital to administration, maintenance, and any potential security compromise. Security documentation, along with other forms of documentation—including network diagrams and configurations—should be well guarded to minimize any potential security risk.

A network environment might have many security mechanisms in place, but if the information—such as logs and events obtained from them—isn't reviewed, security is more relaxed. Monitoring and management solutions can help consolidate this information into reports that can be generated on a periodic basis. These reports are essential to the process of continuously evaluating the network's security.

In addition, management should be informed of any unauthorized access or attempts to compromise security. Business policy can then be made to strengthen the environment's security.

Change Control

Although the documentation of policies and procedures to protect the system from external security risks is of utmost importance, internal procedures and documents should also be established. Developing, documenting, and enforcing a change control process helps protect the system from well-intentioned internal changes.

In environments where there are multiple administrators, it is very common to have the interests of one administrator affect those of another. For instance, an administrator might make a configuration change to limit mailbox size for a specific department. If this change is not documented, a second administrator might spend a significant amount of time trying to troubleshoot a user complaint from that department. Establishing a change control process that documents these types of changes eliminates confusion and wasted resources. The change control process should include an extensive testing process to reduce the risk of production problems.

Procedures

Although security policies and guidelines comprise the majority of security documentation, procedures are equally as important. Procedures include not only the initial configuration steps, but also maintenance procedures and more important procedures that are to be followed in the event of a security breach.

Additional areas regarding security that can be documented include, but are not limited to, the following:

- ▶ Auditing policies including review
- ▶ Service packs (SPs) and hot fixes
- ▶ Certificates and certificates of authority
- ▶ Antivirus configurations
- ▶ Encrypting File System (EFS)
- ▶ Password policies (such as length, strength, age)
- ▶ Group Policy Object (GPO) security-related policies
- ▶ Registry security
- ▶ Lockdown procedures

Training Documentation

Training documentation for a project can be extensive and ranges from user training to technical training. The most important aspect of training documentation is to make sure that it meets the needs of the individual being trained. The two key documents created and used in organizations are focused for the benefit of end users, and technical documents are focused toward administrators.

End User

Proper end-user training is critical to the acceptance of any new application. Developing clear and concise documentation that addresses the user's needs is key in providing proper training. As discussed earlier, developing specific documentation goals and conducting an audience analysis are especially important to the development of useful training materials.

Technical

Administrators and engineers are responsible for the upkeep and management of the Exchange environment. As a result, they must be technically prepared to address a variety of issues, such as maintenance and troubleshooting. Training documentation should address why the technologies are being taught and how the technologies pertain to the Exchange environment. In addition, the training documentation should be easy to use and function as a reference resource in the future.

Summary

The development of documentation for the Exchange Server 2007 environment is important not only to establishing the environment, but also to the health, maintenance, and ongoing support of the system. After this documentation is developed, it must be thoroughly tested—preferably by a disinterested party—and maintained. Every change that is made to the environment should be changed in the documentation.

Best Practices

The following are best practices from this chapter:

- ▶ Determine the business needs for documentation.

- ▶ Determine the goals of each document.

- ▶ Determine the audience and the need for each document.

- ▶ Validate and test the documentation.

- ▶ Develop audience-level specific training materials.

- ▶ Establish a documentation update process.

PART VII

Unified Communications in an Exchange Server 2007 Environment

IN THIS PART

CHAPTER 23

Designing and Implementing Mobility in Exchange Server 2007

Microsoft Exchange Server 2007 was specifically designed to expand beyond the traditional boundaries that previously defined the messaging experience. No longer are users limited to receiving and responding to messages while in the office. Today's fast-paced information society requires more immediate capabilities of gaining access to mail data, enabling information workers to get anytime, anywhere access to their messages.

Exchange Server 2007 greatly enhances the capabilities of information workers to stay in touch, through enhancements to the ways that they receive and respond to emails. Exchange now allows for an unprecedented seamless integration between handheld Windows Mobile devices such as Pocket PCs and Smartphones, and an Exchange mailbox, through an improved Exchange ActiveSync application.

This chapter covers the details of deploying Microsoft Exchange ActiveSync with Exchange Server 2007 and Windows Mobile devices. Step-by-step examples of ActiveSync deployments are outlined, and varying approaches are compared.

Understanding Mobility Enhancements in Exchange Server 2007

Microsoft Exchange ActiveSync is a technology that allows information workers to gain access to their messaging data, calendaring, and other information from a handheld device. ActiveSync works by tunneling the data over Hypertext Transfer Protocol (HTTP), the same one used for web traffic on the Internet.

Using ActiveSync in an Exchange 2007 environment gives organizations unprecedented control over the management of the remote devices and over their security, allowing for lost or stolen devices to be *wiped*, and enforcing policies that require encryption of data and passwords to be used.

Outlining the History of Exchange Mobility Enhancements

ActiveSync was originally released as an add-on product to Exchange 2000 Server known as Mobile Information Server (MIS). MIS was the first foray Microsoft had into syncing handheld devices and saw limited deployment.

Exchange Server 2003 was the first release of the Exchange messaging platform that included built-in ActiveSync functionality, though it had to be enabled in a separate step. The first versions of the software in 2003 did not support automatically pushing emails out to the handhelds, with the exception of a concept called *Always Up to Date* that would notify the device via a short message service (SMS) text message. The device would then dial in and sync. This was time and battery consuming and costly.

Service Pack 2 for Exchange Server 2003 introduced the concept of Direct Push technology, similar to BlackBerry style technology, where messages were automatically pushed out to a handheld as they were received. This improvement was warmly received.

At the same time, Windows Mobile, the handheld operating system formerly known as Windows CE and PocketPC, was evolving. The Messaging Security and Feature Pack (MSFP) for Windows Mobile 5.0 allowed for built-in, file-level encryption for the devices, and integrated them with 2003 SP2's abilities to provision and deprovision devices over the air.

Exchange Server 2007 expands even further beyond 2003 SP2's Direct Push technology, allowing for other improvements, such as the ability to automatically configure a handheld, encrypt connections, reset passwords, and view file data on a SharePoint server.

Exploring Exchange ActiveSync

Exchange ActiveSync is a service that runs on a client access server (CAS) in an Exchange 2007 topology. It uses the same virtual server that other HTTP access methods to Exchange use, such as Outlook Web Access and Outlook Anywhere. In ActiveSync's case, however, it uses its own virtual directory, named Microsoft-Server-ActiveSync.

Because it uses the same type of access mechanism as Outlook Web Access (OWA) does, ActiveSync can be designed using the same CAS considerations that OWA and Outlook

Anywhere does. In most cases, it is deployed as an ancillary service to these offerings. In any case, when it is deployed, it becomes a vital service to the organization.

Enabling ActiveSync in Exchange Server 2007

In Exchange 2007 ActiveSync, the application itself has become more integrated with the rest of Exchange functionality. After the CAS role has been assigned to a server, the server is closely positioned to enable ActiveSync support. That said, several configuration steps can be taken to improve and streamline ActiveSync access, per Microsoft best practices.

Working with ActiveSync Settings in the Exchange Management Console

Many of the ActiveSync settings on a CAS can be modified within the Exchange Management Console, from the Client Access node, as shown in Figure 23.1. The console allows for ActiveSync to be disabled, or for individual ActiveSync settings to be modified on individual recipient mailboxes.

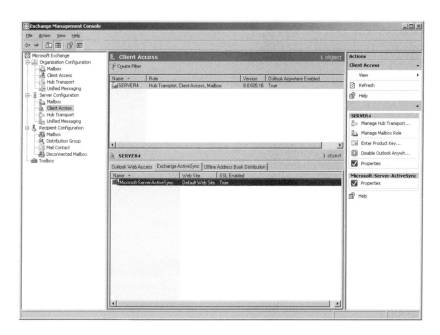

FIGURE 23.1   Administering ActiveSync settings.

Right-clicking on the Microsoft-Server-ActiveSync listing in the details pane and choosing Properties allows for several other ActiveSync settings to be modified, such as the following:

▶ **External url**—This setting allows an administrator to enter in the fully qualified domain name (FQDN) that will be used to access ActiveSync from the Internet. An example of this is http://mail.companyabc.com/Microsoft-Server-ActiveSync.

▶ **Authentication**—Authentication methods for the ActiveSync virtual directory can be entered here. This tab allows an administrator to configure the server to use Basic authentication, which is commonly used with Secure Sockets Layer (SSL) encryption. There is also an option to define whether dual-factor authentication using client certificates is required or accepted.

▶ **Remote File Servers**—This tab, shown in Figure 23.2, introduces some of the new functionality in Exchange 2007 in regard to Windows Mobile access to file data in shares via Universal Naming Convention (UNC) paths, or on Windows SharePoint Services Sites.

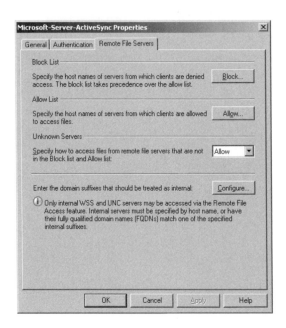

FIGURE 23.2   Configuring Remote File Servers options in ActiveSync.

NOTE

The functionality on the Remote File Servers tab can only be taken advantage of if the Windows Mobile device supports it. Currently, only the 6.0 version of the product supports this functionality.

Configuring Per-User ActiveSync Settings

Individual mailbox settings can be configured for ActiveSync in the Mailbox node under Recipient Configuration in the console pane, shown in Figure 23.3. Enabling and disabling ActiveSync on an individual mailbox can be controlled from here, as well as the ability to add a mailbox to a specific ActiveSync mailbox policy, a concept further defined in the section titled "Working with ActiveSync Policies."

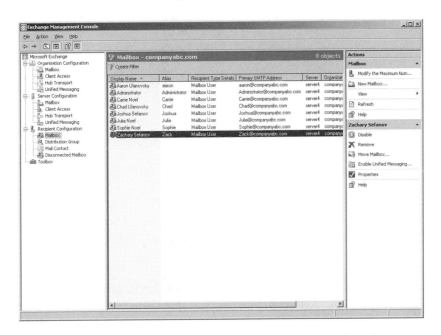

FIGURE 23.3   Viewing mailboxes in Exchange Management Console.

Right-clicking on an individual mailbox and choosing Properties invokes the Properties dialog box. Choosing the Mailbox Features tab, shown in Figure 23.4, allows for Exchange ActiveSync to be enabled or disabled for that particular mailbox. In addition, clicking the Properties button gives the option to join the mailbox to a specific ActiveSync policy, as mentioned earlier.

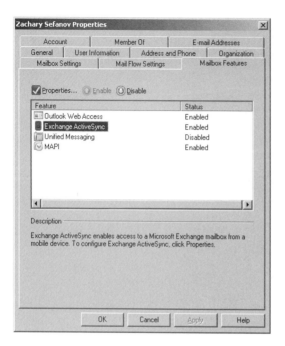

FIGURE 23.4   Enabling or disabling ActiveSync on a mailbox.

Securing Access to ActiveSync with Secure Sockets Layer Encryption

By default, ActiveSync is configured to use Integrated Windows authentication. This form of authentication works fine if access to the server is over a trusted internal network, but is not feasible for access over the Internet, which is where most Mobile devices originate from.

Because of this limitation, a form of authentication that can be sent across the Internet must be used. This effectively limits the ActiveSync server to using Basic authentication, which is supported by most web browsers and devices. The problem with Basic authentication, however, is that the username and password that the user sends is effectively sent in clear text, and can be intercepted and stolen in transit. In addition, mail messages and other confidential information are transmitted in clear text, a huge security issue.

The solution to this problem is to use what is known as Secure Sockets Layer (SSL) encryption on the traffic. SSL encryption is performed using Public Key Infrastructure (PKI) certificates, which work through the principle of shared-key encryption. PKI SSL certificates are widely used on the Internet today, any website starting with an https:// uses them, and the entire online merchant community is dependent upon the security of the system.

For ActiveSync, the key is to install a certificate on the server so that the traffic between the device and the server is protected from prying eyes. There are effectively two options to this approach as follows:

▶ **Use a third-party certificate authority**—A common option for many organizations is to purchase a certificate for ActiveSync (and other Exchange HTTP access methods such as OWA) from a third-party trusted certificate authority (CA), such as VeriSign, Thawte, or others. These CAs are already trusted by a vast number of devices, so no additional configuration is required. The downside to this option is that the certificates must be purchased and the organization doesn't have as much flexibility to change certificate options.

▶ **Install and use your own certificate authority**—Another common approach is to install and configure Windows Server 2003 Certificate Services to create your own CA within an organization. This gives you the flexibility to create new certificates, revoke existing ones, and not have to pay immediate costs. The downside to this approach is that no browsers or mobile devices will recognize the CA, and error messages to that effect will be encountered on the devices unless the certificates are trusted.

Each of these options are outlined in the subsequent sections of this chapter.

Installing a Third-Party CA on a CAS

If a third-party certificate authority will be used to enable SSL on a CAS, a certificate request must first be generated directly from the CAS. After this request has been generated, it can be sent to the third-party CA, who will then verify the identity of the organization and send it back, where it can be installed on the server.

When deciding which CA to use, keep in mind that Windows Mobile devices automatically trust the certificate authorities of the following organizations:

▶ VeriSign

▶ Thawte

▶ GTE CyberTrust

▶ GlobalSign

▶ RSA

▶ Equifax

▶ Entrust.net

▶ Valicert (Windows Mobile 5.0 and up only)

If an internal CA will be utilized, this section and its procedures can be skipped, and you can proceed directly to the subsequent section titled "Using an Internal Certificate Authority for OWA Certificates."

To generate an SSL certificate request for use with a third-party CA, perform the following steps:

1. From the CAS, open IIS Manager (Start, All Programs, Administrative Tools, Internet Information Services [IIS] Manager).

2. In the console tree, expand SERVERNAME (local computer) – Web Sites, right-click the OWA Virtual Server (typically named Default Web Site), and click Properties on the shortcut menu.

3. Select the Directory Security tab.

4. Under Secure Communications, click the Server Certificate button.

5. On the welcome screen, click Next to continue.

6. From the list of options displayed, select Create a New Certificate, and click Next to continue.

7. From the Delayed or Immediate Request dialog box, select Prepare the Request Now, But Send It Later, and then click Next.

8. Type a descriptive name for the certificate, such as the one shown in Figure 23.5, leave the bit length at 1024, and click Next to continue.

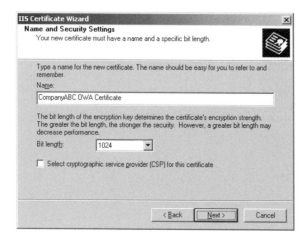

FIGURE 23.5   Generating an SSL certificate request for an OWA virtual server.

9. Enter the name of the organization and what OU will be associated with the certificate. These fields will be viewable by external users, and should accurately reflect the organizational structure of the requestor.

10. Enter a common name for the OWA website in the form of the FQDN. An example of this is mail.companyabc.com. Click Next to continue.

> **NOTE**
>
> If the ActiveSync site will be made accessible from the Internet, the common name of the site needs to be made accessible from the Internet via a DNS A record.

11. Enter the appropriate information into the Geographical Information dialog box, such as state, city, and country. Abbreviations are not allowed. Click Next to continue.

12. Enter a filename for the certificate request, such as `C:\owacert.txt`, and click Next to continue.

13. In the Request File Summary dialog box, review the summary page for accuracy, and click Next to continue.

14. Click Finish to end the Web Server Certificate Wizard.

After the certificate request has been generated, the text file, which will look similar to the one shown in Figure 23.6, can then be emailed or otherwise transmitted to the certificate authority via their individual process. Each CA has a different procedure, and the exact steps need to follow the individual CA's process. After an organization's identity has been proven by the CA, they will send back the server certificate, typically in the form of a file, or as part of the body of an email message.

FIGURE 23.6   Viewing a certificate request file.

The certificate then needs to be installed on the server itself. If it was sent in the form of a `.cer` file, it can simply be imported via the process described next. If it was included in the body of an email, the certificate itself needs to be cut and pasted into a text editor such as Notepad and saved as a `.cer` file. After the `.cer` file has been obtained, it can be installed on the CAS using the following process:

1. From the CAS, open IIS Manager (Start, All Programs, Administrative Tools, Internet Information Services [IIS] Manager).

2. In the console tree, expand SERVERNAME (local computer) – Web Sites, right-click the OWA Virtual Server (typically named Default Web Site), and then click Properties on the shortcut menu.

3. Select the Directory Security tab.

4. Under Secure Communications, click the Server Certificate button.

5. On the welcome screen, click Next to continue.

6. From the Pending Certificate Request dialog box, select Process the Pending Request and Install the Certificate, and click Next to continue.

7. Enter the path and filename where the .cer file was saved to (the Browse button can be used to locate the file), and click Next to continue.

8. Click Finish to finalize the certificate installation.

At this point in the process, SSL communication to the CAS can be allowed, but forcing SSL encryption for the ActiveSync traffic requires more configuration, which is outlined in the subsequent section titled "Forcing SSL Encryption for ActiveSync Traffic."

Using an Internal Certificate Authority for OWA Certificates

If a third-party certificate authority is not utilized, an internal CA can be set up instead. There are several different CA options, including several third-party products, and it might be advantageous to take advantage of an existing internal CA. Windows Server 2003 also has a very functional CA solution built in to the product, and one can be installed into an organization.

> **CAUTION**
>
> Proper design of a secure PKI is a complex subject, and organizations might want to spend a good amount of time examining the many factors that can influence CA design. This step-by-step scenario assumes a very basic design, with an enterprise CA installed directly into a domain.

To set up an internal certificate authority, on a domain member server or, more commonly, on a domain controller, the Certificate Authority component of Windows Server 2003 can be installed using the following procedure:

1. Click Start, Control Panel, Add or Remove Programs.

2. Click Add/Remove Windows Components.

3. Check the Certificate Services check box.

4. At the warning message box, shown in Figure 23.7, click Yes to acknowledge that the server name cannot be changed.

FIGURE 23.7   Installing a local CA.

5. Click Next to continue.

6. From the subsequent dialog box, shown in Figure 23.8, select which type of CA will be set up. Choosing each type of CA has different ramifications and is useful in different situations.

The following types of CAs are available for installation:

▶ **Enterprise Root CA**—An enterprise root CA is the highest level CA for an organization. By default, all members of the forest where it is installed trust it, which can make it a convenient mechanism for securing OWA or other services within a domain environment. Unless an existing enterprise root CA is in place, this is the typical choice for a homegrown CA solution in an organization.

▶ **Enterprise Subordinate CA**—An enterprise subordinate CA is subordinate to an existing enterprise root CA, and must receive a certificate from that root CA to work properly. In certain large organizations, it might be useful to have a hierarchy of CAs, or the desire might exist to isolate the CA structure for OWA to a subordinate enterprise CA structure.

▶ **Stand-alone Root CA**—A stand-alone root CA is similar to an enterprise root CA, in that it provides for its own unique identity, and can be uniquely configured. It differs from an enterprise root CA in that it is not automatically trusted by any forest clients in an organization.

▶ **Stand-alone Subordinate CA**—A stand-alone subordinate CA is similar to an enterprise subordinate CA, except that it is not directly tied or trusted by the forest structure, and must take its own certificate from a stand-alone root CA.

After choosing the type of CA required, continue the CA installation process by performing the following steps:

1. In this example, choose Enterprise Root CA. Click Next to continue.

2. Enter a common name for the CA, such as that shown in Figure 23.9. Click Next to continue.

3. Enter locations for the certificate database and the database log (the defaults can normally be chosen), and click Next to continue.

4. Click Yes when warned that the IIS Services will be restarted.

5. Click Finish after the installation is complete.

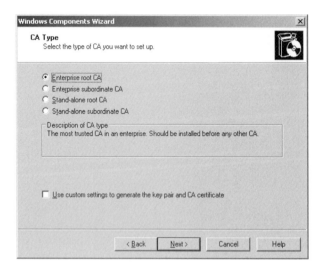

FIGURE 23.8   Selecting a CA type to install.

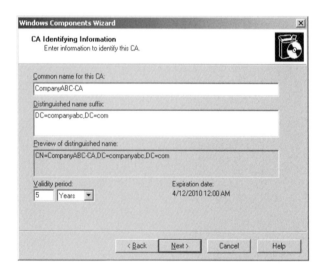

FIGURE 23.9   Entering a common name for the CA.

After the internal CA is in place, the CAS can automatically use it for generation of certificates. To generate and install a certificate on a CAS using an internal CA, use the following technique:

1. From the CAS, open IIS Manager (Start, All Programs, Administrative Tools, Internet Information Services [IIS] Manager).

2. In the console tree, expand SERVERNAME (local computer) – Web Sites, right-click the ActiveSync Virtual Server (typically named Default Web Site, it is typically the same one used for OWA), and then click Properties on the shortcut menu.

3. Select the Directory Security tab.

4. Under Secure Communications, click the Server Certificate button.

5. On the welcome screen, click Next to continue.

6. Select Create a New Certificate, and then click Next to continue.

7. From the Delayed or Immediate Request dialog box, select Send the Request Immediately to an Online Certification Authority, and click Next to continue.

8. Enter a name for the certificate, such as CompanyABC OWA Certificate, leave the bit length at 1024, and click Next to continue.

9. Enter the organization and OU name, keeping in mind that they should accurately reflect the real name of the requestor. Click Next to continue.

10. Enter the FQDN of the CAS, such as `mail.companyabc.com`.

11. In the Geographical Information dialog box, enter an unabbreviated state, city, and country, and click Next to continue.

12. Specify the SSL port (443 is the default) that the server will use, and click Next to continue.

13. In the Choose a Certification Authority dialog box, shown in Figure 23.10, select the CA that was set up in the previous steps, and click Next to continue.

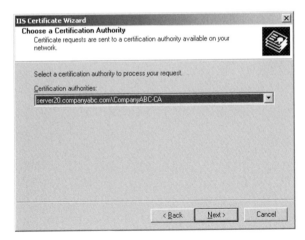

FIGURE 23.10   Installing a local CA certificate on a CAS.

14. Review the request in the Certificate Request Submission dialog box, and click Next to continue.

15. Click Finish.

After installation, the certificate can be viewed by clicking the View Certificate button on the Directory Services tab in the Virtual Server properties dialog box.

After being placed on a server, SSL encryption will be made available on the CAS. If the enterprise CA was installed in an Active Directory domain, all of the domain members will include the internal CA as a trusted root authority and connect to OWA via SSL with no errors. External or nondomain members, however, will need to install the enterprise CA into their local trusted root authorities. This includes Windows Mobile devices as well. The procedure for installing a third-party certificate for a Windows Mobile device is covered in the upcoming section of this chapter titled "Installing a Root Certificate on a Windows Mobile Device."

Forcing SSL Encryption for ActiveSync Traffic

After either a third-party or a local internal certificate has been installed on a CAS, it is typical to then set up the CAS to have ActiveSync traffic forced to use SSL encryption, rather than allow that traffic to use the unencrypted HTTP. To solve this problem, SSL encryption must be forced from the CAS via the following procedure:

1. On the CAS, open IIS Manager (Start, All Programs, Administrative Tools, Internet Information Services [IIS] Manager).

2. Navigate to Internet Information Services, Web Sites, OWA Web Site (usually named Default Web Site).

3. Right-click on the Microsoft-Server-ActiveSync virtual directory (under the Virtual Server), and choose Properties on the shortcut menu.

4. Click the Directory Security tab.

5. Under Secure Communications, click the Edit button.

6. From the Secure Communications dialog box, shown in Figure 23.11, check the Require Secure Channel (SSL) and Require 128-bit Encryption check boxes.

7. Click OK and then click OK again.

Installing a Root Certificate on a Windows Mobile Device

If a third-party or self-generated certificate authority is used for ActiveSync, Windows Mobile devices must be configured to trust that CA. If they are not configured like this, they will error out with something similar to the error shown in Figure 23.12 when attempting to connect via ActiveSync.

For Windows desktops and laptops, this task is relatively straightforward, and involves simply installing the enterprise root CA for this third-party certificate into the Trusted Root Certificate Authority group for the machine. For Windows Mobile devices, however, the enterprise root certificate must first be exported to a .cer file, which then needs to be copied physically to the device, either via a memory card or with ActiveSync. After being copied, the .cer file can be installed by clicking on it. To export the Enterprise Certificate, perform the following steps:

FIGURE 23.11   Forcing SSL encryption on the ActiveSync virtual directory.

FIGURE 23.12   Viewing the third-party certificate error on a Windows Mobile device.

1. On the CAS, open IIS Manager (Start, All Programs, Administrative Tools, Internet Information Services [IIS] Manager).

2. Navigate to Internet Information Services, Web Sites, OWA Web Site (usually named Default Web Site).

3. Right-click on the virtual server, and choose Properties.

4. Select the Directory Security tab.

5. Under Secure Communications, click View Certificate.

6. Under the Certification Path, select the root certificate from the path, such as that shown in Figure 23.13, and click View Certificate.

FIGURE 23.13   Viewing the certification path.

NOTE

Be sure to select the root certificate, and not the actual certificate used for the virtual server (that is, `mail.companyabc.com` in this example).

---

7. Click the Details tab.

8. Click the Copy to File button.

9. In the Certificate Export Wizard, click Next on the welcome screen.

10. Select to export the certificate into a DER encoded binary form, as shown in Figure 23.14. Click Next to continue.

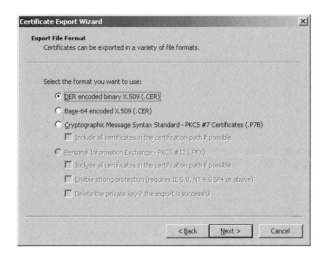

FIGURE 23.14   Exporting the root certificate to a .cer file.

11. Enter a filename for the .cer file, and click Next.

12. Click Finish upon completion of the wizard.

After the certificate has been exported, it must be copied to the Windows Mobile device, either through the Explore button in Microsoft ActiveSync (while the device is cradled), or via a memory chip.

After the .cer file is installed, clicking on it using the File Explorer in Windows Mobile (Start, Programs, File Explorer) invokes a dialog box similar to the one shown in Figure 23.15 warning that you are about to install the certificate. Click Yes and the certificate will be automatically installed and ActiveSync over SSL can be performed.

FIGURE 23.15   Installing a third-party certificate on Windows Mobile.

Securing Access to ActiveSync Using Internet Security and Acceleration (ISA) Server 2006

Allowing your information workers access to a technology like ActiveSync can do wonders for productivity, but can also potentially expose your organization to threats from the outside. Just like Outlook Web Access or Outlook Anywhere, ActiveSync requires a web connection to be available to a CAS. Because ActiveSync is meant to be used when out of the office, the web traffic must go over the Internet and must be accessible without requiring a specific virtual private network (VPN) client to be utilized.

This creates somewhat of a dilemma, as the HTTP used by ActiveSync can be subject to attack, potentially exposing your organization to unnecessary risk. Fortunately, however, Microsoft Exchange Server 2007 can be readily secured against these types of attack with the use of an Application-layer inspection product such as the Internet Security and Acceleration (ISA) Server 2006 product available from Microsoft.

Understanding How ISA Server 2006 Can Protect ActiveSync

ISA Server 2006 is an Application-layer aware firewall that can filter HTTP traffic for exploits and scumware. It can reside inline to the ActiveSync traffic (as a traditional firewall), or as a dedicated reverse proxy system that sits in the demilitarized zone (DMZ) of a packet-filter firewall, similar to the scenario shown in Figure 23.16.

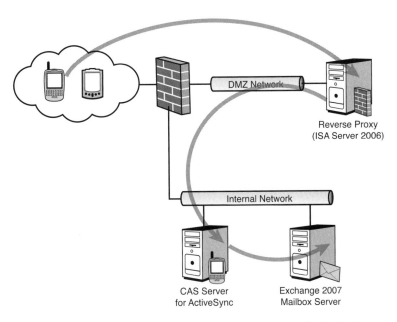

FIGURE 23.16   Understanding ISA securing concepts for ActiveSync.

In this scenario, the client believes it is directly accessing the CAS, but it is instead being secretly authenticated and scanned at the ISA server itself. Using this scenario or the inline firewall scenario with ISA Server 2006 is a highly useful way to secure the ActiveSync traffic.

Creating an ActiveSync Securing Rule in ISA Server 2006

This section of the chapter briefly explains how to create a web publishing rule with ISA Server 2006 for ActiveSync. For more detailed information on using ISA Server with Exchange 2007, reference Chapter 13, "Securing Exchange Server 2007 with ISA Server."

To create the rule in the ISA Server console, perform the following steps:

1. Open the ISA Management Console and navigate to the Firewall Policy node in the console pane.

2. On the Tasks tab of the tasks pane, click the Publish Exchange Web Client Access link.

3. Enter a descriptive name in the welcome dialog box, such as "ActiveSync Rule," and click Next.

4. In the Select Services dialog box, shown in Figure 23.17, change the Exchange version to Exchange Server 2007, and then check the Exchange ActiveSync check box. Click Next to continue.

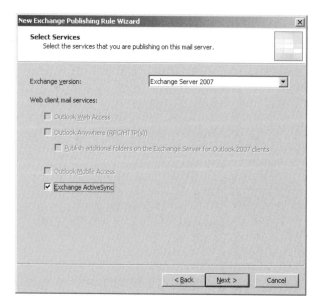

FIGURE 23.17   Creating an ActiveSync rule with ISA Server 2006.

5. In the Publishing Type dialog box, click the Publish a Single Web Site or Load Balancer, and click Next to continue.

6. In the Server Connection Security dialog box, shown in Figure 23.18, click the Use SSL to Connect to the Published Web Server or Server Farm option. This creates an end-to-end SSL connection. Click Next to continue.

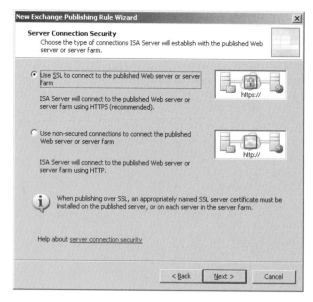

FIGURE 23.18   Securing the ISA rule with SSL.

7. For the internal site name, enter the FQDN that clients use to connect to the CAS, as shown in Figure 23.19. In this case, the name should match what the external clients use, as problems can be encountered when using SSL if the names do not match. If internal DNS does not forward that FQDN to the CAS, you might need to fool the ISA server by using a hosts file to make it resolve the FQDN to the CAS. Click Next to continue.

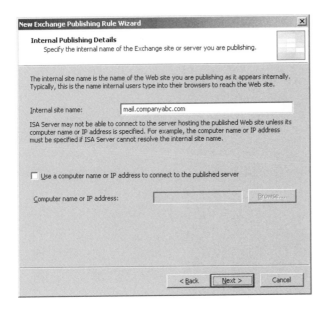

FIGURE 23.19   Creating an ActiveSync securing rule with ISA.

8. Under Public Name Details, enter "This domain name," and then type in the FQDN of the public name, such as mail.companyabc.com. Click Next to continue.

9. For Web Listener, either choose an existing listener that can be used for OWA or Outlook Anywhere, or click the New button. This scenario assumes you are creating a new listener. Click the New button.

10. At the start of the Web Listener Wizard, enter a descriptive name for the listener, such as Exchange HTTP/HTTPS Listener, and click Next to continue.

11. A prompt appears to choose between SSL and non-SSL. This prompt refers to the traffic between the client and ISA, which should always be SSL whenever possible. Click Next to continue.

12. Under Web Listener IP addresses, select the External Network, and leave it at All IP Addresses. Click Next to continue.

13. Under Listener SSL Certificates, click Select Certificate.

14. Select the `mail.companyabc.com` certificate. If the certificate is not on the ISA server, it must be installed into the Certificates store of the ISA server via a process outlined in Chapter 3, "Understanding Core Exchange Server 2007 Design Plans."

15. Click Next to continue.

16. For the type of authentication, choose HTTP Authentication and then check the Basic check box, as shown in Figure 23.20. Leave Windows (Active Directory) selected, and click Next.

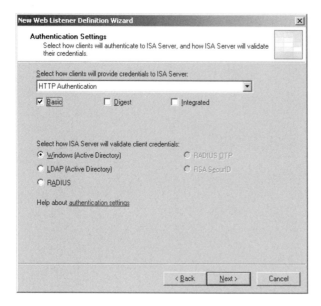

FIGURE 23.20   Selecting Basic authentication for the ISA ActiveSync rule.

17. Click Next at the Single Sign on Settings dialog box. SSO is not available with Basic authentication.

18. Click Finish to end the wizard.

19. Click Next after the new listener is displayed in the Web Listener dialog box.

20. Under Authentication Delegation, choose Basic from the drop-down list. Basic is used as the secured transport mechanism chosen. Click Next to continue.

21. Under User Sets, leave All Authenticated Users selected. In stricter scenarios, only specific AD groups can be granted rights to OWA using this setting. In this case, the default is fine. Click Next to continue.

22. Click Finish to end the wizard.

23. Click Apply in the details pane, and then click OK when you are finished to commit the changes.

The ActiveSync Policy will then show up in the details pane, as shown in Figure 23.21. Further customization of the rule can take place if necessary.

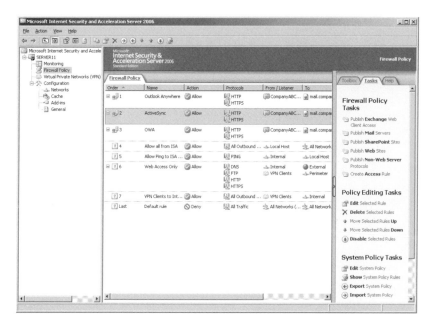

FIGURE 23.21   Viewing the ActiveSync rule in ISA Server 2006.

Working with ActiveSync Policies

ActiveSync in Exchange 2007 allows for an unprecedented level of control over the security and management of devices. It allows an administrator to create ActiveSync mailbox policies that force devices to comply with specific restrictions, such as requiring a complex password, or requiring file encryption.

In addition, Exchange 2007 ActiveSync now allows an administrator to create multiple policies in an organization. This allows specific types of users to have more restrictive policies placed on their handheld devices, while other users are not as restricted. For example, a hospital could stipulate that all of the devices that have confidential patient data on them be forced to be encrypted and password protected, while other users are not forced to the same standards.

Creating ActiveSync Mailbox Policies

Creating a new ActiveSync mailbox policy in Exchange Server 2007 is not a complex task. To do so, follow this procedure:

1. From Exchange Management Console, expand Organization Configuration in the console pane, and click Client Access.

2. In the tasks pane, click the New Exchange ActiveSync Mailbox Policy link.

3. Enter a descriptive name for the policy, such as Manager's ActiveSync Mailbox Policy. Set password settings, such as that shown in Figure 23.22, and click New.

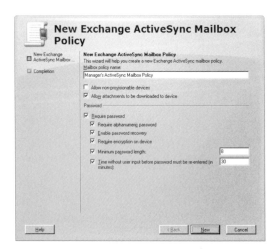

FIGURE 23.22   Creating an ActiveSync mailbox policy.

4. Click Finish.

Applying Mailbox Policies to Users

After a specific policy has been created, it can be added to mailboxes, either during the provisioning process or after the mailbox has already been created. For existing mailboxes, perform the following steps:

1. From the Exchange Management Console, expand Recipient Configuration, and then click Mailbox.

2. Right-click on the mailbox to be added, and click Properties.

3. Select the Mailbox Features tab, click Exchange ActiveSync, and then click the Properties button.

4. Check the Apply an Exchange ActiveSync Mailbox Policy check box, and then click the Browse button.

5. Select the policy from the list, such as that shown in Figure 23.23, and then click OK.

6. Click OK two more times to save the changes.

Adding multiple mailboxes to a specific mailbox policy is best done from the scripting console.

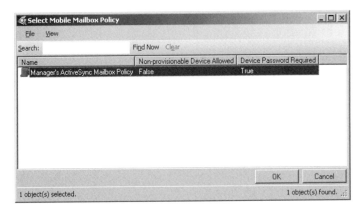

FIGURE 23.23   Applying an ActiveSync mailbox policy to a mailbox.

Wiping and Resetting ActiveSync Devices

One of the advantages to Exchange 2007's ActiveSync is the optimized management capabilities available. With ActiveSync and the proper Windows Mobile devices, passwords can
be reset remotely, and devices can be wiped clean of data in the event that they are lost or
stolen. This concept—combined with the encryption capabilities of the Messaging
Security Feature Pack—allows an organization to deploy ActiveSync without fear of data
compromise.

Figure 23.24 shows a specific device that was wiped, with verification settings and other
information clearly given. The device can be removed from the user by clicking Remove,
or it can be cleared by selecting Clear and then clicking Clear.

FIGURE 23.24   Viewing the ActiveSync device settings for a user.

Invoking this dialog box is as simple as right-clicking on a mailbox user under the Mailbox area of the Recipient Configuration node and choosing Manage Mobile Device.

Working with Windows Mobile Pocket PC and Smartphone Editions

Exchange Server 2007 ActiveSync supports synchronization with multiple client types, including some non-Microsoft device operating systems. In general, however, the best feature set support comes from the Windows Mobile 5.0/6.0 devices. Windows Mobile 5.0 devices can be integrated with the Messaging Security Feature Pack to encrypt data and to allow for remote password reset and remote wipe capabilities. Windows Mobile 6.0 has added capabilities, such as the ability to access file data via UNC paths and document management capabilities via Microsoft Office SharePoint Server 2007 Document libraries.

There are two *flavors* of Windows Mobile available that can be synchronized with Exchange. Windows Mobile Pocket PC Edition is for full Pocket PC devices, many equipped with a stylus and/or a keyboard. The other version supported is the Windows Mobile Smartphone Edition, which is limited to traditional smaller phones, such as clamshell flip phones and non-keyboard units. The configuration steps for both versions of the OS are outlined in this section.

Setting Up Windows Mobile Pocket PC Edition for ActiveSync

Windows Mobile Pocket PC Edition is widely used on many cutting-edge devices and provides for a larger screen than most cell phones. Many of the systems also have a full-sized keyboard. To configure a Windows Mobile Pocket PC Edition phone for ActiveSync to an Exchange server, perform the following steps:

1. From the Windows Mobile screen, click Start, Programs.

2. Select ActiveSync.

3. When prompted about syncing options, choose the Set Up Your Device to Sync with It link.

4. Enter the FQDN of the ActiveSync server into the dialog box shown in Figure 23.25 and make sure the This Server Requires an Encrypted (SSL) Connection check box is checked. The FQDN should match the name on the certificate. Click Next to continue.

5. Enter a valid username, password, and domain, and then choose to save the password. Click Next to continue.

6. Choose which types of data will be synchronized from the dialog box shown in Figure 23.26. Clicking on Calendar or E-mail and choosing Settings allows for customization of the amount of data to be synchronized. Click Finish when you are done.

FIGURE 23.25   Configuring server settings with ActiveSync.

FIGURE 23.26   Syncing calendar, mail, and contact information with ActiveSync.

7. Click the Sync button to connect to the Exchange server.

The Mobile device will start synchronizing automatically. Synchronizing can be enacted manually, or if the Windows Mobile device supports Direct Push, the emails will be automatically pushed out to the phone.

Setting Up Windows Mobile Smartphone Edition for ActiveSync

Many traditional-style mobile phones (no keyboard, stylus, or large Pocket PC display) are configured with the Windows Mobile 5.0 Smartphone Edition operating system, which allows the operator to synchronize the phone with Exchange 2007 and ActiveSync. The procedure for setting up this type of synchronization is very similar to the procedure for Windows Mobile 5.0 Pocket PC Edition, with a few minor exceptions as follows:

> **NOTE**
>
> The hardware on many smartphones is different, and some of the button options in this step-by-step procedure might vary. The overall concept should apply to any Windows Mobile 5.0 Smartphone Edition system, however.

1. From the smartphone, press the button corresponding to the Start command.

2. Navigate to ActiveSync and press Select/Enter.

3. When prompted with the dialog box shown in Figure 23.27, select the Set Up Your Device to Sync with It link.

FIGURE 23.27   Setting up Windows Smartphone Edition for ActiveSync.

4. Enter the FQDN of the ActiveSync server, such as `mail.companyabc.com`. Check the box to require SSL, and press Next.

5. Enter a valid username, password, and domain, and check the Save Password check box, as shown in Figure 23.28. Press Next.

FIGURE 23.28   Entering credentials for ActiveSync.

6. Select which data will be synchronized from the subsequent dialog box, such as contacts, calendar, email, or tasks. Press Finish.

The phone will then begin syncing with the ActiveSync server.

Installing and Working with the Windows Mobile 5.0 Device Emulator

Microsoft has released a software emulator for Windows Mobile 5.0 that can be used for testing, troubleshooting, and code development on the platform. This tool, shown in Figure 23.29, allows for different Windows Mobile *skins* to be used for testing purposes and is an excellent way to test out an ActiveSync deployment in a lab environment.

The device emulator can be downloaded from Microsoft at the following URL:

http://www.microsoft.com/downloads/details.aspx?FamilyID=c62d54a5-183a-4a1e-a7e2-cc500ed1f19a&DisplayLang=en

FIGURE 23.29   Viewing the Pocket PC emulator.

In addition, it is recommended to download and install the Virtual Machine Network Driver to allow the emulator to latch on to the physical machine's network adapter for testing purposes. The Virtual Machine Network Driver is available for download at the following URL:

http://www.microsoft.com/downloads/details.aspx?familyid=DC8332D6-565F-4A57-BE8C-1D4718D3AF65&displaylang=en

Summary

The concept of the "office without walls" is fast becoming a reality, as information workers now have a myriad of options available to connect with their co-workers using Exchange Server 2007 technologies such as ActiveSync. ActiveSync in Exchange 2007 also allows for unprecedented management and security capabilities, allowing organizations to take advantage of the improved productivity these devices give, but without sacrificing security in the process.

Best Practices

The following are best practices from this chapter:

- ▶ Always use SSL encryption with ActiveSync technologies.

- ▶ Consider the use of ActiveSync mailbox policies to gain granular control over password and encryption settings of the mobile devices.

- ▶ If using a smartphone or phone PDA device to sync a mailbox to ActiveSync, consider purchasing an unlimited data plan from the mobile phone provider as the amount of data to be transferred can be great.

- ▶ Consider the use of a third-party trusted root CA for SSL with ActiveSync to avoid having to install a certificate on every mobile device.

- ▶ Secure the ActiveSync HTTP traffic to CAS Systems by implementing ISA Server 2006 to monitor the traffic with Application-layer inspection capabilities.

23

CHAPTER 24

Designing and Configuring Unified Messaging in Exchange Server 2007

Microsoft Exchange Server 2007 unified messaging (UM) delivers voice messaging, fax, and email into a unified Inbox. These messages can be accessed from a telephone or a computer. Exchange Server 2007 unified messaging integrates with the telephony systems, operating fundamentally as a voice mail server using the Exchange Information Store as a repository for the messages.

The concept of unified messaging is new to the Exchange product line, and its introduction brings with it new telephony concepts that might not be familiar to an Exchange administrator. This chapter focuses on the design and configuration of the new unified messaging capabilities built in to Exchange 2007. This includes telephony concepts, server specifications, installation and configuration considerations, and monitoring of the unified messaging services.

Unified Messaging Features

Exchange Server 2007 introduces a brand-new set of features with the addition of the Unified Messaging server role. Unified messaging seamlessly integrates voice messaging, faxing, and electronic mail into a single Inbox. This frees up the user from having to manage separate accounts and Inboxes for these three types of messages. With the new role, there are a number of new features.

Telephony Integration

With unified messaging, Exchange is now integrated into the telephony world. This integration takes place between the Exchange Unified Messaging server and gateways or Private Branch Exchanges (PBXs).

In a classic set of telephony and electronic mail systems, shown in Figure 24.1, there are two separate networks that deliver voice messages and electronic messages (email). In the telephony system, there are separate components for the PBX, voice mail, external lines, and phones. As shown in the figure, calls from the Public Switched Telephone Network (PSTN) come into a PBX device. Typically, an incoming call is routed by the PBX to the telephone. If the phone does not answer or is busy, the call is routed to the voice mail system. Similarly, email from the Internet arrives at the Exchange messaging server. Note that in the classic system, there is no integration or connectivity between the telephony and electronic mail systems.

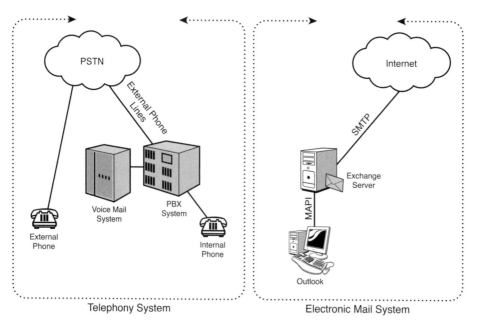

FIGURE 24.1   Classic telephone and electronic mail systems.

With the advent of Exchange Server 2007 and unified messaging, these two disparate systems are integrated, as shown in Figure 24.2. Although the UM server does not connect directly with a traditional PBX, it does integrate with PBXs via gateways. The combination of the PBX and the Internet Protocol (IP) gateway can also be replaced by an IP-PBX, which provides both sets of functionality.

Notice that, in effect, the Unified Messaging server has replaced the voice mail server in the classic system. The new Microsoft Exchange Server 2003 Unified Messaging server is a voice mail server.

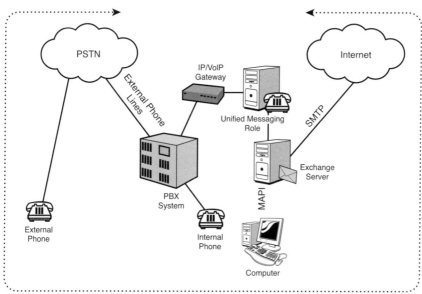

FIGURE 24.2   New integrated system.

The more detailed view with all the Exchange 2007 server roles is shown in Figure 24.3. This figure also includes the various ways that a user can interact with the integrated system.

This diagram is discussed in more detail in later sections of this chapter.

Single Inbox

The Unified Messaging server enables the true unification of email messages, voice mail messages, and fax messages into a single Inbox. Messages from all these disparate sources are stored in the user's Inbox and are accessible through a wide variety of interfaces, such as Outlook, a telephone, a web browser, or even a mobile PDA.

The Inbox can be managed just like a traditional email Inbox, with folders, Inbox rules, message retention, and so on. Exchange administrators can back up and restore Inboxes with all these forms of data just as they do with email data. This reduces the complexity and ease of use for both users and administrators.

Call Answering

Call answering picks up incoming calls for a user who does not answer their phone. It plays their personal greeting, records voice messages, and converts the voice messages to an email message to be submitted to the user's Exchange mailbox.

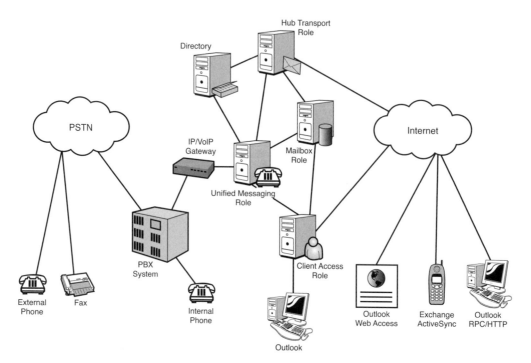

FIGURE 24.3   Detailed architecture diagram.

Fax Receiving

If the incoming call is from a fax machine, the server can recognize this and accept the fax. The fax is then converted to an email message and submitted to the user's Exchange mailbox. The user can then read the fax as an attachment to the message.

Subscriber Access

The subscriber access feature is an exciting new capability that allows a user to access their Exchange mailbox using a phone. This access mechanism is called Outlook Voice Access.

With Outlook Voice Access, a user can access their Exchange Inbox with the telephone to do the following:

▶ Listen to and forward voice mail messages.

▶ Listen to, forward, and reply to email messages.

▶ Listen to calendar information.

▶ Access or dial contacts.

▶ Accept or cancel meeting requests.

▶ Notify attendees that the user will be late.

- ▶ Set a voice mail Out-of-Office message.

- ▶ Set user security preferences and personal options.

This, in effect, gives the user working access to their Exchange Inbox while out in the field with only a telephone.

The system not only recognizes dual tone multiple frequency (DTMF) key presses from the phone, but also understands voice commands. The system guides the user through the prompts responding to voice commands, giving the user complete hands-free operation.

For example, a user might be on the freeway running late for a lunch meeting. Not remembering the exact time, the user calls into the subscriber access and says "Today's Calendar." The unified messaging system speaks the summary of the next meeting, which is at 12 p.m. Recognizing that the traffic will force him to be 20 minutes late, the user says "I'll be 20 minutes late for this appointment." The unified messaging system confirms and then sends a message to all the attendees, which is shown in Figure 24.4.

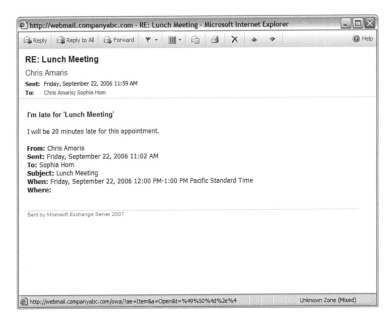

FIGURE 24.4   Late to meeting email.

The speech recognition is remarkably effective and able to recognize commands even over cell phones and with background noise.

> **NOTE**
>
> For this release of the product, speech recognition is enabled only for the main menu and for calendar access menus for unified messaging subscribers. The speech recognition feature is unavailable in this release when subscribers access unified messaging menus such as contacts or voice mail or when they perform a directory search.

Outlook Play on Phone

The Exchange 2007 Outlook Web Access client and the Outlook 2007 client both support a new feature called Play on Phone. This feature allows users to play voice mail on an internal phone rather than through the computer. The user opens the voice mail message, selects the Play on Phone option, enters the extension to play the message on, and clicks the Dial button, as shown in Figure 24.5. The phone at the extension 102 will then ring.

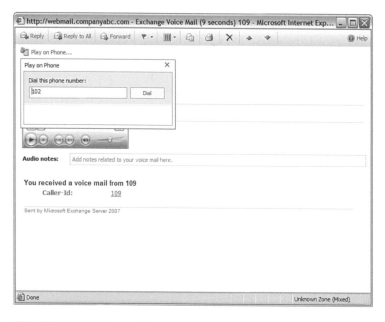

FIGURE 24.5   Play on Phone.

This allows the user to send the audio stream of the voice mail message to an internal phone for better sound quality, for more privacy, or to allow a third party to hear the message. The system even provides prompts over the phone following the playback with message handling options.

Auto Attendant

The auto attendant is like a secretary, providing voice prompts to guide an external or internal caller through the voice mail system. The system can respond to either telephone keypad presses or voice commands.

The auto attendant features include the following:

- A customizable set of menus for external users
- Greetings for business hours and nonbusiness hours
- Hours of operation and holiday schedules
- Access to the organization's directory
- Access for external users to the operator

The voice prompts that provide the preceding information can be customized to suit the organization.

Unified Messaging Architecture

The Exchange 2007 unified messaging features and telephony integration bring a whole new set of concepts, terminology, and architectural elements to the Exchange platform. This section explores these different components, objects, protocols, and services.

Unified Messaging Components

The central repository for all the unified messaging components is Active Directory. The schema extensions that are installed as part of the Exchange 2007 prerequisites add a variety of objects and attributes that support the UM functionality. These objects are as follows:

- Dial plan objects
- IP gateway objects
- Hunt group objects
- Mailbox policy objects
- Auto Attendant objects
- Unified Messaging server objects

The objects and their relationships are illustrated in the example shown in Figure 24.6. The example consists of two locations, San Francisco (SFO) and Paris (PAR), with an integrated Exchange 2007 unified messaging infrastructure. The unified messaging objects are shown with a dotted line around them to separate them from the telephony objects.

When a UM hunt group is created manually, not only does the associated UM IP gateway and the associated UM dial plan get specified, but also a pilot identifier is specified.

This diagram is referenced in the subsequent sections describing the various unified messaging objects and components.

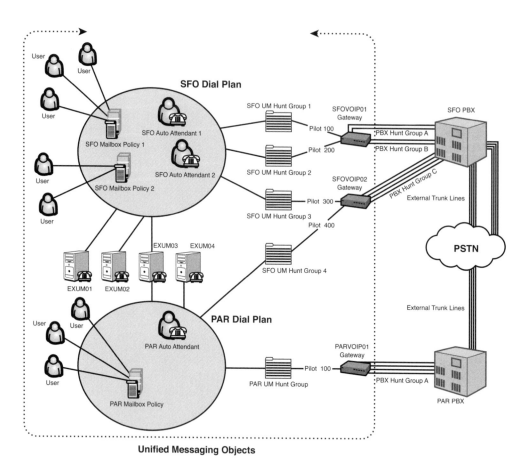

FIGURE 24.6   Unified messaging objects and relationships.

Dial Plan Objects

Dial plans are the central component of the Exchange 2007 unified messaging architecture. A UM dial plan essentially logically corresponds to PBX or subsets of extensions within a PBX. The UM dial plan objects can be found in the Exchange Management Console on the UM Dial Plan tab of the Organization, Unified Messaging container.

Different PBXs with an organization, such as between SFO and PAR in Figure 24.6, can have overlapping extensions. For example, a user in San Francisco might have extension 150 and a user in Paris might also have extension 150. Because the two users are on different PBXs, there is no inherent conflict. However, when Exchange 2007 Unified Messaging is deployed and the telephony infrastructure is unified in Active Directory, then there would be a conflict.

Dial plans ensure that all extensions are unique within the architecture by mapping a dial plan to a PBX. Extensions within a dial plan must be unique. However, extensions between different dial plans do not have to be unique. A user can only belong to a single dial plan and will have an extension number that uniquely identifies him within the dial plan.

In the figure, there is one dial plan for each location. In the example, San Francisco is the large office with more users and Paris is smaller. There could be multiple dial plans per location.

Dial plans also provide a way to set up common settings among a set of users, such as the following :

- ▶ Number of digits in an extension
- ▶ Ability to receive faxes
- ▶ Subscriber greetings
- ▶ Whom caller can contact within the dial plan
- ▶ Call durations
- ▶ Users call restrictions (international calls)
- ▶ Languages supported

These settings should not be confused with UM mailbox policies, which are covered in the "Mailbox Policy Objects" section later in this book.

> **NOTE**
>
> When a new UM dial plan object is created, a default UM mailbox policy object is also created and associated with the dial plan.

The dial plan also associates the extension for the subscriber access to Outlook Voice Access.

There can be multiple dial plans within an architecture and even associated with the same PBX.

UM IP Gateway Objects

The UM IP gateway object is the logical representation of the physical IP/VoIP gateway. The UM IP gateway object is a critical component, in that it specifies the connection between the UM dial plan and the physical IP/VoIP gateway. The major configuration of the UM IP gateway object is the IP address of the IP/VoIP gateway device it represents and the associated dial plan. The UM IP gateway objects can be found in the Exchange Management Console on the UM IP Gateway tab of the Organization, Unified Messaging container.

The UM IP gateway is created as enabled. The gateway can be disabled, either immediately (which disconnects any current calls) or specifying to disable after completing calls.

The latter mode disables the gateway for any new calls but does not disconnect any current calls.

If a UM IP gateway object is not created or is deleted, the Unified Messaging servers in the dial plan will not be able to accept or process calls.

Within the same Active Directory, there can only be one UM IP gateway object for each physical IP/VoIP gateway, and it is enforced through the IP addresses.

UM IP gateway objects can be associated with multiple dial plans. This is accomplished by creating multiple hunt groups, as discussed in the following section.

Hunt Group Objects

In the telephony world, hunt groups are collections of lines that a PBX uses to organize extensions. The hunt group collections allow the system to treat the extensions as a logical group. Hunt groups are used for incoming lines, for outgoing lines, and to route calls to groups of users such as the Sales department. The UM hunt group objects can be found in the Exchange Management Console on the UM IP Gateway tab of the Organization, Unified Messaging container. They are listed under each of the UM IP gateways.

Calls with a hunt group can be routed using different methods or algorithms, such as the following:

▶ **Rollover**—The PBX starts with the lowest numbered line each time and increments until it finds a free line.

▶ **Round-robin**—The PBX rotates equally among all the lines when starting and then rolls over from that starting point. This ensures that the calls are distributed evenly within the hunt group.

▶ **Utilization**—The PBX tracks extension utilization and routes the call to the least utilized line first, and then rolls over to the next least busy line.

These algorithms basically encode what the organization deems the appropriate behavior for the routing.

Each hunt group has an associate pilot number, which is the extension that is dialed to access the hunt group. This is frequently the lowest numbered extension in the set of extensions because the most common implementation of a hunt group is rollover.

Within Exchange 2007, the UM hunt group object performs a different function. Essentially, the UM hunt group object maps the IP/VoIP gateway and an extension to a UM dial plan.

> **NOTE**
>
> If a default hunt group is created when the UM IP gateway object is created, that UM hunt group will not have a pilot extension associated with it. This creates call routing problems if you create additional hunt groups, so it is best to remove the default hunt group. When a new UM hunt group is created after that, the pilot identifier must be specified.

Additional UM hunt groups can be created to route different incoming extensions to different UM dial plans.

There is no limit to the number of UM hunt group objects that can be created. There must be at least one hunt group per UM IP gateway object for calls to be routed to a dial plan.

Mailbox Policy Objects

Mailbox policy objects control unified messaging settings and security for users. The UM mailbox policy objects can be found in the Exchange Management Console on the UM Mailbox Policies tab of the Organization, Unified Messaging container.

These settings include the following:

- ▶ Maximum greeting duration
- ▶ Message text for UM generated messages to users
- ▶ PIN policies
- ▶ Dialing restrictions

Mailbox policies are created to control security and provide customized messages to users. For example, in Figure 24.6 the SFO Mailbox Policy 1 is a general user policy with default PIN settings that require a minimum of 6 characters. The second policy, SFO Mailbox Policy 2, is for executives with higher security requirements and more secure PIN settings that require a minimum of 10 characters.

The UM mailbox policy is associated with one and only one UM dial plan, but dial plans can be associated with multiple mailbox policies. This allows the dial plan to be associated to the users associated with the mailbox policy. Each user will be associated with one and only one UM mailbox policy object, but many users can be associated with a single mailbox policy object.

There is no limit to the number of UM mailbox policy objects that can be created.

Auto Attendant Objects

The auto attendant provides an automated phone answering function, essentially replicating a human secretary. The auto attendant answers the incoming calls, provides helpful prompts, and directs the caller to the appropriate services. The UM auto attendant objects can be found in the Exchange Management Console on the UM Auto Attendant tab of the Organization, Unified Messaging container.

The auto attendant supports both phone key press (DTMF) and voice commands. This sophisticated voice recognition technology allows the caller to navigate the menus and prompts with nothing more than their voice if they want to.

The auto attendant objects support the following configurable features:

- ▶ Customized greetings and menus for business hours and nonbusiness hours

- ▶ Predefined and custom schedule to specify business hours and time zone

- ▶ Holiday schedule for exceptions to the business hour schedule

- ▶ Operator extension and allowing transfer to operator during business and nonbusiness hours

- ▶ Key mapping to enable the transfer of callers to specific extensions or other auto attendants based on hard-coded key presses or voice commands.

> **NOTE**
>
> Everyone has felt the frustration of moving through an automated call system and not being able to reach an operator or a live person. With Unified Messaging, the Exchange administrator now has control over that behavior.
>
> The auto attendant can allow or disallow transfer to the operator by specifically allowing or disallowing transfer to the operator during business and nonbusiness hours.
>
> The author's recommendation is to allow transfers to the operator at least during business hours to reduce caller frustration.

Each auto attendant can be mapped to specific extensions to provide a customized set of prompts. For example, an organization could set up one auto attendant to support the sales organization calls with specific prompts for handling calls to sales. The organization could then set up a second auto attendant to support the service organization with specific prompts for technical support and help. These would service different pilot numbers, depending on the number that the caller used.

A front-end menu can be created with key mapping and an auto attendant with customized prompts. This allows the organization in the previous example to create a top-level auto attendant that would prompt callers to "Press or say 1 for Sales or 2 for Service" and then perform the appropriate transfer. Figure 24.7 shows the key mapping configuration, which would be accompanied by customized prompts.

There is no limit to the number of auto attendants that can be created in Active Directory. An auto attendant can only be associated with a single dial plan, though a dial plan can be associated with multiple auto attendants.

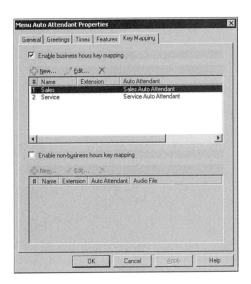

FIGURE 24.7   Key mapping example.

Unified Messaging Server Objects

In Active Directory, the Unified Messaging server object is a logical representation of the physical Exchange 2007 Unified Messaging server. The UM server objects can be found in the Exchange Management Console in the Server Configuration, Unified Messaging container.

The Microsoft Exchange Unified Messaging service (umservice.exe) is the service that instantiates the unified messaging functionality that runs under the Local System account. It is dependent on the Microsoft Exchange Active Directory Topology service and the Microsoft Exchange Speech Engine service.

The major configuration task for the Unified Messaging server object is to specify the associated dial plans, of which there can be more than one as per the diagram in Figure 24.7. The Unified Messaging server must be associated with a dial plan to function. The other configurable parameters for the service are the maximum concurrent calls (default is 100) and maximum concurrent faxes (default is 100).

The Unified Messaging server checks for changes when the service is started and every 10 minutes thereafter. Changes take effect as soon as they are detected by the server. After determining the dial plans for which it is associated, the server then locates and establishes communications with the appropriate IP/VoIP gateways.

Much like the UM IP gateway, the Unified Messaging server is created as enabled. The server can be disabled via the Exchange Management Console or via the Exchange Management Shell for graceful shutdown or maintenance. This can be executed either immediately (which disconnects any current calls) or specifying to disable after completing calls. The latter mode disables the server for any new calls but does not disconnect any current calls. The current calls will be allowed to complete.

Unified Messaging Users

There is actually not an Active Directory object for unified messaging users. Rather, the unified messaging properties are stored in the Active Directory user account and the Exchange 2007 mailbox. Voice mail messages and fax mail messages are stored in the user's mailbox.

These properties can be found in the Exchange Management Console in the properties of the users account in the Recipient Configuration, Mailbox folder. Within the user account properties, the unified messaging settings are under the Mailbox Features tab in the properties of the Unified Messaging feature. After navigating to the Unified Messaging feature, the properties button is clicked to access the feature properties.

When enabling a user for unified messaging, the associated UM mailbox policy and extension must be specified. The link to the mailbox policy provides a one-to-one link to the UM dial plan.

The user's mailbox quotas apply to both voice mail messages and fax messages. If the user's quota settings prevent the user from receiving email (that is, the user's mailbox is full), then unified messaging functionality will be impacted. Callers attempting to leave a message will not be allowed to leave a message and will be informed that the user's mailbox is full.

> **NOTE**
>
> Interestingly, if a user's mailbox is almost full, a caller will be allowed to leave a message for the user even if that message will cause the mailbox to exceed its quota. For example, consider a user who only has 25KB before they exceed their quota and are prevented from receiving messages. A caller could leave a minute long 100-KB voice message. However, the next caller would not be able to leave a message for the user.

Exchange 2007 unified messaging includes a number of features to control the size of voice mail messages to help control the storage impacts.

UM Web Services

A component that is not represented in Active Directory is the UM Web Services. This is a web service that is installed on Exchange 2007 servers that have the Client Access role.

The service is used for the following:

- Play on Phone Feature for both Outlook 2007 and Exchange 2007 Outlook Web Access
- PIN Reset feature in Exchange 2007 Outlook Web Access

This service requires that at least one Exchange 2007 server run the Client Access, Hub Transport, and Mailbox server roles in addition to the Unified Messaging role.

Audio Codecs and Voice Message Sizes

Codec is a contraction of coding and decoding digital data. This is the format in which the audio stream is stored. It includes both the number of bit rate (bits/sec) and compression that is used.

The codec that is used by the Unified Messaging server to encode the messages is one of the following three:

- Windows Media Audio (WMA)—16-bit Compressed
- GSM 06.10 (GSM)—8-bit Compressed
- G.711 PCM Linear (G711)—16-bit Uncompressed

The Exchange 2007 unified messaging default is WMA, which provides a good balance between audio quality and storage. The Audio Codec setting is configured on the UM dial plan on the Settings tab.

NOTE

A dirty little secret is that the digital compression can result in loss of data. When the data is compressed and decompressed, information can be lost. That is, bits of the conversation or message can be lost. This is a trade-off that the codec makes to save space. This is why the G.711 codec is available, which doesn't compress data and doesn't lose data but at a heavy cost in storage.

These are stored in the message as attachments using the following formats:

- Windows Media Audio Format (.wma)—For the WMA codec
- RIFF/WAV Format (.wav)—For GSM or G.711 codecs

The choice of the audio codec impacts the audio quality and the size of the attached file. Table 24.1 shows the approximate size of data in the file attachment for each codec.

TABLE 24.1   Audio Size for Codec Options

Codec Setting	Approximate Size of 10 Sec of Audio
WMA	11,000 bytes
G.711	160,000 bytes
GSM	16,000 bytes

The G.711 audio codec setting results in a greater than 10:1 storage penalty when compared to the WMA audio codec setting. Although the GSM audio codec setting results in approximately the same storage as the WMA codec setting, this comes at a cost of a 50% reduction in audio quality. Clearly, the WMA audio codec setting provides a much smaller file size with a much better audio quality.

> **NOTE**
>
> The .wma file format has a larger header (about 7KB) than the .wav format (about 0.1KB). So for small messages, the GSM files will be smaller. However, after messages exceed 15 seconds, the WMA files will be smaller than the GSM files.

With the clear superiority of the WMA audio codec, the primary reason for the availability of the G.711 and GSM codec is for compatibility with other telephony systems.

Operating System Requirements

This section discusses the recommended minimum hardware requirements for Exchange 2007 servers.

Exchange 2007 unified messaging supports the following processors:

▶ x64 architecture-based Intel Xeon or Intel Pentium family processor that supports Intel Extended Memory 64 Technology

▶ x64 architecture-based computer with AMD Opteron or AMD Athlon 64-bit processor that supports AMD64 platform

The Exchange 2007 unified messaging memory requirements are as follows:

▶ 1GB of RAM minimum

▶ 2GB of RAM recommended

The Exchange 2007 unified messaging disk space requirements are as follows:

▶ A minimum of 1.2GB of available disk space

▶ Plus 500MB of available disk space for each unified messaging language pack

▶ 200MB of available disk space on the system drive

A new requirement with Exchange 2007 is for a:

▶ DVD drive

As features and complexity of the applications such as Exchange 2007 have grown, the installation code bases have grown proportionally. Luckily, so have the hardware specifications of the average new system, which now typically includes a DVD drive.

Exchange 2007 unified messaging supports the following operating system and Windows components:

▶ Windows Server 2003, x64 Standard Edition

▶ Windows Server 2003, x64 Enterprise Edition

Unified Messaging Architecture   809

▶ Windows Server 2003, x64 R2 Standard Edition

▶ Windows Server 2003, x64 R2 Enterprise Edition

Exchange 2007 unified messaging requires the following components to be installed:

▶ Microsoft .NET Framework Version 2.0

▶ Windows PowerShell (formerly code-named Monad)

▶ Microsoft Management Console (MMC) 3.0

Out of the box, an Exchange 2007 Unified Messaging server is configured for a maximum of 100 concurrent calls. This is enough to support potentially thousands of users, given that the number of calls and voice messages per day is a fraction of the number of users and is spread out throughout the day.

Supported IP/VoIP Hardware

Exchange Server 2007 unified messaging relies on the ability of the IP/VoIP gateway to translate time-division multiplexing (TDM) or telephony circuit-switched based protocols, such as Integrated Services Digital Network (ISDN) or QSIG, from a PBX to protocols based on voice over IP (VoIP) or IP, such as Session Initiation Protocol (SIP), Real-Time Transport Protocol (RTP), or T.38 for real-time facsimile transport.

Although there are many types and manufacturers of PBXs, IP/VoIP gateways, and IP/PBXs, there are essentially two types of IP/VoIP gateway component configurations:

▶ **IP/VoIP Gateway**—A legacy PBX and an IP/VoIP gateway provisioned as two separate devices. The Unified Messaging server communicates with the IP/VoIP gateway.

▶ **IP/PBX**—A modern IP-based or hybrid PBX such as a Cisco CallManager. The Unified Messaging server communicates directly with the PBX.

Table 24.2 lists the currently supported IP/VoIP gateways.

TABLE 24.2   Supported IP/VoIP Gateways for Exchange 2007 UM

Manufacturer	Model	Supported Protocols
Intel	PIMG80PBXDNI	Digital
Intel	PIMGG80LS	Analog with In-Band or SMDI
Intel	TIMG300DTI and TIMG600DTI	T1 with Channel Associated Signaling (CAS) or Q.SIG, E1 with Q.SIG
AudioCodes	MediaPack 114, MediaPack 118	Analog with In-Band or SMDI
AudioCodes	Mediant 2000	T1/ or E1 with CAS—In-Band or SMDI, T1/E1 with Primary Rate Interface (PRI) and Q.SIG

To support Exchange Server 2007 unified messaging, one or both types of IP/VoIP device configurations are used when connecting a telephony network infrastructure to a data network infrastructure.

All these solutions must communicate with the unified messenger via SIP.

Telephony Components and Terminology

With the integration of Exchange 2007 into the telephony world, it is important for the Exchange administrator to understand the various components and terminology of a modern telephone system.

The following are some of the common components and terms that are critical to understand:

- ▶ **Circuit**—A circuit is a connection between two end-to-end devices. This allows the device to communicate. A common example of this is a telephone call where two people are talking, in which a circuit is established between the two telephones.

- ▶ **Circuit-switched networks**—Circuit-switched networks consist of dedicated end-to-end connections through the network that support sessions between end devices. The circuits are set up end-to-end through a series of switches as needed and torn down when done. While the circuit is set up, the entire circuit is dedicated to the devices. A common example of a circuit-switched network is the PSTN.

- ▶ **DTMF**—The Dual Tone Multiple frequency (DTMF) signaling protocol is used for telephony signaling and call setup. The most common use is for telephone tone dialing and is known as Touch-Tone. This is used to convey phone button key presses to devices on the network.

- ▶ **IP/PBX**—With the advent of high-speed ubiquitous packet-switched networks, many corporations have moved from legacy PBXs to modern IP-based PBXs known as Internet Protocol/Private Branch Exchange (IP/PBX). These devices come in a myriad of forms, including true IP/PBXs that only support IP protocols to hybrid devices that support both circuit-switched and packet-switched devices. A major advantage of the IP/PBXs is that they are typically much easier to provision and administer. Rather than having to add a separate physical line to plug a phone into, IP phones are simply plugged into the Ethernet jack. Rather than being provisioned by the physical line they are plugged into, the IP phones are provisioned by their own internal characteristics such as the MAC address. This allows for more flexibility.

- ▶ **IP/VoIP gateways**—Connecting legacy circuit-switched networks to packet-switched networks, IP/VoIP gateways provide connections between the new packet-switched VoIP protocols and the circuit-switched protocols. These gateways can connect the PSTN to an IP/PBX or a legacy PBX to VoIP devices. In the case of Exchange 2007 unified messaging, the IP/VoIP gateway connects the Unified Messaging server to the legacy PBX. This is not typically needed if the PBX that the Unified Messaging server is connecting to is an IP/PBX.

▶ **Packet-switched networks**—In packet-switched networks, there is no dedicated end-to-end circuit. Instead, the sessions between devices are disassembled into packets and transmitted individually over the network, then reassembled when they reach their destination. All sessions travel over the shared network. A common example of a packet-switched network is the Internet.

▶ **PBX**—In all but the smallest companies, there is a device that takes incoming calls from the circuit-switched telephone network and routes them within the company. This device is called a Private Branch Exchange or PBX. In the old days, this was done by an operator who plugged in the lines manually. The PBX also routes internal outgoing calls, calls between internal phones, and calls to other devices such as the voice mail system.

▶ **POTS**—The Plain Old Telephone System (POTS) is the original analog version of the PSTN. The term originally referred to Post Office Telephone Service, but morphed into the current definition when control of the telephone systems was removed from national post offices.

▶ **PSTN**—The Public Switched Telephone Network (PSTN) is the circuit-switched network to which most telephones connect. It can be either analog, digital, or a combination of the two.

▶ **TDM**—Time-division multiplexing (TDM) is a digital, multiplexing technique for placing multiple simultaneous calls over a circuit-switched network such as the PSTN.

▶ **VoIP**—Voice over Internet Protocol (VoIP) is the use of voice technologies over packet-switched networks using TCP/IP transport protocols rather than circuit-switched networks like the PSTN. This takes advantage of and reflects the trend toward a single, ubiquitous packet-switched network. The local area network (LAN) and wide area network (WAN) are used not only for data traffic, but also for voice traffic. VoIP is not a single technology, but rather a collection of different technologies, protocols, hardware, and software.

Unified Messaging Protocols

The Exchange 2007 Unified Messaging servers use several telephony-related protocols to integrate and communicate with telephony devices. These protocols are listed and discussed in the following list:

▶ **SIP**—Session Initiation Protocol (SIP) is the signaling protocol that is used to set up and tear down VoIP calls. These calls include voice, video, instant messaging, and a variety of other services. The SIP protocol is specified in RFC 3261 produced by the Internet Engineering Task Force (IETF) SIP Working Group. SIP is only a signaling protocol and does not transmit data per se. After the call is set up, the actual communications take place using the RTP for voice and video or T.38 for faxes.

> **NOTE**
>
> Exchange 2007 only supports SIP over TCP. SIP can be configured to run over User Datagram Protocol (UDP) or Transmission Control Protocol (TCP). UDP is connection-less and does not provide reliability guarantees over the network. TCP is connection-oriented and provides reliability guarantees for its packets.

▶ **RTP**—Real-Time Transport Protocol (RTP) is a protocol for sending the voice and video data over the TCP/IP network. The protocol relies on other protocols, such as SIP or H.323, to perform call setup and teardown. It was developed by the IETF Audio-Video Transport Working Group and is specified in RFC 3550. There is not a defined port for the RTP protocol, but it is normally configured to use protocols 16384–32767. The protocol uses a dynamic port range, so it is not ideally suited to traversing firewalls.

▶ **T.38**— The Real-Time Facsimile Transport (T.38) protocol is an International Telecommunication Union (ITU) standard for transmitting faxes over TCP/IP. The protocol is described in RFC 3362. Although it can support call setup and teardown, it is normally used in conjunction with a signaling protocol such as SIP.

It is important to note that the Exchange 2007 Unified Messaging server is also a Windows server, a web server, and a member of the Active Directory domain. There are a myriad of protocols, including domain name system (DNS), Hypertext Transfer Protocol (HTTP), Lightweight Directory Access Protocol (LDAP), remote procedure calls (RPC), and Simple Mail Transfer Protocol (SMTP) among others, that the servers uses to communicate with other servers in addition to the telephony communications.

Unified Messaging Port Assignments

Table 24.3 shows the IP ports that unified messaging uses for each protocol. The table also shows if the ports can be changed and where.

TABLE 24.3   Ports Used for Unified Messaging Protocols

Protocol	TCP Port	UDP Port	Can Ports Be Changed?
SIP-UM Service	5060		Ports are hard-coded.
SIP-Worker Process	5061 and 5062		Ports are set by using the Extensible Markup Language (XML) configuration file.
RTP		Port range above 1024	The range of ports can be changed in the Registry.
T.38		Dynamic port above 1024	Ports are defined by the system.
UM Web Service	Dynamic port above 1024		Ports are defined by the system.

Unified Messaging Installation

The installation of Exchange 2007 is surprisingly easy, although the configuration can be tricky. This section covers the installation and configuration of a basic system to illustrate the concepts.

The installation of the Unified Messaging server role assumes that Exchange 2007 is already installed on the target server. For detailed instructions on installing Exchange Server 2007, see Chapter 7, "Installing Exchange Server 2007."

Installation of the Unified Messaging server role modifies the base installation of Exchange 2007 and is done in what is termed Maintenance mode. The procedures in this section step through the build of a basic Exchange 2007 unified messaging system, as shown in Figure 24.8.

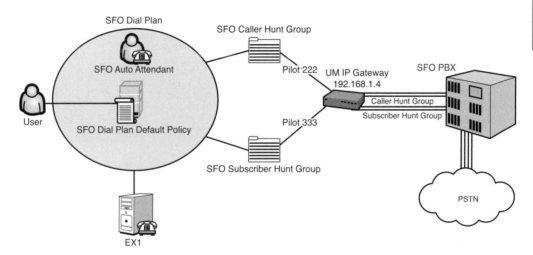

FIGURE 24.8   Sample Exchange 2007 UM system.

Installation Prerequisites

Before starting the installation, it is important that the user's mailboxes that will be serviced by the Unified Messaging server are on Exchange 2007 servers. Earlier versions of Exchange are not supported, as the new unified messaging functionality depends on the Exchange 2007 Hub Transport server and the Mailbox server roles.

Of course, the requirements (such as PowerShell) for any Exchange 2007 server role apply to the Unified Messaging server.

Telephony Prerequisites

As the Exchange 2007 Unified Messaging server is essentially a voice mail system, all the other components must be in place and operational before introducing it. This includes the following:

▶ **PBX**—The existing PBX must be configured with the appropriate hunt groups to route calls correctly.

▶ **Hunt groups**—The hunt groups and pilot numbers should be provisioned in the PBX. The Auto Attendant pilot numbers and the subscriber access pilot numbers should be part of a rollover group, so that if one number is busy, the call will roll over to the next line.

NOTE

Set up separate hunt groups and pilot access numbers on the PBX for the Auto Attendant and the subscriber access lines.

▶ **IP/VoIP gateway**—The IP gateway must be configured to route calls from the pilot extensions to the Exchange 2007 UM server IP address. The gateway must also be configured to use SIP over TCP, rather than SIP over UDP. Some gateways will attempt UDP first and then try TCP, resulting in strange connection behavior such as delays in initiating calls.

▶ **Phones**—The phones must be provisioned and assigned to users. At the very least, at least two test phones should be available.

▶ **External lines**—External lines must be provisioned within the PBX.

See the documentation for the specific manufacturer for the details of the configuration for each of the telephony components.

Installing the Unified Messaging Role

The first step is to install the Unified Messaging role. This procedure assumes that the Exchange 2007 server has already been installed. To add the Unified Messaging server role, complete the following steps:

1. In Control Panel, select Add or Remove Programs.

2. Select Microsoft Exchange Server 2007.

3. Click the Change button to enter Exchange Maintenance mode.

4. Click Next.

5. Select the Unified Messaging Role check box, as shown in Figure 24.9, and click Next.

6. The installer conducts readiness checks.

7. Click the Install button to install the Unified Messaging server role.

8. After the installation has successfully completed, click Finish.

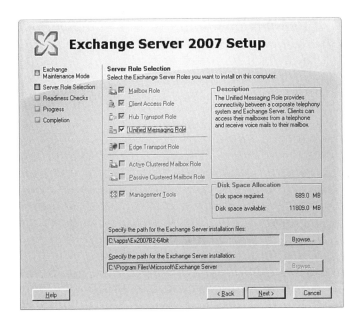

FIGURE 24.9   Choosing the Unified Messaging Role from the setup screen.

The basic software has been installed, but the UM server needs to be configured post-installation to function properly.

Postinstall Configuration

After the server has the Unified Messaging server role installed, you need to complete several postinstall configuration tasks for a basic installation:

- ▶ Create a UM dial plan.

- ▶ Associate subscriber access numbers.

- ▶ Create a UM IP gateway.

- ▶ Associate the UM server with the dial plan.

- ▶ Create a UM Auto Attendant.

- ▶ Create the hunt groups.

- ▶ Enable mailboxes for UM.

- ▶ Test functionality.

Following these tasks results in a functioning Exchange 2007 Unified Messaging system. The remainder of this section details the installation steps for each task.

Creating a UM Dial Plan

The first task is to create the central organizing element of the Exchange 2007 UM infra-structure—the dial plan shown in Figure 24.10.

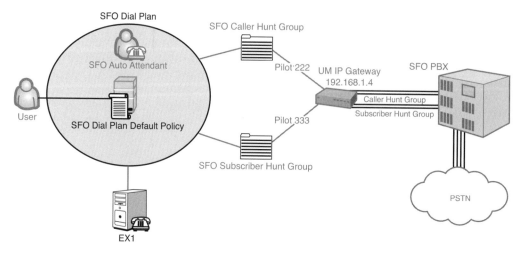

FIGURE 24.10   Creating the dial plan.

To create a dial plan, execute the following steps:

1. Launch the Exchange Management Console.

2. Under the Organization Configuration folder, select the Unified Messaging container.

3. Select the UM Dial Plan tab.

4. In the Action menu, select New UM Dial Plan.

5. Enter the dial plan name, such as SFO Dial Plan.

6. Enter the number of digits in the PBX extensions, such as 3.

7. Click New to create the UM dial plan.

8. Click Finish to close the wizard.

The newly created dial plan should be shown in the results pane. Notice in the figure that the default mailbox policy (SFO Dial Plan Default Policy) was automatically created at the same time.

Associating Subscriber Access Numbers

For subscribers to access their mailbox, one or more subscriber access numbers must be specified in the dial plan. This should be the pilot number for the PBX hunt group that the subscribers will use.

To associate a subscriber access extension to the dial plan, execute the following steps:

1. Launch the Exchange Management Console.

2. Under the Organization Configuration folder, select the Unified Messaging container.

3. Select the UM Dial Plan tab.

4. Select the dial plan in the results pane, such as SFO Dial Plan.

5. In the Action menu, select Properties.

6. Select the Subscriber Access tab.

7. Enter the extension that subscribers will use to access their mailboxes, such as 333.

8. Click Add.

9. Click OK to close the window.

The UM server will now recognize that subscribers will use the extension to access their mailboxes.

Creating a UM IP Gateway

The next task is to create an UM IP gateway to link the dial plan with the IP/VoIP gateway and the PBX. This is shown in Figure 24.11.

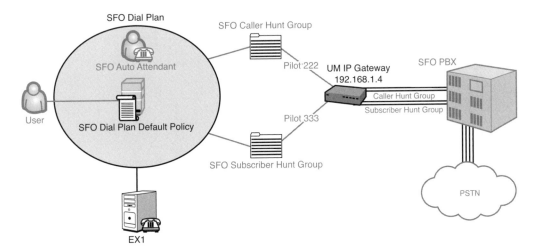

FIGURE 24.11   Creating an IP gateway.

To create the UM IP gateway, execute the following steps:

1. Launch the Exchange Management Console.

2. Under the Organization Configuration folder, select the Unified Messaging container.

3. Select the UM IP Gateway tab.

4. In the Action pane, click New UM IP Gateway.

5. Enter the IP gateway name, such as SFO IP Gateway.

6. Enter the IP address for the IP gateway, such as 192.168.1.4 shown in Figure 24.12.

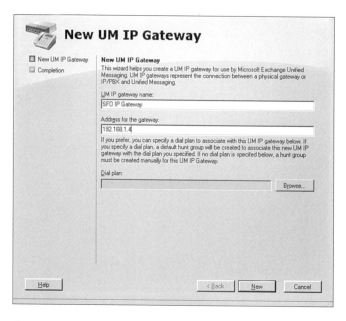

FIGURE 24.12   New UM IP gateway.

7. Click Browse.

8. Select a dial plan to associate the IP gateway with, such as the SFO Dial Plan.

9. This also creates a default hunt group (which will be deleted later).

10. Click OK.

11. Click New to create the UM IP gateway.

12. Click Finish to close the wizard.

The newly created UM IP gateway should be shown in the results pane. The default hunt group will be removed and a new one created in a later task.

Associating the UM Server with the Dial Plan

The dial plan needs to be associated with the UM server that was installed in the first task. This eventually causes the UM server to register with the IP/VoIP gateway to receive calls.

To associate the UM server with the new dial plan, execute the following steps:

1. Launch the Exchange Management Console.
2. Under the Server Configuration folder, select the Unified Messaging container.
3. Select the Unified Messaging server.
4. In the actions pane, click Properties.
5. Select the UM Settings tab.
6. Click Add.
7. Select the dial plan to associate, such as the SFO Dial Plan.
8. Click OK.
9. Click OK to close the Properties dialog box.

The pilot number will now be associated to the dial plan for subscriber access.

Create a Unified Messaging Auto Attendant

For the UM server to answer callers, a UM Auto Attendant must be created and associated with a dial plan. This allows incoming calls to be answered and directed to the appropriate voice mailbox.

To create an Auto Attendant and associate it with a dial plan, execute the following tasks.

1. Launch the Exchange Management Console.
2. Under the Organization Configuration folder, select the Unified Messaging container.
3. Select the UM Auto Attendant tab.
4. In the actions pane, click New UM Auto Attendant.
5. Enter the name of the Auto Attendant, such as SFO Auto Attendant.
6. Click Browse.
7. Select a dial plan, such as the SFO Dial Plan.
8. Click OK.
9. Enter the pilot extension number, such as 222, and click Add.
10. Check the Create Auto Attendant as Enabled check box.

11. Check the Create Auto Attendant as Speech-Enabled check box, shown in Figure 24.13, if you want the Auto Attendant to accept voice commands.

FIGURE 24.13   Creating an Auto Attendant.

12. Click New.

13. Click Finish to close the wizard.

The newly created auto attendant should be shown in the results pane.

NOTE

If the Auto Attendant is created as speech-enabled, a secondary fallback Auto Attendant that is not speech-enabled should be created and that option configured on the primary Auto Attendant. If a user cannot use voice commands, he can use DTMF commands on the secondary Auto Attendant.

Creating the Hunt Groups

The default hunt group that is created with the UM IP gateway does not contain a pilot number. To have the system handle incoming calls correctly, the default hunt group should be deleted and new ones created for the caller and subscriber hunt groups.

To accomplish the creation of the hunt groups, execute the following steps:

1. Launch the Exchange Management Console.

2. Under the Organization Configuration folder, select the Unified Messaging container.

3. Select the UM IP Gateway tab.

4. Select the DefaultHuntGroup in the results pane.

5. In the actions pane, click Remove.

6. At the prompt, click Yes.

7. Select the UM IP gateway, such as SFO IP Gateway.

8. In the actions pane, click New UM Hunt Group.

9. Enter the caller hunt group name, such as SFO Caller Hunt Group.

10. Click Browse.

11. Select the dial plan to associate, such as SFO Dial Plan.

12. Click OK.

13. Enter the hunt group pilot number, such as 222.

14. Click New.

15. Click Finish.

16. Repeat steps 7 through 14, using SFO Subscriber Hunt Group as the name and 333 as the hunt group pilot.

The result of the configuration is shown in Figure 24.14, including the new hunt groups.

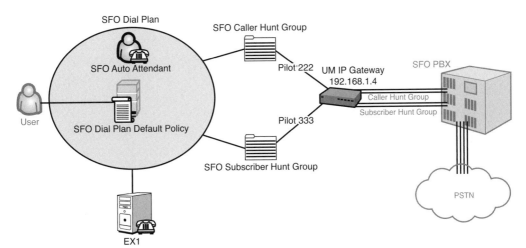

FIGURE 24.14   Creation of hunt groups.

The system is now configured and ready for the final configuration step in the basic configuration—the enabling of a user for unified messaging.

Enabling Mailboxes for UM

The last task is to enable a user's mailbox. This associates the user with a mailbox policy and, therefore, to the rest of the unified messaging infrastructure all the way to the PBX.

To enable a user, execute the following steps:

1. Launch the Exchange Management Console.

2. Under the Recipient Configuration folder, select the Mailbox folder.

3. In the results pane, select the user to be enabled.

4. In the actions pane, select Enable Unified Messaging.

5. Click Browse.

6. Select the UM policy, such as the SFO Dial Plan Default Policy.

7. Click OK.

8. Enter the extension, such as 102, shown in Figure 24.15.

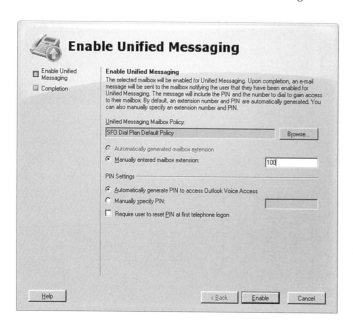

FIGURE 24.15   Enabling a user for unified messaging.

9. Click Enable.

10. Click Finish to close the wizard.

A simple welcome email message with the extension and their confidential PIN will be automatically sent to their Exchange mailbox.

Testing Functionality

The final step is to make sure that it is all working. This could be the most difficult testing tasks for an average Exchange administrator, as they will be the least familiar with the telephony elements of the infrastructure.

It is important to make sure that these critical functions be tested:

- ▶ The UM server is operating.

- ▶ The UM server can connect to the gateway and PBX.

- ▶ The UM server can be reached from an internal phone.

- ▶ The UM server can be reached from an external phone.

Figure 24.16 shows the paths of the critical tests.

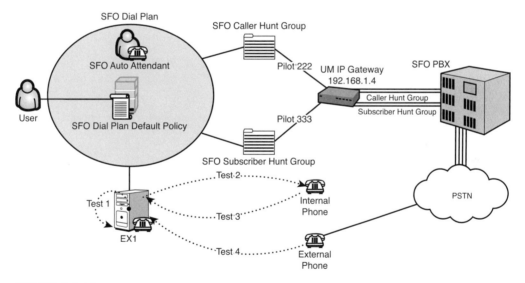

FIGURE 24.16   Testing the UM server.

The specific commands and steps for testing are discussed in the following sections.

Testing Unified Messaging Server Operation

The Unified Messaging server operations test needs to run on the local UM server in the Exchange Management Shell. The shell command is:

```
Test-UMConnectivity
```

This command attempts a diagnostic SIP call and reports back on the success. Figure 24.17 shows the result of a successful test. Specifically, the value of EntireOperationSuccess is True.

FIGURE 24.17   Testing the UM server.

Testing Unified Messaging Server Connectivity

This test shows if the UM server can communicate with the PBX and access a phone. Specifically, it causes the internal phone to ring.

The command needs to be run from the Exchange Management Shell. The command syntax is:

```
Test-UMConnectivity -IPGateway "IP Gateway Name" -Phone extension
```

For example, the command might be:

```
Test-UMConnectivity -IPGateway "SFO IP Gateway" -Phone 102
```

The results for a successful test are shown in Figure 24.18. The phone at the extension should ring. If the test is successful, it will show that "The call was disconnected by the other party" at the end of the test.

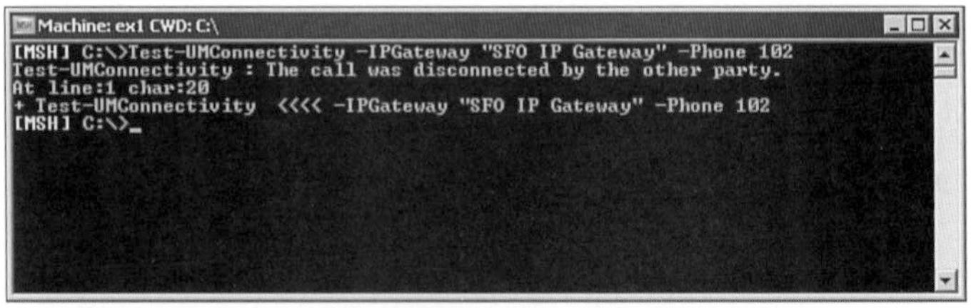

FIGURE 24.18   Connectivity success.

To show the results of an unsuccessful test, enter the command:

```
Test-UMConnectivity -IPGateway "SFO IP Gateway" -Phone 104
```

This command specifies a nonexistent extension. The results are shown in Figure 24.19. It shows that the requested operation failed.

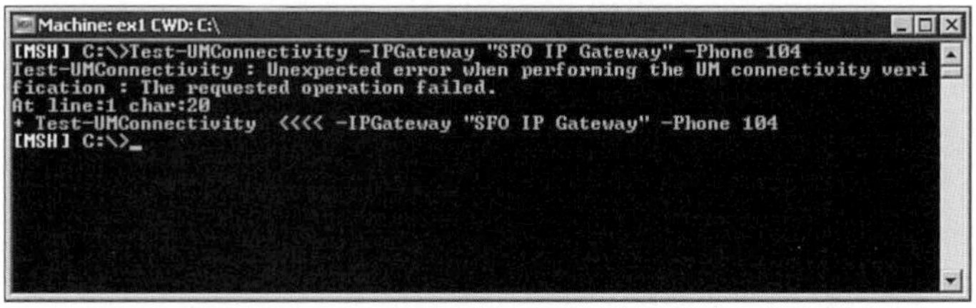

FIGURE 24.19   Connectivity failure.

Testing Unified Messaging Server with an Internal Phone

To test the Unified Messaging server from a phone, pick up a phone from within the dial plan and dial the pilot number.

For example, from the phone at extension 102, dial the pilot number 222. The Auto Attendant should pick up and prompt the caller.

Leave a message for a test user and then hang up.

Dial the pilot number for subscriber access (for example, extension 333) and check the message. Alternatively, check the message using Outlook or Outlook Web Access.

Testing Unified Messaging Server with an External Phone

Use an outside line to call the company number that the PBX routes to the caller hunt group. Say the user's name. Press # to leave a message and leave a message for the user.

To verify the message was received, dial the external number for subscriber access and check the message. Alternatively, check the message using Outlook or Outlook Web Access.

Data Storage in Unified Messaging

Unified messaging stores data in a variety of locations and formats. The different types of data include custom audio prompts, incoming calls, configuration, and setup.

It is important to understand where the data is stored, the relative importance of backing it up, and the method of restoring the data. Tables 24.4, 24.5, 24.6, and 24.7 list the relevant data storage information for each type of data.

TABLE 24.4   Custom Audio Prompt Data

Data Type	Custom audio files (.wav) for UM dial plans and UM Auto Attendants
	Custom audio files (.wav) for telephone user interface (TUI) and Outlook Voice Access
Storage	File system in \UnifiedMessaging\Prompts
Backup	File-level backup is only needed on the prompt publishing server
Restore	File-level restore is only needed on the prompt publishing server

TABLE 24.5   Incoming Call Data

Critical Data	Incoming calls: .eml and .wma files for each voice mail
Storage	File system \UnifiedMessaging\temp
Backup	None
Restore	None

TABLE 24.6   Server Configuration Data

Critical Data	Server configuration data, including all objects and settings
Storage	Active Directory configuration container
Backup	Backup method is domain controller replication or Active Directory backup
Restore	This data is reapplied to the server during a setup /m:recoverserver restore

TABLE 24.7   Setup Data

Critical Data	Limited information is stored in the Registry by Setup that is not essential to server restore
Storage	HKLM\SOFTWARE\Microsoft\Exchange
	HKLM\SYSTEM\currentcontrolset\Services
Backup	Backup method is System State backup or Registry export
Restore	Restore method is System State restore or Registry import

Monitoring and Troubleshooting Unified Messaging

A number of tools are built in to the Exchange 2007 unified messaging platform to support the troubleshooting and monitoring of the services.

First and foremost, it is highly recommended that administrators deploy Microsoft Operations Manager (MOM) 2005 to monitor the Exchange 2007 infrastructure. There is a management pack specific to the Exchange 2007 platform with a wealth of knowledge built in. See Chapter 20, "Using Microsoft Operations Manager to Monitor Exchange Server 2007," for more details on MOM and Exchange 2007.

That said, it is still important for the Exchange administrator to have a good knowledge and familiarity with the tools that are available to monitor Exchange 2007 unified messaging. These tools include the following:

- Exchange Management Shell test cmdlets

- Performance Monitor objects and counters

- Event log messages

- Removing the first UM server

These tools and techniques are covered in the next sections.

Active Calls

The system can provide information on active calls, which is very useful for monitoring and troubleshooting the unified messaging system. The Get-UMActiveCalls cmdlet returns information about the calls that are active and being processed by the Unified Messaging (UM) server. The syntax for the cmdlet is given in Table 24.8.

TABLE 24.8   Get-UMActiveCalls cmdlets

Syntax
Get-UMActiveCalls [-Server <ServerIdParameter>]
Get-UMActiveCalls -InstanceServer <UMServer>
Get-UMActiveCalls -DialPlan <UMDialPlanIdParameter>
Get-UMActiveCalls -IPGateway <UMIPGatewayIdParameter>

Figure 24.20 shows two instances of the command. In the first execution of the command, it shows an active call with the DialedNumber of 333, indicating that it has come in via the subscriber access line configured in the example installation. In the second execution of the command, it shows that the caller has dialed extension 102.

Connectivity

Connectivity to the IP/VoIP gateway can be one of the most troublesome aspects of the deployment and support of a unified messaging system. The Test-UMConnectivity cmdlet can be used to test the operation of a computer that has the Unified Messaging server role installed. The syntax for the cmdlet is given in Table 24.9.

TABLE 24.9   Test-UMConnectivity cmdlet

Syntax
test-UMConnectivity [-Fax <$true | $false>] [-ListenPort <Int32>]
➥[-MonitoringContext <$true | $false>] [-Secured <$true | $false>] [-Timeout <Int32>]
test-UMConnectivity -IPGateway <UMIPGatewayIdParameter> -Phone <String>
➥[-Fax <$true | $false>] [-ListenPort <Int32>] [-MonitoringContext <$true | $false>]
➥[-Secured <$true | $false>] [-Timeout <Int32>]

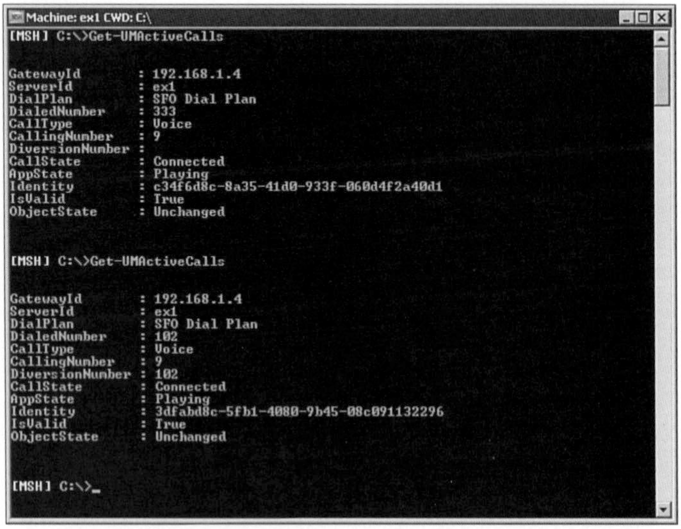

FIGURE 24.20   Active calls.

This test was used in the installation section of this chapter to test the functionality of the UM server. See the section "Testing Functionality" earlier in this chapter for details of the command usage.

Performance Monitors

Unlike many applications, the Exchange 2007 unified messaging application is very well instrumented.

Tables of the counters for each of the monitored objects are noted in the balance of this section.

General Performance Counters for Unified Messaging

The counters listed in Table 24.10 are under the MSExchangeUMGeneral performance object and are useful for monitoring and troubleshooting general problems with the Exchange 2007 UM server.

TABLE 24.10   Counters for the MSExchangeUMGeneral Object

Performance Counter	Description
Total Calls	The number of calls since the service was started.
Total Calls per Second	The number of new calls that arrived in the last second.
Calls Dropped by User Failure	The total number of calls disconnected after too many user entry failures.
Calls Rejected	The total number of new call invitations that have been rejected.

TABLE 24.10   Continued

Performance Counter	Description
Calls Rejected per Second	The number of new call invitations that have been rejected in the last second.
Current Calls	The number of calls currently connected to the UM server.
Current Voice Calls	The number of voice calls currently connected to the UM server.
Current Fax Calls	The number of fax calls currently connected to the UM server. Voice calls become fax calls after a fax tone is detected.
Current Subscriber Access Calls	The number of logged-on subscribers who are currently connected to the UM server.
Current Auto Attendant Calls	The number of Auto Attendant calls that are currently connected to the UM server.
Current Play on Phone Calls	The number of outbound calls initiated to play back messages.
Current Unauthenticated Pilot Number Calls	The number of voice calls to the pilot number that have not yet been authenticated.
Total Play to Phone Calls	The total number of Play to Phone calls that were initiated since the service was started.
Average Call Duration	The average duration, in seconds, of calls since the service was started.
Average Recent Call Duration	The average duration, in seconds, of the last 50 calls.
User Response Latency	The average response time, in milliseconds, for the system to respond to a user request. This average is calculated over the last 25 calls. This counter is limited to calls that require significant processing.
Delayed Calls	The number of calls that experienced one or more delays longer than 2 seconds.
Call Duration Exceeded	The number of calls that were disconnected because they exceeded the UM maximum call length. This number includes all types of calls, including fax calls.
Current CAS Connections	The number of connections that are currently open between the UM server and client access servers.

Call Answering Performance Counters for Unified Messaging

The counters listed in Table 24.11 are under the `MSExchangeUMCallAnswering` performance object and are useful for monitoring and troubleshooting call answering problems with the Exchange 2007 UM server.

TABLE 24.11   Counters for the MSExchangeUMCallAnswering Object

Performance Counter	Description
Call Answering Calls	The number of diverted calls that were answered on behalf of subscribers
Call Answering Voice Messages	The total number of messages that were submitted because the calls were answered on behalf of subscribers
Call Answering Voice Messages per Second	The number of messages that were submitted because the calls were answered on behalf of subscribers
Call Answering Missed Calls	The number of times a diverted call was dropped without a message being left
Call Answering Escapes	The number of times a caller pressed the * key to connect to another user rather than leaving a message
Average Voice Message Size	The average size, in seconds, of voice messages left for subscribers
Average Recent Message Size	The average size, in seconds, of the last 50 voice messages left for subscribers
Average Greeting Size	The average size, in seconds, of recorded greetings that have been retrieved by the UM server
Calls Without Personal Greetings	The number of diverted calls received for subscribers who did not have recorded greeting messages
Fetch Greeting Failure	The number of diverted calls for which the subscriber's personal greeting could not be retrieved within the time allowed
Hung Up After Delay	The number of callers who disconnected after encountering a significant delay
Diverted Extension Not Provisioned	The number of calls received for which the diverted extension supplied with the call is not a UM subscriber extension

Fax Answering Performance Counters for Unified Messaging

The counters listed in Table 24.12 are under the MSExchangeUMFax performance object and are useful for monitoring and troubleshooting fax problems with the Exchange 2007 UM server.

TABLE 24.12   Counters for the MSExchangeUMFax Object

Performance Counter	Description
Fax Messages	The total number of fax messages received
Average Fax Message Size	The average size, in kilobytes, of fax messages received
Average Recent Fax Message Size	The average size, in kilobytes, of the last 20 fax messages
Fax Call Duration Exceeded	The number of fax calls that were disconnected because they exceeded the UM maximum call length
Fax Incomplete	The number of fax calls that were dropped before completion

TABLE 24.12   Continued

Performance Counter	Description
Fax Calls to Non Provisioned Mailboxes	The number of calls to extensions that resolved to mailboxes that are not enabled for fax

Subscriber Access Performance Counters for Unified Messaging

The counters listed in Table 24.13 are under the MSExchangeUMSubscriberAccess performance object and are useful for monitoring and troubleshooting subscriber access problems with the Exchange 2007 UM server.

The variety of counters in the subscriber access area is impressive and can really aid in the understanding of the behavior of the subscribers.

TABLE 24.13   Counters for the MSExchangeUMSubscriberAccess Object

Performance Counter	Description
Subscriber Logon	The number of UM subscribers who have successfully authenticated since the service was started.
Subscriber Logon Failures	The number of authentication failures since the service was started. This number is incremented once when all three per-call logon attempts fail.
Average Subscriber Call Duration	The average duration, in seconds, that subscribers spent logged on to the system. This timer starts when logon completes.
Average Subscriber Recent Call Duration	The average length of time, in seconds, that subscribers spent logged on to the system for the last 50 subscriber calls.
Voice Message Queue Accessed	The number of times subscribers accessed their voice message queues using the telephone user interface.
Voice Messages Heard	The number of voice messages played to subscribers. This count is incremented as soon as playback starts. The subscriber does not need to listen to the entire message.
Voice Messages Sent	The number of voice messages sent by authenticated UM subscribers.
Average Sent Voice Message Size	The average size, in seconds, of voice messages that are sent. This size does not include any attachment data.
Average Recent Sent Voice Message Size	The average size, in seconds, of the last 50 voice messages that were sent.
Voice Messages Deleted	The number of voice messages that were deleted by authenticated subscribers.
Reply Messages Sent	The number of replies sent by authenticated subscribers.
Forward Messages Sent	The number of messages forwarded by authenticated subscribers.
Email Message Queue Accessed	The number of times subscribers accessed their email message queue using the telephone user interface.

24

TABLE 24.13   Continued

Performance Counter	Description
Email Messages Heard	The number of email messages heard by authenticated subscribers.
Email Messages Deleted	The number of email messages deleted by authenticated subscribers.
Calendar Accessed	The number of times subscribers accessed their calendars using the telephone user interface.
Calendar Items Heard	The number of calendar items heard by authenticated subscribers.
Calendar Late Attendance	The number of messages sent to inform the organizer of a meeting that the subscriber will be late.
Calendar Items Details Requested	The number of times a subscriber requested additional details for a calendar item.
Meetings Declined	The number of Meeting Declined messages sent by subscribers.
Meetings Accepted	The number of Meeting Accepted messages sent by subscribers.
Called Meeting Organizer	The number of times subscribers called the meeting organizer.
Replied to Organizer	The number of times subscribers sent reply messages to meeting organizers.
Contacts Accessed	The number of times subscribers accessed the Main Menu Contacts option using the telephone user interface.
Contact Items Heard	The number of times authenticated subscribers listened to directory details.
Hung Up During Delay	The number of times subscribers disconnected during a system delay.
Launched Calls	The number of subscriber calls that resulted in an outbound call being placed.
Directory Accessed	The number of times subscribers accessed the Main Menu Directory option using the telephone user interface.
Directory Accessed by Extension	The number of directory access operations in which the user supplied the extension number.
Directory Accessed by Dial by Name	The number of directory access operations where the subscriber used the Dial by Name feature.
Directory Accessed Successfully by Dial by Name	The number of dial by name directory access operations that completed successfully on behalf of subscribers.
Directory Accessed by Spoken Name	The number of directory access operations in which the subscriber spoke a recipient name.
Directory Accessed Successfully by Spoken Name	The number of speech-recognition directory access operations that completed successfully on behalf of subscribers.

Unified Messaging Auto Attendant Performance Counters

The counters listed in Table 24.14 are under the `MSExchangeUMAutoAttendant` performance object and are useful for monitoring and troubleshooting Auto Attendant problems with the Exchange 2007 UM server.

The variety of counters in the Auto Attendant area is impressive and can really aid in the understanding of the behavior of the callers, the menu choices they make, how long they stay in the system, and their preferred method of access to the menus.

TABLE 24.14   Counters for the `MSExchangeUMAutoAttendant` Object

Performance Counter	Description
Total Calls	The number of calls that have been processed by this Auto Attendant.
Business Hours Calls	The number of calls processed by this Auto Attendant during business hours.
Out of Hours Calls	The number of calls processed by this Auto Attendant outside of business hours.
Disconnected Without Input	The number of calls that were dropped without any input being offered to the Auto Attendant prompts.
Transferred Count	The number of calls that were transferred by this Auto Attendant. This number does not include calls that were transferred by the operator.
Directory Accessed	The number of directory access operations performed by this Auto Attendant.
Directory Accessed by Extension	The number of directory access operations in which the user supplied the extension number.
Directory Accessed by Dial by Name	The number of directory access operations in which the subscriber used the Dial by Name feature.
Directory Accessed Successfully by Dial by Name	The number of successful directory access operations in which the caller used the Dial by Name feature.
Directory Accessed by Spoken Name	The number of directory access operations in which the subscriber spoke a recipient name.
Directory Accessed Successfully by Spoken Name	The number of successful directory access operations in which the caller used the Dial by Name feature.
Operator Transfers	The number of calls that were transferred to the operator.
Menu Option 1 Used	The number of times that a caller has chosen option 1 from the custom menu. This value is always zero if no menu or option is defined.
Menu Option 2 Used	The number of times that a caller has chosen option 2 from the custom menu. This value is always zero if no menu or option is defined.
Menu Option 3 Used	The number of times that a caller has chosen option 3 from the custom menu. This value is always zero if no menu or option is defined.

TABLE 24.14   Continued

Performance Counter	Description
Menu Option 4 Used	The number of times that a caller has chosen option 4 from the custom menu. This value is always zero if no menu or option is defined.
Menu Option 5 Used	The number of times that a caller has chosen option 5 from the custom menu. This value is always zero if no menu or option is defined.
Menu Option 6 Used	The number of times that a caller has chosen option 6 from the custom menu. This value is always zero if no menu or option is defined.
Menu Option 7 Used	The number of times that a caller has chosen option 7 from the custom menu. This value is always zero if no menu or option is defined.
Menu Option 8 Used	The number of times that a caller has chosen option 8 from the custom menu. This value is always zero if no menu or option is defined.
Menu Option 9 Used	The number of times that a caller has chosen option 9 from the custom menu. This value is always zero if no menu or option is defined.
Menu Option Timed Out	The number of times that the system has timed out waiting for a caller to select an option from the custom menu. This value is always zero if no menu is defined.
Average Call Time	The average length of time that callers interacted with the Auto Attendant.
Average Recent Call Time	The average length of time, in seconds, of the last 50 Auto Attendant calls.
Speech Calls	The total number of calls during which the caller is determined to have spoken at least once.
Ambiguous Name Transfers	The number of times that a caller was transferred to the operator because the name that they spelled or spoke was too common in the search results.

System Resources and Availability Counters for Unified Messaging
The counters listed in Table 24.15 are under the MSExchangeAvailability performance object and are useful for monitoring and troubleshooting system resource and availability problems with the Exchange 2007 UM server.

TABLE 24.15   Counters for the `MSExchangeAvailability` Object

Performance Counter	Description
Directory Access Failures	The number of times that attempts to access Active Directory failed.
Bridgehead Access Completed	The number of times that the bridgehead server was accessed successfully.
Bridgehead Access Failures	The number of times that attempts to access a bridge-head server failed. This number is only incremented if all bridgehead servers were unavailable.
Mailbox Server Access Failures	The number of times the system failed to access a Mailbox server.
Maximum Calls Allowed	The length of time, in seconds, that the server was concurrently processing the maximum number of calls allowed.
Worker Process Recycled	The number of times a new UM worker process has been started.
Failed to Redirect Call	The number of times the unified messaging service failed to redirect calls to a UM worker process.
Total Worker Process Call Count	The total number of calls handled by this UM worker process.
Unhandled Exceptions	The number of calls that encountered an unhandled exception.
Unhandled Exceptions per Second	The number of calls that encountered an unhandled exception in the last second.
Incomplete Signaling Information	The number of calls for which the signaling information was missing or incomplete.
Calls Dropped by System Failure	The total number of calls disconnected after a system failure.
Calls Dropped by System Failure per Second	The number of calls disconnected after a system failure in the last second.
Call Answer Queued Messages	The number of messages created and not yet submitted for delivery.
Spoken Name Accessed	The number of times the system retrieved the recorded name of a user.
Name TTSed	The number of times the system used text-to-speech to create an audio version of the display name of a subscriber.

Unified Messaging Performance Monitoring Counters

The counters listed in Table 24.16 are under the `MSExchangeUMPerformance` performance object and are useful for monitoring and troubleshooting server latency problems with the Exchange 2007 UM server. These counters measure the time in number of seconds that server operations took. This is an important measure of the time that callers are waiting for the UM server to complete a task.

TABLE 24.16   Counters for the `MSExchangeUMPerformance` Object

Performance Counter	Description
Operations over Two Seconds	The number of all UM operations that took between 2 and 3 seconds to complete. This is the time during which a caller was waiting for UM to respond.
Operations over Three Seconds	The number of all UM operations that took between 3 and 4 seconds to complete. This is the time during which a caller was waiting for UM to respond.
Operations over Four Seconds	The number of all UM operations that took between 4 and 5 seconds to complete. This is the time during which a caller was waiting for UM to respond.
Operations over Five Seconds	The number of all UM operations that took between 5 and 6 seconds to complete. This is the time during which a caller was waiting for UM to respond.
Operations over Six Seconds	The number of all UM operations that took more than 6 seconds to complete. This is the time during which a caller was waiting for UM to respond.

Event Logs

Event logs are important for troubleshooting Microsoft Exchange unified messaging. Each of the different aspects of a Unified Messaging server generate their own set of error messages. The tables of events show the errors and events that could be generated for each of the following categories:

▶ Call answering

▶ Fax answering

▶ Subscriber access

▶ Auto Attendant

▶ Administrative

▶ System

▶ Performance

The event log messages are very detailed and specific to many conditions, making it very easy to understand, audit, troubleshoot, and instrument the Unified Messaging server.

Table 24.17 shows the error events that can be generated for call answering.

TABLE 24.17   Call Answering Errors and Events

Description	Event Type
A diverted call was received for extension that is not enabled for unified messaging.	Informational
The call is being refused because Active Directory is not available. The call is from calling party calling-number and dialed called-number.	Warning
The call is being refused because the bridgehead server is unavailable. The call is from calling party calling-number and dialed called-number.	Warning
The bridgehead server is not available at the point of submission. The message is being stored locally.	Warning
The call is being refused because the spooler has reached the maximum of n messages. The call is from calling party calling-number and dialed called-number.	Warning
Mailbox is unavailable. A greeting is being synthesized for this mailbox.	Informational
The session was terminated because the message is too long.	Informational
The caller was not able to leave a message because the target mailbox is full.	Informational
The message was not delivered because it is shorter than the minimum message length.	Informational

Table 24.18 shows the error events that can be generated for fax calls.

TABLE 24.18   Fax Answering Errors and Events

Description	Event Type
A fax tone was detected for mailbox, which is not enabled for fax.	Informational
A fax tone was detected on a system that is not enabled for fax. The call was for mailbox.	Informational
A fax tone was detected after a voice mail message was recorded. Two messages will be submitted for mailbox.	Informational
A fax tone was detected, but the call is being dropped because the number of concurrent fax calls has reached the maximum allowed. The call was for mailbox.	Warning
A fax protocol error caused the call to terminate prematurely. The call was for mailbox.	Warning
The bridgehead server is not available at the point of submission. The message is being stored locally.	Warning
The call is being refused because the spooler has reached the maximum of n messages. The call is from calling party calling-number and dialed called-number.	Warning
The fax call was refused because the target mailbox is full.	Informational

24

Table 24.19 shows the error events that can be generated for fax calls.

TABLE 24.19   Subscriber Access Errors and Events

Description	Event Type
The user failed to log on n times. The mailbox is now locked out.	Warning
The call-id was disconnected because the logon failed n times for mailbox.	Informational
User was disconnected after n incorrect responses.	Informational
The message that user attempted to send failed because their mailbox is full.	Informational
User reset their PIN.	Informational
User attempted to access their mailbox, which is locked out.	Informational
User failed to log on because their PIN checksum has been tampered with.	Warning
Language associated with mailbox is not installed.	Warning

Table 24.20 shows the error events that can be generated by the Auto Attendant.

TABLE 24.20   Auto Attendant Errors and Events

Description	Event Type
The caller was disconnected after n incorrect responses.	Informational
The referenced critical audio file was missing.	Error
The referenced audio file was missing.	Warning
The language referenced by the automated attendant is not installed.	Warning
The Auto Attendant name referenced an operator extension that is missing.	Error

Table 24.21 shows the administrative events that can be generated by the Unified Messaging server. These events make it easy to track what administrative changes are being made within the UM system.

TABLE 24.21   Administrative Errors and Events

Description	Event Type
The account for user was enabled.	Informational
The account for user was disabled.	Informational
The settings for user were modified.	Informational
The account was locked out.	Warning
The account was reenabled.	Informational
The PIN for user was changed.	Informational
User PIN policies were changed.	Informational
A server property was changed for server.	Informational
A dial plan property was changed for dial plan dial plan.	Informational
A new dial plan object dial plan was created.	Informational
Dial plan dial plan was removed.	Informational
An IP gateway property was changed for gateway.	Informational
A new IP gateway object gateway was created.	Informational

TABLE 24.21   Continued

Description	Event Type
Gateway was removed.	Informational
Auto attendant AA was removed.	Informational
A UMAutoAttendant property was changed for auto attendant auto attendant.	Informational
A new auto attendant auto attendant was created.	Informational

Table 24.22 shows the system error events that can be generated by the Unified Messaging server.

TABLE 24.22   Unified Messaging System Errors and Events

Description	Event Type
The service is starting.	Informational
The service failed to start. The startup operation returned an error.	Error
The service started successfully.	Informational
The service started, but no IP gateway is defined for the dial plans associated with this server.	Warning
The service started, but the server is not associated with any dial plans.	Warning
Communication was established with IP gateway x.	Informational
The attempt to communicate with IP gateway x failed.	Error
TTS operation for language is being initialized.	Informational
TTS for language was initialized.	Informational
TTS for language failed.	Error
The Fax service was loaded.	Informational
Auto Attendant name is enabled.	Informational
Auto Attendant name is missing audio prompts.	Warning
The Operator extension is missing.	Warning
The UM server is preparing to shut down and is not accepting new calls.	Informational
The service is being stopped.	Informational
The service could not be stopped.	Warning
The UM server is shutting down immediately. X current calls will be disconnected.	Warning
The UM service encountered an unhandled exception during call ID. The call has been disconnected.	Error
The conversion request was denied because the TTS concurrent sessions limit was exceeded.	Warning
The TTS engine threw an exception.	Error
TTS engine error. TTS failed to convert text.	Error
A new call arrived without any call signaling information.	Warning
A UM working process is shutting down and not processing new calls.	Informational
A UM working process is shutting down immediately and dropping x existing calls.	Error
A new UM server worker process was created.	Informational

24

Table 24.23 shows the performance warning events that can be generated by the Unified Messaging server.

TABLE 24.23   Unified Messaging Performance Errors and Events

Description	Event Type
The operation has exceeded 4 seconds. The calling number was X, the called number was Y. The mailbox Z was performing the operation.	Warning
TTS conversion failed to return audio within x seconds.	Warning

Removing the First UM Server in a Dial Plan

The unified messaging prompt publishing point for a dial plan is automatically set at the time that the first Unified Messaging server joins the dial plan. Before you can remove the first Unified Messaging server, you need to migrate all of the custom prompts and then set the new server as the prompt publishing point.

For each dial plan that has a prompt publishing point on the server to be removed, run the following Exchange Management Shell command:

```
Set-UMDialPlan -Identity <Dial_Plan_Name> -PromptPublishingPoint
<UNC_Path_to_PromptPublishingPoint_Share_On_New_Server>
```

Then copy all of the contents of the old Universal Naming Convention (UNC) path to the new UNC path. The first Unified Messaging server can now be removed safely.

Unified Messaging Shell Commands

Sometimes, just finding commands in the Exchange Management Shell can be a daunting task. In this section, each of the unified messaging commands is listed by verb.

For each of the commands, the detailed syntax can be obtained by executing the command `help cmdlet`. For example, to get help on the cmdlet Add-ADPermission, execute the command `help adpermission` in the Exchange Management Shell interface shown in Figure 24.21.

Add/Remove Verb Cmdlets

Table 24.24 lists all the Exchange 2007 unified messaging specific add/remove verb cmdlets.

TABLE 24.24   Add/Remove Cmdlets

Verb	Noun	Cmdlet Name
Add	ADPermission	Add-ADPermission
Add	ExchangeAdministrator	Add-ExchangeAdministrator
Remove	ADPermission	Remove-ADPermission
Remove	UMAutoAttendant	Remove-UMAutoAttendant

TABLE 24.24   Continued

Verb	Noun	Cmdlet Name
Remove	UMDialPlan	Remove-UMDialPlan
Remove	UMHuntGroup	Remove-UMHuntGroup
Remove	UMIPGateway	Remove-UMIPGateway
Remove	UMMailboxPolicy	Remove-UMMailboxPolicy

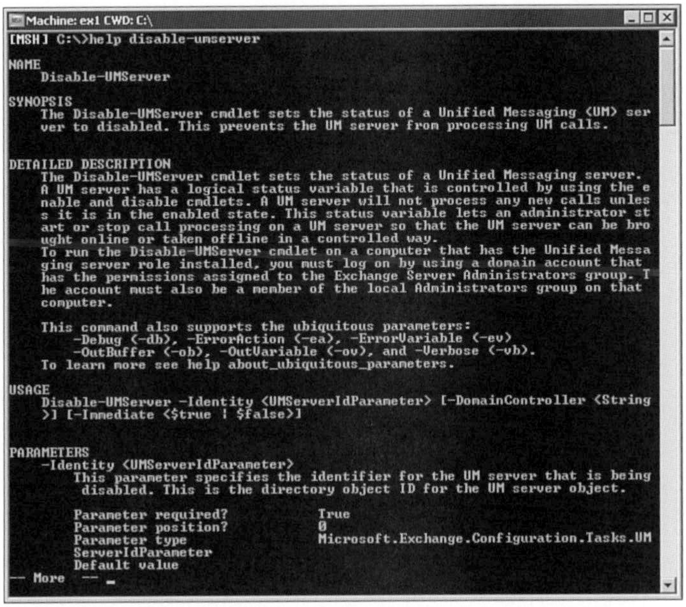

FIGURE 24.21   Exchange Management Shell Help.

Get/Set Verb Cmdlets

Table 24.25 lists all the Exchange 2007 unified messaging specific get/set verb cmdlets.

TABLE 24.25   Get/Set Cmdlets

Verb	Noun	Cmdlet Name
Get	ADPermission	Get-ADPermission
Get	UMActiveCalls	Get-UMActiveCalls
Get	UMAutoAttendant	Get-UMAutoAttendant
Get	UMDialPlan	Get-UMDialPlan
Get	UMHuntGroup	Get-UMHuntGroup
Get	UMIPGateway	Get-UMIPGateway
Get	UMMailbox	Get-UMMailbox
Get	UMMailboxPIN	Get-UMMailboxPIN

TABLE 24.25   Continued

Verb	Noun	Cmdlet Name
Get	UMMailboxPolicy	Get-UMMailboxPolicy
Get	UmServer	Get-UmServer
Set	EventLogLevel	Set-EventLogLevel
Set	UMAutoAttendant	Set-UMAutoAttendant
Set	UMDialPlan	Set-UMDialPlan
Set	UMIPGateway	Set-UMIPGateway
Set	UMMailbox	Set-UMMailbox
Set	UMMailboxPIN	Set-UMMailboxPIN
Set	UMMailboxPolicy	Set-UMMailboxPolicy
Set	UmServer	Set-UmServer

Test Verb Cmdlets

Table 24.26 lists all the Exchange 2007 unified messaging specific test verb cmdlets.

TABLE 24.26   Test Cmdlets

Verb	Noun	Cmdlet Name
Test	SystemHealth	Test-SystemHealth
Test	UMConnectivity	Test-UMConnectivity

Enable/Disable Verb Cmdlets

Table 24.27 lists all the Exchange 2007 unified messaging specific enable/disable verb cmdlets.

TABLE 24.27   Enable/Disable Cmdlets

Verb	Noun	Cmdlet Name
Enable	UMAutoAttendant	Enable-UMAutoAttendant
Enable	UMIPGateway	Enable-UMIPGateway
Enable	UMMailbox	Enable-UMMailbox
Enable	UMServer	Enable-UMServer
Disable	UMAutoAttendant	Disable-UMAutoAttendant
Disable	UMIPGateway	Disable-UMIPGateway
Disable	UMMailbox	Disable-UMMailbox
Disable	UMServer	Disable-UMServer

Copy Verb Cmdlet

Table 24.28 lists the only Exchange 2007 unified messaging specific copy verb cmdlet.

TABLE 24.28   Copy Cmdlet

Verb	Noun	Cmdlet Name
Copy	UMCustomPrompt	Copy-UMCustomPrompt

New Verb Cmdlets

Table 24.29 lists all the Exchange 2007 unified messaging specific new verb cmdlets.

TABLE 24.29   New Cmdlets

Verb	Noun	Cmdlet Name
New	UMAutoAttendant	New-UMAutoAttendant
New	UMDialPlan	New-UMDialPlan
New	UMHuntGroup	New-UMHuntGroup
New	UMIPGateway	New-UMIPGateway
New	UMMailboxPolicy	New-UMMailboxPolicy

SIP Protocol

Session Initiation Protocol (SIP) is an Application-layer signaling protocol for creating, modifying, and terminating sessions with one or more participants.

Given the importance of SIP in the Exchange 2007 unified messaging system, it is important to understand the protocol in some detail. This assists in troubleshooting integration problems between the Unified Messaging server and the IP/VoIP gateway, which is a frequent source of problems.

SIP Terminology

SIP uses specific terminology to define the elements and devices in a SIP call. Table 24.30 lists the various SIP terms and definitions.

TABLE 24.30   SIP Terminology

Term	Description
Methods	SIP commands and messages
Result codes	Responses to SIP methods indicating success, failure, or other information
User Agent	Endpoint devices that can issue or respond to SIP protocol methods (such as the UM server or IP gateway)
User Agent Client	Devices such as phones or PDAs
Server	An application that can accept or respond to SIP methods (for example a UM server)

844   CHAPTER 24   Designing and Configuring Unified Messaging in Exchange Server 2007

TABLE 24.30   Continued

Term	Description
Gateway	A gateway that can convert SIP methods and result codes to another protocol (for example an IP gateway)
Proxy server	A server that can make requests on behalf of other clients

SIP Methods

SIP uses a number of commands or methods within the protocol. Table 24.31 lists the methods that SIP uses.

TABLE 24.31   SIP Methods

Method	Description
REGISTER	Registers a user with a registrar.
INVITE	Session setup request or media negotiation. Used also to hold and retrieve calls.
CANCEL	Used to cancel an in-progress transaction.
ACK	Acknowledgement for an INVITE transaction.
BYE	Terminates a session.
OPTIONS	Used to the remote device status and capabilities.
INFO	Used for mid-call signaling information exchange.
SUBSCRIBE	Request notification of call events.
NOTIFY	Event notification after a subscription.
REFER	Call transfer request.

This table can be useful when doing a protocol trace of a SIP session to determine what the session is doing.

SIP Response Codes

SIP uses a number of response codes, both informational and error related. Table 24.32 lists the response codes that SIP uses.

TABLE 24.32   SIP Response Codes

Response Code	Description
100	Trying
180	Ringing
181	Call is being forwarded
182	Call is being queued
183	Session progress
200	OK
302	Moved temporarily, forward call to a given contact
305	Use proxy: repeat same call setup using a given proxy

TABLE 24.32   Continued

Response Code	Description
400	Bad Request
401	Unauthorized Request
404	Not Found
408	Request Timeout
486	Busy
5xx	Server Failure
6xx	Global Failure

Basic Call Example

The SIP protocol is used to set up calls between and then hands the communication over to the RTP protocol. A basic call sequence for a SIP call setup and teardown in unified messaging looks like the example in Table 24.33.

TABLE 24.33   Basic SIP Call Example

IP Gateway	Direction	UM Server
INVITE	——>	
	<——	180 Ringing
	<——	200 OK
ACK	——>	
RTP	<——>	RTP
	<——	BYE
200 OK	——>	

Notice that after the IP gates sends an SIP ACK method back to the Unified Messaging server, the call is handed off to the RTP protocol. After the call is complete, the Unified Messaging server sends a SIP BYE method to terminate the communication.

Summary

The new features of Microsoft Exchange 2007 unified messaging provide a range of new features for integrating telephony into the Exchange platform, creating a single unified Inbox for all messages. This brings not only a host of new telephony concepts and technologies for the Exchange administrator to master, it also brings a wealth of new and exciting features that provide a rich experience to the Exchange users.

Best Practices

The following are best practices from this chapter:

▶ Allow transfers to the operator at least during business hours to reduce caller frustration.

▶ Be careful when implementing mailbox quotas because it can impact the ability of users to receive voice mail.

▶ Create a secondary Auto Attendant that is not speech-enabled and configure the primary Auto Attendant to fallback to it.

▶ Create separate PBX hunt groups for the caller lines and the subscriber lines with separate pilot numbers.

▶ Have two test internal phones available for testing the new unified messaging system.

▶ Leave the audio codec setting on WMA for optimal storage and playback quality.

▶ Move users' mailboxes to an Exchange 2007 Mailbox server in advance of the unified messaging deployment.

▶ Remove the default hunt groups and create specific ones for maximum control over call routing.

▶ Use key mapping to create helpful front-end menus for callers.

▶ Use the disable after completing call feature when disabling UM IP gateways or UM servers.

CHAPTER 25

Collaborating Within an Exchange Environment Using Microsoft Office SharePoint Server 2007

Exchange is the messaging component of the Microsoft product stack; it focuses on providing tools for knowledge workers to communicate with each other using email and other unified messaging capabilities. Collaboration is not only limited to messaging, however, and many organizations are looking into document management and workflow solutions to provide for a higher degree of collaboration in their messaging environments.

The Microsoft product line that provides for a near seamless integration of document management into a Microsoft Exchange Server 2007 environment is composed of several technologies collectively referred to as SharePoint. This chapter focuses on understanding what the latest SharePoint products, formally named Microsoft Office SharePoint Server (MOSS) 2007 and Windows SharePoint Services (WSS), are and how they can integrate into an Exchange 2007 environment.

Understanding the History of SharePoint Technologies

SharePoint technologies have a somewhat complicated history. Multiple attempts at rebranding the applications and packaging them with other Microsoft programs has further confused administrators and users alike.

Consequently, a greater understanding of what the SharePoint products are and how they were constructed is required.

WSS's Predecessor: SharePoint Team Services

In late 1999, Microsoft announced the digital dashboard concept as the first step in its knowledge management strategy, releasing the Digital Dashboard Starter Kit, the Outlook 2000 Team Folder Wizard, and the Team Productivity Update for BackOffice 4.5. These tools leveraged existing Microsoft technologies, so customers and developers could build solutions without purchasing additional products. These tools, and the solutions developed using them, formed the basis for what became known as SharePoint Team Services (STS), the predecessor of Windows SharePoint Services (WSS).

With the launch of Office XP, SharePoint Team Services was propelled into the limelight as the wave of the future, providing a tool for non-IT personnel to easily create websites for team collaboration and information sharing. Team Services, included with Office XP, came into being through Office Server Extensions and FrontPage Server Extensions. The original server extensions were built around a web server and provide a blank default web page. The second generation of server extensions provided a web authoring tool, such as FrontPage, for designing web pages. Team Services was a third-generation server extension product, with which a website could be created directly out of the box.

Understanding the Original MOSS Application

Microsoft Office SharePoint Server (MOSS) 2007 is the enterprise-level entry of the SharePoint product, building on top of the base Windows SharePoint Services 3.0 functionality. MOSS 2007 further extends the capabilities of WSS, allowing for multiple WSS sites to be indexed and managed centrally.

In 2001, Microsoft released the predecessor to MOSS 2007, SharePoint Portal Server 2001. The intent was to provide a customizable portal environment focused on collaboration, document management, and knowledge sharing. The product carried the "Digital Dashboard" Web Part technology a step further to provide an out-of-the-box solution. SharePoint Portal Server was the product that could link together the team-based websites that were springing up.

Microsoft's initial SharePoint Portal product included a document management system that provided document check-in/check-out capabilities, as well as version control and approval routing. These features were not available in SharePoint Team Services. SharePoint Portal also included the capability to search not only document libraries, but also external sources such as other websites and Exchange public folders.

Because the majority of the information accessed through the portal was unstructured, the Web Storage System was the means selected for storing the data, as opposed to a more structured database product such as Structured Query Language (SQL), which was being used for SharePoint Team Services. The Web Storage System, incidentally, is the same technology that is used by Microsoft Exchange. Further SharePoint implementations use the same SQL database as WSS does, however.

Differences Between the Two SharePoint Products

As SharePoint Team Services was available at no extra charge to Office XP/FrontPage users, many organizations took advantage of this "free" technology to experiment with portal usage. STS's simplicity made it easy to install and put into operation. Although functionality was not as robust as a full SharePoint Portal Server solution, knowledge workers were seeing the benefits of being able to collaborate with team members.

Adaptation of SharePoint Portal Server progressed at a slower rate. In a tight economy, organizations were not yet ready to make a monetary commitment to a whole new way of collaborating, even if it provided efficiency in operations. In addition, the SharePoint Portal interface was not intuitive or consistent, which made it difficult to use.

Having two separate products with similar names confused many people. "SharePoint" was often discussed in a generic manner, and people weren't sure whether the topic was SharePoint Portal or SharePoint Team Services, or the two technologies together. Even if the full application name was mentioned, there was confusion regarding the differences between the two products, and about when each was appropriate to use. People wondered why SharePoint Team Services used the SQL data engine for its information store, whereas SharePoint Portal Server used the Web Storage System. It appeared as though there was not a clear strategy for the product's direction.

Examining Microsoft's Next-Generation SharePoint Products: SPS 2003 and WSS 2.0

Microsoft took a close look at what was happening with regard to collaboration in the marketplace and used this information to drive its SharePoint technologies. Microsoft believed that in the world of online technology and collaboration, people need to think differently about how they work. The focus was to develop a suite of products to better handle this collaboration.

In addition to looking closer at how people collaborate, Microsoft also analyzed what had transpired with its SharePoint products. The end result was that Microsoft modified its knowledge management and collaboration strategy. Microsoft began talking about its "SharePoint technology," with a key emphasis on building this technology into the .NET Framework, and, thus, natively supporting XML Web Services.

In 2003, Microsoft released the 2.0 generation of SharePoint Products. SharePoint Team Services was rebranded as Windows SharePoint Services 2.0, the engine for the team-collaboration environment. Windows SharePoint Services included many new and enhanced features, some of which were previously part of SharePoint Portal Server. Windows SharePoint Services was also included as an optional component to the Windows Server 2003 operating system at the same time.

SharePoint Portal Server 2001 was released as Microsoft Office SharePoint Portal Server 2003. It built on the Windows SharePoint Services technology and continued to be the enterprise solution for connecting internal and external sources of information. SharePoint Portal Server allowed for searching across sites, and enabled the integration of business applications into the portal.

Unveiling the Current Generation of SharePoint: MOSS 2007 and WSS 3.0

As adoption of SharePoint technologies increased, Microsoft put more and more emphasis on the product line as collaboration functionality became increasingly important for organizations. Organizations were increasingly excited about the 2003 product line, but there were some functional disadvantages to the platform, which held many organizations back from a full deployment of the product or forced them to purchase third-party add-ons to the suite. Workflow, navigation components, and administration were all weaker than many organizations needed, and Microsoft began work on the 3.0 generation of SharePoint Products.

Along with the new generation came another rebranding of the product. SharePoint Portal Server became Microsoft Office SharePoint Server (MOSS) 2007. Windows SharePoint Services retained the same name and simply incremented the version number to 3.0.

MOSS 2007 and WSS 3.0 introduced several functional enhancements to SharePoint, including the following:

▶ **Integrated business process and Business Intelligence**—A significant portion of the development time for SharePoint was spent focused on improving the business workflow functionality of SharePoint. MOSS 2007 introduces a multitude of business process and Business Intelligence improvements that allow organizations to increase the efficiencies in their tasks.

▶ **Consolidated administrative tools**—Previous versions of SharePoint proved to be a headache to administer, as administrative tools and interfaces were scattered throughout the product. MOSS 2007 consolidates these admin interfaces into a single location, and provides for additional administrative tools as well.

▶ **Improved Office integration**—MOSS 2007 has further improved the tight integration between Office and SharePoint by allowing for advanced functionality, such as direct editing from Microsoft Excel, and offline capabilities in Microsoft Outlook and Groove.

▶ **Extranet and single sign on enhancements**—SharePoint 2007 allows for more secure and functional extranet deployment scenarios, so that internal MOSS sites can be utilized from the Internet without compromising safety or violating governmental regulations.

Identifying the Need for MOSS 2007

SharePoint is one of those services that is greatly misunderstood. Much of the confusion over the previous branding of the product has contributed to this, but a fundamental shift in thinking is required to effectively utilize the platform. An understanding of what SharePoint is and how it can be fully utilized is an important step toward realizing the efficiency the system can bring.

Changing Methodology from File Servers to a MOSS Document Management Platform

MOSS expands beyond its origins as a web team site application into a full-fledged documentation platform with the new functionalities introduced. These capabilities, previously only available with the full-functioned SharePoint Portal Server product, allow MOSS to store and manage documents efficiently in a transaction-oriented Microsoft SQL Server 2000 environment. What this means to organizations is that the traditional file server is less important, and effectively replaced, for document storage. Items such as Microsoft Word documents, Excel spreadsheets, and the like are stored in the MOSS database.

Along with these document management capabilities comes the realization by users that their standard operating practice of storing multiple versions of files on a file server is no longer feasible or efficient. Using MOSS effectively subsequently requires a shift in thinking from traditional approaches.

Enabling Team Collaboration with MOSS

MOSS 2007 and Windows SharePoint Services have demonstrated how web-based team sites can be effectively used to encourage collaboration among members of a team or an organization. Content relevant to a group of people or a project can be efficiently directed to the individuals who need to see it most, negating the need to have them hunt and peck across a network to find what they need.

After being deployed, the efficiency and collaboration realized is actually quite amazing. A good analogy to SharePoint can be found with email. Before using email, it's hard to understand how valuable it can be. After you've used it, however, it's hard to imagine not having it. The same holds true for SharePoint functionality. Organizations that have deployed WSS or the full-functioned MOSS 2007 product have a hard time imagining working without it.

Customizing SharePoint to Suit Organizational Needs

If the default functionality in SharePoint is not enough, or does not satisfy the specific web requirements of an organization, SharePoint can easily be customized. Easily customizable or downloadable Web Parts can be instantly "snapped-in" to a site, without the need to understand Hypertext Markup Language (HTML) code. More advanced developers can use ASP.NET or other programming tools to produce custom code to work with MOSS. Further enhancement of MOSS sites can be accomplished using SharePoint Designer 2007, which allows for a great deal of customization with relative ease. In general, if it can be programmed to work with Web Services, it can interface with SharePoint.

Exploring Basic MOSS Features

A SharePoint deployment can be used to create websites, manage documents, and provide other capabilities. Understanding and testing the features available in MOSS is an important prerequisite step toward effectively using MOSS, and a walk-through of those features should subsequently be performed.

The next sections walk through the features that are readily available to an employee using Microsoft Word 2007 when MOSS 2007 is installed on the network. Note that shared workspaces can be created from other Microsoft Office applications, including Excel, PowerPoint, and Visio.

Creating a Shared Workspace from MOSS

When a document is opened or created in Word 2007, click on the Office button followed by the Publish link and then Create Document Workspace. When selected, the Document Workspace interface appears on the right side of the screen. The user is prompted to name the workspace—the default is the document name—and enter the URL of the SharePoint site where the workspace will reside. The user can then add members to the site by entering either a domain and username, an email address, or both to define who will be included in the workspace. The level of participation for those members can also be set on the site with varying levels of authority, such as Reader, Contributor, Web Designer, or Administrator.

Six tabs in the Shared Workspace area provide information and tools to the user who created the site, as well as other users who open the file:

- **Status**—Provides errors or restrictions regarding the file

- **Members**—Provides a list of the different members of the workspace, and whether they are online

- **Tasks**—Allows the user to view tasks assigned to members of the site or create new ones

- **Documents**—Displays any other documents or folders available in the workspace, and allows the addition of other documents or folders to the workspace

- **Links**—Displays any URL links on the site and allows the addition of new URL links to the workspace

- **Document Information**—Displays basic information about the file such as who created or edited it, and allows viewing of the revision history

These features give the user a "dashboard," providing valuable information about the document, and help other users collaborate on the document.

TIP

Online presence can be enabled on a virtual server basis when Office 2003/2007 and Microsoft Office Communications Server 2007 (previously named Live Communications Server) are installed. Smart Tags using the Person Name object type become active when the mouse pointer is hovering over a site member's name. Additional tools are made available when the down arrow is clicked, such as a notification as to whether the person is online or available for instant messaging. Other options include Schedule a Meeting, Send Mail, or Edit User Information.

Working Within the MOSS Site

A MOSS 2007 environment is composed of multiple WSS sites, which are essentially individual workspaces that contain the knowledge worker content, such as document libraries, lists, document workspaces, and so on. Figure 25.1 illustrates a document workspace in MOSS 2007.

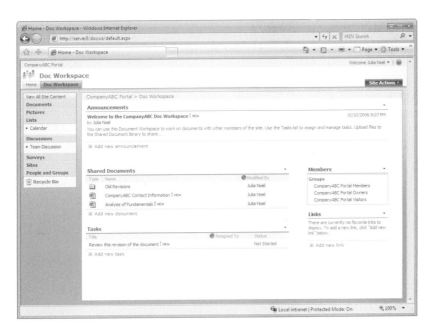

FIGURE 25.1   The MOSS 2007 document workspace.

Understanding Document Libraries

Document libraries may well be the feature most often used, as it is the location where documents and folders can be stored and managed, and document libraries offer a number of features not available in a standard server file share.

The team members who are working on one of the documents in the document library can upload related items to this library for reference purposes. This eliminates the step of printing out copies of supporting documentation for an in-person meeting, or emailing the actual files or hyperlinks via email.

A number of actions can be performed on the document from the Shared Documents page, as shown in Figure 25.2 :

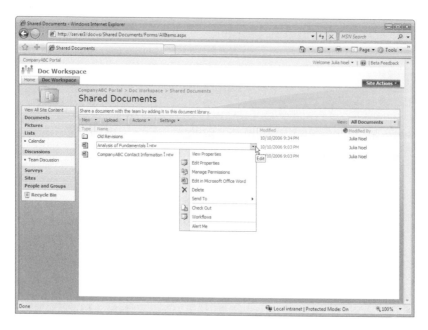

FIGURE 25.2   Available actions at the Shared Documents page.

▶ **View Properties**—Show the document filename and title assigned to the document (if any), who created the document and when, as well as who modified the document and when.

▶ **Edit Properties**—Change the name of the file that SharePoint is storing and the title of the document.

▶ **Manage Permissions**—Change who has rights to the document.

▶ **Edit in Microsoft Word**—Modify a document that the user has editing rights in the Shared Document library. The document can be opened and edited in Microsoft Word. Note that if the document is a Microsoft Office document, the appropriate application will be listed, such as Excel or PowerPoint.

▶ **Delete**—Delete the file if you (the user) have deletion rights in the Shared Document library.

▶ **Send To**—Move the document to another location, email it to someone, create a document workspace, or download a local copy of the document.

▶ **Check Out**—Retrieve a document that is reserved for the individual who has checked it out, and only that person can modify the document. So even if that person doesn't have the document open, no one else can edit it. An administrator of the site can force a document check-in.

> ▶ **Workflows**—Invoke the Workflow Wizard, which allows for special document workflow processes, such as approval routing or feedback collection .

> ▶ **Alert Me**—Notify the user with an email alert if changes are made to the file.

NOTE

Alerts are an extremely powerful feature in MOSS. A user can set an alert on an individual item stored in a SharePoint list, such as a document, so that if the document is changed, users receive an email letting them know of the change. Alternatively, an alert can be set for the whole document library, so if any items are changed, added, or deleted, users receive an email. The emails can be sent immediately, or in a daily or weekly summary. This is the primary way MOSS pushes information to the users of its sites, enhancing the flow of information.

Other capabilities in the Shared Documents page include creating a new document, uploading other documents to the site, creating a new folder, filtering the documents, or editing the list in a datasheet.

Using Picture Libraries

A picture library can include a wide variety of file types, including JPEG, BMP, GIF, PNG, TIF, WMF, and EMF. Examples are photos of members of the team, or screenshots of documents from software applications that might not be available to all users. For instance, a screen capture from an accounting application could be saved to the library in BMP format so that any of the users of the site could see the information.

Similarly, a Visio diagram or Project Gantt chart could be saved to one of these formats, or as an HTML file and then saved to a picture library and thereby made accessible to users of the site who might not have these software products installed on their workstations. By providing a graphical image rather than the native file format, the amount of storage space required can be reduced in many cases, and there is no easy way for users to change the content of the documents.

Maps of how to find a client's office or digital photos of whiteboards can also be included. Some editing features are available using the Microsoft Picture Library tool (if Office 2007 is installed), which include brightness and contrast adjustment, color adjustment, cropping, rotation and flipping, red-eye removal, and resizing.

Pictures can be emailed directly from the library, or a discussion can be started about a photo as with other documents in libraries. Pictures can be sorted using the filter tool by file type, viewed in a slideshow format, and checked out for editing; the version history can be reviewed; or alerts can be set.

Although this type of library might not be useful in every collaborative workspace, it provides a set of tools that are well suited to newsletter creation, complex document publication, or less formal uses, such as company events.

Working with SharePoint Lists

Lists are used in many ways by MOSS, and a number of the Web Parts provided in the default workspace site are, in fact, lists. Some of the list options available are listed as follows:

▶ **Links**—These lists can contain either internal or external URL links, or links to networked drives.

▶ **Announcements**—These lists typically contain news that would be of interest to the employees accessing the site, and can be set to expire at predefined times.

▶ **Contacts**—Contacts can be created from scratch using the provided template, or can be imported from Outlook. This type of list can help clarify who is involved with a particular project or site, what their role is, how to contact them, and can contain custom fields.

▶ **Events**—Events can be created in the site complete with start and stop times, descriptions, location information, and its rate of recurrence. The option to create a workspace for the event is provided when it is created. Events can be displayed in list format or in a calendar-style view. Events can be exported to Outlook, and a new folder will be added to the calendar containing the events. Note that this calendar will be read-only in Outlook.

▶ **Tasks**—Each task can be assigned to a member of the site and can have start/due dates and priority levels set, and the percentage complete can be tracked. These tasks do not link to Outlook, however, so they're specific to the SharePoint site.

▶ **Issue tracking**—Slightly different from tasks, issues include category references, and each receives its own ID number. Individuals assigned to an issue can automatically be sent email notification when an issue is assigned to them, and will receive emails if their assigned issue changes.

▶ **Custom list options**—If one of the template lists doesn't offer the right combination of elements, one can be created from scratch. This allows the individual creating the list to choose how many columns make up the list, determine what kind of data each column will contain, such as text, choices (a menu to choose from), numbers, currency, date/time, lookup (information already on the site), yes/no, hyperlink or picture, or calculations based on other columns. With this combination of contents available and the capability to link to other data contained in the site from other lists, a database of information that pertains to the site can be created that can get quite complex. For example, a custom list could include events from the Events list, tracking the cost of each event and which task corresponds to the event.

▶ **Data imported from a spreadsheet**—Rather than creating a list from scratch, data can be imported from a spreadsheet (ideally Excel). The data can then be used actively within the site without the file needing to be opened in Excel. It can then be exported for use in other applications.

With any list, additional options are available to users of the site. Figure 25.3 shows a simple task list open in Datasheet view (Office 2003/2007 is required for this feature), as well as the additional options available when the Task Pane option is selected.

FIGURE 25.3   Datasheet view task options.

After the list is displayed in Datasheet view, new rows can be added by either selecting this option in the toolbar, or by clicking in the row that starts with the asterisk. Totals of all columns can be displayed by clicking the Totals option.

Using SharePoint Discussions

The next option in the Quick Launch toolbar is for discussions, which are a key component for online collaboration. Although email is well suited to conversations involving a handful of people, it becomes unwieldy when there are too many participants, as multiple threads of conversations can easily get started and the original point of the discussion can get lost. With a bulletin board or threaded discussion, the high-level topics can be viewed at the same time, readers can choose the topics of interest, and can see any responses to the initial item. With email, individuals have no control over which emails they receive, whereas a discussion Web Part in SharePoint allows the user to decide which items to read and which ones to respond to.

Members with the appropriate rights can also manage the discussions to remove topics or responses that are not appropriate to the discussion, or remove threads when they have been completed. This level of control facilitates effective communication and encourages participation by the various team members.

Figure 25.4 shows a sample of a discussion concerning a proposal that is about to be sent out. Other responses have been posted.

FIGURE 25.4   Sample discussion board.

Discussions can also take place on any Office document posted to a SharePoint site. The data is stored in the SharePoint database, not in the document itself. This encourages team members to share their input and thoughts about a document in a controlled environment that is directly associated with the document.

Depending upon which site group participants are members of, they might only be able to view threaded discussions, or they might be able to participate, edit, and even delete portions of the conversation.

The alerts feature is very useful with discussions, as users can choose when and if they want to be alerted about changes to a specific discussion thread. This eliminates the need for participants to check a number of different discussions on a regular basis, as they can receive an email informing them if changes have been made.

Understanding Surveys

An entry for surveys also appears in the Quick Launch area in the document workspace. With MOSS, it's easy to quickly create a survey to request input from site users on any number of topics. They can be configured to request input on any topic imaginable, such as the functionality of the site, the information contained in it, or any business-related topics. As well as collecting the information from the surveys, the results can be viewed individually, displayed graphically, or exported to a spreadsheet for further analysis.

Surveys can be configured to be anonymous, so no information is saved or provided about the individual who responds to the survey, or the information can be displayed. In addition, both multiple responses and single responses are possible. Other options include allowing survey users to see other responses or only their own, or allowing them to edit their own and others' responses (or none at all). Common sense would dictate that users should not be able to edit a survey after it's submitted, but in some situations it might make sense to allow a person to go back and change input at a later date.

Exploring End-User Features in MOSS

The previous versions of SharePoint brought confusion to end users. The user interface was inconsistent, and it was difficult to maneuver between pages. For example, some pages had a Back button, some had menu items on the page that you could click and go back to, and some had nothing to get you "back," and you had to use the browser's Back feature or type in the URL to get back to where you wanted to go. In addition, there were some functions that had to be performed outside of SharePoint, some could only be done from within, and some could be done either way.

MOSS 2007 has a better user interface, and also has tighter integration with Microsoft Office. A user working on a document in Word 2007 can decide that collaboration is necessary and create a shared workspace, invite users to participate, and set up some milestone tasks without ever leaving Office 2007.

MOSS provides the end user with a much better set of features for customizing and personalizing sites. Users can create their own personal sites containing their own documents, their own links, and other content that is meaningful to them, as opposed to having to live with a "generic" website with "generic" content that might not be applicable to their position in the organization.

Some of the new and improved features available for enhancing the end-user experience are discussed in the following sections.

Expanding Document Management Capabilities

Previous versions of SharePoint, particularly the 1.0 versions of the product line, had some limitations with their document management capabilities. MOSS 2007, however, has become much more of an enterprise document management (DM) solution, including features such as the following:

- Document check-in/check-out to ensure that revisions are not overwritten by another user
- Ability to maintain versions of documents for tracking changes
- Ability to require approval when checking a document back in for quality control
- Improved document workflow capabilities

In addition to these features, MOSS provides the user with the flexibility to create a structured document storage environment, as opposed to the relatively flat view of the document space in older versions. MOSS is also more tightly integrated with Microsoft Office 2007, providing enhanced features available directly from the Office interface. Features in these areas include the capability to perform the following tasks:

▶ Create folders within a document library, and view all documents in a library, including those in subfolders.

▶ Create a MOSS document workspace directly from Word 2007, providing a means for easily setting up collaboration sites.

▶ Easily save and retrieve SharePoint documents from Office 2007 applications. Improvements in Microsoft Office 2007 and MOSS make saving documents to a workspace as easy as saving them to a file share.

▶ Access document libraries in the same manner as file shares through HTTP DAV Web Folder support, preventing users from having to learn a whole new set of commands.

▶ View Office documents through the browser without having Office installed on the client computer. This enables the remote and mobile user to view documents stored in SharePoint when on the road from a client's computer, when sitting at an airport kiosk, or when having a cup of coffee at an Internet café.

Introducing Meeting Workspaces

When organizations have meetings, there is generally an agenda for the meeting, some type of document or documents associated with the meeting, and often follow-up tasks. Although email can be used to send out agendas and documents prior to the meeting, and to send out follow-up tasks and meeting notes, a better solution is to have all of the information associated with the meeting available in one place. Meeting workspaces in MOSS provide this capability—a place for managing all of the documentation and tasks associated with a meeting. Meeting workspaces can be created from the site or from the "schedule meeting" function in Outlook 2003/2007. When a meeting is scheduled using Outlook 2003/2007, an option is available for creating a MOSS meeting workspace to store the meeting agenda, a list of attendees, documents relevant to the meeting, and any action items that result from the meeting.

Several meeting templates are available when creating the meeting workspace. In addition to a "standard" single meeting workspace, the other types of meeting workspaces include the following:

▶ Decision meeting workspaces

▶ Social meeting workspaces

▶ Multiple meeting workspaces

Figure 25.5 shows some of the different templates that can be chosen when creating a new site.

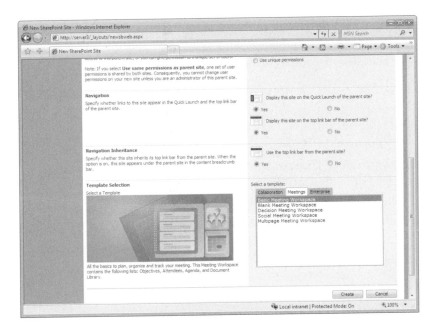

FIGURE 25.5   Templates for new SharePoint sites.

Integrating with Microsoft Office 2007

A key design goal for MOSS 2007 was to have it even more tightly integrated with Microsoft Office. Although SharePoint technologies support earlier versions of Office, such as Office 2000 or Office 2003, improvements and enhancements in both WSS 3.0 and in Microsoft Office 2007 provide a more efficient way for users to access shared document workspaces and team sites. This ease of use for accessing information encourages users to share, collaborate, and communicate together on projects, initiatives, or ideas. For example, instead of simply opening up a document in an older version of Office and working on the document, a user opening the same document off a SharePoint server with Microsoft Office 2007 is presented with not only the document, but also a new task pane that lists the members of the team site where the document is stored (showing presence information about the users), the status of the document, as well as any tasks and links associated with the document. Specifically, Microsoft Office 2007 integration means that

▶ The entire setup of the document workspace can be done from the Word 2007 interface. Using the Shared Workspace task pane, the document workspace can be created, users granted access, links pertaining to the document added, and tasks created.

- ▶ The document workspace is accessible through the task pane whenever the document is opened in Word 2007. The status of the members is displayed (such as whether they are online); messages can be sent to the members, links browsed to, and tasks viewed and updated.

- ▶ When a meeting is created using Outlook 2007, a SharePoint meeting workspace can also be created for storing content related to the meeting.

- ▶ SharePoint contacts can be viewed directly from Outlook 2007.

- ▶ Metadata and file properties are copied from Office documents to SharePoint libraries—therefore, file information doesn't have to be reentered into SharePoint if it has already been entered in Office.

- ▶ SharePoint documents can be attached to mail messages as shared attachments. When the user receives the message, there is a link to the workspace where the shared attachment can be accessed.

- ▶ MOSS sites can be searched from the Office 2007 Research and Reference tool pane.

- ▶ Documents stored in SharePoint picture libraries can be edited with an Office 2007 picture editing tool.

Personalizing MOSS 2007

MOSS 2007 includes many ways in which users can personalize a SharePoint environment. Some forms of personalization can originate from Office 2007, and some features are accessed directly through MOSS. The following list includes various ways in which users can personalize the SharePoint experience:

- ▶ Users can create private sites and private views with their own personalized look and feel, in a way that makes sense for the way they work. Changes to team sites are stored with the user's profile and will be applied each time the user visits the site.

- ▶ News can be targeted to users based on their audience affiliation. Considering the amount of information available, this is an efficiency feature that streamlines the content based on user interest.

- ▶ Users can be given the capability to create sites without involving IT personnel. A typical scenario in today's world, where the organization does not have a portal application such as MOSS, might go something like this:

  A user decides that a website would be helpful for collaborating on a project. The user presents the justification of the website to and obtains the approval of the department manager. The department manager submits a request to the IT department to have the site created. The IT manager reviews the request and places it low on the priority list because it will take time to develop the site, and the users can collaborate in the current environment using email and shared network drives. By the time IT gets to the project, the users have already completed the work and no longer need the collaboration site.

If users can create shared sites and workspaces on their own, and don't have to wade through the red tape of getting IT personnel to create them, they will be more likely to use them and realize the benefits they can provide.

Using Lists with MOSS

Each list in MOSS is a Web Part; therefore, they can be easily customized from the browser. Lists have been enhanced in many ways, including support for additional field types such as rich text, multivalue fields, and calculated fields. Field values can also be calculated. Field types can be changed after the list has been created, thus providing a means for accommodating data that is not particularly stable.

MOSS also has many new options for viewing lists. Filtered list views can also be created based on a calculation. For example, all events within the next week can be viewed by setting up a filter based on the date being greater than the current date plus seven. Another new view is the Event Calendar view, which enables displaying any list that has a date and time field in it using the daily, weekly, or monthly calendar view. Aggregated views enable totaling data into a number field and displaying the value. Totals can be based on the entire view or a subset of it. Group-by views enable grouping by one column, and then sorting within each group.

A picture library is a new kind of list. Graphics and photos can be stored in a picture library and optionally viewed as a filmstrip or as thumbnails in views automatically generated by SharePoint.

For Microsoft Office 2003/2007 users, lists can be edited in Datasheet view. This option presents the data in spreadsheet style, and provides spreadsheet types of editing features, such as copy and paste, adding rows, and fill options. Using the Datasheet view can be faster then the traditional SharePoint list editing style for some types of data entry and editing.

MOSS includes security features for lists. Permissions can be applied to the list so that only specific people can change it. Also included is the capability for the list owner to approve or reject items that are submitted to the list.

Other new list features include the following:

▶ Users can create their own personal lists that are not visible to other users.

▶ Alert notifications for lists include the name of the user who made the change to the list and which item in the list was changed.

▶ Attachments can be added or removed from a list item dependent on whether the attachment is required or not.

▶ Recurring events can be set up on an event list when a event occurs on a regularly scheduled basis.

25

Improving on SharePoint Alerts

Alerts in MOSS 2007 are what used to be called notifications in previous versions. Alerts have been improved to identify whether the alert was sent because content was changed or added, and now include the tracking of additional items. Prior versions of SharePoint tracked search queries and documents. In addition to these items, MOSS alerts track the following:

- News listings

- Sites added to the site directory

- SharePoint lists and libraries

- List items

- Site users

- Backward-compatible document library folders

Microsoft Outlook 2007 can be used to view MOSS alerts, and it includes rules to sort and filter them into special folders.

Exploring Additional New/Enhanced End-User Features

Many other new and enhanced features improve the end-user experience. These include the following:

- A site directory that lists all MOSS sites.

- The capability for users to create a SharePoint site from the Sites Directory page, to indicate whether they want the site added to the directory, and whether they want the site content to be indexed. This provides a level of security for protecting sensitive information, such as human resources data.

- Support for multiple file uploads. Older versions required files to be uploaded individually. MOSS supports multiple file uploads (such as an entire directory or folder). This is a great time-saver for organizations that are migrating large numbers of documents to SharePoint.

- The capability to select from one of several site templates when creating a new site. Organizations can also create their own site templates (such as with the organization logo and color theme) for providing a level of consistency among different types of sites within the site.

- The capability to create surveys and have the results automatically calculated and made available.

- Additional improvements in the survey process. The survey feature now supports responding to a question using a scale, and the capability for users to select all answers that might apply to a survey question.

▶ Everywhere a member name appears in a MOSS site, a user presence menu is available. The presence menu can be integrated with Active Directory, Exchange 2007, and Office Communications Server 2007 for providing information such as office location and free/busy status. It can be used for scheduling meetings and sending email.

▶ Team discussions that can be expanded and collapsed.

Customizing and Developing MOSS Sites

MOSS has many out-of-the-box new features that make it easier to customize using the browser interface. This provides nonprogrammers with a mechanism to create and customize sites to meet their needs.

For developers, the following provides an overview of the SharePoint technical structure. MOSS is built on the .NET platform. Use of the .NET platform enables SharePoint to assimilate information from multiple systems into an integrated solution. ASP.NET contains many new features, and it is more responsible, secure, and scalable than ASP. Using ASP.NET reduces the amount of code that needs to be written over similar ASP solutions.

SharePoint's SQL back end provides access to internal database components using industry-standard tools. From an application standpoint, integration with BizTalk provides access to over 300 application connectors using Web Services calls.

In MOSS, sites and lists can be saved as templates, stored in a Site or List Template library, and then made available to all sites in the collection. There is also a library for Web Parts that can be shared across all sites in the collection.

Features such as these provide an environment for developing fully customized MOSS solutions. Additional customization and development features are highlighted in the following sections.

Using the Browser to Customize SharePoint

Through the browser, you can add a logo to the team site, apply a theme, modify a list, or create a new Web Part page.

In SharePoint Team Services, there was a template that contained three "zones" for placing Web Parts, producing a three-column view. In MOSS, there are additional zone layouts to choose from, making customization much more user friendly.

The new Web Part tool pane is a feature that enables users to easily customize sites. It provides the ability to do the following:

▶ Drag/drop Web Parts onto a page

▶ Customize Web Parts

▶ Change the home page site logo

The site administrator can control what goes into the Web Part libraries and who has access to the libraries for adding Web Parts to a site. Figure 25.6 illustrates the Web Part tool pane with its various Web Part libraries and the capability to display the contents of the library.

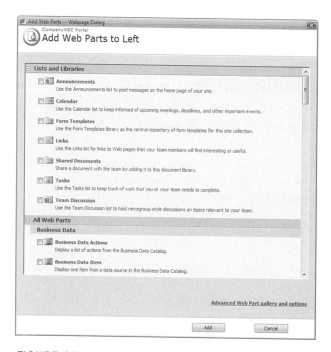

FIGURE 25.6   Displaying the Web Part tool pane for access to Web Part libraries.

Development Enhancements for Site Templates

MOSS includes multiple templates that can be used when you create a new site. Each template includes a set of features from MOSS to satisfy a specific collaboration need. Templates are included for the following:

- ▶ Document collaboration
- ▶ Team collaboration
- ▶ Wiki sites
- ▶ Blogs
- ▶ Records repositories
- ▶ Publishing sites
- ▶ Basic meetings
- ▶ Decision meeting workspaces
- ▶ Social meeting workspaces

- ▶ Multipage meeting workspaces

- ▶ Document centers

- ▶ Personalization sites

- ▶ Report center sites

If these don't satisfy the organization's requirements, customized templates can easily be put together using the browser-based customization features, using SharePoint Designer 2007 or some other web design tool, or using programming. For example, if an organization always put its company logo on the home page and used specific Web Parts that were unique to their organization, it could save the site as a template and then just duplicate the template when necessary to maintain consistency and security.

Editing MOSS 2007 with SharePoint Designer 2007

With SharePoint Team Services, it was difficult to modify SharePoint sites. SharePoint 2003 made it easier with the use of FrontPage 2003, but performance was affected by editing sites directly. With MOSS 2007, a new product, SharePoint Designer 2007, shown in Figure 25.7, is more tightly integrated with Windows SharePoint Services and Microsoft Office SharePoint Server 2007 and fully supports Web Parts, Web Part pages, and Web Part zones. This means that Web Parts can be added and customized using SharePoint Designer 2007 to provide the look, feel, and content to meet organizational requirements.

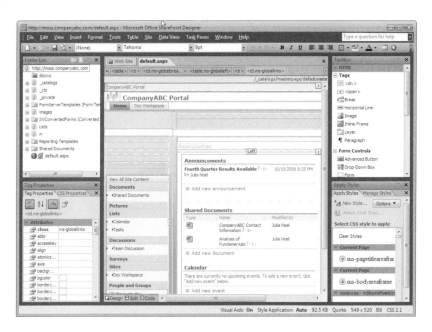

FIGURE 25.7   Working with SharePoint Designer 2007.

Web Parts can be previewed in SharePoint Designer before being published to the SharePoint site, thus providing an "audit" to ensure that the changes have the desired effect. The SharePoint Designer client can be used to back up and restore MOSS sites, providing a much-needed feature that was lacking in older versions of the product.

Other features provided in SharePoint Designer 2007 include the ability to do the following:

- ▶ Deploy a site throughout the organization using solution packages. This provides a means for implementing changes and modifications to organizations that have multiple sites and servers.

- ▶ Search Web Part libraries directly. This enables the product to be a complete editing source for web pages, as opposed to a two-step process in which the Web Parts would be added using the MOSS interface, and then further modifications made in SharePoint Designer.

- ▶ Create list templates and create, edit, and delete SharePoint list views. For experienced SharePoint Designer users, the SharePoint interface might be cumbersome for performing functions such as these. Therefore, SharePoint Designer can be more efficient for these users when creating templates and managing list views.

- ▶ Connect Web Parts across pages or on the same page to create a new user interface. Because SharePoint Designer is a web development tool, it has more capabilities and is more flexible than SharePoint; thus, features such as these are available for more complete customization.

- ▶ Use an Extensible Stylesheet Language (XSL) data view Web Part that can bring data from external sources into SharePoint sites. This is a great new integration feature that shows Microsoft's commitment toward a truly integrated Office solution.

Summary

Microsoft Office SharePoint Server 2007 is an excellent way to extend the capabilities of an Exchange Server 2007 messaging environment. Installation of MOSS 2007 allows a server to become an enterprise-level document management and collaboration system. Enhanced capabilities within MOSS and strong integration with Microsoft Office 2007 allow organizations to realize improvements in productivity and quality quickly. In addition, the scalability of MOSS and its reliability on the robust Microsoft SQL database provide strong incentive to deploy and utilize MOSS technology.

Best Practices

The following are best practices from this chapter:

- ▶ Consider using a full version of SQL Server 2000/2005 for any MOSS 2007 implementation with greater than 10 sites.

▶ Use document versioning sparingly in MOSS document libraries to ensure that the SQL database does not grow too large.

▶ Keep a MOSS server up to date with all Windows Server 2003 and SQL Server patches and updates to reduce the risk of attacks or malfunctions.

▶ Deploy MOSS server(s) to replace file servers for document storage to take advantage of the newly integrated document management features MOSS offers.

▶ Keep the number of virtual servers created per MOSS server to 10 or fewer to avoid performance degradation.

▶ Use SharePoint Designer 2007 to provide advanced administration, site maintenance, and backup and restore capabilities.

25

CHAPTER 26

Extending the Real-Time Communications Functionality of Exchange Server 2007

Microsoft Exchange Server 2007 is the messaging muscle to the Microsoft collaborations platform. In addition to messaging functionality, however, many organizations are looking to improve the ability of their knowledge workers to collaborate between themselves, particularly when they might be remote. They have found that email, although a time-saving and ideal mechanism for certain types of communications, is not the best medium to transmit real-time conversations between knowledge workers.

In the Microsoft suite of applications, the Real-Time Communications (RTC) product suite that includes products such as Office Communications Server (OCS) 2007 and Office Live Meeting provides for this extra layer of collaboration through its inclusion of instant messaging, web conferencing, and user presence information. At the same time, although it handles all of these functions, it also provides for mechanisms to secure and audit these activities.

This chapter covers the products that comprise the Microsoft RTC strategy: Office Communications Server 2007, Office Live Meeting, and the Communicator 2007 client. Step-by-step guides on how to install, use, and administer these applications are presented, and best practices in their deployment and architecture are outlined.

Understanding Microsoft's Unified Communications Strategy

Microsoft has placed considerable emphasis on its unified communications (UC) strategy in Exchange Server 2007. Microsoft is looking to position several products as solutions to the various types of communications that knowledge workers use, such as phone, email, instant messaging, videoconferencing, and voice mail. By default, Exchange 2007 includes built-in support for email, voice mail, and phone through the Unified Messaging server role and Mailbox role. Instant messaging and videoconferencing, however, require the use of specific add-on products as described in this chapter.

These products in the RTC suite work very closely with Exchange 2007 to further extend the capabilities of the environment and to further improve the efficiencies gained when communications barriers are broken down in an organization.

Outlining the History of the Unified Communications Products

Microsoft has made several forays into the videoconferencing and instant messaging space, which have eventually led to the current state of the product today. What we now know as the Office Communications Server (OCS) 2007 product was originally part of the Exchange 2000 Beta Program (Platinum) but was removed from the application before it went to market. It was then licensed as a separate product named Mobile Information Server (MIS) 2000. MIS has some serious shortcomings, however, and adoption was not high.

Microsoft rebranded the application upon the release of Exchange Server 2003 by naming it Live Communications Server (LCS) 2003. This version was deployed much more extensively than the previous versions, but still suffered from some integration problems with Exchange.

The LCS product was rereleased two years later as Live Communications Server 2005, with an SP1 version coming later that added some additional functionality. This version of the product was widely deployed, and was the most solid implementation to date.

Timed to release with Exchange 2007, the new version of LCS was named the Office Communications Server (OCS) 2007. This version marked the ascension of the technology as a core component to many organizations' collaboration designs.

Exploring the Office Communications Server (OCS) 2007 Product Suite

OCS 2007 builds upon some impressive capabilities of its predecessors, while at the same time adding additional functionality. The following key features of the application exist:

- ▶ **Web conferencing**—OCS has the capability to centrally conference multiple users into a single virtual web conference, allowing for capabilities such as whiteboard, chat, and application sharing. In addition, these conferences can be set up and scheduled from within the users' Outlook clients.

▶ **Videoconferencing**—In addition to standard web conferencing, OCS allows for videoconferencing between members of a conference. The OCS server can act as the bridge for this type of conferencing, or it can redirect users to a third-party bridge as necessary.

▶ **Instant messaging**—The OCS server also acts as an instant messaging server, providing for centralized IM capabilities as well as the ability to archive IM traffic and to filter it for specific information. OCS allows an organization to gain more control over the instant messaging traffic that is being used.

▶ **Presence information**—Tied into the instant messaging functionality of OCS is the ability of the software to provide presence information for users. For example, within an Outlook message, a user can determine whether the sender of the message is online by hovering over their name.

▶ **Public IM Connectivity**—Microsoft Yahoo!, and AOL recently agreed to make it easier to interoperate between their various IM tools. In response to this agreement, Microsoft made it possible to integrate a corporate IM platform on OCS with external private IM clients on the MSN, Yahoo!, or AOL platforms. The way that OCS does this is through the concept of a Public IM Connectivity (PIC) license.

▶ **IM federation**—OCS also has the ability to tie a corporate IM environment into the OCS or LCS environment at another organization, through a process known as IM federation. Externally facing OCS Federation Proxy servers are used for this capability.

▶ **Contact management**—OCS integrates Exchange contacts with IM contacts, providing the ability to integrate them into a common list.

▶ **Outlook integration**—OCS now offers the ability for the IM functionality to be tied into the Free/Busy and Out of the Office functionality of Outlook and Exchange 2007. This allows users to determine the status of a user directly from the IM client.

The product is available in the following two versions:

▶ **Standard Edition**—The Standard Edition of OCS 2007 allows for a single server to be deployed using a Microsoft SQL Server Desktop Engine (MSDE) database. It supports up to 15,000 concurrent users.

▶ **Enterprise Edition**—The Enterprise Edition allows for pool's of servers connected to a common Structured Query Language (SQL) database to be utilized, allowing for up to 120,000 users.

Server roles are defined for OCS servers, just as Exchange 2007 defines server roles. A single server can hold multiple roles, and multiple servers can be deployed with a single role, as necessary. The following server roles exist in OCS:

▶ **Server**—The default server for OCS handles IM, web conferencing, and presence information.

▶ **Archiving server**—An OCS Archiving server archives instant messages and specific usage information and stores it in a SQL database.

▶ **Proxy server**—An OCS Proxy server allows for requests to be forwarded when those requests do not require authentication and/or user registration.

▶ **Edge server**—An OCS Edge server creates an encrypted, trusted connection point for traffic to and from the Internet. It serves as a method of protecting internal servers from direct exposure and is often placed into a demilitarized zone (DMZ) of a firewall.

The OCS product is central to Microsoft's unified communications strategy, as it serves as a mechanism to unite the various products such as Exchange and SharePoint by providing information about when a user is online, and providing ideal mechanisms to communicate with them.

> **NOTE**
>
> OCS 2007 has the capability to connect an organization's IM clients into a Yahoo! or AOL instant messaging client infrastructure as the three companies have resolved their differences and are now collaborating in this space.

Viewing the Communicator 2007 Client

On the client side of the unified communications equation, Microsoft has released a new version of the corporate instant messaging client. This version is known as Communicator 2007. The Communicator client provides the end user with a mechanism to conduct instant messaging conversations with users, to share their desktop with another user or with a group of users, and to transfer files and view video content.

The Communicator client serves as a replacement for free Internet instant messaging clients, which can serve as a conduit for viruses and spyware. In addition, the Communicator client does not include any type of advertising in its console, as do the public IM clients for MSN, Yahoo!, and AOL. More information on installing and using the Communicator client are provided in later sections of this chapter.

Exploring Office Live Meeting

For those organizations that need to extend the same basic functionality provided by OCS to any number or set of external users, Microsoft provides for a hosted product known as Microsoft Office Live Meeting. Live Meeting provides for a centralized service that can be used to set up conferences between any number of users worldwide.

More information on how to use the Office Live Meeting product is presented in later sections of this chapter.

Installing OCS 2007

OCS 2007 has a surprisingly complex installation process at first glance. What Microsoft has done, however, has been to divide up the installation process into multiple sections, providing for checks along the way so that there is less room for error. Because the installation requires an Active Directory schema upgrade, it is important that the process run smoothly, so it is good that this process is designed the way it is.

This section of the chapter focuses on the installation of the Standard Edition of OCS 2007. The Enterprise Edition installation routine is similar, but with more emphasis on multiple server deployment and on the use of a full SQL database.

Extending the Active Directory (AD) Schema

OCS 2007 integrates deep into an existing AD environment. It integrates so deeply, in fact, that an extension of the underlying AD schema is required before the product can be installed. AD schema upgrades are no small thing, of course, so it is wise to become familiar with the consequences of extending the schema and to make sure that a backup of the domain takes place first. To start the installation process, perform the following steps:

1. Run the OCS 2007 setup program from the media. Click on the `deploy.exe` file.

2. From the Deployment Wizard, click the Deploy Standard Edition Server link.

3. Review the steps on the subsequent dialog box for the Deployment Wizard, shown in Figure 26.1. Click Prepare Active Directory.

FIGURE 26.1   Deploying OCS 2007.

CAUTION

Installation of Office Communications Server 2007 requires an AD schema upgrade to the AD forest. It is important to fully understand the consequences of a schema upgrade in advance, as an upgrade will replicate to all domain controllers in a forest.

---

4. In the subsequent dialog box, shown in Figure 26.2, click Run to start the schema upgrade process.

FIGURE 26.2   Starting the schema upgrade process.

5. At the Schema Preparation Wizard welcome screen, click Next to begin the process.

6. In the Schema File Location dialog box, leave the default location selected, and click Next.

7. At the review screen, review the settings and, keeping in mind the caution previously given about schema upgrades, click Next to continue.

8. The schema upgrade process will begin, as shown in the dialog box in Figure 26.3. When it is complete, click Finish.

After the schema update has run, be sure you wait until the new schema extensions have replicated to all domain controllers in the forest. After this has been verified, return to the Deployment Wizard to continue.

Preparing the AD Forest

After the schema extension is complete, perform the following steps:

1. Return to the Deployment Wizard and click Run under Step 3: Prep Forest, as shown in Figure 26.4.

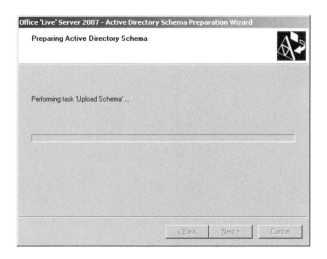

FIGURE 26.3   Extending the schema.

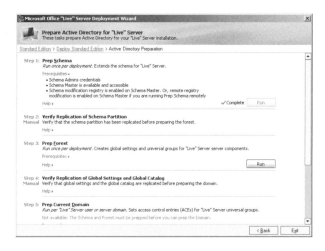

FIGURE 26.4   Prepping the forest.

2. Click Next at the welcome screen of the Forest Preparation Wizard.

3. The subsequent dialog box, shown in Figure 26.5, gives you the option to choose between storing the global settings in the root domain, or in the configuration partition. In most cases, install in the root domain.

4. Under Domain, choose the domain where OCS will create the groups used by the server. This is typically the main resource domain where the servers are installed into. Click Next to continue.

5. At the review screen, click Next to continue.

6. Click Finish.

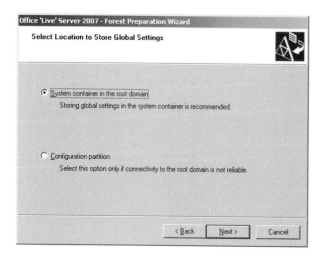

FIGURE 26.5   Choosing where to store global settings.

After this step is complete, ensure that replication of the newly created objects has occurred on all domain controllers in the forest and proceed to the next step.

Prepping the Domain

The following procedure must be run on each domain in the forest where OCS will be installed:

1. Click Run under the Prep Current Domain listing in the Deployment Wizard.

2. From the Domain Preparation Wizard, click Next to continue.

3. From the Domain Preparation Information dialog box, review the warning illustrated in Figure 26.6, and click Next to continue.

4. Click Next at the review dialog box.

5. Click Finish.

Once again, make sure replication takes place before advancing to the next step in the installation process.

Delegating Setup and Administrative Privileges

To continue the installation process, perform the following steps:

1. From the Deployment Wizard, click on Delegate Setup and Administration under Step 7.

2. Click the Run button underneath Delegate Setup Tasks.

3. At the Setup Delegation Wizard welcome dialog box, click Next to continue.

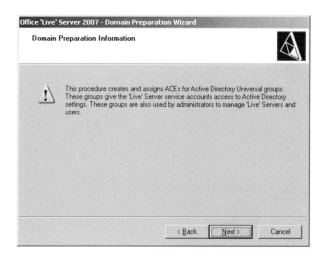

FIGURE 26.6   Prepping the domain.

4. At the Authorize Group dialog box, shown in Figure 26.7, choose the Trustee domain and enter a name of an existing Universal Security group. Members of that group will receive permissions to activate the server. Click Next to continue.

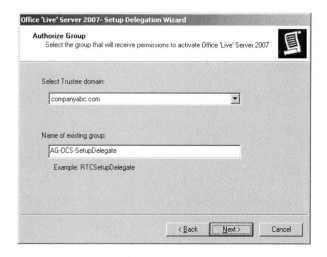

FIGURE 26.7   Delegating setup and administrative privileges.

NOTE

The group chosen must be a Universal Security group, or installation will fail.

5. At the OU Location dialog box, enter the full distinguished name (DN) of the organizational unit (OU) where the OCS Server computer accounts will be located. For example, the following DN was entered in this example:

```
OU=OCS,OU=Servers,OU=Computers,OU=Resources,DC=companyabc,DC=com
```

6. After entering the DN of the server's OU, click Next to continue.

7. Enter the name of service accounts that will be used for the session initiation protocol (SIP) and components services, such as that shown in Figure 26.8. These accounts should be created in advance in AD.

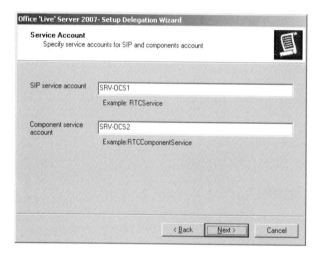

FIGURE 26.8   Entering in service account information.

8. Review the information in the subsequent dialog box, and then click Next to begin setup.

9. Click Finish.

At this point, setup of the Active Directory portion of the OCS Enterprise is complete, and individual servers can now be deployed.

Configuring IIS on the Server

The installation of the server portion of the process requires that the WWW Service of Internet Information Services (IIS) be installed on the server. To install the IIS component, perform the following actions:

1. From the server that OCS will be installed on, click Start, Control Panel, Add or Remove Programs.

2. Click Add/Remove Windows Components.

3. Select Application Server from the list (only click on the name to highlight it, do not check the box), and click the Details button.

4. Select Internet Information Services (IIS) from the list (again, only select it, do not check the box), and then click the Details button.

5. Scroll down and check the box for World Wide Web Service, as shown in Figure 26.9, and click OK.

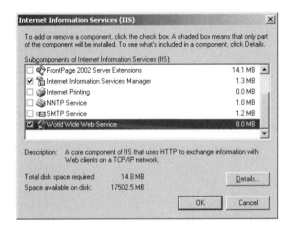

FIGURE 26.9   Installing the WWW Service.

6. Click OK again and then click Next.

7. If prompted for the CD-ROM, enter the media and click OK.

8. Click Finish.

Deploying an OCS 2007 Server

After all of the prerequisites have been satisfied and the AD schema has been extended, the process for installing an OCS 2007 standard server can begin. This process will be the same for as many OCS servers as will need to be deployed. To begin this process, perform the following steps:

1. From the Deployment Wizard, click Deploy Standard Edition Server.

2. Under Step 2, click Run, as shown in Figure 26.10.

3. At the welcome screen, click Next.

4. Leave the installation folder at the default, and click Next to continue.

5. At the account information field, shown in Figure 26.11, select Use an Existing Account, and enter the service account information entered in the previous steps for delegation.

FIGURE 26.10   Deploying server components.

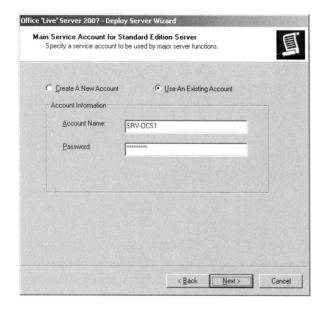

FIGURE 26.11   Specifying service account settings.

6. At the Component Service Account dialog box, choose Use an Existing Account, and then enter the second service account created during the delegation steps (that is, SRV-OCS2) and its password. Click Next to continue.

7. In the Web Farm FQDNs dialog box, shown in Figure 26.12, enter the external FQDN of the farm as it will be made available to Internet users (if applicable). Click Next to continue.

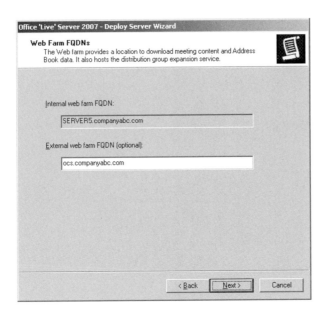

FIGURE 26.12   Entering web farm FQDN settings.

8. Enter the database and log information into the fields in the Database File dialog box. Click Next to continue.

NOTE

For best performance, separate the database and logs onto physically separate drive sets.

9. Click Next at the Ready to Deploy dialog box.

10. Click Finish.

Configuring the Server

After the server software has been installed, OCS services are not started by default. Instead, the Deployment Wizard encourages administrators to configure certain settings first before doing so. To configure these settings, follow this procedure:

1. From the Deployment Wizard, click Run under Step 3 (Configure Server).

2. Click Next at the welcome screen.

3. Select the installed server from the drop-down list shown in Figure 26.13, and click Next to continue.

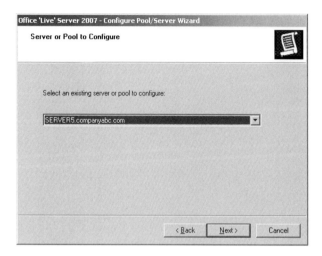

FIGURE 26.13   Configuring the OCS server.

4. If any additional SIP domains are needed in the environment, enter them in the subsequent dialog box. If not, accept the default of the domain name (for example, companyabc.com), and click Next.

5. Under Client Logon Settings, select that all clients will use DNS SRV records for auto logon, and click Next to continue.

6. Check the domain or domains that will be used for SIP automatic logon, such as that shown in Figure 26.14, and click Next to continue.

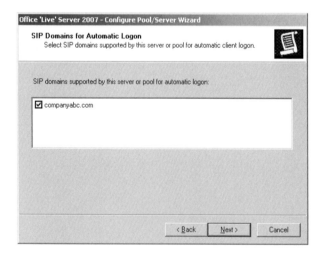

FIGURE 26.14   Selecting SIP domains for automatic logon.

7. In the External User Access Configuration dialog box, select to not configure external user access now. External user access can be configured at a later date from the Admin tool. Click Next to continue.

8. Click Next at the Verification dialog box.

9. Click Finish.

Configuring Certificates for OCS

Communications to and from the OCS server should ideally be encrypted and the user should also be able to trust that they are actually accessing the server that they expect. For this reason, Microsoft made it part of the installation process to install certificates onto the OCS server. To start the process of installing a certificate on the server, perform the following steps:

1. From the Deployment Wizard, click Run under Step 4 (Configure Certificate).

2. Click Next at the welcome screen.

3. From the list of available tasks, shown in Figure 26.15, select Create a New Certificate, and click Next.

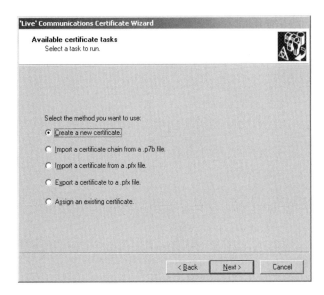

FIGURE 26.15   Creating a new certificate for the OCS server.

4. Select Send the Request Immediately to an Online Certification Authority, and click Next to continue.

NOTE

This step assumes that an internal Windows certificate authority exists in the organization. If not, the request must be sent off to a third-party CA, such as VeriSign or Thawte.

5. Type a descriptive name for the certificate, leave the bit length at 1024 and the certificate as exportable, and click Next to continue.

6. Enter the organization and OU of your organization. It should exactly match what is on file with the CA. Click Next to continue.

7. At the Your Server's Subject Name dialog box, enter the subject name of the server (FQDN in which it will be accessed), such as that shown in Figure 26.16. Enter any subject alternate names as well. It is recommended to check Automatically Add Local Machine Name to Subject Alt Name check box. Click Next to continue.

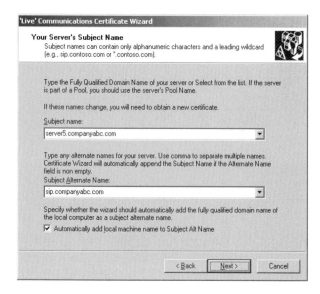

FIGURE 26.16   Entering the server's subject name.

8. Enter the appropriate country, state, and city information into the Geographical Information dialog box, bearing in mind that abbreviations cannot be used. Click Next to continue.

9. Select the local CA from the drop-down list, and click Next to continue.

10. Click Next at the Verification dialog box.

11. In the Success dialog box, click Assign.

12. Click OK to acknowledge that the settings were applied.

13. Click Finish to exit the wizard.

After the certificate is installed, check to make sure that the changes have replicated.

Starting the OCS Services on the Server

After the certificate has been installed, the services for OCS can be started via the Deployment Wizard via the following process:

1. From the Deployment Wizard, click Run under Start Services.

2. On the wizard welcome screen, click Next.

3. Review the list of services to be started, as shown in Figure 26.17. Click Next to continue.

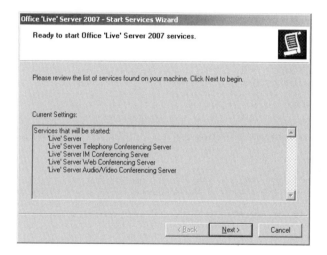

FIGURE 26.17   Starting the services.

4. Click Finish when the wizard is complete.

Validating Server Functionality

The Deployment Wizard contains a useful mechanism for running a series of tests against the server to ensure that everything was set up properly. To run this wizard, do the following:

1. From the Deployment Wizard, click Run under Step 7 (Validate Server Functionality).

2. Click Next at the welcome screen for the Validation Wizard.

3. Select the check boxes to validate the local server configuration, connectivity, and SIP logon, and click Next to continue.

4. Enter an account for testing logon functionality, as shown in Figure 26.18. Click Next to continue.

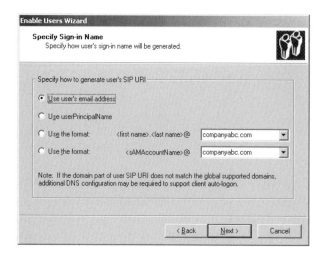

FIGURE 26.18   Testing logon functionality.

5. Enter a second user account to test two-party IM functionality, and click Next when you are ready.

6. On the subsequent Federation dialog box, select whether to test federation, if it is enabled. Click Next to continue.

7. Click Finish and review the logs for any errors.

Installing the Admin Tools

Administrative tools for OCS 2007 can be installed on a separate server from the OCS server itself. The system in question need only be either Windows Server 2003 SP1 or R2 edition, or Windows XP Professional XP2. To install Admin tools on a different system, do the following:

1. From the initial Deployment Wizard screen, click the Administrative Tools link.

2. Click Next at the welcome screen.

3. Select I Accept for the license terms, and click Next.

4. Click Next to start the installation.

5. After installation, click Close to exit.

Exploring Office Communications Server Tools and Concepts

After OCS 2007 has been installed in an organization, the job of administering the environment comes into play. OCS functionality is not difficult to grasp, but it is important to have a good grasp on several key concepts in how to administer and maintain the OCS environment. Key to these concepts is a familiarity with the OCS Admin tools, as illustrated in the following sections.

Administering Office Communications Server

Administration of an OCS 2007 environment is composed of two components, user administration and server administration. User administration is primarily concerned with enabling users for OCS access, giving them a SIP account, moving them from one server to another, and enabling or disabling public IM connectivity and federation.

Adding Users to OCS

The Office Communication Server 2007 Admin tool allows for both user and server administration. Enabling a user account for OCS access, however, requires the use of the Active Directory Users and Computers (ADUC) tool, which can be downloaded from Microsoft as part of the Windows Server 2003 Service Pack 1 Admin Pack (`adminpak.msi`). Installing it on the server that runs OCS allows for additional tabs for OCS to be displayed, and allows for new drop-down menu options that enable and disable OCS access.

To enable a user account for OCS access, perform the following steps from the ADUC tool on the OCS server:

1. From Active Directory Users and Computers, right-click on the user to be enabled, and choose Enable Users for Office Communications.

2. Click Next at the welcome screen.

3. Select the server pool from the list, and click Next to continue.

4. In the dialog box shown in Figure 26.19, specify how to generate the SIP address for the user. Click Next to continue.

5. Click Finish.

Configuring User Settings from the OCS Admin Tool

After a user account has been provisioned for OCS access using the ADUC tool, it will show up in the Users container underneath the server name icon in the console pane of the Admin tool. Right-clicking on the user and selecting Properties invokes the dialog box shown in Figure 26.20.

26

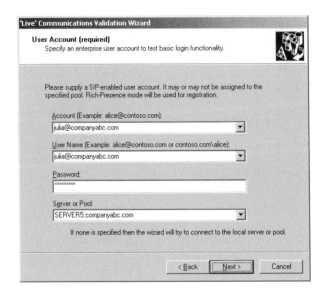

FIGURE 26.19   Enabling a user for OCS.

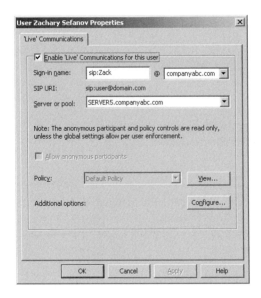

FIGURE 26.20   Modifying user settings in OCS 2007.

Clicking on the Configure button also opens up advanced options, such as Federation and Public IM options. The OCS console allows for OCS users to be deleted or moved to other servers.

Configuring Server Settings from the OCS Admin Tool

Server-specific settings can be configured from the OCS Admin tool by right-clicking the server name and choosing Properties, <Server Role> (where *Server Role* is the role that will be configured, such as Front End, Web Conferencing, A/V, or Web Component). The dialog box shown in Figure 26.21 displays some of the settings that can be manipulated here.

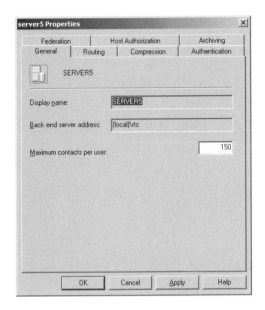

FIGURE 26.21   Changing server settings in the OCS Admin tool.

Using the Instant Messenger Filter in OCS 2007

OCS 2007 also includes a built-in instant messenger filter, shown in Figure 26.22, that gives organizations control over what type of traffic is being sent through IM. This allows administrators to limit the risk that IM clients can pose, particularly with spyware and other vulnerabilities. It also includes a file transfer filter that can be modified to block specific file extensions.

Together with a Public IM Connectivity (PIC) license running on an OCS Edge Proxy server, this allows an organization to let employees use the IM client for external IM functionality, but without exposing them to unnecessary risks.

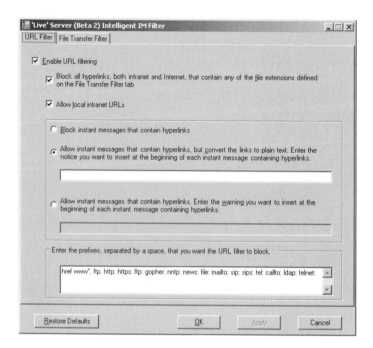

FIGURE 26.22   Viewing the IM filter in OCS.

Installing and Using the Communicator 2007 Client

The client component of an OCS 2007 implementation is the Communicator 2007 client. This client is essentially the business version of Microsoft's IM client, which provides for instant messaging capabilities as well as conferencing, video, and audio capabilities.

The Communicator client, shown in Figure 26.23, communicates to the OCS 2007 server via an encrypted Transport Layer Security (TLS) channel, securing the traffic from prying eyes. Users can set their presence information directly from the client, allowing other users in the OCS system to view whether they are online and available for conversations.

Installing the Communicator 2007 Client

The Communicator 2007 client can be installed as part of a deployment package in an application such as Systems Management Server (SMS) 2003 or System Center Configuration Manager 2007, or it can be manually deployed to desktops. The following procedure illustrates how to manually install the client on a desktop:

1. Run the Communicator 2007 client setup from the client media.

2. Click Next at the welcome screen.

3. Select I Accept for the license terms, and click Next.

FIGURE 26.23   Viewing the Communicator 2007 client.

4. Enter a patch for the application (typically accept the default path given), and click Next to continue.

5. Click Finish.

Web Conferencing with Office Live Meeting

For organizations requiring web conferencing and application sharing on a broader scale, and beyond the borders of their organization, Microsoft offers a hosted product known as Office Live Meeting. The Live Meeting product allows an organization to quickly and easily set up or schedule a web conference, and invite any number of users into that conference. Live Meeting scales to thousands of users, and is a critical component in Microsoft's Real-Time Communications strategy.

Installing the Live Meeting 2007 Client

Live Meeting 2007 sessions can be attended with the use of a full client, or via the web-only console. The web console does not require the installation of any specialized client software, which can be useful in situations where the user does not have the ability to install the full client.

The best experience in a Live Meeting session is had when using the full client, so it is recommended to install the client when prompted. When a meeting is set up for the first time on a system, you will be prompted to install the software. After you click the link to Install and Join, the client will be automatically downloaded and installed.

Working with Live Meeting

A Live Meeting session, shown in Figure 26.24, allows for a presenter to share applications with end users, chat with them over text or audio, stream video to the users, and interact with them over a question-and-answer format.

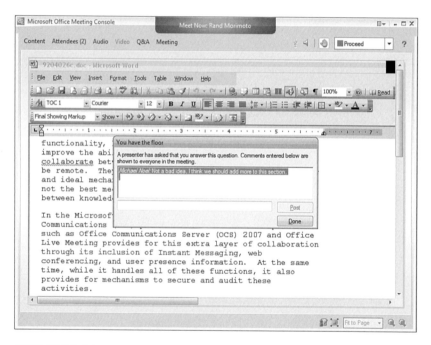

FIGURE 26.24   Viewing an Office Live Meeting session.

Invitations to the Live Meeting conference can be easily sent via email, and attendees need only click on the link in the email to join. The presenter then has the choice to accept new users automatically, or to place them in the *lobby* until verification of their identity is complete.

Users who have attended Microsoft Webcasts in the past might recognize many of the features, as similar technology has been used for this purpose. Office Live Meeting enables organizations to quickly and easily hold online web conferences on the fly.

Summary

The Real-Time Communications functionality that Microsoft has designed into Office Communications Server 2007, Office Live Meeting, and the Communicator 2007 client are ideal for organizations looking to get more productivity out of their Exchange 2007 environment. Tight integration with Exchange 2007, Outlook 2007, and other Microsoft technologies makes them an ideal match for organizations because they allow for improved efficiencies in communications between knowledge workers.

Best Practices

The following are best practices from this chapter:

- ▶ Take care when installing OCS 2007 because it extends the AD schema. Be sure to fully understand the implications of a schema change before doing so.

- ▶ Deploy the Enterprise Edition of OCS 2007 if greater than 15,000 users will be using the environment or if redundancy of server components is required.

- ▶ Use the instant messaging filter in OCS 2007 to filter out potential spyware and unwanted files from users.

- ▶ Consider the use of a Public IM Connectivity (PIC) license to allow internal corporate IM users access to public instant messaging clients, such as MSN, Yahoo!, and AOL.

- ▶ Use the hosted Office Live Meeting to establish web conferences with individuals both inside and outside of an organization.

26

PART VIII

Client Access to Exchange Server 2007

IN THIS PART

CHAPTER 27

Getting the Most Out of the Microsoft Outlook Client

Microsoft Outlook is the common client software used to access Microsoft Exchange for messages, calendar appointments, contacts, and general communications. With the evolution of the Outlook client over the years, the newer versions of the client software have more features and functions than older versions of the Outlook client. This chapter details the capabilities of the current Outlook client (Microsoft Outlook 2007) as well as how older versions of the Outlook client interact with the new Exchange 2007 messaging system.

Common Functions of All Versions of Outlook

In the early days of Microsoft, the Office team of developers didn't work with the Exchange developers. This resulted in the Office suite focusing on individual productivity while Exchange was being built as an enabler for collaboration. Starting with Outlook 98, these two groups started to work more closely together and Outlook began to take on an identity of a collaboration tool. This new era of collaboration eventually resulted in the release of Outlook 2007, which, fortuitously coincides with the release of Exchange Server 2007. This sends a very clear message that the two teams now work very closely with each other with a common goal of enabling knowledge workers to more easily collaborate with each other. This need for better collaboration was further bolstered with focused feedback from the end-user community to the design teams. The results are self-evident with Outlook 2007 because

Exchange and Outlook now have greater integration, enhanced functionality for the end user, and improved collaborative tools, creating a better business communication client. Outlook 2007 has gone beyond even Exchange and offers improved integration with SharePoint as well.

Comparing Outlook 9x, 200x, and Outlook 2007

As Outlook clients have been updated over the years, most of the changes have been evolutionary. That is, functions have been added to react to the new needs of the user community. Functions that existed in older versions of Outlook have either remained or have been upgraded. Each new version of Outlook has also added entirely new functions and integrations. Early versions of Outlook were focused almost entirely on messaging and calendaring. Newer generations of Outlook have added collaboration tools such as forms and rules to manage messages or integrate into applications such as instant messaging or SharePoint.

To meet current needs, the past few versions of Outlook have focused more on improving security. This trend began with Outlook XP and Outlook 2003 and has continued with Outlook 2007. Outlook 2007 offers impressive functions such as Information Rights Management, which allows an email sender to enforce options such as making a message expire or preventing someone from forwarding a message. With the increase in concern about phishing and spam, Outlook 2007 offers new functionality in the way of blocking these nuisances. New functions in the area of calendaring include improvements in the prioritizing of to-do items and the ability to create Internet calendars. In addition to these areas, a focus on views, the user interface, and more powerful searching of mail items have also become a key focus in Outlook 2007. Regardless of the Outlook version, the underlying focus has always been to streamline, add new functionality, and make Outlook a more collaborative business tool. Outlook 2007 is no exception to this philosophy and has made Outlook even easier to use and more powerful in its integration with other Microsoft applications. Although Outlook 2007 is a powerful application by itself, it becomes more valuable to a business when it is matched up with applications such as Exchange 2007 and SharePoint.

The Basic Features of Outlook

In the history of Outlook, the basic features of messaging, calendaring, and task tracking have always been available. Each version has improved upon these basic functions and has sought to add to them. Outlook has long supported protocols such as Messaging Application Programming Interface (MAPI), Internet Message Access Protocol version 4 (IMAP4), and Post Office Protocol version 3 (POP3) to allow users to access messaging functions. Storage in local files as well as local archival has existed in each version of Outlook. As Outlook has evolved, it has become easier to access these functions and they have become more powerful.

Outlook has always offered contact management from both a local and centralized standpoint. Later versions of Outlook have offered users the ability to search and archive their messages. As Outlook has evolved, these functions have become faster and easier to access.

Security in Outlook

Security has always been a concern for Information Technology (IT) departments and Outlook has always offered cutting-edge security functions to help protect users. These functions range from support for Secure/Multipurpose Internet Mail Extensions (S/MIME) encrypted messaging to integrated antiphishing technologies. Outlook has always made an effort to reduce the exposure of the user by blocking Hypertext Markup Language (HTML) content and preventing embedded scripts from launching when content is previewed. The past few versions of Outlook have prevented third-party applications from accessing it to help protect a user's email as well as the Exchange server itself.

Collaborating with Outlook

Collaboration is a major reason companies leverage the Outlook client as their standard calendaring and messaging application. With each new version, the collaborative power of Outlook has grown. Although many tools are available for an Outlook user with just an Exchange server, integration with Microsoft Office and Microsoft's SharePoint Portal product has greatly increased the possibilities for collaboration with Outlook 2007 and Exchange Server 2007.

Other Enhancements in Outlook

Each new version of the Outlook client has introduced new or improved features to enhance functionality and enhance the end-user experience. Whether making it faster, sleeker, or more intuitive, each iteration of Outlook has surpassed the previous version in usability and integration with Exchange as well as other applications. Outlook 2007 is no exception to this trend. This chapter covers many of the most popular features available with Outlook 2007. It also shows the user how to leverage some of the existing features when using this new client with Exchange Server 2007.

What's New in Outlook 2007

As mentioned earlier, new versions of Outlook continue to provide new features and functionality, in addition to enhancing existing features. In this section, administrators can find information covering some of the new features that organizations might find beneficial along with new tools for the end user.

Understanding the Outlook 2007 Interface

The new Outlook 2007 interface incorporates several changes that have been requested by users and administrators over time.

To meet some of these requests, the four-pane view is much more user-friendly, and the preview pane now allows the user to preview attachments in the same interface by simply right-clicking the attachment. Also, the new buttons in the shortcut pane below the folder pane provide a quick new way to access the different features of Outlook. These new features provide an enhanced way to quickly view and organize email. Familiar "right-click" functions still exist to simplify the management of folders and modification of permissions of various folders.

Similarities with Outlook Web Access

The updated Outlook 2007 graphical user interface (GUI) is extremely similar to the GUI that Outlook Web Access (OWA) users using Exchange Server 2007 experience. Although Outlook 2007 provides some features that OWA does not, it does serve to ease the transition between Outlook and OWA for the end users. By keeping the interfaces similar, there is a reduced level of training necessary to teach users how to use OWA. The similarities between Outlook 2007 and OWA 2007 are a result of close work between the two development teams.

> **NOTE**
>
> Outlook Web Access is covered in greater detail in Chapter 28, "Leveraging the Capabilities of the Outlook Web Access (OWA) Client."

Methods for Highlighting Outlook Items

Each new version of Outlook has improved the methods for organizing and finding messages. As email becomes a more and more common way of sharing information, the volume of mail received by end users will continue to increase. With Outlook 2007, users are given enhanced methods for organizing, categorizing, and flagging messages when working with Outlook and Exchange.

Using Quick Flags to Tag Messages

Using quick flags has changed in Outlook 2007. End users used to assign a colored flag to a message to help them organize messages. In previous versions of Outlook, these flags had no predetermined meanings. This meant the user was free to use them in whatever manner they wanted. In Outlook 2007, the flags now have some predefined meanings for follow-up tasks. Flags can be set for when a message must be dealt with and setting these flags results in a new entry in the Tasks area. The old functionality of flags has been replaced with a category option. Right-clicking the rounded square to the left of the flag gives you the option to tag the message with a color. These colors have no predefined meanings, so the user is free to associate any meaning with the color they want. By right-clicking the Arrange By option at the top of the message pane, the user can sort messages by these categories.

To set quick flags in the Outlook 2007 client, complete the following:

1. Right-click on the gray flag icon on the far-right side of the email message in the Inbox to access the flag options.

2. Choose the flag you need to use.

Flags can also be used to configure a reminder. The option for using reminders with flags allows users to configure information and a due date associated with each flag. To configure a reminder, complete these steps:

1. Flag the message.

2. Right-click on the flag and choose Add Reminder.

3. Choose the reason to flag the message and then choose a due date.

4. Choose the date and time for the reminder, and click OK when you are finished.

If you have the To-Do Bar enabled, you will now see your flagged message in the task area, similar to that shown in Figure 27.1, showing the flag, the category, and a bell to represent that there is a reminder set.

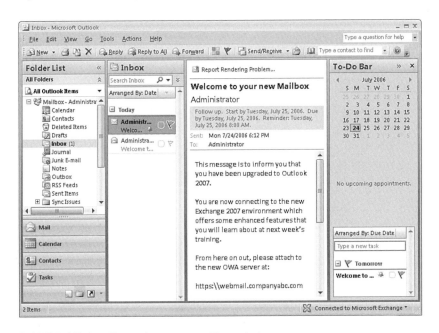

FIGURE 27.1   Flagged message with reminder.

NOTE

A flag with an associated reminder provides the end user a standard Outlook reminder pop-up balloon when the preconfigured reminder comes due.

Like any column in Outlook, the flag column can be used as a sorting point for arranging messages. Simply clicking the arrow at the top of the flag column arranges the messages by the presence of flags.

Making Key Appointments Stand Out with Color

Using the Outlook 2007 calendar, this new feature allows for the customization and organization of appointments using colors, allowing end-user appointments to stand out when viewing the calendar.

To choose a color and label an appointment, follow these steps:

1. Open the appointment in the calendar.

2. Click the multicolored button labeled Categorize.

3. Choose the color you want to use.

4. Close the calendar item.

The calendar item will now appear with the color you selected, similar to what is shown in Figure 27.2.

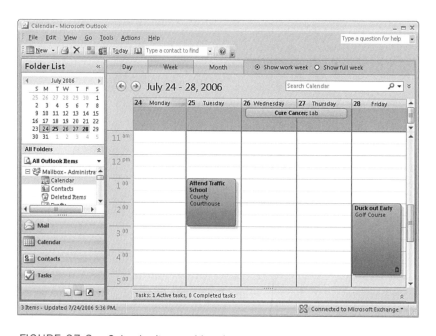

FIGURE 27.2   Calendar items with color.

Creating Meetings Based on Time Zone

Another new feature in the calendar allows meeting creators to more easily set meetings in other locations. A common complaint about Outlook was that meetings were created at the unintended time when a user was going to be traveling to another time zone. In Outlook 2007, there is an option to enable a time zone drop-down to more easily and accurately pick times for meetings created in advance for other locations. Begin by creating a new meeting request and complete the following:

1. Toward the right side of the main set of buttons, find the Globe icon labeled Time Zones.

2. Click the Time Zones icon and a new drop-down is created next to the start and end times.

3. Via the drop-down, select the time zone where the meeting is going to occur.

4. Select the start and stop times as usual.

5. Invite your attendees and click Send when you are finished.

Using the New Search Functionality

Outlook 2007 makes it easier than ever to search through large mailboxes and calendars. Users can save searches that are commonly used and can leverage the flag and category functions mentioned earlier to provide very powerful ways of managing messages, appointments, or tasks.

Using the Query Builder

The query builder is easily accessible from the top of the toolbar above the message pane. To perform a search, do the following:

1. Enter the word(s) to search for in the Search Inbox box and matches will immediately highlight.

2. Click the double-down arrow next to Search Inbox to expand the query builder.

3. Click Add Criteria to add additional fields to search against.

Typing in the search area updates the results in near real time.

Saving Commonly Used Searches

To save a search, the search must be started from within the Folder list under Search Folders. To do so, complete the following steps:

1. Right-click on Search Folders and choose New Search Folder.

2. Within the New Search Folder pop-up window, choose the search folder and criteria for your search. Depending on what selection is made, the user might be presented with more options to complete before commencing the search. Choose also what part of Outlook to search.

3. Click OK when you are finished.

4. The search completes and the results are displayed in the center pane. In addition, the search is saved under the Search Folders area in the Folder list.

5. To delete the saved search, click on it and choose Delete.

27

> **TIP**
>
> Saved searches are also available when using Outlook Web Access (OWA). For saved searches to be accessed via Outlook Web Access, a user must create the saved search in Outlook 2007 first.

Managing Multiple Email Accounts from One Place

Outlook 2007 allows the end user to access multiple email accounts from the same Outlook client, including IMAP, POP3, and Hypertext Transfer Protocol (HTTP) mail accounts. This allows for multiple mail account configurations for the same user.

To configure Outlook to access multiple mailboxes, do the following:

1. Go to Tools, Options.

2. Click the Mail Setup tab.

3. Click E-Mail Accounts.

4. Click New E-Mail Account.

5. Select the type of account (for example, POP3, HTTP, Exchange, IMAP).

6. Click Next.

7. Enter the appropriate information for the email account so that it can be properly connected.

   If your server does not support autodiscovery (that is, Exchange 2000 or Exchange 2003), you need to check the box for Manually Configure Server Settings.

8. Click Next.

9. Click Finish, completing the account setup.

Taking Advantage of the Trust Center

Outlook 2007 adds a new function called the Trust Center, shown in Figure 27.3. The Trust Center is a centralized location for the management of security-related functions in Outlook 2007. This includes the following:

▶ Trusted Publishers

▶ Add-ins

▶ Privacy Options

▶ E-Mail Security

▶ Attachment Handling

▶ Automatic Download

- ▶ Macro Security

- ▶ Programmatic Access

By placing these functions under a single interface, it is much easier to manage the security functions in Outlook 2007. Each of these areas is further addressed later in this chapter.

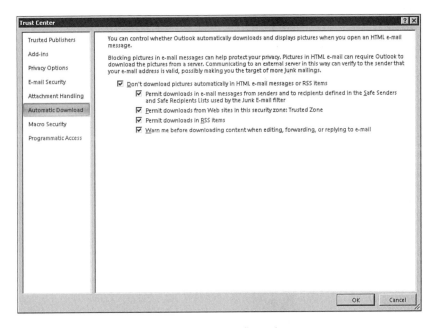

FIGURE 27.3 Microsoft Trust Center configuration screen.

Introducing RSS feeds

New to Outlook 2007 is the ability to subscribe to RSS feeds. RSS stands for Really Simple Syndication. Many blogs and news sites are offering RSS feeds as a way to disseminate information. RSS feeds are a concept similar to the old Network News Transfer Protocol (NNTP).

To subscribe to an RSS feed, simply do the following:

1. Click tools and then click Options.

2. Select the Mail Setup tab and click E-Mail Accounts.

3. From the Account Settings window, click the RSS Feeds tab.

4. Click New.

5. Enter the uniform resource locator (URL) to the RSS feed you want to add, and click Add.

6. If the URL is valid, you will see the RSS Feed Options page. Choose the settings you want for this feed, similar to that shown in Figure 27.4, and click OK.

FIGURE 27.4   Sample RSS Feed Options page.

7. Click Close and then click OK.

Security Enhancements in Outlook 2007

Microsoft announced its Secure Computing initiative in 2002 and has continued to improve the security of their products ever since. For Outlook 2007, this means a great increase in the number of security and antispam features available when using the Outlook 2007 client and Exchange Server 2007. Similarly, improvements have been made in the area of preventing unwanted viruses or malicious scripts from executing when a message is received or previewed. Microsoft continues to integrate advanced email security features such as digital signing of messages, mail encryption, and Information Rights Management.

Support for Secured Messaging

Microsoft's Outlook 2007 development team has taken the feedback from IT groups as well as from end users and has recognized the ever-increasing need for secured messaging. To stay ahead of competitors, Outlook 2007 expanded its support for secured messaging, including S/MIME, digital signing, message encryption, and smart card support.

S/MIME Support, Digital Signatures, and Email Encryption

Though S/MIME support has been available in previous versions of Outlook, Outlook 2007 provides updated support for the latest S/MIME functionality. Using S/MIME, email messages are encrypted by the recipient's public key and can be decrypted, and, therefore, made accessible, only with the recipient's private key. This private/public key exchange is critical for secure email correspondence.

Use of S/MIME support requires that the Outlook 2007 client have a certificate for cryptography on the client computer (and is stored locally either in the Microsoft Windows certificate store or on a smart card), and can be pushed through Registry settings or via Group Policy to easily implement S/MIME throughout an organization. This type of internal certificate use is usually performed via an internal Public Key Infrastructure (PKI). The creation of an internal PKI goes beyond the scope of this book and is not included here.

S/MIME support also includes digital signing. Digital signing allows for security labels and signed secure message receipts. This is a way for a message recipient to be sure that the message came from the person who claimed to send it. Using Outlook 2007, enterprisewide security labels are enforced such as "For Internal Use Only" or labeling messages to restrict the forwarding or printing of messages through Information Rights Management. In addition, users can now request S/MIME affirmation of receipt of a message. By requesting a receipt, the sender confirms that the recipient recognized and verified the digital signature because no receipt is received unless the recipient, who should have received the message, actually does receive the message. Only then does the sender receive the digitally signed read receipt. This allows email users to more safely trust the information they receive via email. This can be especially valuable when email is used for workflow or approval processes.

Setting Email Security on a Specific Message
Security such as payload encryption or digital signing can be set for an individual email using the options available when creating an email message. Clicking on the Options button opens the Message Options dialog box. There, the user clicks can access the Security Properties page to set the security for the message. The user can choose to encrypt the message and/or add a digital signature, request S/MIME receipt, and configure the security settings.

To do this, follow these steps:

1. Open a new message.

2. Click the Options tab and click More Options.

3. Click the Security Settings button.

4. Add security settings as desired, similar to the ones shown in Figure 27.5.

5. Click OK when you are finished.

6. Continue with the email as normal.

Setting Email Security on the Entire Mailbox
Security settings can also be globally configured for the entire mailbox so that they apply at all times.

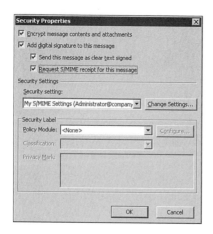

FIGURE 27.5   Security Properties page in Outlook.

To do this, follow these steps:

1. Go to Tools, Trust Center.

2. Select Email Security from the left pane.

3. Enable the choices desired for security for the entire mailbox:

   ▶ Encrypt Contents and Attachments for Outgoing Messages

   ▶ Add Digital Signature to Outgoing Messages

   ▶ Send Clear Text Signed Messages When Sending Signed Messages (picked by default). (This allows users who don't have S/MIME security to read the message.)

   ▶ Request S/MIME Receipt for All S/MIME Signed Messages

4. For all choices (except the third choice) to work properly, the user must get a digital certificate provided by the administrator. This can be imported by clicking on the Import/Export button at the bottom of the window beneath Digital IDs (Certificates) or by clicking on Get a Digital ID.

5. After you import the digital certificate, the security functionality is complete.

6. Click OK when you are finished.

Attaching Security Labels to Messages

Also a feature in Outlook 2007, security labels can be configured by the administrator and used by the end user to add security messages to the heading of any email messages. Security labels require digital certificates and denote the sensitivity and security of an email. This functionality leveraged Information Rights Management functions made possible by Exchange and Active Directory. Security labels include information in the email header such as "Do not forward outside of the company" or "Confidential." They can be configured on a message-by-message basis or for the entire mailbox.

To configure a security label for a single message, follow these steps:

1. Open a new message.

2. Click the Options tab and click More Options.

3. Click Security Settings from the Message Options window.

4. Click the Add Digital Signature to This Message check box.

5. Choose the security label, classification, and privacy mark that apply to the message.

6. Click OK when you are finished.

To configure a security label for all messages in the mailbox, follow these steps:

1. Go to Tools, Trust Center.

2. Click E-Mail Security in the left pane.

3. Click Settings.

4. Click Security Labels.

5. Choose the policy module, classification, and privacy mark that will apply to all messages.

6. Click OK three times when you are finished.

Using Junk Email Filters to Reduce Spam

Improved antispam and antiphishing have now been integrated into both Outlook 2007 and Exchange Server 2007. With this feature, the end user can configure the level of anti-spam filtering desired and control the level of restriction in which messages will be checked. These local functions work in tandem with antispam settings on the Exchange 2007 server.

In today's workplace, it is commonplace for 90% of incoming mail to be spam. Rather than burden the end user with the task of reviewing and deleting spam messages, Outlook 2007 is able to determine if a message is spam and prevent the user from having to deal with it. This can be especially helpful as spam messages are often infected with viruses or contain materials that would be inappropriate in the workplace. Occasionally, Outlook 2007 misses some messages that are actually spam, but the user has the ability to help improve the system when using Exchange 2007. By tagging a message as spam, Exchange will be more likely to catch a similar spam message in the future. This can benefit an entire network when users tag spam messages in this way.

27

With the Outlook 2007 Junk E-mail filter, messages are reviewed when the client receives them to determine if the message should be treated as junk or valid email. To do this, the filter analyzes each message based on a class or criteria and imported spammer list. When Outlook is initially installed, the default setting is Low, which catches only the most obvious junk email. This setting is configurable by the end user and can be changed to increase the level of sensitivity on the junk email feature. This catches more unwanted email but increases the chance of false positives. False positives are valid messages that are mistakenly junked. It is important to occasionally check the Junk Mail folder to ensure that no valid messages were accidentally junked. Messages caught by the filter and determined to be junk mail are moved to a Junk E-mail folder in the Outlook 2007 client. The end user can and should review emails checking for false positive emails that were accidentally specified as junk. Optionally, the end user can configure the option to permanently delete junk email messages as they arrive and not save them to the folder at all. This setting should be used with caution.

To configure junk email filtering, follow these steps:

1. In Outlook 2007, go to Tools, Options, Preferences tab.

2. Under Email, click on the Junk Email button.

3. On the Options tab shown in Figure 27.6, choose the level of blockage desired.

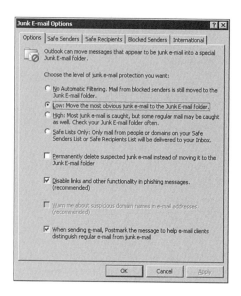

FIGURE 27.6   Junk mail options.

4. Click OK when you are finished.

Utilizing the Safe Senders List

If the Outlook 2007 Junk E-mail filter incorrectly determines that a message is junk, the end user can add the sender's email address to a Safe Senders list. This list prevents the filter from identifying any new emails from that sender to be classified as junk mail. This function is also referred to as a "white list." The Safe Senders list supports both email addresses and wildcard domains for safe senders. So, a user could add andrew@companyabc.com to allow that one user to send them messages, or a user could add @companyabc.com to allow any user from companyabc.com to send them a message without any chance of the message being flagged as spam. By default, all email addresses in the end user's contacts list are automatically included in the Safe Senders list, as are any names listed in the Exchange 2007 Global Address List. The option to Automatically Add People/E-Mail to the Safe Senders List can be very useful in reducing the amount of manual interaction with the Safe Senders list.

Utilizing the Safe Recipients List

The Safe Recipients list performs a very similar function to the Safe Senders list. The Safe Recipients list allows the user to configure email lists or mail-enabled groups of which they are a member. Any messages sent from these email groups are automatically considered as "safe."

Utilizing the Blocked Senders List

The opposite of the Safe Senders list is the Blocked Senders list. This concept is often referred to as a "black list." By entering email addresses or wildcard domains, a user can tell Outlook 2007 to automatically junk any and all messages received from the blocked senders.

TIP

It is important to understand that Blocked Sender rules are based only on the Reply-to addresses given in the email. Reply-to addresses can be forged in an attempt to slip around antispam systems.

Utilizing the International List

Outlook 2007 also has the ability to flag messages as junk based on where they came from. The International tab allows a user to block entire top-level domains (shown in Figure 27.7) or to block messages in particular languages. This is a more encompassing option than blocking by domain name.

To add users to the Safe Senders, Safe Recipients, Blocked Senders, or International lists, do the following:

1. Select Tools, Options, and go to the Preference List tab. Click the Junk E-mail button.

2. Choose one of the tabs (Safe Senders, Safe Recipients, or Blocked Senders), and then click Add to insert the user to the appropriate list.

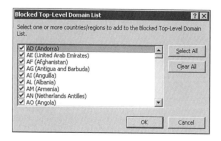

FIGURE 27.7   Blocked top-level domains.

3. Type in the SMTP email address of the user, group, or domain (such as `jdoe@companyabc.com` or `@companyabc.com`).

4. Click OK when you are finished.

TIP

Many services provide lists of junk senders for import into a Blocked Senders list. These lists are created based on known spammers. If your organization wants to provide the end users with a list of trusted or junk senders, the end user can easily import the list by clicking on the Import from File button.

Avoiding Web Beaconing

Web beaconing refers to the use of references to external content via email to identify a message as having been read. This allows a spammer to validate their list of addresses by identifying the messages that reached a valid user and were opened. When the end user opens the message or views it in the preview pane, the computer retrieves this external content. Outlook 2007 has the ability to block web beaconing, which can help reduce the chances of a user getting onto more spam lists.

To enable web beacon filtering, from Outlook 2007, do the following:

1. Click Tools and then click Trust Center.

2. Select Automatic Download in the left pane.

3. Check the Don't Download Pictures Automatically in HTML E-Mail Messages or RSS Items check box.

4. Click OK when you are finished.

Understanding RPC Over HTTPS in Outlook 2007

RPC over HTTPS allows Outlook 2007 to connect to Exchange Server 2007 using the MAPI protocol tunneled over an Internet connection via Hypertext Transfer Protocol Secure

(HTTPS). This allows the user to connect to Exchange and benefit from all the native MAPI functions without having to use a separate virtual private network (VPN) client. RPC over HTTPS has the benefit of not suffering from high-latency connections as HTTP protocols are designed for poor connectivity. MAPI, on the other hand, quickly falls apart when latency breaks 250ms or so.

Installing and Configuring RPC Over HTTPS on the Server Side

RPC over HTTPS requires additional configuration on the Exchange server to support HTTP proxy. Three items must be configured on the Exchange 2007 front-end server for the remote connection:

▶ Install the RPC over HTTP proxy Windows component.

▶ Configure Internet Information Services (IIS) to support RPC over HTTP secured communications.

▶ Configure Transmission Control Protocol (TCP) proxy ports for directory and mailbox connections.

Installing the RPC Over HTTP Windows Component

To be able to run RPC over HTTPS, the RPC over HTTP Windows component needs to be installed. To install the component, do the following:

1. From the Windows 2007 front-end server that will host the RPC over HTTP client connections, click Start, Settings, Control Panel, Add or Remove Programs.

2. Select Add/Remove Windows Components.

3. Highlight the Network Services component, and then click Details.

4. Select the RPC over HTTP Proxy option, and then click OK.

5. Click Next to begin the installation, and then click Finish when you are done.

Configuring IIS to Support RPC Over HTTPS

After the RPC over HTTP proxy component has been installed, IIS needs to be configured to support remote procedure calls (RPC) secured communications. To do so, do the following:

1. Select Start, Programs, Administrative Tools, Internet Information Services (IIS) Manager.

2. Traverse the IIS tree past the server, Web Sites, RPC. Right-click on the RPC container, and select Properties.

3. Select the Directory Security tab, and click Edit.

4. Deselect the Enable Anonymous Access option.

27

5. Select the Basic Authentication option (the Integrated Windows Authentication option should also be selected by default). Click OK.

6. Click Edit and select both Require Secure Channel (SSL) and Require 128-bit Encryption. Click OK.

> **NOTE**
>
> To support Secure Sockets Layer (SSL; HTTPS), you need to request and install an SSL certificate on the edge system hosting the RPC proxy. If this certificate is tied to a nonpublic root, the root certificate needs to be imported by users before RPC over HTTPS will operate correctly.

Further detail on the process of setting up edge services like RPC over HTTPS can be found in Chapter 8, "Implementing Edge Services for an Exchange Server 2007 Environment."

Installing and Configuring RPC Over HTTP on Outlook 2007

After RPC over HTTP is configured on the edge server, the end user's workstation needs to be configured to support RPC over HTTPS.

For Outlook 2007 to use RPC over HTTPS, the workstation must be running a supported operating system. At this time, the only supported operating system is Windows XP SP1 or higher. In addition, the client system must have installed the following hot fix to enable RPC over HTTP.

> **TIP**
>
> The required hot fix can be downloaded from Microsoft at: http://support.microsoft.com/default.aspx?scid=KB;EN-US;331320.
>
> As a best practice, install all security updates and required patches to ensure proper functionality when accessing Exchange over the Internet. Systems that will access Exchange from outside the network are especially susceptible to viruses and spyware and should be well protected.

To install the required patch and configure the Outlook 2007 client for RPC over HTTP access, complete the following:

1. Install the patch listed in the preceding Tip.

2. Reboot the PC.

3. Launch Outlook 2007.

4. Go to Tools, Options, Mail Setup, and click E-Mail Accounts.

5. Highlight the Exchange Server connection, and click Change.

6. On the Change E-Mail Account screen, click More Settings.

7. Click the Connection tab.

8. Click the Connect to My Exchange Mailbox Using HTTP check box.

9. Click Exchange Proxy Settings.

On the Exchange Proxy Settings screen, configure the following:

1. For Connection Settings, enter the URL of the Exchange server that has been configured as the RPC proxy server.

2. Click Connect Using SSL Only.

3. Click the two boxes to use HTTP as the first choice for both fast and slow connections, as shown in Figure 27.8, and then click OK.

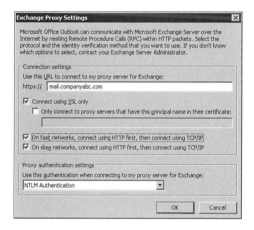

FIGURE 27.8   RPC proxy settings.

4. Click OK to accept the information box about restarting Outlook.

5. Click Next, click Finish, and then click Close.

6. Click OK to exit the options screen.

7. Close Outlook and launch Outlook again.

TIP

To ensure that Outlook 2007 is now using RPC over HTTPS, hold the Ctrl key and right-click the Outlook icon in the taskbar. Click Connections. This screen shows you the connection type to the Exchange server.

The most secure method of connecting uses the following settings, which are also the default settings when RPC over HTTP is first configured:

▶ Connect with SSL Only

▶ Mutually Authenticate the Session When Connecting with SSL

▶ Password Authentication Is NTLM

Deploying Outlook 2007

To take advantage of all the features of Outlook 2007, you need to deploy Outlook 2007 to your users. The deployment can be performed with many tools such as Systems Management Server 2003 or though Group Policy Objects. This section focuses on how to preconfigure Outlook 2007 so that it will be deployed with the functions and settings that you need.

Utilizing the Office Customization Tool

The Office Customization Tool (OCT) is a new application included in Office 2007. The OCT allows an administrator to preconfigure components and settings within the Office 2007 suite to simplify deployments of Office 2007 applications.

The OCT is accessed in the following manner:

1. Launch a command prompt.

2. Browse to the drive containing the Office install files.

3. Browse to the directory containing the `setup.exe` file.

4. Type `Setup.exe /admin`.

Running the OCT in this way allows you to either create a new setup customization file or to modify an existing one. If you are creating a new file, the OCT displays a list of the products available on the network installation point. You must select a single product that you want to customize.

After running the wizard, you can save your customizations in the Updates folder. Setup will look into this folder to find customizations when you run the setup.

Alternatively, you can save your customizations in another location and reference them during the install. For example:

```
Setup.exe /adminfile \\server\share\OCT\remoteusers.msp
```

This is an exceptionally powerful ability as you can create different custom settings for different types of users.

Taking Advantage of OCT for Outlook 2007

Although the OCT offers customizations for all Office 2007 components, this section examines some of the settings available specifically for Outlook 2007. Some of the more useful settings include the following:

- **Use existing profile**—This setting retains the existing profile or prompts the user to create a profile the first time Outlook is started.

- **Modify profile**—This setting modifies the default profile or makes changes to profiles that you specify. If there isn't a default profile or no profile by the name that you specify, Outlook creates a profile based on settings you choose in the other areas of the OCT.

- **New profile**—This setting creates a new profile and sets it as the default profile. If a profile already exists, it is not removed and is still available to the user. You need to enter a name in the Profile name box, which appears in the E-Mail Accounts dialog box in Outlook. The new profile is created based on the options you choose in the other areas of the OCT.

- **Apply PRF**—This setting imports an Outlook profile (PRF) file to define a new default profile. You can use any profile created for Outlook 2007. Enter a name and path for the profile in the Apply the Following Profile (PRF File) field. If you created a PRF file for a previous version of Outlook, you can import it to Office Outlook 2007, provided it uses only MAPI services.

- **Do not configure Cached Exchange mode**—This setting configures Outlook 2007 to only attach to the Exchange mailboxes directly from the Exchange server, as opposed to being cached on users' computers in an Offline Folder file (OST file).

- **Configure Cached Exchange mode**—This setting creates an OST file or uses an existing OST file. This results in users working with a local copy of their Exchange mailbox. When selecting Use Cached Exchange mode, you can configure the following options.

  - **Download only headers**—Download copies of headers only from users' Exchange mailboxes.

  - **Download headers followed by the full item**—Download copies of headers from users' Exchange mailboxes, and then download copies of messages.

  - **Download full items**—Download copies of full messages (headers and message bodies) from users' Exchange mailboxes.

  - **On slow connections, download only headers**—When a slow network connection is detected, download copies of headers only from users' Exchange mailboxes.

  - **Download Public Folder Favorites**—Download the list of public folder favorites .

Using Outlook 2007 Collaboratively

Like every evolution of Outlook, Outlook 2007 expands on the collaborative tools available to the end user when connecting to an Exchange server. This section covers many of these collaborative tools and new collaborative features available in the Outlook 2007 client.

Viewing Shared Calendars in Multiple Panes

Tracking appointments and setting meetings have quickly become high priorities for employees in today's business world. To simplify these types of functions, Outlook 2007 allows a user to view multiple Exchange calendars in a shared pane. In previous versions of Outlook, an additional calendar would be opened in a new window. In Outlook 2007, if a user has configured their calendar with View rights, other users can view those calendars as well as their own at the same time lined up side by side to view or compare them.

To open additional calendars, perform the following steps:

1. Choose File, Open, Other User's Folder.

2. Choose the name of the user and select Folder Type: Calendar. The calendar opens in the main window and automatically removes the mailbox owner's calendar.

   New to Outlook 2007 is a prompt to allow a user to request access to a calendar to which they don't currently have access.

3. To view both your own calendar and the additional calendar, look at the left pane. There is an area under the monthly calendar that provides check boxes for what calendars the end user wants to view. This is split into My Calendars and Peoples Calendars. Check the My Calendar check box and another check box to view both your own calendar and an additional calendar.

TIP

When viewing multiple calendars, keep in mind that each additional calendar is shown in a different color; also note that the corresponding check box on the left is seen in the same color.

---

4. Continue to add the desired calendars, and click on the check boxes to remove or add calendars to the view.

5. When you are finished, click the My Calendar check box and deselect all the additional calendars.

TIP

When in the Calendar view, you can click the Open a Shared Calendar hyperlink and you will be prompted to enter the name of the user whose calendar you want to view. Enter the name of the calendar to open and click OK. This automatically shows both the mailbox owner's calendar and the new calendar(s).

Enabling Calendar Sharing in Outlook 2007

By default, calendars are not shared. This is for the security of the user. It is up to the calendar owner to specify which users should be able to read or write to their calendar.

To enable the mailbox owner's calendar to be shared, follow these steps:

1. From the Folder List view, right-click Calendar in the left pane.

2. Click Change Sharing permissions.

3. From the Calendar Properties page, click Add.

4. Browse or enter the name or group to get access to the calendar, and click Add.

5. Click OK when the users have been added.

6. The end user must now assign the permissions for other users to have to the calendar. Outlook provides predefined roles for permissions that appear in the Permission Level box. Clicking the drop-down menu and choosing a predefined permission level shows what permissions are being granted, making it easy to choose the desired permissions. To create a unique set of permissions, choose an initial permission level and then check the boxes and radio buttons to assign the unique permissions, as shown in Figure 27.9.

7. Click OK when you are finished. The user(s) specified will have those rights to the end user's calendar until the end user specifically removes them by going through the same process mentioned, and then clicking on the user or group with permissions to the calendar and choosing Remove.

NOTE

When you grant another user Read access to your calendar, they will be able to read your calendar entries. They will not, however, be able to read calendar items that are marked as Private.

Sharing Other Personal Information

Outlook 2007 allows users to share their personal information (such as the Inbox, contacts, and tasks) with other users. This is done via the same method listed previously with the difference being that the permissions are set for the Inbox, Contacts, or Tasks folders.

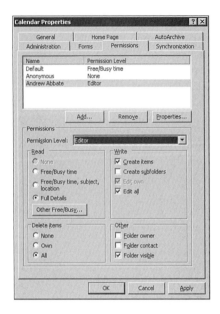

FIGURE 27.9   Changing sharing permissions.

To enable Inbox sharing, for example, follow these steps:

1. Right-click on the Inbox in the Folder view.

2. Choose Change Sharing Permissions.

3. Add the users or groups and set their permissions as described previously in the "Enabling Calendar Sharing in Outlook 2007" section.

Delegating Rights to Send Email "On Behalf Of" Another User

In some situations, such as when a user has an administrative assistant, they might want to give someone the ability to send messages or meeting requests on their behalf. This results in a message that will come from "user B on behalf of user A." To enable a user to send email on someone else's behalf, follow these steps:

1. Go to Tools, Options, and select the Delegates tab.

2. Click Add.

3. Add the name of the user or group that needs the rights.

4. Click OK.

5. Choose the permission level for each component of Outlook.

6. Click OK when you are finished.

7. To send the delegates a summary message of their rights, click the Automatically Send a Message to Delegate Summarizing These Permissions check box, as shown in Figure 27.10, before clicking OK.

FIGURE 27.10   Adding delegates.

8. To enable the delegates to see private items, click the Delegate Can See My Private Items check box before clicking OK.

Sharing Information with Users Outside the Company

In response to more advanced needs of users, Outlook 2007 has provided functions to help extend familiar collaboration tools into unfamiliar areas. Much of the functionality available among users of the same Exchange environment is now available across the Internet. This is a great enabler for users because it is now easier to collaborate with colleagues from other companies.

Configuring Free/Busy Time to Be Viewed via the Internet

In the past, it required specialized software and connectors to exchange free/busy information with another Exchange organization. Free/busy information is what tracks the availability of users in terms of having appointments, being in meetings, or having free time available. Exchange administrators and mailbox owners can publish this free/busy information outside of their Exchange environment to more easily set up meetings with other organizations. If this functionality is needed, this information can be published to a web server available to both organizations. In the past, you could use a service provided by Microsoft called the Microsoft Office Internet Free/Busy Service, but this service is no longer available. This service has been replaced by Office Online. By publishing free/busy information to a shared website, users outside of the Exchange organization can view published free/busy information over the Internet. They can also use the same website to schedule meetings with recipients from the participating organizations. This option is available for users accessing Exchange with the Outlook 2002 or later clients.

To configure free/busy time to be displayed on the Internet with a custom server, follow these steps:

1. Right-click the calendar to be shared.

2. Choose Publish to Internet and Publish to Custom Server.

3. Enter the URL to which you will publish your information.

4. Choose the time frame you want to publish as well as the options and upload method, similar to that shown in Figure 27.11.

5. Click OK.

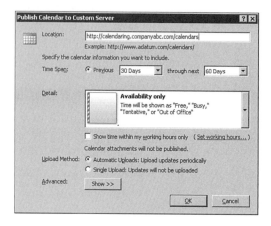

FIGURE 27.11   Publishing calendars.

To stop sharing this information on the custom server, complete the following steps:

1. Right-click the shared calendar.

2. Choose Publish to Internet.

3. Choose Remove from Server.

4. Click Yes.

To configure which service will publish the free/busy information, follow these steps:

1. To use a locally provided website, click Publish at My Location, and enter the URL to the location.

2. Click OK.

3. You might be prompted to install some files to complete the installation of the added functionality.

4. Click Yes to install. The Outlook feature is installed.

5. Click OK two more times.

To publish a calendar to Office Online, follow these steps:

1. From the navigation pane, right-click the calendar you want to share.

2. Choose Publish to Internet and then click Publish to Office Online.

3. Register for Office Online if you do not already have a Windows Live ID.

4. Specify how much information you want to upload (in days).

5. Choose your options, permissions, and upload method.

6. Click OK and information will be published.

7. Optional: Send invites to contacts to share your information.

To stop sharing this information on Office Online:

1. Right-click the shared calendar.

2. Choose Publish to Internet.

3. Choose Remove from Server.

4. Click Yes.

Viewing Free/Busy Time via the Internet

If granted necessary permissions, Outlook users from one organization can view free/busy information from another organization's users via the shared website. The user can send meeting requests, add the user to a group schedule, and see free/busy time just as they could with users from their own organization. To do this, the end user must access the free/busy information website, click on View Free/Busy Times on the Web, and enter the email address of the user whose free/busy time is to be viewed.

The user also has the option to see a free/busy search path for their contacts. To do so, follow these steps:

1. In the navigation pane, click Contacts, and then double-click an entry to open a contact.

2. Click the Details tab.

3. Under the text that reads Internet Free-Busy, type the fully qualified path of the location that you want to search for this contact's free/busy information in the Address box. You can use any valid URL format, such as: http://..., file://\\..., or ftp://...., as shown in Figure 27.12.

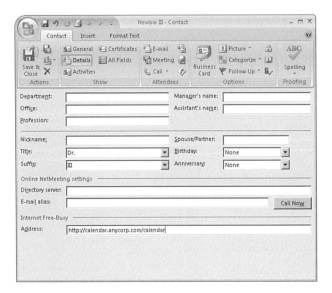

FIGURE 27.12   External Free/Busy path.

To let other users know about your shared calendar information, you can do the following:

1. Right-click the shared calendar.

2. Click Publish to Internet.

3. Click Share Published Calendar.

4. Enter the email addresses of the people with whom you want to share your free/busy information.

5. Click Send.

The person who will be accessing the shared calendar will also need a Windows Live logon.

They will receive a message stating the following:

```
Andrew Abbate has invited you to add the "Andrew_Abbate_Calendar" Internet Calendar
subscription to Microsoft Office Outlook.
You can open this calendar on any computer with an Internet calendar compatible
program installed, such as Microsoft Office Outlook 2007.
```

Sending Contact Information to Others

As the business world becomes more and more electronic, old customs such as the exchange of paper business cards are being replaced by more modern methods. Virtual Business Cards, or vCards have greatly increased in popularity. These vCards enable an

Outlook user to send anyone a small file containing their contact information. Because of the vCard format, this contact information can then be imported into the recipient's contact list. The vCard can contain common information such as the following:

- Name
- Address
- Phone numbers
- Email address
- Job title

Going beyond the concepts of a typical business card, a vCard can also include the following:

- A picture of the contact
- A public key for encryption or digital signing
- A link to Internet published free/busy information

vCards can be emailed as attachments or they can be automatically attached to outgoing messages as part of a signature file.

To email a vCard, follow these steps:

1. Open the contact that will become the vCard.
2. Click Actions, Send as Business Card.
3. Input information into the email and send the email.

When the user receives the card, he can open it and Save and Close into his own contacts area.

To include a vCard in an AutoSignature, follow these steps:

1. Click Tools, Options.
2. Click the Mail Format tab and click Signatures.
3. Edit an existing AutoSignature or create a new one.
4. In the toolbar above the text window, click the Business Card icon.
5. Select the business card from your contacts, and click OK.
6. Click OK.

27

Using Public Folders to Share Information

Public folders have long been a staple of collaborative work via Outlook. Outlook 2007 continues to support easy access of public folders. Public folders are often used where mailing lists would be overkill. Rather then flooding mailboxes of dozens of users with back-and-forth discussions, public folders are used as a single storage point for these types of messages and various users are granted access to read or write to these folders. Public folders are also a great place to store common contacts or common calendar items. This makes it easier to share information within a subset of users in Exchange. Outlook 2007 makes it easy to access this information centrally without it cluttering the global resources.

Using Group Schedules

Group schedules are a fairly new feature and are only available to Outlook 2003 and 2007 clients. Group schedules enable the user to create groups of users enabling a quick view of their calendars. The Group Schedules features also allow a user to send all the members of the Group Schedule email or a meeting request using a single address. This makes it very easy for a user to group together commonly used resources for a quick view of availability. This might include a list of conference rooms in a given building or could be members of a team for a project they are working on. By arranging these resources together into a group schedule, the user can avoid the tedious process of inviting all of the resources individually to a meeting to see when they are available.

Configuring Group Schedules

Users can create multiple group schedules to help them organize resources into logical groups.

To create a new group schedule, follow these steps:

1. From the Calendar view, click Action, View Group Schedules. The Group Schedules dialog box opens.

2. Click New.

3. Name the group schedule.

4. Click OK.

5. The Customized Group Schedules dialog box opens.

6. Click Add Others.

7. Type the name of the user(s) in the Type Name or Select from List box, and click To after the user has been selected. Note that more than one user at a time can be selected and added to the To area.

8. When all users are selected, click OK.

9. Click Save and Close.

After the group schedule has been created, to view it and work with it, follow these steps:

1. Click on the View Group Schedules button.

2. Select the group schedule to view.

3. Click Open to show a screen similar to the one shown in Figure 27.13.

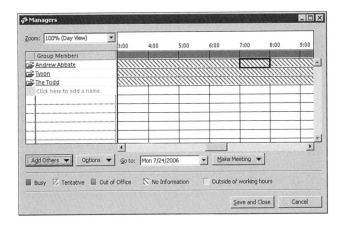

FIGURE 27.13   Group views.

Sending Email or Meeting Requests to Group Schedules

Organizing subsets of user or resources into group schedules can also be very useful for sending emails or meeting requests. In this sense, the group schedule acts similarly to a distribution group.

To schedule a meeting, follow these steps:

1. Click Make Meeting from within the Group Schedule view for the specific group.

2. Choose New Meeting to just send the meeting request to one member.

3. Choose New Meeting with All to send the meeting request to all members of the group schedule.

4. Fill out the meeting request as you normally would.

To send an email, follow these steps:

1. Click Make Meeting.

2. Choose New Mail Message to send to an individual member of the group.

3. Choose New Mail Message to All to send to the whole group.

4. Fill out the email message as you normally would, and send the message.

NOTE

It is important to realize that group schedules created in this way are only available to the user who created them. Other members of the group schedule who wanted similar functionality would have to create their own group schedule.

Using Cached Exchange Mode for Offline Functionality

Outlook 2007 continues to support Cached Exchange mode. Cached Exchange mode, or Cached mode for short, refers to a configuration where Outlook is storing the messages and calendar items locally. Unlike the old Personal folder file (PST) storage method, Cached mode utilizes an OST file. This file is synchronized with the Exchange server on a regular basis. This means that there are two copies of the mailbox at all times. One copy lives on the Exchange server and one copy lives on the Outlook client.

This configuration has many advantages in terms of performance and reliability. For example, imagine that a user is connecting to their Exchange server over a dial-up connection and isn't running Cached mode. The user receives a message with a large attachment. The user sees the new message and opens the attachment. Now, the message has to be downloaded to the user's computer. This takes several minutes because of the size of the file and the relatively slow link speed. This usually results in unhappy users because they had to wait several minutes between wanting to open the attachment and the attachment actually opening.

Now, let's view this same scenario with Cached mode. In Cached mode, the attachment is downloaded in the background when the message arrives, assuming the Outlook client is attached to the server. The message with the attachment doesn't appear in the mailbox until the contents have been downloaded and cached locally. Now, when the user sees the message appear in the Inbox, the files associated with the attachment are already on the local system. The user opens the attachment and it opens immediately. This results in a happier user.

The truth of the matter is that the download time of the message was exactly the same in both scenarios. However, the perceived difference is that the Cached mode situation was faster because the user doesn't know when the message was sent. This situation also takes great advantage of the idle time of the user. Most messages arrive and are fully downloaded to the client while the user is away from their system or doing other things. This means that when the user is actively working with email, there aren't any delays in moving data.

Because the data downloaded is only a mirror of the Exchange mailbox, the content available via OWA is exactly the same. Similarly, if the user were to get another computer or a new computer, Outlook simply creates another copy of the data locally to keep in sync.

With the OST file locally stored, the user is able to work with the contents of their mailbox even when not connected to the Exchange server. Changes made locally will sync back to the Exchange server. Like most replication performed by Microsoft, the newest copy always wins and overwrites older changes. This allows a traveling user to reply to messages, organize folders, and create calendar entries while away from the office. Upon connecting to the Exchange server, their local changes get applied to the Exchange server copy. This is really an optimal configuration for traveling users and users who have limited connectivity.

The User Experience in Cached Exchange Mode

When the user is connected to the Exchange server, the phrase "Connected to Microsoft Exchange" appears in the lower-right corner of the Outlook 2007 window. The message "All Folders Are Up to Date" should also be displayed when synchronization is up to date.

When connectivity is lost, the message says "Disconnected" and gives the date and time the offline folders were last updated.

When connectivity is first restored, the message says "Trying to Connect." As connectivity is reestablished, the phrase "Connected to Microsoft Exchange" reappears, and to the left are updates informing the user what is automatically occurring to get the mailbox up to date.

These messages could be any of the following:

▸ Waiting to Update the Full Items in Inbox

▸ Sending Complete

▸ All Folders Are Up-to-Date

The user might occasionally find that people appear to be missing from the Global Address List (GAL). While running in Cached mode, Outlook 2007 no longer gets its GAL from the global catalog. The client downloads the Offline Address Book. This is what allows the user to look up addresses while not connected to the network. The user can trigger a download of the OAB at any time. Important to realize is that, by default, Exchange only updates the OAB every 24 hours. As such, it's possible for a user to be added to Exchange after the OAB generation has occurred. Users not running in Cached mode would see the new user in the GAL but the Cached mode users wouldn't see them until the OAB was updated and they downloaded the latest copy.

Deploying Cached Exchange Mode

Cached mode can be deployed by using the Office Customization Tool or through enabling this option using domain Group Policy. Be aware that setting it via Group Policy on a large number of users drastically increases network traffic to the Exchange server. Outlook in Cached mode has to download the entire mailbox. Environments where mailbox size limits aren't set are especially impacted by this. Imagine 200 users log on on Monday morning and a GPO sets their Outlook to Cached mode. If each user had 100MB of mail in their mailbox, there would be 20GB of data being copied from the Exchange server. This could be especially impacting if some of those users were coming across WAN connections to get to Exchange.

If possible, only set a user to Cached mode when they are on the same LAN of the Exchange server or when they are first created in Exchange. This reduces the traffic at the Exchange server.

Deploying Cached Exchange Mode Manually

When configuring a user's Outlook profile manually, it's possible to configure Cached mode at that time.

To configure Cached mode manually, do the following:

1. Begin configuring a user profile in the standard manner.

2. When the E-Mail Accounts page is reached, make sure the Use Cached Exchange Mode check box is checked.

3. Finish configuring the Outlook profile.

Deployment Considerations for Cached Exchange Mode

Because enabling Cached mode forces the end users to synchronize a full copy of their mailbox to a local OST file as well as a full copy of the OAB, the demand on an Exchange server can be quite high. If a large number of users must be configured to use Cached mode at one time, the best choices for configuring Cached mode are as follows:

▶ Only enable Cached mode if the user will benefit from it. This would include traveling users or users who are on slow connections.

▶ Deploy Cached mode to groups of users at a time rather than to the whole enterprise.

▶ Encourage users to clean up their mailboxes prior to enabling Cached mode. Sent and Deleted items often account for 50% of the size of a mailbox.

▶ Deploy Cached mode sooner rather then later. The smaller the mailbox at the time of the OST creation, the less data needs to be moved.

Using Cached Exchange Mode

Because Cached mode acts somewhat differently from a traditional mailbox, an administrator might consider some additional user training for those with Cached mode. This helps users recognize those differences and should result in fewer calls to the help desk. Some of these differences are mentioned in the following sections.

The Send/Receive Button

For users in Cached mode, it is unnecessary to click the Send/Receive messages button regularly when synchronizing with the new Cached mode functionality. This now happens automatically and clicking Send/Receive doesn't accomplish anything.

RPC Over HTTPS and the Cached Exchange Mode

It is recommended that users running RPC over HTTPS also run Cached Exchange mode enabled. This is because Exchange Cached mode deals better with "slow links and disconnections" to Exchange. Because RPC over HTTPS accesses Exchange information via the Internet, these users are more likely to experience network latency and slowness.

Slow-Link Connection Awareness

Cached mode was originally designed to address the challenges associated with links 128Kbps or slower. When slow-link connection awareness is enabled, it automatically implements the following email-synchronization behaviors:

▶ OAB is not downloaded (neither partial nor full download).

▶ Mail headers only are downloaded.

▶ The rest of the mail message and attachments are downloaded when the user clicks on the message or attachment to open it.

To change the slow-link configuration, perform the following steps:

1. Click File.

2. Choose Cached Exchange Mode.

3. Uncheck On Slow Connections Download Only Headers.

Cached Exchange Mode and OSTs and OABs

Using Cached mode downloads a full copy of the user's mail to the OST file stored locally on the user's hard drive. However, administrators need to be aware of some considerations regarding OSTs and Cached mode to plan and make their configuration choices for these Exchange clients allowing optimal performance and efficient connectivity.

Cached Exchange Mode OST Considerations

OST files in Outlook 2007 use the new Unicode format. This allows them to go beyond the 2-GB limitation of the old American National Standards Institute (ANSI) format. However, be sure to account for the potential size of the OST file when planning your desktop or laptop images. Older notebooks might not have enough space locally to support a large OST file if you aren't limiting the size of mailboxes on the Exchange server.

Cached Exchange Mode and Outlook Address Book (OAB) Implications

When using Cached mode, it is possible to download a No Details Outlook address book. However, users in Cached mode should download the Full Details OAB. This is because they can experience significant delays when they access the OAB when the full details are not locally accessible. When this situation occurs, the user's workstation must contact the Exchange server to provide full data for the OAB. This results in delays for the user during the download.

When Cached mode is enabled, the OAB is synchronized every 24 hours, by default. If there are no updates to the server OAB, there will be no updates to the offline OAB. When there are changes to the OAB, only the differences are downloaded. This results in a faster update to the OAB for the Cached mode user.

Outlook Features That Decrease Cached Exchange Mode's Effectiveness

Cached Exchange mode is easy to configure and provides many benefits to the occasionally offline user. It is important to try to keep the Cached mode experience as positive as possible for the user. Thus, it is useful to know that several Outlook 2007 features can actually decrease the effectiveness of Cached mode. The features discussed in the following sections all result in Outlook 2007 sending calls to the Exchange server for information when in Cached mode. For users using Cached mode, these calls can greatly decrease the effectiveness and performance of the client and, therefore, should be avoided if possible.

Delegate Access and Accessing Shared Folders or Calendars

These two items both require access to the Exchange server to view other users' Outlook items. Cached mode does not download another user's data to the local OST, so this nullifies the use of Cached mode when the functionality is required. These functions will work while the Cached mode user is connected to the Exchange server, but it can result in attempted external connections that will fail when the user is offline. This results in the interface waiting for a timeout before continuing with its processes.

Outlook Add-ins

Outlook add-ins such as ActiveSync can result in Outlook not utilizing important items, such as the Download Headers Only functionality that allows Cached mode to work so well. They also can cause excessive calls to the Exchange server or network. Avoid Outlook add-ins, if possible. Third-party add-ins should be tested with Cached mode for both online and offline behaviors to see if they are making calls to nonlocal data that could impact Cached mode users while they are offline.

Digital Signatures

Verification of digital signatures requires Outlook to verify a valid signature for messages sent using digital encryption, requiring a server call as well. Be sure to test such configurations to ensure that signed or protected content can still be accessed while a user is offline.

Noncached Public Folders

This, too, requires bandwidth and a call to the server. Consider synchronizing frequently used public folders to the OST through the use of Public Folder Favorites. Be careful not to cache too much public folder information because it inflates the size of the OST file.

Including Additional Searchable Address Books

If the enterprise includes custom address books and contact lists that are enabled to be searchable and usable for email addressing, this results in the client/server communications. These types of address lists are not cached by Outlook.

Customizing the User Object Properties

If the enterprise has created customized items on the General tab of the properties box of a user, this always requires a call to the server: When user properties are displayed, the General tab is always displayed first. Therefore, if these are necessary, consider placing any customized fields on a different tab on the user properties pages requiring a call to the server only when that tab is accessed, not every time the user properties are accessed.

Summary

As you have seen, Outlook 2007 has continued the tradition of improving user experiences through new functionality, improvements to existing concepts, and by giving a similar experience both on and off the network.

Users will enjoy the new collaboration functions of Outlook 2007, which have made incredible strides in the area of calendar interactions. In the past, it was always difficult to schedule meetings with users from other Exchange organizations without having to set up complex connectors and deal with the politics of connecting two environments. Through the enhancements in Internet-based calendaring, users can empower themselves to make their free/busy information available to collaborative partners and just as easily revoke access to that information when the project is completed.

Search functionality has become even simpler than ever and much more powerful. Near real-time searches of the entire mailbox are made possible through configurable indexing to make finding that missing message a snap. Searching of calendar items and tasks further strengthens the abilities of Outlook 2007's search functions.

As spam and phishing become more and more of an issue as time goes by, Outlook 2007 adds improved abilities to help the user avoid these annoying and potentially dangerous email messages. By integrating with the message filtering functions of Exchange 2007, Outlook 2007 allows the end users to do their part to help protect the company as a whole by acting as a secondary layer in the spam blocking by flagging messages that snuck through the primary filter.

Entirely new functions such as the ability to subscribe to RSS (Really Simple Syndication) feeds gives the Outlook 2007 user access to whole new worlds of information.

Security enhancements in Outlook 2007 include improvements for encrypted client-to-server communications by using RPC over HTTPS and making the configuration even

27

easier than before. The capability to add security to specific messages through Information Rights Management and the capability to set security for an entire mailbox give users a much more secured environment for enabling business processes.

Finally, a Cached mode method of access enables a user to access mail, calendar appointments, and other content within Outlook, regardless of whether they are connected to Exchange. Cached mode access provides remote and roving users an improved user experience by placing data local to their system making accessing large attachments significantly faster than if they were accessing them from the Exchange server.

All of the new capabilities of Outlook 2007, as well as the capability to leverage existing features in earlier versions of Outlook, provide a compelling argument to upgrade users to the latest and truly greatest version of Outlook.

Best Practices

▶ Previous versions of the Outlook client are sufficient for most email users, but those who want to get the most out of Exchange Server 2007—especially remote or traveling users who need to access their mail from outside the network—should upgrade to Outlook 2007.

▶ Quick flags should be used to flag messages that require follow-up or other attention.

▶ Key appointments can be categorized with colors to draw attention to appointments in user calendars.

▶ Using the new search capabilities of Outlook 2007 can drastically improve the time it takes for a user to find messages or information within Outlook.

▶ Instead of establishing a VPN before accessing an Exchange server from a remote Outlook 2007 client, the RPC over HTTPS should be enabled to provide SSL-based 128-bit encrypted end-to-end communication from client to server.

▶ For easier deployment of RPC over HTTPS, use an SSL certificate from a major provider that is already preloaded into the user's certificate trust list.

▶ RPC over HTTPS provides the best performance on unreliable or high-latency links. However, RPC over HTTPS takes roughly twice the bandwidth to move the same amount of data. Take this into consideration when deploying RPC over HTTPS.

▶ Calendars can be set up in group schedules to provide a side-by-side view of appointment calendars for individuals or groups of users.

▶ Free/busy times can be configured to be viewable from the Internet, to provide external users access and views to appointment schedules.

▶ Cached mode can be used to support users accessing Exchange across WAN links, saving bandwidth for other network needs such as business application access.

▶ Cached mode for the Outlook client can improve performance for remote users across slow, unreliable, or failed client-to-server connections.

CHAPTER 28

Leveraging the Capabilities of the Outlook Web Access (OWA) Client

Outlook Web Access (OWA) has become a commonly used and highly valuable feature of Exchange. In older versions, OWA was often attacked for being a watered-down version of the Outlook client. With newer versions of OWA, functionality is so similar to the full client that often a user can forget that they aren't using the full client.

With this latest version, Microsoft has incorporated the most frequent user and administrator requests for changes into OWA 2007. This chapter focuses on helping Exchange Server 2007 administrators and OWA users to become intimately familiar with OWA and learn how to best leverage the capabilities of OWA in a business environment. The information in this chapter is useful for both new users and users familiar with OWA. It includes instructions for basic and advanced functions of OWA so that both new users and power users can gain useful knowledge from this chapter.

One of the key goals with OWA in Exchange 2007 was to make the OWA client a viable choice for companies to deploy as a client of choice by giving it all the functionality that the users are likely to need.

Understanding Microsoft's Direction on OWA

As with the previous version of OWA in Exchange 2007, the goal has been to try to keep the experience as similar as possible while offering new functionality and new technology to users and administrators alike. This allows administrator to offer new functions to users without incurring the costs of having to retrain the users on a new technology or interface. Microsoft understands that OWA is rapidly becoming the client of choice for users who need external access or who don't travel with a portable computer. By providing the roaming client with all the functionality they need without adding complexity to an information technology (IT) environment, they are able to further cement Exchange as the email system of choice for corporate America.

Leveraging a Common Interface

The first thing a user is likely to notice in OWA 2007 is the new look. Although updated, it is nearly identical to the full Outlook 2007 client. Although there are still some differences between Outlook 2007 and OWA, the overall look, feel, and functionality are designed to be the same. Using the OWA client along with the latest Exchange service packs provide enhanced elements in areas such as spelling and grammar checking, keyboard shortcuts, rule configurations, reading panes, and other improvements that help OWA seem familiar to end users. This results in a very smooth transition from the full client to the use of OWA when users will be away from their workstations.

> **NOTE**
>
> Though OWA 2007 provides a very robust client access solution with many of the features of the full Outlook 2007 client, many features are only available with Outlook 2007. For information on using the full client and all its features, see Chapter 27, "Getting the Most Out of the Microsoft Outlook Client."

Providing a Feature-Rich Web Client

Thanks to the inclusion of the most useful functions of Outlook, OWA is now a viable choice for the primary email and calendaring client for end users. With Exchange Server 2007 and the latest service packs, OWA is no longer regarded as merely a remote access solution, but can be used day in and day out by users accessing mailbox information both in the office and from the Internet. Some organizations might not deploy the full Outlook 2007 at all and use OWA exclusively as their standard Exchange client. It should be noted, however, that limiting clients to OWA only restricts some of the potential benefits to the users. For example, OWA has no provisions for allowing a user to access their mail or calendar data while offline. There is also reduced integration with other applications such as SharePoint or Microsoft Office 2007. As such, administrators should consider leveraging both solutions to provide users with the solution that best meets their needs and restrictions. Administrators should always plan to support both types of clients, and expect the use of OWA to grow as users become aware of its benefits.

Integrating Extensible Markup Language (XML) in the Client Interface

Microsoft has continued to take steps to further integrate XML into the OWA client interface. The integration of XML into all Microsoft products, which leverages web technologies, is a priority for Microsoft. The benefit is that OWA can more effectively integrate data and that a compatible language is used throughout Exchange as well as other Microsoft products that are served by web-based technology. This is somewhat in response to criticism that Microsoft tends to not use open standards but regardless of the driver, it is the end user who benefits. OWA utilizing XML paired with the latest version of Internet Information Services (IIS) is able to provide enhanced levels of both security and compatibility.

What's New in OWA 2007?

As has always been the case with new versions of Exchange, Exchange 2007 brings with it many new functions to the OWA client. These improvements run the gamut from smarter calendaring to management of mobile devices to a greatly improved address book. By learning and leveraging these new functions, end users can become even more effective when they are accessing their mail from outside the network. Being at an airport kiosk is just as effective as being at the office when it comes to dealing with email, calendaring, and unified messaging.

Smarter Meeting Booking via OWA

OWA 2007 makes setting meetings easier by offering some functions that were previously unavailable. The first function is the Scheduling Assistant. When creating a new meeting request via OWA, the user is able to click the Scheduling Assistant tab and add both rooms and attendees to a meeting request. The second function is a Suggested Times display for the meeting that shows potential dates for the meeting. The third function rates the potential meeting times as Great, Good, or Poor depending on how many of the attendees are available.

To schedule a meeting using the Scheduling Assistant, perform the following steps:

1. From OWA, click the Calendar button in the Outlook toolbar.

2. Click New Meeting Request.

3. Click the Scheduling Assistant tab; you'll see a screen similar to the one shown in Figure 28.1.

4. Click Select Attendees and add meeting attendees and resources.

5. Click OK when all attendees and resources have been added.

6. Choose a Suggested Time from the lower-right pane.

7. Return to the appointment pane, and enter meeting information as you normally would.

8. Click Send.

28

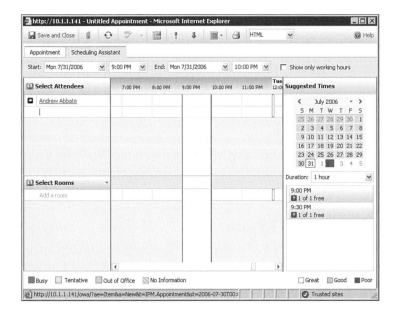

FIGURE 28.1   The Scheduling Assistant.

Windows SharePoint Services Integration

As part of a push to replace public folders with SharePoint, OWA 2007 has introduced a new interface to simplify access of SharePoint information. In the shortcut bar, there is a new item called Documents. This new window is used to access Microsoft Windows SharePoint Services servers or even Windows file servers from OWA.

From this interface, a user can click Open Location, is prompted with a screen similar to the one shown in Figure 28.2, and is asked to enter an address to a SharePoint Services server or Windows file share that they want to open.

Opening a file location gives the OWA user access to the files located in that share. Opening a path to a SharePoint Services server gives the client access to the SharePoint site, assuming they have the necessary rights.

Using OWA to Manage Your Mobile Devices

OWA 2007 allows users to self-manage their Windows Mobile 5.0 or higher devices. This includes functions such as a remote wipe of a lost device, removing old mobile devices from the account, displaying the device password, or retrieving the synchronization log.

Windows Mobile phones often carry potentially sensitive data on them in the form of emails containing corporate information. If a device is ever lost or replaced, it should be wiped. A simple way to do this is the following:

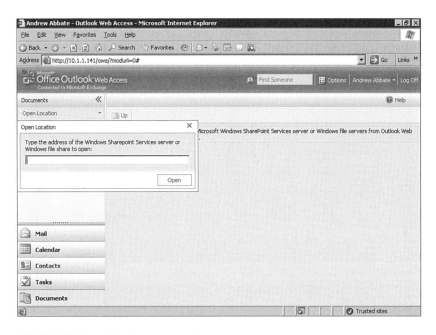

FIGURE 28.2   The Documents Connector.

1. Log on to OWA.

2. In the upper right of the OWA interface, click Options.

3. In the upper portion of the left pane, under Options, click Mobile Devices to get a screen similar to the one shown in Figure 28.3. You might have to scroll down in the menu.

4. Highlight your device.

5. Click Wipe All Data from Device.

6. Click Yes.

If you have a device that will no longer be synced with Exchange, you can remove that device from your ActiveSync profile via the following steps:

1. Log on to OWA.

2. In the upper right of the OWA interface, click Options.

3. In the upper portion of the left pane, under Options, click Remote Devices. You might have to scroll down in the menu.

4. Highlight your device.

5. Click Remove Device from List.

6. Click Yes.

28

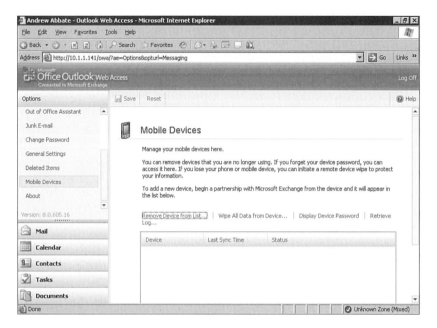

FIGURE 28.3   Managing mobile devices.

If you lose the password on your device and your administrator has previously enabled the Recovery Password feature on your mobile device, which is running Mobile 5.0 or higher with the Messaging and Security Feature Pack installed, you can recover your password with the following steps:

1. Log on to OWA.

2. In the upper right of the OWA interface, click Options.

3. In the upper portion of the left pane, under Options, click Remote Devices. You might have to scroll down in the menu.

4. Highlight your device.

5. Click Display Device Password.

6. Click Yes.

OWA gives you a password that is not your original password. It is a recovery password designed by resetting the existing password. At the time this recovery password is displayed, you should use it to log on to the mobile device. When you do so, the device prompts you to create a new password.

Leveraging Improvements in Search

Searching through your Inbox or your tasks is much easier with the improvements to the search functions in OWA 2007. An interface very similar to that in Outlook 2007 gives the user the ability to search through subjects as well as message bodies. The search can be filtered by who it was sent from or to, allowing greater granularity. Even the category colors set on messages are a field that can be searched upon. After the results are generated, they can be sorted by any attribute, such as date, size, importance, or even message flags.

Using the Outlook Web Access Address Book

One of the biggest complaints about previous versions of OWA was the difficulty of using the address book. Users had to guess at first or last names and then search the address book rather then simply browse the list the way they did in the full client. OWA 2007 finally offers a consistent interface for the address book when compared with the full client. When a user accesses the address book, they will see a view where all addresses are listed; by default, they are arranged by name. From this interface, the user has the ability to type part of a name into the search bar and click the magnifying glass to search based on the parameters they entered.

One of the most impressive enhancements to the address book view is that when a user in the address book is highlighted, a screen similar to the one shown in Figure 28.4 appears, where the pane to the right is filled with information about the user, including their availability based on the current time.

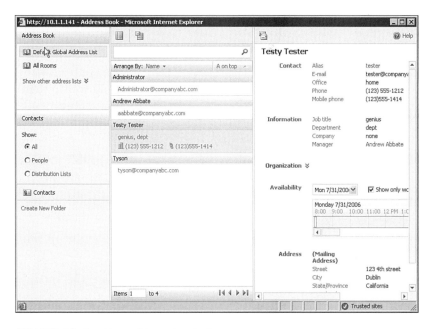

FIGURE 28.4   New address book view.

This is exceptionally helpful if you want to quickly see if someone is available. In previous versions of OWA, you had to go through the process of creating a meeting request to see the user's availability. This new interface for the address book is a significant improvement over Exchange Server 2003 and is likely to generate the most positive comments from end users.

Out of Office Enhancements

The Out of Office rules have been enhanced in Exchange 2007 and OWA supports them. Users now have the ability to set different rules and messages for internal senders versus external senders. This is an improvement that administrators have been wanting for some time as there has always been a debate over how much information should be included in the Out of Office response. Now users can fully inform co-workers about their absence without having to give the same information to outside senders.

Regional Settings

OWA 2007 introduces the ability to run OWA in a language other than that of the browser. This means that a worker from the United States could access OWA from a system in another country that was running Windows and Microsoft Internet Explorer in another language and still get the OWA interface and their messages in English. This is a great step forward for traveling users who might not always have their personal notebook with them.

Opening Another User's Mailbox

One of the more handy functions of Outlook that was never easily available in OWA was the ability to open another user's mailbox. Although an advanced user could type in the full path to the user's mailbox, assuming they knew it, this was beyond the abilities of a typical user. In OWA 2007, the user can simply perform the following steps to access another mailbox to which they have rights:

1. In the main Office OWA bar, click the button between Options and Log Off, where your name appears, and a screen similar to the one shown in Figure 28.5 appears.

2. Type in the name of the mailbox you want to open in the Select Mailbox area. This field potentially autofills if the mailbox is one you have sent mail to in the past.

3. Click Open.

You can now access the mailbox via OWA.

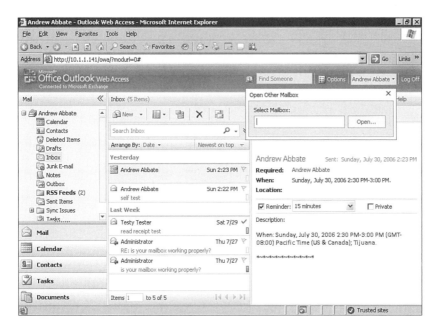

FIGURE 28.5   Opening another user's mailbox.

Logging On to OWA 2007

To take advantage of all the functions of OWA 2007, the user must first log on to the system. OWA is traditionally published to the Internet so that users can log in from basically anywhere and access their mailbox. In most situations with OWA 2007, the user will be logging on through what is called the forms-based authentication (FBA). This means they'll see a web page with several options from which they can choose. These options determine some basic behaviors of the client as well as determine the functions to which the user will have access. These are usually referred to as the user modes and the security levels.

Understanding User Modes

If your Exchange server has been set up to use FBA on the OWA site, the OWA logon will look like the screen shown in Figure 28.6.

Unlike the previous version of Exchange, the choice between the Premium and the Light modes is picked in a different way. The default setting is to run the full OWA client and the user must check the Use OWA Light check box to use the more basic client.

28

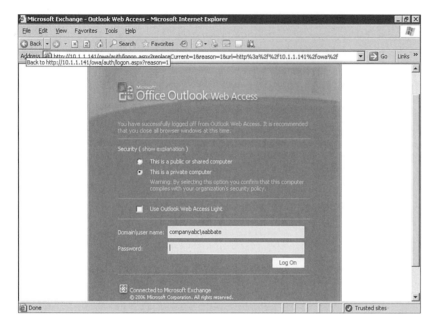

FIGURE 28.6   The forms-based logon.

Using the OWA Standard Authentication Mode

The standard authentication mode of OWA provides the end user with an experience that is nearly identical to Outlook 2007 for almost all functions. The only potential drawback to using the full OWA client is that the bandwidth requirements are higher than those for users using the Light OWA client. If users have reasonable network connectivity, for example, 64Kbps or higher, they should be encouraged to use the standard authentication mode. Although the full OWA client has a higher bandwidth requirement, this can be offset by enabling GZIP compression at the Exchange server. Administrators should be aware that this increases the processor load on the client access server and should be taken into account when the server is designed. The reduction in bandwidth used can be as much as 50%, so it is worthwhile to test the system with compression enabled to see if it is supportable.

To enable GZIP compression on the OWA site, an administrator must perform the following steps on the client access server:

1. Click Start, All Programs, Microsoft Exchange Server 2007, and select Exchange Management Shell.

2. From the Exchange Management Shell prompt, type `get-owavirtualdirectory`.

3. Record the identity of the OWA virtual directory.

4. Type `set-owavirtualdirectory –identity "Owa (Default Web Site) –gziplevel high`.

5. Type Exit.

6. Launch the DOS prompt.

7. Type iisreset /noforce.

8. Type Exit.

Using the Light Client

As in the past, the Light client, which replaces the former Basic client, doesn't utilize ActiveX controls and, therefore, is the only choice for web browsers that do not support ActiveX. The official statement of supported browsers is that the user must run Internet Explorer 6.01 or higher to use the FBA client.

With significantly fewer options and features available to the users accessing OWA, the Light client mode can still be used to access mail and calendaring information through the OWA forms-based interface. There are some advantages to using the Light client such as the reduction in bandwidth needed. The Light client is also a good choice if the user needs to access OWA through a restricted browser as is often found in public locations. A sample of the Light client is shown in Figure 28.7.

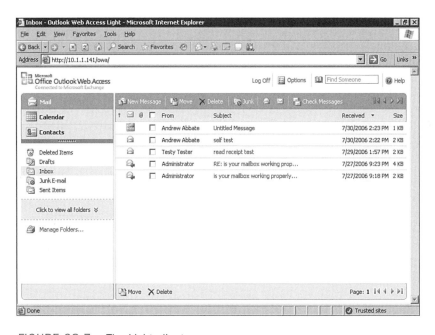

FIGURE 28.7   The Light client.

> **NOTE**
>
> This chapter is written from the point of view of a user who is accessing OWA via the standard authentication mode client. The experience for a user accessing OWA via the Light client will vary from the descriptions in this chapter.

Understanding Security Settings

When the user logs on to OWA via FBA, they are presented with two options as to how they are connecting. These options are Public Computer and Private Computer. Users should be taught to select the mode that is most appropriate for their situation because email is considered intellectual property and should be protected accordingly.

Public Mode

When a user sets the Public or Shared Computer option, they are telling the Exchange server that they are on a computer with a low level of trust. This means that Exchange will take a more restrictive stance in some areas of security. Most notably, the user's session will time out after several minutes of inactivity. This is to reduce the chances of the user forgetting to log off and an unauthorized party having access to the mailbox. The timeout for disconnect is only enforceable on sessions using FBA.

Private Mode

If a user selects Private Computer when logging on to OWA via FBA, they will have fewer restrictions placed on them than they would in Public mode. Most notably, they will be able to be inactive for hours without having to authenticate again to OWA. This is allowed because the computer is assumed to have a higher level of assurance.

Getting to Know the Look and Feel of OWA 2007

As stated previously, the user interface (UI) of the new OWA client, shown in Figure 28.8, looks and feels almost exactly like the full Outlook 2007 client, lacking only the To-Do bar. It has the same basic pane structure, the same color scheme, the full folder tree, and the ability to change the widths of the columns. It includes many similar elements and components found in Outlook 2007 to allow users to retain the same level of familiarity with the tools and options when moving from the full Outlook 2007 to OWA 2007.

Using Multiple Panes

By default, the OWA standard authentication mode client offers a very familiar pane when working within the UI. When users initially open OWA, they are presented with five basic panes. These panes are meant to organize the information presented in OWA and to take the best advantage of the available space.

The five panes are as follows:

- Folder list
- Shortcut bar
- Middle pane (message list)
- Infobar
- Reading pane

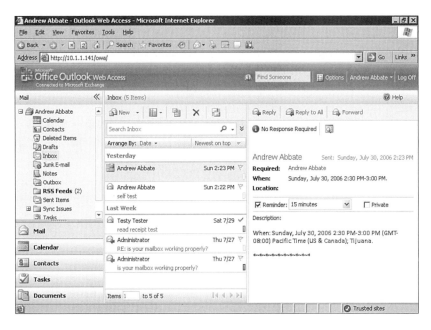

FIGURE 28.8   OWA panes.

The Folder list is the upper-left pane, which lists all the folders available in the user's mailbox. This includes Calendar, Contacts, Deleted Items, Drafts, Inbox, Junk E-Mail, Notes, Outbox, Sent Items, Sync Issues, Tasks, and any custom created folders.

To simplify navigation within OWA, there is a shortcut bar that is located below the Folder list. This shortcut bar lists shortcut icons to the Inbox, Calendar, Contacts, Tasks, and Documents. Another helpful feature is the new mail notification pop-up. When a new message arrives, a vertical pop-up appears in the lower-left corner of OWA that notifies the user that they have new mail. The user can then click that button to refresh OWA and view the new message.

28

> **NOTE**
>
> Users familiar with OWA from Exchange 2003 might notice that the Options button is no longer in the shortcut bar. The Options button has moved to the upper-right portion of the interface near the Log Off button.

The middle pane changes slightly as the user goes between mail, calendaring, and contacts. The pane lists the contents of whatever Exchange feature is selected in the Folder list or icon in the shortcut bar. For example, if Inbox is selected in the Folder list, the middle pane displays the existing and new messages in the Inbox just as it would in the full Outlook 2007 client. When using other options, such as the Calendar, there is one pane shown in the middle, not a split screen, as shown when the Inbox is highlighted. The middle pane has been designed to always provide the best experience for the given folder type rather than trying to keep its behavior the same.

In addition, an optional pane called the reading pane is available (shown on the far right of Figure 28.8). The reading pane is turned on by default and shown when viewing the Inbox. This pane shows the content or body of the message highlighted in the center pane. This reading pane can also be configured to sit below the middle pane rather than to the right. This allows the user to further customize their own experience to their personal preferences.

The toolbar across the top is called the Infobar. Like Outlook, it provides choices that are available while you view the information in the middle pane. The choices change depending on what a user is viewing when working within OWA. Different options are available when working with the Inbox, Calendar, and other options.

Changing the Size of the Panes

To customize the OWA UI, a user can easily configure the width or height of the panes available. With OWA 2007, the adjustments of pane sizing can be saved when a user logs off. These sizing adjustments are remembered and restored when a user logs back on to OWA.

1. To change the size of work area panes within OWA, hover the mouse pointer over the border between the panes, and wait for the double arrow or horizontal double arrow to appear.

2. When the arrow appears, hold down the left mouse button and move the border right/left or up/down to resize the pane to the size you want.

3. When the pane is in the proper place, release the left mouse button, and the pane will maintain the newly created size.

Using Pull-Down Menus

Some icons in OWA allow a user to perform several different tasks. Icons that contain a downward facing arrow next to them allow users to choose different options. To view the choices available with these options, click the arrow to the right of the icon or the icon to see a menu similar to the one shown in Figure 28.9. To choose an option, move the mouse pointer down the list and view the choices as they are highlighted. To choose an option, highlight the option and click the desired choice.

If there is no arrow next to the icon, the icon provides only a single choice, by clicking it.

Moving Through the OWA Features

You can move through the different OWA features in a couple of ways. The first is by clicking the buttons that represent the feature you want to access. For example, the short-cut bar presents you with labeled icon buttons for options, such as the Contacts or the Inbox. By clicking once on the icon button, you can access the feature as it is opened in the center pane.

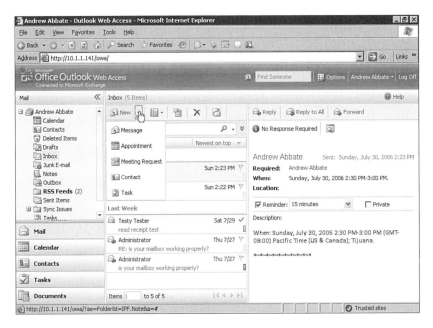

FIGURE 28.9   Pull-down menu in OWA.

Another option is to select the desired options in the folder tree located in the folder pane. Clicking the Inbox or any other folder in the list also allows the feature to be opened in the center pane. In fact, if you select an option in this manner you will see that the same option is now highlighted in the shortcut bar.

Moving Through Email Pages

When the Inbox folder is selected, email messages are displayed in the middle pane with the body of the message in the reading pane. When working with the Inbox, you can now configure how many email messages are displayed on the screen at one time. To modify the number of messages shown per screen, complete the following steps:

1. Click Options in the upper-right portion of the screen.

2. Select Messaging from the left pane.

3. In Message Options, shown in Figure 28.10, set the Number of Items to Display per Page option to the value you want.

4. Click Save.

When users have large numbers of messages, it can be difficult to get to the page containing the message they want. To move through the pages of messages, click the left or right arrow button at the bottom of the middle pane to navigate between pages. To go to the end or beginning of the pages of messages, click the arrow with the vertical line next to it. The arrow pointing left displays the beginning of the email pages; the arrow to the right displays the end.

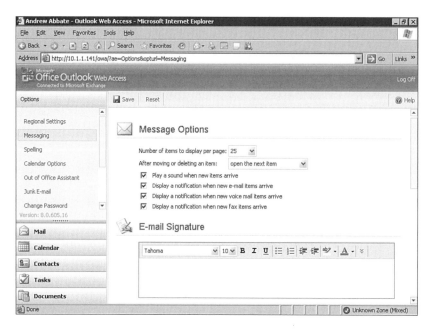

FIGURE 28.10   The Message Options settings.

Often, a simpler way to organize the messages when trying to find a particular one is to use the Description bar, organizing emails by the From, Subject, Date Received, and more field options when the pane is moved over. Click the options to sort messages based on these criteria. This can simplify the process of trying to find a message that came from a particular user.

Also keep in mind that you still have access to the search features if you feel you have enough information to search on rather than just scanning through a large pile of messages to find the one you are looking for.

Changing the Viewing Order and Using the Two-Line View

Users can change the viewing order of email messages in the Inbox or other email folders by using these selections. The default initial configuration is to display the most recent messages received by the users at the top of the email list. To change the view so the new messages go to the bottom of the list, click the phrase Newest on Top in the middle pane with a down-pointing arrow next to it. This rearranges the messages so the oldest received email is at the top. The clickable phrase will now read Oldest on Top.

Users can also choose to turn off the two-line view, thus consolidating the information about the email message into a single line. This allows a user to show more messages per page in OWA.

The two-line view is configured as on by default. To change the two-line view to a different view, click the Single Line/Multiple Line button located just to the left of the Delete button.

Using the Reading Pane

As was the case with previous versions of the OWA client, the reading pane is an option that can be toggled on or off. Turning on the reading pane opens a vertical pane on the far-right side of the OWA user interface that shows the content of the message. The ability to scroll through the contents of the message in the reading pane enables you to view the whole message without having to physically open it. The location of the reading pane is customizable and can be located either on the right vertical pane, or as a horizontal pane at the bottom of the page. If the reading pane is toggled off, OWA removes the pane entirely, allowing for more space for the middle pane.

To configure the reading pane, complete the following steps:

1. Click the reading pane icon. The drop-down menu provides choices as to where to put the reading pane (the default location is the right side of the OWA UI).

2. Choose Right to configure the vertical pane on the right side; choose Bottom to configure the horizontal pane.

3. Choose Off to turn the reading pane off. When the reading pane is removed, the middle pane expands to take up the space the reading pane used.

Attachments can also be accessed via the reading pane, using the methods discussed later in this chapter in the section "Using OWA Mail Features."

Reading a message via the reading pane acts much the same as double-clicking a message to open it. Both methods update the mailbox to know that a message has been read. This results in a new message changing its appearance in the middle pane from bold to not bold. This signifies that the message has been read. One difference to be aware of is that when viewing messages via the reading pane, even though you have read the message, a read receipt would not be generated if the sender had requested one. That only occurs via OWA if the message is double-clicked and read.

Creating New Folders

To further organize a mailbox, users can create folders and subfolders in their mailbox or Inbox while using OWA. You can easily create a type of additional folder that can be viewed and accessed in the Folder list:

1. To create a new folder, click the location in the Folder tree in the left pane where you want the folder to be created.

2. Right-click the parent folder (which includes Mailbox) in the folder tree, and choose Create New Folder, as shown in Figure 28.11.

3. Name the folder and press Enter.

After being created, the new folder is immediately accessible for use and appears in the location where it was placed in the Folder list.

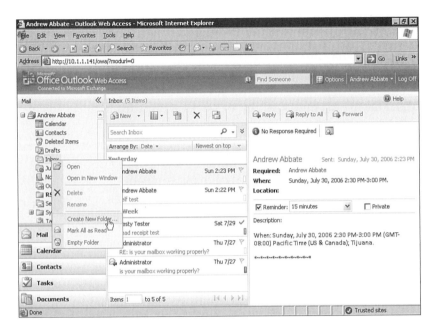

FIGURE 28.11   Creating a new folder.

Changes to Public Folders in OWA 2007

There is one major change to the way that OWA views public folders in OWA 2007. It doesn't. Microsoft is no longer offering the ability to access public folders via OWA. This is part of Microsoft's shift in focus from public folders in Exchange to SharePoint. As seen in the previous "What's New in OWA 2007?" section, companies are encouraged to migrate their public folder data to SharePoint to integrate the views via OWA.

Using OWA Help

As with all Microsoft applications, help is also available to users in OWA by clicking Help from the menu bar. The Help pages allow users access to information on features as well as step-by-step instructions for completing various tasks. Unfortunately, this Help feature does not enable searching or viewing by index as with the full Outlook 2007 client. OWA Help topics are organized by groups according to the topic headings for simple access to any available topic. For example, if your question deals with meetings, you can navigate to the calendar area and expand it to working with meetings and see all the topics dealing with meetings. By clicking the plus sign (+), you can expand all the topics under the contact heading, as shown in Figure 28.12, enabling a view of all subheadings that become available. When you click a subheading, the Help information appears in the right pane.

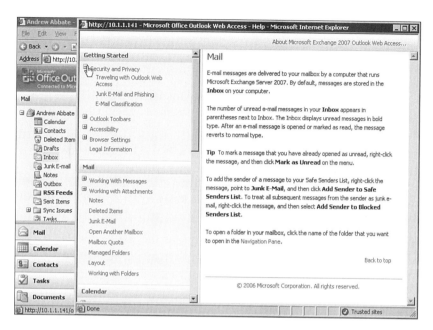

FIGURE 28.12   Viewing help in OWA 2007.

Logging Off OWA 2007

When a user has logged on to OWA with FBA, they will find a Log Off button located on the right of the Infobar. By having this Log Off button available, it is easy for the user to securely log off OWA and close the session. This prevents another user from navigating back to the mailbox and impersonating the user. This is especially important when a user is attaching to OWA via a public or shared computer. A user needs to click the Log Off button to log off from OWA.

Using OWA Mail Features

Although OWA is a feature-rich interface into Exchange, the primary reason people use it is for the ability to access their email quickly and easily via the Internet. The new version of OWA makes using the email portion of OWA easier and more robust than it has been previously. The following sections cover how to create and send email messages, including new features in OWA 2007 and advanced features available for dealing with sending and receiving email.

Creating an Email

Several methods exist for creating a new email message. The most common way to create a message is to be in the Inbox view and simply click the New icon in the toolbar. This icon has a picture of a mail message on it. The other method is available from any view and is based on the same New icon. Instead of clicking the main icon, you can click the down arrow next to it to be presented with several options. Select Message and you will generate a new email message.

Addressing an Email

You can add recipients to an OWA email message in a few different ways. When the new message is created, the To, CC, and BCC fields appear and are blank. These areas are used to enter recipient names to which the message will be sent.

When sending a message, the primary recipients' names go into the To field of the message. Secondary recipients go in the CC (carbon copy) field. The BCC field stands for blind carbon copy, which means that the BCC recipient is invisible to all other recipients receiving the same message. In addition, when you use the Reply to All option, the recipient in the BCC box does not receive the reply.

As general email etiquette, place a recipient in the To field if the message is directed at them or if are you expecting them to reply. Use the CC field for people who are being "kept in the loop" on information and who won't likely be replying.

> **NOTE**
>
> Interesting to note is that if you BCC a recipient who has their out of office reply set, it replies back to all users on the original distribution. If you were using the BCC field to prevent primary recipients from knowing that a third-party was being copied, this behavior could potentially give you away.

To address an email, type a name (for example, John Doe) or an email address (for example, JDoe@companyabc.com) into one of the three boxes. Note that multiple names can be entered into any of the fields; each name or address must be separated by a semicolon (;).

> **NOTE**
>
> When a name is entered and before it has been checked by Exchange and verified, it appears as a single line of text with no underline. After Exchange has checked the name—either against the Global Address List (GAL) or contact list—or has confirmed that it is a legitimately formatted email address, the name becomes underlined, ensuring that Exchange regards the address as valid. Any subsequent, unverified addresses go into the bottom box on the screen until they are checked, and then they are moved to the upper box.

After names or partial names have been entered, you can click the Check Names button to have OWA check against the Global Address List (GAL) to find the closest match. If several matches are available, they will be displayed and the user is able to click the correct address.

When typing in the name of a previously used recipient, OWA provides a shortcut to the full name, as shown in Figure 28.13. This functionality was previously only available in the full Outlook client.

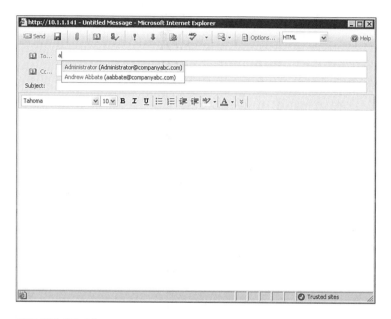

FIGURE 28.13   The type ahead feature.

Alternatively, you can use the Find Names option to populate the fields:

1. Click the To button to the left of the box area. This causes the Address Book dialog box to appear.

2. Enter the partial or full name of the recipient (for example, John), and click the magnifying glass.

3. Click the recipient to highlight the name.

4. Click To, CC, or BCC.

5. Click OK.

The final method is to trigger the new message via the address book. By clicking the icon for the address book, you are able to search for a user or contact by name. From here, you can right-click the name from the address book, choose New Message, and a new message appears with the user chosen already in the To field.

Removing a User from the To, CC, or BCC Fields in a Message

If you find that you have accidentally added an incorrect recipient or if you change your mind about a recipient, you don't have to cancel the message. You can remove a recipient from any of the three fields by right-clicking the recipient name or email address that needs to be removed, and then click Remove on the shortcut menu, or context menu. When removing names in the manner, it is important to know that there is no confirmation pop-up box; the name is immediately removed.

Adding Attachments

Many users need to be able to attach files to their messages. This function is supported when sending messages via OWA. When you send attachments, an upload of the file or attachment is required and can be affected when doing so over a slow link. In addition, if attachment size limits are enabled at the server, this prevents you from sending very large attachments from OWA. To add an attachment, the email being composed must be open:

1. Click the paper clip icon on the toolbar at the top of the message. The Attachment dialog box opens.

2. Browse to the file to be attached, highlight it, and then click Open.

3. To add more attachments, click the Choose More Files option. This creates additional entries, as shown in Figure 28.14.

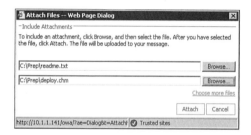

FIGURE 28.14   Adding attachments.

4. When all attachments have been selected, click Attach.

As shown in Figure 28.15, notice that all the attachments are listed below the Subject line, and the word *Attachments* is shown as an icon next to the attachment name.

Sending an Email

After the information, attachments, and recipients have been entered in to the message, you can send the email by clicking the Send button with the envelope on it. At this time, if there are any issues with the names in the To, CC, or BCC boxes, OWA presents a dialog box highlighting the irresolvable address names. At this time, you can either delete this recipient from the list or choose a different user from a list by clicking Change To. If neither option is helpful, click Cancel and remove the address manually by using the method previously outlined for removing a user address from the To, CC, or BCC field list in the message.

After all changes are made to addresses, click OK and the message is immediately sent.

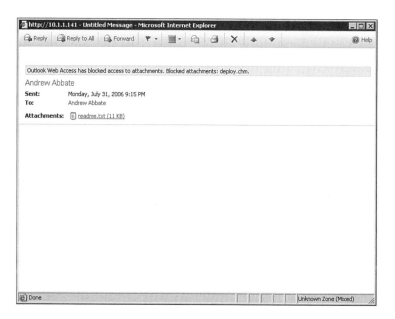

FIGURE 28.15   Attachments in OWA.

Reading an Email

When an Inbox receives a new email message, a notification box appears in two places. A message window appears in the lower-right of the screen, and a message box appears in the shortcut bar. Both notify the user that a new message has arrived.

You can also force OWA to look for new email; to do this, click the Send/Receive Email button in the Infobar. This initiates a check with Exchange and updates OWA that a message has arrived. A refresh of the browser screen also updates the UI with any new messages. The Inbox folder in the folder tree includes the number of unread messages in parentheses. This value updates when a new message arrives.

If the new message that arrives was classified as junk and was placed into the Junk E-Mail folder, the new message pop-up window would not be triggered.

To read an email, double-click the message in the message list. This opens the email message in its own window, enabling you to view the contents and access any attachments. Alternatively, you can just highlight the message and view the contents in the reading pane.

Reading Attachments

If a message arrives with an attachment, it is indicated in the message list pane as a paper clip icon.

In the reading pane or in an opened email, an attachment can be identified to the left of the message list or listed below the Subject line and below the word "Attachment." To read the attachment, three options are available:

▶ The first option is to right-click on the underlined attachment name and choose Open. If allowed, the attachment will open in a new window.

▶ The second option is to right-click on the underlined attachment and choose Save Target As. This method downloads the attachment to the client accessing Exchange and allows the user to choose a location to save the file. After the file has been saved, the user can browse to that location on the local client system and open the attachment there.

▶ The third option is to double-click on the underlined attachment, and if allowed, the attachment opens in a new window. Certain attachment types will not support this behavior depending on how their viewers are spawned.

Some attachments that are at a high risk of containing viruses (such as executables) must be saved to a hard disk first, and cannot be opened directly from OWA. This is an intended security feature built in to OWA and keeps users from inadvertently opening a spamming virus that would exploit the user's computer. Forcing the file to be saved to disk provides another level of virus protection because generally, saving a file to a hard disk brings the machine's antivirus software into play, providing yet another assurance that the attachment isn't infected with a true virus. When an attachment is considered high risk, OWA notifies the user that the attachment cannot be opened directly. The user then is forced to choose the Save Target As option. Saving the file locally to the disk can be helpful for users who use OWA as their primary Outlook client as they would have access to the attached files while offline.

Replying or Forwarding an Email

Just as in the full Outlook 2007 client, OWA provides many options for emails to be replied to or forwarded. Three methods are available when choosing to reply or forward an email.

When a message is open, three buttons are available on the message dialog box toolbar. To reply to just the sender, click Reply, type your reply, and click Send. To reply to all the recipients in the list, use Reply to All instead. Note that when the Reply to All option is used, it does not reply to any recipients listed in the BCC field. To forward the message to a different user not in the current recipient list, click Forward, as shown in Figure 28.16, and then enter the new recipient's address in the To field, using one of the addressing methods listed previously for addressing an email. When the message is properly addressed and any comments added, click Send.

Another option is to right-click a message in the message list and choose Reply, Reply to All, or Forward from the shortcut menu.

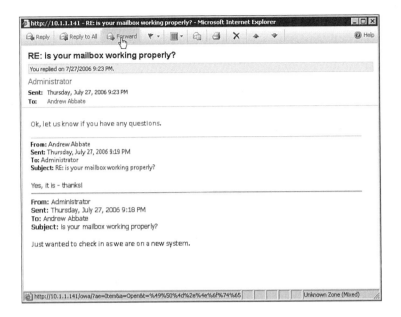

FIGURE 28.16   Reply, Reply to All, and Forward menu options.

The final method is to click a message once in the message list to highlight it and click one of the three envelope icons in the Infobar. Doing this allows a message to be replied to without actually opening the message. The left button is the Reply option, the middle is the Reply to All button, and the right button is the Forward button.

This is yet another example of how Microsoft provides several ways of performing the same task so that a user can adopt the methods with which they find most comfortable.

Deleting Email

To delete a message while it's not open, simply highlight the email to be deleted and either press the Delete key or click the black X Delete button on the toolbar.

To delete more than one message at a time, press and hold the Ctrl key and click each message being selected, highlighting all the selected messages. After all have been highlighted, click the X button or press Delete.

To choose multiple consecutive messages, press and hold the Shift key and click the top message; while still holding down the Shift key, click the bottom message of the group you want to select. When all are highlighted, delete the messages, using one of the two methods listed previously.

To delete an email while it's open, click the black X Delete button in the open email message.

28

Configuring Message Options: Importance, Sensitivity, and Tracking Options

Certain options are available that can be applied to the current email message being created.

To access the options while the message is open, click the Options button in the toolbar of the message. The Message Options dialog box opens, as shown in Figure 28.17. Here, message sensitivity and tracking options for this particular message can be configured. Click OK when the options for the message are completed.

FIGURE 28.17   Message Options dialog box.

Importance

Importance can be configured as Low, Normal, or High. By default, messages are marked as Normal. Configuring a message as Low Importance causes a down-pointing blue arrow icon to appear to the left of the message when the recipient receives the message.

Configuring an email message as High Importance attaches a red exclamation mark (!) icon to the message that appears in the message list when the user receives the message. These choices don't actually speed up the delivery of the message, but provide a visual clue as to the message importance.

Sensitivity

Setting sensitivity options is a simple way for the sender to provide information about the message to any recipient receiving the message. Note that this option adds no security to the email message. When set, a visual clue appears at the top of the message (above the To and From boxes), suggesting the extra security assigned by the sender. The sensitivity setting also appears in the reading pane when the message is highlighted and is displayed in the Infobar when highlighted.

The choices for sensitivity settings are Normal, Personal, Private, and Confidential:

▶ **Normal**—Normal is the default setting for sensitivity: No message appears.

▶ **Personal**—The message reads: Please treat this as Personal.

▶ **Private**—The message reads: Please treat this as Private.

▶ **Confidential**—The message reads: Please treat this as Confidential.

Figure 28.18 is an example of a message that was marked Confidential and received.

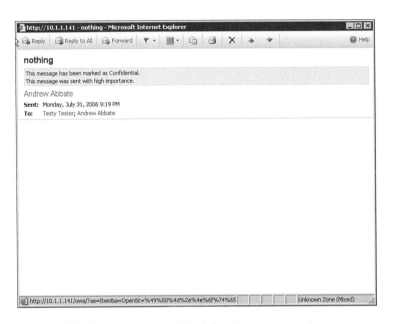

FIGURE 28.18   Treat-as-confidential notice on an email message.

Tracking Options

Tracking options enable you to determine when the message has been delivered to a mailbox (which usually happens immediately) and request a read receipt be sent to the sender when the recipient(s) has read the message. If you enable these options, you receive a message when each recipient receives and/or opens the message.

However, the recipient also has the choice of whether to send a read receipt confirmation message. If the recipient chooses not to send the receipt, the sender does not receive a notification that the message was read.

In addition, if the recipient deletes an email configured with a read receipt without opening it, the sender receives a message stating that the message was deleted without being read.

If the recipient reads the message via the reading pane in OWA, the client does not send a read receipt.

Changing the Look of the Text in an Email Message

The look of the text in an email can be easily changed and formatted. The choices for manipulating text include changing the font, font size, and font color; applying formatting, such as spacing, indentation and bullets, paragraph left/right, show paragraph markers, indent, and underline; and applying styles.

To manipulate the text while the Create Message dialog box is open, highlight the text to be changed. Choose any of the options found on the Formatting toolbar below the Attachments area. There is no need to click an Apply or OK button because these types of changes are immediately applied to the highlighted text.

> **NOTE**
>
> Unless the message is created in OWA as a Hypertext Markup Language (HTML) message, you cannot access many of the font or formatting options. More specifically, if the message is set as Plain Text, the formatting toolbar is not present.

Taking Advantage of Advanced OWA Features

Many advanced features in OWA make finding users and user information and manipulating messages easier than in previous versions of OWA. Many of the features listed and discussed in this section are not available when using Light version of OWA.

Moving Email Messages to Folders

You have the same visual folder view in OWA available as in Outlook 2007, meaning that all your folders and subfolders are available in OWA that are available in Outlook 2007. To move a message between folders, click the message once to highlight it, and use the drag-and-drop functionality to move it into the desired folder. When moving messages and email items, there is no confirmation message displayed confirming that the message moved successfully, so to confirm the move was successfully completed, you must open the folder to verify the message is there.

Using the Address Book

The address book has a much more robust search address book feature, which is new to OWA 2007. You can now use the search feature to look for names and addresses listed in the Global Address List and any other address books configured in your mailbox. To access the address book, click the Open Address Book icon located on the Infobar.

After clicking the icon, the Find Names dialog box opens. You can perform searches using any of the following criteria:

▶ Display name

▶ Last name

▶ First name

▶ Office

When you input information into the search field and click the magnifying glass icon, as shown in Figure 28.19, OWA searches are performed against whatever information was entered and returns all the matches found. If multiple matches are found, they are listed in the middle pane. Highlighting a result in the middle pane shows the address book entry for the mailbox in question in the reading pane.

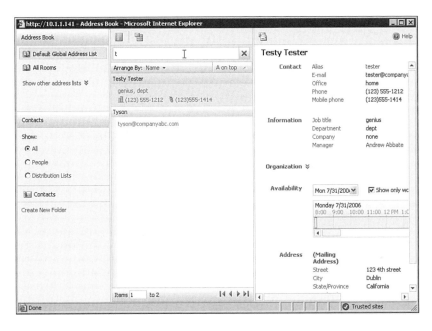

FIGURE 28.19   Finding a name in OWA.

To search a contact list or other custom list available in the GAL, simply select that list from the far left pane before performing the search, as shown in Figure 28.20.

To create a new email message directly to a user found in the address book, right-click the user and select New Message.

Marking Messages Read/Unread

Additional organization of messages can be completed by marking a message read/unread (bold/not bold). To do so, right-click the message once to highlight it, and choose Mark as Read, as shown in Figure 28.21.

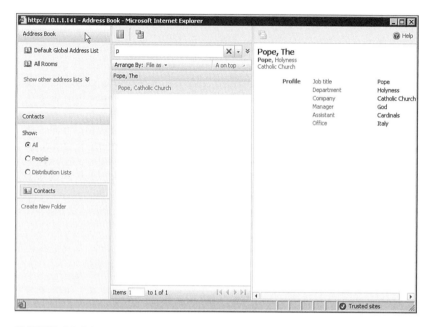

FIGURE 28.20   Finding a contact.

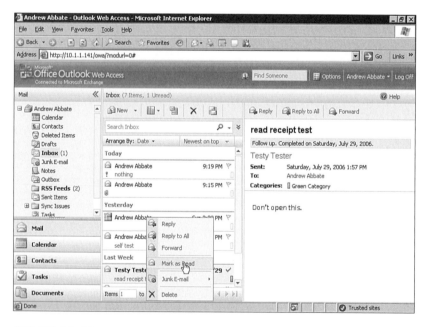

FIGURE 28.21   Marking a message as read.

Viewing User Property Sheets

To take advantage of the information provided through the Exchange Global Address List, OWA users can now view a great deal of information about address entries by viewing property sheets of names in the address list. Limited information is also available for senders from other organizations by viewing the properties of the addresses listed in the From field of any message received by a user.

To view property sheets of a user, sender, or any other type of recipient in a mail message, a username or address must be visually apparent. You can simply open an email message so the sender or recipients are displayed in the window or find the user in the address book. When viewing these Properties pages of an address in a mail message, this functionality is not available through the reading pane and can only be performed when the message is opened.

To view this information using the address book, click the name of the user and choose Properties. If the user is in an email message, double-click the username in the sender or recipients list.

The Properties page opens, as shown in Figure 28.22, which lists the following information about the user:

- ▶ Name (first and last)
- ▶ Alias
- ▶ Email address
- ▶ Office
- ▶ Phone numbers
- ▶ Job title
- ▶ Department
- ▶ Company
- ▶ Manager
- ▶ Availability (if calendar path is known and published)
- ▶ Mailing address

New to OWA 2007 is the option to generate a map to the sender's address if the information is present in the property page.

When viewing properties information, the data viewed is pulled directly from Active Directory if the user is viewable in the GAL. If the user is viewing a user object in the Contacts list, the data viewed is only information configured for that contact in the user's Contacts list.

28

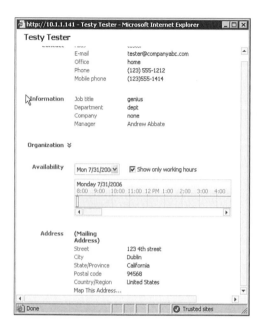

FIGURE 28.22   The Properties page detailing information about a user.

Note that user information in the Contacts list can be modified though OWA by clicking the Add to Contacts button while the properties sheet is open. Clicking Add to Contacts opens an Untitled Contact sheet, which enables the user to add/change any additional information.

After adding or modifying information, click Save and Close. When the contact closes, the Properties box must be closed by clicking Close. When completed, click Close again.

Using the OWA 2007 Spell Check

One of the most underutilized features of OWA has always been the Spell Check feature. With Exchange Server 2007, this feature has been improved yet again.

This functionality in OWA 2007 is very similar to the spelling checker feature found in all Microsoft products, and should feel very familiar to users. Currently, it includes some enhanced features making the spelling checker more effective when using it with OWA:

1. To enable Spell Check while creating a message in a Create Message dialog box, click the Spell Check icon on the toolbar.

2. The first time Spell Check is used, a dialog box opens requesting a language selection. Choose the language by using the drop-down menu.

3. When completed, click Check Document.

4. Spell Check then checks the message. If it finds any errors, it highlights the error in the main text box. In the Suggestions box, it provides the recommended changes or suggestions of what OWA thinks the word should be.

5. Ignore the word and move to the next one, by clicking Ignore.

6. Manually change the word to a different spelling by entering the change in the Change To box. Then click Change.

7. Click a suggested word and click Change.

8. Spell Check will continue until it has checked the whole message. When completed, the Spelling dialog box closes.

TIP

Users can take advantage of specific options available regarding the functionality of the Spell Check feature (for example, configuring Spell Check to automatically occur before sending a message). OWA 2007 also scans a message as content is typed and automatically underlines words that OWA deems as suspicious. By right-clicking the word, you will be prompted to choose a different word from the dictionary, as shown in Figure 28.23.

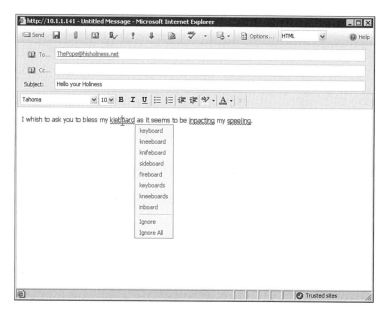

FIGURE 28.23   Spell-checking a message.

To configure preferences for spelling options, you can access these settings by clicking Options and selecting Spelling in the left pane. Don't forget to click Save when you are done!

Configuring Rules Using the Rules Editor

Unlike the previous version of OWA, OWA 2007 no longer supports creation or modification of rules. To create or modify rules other than the Out of Office response, you must connect to your mailbox with the full Outlook client to use the Rules Editor. Because all rules are server side, they will continue to process properly while you are using OWA.

Displaying Context Menus

Message context menus are a new feature in OWA 2007. The context menus are available to perform a task or next step and can be accessed by right-clicking a message in the message list in the middle pane. The context list then provides the following choices:

- ▶ Reply
- ▶ Reply to All
- ▶ Forward
- ▶ Mark as Read
- ▶ Delete

When you move the mouse over the desired choice and click once, the action is then taken. Each of these options is discussed in this chapter.

The options for setting flags and categories are now performed by hovering the mouse pointer over the flag or rectangle at the far right of the message in the middle pane and right-clicking them for the full list of actions.

Enabling Categories for Easier Reminders

Continuing to improve on management tools, OWA supports category settings. Using this feature is an easy way to configure reminder notifications to follow up on emails, including specifying levels of importance for each of them, classifying each by one of seven colors. The category squares can also be cleared and marked Complete.

Categories can be configured on email messages by right-clicking the narrow rectangle at the far right of the message and selecting the color to assign to the message.

In a full mailbox, this feature can be very helpful to identify follow-up emails and emails you need to track.

> **NOTE**
>
> The colors used for categories have no assigned significance within OWA or Outlook. Each user or organization can choose to designate certain colors for different levels of importance, priority, or even classification. The colored rectangles merely designate similarities or differences between messages, not specific priority.

When a categorized message no longer needs to be identified, right-click the colored rectangle and choose Clear Categories, which returns it to a grayed out rectangle.

Performing Searches with Outlook

Using saved searches are possible in OWA; however, it is the full Outlook 2007 client that makes this possible. By creating and saving frequently used searches in Outlook, a user is not required to input all the search criteria multiple times. These saved searches are then stored in the Folder list in a folder called Search Folder. Remember, the search folders and searches must be created in Outlook 2007 (not OWA) for a user in OWA to be able to use them.

To use already created searches, go to the Folder list, click Search Folder, and access the previously used searches to run them again.

Search functionality is available in OWA throughout the entire mailbox—and in every folder. The only limitation is that searches can't be saved in OWA. To use searches in OWA, follow these steps:

1. Click the folder in the folder tree you want to search.

2. Type the search criteria into the Search area in the middle pane, and click the magnifying glass.

You cannot save a new search in OWA, but you can delete a saved search that was created in Outlook 2007. Highlight the saved search item and then click the X in the upper-right corner to delete a saved search located in the search folder.

Using Keyboard Shortcuts to Save Time

A significant improvement, which makes many sophisticated typists happy, is that many of the familiar keyboard shortcuts used in Microsoft Office now also work while in OWA. Table 28.1 lists the keyboard shortcuts that can now be used in the OWA client.

TABLE 28.1   Keyboard Shortcuts Available in the OWA Client

Shortcut	Option
In Inbox View	
Ctrl+N	Open a new message window
Ctrl+Q	Mark message as read
Ctrl+U	Mark message as unread
Ctrl+R	Reply to message
Ctrl+Shift+R	Reply to all selected messages
Ctrl+Shift+F	Forward the selected message
In Message View	
Ctrl+>	View the next message in the list
Ctrl+<	View the previous message in the list

TABLE 28.1   Continued

Shortcut	Option
In Opened Message, While Creating a Message	
Ctrl+S	Save the message
Ctrl+Enter or Alt+S	Send the message
[F7]	Activate Spell Check
Ctrl+K	Check names in the address boxes
Alt+T or Alt+C or Alt+B	Find names (look in address book)
In Contacts View	
Ctrl+Shift+L	Create a new contact distribution list
In Task View	
Ctrl+N	Create a new task

Customizing OWA Options

OWA enables you to customize and configure certain features universally for your OWA Inbox. When the options are saved, they apply until they are changed, whether you are in OWA or in Outlook 2007. To access the options area, click the Options button on the Infobar. A list of options becomes available for customization and configuration. To save the configuration changes, click Save on the toolbar at the top of the Options page; otherwise, the options are discarded when the Options page is exited.

Configuring the Out of Office Assistant

The Out of Office Assistant, shown in Figure 28.24, enables you to create a message that will automatically and instantly be sent to any senders who have sent a message to you while the Out of Office Assistant is enabled. When a user enables the Out of Office Assistant, it remains on until you turn it off. OWA 2007 enhances the functionality of the Out of Office message function by allowing the user to configure two different messages and behaviors—one for messages received from inside the company and one for responding to external messages. This allows a user to safely provide information to internal users that might be inappropriate to send to an external recipient. The enabling of and disabling of the Out of Office Assistant is performed as follows:

1. Click Options in the upper-right portion of the toolbar.

2. Click Out of Office Assistant in the left pane.

3. Select Send Out of Office Auto-Replies.

4. Click the Send Out of Office Auto-Replies Only During This Time Period check box if you want to limit the times where this rule is effective.

5. Enter the time frame if this option was desired.

6. Enter the auto-reply message for senders inside your own organization.

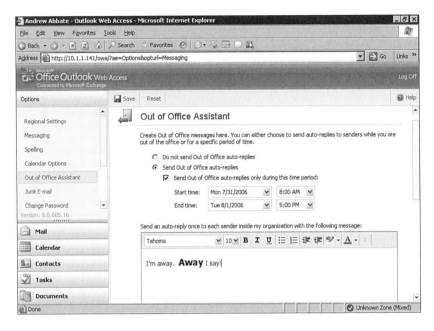

FIGURE 28.24   Sample internal Out of Office response.

7. Check the Send Out of Office Auto-Replies to External Senders check box, if so desired.

8. Choose between replying to any message or only to senders who are also in your Contacts list.

9. Enter the auto-reply message for senders outside your organization, as shown in Figure 28.25.

10. Click Save.

If a sender sends an email to a recipient with the Out of Office Assistant configured, the sender receives the Out of Office notification only once, even if he sends repeated messages or sends to a distribution list of which the out-of-office recipient is a member.

Configuring Items per Page

You can control how many items per page are shown. By default, OWA only displays 25 items, but this can be changed to show up to 100 objects per page, making visual searching for messages much easier. To change this setting:

1. Click Options in the upper-right portion of the toolbar.

2. Click Messaging in the far-left pane.

3. Click the Number of Items to Display per Page drop-down.

4. Click Save.

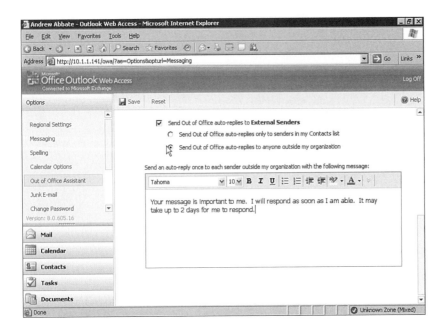

FIGURE 28.25   Sample external Out of Office response.

Setting Default Signatures

Another option available in the OWA Messaging options is the creation of an automatic signature. A signature is text composed in advance that appears at the bottom of new email messages. Signatures usually provide personal information about the sender—such as name, company, title, and phone number—enabling you to preconfigure the information so it doesn't have to be typed every time a message is created. You can also configure a signature to be automatically included in every message you send or to be added on a message-by-message basis:

1. Click Options in the upper-right portion of the toolbar.

2. Click Messaging in the far-left pane.

3. In the E-Mail Signature area, enter the text in the font you desire.

4. Check the Automatically Include My Signature on Outgoing Messages check box.

5. Click Save.

When an initial signature is saved, its font size, choice of font, color, and choices such as bold, italic, and underline can be changed without opening the signature again. Click Choose Font under Messaging Options. Choose the desired options and then click OK.

If the Automatically Include My Signature on Outgoing Messages check box is checked, the signature appears on any messages created from scratch, forwarded, and replied to. If that option is not checked, you can add the signature on a message-by-message basis from within an open message you compose. To add the signature manually, click Insert Signature (the icon with a piece of paper and hand with a pen) on the Standard toolbar within an open email message. It automatically inserts the signature after the button is clicked.

Reading Pane Options

The Reading Pane Options, shown in Figure 28.26, deal with the message list when AutoPreview is enabled. You must determine how long to wait with a message being previewed before it is marked as read. Choose from among the following options:

- ▶ **Mark Item Displayed in Reading Pane as Read**—After a specified amount of time that the message is viewed in the reading pane, the message becomes marked as read.

- ▶ **Mark Item as Read when the Selection Changes**—This option marks the message as read when the user clicks on a new message, no matter how long it was in the reading pane.

- ▶ **Do Not Automatically Mark Items as Read**—If configured, the messages are marked as read only when they are physically clicked on and opened.

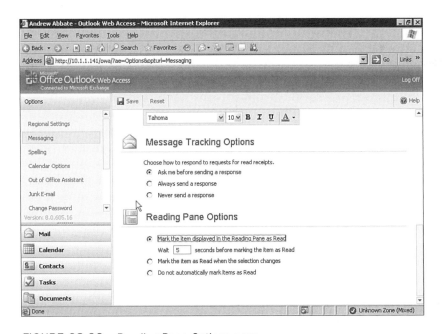

FIGURE 28.26   Reading Pane Options page.

Spelling Options

The Spelling Options section provides configuration options for the Spell Check feature. If you check the Always Check Spelling Before Sending check box, the spell checker automatically launches after Sent is clicked on a message but before it is sent.

A default language can also be configured in this location. OWA supports the following 10 language groups: English (Aus, UK, US, Canada), French, German (pre- and post-reform), Italian, Korean, and Spanish.

In OWA 2007, you also have the ability to have the spell checker ignore words in uppercase as well as ignore words with numbers. This is the same functionality you get in other Office applications.

Privacy and Junk Email Prevention

OWA gives you many choices as to what to do with junk email, as shown in Figure 28.27, and provides default options, which are the minimum configuration suggested by Microsoft for spam control.

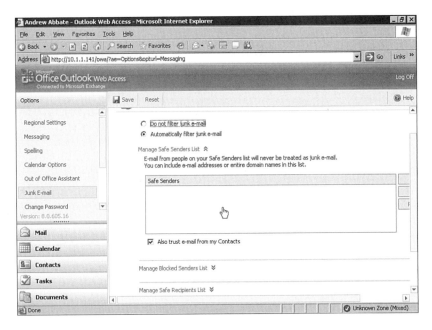

FIGURE 28.27   Privacy and Junk E-mail Options page.

To filter junk email, click the Automatically Filter Junk E-mail check box. When configured, Exchange moves any mail it considers junk to your Junk E-Mail Folder in the Folder list. When checked, you also must specify what is considered junk email by filling out the Manage Junk E-Mail Lists dialog box. Specify Safe Senders, Safe Recipients, or Blocked Senders by adding their names or email addresses in the proper list.

The option to always trust email from contacts from your personal Contacts list is checked by default.

> **NOTE**
>
> Users in the GAL are not considered as coming from junk email addresses; therefore, there is no reason to manage addresses from the GAL unless you specifically want to flag messages from an individual or individuals.

The final option in the junk email options is whether to block external content, the implications of which are discussed in the section "Understanding Spam Beacon Blocking" later in this chapter.

Color Scheme Appearance

The color scheme of OWA is configurable as well. The default is blue, but numerous choices are available. To choose a scheme, go to the general settings via the Options button and click the drop-down list under Appearance. Choose the color scheme desired. Note that the color doesn't change until Save is clicked.

Configuring Date and Time Formats

The Date and Time Formats options are accessible under the Regional Settings under Options. This enables you to configure the time zone, time style, and date style.

Changing the time zone can be useful if you move to a different time zone and want OWA to reflect the new zone. To configure the time zone, click the drop-down list arrow and choose the proper time zone.

Don't forget to click Save for this to take effect!

Configuring Calendar Options

The Calendar Options, shown in Figure 28.28, enable you to choose the day and times that describe a week in the calendar. By default, the week begins on Sunday, the day start time is 8:00 a.m., and the end time is 5:00 p.m. This can be changed by clicking the drop-down menus to the right of the titles in the Calendar Options area in the Options menu.

The work week defaults to Monday through Friday, 8:00 a.m. to 5:00 p.m. and can be configured via the drop-down menus as well.

Configuring Reminder Options

Reminder Options specify the default time of how soon before meetings, appointments, and tasks dates you are reminded. By default, all the configuration boxes are checked, and the default reminder time, which appears when you create a calendar or task item with a reminder, is 15 minutes. Configure any changes to reminders in this area by unchecking or checking the boxes or changing the reminder time by using the drop-down menus.

28

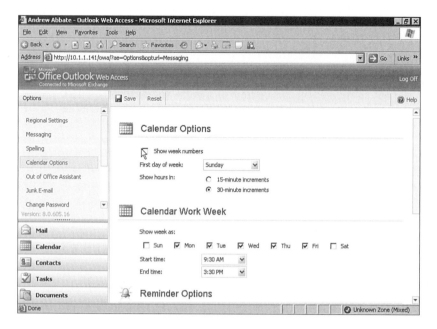

FIGURE 28.28   Configuring Calendar Options.

Configuring E-mail Name Resolution Options

Configuring E-Mail Name Resolution Options enables you to determine where OWA checks first for resolution of addresses in the address boxes in emails. By default, OWA checks the GAL first. To configure OWA to check your contacts first before the GAL, click the Contacts option button. Don't forget to click Save if you change the default options.

Changing the Active Directory Password

You can change your Active Directory password via OWA. This is extremely useful for mobile users who rarely come into the office. If you are on the road and your password expires, OWA enables you to access OWA and then forces you to change your password immediately. To change the password before being prompted, complete the following steps:

1. Access the Outlook options via the Options button in the upper-right portion of the toolbar.

2. Choose Change Password in the left pane to get a screen similar to the one shown in Figure 28.29.

3. Type the old password.

4. Enter and then confirm the new password.

5. Click Save.

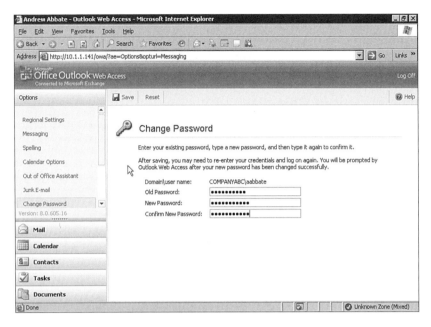

FIGURE 28.29   Changing a password from within OWA.

Using the Calendar in OWA

Outlook 2007 provides a fully functional calendar for managing personal meeting appointments, group appointments, and recurring events. The Calendar feature in OWA includes the same functionality, including the new available features available with the full Outlook client. These options include appointment views, creation, and changes, and even changing meeting times as a meeting attendee.

Using Views

You can view your calendar in many different ways, either by day, week, or month. To choose the view, click the icons in the Infobar that show Today, Day, Work Week, and Week:

▶ **Today view**—The Today view goes to today's date in the single day view.

▶ **Day view**—The Day view displays one day at a time. Users can move from day to day by clicking the day they want on the calendar in the right pane.

▶ **Work Week view**—The Work Week view displays one week at a time in five split panes in the middle pane. These days are determined by the Calendar Work Week option settings for workdays. Brief descriptions of the day's appointments are shown in the seven panes.

▶ **Week view**—The Week view displays one week at a time in seven split panes in the middle pane. Brief descriptions of the day's appointments are shown in the seven panes.

Creating an Appointment in Calendar

In OWA, all calendar objects are initially called appointments, whether they are meeting requests with multiple invitees or appointments meant only for the individual user. To create a new appointment, complete the following steps:

1. Click the drop-down list arrow next to the New button on the toolbar, and choose Appointment to see a screen similar to the one shown in Figure 28.30.

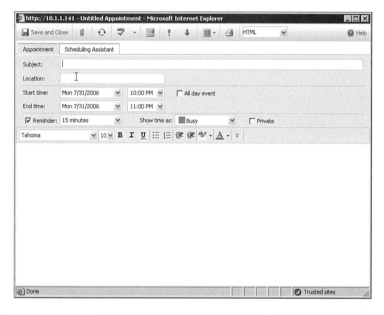

FIGURE 28.30   New Calendar Appointment page.

2. To maintain the appointment as an appointment and not a meeting request (meaning no one else is invited), use the default Appointments dialog box that opens. Enter the subject of the appointment in the Subject box.

3. Enter the location of the appointment in the Location box.

   To specify a start time, there are two choices:

   ▶ To manually enter the time, type the time in the Start Time and End Time boxes.

   ▶ To use the OWA calendar, click the drop-down menu boxes to the right of Start Time and End Time. From the calendar that is presented, click the date in the calendar to choose the date of the appointment.

To configure the time in a similar way, complete the following steps:

1. Click the drop-down menu to the right of Start Time and End Time and choose the start and end times.

2. It is optional to add text in the text area and to add attachments using the method discussed earlier in this chapter. If you want to do so, make these additions now.

3. To mark the appointment as important, click the ! icon located on the toolbar.

4. When you are finished, click Save and Close.

Creating a Meeting Request in Calendar

When creating a new meeting, the same Appointment dialog box is used, but includes the ability to invite other users to the appointment:

▶ To create a new meeting request, click the drop-down list arrow next to the New button on the toolbar and choose Appointment. Input the subject of the meeting.

▶ To invite attendees, click the Scheduling Assistant tab to display a page similar to Figure 28.31. The Appointment dialog box then changes appearance to add the Select Attendees and Select Rooms boxes.

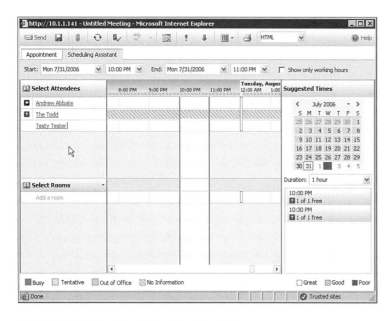

FIGURE 28.31   Scheduling Assistant tab.

Inviting Attendees

Adding attendees to the meeting requires some extra steps. To add attendees, you have two choices:

▸ Enter the names directly under Select Attendees and press Enter after each for a name lookup.

▸ Click the address book icon next to Select Attendees to look up names from the address book and add them there as Required, Optional, or Resources.

If you add users through the first method, they default to Required. You can change them to Optional by clicking the small icon to the left of the name.

As you invite people or resources to the meeting, you can view their availability in the main pane. This shows the schedules of the attendees by showing free time, busy time, or out-of-office time (not the details of what the attendees will be doing during those times, but whether they're available). If the attendees are busy at the specified time, you can choose a new time while viewing attendee availability.

The Scheduling Assistant also suggests times when the attendees are available. This appears in the lower-right portion of the screen.

To enter the new start and end times while viewing attendee availability, click the drop-down menus to the right of Start Time and End Time and Date and choose a new time. Another option is to click the actual calendar and move the start times and date by clicking and dragging the green and red vertical lines. The green line shows the start time, and the red line shows the end time.

Click the Appointment tab to complete the rest of the meeting request. Click Send to exit the meeting request and send the request to all invited attendees.

Setting Recurring Appointments/Meetings

If a meeting or appointment occurs with regularity, OWA enables the creation of multiple appointments with a single meeting request or appointment. To enable recurring appointments, while the Appointment dialog box is open, click the Recurrence button. The Recurrence dialog box opens, as shown in Figure 28.32.

To set the recurrence pattern, choose whether the meeting is Daily, Weekly, Monthly, or Yearly by clicking the option button to the left of the appropriate choice.

Depending on which of those buttons is clicked, the items to the right change. The Weekly recurrence gives the options of what days the appointment occurs upon, as well as how often—for example, Every X Week(s). If Daily is chosen, the options display daily choices, such as Every X Days, or Every Week Day.

Range of recurrence enables the configuration of an end date for the recurrences. A specific end date can be specified, or the recurrence can be configured with No End Date or to End After X Occurrences, where X is the number of times the event will occur.

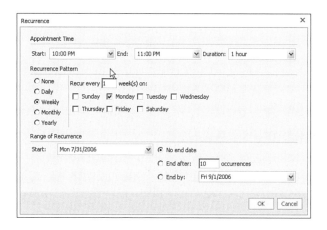

FIGURE 28.32   Recurrence dialog box.

When you are finished, click OK. To exit the Recurrence dialog box without saving the recurrence configuration, click Remove Recurrence. The Appointment dialog box reappears. Complete the appointment or meeting request as needed and click Save and Close when you are finished.

New to the calendaring functions in OWA 2007 is a consolidated view to see who has responded to your meeting request. In OWA 2003, the meeting organizer would receive individual responses from each invitee and would use these to track the responses. In OWA 2007, you can open an existing meeting request and choose the Tracking tab, as shown in Figure 28.33. This view shows you who has responded so far.

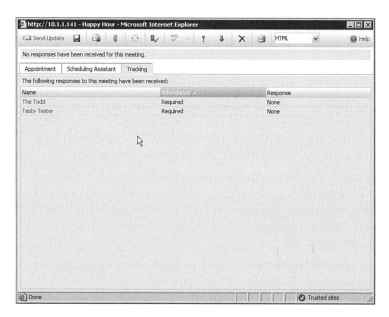

FIGURE 28.33   Tracking meeting responses.

Gaining Functionality from the Meeting Invitation Functions

The meeting invitation function enables you to forward a meeting request to others, reply to the meeting request, set reminder times, launch an invitation, or receive task and calendar reminders.

Forwarding and Replying to Meeting Requests

When forwarding or replying to a meeting request, users have the option of accepting, tentatively accepting, or rejecting the meeting request. To use these options, click the Forward To or Reply To context menus or the buttons on the Infobar. If the request is opened normally, the recipient cannot reply to or forward the meeting request without accepting or rejecting the request. By forwarding or replying to a request, you can create a discussion of the invitation or share its information with others without accepting or rejecting the original invitation.

Setting Preferred Reminder Time Changes

When creating or setting reminders, the preferred reminder time is set to 15 minutes by default. This means that if you create a new Outlook item that uses a reminder time, 15 minutes prior to the reminder time, a notification is displayed to remind the users of the upcoming item. This is a configurable option and can be changed in the Options section of OWA, as discussed previously in this chapter.

To change the reminder time provided by a meeting invitation, open the event and click in the drop-down menu that displays the reminder time. Choose the desired reminder time.

Launching an Invitation in Its Own Window

To accept, request a change, or deny a meeting request, the request must be opened. To open it, double-click the invitation that arrives in the message Inbox pane.

The invitation then opens in its own separate window, enabling the invitees to accept the meeting, tentatively accept the meeting, or deny the request. This can be done by clicking the corresponding buttons on the toolbar in the meeting request box, and then clicking Send.

By accepting a meeting request, the meeting is automatically placed into your calendar with a dark blue heading on the left side of the meeting title. This can be seen in the Calendar view pane. Tentatively accepting the request also places the meeting in your calendar, but it appears in a light blue heading, indicating that the meeting is tentative. Denying the request doesn't alter your calendar at all.

All three choices result in an email being sent back to the original sender of the meeting request, stating the status that each attendee has placed for the meeting .

Receiving Task and Calendar Reminders

When reminders occur in Tasks or your Calendar, a message appears in the shortcut bar and appears as a dialog box listing the reminders on your screen. You then can launch the task or appointment by clicking Open Item. You have three options:

- ▶ Dismiss all reminders at one time by clicking Dismiss All.

- ▶ Dismiss items individually by clicking once on the item and then clicking Dismiss.

- ▶ Snooze the reminder, and choose the amount of time to snooze by highlighting the reminder and clicking Snooze. In the time specified in the snooze time, the reminder will appear again.

To view any reminders at any time, click the alarm icon button in the Infobar while in the Calendar view. The Reminder box appears after the button has been clicked.

Using Tasks in OWA

The Tasks option in OWA is similar to a to-do list. Tasks can be created, viewed, and organized.

Creating Tasks

You can create tasks in OWA 2007 just as you do in Outlook 2007. Tasks are used to remind you of jobs that must be completed by a certain date or time. Tasks also enable you to set due dates and reminders and to follow the progress or percent of tasks that have been completed along with their status, enabling you to monitor areas such as works in progress. To make them even more effective, all criteria inside them can be easily changed when the task is saved, such as enabling frequent updates to the task's status and specifics about the tasks.

The Subject, Due Date, and Completion Status criteria can be sorted in the middle pane view while accessing tasks, making it easy to sort and view tasks.

To access tasks, click the Tasks button in the shortcut bar, or click New, Task in the Infobar. The New Task dialog box opens.

The methods used to input the subject, set the due dates and start dates, set a reminder, add attachments, complete text in the text box, and configure the task as recurring have been discussed earlier in the chapter and are applicable to configuring tasks.

When the task has been configured, click Save and Close to finish the task and save it to your Tasks list. The task then appears on the list of tasks. The default order of the tasks is by due date, and tasks with no due date appear first.

28

Task Views

Like other OWA functions, tasks provide you with multiple views that can make the organization and viewing of tasks easier:

- ▶ **All**—The simple list provides a one-line list by subject and due date, and indicates whether the task is completed.

- ▶ **Active**—The Active list provides the same detail as the All list, but only shows incomplete items.

- ▶ **Overdue**—Similar to the Active list but with only overdue items listed.

- ▶ **Complete**—This view shows tasks that have been marked as completed.

Using Contacts in OWA

Contacts enable you to create your own lists of users who might not be within the GAL. By entering them into the Contacts list, you can easily send emails and appointments to those contacts and create distribution lists made up of users in the GAL and those in your personal Contacts list.

Creating Contacts

Creating contacts is a simple, three-step process:

1. Click New/Contact in the Infobar. The New Contact dialog box opens, as shown in Figure 28.34.

2. Enter all pertinent information about the contact. The top-level tabs allow you to jump directly to a specific type of information.

3. When completed, click Save and Close to save the contact in the Contacts list.

Editing Contacts

To edit an already created contact, double-click the contact. Edit the contact sheet as needed, and then click Save and Close when you are finished.

Mapping Addresses from Contacts

When you view a contact, if you have access to the Internet, you can select Map This Address from the detail view of the user and it will pull up a map of the location stated in the Address portion of the Contacts sheet.

Changing Contact Views

Just as the Inbox provides you with multiple views for email, Contacts provides three views for contacts:

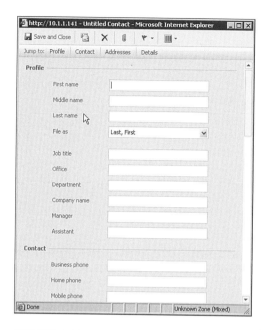

FIGURE 28.34   New Contact dialog box.

▸ **All**—This view shows the entire contents of the Contacts folder. This includes both people and distribution lists. As this list can be very large, you have the standard options for searching or filtering the results.

▸ **People**—This view limits the Contacts list to only people. This list can be searched or filtered to further refine the view.

▸ **Distribution Lists**—This view shows only distribution lists that were created by the user and stored as personal contacts.

Users should be aware that while they can view their distribution lists through OWA, they cannot edit them or create new ones.

Deleting Contacts

To delete a contact, click the contact to highlight it, and click Delete in the Infobar or press the Delete key.

Finding Names

To find names in contacts, click the Contacts folder in the shortcut bar. Choose the appropriate view, for example, All. Type in part of the name that you are looking for in the Search Contacts box, and click the magnifying glass. The closest matches appear in the middle pane.

Sending Mail from Contacts

If a contact sheet is open, email can be sent directly to the contact if a correct email address is configured for the contact. To send an email directly, click the New Message to Contact button on the toolbar.

OWA then opens a new email dialog box with the addressee information already completed, listing the contact as the intended recipient. Complete the email and send it.

Creating New Distribution Lists

OWA 2007 no longer supports the creation of distribution lists. These lists would have to be created through the full Outlook client.

Understanding OWA Security Features

OWA has several enhancements for security, including support for message classification, spam beacon blocking, attachment blocking, cookie authentication, and clearing user credentials during the logoff process.

Utilizing Message Classification

OWA 2007 allows a user to take advantage of the message classification rules that are configured on the Exchange 2007 server. These configurations in Exchange 2007 allow specific message types to be handled in specific ways. For example, a "Company Confidential" message might have a standard disclaimer applied to it before it is sent or an "A/C Privileged" message might be routed through an encrypted connection to the recipient's server. By clicking the Message Classification icon in the toolbar of a new message, the OWA user can set these values.

Understanding Spam Beacon Blocking

OWA 2007 provides additional security against spam. If configured, OWA does not enable spam beaconing technology to function in OWA; it blocks links to external content on the Internet from being accessed from the OWA interface. This greatly increases the anti-spam features of OWA by disabling the spammer's ability to hide beacons in unwanted spam messages. Those spam beacons automatically contact the spammers when the email messages are opened, letting the spammers know they have reached a live email address. By blocking this functionality, one more method of finding live addresses is eliminated from the spammer's arsenal.

Understanding Attachment Blocking

OWA also provides built-in and configurable functionality to block Internet attachments, such as links to websites, music, and other Internet technologies available only outside the firewall (on the Internet).

OWA built on Exchange Server 2007 contains a block list. Any attachments with an extension type in the block list are automatically blocked when sent to a user in Outlook or OWA. The latest service packs now also include blocking of XML MIME applications and test files.

When changing or modifying these options, only administrators can configure these options; this is not configured by users in OWA. When one of these type of files are blocked, users are sent a message notifying them that the attachment is blocked.

Understanding Cookie Authentication Timeout and Timed Logoff

OWA 2007 uses cookies to hold the user authentication information. When a user logs off of OWA 2007, the cookie automatically expires, so a hacker can't use the cookie to gain authentication. In addition, the cookie is configured to automatically expire—after 20 minutes of inactivity in OWA if the user specified a private computer, or 10 minutes if the user specified a shared or public computer.

After timed logoff has occurred and a user tries to access OWA, he has to reenter user credentials.

Clearing User Credentials at Logoff

For users who access OWA 2007 via Internet Explorer 6.0 SP1 or higher and FBA, the user's logon credentials cache automatically clears when the user logs off from OWA 2007. It is no longer necessary to close the browser window to clear the cache. For users accessing OWA via other Internet browsers or via OWA servers that aren't configured to use FBA, users must still close the browser window to clear the cache and will be prompted to do so.

Tips for OWA Users with Slow Access

Some users might need to access OWA through a slow, dial-up connection. OWA provides them with many ways to enhance performance and speed to improve the overall OWA experience. Leveraging options built in to the Exchange operating systems and toggling off some OWA options can ensure that users accessing OWA experience a friendly, easy-to-use client.

When using forms-based authentication, making additional changes to the Exchange server can improve OWA performance. This option provides data compression on two levels when communicating with OWA and can improve the overall performance of OWA by up to 50%.

28

> **TIP**
>
> When enabling compression on the Exchange virtual server, test performance to validate that the change is addressing your performance concerns. Ensure that compression isn't placing too high a CPU load on the system.

To enable compression on the Exchange virtual server, perform the following steps:

1. Click Start, All Programs, Microsoft Exchange Server 2007, and select Exchange Management Shell.

2. From the Exchange Management Shell prompt, type `get-owavirtualdirectory`.

3. Record the identity of the OWA virtual directory.

4. Type `set-owavirtualdirecotry -identity "Owa (Default Web Site) -gziplevel high`.

5. Type `Exit`.

6. Launch the DOS prompt.

7. Type `iisreset /noforce`.

8. Type `Exit`.

There are options that can be configured from the server and through Group Policy to improve access speeds, but users can help speed up their access regardless of whether the server-side improvements are implemented. Major options are as follows:

▶ Choose Basic Mode when Logging into OWA

▶ Set Low Number of Messages to Be Displayed on the Page

▶ Turn Off the Reading Pane

▶ Turn On Two-Line Viewing

▶ Enable the Blocking of Internet Content

Summary

OWA in Exchange Server 2007 is more than just an alternative means of access when the user does not have the ability to connect with the full Outlook client. Because of significant enhancements added to OWA 2007, along with forms-based authentication, many organizations are finding the security and features of the premium OWA client robust enough to use OWA as a primary client for internal users as well. Because of continuous improvements available with service pack revisions, spell checker, preview mode, filters, and address book lookup capabilities provide a robust set of features users leverage on a regular basis. When planning and deploying client access solutions, OWA deserves much more consideration, so that it can also be used as a primary messaging client solution. You will find that more and more of your users will take advantage of OWA as they discover just how useful it is.

Best Practices

The following are best practices from this chapter:

▶ Use the Light version of the OWA client when client bandwidth access is limited.

▶ Use the standard authentication mode OWA client when full functionality is desired.

▶ Take advantage of the Scheduling Assistant to pick the best times for meetings.

▶ Leverage compression on the Exchange server to improve performance by up to 50% when accessing OWA.

▶ Always back up or copy OWA files before making any changes.

▶ Change pane size to customize the OWA view and meet your needs.

▶ Use Ctrl or Shift when selecting emails for deletion; this speeds up the process of deleting several messages at the same time.

▶ Use categories or flags to create reminders or to bring attention to a message for Outlook users.

▶ Use keyboard shortcuts to simplify menu button tasks or functions.

▶ Customize task views to give users the ability to see pertinent task information.

▶ Send mail to an email contact by selecting the contact and choosing to send the email to the contact.

▶ In contact distribution lists, include only recipients from the GAL, not from the user's contact list.

▶ Because S/MIME attachments are supported by OWA, use them to extend encryption and digitally signed messages for enhanced security.

28

CHAPTER 29

Using Non-Windows Systems to Access Exchange Server 2007

In today's business networks, Exchange 2007 administrators are challenged with a variety of compatibility issues. One of the biggest challenges is the need to support today's complex, mixed-Exchange client platforms often found when implementing or upgrading to Microsoft Exchange Server 2007. With a diversity of different client needs attached to Exchange data, administrators and information technology (IT) managers are constantly challenged with the complexities of providing client access to corporate mail systems for a variety of different clients, including those running non-Windows–based client operating systems.

When administrators need to meet these specific requirements and the many challenges involved with connecting non-Windows–based clients to Exchange Server 2007 mail information, they can become overwhelmed with using the built-in functionality of Windows Server 2003 and Exchange 2007 technologies. Combining Microsoft technologies, administrators can provide support and establish compatibility to alternative messaging clients using remote technologies, Internet solutions, and Microsoft-developed alternative clients. This makes Exchange 2007 an effective all-in-one corporate mail solution to support non-Windows-based client operating systems, such as Apple's Mac platform and UNIX-based platforms.

Using the information in this chapter, administrators will learn the options available for connecting these non-Windows–based client systems and the applications available to provide access to Microsoft Exchange 2007 mailbox information.

This chapter discusses applications—such as Outlook Web Access (OWA), Mac OS X Mail, Outlook Express, Post Office Protocol 3 (POP3)/Internet Message Access Protocol (IMAP) clients, and Entourage for the Mac—that provide connectivity for non-Windows–based clients to Exchange 2007 mail data. Each option is reviewed and discussed in detail to determine the different functions available with each solution and the compatibility when being used to connect Exchange 2007 with the different alternative operating systems.

In addition to functionality and the conventional client/server connectivity methods, this chapter also provides systems administrators with the step-by-step instructions to configure access to Exchange 2007, using concepts such as Remote Desktop and Windows 2003 Terminal Services.

Understanding Non-Windows–Based Mail Client Options

In most enterprise network environments today, the need to support non-Microsoft Windows client operating systems is almost guaranteed; administrators must plan and support alternative means of access to Exchange mail information.

To accomplish this goal, administrators can use several options available to provide Exchange data and calendaring information to a variety of alternative non-Windows–based clients systems. Leveraging the built-in compatibility and functionality of Exchange Server 2007, access can be accomplished using any one or combination of multiple familiar client options, depending on the operating system being used and the functionality needed by the individual client.

Using Exchange client options such as Mac OS X Mail, Entourage 2004, Outlook Web Access, Windows-based Remote Desktop, and others listed later in this chapter, administrators can identify the best solution available to provide Exchange 2007 server connectivity based on the operating system being used and functionality of each solution.

In addition, because these types of clients are usually the minority in most Microsoft Exchange environments, administrators can evaluate the functionality available with each of these client solutions and implement any specific one based on the requirements of the client accessing Exchange information.

Supporting Mac Clients with Microsoft Solutions

When determining which Exchange client is best for supporting Mac users and desktops, the most important consideration is the required functionality of the client user and the limitations involved with each available option.

To support Mac desktops with Exchange Server 2007, Microsoft provided a few options, including Entourage 2004 and Outlook Express clients designed specifically for the Macintosh desktop operating system. A very popular option for Macintosh support to Exchange is to use the built-in Mac OS X Mail client that comes with OS X and fully supports access to Exchange.

Using any of these options, administrators can support internal network access and remote connectivity to Exchange 2007 using applications installed directly on the client desktop using protocols already enabled to support their Windows-based Outlook client cousins.

Supporting Outlook Options

For additional information on Entourage 2004 and support for Mac clients in an Exchange 2007 environment, Microsoft provides comprehensive information and instructions through the Mactopia support website at www.Microsoft.com/Mactopia.

Though most Windows users are familiar with the name Outlook and Outlook Express, Microsoft also provides another very powerful client option for connecting Macintosh clients to Exchange 2007. Using the Entourage 2004 client, Mac users can get a robust set of client options such as mail and calendaring synchronization, junk email filtering, and contact management with the look and feel more familiar to Macintosh users. Not the Outlook client, this alternative to Outlook is available individually or as part of the Office 2004 Mac client suite or can be downloaded independently.

Providing Full Functionality with Virtual PC and Remote Desktop for Mac

What is probably the simplest and most popular option when supporting Mac clients in a predominantly Windows-based environment is using the Microsoft Virtual PC and Remote Desktop Client for Mac. Using these Mac client options provides any Mac user the full functionality of the Windows-based Outlook 2007 and Outlook 2003 clients on the Mac desktop. These are two options that can be easily implemented and allow Mac users full access to Windows client tools and functionality. Using this option, administrators can not only provide access to Microsoft Outlook, but they can also provide full functionality to Windows desktop applications and tools directly to the Mac client.

Using the Virtual PC for Mac, users can launch and work in a fully functional virtual Windows-based PC loaded on the Mac desktop. Effective for Mac users with Windows experience, Virtual PC provides cross-platform functionality for users by allowing features such as access to Mac desktop peripherals, cut-and-paste features between the Virtual PC and the Mac OS, no-configuration printing, and access to Windows network-based shares.

NOTE

Unlike the RDP client, Virtual PC runs the applications on the local Mac client. This means that any data, including saved files and Offline Folders, is also stored on the local Mac desktop.

To get more information on Virtual PC, including updates, visit the Microsoft web page at: http://www.microsoft.com/mac/products/virtualpc/virtualpc.aspx?pid=virtualpc.

29

Using the Remote Desktop Client, Mac users can access a Windows desktop functionality through sessions based on Terminal Services functionality, allowing full functionality in Windows through a remote connection. This function also gives Mac clients the ability to cut and paste information from the Remote Desktop Connection to the Mac operating system, full printing functionality to local connected Mac printers, and the ability to provide network access to shared Windows resources. The difference in these two options is the default storage of Exchange data and saved work; with the RDP client, when the RDP session is disconnected, all saved information remains on the network and not on the attached client.

Using the Internet for Exchange Connectivity

When access to Exchange information is all that is required, the most effective option available is leveraging the Outlook Web Access (OWA) functionality built in to the Exchange Server 2007 operating system. Because using this option is normally enabled for standard Windows-based remote access from the Internet, Mac users and UNIX/Linux users can also access OWA as they access a web page from both the internal network and the Internet.

By using web-based access to provide Exchange 2007 client functionality, administrators can consider this solution for a variety of different non-Windows–based client systems with Internet browsing enabled. Although OWA provides a limited set of Outlook functions, the Outlook 2007 and Outlook 2003 versions provide all the basic needs, including spell checking, calendar appointments, the Rules Wizard, and more. Even more important, this option requires no additional client software to be installed on any non-Windows–based client.

> **NOTE**
>
> Enabling web access to support non-Windows–based clients for both internal network access and access from the Internet requires additional configuration of the Exchange 2007 server and network firewall.
>
> For detailed information on how to design and configure Microsoft Outlook Web Access in Exchange 2007 for web access support, see Chapter 28, "Leveraging the Capabilities of the Outlook Web Access (OWA) Client."

Comparing Client Functionality and Compatibility

With each option and method of access to Exchange 2007, different options and functionality are available. As mentioned in the review of each method of access, some methods enable full functionality and others are limited.

Review the operating system requirements in Table 29.1 to determine whether the Mac operating systems meet the required revision for the method of access being considered.

TABLE 29.1   Client Compatibility

Outlook Express	Remote Desktop	Entourage	Outlook Web Access	VirtualPC
OS 8.1 or higher	OS X 10.1 or higher	OS X 10.1 or higher	Internet Explorer for Mac	OS 10.2.8 or higher

Determine the required functionality by using Table 29.2 to compare the features of each client access method. Review the functionality of each method and compare the result with the Mac OS you are working with.

TABLE 29.2   Client Functionality

Requirement	Outlook Express	Remote Desktop	Entourage 2004	OWA
Email	x	x	x	x
Calendaring	No	x	x	x
Contacts	x	x	x	x
Directory search	x	x	x	x
Offline access	x	x	x	No
PST archive	No	x	x	No
PST import/export	No	x	x	No
Junk mail filtering	No	x	x	x
SSL security	No	x	x	x

Outlook Express

A common client used by many users to access Exchange from a non-Windows perspective has been the use of the Outlook Express client shown in Figure 29.1. However, a few years ago, Microsoft chose to abandon the further development of Outlook Express and focused their support in development of the Outlook client for Windows as well as a better OWA client for non-Windows users. Outlook Express remains a viable remote client solution for Exchange supporting IMAP and POP3 access, and Outlook Express is available for Macintosh, UNIX/Linux, and Windows support.

With Microsoft not advancing the development of Outlook Express, organizations can choose other IMAP or POP3 clients available on the marketplace, such as the free Mac Mail utility found directly in the operating system on Macintosh systems, or any of a number of IMAP/POP3 clients for Linux (see http://www.emailman.com/unix/clients.html for a series of mail clients downloadable off the Internet).

However, because Outlook Express is still a commonly used client, some features/functions of Outlook Express are covered here in this section. Outlook Express offers support with the basic needs for mail and address books, such as the following:

▶ **Email support**—Access to Exchange email using the Simple Mail Transfer Protocol (SMTP) and Post Office Protocol (POP).

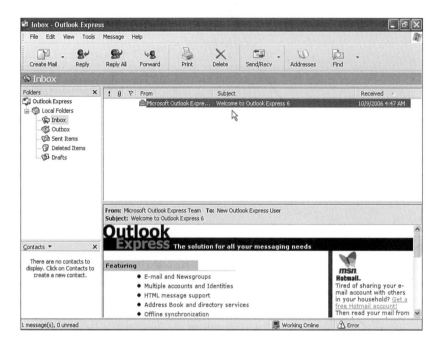

FIGURE 29.1   Microsoft Outlook Express.

▶ **Address books**—Email addresses are stored in address books locally and within the Outlook Express client.

NOTE

Messages accessed through Outlook Express via POP3 are downloaded to the local client and, by default, are removed from the local server. Because client messages, by default, are downloaded and stored on the local client only if a user wants to keep their mail on the Exchange server, choose the option in Outlook Express (varies by Outlook Express versions) that typically resides in the account settings or profile configuration option of Outlook Express to Keep a Copy of Mail on the Server.

▶ **Contact address list**—Outlook Express supports contacts and address lists, which can be used to select addresses when creating and sending messages and to store personal contact information.

▶ **LDAP support**—Lightweight Directory Access Protocol (LDAP) support enables an Outlook Express client's access to view information such as the Global Address List (GAL) of an Exchange 2007 organization.

▶ **POP support**—POP is the primary method of supporting Outlook Express clients when accessing Exchange from the Internet. This option requires POP to be enabled on Exchange 2007 and might require additional configuration of the firewall to enable pass-through of POP.

▶ **Password support**—Usernames and passwords can be configured in advance, enabling users to open Outlook Express and access mail with a preconfigured account name and password.

Installing and Enabling Support for Outlook Express

This section reviews the tasks required to configure Outlook Express to support communication with Exchange 2007 from the internal network location and the Internet. Although each version of Outlook Express, depending on the operating system, is slightly different, the instructions might also be a little different; however, for the most part, these instructions provide general installation and configuration guidance.

One common task when enabling support for Outlook Express is to enable support for the client to use TCP/IP to communicate with and access Exchange mail.

NOTE

Using TCP/IP enables client access from the internal network and from the Internet. This configuration is not the same as the protocol that will be used to access Exchange 2007 mail.

When installing Outlook Express, the installation file can be downloaded free from the Microsoft website at:

http://www.microsoft.com/downloads/Search.aspx?displaylang=en

Configuring POP Access with Outlook Express

In this scenario, you can configure the Outlook Express client to connect to Exchange 2007 through an Internet connection using the Post Office Protocol. This enables Outlook Express to access the Exchange 2007 server and authenticate downloading messages.

NOTE

Before configuring client connectivity to Exchange 2007 using POP, additional configuration of the Exchange server is required to enable the protocol for the individual mail and server. In addition, if accessing with POP from the Internet, the network firewall should be configured to enable POP access and the domain name for the Exchange 2007 POP server should be populated to the Internet.

For more information on domain name system (DNS), see Chapter 6, "Understanding Network Services and Active Directory Domain Controller Placement for Exchange Server 2007."

For information on configuring your firewall and security best practices when enabling support with POP, consult the firewall manufacturer's product information.

29

To configure Outlook Express to connect an Exchange 2007 server using POP, begin by opening Outlook Express and follow these steps:

1. From the Tools menu, select Accounts.

2. On the Internet Accounts tab, click the Mail tab and select New.

3. To create a new email account, enter the name for the account in the Display Name dialog box, enter the name for the account being created, and click Next.

4. On the email screen, select the I Already Have an Email Address That I'd Like to Use option, and enter the email address for the user being configured. Click Next to continue.

5. At the Email Server Information page, type "POP" under the My Incoming Mail Server selection.

6. Enter the fully qualified mail server name as listed in the following example. Then click Next to continue.

   Example:

   Incoming Mail Server = Mail.CompanyABC.com

   Outgoing Mail Server = SMTP.CompanyABC.com

NOTE

The incoming and outgoing mail server names should be added and populated to the Internet for proper DNS name resolution.

When configuring this option for Internet access, the outgoing mail server might need to be configured to point to the outgoing mail server of the Internet service provider (ISP) being used.

---

7. At the authentication screen, enter the logon name and password for the account accessing the Exchange 2007 POP server, as shown in the following example.

   Example:

   Account Name = User@CompanyABC.com

   Password = ***********

8. To enhance security and limit the ability of others to access the Exchange POP account, uncheck the Save Password check box and click Next to continue.

Password and Best Practices

To enhance security, leave the password entry blank; this requires users to enter the password each time they access Exchange.

In addition, when accessing Exchange through POP, it is best practice to use strong passwords to enhance security. Use the Active Directory Users and Computers management console to create a strong password for accounts using this method of access.

---

9. Complete the installation by entering the account name for the account being used, and then click Next to complete the installation.

10. Test accessing the Exchange 2007 POP services by selecting Send/Receive on the Outlook Express toolbar.

Migrating and Backing Up Personal Address Books

One of the most common tasks when managing Outlook Express clients is backing up the contacts from the Outlook Express 5 client. When performing this task, administrators can export contact information and create comma-separated files for import into other mail programs and Outlook clients.

To complete the export of contact information for backup and migration reasons, follow the example in the next section. In this scenario, you back up the Outlook Express 5 contacts to a comma-delimited CSV file.

Backing Up Outlook Express Contacts

To begin, open the Outlook Express 5 client and complete the following steps to create a full backup of all the contact information:

1. From the File menu, select the Export Contact option.

2. In the Save dialog box, select the location where the export file will be saved by modifying the default Desktop location.

3. In the Name dialog box, enter the name for the Export file to create.

> **NOTE**
>
> By default, export files are created as comma-delimited files only and are placed on the desktop.

4. Click the Save button to create the export file and back up the Outlook Express contacts.

Mac OS X Mail

With the release of OS X, users of Macintosh computers can use the built-in OS X Mail client that provides support for email access and synchronization of email messages, address book information, and calendar information.

Mac OS X Mail uses IMAP as the standard communication method between Mac Mail and Exchange. A Macintosh user can access Exchange content, transfer the information to the Macintosh, or download the information and leave a copy of the information on the Exchange server.

> **NOTE**
>
> Usually, users download their information to their Mac Mail and leave a copy on the Exchange server so that if the user needs to access their email from the Microsoft Exchange OWA client, or uses a different mail client on a different system, all of the user's information remains on the Exhange server for subsequent download and access.

Understanding Mac Mail Support for Exchange

Mac OS X Mail is simply an IMAP mail client for Exchange and requires the Macintosh computer to have TCP/IP connectivity to the Exchange server and Active Directory authentication to the Active Directory network in which Exchange resides. This allows for the support of Mac-to-Exchange integration while a Macintosh is on the local area network (LAN) backbone or while the Macintosh user is mobile.

To access the Exchange server on the LAN, a user needs to have TCP/IP access to the Exchange server, whether that is directly on the network subnet as the Exchange server, or with appropriate routes from where the user is connected to the Exchange server.

While mobile, the TCP/IP access of the Macintosh user is handled through the same network connection address as OWA. OWA should be configured with Secure Sockets Layer (SSL)–encrypted access for improved security. As long as users can access their mailbox externally using OWA, they can configure their Macintosh to access the OWA port to download and synchronize mail to the Mac OS X Mail client.

Configuring Mac Mail Support on Exchange Server 2007

To configure support for Mac Mail on the Exchange 2007 side, all the organization needs to do is set up Exchange 2007 to support OWA and enable IMAP on Exchange. OWA is configured by default in Exchange 2007, and most organizations already have OWA operating in the environment. With OWA already functional in an Exchange 2007 environment, all that needs to be done is to configure and enable IMAP support on Exchange.

Unlike previous versions of Exchange that supported IMAP from the graphical user interface (GUI), Exchange 2007 does not have a GUI option within the Exchange Management Console to enable IMAP support. Configuration of a user client in Exchange 2007 requires the use of the Exchange Management Shell. The script to enable a user's mailbox to support IMAP is as follows:

```
set-CASMailbox testmbx -ImapEnabled:$True
```

where *testmbx* is the name of the mailbox being enabled for IMAP support.

Configuring Mac Mail on a Mac OS X System

With IMAP support enabled on Exchange 2007, the user just needs to configure the Mac Mail client on OS X. To configure the Mac Mail client on Mac OS X, do the following:

1. Launch Mac Mail on an OS X system.

2. Click Mail, Preferences, and then click Accounts.

3. Click Add Account.

4. When prompted to choose an account type, click up and down on the scroll option and select Exchange, similar to what is shown in Figure 29.2.

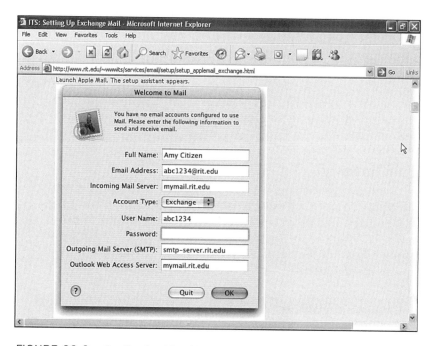

FIGURE 29.2   Configuring Mac Mail for Exchange support.

5. On the Accounts Information page, type the name of the Outlook Web Access server used by users to access Outlook Web Access in the Incoming Mail Server field (such as owa.companyabc.com).

6. Enter the user's logon name and password to access Exchange.

7. In the Outlook Web Access Server field, type the name of the Outlook Web Access server, which will likely be the exact same name as referenced in step 5.

8. Click OK and then click OK again to save the settings.

After the Mac Mail configuration settings have been set, the user can now synchronize with the Exchange server to download Exchange content information with the network.

Because of the simplicity of the Mac Mail client, and also because it is included free with the Mac OS X operating system and provides direct support right to Exchange, most organizations use the Mac Mail client as a simple and effective mail client for Exchange.

29

Configuring and Implementing Entourage for the Mac

Understanding the need for a more comprehensive functional solution for Mac, Microsoft provides a powerful Exchange client for the Macintosh as part of their Office 2004 package called Entourage 2004. This option is very effective for Mac users' internal and external connectivity needs because it provides the same look and feel that Mac users are familiar with and many of the enhanced functions of the latest Windows-based Outlook client.

The most compatible platform with the Mac operating system, Entourage 2004 provides support for email, calendaring, contact management, junk email filtering, synchronization, and even support for handheld devices when combined with Exchange Server 2007. Exchange administrators can now leverage the Entourage client to provide Mac users a familiar look and feel while delivering full integration with added features and access to Exchange 2007 data.

Features and Functionality

The Entourage 2004 client software combined with the Exchange 2007 platform and latest service packs can provide enhanced functionality for the Mac user in many areas not before available. The Exchange update is required for Entourage to work in an Exchnage environment. To download the Exchange update, go to http://www.microsoft.com/mac/otherproducts/officex/officex.aspx?pid=officex&type=exchangeupdate and follow the instructions and requirements for the installation of the update.

> **CAUTION**
>
> The Entourage 2004 client and Exchange updates are available from Microsoft and have been fully certified for use on the Microsoft Exchange 2007 platform. Test all components and functionality of Entourage in a lab environment before connecting any Entourage 2004 clients to the Exchange 2007 organization.

When combined with the Exchange update, Entourage provides extensive support and enhanced functionality in the following areas:

▶ **Message format support**—Hypertext Markup Language (HTML) and plain text email format are fully supported, providing seamless integration with Windows-based Outlook clients.

▶ **Rules support**—As with the Outlook, Entourage 2004 supports the creation of email rules at the client level.

▶ **Junk email filtering**—With today's unsolicited email issues, users can now filter junk mail by using three levels of filtering: Low, High, and Exclusive. This option also includes an exempt feature for all contacts that are stored and associated with the Entourage client.

- ▶ **Outlook functions**—As with Outlook, Entourage 2004 provides full support for Exchange calendaring, scheduling appointments, contacts, and scheduled tasks.

- ▶ **Offline synchronization**—To support roaming users, Entourage can fully synchronize mailbox data between Exchange 2007 and the client.

- ▶ **Offline address book**—Entourage 2004 provides full synchronization of the Exchange 2007 offline address list.

- ▶ **LDAP support**—Using the Entourage client, Mac users can now access the GAL and Active Directory through LDAP lookups.

- ▶ **Palm support**—Sync and update information from the Entourage 2004 client to Palm handheld devices.

- ▶ **PST support**—Administrators can use the PST Import tool to export and import Exchange data to Entourage 2004 from Outlook for Mac and the previous version of Entourage.

- ▶ **Integrated upgrade support**—With the 2004 version, administrators can complete an upgrade directly from Outlook, Outlook Express 5, and the previous version of Entourage, saving mail information, contacts, and identities using the built-in wizard available with the Office 2004 suite for Mac.

Deploying Entourage 2004

Requirements for installing Entourage 2004 vary slightly from the requirements of Outlook and other Exchange solutions. Before installing and configuring Entourage 2004 clients, administrators must ensure that minimum hardware requirements at the Mac desktop are met and the Exchange 2007 prerequisites have been configured. In addition, the client must be updated and installed with the required updates and software to ensure proper functionality and connectivity when accessing Exchange mail data.

Before installing Entourage, ensure that the following requirements and configurations have been enabled on the Exchange server:

- ▶ Microsoft Exchange 2007 with the latest service pack

- ▶ IMAP/HTTP DAV/SMTP/LDAP

- ▶ Outlook Web Access

Though most of these settings are already enabled to support Windows-based client connectivity to Exchange Server, review and address any of the hardware and software requirements for installing Entourage by reviewing Table 29.3 and the software prerequisites for Exchange 2007.

Verify that the Mac client desktop hardware you are installing meets the minimum hardware requirements to install Entourage 2004, as listed in Table 29.3. If you do not know what hardware is installed on the Mac client, use the Mac System Profiler available on the

29

Tools menu of the Mac desktop to display and evaluate the hardware installed on the Mac desktop.

TABLE 29.3   Entourage 2004's Mac Hardware Requirements

Processor	Memory	Hard Disk Space
G3, Mac OS X–compatible	256MB	250MB available disk space

After the Exchange server has been prepared and the hardware requirement for Entourage has been addressed, the next components to support Entourage are the updates and software requirements for the Mac client. Before the installation of Entourage 2004 can be completed, the following components must be installed or updated in the Mac client:

▶ **Office 2004 for Mac**—To install Entourage 2004, the Microsoft Office 2004 for Mac suite must be installed.

▶ **Install Updates**—Because upgrades can be completed after the installation of Office 2004 for Mac, administrators can install any available updates before running the Upgrade Wizard or configuring any identities.

▶ **Microsoft Exchange Update**—When connecting Entourage 2004 to Exchange 2007, be sure to install the Office 2004 Service Pack 1 update for Mac on the client computer. For download and additional information, go to:

http://www.microsoft.com/mac/downloads.aspx?pid=download&location=/mac/download/office2004/update_11.1.1.xml&secid=4&ssid=14&flgnosysreq=True

---

TIP

To address Office 2004 updates, Microsoft provided an autoupdate feature for the Office for Mac suite. Download and install the latest update version from Microsoft at: http://www.microsoft.com/mac/downloads.aspx?pid=download&location=/mac/download/office2004/mau.xml&secid=4&ssid=11&flgnosysreq=True.

To provide functionality for junk email filtering with the latest definition files, install the junk email filter update from Microsoft at: http://www.microsoft.com/mac/downloads.aspx.

After all updates have been completed and requirements met, the installation of Entourage 2004 can be completed and the Entourage client can be connected to Exchange. To configure the Entourage client for Exchange support, follow these steps:

Enhancing Authentication with NTLM V2

To further leverage the available features of Windows and Exchange, administrators can enable NTLM version 2 for authentication of Mac users when connecting with Entourage clients.

To encrypt a password using NTLM V2, select the properties of the Exchange mail account and select the Advanced Features tab. Enable password encryption by selecting the Always Use Secure Passwords option.

Entourage 2004 does not support NTLM version 1; ensure that the default domain policy is configured to support NTLM version 2 before connecting Entourage 2004 clients.

1. Launch the Entourage 2004 client, and select Tools, Accounts.

2. Select the Mail tab, select New from the New drop-down box, and enter the account type for connecting to Exchange 2007.

3. Enter the user information for the account connecting to Exchange with the client:

   ▶ **Account Name**—Enter the name of the account created in Active Directory for the Mac user to connect to Exchange 2007.

   ▶ **Password**—Provide the password for the Active Directory account or leave this entry blank to prompt the user to log on when connecting to Exchange.

   ▶ **Domain Name**—Enter the name of the Active Directory domain where the account is a member.

Terminal Server Client for Mac

The Terminal Server Client for Mac, shown in Figure 29.3, can be considered and planned in the same manner as its Windows counterpart. When the prerequisites are met, administrators can use the Terminal Server Client to provide full Windows and application functionality to Mac users requiring Exchange services and more.

FIGURE 29.3   Terminal Server Client for the Macintosh.

Through Terminal Services technology, Mac users are able to fully access the Windows client and Outlook application with all the features and functionality of Windows-based users, including network shares and printers.

Compatibility, Features, and Functionality

Because this Remote Desktop Connection for Mac uses Windows Terminal Services, the only compatibility concern to be considered is the actual connection manager. All applications, when being run, are executed remotely and do not require additional compatibility between Windows-based applications, such as Outlook and the Mac client.

The Remote Desktop Connection manager is compatible with the Mac OS X 10.1 version or later. If required on an earlier version of the Mac client, upgrade the Mac operating system to meet the operating system requirements. Also ensure that the Mac client hardware meets the minimum hardware requirements for installing the Remote Desktop Connection for Mac, as shown in Table 29.4.

TABLE 29.4   Remote Desktop Hardware Requirements

Processor	Memory	Hard Disk Space
Mac PowerPC	128MB	3MB for installation 1.1MB after installation

One of the biggest benefits to the Remote Desktop Connection client for the Mac is its integration with Windows and Mac clients. Because of this compatibility, Mac users are able to leverage the functionality and features of Microsoft Outlook when accessing Exchange information and also leverage some of the following enhanced features when integrating Mac clients into a Windows Terminal Services environment:

▶ **Access to Windows**—The Remote Desktop Connection for Mac provides full access for Mac users into the Windows environment. This connection can be configured to the Windows desktop or restricted to an application such as Outlook.

▶ **Printing**—Through the Terminal Services connection, Mac users can access network printing and print information from applications to a networked Windows printer. To further enhance this feature, Mac users can print Windows information to the local Mac printer.

▶ **Access to Data**—Through the copy feature, Mac users are fully enabled to copy and paste data between the Mac client and the Windows Terminal Services session.

Before beginning any installation of the Remote Desktop Connection for Mac, Microsoft Windows Terminal Services and remote access must be enabled for supporting a remote connection with one or more of the following Microsoft Windows operating systems:

▶ **Windows XP**—Supported only through the Remote Desktop Connection feature of Windows XP, this method is limited to one concurrent connection.

▶ **Windows 2003**—Supported in all versions of Windows Server 2003, Terminal Services can be enabled to support remote access for multiple, simultaneous connections.

▶ **Windows 2000**—Included in Windows 2000 Enterprise, Standard, and Datacenter Editions, the Terminal Service Application mode component must be enabled and will support multiple, simultaneous connections.

TIP

When using Terminal Services for multiple client connections from Mac and Windows users, performance is dependent on the total amount of simultaneous connections and the total amount of available hardware resources installed in the server.

Installing the Terminal Server Client

To install and configure the Remote Desktop Connection for Mac, let's begin with a simple scenario of creating a one-to-one connection. In this scenario, you configure a Windows XP desktop and a Mac client to provide remote desktop connectivity to Microsoft Outlook.

To begin, enable the Remote Desktop feature of the Windows XP client by following these steps:

1. From the Windows XP desktop, select Start, My Computer and open the Properties page by right-clicking the Remote Desktop icon and selecting Properties.

2. Select the Remote tab and check the Allow Users to Connect Remotely to This Computer check box.

3. Next, assign the account that may access the desktop remotely by clicking the Select the Remote Users button. Assign or create an account for the Mac users to authenticate with when accessing the Windows XP system remotely.

After the remote desktop configuration is complete and the client permissions to access Windows remotely have been configured, begin the installation of the Remote Desktop Connection for Mac by ensuring that the Mac client can communicate via TCP/IP on the network. Follow these steps to configure TCP/IP on the Mac client.

1. From the Apple menu, select Control, TCP/IP properties.

2. In the TCP/IP dialog box, configure the TCP/IP properties. In this scenario, configure the TCP/IP properties using a Static setting. Select the Connect Via option and select Ethernet.

3. From the Configure tab, select Manual.

4. Enter the TCP/IP properties for the client and the DNS address being used on your network.

5. Close the TCP/IP properties and reboot the Mac system.

To install the Remote Desktop Connection for Mac, download the installation file from Microsoft and place the file on the local Mac client where it will be installed.

To install the client, complete the following steps:

1. Expand the downloaded installation file by double-clicking it.

2. Go to the Mac desktop and open the Remote Desktop Connection volume. Copy the Remote Desktop Connection folder into the local disk of the Mac client.

3. Remove the Remote Desktop Connection volume and the original installation file by placing them in the Desktop Trashcan.

4. Launch the Remote Desktop Connection from the Remote Desktop Folder, and enter the name of the system to which you are connecting. Click Connect to establish the remote connection.

5. When prompted, enter the name and password of the account you configured to allow remote access to this desktop system.

Understanding Other Non-Windows Client Access Methods

In addition to the Mac operating systems, Exchange 2007 can support a variety of clients by using virtual machines on the Mac client and leveraging support for IMAP, SMTP, and POP. Using these protocols, Exchange administrators can provide limited email functionality and support a variety of clients throughout the Exchange environment for email and communication purposes.

Virtual PC Access to Exchange

Most effective for users who are familiar with operating and working within Windows PC–based operating systems, the Virtual PC for Mac provides the same full functioning of a Windows PC client on the Mac OS desktop. Using this option allows Mac users who are comfortable working in Windows Microsoft Office and Outlook applications the ability to use a Microsoft client from the Mac. Running within a virtual machine, a Windows domain client PC can allow the same features to a Mac desktop as any Windows domain client.

With a virtual PC machine, the latest version of Outlook for Windows can be used on the Mac client desktop, accessing Exchange 2007 data with full Windows-based support in areas such as offline files, multiple profiles, and Windows domain network resources. For more information regarding Virtual PC, go to the Mactopia web page: http://www.microsoft.com/mac/products/virtualpc/virtualpc.aspx?pid=virtualpc.

POP3 Access to Exchange

POP3 is one of the most popular methods of providing mail services on the Internet today. POP is highly reliable but has limited functionality. Users who access email using POP3 are limited to downloading all messages to the local client and can only send and receive messages when a connection is established with the POP server.

Unlike previous versions of Exchange that supported POP3 from the GUI, Exchange 2007 does not have a GUI option within the Exchange Management Console to enable POP3 support. Configuration of a user client in Exchange 2007 requires the use of the Exchange Management Shell. The script to enable a user's mailbox to support POP3 is as follows:

```
set-CASMailbox testmbx -PopEnabled:$True
```

where *testmbx* is the name of the mailbox being enabled for POP3 support.

When enabled with Exchange 2007, POP can be leveraged to provide email support to additional non-Windows–based clients' platforms. Through the common method of sending mail, multiple client platforms can communicate over email regardless of the actual desktop operating system and client mail software being used.

The POP3 functionality of Exchange Server 2007 can support multiclient environments, including the Eudora Mail client, the Netscape Mail client, and other POP-compatible nonspecific client platforms. This protocol is best used when supporting single-client systems that download mail and store mail information locally.

IMAP Access to Exchange

As covered in the section "Mac OS X Mail," IMAP is a fully supported method that allows access from non-Windows–based client systems to access Exchange 2007 information. Designed to allow access to Information Stores located on a remote system, IMAP can also be used to support the Linux-based Netscape Mail clients.

Using the Netscape Mail client, Netscape users can access, collaborate, and store information on the Exchange 2007 server with the IMAP support built in to Netscape Communicator. With this functionality, networks can now incorporate additional operating systems, such as Linux with Netscape Mail, and still support email functionality between all network users.

Use the Preferences option on the Netscape Mail client to configure and enable support for IMAP communication with Exchange 2007.

Windows Mobile/Pocket PC Access

Client mobile access is now fully integrated and supported when the Exchange 2007 server is installed. Remote and mobile users can use the Outlook Mobile version to send, receive, and synchronize mail, calendaring, and task information, using the Windows Mobile and Pocket PC platform over mobile information services built in to Exchange 2007.

29

For more information regarding the options and configuration to support Windows Mobile and Pocket PC access to Exchange 2007, see Chapter 23, " Designing and Implementing Mobility in Exchange Server 2007."

HTML Access

Another feature with Exchange 2007 is HTML access. With this feature, administrators can use Internet-ready cellular telephones to provide HTML access to Exchange information for mobile users regardless of where they might be.

By providing additional mobile services and client permissions through Active Directory, alternate access can be granted to email and Exchange using Internet-ready mobile phone devices over HTML access.

For more information regarding HTML access options and configurations, see Chapter 23.

Outlook Web Access

Another very effective method of allowing access to Exchange information is OWA. Enhanced greatly in Exchange 2007, OWA can be used to provide HTML browser access to Exchange mailboxes from inside the network and from the Internet.

Probably the biggest benefit to using the OWA solution to support non-Windows–based clients is that it is nondiscretionary as to which type of Internet browser can be used to access it. Effective in functionality just like the full Outlook client, Linux-based users and others using non-Windows–based systems can access OWA for email and calendar management in the same fashion as any Windows-based users.

For more information regarding OWA and enabling support, see Chapter 28.

Summary

In a Microsoft-centric environment, administrators of networks often focus solely on Windows-based connections to Exchange spending little time on options for non-Windows–based users. When accessing Exchange 2007, many options are available for non-Windows users, including a whole suite of clients for the Macintosh—such as Entourage 2004, Outlook Express, and the Remote Desktop Connection. In addition, Outlook Express is still available on other non-Windows platforms. For UNIX and Linux clients, several mail clients are available that support IMAP and POP3, that can access Exchange 2007 or OWA from any browser, and that provide full support for email, calendars, and contacts.

By choosing any one of a variety of client applications to access Exchange, an organization can leverage the capabilities of Exchange 2007 beyond just Windows-based users and provide seamless messaging communications throughout an entire enterprise. Depending on the client application selected, some options provide just email communications and others provide the full suite of Outlook and Exchange business productivity functions, such as calendaring, contacts, notes, to-do lists, journals, public folder access, offline files, junk email filtering, and more.

Using the information in this chapter, an organization should not be limited in its ability to extend Exchange 2007 to all users within the enterprise, and with the implementation of new client access capabilities, an organization can greatly improve its reach to all users in an organization well beyond Windows.

Best Practices

The following are best practices from this chapter:

▶ When choosing a client configuration for Exchange, an organization should evaluate the different solutions available for non-Windows client connectivity.

▶ To achieve the full Outlook functionality of Windows users, a non-Windows client might consider using a Terminal Services or the Virtual PC for Mac, which provides complete support to a full Windows client that is identical to the one Windows users access.

▶ Users who want calendar integration access or are using a system running Mac OS X will not want to use Outlook Express, which lacks calendar support, and should consider one of the other client applications when calendaring is required.

▶ An effective client for Mac OS X users to use is the built-in Mac Mail client because it has direct Exchange support and synchronizes mail, calendar, and address book information.

▶ For IMAP or POP3 to work in Exchange 2007, the functions need to be enabled using the Exchange Management Shell. However, if IMAP and/or POP3 will not be used, the services should be disabled on Exchange to minimize any security risk to unauthorized access to Exchange 2007.

▶ To improve security, leave the password entry on any client options configuration page blank so that the user will be prompted for a password every time logon is executed.

▶ Because different versions of client software for the Macintosh have different support requirement for various versions of the Mac OS, make sure to verify compatibility before installing any client software.

▶ To provide authentication to Entourage clients, NTLM v2 must be enabled on the default domain policy for access to the Exchange 2007 server.

29

CHAPTER 30

Deploying the Client for Microsoft Exchange

W hether you are implementing a new Microsoft Exchange Server 2007 environment or upgrading your organization from a previous version of Microsoft Exchange Server, deploying the email client to your user community is a task that must be accomplished to provide full email functionality.

Many options are available for deploying the Microsoft Exchange Outlook client, and administrators can utilize one or all of them to distribute the client software to their user community.

This chapter is intended to assist administrators with the planning and deploying of the Outlook client. It provides information about possible deployment alternatives and shares best practices to ease the process.

Outlook 2007 Auto Account Setup

Regardless of the method used to get Outlook to the desktop, when an administrator combines Exchange Server 2007 and Outlook 2007, the configuration of the Outlook client is easier than ever before.

The first time a user opens Outlook 2007 on a workstation, the client utilizes a new technology called the Autodiscover service to help with the client configuration. The Outlook client checks the credentials of the logged-on user and automatically fills in the username and email address, as shown in Figure 30.1.

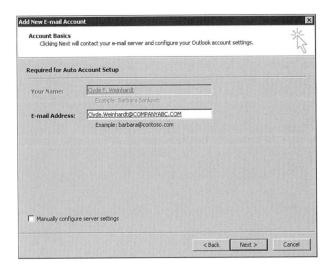

FIGURE 30.1   Autodiscover of username and email address.

After the username and mailbox have been selected, the user clicks Next, and the
Autodiscover feature continues with the client setup—establishing a network connection
to the Exchange server, searching for the username, and logging on to the messaging
server. All remaining client configuration is completed automatically, as shown in
Figure 30.2.

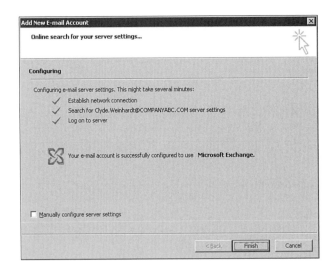

FIGURE 30.2   Email client configuration.

Users no longer have to remember complicated server names because the location of the
user mailbox is automatically managed by Outlook and Exchange. Even if a user mailbox

is moved to a new location, all user configuration information is updated automatically thanks to the autodiscover technology.

Understanding Deployment Options

When deploying the Outlook client, administrators can take advantage of several existing Microsoft technologies that have been designed for software distribution. In addition, by utilizing tools found in the Microsoft Office Resource Kit (ORK), custom installations and settings can be preconfigured and deployed using one of several software distribution methods.

As organizations begin the planning process, administrators can pick and choose from the available deployment methods and can implement custom client installations that are based on the specific need for each type of client desktop. This chapter explores the different options available for deploying the Exchange Outlook client software to desktops in the enterprise.

Available Methods of Deployment

With Outlook 2003 and Outlook 2007, the installation of the client software to the desktop can be performed in ways not available for previous versions. By implementing the tools available in the Microsoft ORK, administrators can elect to use one or more of the following methods for deploying the Outlook client:

- ▶ **Manual installation**—Manual installation enables administrators to incorporate wizards, profile generation tools, and configuration files into the client installation process. Using these methods, administrators can define baseline settings and standard configuration settings, and they can manually test the installation when complete.

- ▶ **Windows 2003 Group Policy**—Leveraging Windows Group Policy Software deployment technologies and Microsoft Office Security Templates, Outlook clients and client updates can be pushed to desktop systems on the network. Using Group Policy, administrators can also centrally configure Outlook security and user options to enforce a baseline configuration to all client systems on the enterprise.

- ▶ **Imaging technologies**—Whether upgrading to a newer version of Outlook or deploying Outlook in a new environment, organizations can image the Outlook clients to the desktop or refresh the entire desktop image to implement updates or the latest company standards.

- ▶ **Systems Management Server**—Using Microsoft Systems Management Server (SMS), you can centrally deploy and push the Outlook client and updates to large numbers of desktop systems in multiple locations throughout the enterprise. This option also enables tracking and reporting information to manage a full Exchange Outlook client deployment.

30

Outlook Profile Generation

Often, one of the biggest challenges Exchange administrators face when deploying Outlook is configuring the profiles to communicate with the Exchange server. To automate this task, profiles can be scripted using tools available with the ORK from Microsoft.

Outlook 2003 client profiles and their associated Exchange server settings can be configured using the Office 2003 Custom Installation Wizard (CIW) and configuration files can be created with Outlook option settings.

Outlook 2007 can be similiarly prepared utilizing the new Office Customization Tool (OCT). The OCT is a new application that is included with Microsoft Office 2007. With the OCT, administrators can preconfigure components and settings within the Office 2007 suite to simplify deployments.

Creating Custom Profiles by Using PRF Files

By creating an Outlook profile (PRF) file, administrators can quickly create Messaging Application Programming Interface (MAPI) profiles for Microsoft Office Outlook users. A PRF file is a text file that contains syntax that Microsoft Outlook uses to generate a profile. By utilizing a PRF file, an administrator can configure new profiles, or modify existing ones, without affecting other parts of your Outlook (or Office) installation. PRF files can be manually edited to include custom Outlook settings or MAPI services that are not included in the Custom Installation Wizard interface.

Because Outlook PRF files are executable, administrators can update profiles by double-clicking the filename to run the file directly. When executing a PRF file, Outlook ensures that services that should be unique are not added more than once.

The easiest way to create a PRF file is by using the Custom Installation Wizard (CIW) for Office 2003, or the OCT for Office 2007. Administrators can specify the settings desired, and then export the settings to a PRF file. The PRF file can then be manually edited if the need should arise, for example, if your organization wants to add a new service that is not included in the CIW or OCT. The PRF file can be manually edited in any text-editing application (such as notepad.exe).

PRF files can be applied to Outlook in several ways:

▶ Import the PRF file in the CIW or the OCT to specify profile settings in a transform, and then include the transform when you deploy Outlook.

▶ Specify the PRF file as a command-line option for outlook.exe, without prompting the user, as follows:

```
outlook.exe /importprf \\server1\share\outlook.prf
```

▶ Specify the PRF file as a command-line option for outlook.exe, but prompt the user before importing the PRF file, as follows:

```
outlook.exe /promptimportprf \\localfolder\outlook.prf
```

> **NOTE**
>
> Although the PRF file can be located on a network share (as shown in the first example), it will not be applied if the file is not found or if the user account used to execute the installation process does not have the appropriate permissions to access the file.

▶ Because the PRF file is an executable file, administrators can launch the file directly on a user's computer by double-clicking the file.

▶ Administrators can also configure the Registry to trigger Outlook to import the PRF file upon startup. Both the CIW and the Custom Maintenance Wizard contain a feature that allows you to Add/Remove Registry Entries.

Using the CIW or the OCT to preconfigure Outlook options and apply the initial profile configuration through PRF files is a very effective means of deploying Outlook.

> **NOTE**
>
> The CIW and Microsoft Exchange Profile Update tool, along with additional utilities, can be found in the the ORK, which can be downloaded from Microsoft.

Configuring Outlook Client Options

Even after the Outlook client software has been installed, administrators can define configuration settings and apply them dynamically to the existing clients. This task can be accomplished in one of several ways.

Custom Installation Wizard

To deploy the Outlook 2003 client to desktops on the network with configuration options predefined, powerful tools such as the CIW, along with Office configuration files such as PRF files, can be leveraged to define Outlook client options for large deployments that have the need to specify client user options. Using these tools can potentially eliminate the need for administrators to visit each desktop to configure profile settings and Outlook options.

Office Customization Tool

What the CIW is to Office 2003, the OCT is to Office 2007. Administrators can preconfigure components and settings to simplify the deployment of the product.

Windows Server Group Policy

Another effective configuration option is the centralized management available through security templates for Outlook. With the Group Policy feature of Windows Server 2003, standard and advanced options can be configured and established after the client software has been deployed.

30

This option can also be useful when deploying new settings to existing clients after a policy change.

Transforms

The final option for defining Outlook client setting and configuration options is the use of Office transforms. Transforms are configuration files that can be used with the Windows Installer and contain information and modifications that will be applied to the Outlook client during installation.

Office transforms are created using the CIW or the OCT and have a .MST file extension.

Deploying Non-Windows Systems

In organizations with non-Windows–based systems, such as a Macintosh desktop, special considerations must be made for accessing an Exchange environment. To understand the installation and configuration process for non-Windows systems, refer to Chapter 29, "Using Non-Windows Systems to Access Exchange Server 2007."

Planning Considerations and Best Practices

Before deploying the Microsoft Outlook client, organizations should carefully evaluate their messaging needs and take a good look at their existing environment. There are many facets to the deployment of any software solution, and organizations with complex environments and messaging needs will only be successful in their implementation if they plan accordingly.

Identifying and documenting various client needs, reviewing the overall network topology, and reviewing recommended best practices can allow administrators to greatly enhance the performance of each deployment and ensure a transparent client installation.

Network Topology Bandwidth Consideration

When planning the deployment of Outlook clients to end users, administrators should take their existing network environment into account to avoid network disruptions or bandwidth saturation that could impact their user community.

When evaluating the network environment in a single-site deployment, the primary focus should be on ensuring adequate bandwidth for the client deployment. By planning the deployment in small groups, or after normal business hours, administrators can avoid negatively impacting their user community.

With multisite organizations, administrators must review the available network bandwidth on wide area network (WAN) links. Because these types of connections are generally significantly slower than local area network (LAN) connections, it can be challenging to deploy multiple Outlook clients simultaneously without negatively impacting the overall WAN performance. If this is done during normal working hours, or during periods of high network utilization (during the evenings when network backups are being performed, for example), communication problems can result.

One way to avoid passing large amounts of data across the WAN is through the use of administrative distribution points that contain copies of the files necessary for installation. By placing an administrative distribution point at each remote location, deployments can be managed centrally while minimizing the traffic across the WAN link. This can help avoid bandwidth saturation and can improve overall implementation times.

Planning Best Practices

To assist in the planning process when deploying the Outlook client, the following best practices are offered for review:

▶ Deploy the Outlook client with the Microsoft Office suite to provide enhanced functionality, such as the ability to utilize Microsoft Word as the Outlook client email editor.

▶ Be sure to document all profile settings and configuration options for each transform, PRF, and custom installation file.

▶ Always test deployment options and profile generations in a lab environment prior to deploying to actual clients.

▶ Deploy Outlook and preconfigured settings to a pilot group prior to full deployment. Administrators should work with these pilot users on testing all aspects of the application prior to widespread distribution.

▶ Break users into small, easily managed groups for deployment. Deploy the client software in phases to these groups to ensure "morning-after" supportability.

▶ When creating and naming configuration files, use unique naming conventions based on the group or configuration options being focused on. For example, when configuring options for workstations in the Public Relations department, you can name the file *public_relations.prf* to avoid confusing it with other configuration files.

Addressing Remote and Mobile Client Systems

When planning the Outlook client deployment, special attention must be paid to the needs of remote and mobile clients. With remote and mobile users accessing the business network environment using many different methods, administrators should consider what might happen to clients who access the network over low-bandwidth links, such as virtual private network (VPN) or Remote Access Server (RAS) dial-up links.

One method to avoid this problem is to schedule remote and mobile users to come to a location where administrators can perform the installation manually. This can be accomplished during monthly or quarterly meetings or during sales calls near a corporate office. Alternatively, user workstations can be shipped to a central location where administrators can install the application and return the machine to the user. This method is often used during full software upgrades, or in situations where the installation process requires special know-how beyond the average end user.

As an additional alternative, rarely used except with senior executives, administrators can travel to the client location to perform the needed work.

Managing the Outlook Deployment

Managing the deployment of Outlook clients can be much easier when utilizing a software deployment tool, such as Microsoft Systems Management Server (SMS). With Microsoft SMS, deployments can be tracked and managed down to the desktop level. Administrators can identify which desktops need the Outlook client, deploy the Outlook client, and even identify and track any failed installations utilizing the reporting functionality built in to SMS 2003.

When options such as SMS are not available, it can be extremely difficult to track the deployment of the client and determine overall progress. The tools available in the ORK do not present any evidence on the installation progress, nor does the use of Windows 2003 Server Group Policy. However, you can use the following methods to gather a limited amount of information:

▶ When using Windows Server Group Policy, administrators can filter the server Application Event Logs to search for any events generated by the MSI Installer.

▶ On the local machine, administrators can use the Add or Remove Programs application in Control Panel to determine if the Outlook update package is listed. By utilizing the Remote Desktop feature built in to Windows XP, this option can be accomplished remotely.

Preparing the Deployment

As the planning phase of the deployment comes to a close, administrators can focus on preparing the different areas of the Outlook client deployment.

Each of the different methods that will be utilized to deploy the software should be reviewed and tested to ensure a seamless installation.

Outlook Systems Requirements

Prior to deploying the Outlook client to user desktop systems on the network, the desktop hardware must be evaluated to determine whether it meets the recommended Microsoft hardware and software requirements to support the client.

> **TIP**
>
> Utilizing Microsoft Systems Management Server (SMS), administrators can conduct remote hardware inventories on managed systems. SMS can then create a report detailing the current status of all hardware, software, and available drive space on these systems.

Ensure that the desktop systems meet the minimum installation requirements by reviewing Table 30.1.

TABLE 30.1   Outlook System Requirements

Requirement	Outlook 2003	Outlook 2007
Client operating system	Microsoft Windows 2000 SP3 or later	Microsoft Windows Vista, Windows XP2 or later
Processor speed	233-MHz processor or higher	500-MHz processor or higher
Memory	128MB of RAM or higher	256MB of RAM or higher
Hard disk space	400MB	2GB required for installation
Messaging system	Microsoft Exchange Server 5.5 or greater	Microsoft Exchange 2000 Server or greater
Monitor resolution	800x600 or higher recommended	Minimum 800x600; 1024x768 recommended
Additional components	Microsoft Internet Explorer 5.01 or higher	Microsoft Internet Explorer 6.0 or higher

Although the installation of Outlook 2007 requires 2GB of hard disk space, a portion of that space will be released after installation if the original download package is removed from the hard drive.

> **NOTE**
>
> If installing Microsoft Office Outlook 2007 with Business Contact Manager, a 1-GHz processor and 512MB of RAM or higher is required. Also, prior to installing Outlook 2007 with Business Contact Manager, administrators will first have to install Outlook 2007.

Planning Predefined Configuration Options

Another area to understand when planning for the deployment of the Outlook client is what options can be configured using the CIW and transform configuration files.

Understanding how to utilize PRF files, transforms, and various ORK utilities enables Exchange administrators to create a baseline plan detailing what options will be used prior to actually creating the individual configuration files.

Using the CIW, you can configure the following features:

▶ **Outlook User Profile Settings**—Administrators can specify how users' profiles will be created. Using this option, administrators can set new profiles, modify existing profiles, or add additional user profiles.

▶ **Exchange Server Settings**—Settings defining Exchange server names and specific options, such as Exchange connection options, can also be defined.

30

▸ **Installation States for Outlook and Features**—Using the installation options, administrators can define installation states to make individual features available, available at first use, or not available.

▸ **Mail Options**—Options such as PST and OST settings and synchronization options can be defined using the CIW.

▸ **Settings and Options**—Many of the options available when configuring Outlook from within the application can be defined when creating custom installation files.

▸ **Installation Path**—Ensure that the installation directory path on the desktop where the Outlook client will be installed contains enough free disk space to complete the installation.

Using the OCT, the following features are configurable:

▸ **Outlook User Profile Settings**—Administrators can specify how users' profiles will be created. Using this option, administrators can set new profiles, modify existing profiles, or add additional user profiles.

▸ **Apply PRF**—This setting imports an Outlook PRF file to define a new default profile. You can use any profile created for Outlook 2007.

▸ **Do Not Configure Cached Exchange Mode**—This setting configures Outlook 2007 to only attach to the Exchange mailboxes directly from the Exchange server.

▸ **Configure Cached Exchange Mode**—This setting creates an OST file or uses an existing OST file. This results in users working with a local copy of their Exchange mailbox.

Creating Administrative Installation Points

If the deployment requires administrative installation points, administrators can create them using the `setup.exe` program of the Outlook or Office installation software and utilizing the `/a` switch.

To create the administrative installation point, complete these steps:

> **NOTE**
>
> In the following example, the administrative installation point is created using the Microsoft Office 2003 installation media.

1. Insert the installation CD-ROM into the systems where the installation point will be created. Click Start, Run, type `setup.exe /a` in the Open text box, and then click OK to continue.

2. When prompted, enter the product key that came with the Office 2003 installation software, and click Next to continue.

> **NOTE**
>
> Use the Install Location option on this screen to change the installation path that Outlook will use when being deployed.

3. Accept the End User License Agreement (EULA) and select Install; this begins the installation process.

4. Select the installation state for Outlook and Outlook options; click Next to continue.

Automating Outlook Profile Settings

You have multiple options for configuring Outlook profiles when deploying. The most commonly used are the PRF files that generate Outlook profiles and apply Outlook settings.

To configure profile settings using PRF files, administrators can use the CIW or the OCT. Profile settings are defined on the Outlook: Customize Default Profile page. This section guides administrators through the standard configuration of the PRF file to generate a user's profile dynamically after the Outlook client installation has completed. In this scenario, you configure a single PRF file and create the Outlook profile for any user when the Outlook client is launched for the first time.

To create a new profile, open the CIW by selecting Start, Run, Microsoft Office, Microsoft Office Tools, Microsoft Office ORK, Custom Installation Wizard. Then follow these steps:

1. Select the default options until the Outlook: Customize Default Profile page appears. Select the New Profile option, enter Outlook for the profile name, and click Next.

> **TIP**
>
> To configure the PRF file to run when Outlook is launched for the first time, use the Add/Remove Registry Entries page of the Custom Installation Wizard.
>
> To enable the run-once option, make the following Registry changes:
>
> 1. Delete the following key:
>
>   `HKEY_CURRENT_USER\Software\Microsoft\Office\10.0\Outlook\Setup\First-Run`
>
> 2. Expand the Registry tree to the following:
>
>   `HKEY_CURRENT_USER\Software\Microsoft\Office\10.0\Outlook\Setup`
>
> 3. Add the string value and enter the path of the PRF file share created earlier.

2. To configure the PRF file to dynamically configure each user profile, enter the %username% variable in the User Name field. Also, enter the name of your Exchange server.

30

3. Because this PRF file is a default profile configuration file, click Next at the Add Accounts screen.

4. On the Remove Accounts and Export Settings screen, select the Export Profile Settings option. Enter the name "Outlook" for the name of the new PRF file and save the file to the desired location. Select Finish to complete the PRF file creation.

> **NOTE**
>
> Microsoft PRF files can also be configured with additional Outlook profile settings, such as Personal folders and Outlook option settings. To understand more about configuring PRF files, go to http://www.microsoft.com/office/ork and search for .PRF.

Creating Transforms and Profile Files

Several different types of configuration files can be used to deploy Outlook client configurations to the desktop. In this section, you complete the steps needed to configure Outlook using the CIW to create transforms and PRF files.

Creating Transforms

Transform files, designated with a .MST extension, are created using the Office CIW or the Office OCT. Transforms can be used to create detailed custom settings when installing and configuring the Outlook client.

> **NOTE**
>
> Use the Transform option when extensive settings are required for the Outlook deployment and when deploying Outlook with the Office application suite. Transforms can be configured with custom settings and Outlook profile information, making this option the most comprehensive of all configuration options when deploying.
>
> Be sure to document all settings expected to be used when creating configuration transform files.

To create a transform file, download and install the appropriate ORK, launch the utility, and then follow these steps:

1. From the Welcome to Microsoft Office Custom Installation Wizard screen, click Next.

2. On the Open the MSI File page, enter the path and filename for the Outlook MSI Installation package. Use the Browse button to locate the MSI installation package being used for this Microsoft Transform file. Click Next to continue.

3. Because this scenario is creating a new Transform file, on the Open the MST File page, click the Create a New MST File option, and click Next.

4. Select the location where the new MST file will be created, and click Next.

5. Enter the location where the Outlook installation will be placed on the desktop when the client is deployed, and then enter the name of the organization that will be used for registration information.

6. If previous installations of Outlook and Microsoft Office exist on the desktop, select which installation version to remove.

7. On the Set Feature Installation States page, select the Outlook components that will be installed. Select the Microsoft Outlook for Windows and the Run from My Computer options.

8. Use the Custom Default Application Settings page to define and add an Office Application Settings (OSP) file. If upgrading, select the Migrate User's Settings check box to maintain the existing user-defined options after the upgrade.

9. Use the Change the Office User Settings page to define the settings and options to be applied to Outlook after the installation is finished.

10. Use the Options pages to modify the Outlook installation; continue through the configuration pages to create the transform files.

Continue through the installation and configure the following:

1. Add/remove additional custom installation files.

2. Add/remove custom Registry entries.

3. Modify shortcuts and Outlook icons.

4. If deploying across WAN links, select an additional installation point for the deployment.

5. Establish Outlook security settings.

6. Add additional programs to be installed with Outlook.

30

Configuring Profiles with Transforms

Customizing the configuration of a profile during the installation can be accomplished using the Customize Default Profiles page. Using the options available, administrators can select the method in which to create the client profile with the Outlook Deployment tool.

For this transform, select Apply PRF File and select the PRF file created in the previous section. If you want to use an existing profile, modify an existing profile, or create a new profile, you can select one of those options instead.

▶ **Use Existing Profile**—Use when upgrading the Outlook client; this option maintains the existing settings.

> **NOTE**
>
> When Use Existing Profile is selected and no profile is found on the client desktop, this option prompts the user to create the profile.

▶ **Modify Profile**—Select this option to customize profile information and Exchange Outlook options.

▶ **New Profile**—Use this option to create a single new profile and configure connection settings.

Additional options are available, such as Send and Receive Options and Mail settings; continue through the configuration screens by choosing the desired options for your organization's deployment. The creation of the PRF file can be completed at any time by clicking the Finish button on any setup screen.

After the PRF has been created, the command syntax required to implement the transform file will be shown for you. Copy the command as it is shown for future reference.

Installing the Exchange Client

The option that requires the most administrative attention—manually installing the Outlook client—is often a necessary choice for deploying the Outlook client. After considering all available options, administrators must determine which option best fits the deployment needs by determining the overall effort required for each.

Any or all of the options can be utilized for an organizationwide deployment—utilizing each where it best fits. In this section, you review the basic steps for installing the Outlook client to desktop systems using transforms, PRF files, and the switches available when using these options.

Using Transforms and PRF Files When Installing Outlook

When the options are not available to push the installation to client systems, administrators can still install the Outlook client and save valuable keystrokes and time by predefining profile information. Using these options with a manual installation scenario can greatly reduce the overall amount of time required to install the Outlook client manually. Administrators can now incorporate the manual installation process with preconfiguration files, such as PRF files and transforms, and save time on each installation by avoiding the necessity of manually configuring each installation after completion.

When the required functionality is the client profile configuration setting and limited configuration options, the manual installation can easily be completed by using a simple PRF file. PRF files are simple to incorporate into the installation and require only the addition of a command-line switch with the `setup.exe` installation program to deploy.

With more complex installation needs, administrators can create MST files to define Outlook settings, security profiles, and user options. This option is most effective and enables administrators to continue with installations rather than manually configure each client setting individually.

Installing the Outlook Clients with PRF Files

After creating a PRF file by following the steps detailed in the previous section, administrators can copy the file to an installation share for use when manually installing Outlook. This allows administrators to avoid the necessity of manually configuring each Outlook profile after installation.

To understand more about using PRF files when using the Windows installation program, complete these steps:

1. Create a folder share and place the `Outlook.PRF` file in the folder where it can be accessed from any location on the network.

> **TIP**
>
> When creating shares to support installs and PRF configuration file access, grant the account being used to install the client with Full Control permissions to the PRF file and installation share.

2. To open a command prompt and begin an installation in Outlook using PRF files, begin by selecting Start, Run, enter "command" in the Open text box, and then click OK to continue.

3. At the command prompt, type

```
d:\setup.exe /ImportPRF \\Outlook Files\Outlook.PRF
```

where *d:* represents the location of the Outlook installation files and *Outlook Files* is the name of the folder share created to host the PRF configuration files.

When errors occur or it appears that the Outlook profile has not been set correctly, the PRF file can be run by using the Open command and manually installing the configuration information.

30

Manually Installing Outlook with Transforms

Transforms offer administrators the most functionality and flexibility when predefining Outlook settings and profile information. By utilizing transforms, administrators can leverage multiple options and even combine multiple transforms to configure Outlook clients. To understand the command lines and syntax used when installing the Microsoft Outlook client with MST files, review the examples listed in the following sections.

Applying Transforms with the Outlook Setup.exe

In these examples, administrators should use the `OutlookSet1.MST` transform filename to customize the Outlook installation. To incorporate transforms into the Outlook installation, use the following command:

```
Example: D:\setup.exe TRANSFORMS=OutlookSet1.mst
```

Administrators can also use multiple transforms when necessary. At times, organizations create individual transforms to configure specific settings. By combining these individual transforms, administrators can "pick and choose" which settings they do or do not want to apply.

For example, an organization creates a baseline transform that defines settings to be applied to all users. They then create individual transforms for specific settings for particular departments. These transforms can be applied to a single installation, creating customized Outlook settings that are configurable and easily redeployed if necessary. Using a `Setup.ini` file with the proper syntax, administrators can link and apply transforms in a very effective manner.

Pushing Client Software with Windows Server 2003 Group Policies

Using Windows Server 2003 Group Policy management tools, administrators can easily and inexpensively deploy the Outlook client to desktops throughout their organization by minimizing the tasks that require manual intervention.

Group policies can provide extremely powerful administration and management options when deploying the Outlook client. Use the information provided in this section to set up and deploy the `Outlook.MSI` package.

Deploying Outlook with Group Policy Overview

Using Group Policy to deploy the Outlook client is one of the most effective and flexible options administrators can leverage.

However, before creating deployment packages, administrators should understand the basic functionality of Group Policy in Windows Server 2003. Review the information and overview provided in the next sections before planning and setting up Windows Server 2003 Group Policy to support the Outlook client deployment.

Exchange Client Policy Options

When utilizing Group Policy functionality to deploy Outlook clients, the ORK provides predefined security templates for managing Outlook on the domain.

This template enables administrators to centrally manage and configure many of the security functions and preferences normally required to be configured at each individual Outlook client. Using the security template, administrators can fully manage and configure the following areas defined by domain clients:

▶ **Outlook preferences**—The preferences options available with the security template can be enabled in the same manner as using the Options tab available on the Tools menu of the Outlook desktop client. When defining preferences, administrators can control the standard look and feel of each component available with Outlook. Options include areas for enforcing items, such as spell check and email format, calendaring views, contacts options, and more.

▶ **Exchange settings**—Configuration items, such as Outlook user profile configurations and auto archiving, can now be centrally configured.

▶ **Intranet and SharePoint Portal Server settings**—In addition to the Outlook client settings, using the templates enables administrators to configure access to internal business information and SharePoint Portal Server resources through Outlook client folders.

Though the template enables you to configure many important options and preferences with the Outlook Exchange client, not all areas are available using the template.

Adding the Outlook Administrative Template

Because the additional administrative templates are not configured by default when Windows Server 2003 is installed, administrators must download or install the administrative Outlook template manually. For Outlook 2003, this file is called Outlook11.adm and is available in the ORK. During installation, Outlk11.adm is placed on the local drive of the systems on which the ORK is installed.

To begin setting up the Outlook security template Outlk11.adm, start by installing the Group Policy Management Console (GPMC) on the domain controller on which the policy will be administered.

Next install the Microsoft ORK on a system on which the template can be accessed from a domain controller for import into the Domain Group Policy.

> **NOTE**
>
> Both the GPMC and the ORK can be downloaded from Microsoft at: http://www.microsoft.com/downloads.
>
> In the Search field, simply type "Office Resource Kit" or "GPMC" to find the latest revisions.

30

After the ORK is installed, the Outlk11.adm file is automatically extracted and placed in the C:\Windows\Inf directory (where *C:* represents the system root where the Windows installation resides) on the local system drive where the ORK was installed.

To import the Outlook security template Outlk11.adm into the Domain Group Policy using the GPMC, use the following steps:

NOTE

When importing the Outlk11.adm security template, it is a best practice to import the template to the default Domain Group Policy. Review the event logs on additional domain controllers or use the Replmon tool available with Windows 2003 support tools to ensure the replication of the domain policy to all domain controllers occurs correctly.

---

1. From a domain controller in the domain where the policy will be applied, open the Group Policy snap-in by selecting Start, All Programs, Administrative Tools, Group Policy Management.

2. Select the location Default Domain Policy where Outlk11.adm will be imported to, as shown in Figure 30.3.

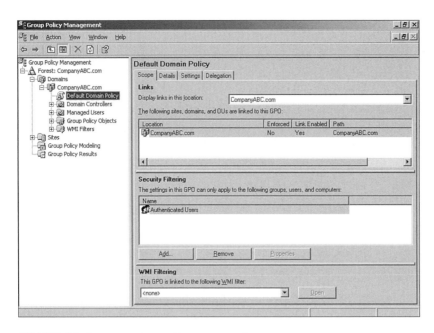

FIGURE 30.3   Group Policy Management Console.

3. On the Action menu, select Edit; this opens the Group Policy Object Editor window.

4. In the Group Policy Object Editor, right-click Administrative Templates under the User Configuration option and choose Add/Remove Templates, as shown in Figure 30.4.

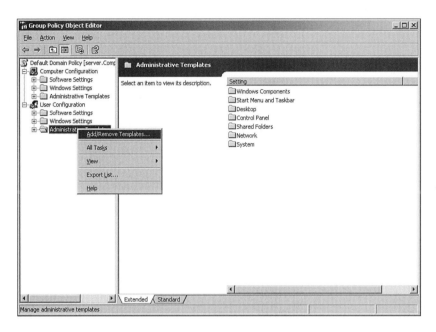

FIGURE 30.4   Group Policy Object Editor.

5. From the Add/Remove Templates dialog box, click the Add button.

6. Navigate to the location where Outlk11.adm was placed, as noted in step 2. Select the template to import Outlk11.ADM and click the Open button.

7. Ensure that the OUTLK11 template has been added to the Add/Remove Templates dialog box, and click Close to continue.

You should now see the Microsoft Outlook 2003 template under the Administrative Templates folder in the Group Policy Object Editor.

Administrative Options

Delegating the proper rights for administrators to manage and manipulate Group Policy when deploying Outlook clients is important. With the Delegation Wizard available in the Windows Group Policy snap-in, administrative rights can be assigned to Exchange administrators to manage and control the deployment of Outlook to the desktop without interfering with the day-to-day operations of the Windows systems. By using the Delegation Wizard to assign rights, administrators can grant permissions to individual accounts, groups, and Exchange server administrators.

30

Deployment Options

With Group Policy, the Outlook client can be deployed to the desktop using any of the following deployment methods:

▶ **Assigned to Computers**—This method of installation creates an Outlook installation package that is applied to workstations when a user logs on to the desktop. Using this option, all users have access to the Exchange client software after it's installed.

▶ **Assigned to Users**—When the installation package is assigned to users, application shortcuts are placed on the desktop of the user's profiles and in the Start menu of the individual user's profile. When these shortcuts are selected, the application installation is launched and completed.

▶ **Publishing the Installation**—When Outlook client software packages are published, the installation package is displayed in the Add/Remove Programs Group in the local desktop system Control Panel. Users can then initiate the installation by selecting the Install option.

With each method, Exchange 2003 administrators use the MSI installation file format to push the Outlook client's software packages from a central location or from administrative installation points to the workstations or users on the network.

Pushing Outlook Client

The steps in this scenario enable administrators to push the Exchange Outlook client package to workstations on the domain.

> **NOTE**
>
> To enhance functionality when using Windows Server 2003 Group Policy, download and install the Microsoft Group Policy Management Console (GPMC) from Microsoft.

Open the Group Policy Management Console by selecting Start, All Programs, Administrative Tools, Group Policy Management. To create Outlook client software Group Policy Objects (GPOs), complete the following steps:

1. Select the Default Domain Policy for your domain by selecting Forest, Domains, YourCompanyDomain, Group Policy Objects.

2. Select the Default Domain Policy, click Action, and then click Edit. This opens the Group Policy Object Editor to create the software push.

3. Select Computer Configuration and then Software Installation.

4. From the Action menu, select New, Package.

5. Navigate the Open dialog box to the network share where the `Outlook.MSI` was placed, and select the MSI package being applied. Select Open to continue.

> **NOTE**
>
> If prompted that the Group Policy Object Editor cannot verify the network location, ensure that the share containing the installation files has the permissions configured to allow user access. Select Yes to continue when confirmed.

6. At the Deploy Software dialog box, select Advanced and click OK to continue. Windows Server 2003 will verify the installation package; wait for the verification to complete before continuing to the next step.

7. After the package is visible in the right pane of the software installation properties, highlight the install package and click Action/Properties.

8. On the Package properties page, select the Deployment tab. Review the configuration, click Assign, and ensure that the Install this Package at Logon option is selected. Click OK when you are finished.

When the new package is ready to deploy, test the update by logging on to a workstation and verifying that the package has installed correctly using the steps listed in the section "Configuring the SMS Package for an Unattended Installation" later in this chapter. If problems exist, redeploy the package by selecting the software update; click Action, All Tasks, Redeploy Application to force the deployment.

Testing the Outlook Client Deployment

When using Group Policy, administrators cannot determine whether a software package was pushed successfully without any additional management software such as Microsoft SMS. Evidence of the success of a client installation using Group Policy can only be determined by reviewing the client desktop. Using the following two areas on the client desktop, administrators can determine whether a software installation was successful:

▶ View the client application logs for MSI Installer events.

▶ On the local machine, view Add/Remove Programs to see whether the Outlook update package is listed.

Updates and Patch Management with Group Policies

One other advantage to using Group Policy is the centralized deployment options available to distribute the Exchange Outlook client updates and patches to domain workstations. Using any one of the following options, including a combination of each, Exchange administrators can use Group Policy to deploy updates using Microsoft MSI installation packages or Windows Updates security templates to push updates to the Microsoft Outlook client. Using GPOs, installation of software updates can be deployed from the centralized administrative installation point to a predefined set of workstations or, in the case of a WAN, from any remote installation point or Windows Update site configured in the GPO settings.

30

Deployment Options When Updating Exchange Clients

Using Group Policy, the Outlook client can be upgraded and patched using one of the following deployment methods:

▶ **Assigned to Computers**—This method of installation uses the Outlook Installation package on the workstation and is available when the workstation is restarted. Using this option, all users have access to the Exchange client software after it is installed.

▶ **Assigned to Users**—When the installation package is assigned to users, application shortcuts are placed on the desktop of the user's profile and on the Start menu. When these shortcuts are selected, the application installation will be completed.

▶ **Publishing the Installation**—This option requires additional configuration at the desktop level to allow users the ability to install published packages on client systems. When a software package is published, the installation package is displayed in the Add/Remove Programs group in the local desktop system Control Panel. Users can then initiate the installation by selecting the update.

▶ **Using Windows Update Services**—This might be the most common method of deploying software updates to client desktop systems on any enterprise. Using Windows Server Update Services technology and Group Policy, security updates, patches, and critical updates can be deployed for Microsoft Office platforms to the client workstation.

Each method enables Exchange Server administrators to deliver update packages to the Outlook client using a push or pull method. These updates can be configured for deployment from a central location or from an administrative installation point located on the network to allow for ease of download to the workstation anywhere in the enterprise.

CAUTION

When deploying updates with GPOs, do not assign the option to install updates to users and computers at the same time. Assigning both options can create conflicts as to how updates are installed and possibly corrupt the installation of the Outlook client.

Group Policy Best Practices

As with all aspects of Group Policy, the choices and configuration options available when deploying clients or updates are numerous. Regardless of which type of package is being pushed, some basic best practices apply and can help make the process easier and less troublesome:

▶ When configuring clients to use update methods such as Windows Server Update Services, configure clients to use installation points that will allow clients to update systems from the local LAN rather than over WAN links.

▶ Software packages pushed with GPOs must be in the format of an MSI package. Any other format type than an MSI cannot be pushed using Group Policy. Using additional tools such as Marovision's Admin Studio can help administrators convert other update formats such as .exe files to customized MSI installation packages as well as custom configuration of predefined installation choices.

▶ When configuring software pushes using GPOs, configure the GPO at the highest levels possible in the domain tree. If the push is going out to more than one group or OU, the software update should be configured to be pushed at the domain level. If the software update is being pushed to only a few groups or one OU, or if multiple update packages are being pushed, configure the push at the group or OU level.

▶ Configure software pushes to the Computer Configuration settings rather than the User Configuration settings. This way, if users log on to multiple computer systems, updates are not applied more than once to the same system.

▶ When pushing updates to multiple locations, use technologies such as administrative distribution points and distributed file system (DFS). This allows software updates to be installed from packages and sources close to the client being updated.

Pushing Client Updates

With the options available and a good understanding of the best practices for deploying software using GPOs, the next step is to configure a GPO to push an update directly to the Outlook client. The steps in this scenario enable administrators to push a small update package to the Exchange Server 2003 Outlook client workstations on the domain.

Begin by downloading an update to use for this exercise ensuring an MSI format. Also, create a share on the network folder where the update will be placed and deployed. To begin, open the GPMC by selecting Start, All Programs, Administrative Tools, Group Policy Management. With the GPMC open, create an Outlook client software update GPO by following these steps:

1. Select the Default Domain Policy for your domain by selecting Forest, Domains, YourCompanydomain, Group Policy Objects.

2. Select Default Domain Policy, click Action, and then click Edit. This opens the Group Policy Object Editor to create the software push.

3. Select Computer Configuration and select Software Settings, Software Installation.

4. On the Action menu, select New, Package.

5. Navigate the Open dialog box to the network share where the MSI was placed, and select the MSI package being applied. Select Open to continue.

30

> **NOTE**
>
> If prompted that the Group Policy Object Editor cannot verify the network location, ensure that the share created earlier in these steps has permissions allowing user accounts in the domain access to the share. Select Yes to continue after confirming.

6. At the Deploy Software dialog box, select Advanced and click OK to continue. Windows verifies the installation package; wait for the verification to complete before continuing to the next step.

7. When the package is visible in the right pane of the software installation properties, highlight the install package, and click Action, Properties.

8. On the Package properties page, select the Deployment tab. Review the configuration, click Assign, and ensure that the Install This Application at Logon option is selected, as shown in Figure 30.5. Click OK when you are finished.

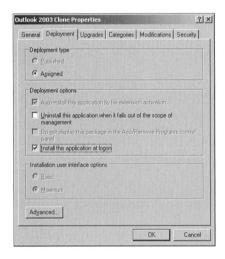

FIGURE 30.5   Outlook Update properties.

The new package is now ready to deploy; test the update by logging on to a workstation connected to the domain. Verify that the package has been installed. If problems exist, redeploy the package by selecting the software update in the GPMC and clicking Action, All Tasks, Redeploy Application to force the deployment.

Determining the Success of a Push

Without additional management software such as Systems Management Server 2003, administrators cannot determine whether a software package was pushed successfully to a client system with a GPO. This is because all evidence of software pushes is only evident locally on the client machines on which the update logs are stored. To check and verify if an update has been installed successfully, you can check several areas:

- Look for MSI Installer events that are written into the application event logs.

- On the local machine, view Add/Remove Programs to see whether the Outlook update package is listed.

- If using Windows Server Update Services, review the Windows Update log located in the `Program Files\Windows Update` directory on the local machine.

Deploying with Microsoft Systems Management Server

The most comprehensive option to deploy the Outlook client is Microsoft Systems Management Server (SMS). With the powerful software deployment functionality and management tools incorporated with SMS, this method becomes the best solution for deploying the Outlook client software to medium and large organizations.

Planning and Preparing Outlook Deployments with SMS

To prepare the Outlook client installation for use with SMS, administrators must plan and prepare the deployment in many of the same ways as when using other options.

This section reviews and outlines the following options and deployment preparation tasks involved with using SMS:

- **Software distribution**—Plan and create administrative installation points to support software pushes in remote locations and on separate subnets. SMS site servers and remote distribution points can be used to support software distribution, while preventing pushes over WAN links.

- **Evaluate client needs**—Determine the specific client installation needs and document the deployment plan.

- **Inventory using SMS collections**—Leveraging the powerful functionality of SMS collections, administrators can perform detailed inventories of desktop hardware and software.

Deploying with Systems Management Server

When deploying the Outlook client with Microsoft Systems Management Server, SMS leverages the Windows Installer to enhance the functionality of the deployment. Furthermore, SMS incorporates the ability to recover from failed installations.

When leveraging Windows Installer and SMS to push client software, the following options are available:

- **Predefined Configuration Support**—Administrators can incorporate transforms and PRF files with the distribution of the MSI package.

30

▶ **Per System Pushes**—Users can establish a connection to the website without providing credentials.

▶ **Unattended Installation**—Using the /qb option with the installation syntax for the MSI package, administrators can force an unattended installation to the Outlook client.

▶ **Administrative Installation Points**—As with other options, remote locations and alternate locations can be defined to support client pushes over slower connections.

▶ **Advertised and Silent Installation**—Administrators can choose between the options of advertising the installation package in the SMS Advanced Client or forcing the installation without user intervention.

Configuring the SMS Package for an Unattended Installation

Using the property pages of the Outlook MSI package used with SMS to deploy Outlook clients, administrators can define the options to be used and how the package will be installed.

In this scenario, an administrator can configure the basic installation package for an unattended installation with SMS:

1. Select the Outlook MSI file and open the Programs property page. Modify the Installer package properties by adding the command-line switch /qn.

2. To complete configuring the unattended installation for the MSI package, click the Environment tab and uncheck the User Input Required check box.

> **NOTE**
>
> To add a PRF file for use with the SMS package, add this command:
>
>   /ImportPRF \\Outlook Files\Outlook.PRF
>
> after the /qn switch (where *Outlook Files* represents the share location where the packages can be found).

Now that the installation package has been prepared, SMS can be configured to push Microsoft Outlook clients to the desktop.

Managing Postdeployment Tasks

Overall, without deployment and management software such as SMS, administrators are very limited in options for managing and validating Outlook client deployments. This section reviews methods and functionality of Exchange Server that can be leveraged to help determine the overall success of a deployment and troubleshoot common deployment issues.

Validating Successful Installations

When SMS is not available for managing and determining the success of the Outlook client deployments, administrators must use the standard tools and functionality available with Windows Server and Exchange Server. Administrators can use several methods to review and validate client installations and ensure that the client can authenticate after the Outlook client is deployed into the production environment.

Review the following options to determine methods and tricks that can assist in validating Outlook client functionality after the deployment is complete:

▶ Installations can be validated by reviewing the Application Event Logs of the client systems and identifying MSI Installer events that are written into the event logs.

▶ On the local machine, view Add/Remove Programs to see whether the Outlook update package is listed.

▶ Enable diagnostic logging on the Exchange server to monitor `MSExchangeIS` events when deploying clients.

Summary

When planning a deployment of Outlook clients, organizations can leverage different options depending on the type of client and the specific needs identified during the discovery. If using manual installation or Windows Server 2003 Group Policy and SMS, extensive planning and testing of Outlook client transforms and Outlook profiles should be performed prior to deploying any clients to the production environment.

Regardless of the deployment method, configuration settings and procedures should be documented and the deployment of Outlook clients should be staged in groups for manageability.

Best Practices

The following are best practices from this chapter:

▶ Use the Group Policy Management Console (GPMC) to plan and test policies prior to installation, as well as to debug policy problems after implementation.

▶ The Resultant Set of Policies (RSoP) should be used to analyze policy enforcement.

▶ Administrators should delegate rights to distribute the management and enforcement of group policies.

▶ Document configuration settings being applied to Outlook transform and PRF files.

▶ With Microsoft Systems Management Server (SMS), inventories can be conducted on network desktop systems to identify hardware and software installed on each.

30

▶ To enhance functionality when using Windows Server 2003 Group Policy, download and install the GPMC from Microsoft.

▶ Enable diagnostic logging on the Exchange server to monitor MSExchangeIS events when deploying clients.

▶ Leverage built-in functionality such as Remote Desktop and the Computer Management snap-in to review the success and failures of client installations.

PART IX

Data Protection and Disaster Recovery of Exchange Server 2007

IN THIS PART

CHAPTER 31

Continuous Backups, Clustering, and Network Load Balancing in Exchange Server 2007

One of the most anticipated features of Microsoft Exchange Server 2007 is Cluster Continuous Replication (CCR). Exchange Server 2007 goes beyond the clustering abilities of Exchange 2003 in that it no longer requires shared storage between the two nodes—each node maintains an independent copy of the Exchange databases. The identity of the mail server is maintained by the cluster resources and can move back and forth between the cluster nodes. The net result is the ability to perform clustering with simple hardware and to failover to a second copy of the Exchange databases in the event of a server failure. This replication can be performed between multiple locations, giving administrators a level of redundancy never before available in Exchange.

Another very useful feature introduced in Exchange Server 2007 is the concept of a Local Continuous Replication (LCR). LCR follows a similar concept to CCR but only requires a single server. By maintaining a second set of logs and databases, the system can very quickly recover from a media failure of the databases.

Network Load Balancing (NLB) is as important as ever in the Exchange Server 2007 world because it allows various services such as Post Office Protocol version 3 (POP3), Internet Message Access Protocol version 4 (IMAP4), or Outlook Anywhere to enjoy redundancy as well.

This chapter further details these various functions and offers advice on how best to utilize them. Step-by-step installation and configuration instructions are included where appropriate.

Understanding Clustering

Before implementing clustering technologies, it is important to understand that Windows Server 2003 clustering comes in different levels of availability or options. Determine which fault-tolerant option is best; the following list describes some of those options, how they work, and a few terms used to describe the way clustered Exchange 2007 operates:

- ▶ **Active/Active**—In Active/Active clustering, all servers in the cluster are live and servicing clients at the same time. Active/Active clustering is limited to two clustered nodes and is not supported for CCR.

- ▶ **Active/Passive**—In Active/Passive clustering, clustering is available when two or more nodes are available. Only one server in the cluster can service end users at a time. Active/Passive clusters are also limited to a per-application basis while the other server(s) wait in a standby or offline mode until a failure occurs. If a failure occurs, the passive node then begins to service clients. In this configuration, one virtual server is configured and shared by both nodes. Exchange Server 2007 CCR supports a two-node Active/Passive configuration.

- ▶ **Exchange virtual server**—An Exchange virtual server is really a cluster-configured resource group that contains all resources for Exchange to operate on the cluster. This includes a NetBIOS name of the virtual server, a TCP/IP address for the virtual server and all disk drives, and vital Exchange services required to operate in a clustered configuration. In an Active/Active two-node cluster, one Exchange virtual server is created per node while the NetBIOS name and TCP/IP address of the cluster form the virtual server. When failover occurs in this configuration, the entire Exchange virtual server fails over to the surviving node in the cluster dynamically. This is also referred to simply as a mailbox cluster in Exchange Server 2007.

- ▶ **Resource DLL or `Exres.dll`**—`Exres.dll` is the gateway responsible for communications between the cluster service and the Exchange services. This `.dll` is responsible for reporting failures in the cluster and bringing resources online and offline.

- ▶ **Heartbeat**—A single User Datagram Protocol (UDP) packet is sent every 500 milliseconds between nodes in the cluster across the internal private network that relays health information of the cluster nodes and on the health of the clustered application. If there is no response during a heartbeat, the cluster begins a failover. In Exchange Server 2007, this interval can be changed. This is useful when utilizing a geographically disparate CCR.

- ▶ **Failover**—Failover is the process of one node in the cluster changing states from offline to online, resulting in the node taking over responsibility for the Exchange virtual server.

▶ **Failback**—Failback is the process of moving Exchange virtual server applications that failed over in the cluster back to the original online node.

▶ **Quorum resource**—This is the shared disk that holds the cluster server's configuration information. All servers must be able to contact the quorum resource to become part of an Exchange Server 2007 cluster.

▶ **Resource group**—A resource group is a collection of cluster resources, such as the Exchange NetBIOS name, TCP/IP address, and services of the Exchange cluster. A resource group also defines which items fail over to the surviving nodes during failover. This also includes cluster resource items, including cluster disk. A resource group is owned by only one node in the cluster at a time.

▶ **Cluster resource**—Cluster resources are vital information of the Exchange virtual server and include its network TCP/IP addresses, NetBIOS name, disks, and Exchange services—such as the System Attendant. These cluster resources are added to cluster group when the virtual server is created to form Exchange virtual servers.

▶ **Dependency**—Dependencies are specified when creating the cluster resources. Similar to dependencies on Exchange services, a cluster resource that is specified as a dependency defines a mandatory relationship between resources. Before a cluster resource is brought online, whatever resource is defined as dependent must be brought online first. For instance, the virtual server NetBIOS name is dependent on the TCP/IP address; therefore, the TCP/IP address of the virtual server must be brought online before the NetBIOS name is brought online.

▶ **Majority node cluster**—In this configuration, each node is responsible for contributing one local disk to the quorum disk set that is used as storage disks. This configuration limits the majority-of-node-resource to one owner at a time. This configuration requires a minimum of two nodes to be available at all times.

▶ **Quorum-device cluster**—Using the quorum type resource requires the cluster storage resource to be connected with a Fibre Channel or small computer system interface (SCSI) bus. In this configuration, any physical disk can be configured as a quorum disk.

> **NOTE**
>
> In Exchange Server 2007, only the Mailbox role can be clustered; therefore, a multiple role server cannot be clustered.

Deploying a Cluster Continuous Replication Mailbox Cluster

Deployment of a Cluster Continuous Replication (CCR) mailbox cluster is a fairly straightforward process but it does have several steps that must occur in the correct order. By becoming familiar with the requirements and the process, the implementation should be fairly uneventful.

Be aware that a two-node CCR now supports the concept of a file share witness to act as the local quorum. This means that rather than using a shared drive to track the status of the cluster, this function is performed on a file share to which both nodes have access. This is a useful change because in the past, you needed at least three nodes in a cluster to utilize a majority node set (MNS) quorum. By using the file share witness, you can run with only two nodes and not be at risk of split brain syndrome, where the two nodes each believe they should own the cluster resources.

Requirements for CCR

You will need two servers that are capable of supporting the Exchange Server 2007 Mailbox role. You don't need shared storage with a CCR because the transactions are shipped to the passive node and applied locally. This results in two independent databases and sets of log files on two different servers with independent media. You will want to follow the same standards as you would with a normal Mailbox server in terms of database sizes, separation of logs, and databases and hardware specifications to support your anticipated user load.

To set up a CCR, you need the following:

- ▶ Two servers running Windows Server 2003, Enterprise Edition

- ▶ Two network interfaces per server

- ▶ Three hard drives per server (OS/Logs/Databases)

- ▶ Hotfix 921181—support for file share witness

Hotfix 921181 can be downloaded from http://www.microsoft.com/downloads/details. aspx?familyid=C62E21D9-192C-44DD-9C80-403BDA97990C&displaylang=en

You will also need to create the file share that will be used as the file share witness by the cluster. It is recommended that you place this file share on the local Hub Transport server.

Preparing the Operating System

The CCR mailbox cluster is based on a Windows Server 2003 cluster with Exchange Server 2007 running on both nodes. To prepare those nodes to participate in a Windows cluster, perform the following items on each node:

1. Install Windows 2003 x64 normally.

2. Join the nodes to the domain that will host the Exchange servers.

3. Create a heartbeat network between the two nodes by addressing a network interface card (NIC) on a different Internet Protocol (IP) space from the production network. Isolate these heartbeat NICs to an isolated virtual local area network

(VLAN) or a separate network switch. This is the network that will be used by the cluster nodes to communicate with each other.

4. Download hotfix 921181:

   http://www.microsoft.com/downloads/details.aspx?familyid=C62E21D9-192C-44DD-9C80-403BDA97990C&displaylang=en

   and install on each node. This allows the cluster to use a file share witness for the majority node set quorum.

5. Install IIS on each node via the following process:

   a. Click Start, Control Panel, Add or Remove Programs.

   b. Click Add/Remove Windows Components.

   c. When the menu appears, highlight Application Server, and click Details.

   d. Select Internet Information Services (IIS), and click OK.

   e. Click Next and then click Finish.

   f. Close the Add/Remove Programs interface.

6. Install the updated `msdaps.dll` for use with 64-bit Windows:

   a. Open a web browser and go to http://go.microsoft.com/fwlink/?linkid=55328.

   b. Download the update.

   c. When the security warning appears, click Run.

   d. When the second warning appears, click Run.

   e. When the wizard appears, click Next.

   f. When the license agreement appears, click I Agree, and then click Next.

   g. When the installation is completed, click Finish.

When this process has been completed on both nodes, the systems are ready for the rest of the configuration process to continue.

Creating the File Witness Share

The file witness share is the replacement for a shared quorum drive that allows a two-node majority node set cluster to operate without suffering from split brain syndrome, where the cluster is split into two or more partitions that cannot communicate with each other. The quorum is used to guarantee that any cluster resource is brought online on only one node. To create this share, follow these steps:

1. Create a directory on the Hub Transport server.

2. Right-click the directory, and choose Sharing and Security.

3. Click Share This Folder and enter a share name.

4. Click the Permissions button, and then click Add.

5. Type in the name of the account under which the cluster service will run, and then click OK.

6. Grant the service account Full Control, and click OK.

7. Click the Security tab.

8. Grant the service account Full Control, and click OK.

This creates the share with the correct permissions for the cluster to later utilize it for the file share witness.

Creating the Cluster

Now that the nodes are prepared and the file witness share is created, the cluster can be created. Be sure to have the following items ready for the cluster configuration:

▸ Unique names for each node

▸ Unique name for the cluster identity

▸ Unique name for the Exchange virtual server

▸ Unique IP addresses for each of the names created previously

NOTE

All the IPs listed must be from the same network range.

With these items ready, complete the following steps to create the cluster:

1. From the Start menu, click Program Files, Administrative Tools, Cluster Administrator.

2. Under Action, choose Create New Cluster, and click OK.

3. The New Server Cluster Wizard launches. Click Next.

4. Choose the domain that will host the cluster in the drop-down menu, and then enter the name of the cluster. This is the name of the cluster itself and doesn't affect the Exchange virtual name. Click Next.

5. Enter the name of the first node that will participate in the cluster. Click Next.

6. The New Server Cluster Wizard analyzes the node to see if it can become a cluster node. A warning appears about the lack of a shared quorum device. Disregard this message as you will be using a majority node set quorum. Click Next.

7. Enter the IP address that will be used to manage the cluster. This needs to be a unique and reachable IP address. Click Next.

8. Enter the name and password of the account under which the cluster service will run. This account needs to have local Administrator rights to each node of the cluster. Click Next.

9. At the Proposed Cluster Configuration screen, click Quorum, and change the option to Majority Node Set via the drop-down options, as shown in Figure 31.1. Click OK and then click Next.

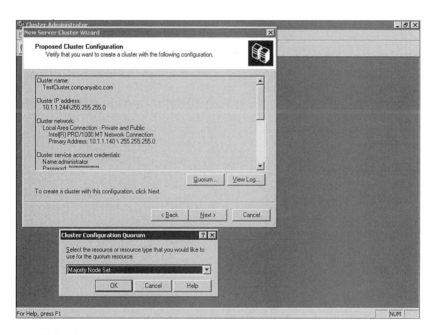

FIGURE 31.1   Setting the Quorum type.

10. When the New Server Cluster Wizard completes its tasks, click Next and then click Finish.

Adding the Second Node to the Cluster

Now that the cluster has been established by the first node, you can join the second node to the cluster. To do this, perform the following steps:

1. Right-click NodeA in the left pane of the Cluster Administrator.

2. Click New and then click Node.

3. When the Add Nodes Wizard launches, click Next.

4. Type the name of the second node, as shown in Figure 31.2, click Add, and then click Next.

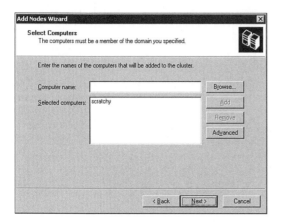

FIGURE 31.2   Selecting the second node.

5. The analysis runs to see if the node selected is a viable cluster node. When it completes, click Next.

6. Type the password of the Cluster Service Account, and click Next.

7. Review the Proposed Cluster Configuration; if it is correct, click Next.

8. When the Add Nodes Wizard is complete, click Next, and then click Finish.

9. Close the Cluster Administrator.

Configuring the MNS Quorum

With the cluster built and configured to use an MNS quorum, the cluster needs to be updated to use the file share witness as its quorum. To do this, follow these steps:

1. Open a command prompt on the node that currently owns the cluster resources.

2. Type the following:

```
Cluster res "Majority node set" /priv mnsfileshare=\\server\share
```

This should point to the share created on the Hub Transport server earlier. You can ignore the warning as it simply means you need to take the resources offline and back online for the changes to take effect. You do this by typing:

```
Cluster group "cluster group" /move
Cluster res "Majority Node Set" /priv
```

At this point, the cluster is using the file share witness and you've verified the setting.

3. Close the command prompt.

Installing Exchange Server 2007 on the Active Node

Now that the cluster is established and is correctly functioning with the file share witness, it is time to install the Exchange Server 2007 mailbox components on the nodes. This process will be broken out by node, and you will start with the node that currently owns the cluster resources. This is referred to as the active node. To install the clustered mailbox role, follow these steps:

1. Insert the Exchange Server 2007 media in the CD-ROM drive.

2. Run Setup.exe.

3. Following the Exchange 2007 Installation Wizard, you are prompted to install the .NET Framework 2.0. and MMC 3.0 on the system. Follow the wizard as prompted through the installation of the .NET Framework and MMC components.

4. The installation then takes you to the Microsoft website. Click Download when prompted, and then choose Run. The files download and a security warning appears. Click Run.

5. When the Update Wizard appears, click Next.

6. After reading the license agreement and agreeing to the content, click I Agree, and then click Next.

7. When the update is completed, click Finish.

8. Return to the setup interface, and click Install Microsoft Command Shell.

9. Click Open when prompted. The files decompress and open a window. Double-click Msh_Setup.msi.

10. When the security warning appears, click Run.

11. When the Command Shell (x64) Setup Wizard appears, click Next.

12. At the license agreement, click I Accept the Terms in the License Agreement, and then click Next.

13. Accept the default destination folder, and click Next.

14. At the Start Installation screen, click Install.

15. When the Setup Wizard completes, click Finish.

16. Return to Setup.exe and click Install Microsoft Exchange. Files copy and the Exchange Server 2007 setup launches. Click Next.

17. Upon reviewing the license agreement, if you are in agreement with the terms, click to accept the license agreement, and then click Next.

18. Leave the error reporting options set to Yes, and click Next.

19. Choose Custom Exchange Server Installation, and click Next.

20. Under Server Role Selection, choose Active Clustered Mailbox Role, and click Next.

21. Leave the Cluster Settings as Cluster Continuous Replication, and enter a name for the clustered Mailbox server. This name is different than the cluster name. This is the name that Outlook will connect to. Enter a unique IP address as well. Click Next.

22. The Setup Wizard performs a readiness check and if it passes, the role can be installed.

23. Click Install.

24. When the setup is completed, click Finish.

25. At the setup interface, click Get Critical Updates for Microsoft Exchange.

26. The Microsoft Update site launches. Click Express to get recommended updates.

27. Click Install Updates if any updates are available.

At this point, the installation of the first node of the Exchange Server 2007 mailbox cluster is complete. Verify that the Exchange Server 2007 services start correctly and that the virtual server is seen in the Exchange Management Console. If these services are started correctly, you can move on to installing the second node.

Installing Exchange Server 2007 on the Passive Node

With the active node installed and functioning as an Exchange Server 2007 Mailbox server, you can now install Exchange Server 2007 on the second node to complete the CCR cluster. Follow these steps:

1. Insert the Exchange Server 2007 media in the CD-ROM drive.

2. Run Setup.exe.

3. Following the Exchange 2007 Installation Wizard, you are prompted to install the .NET Framework 2.0 and MMC 3.0 on the system. Follow the Setup Wizard as prompted through the installation of the .NET Framework and MMC components.

4. The installation then takes you to the Microsoft website. Click Download when prompted, and then choose Run. The files download and a security warning appears. Click Run.

5. When the Update Wizard is complete, click Finish.

6. Return to the setup interface, and click Install Microsoft Command Shell.

7. Click Open when prompted. The files decompress and open a window. Double-click `Msh_Setup.msi`.

8. When the security warning appears, click Run.

9. When the Command Shell (x64) Setup Wizard appears, click Next.

10. At the license agreement, click I Accept the Terms in the License Agreement, and click Next.

11. Accept the default destination folder, and click Next.

12. At the Start Installation screen, click Install.

13. When the Setup Wizard completes, click Finish.

14. Return to `Setup.exe` and click Install Microsoft Exchange.

15. Files copy and the Exchange Server 2007 setup launches. Click Next.

16. Accept the license agreement, and click Next.

17. Leave the error reporting options set to Yes, and click Next.

18. Choose Custom Exchange Server Installation, and click Next.

19. Under Server Role Selection, choose Passive Clustered Mailbox Role, and then click Next.

20. When the readiness checks are complete, click Install.

21. When the setup is completed, click Finish.

22. At the setup interface, click Get Critical Updates for Microsoft Exchange.

23. The Microsoft Update site launches. Click Express to get recommended updates.

24. Click Install Updates if any updates are available.

The cluster is now ready for use.

> **NOTE**
>
> It is of value to point out that the use of the terms *Active* and *Passive* in this chapter and in the setup reference the status of the two nodes at the time of cluster inception. After the cluster is established, *Active* simply refers to the node that currently owns the cluster and Exchange resources.

Special Considerations for CCR

There are a few items that must be addressed when implementing a CCR cluster that are outside the cluster itself.

One of the items discussed in the cluster installation was the heartbeat and the heartbeat network that must be configured. The limitation of the heartbeat network in Windows Server 2003 is that the heartbeat subnet must be local to the nodes. Normally, this is easy to achieve because the two nodes might be in the same rack or at least in the same data center. If, on the other hand, you plan to deploy the CCR nodes in geographically disperse locations, you must stretch a VLAN across the wide area network (WAN) to make the heartbeat ports on the switches appear to be on the same VLAN. This is usually achieved through port tagging on the switch. Windows Longhorn will not have this limitation in its clustered configuration.

Another item that needs to be enabled for CCR is the transport dumpster function on the Hub Transport servers. This needs to be enabled on the Hub Transport servers in all sites because it is disabled by default.

The Hub Transport server maintains a queue of mail that was recently delivered to a clustered Mailbox server. In the event of a failover that is not lossless, CCR automatically requests every Hub Transport server in the site to resend mail from the transport dumpster queue. The Information Store automatically deletes duplicate messages and redelivers mail that was lost. You can use the Set-TransportConfig cmdlet to enable and configure the transport dumpster, which is controlled at the storage group level. It is recommended to configure the MaxDumpsterSizePerStorageGroup parameter, which specifies the maximum size of the transport dumpster queue for each storage group, to a size that is 1.25 times the size of the maximum message that can be sent. For example, if the maximum size for messages is 10MB, you should configure the MaxDumpsterSizePerStorageGroup parameter with a value of 12.5MB. It is also recommended to configure the MaxDumpsterTime parameter, which specifies how long an email message should remain in the transport dumpster queue, to a value of 07:00:00, or 7 days. This is sufficient to allow for an extended outage to occur without loss of email.

When using the transport dumpster feature, additional disk space is needed on the Hub Transport server to host the transport dumpster queues. The amount of storage space required is roughly equal to the value of MaxDumpsterSizePerStorageGroup times the number of storage groups. Be sure to plan for this additional space when planning out an Exchange Server 2007 deployment that will utilize CCR mailbox clusters.

To enable the transport dumpster, follow these steps:

1. Open the Exchange Command Shell.

2. Run the following command:

```
Set-transportconfig -MaxDumpsterSizePerStorageGroup <size> -MaxDumpsterTime
➥<timespan>
```

For example, to configure the maximum size of the dumpster per storage group to 20MB with a dumpster life of 7 days, use the following command:

```
Set-transportconfig -MaxDumpsterSizePerStorageGroup 20MB -MaxDumpsterTime
➥07.00:00:00
```

> **NOTE**
>
> Interesting to note is that the two nodes in a CCR do not have to be identical. It is fully supported to run different hardware for the two nodes. This allows an environment to repurpose servers as the passive nodes of CCRs to save money. Be sure that the mismatched node is capable of supporting a level of performance that is within your service level agreement.

Other Advantages of Clustering

Utilizing clustered mailboxes can provide benefits beyond just the obvious disaster recovery abilities. Having a clustered mailbox gives the administrator increased flexibility in dealing with the Mailbox servers.

Imagine a situation in which you need to take down a Mailbox server to perform maintenance or to perform an upgrade. Normally, you schedule the outage, let the user population know that mail will be unavailable during that time, and hope that they get their work done during that outage window. Meanwhile, processes and users who are dependent on the mailboxes are unable to perform their normal tasks. If, on the other hand, you could simply fail the Mailbox role over to the passive node, you could perform the maintenance or upgrade on the previously active node without interrupting the Exchange services. Users and applications would still be able to access the mailboxes and there wouldn't be a constraint around when you could do the work.

Another very common example of this is in the area of patch management. With clustered mailboxes, an administrator can patch the passive node, fail the Exchange services over to it, and then patch the remaining node. This greatly reduces the downtime associated with installing patches on Exchange Server 2007 servers.

Single Copy Clusters

The old model of Exchange clustering, where two nodes have shared resources that hold the Exchange databases and logs, is still available in Exchange Server 2007. This model is now called the Single Copy Cluster (SCC).

Requirements of SCC

Single copy clustering is the method of clustering where two or more nodes have the ability to control a single set of media that holds the application data. In the case of Exchange Server 2007, this refers to a cluster where there is only a single copy of the logs and databases but there are two nodes available to control that data.

This means that to run a Single Copy Cluster, you need to provide the cluster with shared media. The most common ways to provide this are via storage area networks (SAN), network attached storage (NAS), or dual-connected SCSI.

To set up an SCC, you need the following:

▶ Two servers running Windows Server 2003, Enterprise Edition

▶ Two network interfaces per server

▶ Two shared hard drives (Logs/Databases)

▶ One local hard drive per server (OS)

Preparing the Operating System

Creating a Single Copy Cluster starts out as a standard installation of Windows Server 2003, x64 Enterprise Edition. Follow these steps to build the operating system:

1. Install Windows 2003 x64 normally.

2. Join the nodes to the domain that will host the Exchange servers.

3. Create a heartbeat network between the two nodes by addressing a NIC on a different IP space from the production network. Isolate these heartbeat NICs to an isolated VLAN or a separate network switch. This is the network that will be used by the cluster nodes to communicate with each other.

4. Install IIS on each node via the following process:

    a. Click Start, Control Panel, Add or Remove programs.

    b. Click Add/Remove Windows Components.

    c. When the menu appears, highlight Application Server, and click Details.

    d. Select Internet Information Services (IIS), and click OK.

    e. Click Next and then click Finish.

    f. Close the Add/Remove Programs interface.

5. Install the updated `msdaps.dll` for use with 64-bit Windows:

    a. Open a web browser and go to http://go.microsoft.com/fwlink/?linkid=55328.

    b. Download the update.

    c. When the security warning appears, click Run.

    d. When the second warning appears, click Run.

    e. When the Setup Wizard appears, click Next.

    f. When the license agreement appears, click I Agree, and then click Next.

    g. When the installation is completed, click Finish.

6. Install the updated `mountmgr.sys` for use with 64-bit Windows:

   a. Open a web browser and go to http://go.microsoft.com/fwlink/?linkid= 3052&kbid=898790.

   b. Download the update.

   c. Follow the installation instructions to complete the installation of the hotfix.

Configuring the Shared Storage

In the case of a two-node active/passive shared storage cluster, you need to configure several drives that will be accessible by both nodes. These would include the quorum drive, the Microsoft Distributed Transaction Coordinator (MSDTC) distributed transaction coordinator drive, the log drive, and the database drive.

You can generally accomplish this shared storage in three ways:

▶ **Network attached storage**—Usually connected to the server via Internet SCSI (iSCSI) or Virtual Logical Disk drivers

▶ **Storage area network**—Connected by Fibre Channel

▶ **Shared SCSI**—Connected via a separate SCSI controller and attached to a dual-termination enclosure

> **NOTE**
>
> If using storage area networks to attach the shared resources, be sure to zone the LUNs (virtual partitions or volumes) such that only the potential owner nodes and the disks are present in that zone. If another Windows system were to see the LUN, it might try to write its own signature to the "disk" and that would break the access from the point of view of the cluster nodes.

Creating the Cluster

Now that the nodes are prepared and the shared storage is created, the cluster can be formed. Be sure to have the following items ready for the cluster configuration:

▶ Unique names for each node

▶ Unique name for the cluster identity

▶ Unique name for the Exchange virtual server

▶ Unique IP addresses for each of the names created previously

NOTE

All the IPs listed must be from the same network range.

With these items ready, complete the following steps to create the cluster:

1. Right-click My Computer, and choose Manage.

2. Click the Disk Management icon.

3. When the Initialize and Convert Wizard appears, click Next.

4. Click Next twice to initialize but not convert the disks, which results in a screen that shows Basic disks similar to the one shown in Figure 31.3.

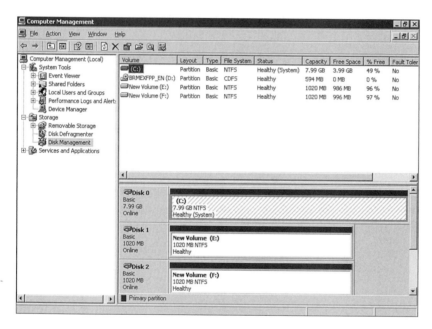

FIGURE 31.3   Shared disks as Basic disks.

NOTE

Disks made available to a cluster must be configured as Basic disks. A Windows 2003 cluster can't access a Dynamic disk.

5. Click Finish.

6. Right-click each disk that is currently not partitioned and create a partition in the size you need. Be sure to create them as primary partitions and format them as NTFS.

7. From the Start menu, click Program Files, Administrative Tools, Cluster Administrator.

8. Under Action, choose Create New Cluster, and click OK.

9. The Setup Wizard launches. Click Next.

10. Choose the domain that will host the cluster in the drop-down menu, and enter the name of the cluster. This is the name of the cluster itself and doesn't affect the Exchange virtual name. Click Next.

11. Enter the name of the first node that will participate in the cluster. Click Next.

12. The Setup Wizard analyzes the node to see if it can become a cluster node. Click Next.

13. Enter the IP address that will be used to manage the cluster. This needs to be a unique and reachable IP address. Click Next.

14. Enter the name and password of the account under which the cluster service will run. This account needs to have local Administrator rights to each node of the cluster. Click Next.

15. At the Proposed Cluster Configuration screen, click Quorum, and select the shared disk that was created to host the quorum. Click OK and then click Next.

16. When the Setup Wizard completes its tasks, click Next, and then click Finish.

Adding the Second Node

Now that the cluster has been established by the first node, you can join the second node to the cluster. To do this, perform the following steps:

1. Right-click NodeA in the left pane of the Cluster Administrator.

2. Click New and then click Node.

3. When the Setup Wizard launches, click Next.

4. Type the name of the second node, click Add, and then click Next.

5. The analysis runs to see if the node selected is a viable cluster node. When it completes, click Next.

6. Type the password of the Cluster Service Account, and click Next.

7. Review the Proposed Cluster Configuration, and if it is correct, click Next.

8. When the Add Nodes Wizard is complete, click Next, and then click Finish.

9. Close the Cluster Administrator.

Creating the Distributed Transaction Coordinator

To create the MSDTC resource, perform the following steps:

1. Click Start, Program Files, Administrative Tools, Cluster Administrator.

2. Right-click the cluster resource, choose New, and then click Resource.

3. In the New Resource dialog box, enter Microsoft Distributed Transaction Coordinator for the name, select a resource type of Distributed Transaction Coordinator, and assign it to the cluster group similar to what is shown in Figure 31.4. Click Next.

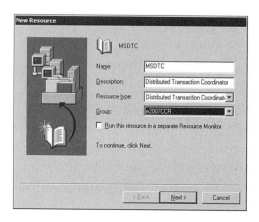

FIGURE 31.4   Creating a Distributed Transaction Coordinator.

4. Verify that all nodes are listed as potential owners, and click Next.

5. Add the storage resource that will host the Distributed Transaction Coordinator (DTC), and choose the options to add the storage resource as a dependency as well as the cluster network name. Click Next.

6. Click OK when the successful status window appears.

Installing Exchange Server 2007 on the Active Node

Now that the cluster is established and both nodes are able to control the resources, it is time to install the Exchange Server 2007 mailbox components on the cluster. This process will be broken out by node, and you will start with the node that currently owns the cluster resources. This is referred to as the active node. To install the Exchange Server 2007 Single Copy Cluster, follow these steps:

1. Insert the Exchange Server 2007 media in the CD-ROM drive.

2. Run Setup.exe.

3. Following the Exchange 2007 Installation Wizard, you are prompted to install the .NET Framework 2.0. and MMC 3.0 on the system. Follow the Setup Wizard as prompted through the installation of the .NET Framework and MMC components.

4. The installation then takes you to the Microsoft website. Click Download when prompted, and then choose Run. The files download and a security warning appears. Click Run.

5. When the Update Wizard is complete, click Next.

6. After reading and agreeing to the license agreement, click I Agree, and click Next.

7. When the update is completed, click Finish.

8. Return to the setup interface, and click Install Microsoft Command Shell.

9. Click Open when prompted. The files decompress and open a window. Double-click Msh_Setup.msi.

10. When the security warning appears, click Run.

11. When the Command Shell (x64) Setup Wizard appears, click Next.

12. After reading and agreeing to the license agreement, click I Accept the Terms in the License Agreement, and click Next.

13. Accept the default destination folder, and click Next.

14. At the Start Installation screen, click Install.

15. When the Setup Wizard completes, click Finish.

16. Return to Setup.exe and click Install Microsoft Exchange.

17. Files copy and the Exchange Server 2007 setup launches. Click Next.

18. Accept the license agreement, and click Next.

19. Leave the error reporting options set to Yes, and click Next.

20. Choose Custom Exchange Server Installation, and click Next.

21. Under Server Role Selection, choose Active Clustered Mailbox Role, as shown in Figure 31.5, and click Next.

22. Select Single Copy Cluster, and enter a name for the clustered Mailbox server. This name is different than the cluster name. This is the name that Outlook will connect to. Enter a unique IP address as well. Click Next.

23. The Setup Wizard performs a readiness check and if it passes, the role can be installed.

NOTE

In the case of Windows Server 2003, x64 Enterprise Edition SP1, you will need to install a hotfix from KB898790. This upgraded Mountmgr.sys is included in SP2.

FIGURE 31.5   Choosing server roles.

24. Click Install.

25. When the setup is completed, click Finish.

26. At the setup interface, click Get Critical Updates for Microsoft Exchange.

27. The Microsoft Update site launches. Click Express to get recommended updates.

28. Click Install Updates if any updates are available.

At this point, the installation of the first node of the Exchange Server 2007 mailbox cluster is complete. Verify that the Exchange Server 2007 services start correctly and that the virtual server is seen in the Exchange Management Console. If these services are started correctly, you can move on to installing the second node.

Installing Exchange Server 2007 on the Passive Node

With the active node installed and functioning as an Exchange Server 2007 Mailbox server, you can now install Exchange Server 2007 on the second node to complete the Single Copy Cluster. Follow these steps:

1. Insert the Exchange Server 2007 media in the CD-ROM drive.

2. Run Setup.exe.

3. Following the Exchange 2007 Installation Wizard, you are prompted to install the .NET Framework 2.0 and MMC 3.0 on the system. Follow the wizard as prompted through the installation of the .NET Framework and MMC components.

4. The installation then takes you to the Microsoft website. Click Download when prompted, and then choose Run. The files download and a security warning appears. Click Run.

5. When the Update Wizard is complete, click Next.

6. After reading and agreeing to the license agreement, click I Agree, and click Next.

7. When the update is completed, click Finish.

8. Return to the setup interface, and click Install Microsoft Command Shell.

9. Click Open when prompted. The files decompress and open a window. Double-click Msh_Setup.msi.

10. When the security warning appears, click Run.

11. When the Command Shell (x64) Setup Wizard appears, click Next.

12. After reading and agreeing to the license agreement, click I Accept the Terms in the License Agreement, and click Next.

13. Accept the default destination folder, and click Next.

14. At the Start Installation screen, click Install.

15. When the wizard completes, click Finish.

16. Return to Setup.exe and click Install Exchange Server 2007.

17. Files copy and the Exchange Server 2007 setup launches. Click Next.

18. After reviewing the license agreement, click to accept the terms, and click Next.

19. Leave the error reporting options set to Yes, and click Next.

20. Choose Custom Exchange Server Installation, and click Next.

21. Under Server Role Selection, choose Passive Clustered Mailbox Role, and click Next.

22. When the readiness checks are complete, click Install.

> **NOTE**
>
> In the case of Windows Server 2003, x64 Enterprise Edition SP1, you need to install a hotfix from KB898790. This upgraded Mountmgr.sys is included in SP2.

23. When the setup is completed, click Finish.

24. At the setup interface, click Get Critical Updates for Microsoft Exchange.

25. The Microsoft Update site launches. Click Express to get recommended updates.

26. Click Install Updates if any updates are available.

The cluster is now ready for use.

> **NOTE**
>
> It is of value to point out that the use of the terms *Active* and *Passive* in this chapter and in the setup reference the status of the two nodes at the time of cluster inception. After the cluster is established, *Active* simply refers to the node that currently owns the cluster and Exchange resources.

The default installation options place the first storage group and the associated database on the C drive. You should move these resources to the shared disks to allow correct failover of the resources.

Administrators who are familiar with clustering in Exchange 2003 will find that this process is very similar but has the advantage of not needing to manually create the System Attendant or the Exchange virtual server.

Special Considerations for SCC

A few items must be taken into consideration when preparing to use a Single Copy Cluster. The single biggest challenge for most administrators is the configuration of the storage. Important things to keep in mind are the distribution of disks and the methods of connection. For example, if an Exchange Server 2007 cluster is going to be formed using a shared SCSI enclosure, each node needs a dedicated controller for this shared storage. Any local disks for the operating system must use a different controller. A multi-channel controller does not work for this differentiation; the controllers must be physically different and the controllers for each node must use a different SCSI ID.

When it comes time to partition out the drives for the cluster, be sure to provide drives for the quorum, the Distributed Transaction Coordinator, the logs, and the databases.

If the drives are going to be partitioned on a SAN, be sure to zone the LUNs and the host bus adapters (HBAs) such that only the cluster nodes can see the drives; otherwise, you run the risk of another Windows system writing a signature to the drive and rendering it unusable by the cluster.

Other Advantages of SCC

Utilizing clustered mailboxes can provide benefits beyond just the obvious disaster recovery abilities. Having a clustered mailbox gives the administrator increased flexibility in dealing with the Mailbox servers.

Imagine a situation in which you need to take down a Mailbox server to perform maintenance or to perform an upgrade. Normally, you schedule the outage, let the user population know that mail will be unavailable during that time, and hope that they get their work done during that outage window. Meanwhile, processes and users who are dependent on the mailboxes are unable to perform their normal tasks. If, on the other hand, you could simply fail the mailbox role over to the passive node, you could perform the maintenance or upgrade on the previously active node without interrupting the Exchange services. Users and applications would still be able to access the mailboxes, and there wouldn't be a constraint around when you could do the work.

Another very common example of this is in the area of patch management. With clustered mailboxes, an administrator can patch the passive node, fail the Exchange services over to it, and then patch the remaining node. This greatly reduces the downtime associated with installing patches on Exchange Server 2007 servers.

Comparing and Contrasting CCR Versus SCC

There are a few differences between a CCR cluster and an SCC cluster that might make one a more appropriate choice for a particular environment.

One advantage that CCR brings to the table is the fact that there are two independent copies of all the logs and database. This means that in the case of a media failure, the passive node can be made active and the logs and databases are available to the end users. In the case of an SCC cluster, there is no protection against the loss of those files other than disk-level redundancy.

CCR has an advantage in the area of geographic clustering in that through log shipping, the two nodes can be located in different locations, assuming the heartbeat network can be "stretched" to appear to be the same subnet. Although a SAN-attached SCC could theoretically be geographically disparate as well, the cost of running fiber over long distances makes this a somewhat unrealistic option for most environments.

SCC has an advantage in the area of cost. Because it only requires one set of shared disks, as opposed to a mirror configuration of disks on the second node, it might be less expensive to implement an SCC cluster as opposed to a CCR cluster.

CCR has some advantages in the area of the disk technology used. Because the clustering is fed by replication, it is possible to use directly attached disks on both nodes. Locally attached disks are significantly less expensive than network or SAN-attached disks and this can make a configuration less expensive.

An SCC cluster on Windows Server 2003, x64 Enterprise Edition can scale up to 8 nodes. This can be any combination of active and passive nodes. For example, it is not unusual to see an 8-node Exchange cluster where there are 6 active nodes and 2 passive nodes and there are six virtual servers available between those nodes. In a CCR cluster, they must be configured in pairs so to get six virtual servers, you need 12 nodes.

As you can see, it is very important to understand exactly what your requirements are before deciding to use one type of cluster versus the other. Although CCR is usually more expensive when creating very large farms of Exchange servers, it has the significant benefit of providing two independent copies of the data. This means that data maintenance can be performed without taking down Exchange from the point of view of the users. This isn't possible with an SCC cluster without additional NAS- or SAN-level replication and manual interaction to point the databases and storage groups at the replica files.

Managing a Windows Server 2003 Cluster

The majority of the functions you need to access for managing the cluster are available in the Cluster Administrator snap-in. Those functions are also available from the command line, which allows clever administrators to easily automate common functions.

Managing the Cluster from the Command Line

Most any cluster management function that can be done from the graphical user interface (GUI) can be done from the command line. This can be quite useful when deploying multiple clusters because it allows you to write a batch file that contains all the necessary commands to create and configure the cluster. This is beneficial because it guarantees that the clusters will be created identically.

These commands all stem from `cluster.exe`.

For example, the command

```
Cluster /cluster:ClusterOne /create /ipaddr:10.1.1.1,255.255.255.0,publicnic
➥/pass:Password /user:Companyabc.com\Clusteracccount /node:NodeA /verb
```

creates a new cluster called ClusterOne. It assigns the IP address of 10.1.1.1 to the cluster resource with a subnet mask of 255.255.255.0. The cluster service is configured to run with the `Companyabc.com\Clusteraccount` account and the password is set to `Password`. The node is NodeA and the output of the process is logged to the cluster log.

Other useful commands are as follows:

```
Cluster /cluster:Clustername node Nodename /start
Cluster /cluster:Clustername node Nodename /stop
```

These commands can be used to start and stop the cluster service on a particular node of a given cluster. These commands can be run from any system that has the `cluster.exe` file present and where the user running it has sufficient rights to start and stop the services on the cluster.

Some more commonly used commands include the following:

```
Cluster /cluster:Clustername group Groupname /ren:NewGroupName
```

This command renames an existing group on the cluster specified:

```
Cluster /cluster:Clustername group Groupname /move:Nodename
```

This command moves the resources in a particular group on the specified cluster to the node you choose.

```
Cluster /cluster:Clustername group Groupname /on:Nodename
Cluster /cluster:Clustername group Groupname /off:Nodename
```

These commands allow an administrator to take a group offline on a given node or to bring it online. This is very useful for remote maintenance.

By combining these types of commands, a clever administrator can write simple batch scripts that will create clusters, define resources, organize the resources into groups, and even allow them to remotely move the resource groups between nodes. This enables an administrator to easily deploy Windows Server 2003, x64 Enterprise Edition clusters for use with Exchange Server 2007 without having to worry about inconsistent configurations of the clusters in the environment.

Managing the Cluster from the GUI

Some administrators feel more comfortable having a GUI for managing their applications. For this purpose, Microsoft provides the Cluster Administrator for managing Windows Server 2003, x64 Enterprise Edition clusters. This tool is accessed by clicking Start, Programs, Administrative Tools, Cluster Administrator.

This tool allows the administrator to perform all the necessary functions of managing the cluster.

Moving Resources Between Groups

To move a resource to a different group, perform these steps:

1. Open the Cluster Administrator.

2. Expand the cluster name.

3. Click Resources in the left pane, and highlight the resource you want to move in the right pane.

4. Right-click the resource in the right pane, and choose Change Group, as shown in Figure 31.6, and then choose the group to which you want to move the resource.

Creating New Resources

To create a resource for a cluster, perform these steps:

1. Open the Cluster Administrator.

2. Right-click the cluster name, choose New, and click Resource.

3. Enter the Name and Description of the resource. Choose the appropriate Resource Type in the drop-down, and choose the group that should own the resource. Click Next.

4. Verify the possible owners; add any that are missing that you want to be possible owners of the new resource. Click Next.

5. Add any dependencies that the resource needs. In most cases, the wizard tells you that you needed one when you click Next.

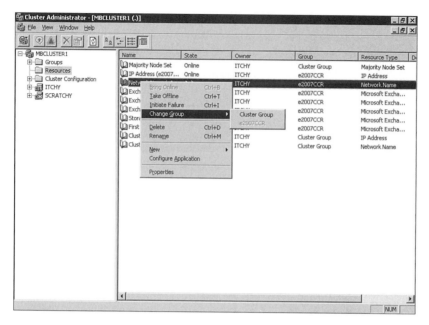

FIGURE 31.6   Moving resources.

6. Enter any additional resource-specific information (some resource types require additional dialog boxes).

7. Click Finish.

Moving Groups Between Nodes

To move a group between nodes for a cluster, perform these steps:

1. Open the Cluster Administrator.

2. Expand the cluster name.

3. Expand Groups.

4. Right-click the group you want to move, and select Move Group, as shown in Figure 31.7.

Adding New Nodes to a Cluster

To add new nodes to a cluster, perform these steps:

1. Open the Cluster Administrator.

2. Right-click the cluster name, choose New, and then click Node.

3. The Add Nodes Wizard launches. Click Next.

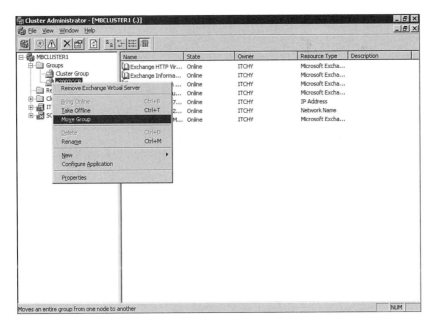

FIGURE 31.7   Moving groups between nodes.

4. Enter the name of the system that will be added to the cluster, and click Add. Click Next.

5. The Analyzing Configuration screen launches, as shown in Figure 31.8. When it completes successfully, click Next.

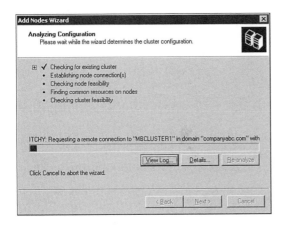

FIGURE 31.8   Analyzing the configuration.

6. When the node has been added, click Finish.

Renaming Resources

To rename a resource in a cluster, perform these steps:

1. Open the Cluster Administrator.

2. Expand the cluster name.

3. Click Resources in the left pane.

4. Right-click a resource in the right pane, and choose Rename.

5. The name of the resource can now be retyped. Type the new name of the resource, and press Enter.

Renaming Groups

To rename a group in a cluster, perform these steps:

1. Open the Cluster Administrator.

2. Expand the cluster name.

3. Expand the Groups container.

4. Right-click a group in the left pane, and select Rename.

5. The name of the group can now be retyped. Type the new name of the group, and press Enter.

Taking Resources Offline

To take a resource offline, perform these steps:

1. Open the Cluster Administrator.

2. Expand the cluster name.

3. Click Resources in the left pane.

4. Right-click a resource in the right pane, and choose Take Offline.

Backing Up the Cluster

Backing up a clustered Mailbox server pair is very similar to backing up a normal Exchange Server 2007 Mailbox server. The main thing to keep in mind is that you will be backing up the clustered mailbox name, not either of the node names, when backing up the Exchange data. The individual nodes don't necessarily need to be backed up because a restore of the cluster pair would likely use the setup /recoverserver option and, therefore, the System State would be unnecessary.

For example, if you had two CCR nodes named Itchy and Scratchy, the cluster was called ExchangeCCR, and the mailbox cluster was called E2007CCR, you would point your backup software at E2007CCR and select your storage groups to back up. Be aware that in the event of a geographically separated CCR pair, if the remote node holds the cluster resources, your backup occurs over the WAN rather than on the local server.

Load Balancing in Exchange Server 2007

Another high-availability technology provided with the Windows Server 2003 platform is Network Load Balancing (NLB). NLB clusters provide high network performance and availability by balancing client requests across several server systems. When the client load increases, Windows NLB clusters can easily be scaled out by adding more nodes to the NLB configuration, to maintain an acceptable client response time to client requests.

Using NLB offers administrators the ability to leverage two dynamic features: First, to implement Windows NLB clusters, no proprietary hardware is required and NLB clusters can be implemented and configured through Windows management interfaces fairly easily and quickly.

NLB clusters are most effectively used to provide front-end support for web applications, virus scanning, and Simple Mail Transfer Protocol (SMTP) gateways. Because they are a very effective solution when used for web application functionality, NLB technology is a very effective solution for front-end access to Exchange Outlook Web Access and terminal servers maintaining Exchange client software.

NLB clusters can grow to 32 nodes, and if larger cluster farms are necessary, the Microsoft Application Center server can be considered as an option for server platform support, along with technologies such as domain name system (DNS) round-robin to meet larger client access demands.

NLB Modes and Port Configuration Overview

In Unicast mode, clients and servers maintain a one-to-one relationship when communicating. In Multicast mode, servers respond by broadcasting a single, multicast address, which clients attach to when accessing information such as websites.

Another option when configuring NLB with Outlook Web Access is the ability to define the ports in which NLB cluster members will respond to client requests. This option is effective for the scenario because administrators can restrict and allow access to ports such as Hypertext Transfer Protocol (HTTP) port 80 and Secure Sockets Layer (SSL) port 443.

NLB Network Card Configurations

One of the first steps when configuring NLB cluster nodes is the configuration of the NICs in each server. A configuration of network cards can be completed using the NLB Manager and the TCP/IP properties of each node's network interface. One other option for configuring NICs is the command-line tool `nlb.exe`. This utility enables administrators to configure TCP/IP properties on NLB cluster nodes remotely and through the command line.

Configuring Network Load Balancing with Client Access Servers

Using the NLB Manager is the simplest method in configuring Client Access servers into a load-balanced cluster configuration. When using the Network Load Balancing Manager, all information regarding the NLB cluster and load-balancing TCP/IP addresses is added dynamically to each cluster node when configured. Using the NLB Manager also simplifies the tasks of adding and removing nodes by enabling administrators to use the NetBIOS name or TCP/IP address to identify nodes.

> **TIP**
>
> To effectively manage NLB clusters on remote servers, install and configure two NICs on the local NLB Manager system.
>
> For more information regarding Network Load Balancing services with Windows Server 2003, go to http://www.microsoft.com/windowsserver2003/default.mspx.

In the following example, NLB services will be implemented to provide support with two separate Outlook Web Access servers. This scenario assumes that each Outlook Web Access server has already been installed and configured and is functioning.

To begin, configure the network cards for each Outlook Web Access system that you plan to configure in the NLB cluster:

1. Log on to the local console of a cluster node using an account with local Administrator privileges.

2. Select Start, Control Panel, and then double-click network connections.

3. Right-click the network adapter icon for the network adapter device managing the NLB cluster interface and choose properties.

4. Choose the Network Load Balance option and click the Properties button.

5. Modify the properties by setting the binding for the appropriate cluster and dedicated IP addresses to each node's network card; use the advanced pages accessed through the General tab of the TCP/IP property page.

> **TIP**
>
> It is a good practice to rename each network card so you can easily identify it when configuring interfaces and troubleshooting problems.

After the TCP/IP properties of the network card for the two OWA servers have been configured and tested, configure the NLB cluster by accessing the NLB Manager in the Administrative Tools of the Windows 2003 server. To begin, open the NLB Manager and complete the following steps:

1. From the NLB Manager menu bar, click Cluster, and then click New.

2. Enter the cluster IP address and subnet mask of the new cluster that will be used for both OWA servers' cluster members, similar to what is shown in Figure 31.9.

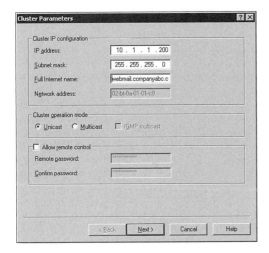

FIGURE 31.9   Creating the NLB cluster.

    a. Enter the fully qualified domain name for the cluster in the Full Internet Name text box.

    b. Choose the Cluster Operation Mode (change the default to Multicast because this is a web functional configuration).

    c. Configure a remote control password if you will be using the command-line utility (nlb.exe) to remotely manage the NLB cluster.

3. Click Next to continue.

4. Enter any additional TCP/IP addresses that will be load-balanced and click Next to continue.

5. Configure the appropriate port rules for each IP address in the cluster. For CAS services being accessed from the Internet only, click the Edit tab and configure the port range to be 443, allowing HTTPS traffic between cluster NLB servers.

6. On the Connect page, type the name of the server you want to add to the cluster in the Host text box, and click Connect. Review the server information and highlight the network interface to be used for the server; click Next to continue.

7. On the Host Parameters page, set the cluster node priority. Each node requires a unique host priority, and because this is the first node in the cluster, leave the default of 1; click Finish when you are done.

Additional CAS servers can be added to the NLB cluster by repeating these steps at any time. Validate that the state of the clustered NLB system is listed in the NLB Manager as Started, and close the Manager to complete the configuration of additional servers.

Local Continuous Replications in Exchange Server 2007

Local Continuous Replication (LCR) is another way in which Exchange Server 2007 provides improved resiliency against failure. LCR works similarly to CCR in that a secondary copy of the databases and log exist on separate storage. In the case of LCR, the secondary copy exists on the same server. This helps protect against media failures because the administrator can quickly switch over to the secondary copy of the logs and databases.

Configuring LCR

Setting up LCR is a fairly simple process and must be performed on each storage group that is to utilize LCR. To enable Local Continuous Replication on a storage group, complete the following steps:

1. Click Start, Programs, Exchange, Exchange Management Console.

2. In the left pane, expand Server Configuration.

3. Click Mailbox.

4. In the center pane, click the storage group for which you intend to enable LCR.

5. From the Action bar, click Enable Local Continuous Replication.

6. When the Setup Wizard launches, click Next.

7. Browse to the paths that will host the replica logs and system files. This should be a different disk than the original storage group location. Click Next.

8. Browse to the path that will host the replica database. This should be a disk other than the one that hosts the primary copy of the database. Click Next.

9. Review the configuration. If it is correct, click Enable.

10. When the configuration completes successfully, click Finish.

Recovering a Storage Group with LCR

In the event of a failure of either the primary database disks or the primary log disks, you can switch over to the secondary copy via the following process:

1. Verify that the corruption is not the result of an offline log drive, offline database drive, or a disk volume configuration error. If the log volume of the production

storage group is not available (and could be available) at the time of the failover, more data might be lost than necessary.

2. Assess if the data in the passive copy of the database is acceptable. Typically, the system should be able to recover with all data from the active copy of the database. Thus, the assessment should show that all necessary log files are available. If this is not the case, you should investigate why some or all log files are unavailable.

3. Disable LCR for the storage group containing the corrupt data.

4. Dismount the corrupt database. You can use the `Dismount-Database` cmdlet in the Exchange Management Shell or the Dismount shortcut menu option for the database in the Exchange Management Console.

5. If you determine the passive copy of the database is acceptable, activate it using either of the following methods:

   ▶ If you are using the NTFS file system volume mount points for your production and LCR storage group and database files, use the `Restore-StorageGroupCopy` cmdlet to copy all remaining logs and make the database mountable. Remove the existing drive letter assignments for the mount points that contain the storage group and database files. Create new drive letter assignments that point to the mount points that contain the storage group and database files. Continue to step 6.

   ▶ If you are not using NTFS file system volume mount points for your production and LCR storage group and database files, move the corrupted files to a safe location. Use the `Restore-StorageGroupCopy` cmdlet with the `ReplaceLocations` parameter to push the copy's locations into the product locations. This automatically attempts to copy the final logs. Continue to step 6.

6. Use the `Restore-StorageGroupCopy` cmdlet as follows:

```
Restore-StorageGroupCopy -Identity:<Server>\<StorageGroupName>
➡-ReplaceLocations:$true
```

7. At the confirmation prompt, type Y, and then press Enter.

8. The database can now be mounted.

9. The `Restore-StorageGroupCopy` cmdlet automatically disables LCR for the storage group. LCR must be reenabled after the recovery is complete.

Limitations of LCR

When using LCR on a storage group, that storage group is limited to a single database. This means that if you planned to use more than 20 databases, you need to either put multiple databases on a single hard drive or you need to mount the hard drives as logical mount points. By using logical mount points, you can get around the limitations on available drive letters.

To take full advantage of the redundancy offered by LCR, you must place the local replica of the logs and databases on drives other than those that host the primary copy. This way, if a drive fails, the replica data is still safe and usable.

If an Exchange Server 2007 Mailbox server is configured as a CCR cluster, it will be unable to utilize LCR for local redundancy.

Summary

As you have seen in this chapter, Microsoft has offered two new ways to increase the availability of Exchange. By duplicating the logs on the same server and maintaining a secondary copy of the databases and logs, Local Continuous Replication gives administrators a very rapid way to restore an entire database and gets its mailboxes up and running. In the past, you had to resort to running a restore to get this information back. In the case of a tape backup, this could potentially take hours, whereas the LCR backup can be restored in literally seconds. This is a huge boon to administrators who worry about the impact of Exchange downtime on their users.

Microsoft has also provided an all new method of performing replication and clustering between Exchange servers in the form of Cluster Continuous Replication. CCR not only protects the identity of the Exchange server through clustering, it protects the logs and databases by shipping the logs to the remote server each minute to ensure that the passive node has an accurate log and database that can be brought into use within minutes should the active node fail.

The method of clustering that was prevalent in Exchange 2003 is still available in the form of single copy clustering. SCC provides two nodes that can access the same copy of the Exchange Server 2007 logs and databases through shared media. SSC clusters can support up to eight nodes with any distribution of active and passive nodes.

This gives administrators unprecedented flexibility in providing maximum uptime with minimal interruptions for maintenance or upgrade tasks. Microsoft has continued to make progress in the area of resiliency and recoverability for Exchange Server 2007.

Best Practices

The following are best practices from this chapter:

- ▶ Prioritize the heartbeat NICs on the cluster nodes.

- ▶ Purchasing compatible server and network hardware is a good start to building fault-tolerant systems, but the proper configuration of this hardware is equally important.

- ▶ Create disk subsystem redundancy using hardware-based RAID technologies.

- ▶ Always plan for a sufficient amount of TCP/IP addresses in advance to support current and future cluster needs.

▶ Do not run both clustering and NLB on the same computer; it is unsupported by Microsoft because of potential hardware-sharing conflicts between MSCS and NLB.

▶ Active/Passive mode is easiest to manage and maintain, and the licensing costs are generally lower.

▶ To avoid unwanted failover, power management should be disabled on each of the cluster nodes, both in the motherboard BIOS and in the power applet in Control Panel.

▶ Carefully choose whether to use a shared disk or a nonshared approach to clustering.

▶ Use the same type of card and driver when implementing multiple network cards in each node. This helps to ensure that one card can be dedicated to internal cluster communication and each functions properly.

▶ To avoid unplanned interruptions in service, disable the ability for the cluster to failback automatically.

▶ Thoroughly test failover and failback mechanisms after the configuration is complete and before adding mailboxes and public folders to a clustered Exchange Server 2007 Mailbox server.

▶ Do not change the cluster service account password using the Active Directory Users and Computers tool or the Windows security box if logged on with the same account.

▶ Perform backups periodically and immediately following any hardware changes to a cluster node, including changes on a shared storage device or local disk configuration.

▶ When possible, on internal network devices, create a port rule that allows only specific ports to the clustered IP address, and an additional rule blocking all other ports and ranges.

CHAPTER 32

Backing Up the Exchange Server 2007 Environment

Although the key to implementing technologies is to install the software in a production environment, making sure the new technology environment is being properly backed up is just as important for the organization. This chapter covers the proper planning, implementing, testing, and support of a properly backed-up environment. Organizations should spend as much time planning and implementing their backup processes as they do implementing the core environment. This will ensure that if there are any problems with the systems, servers, and sites, that a successful recovery process can be initiated.

Understanding the Importance of Backups

Through various improvements and changes in the JET database engine and storage, Microsoft Exchange Server 2007 offers the most stable and resilient database of any Exchange implementation to date. The database is able to recover from dirty shutdowns, hardware failures, and power outages. The database allows both users and administrators to recover recently deleted items. However, even with all of this functionality, it is still necessary to perform backups of the Exchange server.

Traditionally, backups are performed and maintained for three primary purposes:

▶ Recovering deleted items past the retention period

▶ Offline extraction of messages

▶ Disaster recovery

To be able to support these functions, it is critical to not only perform the regular backups, but to also understand what it is you are backing up, how often you are backing it up, and exactly what recovery scenarios you can support.

The goal of this chapter is to show an administrator how to do the following:

- ▶ Evaluate their needs for backup

- ▶ Capture all the necessary information for disaster recovery

- ▶ Properly document their environment

- ▶ Determine a reasonable service level agreement (SLA)

- ▶ Design their backup strategy to support that SLA

- ▶ Build policies and procedures around backup processes

- ▶ Determine what data to back up

- ▶ How to take advantage of new backup technologies available in Exchange 2007

The process of restoring data within Exchange 2007 is covered in Chapter 33, "Recovering from a Disaster in an Exchange Server 2007 Environment."

> **NOTE**
>
> The backup processes in this chapter focus on the use of NTBackup, the built-in backup utility provided with Windows Server 2003. The installation of Exchange 2007 includes updates to NTBackup to allow it to properly back up Exchange 2007. If you plan to use a third-party backup application, be sure that it supports Exchange 2007, or you could get undesired results!

Establishing Service Level Agreements

The most common question from Exchange administrators is "How should I be doing my backups?" The answer to this question is quite simple. You should be doing them such that they support your service level agreements around recoverability for Exchange services.

Based on this concept, it quickly becomes apparent that the first step in planning out your backups is to determine exactly what you've committed yourself to. This is commonly referred to as a service level agreement or simply an SLA.

Establishing a Service Level Agreement for Each Critical Service

Exchange 2007 is often deployed such that roles are distributed across multiple servers. This distribution of roles might vary from site to site. However, the SLAs will likely remain constant across the enterprise.

It is important to understand the implication of SLAs for each aspect of Exchange 2007 as the SLA drives your design and must be considered up front and not as an afterthought to a deployed Exchange 2007 environment.

Determining SLAs for Mailbox Servers

One of the most important aspects of Exchange 2007 is the Mailbox server. If the Mailbox server isn't up, users can't access their mail. This is usually the first thing that triggers the help desk phone to ring. Most companies start their SLAs around the Mailbox servers. In most environments, a 2-hour recovery for a mailbox database is acceptable. This means that if your database fails, you need to be able to recover that data within 2 hours. If you know that your system is capable of restoring 10GB of data per hour, you know that, based on your backup process, you can only support 20GB per database.

If your SLA for an entire Mailbox server recovery is 4 hours and you know that it takes 2 hours to rebuild a new server with Exchange 2007, then you only have 2 hours to restore data, which, based on the preceding example, means you can only have 40GB of data on the server. If you had planned to allow users 200MB of storage each, this limits the server to 100 users. If you wanted to support more users per server, you either have to alter the SLA or you have to change your backup strategy to allow you to restore more data in the same period of time. This is what allows you to safely support large numbers of users with good SLAs. This is where you have to balance the costs of the backup/restore system with the cost of adding additional servers.

Determining SLAs for Client Access Servers

Another major component of Exchange 2007 is the Client Access server (CAS). These are the systems that allow mobile devices and web browsers to access users' email. When determining SLAs for this function, it is helpful to view the service and the servers as two entities. Although you likely want very high availability on the service, you can likely worry less about the servers individually if they are designed with redundancy in mind. So, if you have two or more CASs, you have plenty of time to rebuild one server if it fails because there is already another that is taking up the load. Keep this in mind when designing your Exchange environment. Also keep in mind that the data on a CAS is mostly static. Building a new CAS might be faster than restoring an existing one.

Determining SLAs for Edge Transport Servers

For systems like the Edge Transport servers in Exchange 2007, it is more useful to view the SLA for this role as being for the service as opposed to the servers themselves. In the case of Edge Transport servers, the service they provide is sending and receiving external email to and from the Internet. In this sense, most companies try to enforce a fairly aggressive SLA on the service itself. For example, if Internet mail connectivity were to fail, they'd want the service restored within an hour or two. In most environments, this is fairly easy to accomplish because there is typically two or more Edge Transport servers to provide redundancy and minimize wide area network (WAN) traffic. In the case of the SLAs on the servers themselves, typically a 1-day recovery is acceptable. Because the Edge Transport servers don't hold any unique data, they can easily be replaced in the event of a failure.

Determining SLAs for Hub Transport Servers

The role of the Hub Transport server is to transfer mail from one site to another connected site. As such, when a Hub Transport server fails, the site it served is effectively cut off from other sites. As such, a company would most likely want a fairly aggressive SLA on the Hub Transport servers. In most environments, the Hub Transport server role is combined with other roles because, in most cases, it won't justify being on an isolated server. As such, the SLA for recovery is often overwritten by the SLA for another role that it supports. As such, it is recommended that, when possible, two or more systems per site should host the Hub Transport server role.

Supporting Backups with Documentation

Performing trustworthy backups is a critical process in any Exchange environment. One of the simplest ways to ensure that your backups are being done properly is to document your requirements and your processes.

A mechanism needs to be in place to track the success of backups and a process to follow if a backup fails. Sticking to this process and not conflicting with the set policies ensures that backups are valid and recoverable in the event of a failure.

Documenting Backup Policy and Procedures

When building your documentation around your backups, it is best to start with a policy that will support not only the SLAs for your Exchange environment but one that complies with any existing rules from your Information Security group or Regulatory Compliance group.

Management should review and approve your backup policies to ensure that they are in line with any established SLAs. Policies should include items such as the following:

▶ Frequency and type of backups

▶ Acceptable standards for offsite storage and retrieval

▶ Escalation path for failed backups

▶ Decision criteria for overrun jobs

▶ Clear statement of what is and isn't backed up

▶ Whether the backups are password protected

▶ Data retention periods

In this way, everyone knows what is and isn't covered by Exchange backups and there are no surprises in the future. Having this policy documented is also very helpful if you are required to pass any audits or verify regulatory compliance.

Maintaining Documentation on the Exchange Environment

Systems like Exchange often outlast the employees who built them. This means that it's easy to lose track of exactly how systems are deployed, where various roles are located, and the specific needs of each participating system. For this reason, it is very important to maintain accurate documentation regarding the server configurations, the network, and the path of mail flow. In addition, it is also important to track the configuration of firewalls and switches that could potentially impact the overall Exchange environment if they were to fail and need to be replaced.

Server Configuration Documentation

Server documentation is essential for any environment regardless of size, number of servers, or disaster recovery budget. A server configuration document contains a server's name, network configuration information, hardware and driver information, disk and volume configuration, or information about the applications installed. This complete server configuration document contains all the necessary configuration information a qualified administrator would need if the server needed to be restored and the operating system could not be restored efficiently. A server configuration document can also be used as a reference when server information needs to be collected.

> **TIP**
>
> To assist with gathering information, administrators can use the WINMSD tool to collect server data and configuration information to assist in producing server build documents. In the Run dialog box, type winmsd in the Open text box, and click OK to view the Systems Information screen in Windows Server 2003.

The Server Build Document

A server build document contains step-by-step instructions on how to build a particular type of server for an organization. The details of this document should be tailored to the skill of the person intended to rebuild the server. For example, if this document was created for disaster recovery purposes, it might be detailed enough that anyone with basic computer skills could rebuild the server. This type of information could also be used to help information technology (IT) staff follow a particular server build process to ensure that when new servers are added to the network, they all meet company server standards.

Hardware Inventory

Documenting the hardware inventory of an entire network might not be necessary. If the entire network does need to be inventoried, and if the organization is large, the Microsoft Systems Management Server can help automate the hardware inventory task. If the entire network does not need to be inventoried, hardware inventory can be collected for all the production and lab servers and networking hardware, including specifications such as serial numbers, amount of memory, disk space, processor speed, and operating system platform and version.

Network Configurations

Network configuration documentation is essential when network outages occur. Current, accurate network configuration documentation and network diagrams can help simplify and isolate network troubleshooting when a failure occurs.

WAN Connection

WAN connectivity should be documented for enterprise networks that contain many sites to help IT staff understand the enterprise network topology. This document is very helpful when a server is restored and data should be synchronized enterprisewide after the restore. Knowing the link performance between sites helps administrators understand how long an update made in Site A will take to reach Site B. This document should contain information about each WAN link, including circuit numbers, Internet service provider (ISP) contact names, ISP technical support phone numbers, and the network configuration on each end of the connection, and can be used to troubleshoot and isolate WAN connectivity issues.

Router, Switch, and Firewall Configurations

Firewalls, routers, and, sometimes, switches can run proprietary operating systems with a configuration that is exclusive to the device. During a system recovery, certain gateway connections, configuration routing information, routing table data, and other information might need to be reset on the restored server. Information should be collected from these devices, including logon passwords and current configurations. When a configuration change is planned for any of these devices, the newly proposed configuration should be created using a text or graphical editor, but the change should be approved before it is made on the production device. A rollback plan should be created first to ensure that the device can be restored to the original state if the change does not deliver the desired results.

Updating Documentation

One of the most important, yet sometimes overlooked, areas around documentation is maintaining their accuracy as changes are applied to server systems. Documentation is tedious, but outdated documentation can be worthless if changes have occurred to a server's software configuration since the document was created. For example, if a server configuration document was used to re-create a server from scratch but many changes were applied to the server after the document was created, the correct security patches might not be applied, applications might be configured incorrectly, or data restore attempts could be unsuccessful. Whenever a change will be made to a network device, printer, or server, documentation outlining the previous configuration, proposed changes, and rollback plan should be created before the change is approved and carried out on the production device. After the change is carried out and the device is functioning as desired, the documentation associated with that device or server should be updated.

Logging Daily Backup Results and Evaluation

When running regular backups of mission-critical systems, it is important to monitor the process to ensure that backup jobs are running properly. It is equally important to ensure that the data being backed up can actually be restored.

Tracking Success and Failure

32

Most third-party backup software packages have the ability to send a summary of the result of the backup job to the administrator. This is a critical function because failures or inconsistent results need to be immediately brought to the attention of the administrator who is responsible for backups.

The results of these nightly backups should be reviewed each day to ensure not only the success of the backup process, but also to sanity check the results. For example, if your backup normally ran for 6 hours and filled up 80GB of space, you should be suspicious of a 16-hour job of the same size or a 1-hour job that only backed up 12GB of data. Because either of those results could show up as a successful run of the backup job, it is critical for an administrator to review the results.

In the case of NTBackup, the built-in backup utility included in Windows, the ability to get the results of the backup job is fairly limited. Luckily, this information is posted into the event log of the server and can be easily checked each morning.

The status of the backup will appear as an event 8019.

Validating Your Backups

The benefit of backing up data to a remote location or media is the ability to recover the data at a later time. As such, it is very important to regularly validate that your backups are valid and can be successfully restored. It is recommended that you adopt a practice of randomly pulling backups and picking random directories and files and performing a restore to a nonproduction location. After the restore, verify that you can access the data successfully. This process helps ensure that your data can be restored in the event of an emergency. For more information on restoring Exchange data specifically, see Chapter 33.

Roles and Responsibilities

With any process that is likely to include more than one person, it is useful to clearly define the roles and responsibilities of those people. This ensures that the people involved know what is expected of them and they know who to go to in various situations.

Separation of Duties

A typical Exchange environment involves members from potentially many groups. For example, one group might be responsible for Exchange services and configuration, whereas another group might be tasked with management of Windows and security patches. Often, yet another group is responsible for performing backups of the systems. It is very important for each of these groups to be aware of what other groups are doing. For example, if the Windows group needed to install Windows patches on the Exchange servers, the backup group would also need to be aware of this because they might need to change the scheduling of the backup job. This type of interdependency must be taken into account when configuring the backup schedule.

Escalation and Notification

If a backup job fails, it is critical for the support staff to know what they are supposed to do and who they should contact. It is recommended to build a matrix of common issues and create an escalation path for various events. It is also quite useful to have those events automatically notify the responsible party. For example, the server monitoring group might be told that in the event of a backup failure, they should do the following:

▶ Contact the backup group to alert them of the failed job.

▶ Contact the Exchange group to alert them of the failed job.

▶ If neither group contacts you within 30 minutes, contact the IT manager.

▶ If the IT manager doesn't contact you within 60 minutes, contact the IT director.

By knowing who to call, it is easier to get a qualified party to look at the issue and potentially fix the issue in time to allow another backup job to be attempted before the backup window is expired.

Developing a Backup Strategy

Developing an effective backup strategy involves detailed planning around the logistics of backing up the necessary information or data via backup software, media type, and accurate documentation. To truly be effective, organizations should not limit a backup strategy by not considering the use of all available resources for recovery.

Along with planning and documentation, other aspects of a backup strategy include assigning specific tasks and responsibilities to individual IT staff members, considering the best person to be responsible for backing up a particular service or server and ensuring that documentation is accurate and current depending on their strengths and area of expertise.

What Is Important to Exchange Backups?

In general, the critical thing to capture in an Exchange backup is any unique data whose loss would impact users. This typically means that you need to back up the mailbox databases, public folder databases, and the log files that go with them. Files such as the operating system itself or the System State data are less important. As you'll find out in Chapter 33, this information can be easily recovered because it is stored in Active Directory (AD).

Creating Standard Backup Procedures

Creating a regular backup procedure helps ensure that the entire enterprise is backed up consistently and properly on a regular basis. When a regular procedure is created, the assigned staff members soon become accustomed to the procedure because they are given a guide that walks through each required step. If there is no documented procedure, certain items might be overlooked and not be backed up, which can be a major problem if a failure occurs. For example, a regular backup procedure for an Exchange 2007 server might back up the Exchange databases on the local drives every night, and perform an Automated System Recovery (ASR) backup once a month and whenever a hardware change is made to a server. These differences might be overlooked if no one is following regular change control and documented procedures.

> **TIP**
>
> It is a best practice to add documentation updates into standard server change control processes. This ensures that any modifications to server configurations also get added into server build documents.

Protecting Data in the Event of a System Failure

Server failures are the primary concern most organizations plan for, because a complete system failure creates the most impact and, ultimately, a scenario where data needs to be restored from backup tape. Server hardware failures include failed motherboards, processors, memory, network interface cards, disk controllers, power supplies, and, of course, hard disks. Each of these failures can be minimized through the implementation of RAID-configured hard disk drives, error correcting memory, redundant power supplies, or redundant controller adapters. In a catastrophic system failure, however, it is likely that the entire data backup would have to be restored to a new system or repaired server.

Because data is read and written to hard drives on a constant basis, hard drives are frequently singled out as the most possible cause of a server hardware failure. To address this, Windows Server 2003 supports hot-swappable hard drives and RAID storage systems, allowing for the replacement of the drive without server downtime. However, this is only if the server chassis and disk controllers support such a change. Windows Server 2003 supports two types of disks: Basic disks, which provide backward compatibility, and Dynamic disks, which enable software-level disk arrays to be configured without a separate disk controller. Both Basic and Dynamic disks, when used as data disks, can be moved to other servers easily. This provides data or disk capacity elsewhere if a system hardware failure occurs and the data on these disks needs to be made available as soon as possible.

> **NOTE**
>
> If hardware-level RAID is configured, the controller card configuration should be backed up using a utility available through the vendor.
>
> With most array controllers today, dynamic reading of the disk configuration can be done as long as the disks are placed into a new system using the same disk order. If

this is not supported, the controller can be moved to the new systems or the configuration might need to be re-created from scratch to complete a successful disk move to a new machine.

This process should always be tested, verified, and documented in a lab environment before being considered as a valid recovery option.

To protect against a system failure, organizations need to have a full image backup that can then be restored in its entirety to a new or repaired server system. This also requires completing and documenting these steps in advance to ensure that it can be completed and administrators understand the steps involved.

Protecting Data in the Event of a Database Corruption

Data recovery also is needed in the event of a database corruption in Exchange. Unlike a catastrophic system failure, which can be restored from the last tape backup, data corruption creates a more challenging situation for information recovery. If data is corrupt on the server system, a restore from the last backup might also contain corrupt information in its database, so a data restore needs to predate the point of corruption. This typically requires the ability to restore the database from an older full backup tape and then recover incremental data since the clean database restoral.

Providing the Ability to Restore a Message, Folder, or Mailbox

In other situations, an organization might need to recover a single message, folder, or mailbox rather than a full database. With most full backups of an Exchange server, the restore process requires a full restore of all messages, folders, and mailboxes. If an administrator has to work with only a full image backup, typically a full restore must be performed on a spare server and information extracted from the full restore as necessary.

If message, folder, or mailbox recovery is required on a regular basis, the organization might elect to back up information in a format or process that provides an easier method of information recovery. This might involve the purchase and use of a third-party tape backup system, or a combination of various utilities available in Exchange 2007 to restore individual sets of information.

Assigning Tasks and Designating Team Members

Each particular server or network device in the enterprise has specific requirements for backing up and creating documentation around hardware and the service it provides. To make sure that a critical system is being backed up properly, IT staff should designate a single individual to monitor that device and ensure the backup is completed and documentation is accurate and current at all times. Assigning a secondary staff member who has the same set of skills to act as a backup if the primary staff member is unavailable is a wise decision, to ensure that there is no point of failure among IT staff performing these tasks.

Assigning only primary and secondary resources to specific devices or services helps improve the overall security and reliability of the device and services provided to network users. By limiting who can back up and restore data—and even who can manage servers and devices—to just the primary and secondary qualified staff members, the organization can rest assured that only competent, trained individuals are working on systems they are assigned to manage. Even though the backup and restore responsibilities lie with the primary and secondary resources, the backup and recovery plans should still be documented and available to the remaining IT staff for additional training and a final means of support if needed.

Selecting the Best Devices for Your Backup

Each device used on any network could have specific backup requirements. As mentioned earlier, each assigned IT staff member should also be responsible for researching and learning the backup and recovery requirements of each device to ensure that all backups will have everything that is necessary to also recover from a device failure.

As a rule of thumb for network devices, the device configuration should be backed up whenever possible—using the device manufacturer's configuration software whenever possible or just by documenting the configuration for use as a reference should a device require reconfiguration.

> **TIP**
>
> It is also a best practice to evaluate the hardware used in your environment to determine which areas might be the most likely points of failure. Having spare devices can reduce the overall downtime in case of a failure. When dealing with Exchange 2007 considerations, these spare hardware devices can be pieces such as hard drives to support a failed drive in a RAID configuration.

Understanding How Devices Affect Backups

Depending on how a given environment is architected, there might be several different options on how it will be backed up. Administrators lucky enough to have network attached storage (NAS) or storage area networks (SANs) for their Exchange 2007 servers might have significantly faster options for performing backups than administrators who are using direct attached storage (DAS). Many times, the NAS or SAN devices are able to perform local snapshots, or the SAN might be able to be backed up by a tape device that is plugged directly into the Fibre Channel fabric. This has great advantages when compared to backing up an Exchange 2007 server over the network. For example, Gigabit Ethernet allows for 1Gb/sec of throughput. Fibre Channel not only offers speeds of 4Gb/sec, but is also a more efficient protocol.

Determining Backup Speeds and Times

The time needed to perform a backup of Exchange 2007 is influenced mostly by the speed of the backup device itself. Although vendors quote values for MB per minute that their device can backup, this isn't always an accurate value when backing up an Exchange 2007 server. It is always recommended to perform test backups of Exchange servers to determine the speed at which they can be backed up. By knowing how long jobs will take, an administrator can better select the backup window in which the backups will occur. As Exchange servers grow in terms of the storage used by mail data, the backups take longer to occur. Pay careful attention to the network utilization and to the backup device utilization so that you can watch for bottlenecks that cause backup jobs to take too long.

TIP

Consider backing up Exchange 2007 to a backup server that is using disks as the media for the backup. This is typically the fastest media that you will be able to utilize for "over the network" backups. Then take the locally stored backup and back that up to tape. Because you are backing up "cold" data, there is no concern about performing the backup during the day. This allows you to keep your backup window relatively short. The side benefit is that if you ever experience a failure that requires you to restore from the backups, you'll be doing a disk-to-disk restore, which is much faster than a tape-to-disk restore.

Validating the Backup Strategy in a Test Lab

Regardless of what methodology you choose for backups of your Exchange 2007 environment, it is critical to test the processes in a lab environment. The goal of this validation is not only to prove that data can be backed up and restored, but also to refine and document the exact steps used. It is much easier to figure out how to perform a restore in the lab than it is in production when hundreds or thousands of mailbox users are down. The goal of a production restore is to be able to follow accurate, validated instructions and not have to figure out what you need to do on the fly.

What to Back Up on Exchange Servers

With the various roles available on Exchange servers, the process of backing them up is no longer a one-size-fits-all proposition. Different Exchange 2007 roles have different needs and different options on what to back up and how to back it up. This section highlights the needs of the various Exchange roles.

What to Back Up on Mailbox Servers

When planning backups for an Exchange server, you must first determine the critical data that is stored on that particular system. For a Mailbox server, the critical data present is as follows:

- Exchange database files—mailboxes
- Exchange database files—public folders
- Exchange transaction log files
- Full-text indexing information
- Free/busy information
- Offline Address Book

Of these items, the index information, the free/busy information, and the Offline Address Book can all be regenerated so they do not need to be backed up. This leaves the databases and the transaction logs. If you are using a certified Exchange 2007–compatible backup software product, you will always back up the databases and the log files as logical devices.

If you should ever need to back up the databases or log files at a flat-file level, be sure to stop all the Exchange services. These files can be found by running the Exchange Management Shell and typing the following:

```
Get-storagegroup –server <server_name> | fl name,systemfolderpath,logfolderpath
```

To back up the databases and log files while the server is online via NTBackup, follow these steps:

1. At the Run line, type ntbackup and press Enter.

2. When the Backup Wizard launches, click Next.

3. Choose Back Up Files and Settings, and then click Next.

4. Choose Let Me Choose What to Back Up, and then click Next.

5. In the left pane, expand Microsoft Exchange Server.

6. Expand the server you want to back up, and an Items to Back Up dialog box opens, similar to the one shown in Figure 32.1.

7. Check the Microsoft Information Store check box to back up all mailbox databases and the associated log files. If you only want to back up specific databases, you can be more granular.

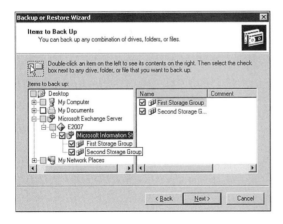

FIGURE 32.1   Selecting items to back up.

8. Click Next.

9. Choose the location and name of the backup file, and click Next. You might have to browse to the location where you want to store the backup.

10. Review the settings chosen for the backup, and click Finish.

Before clicking Finish, you can access advanced options by clicking Advanced:

1. Choose the type of backup. A Normal backup truncates the log files after the backup. Click Next.

2. Choose whether to verify the backup. This takes nearly as long as the backup itself. Click Next.

3. Choose to append or replace any existing backups. Click Next.

4. If you want to run the job later, you can schedule the job for another time. Click Next.

5. Click Finish and the job will run.

It is highly recommended to back up the databases and log files nightly. By performing full backups, the log files that have already been committed to the databases will be removed. This prevents the log drive from becoming full. If the log drives fill to capacity, the Exchange 2007 services will shut down.

What to Back Up on Hub Transport Servers

When planning for backups on a Hub Transport server, the critical data located on this role includes the following:

▶ Message tracking logs

▶ Protocol logs

The logs contained on the Hub Transport server are not critical for a restore of an Exchange 2007 environment; however, these logs might be useful for troubleshooting or for forensics and can be backed up at a file level. The logs are located below the directory where Exchange was installed in \Transportroles\logs

To back up these files using NTBackup, follow these steps:

1. At the Run line, type ntbackup and press Enter.

2. When the Backup Wizard launches, click Next.

3. Choose Back Up Files and Settings, and then click Next.

4. Choose Let Me Choose What to Back Up, and then click Next.

5. In the left pane, expand My Computer and then the drive containing the installation of Exchange, and navigate to `\transportroles` and check the Logs check box, as shown in Figure 32.2.

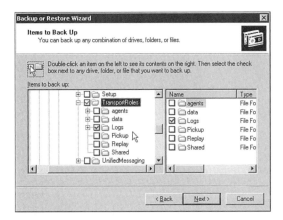

FIGURE 32.2   Selecting the log files for backup.

6. Click Next.

7. Choose the location and name of the backup file, and click Next. You might have to browse to the location where you want to store the backup.

8. Review the settings chosen for the backup, and click Finish.

What to Back Up on Client Access Servers

Generally speaking, there is no need to back up the CAS. This is because the CAS merely acts as a pass-through to get to Exchange data. This was also the case in previous versions of Exchange. Typically, multiple CAS servers are deployed for redundancy so rapid restoration is rarely needed. Typically, if a CAS server fails, it would be rebuilt from scratch and would not need any data restored to it.

If there is only a single CAS server in the environment, it might be worthwhile to back up the POP/IMAP configuration stored in `\ClientAccess\PopImap`. Optionally, you could just document the Post Office Protocol (POP) and Internet Message Access Protocol (IMAP) settings and reset them if a CAS were rebuilt.

What to Back Up on Edge Transport Servers

When backing up the Edge Transport server, the following unique data should be captured:

▶ Protocol logs

To back up the protocol logs, follow the steps given for Hub Transport servers in the previous section.

What to Back Up on Unified Messaging Servers

When planning for backups on a Unified Messaging server, the critical data located on this role includes the following:

▶ Custom audio prompts

This information is stored under the Exchange file structure in `\UnifiedMessaging\Prompts` and is only needed on the prompt publishing server. Not unlike a CAS server, its configuration is stored in AD and it acts as a pass-through to the `.wav` files stored in the users' mailboxes.

To back up the prompts directory via NTBackup, perform the following:

1. At the Run line, type ntbackup and press Enter.

2. When the Backup Wizard launches, click Next.

3. Choose Back Up Files and Settings, and then click Next.

4. Choose Let Me Choose What to Back Up, and then click Next.

5. In the left pane, expand My Computer and then the drive containing the installation of Exchange, and navigate to `\UnifiedMessaging` and check the Prompts check box, as shown in Figure 32.3.

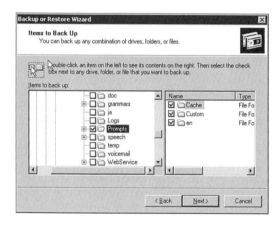

FIGURE 32.3   Selecting voice mail prompts to back up.

6. Click Next.

7. Choose the location and name of the backup file, and then click Next. You might have to browse to the location where you want to store the backup.

8. Review the settings chosen for the backup, and click Finish.

Directory Server Data

As was the case with the previous version of Exchange, Exchange 2007 stores the vast majority of its configuration information in Active Directory. This allows Exchange 2007 servers to easily read the configurations of other systems in the environment and it provides an easy mechanism to restore the configuration of a rebuilt server. For this reason, it is critical to ensure that at least one domain controller in the root of the forest is being backed up regularly.

To back up a domain controller, run the following from the domain controller:

1. At the Run line, type ntbackup and press Enter.

2. When the Backup Wizard launches, click Next.

3. Choose Back Up Files and Settings, and then click Next.

4. Choose Let Me Choose What to Back Up, and then click Next.

5. In the left pane, expand My Computer and then check the System State check box, as shown in Figure 32.4.

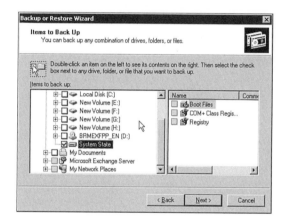

FIGURE 32.4   Selecting items to back up.

6. Click Next.

7. Choose the location and name of the backup file, and click Next. You might have to browse to the location where you want to store the backup.

8. Review the settings chosen for the backup, and click Finish.

Common Settings and Configuration Data

Be aware of any additional dependencies that would need to be backed up to fully restore the Exchange environment. This could include things such as the following:

- ▶ SSL certificates

- ▶ S/MIME certificates

- ▶ IIS metabase

- ▶ Custom Outlook Web Access pages

- ▶ Third-party applications

Leveraging Local Continuous Replication

Exchange 2007 has introduced a new concept in backups for the storage groups. This concept is called Local Continuous Replication (LCR). The goal of LCR is to provide a single-server implementation of log shipping to establish a second set of mail databases located on separate disks. The advantage of this is that the local server has an up-to-date copy of the database that can be used in the event of a disk failure on the primary databases.

> **NOTE**
>
> When utilizing LCR, you might notice that your backup behavior is slightly different than what you are accustomed to. The log files might not truncate as completely as you expect. This is because the LCR mechanism prevents logs from being deleted until they have been committed to the secondary database as well.

To enable LCR on a storage group, complete the following steps:

1. Click Start, Programs, Exchange, Exchange Management Console.

2. In the left pane, expand Server Configuration.

3. Click Mailbox.

4. In the center pane, click the storage group for which you intend to enable LCR.

5. From the Action bar, click Enable Local Continuous Replication.

6. When the Setup Wizard launches, click Next.

7. Browse to the paths that will host the replica logs and system files. This should be a different disk than the original storage group location. Click Next.

8. Browse to the path that will host the replica database. This should be a disk other than the one that hosts the primary copy of the database. Click Next.

9. Review the configuration, as shown in Figure 32.5. If it is correct, click Enable.

10. When the configuration completes successfully, click Finish.

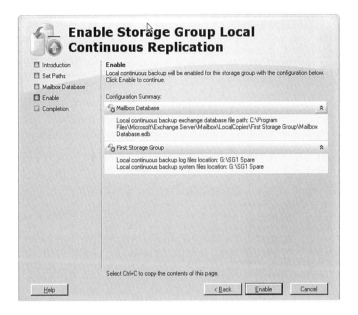

FIGURE 32.5   Reviewing the LCR configuration.

TIP

When enabling LCR, be sure that the Information Store service is started and the databases are mounted or the seeding of the replica will fail.

After you have enabled your local backup, you can verify the success of the configuration by looking in the directory where you placed the replica database. You will find a file called `seeder.txt`. Open the file and search for "was seeded successfully" to ensure that your storage group was seeded properly.

Introducing Cluster Continuous Replication

Another new feature available in Exchange 2007 is Cluster Continuous Replication (CCR). The concept with CCR is to be able to maintain a second Exchange server with the same data as the primary Exchange server. This allows an administrator to run an Exchange 2007 cluster without having to utilize shared storage. This means that the secondary node can be located at a different physical location to provide for easy failover if a major site catastrophe should occur. CCR utilizes log shipping to allow the second server to process the same transactions that are performed on the primary copy. This functionality is described in depth in Chapter 31, "Continuous Backups, Clustering, and Network Load Balancing in Exchange Server 2007."

Using and Understanding the Windows Backup Utility (`Ntbackup.exe`)

Windows Server 2003 includes several tools and services to back up and archive user data, but when it comes to backing up the entire operating system and disk volumes, Windows Server 2003 Backup is the program to use. Windows Server 2003 Backup is included on all the different versions of the Windows platform. Some Windows Server 2003 services provide alternative backup utilities, but they still can be backed up using `Ntbackup.exe`.

Windows Server 2003 Backup provides all the necessary functions to completely back up and restore a single file or the entire Windows Server 2003 system. Third-party, or even other Microsoft, applications installed on a Windows 2003 server system should be researched to ensure that no special backup requirements or add-ons are necessary to back up the application data and configuration.

Windows Server 2003 Backup is capable of many types of backups; however, it is primarily used to back up the local server, but can also be used to back up remote server volumes. Although, in the case of backing up remote server volumes, open files are always skipped. Another limitation is that System State can only be backed up from the local server.

Modes of Operation

The Windows Backup utility can run in two separate modes: Wizard and Advanced. Wizard mode provides a simple interface that enables a backup to be created in just a few easy steps:

1. Choose to back up or restore files and settings.

2. Choose to back up everything or specify what to back up.

3. Choose what data to back up only if you do not choose the option to back up everything.

4. Specify the backup media, tape, or file.

That is all it takes to use Wizard mode, but features such as creating a scheduled backup or choosing to use Volume Shadow Copy Service can be performed only using Advanced mode.

Advanced mode provides greater granularity when it comes to scheduling and controlling backup media security and other backup options. In the following sections concerning Windows Server 2003 Backup, you use Advanced mode.

Using the Windows Backup Advanced Mode

Running the Windows Server 2003 Backup utility in Advanced mode enables administrators to configure all the available options for backups including using Volume Shadow Copy Service (VSS). Scheduled backups can be created; specific wizards can be started; and advanced backup options can be configured, such as verifying backup, using volume shadow copies, backing up data in remote storage, and automatically backing up system-protected files.

To create a backup in Advanced mode, use the following steps:

1. Click Start, All Programs, Accessories, System Tools, Backup.

2. If this is the first time you've run Backup, it opens in Wizard mode. Choose to run it in Advanced mode by clicking the Advanced Mode hyperlink.

3. Click the Backup Wizard (Advanced) button to start the Backup Wizard.

4. Click Next on the Backup Wizard welcome screen to continue.

5. On the What to Back Up page, select Back Up Selected Files, Drives, or Network Data, and click Next to continue.

6. On the Items to Back Up page, expand Desktop, My Computer in the left pane, choose each of the local drives and the System State, and then click Next to continue.

7. Choose your backup media type and choose the correct media tape or file. If you're creating a new file, specify the complete path to the file, and the backup will create the file automatically. Click Next to continue.

8. If the file you specified resides on a network drive, click OK at the warning message to continue.

9. If you chose tape for the backup, choose the media for the backup and choose to use a new tape.

10. Click the Advanced button on the Completing the Backup Wizard page to configure advanced options.

11. Choose the backup type and choose whether to back up migrated remote storage data. The default settings on this page will fit most backups, so click Next to continue.

12. Choose whether a verify operation will be run on the backup media and click Next. Disabling Volume Shadow Copy would be an option if a backup were just backing up local volumes, not the System State.

13. Choose the Media Overwrite option of appending or replacing the data on the media, and click Next.

14. On the When to Back Up page, choose to run the backup now or to create a schedule for the backup. If you chose Now, skip to step 18.

15. If you chose to create a schedule, enter a job name and click the Set Schedule button.

16. On the Schedule Job page, select the frequency of the backup, start time, and start date, and click OK when you are finished. You can set additional configurations using the Settings tab as shown in Figure 32.6.

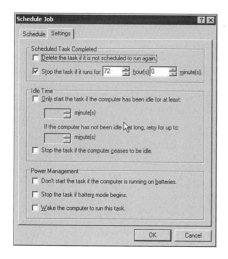

FIGURE 32.6   Changing the settings for a schedule job.

17. On the Set Account Information page, enter the user account name and password that should be used to run the scheduled backup, and click OK when you are finished.

18. On the When to Back Up page, click Next to continue.

19. Click Finish to save the scheduled backup or immediately start the backup job.

20. When the backup is complete, review the backup log for detailed information and click Close on the Backup Progress window when you are finished.

Automated System Recovery

Automated System Recovery (ASR) is a backup option that is used to back up a system to recover from a complete server failure. An ASR backup contains disk volume information and a copy of all the data on the boot and system volumes, along with the current System State. ASR can be used to restore a system from scratch, and it will even re-create disk volumes and format them as previously recorded during the ASR backup. ASR does not back up the data stored on volumes that are solely used for data storage.

To perform an ASR backup, you start with a blank floppy disk and a backup device—either a tape device or disk will suffice. One point to keep in mind is that an ASR backup will back up each local drive that contains the operating system and any applications installed. For instance, if the operating system is installed on drive C: and Microsoft Office is installed on drive D:, both of these drives will be completely backed up because the Registry has references to files on the D: drive. Although this can greatly simplify restore procedures, it requires additional storage and increases backup time for an ASR backup. Using a basic installation of Windows Server 2003, Enterprise Edition with only basic services installed, an ASR backup can average 1.3GB to less than 4GB or 5GB.

ASR backups should be created for a server before and after any hardware changes are performed or when a major configuration change occurs with the system. ASR backups contain disk information, including basic or dynamic configuration and volume set type. They save volume or partition data so that when an ASR restore is complete, only the data stored on storage volumes needs to be recovered.

Creating an ASR Backup

An ASR backup can currently be created only from the local server console using the graphical user interface (GUI) version of the Windows Server 2003 Backup utility.

To create an ASR backup, follow these steps:

1. Log on to the server using an account that has the right to back up the system. (Any local administrator or domain administrator has the necessary permissions to complete the operation.)

2. Click Start, All Programs, Accessories, System Tools, Backup.

3. If this is the first time you've run Backup, it opens in Wizard mode. Choose to run it in Advanced mode by clicking the Advanced Mode hyperlink.

4. Click the Automated System Recovery Wizard button to start the Automated System Recovery Preparation Wizard.

5. Click Next after reading the Automated System Recovery Preparation Wizard welcome screen.

6. Choose your backup media type and choose the correct media tape or file. If you're creating a new file, specify the complete path to the file, and the backup will create the file automatically. Click Next to continue.

7. If you specified a file as the backup media and it resides on a network drive, click OK at the warning message to continue.

8. If you chose tape for the backup, choose the media for the backup and choose to use a new tape.

9. Click Finish to complete the Automated System Recovery Preparation Wizard and start the backup. As the ASR backup process begins, you will see the ntbackup utility processing the backup, similar to what is shown in Figure 32.7.

10. After the tape or file backup portion completes, the ASR backup prompts you to insert a floppy disk to hold the recovery information. Insert the disk and click OK to continue.

11. Remove the floppy disk as requested and label the disk with the appropriate ASR backup information. Click OK to continue.

FIGURE 32.7   ASR backup in process.

12. When the ASR backup is complete, click Close on the Backup Progress window to return to the backup program or click Report to examine the backup report.

> **NOTE**
>
> The information contained on the ASR floppy disk is also stored on the backup media. The ASR floppy contains only two files, `asr.sif` and `asrpnp.sif`, which can be restored from the backup media and copied to a floppy disk if the original ASR floppy cannot be located.

Tips on Using ASR

One tip on using ASR is to ensure an ASR backup is completed after the server is built, updated with service packs, reconfigured, and security changes are applied. Also, an ASR backup should be performed when hardware configurations change and periodically otherwise. On domain controllers, this period should be less than 30 days to ensure that the domain can be up and running again if an Active Directory authoritative restore is necessary, but best practices would say much sooner depending on the total amount of additions and changes occurring in Active Directory on a daily basis.

ASR backs up only the system and boot partitions. ASR will not back up the Exchange databases if they are installed on a separate drive. A normal tape backup of the drive(s) storing the Exchange databases or any other drive volume with critical data should be backed up separately. ASR backups, on average, are 1.3GB to 5GB in size, so be sure to place the data in a location that can hold several copies of an ASR backup. To prevent ASR backups from getting too large, user data and file shares should be kept off the system and boot volumes.

Backing Up the Windows Server 2003 and Exchange Server 2007

The Windows Server operating system and the Exchange Server 2007 messaging system contain several features to enhance operating system stability, provide data and service redundancy, and deliver feature-rich client services.

And now, Windows Server 2003 provides additional services such as Volume Shadow Copy Service, or VSS, which works to enhance backup capabilities when organizations use third-party backup products. Additional information about working with VSS is covered in the "Volume Shadow Copy Service and Exchange Server 2007" section later in this chapter.

Though other options have been mentioned, this section discusses ways to back up a Windows Server 2003 system, including key components of Exchange Server 2007 using the built-in backup utilities available with the Windows Server 2003 operating system. Also, additional Windows services are discussed, including built-in tools that aid in the backup and recovery process.

By preparing for a complete server failure and using the information in this section, an organization is more likely to successfully recover from a failed server, restoring it to its previous state.

Backing Up Boot and System Volumes

A backup strategy for every Exchange 2007 system should always include the boot and system disk volumes of the server. For most Exchange server installations, the boot and system volume are the same, but in some designs they are located on completely separate volumes—as usually is the case for dual-boot computers. For the rest of this section and discussion, assume that they are both on the same partition. This volume contains all the files necessary to start the core operating system. It should be backed up before and after a change, such as the application of service packs, is made to the operating system and once every 24 hours, if possible.

When Exchange Server is installed on a Windows 2003 server, the installation, by default, will install on the system partition unless a different location is specified during installation. On average, the amount of information stored on the system volume, with applications, services, and all service packs installed, is typically less than 2GB.

> **NOTE**
>
> When system volumes are backed up, the System State should also be included in the backup at the same time to simplify recovery and restoration of the system to its original state, if a server needs to be recovered from scratch.

Backing Up Windows Server 2003 Services

Many Windows Server 2003 services store configuration and status data in separate files or databases located in various locations on the system volume. If the service is native to Windows Server 2003, performing a complete server backup on all drives and the System State almost certainly backs up the critical data. A few services provide alternative backup and restore options. The procedures for backing up these services are outlined in the "Backing Up Specific Windows Services" section later in this chapter.

Backing Up the System State

The System State of a Windows Server 2003 system contains, at a minimum, the system Registry, boot files, and the COM+ class registration database. Backing up the System State creates a point-in-time backup that can be used to restore a server to a previous working state. Having a copy of the System State is essential if a server restore is necessary.

How the server is configured determines what will be contained in the System State, other than the three items listed previously. On a domain controller, the System State also contains the Active Directory database and the SYSVOL share. On a cluster, it contains the cluster quorum data. When services such as Certificate Services and Internet Information Services, which contain their own service-specific data, are installed, these databases are not listed separately but are backed up with the System State.

Even though the System State contains many subcomponents, using the programs included with Windows Server 2003, the entire System State can be backed up only as a whole. When recovery is necessary, however, there are several different options. Recovering data using a System State backup is covered in Chapter 33.

The System State should be backed up every night to prepare for several server-related failures. A restore of a System State is very powerful and can return a system to a previous working state if a change needs to be rolled back or if the operating system needs to be restored from scratch after a complete server failure.

Using the Active Directory Restore Mode Password

When a Windows Server 2003 system is promoted to a domain controller, one of the configurations is to create an Active Directory Restore mode password. This password is used only when booting into Active Directory Restore mode. Restore mode is used when the Active Directory database is in need of maintenance or needs to be restored from backup. Many administrators have found themselves without the ability to log on to Directory Restore mode when necessary and have been forced to rebuild systems from scratch to restore the System State data. Many hours can be saved if this password is stored in a safe place, where it can be accessed by the correct administrators.

The Restore mode password is server-specific and created on each domain controller. If the password is forgotten, and the domain controller is still functional, it can be changed using the command-line tool ntdsutil.exe, as shown in Figure 32.8. The example in Figure 32.8 changes the password on the remote domain controller named dc.companyabc.com.

Volume Shadow Copy Service and Exchange Server 2007

Before discussing the backup process using Window NT backup, it is important for Exchange administrators to understand what Windows 2003 Volume Show Copy Service is used for. With many third-party options available today, most Exchange Server 2007 organizations use these third-party backup products.

The Volume Shadow Copy Service is a server service in Windows 2003 and is available as part of the operating system. Alone, VSS is a service, but when combined with backup applications, VSS become a vital part of every organization's backup strategy and recovery plan.

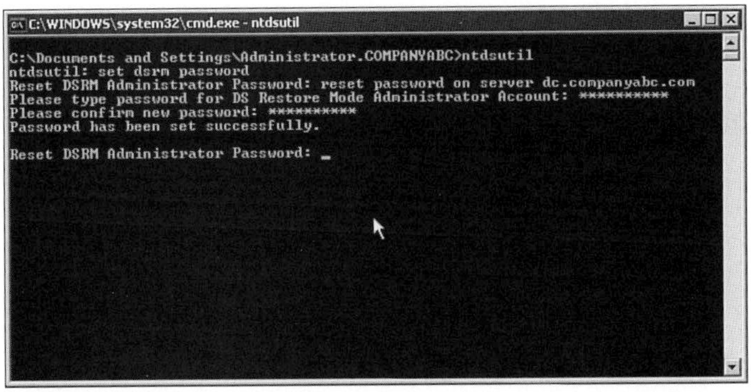

```
C:\WINDOWS\system32\cmd.exe - ntdsutil                          _ □ X

C:\Documents and Settings\Administrator.COMPANYABC>ntdsutil
ntdsutil: set dsrm password
Reset DSRM Administrator Password: reset password on server dc.companyabc.com
Please type password for DS Restore Mode Administrator Account: **********
Please confirm new password: **********
Password has been set successfully.

Reset DSRM Administrator Password: _
```

FIGURE 32.8   Changing the Active Directory Restore mode password (using `ntdsutil.exe`).

What Role VSS Plays in Backup

Microsoft has created VSS to provide application platforms and infrastructures to enhance functionality when working with Microsoft services such as Exchange Server 2007. The key to VSS is its ability to act as a go-between or coordinator for service providers (backup applications) and service writers (Exchange 2007 databases).

It is important to know that VSS does not function alone; VSS is designed to provide application developers a platform in which to build applications to create Exchange snapshots.

Shadow Copies and Snapshots

This ability enabled third-party backup applications to create shadow copies or mirrors of the Exchange database and allowed for administrators to design more dynamic backup strategies and reduce the overall cost of restoring servers. Using Show Copies (Mirror Copies) and Snapshots (Point in Time Mirror Copies), daily backups can be much smaller and for vital messaging systems, snapshots can be taken several times a day.

VSS Requirements and Prerequisites

When looking at third-party products as an option for backups with VSS technology, you must evaluate the products to ensure that they are compatible with VSS. Compatibility is based on three specific areas:

- ▶ First, backups of the Exchange 2007 database, logs, and checkpoint files must be completed by the application writer (Exchange 2007).

- ▶ Second, the application must complete a full validation of the backup.

- ▶ Last, when restoring data in Exchange, this must also be completed by the application writer (Exchange 2007).

VSS and third-party applications also require hardware compatibility. This is especially true when backing up to disk subsystems, such as NAS and SAN solutions. To verify this information, review the application vendor support pages and verify that the application and hardware meet all requirements.

TIP

For more information regarding Volume Shadow Copy Service and compatibility requirements, see the Microsoft article on the Microsoft web page at: support.microsoft.com/?kbid=822896.

Backing Up Specific Windows Services

Most Windows Server services that contain a database or local files are backed up with the System State but also provide alternate backup and restore options. Because the System State restore is usually an all-or-nothing proposition, except when it comes to cluster nodes and domain controllers, restoring an entire System State might deliver undesired results if only a specific service database restore is required. This section outlines services that either have separate backup/restore utilities or require special attention to ensure a successful backup.

Disk Configuration (Software RAID Sets)

Disk is not a service but should be backed up to ensure that proper partition assignments can be restored. When Dynamic disks are used to create complex volumes—such as mirrored, striped, spanned, or RAID-5 volumes—the disk configuration should be saved. This way, if the operating system is corrupt and needs to be rebuilt from scratch, the complex volumes need to have only their configuration restored, which could greatly reduce the recovery time. Only an ASR backup can back up disk and volume configuration.

Certificate Services

Installing Certificate Services creates a certificate authority (CA) on the Windows Server 2003 system. The CA is used to manage and allocate certificates to users, servers, and workstations when files, folders, email, or network communication needs to be secured and encrypted. In many cases, the CA is a completely separate secured CA server; however, many organizations use their Exchange server as a CA server. This might be because of a limited number of servers with several different roles and services installed on a single server, or because the organization wants to use Secure Sockets Layer (SSL) and forms-based authentication (FBA) for secured Outlook Web Access, so they install Certificate Services on an Exchange server. Whatever the case, the CA needs to be backed up whether on the Exchange server or on any other server; if the CA server crashes and needs to be restored, it can be restored so users can continue to access the system after recovery.

CAUTION

For security purposes, it is highly recommended that Certificate Services be enabled on a server other than the Exchange server. Definitely do not have the CA services on an Outlook Web Access server that is exposed to the Internet. The integrity of certificate-authenticated access depends on ensuring that certificates are issued only by a trusted authority. Any compromise to the CA server invalidates an organization's ability to secure its communications.

When the CA allocates a certificate to a machine or user, that information is recorded in the certificate database on the local drive of the CA. If this database is corrupted or deleted, all certificates allocated from this server become invalid or unusable. To avoid this problem, the certificates and Certificate Services database should be backed up frequently. Even if certificates are rarely allocated to new users or machines, backups should still be performed regularly.

Certificate Services can be backed up in three ways: backing up the CA server's System State, using the CA Microsoft Management Console (MMC) snap-in, or using the command-line utility `Certutil.exe`. Backing up Certificate Services by backing up the System State is the preferred method because it can be easily automated and scheduled. But using the graphic console or command-line utility adds the benefit of being able to restore Certificate Services to a previous state without restoring the entire server System State or taking down the entire server for the restore.

To create a backup of the CA using the graphic console, follow these steps:

1. Log on to the CA server using an account with local Administrator rights.

2. Open Windows Explorer and create a folder named `CaBackup` on the C: drive.

3. Select Administrative Tools, Certificate Authority.

4. Expand the Certificate Authority server, and select the correct CA.

5. Select Actions, All Tasks, Back Up CA.

6. Click Next on the Certification Authority Backup Wizard welcome screen.

7. On the Items to Back Up page, check the Private Key and CA Certificate check box and the Certificate Database and Certificate Database Log check box, as shown in Figure 32.9.

8. Specify the location to store the CA backup files. Use the folder created in the beginning of this process. Click Next to continue.

9. When the CA certificate and private key are backed up, this data file must be protected with a password. Enter a password for this file, confirm it, and click Next to continue.

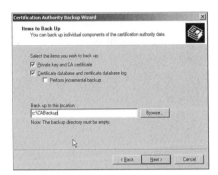

FIGURE 32.9   Selecting items for the certificate authority backup.

> **NOTE**
>
> To restore the CA private key and CA certificate, you must use the password entered in step 9. Store this password in a safe place, possibly with the master account list.

10. Click Finish to create the CA backup.

Internet Information Services (IIS)

Internet Information Services (IIS) is the Windows Server 2003 web and FTP services that support websites like OWA. It is included on every version of the Windows Server 2003 platform. IIS storesconfiguration information for web and FTP site configurations and security, placing the information into the IIS metabase. The IIS metabase can be backed up by performing a System State backup of the server running IIS, but it can also be backed up using the IIS console. Best practices say that the IIS metabase should be backed up separately before and after any IIS configuration change is made. This is to ensure a successful rollback is available should issues occur and also to have the latest IIS configuration data backed up after the change.

To back up the IIS metabase using the IIS console, use the following steps:

1. Log on to the IIS server using an account with local Administrator access.

2. Click Start, All Programs, Administrative Tools, Internet Information Services (IIS).

3. If the local IIS server does not appear in the window, right-click Internet Information Services in the left pane, and select Connect.

4. Type in the fully qualified domain name for the IIS server, and click OK.

5. Right-click the IIS server in the left pane, and select All Tasks, Backup/Restore Configuration.

6. The Configuration Backup/Restore window lists all the automatic IIS backups that have been created. Click the Create Backup button.

7. Enter the backup name and, if necessary, check the Encrypt Backup Using Password check box, enter and confirm the password, and click OK when you're finished, as shown in Figure 32.10.

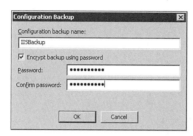

FIGURE 32.10   Creating an IIS configuration backup.

8. When the backup is complete, it is listed in the Configuration Backup/Restore window. Click Close to return to the IIS console.

Before a change is made to the IIS configuration, a backup should be manually created. When the change is completed, the administrator should either perform another backup or choose the option to save the configuration to disk. The administrator can save new IIS configuration changes to disk by right-clicking the IIS server, selecting All Tasks, and then choosing Save Configuration to Disk. This option works correctly only after a change has been made that has not yet been recorded in the IIS metabase.

Managing Media in a Structured Backup Strategy

Windows Server 2003 uses the Removable Storage service to allocate and deallocate media. The media can be managed using the Removable Storage console in the Computer Management administrative tools, as shown in Figure 32.11. The Removable Storage service allocates and deallocates media for these services by enabling each service to access media in media sets created for the respective program.

Media Pools

The Windows Server 2003 Removable Storage service organizes media so that policies and permissions can be applied and different functions can be performed. For example, the backup media pool is allocated for media created using Windows Server 2003 Backup. Only users granted the privilege to back up or restore the system, or administer the removable media service, will be granted access to this media pool.

Free Pool

Media that can be used by any backup or archiving software that uses the Windows Server 2003 Removable Storage service is known as a free pool. Media in this pool are usually blank media or media marked as clean, and can be overwritten and reallocated.

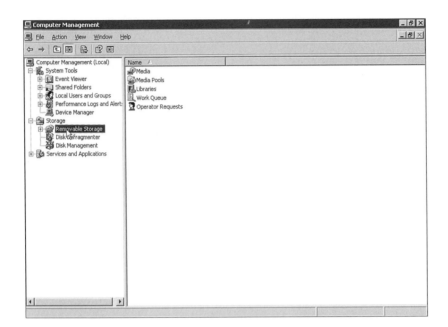

FIGURE 32.11   Removable Storage console.

Remote Storage Pool

Use on a server only if the Remote Storage server has been installed. This pool stores media allocated for the Remote Storage service. If no tape is found, the device reallocates media from the free pool.

Imported Pool

When media is inserted into a tape device and an inventory is run, if the media is not blank and not already allocated to the remote storage pool or backup media pool, this media is then stored in an imported media pool. If the media is known to have been created with Windows Server 2003 Backup, opening the backup program and performing a catalog should be sufficient to reallocate this media into the backup pool set.

Backup Pool

This pool of media is clear and simple; it contains all the media allocated to the Windows Server 2003 Backup program.

Custom Media Pools

Custom media pools can be created if special removable media options are required. Media pool options are very limited in Windows Server 2003, and there should be no compelling reason to create a custom media pool.

Summary

As you have seen in this chapter, Microsoft has done an excellent job in shoring up some of the inadequacies that existed in previous versions of Exchange in the area of backup. Administrators finally have some very viable options for performing geographic clusters or simply flipping over to backup copies of the Exchange databases. This means that administrators will be able to avoid restoring from slow tapes in more situations.

Exchange 2007 has taken a philosophy of improving the overall backup process by offering more scenarios where you can restore or recover data without having to resort to restoring from tape. This means that Exchange 2007 administrators can put more faith into the stability and recoverability of Exchange 2007.

Although the backup mechanisms are mostly unchanged, this means that it is still very easy to back up Exchange 2007 data to disk or tape for long-term storage. VSS is still utilized for backups and is the interface of choice for third-party backup applications. Advanced features such as backing up the local replica give administrators increased flexibility with the ability to back up Exchange 2007 servers during business hours with greatly reduced impact to end users. This can be especially helpful in situations in which a backup job fails and the administrator has to make a choice between impacting end users' performance or skipping a backup.

Backups continue to be the safety net that allows administrators to operate knowing that in any situation they can restore a message, a mailbox, or an entire server. Careful planning and constant verification of backups allow an administrator to sleep at night knowing their Exchange environment is safe.

Best Practices

The following are best practices from this chapter:

- ▶ When space allows, implement Local Continuous Replication on Mailbox servers.

- ▶ Try to run the Hub Transport role on more than one server per site.

- ▶ Mailbox servers should be backed up nightly.

- ▶ Always check the status of backup jobs to ensure they are running properly.

- ▶ Maintain a list of who to contact if errors occur during the backup process.

- ▶ Always follow the documented process for performing backups. If the process changes because of a change in the environment or backup product, be sure to update the documentation.

- ▶ Always perform a full backup before making major changes to an Exchange server.

- ▶ Perform a monthly ASR backup of key systems to enable rapid restore in the case of a major failure.

- ▶ When possible, perform nightly backups to disk for speed and spool them to tape during the day.

▶ Define your SLAs before determining your backup strategy because the SLA will heavily influence your choices.

▶ Clearly define the roles and responsibilities of the people who are involved in backups of Windows and Exchange.

▶ Always take your third-party Exchange 2007 applications into account when planning your backup strategy.

▶ Be sure to update your backup jobs when new storage groups or databases are added.

CHAPTER 33

Recovering from a Disaster in an Exchange Server 2007 Environment

As time goes by, companies become more and more dependent on email as a business-critical communication and collaboration tool. As such, when an Exchange server or environment isn't working properly, there is an urgent need to get the Exchange system back up and running as quickly as possible. Depending on the type of failure that took down all or part of the Exchange environment, you can use one of several approaches to recover the environment and restore the flow of mail and access to existing messages.

Unfortunately, most organizations do not proactively create an environment with disaster-recovery processes in place. As a result, this chapter takes into account the information in Chapter 31, "Continuous Backups, Clustering, and Network Load Balancing in Exchange Server 2007," and Chapter 32, "Backing Up the Exchange Server 2007 Environment," and also provides recommendations based on possible disaster scenarios.

Identifying the Extent of the Problem

Before attempting to perform a recovery, it is important to first determine the type and extent of the problem. If the problem is not properly identified, you run the risk of performing an incorrect action that could actually make the problem worse. Equally important is to choose the most appropriate solution available. For example, restoring an entire server when only a single database failed would impact users who otherwise could have continued to use Exchange, and it would take significantly longer than restoring just the necessary database. Even though both plans of action would fix the issue, one is much simpler with less impact than the other.

Database Improvements Minimizes Corruption

Exchange Server 2007 brings a new version of the JET database called Jet Blue, which includes error correcting codes (ECC) enhancements that help minimize the number of errors in the database. The ECC automatically identifies and fixes minor errors. The enhancements to Jet Blue also improve the indexing and search functions.

Mailbox Content Was Deleted, Use the Undelete Function of Exchange and Outlook

When information is deleted from a user's mailbox, whether it is an email message, a calendar appointment, a contact, or a task, the information is not permanently deleted from the Exchange server. Deleted items go into the Deleted Items folder in the user's Outlook mailbox. The information is actually retained on the Exchange server for 30 days after deletion, even when it is supposedly permanently deleted from the Deleted Items folder.

NOTE

The Mail Retention feature needs to be enabled on the Exchange server for Outlook information to be retained on the Exchange server.

With a little training and documentation, end users can recover their own deleted mail items with ease. To recover mailbox items that have been deleted within Outlook, do the following:

1. Highlight the Deleted Items folder.

2. Click Tools, Recover Deleted Items.

3. In the Recover Deleted Items From – Deleted Items window, select the items that you want to restore.

4. Click the Recover Selected Items button.

If the item was "Shift-deleted," which bypasses the Deleted Items folder, the message is not lost. Follow these instructions to recover hard-deleted items:

1. Click Start, Run, type Regedt32.exe in the Open text box, and then click OK.

2. Browse to the following key in the Registry:

   HKEY_LOCAL_MACHINE\SOFTWARE\Microsoft\Exchange\Client\Options

3. On the Edit menu, click Add Value, and then add the following Registry value:

   Value name: DumpsterAlwaysOn

   Data type: DWORD

   Value data: 1

4. Quit Registry Editor.

With this key set, you can highlight any folder in Outlook and use the Recover Deleted Items tool.

Data Is Lost, Must Restore from Backup

If data is lost and the undelete function does not recover the information, the information might need to be restored from a backup. Depending on how much information was lost, this might involve a full recovery of the Exchange server from tape or snapshot, or it might involve restoring just a single mailbox, folder, or message. The key to restoring information is determining what needs to be restored. If just a single message needs to be restored, there is no reason to recover the entire server in production. In many cases, when full tape backups have been conducted of an Exchange server, a restore of the storage group containing the missing data can be performed via the recovery storage group and the missing content merged back into the production databases. This function is explained in detail later in this chapter.

The process of restoring all or partial data from tape is covered in the sections "Recovering from a Complete Server Failure" and "Recovering from Database Corruption," later in this chapter.

Data Is Okay, Server Just Doesn't Come Up

The failure of a server does not necessarily mean that the data needs to be restored completely from tape. Often, a server goes down because of a failure with the power supplies, a motherboard failure or even a processor failure. In a situation where the hard drives on a dead server are still operational, the hard drives should be moved to an operational server or, at the very least, the data should be transferred to a different server. By preserving the data on the drives, an organization can minimize the need to perform more complicated data reconstruction from a tape restore, which could result in the loss of data from the time of the last backup. Restoring from tape should always be considered a final option.

The process of recovering data from a drive and recovering a failed server is covered in the section "Performing a Restore of Only Exchange Database Files," later in this chapter.

Data Is Corrupt—Some Mailboxes Are Accessible, Some Are Not

Data corruption typically occurs on Exchange servers when the time period since the last database maintenance is too long or maintenance has been neglected altogether. Without periodic maintenance, covered in Chapter 19, "Exchange Server 2007 Management and

Maintenance Practices," the databases in Exchange are more susceptible to becoming corrupt. Exchange database corruption that is not repaired can make individual messages or entire portions of mailboxes stored on an Exchange server to become inaccessible.

When a mailbox or multiple mailboxes are corrupt, the good data in the mailboxes can be extracted with minimal data loss. By isolating the corruption and extracting good data, an organization that might not need to recover the lost data can typically continue to operate with minimal downtime.

The process of extracting mail from an Exchange database is covered in the section "Recovering from Database Corruption," later in this chapter.

Data Is Corrupt, No Mailboxes Are Accessible

Depending on the condition of an Exchange database, the information might be so corrupt that none of the mailboxes are accessible. Recovering data from a corrupt database that cannot be accessed is a two-step process. The first step is to conduct maintenance to attempt to repair the database; the second step is to extract as much information from the database as possible.

The process of performing maintenance and extracting data from a corrupt database is covered in the section "Recovering from Database Corruption," later in this chapter.

Exchange Server Is Okay, Something Else Is Preventing Exchange from Working

If you know that the Exchange server and databases are operational and something else is preventing Exchange from working, the process of recovery focuses on looking at things such as Active Directory, Internet Information Services (IIS), the domain name system (DNS), and the network infrastructure, as with site-to-site connectivity for replication.

The process of analyzing the operation of other services is covered in the sections "Recovering Windows Server 2003 Domain Controllers" and "Recovering Active Directory," later in this chapter.

Mail Is Not Flowing Between Sites

If users are able to access their mailboxes normally and mail can be sent between users of the same site, odds are the issue is with the Hub Transport server. In larger implementations of Exchange 2007, the Hub Transport server role is likely to be run on a system that doesn't host mailboxes. Generally speaking, backups are not performed on a Hub Transport server as it contains no unique information. To restore these services, simply rebuild the Hub Transport server. Installing with a /recoverserver switch allows the server to recover its configuration from Active Directory, saving some configuration steps. This assumes the server is built with the same name.

If you need the transport services up very rapidly, consider adding the Hub Transport server role to an existing system. To add this role, follow these steps:

1. From an existing Exchange 2007 server, open a command prompt.

2. Navigate to Program Files, Microsoft, Exchange Server, bin.

3. Type `exsetup.exe /mode:install /role:hub`.

Internet Mail Is Not Flowing

If you are unable to send mail to the Internet or receive mail from the Internet, there is a very good chance that the issue is a failure with the Edge Transport server. Most environments should run more than one Edge Transport server, preferably in different locations. But if an Edge Transport server fails, it should be rebuilt as they are typically not backed up. Installing with a `/recoverserver` switch allows the server to recover its configuration from Active Directory, saving some configuration steps. This assumes the server is built with the same name.

If you need the transport services up very rapidly, consider adding the Edge Transport server role to an existing system. To add this role, follow these steps:

1. From an existing Exchange 2007 server, open a command prompt.

2. Navigate to Program Files, Microsoft, Exchange Server, bin.

3. Type `exsetup.exe /mode:install /role:et`.

> **NOTE**
>
> If you place the Edge Transport role on a new system, you need to make sure that incoming Simple Mail Transfer Protocol (SMTP) mail from the Internet reaches this system. This might involve a change in configuration of MX records, firewall rules, Network Address Translation (NAT), or your antispam/antivirus gateway. Be sure you understand the implications of putting the Edge Transport role on another system before attempting this fix.

What to Do Before Performing Any Server-Recovery Process

If a full server recovery will be performed, or if a number of different procedures will be taken to install service packs, patches, updates, or other server-recovery attempts as an attempt to recover the server, a full backup should be performed on the server.

At first, it might seem unnecessary to back up a server that isn't working properly, but during the problem-solving and debugging process, it is quite possible for a server to end up in even worse shape after a few updates and fixes have been applied. The initial problem might have been that a single mailbox couldn't be accessed, and after some problem-solving efforts, the entire server might be inaccessible. A backup provides a rollback to the point of the initial problem state. When making changes in an attempt to fix a server, you always want a way to roll back a change in case it turns out to make the situation worse. When the backup is complete, verify that the backup is valid, ensuring that no open files are skipped during the backup process or that, if the files are skipped, they are backed up in other open file backup processes. This way, you will always have the ability to return to your starting point in case you need to try a different method to fix the server.

> **CAUTION**
>
> When performing any recovery of an Exchange server or resource, be careful what you delete, modify, or change. As a rule of thumb, *never* delete objects that are known throughout the directory; otherwise, you will not be able to restore the object because of the uniqueness of each object. As an example, if you plan to restore an entire server from tape, you do not want to first delete the server and then add the server back during the restoration process. The restoration process requires the existence of the old server in the directory. Deleting the server object and then adding the object again later gives the object a completely different globally unique identifier (GUID). Even though you restore the entire Exchange server from tape, the ID of the server and all of the objects in the server will be different, making it more difficult to recover the server. Other replicable objects that should not be deleted include public folders, public folder trees, groups, and distribution lists.

Validating Backup Data and Procedures

Another very important task that should be done before doing any maintenance, service, or repairs on an Exchange server is to validate that a full backup exists on the server, test the condition of the backup, and then secure the backup so that it is safe. Far too many organizations proceed with risky recovery procedures, believing that they have a fallback position by restoring from tape, only to realize that the tape backup is corrupt or that a complete backup does not exist. Equally important is to be sure that the tape you might need is actually onsite. Many companies send tapes offsite for storage. If you are depending on a particular backup tape for your rollback, be sure it is readily accessible.

If the administrators of the network realize that there is no clean backup, the procedures taken to recover the system might be different than if a backup had existed. If a full backup exists and is verified to be in good condition, the organization has an opportunity to restore from tape if a full restore is necessary.

Preparing for a More Easily Recoverable Environment

Steps can be taken to help an organization more easily prepare for a recoverable environment. This involves documenting server states and conditions, performing specific backup procedures, and setting up new features in Exchange Server 2007 that provide for a more simplified restoration process. By maintaining these processes and performing regular test restores, a company can feel confident that they can quickly and easily recover from a disaster.

Documenting the Exchange Environment

Key to the success of recovering an Exchange server or an entire Exchange environment is having documentation on the server configurations. Having specific server configuration information documented helps to identify which server is not operational, the routing of information between servers, and, ultimately, the impact that a server failure or server recovery will have on the rest of the Exchange environment. By having a complete understanding of the Exchange environment as a whole, an administrator can often bring up temporary services to alleviate a failure and give themselves more time to fix the issue and determine the root cause.

> **NOTE**
>
> A utility called ExchDump can assist an administrator with baselining and improving the environment. Use ExchDump to export and document a server's configuration. The ExchDump utility can be downloaded from the Microsoft Exchange download page at http://www.microsoft.com/exchange/downloads/2003/default.mspx.
>
> Although this utility was originally written for Exchange Server 2003, it works fine for extracting the same information from an Exchange 2007 server.

Some of the items that should be documented include the following:

- Server name
- Server roles held
- Version of Windows on servers (including service pack)
- Version of Exchange on servers (including service pack)
- Organization name in Exchange
- Site names
- Storage group names
- Database names
- Location of databases
- Size of databases
- When database maintenance was last run
- Public folder tree name
- Replication process of public folders
- Security delegation and administrative rights
- Names and locations of global catalog servers

Documenting the Backup Process

To simplify a restore of an Exchange environment, it is important to start with a clean backup. A clean backup is performed when the proper backup process is followed. Create a backup process that works, document the step-by-step procedures to back up the server, follow the procedures regularly, and then validate that the backups have been completed successfully.

Also, when configurations change, the backup process as well as system configurations should be documented and validated again, to make sure that the backups are being completed properly.

Documenting the Recovery Process

An important aspect of recovery feasibility is knowing how to recover from a disaster. Just knowing what to back up and what scenarios to plan for is not enough. Restore processes should be created and tested to ensure that a restore can meet service level agreements (SLAs) and that the staff members understand all the necessary steps.

When a process is determined, it should be documented, and the documentation should be written to make sense to the desired audience. For example, if a failure occurs in a satellite office that has only marketing employees and one of them is forced to recover a server, the documentation needs to be written so that it can be understood by just about anyone. If the information technology (IT) staff will be performing the restore, the documentation can be less detailed, but it assumes a certain level of knowledge and expertise with the server product. The first paragraph of any document related to backup and recovery should be a summary of what the document is used for and the level of skill necessary to perform the task and understand the document.

The recovery process involved in resolving an Exchange problem should also be focused not only on the goal of getting the entire Exchange server back up and operational, but also on considering smaller steps that might help minimize downtime. As an example, if an Exchange server has failed, instead of trying to restore 100GB of mail back to the server, which can take hours, if not days, to complete, an organization can choose to restore just the user Inboxes, calendars, and contacts. After a faster system recovery of core information on a server, the balance of the information can be restored over the next several hours.

The other advantage of having a properly documented restore procedure is that it greatly reduces the chances of human error occurring during a restore. Recovering a failed server while hundreds or possibly thousands of email users are affected is a stressful situation. This isn't the time to learn how to perform a restore. The goal in this situation is for the administrator to be able to follow a clearly documented and well-tested process to ensure that no steps are missed and that no information is entered incorrectly. Having well-documented steps can greatly reduce the stress of this situation and increase the chances of a successful restore.

Including Test Restores in the Scheduled Maintenance

Part of a successful disaster recovery plan involves periodically testing the restore procedures to verify accuracy and to test the backup media to ensure that data can actually be recovered. Most organizations or administrators assume that if the backup software reports "Successful," the backup is good and data can be recovered. If special backup consideration is not addressed, the successful backup might not contain everything necessary to restore a server if data loss or software corruption occurs.

Restores of file data, application data, and configurations should be performed as part of a regular maintenance schedule to ensure that the backup method is correct and that disaster recovery procedures and documentation are current. Such tests also should verify that the backup media can be read from and used to restore data. Adding periodic test restores to regular maintenance intervals ensures that backups are successful and familiarizes the administrators with the procedures necessary to recover so that when a real disaster occurs, the recovery can be performed correctly and efficiently the first time.

These test restores should occur in a lab environment where end users won't be affected. The restores should vary in type, testing single mailbox restores, complete server restores, and full site restores where even domain controllers might need to be restored from scratch. This helps ensure that staff members are comfortable with the process and will have no problem performing a restore in production should the occasion ever arise.

Recovering from a Site Failure

When a site becomes unavailable because of a physical access limitation or a disaster such as a fire or earthquake, steps must be taken to provide the recovery of the Exchange server in the site. Exchange does not have a single-step method of merging information from the failed site server into another server, so the process involves recovering the lost server in its entirety.

To prepare for the recovery of a failed site, an organization can create redundancy in a failover site. With redundancy built in to a remote site, the recovery and restore process can be minimized if a recovery needs to be performed.

For environments where SLAs offer very little time to bring up a recovery location, administrators should strongly consider implementing Cluster Continuous Replication, a new feature of Exchange 2007. For details on building this type of Exchange cluster, see Chapter 31, "Continuous Backups, Clustering, and Network Load Balancing in Exchange Server 2007."

Creating Redundant and Failover Sites

Redundant sites are created for a couple of different reasons. First, a redundant site can have a secondary Internet connection and bridgehead routing server so that if the primary site is down, the secondary site can be the focus for inbound and outbound email communications. This redundancy can be built, configured, and set to automatically provide failover in case of a site failure. See Chapter 7, "Installing Exchange Server

2007," for details on creating Send/Receive Connectors and configuring Hub Transport servers.

The other reason for redundant site preparation is to provide a warm spare server site so that a company will be prepared to perform a restore of a site server in case of a site failure. The site recovery can simply be having server documentation available in another site or having a full image of server information stored in another site. The more preparatory work is conducted up front, the faster the organization will be able to recover from a system failure.

If you plan to utilize warm spares, be sure to update those warm spares with patches and applications as you apply them to the production systems. This eliminates several steps when it comes time to put them into use.

Creating the Failover Site

When an organization decides to plan for site failures as part of a disaster recovery solution, many areas need to be addressed and many options exist. For organizations looking for redundancy, network connectivity is a priority, along with spare servers that can accommodate the user load. The spare servers need to have enough disk space to accommodate a complete restore. As a best practice, to ensure a smooth transition, the following list of recommendations provides a starting point:

- ▶ Allocate the appropriate hardware devices, including servers with enough processing power and disk space to accommodate the restored machines' resources.

- ▶ Host the organization's DNS zones and records using primary DNS servers located at an Internet service provider (ISP) collocation facility, or have redundant DNS servers registered for the domain and located at both physical locations.

- ▶ Publish the recovery site's IP address as a lower-priority MX record. This way, when the recovery server comes online you won't have to wait for DNS propagation to advertise the new MX record.

- ▶ For the Exchange servers, ensure that the host records in the DNS tables are set to low Time to Live (TTL) values so that DNS changes do not take extended periods to propagate across the Internet. The Microsoft Windows Server 2003 default TTL is 1 hour.

- ▶ Ensure that network connectivity is already established and stable between sites and between each site and the Internet.

- ▶ Create at least one copy of backup tape medium for each site. One copy should remain at one location, and a second copy should be stored with an offsite data storage company. An optional third copy could be stored at another site location and can be used to restore the file to spare hardware on a regular basis, to restore Windows if a site failover is necessary.

▶ Have a copy of all disaster recovery documentation stored at multiple locations as well as at the offsite data storage company. This provides redundancy if a recovery becomes necessary.

Allocating hardware and making the site ready to act as a failover site are simple tasks in concept, but the actual failover and failback process can be troublesome. Keep in mind that the preceding list applies to failover sites, not mirrored or redundant sites configured to provide load balancing.

Failing Over Between Sites

Before failing over between sites can be successful, administrators need to be aware of what services need to failover and in which order of precedence. For example, before an Exchange server can be restored, Active Directory domain controllers, global catalog servers, and DNS servers must be available.

To keep such a cutover at a high level, the following tasks need to be executed in a timely manner:

1. Update Internet DNS records pointing to the Exchange server(s) if the recovery site wasn't already advertised.

2. Restore any necessary Windows Server 2003 domain controllers, global catalog servers, and internal DNS servers.

3. Restore the Exchange server(s).

4. Test client connectivity, troubleshoot, and provide remote and local client support as needed.

Failing Back After Site Recovery

When the initial site is back online and available to handle client requests and provide access to data and networking services and applications, it is time to consider failing back the services. This can be a controversial subject because failback procedures are usually more difficult than the initial failover procedure. Most organizations plan on the failover and have a tested failover plan that might include database log shipping to the disaster recovery site. However, they do not plan how they can get the current data back to the restored servers in the main or preferred site.

Questions to consider for failing back are as follows:

▶ Will downtime be necessary to restore databases between the sites?

▶ When is the appropriate time to fail back?

▶ Is the failover site less functional than the preferred site? In other words, are only mission-critical services provided in the failover site, or is it a complete copy of the preferred site?

The answers really lie in the complexity of the failed-over environment. If the cutover is simple, there is no reason to wait to fail back.

Providing Alternative Methods of Client Connectivity

When failover sites are too expensive and are not an option, it does not mean that an organization cannot plan for site failures. Other lower-cost options are available but depend on how and where the employees do their work. For example, many times users who need to access email can do so without physically being at the site location. Email can be accessed remotely from other terminals or workstations.

The following are some ways to deal with these issues without renting or buying a separate failover site:

▶ Consider renting racks or cages at a local ISP to colocate servers that can be accessed during a site failure.

▶ Have users dial in from home to a terminal server hosted at an ISP to access Exchange.

▶ Set up remote user access using Terminal Services or Outlook Web Access at a redundant site so that users can access their email, calendar, and contacts from any location.

▶ Rent temporary office space, printers, networking equipment, and user workstations with common standard software packages such as Microsoft Office and Microsoft Internet Explorer. You can plan for and execute this option in about 1 day. If this is an option, be sure to find a computer rental agency first and get pricing before a failure occurs and you have no choice but to pay the rental rates.

Recovering from a Disk Failure

Organizations create disaster recovery plans and procedures to protect against a variety of system failures, but disk failures tend to be the most common in networking environments. The technology used to create processor chips and memory chips has improved drastically over the past couple decades, minimizing the failure of system boards. And although the quality of hard drives has also drastically improved over the years, because hard drives are constantly spinning, they have the most moving parts in a computer system and tend to be the items of most failure.

Key to a disk fault-tolerant solution is creating hardware fault tolerance on key server drives that can be recovered in case of failure. Information is stored on system, boot, and data volumes that have varying levels of recovery needs. Many options exist such as storage area networks (SANs) or various RAID levels to minimize the impact of drive failures.

Hardware-Based RAID Array Failure

Common uses of hardware-based disk arrays for Windows servers include RAID 1 (mirroring) for the operating system and RAID 5 (striped sets with parity) for separate data volumes. Some deployments use a single RAID-5 array for the OS, and data volumes for RAID 0+1 (mirrored striped sets) have been used in more recent deployments.

RAID controllers provide a firmware-based array-management interface, which can be accessed during system startup. This interface enables administrators to configure RAID controller options and manage disk arrays. This interface should be used to repair or reconfigure disk arrays if a problem or disk failure occurs.

Many controllers offer Windows-based applications that can be used to manage and create arrays. Of course, this requires the operating system to be started to access the Windows-based RAID controller application. Follow the manufacturer's procedures on replacing a failed disk within hardware-based RAID arrays.

> **NOTE**
>
> Many RAID controllers allow an array to be configured with a *hot spare disk*. This disk automatically joins the array when a single disk failure occurs. If several arrays are created on a single RAID controller card, hot spare disks can be defined as global and can be used to replace a failed disk on any array. As a best practice, hot spare disks should be defined for arrays.

System Volume

If a system disk failure is encountered, the system can be left in a completely failed state. To prevent this problem from occurring, the administrator should always try to create the system disk on a fault-tolerant disk array such as RAID 1 or RAID 5. If the system disk was mirrored (RAID 1) in a hardware-based array, the operating system will operate and boot normally because the disk and partition referenced in the boot.ini file will remain the same and will be accessible. If the RAID-1 array was created within the operating system using Disk Manager or diskpart.exe, the mirrored disk can be accessed upon bootup by choosing the second option in the boot.ini file during startup. If a disk failure occurs on a software-based RAID-1 array during regular operation, no system disruption should be encountered.

Boot Volume

If Windows Server 2003 has been installed on the second or third partitions of a disk drive, a separate boot and system partition will be created. Most manufacturers require that for a system to boot up from a volume other than the primary partition, the partition must be marked active before functioning. To satisfy this requirement without having to change the active partition, Windows Server 2003 always tries to load the boot files on the first or active partition during installation, regardless of which partition or disk the system files will be loaded on. When this drive or volume fails, if the system volume is still intact, a boot disk can be used to boot into the OS and make the necessary modification after changing the drive.

Data Volume

A data volume is by far the simplest of all types of disks to recover. If an entire disk fails, simply replacing the disk, assigning the previously configured drive letter, and restoring the entire drive from backup will restore the data and permissions.

A few issues to watch out for include the following:

▶ Setting the correct permissions on the root of the drive

▶ Ensuring that file shares still work as desired

▶ Validating that data in the drive does not require a special restore procedure

Recovering from a Boot Failure

Occasionally, a Windows Server 2003 system can suffer a service or application startup problem that could leave a server incapable of completing a normal bootup sequence. Because the operating system cannot be accessed in this case, the system remains unavailable until this problem can be resolved.

Windows Server 2003 includes a few alternative bootup options to help administrators restore a server to a working state. Several advanced bootup options can be accessed by pressing the F8 key when the boot loader screen is displayed. If the Recovery Console was previously installed, it is listed as an option in the boot loader screen. The advanced boot options include the following:

▶ **Safe Mode**—This mode starts the operating system with only the most basic services and hardware drivers, and disables networking. This allows administrators to access the operating system in a less functional state to make configuration changes to service startup options, some application configurations, and the system Registry.

▶ **Safe Mode with Networking**—This option is the same as Safe Mode, but networking drivers are enabled during operation. This mode also starts many more operating system services upon startup.

▶ **Safe Mode with Command Prompt**—This option is similar to the Safe Mode option; however, the Windows Explorer shell is not started by default.

▶ **Enable Boot Logging**—This option boots the system normally, but all the services and drivers loaded at startup are recorded in a file named ntbtlog.txt, located in the %systemroot% directory. The default location for this file is C:\Windows\ntbtlog.txt. To simplify reading this file, the administrator must delete the existing file before a bootup sequence is logged so that only the information from the last bootup is logged.

▶ **Enable VGA Mode**—This mode loads the current display driver, but it displays the desktop at the lowest resolution. This mode is handy if a server is plugged into a different monitor that cannot support the current resolution.

▶ **Last Known Good Configuration**—This mode starts the operating system using Registry and driver information saved during the last successful logon.

▶ **Directory Services Restore Mode**—This mode is only for domain controllers and allows for maintenance and restoration of the Active Directory database or the SYSVOL folder.

▶ **Debugging Mode**—This mode sends operating system debugging information to other servers through a serial connection. This requires a server on the receiving end with a logging server that is prepared to accept this data. Most likely, standard administrators will never use this mode.

▶ **Start Windows Normally**—As the name states, this mode loads the operating system as it would normally run.

▶ **Reboot**—This option reboots the server.

▶ **Return to OS Choices Menu**—This option returns the screen to the boot loader page so that the correct operating system can be chosen and started.

The Recovery Console

The Recovery Console provides an option for administrators to boot up a system using alternate configuration files to perform troubleshooting tasks. Using the Recovery Console, the bootup sequence can be changed, alternate boot options can be specified, volumes can be created or extended, and service startup options can be changed. The Recovery Console has only a limited number of commands that can be used, making it a simple console to learn. If Normal or Safe Mode bootup options are not working, the administrator can use the Recovery Console to make system changes or read the information stored in the boot logging file using the `type` command. The boot logging file is located at `C:\Windows\ntbtlog.txt` by default and exists only if someone tried to start the operating system using any of the Safe Mode options or the boot logging option.

Recovering from a Complete Server Failure

Because hardware occasionally fails and, in the real world, operating systems do have problems, a server-recovery plan is essential, even though it might never be used. The last thing any administrator wants is for a server failure to occur and to end up on the phone with Microsoft technical support asking for the server to be restored from backup when no plan is in place. To keep from being caught unprepared, the administrator should have a recovery plan for every possible failure associated with Windows Server 2003 systems.

Restoring Versus Rebuilding

When a complete system failure occurs, whether it is because of a site outage, a hardware component failure, or a software corruption problem, the method of recovery depends on the administrator's major goal. The goal is to get the server up and running, of course, but behind the scenes, many more questions should be answered before the restore is started:

▶ How long will it take to restore the server from a full backup?

▶ If the server failed because of software corruption, will restoring the server from backup also restore the corruption that actually caused the failure?

▶ Will reloading the operating system and Exchange manually followed by restoring the System State be faster than doing a full restore?

Loading the Windows Server 2003 operating system and Exchange Server 2003 software can be a relatively quick process. This ensures that all the correct files and drivers are loaded correctly and all that needs to follow is a System State restore to recover the server configuration and restore the data. One of the problems that can occur is that, upon installation, some applications generate Registry keys based on the system's computer name, which can change if a System State restore is performed.

Exchange Server 2007 has a `setup /recoverserver` installation option and does not need the server's System State restore—just the original computer name and domain membership, as long as computer and user certificates are not being used. Using this switch also prevents the Exchange computer from creating the default storage groups and databases. This simplifies the process of restoring the server later.

The key to choosing whether to rebuild or restore from backup is understanding the dependencies of the applications and services to the operating system, and having confidence in the server's stability at the time of the previous backups. The worst situation is attempting a restore from backup that takes several hours, only to find that the problem has been restored as well.

Manually Recovering a Server

When a complete server system failure is encountered and the state of the operating system or an application is in question, the operating system can be recovered manually. Locating the system's original configuration settings is the first step. This information is normally stored in a server build document or wherever server configuration information is kept.

Because each system is different, as a general guideline for restoring a system manually, perform the following steps:

1. Install a new operating system on the original system hardware and disk volume, or one as close to the original configuration as possible. Be sure to install the same operating system version—for example, Windows Server 2003, Enterprise or Standard Edition.

2. During installation, name the system using the name of the original server, but do not join a domain.

3. Do not install additional services during installation, and proceed by performing a basic installation.

4. When the operating system completes installation, install any additional hardware drivers as necessary and update the operating system to the service pack and security patches that the failed server was expected to have installed. To reduce compatibility problems, install the service packs and updates as outlined in the server build document to ensure that any installed applications will function as desired. During a restore is not the time to roll out additional system changes. The goal is to get the system back online, not to upgrade it.

5. Using the Disk Management console, create and format disk volumes and assign the correct drive letters as recorded in the server build document.

6. If the server was originally part of a domain, join the domain using the original server name. Because many Windows Server 2003 services use the server name or require the service to be authorized in a domain, perform this step before installing any additional services or applications.

7. Install any additional Windows Server 2003 services as defined in the server build document.

8. Install Exchange Server 2007 using the same version of Exchange (Standard or Enterprise) that was originally installed. Apply any Exchange service packs and updates that were expected to be on the original server as well. When installing Exchange, use the setup /recoverserver installation process that will install Exchange but will not add new databases.

9. Restore Exchange data to the new server.

10. Test functionality, add this system to the backup schedule, and start a full backup.

> **NOTE**
>
> If certificates were issued to the previous server, the new server must import the same certificates or enroll with the certificate authority (CA) for a new certificate before encrypted communication can occur.

Restoring a Server Using a System State Restore

The restoration of an Exchange Server 2007 system into an existing Active Directory domain does not require the installation of the System State because the procedures covered in the previous section will recover the server and database for the server replacement. However, if the failure of Exchange also included the loss of the Active Directory global catalog and there is no other global catalog in the organization, a System State restore of the global catalog needs to be performed before Exchange can be restored.

Exchange Server 2007 requires a valid Active Directory to be in place. This process might be required if the Exchange server was the only server in the network and, thus, the loss of the Exchange server also meant the loss of the only global catalog server. This also might be the case if there was a site failure and all servers, including the Exchange server and Active Directory global catalog server, were lost.

To recover the System State, follow these steps:

1. Shut down the original server or build a new server hardware system.

2. Install a new copy of Windows Server 2003 on the system hardware and disk volume, or one as close to the original configuration as possible. Be sure to install the same operating system version—for example, Windows Server 2003, Enterprise or Standard Edition.

3. During installation, name the system using the name of the original server, but do not join a domain.

> **NOTE**
>
> If the machine is joined to the original domain during the clean installation, a new security identifier (SID) will be generated for the machine account. A System State restore after this restores an invalid computer SID, and many services and applications will fail.

4. Do not install additional services during installation, and proceed by performing a basic installation.

5. When the operating system completes installation, install any additional hardware drivers as necessary and update the operating system to the latest service pack and security patches. To reduce compatibility problems, install the service packs and updates as outlined in the server build document, to ensure that any installed applications will function as desired.

6. Using the Disk Management console, create and format disk volumes and assign the correct drive letters as recorded in the server build document.

7. After the installation, restore any necessary drivers or updates to match the original configuration. This information should be gathered from a server configuration document (server build document). Then reboot as necessary.

After all the updates have been installed, restore the previously backed-up System State data; afterward, restore any additional application or user data.

System State Restore

This section outlines how to restore the System State to a member or standalone Windows Server 2003 system. To restore the System State, perform the following steps:

1. Click Start, All Programs, Accessories, System Tools, Backup.

2. If this is the first time you've run Backup, it opens in Wizard mode. Choose to run it in Advanced mode by clicking the Advanced Mode hyperlink.

3. Click the Restore Wizard (Advanced) button to start the Restore Wizard.

4. Click Next on the Restore Wizard welcome screen to continue.

5. On the What to Restore page, select the appropriate cataloged backup medium, expand the catalog selection, and check System State. Click Next to continue.

6. If the correct tape or file backup medium does not appear in this window, cancel the restore process. Then, from the Restore Wizard, locate and catalog the appropriate medium and return to the restore process from step 1.

7. On the Completing the Restore Wizard page, click Finish to start the restore. The restore will look similar to Figure 33.1.

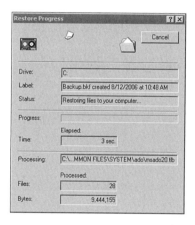

FIGURE 33.1   Performing a restore on an Exchange server.

8. When the restore is complete, review the backup log for detailed information, and click Close on the Restore Progress window when finished.

9. Reboot the system as prompted.

10. When the system restarts, log on using an account with local and/or domain Administrator rights, as necessary.

11. After the System State is restored, Exchange Server 2007 can be installed.

Restoring a System Using an Automated System Recovery Restore

When a system has failed and all other recovery options have been exhausted, an Automated System Recovery (ASR) restore can be performed, provided that an ASR backup has been previously performed. The ASR restore will restore all disk and volume configurations, including redefining volumes and formatting them. This means that the data stored on all volumes needs to be restored after the ASR restore is complete. This restore brings a failed system back to complete server operation, except for certain applications that require special configurations after the restore. For example, the Remote Storage service data needs to be restored separately.

> **NOTE**
>
> An ASR restore re-creates all disk volumes, but if a new or alternate system is being used, each disk must be of equal or greater size to the disks on the original server. Otherwise, the ASR restore will fail.

To perform an ASR restore, follow these steps:

1. Locate the ASR floppy created for the failed node, or create the floppy from the files saved in the ASR backup medium. For information on creating the ASR floppy from the ASR backup medium, refer to Help and Support from any Windows Server 2003 Help and Support tool.

2. Insert the Windows Server 2003 operating system medium in the CD-ROM drive of the server to which you are restoring, and start the installation from this CD.

3. When prompted, press F6 to install any third-party storage device drivers, if necessary. This includes any third-party disks or tape controllers that Windows Server 2003 will not natively recognize.

4. Press F2 when prompted to perform an Automated System Recovery.

5. Insert the ASR floppy disk into the floppy drive, and press Enter when prompted. If the system does not have a local floppy drive, one must temporarily be added; otherwise, an ASR restore cannot be performed.

6. The operating system installation proceeds by restoring disk volume information and reformatting the volumes associated with the operating system. When this process is complete, the operating system will restart after a short countdown, the graphic-based OS installation will begin, and the ASR backup will attempt to reconnect to the backup medium automatically. If the backup medium is on a network drive, the ASR backup reconnection will fail. If it fails, specify the network location of the backup medium using a Universal Naming Convention (UNC) path, and enter authentication information, if prompted.

7. When the medium is located, open the medium, click Next, and then click Finish to begin recovering the remaining ASR data.

8. When the ASR restore is complete, if any local disk data was not restored with the ASR restore, restore all local disks.

9. Click Start, All Programs, Accessories, System Tools, Backup.

10. If this is the first time you've run Backup, it opens in Wizard mode. Choose to run it in Advanced mode by clicking the Advanced Mode hyperlink.

11. Click the Restore Wizard (Advanced) button to start the Restore Wizard.

12. Click Next on the Restore Wizard welcome screen to continue.

13. On the What to Restore page, select the appropriate cataloged backup medium, expand the catalog selection, and check the desired data on each local drive. Click Next to continue.

14. On the Completing the Restore Wizard page, click Finish to start the restore. Because you want to restore only what ASR did not, you do not need to make any advanced restore configuration changes.

15. When the restore is complete, reboot the server, if prompted.

16. After the reboot is complete, log on to the restored server and check server configuration and functionality.

17. If everything is working properly, perform a full backup and log off the server.

Restoring the Boot Loader File

When a Windows Server 2003 system is recovered using an ASR restore, the boot.ini file might not be restored. This file contains the options for booting into different operating systems on multiboot systems and booting into the Recovery Console if it was previously installed. To restore this file, simply restore it from backup to an alternate folder or drive. Delete the boot.ini file from the C:\ root folder and move the restored file from the alternate location to C:\ or whichever drive the boot.ini file was previously located on.

Recovering Exchange Application and Exchange Data

To recover an Exchange server, there are several different ways of rebuilding the core Exchange server and restoring the Exchange data. The restoration of Exchange databases must be done to a server with the exact same server name as the original server from which the databases were backed up.

After the Active Directory and base Windows server(s) have been installed, the first process is installing or restoring the Exchange application software; the second process is installing the data files for Exchange.

Recovering Using Ntbackup.exe

When program and data files are corrupt or missing, or a previously backed-up copy is needed, the information can be restored using Ntbackup.exe if a previous backup was performed using this utility. The following process should be followed:

1. Log on to the server using an account that has at least the privileges to restore files and folders. Backup Operators and Local Administrator groups have this right, by default.

2. Click Start, All Programs, Accessories, System Tools, Backup.

3. If this is the first time you've run Backup, it opens in Wizard mode. Click Next to continue with a restore.

4. Select Restore Files and Settings, and then click Next.

5. On the What to Restore page, select the appropriate cataloged backup medium, expand the catalog selection, and select to restore all applicable volumes (C:, D:, E:, and so on), Information Stores, and the System State. Then click Next.

> **NOTE**
>
> To restore the Information Stores via Ntbackup, the Exchange services must be up and running.

6. If the correct tape or file backup medium does not appear in this window, cancel the restore process. Then, from the Restore Wizard, locate and catalog the appropriate medium and return to the restore process from step 4.

7. On the Completing the Restore Wizard page, click Finish to start the restore.

8. When the restore is complete, review the backup log for detailed information, and click Close on the Restore Progress window when finished.

9. Reboot the server. The system should come up as a complete replacement of the original server system.

> **NOTE**
>
> Third-party backup products for Exchange Server 2003 offer various backup and restore options that go beyond ntbackup's functionality, including individual mailbox or message restores as well as integration with Volume Shadow Copy Services (VSS).

Performing a Restore of Only Exchange Database Files

If Exchange Server program files have been corrupt or the restore of the full backup information from tape might restore corruption and server instability, an administrator can choose to install Exchange Server 2007 from scratch and restore just the database files. This process involves installing the Exchange program files from CD-ROM and then restoring a copy of the Exchange databases.

To install Exchange and restore the Exchange database files, do the following:

1. Log on to the server using an account that has administrative privileges to install application software as well as restore data from tape.

2. Ensure that the server has the exact same server and that the version of Windows is the same version. Also be sure that all the same services are installed. This would include things like IIS or any audio Codecs installed for unified messaging functions.

3. In Active Directory Users and Computers, reset the computer account for the server you are rebuilding.

4. Join the domain.

5. Install Microsoft Command Shell from http://go.microsoft.com/fwlink/?linkid= 64457&clcid=0x409.

6. Install Microsoft Management Console 3.0 from http://www.microsoft.com/ downloads/details.aspx?familyid=b65b9b17-5c6d-427c-90aa-7f814e48373b& displaylang=en.

7. Install Exchange Server 2007 using the setup /recoverserver command, which will run through a script displaying a screen similar to the one shown in Figure 33.2.

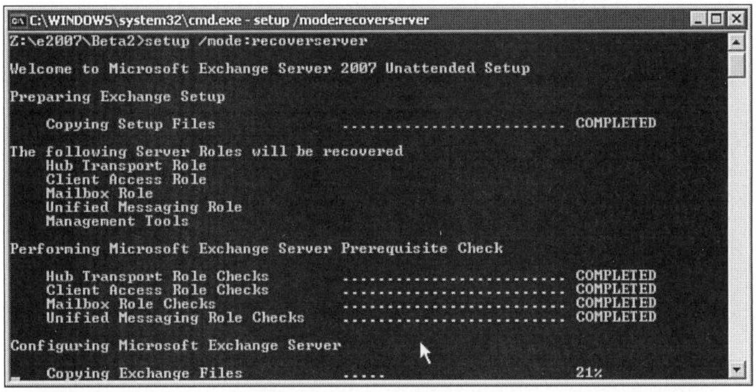

FIGURE 33.2   Selecting the Recover Server method of installation.

8. After Exchange Server 2007 has been installed, restore data files to the Exchange server.

Restoring Exchange Data Files from Tape

If the Exchange data files are stored on tape, restore just the Exchange database files by doing the following:

1. Click Start, All Programs, Accessories, System Tools, Backup.

2. If this is the first time you've run Backup, it opens in Wizard mode. Choose to run it in Advanced mode by clicking the Advanced Mode hyperlink.

3. Click the Restore Wizard (Advanced) button to start the Restore Wizard.

4. Click Next on the Restore Wizard welcome screen to continue.

5. On the What to Restore page, select the appropriate cataloged backup medium, expand the catalog selection, and select the Information Stores for restoration.

6. If the correct tape or file backup medium does not appear in this window, cancel the restore process. Then, from the Restore Wizard, locate and catalog the appropriate medium and return to the restore process from step 4.

7. On the Completing the Restore Wizard page, click Finish to start the restore.

8. When the restore is complete, review the backup log for detailed information, and click Close on the Restore Progress window when finished. Reboot the Exchange server to restart all services. (Alternatively, after a restore of data, the individual databases can just be mounted to get the Exchange server back and operational.)

> **NOTE**
>
> If you restore a storage group that was utilizing Local Continuous Backup, you need to break and reestablish this mirror. Steps for performing this can be found in Chapter 32.

Recovering from Database Corruption

If an Exchange database is corrupt, it is not extremely effective to restore the corrupt database to a production server. The server might continue to operate, but database corruption never goes away on its own, and you eventually will have to repair the database. In fact, when minor database corruption is not repaired, the corruption can get to the point that entire sections of the Exchange database become inaccessible.

A couple of methods can be used to repair a corrupt Exchange database, or at least restore the database and extract good information from the database. Key to the successful recovery of as much information as possible is using the right tool. In many cases, administrators jump right into using the ESEUTIL /p repair command; instead of repairing the Exchange database to 100% condition, the utility finds a corrupt section of the database and deletes all information from that portion of the database on. So, although the Exchange system becomes 100% clean, the utility deleted 20%–30% of the data that was in the database to get the database to a clean state. The ESEUTIL /P command is the task of last resort: Other tools work around corrupt database areas and allow the administrator to recover as much of the data as possible.

Going all the way back to the start of the chapter in the "What to Do Before Performing Any Server-Recovery Process" section, this is where having a complete backup of the databases in Exchange is really important. If a process to repair or recover information causes more harm to the database than good, there is still a backup copy to restore and start again.

Exchange 2007 makes this process easier for the new administrator by introducing the Database Recovery Management tool that will analyze the failed databases for the administrator and choose what tools to run against them.

Using the Database Recovery Management Tool

Exchange 2007 brings several new tools to make life easier for the Exchange administrator. The new Database Recovery Management tool automates many of the processes of evaluating corrupted databases and repairing them. To utilize this tool with a corrupted database, perform the following steps:

1. Open EMC.

2. Expand tools.

3. Choose Database Recovery Management.

4. Let the tool check for updates.

5. Choose the Go to Welcome screen.

6. Type in a label for this activity.

7. Enter server and domain controller names, and click Next.

8. If the connectivity tests are acceptable, click Gather Database Information from AD.

9. Click Troubleshoot Database Mount Problem.

10. Select the storage group you want to troubleshoot, and click Next.

11. Select the database you are troubleshooting, and click Analyze Selected Databases.

12. View the information given.

13. Click Go Back to Task Center.

14. Click Repair Database Wizard.

15. Select the storage group, and click Next.

16. Select the database and click Next.

17. View the repair results as shown in Figure 33.3.

18. Click Go Back to Task Center.

19. Close the Troubleshooting Assistant.

Flat-File Copying the Exchange Databases

One of the best techniques Exchange experts use when working to recover corruption in a database is to make a flat-file copy of the Exchange databases. A flat-file copy is merely an exact copy of the Exchange databases copied to another portion of the server hard drive or to another server. To do a manual copy of the databases, do the following:

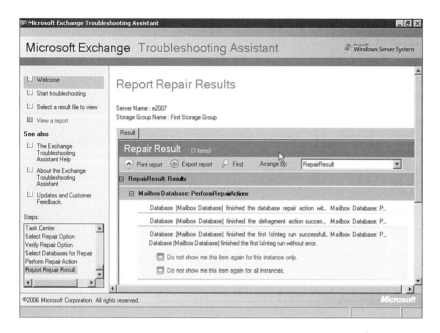

FIGURE 33.3   Viewing the repair results.

1. Dismount the Exchange database stores by going into the Exchange System Manager. Traverse the tree past Administrative Groups, Servers, Storage Group. Right-click on the mailbox store, and select Dismount Store.

2. Dismount the store for all mailbox stores you will be working on.

3. Copy (using Windows Explorer, or XCOPY) the *.edb files to a safe location.

NOTE

If the databases need to be manually restored, a simple XCOPY (or Windows Explorer copy) of the databases back to the original subdirectories will bring the data back to the condition the databases were in at the time the databases were copied off the system. If the Exchange databases were properly dismounted before they were copied, the logs would have already been committed to the database and the database can be remounted exactly where it left off.

Moving Mailboxes to Another Server in the Site

One way of extracting mail from a corrupt database is to move the mailbox or mailboxes to a different server in the site. Instead of trying to run utilities to fix the corruption in the database, which can take several hours (or even days, depending on the size of the database and the amount of corruption that needs to be fixed), an administrator can set up another server in the Exchange site and move the mailboxes to a new server.

Moving mailboxes grabs all of the mail, calendar, contacts, and other mailbox information from one server and moves the information to a new server. As the information is written to the new server, the information is automatically defragmented and corruption is not migrated. In addition, mailboxes can be moved from one server to another without ever having to bring down the production server. A mailbox user must be logged off Outlook and must not be accessing Exchange before the mailbox can be moved. However, if mailboxes are moved when individuals are out of the office, at lunch, or on weekends, the mailboxes can be moved without users ever knowing that their information was moved from one system to another.

The two caveats to moving mailboxes are these: Corrupt mailboxes will not move, and user Outlook profiles will be changed. For Outlook profiles, because a user's Outlook profiles point to a specific server, when a mailbox is moved from one server to another, the user's profile also needs to point to the new server. Fortunately, with Exchange and Outlook, when a user's mailbox is moved, Outlook tries to access the mailbox on the original server, and the server notifies Outlook that the mailbox has been moved to a new Exchange server. The user's Outlook profile automatically changes to associate the profile to the new server where the user's mailbox resides. So, as long as the old server remains operational and the user attempts to access email from the old server, the profiles will be automatically changed the next time the user tries to access email. Typically, within 1 to 2 weeks after moving mailboxes from one server to another, the user profiles are all automatically changed.

As for corrupt mailboxes, unfortunately, Exchange typically does not move a corrupt mailbox. So, if a user's mailbox has been corrupted, the mailbox will remain on the old server. Moving the data from the corrupt mailbox will need to be handled in a manner specified in the following section, "Recovering Data with a Recovery Storage Group." However, if 80%–90% of the user mailboxes can be moved to a new server, the administrators are trying to recover only a handful of mailboxes instead of all mailboxes on a server. This could mean far less downtime for all users who had mail on the server and could limit the exposure of data loss to a limited number of users. It will also result in much faster results when running the database recovery tools as the database will be much smaller.

To move mailboxes between servers in a site, do the following:

1. Open the Exchange Management Console.

2. Expand Recipient Configuration and click Mailbox.

3. Highlight the mailboxes to be moved.

4. From the Action menu, choose Move Mailbox.

5. The Move Mailbox tool launches. Select the destination for the mailbox to be moved, and click Next.

6. Choose how you want the tool to deal with corrupted messages, and click Next.

7. Choose to either move the mailbox immediately or to be scheduled for a later time. Click Next.

8. Review the proposed changes and if you are satisfied that they are correct, click Move.

9. Review the results of the mailbox move, and click Finish to complete the move.

Running the ISINTEG and ESEUTIL Utilities

When a database is determined to be corrupt, usually an administrator is directed to run the built-in utilities on Exchange to run maintenance on the databases. The utilities are the ISINTEG ("eye-ess-in-tehg") and ESEUTIL ("ee-ess-ee-u-tihl"). However, depending on the condition of the database, a very corrupt database can take several hours to run, only to result in the loss of data. Some administrators are incorrectly told to never run the utilities because they will always result in loss of data. It's typically just a lack of knowledge of how the utilities work that leads to misunderstanding the potential results of the databases.

As noted in the previous two sections, there might be better options for recovering information from a corrupt database. Instead of trying to fix a known corrupt database, simply migrating the information off a server or extracting information from corrupt databases is frequently a better fix. However, if the determination is to run the utilities, a few things should be noted:

▶ The ISINTEG utility is a high-level utility that checks the consistency of the database, validating the branches of the database that handle data, data directory tables, attachment objects, and the like. Fixing the database table makes way for a more intensive data integrity check of the database.

▶ The ESEUTIL utility is a low-level utility that checks the data within the database. ESEUTIL does not differentiate between a corrupt section of the database and how that section impacts mailboxes or messages. So, when a complete repair is performed using ESEUTIL, entire mailboxes can be deleted or all attachments for the entire database can be eliminated to fix the corruption. This is why running ESEUTIL to repair a database is a function of last resort.

▶ To run ISINTEG on a database takes around 1 hour for every 10GB being scanned for a moderately corrupt database. The repairs are done relatively quickly, and the database is ready for more extensive scanning.

▶ Running ESEUTIL on a database takes anywhere from 1 hour for every 10GB to up to 1 hour per 1GB, depending on the level of repair being performed. It is not unreasonable to see a relatively corrupt 30-GB database take more than 24 hours to complete the repair.

▶ ISINTEG and ESEUTIL can be performed only offline, meaning that the Exchange server is offline during the process. Users cannot access their mailboxes during the ISINTEG and ESEUTIL processes. Thus, if it takes 20 to 40 hours of downtime to complete the repair of a database, the Move Mailbox method that can be run without bringing servers offline is frequently a more palatable solution.

▶ However, if run on a regular basis, the ISINTEG and ESEUTIL utilities can clean up an Exchange database before serious corruption occurs. Administrators who get scared off performing maintenance because of the potential threat of losing data could actually minimize their chance of data corruption if the utilities are run regularly. See Chapter 19 for recommended maintenance practices.

The common parameters used for the ISINTEG and ESEUTIL utilities are as follows. For regular maintenance such as checking the database structure's integrity and performing defragmentation of the database, the following commands should be run:

```
isinteg -s SERVERNAME -test allfoldertests
eseutil /d priv1.edb
```

When run against an Exchange server, the ISINTEG utility produces a summary similar to the one in Figure 33.4.

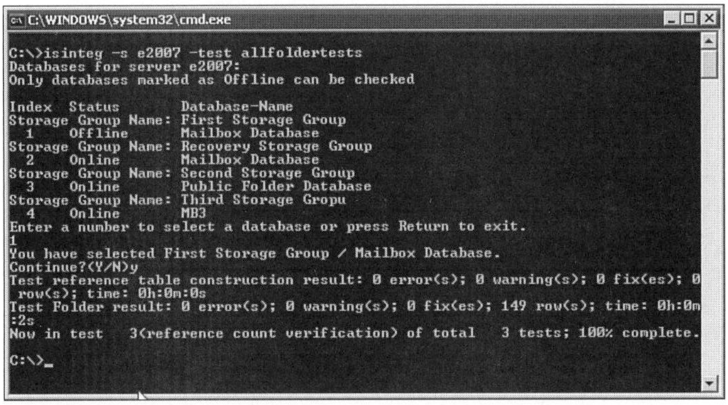

FIGURE 33.4   Results from an ISINTEG utility run.

> **NOTE**
>
> The ISINTEG and ESEUTIL utilities typically reside in the \Program Files\ Exchsrvr\Bin directory of the Exchange server. The databases that are typically specified in ESEUTIL are the priv1.edb and pub1.edb. However, if an organization has multiple database and storage groups, several databases might need to be checked separately for integrity.

When a database needs to be repaired, eseutil /p priv1.edb can be run. Beware: The /p repair command is a brute-force repair and deletes sections of the database to make the integrity of the database clean. A message provides an additional warning about ESEUTIL, as shown in Figure 33.5. When running the /p command in ESEUTIL, entire sections of the database might be deleted to repair and recover the state of the database.

FIGURE 33.5   Running `ESEUTIL` /p.

> **NOTE**
>
> Prior to a disaster, if the `ISINTEG` or `ESEUTIL` utilities have not been run against an
> Exchange database for a long period of time, restore the database from tape to an
> Exchange server in a lab environment to run tests. These tests can tell you how much
> corruption might be present as well as give an indication of how long it might take to
> repair the database.

Using the Recovery Storage Group in Exchange Server 2007

When an administrator wants to recover a mail message, a calendar appointment, a contact, a folder, or entire user mailboxes, Exchange Server 2007 has a recovery storage group function and wizard that provides a recovery mechanism. Prior to Exchange 2003, if an administrator wanted to recover a mailbox or information, the administrator would have to build a brand-new Exchange server with the exact same server name in the lab and then restore a database to the lab server. After the restore, the administrator could run the ExMerge utility to export the desired mailbox or information, and then transfer the information to the production server and ExMerge the information back into the production server.

The recovery storage group in Exchange Server 2007 facilitates the restore of any database, including an Exchange 2000 SP3 or higher database from any server in the Exchange organization. So, an Exchange database can be restored to the recovery storage group, and then information can be extracted without ever having to bring up another server or shut down the production server. The Disaster Recovery Management (DRM) tool makes this process even easier by intelligently offering alternate options to the administrator. DRM even goes as far as to offer to create a dial-tone recovery storage group for rapid restoration of send and receive functionality.

Recovering Data with a Recovery Storage Group

A recovery storage group is created on any Exchange Server 2007 system. To create a recovery storage group, do the following:

1. Launch the Exchange Management Console.

2. Click the Toolbox and double-click Database Recovery Management.

NOTE

The server that will host the recovery storage group must have enough disk space to allow for the full restore of the database that will be hosted on the system.

3. Click Go to Welcome screen.

4. Enter a label to identify your activity. Enter the server and domain controller names, and click Next.

5. Click Gather Database Information from AD.

6. From the Manage Recovery Storage Group options, click Create a Recovery Storage Group.

7. Choose the storage group that contains the database you plan to recover, and click Next.

8. Click Create Recovery Storage Group.

9. When the recovery storage group is created successfully, click Go Back to Task Center.

10. Close the Task Center.

11. From the Run command, run Ntbackup.

12. The Backup or Restore Wizard launches; click Next.

13. Choose restore files and settings, and click Next.

14. Expand the media and select the Information Store associated with the storage group you selected when creating the recovery storage group. Click Next.

15. On the Restore To line, enter the name of the server that is hosting the recovery storage group. For Temporary Location for Log and Patch Files, choose a local directory with sufficient space. Check the Last Restore Set check box. Click Next.

16. Click the Advanced button.

17. Choose to restore files to an alternate location. Browse to the directory created by the recovery storage group, and click Next.

18. Leave the check in place for the Preserving Existing Volume Mount Points check box, and click Next.

19. Click Finish and the restore will begin.

20. When the files restore successfully, click Close and return to the Database Recovery Management tool.

21. Choose Mount or Dismount Databases in the Recovery Storage Group.

22. Check the box for the database you plan to mount, and click Mount Selected Database.

23. Click Go Back to Task Center.

24. Click Merge or Copy Mailbox Contents.

25. Select the source database, and click Gather Merge information.

26. In this scenario, do not check the box for Swap Database Configurations. That is used in dial-tone recovery. Click Next.

27. If you do not need to do custom GUID matching, click Perform Pre-merge Tasks.

28. Check the mailboxes you want to merge with the production mailboxes, and click Perform Merge Actions.

29. When the merge is complete, close the Database Recovery Management tool.

Recovering Internet Information Services

When Internet Information Services (IIS) data is erased or the service is not functioning as desired, restoring the configuration might be necessary. To restore the IIS metabase data, perform the following steps:

1. Log on to the desired IIS server using an account with local Administrator privileges.

2. Click Start, Programs, Administrative Tools, Internet Information Services (IIS) to start the IIS Manager.

3. Select the web server in the left pane.

4. Select Action, All Tasks, Backup/Restore Configuration.

5. A listing of automatic backups that IIS has already performed appears on the Configuration Backup/Restore page. Select the desired backup and click the Restore button to perform a manual restore.

6. A pop-up window opens stating that all Internet services will be stopped to restore the data and restarted afterward. Click Yes to begin the restore.

7. When the restore is complete, a confirmation pop-up window is displayed. Click OK to close this window.

8. Click Close on the Configuration Backup/Restore page.

9. Back in the IIS Manager window, verify that the restore was successful, close the window, and log off the server when you're finished.

Backups are stored in `%systemroot%\system32\Inetsrv\MetaBack`, by default.

Recovering IIS Data and Logs

IIS web and FTP folders are stored in the `C:\InetPub\` directory. The default location for the IIS logs is `C:\Windows\system32\LogFiles`. To recover the IIS website, FTP site, or IIS logs, restore the files using either shadow copy data or a backup/restore tool such as `Ntbackup.exe`.

Recovering the Cluster Service

Cluster nodes require that special backup and restore procedures be followed to ensure a successful recovery if a cluster failure is encountered. For detailed information on backing up and restoring a cluster node, refer to Chapter 31, or use the Windows Server 2003 Help and Support tool.

Recovering Windows Server 2003 Domain Controllers

When a Windows Server 2003 domain controller fails, the administrator needs to either recover this server or understand how to completely and properly remove this domain controller from the domain. The following are some questions to consider:

▶ Did this domain controller host any of the domain or forest Flexible Single Master Operations (FSMO) roles?

▶ Was this domain controller a global catalog (GC) server, and, if so, was it the only GC in a single Active Directory site?

▶ If the server failed because of Active Directory corruption, has the corruption been replicated to other domain controllers?

▶ Is this server a replication hub or bridgehead server for Active Directory site replication?

Using the preceding list of questions, the administrator can decide how best to deal with the failure. For example, if the failed domain controller hosted the PDC emulator FSMO role, the server could be restored or the FSMO role could be manually seized by a separate domain controller. If the domain controller was the bridgehead server for Active Directory site replication, recovering this server might make the most sense so that the desired primary replication topology remains intact. The administrator should recover a failed domain controller as any other server would be recovered, restore the OS from an ASR restore, or build a clean server, restore the System State, and perform subsequent restores of local drive data as necessary.

Recovering Active Directory

When undesired changes are made in Active Directory or the Active Directory database is corrupted on a domain controller, recovering the Active Directory database might be necessary. Restoring Active Directory can seem like a difficult task, unless frequent backups are performed and the administrator understands all the restore options.

The Active Directory Database

The Active Directory database contains all the information stored in Active Directory. The global catalog information is also stored in this database. The actual filename is `ntds.dit` and, by default, is located in `C:\Windows\NTDS\`. When a domain controller is restored from server failure, the Active Directory database is restored with the System State. If no special steps are taken when the server comes back online, it will ask any other domain controllers for a copy of the latest version of the Active Directory database. This situation is called a *nonauthoritative restore* of Active Directory.

When a change in Active Directory needs to be rolled back or the entire database needs to be rolled back across the enterprise or domain, an authoritative restore of the Active Directory database is necessary.

Active Directory Nonauthoritative Restore

When a domain controller is rebuilt from a backup after a complete system failure, simply recovering this server using a restore of the local drives and System State is enough to get this machine back into the production network. When the machine is back online and establishes connectivity to other domain controllers, any Active Directory and SYSVOL updates will be replicated to the restored server.

Nonauthoritative restores are also necessary when a single domain controller's copy of the Active Directory database is corrupt and is keeping the server from booting up properly. To restore a reliable copy of the Active Directory database, the entire System State needs to be restored; if additional services reside on the domain controller, restoring the previous configuration data for each of these services might be undesirable. In a situation like this, the best option is to try to recover the Active Directory database using database maintenance and recovery utilities such as `Esentutl.exe` and `Ntdsutil.exe`. These utilities can be used to check the database consistency, defragment, and repair and troubleshoot the Active Directory database. For information on Active Directory maintenance practices with these utilities, refer to Windows Server 2003 Help and Support.

To restore the Active Directory database to a single domain controller to recover from database corruption, perform the following steps:

1. Power up the domain controller and press the F8 key when the boot loader is displayed on the screen.

2. When the advanced boot options are displayed, scroll down, select Directory Services Restore Mode, and then press Enter to boot the server. This mode boots the Active Directory database in an offline state. When you choose this boot option, you can maintain and restore the Active Directory database.

3. When the server boots up, log on using the username Administrator and the Restore mode password specified when the server was promoted to a domain controller. To change the Restore mode password on a domain controller running in Normal mode, use the `Ntdsutil.exe` utility; this process is covered in Chapter 31.

4. Click Start, Run.

5. Type `Ntbackup.exe` and click OK.

6. When the Backup or Restore window opens, click the Advanced Mode hyperlink.

7. Select the Restore and Manage Media tab.

8. Select the appropriate backup medium, expand it, and check the System State. If the correct medium is not available, the file must be located or the tape must be loaded in the tape drive and cataloged before it can be used to restore the System State.

9. Choose to restore the data to the original location, and click the Start Restore button in the lower-right corner of the backup window.

10. A pop-up window indicates that restoring the System State to the original location will overwrite the current System State. Click OK to continue.

11. A Confirm Restore window opens in which you can choose advanced restore options. Click OK to initiate the restore of the System State.

12. When the restore is complete, a system restart is necessary to update the services and files restored during this operation. Because only a nonauthoritative restore of the Active Directory database is necessary, click Yes to restart the server.

13. After the server reboots, log on as a domain administrator.

14. Check the server event log and Active Directory information to ensure that the database has been restored successfully. Then log off the server.

Active Directory Authoritative Restore

When a change made to Active Directory is causing problems, or when an object is modified or deleted and needs to be recovered to the entire enterprise, an Active Directory authoritative restore is necessary.

To perform an authoritative restore of the Active Directory database, follow these steps:

1. Power up the domain controller, and press the F8 key when the boot loader is displayed on the screen.

2. When the advanced boot options are displayed, scroll down, select Directory Services Restore Mode, and press Enter to boot the server. This mode boots the Active Directory database in an offline state. When you choose this boot option, you can maintain and restore the Active Directory database.

3. When the server boots up, log on using the username Administrator and the Restore mode password specified when the server was promoted to a domain controller. To change the Restore mode password on a domain controller running in Normal mode, use the `Ntdsutil.exe` utility; this process is covered in Chapter 31.

4. Click Start, Run.

5. Type `Ntbackup.exe` and click OK.

6. When the Backup or Restore window opens, click the Advanced Mode hyperlink.

7. Select the Restore and Manage Media tab.

8. Select the appropriate backup medium, expand it, and check the System State. If the correct medium is not available, the file must be located, or the tape must be loaded in the tape drive and cataloged before it can be used to restore the System State.

9. Choose to restore the data to the original location, and click the Start Restore button in the lower-right corner of the backup window.

10. A pop-up window indicates that restoring the System State to the original location will overwrite the current System State. Click OK to continue.

11. A Confirm Restore window opens in which you can choose advanced restore options. Click OK to initiate the restore of the System State.

12. When the restore is complete, a system restart is necessary to update the services and files restored during this operation. Because only a nonauthoritative restore of the Active Directory database is necessary, click No.

13. Close the backup window, and click Start, Run.

14. Type cmd.exe and click OK to open a command prompt.

15. At the command prompt, type ntdsutil.exe and press Enter.

16. Type Authoritative restore and press Enter.

17. Type Restore Database and press Enter to restore the entire database. The respective Active Directory partitions, such as the schema partition and the domain-naming context partition, are replicated to all other appropriate domain controllers in the domain and/or forest.

18. An Authoritative Restore Confirmation dialog box appears; click Yes to start the authoritative restore.

19. The command prompt window displays whether the authoritative restore was successful. Close the command prompt and reboot the server.

20. Boot up the server in Normal mode, log on, and open the correct Active Directory tools to verify whether the restore was successful. Also, check on other domain controllers to ensure that the restore is being replicated to them.

21. When you're done, perform a full backup of the domain controller or at least the System State; then log off the server when the backup is complete.

Partial Active Directory Authoritative Restore

Most Active Directory authoritative restores are performed to recover from a modification or deletion of an Active Directory object. For example, a user account might have been deleted instead of disabled, or an organizational unit's security might have been changed and the administrator is locked out. Recovering only a specific object, such as a user account or an organizational unit or a container, requires the distinguished name (DN) of that object. To find the DN, the administrator can use the Ntdsutil utility; however, if an LDIF dump of Active Directory exists, this file is more helpful. If no LDIF file exists and the DN of the object to be recovered is unknown, the recovery of the single object or container is not possible.

To simplify the steps to partial recovery, you will recover a single user account using the logon john that was previously contained in the Users container in the Companyabc.com domain. To restore the user account, follow these steps:

1. Power up the domain controller, and press the F8 key when the boot loader is displayed on the screen.

2. When the advanced boot options are displayed, scroll down, select Directory Services Restore Mode, and press Enter to boot the server. This mode boots the Active Directory database in an offline state. When you choose this boot option, you can maintain and restore the Active Directory database.

3. When the server boots up, log on using the username Administrator and the Restore mode password specified when the server was promoted to a domain controller. To change the Restore mode password on a domain controller running in Normal mode, use the Ntdsutil.exe utility; this process is covered in Chapter 31.

4. Click Start, Run.

5. Type Ntbackup.exe and click OK.

6. When the Backup or Restore window opens, click the Advanced Mode hyperlink.

7. Select the Restore and Manage Media tab.

8. Select the appropriate backup medium, expand it, and check the System State. If the correct medium is not available, the file must be located, or the tape must be loaded in the tape drive and cataloged before it can be used to restore the System State.

9. Choose to restore the data to the original location, and click the Start Restore button in the lower-right corner of the backup window.

10. A pop-up window indicates that restoring the System State to the original location will overwrite the current System State. Click OK to continue.

11. A Confirm Restore window opens in which you can choose advanced restore options. Click OK to initiate the restore of the System State.

12. When the restore is complete, a system restart is necessary to update the services and files restored during this operation. Because only a nonauthoritative restore of the Active Directory database is necessary, click No.

13. Close the backup window and click Start, Run.

14. Type cmd.exe and click OK to open a command prompt.

15. At the command prompt, type ntdsutil.exe and press Enter.

33

16. Type `Authoritative restore` and press Enter.

17. Type `Restore Object "cn=John,cn=Users,dc=companyabc,dc=com"`, and press Enter.

18. The success or failure status of the restore appears in the command prompt. Now type `quit` and press Enter. Repeat this step until you reach the `C:` prompt.

19. Close the command prompt windows and reboot the server.

20. Log on to the server with a domain Administrator account, and verify that the account has been restored. Then log off the server.

Global Catalog

No special restore considerations exist for restoring a global catalog server other than those outlined for restoring Active Directory in the previous sections. The global catalog data is re-created based on the contents of the Active Directory database.

Restoring the SYSVOL Folder

The SYSVOL folder contains the system policies, group policies, computer startup/shutdown scripts, and user logon/logoff scripts. If a previous version of a script or Group Policy Object is needed, the SYSVOL folder must be restored. As a best practice and to keep the process simple, the SYSVOL folder should be restored to an alternate location where specific files can be restored. When the restored files are placed in the SYSVOL folder, the File Replication Service recognizes the file as new or a changed version and replicates it to the remaining domain controllers. If the entire SYSVOL folder needs to be pushed out to the remaining domain controllers and the Active Directory database is intact, a primary restore of the SYSVOL is necessary.

To perform a primary restore of the SYSVOL folder, follow these steps:

1. Power up the domain controller, and press the F8 key when the boot loader is displayed on the screen.

2. When the advanced boot options are displayed, scroll down, select Directory Services Restore Mode, and press Enter to boot the server. This mode boots the Active Directory database in an offline state. When you choose this boot option, you can maintain and restore the Active Directory database.

3. When the server boots up, log on using the username Administrator and the Restore mode password specified when the server was promoted to a domain controller. To change the Restore mode password on a domain controller running in Normal mode, use the `Ntdsutil.exe` utility; this process is covered in Chapter 31.

4. Click Start, Run.

5. Type `Ntbackup.exe` and click OK.

6. When the Backup or Restore window opens, click the Advanced Mode hyperlink.

7. Select the Restore and Manage Media tab.

8. Select the appropriate backup medium, expand it, and check the System State. If the correct medium is not available, the file must be located, or the tape must be loaded in the tape drive and cataloged before it can be used to restore the System State.

9. Choose to restore the data to the original location, and click the Start Restore button in the lower-right corner of the backup window.

10. A pop-up window indicates that restoring the System State to the original location will overwrite the current System State. Click OK to continue.

11. A Confirm Restore window opens in which you can choose advanced restore options. Click the Advanced button to view the advanced restore options.

12. Check the When Restoring Replicated Data Sets, Mark the Restored Data as the Primary Data for All Replicas check box, as shown in Figure 33.6.

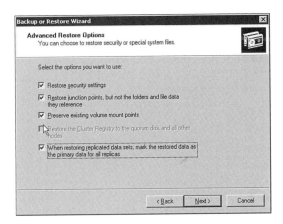

FIGURE 33.6   Choosing to perform a primary restore.

13. Click OK to return to the Confirm Restore page, and click OK to start the restore.

14. When the restore is complete, a system restart is necessary to update the services and files restored during this operation. Because only a nonauthoritative restore of the Active Directory database is necessary, click Yes to restart the server.

15. After the server reboots, log on using an account with domain Administrator access.

16. Check the server event log and the SYSVOL folder to ensure that the data has been restored successfully. Log off the server when you're finished.

Summary

As you've seen in this chapter, Exchange 2007 offers a number of different ways to recover from different types of disasters. Dealing with these disasters is much like being a doctor. You start off with preventative measures to try to greatly reduce the risk of having a failure. If you do encounter a failure, you always start with the least intrusive actions so as not to make the problem worse. Only when other options have been exhausted do you revert to a tape backup. In this way, you are able to reduce the impact of the failure and improve your chances of not losing any data.

Recovering from a disaster can often go beyond the scope of just the Exchange server as it may have been a full site failure. By having written procedures that have been well tested and practiced, you can quickly recover from major failures.

You've also seen how to deal with minor issues such as corrupted messages in otherwise healthy servers and have seen how similar processes can allow for easy extraction of archived messages or how to recover something that was accidentally deleted.

By utilizing the advanced data protection features of Exchange 2007 such as Local Continuous Replication or Cluster Continuous Replication as well as maintaining a reasonable retention period for deleted items, Exchange administrators can greatly reduce the chances of having to restore from tape. By maintaining best practices around database maintenance and isolation of log files from database files, you can also greatly reduce your chances of encountering corrupted data in Exchange. Coupling this with the enhancements in the Jet Blue database, managing an Exchange 2007 environment should be more uneventful than ever.

Best Practices

The following are best practices from this chapter:

- ▶ Always separate your logs and databases onto different physical drives. This way, if you have to restore a database from the night before, the logs can be replayed to bring the database back to current.

- ▶ Consider multiple alternatives beyond restoring an entire server or running the built-in Exchange utilities when analyzing recovery methods.

- ▶ Have good documentation on the Exchange environment to make for an easier time in recovering from system failures.

- ▶ Use the setup /disasterrecovery command to greatly simplify the recovery process in Exchange.

- ▶ Perform an offline copy of the database using XCOPY before performing any maintenance.

- ▶ Move mailboxes from an old server with corrupt databases to a new server in the same site to minimize downtime.

- ▶ Run the ISINTEG and ESEUTIL utilities on a regular basis to maintain the integrity of Exchange databases.

- Use a recovery storage group whenever possible to simplify the recovery of information from backup.

- Take advantage of the new Database Recovery Management tool.

- Enable Local Continuous Replication if space allows.

- Enable Cluster Continuous Replication if budget allows.

- Utilize the "swap databases" function if you need to merge new data after a dial tone recovery.

- Test Active Directory recovery in a lab.

33

PART X

Optimizing Exchange Server 2007 Environments

IN THIS PART

CHAPTER **34**

Optimizing an Exchange Server 2007 Environment

Microsoft Exchange Server 2007 offers many enhancements over previous versions of Exchange. These enhancements can improve the messaging environment's reliability, availability, and scalability. To be able to make use of these features, however, you must carefully plan the deployment and implementation of Exchange Server 2007. Any good implementation of Exchange 2007 includes an optimization phase. This involves baselining the performance of the "out-of-the-box" build and applying best practices to improve the performance of the environment. Through careful analysis of capacity and testing with the available tools, a clever administrator can wring additional performance out of an Exchange 2007 environment.

Capacity analysis, stress testing, and performance optimization processes and procedures are, most often, low-priority tasks for most IT organizations. This is frequently because productivity is regularly measured by what can be achieved now and not always what can be properly planned or designed. The benefits of capacity analysis and performance monitoring can be obtained in the short term, but they are more important when established over longer periods of time. As a result, the main focus of most Information Technology (IT) departments shifts to the more immediate and more tangible day-to-day processes and IT needs. Companies that focus on the performance optimization of their Exchange 2007 environment will find that it requires upgrades less often and it offers a better experience to the user community.

The results of capacity analysis and performance optimization save organizations of all sizes time, effort, and expenditures. This chapter is designed to provide best practices for properly and proactively performing capacity analysis and performance optimization so that IT personnel and end users can work more effectively and efficiently.

Examining Exchange Server 2007 Performance Improvements

Before delving into ways to tweak Exchange Server 2007 performance, it is important to have an understanding of the performance improvements that have been made since its predecessor, Exchange Server 2003. Although some of these performance improvements are more noticeable than others, Exchange Server 2007 has been designed to scale into the enterprise and beyond.

Architectural Improvements

One of the largest and most apparent changes in Exchange 2007 is the move to a 64-bit architecture. This provides Exchange 2007 with new opportunities for scalability and performance that were not available with 32-bit code. By eliminating the legacy limitation of a 3-GB memory space, the Exchange engine is no longer as limited in how much information it can cache. This means that Exchange is no longer as limited by disk input/output (I/O) performance. When configured with sufficient memory, Exchange 2007 can reduce its disk I/O requirements by as much as 75%. This allows administrators to be much more efficient in their use of disks.

The 64-bit architecture of Exchange 2007 also allowed Microsoft to raise the limits on the number of databases that could be hosted by a single Exchange server. Whereas Exchange 2003 was only capable of a total of 20 databases (spread out across four storage groups), Exchange 2007 is able to host as many as 50 databases (spread out across 50 storage groups). This again offers administrators greater flexibility in how they design their Exchange 2007 servers, which can result in increased performance if it is designed correctly. This topic is covered in greater detail later in this chapter.

Database Engine Improvements

Microsoft has continued to make great strides with the JET database. JET is the database used by Exchange 2007, as well as in previous versions of Exchange, to store mailbox data and public folder data. In the new 64-bit version of JET offered by Exchange 2007, the JET engine is able to take advantage of the lift in restrictions on memory space and it allows JET to allocate significantly more cache for the Exchange store. This means that users have access to more cache and this greatly increases the likelihood that data requested by a user is already in memory and doesn't have to be read from disk. This results in quicker response times for the end users. Similarly, the database page size in Exchange 2007 has been increased from 4KB to 8KB. Although this might not seem significant, the result is that more messages are able to fit into a single database page and, as a result, the Exchange server needs only one I/O operation rather than two to retrieve the message.

This also helps to significantly reduce the overall I/O requirements of the Exchange 2007 server.

Transport Pipeline Improvements

The transport pipeline refers to the collection of server roles as well as various queues, components, and connections within Exchange that work together to transport messages to the message categorizer in the Hub Transport server. The job of this categorizer is to deliver mail to the appropriate location within the Exchange environment. This process has been greatly improved in Exchange 2007 and is able to handle significantly more messages than earlier versions of Exchange.

Analyzing Capacity and Performance

Capacity and performance analysis for an Exchange Server 2007 environment requires a well-established understanding of the business and messaging needs of the organization and a well-documented outline of the organization's expectations of its messaging environment. The capacity of an Exchange environment is directly dependent on the expected level of performance. It is important to understand exactly what it is you are expecting from the system in terms of storage per user, level of responsiveness of the server, and room for anticipated expansion. When armed with these concepts, you can more accurately determine what your current capacity is.

The first step in capacity analysis is to grasp an understanding of these concepts and define performance expectations. This can be done by establishing policies and service level agreements (SLAs). It is in these policies and SLAs that an administrator can outline acceptable performance thresholds and more accurately gauge the capacity needs of Exchange Server 2007. These thresholds can also be used to accurately establish performance baselines from which to analyze the requirements against available resources.

To help develop the policies and SLAs, use questionnaires, interviews, business objectives, and the like along with performance measurements via the Performance Monitor, Exchange Best Practices Analyzer, or third-party analysis tools. This allows you to combine realistic expectations with concrete data to see where you are relative to where you want to be.

Establishing Baselines

The importance of establishing meaningful baselines of the messaging environment cannot be underscored enough. Baselines are particularly important in the sense that they are the measurable tools that can be used to balance what is required of Exchange Server 2007 with what resources are needed to fulfill those requirements. Achieving this balance can be made simpler if an administrator consults performance metrics, such as industry-standard benchmarks. By starting with an accurate baseline of system performance, you can quickly and easily test changes in the environment to see if they have made things better or worse. Accurate baselines are also very helpful when troubleshooting problems and you can quickly determine which subsystems are not performing the way they normally do. A clear baseline allows you to determine whether a server that "seems slow" really is slower than the way it usually runs.

> **NOTE**
>
> Use ExchDump to assist with baselining the environment. ExchDump exports a server's configuration, which can be useful to determine whether the build follows company standards. This is particularly important with Exchange clusters because each node in the cluster should be a replica of the other.

To establish an accurate baseline of Exchange Server 2007, a number of tools can help an administrator in this process. These tools are discussed in detail in the following sections. Some of these capacity analysis tools are built in to Windows Server 2003, and others are built in to Exchange Server 2007. Many third-party tools and utilities are also available for the careful measurement of Exchange Server 2007 capacity requirements and performance analysis.

Using the Exchange Best Practices Analyzer Tool

The Exchange Best Practices Analyzer (ExBPA) is a utility provided by Microsoft that analyzes an Exchange server's configuration and informs administrators on possible configuration changes that can be made to improve performance or mitigate problems. More specifically, ExBPA can be used to perform a health check, a health and performance check, a connectivity test, and a baseline test. This tool, which was a download in previous versions of Exchange, is now a built-in tool. To access the Best Practices Analyzer, perform the following steps:

1. Launch Exchange Management Console.
2. If the left pane, scroll down and select Toolbox.
3. In the action pane, click Open Tool from under the Best Practices Analyzer option.
4. When the Best Practices Analyzer tool launches, check the Check for Updates on Startup check box, and click Check for Updates Now.
5. If there are updates available, click Download the Latest Updates.
6. After being updated, the tool closes, and you have to click it again.
7. Choose Go to Welcome Screen.
8. Click Select Options for a New Scan.
9. Type the name of your closest global catalog, and click Connect to the Active Directory Server.
10. Enter a label for this scan, choose the systems you want to scan, choose Health Check, and click Start Scanning.
11. When the tool has finished, click View a Report of This Best Practices Scan to display an output similar to the one shown in Figure 34.1.

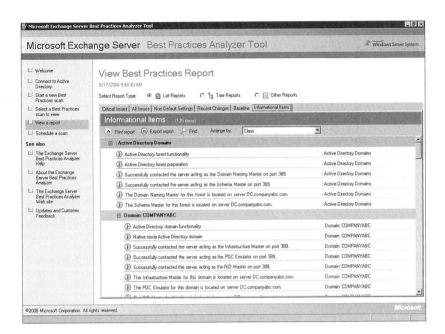

FIGURE 34.1   Viewing ExBPA reports.

When viewing the report, an administrator is able to see any critical issues, nondefault settings, or recent changes to the system. This quickly identifies configuration settings that might be detrimental to the overall performance of the system. Be sure to always update the Best Practices Analyzer before running it because Microsoft is constantly adding new information to this tool.

The Informational Items tab offers a convenient and consolidated view of information that is typically captured in Exchange documentation. Take advantage of this view when tracking the configuration of your Exchange 2007 servers.

Using the LoadSim Tool

Loadsim is a "stress test" tool written by Microsoft to allow an administrator to simulate the load of multiple users against an Exchange server. This can be especially helpful in validating the performance and capacity of a system by testing it prior to attaching live users to it. LoadSim can be downloaded from the Microsoft website at http://www. microsoft.com/downloads/details.aspx?familyid=92EB2EDC-3433-47CA-A5F8-0483C7DDEA85&displaylang=en.

To simulate a load against an Exchange server, follow these steps:

1. Launch the Loadsim application.

2. Click Configuration from the menu bar, and select Topology Properties.

3. In the left pane, expand the server that you plan to test, and select a storage group.

4. In the right pane, double-click the database, and enter the number of users you want to simulate.

5. Repeat this process for each storage group and database.

6. Use the Distribution Lists and Public Folders tabs to simulate the use of these objects as well.

7. When finished with defining the user loads, click OK.

8. Click Configuration in the menu bar, and select Test Properties.

9. Choose the duration for the test to run.

10. In the bottom pane, click Add to add user groups. These user groups define the protocols and "user type" of the test users. This allows you to run multiple profiles of users on the same database. Click OK.

11. From the Test Properties page, click OK.

12. Click Run in the menu bar, and select Create Topology. This creates the test user and distribution list objects in Active Directory (AD).

13. Click Run in the menu bar, and select Initialize Test. Click Yes to initialize public folders from this system.

14. Click Run in the menu bar, and select Run Simulation.

While the load simulation is running, you can monitor the performance counters on the Exchange 2007 server and see how the system is handling the load. This allows you to validate your design in terms of how the server is configured versus the anticipated user load.

Don't forget to delete the user and distribution list objects from Active Directory when you are finished with your testing.

Planning for Growth

One of the easiest ways to maintain the performance of an Exchange 2007 server is to plan ahead for the growth of the environment. Too many administrators have a tendency to build an Exchange infrastructure that meets the storage and performance requirements of today but that fails to account for the growth of the company.

Typically, when designing an Exchange 2007 infrastructure, you should try to look ahead roughly 3 years to predict the size to which the company will grow. This is a good time to talk to groups such as Human Resources and Finance to see the rate at which the company has grown historically. This will give you a good idea of how many employees would be utilizing the Exchange environment in 3 years. This process should also uncover specific expansion plans for the company. For example, if the company were going to grow from 10,000 employees to 13,000 employees in 3 years, you would naturally consider that a 30% growth and would allow for an extra 30% capacity on servers. However, if the case were that 2,000 of those employees would be in a new facility in

Japan that was going to be online in 2 years, it would really be a 10% growth across the enterprise and potentially a very large increase in capacity needs in Asia or perhaps an entirely new Exchange site in Japan.

Understanding these types of growth allow you to more easily plan for capacity growth and understand how the increase in user load will affect the performance of your Exchange 2007 servers in various sites.

The other thing to consider when planning for growth is the increases in usage of the Exchange environment. It is common to see companies increase the storage limits for users without changing the number of users on a server. There are also third-party technologies that might be in your 3-year plan that will leverage Exchange 2007 as a storage or transport. Voice mail system, Structured Query Language (SQL), or Oracle implementations could quickly increase the loads placed on your Exchange 2007 servers.

The reason it is important to predict, as best you can, these anticipated growths is because it is often easier to account for these needs at the time of the Exchange 2007 design. Most companies are using storage area networks (SANs) or network attached storage (NAS) for the mailbox stores in Exchange. Although these systems do have the ability to resize their LUNs to offer additional storage, this is a very time-consuming process and it directly impacts the users on the server. Similarly, because these are usually shared storage devices, there is likely not enough spare capacity on the shelf or device to allocate more space to the Exchange servers. This results in the SAN or NAS administrator having to allocate additional space in a nonoptimal way, which can affect the performance of all the applications that attach to the NAS or SAN.

Optimizing Exchange 2007 Servers

With the separation of various roles in Exchange 2007, individual optimimizations vary from role to role. The following sections address the various roles in Exchange 2007 and how to optimize the performance of those roles.

Optimizing Mailbox Servers

Of all the servers in an Exchange 2007 environment, the Mailbox server role is the one that will likely benefit the most from careful performance tuning.

Mailbox servers have traditionally been very dependent on the disk subsystem for their performance. Although this has changed in Exchange 2007, it is important to understand that this change in disk behavior is very dependent on memory. As such, the general rule for performance on an Exchange 2007 Mailbox server is to configure it with as much memory as you can. For example, in Exchange 2003, if you had a load of 2,000 users that generated an average of 1 disk I/O per second and you were running a RAID 0+1 configuration, you would need 4GB of memory and 40 disks (assuming 10k RPM disk and 100 random disk I/O per disk) to get the performance you'd expect out of an Exchange server. In Exchange 2007, you could reduce the number of disks required by roughly 70% if you increased the system memory to 12GB of memory.

As you can see, with a Mailbox server, the trick is to balance costs against performance. In large implementations, it is less expensive to replace high-performance disks with memory. This makes direct attached disks a viable choice for Exchange 2007 Mailbox servers.

Another area where a Mailbox server benefits in terms of performance is the disk subsystem. Although you've just seen that the disk requirements are lower than previous versions of Exchange, this doesn't mean that the disk subsystem is unimportant. This is another area where you must create a careful balance between cost, performance, and recoverability. The databases benefit the most from a high-performance disk configuration. Consider using 15k RPM drives because they offer more I/O performance per disk; generally 50% more random I/O capacity versus a 10k RPM disk. Given the reduction in disk needed to support the databases, you should consider using RAID 0+1 rather then RAID 5 so as not to incur the write penalties associated with RAID 5. The log files also need fast disks to be able to commit information quickly, but they have the advantage of being sequential I/O rather than random. That is, the write heads don't have to jump all around the disk to find the object to which they want to write. The logs start at one point on the disk and they write sequentially without having to modify old logs.

In a perfect world, the databases and logs are all on their own dedicated disks. Although this isn't always possible, it does offer the best performance. In the real world, you might have to occasionally double up databases or log files onto the same disk. Be aware of how this affects recoverability. For performance, always separate the logs from the databases as their read/write patterns are very different. It also makes recovery of a lost database much easier.

Mailbox servers also deal with a large amount of network traffic. Email messages are often fairly small and as a result, the transmission of these messages isn't always as efficient as it could be. Whenever possible, equip your Mailbox servers with Gigabit Ethernet interfaces. If possible, and if you aren't clustering the Mailbox servers, try to run your network interfaces in a teamed mode. This improves both performance and reliability.

As Mailbox servers also hold the public folder stores, consider running a dedicated public folder server if your environment heavily leverages public folders. Public folder servers often store very large files that users are accessing, so separating the load of those large files from the Mailbox servers results in better overall performance for the user community.

For companies that only lightly use public folders, it requires some investigation of the environment to see if it is better to run a centralized public folder server or if it is better to maintain replicas of public folders in multiple locations. This is usually a question of wide area network (WAN) bandwidth versus usage patterns.

Optimizing Mailbox Clusters

Mailbox servers in Exchange 2007 offer a new function known as Cluster Continous Replication. Mailbox servers clustered in this way can be optimized in much the same way as standalone Mailbox servers. One of the key differences is that network interfaces should not be teamed on a Windows cluster. This is because the small amount of latency introduced in the load-balancing algorithm of the teaming can cause the cluster to believe that a node is not available and trigger an unnecessary failover of resources.

Mailbox clusters in Exchange 2007 should always be configured with multiple network interface cards (NICs) and a NIC should be dedicated to cluster traffic only. This helps ensure that the cluster heartbeat is always working properly. In the case of "local clusters," you should always use a hub between the heartbeat NICs, so that link state is not lost if you reboot a system.

On a mailbox cluster, it is very important that the log files be placed on a fast disk subsystem. This is because in addition to storing transactions for the database, the logs are also shipped to the remote node for reprocessing. This is how the two nodes maintain similar information so that a failover can be accomplished without the need for shared storage.

Optimizing Client Access Servers

Client Access servers (CASs) tend to be more dependent on CPU and memory than they are on disk. Because their job is to simply proxy requests back to the Mailbox servers, they don't need much in the way of local storage. The best way to optimize the Client Access server is to give it enough memory that it doesn't need to page very often. By monitoring the page rate in the Performance Monitor, you can ensure that the CAS is running optimally. If it starts to page excessively, you can simply add more memory to it. Similarly, if the CPU utilization is sustained above 65% or so, it might be time to think about more processing power.

Unlike Mailbox servers, Client Access servers are usually "commodity" class servers. This means they aren't likely to have the capacity for memory or CPU that a Mailbox server might have. It is typical to increase the performance of the Client Access servers by simply adding more servers into a load-balanced group.

This is a good example of optimizing a role as opposed to a server that holds a role. As you start to add more services to your Client Access servers, such as Outlook Anywhere or ActiveSync, you will see an increase in CPU usage. Be sure to monitor this load because it allows you to predict when to add capacity to account for the increased load. This prevents your users from experiencing periods of poor performance.

Optimizing Hub Transport Servers

The goal of the Hub Transport server is to transfer data between different Exchange sites. Each site must have a Hub Transport server to communicate with the other sites. Because the Hub Transport server doesn't store any data locally, its performance is based on how quickly it can determine where to send a message and send it off. The best way to optimize the Hub Transport role is via memory, CPU, and network throughput. The Hub Transport server needs ready access to a global catalog server to determine where to route messages based on the recipients of the messages. Placing a global catalog (GC) in the same site as a busy Hub Transport server is a good idea. Ensure that the Hub Transport server has sufficient memory to quickly move messages into and out of queues.

Monitoring available memory and page rate gives you an idea if you have enough memory. High-speed network connectivity is also very useful for this role. If you are running a dedicated Hub Transport server in a site and you find that it's overworked even though it has a fast processor and plenty of memory, consider simply adding a second Hub Transport server to the site because they automatically share the load.

Optimizing Edge Transport Servers

The Edge Transport server is very similar to the Hub Transport server, with the key difference being that it is the connection point to external systems. As such, it has a higher need for processing power because it needs to convert the format of messages from Simple Mail Transfer Protocol (SMTP) to Messaging Application Programming Interface (MAPI) for internal routing. Edge Transport servers are often serving "double duty" as antivirus and antispam gateways, thus increasing the need for CPU and memory. The Edge Transport role is one where it is very common to optimize the service by deploying multiple Edge Transport servers. This not only increases a site's capacity for sending mail into and out of the local environment, but it also adds a layer of redundancy.

To fully optimize this role, consider running Edge Transport servers in two geographically disparate locations. Utilize multiple MX records to balance out the load of mail coming into the company. Use your route costs to control the outward flow of mail such that you can reduce the number of hops needed for mail to leave the environment.

Keep a close eye on CPU utilization as well as memory paging to know when you need to add capacity to this role. Utilizing content-based rules or running message filtering increases the CPU and memory requirements of this role.

Optimizing Unified Messaging Servers

The Unified Messaging server is a new role in the Exchange world. In the past, this type of functionality was always performed by a third-party application. In Exchange 2007, this ability to integrate with phone systems and voice mail systems in built in. As you might expect, to optimize this role, you must optimize the ability to quickly transfer information from one source to another. This means that the Unified Messaging role needs to focus on sufficient memory, CPU, and network bandwidth. To fully optimize Unified Messaging services, strongly consider running multiple network interfaces in the Unified Messaging server. This allows one network to talk to the phone systems and the other to talk to the other Exchange servers. Careful monitoring of memory paging, CPU utilization, and NIC utilization allows you to quickly spot any bottlenecks in your particular environment.

General Optimizations

Certain bits of advice can be applied to optimizing any server in an Exchange 2007 environment. For example, the elimination of unneeded services is one of the easiest ways to free up CPU, memory, and disk resources. Event logging should be limited to the events you care about and you should be very careful about running third-party agents on your Exchange 2007 servers.

Event logs should be reviewed regularly to look for signs of any problems. Disks that are generating errors should be replaced and problems that appear in the operating system should be addressed immediately.

You should regularly review the performance counters identified in this chapter to see how your systems are running compared to what you'd expect. Always investigate any anomalies to determine if things have been changed or if you are suffering a potential problem. By staying on top of your systems and knowing how they should run, you can more easily keep them running in an optimal manner.

Optimizing Active Directory from an Exchange Perspective

As you likely already know, Exchange 2007 is very dependent on Active Directory for routing messages between servers and for allowing end users to find each other and to send each other mail. The architecture of Active Directory can have a large impact on how Exchange performs its various functions.

When designing your Exchange 2007 environment, consider placing dedicated global catalog servers into an Active Directory site that contains only the GCs and the local Exchange servers. Configure your site connectors in AD with a high enough cost that the GCs in this site won't adopt another nearby site that doesn't have GCs. This ensures that the GCs are only used by the Exchange servers. This can greatly improve the lookup performance of the Exchange server and greatly benefits your OWA users as well.

In the case of a very large Active Directory environment, for example 20,000 or more objects, consider upgrading the domain controllers to run Windows Server 2003 64-bit. This is because a directory this large can grow to be larger than 3GB. When the Extensible Storage Engine database that holds Active Directory grows to this size, it is no longer able to cache the entire directory. This increases lookup and response times for finding objects in Active Directory. By running a 64-bit operating system on the domain controller, you can utilize the larger memory space to cache the entire directory. The nice thing in this situation is that you retain compatibility with 32-bit domain controllers, so it is not necessary to upgrade the entire environment, only sites that will benefit from it.

Monitoring Exchange Server 2007

A variety of built-in Microsoft tools are available to help an administrator establish the baseline of the Exchange Server 2007 environment. Among these, the Performance Monitor Microsoft Management Console (MMC) snap-in is one of the most common tools used to measure the capacity requirements of Exchange Server 2007. This MMC tool is built in to Windows Server 2003.

Using the Performance Monitor Console

The Performance snap-in enables an in-depth analysis of every measurable aspect of the Exchange server. The information that is gathered using the Performance snap-in can be presented in a variety of forms, including reports, real-time charts, or logs, which add to the versatility of this tool. The resulting output formats enable an administrator to present a baseline analysis in real time or through historical data. The Performance snap-in, shown in Figure 34.2, can be launched from the Start, Administrative Tools menu.

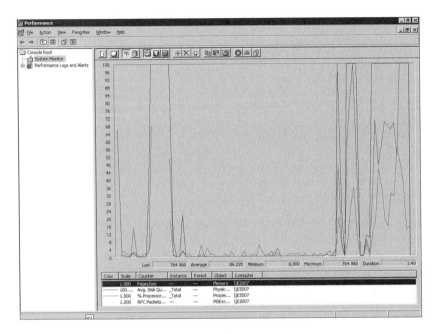

FIGURE 34.2   The Performance snap-in.

Using Network Monitor

The Network Monitor, as illustrated in Figure 34.3, is a reliable capacity-analysis tool used specifically to monitor network traffic. Two flavors of the Network Monitor are available: one that is built in to Windows Server 2003 and one that is provided in Systems Management Server (SMS). The one included with Windows Server 2003 is a more down-scaled version. It is capable of monitoring network traffic to and from the local server on which it runs. The SMS version monitors network traffic coming to or from any computer on the network and enables you to monitor network traffic from a centralized machine. This facilitates gathering capacity-analysis data, but it is also important to note that it could present possible security risks because of its ability to promiscuously monitor traffic throughout the network.

The one built in to Windows can be installed via the Add/Remove Programs interface and is accessible via the Administrative Tools.

There are also third-party network monitoring tools, such as Ethereal, that are very useful for monitoring network performance because they pick up things such as excessive retransmits between hosts, CRC errors, or odd protocol transmissions that could affect the performance of Exchange 2007 servers.

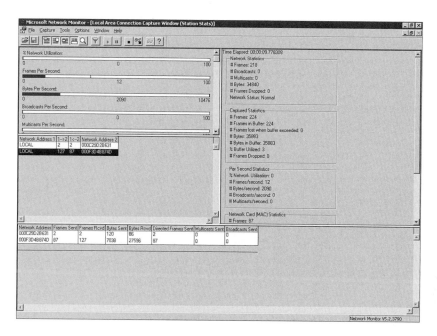

FIGURE 34.3   The Network Monitor interface.

> **NOTE**
>
> Ethereal is a free tool that can be downloaded from http://www.ethereal.com/
> download.html.

Using Task Manager

Task Manager displays real-time performance metrics, so an administrator can quickly get an overall idea of how the Exchange 2007 server is performing at any given time. Its biggest downfall, however, is that it does not store any historical data, so it not a suitable tool for capacity-analysis purposes. Task Manager is typically used as a quick check to see if anything is out of the ordinary. If a server appears to be running slow, using Task Manager and using the Processes tab allows you to sort the processes by CPU or Memory use and quickly see if something is noticeably different from its baseline value. This is a quick way to spot common issues like an antivirus scanner taking up all the CPU time or an lsass.exe process using an excessive amount of memory.

Analyzing and Monitoring Core Elements

The capacity analysis and performance optimization process can be intimidating because there can be an enormous amount of data to work with. In fact, it can easily become unwieldy if not done properly. The process is not just about monitoring and reading counters; it is also an art.

As you monitor and catalog performance information, keep in mind that more information does not necessarily yield better optimization. Tailor the number and types of counters that are being monitored based on the server's role and functionality within the network environment. It's also important to monitor the four common contributors to bottlenecks: memory, processor, disk, and network subsystems. When monitoring Exchange Server 2007, it is equally important to understand the various Exchange roles to keep the number of counters being monitored to a minimum.

Memory Subsystem Optimizations

At the risk of sounding cliché, forget everything you knew about memory optimization in 32-bit Windows. Because Exchange 2007 is a 64-bit application, it requires a 64-bit operating system. 64-bit Windows 2003 deals with memory in an entirely different way than Windows 2003 32-bit did. The concepts of Physical Addressing Extensions (PAE) have gone away, as there are now enough bits to natively address memory, and the old tricks such as "/3GB" and "/USERVA=3030" in the boot.ini files have gone away. Table 34.1 summarizes some of the key improvements in memory management that will greatly enhance the performance of Exchange 2007.

TABLE 34.1   Key Improvements in Memory Management with 64-bit Windows

Architectural Component	64-bit Windows	32-bit Windows
Virtual memory	16TB	4GB
Paging file size	512TB	16TB
Hyperspace	8GB	4MB
Paged pool	128GB	470MB
Non-paged pool	128GB	256MB
System cache	1TB	1GB
System PTEs	128GB	660MB

Virtual memory refers to the memory space made from a combination of physical memory and swap file space. Each process in Windows is constrained by this virtual memory size. In 32-bit Windows, this meant that the store.exe, traditionally the largest consumer of memory in Exchange, was limited to 4GB of address space. In 64-bit Windows, store.exe can access 16TB of address space. This gives store.exe 4,096 times as much memory space as before. This means Exchange 2007 can utilize significantly more physical memory and use the page file, consisting of much slower disks, less often. By being able to cache more of the Exchange database in this larger memory space, the requirements for disk I/O are greatly reduced.

The page file refers to the disk space allocated for scratch space where the operating system will place "memory pages" when it no longer has room for them and they aren't being actively used. This increased value allows for the support of the greater virtual memory size.

Hyperspace is the special region that is used to map the process working set list. It is also used to temporarily map other physical pages for such operations as zeroing a page on the free list, invalidating page table entries in other page tables, and for setting up the address space of a new process.

Paged pool is the region of virtual memory that can be paged in and out of the working set of the system process. It is used by Kernel mode components to allocate system memory.

Non-paged pool is the memory pool that consists of ranges of system virtual addresses. These virtual addresses are guaranteed to be resident in physical memory at all times. Thus, they can be accessed from any address space without incurring paging I/O to the disks. This pool is also used by Kernel mode components to allocate system memory.

System cache refers to the pages that are used to map open files in the system cache.

System PTEs are the Page Table Entries that are used to map system pages. 64-bit programs use a model of 8TB for User and 8TB for Kernel, whereas 32-bit programs use 2GB for User and 2GB for Kernel.

With the Performance Monitor console, a number of important memory-related counters can help in establishing an accurate representation of the system's memory requirements. The primary memory counters that provide information about hard pages (pages that are causing the information to be swapped between the memory and the hard disk) are as follows:

▶ **Memory—Pages/sec**—The values of this counter should range from 5 to 20. Values consistently higher than 10 are indicative of potential performance problems, whereas values consistently higher than 20 might cause noticeable and significant performance hits. The trend of these values is impacted by the amount of physical memory installed in the server.

▶ **Memory—Page Faults/sec**—This counter, together with the Memory—Cache Faults/sec and Memory—Transition Faults/sec counters, can provide valuable information about page faults that are not committed to disk. They were not committed to disk because the memory manager allocated those pages to a standby list. Most systems today can handle a large number of page faults, but it is important to correlate these numbers with the Pages/sec counter as well to determine whether Exchange is configured with enough memory.

Figure 34.4 shows some of the various memory-related and process-related counters.

Improving Virtual Memory Usage

Calculating the correct amount of virtual memory is one of the more challenging parts of planning a server's memory requirements. While trying to anticipate growing usage demands, it is critical that the server has an adequate amount of virtual memory for all applications and the operating system. This is no different for Exchange Server 2007.

FIGURE 34.4   Memory-related counters in Windows Server 2003.

Virtual memory refers to the amount of disk space that is used by Windows Server 2003 and applications as physical memory gets low or when applications need to swap data out of physical memory. Windows Server 2003 uses 1.5 times the amount of random access memory (RAM) as the minimum paging file size by default, which for many systems is adequate. However, it is important to monitor memory counters to determine whether this amount is truly sufficient for that particular server's resource requirements. Another important consideration is the maximum size setting for the paging file. As a best practice, this setting should be at least 50% more than the minimum value to enable paging file growth, should the system require it. If the minimum and maximum settings are configured with the same value, there is a greater risk that the system could experience severe performance problems or even crash.

The most indicative sign of low virtual memory is the presence of 9582 warning events logged by the Microsoft Exchange Information Store service that can severely impact and degrade the Exchange server's message-processing abilities. These warning events are indicative of virtual memory going below 32MB. If unnoticed or left unattended, these warning messages might cause services to stop or the entire system to crash.

TIP

Use the Performance snap-in to set an alert for Event ID 9582. This helps proactively address any virtual memory problems and possibly prevent unnecessary downtime.

To get an accurate portrayal of how Exchange Server 2007 is using virtual memory, monitor the following counters within the MSExchangeIS object:

► **VM Largest Block Size**—This counter should consistently be above 32MB.

► **VM Total 16MB Free Blocks**—This counter should remain over three 16MB blocks.

► **VM Total Free Blocks**—This value is specific to your messaging environment.

► **VM Total Large Free Block Bytes**—This counter should stay above 50MB.

Other important counters to watch closely are as follows:

▶ **Memory—Available Bytes**—This counter can be used to establish whether the system has adequate amounts of RAM. The recommended absolute minimum value is 4MB.

▶ **Paging File—% Usage**—% Usage is used to validate the amount of the paging file used in a predetermined interval. High usage values might be indicative of requiring more physical memory or needing a larger paging file.

Monitoring Processor Usage

Analyzing the processor usage can reveal valuable information about system performance and provide reliable results that can be used for baselining purposes. Two major Exchange-related processor counters are used for capacity analysis of an Exchange Server 2007:

▶ **% Privileged Time**—This counter indicates the percentage of nonidle processor time spent in privileged mode. The recommended ideal for this value is under 55%.

▶ **% Processor Time**—This counter specifies the processor use of each processor or the total processor use. If these values are consistently higher than 50%–60%, consider upgrade options or segmenting workloads.

Tracking these values long term, for trend analysis, makes it much easier to spot account-able anomalies, such as a processor time spike during the online defragmentation or inter-actions with other systems. Tracking a "weighted average" of these processor values allows you to predict the point in time at which a system needs to upgraded or when an additional system needs to be deployed to share the load.

Monitoring the Disk Subsystem

Exchange Server 2007 relies heavily on the disk subsystem and it is, therefore, a critical component to properly design and monitor. Although the disk object monitoring counters are, by default, enabled in Windows Server 2003, it is recommended that these counters be disabled until such time that an administrator is ready to monitor them. The resource requirements can influence overall system performance. The syntax to disable and reen-able these counters is as follows:

```
diskperf -n (to disable)
diskperf -y [\\computer_Name] (to reenable)
```

Nevertheless, it is important to gather disk subsystem performance statistics over time.

The primary Exchange-related performance counters for the disk subsystem are located within the Physical and Logical Disk objects. Critical counters to monitor include, but are not limited to, the following:

▶ **Physical Disk—% Disk Time**—This counter analyzes the percentage of elapsed time that the selected disk spends on servicing read or write requests. Ideally, this value should remain below 50%.

▶ **Logical Disk—% Disk Time**—This counter displays the percentage of elapsed time that the selected disk spends fulfilling read or write requests. It is recommended that this value be 60%–70% or lower.

▶ **Current Disk Queue Length (Both Physical and Logical Disk Objects)**—This counter has different performance indicators depending on the monitored disk drive (Database or Transaction Log volume). On disk drives storing the Exchange database, this value should be below the number of spindled drives divided by 2. On disk drives storing transaction log data, this value should be below 1.

If there appears to be an excessive load on the disks, consider adding more memory to the Exchange 2007 server. Improvements in cache in the Exchange database engine allow more information to be read and cached into memory. This decreases the workload on the disks and might alleviate the need to add more disks. For large Exchange 2007 servers, it is usually less expensive to add more memory than to add more disks to address this type of issue.

Monitoring the Network Subsystem

The network subsystem is one of the more challenging elements to monitor because a number of factors make up a network. In an Exchange messaging environment, site topologies, replication architecture, network topologies, synchronization methods, the number of systems, and more are among the many contributing factors.

To satisfactorily analyze the network, all facets must be considered. This most likely requires using third-party network monitoring tools in conjunction with built-in tools such as the Performance snap-in and Network Monitor.

From a performance standpoint, consider implementing Gigabit Ethernet adapters in your Exchange 2007 servers. Given the amount of memory and disk likely to be in the server, it would easily saturate a 100-MB connection. If your server hardware offers it, consider using fault-tolerant configurations for your Ethernet connections that will not be participating in clusters or load-balance groups. Most of the fault-tolerant configurations on the market today separate out input and output to different interfaces, resulting in better overall throughput for the network interfaces.

If you are connecting your storage via NAS, strongly consider running dedicated Gigabit Ethernet interfaces for the connection to the NAS network. This separates the load of the NAS from the load for the users and results in better overall performance for the users.

Properly Sizing Exchange Server 2007

Before delving into recommended configurations for Exchange Server 2007, it is essential to not only understand the fundamentals of this messaging system, but to also understand the dependencies and interactions those components have with the underlying operating system (that is, Windows Server 2003). Being a client/server messaging application, maximizing Exchange Server 2007 involves fine-tuning all of its core and extended components. Optimization of each of these components affects the overall performance of Exchange.

The core components of Exchange Server (for example, the Information Stores, connectors, transaction logs, and more) have a direct bearing on gauging resource requirements. The number of users in a messaging environment and the various Exchange functions are equally influential.

Optimizing the Disk Subsystem Configuration

Many factors, such as the type of file system to use, physical disk configuration, database size, and log file placement, need to be considered when you are trying to optimize the disk subsystem configuration. The desire for performance must also be balanced with the requirements for redundancy and revocability.

Choosing the File System

Among the file systems supported by Windows Server 2003 (that is, FAT and NTFS), it is recommended to use only NTFS on all Exchange 2007 servers. NTFS provides the best security, scalability, and performance features. For instance, NTFS supports file- and directory-level security, large file sizes (files of up to 16TB), large disk sizes (disk volumes of up to 16TB), fault tolerance, disk compression, error detection, and encryption.

Choosing the Physical Disk Configuration

Windows Server 2003, like its predecessors, supports RAID (Redundant Array of Inexpensive Disks). The levels of RAID supported by the operating system are as follows:

- RAID 0 (Striping)
- RAID 1 (Mirroring)
- RAID 5 (Striping with parity)

Various other levels of RAID can be supported through the use of hardware-based RAID controllers.

The deployment of the correct RAID level is of utmost importance because each RAID level has a direct effect on the performance of the server. From the viewpoint of pure performance, RAID level 0 by far gives the best performance. However, fault tolerance and the reliability of system access are other factors that contribute to overall performance. The skillful administrator strikes a balance between performance and fault tolerance without sacrificing one for the other. The following sections provide recommended disk configurations for Exchange Server 2007.

> **NOTE**
>
> As mentioned earlier, various levels of RAID are available, but for the context of Exchange Server 2007, there are two recommended basic levels to use: RAID 1 and RAID 5. Other forms of RAID, such as RAID 0+1 or 1+0, are also optimal solutions for Exchange Server 2007. These more advanced levels of RAID are supported only when using a hardware RAID controller. As a result, only RAID 1 and 5 are discussed in this chapter.

Disk Mirroring (RAID 1)

In this type of configuration, data is mirrored from one disk to the other participating disk in the mirror set. Data is simultaneously written to the two required disks, which means read operations are significantly faster than systems with no RAID configuration or with a greater degree of fault tolerance. Write performance is slower, though, because data is being written twice; once to each disk in the mirror set.

Besides adequate performance, RAID 1 also provides a good degree of fault tolerance. For instance, if one drive fails, the RAID controller can automatically detect the failure and run solely on the remaining disk with minimal interruption.

The biggest drawback to RAID 1 is the amount of storage capacity that is lost. RAID 1 uses 50% of the total drive capacity for the two drives.

> **TIP**
>
> RAID 1 is particularly well suited for the boot drive and for volumes containing Exchange Server 2007 log files.

Disk Striping with Parity (RAID 5)

In a RAID-5 configuration, data and parity information is striped across all participating disks in the array. RAID 5 requires a minimum of three disks. Even if one of the drives fails within the array, the Exchange Server 2007 server can still remain operational.

After the drive fails, Windows Server 2003 continues to operate because of the data contained on the other drives. The parity information gives details of the data that is missing because of the failure. Either Windows Server 2003 or the hardware RAID controller also begins the rebuilding process from the parity information to a spare or new drive.

RAID 5 is most commonly used for the data drive because it is a great compromise among performance, storage capacity, and redundancy. The overall space used to store the striped parity information is equal to the capacity of one drive. For example, a RAID-5 volume with three 200-GB disks can store up to 400GB of data .

Although RAID 5 has a significant performance penalty for disk activity that has a large percentage of writes, this can be mostly compensated for via caching on the RAID controller. This allows the writes to be done in cache and later be committed to disk. If you are going to utilize write caching on your RAID controller, ensure that the cache is protected by a battery. Otherwise a system failure could result in cached information never getting written to disk. This is a sure way to corrupt a database.

Hardware Versus Software RAID

Hardware RAID (configured at the disk controller level) is recommended over software RAID (configurable from within the Windows Server 2003) because of faster performance, greater support of different RAID levels, support for caching, and capability of recovering from hardware failures more easily.

Database Sizing and Optimization

As mentioned throughout this book, Exchange Server 2007 is available in two versions: Standard and Enterprise. The Standard Edition supports one storage group with one private and one public Information Store. The maximum Information Store (database) size is 75GB with Exchange Server 2007, Standard Edition. The Enterprise Edition provides support for up to 50 storage groups with a combined total of 50 usable databases per server with practically unlimited database size. Technically, the databases are limited to 16,000GB but it's unlikely that you'll grow them that large. Unlike with previous versions of Exchange, it is currently recommended that for performance and recoverability purposes, you should only place one database into each storage group.

The flexibility with the Enterprise Edition is beneficial not just in terms of growth but also in terms of performance and manageability. More specifically, the advantages for segmenting can include the following:

▶ Administrators are enabled to segment the user population on a single Exchange server.

▶ Multiple mailboxes can more evenly distribute the size of the messaging data and help prevent one database from becoming too large and possibly unwieldy for a given system.

▶ Multiple databases present greater opportunities for faster enumeration of database indexing.

▶ Multiple databases can be segmented onto different RAID volumes and RAID controller channels.

▶ Transaction logs can be segmented from other log files using separate RAID volumes.

▶ Failures such as database corruption affect a smaller percentage of the user population.

34

▶ Offline maintenance routines require less scheduled downtime, and fewer users are affected.

TIP

If using the Enterprise Edition, the recommended best practice is to keep database sizes in the 10GB–20GB range. An administrator can use this guideline to gauge or plan for the number of users each database should optimally contain. This best practice is also useful in determining the appropriate number of Exchange Server 2007 Mailbox servers that are required to support the number of users in the organization.

Determining the number of storage groups and databases for Exchange Server 2007 Mailbox servers should also be based on workload characterization. Users can be grouped based on the how they interact with the messaging system (for example, in terms of frequency, storage requirements, and more). Users placing higher demands on Exchange Server 2007 can be placed into a separate storage group and separate databases so that the greater number of read/write operations do not occur in the same database and are more evenly distributed. This is beneficial to performance only if the storage groups and databases are located on physically different disks.

If a deployment calls for a large number of storage groups and databases, it is necessary to mount disks as mount points rather than as drive letters or you would quickly run out of drive letters before utilizing all 50 of your potential storage groups.

Optimizing Exchange Logs

Similar to the previous versions of Exchange, transaction log files should be stored on separate RAID volumes. This enables significant improvements in disk input/output (I/O) operations. Transaction logs are created on a per–storage group level rather than per database. Therefore, when you have multiple storage groups, multiple log files are created that enable simultaneous read and write operations. If the transaction logs are then placed on separate RAID volumes, there can be significant improvements to performance.

TIP

Because transaction logs are as important to Exchange Server 2007 as the data contained in the databases, the most suitable RAID configuration to use for transaction log files is RAID 1. This provides suitable performance without sacrificing fault tolerance. Because the logs are written sequentially, they require significantly fewer disks than a database would to achieve sufficient I/O capacity.

Sizing Memory Requirements

The recommended starting point for the amount of memory for an Exchange Server 2007 server is 2GB of RAM per server + 5MB of RAM per user. The specific memory requirements naturally vary based on server roles, server responsibilities, and the number of users to support. In addition, some organizations define certain guidelines that must be followed for base memory configurations. A more accurate representation of how much memory is required can be achieved by baselining memory performance information gathered from the Performance snap-in or third-party tools during a prototype or lab testing phase.

Another important factor to take into consideration is when the organization adds functionality to Exchange Server 2007 or consolidates users onto fewer servers. This obviously increases resource requirements, especially in terms of adding more physical memory. In these scenarios, it is recommended to use the base amount of memory (for example, 8GB) and then add the appropriate amount of memory based on vendor specifications. It is also important to consult with the vendor to determine what the memory requirements might be on a per user basis. This way, the organization can plan ahead and configure the proper amount of memory prior to needing to scale to support a larger number of users in the future.

Sizing Based on Server Roles

Server roles can have a considerable bearing on both the performance and capacity of Exchange Server 2007. Based on the various roles of the Exchange servers, the strategic placement of Exchange services and functionality can greatly improve performance of the overall messaging system while reducing the need for using additional resources. By the same token, a misplaced Exchange service or functional component can noticeably add to network traffic and degrade the overall performance of the messaging system.

Servers are divided into five roles: Client Access servers, Mailbox servers, Hub Transport servers, Edge Transport servers, and Unified Messaging servers.

Mailbox Server Sizing

Various factors affect the performance of a Mailbox server, including the following:

▶ The number and type of protocols supported

▶ The number of users supported

▶ The authentication methods supported

▶ Encryption requirements

Table 34.2 shows the recommended resource requirements of Mailbox servers. It is important to note that these guidelines are minimum recommendations, and actual requirements might vary depending upon the organization.

TABLE 34.2   Recommended Minimum Mailbox Server Configurations

Resource	Description
RAM	2GB + 5MB/user
Processor	Pentium IV 3.0GHz or higher processor with E64MT support or equivalent AMD processor

TABLE 34.2   Continued

Resource	Description
Hard disk	RAID 1 for Windows Server 2003
	RAID 0+1 for mailbox data
Network	Gigabit Ethernet NIC(s)
Other considerations	If connections to this server are over SSL, consider using a NIC that off-loads SSL processing

Client Access Server Sizing

Various factors affect the performance of a Client Access server, including the following:

- ▶ The number and type of protocols supported
- ▶ The number of type of applications supported
- ▶ The number of users supported
- ▶ The authentication methods supported
- ▶ Encryption requirements

Table 34.3 shows the recommended resource requirements of Client Access servers. It is important to note that these guidelines are minimum recommendations, and actual requirements might vary depending upon the organization.

TABLE 34.3   Recommended Minimum Client Access Server Configurations

Resource	Description
RAM	1GB
Processor	Pentium IV 3.0GHz or higher processor with E64MT support or equivalent AMD processor
Hard disk	RAID 1 for Windows Server 2003 and Exchange Server 2007
Network	Gigabit Ethernet NIC(s)
Other considerations	If connections to this server are over SSL, consider using a NIC that off-loads SSL processing

Hub Transport Server Sizing

Various factors affect the performance of a Hub Transport server, including the following:

- ▶ The number and type of protocols supported
- ▶ The number of users supported
- ▶ The authentication methods supported
- ▶ Encryption requirements

Table 34.4 shows the recommended resource requirements of a Hub Transport server. It is important to note that these guidelines are minimum recommendations, and actual requirements might vary depending upon the organization.

TABLE 34.4   Recommended Minimum Hub Transport Server Configurations

Resource	Description
RAM	1GB
Processor	Pentium IV 3.0GHz or higher processor with E64MT support or equivalent AMD processor
Hard disk	RAID 1 for Windows Server 2003 and Exchange Server 2007
Network	Gigabit Ethernet NIC(s)
Other considerations	If connections to this server are over SSL, consider using a NIC that off-loads SSL processing

Edge Transport Server Sizing

Various factors affect the performance of an Edge Transport server, including the following:

▶ The number of messages sent and received

▶ The types of rules implemented

▶ The types of filtering performed

▶ Encryption requirements

Table 34.5 shows the recommended resource requirements of an Edge Transport server. It is important to note that these guidelines are minimum recommendations, and actual requirements might vary depending upon the organization.

TABLE 34.5   Recommended Minimum Edge Transport Server Configuration

Resource	Description
RAM	1GB
Processor	Pentium IV 3.0GHz or higher processor with E64MT support or equivalent AMD processor
Hard disk	RAID 1 for Windows Server 2003 and Exchange Server 2007
Network	Gigabit Ethernet NIC(s)
Other considerations	If extensive content rules will be applied, consider a dual-core processor

34

Unified Messenger Server Sizing

Various factors affect the performance of a Unified Messaging server, including the following:

▶ The number and type of codecs supported

▶ The number of users supported

▶ The type of phone system integrated with

Table 34.6 shows the recommended resource requirements of a Unified Messaging server. It is important to note that these guidelines are minimum recommendations, and actual requirements might vary depending upon the organization.

TABLE 34.6   Recommended Minimum Unified Messaging Server Configurations

Resource	Description
RAM	1GB
Processor	Pentium IV 3.4GHz or higher processor with E64MT support or equivalent AMD processor
Hard disk	RAID 1 for Windows Server 2003 and Exchange Server 2007
Network	Gigabit Ethernet NIC(s)
Other considerations	Use of very high-compression audio codecs might increase the minimum CPU requirements

Combined Role Server Sizing

Various factors affect the performance of an Exchange 2007 server with combined roles, including the following:

▶ The number and type of protocols supported

▶ The number of users supported

▶ The authentication methods supported

▶ Encryption requirements

Table 34.7 shows the recommended resource requirements of a combined role Exchange 2007 server. It is important to note that these guidelines are minimum recommendations, and actual requirements might vary depending upon the organization.

TABLE 34.7   Recommended Minimum Combined Server Configuration

Resource	Description
RAM	3GB +5MB per user
Processor	Pentium IV 3.4GHz or higher processor with E64MT support or equivalent AMD processor
Hard disk	RAID 1 for Windows Server 2003 and Exchange Server 2007 RAID 0+1 for mailbox data

TABLE 34.7   Continued

Resource	Description
Network	Gigabit Ethernet NIC(s)
Other considerations	If there will be a large number of functions run on this system, consider implementing a dual-core processor for added processing power

Optimizing Exchange Through Ongoing Maintenance

Through typical usage, Exchange databases become fragmented. This fragmentation gradually slows server performance and can also lead to corruption over extended periods of time. To ensure that an Exchange server continues to service requests in an optimized manner and the chances of corruption are minimized, it is important to perform regular maintenance on Exchange.

Although Exchange Server 2007 performs online maintenance tasks on a nightly basis, this accounts for roughly only 60%–70% of the maintenance tasks that are recommended. Offline maintenance, on the other hand, achieves the true optimization of the Information Stores, as well as prevents and fixes corruption. Offline optimization routines help keep the messaging server operating like a well-oiled engine and ensure that Exchange provides the highest serviceability and reliability.

CAUTION

It is of utmost importance to perform a full backup of Exchange Server 2007 prior to and immediately after running offline maintenance. After the backup has completed, it is equally important to verify the backups.

Because offline maintenance procedures require at least one database or that the entire server is offline, it is also important to schedule maintenance during the off-peak hours and notify the end users in advance.

NOTE

If Exchange Server 2007, Enterprise Edition is being used, you can perform maintenance on a single database and not affect other data that is stored within other databases. In addition, the entire server does not have to be offline.

The utilities to use for offline maintenance are ESEUTIL (ESEUTIL.EXE) and the Integrity Checker (ISINTEG.EXE). These utilities perform a number of functions, including, but not limited to, checking database and table integrity, identifying and correcting corruption, and defragmenting databases. For further information on the recommended best practices

on maintaining Exchange Server 2007 and step-by-step instructions for offline maintenance, refer to Chapter 19, "Exchange Server 2007 Management and Maintenance
Practices."

Monitoring Exchange with Microsoft Operations Manager

Microsoft Operations Manager (MOM) is an application that can be used to actively
monitor Exchange Server 2007. Employing MOM in an Exchange messaging environment
offers administrators the following benefits:

▶ MOM has the capability of detecting even the smallest of problems that, if unnoticed, can lead to more complicated issues. Early detection of problems enables an
administrator to troubleshoot the problem areas well in advance.

▶ MOM can monitor all Exchange-related system health indicators.

▶ The Exchange Server 2007 Management Pack leverages all the new features of
Exchange Server 2007.

▶ The Exchange Server 2007 Management Pack also includes the Microsoft Knowledge
Base, which can be used for fast and reliable resolution of issues.

▶ MOM can centrally manage a large number of Exchange Server 2007 servers over
widely dispersed deployments.

▶ MOM can actively monitor server availability by verifying that services are running,
databases are mounted, messages are flowing, and users are able to log on.

▶ MOM can actively monitor server health by monitoring free disk space thresholds,
mail queues, security, performance thresholds, and more.

▶ MOM provides detailed reports on database sizes, traffic analysis, and more.

▶ Alerts can be sent based on customized thresholds and events.

In short, MOM is an excellent tool that administrators can use to proactively monitor the
Exchange environment from a centralized location.

Summary

Despite all the performance, reliability, scalability, and availability enhancements of
Exchange Server 2007, capacity analysis and performance optimization are still a necessity. The techniques and processes described in this chapter not only help you determine
how to size a server or tweak it to operate optimally; they also reflect a methodology for
continually monitoring a changing environment. By keeping one step ahead of the
system, an organization can use resources more efficiently and effectively and in return
save time, effort, and costs associated with supporting Exchange Server 2007.

Capacity must always be monitored and growth must be planned for. An efficient administrator will have a playbook built up for expanding the Exchange 2007 environment in a logical and effective manner. This includes plans for increasing capacity on existing servers, increasing capacity from a storage standpoint, and bringing up new Exchange 2007 sites when expansion requires is. By tying capacity expansion to company growth and expansion, Information Technology is able to stay in step with the needs of the business and fulfill its role as a business enabler rather then just being a support cost.

Best Practices

The following are best practices from this chapter:

- ▶ Begin capacity analysis and performance optimization sooner rather than later.

- ▶ Create performance baselines in which to gauge the changing requirements and performance levels of Exchange Server 2007.

- ▶ Use existing baselines to recognize changes in the performance or behavior of a server.

- ▶ Establish SLAs and other policies that reflect the business expectations of the messaging environment.

- ▶ Monitor only those counters that are pertinent to the server's configuration.

- ▶ Always monitor the four common contributors to bottlenecks: memory, disk subsystem, processor, and network.

- ▶ Run performance and stress tests in a lab environment prior to implementing in a production environment.

- ▶ Establish regular maintenance routines, including those for offline maintenance tasks.

- ▶ Set an alert for Event ID 9582 to proactively address any memory or virtual memory problems.

- ▶ Use enough physical memory in Mailbox servers to reduce the requirement on the disk subsystem.

- ▶ Keep Exchange Server 2007 database sizes in the 10GB to 20GB range whenever possible.

- ▶ Choose hardware RAID over software RAID whenever possible.

- ▶ Use separate, hardware-based RAID-1 volumes for system files and transaction logs.

34

Designing and Optimizing Storage (SAN/NAS) in an Exchange Server 2007 Environment

A few years ago, storage area network (SAN) and network attached storage (NAS) devices were only found in very high-end data centers and were generally only used in very high-performance scenarios. Now, use of SAN and NAS devices has become much more common. SANs are extremely high-performance collections of disks that can be sliced and diced dynamically and attached to remote systems as though they were directly attached. SANs differ from traditional direct attached storage (DAS) in that the disks are no longer attached to the local system through SCSI or IDE connections. The SAN is viewed as a cloud and is literally a separate, high-speed network with the sole purpose of connectivity between hosts and high-speed disks. From the server's point of view, the remote disk acts exactly the same as the locally attached disk. By consolidating the disks into a central location, you are able to take advantage of situations that just weren't possible in the past. NAS is very similar with the key difference being that the disks are presented via Ethernet rather then Fibre Channel. Many disk consolidation devices available today are a hybrid of the two, offering Fibre Channel Protocol in addition to Internet SCSI (iSCSI) for connectivity. This gives you more options and allows you to control costs by only using the more expensive Fibre Channel when the situation calls for it.

Many applications can take advantage of the performance and large number of spindles that are typically only offered via a SAN or NAS. Microsoft Exchange Server 2007 is one such application. Although administrators of Exchange 2007 have the option of adding additional memory to offset the input/output (I/O) requirements, there are still many advantages to running a SAN or NAS back end.

This chapter highlights advantages of SANs and NAS, and shows you when to take advantage of one technology over another. This chapter explains the requirements of each technology to help you avoid common mistakes when choosing a storage technology. It also touches on industry best practices for using NAS and SAN technologies with Exchange 2007.

Defining the Technologies

To understand how and when to use technologies such as NAS or SAN, it is important to understand what they are and what they offer. The technologies differ in how they are used and what advantages they provide. Many administrators assume that they need a SAN when often a NAS will suffice. Because information technology (IT) budgets are far from limitless, it is to your advantage to know that you aren't overbuying for your solution. By the same token, it is often less expensive to buy your solution all at once rather than trying to expand it later.

What Is a SAN?

A SAN is a high-speed, special-purpose network or subnetwork that connects various data storage devices with associated data servers on behalf of a larger network of users. Typically, a SAN is but part of an overall network of computing resources for an enterprise. A SAN is usually located in relative proximity to other computing resources such as databases and file servers but might also extend to remote locations for backup and archival storage. These remote locations are traditionally connected via wide area network (WAN) carrier technologies, such as asynchronous transfer mode (ATM) or Synchronous Optical Networks (SONETs).

It is very important to understand that the SAN is more than just the chassis that contains the disks. It includes the redundant array of inexpensive or independent disks or drives (RAID) controllers for the disks, the Fibre Channel switching fabric, and the host bus adapters (HBAs) that reside in the data servers. SANs are traditionally connected to hosts via Fibre Channel and talk via Fibre Channel Protocol. Although it can be fairly easy to support dual-arbitrated fiber loops in a corporate environment, keep in mind that one of the primary benefits of SAN is the ability to do block-level mirroring to another SAN. If this SAN is located remotely, up to 1,000km away with current fiber technology, a company needs to have fiber between the two locations. A fiber connection across those kinds of distances can be quite expensive.

SAN technologies excel in the area of disk performance. Fibre Channel networks regularly push 4Gb/sec of throughput. Although SCSI technologies can move data at up to 320Mb/sec and can be bonded together for higher throughput, they are limited to less than 25 feet of distance. SAN, not unlike SCSI, is seen by the host system as raw disk space. This is also referred to as a block-level technology. In the past, database applications required block-level access to the disk as well as the "near 0 latency" offered by SAN.

> **TIP**
>
> Although most SAN manufacturers refer to the performance of their products as having *zero latency*, it is important not to misinterpret this. Zero latency refers to the fact that Fibre Channel has extremely low overhead and doesn't add additional latency. The laws of physics, on the other hand, are still in effect. A 1,000-km fiber run between remote locations still takes 7 milliseconds round-trip.

What Is NAS?

NAS is a hard disk storage technology that uses an Ethernet connection rather than being attached directly to the host computer that is serving applications or data to a network's users. By removing storage access and its management from the host server, both application programming and files can be served faster because they are not competing for the same processor time. The NAS device is attached to a local area network (LAN) via Ethernet and given an IP address. File requests are mapped by the host server to the NAS device.

NAS consists of hard disk storage, including multidisk RAID systems and software for configuring and mapping file locations to the network-attached device. NAS software can usually handle a number of network protocols, including Microsoft's Internetwork Packet Exchange, Common Internet File System, and NetBEUI; Novell NetWare Internetwork Packet Exchange; and Sun Microsystems Network File System. Configuration, including the setting of user access priorities, is usually possible using a web browser though many NAS offerings require command-line configuration. Most NAS manufacturers include specialized software for allowing specific applications such as Structured Query Language (SQL) or Exchange to take advantage of special functions provided by the NAS. These functions include things like mirroring, failover, automated recovery, and snapshotting.

NAS has the advantage of using existing Ethernet technologies that are much less expensive than fiber technologies. With the availability of 10Gb Ethernet, NAS is able to compete with Fibre Channel–based technologies even with the added overhead of Ethernet over Fibre Channel. In most scenarios, Gigabit Ethernet is sufficient for Exchange 2007 servers, especially if multiple connections are employed.

When Is the Right Time to Implement NAS and SAN Devices?

There are many reasons to implement a NAS or SAN solution in favor of direct attached storage. In the case of Exchange 2007, if the requirements for storage consolidation, reduction in mailbox server count, centralized management of disk resources, service level agreement (SLA) recoverability times, or near real-time mirroring of data justify the cost

35

of a SAN or NAS solution, it is time to explore those options. To make an informed decision about when to make the switch within your Exchange 2007 environment, it is important for you to pass through several phases:

1. **Analyze**—Gather usage metrics and performance metrics. Determine how storage is being used and how it affects the business processes. Determine if disk throughput is the bottleneck in your Exchange deployment.

2. **Plan**—Determine the current limitations of your storage solutions. Prioritize the problems and determine if there is a better way. Don't fall into the trap of doing things just because they were always done a particular way.

3. **Develop**—Build the proposed solution for testing. Perform benchmarking to show improvements over the old methods. Experiment with various functions of Exchange 2007 on different types of disks. Get a feel for the improvement versus the costs.

4. **Pilot**—Test the solution and improve it based on user feedback. Educate the user population on how to take full advantage of the new functions and determine the improvements in efficiencies.

5. **Deploy**—Deliver the solution to the masses.

Following this methodology not only streamlines the process of implementing new and more efficient storage technologies, but also provides valuable data to help upper management buy into the upgrades and support the storage program for the Exchange environment.

Analyzing Your Storage Needs

The first phase of any good project is an in-depth analysis of the environment and its needs. In the case of storage systems, it is critical to identify any systems with special requirements. This includes systems that require multiple layers of redundancy, systems that are under extremely tight SLAs, and systems that cannot tolerate a loss of data. In the case of Exchange 2007 that is deployed by role, it is most likely only the Mailbox server role that will benefit significantly from using SAN or NAS technologies. Similarly, you might determine that it is less expensive to take advantage of the additional memory that can be used by Exchange 2007 because of its 64-bit architecture, to increase the caching of database transactions and, therefore, reduce the necessary number of disks. NAS and SAN solutions can be very expensive compared to purchasing memory for a server. If the driving force toward a SAN or NAS is performance based, consult Chapter 34, "Optimizing an Exchange Server 2007 Environment," for more information on the reduction in disk I/O that can be gained by increasing system memory. If your driving force is centralized disk management, enhanced capacity, or rapid restoration of data, SAN or NAS might be for you .

Another key area to understand is the capacity requirements of the enterprise. If an investment is going to be made in storage, it is a good idea to plan for several years of growth. Look at the number of servers in the environment. If additional servers have been added simply because that is the way things were always done, it is time to look at shifting the philosophy to doing things because it is the right way to do it.

TIP

Disk drives get larger, faster, and less expensive each year. When planning for the future, keep expandability in mind. By buying a partially filled chassis now and adding additional disks later, you can take advantage of falling disk prices and save money over the long run and still get the full capacity they need and the benefits of fewer chassis.

Planning the Storage Solution

Storage technologies can be very confusing. In most situations, valid arguments can be made for using any of the available technologies. This is a situation in which it makes a lot of sense to get your vendors involved. Contact your potential vendors and let them know what your storage requirements are. Often, they have worked with other companies with similar needs and can provide valuable insight into what worked and what didn't. Given the costs of a large storage system, you can't afford to do it wrong.

After you have an idea of what you want to implement, find out if you can contact references to determine if they were happy with the solution they implemented. Some companies try to get you to commit to the latest and greatest versions of their software and firmware. Large storage environments are a big investment and business processes depend heavily on it. Ensure that you are implementing a stable and well-tested solution.

TIP

A tremendous number of options are available when it comes to storage solutions. When in doubt about a decision, always refer to the original goals of the project and ask yourself, "Does this decision support the goals of the project?"

Developing the Storage Solution

After you have determined the needs, explored the options, and come up with a plan, the real fun can begin. Any solution that will become part of the critical path of business must be developed and tested in a controlled lab environment. This is the part of the project where policies and procedures start to take form. Practice runs of mirroring, failing over of resources, and recovery of systems ensure that the solution will be able to support the needs of the company.

During this development phase, practice connecting your servers to the SAN or NAS. Develop and document standards around HBAs or network interface cards (NICs), the versions of firmware that will be used, and the version of the drivers that will be used. Most SAN and NAS manufacturers provide a detailed list of supported combinations of hardware, firmware, and software. Deviate from these approved lists at your own risk. The last thing you want to implement is an unstable storage environment because you chose not to follow the recommended configurations.

The development phase will identify several requirements that are not usually thought of during the planning phase. Most specifically, these requirements are in the area of facilities. Most SAN devices are fairly large. An EMC Symetrix and Connectix, for example, will take up a full rack each. With heat generation more than 3,000BTUs, HVAC resources will need to be considered. Also keep in mind that most SAN and NAS solutions require 220V to run them. Ensure that planned data center locations have appropriate space, cooling, and power. Power should include not only the standard AC feed, but battery backup as well. Be aware of any special requirements of the SAN or NAS. Some SAN devices on the market void their warranty if they are placed within 5 feet of any solid objects.

> **TIP**
>
> Be sure to carefully document the entire installation and configuration process. It not only makes troubleshooting easier, but it also provides the full road map for pilot implementation.

Designing the Right Data Storage Structure for Exchange Server 2007

Exchange 2007 provides administrators with a lot more options on how to configure their environment than previous versions of Exchange. When considering SAN or NAS for Exchange 2007, it is important to understand the strengths and weaknesses of a given disk solution and ensure that you are addressing all of the potential concerns and gaining all of the potential benefits. This includes decisions regarding disk type, methods of connectivity, and the distribution of aggregates and logical unit numbers, or LUNs.

Choosing the Right Connectivity for NAS

All the high-speed disks in the world won't amount to much if you can't get the data to and from the Exchange servers quickly. In a NAS environment, the network itself is the biggest concern for performance. Most NAS devices on the market use very fast *heads* that are literally dedicated computers with high-performance processors and loads of memory. With SCSI RAID controllers on board, they can easily saturate multiple 100-Mb Ethernet connections. Attaching such a device to a low-end switch would result in the NAS running in an extremely restricted manner. Strongly consider using a switch that will enable you to use a gigabit connection.

Consider creating a separate network for the NAS environment. Suppose, for example, that the NAS is going to support a number of Exchange servers. By multihoming the Exchange servers, one Ethernet connection can face the users and provide connectivity to the mail clients, whereas the other interface can be dedicated to NAS traffic. This allows each interface to run unfettered by the traffic associated with the other network. This also enables you to upgrade only a subset of the network to improve performance and save money. The traffic of the database transaction back to the NAS device by Exchange would be much greater than the traffic associated with users viewing their mail because the traffic that would normally go to the local disk would now be traveling across the Ethernet via the virtual disk driver that connects the NAS to the Exchange server.

When selecting network gear for a NAS *out-of-band* network, focus on packets per second. Whenever possible, build this NAS network with multiple switches that are cross-connected. Connect each server to both switches with the NICs in a Teamed mode. This not only adds bandwidth, but also creates redundancy for the Network layer. Odds are if the application warranted the use of a NAS device, it deserves redundancy at the network level as well.

When selecting NICs for the servers, strongly consider the use of NICs that support Transmission Control Protocol (TCP) offload processing. This means that the work involved with network transfers is performed by the NIC itself rather then increasing the load on the server's CPUs. Because the NIC is designed with data transfer in mind, the result is the ability to move huge amounts of data without impacting the overall performance of the Exchange server. Because network overhead is associated with mounting NAS disks, this type of configuration can be very helpful for the Exchange server.

Choosing the Right Connectivity for SANs

When attaching. to a SAN, you will be using HBAs via Fibre Channel rather than NICs via Ethernet. HBAs can be relatively expensive, but they offer much greater throughput than NICs and NAS would offer. Between the higher speeds (4Gb for Fibre Channel versus 1Gb for Ethernet) and the lower overhead involved in the protocol, a HBA-attached SAN can move significantly more data in the same period of time. This can be especially useful in situations where a large number of disks are being accessed.

SANs are generally attached to the HBAs via a Fibre Channel fabric. A Fibre Channel fabric is created by a set of interconnected HBAs, bridges, storage devices, and switches. Strongly consider implementing multiple fabrics for redundancy. Generally, a fabric can be thought of as a set of switches sharing interswitch links along with the devices to which they are connected. A SAN with multiple switches not connected by interswitch links provides multiple fabrics.

The SAN connects to the switch fabric through controllers. These controllers are what combine the disks together into larger aggregates and servers as the entry and exit point for data. SAN controllers generally contain very large caches of memory (typically 2–4GB) to improve performance. Multiple controllers are always recommended for redundancy and performance.

When thinking about the connectivity between the Exchange servers and the SAN, always try to use multiple LUNs and connect them such that half the LUNs prefer Controller A and half prefer Controller B. This helps even out the load across the controllers and increases overall throughput of the SAN. In the event of controller failure or controller maintenance, the connectivity is picked up by the remaining controller.

When planning your SAN storage, be very aware of how your particular SAN and switch fabric deal with zoning. The concept of zoning is similar to the concept of virtual LANs (VLANs) in networking. The objective is to ensure that only the necessary servers can see the disks that will be provisioned to them. Depending on your particular solution, this is performed via LUN masking, hard/soft zoning, port zoning, or through the use of world-wide names. These concepts work as follows:

▶ **LUN masking**—LUN masking is a process that makes particular LUNs available to some hosts but not to others. This process is akin to setting permissions on a resource to determine which hosts are allowed to access them. This is particularly important in Windows environments where a server will attempt to write a signature to a newly discovered disk. This can render an existing LUN unavailable to its originally intended host.

▶ **Hard/soft zoning**—In this context, hard and soft refer to the location of the implementation of this type of zoning. Hard zoning is done at a hardware level and soft zoning is done in software. Hard zoning physically blocks access to a zone from any device outside of the zone. Soft zoning uses filters in the switch fabric that prevent ports from being seen from outside of their assigned zones.

▶ **Port zoning**—Port zoning uses physical ports to define security zones. A user's access to data is determined by what physical port he is connected to. The drawback with port zoning is that zone information must be updated every time a user changes switch ports. In addition, port zoning does not allow zones to overlap. Port zoning is normally implemented using hard zoning, but can also be implemented using soft zoning.

▶ **World Wide Name (WWN) zoning**—WWN zoning uses name servers in the switches to either allow or disallow access to particular WWNs in the fabric. A major advantage of WWN zoning is the ability to modify the fabric without having to redo the zone information. SAN-related devices like HBAs are built with unique WWNs installed into them not unlike Media Access Control (MAC) addresses in network interfaces.

Choosing the Right Type of Disks

When researching SAN and NAS devices, you will discover that you have several types of disks available to you. These disks will vary by architecture (SCSI versus ATA versus Fibre Channel) as well as by size. Current disks are available in sizes ranging from 72GB to 250GB each.

In terms of size, your decisions will be based on three factors:

▶ Price

▶ Capacity

▶ Performance

Generally speaking, the larger the disk, the more you pay for it. Capacity refers to the total amount of space you plan to deploy. If, for example, you needed to deploy 2TB of space, you could use eight 250-GB disks or thirty-two 72-GB disks. Why would you pick one configuration over the other?

If you opted to use eight 250-GB disks, you'd be using less capacity on your SAN or NAS device. If you expected to expand capacity in the future, you'd be able to expand further before needing to purchase additional disk shelves or chassis. The potential downside to this approach is that eight 250-GB disks might be more expensive than thirty-two 72-GB disks. The other more noticeable impact is in the area of I/O performance. Assuming the spindle speeds were the same for both disks, you would get four times more I/O out of the thirty-two 72-GB disks than you would from the eight 250-GB disks. Depending on whether your application needed the additional I/O, this might be a deciding factor.

TIP

If random access disk I/O performance is a concern, pay close attention to the spindle speed of the disks. Traditionally, the largest disks available to SAN or NAS applications operate at a lower revolutions per minute (rpm) than smaller disks. Typical random access I/O per second ratings of hard drives is roughly rpm/100. For example, a 15,000-rpm hard drive offers 150 random access disk I/O per second.

Useful to note is that with sufficient memory in an Exchange 2007 server, disk I/O requirements are roughly one fourth what they were in an Exchange 2003 server with the same number of users. This behavior was specifically engineered into Exchange 2007 to take advantage of the ever-increasing capacity of hard disks. Hard disk capacity is increasing drastically every year with nearly no improvements in I/O performance. According to Seagate, although disk capacity increased 15,000 times from 1987 to 2004, the random I/O performance increased only 11 times during the same period.

In addition to choosing the size of the disks you deploy, you also have a choice in terms of the disk architecture. Your most common choices are as follows:

- Serial ATA (SATA)

- SCSI

- Fibre Channel

SATA is generally the least-expensive option. SATA disks provide excellent throughput, nearly equal to SCSI, at a much better price. High-capacity disks are usually available as SATA first because it is a more common market for disks. Newer implementations of SATA include high-performance functions such as command queuing, which give them performance that approaches that of SCSI.

SCSI disks have been around for decades. It's a very well-proven technology and is known for having very high performance as well as very high reliability. SCSI disks are less expensive than Fibre Channel disks but offer lower throughput through the bus. This results in needing more controllers to manage the disks themselves and lower performance than Fibre Channel disks.

Fibre Channel disks are the highest-performance drives available today. They are also the most expensive and generally trail a full generation behind other formats in terms of capacity. If performance is your number-one concern, the Fibre Channel disk can't be beat.

TIP

Don't be afraid to mix and match disk types for different applications. A typical SAN or NAS supports multiple disk shelves of different types. Consider something like Fibre Channel disks for the databases, SCSI drives for the logs, and Serial ATA disks for archive storage. A similar concept can be applied to disk sizes to maximize capacity where I/O loads will be relatively low.

Slicing and Dicing the Available Disk

Simple physics tells you that you'll get improvements in performance as you add more disks to an array. Because each drive's read/write head can operate simultaneously, you get a fairly linear improvement as drives are added. NAS and SAN offer the advantage of dynamically increasing the size of a volume without taking the volume offline. This allows for the addition of even more spindles.

Although it's possible to later resize a volume from a NAS or SAN, you must be careful not to oversubscribe the device. Devices that support snapshots of the data reserve twice the volume size that they claim for capacity. So, to make 100GB available to a server, the NAS reserves 200GB on itself. This ensures that it is able to complete all transactions. This function can be disabled on most devices, but it is not recommended. This removes the protection from oversubscription of the disks.

When provisioning disk space for an Exchange server, you should consider a few rules of thumb when optimizing performance.

In a perfect world, an entire SAN or NAS would be dedicated to just the Exchange 2007 environment. This would reduce the possibility of contention with other applications. If your budget doesn't allow for this, be very aware of what applications are being shared with your SAN or NAS.

If you can't dedicate a SAN or NAS to your Exchange environment, build your aggregate from disks that are spread out across multiple shelves. This helps distribute the load across multiple backplanes and results in fewer spikes in performances.

Try not to make LUNs larger than they need to be. For example, if you plan to have four storage groups with 50GB of mail each, create four LUNs of 50GB each rather than a single LUN of 200GB. This allows you to separate the LUNs across both controllers and improves the performance of the system. The potential pitfall here is that you could run out of drive letters because Exchange 2007 allows for up to 50 databases in up to 50 storage groups in the Enterprise Edition. To work around this, mount the LUNs as mount points instead of drive letters. This can greatly simplify expansions of Exchange 2007 servers as you can place a storage group on a drive letter and then mount new LUNs as mount points for each new database that you need to bring online. This is exceptionally useful when using snapshot functions in NAS or SAN where the database has to be dismounted for an integrity check because this typically occurs at the LUN level.

To mount a LUN as a mount point rather than a drive letter, perform the following steps:

1. Right-click My Computer and choose Manage on the shortcut menu.

2. Expand Storage and click Disk Management.

3. Right-click the unpartitioned space and select New Partition on the shortcut menu.

4. When the New Partition Wizard launches, click Next.

5. From the Select Partition Type screen, select Primary Partition, and click Next.

6. Choose the size of the partition desired, and click Next.

7. Select Mount in the Following Empty NTFS folder, and click Browse.

8. Select the folder that will host the new mount point, and click OK. Ensure that this folder is empty. Choose to create a new folder, if necessary. Click Next.

9. Choose to format the drive as NTFS. Label it to reflect the name of the data it will house. Click Next.

10. After the drive is formatted, click Finish.

> **NOTE**
>
> When configuring LUNs for a cluster, be sure to create them as basic disk in Windows; otherwise, the cluster will not recognize the disks as potential cluster resources.

Predicting Disk Performance with Exchange Server 2007

When planning the number of disks to use for LUNs for various functions in Exchange 2007, the question that invariably comes up is "How many spindles do I need for good performance?" Although it is fairly straightforward to determine the I/O needs for various functions in Exchange 2007, it can be trickier to predict the effect that the disk configuration will have on the system. One of the most common configurations is to utilize RAID 5 to provide redundancy at the disk level. To understand the impact of RAID 5, consider the following:

RAID-5 performance can be approximated as %Reads*IOPS per disk*(disks-1))+(%Writes*IOPS per disk*((disks-1)/4))= Total IOPS

35

Or, for the more mathematically oriented:

Total IOPS = (R*I(d-1))+(W*I((d-1)/4))

where:

- R = % Reads

- W = % Writes

- I = Input / Output operations per second (IOPS) per disk

- d = number of disks in RAID5

- T = Total IOPS

With typical IOPS performance per disk being:

- 140-150 Random IOPS from 15,000-RPM disks

- 100-120 Random IOPS from 10,000-RPM disks

- 75-100 Random IOPS from 7,200-RPM disks

Adding in Fault Tolerance for External Storage Systems

When implementing centralized storage solutions, you are often placing a large number of very important eggs into a single basket. SAN and NAS manufacturers understand this and have spent a lot of research and development dollars on building in fault tolerance into their offerings. Many options are available to the end user; some of the fault-tolerance options are as follows:

- **RAID configurations**—RAID levels 0+1 and 5 are most common. RAID level 6 offers the ability to lose two drives at a time and not lose data.

- **Triple mirroring**—This enables you to snap off a mirror so that data becomes static for purposes of backup. Meanwhile, the system still has mirrored drives for fault tolerance. This is most commonly used with databases.

- **Log shipping**—Most SAN and NAS devices can copy log files in near real time to another SAN or NAS so that databases can be copied regularly and log files can be kept in sync remotely.

- **Geographic mirroring**—SAN and NAS devices offer in-band and out-of-band options for mirroring data across wide distances. Whereas SCSI has a 25-foot limitation, Fibre Channel can locate a device up to 1,000km away.

- **Snapshotting**—By flagging disk blocks as being part of a particular version of a file and writing changes to that file on new blocks, a NAS or SAN device can take a snapshot of what the data looked like at a point in time. This enables a user to roll back a file to a previous version. It also enables you to roll an entire system back to a point in time almost instantly.

▶ **Clustering**—NAS devices that use heads to serve data offer dual heads so that if one fails, the other continues to serve data from the disks.

▶ **Redundant power systems**—Any good SAN or NAS offers multiple power supplies to protect against failure. Take advantage of the separate power supplies by attaching them to separate electrical circuits.

▶ **Redundant backplanes**—Many NAS and SAN devices offer redundant backplanes to protect against hardware failure.

▶ **Hot standby drives**—By having unused drives available in the chassis, the device can replace a failed disk instantly with one that is already present and ready for use. Be sure to monitor the SAN or NAS device to see if a disk has failed and been replaced. It can be easy to miss because there is no interruption to service.

Although Exchange 2007 offers functions such as Cluster Continuous Replication to provide for server-level fault tolerance, it is still a best practice to provide disk-level redundancy for the individual servers. With the reduced dependence on disk I/O in Exchange 2007 servers equipped with large amounts of system memory, RAID 5 will become a more common configuration on Mailbox servers. If utilizing a caching controller for the RAID controller, be sure that the cache is protected by a battery backup. Failure to do so could result in lost data that was cached in the controller during a failure. If the cache isn't committed to the disk, the data will be in an inconsistent state and most likely will not be usable.

35

TIP

RAID 5 is not recommended for any application that performs write transactions more than about 30% of the time. This is because each write transaction requires reading multiple disks and recalculating and writing of parity bits.

Recommendations for SAN and NAS Solutions

SAN and NAS manufacturers have provided a number of technologies that make it easier to integrate their products with specific software products. Because these products having been available for a number of years, best practices around these implementations have been developed and can help you avoid common pitfalls with SAN and NAS usage.

Recommendations for Exchange with NAS/SAN Environments

When implementing a NAS or SAN solution in a Microsoft Exchange environment, many different interpretations abound on the best way to implement the solution. Some of the recommendedbest practices are as follows:

▶ Run multiple HBAs in each Exchange server with each HBA connected to a different Fibre Channel switch. This allows for failover if one of the Fibre Channel switches should fail.

▶ Ensure that zoning of the SAN is configured correctly so that only the necessary systems can see the LUNs. In the case of a cluster, all nodes that might potentially own the disks should be in the same zone. If an unrelated Windows system sees the disks, it tries to write a new signature to the disk, which makes it unreadable by the intended hosts.

▶ Backups should be performed at the storage group level rather than at the mailbox level. Mailbox-level backups are very processor intensive for the Exchange server.

▶ If available, direct disk backup solutions are significantly faster than storage group level backups.

▶ If you are implementing third-party applications with your NAS or SAN for use with Exchange, make sure they are certified by Microsoft for use with Exchange 2007 and that they use the standard application programming interfaces (APIs) such as Volume Shadow Copy Services.

▶ Separate log files from databases onto different drive sets. This improves overall throughput and improves recoverability in the case of a NAS/SAN failure.

▶ Replicate databases hourly to another device for disaster recovery. Logs should be replicated every few minutes. This limits potential mail loss to one log replication interval.

▶ Always use integrated tools if they are available, such as Network Appliance's SnapManager for Exchange. They greatly simplify management and recoverability of the product for which they were designed.

▶ Always plan for space reservation on a volume. If the database will grow to 80GB and will have snapshots taken for recoverability, reserve 160GB of space on the device.

▶ When possible, expand capacity on the Exchange 2007 server via additional mailbox databases placed on new LUNs. Although LUNs can be dynamically grown, it is usually a very time-consuming process and will impact system performance on the Exchange server.

▶ Avoid placing multiple virtual logical disks or LUNs on the same RAID group. This could result in databases and log files being on the same RAID group. This would complicate system recoveries if the RAID group were to fail.

Consolidating the Number of Exchange Servers via NAS or SAN

Exchange servers were traditionally sized based not only on performance potential, but also on the time needed to recover a system. Administrators knew that if they had a 4-hour SLA for system recovery they could count on using half that time to recover data from tape and half that time to perform the recovery tasks. This meant that they could only have as much local storage as they could recover in 2 hours. So, if a backup/restore system could restore 16GB of data in 2 hours and each user was allowed 100MB of storage, the maximum number of users on the system would be 160. For a company of 1,600 users, this would mean 10 Exchange servers would be required to support the 4-hour SLA.

By placing the mailbox stores onto a NAS or SAN device that can be mirrored and snap-shotted, the recoverability time for a 16-GB database would drop to mere minutes. Now the bottleneck would become the performance of the server itself and possibly the I/O rate of the NAS or SAN. Odds are that the systems that had been purchased for the ability to support 160 users would be dual-processor systems with 1 to 2GB of memory. By reducing the server count to two and fully populating those two systems with memory taken from the retired systems, the two systems with NAS- or SAN-based mailboxes could easily support the 800 users each and still meet the 4-hour recovery time required by the SLA. This would result in the reduction of eight Exchange servers, which would free up OS licenses and hardware as well as reduce the effort required to manage the data center.

TIP

When consolidating Exchange servers, consider taking some of the newly freed up Exchange servers to be used as Cluster Continuous Replication Exchange servers or place them in the lab to be used for recovery and testing of patches.

Making the Best Use of SAN/NAS Disks with Exchange Server 2007

SAN or NAS disks are generally much more expensive than the disks used in DAS. As such, you will generally utilize the SAN/NAS storage only where it makes a significant difference in performance. Many aspects of Exchange 2007 utilize the disks but use them in different ways.

The largest consumer of disk performance is the Mailbox role. In Exchange 2007, it is very common to run servers that are dedicated to doing nothing but hosting mailboxes. On these systems, several different consumers of disk resources would benefit from being placed on SAN or NAS, as discussed in the following sections.

Storage of Transaction Log Files (`.log` Files)

Changes made to the database are first committed to the transaction log. This results in a sequential write to the disk. Because sequential I/O is significantly higher per disk than random I/O, the logs do not benefit as much from being placed on SAN or NAS disks. For performance reasons as well as recoverability reasons, the logs should not be located on the same disks as the database. Similarly, the logs should not be on the same disk as the page file for the operating system.

To create a storage group with log files on a NAS or SAN disk, complete the following steps:

1. From the Start menu, select Programs, Microsoft Exchange, Exchange Management Console.

2. Expand Server Configuration, and then highlight Mailbox.

3. Right-click the Mailbox server, and choose New Storage Group on the shortcut menu.

4. Enter the storage group name in the Storage Group Name field.

5. Next to the Log Files Location field, click Browse.

6. Navigate to the drive letter representing the SAN/NAS disk, and click OK.

7. Next to the System Files Location field, click Browse.

8. Navigate to the drive letter representing the SAN/NAS disk, and click OK.

9. Click New to create a new storage group similar to the one shown in Figure 35.1.

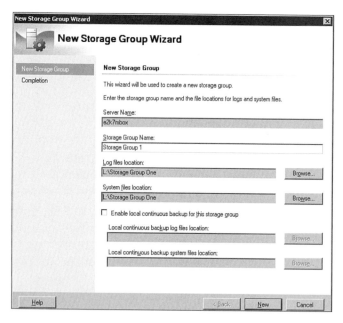

FIGURE 35.1   New Storage Group Wizard.

10. After the wizard has completed, click Finish.

Storage of the JET Database (.edb File)

The Exchange 2007 Mailbox server stores all mail in a JET database. Unlike Exchange Server 2003, there is no longer a .stm file. The JET database is randomly accessed as users access their mail or send and receive new messages. For purposes of performance and recoverability, the disks that contain the databases should be physically separate from the disks that contain the logs.

To create a mailbox database with the files stored on a NAS/SAN disk, perform the following steps:

1. From the Start menu, select Programs, Microsoft Exchange, Exchange Management Console.

2. Expand Server Configuration, and then highlight Mailbox.

3. Right-click the storage group that will host the database, and choose New Mailbox Database on the shortcut menu.

4. Enter the name for the new mailbox database in the Mailbox Database Name field.

5. Next to the Exchange Database File Path field, click Browse.

6. Navigate and highlight the drive letter that represents the SAN/NAS disk.

7. Click New to create a new mailbox similar to the one shown in Figure 35.2.

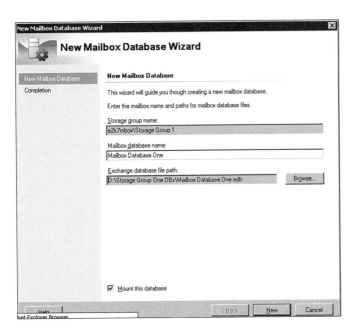

FIGURE 35.2   New Mailbox Database Wizard.

8. When the wizard is completed, click Finish.

Performing Content Indexing

The Search features have been significantly improved in Exchange 2007. Content indexing is a random access workload that should be placed on the same LUN as the database that it is indexing. Content indexing is usually about 5% of the database size. Content indexing runs in the background indexing messages as they arrive and, as such, the disk I/O impact is minimal.

To create a content index on a database that is SAN or NAS attached, perform the following:

1. From the Start menu, click Programs, Microsoft Exchange, Exchange Management Shell.

2. From the Exchange Management Shell, type:

   ```
   New-ContentIndex -Database <databaseIDParameter> -Directory <string>
   ```

   where *databaseIDParameter* is the mailbox database that will be indexed and the *Directory <string>* is the path to the location of the index. By default, this is created in the same path as the database.

3. Press Enter.

When a process requests a page from memory and the system cannot find the page at the requested location, a page fault occurs. If the page is elsewhere in memory, the fault is a soft page fault. If the page must be retrieved from disk, the fault is a hard page fault. Most processors can handle large numbers of soft page faults without consequence. However, hard page faults can cause significant delays. Continuous high rates of disk paging indicate a memory shortage. If memory can not be increased sufficiently to reduce the number of hard page faults, you must improve the speed of the disks that host the page file. In this scenario, the page file location could benefit from the improved performance of a SAN or NAS disk.

If you want to move your page file to a SAN or NAS attached disk, perform the following steps:

1. Right-click My Computer and select Properties on the shortcut menu.

2. Click the Advanced tab.

3. In the Performance section, click Settings.

4. From the Performance Options pane, click the Advanced tab.

5. Near the bottom of the pane in the Virtual Memory section, click Change.

6. Highlight the drive letter that represents the disk that should host the page file.

7. Click the Custom Size option button.

8. Enter an initial size of 1.5*system memory.

9. Enter a maximum size of 1.5*system memory, and then click Set.

10. Highlight the drive letter that previously held the page file.

11. Click the No Paging File option button, and then click Set.

12. Click Yes to accept the warning about the page file on the volume you are modifying, and then click OK.

13. Click OK again to accept the notification that you need to reboot for the settings to take effect.

14. Click OK twice to close the dialog box.

15. Click Yes to reboot if it is acceptable to reboot the system.

You might wonder why the page file was configured with the same value for initial and maximum sizes. By setting the range to a single value, the page file is initially created at a size that will never change. This allows the page file to be contiguous on the drive. A page file that is allowed to grow might grow to a new location on the hard drive. This results in fragmentation of the page file and causes a reduction in page file performance.

In Exchange 2007, significant improvements have been achieved in memory management because of the use of 64-bit code. This allows you to install enough memory to greatly reduce the need for the system to page to disk.

Content Conversion

Most content conversion performed in an Exchange 2007 environment is performed by the client access servers (CASs) and the Hub Transport servers. Legacy WebDAV content conversion, for legacy Outlook Web Access (OWA) clients, occurs on the Exchange 2003 Mailbox server. When a client needs data that must be converted on a CAS, the data is pulled from the Exchange 2003 Mailbox server, converted in the Exchange 2007 Mailbox server's TMP folder, and sent to the CAS. To improve performance, the TMP folder should not be on the same LUN as the page file and operating system. If there is a large amount of legacy OWA clients supported, placement of the TMP folder on a NAS or SAN disk might result in improved performance.

Performing Database Maintenance

The Exchange 2007 Information Store performs periodic online maintenance against each database. The two tasks that impact disk I/O are the hard deletion of messages and mailboxes that are past their retention policy and online database defragmentation. Because a backup job will halt online defragmentation, you must be sure to give both database maintenance and backup jobs exclusive windows of time to finish their tasks or disk contention will result in greatly reduced performance for both tasks. If you are unable to sufficiently separate these two events, the increased I/O load would benefit from the databases being located on SAN or NAS disks.

Backing Up and Restoring Data

Backing up data requires that data be read from both the database and transaction log volumes. This additional I/O can impact user response times and should be avoided during business hours. Placing the databases and log files on faster SAN or NAS disks can often result in faster backup and restore processes, assuming the destination location for the data is not the bottleneck. Backups that attach to the SAN or NAS directly are usually much faster than backing up Exchange 2007 via the network with an Exchange agent.

The process of performing a soft recovery in the case of a database restore requires that the JET engine play back all of the transaction log files. This results in a sequential read stream from the disks containing the associated log files. As a result, the recovery process will be faster if the transaction log files are on a disk with fast sequential disk access, such as SAN or NAS.

In addition to having similar needs for content conversion and paging, CASs also consume disk I/O in the process of protocol logging.

Enabling Protocol Logging

Protocol logging, if enabled, results in a sequential write that is a performance hit and consumes disk space to store the logs. Protocol logging is typically used to verify the performance of a given protocol or when you suspect attacks from the Internet.

Impact from Message Tracking Logs

Edge and Hub Transport servers maintain message tracking logs that result in sequential write traffic for the log files. Because sequential write performance is much higher than random access, these types of logs typically don't require high-performance disks.

Conversion of Incoming Mail

The Hub Transport server converts incoming mail into a Messaging Application Programming Interface (MAPI) format. This occurs in the TMP directory of the Hub Transport server. As such, it is important to ensure that the TMP directory is not located on the same LUN as the page file or the operating system. In environments that receive very large amounts of Internet mail, it is beneficial to place this TMP directory on a SAN or NAS attached disk.

Events Trigged by Agents

Customization of the Transport server is done via bits of code more commonly referred to as agents. These agents run in the common language runtime environment and are triggered by specific events. Some agents write data to a log, which could result in a disk performance hit in addition to consuming disk space. If you find your environment taking performance hits because of agents, consider configuring them to place their logs on higher-performance NAS or SAN disks.

Summary

This chapter has introduced the concepts of network attached storage and storage area networks as options to improve performance and manageability over traditional direct attached storage. You've seen how SAN and NAS can be used to manage data more effectively through the reduction of servers.

Applications like Exchange can be made to support much larger numbers of users through the leveraging of large numbers of disks. Performance scales nearly 1:1 as additional disks are added. Plus, adding additional disks allows an application to support more I/O operations per second, which is critical to database-based applications.

You've seen how advanced technologies like snapshotting enable you to back up Exchange data regularly on the device itself so that users can recover their own data without having to involve administrators. When coupled with new technologies like Cluster Continuous Replication, snapshotting can give administrators great peace of mind that they can recover very quickly from a server or database failure.

NAS implementations work with existing Ethernet infrastructures and impart additional loads on them that must be planned for. You've seen that a strong network is the key to good NAS performance.

This chapter discussed some of the specific functions within Exchange 2007 that work well with both NAS and SAN storage. You've learned that SAN provides block-level access to the disk, whereas NAS provides file-level access. Some applications require SAN, but most can work with NAS.

SAN and NAS offer you greater performance and enable you to perform geographic mirroring that was previously impossible for the application itself. As administrators develop greater confidence in the newer Exchange technologies such as Cluster Continuous Replication, they might replace NAS or SAN replication. However, until that happens, SAN and NAS offer time-proven solutions for geographic redundancy. As Ethernet and Fibre Channel technologies continue to improve and as chassis and disk prices continue to fall, you will find NAS and SAN becoming more common in the IT world.

Best Practices

The following are best practices from this chapter:

▸ Implement a SAN or NAS solution when there is a need for storage consolidation, movement toward centralized management of messaging systems, or for near real-time mirroring of data.

▸ Analyze your storage needs so that you can size the storage system with the appropriate disk space necessary to meet current and project near-term future requirements.

▶ During the development and testing phase, connect and disconnect servers to the SAN and NAS system to confirm your knowledge and the practice of accessing external storage on the network.

▶ Choose the right type of connectivity based on the transaction throughput of data transmission that will allow the SAN or NAS to keep up with the reading and writing of data to and from the servers.

▶ Acquire disks that are fast enough to keep up with the performance demand of the servers and of the network connectivity of the SAN or NAS.

▶ Use the formula in the section "Predicting Disk Performance with Exchange Server 2007" to calculate the I/O per second to determine disk performance as well as disk speed requirements of the disk subsystem.

▶ Add the appropriate fault tolerance to the storage system based on the disaster recovery and business continuity needs of the organization.

▶ Develop a backup strategy that matches the performance capabilities and the recovery time frame desired in the organization.

▶ Place the Exchange database files and the log files on the proper disk location of the SAN and NAS system for optimum performance and desired recoverability in the event of a storage system failure.

Index

Symbols

A

How can we make this index more useful? Email us at indexes@samspublishing.com

installing, 576

   third-party CA, 767-770

MAPI, 564

NLB configurations, 1074-1075

optimizing, 1167

Outlook Anywhere, 571-572

OWA, 566, 570

POP, 575

sizing, 1182

Categorizer, 169

Hub Transport servers, 578

   submission queues, 590

categorizing

appointments via color (Outlook), 904

email, OWA, 970

CC (carbon copy), 956. *See also* **email**

CC fields (email), removing users from (OWA), 957

CCA (Configuration Connection Agreements), Exchange Server 5.5 migrations, 550

CCR (Cluster Continuous Replication), 28, 88, 96, 1099

heartbeats, 1056

mailbox clusters, 1048-1055

SCC versus, 1067

transport dump feature (Hub Transport servers), 1056

CD (connected directory), 109

centralized IT environments, 51

certificate authority. *See* **CA**

Certificate Practice Statement (CPS), 375

certificate servers, adding templates to, 384

Certificate Services

backups, 1108-1109

installing, 380-382

Windows Server 2003, 374-375

certificate templates, 377-378

certificate-based encrypted messaging, 373

certificates, 377

aquiring, 378

Exchange user certificates, configuring with Autoenrollment, 382-384

Office Communications Server, configuring for, 885-887

Outlook, acknowledging, 389

validating that they are working properly, autoenrollment, 385-387

Windows certificate of authority, installing, 380

change control, security documentation, 756-757. *See also* **documentation**

changes in Exchange Server 2007, 74-75

charts, Gantt Chart, 55-56

Checkpoint-Meta IP, 134

circuits, 810

CIW (Custom Installation Wizard), creating transforms (Outlook deployments), 1026-1027

classifying messages, Hub Transport servers, 586-587

client access licenses (CALs), 713

client access points, identifying, 84-85

Client Access rules (Management Pack), 698-699

Client Access server roles, 27-28, 98-99, 649

installing, 215

client access server. *See* **CAS (Client Access Server)**

client authentication, certificate templates, 377

client DNS, examing use for Exchange, 144

Client Performance reports (Metric reports), 707

client-based virus protection, 307

client-level security, 308-309

clients

32-bit RDP clients, accessing with Terminal Services, 714

access, 84-85

   integrating, 104-105

   MAPI compression, 84

   OWA, 85

   SMTP, 85

DNS

   need for, 133

   SMTP, 144

   troubleshooting, 150

integrating client access into Exchange Server 2007, 104-105

Macintosh

   Entourage X, 1004-1007

   Terminal Services Client, 1007-1010

non-Windows access methods, 1010-1012

How can we make this index more useful? Email us at indexes@samspublishing.com

How can we make this index more useful? Email us at indexes@samspublishing.com

mail flow tools, 652

mail notification pop-up (OWA), 949

mailboxes, migrating, 552, 554-556

MAPI conversions, 1208

Message Tracking tool, 641

name resolution, OWA, 978

options, configuring, 962

outbound routing, 150

Outlook

multiple account management, 906

sending and receiving digitally signed and encrypted emails, 387-388

Outlook 2003, 312-314

Outlook Email Postmark, 320

Outlook Express, 997

Outlook security

Blocked Senders List, 913

encryption, 909

International List, 913

junk email filters, 911-914

Safe Recipients List, 913

Safe Senders List, 913

security labels, 911

targeting specific messages, 909

web beaconing, 914

OWA. See OWA

passwords, modifying, 978

privacy, 976

Queue Viewer, 642

read receipts, blocking, 320

reading, 959

marking read/unread, 965

replying, 960-961

restoring, backup strategy development, 1090

routing, 143

searching, 971

security, 147-148

sending, 958

Edge Transport server failures, 1119

Hub Transport server failures, 1118

sending "on behalf of" other users (Outlook collaboration), 922-923

sending digitally signed email, 389-390, 392

sending encrypted email messages, 392-393

signatures, setting default signatures in OWA, 974-975

spam

filtering junk mail, 318-319

tools, 315

Web beaconing, 316-317

spell checking, OWA, 968-969, 976

text

modifying, 964

Spell Check feature, 968

tracking, 963

unified messaging, 614

Unified Messaging Server Role, 649

email addresses, managing, 616

email disclaimers, 445-446

administrative policies, 344-346

Email Postmark validation, 247

Email Postmarks, 373

EMC (Exchange Management Console), 15-16, 601, 649-650

action pane, 603

Anti-Spam tab, 223

components of, 601

console tree, 602-603

databases, 632-633

databases, creating, 631

disaster recovery tools, 651-652

disconnected mailboxes, 625-626

distribution groups

creating, 617-619

delegating management of, 621

distribution list mail flow settings, 622-623

dynamic distribution groups, 620-621

email addresses, managing, 616

email contacts, 623-624

EMS (Exchange Management Shell) versus, 610

ExBPA (Exchange Best Practices Analyzer), 651, 677

Finalize Deployment page, 603

How can we make this index more useful? Email us at indexes@samspublishing.com

G

Active Directory
  authentication, 157
  changing passwords via OWA, 978
ActiveSync with ISA Server 2006, 778-783
administrative roles, 330-331
application-layer filtering, 398-399
assessing risks, 329-330
audit logging, 656-660
breaches, cost of, 397
client-based virus protection, 307
client-level security, 308-309
clients
  lockdown guidelines, 307
  new features, 308-309
  optimizing Windows Server 2003, 299
  patches/updates, 304
  templates, 301-303
documentation, 756-757
Edge Transport, 148
email, modifying passwords, 978
event codes, 658
events, auditing, 333
Exchange Server 2007 implementation, 89-90
Exchange Server 2007 through administrative
  policies. See administrative policies
firewalls, importance of, 397-398
groups, 169, 343-344
  administrative policies, 343-344
HTTP traffic, 399-400
implementing, 89-90
importance of in Exchange Server 2007, 327-328
ISA Server, 396
  Action tab, 409
  Alerts tab, 422, 424
  Application Settings tab, 411
  Authentication Delegation tab, 411
  Bridging tab, 411
  connectivity verifiers, 424, 426
  customizing Dashboard, 421
  From tab, 410

General tab, 409
HTTP traffic security concerns, 399-400
IMAP, 414-415
Link Translation tab, 411
Listener tab, 410
logs, 418-420
MAPI, 411-413
messaging security, 401
outlining the need for, 396-399
OWA (Outlook Web Access), 401-411
Paths tab, 411
POP3, 413-414
Public Name tab, 411
Schedule tab, 411
Services tab, 424
Sessions tab, 424
SMTP (Simple Mail Transfer Protocol),
  416-417
To tab, 410
Traffic tab, 410
Users tab, 411
Kerberos failure codes, 659
layers, 334
message tracking, 664-667
mobile devices Terminal Services, 727-729
multiple forests, 79
NT Status codes, 660
Outlook. See Outlook, security
Outlook 2003. See Outlook 2003, security
Outlook Express, 999
OWA, 321, 948, 988-989
patches and updates, 304-307
proxies, 147-148
Remote Desktop for Administration, 720-723
secure messaging environments, 332
  Windows Server 2003, 332-341
server-level security. See server-level security
servers
  antivirus applications, 351
  hardening, 334-337, 343-344
  patches/updates, 340

Subscriber Access feature, 796-797

telephony, 810-811

circuit-switched networks, 810

circuits, 810

hunt groups, 814

installation prerequisites, 813-814

IP/BPX (Internet Protocol/Private Branch Exchange), 810

IP/VoIP gateways, 810, 814

packet-switched networks, 811

PBX (Private Branch Exchanges), 811, 814

POTS (Plain Old Telephone System), 811

PSTN (Public Switched Telephone Networks), 811

RTP (Real-Time Transport Protocol), 812

SIP (Session Initiation Protocol), 811, 843-845

T.38 (Real-time Facsimile Transport Protocol), 812

TDM (Time-Division Multiplexing), 811

VoIP (Voice over Internet Protocol), 811

telephony integration, 794

testing, 824-825

UMIP gateway objects, 801

unified messaging server objects, 805

user properties, 806

Web Services, 806

Unified Messaging Local Fax Service Availability Summary reports (Service Availability reports), 708

Unified Messaging Local Voice Service Availability Summary reports (Service Availability reports), 709

Unified Messaging Remote Fax Service Availability Summary reports (Service Availability reports), 709

Unified Messaging Remote Voice Service Availability Summary reports (Service Availability reports), 709

Unified Messaging role, 100

Unified Messaging rules (Management Pack), 704

Unified Messaging server, 83

unified messaging server objects, Unified Messaging, 805

Unified Messaging server roles, 28, 649

installing, 215

Unified Messaging Servers

backups, 1096

Exchange Server 2003 migrations, 529

optimizing, 1168

sizing, 1184

Unified Messaging tab (mailbox features properties), 614

universal group caching, 164-165

universal groups, 171

UNIX

components of services, 124

development of services, 123-124

installing services for UNIX R2, 125-128

prerequisites of services, 124-125

synchronizing user information between Active Directory, 128-129

UNIX BIND DNS, 134

UNIX desktops, Exchange Server support for

Outlook Express, 997-1001

OWA, 996, 1012

UNIX R2, installing services for, 125-128

UNIX systems, integrating with Active Directory and Exchange Server 2007, 122-123

Unreachable Queue Length performance counter, 700-701

unread, marking email messages, 965

unread/read, marking email as (OWA), 965

unsupported connectors, 559

updates. See also migration

backup documentation, 1086

link state updates, Exchange Server migrations, 503

Outlook deployments, Group Policies, 1035-1038

security, 304

security patches and updates, 340

servers, 340

Windows Update, 304, 340

WSUS, 340-341

updating

operating systems, 194

Windows 2003 Server Automatic Updates, 90

BOOKS ONLINE
ENABLED

UNLEASHED

Unleashed takes you beyond the basics, providing an exhaustive, technically sophisticated reference for professionals who need to exploit a technology to its fullest potential. It's the best resource for practical advice from the experts, and the most in-depth coverage of the latest technologies.

Microsoft Windows Server 2003 Unleashed (R2 Edition)
ISBN: 0672328984

OTHER UNLEASHED TITLES

Microsoft BizTalk Server 2006 Unleashed
ISBN: 0672329255

Microsoft SharePoint 2007 Development Unleashed
ISBN: 0672329034

Microsoft Exchange Server 2003 Unleashed
ISBN: 0672328070

Microsoft Small Business Server 2003 Unleashed
ISBN: 0672328054

Microsoft Visual C# 2005 Unleashed
ISBN: 0672327767

ASP.NET 2.0 Unleashed
ISBN: 0672328232

Microsoft Visual Studio 2005 Unleashed
ISBN: 0672328194

Microsoft ISA Server 2006 Unleashed
ISBN: 0672329190

Windows Presentation Foundation Unleashed
ISBN: 0672328917

Microsoft Office Project Server 2007 Unleashed
ISBN: 0672329212

Microsoft SharePoint 2007 Administration Unleashed
ISBN: 0672329476

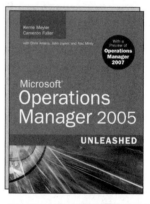

Microsoft Operations Manager 2005 Unleashed
ISBN: 067232928X

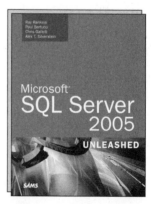

Microsoft SQL Server 2005 Unleashed
ISBN: 0672328240

SAMS

www.samspublishing.com